Lecture Notes in Artificial Intelligence   10102

Subseries of Lecture Notes in Computer Science

More information about this series at http://www.springer.com/series/1244

Chin-Yew Lin · Nianwen Xue
Dongyan Zhao · Xuanjing Huang
Yansong Feng (Eds.)

Natural Language Understanding and Intelligent Applications

5th CCF Conference on Natural Language Processing
and Chinese Computing, NLPCC 2016 and
24th International Conference on Computer Processing
of Oriental Languages, ICCPOL 2016
Kunming, China, December 2–6, 2016
Proceedings

Springer

Editors
Chin-Yew Lin
Microsoft Research Asia
Beijing
China

Nianwen Xue
Brandeis University
Waltham, MA
USA

Dongyan Zhao
Peking University
Beijing
China

Xuanjing Huang
Fudan University
Shanghai
China

Yansong Feng
Peking University
Beijing
China

ISSN 0302-9743   ISSN 1611-3349   (electronic)
Lecture Notes in Artificial Intelligence
ISBN 978-3-319-50495-7   ISBN 978-3-319-50496-4   (eBook)
DOI 10.1007/978-3-319-50496-4

Library of Congress Control Number: 2016959634

LNCS Sublibrary: SL7 – Artificial Intelligence

Printed on acid-free paper

This Springer imprint is published by Springer Nature
The registered company is Springer International Publishing AG
The registered company address is: Gewerbestrasse 11, 6330 Cham, Switzerland

Message from the Program Committee Co-chairs

We are very happy to welcome you to the proceedings of NLPCC-ICCPOL 2016, the 5th International Conference on Natural Language Processing and Chinese Computing and the 24th International Conference on Computer Processing of Oriental Languages. NLPCC is the annual conference of CCF-TCCI (Technical Committee of Chinese Information, China Computer Federation). The previous NLPCC conferences were successfully held in Beijing in 2012, Chongqing in 2013, Shenzhen in 2014, and Nanchang in 2015. This year is the third year when NLPCC became an international conference and for the first time it is held jointly with ICCPOL. As a leading conference in the field of NLP and Chinese computing, NLPCC has been the main forum for researchers and practitioners in NLP from academia, industry, and government to share their ideas, research results, and experiences, and to promote the research and technical innovations in these fields.

We received 335 paper submissions this year covering the advanced topics of fundamental research in language computing, multilingual access, Web mining/text mining, machine learning for NLP, knowledge graph, NLP for social network, search and ads, question answering as well as applications of language computing. Among them, 119 manuscripts were written in Chinese and 216 in English. All submissions were subject to double-blind review by at least three reviewers. The final decisions were made at a meeting with the Program Committee (PC) chairs and area chairs. Finally 61 (18.21%) were accepted as long papers (13 in Chinese and 48 in English) and 42 (12.54%) as posters (one in Chinese and 41 in English). Six papers were nominated for best papers by the area chairs. The final selection of the best paper(s) was made by an independent best paper committee. These proceedings include the accepted English papers, while the accepted Chinese papers are published in 北京大学 学报 (*ACTA Scientiarum Naturalium Universitatis Pekinensis*).

We gratefully acknowledge the contribution of our four distinguished keynote speakers to the conference program: Bin Yu (Fellow of American Academy of Arts and Sciences; IEEE Fellow; Professor, University of California, Berkeley, USA), Jacob Devlin (Senior Research Scientist, MSR, USA), Haizhou Li (IEEE Fellow, Professor, National University of Singapore, Singapore), and Huan Liu (Professor, Arizona State University, USA)

We would like to thank all the people who made NLPCC-ICCPOL 2016 a successful conference. In particular, we would like to thank the area chairs for their hard work in recruiting reviewers, monitoring the review and discussion processes, and carefully rating and recommending submissions. We would like to thank all 188 reviewers for their time and efforts to review the submissions. We are very grateful to Eduard Hovy and Yajuan Lv for their participation in the best paper committee. We are also grateful for the help and support from the general chairs, Eduard Hovy, Min Zhang, and Richard Sproat, and from the Organizing Committee chairs, Dongyan Zhao, Zhengtao Yu, and

Hyukro Park. Special thanks go to Yansong Feng and Xuanjing Huang, the publication chairs for their great help.

Finally, we would like to thank all the authors who submitted their research work to the conference, and thank our sponsors for their contributions to the conference.

December 2016   Chin-Yew Lin
                                                                 Nianwen Xue
                                                                 Akiko Aizawa

Organization

Organization Committee

General Chairs

Eduard Hovy	Carnegie Mellon University, USA
Min Zhang	Soochow University, China
Richard Sproat	Google New York, USA

NLPCC-ICCPOL 2016 Program Co-chairs

Chin-Yew Lin	Microsoft Research Asia, China
Nianwen Xue	Brandeis University, USA
Akiko Aizawa	National Institute of Informatics, Japan

Area Co-chairs

NLP Fundamentals

Zhiguo Wang	IBM, USA
Wanxiang Che	Harbin Institute of Technology, China

Machine Translation

Qun Liu	Dublin City University/CAS ICT, Ireland
Shujian Huang	Nanjing University, China

NLP for Data Science and Text Mining

Jing Jiang	Singapore Management University, Singapore
Rui Xia	Nanjing University of Science and Technology, China

Machine Learning for NLP

Xipeng Qiu	Fudan University, China
Yue Zhang	Singapore University of Technology and Design, Singapore

Knowledge Graph/IE/QA

Gerard de Melo	Tsinghua University, China
Guilin Qi	Southeast University, China

NLP for Social Network

Yizhou Sun   Northeastern University, USA
Nicholas Yuan   Microsoft Research

NLP for IR and Ads

Zhicheng Dou   Remin University of China
Xin Xin   Beijing Institute of Technology, China

Conversational Bot/Discourse/Summarization

Sujian Li   Peking University, China
Man Lan   East China Normal University

ADL/Tutorials Chairs

Jie Tang   Tsinghua University, China
Guodong Zhou   Soochow University, China

Evaluation Chairs

Xiaojun Wan   Peking University, China
Shiqi Zhao   Baidu

Student Workshop Chairs

Yajuan Lv   Baidu
Deyi Xiong   Soochow University, China

Organizing Committee Chairs

Dongyan Zhao   Peking University, China
Zhengtao Yu   Kunming University of Science and Technology, China
Hyukro Park   Chonnam National University, Korea

Sponsor Chairs

Ming Zhou   Microsoft Research Asia
Kam-Fai Wong   The Chinese University of Hong Kong, SAR China

Publicity Chairs

Ruifeng Xu   Harbin Institute of Technology Shenzhen Graduate School,
                      China
Kang Liu   Automation Institute, CAS, China

Publication Chairs

Xuanjing Huang   Fudan University, China
Yansong Feng   Peking University, China

Website Chair

Aixia Jia   Peking University, China

Program Committee

Cao, Hailong	Harbin Institute of Technology, China
Chang, Ching-Yun	Singapore University of Technology and Design, Singapore
Chang, Yung-Chun	Academia Sinica, Taiwan
Che, Wanxiang	Harbin Institute of Technology, China
Chen, Berlin	National Taiwan Normal University
Chen, Boxing	National Research Council Canada
Chen, Jiajun	Nanjing University, China
Chen, Lin	University of Illinois at Chicago, USA
Chen, Ting	Northeastern University, USA
Chen, Wenliang	Soochow University, China
Chen, Yidong	Xiamen University, China
Chen, Zhigang	IFLYTEK, China
Cheng, Gong	Nanjing University, China
Cheng, Li	Xinjiang Branch, Chinese Academy of Science, China
Cui, Lei	Microsoft Research, China
Dai, Xinyu	Nanjing University, China
Dong, Fei	Singapore University of Technology and Design, Singapore
Dou, Zhicheng	Remin University of China
Du, Jianfeng	Guangdong University of Foreign Studies, China
Du, Jinhua	Xi'an University of Technology, China
Duan, Junwen	Harbin Institute of Technology, China
Duan, Nan	Microsoft Research, China
Duan, Xiangyu	Soochow University, China
Fu, Guohong	Heilongjiang University, China
Gao, Wei	Qatar Computing Research Institute, Qatar
Ge, Tao	Peking University, China
Gu, Yupeng	Northeastern University, USA
Guo, Jiafeng	Institute of Computing Technology, CAS, China
Guo, Jiang	Harbin Institute of Technology, China
Han, Jialong	Nanyang Technological University, Singapore
Han, Xianpei	Institute of Software, CAS, China
He, Wei	Baidu
He, Yanqing	Institute of Scientific and Technical Information of China
He, Yifan	New York University, USA
He, Yulan	Aston University, UK
He, Zhongjun	Baidu
Hong, Yu	Soochow University, China
Huang, Dongyan	Institute for Infocomm Research (I2R), Singapore
Huang, Guimin	Guilin University of Electronic Technology, China
Huang, Hongzhao	Facebook

Huang, Jianbin   Xidian University, China
Huang, Minlie   Tsinghua University, China
Huang, Shujian   Nanjing University, China
Huang, Ting-Hao   Carnegie Mellon University, USA
Huang, Xuanjing   Fudan University, China
Huang, Zhongqiang   Raytheon BBN Technologies, USA
Jiang, Jing   Singapore Management University, Singapore
Jiang, Wenbin   Institute of Computing Technology, CAS, China
Jin, Peng   Leshan Normal University, China
Kano, Yoshinobu   Shizuoka University, China
Kit, Chunyu   City University of Hong Kong, SAR China
Kong, Fang   Soochow University, China
Kong, Lingpeng   Carnegie Mellon University, USA
Ku, Lun-Wei   Academia Sinica, Taiwan
Kwong, Oi Yee   The Chinese University of Hong Kong, SAR China
Lan, Man   East China Normal University, China
Lan, Yanyan   Institute of Computing Technology, CAS, China
Lang, Jun   Alibaba Group
Li, Chenliang   Wuhan University, China
Li, Fangtao   Google
Li, Junhui   Soochow University, China
Li, Maoxi   JiangXi Normal University, China
Li, Peng   Institute of Information Engineering,
                        Chinese Academy of Sciences, China
Li, Ru   ShanXi University, China
Li, Shoushan   Soochow University, China
Li, Sujian   Peking University, China
Li, Wenjie   The Hong Kong Polytechnic University, SAR China
Li, Yuan-Fang   Monash University, Australia
Li, Zhenghua   Soochow University, China
Lian, Defu   University of Electronic Science and Technology of China
Liang, Shuailong   Singapore University of Technology and Design, Singapore
Lin, Chenghua   University of Aberdeen, UK
Liu, Bingquan   Harbin Institute of Technology, China
Liu, Cheng-Lin   Institute of Automation, CAS, China
Liu, Jiangming   Singapore University of Technology and Design, Singapore
Liu, Kang   Institute of Automation, Chinese Academy of Sciences, China
Liu, Qi   University of Science and Technology of China
Liu, Qun   Dublin City University, Ireland
Liu, Shujie   Microsoft Research, China
Liu, Yang   Shandong University, China
Liu, Yang   Tsinghua University, China
Liu, Yijia   Harbin Institute of Technology, China
Liu, Yiqun   Tsinghua University, China
Liu, Zhiyuan   Tsinghua University, China
Lu, Bin   City University of Hong Kong, SAR China

Luo, Zhunchen	China Defense Science and Technology Information Center, China
Lv, Chen	Wuhan University, China
Ma, Yanjun	Baidu
Melo, Gerard de	Tsinghua University, China
Ng, Vincent	The University of Texas at Dallas, USA
Peng, Zhaohui	Shandong University, China
Qi, Guilin	Southeast University, China
Qin, Bing	Harbin Institute of Technology, China
Qiu, Xipeng	Fudan University, China
Qu, Weiguang	Nanjing Normal University, China
Ren, Xiang	University of Illinois at Urbana-Champaign, USA
Ren, Yafeng	Singapore University of Technology and Design, Singapore
Shi, Chuan	Beijing University of Posts and Telecommunications, China
Shi, Xiaodong	Xiamen University, China
Song, Ruihua	Microsoft Research, China
Song, Wei	Capital Normal University, China
Su, Jinsong	Xiamen University, China
Sun, Aixin	Nanyang Technological University, Singapore
Sun, Chengjie	Harbin Institute of Technology, China
Sun, Guangzhong	University of Science and Technology of China
Sun, Xu	Peking University, China
Sun, Yizhou	Northeastern University, USA
Tang, Duyu	Harbin Institute of Technology, China
Tang, Jian	Microsoft Research, China
Tang, Zhi	Peking University, China
Teng, Zhiyang	Singapore University of Technology and Design, Singapore
Tseng, Yuen-Hsien	National Taiwan Normal University, Taiwan
Tu, Zhaopeng	Huawei Noah's Ark Lab, Hong Kong, SAR China
Vo, Duy Tin	Singapore University of Technology and Design, Singapore
Wan, Xiaojun	Peking University, China
Wang, Bin	Institute of Information Engineering, Chinese Academy of Sciences, China
Wang, Bo	Tianjin University, China
Wang, Chenguang	Peking University, China
Wang, Haofen	East China University of Science and Technology, China
Wang, Quan	Institute of Information Engineering, CAS, China
Wang, William Yang	Carnegie Mellon University, USA
Wang, Xiaojie	Beijing University of Posts and Telecommunications, China
Wang, Xin	Tianjin University, China
Wang, Zhe	Griffith University, Australia
Wang, Zhiguo	IBM Research, USA
Wei, Zhongyu	The University of Texas at Dallas, USA
Wu, Hua	Baidu
Wu, Le	Hefei University of Technology, China
Wu, Xiaofeng	Dublin City University, Ireland

Wu, Yunfang	Peking University, China
Xia, Rui	Nanjing University of Science and Technology, China
Xia, Yunqing	Tsinghua University, China
Xiao, Tong	Northeastern University, USA
Xiao, Yanghua	Fudan University, China
Xin, Xin	Beijing Institute of Technology, China
Xiong, Deyi	Soochow University, China
Xu, Jinan	Beijing Jiaotong University, China
Xu, Jun	Institute of Computing Technology, CAS, China
Xu, Peng	Google
Xu, Ruifeng	Harbin Institute of Technology, China
Xu, Weiran	Beijing University of Posts and Telecommunications, China
Yang, jie	Singapore University of Technology and Design, Singapore
Yang, Yang	Tsinghua University, China
Yin, Hongzhi	University of Queensland, Australia
Yin, Jianmin	Huaguang
Yu, Bei	Syracuse University, USA
Yu, Liang-Chih	Yangzhou University, China
Yuan, Nicholas	Microsoft Research
Zan, Hongying	Zhengzhou University, China
Zhang, Chengzhi	Nanjing University of Science and Technology, China
Zhang, Dakun	Toshiba
Zhang, Dongdong	Microsoft Research, Asia, China
Zhang, Fuzheng	Microsoft Research, Asia, China
Zhang, Jiajun	Institute of Automation, CAS, China
Zhang, Jing	Tsinghua University, China
Zhang, Joy Ying	Carnegie Mellon University, USA
Zhang, Junsong	Xiamen University, China
Zhang, Min	Tsinghua University, China
Zhang, Qi	Fudan University, China
Zhang, Wei	Institute for Infocomm Research (I2R), Singapore
Zhang, Xiaowang	Tianjin University, China
Zhang, Yue	Singapore University of Technology and Design, Singapore
Zhao, Hai	Shanghai Jiao Tong University, China
Zhao, Tiejun	Harbin Institute of Technology, China
Zhao, Wayne Xin	Renmin University of China, China
Zheng, Kai	University of Queensland, Australia
Zhou, Deyu	Southeast University, China
Zhou, Guodong	Soochow University, China
Zhou, Yu	University of Science and Technology of China
Zhu, Hengshu	Baidu
Zhu, Jiaqi	Institute of Software, CAS, China
Zhu, Jingbo	Northeastern University, USA
Zhu, Kenny	Shanghai Jiao Tong University, China

Organizers

Organized by

China Computer Federation, China

Hosted by

Kunming University of Science
and Technology

State Key Laboratory of Digital Publishing

Publishers

ACTA Scientiarum Naturalium Universitatis Pekinensis

Lecture Notes in Artificial Intelligence Springer

In Cooperation with

Asian Federation of Natural   Chinese and Oriental Language Computer Society
Language Processing

Sponsoring Institutions

Microsoft Research Asia

DeepShare

Baidu Inc.

GridSum

Sogou Inc.

RSVP Technologies Inc.

NiuTrans

Contents

Machine Learning for NLP

Information Extraction, Question Answering and Knowledge Acquisition

Discourse Analysis

NLP for Social Media

Short Papers

Shared Tasks

Short Papers

Fundamentals on Language Computing

Integrating Structural Context with Local Context for Disambiguating Word Senses

Qianlong Du[1,2], Chengqing Zong[1,2(✉)], and Keh-Yih Su[3]

[1] National Laboratory of Pattern Recognition, Institute of Automation,
Chinese Academy of Science, Beijing, China
{qianlong.du, cqzong}@nlpr.ia.ac.cn
[2] University of Chinese Academy of Sciences, Beijing, China
[3] Institute of Information Science, Academia Sinica, Taipei, Taiwan
kysu@iis.sinica.edu.tw

Abstract. A novel word sense disambiguation (WSD) discriminative model is proposed in this paper to handle *long distance sense dependency* and *multi-reference lexicon dependency* (i.e., the sense of a lexicon might depend on several other non-local lexicons under the same subtree) within the sentence. Many WSD systems only adopt local context to independently decide the sense of each lexicon in a sentence. However, the sense of a target word actually also depends on those structure related sense/lexicons that might be far away from it. Therefore, we propose a supervised approach which integrates *structural context* (for long distance sense dependency and multi-reference lexicon dependency) with the local context (for local dependency) to handle the problems mentioned above. As the result, the sense of each word is decided not only based on the local lexicons, but also based on various reference sense/lexicons (might be *non-local*) specified by all its associated syntactic subtrees. Experimental results show that the proposed approach significantly outperforms other state-of-art WSD systems.

1 Introduction

Word sense disambiguation (WSD) is a process of determining the appropriate sense of a word in the given context. It is a fundamental task in natural language processing. Usually, we regard word sense disambiguation as an intermediate step, which could help high-level applications in NLP, such as machine translation (Carpuat and Wu 2005; Carpuat and Wu 2007; Chan et al. 2007), information retrieval (Stokoe et al. 2003) and content analysis (Berendt and Navigli 2006). With the help of WSD, it is expected to get a higher performance in these applications.

Among those proposed WSD systems, supervised approaches have achieved the best performance (Tratz et al. 2007; Hatori et al. 2009; Zhong and Ng 2010). And many of them simply extract lexicon related features from the local context around the target word, and then independently train a classifier on those features for each word (Zhong and Ng 2010). Therefore, the correlation between the senses of various words and the long distance dependency specified by the syntactic relation are not considered by them.

© Springer International Publishing AG 2016
C.-Y. Lin et al. (Eds.): NLPCC-ICCPOL 2016, LNAI 10102, pp. 3–15, 2016.
DOI: 10.1007/978-3-319-50496-4_1

4   Q. Du et al.

Fig. 1. Sample sentence and its dependency tree structure (Color figure online)

However, the senses of words do have influence on each other, and the non-local context also affects the sense selection. Furthermore, the dependency should be considered under the syntactic relation between them, as pointed out by Erk and Padó (2008). Also, the long distance dependency should not be covered by simply adopting a large context window, as it would involve a lot of irrelevant words and thus introduce considerable noise. What we really want is to only utilize those closely related non-local words specified by the syntactic structure, not those irrelevant words that are far away from the target word.

Take the following sentence as an example: "*Tom will join the board of the film company as a nonexecutive director*". The desired sense and the sense incorrectly assigned by Zhong and Ng (2010) of the word "*director*" in that sentence are listed as follows.

(a) *member of a board of directors* (desired sense)
(b) *the person who directs the making of a film* (wrongly assigned sense)

Figure 1 shows this sentence and its dependency tree structure, and we want to disambiguate the sense of the word "*director*" (marked in red color), which should be the sense-(a) illustrated above. After having analyzed this sentence, we found that the most important word (or the key-context-word) for deciding the sense of "*director*" is "*board*" (in blue color), and other words in this sentence are either less relevant or irrelevant for deciding its sense. If only the local context is adopted to disambiguate the senses of "director" in this case (Zhong and Ng 2010), then we need to use a 17-word window (centering on the target word "director") to extract the key word "*board*". In this way, many noisy irrelevant words (e.g. "*film*", "*company*", etc.) would be also involved. As the consequence, it will tag the word "*director*" with the incorrect sense "*the person who directs the making of a film*" because the sense-(b) of "*director*" usually co-occurs with the phrase "*film company*".

To take care of sense dependency, Hatori et al. (2009) had made use of the tree structure in their model. And they achieved a good precision with a small corpus. However, they merely adopted a simple dependency model in which the sense of each target word only depends on the sense of its *reference-head lexicon*. With only one reference sense, as shown in the dependency tree of Fig. 1, the sense of "*director*" will only depend on the sense of "*join*" (as it is the head). As the result, the sense of a head

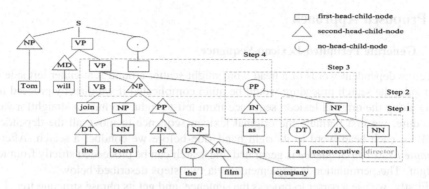

Fig. 2. The corresponding phrase structure tree

lexicon (e.g., "*director*" in Fig. 1) will not depend on any other *non-local lexicons* under the same subtree. Therefore, *multi-reference lexicon dependency* (which denotes that the sense of each word would also depend on its sibling lexicons under the same subtree) is not taken consideration (i.e., "*director*" will not be related to "*board*" in Fig. 2). In addition, they incorporated a large 60-word window which will import many irrelevant words (and involve considerable noisy features).

To handle the problems mentioned above, a novel approach which integrates *structural context* (which are the *head-lexicons* of those *child-nodes* under each associated syntactic subtree) with *local context* to disambiguate the word sense is proposed in this paper. This approach explicitly expresses the structural dependency between various senses via those associated syntactic subtrees, and let each word have one reference sense and various sibling reference lexicons under each associated subtree. Since a head word (e.g., a verb) might be simultaneously involved in several subtrees, it could have a different set of dependent lexicons under each associated subtree (e.g., a verb will be the head lexicon under both "*VP → VP NP*" and "*S → NP VP*" these two subtrees). Therefore, the sense of a head word would be decided via jointly considering all those associated lexicons under various syntactic relations.

Furthermore, we slightly modified the *head-percolation* rules (which specify a specific child-node under each subtree to percolate its head lexicon to the subtree root-node) to make them fit the WSD task better (e.g., for the PP-phrase "*as a nonexecutive director*" in Fig. 2, we regard "*director*", not "*as*", as the head of this *PP* so that "*director*" can be related to "*board*" under an upper level subtree "*VP → VB NP PP*").

In order to investigate the performance of our model, we conduct several experiments on all-words WSD tasks. The results show that our model is significantly better (in statistical sense) than other state-of-the-art approaches. It thus illustrates that the proposed structural context cannot be ignored.

2   Proposed Approach

2.1   Generate Permuted-Lexicon-Sequence

Since the dependent words of a head word might scatter around it at either left side or right side, the search procedure would be quite complicated if we directly proceed the WSD along the original lexicon sequence from left to right. To have a straightforward procedure, we first permute the original lexicon sequence to move all the dependent words of each head word to its right hand side before we conduct a search. After a *Permuted-Lexicon-Sequence* is generated, the search can be proceeded strictly from left to right. The permutation is implemented via two steps described below.

Firstly, we use a parser to process the sentence, and get its phrase structure tree. For each sub-tree, we specify its *first-head-child-node* and *second-head-child-node* according to a few simple pre-specified precedence rules (e.g., $VP > NP > PP > MD$, if they co-occur under the same parent node). The dependence between various *child-nodes* is specified as follows: (1) Let each *non-head-child-node* (if it exists) under the sub-tree depend on both the *first-head-child-node* and the *second-head-child-node* (denoted as *first-reference-lexicon* and *second-reference-lexicon*); (2) Let the *second-head-child-node* depend on the *first-head-child-node*. Afterwards, we generate its corresponding *Permuted-Lexicon-Sequence* by permuting all *child-nodes* into the order "*First-Head < Second-Head < NonHead*" from the left to the right. Furthermore, we move all those monosemous words under each subtree to the left side of its *first-head-child-node* (because they will not depend on any other *child-nodes* under the subtree, as each of them has only one sense under WordNet (WSD is thus not necessary)). Afterwards, we perform the decoding process on this *Permuted-Lexical-Sequence* from left to right.

To illustrate the permutation procedure, Fig. 2 shows the associated phrase structure tree (with the *head-child-nodes* marked) of the sentence given at Fig. 1. After having marked the *head-child-nodes* of each sub-tree, we can extract the associated structural context of the lexicon "*director*" via following 4 steps.

Step 1:   Regard the terminal-node "director" as the *first-head-child-node* of the sub-tree "*NN → director*", and it will be the head-lexicon of *NN*.

Step 2:   As "*JJ*" and "*NN*" are the *second-head-child-node* and the *first-head-child-node*, respectively, of the sub-tree "*NP → DT JJ NN*", "*director*" will be further percolated to the sub-tree root-node "*NP*". Also, the head-lexicon of "*JJ*" (i.e., the word "nonexecutive") will depend on the word "director" (which is the head-lexicon of "*NN*"). Besides, as "*DT*" in this sub-tree is a *non-head-child-node*, its head-lexicon (i.e., the word "*a*") will depend on both "*nonexecutive*" and "*director*" which are the head-lexicons of "*NN*" and "*JJ*", respectively (called as the *first-reference-lexicon* and the *second-reference-lexicon*). Since *NN* is the *first-head-child-node* under "*NP → DT JJ NN*", we will continuously traverse to its parent subtree "*PP → IN NP*"

Step 3:   In the subtree "*PP → IN NP*", "*IN*" and "*NP*" are the *second-head-child-node* and the *first-head-child-node*, respectively. The head lexicon of "*IN*" (i.e., the word "*as*") will depend on the head lexicon of "NP" (i.e., the word

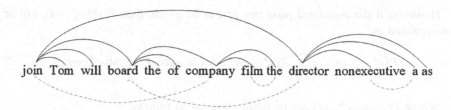

Fig. 3. The *Permuted-Lexical-Sequence* for the sample sentence in Fig. 1.

"*director*"). As "*NP*" is the *first-head-child-node* under "*PP* → *IN NP*", we traverse again to its parent subtree "*VP* → *VB NP PP*".

Step 4:   In the subtree "*VP* → *VB NP PP*", "*VB*" and "*NP*" are the *first-head-child-node* and the *second-head-child-node*, respectively. As "*PP*" is a *non-head-child-node*, the head lexicon of it (i.e., the target word "*director*") will depend on both the head-lexicons of "*VB*" and "*NP*" (the *first-reference-lexicon* and *second-reference-lexicon* of this subtree). Besides, the *second-reference-lexicon* (i.e., the word "*board*") also depends on the *first-reference-lexicon* (i.e., the word "*join*"). As "*PP*" is not the *first-head-child-node* of current subtree, the traversing procedure stops; otherwise, we will keep going until we reach the root of the whole tree.

Based on the method described above, we can find the dependency relationship between various terminal nodes of the parse tree in Fig. 2. Figure 3 shows the associated *Permuted-Lexicon-Sequence* of that sentence, in which the black arc denotes the first reference dependency and the red arc denotes the second reference dependency.

2.2   Proposed Model

The task of WSD is to determine the correct senses of words in the given context. Given a sentence *snt*, let w_1^m denote the sequence of words $(w_1, w_2, \ldots, w_m)$ within the sentence to be assigned their senses, and s_1^m denote the corresponding sense sequence for w_1^m, then the word sense disambiguation problem can be formulated as: $\widehat{s_1^m} = \arg\max_{s_1^m} P(s_1^m | w_1^m, snt)$, where m is the number of words to be assigned senses[1]. In the discriminative model adopted by Zhong and Ng (2010), the above $P(s_1^m | w_1^m, snt)$ is derived as follows.

$$P(s_1^m | w_1^m, snt) = \prod_{i=1}^{m} P(s_i | s_1^{i-1}, w_1^m, snt) \approx \prod_{i=1}^{m} P(s_i | w_i, snt) \qquad (1)$$

---

[1] Which words should be assigned senses depends on the given task.

However, if the associated parse-tree pt can be given, then $P(s_1^m|w_1^m, snt)$ will be re-formulated as:

$$P(s_1^m|w_1^m, snt) = \sum_{pt} P(s_1^m, pt|w_1^m, snt) \approx max_{Pt} P(s_1^m, pt|w_1^m, snt) \qquad (2)$$

Where $P(s_1^m, pt|w_1^m, snt)$ can be further derived as follows.

$$P(s_1^m, pt|w_1^m, snt) = P(s_1^m|w_1^m, snt, pt) \times P(pt|snt) \qquad (3)$$

We will first permute those m lexicons into its corresponding *Permuted-Lexicon-Sequence* LX_1^m according to the dependency relationship specified by the associated *parse-tree*. With LX_1^m specified above, $P(s_1^m|w_1^m, snt, pt)$ can be replaced with $P(LXS_1^m|LX_1^m, snt, pt)$, where LXS_1^m denotes a specific sense sequence assigned to LX_1^m.

It is reasonable to assume that the sense assignment of each lexicon mainly depends on its local context and its structural context specified by the *parse-tree*. In the above formulation, for each permuted lexicon LX_i in LX_1^m, we will find its original location in the given sentence (call it <i>), and then extract its associated local context vector CLX_i which is a window $[w_{<i>-K}^{<i>+K}]$ around $w_{<i>}$ (which is LX_i) with the length "$2K + 1$" (including $w_{<i>}$). Take the following sentence as an example:

(i)   He works in a bank in the capital of his hometown.

For the word "*bank*" in this sentence, if we set K to 3, the local context will be the phrase "*works in a bank in the capital*". We will extract the position, POS, word form and local collocations (specified at (Zhong and Ng 2010)) of each word from them (even they are not specified in WordNet). Take the word at the position <−2> (i.e., the word "*in*" at the left side) as an example, it is not defined in WordNet as it is not a content word; however, it still helps our disambiguation task, because it usually co-occurs with the "*bank*" when its sense is "*a building in which the business of banking transacted*".

Besides the local context, we also extract the *structural context sequence* of each lexicon from all its associated syntactic subtrees. Take the target word "*director*" in Fig. 2 as an example, the procedure of extracting its structural lexicons is described as follows. In the Step 2 specified in the previous section, it shows that the associated context words under the sub-tree "*NP → DT JJ NN*" are "*a*" and "*nonexecutive*" (the head lexicons of "*DT*" and "*JJ*"). In the Step 3, we get only one associated context word "*as*" (the head lexicons of "*IN*") under the sub-tree "*PP → IN NP*". Finally, in the Step 4, the associated context words obtained under the sub-tree "*VP → VB NP PP*" are "*join*" and "*board*" (the head lexicons of "*VB*" and "*NP*"). Those extracted words make up the structural context sequence "*join board as a nonexecutive director*", and we can see that this sequence includes the key-lexicon "*board*" for disambiguating the sense of "*director*" without importing too many irrelevant words (such as "*the*", "*of*", "*the*", "*film*" and "*company*", if a large local context window is adopted). We will pack the lemmas, *POS*es and collocations of those words in this sequence as the *structural-lexicon-dependency* feature (denoted as *SLX*) to improve the performance.

Also, for each permuted lexicon LX_i, and for each subtree that it is involved, the *first-reference-lexicon* and *second-reference-lexicon* under the subtree will also be specified according to the procedure mentioned in Sect. 2.1. For each associated subtree, use the *Reference-Sense-Tuple* <*first-reference-lexicon-sense, second-reference-lexicon,* associated *production-rule*> to denote its corresponding structural context. The associated *structure-reference-information* for LX_i (denoted by $RXSI_i$) is then a set of such tuples derived from all its associated subtrees. Take the word "*director*" in Fig. 2 as an example, its *structure-reference-information* $RXSI_i$ will involve three subtrees (i.e., "*NP → DT JJ NN*", "*PP → IN NP*" and "*VP → VB NP PP*"). And the corresponding tuple for the subtree "*VP → VB NP PP*" would be <*assigned sense of* "*join*", "*board*", " *VP → VB NP PP*">.

Assume that the assignment of the lexicon sense LXS_i (for LX_i) only depends on its *local context vector* CLX_i, *structural lexicon information* SLX_i and its associated *structure-reference-information* $RXSI_i$. Let $RLXI_i$ denote the associated set of *Reference-Lexicon-Tuple* (which is obtained by replacing the first element "*first-reference-lexicon-sense*" of the corresponding *reference-sense-tuple* with "*first-reference-lexicon*"), then $RXSI_i$ can be obtained from $RLXI_i$ after all associated "*first-reference-lexicon-sense*" are given. Let t_1^m denote the corresponding POS-sequence for LX_1^m, then the original probability factor $P(LXS_1^m | LX_1^m, snt, pt)$ can be derived as follows.

$$P(LXS_1^m | LX_1^m, snt, pt)$$
$$\approx P(LXS_1^m | LX_1^m, t_1^m, CLX_1^m, SLX_1^m, RLXI_1^m)$$
$$\approx \prod_{i=1}^{m} P(LXS_i | LX_i, t_i, CLX_i,, SLX_i, LXS_1^{i-1}, RLXI_i)$$
$$\approx \prod_{i=1}^{m} P(LXS_i | LX_i, t_i, CLX_i, SLX_i, RXSI_i)$$
(4)

To enhance the coverage rate of the test set, we will pool the training samples of various word-types (i.e., different LX_i) together by replacing their *LXS* and *first-reference-lexicon-sense* (in the tuple of *RLXI*) with their corresponding *synsets* defined in WordNet 3.1 (i.e., replacing "$P(LXS_i | LX_i, t_i, CLX_i, SLX_i, RXSI_i)$" with "$P(synset_i | t_i, CLX_i, SLX_i, RXSI_i)$" in Eq. (4), in which LX_i has been dropped).

3 Evaluation

3.1 Data Sets

We train various models on Semcor corpus (Miller et al. 1993), and then conduct word sense disambiguation experiments on the test sets of senseval-2 (Palmer et al. 2001) and senseval-3 (Snyder and Palmer 2004). We choose these corpora because they are frequently used in evaluating WSD performance in the literature; and the quality of these corpora is good (Navigli 2009).

Semcor corpus is constructed via annotating a subset of the English Brown Corpus (Kucera and Francis 1967) with WordNet synsets (Miller et al. 1990; Fellbaum 1998). It is the largest publicly available sense-tagged corpus. And we select two all-words test sets from Semantic Evaluation (Palmer et al. 2001; Snyder and Palmer 2004) (i.e., senseval-2 and senseval-3) as the test sets. These two testing sets are from WSJ articles and Brown Corpus.

3.2   Experiments

Experimental Setup. We first use the *Berkeley parser*[2] to process the sentences extracted from the Semcor corpus (Miller et al. 1993) to get the phrase structure trees. As some of the sub-trees we parsed only have one child node, we will use the approach described in (Su et al. 1995) to normalize the trees. After this step, all the sub-trees (except the leaf nodes) in the phrase structure trees will have at least two child nodes.

We then mark the *head-child-node* for each sub-tree in the phrase structure trees. The rules that specify which syntactic label in the sub-tree should be the *head-child-node* are taken from *Penn2Malt*[3]. Afterwards, with the method presented in Sect. 2.1, we will permute the original sentence into its corresponding *Permuted-Lexicon-Sequence*. During the permutation, we also extract the *structural dependency* features and contextual features described in Sect. 2.2 from the phrase structure subtrees. We then use those *structural context* and *local contextual* features to train a *Maximum Entropy Classifier*[4]. When a test sentence is encountered, we will first obtain its *Permuted-Lexicon-Sequence*, as mentioned above, and then proceed the decoding on the *Permuted-Lexicon-Sequence*.

Results and Analysis. Tables 1 and 2 show the performance of our system on senseval-2 and senseval-3 data-sets, respectively. In order to compare with those state-of-the-art systems, we also add those participants that were ranked within Top-2 in SE2 all-words task into Tables 1 and 2 (the WordNet Most Frequent Sense "*MFS*" is also added as the lower bound). Those official scores are extracted from (Taghipour and Ng 2015) and (Tartz et al. 2007). It should be noted that some systems (except IMS, T-CRF and our model) use additional training corpus, while we just use the Semcor corpus (Miller et al. 1993) as our training set. For example, "IMS + adapted CW" (Taghipour and Ng 2015) adopted additional six parallel corpora and DSO corpus (Ng and Lee 1996) as the training set, besides, it used three large corpus to train the required word embedding; and "PNNL" use additional OMWE 1.0 (Chklovski and Mihalcea 2002) and example sentences in WordNet as the training corpus. Therefore, their performances cannot be directly compared with that of ours (i.e., only IMS and T-CRF can be directly compared).

---

[2] http://nlp.cs.berkeley.edu/software.shtml.

[3] http://stp.lingfil.uu.se/ ~ nivre/research/Penn2Malt.html.

[4] http://homepages.inf.ed.ac.uk/lzhang10/maxent.html.

Table 1. SE2 all-words task results. The improvement of our model over the IMS baseline is statistically significant (p < 0.05).

	SE2
IMS	68.75%
Our model	69.59%
Rank-1 system (Palmer et al. 2001)	69.0%
Rank-2 system (Palmer et al. 2001)	63.6%
MFS	61.9%

Table 2. SE3 all-words task results. The improvement of our model over the IMS baseline is statistically significant (p < 0.05).

	SE3
IMS	64.58%
T-CRF (Hatori et al. 2009)	65.40%
Our model	66.04%
IMS + adapted CW (Taghipour and Ng 2015)	68.20%
PNNL (Tartz et al. 2007)	67.00%
MFS	62.37%

From these two tables, we can see that the performance has been improved significantly (p < 0.05) over the baseline on both datasets. This shows that the *structural context* features are very useful for WSD. Table 3 investigates the individual contribution from each set of those adopted feature sets (i.e., *local context* features, *structural sense dependency* features, and *structural lexicon dependency* features), which shows that *local context* feature is the most effective feature set, but other two feature sets are also helpful.

Table 3 shows the effect of each feature on these two datasets. When we adopt just one type of feature, the *local context* feature is the best. This is because the associated *reference-lexicons* are within the *local context* window about 66% of the time (we got the ratio of reference lexicons within the *local context* window are 66.34% and 65.60% on SE2 and SE3, respectively). However, to further improve the performance, the remaining 34% cases with complex *structural dependency* should also be taken care. Besides, when we add the *structural context* features to the model, the improvement on senseval-3 is better than senseval-2 (In Table 3, when we add these two *structural*

Table 3. The performance for each dependency relation on these two datasets

Feature type	SE2	SE3
Local-context (*baseline*)	68.75%	64.58%
Structural-lexicon-dependency	63.20%	63.90%
Structural-sense-dependency	57.50%	61.82%
Local-context + structural-lexicon-dependency	69.04%	64.73%
Local-context + structural-sense-dependency	69.03%	65.84%
Local-context + structural-lexicon + structural-sense	69.59%	66.04%

context features, the improvement on SE3 is *1.46%* while the improvement on SE2 is just *0.84%*). The reason for that is that senseval-3 contains more words whose dependency relation is complex (As we calculated, the ratio of reference lexicons without local context window on SE3 is bigger than the ratio on SE2).

In Table 4, we present the performance of each *POS* on Senseval2 all-words task. From this tables, we find that the influences of structural context on each *POS* category are different. The distribution and size of the samples may have an influence on the results, however, we can still see that it can improve the performance of *noun* and *verb* words significantly. And it also has a little positive influence on *adj* and *adv* words. This is also true for SE3. This phenomenon matches the observation that the *long distance dependency* and *multi-reference dependency* usually exist between *verb* and *noun* words, while the *adj* and *adv* words frequently only depend on the local context. As the use of *structural lexicon dependency* features, we can see the performance of *adj* and *adv* words also improves. In summary, the *structural dependency* we proposed contributes more to the words with complex dependency relations.

Table 4. The performance for each *POS* on SE2 all-words task.

POS	SE2			
	Adj.	Noun	Verb	Adv.
#Tokens	404	1065	535	265
IMS	72.03%	75.39%	46.54%	81.89%
Our model	72.28%	75.96%	48.60%	82.26%
Diff.	+0.25%	+0.57%	+1.06%	+0.37%

4 Related Work

WSD is a well-known topic, and many related papers have been published. Navigli (2009) had given a good survey of this field. Based on the classification method adopted, the task of WSD could be divided into (1) Supervised (Tratz et al. 2007; Hatori et al. 2009; Zhong and Ng 2010; Chen et al. 2014), (2) Unsupervised (Agirre et al. 2014; Chen et al. 2009), and (3) Semi-supervised (Mihalcea 2004) approaches. Among them, the supervised approach gives the best performance so far. As our method is a supervised method for all-words WSD (Hatori et al. 2009; Zhong and Ng 2010; Taghipour and Ng 2015), we will focus and introduce this kind of approaches in the following.

Zhong and Ng (2010) proposed a WSD system based on supervised learning, and achieved state-of-the-art results on several Senseval and Semeval evaluations. They adopted POS tags, content words and collocations in a 7-word local window as features, and used a SVM to perform classification. In comparison with our approach, they ignored the structural dependency and did not consider the correlation between various senses.

On the other hand, Hatori et al. (2009) considered the structural dependency (via a dependency tree) in addition to the local context mentioned above. They described these dependencies on the tree-structured conditional random fields. Furthermore, they incorporated these sense dependencies in combination with various coarse-grained sense tag sets, which are expected to relieve the data sparseness problem, and enable their model to work even for words that do not appear in the training data. Their approach was shown to be comparable to those state-of-the-art systems on Senseval data-sets. In comparison with our approach, they adopted a large 60-word context window, which would involve many irrelevant words and thus introduce additional noisy information. Also, each sense only depends on one reference sense in their model, which is inadequate in many cases.

5 Conclusion

To correctly classify each content word in the sentence, not only *local context* but also *structural context* (which is mainly responsible for handling long distance sense/ lexicon dependency) is required. To take the *structural context* into account without introducing too much additional noisy information, we propose a new approach to describe various syntactic dependency relations between different words. In this approach, after parsing a sentence into its phrase structure tree, we mark two *head-child-nodes* under each sub-tree. Then we can use these *head-child-nodes* and syntactic subtrees to describe the *long distance dependency* and *multi-reference dependency* (which lets each target word be capable of depending on several *non-local* words).

Our contributions include: (1) Proposing a novel model to represent different dependency relations between various senses, which is able to handle the long distance *multi-reference dependency* that has not been touched in those previous WSD tasks. (2) Proposing a way to permute the original lexicon sequence to improve the search efficiency. (3) Showing that the structural dependency relations are useful for distinguish the senses of words with complex dependency relations.

Acknowledgements. The research work has been funded by the Natural Science Foundation of China under Grant No. 61333018.

References

Agirre, E., de Lacalle, O.L., Soroa, A.: Random walks for knowledge-based word sense disambiguation. Comput. Linguist. **40**(1), 57–84 (2014)

Miller, G.A., Beckwith, R., Fellbaum, C.D., Gross, D., Miller, K.: WordNet: an online lexical database. Int. J. Lexicograph **3**(4), 235–244 (1990)

Berendt, B., Navigli, R.: Finding your way through blogspace: using semantics for cross-domain blog analysis. In: Proceedings of American Association for Artificial Intelligence, pp. 1–8 (2006)

Carpuat, M., Wu, D.: Word sense disambiguation vs. statistical machine translation. In: Proceedings of 43rd Annual Meeting of the ACL, pp. 387–394 (2005)

Carpuat, M., Wu, D.: Improving statistical machine translation using word sense disambiguation. In: Proceedings of 2007 Joint Conference on Empirical Methods in Natural Language Processing and Computational Natural Language Learning, pp. 61–72 (2007)

Chan, Y.S., Ng, H.T., Chang, D.: Word sense disambiguation improves statistical machine translation. In: Proceedings of 45th Annual Meeting of the Association of Computational Linguistics, pp. 33–40 (2007)

Chen, P., Ding, W., Bowes, C., Brown, D.: A fully unsupervised word sense disambiguation method using dependency knowledge. In: Human Language Technologies: The 2009 Annual Conference of the North American Chapter of the ACL, pp. 28–36 (2009)

Chen, X., Liu, Z., Sun, M.: A unified model for word sense representation and disambiguation. In: Proceedings of 2014 Conference on Empirical Methods in Natural Language Processing (EMNLP), pp. 1025–1035 (2014)

Chklovski, T., Mihalcea, R.: Building a sense tagged corpus with open mind word expert. In: Proceedings of ACL-2002 Workshop on Word Sense Disambiguation: Recent Successes and Future Directions (2002)

Fellbaum, C.: WordNet: An Electronic Database. MIT Press, Cambridge (1998)

Erk, K., Pado, S.: A structured vector space model for word meaning in context. In: Proceedings of 2008 Conference on Empirical Methods in Natural Language Processing, pp. 897–906 (2008)

Gale, W.A., Church, K.W., Yarowsky, D.: A method for disambiguation word senses in a corpus. Comput. Human. **26**(5–6), 415–439 (1992)

Hatori, J., Miyao, Y., Tsujii, J.: On contribution of sense dependencies to word sense disambiguation. Inf. Med. Technol. **4**(4), 1129–1155 (2009)

Mihalcea, R., Tarau, P., Figa, E.: PageRank on semantic networks, with application to word sense disambiguation. In: Proceedings of 20th International Conference on Computational Linguistics. Association for Computational Linguistics (2004)

Miller, G.A., Leacock, C., Tengi, R., Bunker, R.T.: A semantic concordance. In: Proceedings of Workshop on Human Language Technology (1993)

Navigli, R.: Word sense disambiguation: a survey. ACM Comput. Surv. **41**(2), 1–69 (2009). Article no. 10

Ng, H.T., Lee, H.B.: Integrating multiple knowledge sources to disambiguate word sense: an exemplar-based approach. In: Proceeding of 34th Annual Meeting of the Association for Computational Linguistic (ACL), pp. 40–47 (1996)

Palmer, M., Fellbaum, C., Cotton, S., Delfs, L., Dang, H.T.: English tasks: all-words and verb lexical sample. In: Proceedings of 2nd International Workshop on Evaluating Word Sense Disambiguation Systems (SENESEVAL-2) (2001)

Snyder, B., Palmer, M.: The English all-words task. In: Senseval-3: 3rd International Workshop on the Evaluation of the Systems for the Semantic Analysis of Text (2004)

Stokoe, C., Oakes, M.P., Tait, J.: Word sense disambiguation in information retrieval revisited. In: Proceedings of 26th Annual International ACM SIGIR Conference on Research and Development in Information Retrieval (SIGIR), pp. 159–166 (2003)

Su, K.-Y., Chang, J.-S., Hsu, Y.-L.U.: A corpus-based statistic-oriented two-way design for parameterized MT systems: rationale, architecture and training issues. In: Proceedings of 6th International Conference on Theoretical and Methodological Issues in Machine Translation (TMI-1995), Leuven, Belgium, vol. 2, pp. 334–353 (1995)

Taghipour, K., Ng, H.T.: Semi-supervised word sense disambiguation using word embeddings in general and specific domains. In: The 2015 Annual Conference of the North American Chapter of the Association for Computational Linguistics (2015)

Tratz, S., Sanfilippo, A., Gregory, M., Chappell, A., Posse, C., Whitney, P.: PNNL: a supervised maximum entropy approach to word sense disambiguation. In: Proceedings of 4th International Workshop on Semantic Evaluations (SemEval-2007), pp. 264–267 (2007)

Turing, M.: Computing machinery and intelligence. Mind **54**, 443–460 (1950)

Wasserman-Pritsker, E., Cohen, W.W., Minkov, E.: Learning to identify the best contexts for knowledge-based WSD

Zhong, Z., Ng, H.T.: It makes sense: a wide-coverage word sense disambiguation system for free text. In: Proceedings of ACL 2010 System Demonstrations (2010)

Tibetan Multi-word Expressions Identification Framework Based on News Corpora

Minghua Nuo[1(✉)], Congjun Lun[2,3], and Huidan Liu[3]

[1] College of Computer Science-College of Software Engineering,
Inner Mongolia University, Hohhot, China
nuominghua@163.com
[2] Institute of Ethnology and Anthropology,
Chinese Academy of Social Sciences, Beijing, China
[3] Institute of Software, Chinese Academy of Sciences, Beijing, China
{congjun,huidan}@iscas.ac.cn

Abstract. This paper presents an identification framework for extracting Tibetan multi-word expressions. The framework includes two phases. In the first phase, sentences are segmented and high-frequency word-based n-grams are extracted using Nagao's N-gram statistical algorithm and Statistical Substring Reduction Algorithm. In the second phase, the Tibetan MWEs are identified by the proposed framework which based on the combination of context analysis and language model-based analysis. Context analysis, two-word Coupling Degree and Tibetan syllable inside word probability are three strategies in Tibetan MWE identification framework. In experimental part, we evaluate the effectiveness of three strategies on small test data, and evaluate results of different granularity for Context analysis. On small test corpus, F-score above 75% have been achieved when words are segmented in pre-processing. On larger corpus, the P@N (N is 800) overcomes 85%. It indicates that the identification framework can work well on larger corpus. The experimental result reaches acceptable performance for Tibetan MWEs.

Keywords: Tibetan Multi-word expression · Two-word coupling degree · Inside word probability

1 Introduction

In real-life human communication, meaning is often conveyed by word groups, or meaning groups, rather than by single words. Such word groups or multi-word expressions (MWE hereafter) can be described as *a sequence of words that acts as a single unit at some level of linguistic analysis*. MWEs are frequently used in everyday language, usually to precisely express ideas and concepts that cannot be compressed into a single word. As a consequence, their identification is a crucial issue for applications that require some degree of semantic processing (e.g. machine translation, summarization, information retrieval). Very often, it is difficult to interpret human speech word by word. Consequently, for an MT system, it is important to identify and interpret accurate meaning of such word groups, or multi-word expressions, in a source

© Springer International Publishing AG 2016
C.-Y. Lin et al. (Eds.): NLPCC-ICCPOL 2016, LNAI 10102, pp. 16–26, 2016.
DOI: 10.1007/978-3-319-50496-4_2

language and interpret them accurately in a target language. However, accurate identification and interpretation of MWEs still remains an unsolved problem in Tibetan natural language processing research.

The Tibetan alphabet is syllabic, like many of the alphabets of India and South East Asia. Each letter has an inherent vowel /a/. Other vowels can be indicated using a variety of diacritics which appear above or below the main letter. A syllable contains one or up to seven character(s). Syllables are separated by a marker known as "tsheg", which is simply a superscripted dot. Linguistic words are made up of one or more syllables and are also separated by the same symbol, "tsheg", thus there is a lack of word boundaries in the language. Consonant clusters are written with special conjunct letters. Figure 1 shows the structure of a Tibetan word which is made up of two syllables and means "show" or "exhibition".

terday	man	rich	this	house	expensive	an	bought	did
terday this rich man bought an expensive house.

Fig. 1. Structure of a Tibetan word   **Fig. 2.** A Tibetan sentence and its translation

Tibetan sentence consists of one or more words, phrases or multi-word units. Another marker known as "shad" indicates the sentence boundary, which looks like a vertical pipe. Figure 2 shows a Tibetan sentence. It is segmented in line 2 and word by word translation is given in line 3.

In this paper, we present Tibetan MWE identification framework. The rest of this paper is organized as follows. In Sect. 2 we recall related work on multi-word expression extraction methods. Section 3 describes the outline of our framework. We propose the details of framework in Sect. 4. Then, in Sect. 5 we make experiments for evaluation. Section 6 concludes the paper.

2 Related Work

The issue of MWE processing has attracted much attention from the Natural Language Processing (NLP) community, including [1–13]. Study in this area covers a wide range of sub-issues, including MWE identification and extraction from monolingual and multilingual corpora, classification of MWEs according to a variety of viewpoints such as types, compositionality and alignment of MWEs across different languages. Directly related to our work is the development of a statistical MWE tool at Lancaster for searching and identifying English MWEs in running text [14, 15] Trained on corpus data in a given domain, this tool can automatically identify MWEs in running text or extract MWEs from corpus data from the similar domain. It has been tested and compared with an English semantic tagger [16] and was found to be efficient in identifying domain-specific MWEs in English corpora, and complementary to the semantic tagger which relies on a large manually compiled lexicon. Extraction of Chinese multi-word expressions from corpus resources as part of a larger research effort to improve a machine translation (MT) system is reported in [17].

However, Tibetan MWE processing still presents a tough challenge, and it has been receiving increasing attention. In Tibetan information processing, the shortage of Tibetan language resource leads to the fact that most of the techniques related text processing are still developing. Recently, the focus of Tibetan information processing is gradually transferred from word processing to text processing. The Tibetan text processing started in the early 1990s, mainly analyze statically at the beginning. Since 2003, research on Tibetan syntactic chunks [18–20] is reported. Since 2010, Nuo et al. do research on chunk, multi-word equivalence for Chinese-Tibetan machine translation system. Nuo et al. [21] construct Chinese-Tibetan multi-word equivalence dictionary for Chinese-Tibetan computer-aided translation system. They present an identification framework for extracting Tibetan base noun phrase in [22]. So far, there is no Tibetan parser. We have built large scale Tibetan text resources recently, and we are tagging Part-Of-Speech and labeling role right now, these corpora can form our training set and test data. This paper presents identification of Tibetan MWEs using statistical methods.

3 Brief Description of Tibetan MWE Identification Framework

The proposed Tibetan MWE identification framework consists of three main steps: pre-processing step, context analyzing step, and language model-based analysis for candidate n-grams, which are in boldface in Fig. 3. The two-word coupling degree dictionary and Tibetan syllables inside word probability dictionary are trained from annotated training corpus.

In pre-processing step, Tibetan corpus is word segmented and stored one sentence per line. High-frequency strings are extracted using Nagao's algorithm [23] and Substring Reduction Algorithm [24]. They are initial candidate MWE. These candidates determined to be a MWE based on their internal structure, pragmatic environment in the text and semantic features.

In the context analyzing step, we use adjacent characteristic to capture pragmatic environment in the text. We will calculate adjacent features such as adjacent categories, adjacent pair categories, adjacent entropy etc., if the result is lower than threshold, the candidate n-gram will be filtered as a noise; if higher, goes to the next step.

The final step is language model-based analysis step. Coupling Degree is used to measure internal formation of a MWE; it can help us to examine whether high-frequency string has a complete semantics or not. In this step, firstly, we scan the candidate n-gram string word by word, and search Coupling Degree of pair of adjacent words, if the result is less than the threshold; the word pair regarded as not a MWE but a noise and be removed. Secondly, find inside word probabilities to determine whether candidate string is started with or ended with common function words (i.e. stop words). We combine Coupling Degree of adjacent words with inside word probabilities to analyze candidate n-grams and remove the noises. Then output the remaining meaningful strings to a file, they are MWEs.

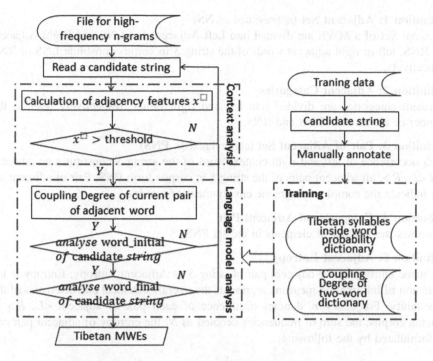

Fig. 3. Flow chart of Tibetan MWE identification framework

In next section, we describe in detail how to identify Tibetan MWEs. Different methods are evaluated, and we will select the method with best performance to generate referable Tibetan MWE.

4   Tibetan MWE Identification Based on the Combination of Context Analysis and Language Model-Based Analysis

In pre-processing stage, corpora text has been formatted and segmented. High-frequency repeated strings from large-scale corpus contain meaningful strings (i.e. MWE) as well as disturbance term (i.e. noises). The essence of extracting MWEs from corpus is to remove those noises from candidate n-grams. This section will detail the core steps of Tibetan MWE identification framework.

4.1   Context Analysis

Acting as a single unit, internal words in MWE are tightly related; external (or context) words of MWE are loosely related. Meaningful string as an independent language unit has a variety of different contexts in the real text. In order to describe the flexibility of the string S's context, we define a series of adjacent feature measures.

Definition 1: Adjacent Set (abbreviated as **NS**)
Adjacent Set of a MWE are divided into Left Adjacent Set LNS and Right Adjacent Set RNS, left or right adjacent words of the string S in corpus constitute LNS or RNS respectively.

Definition 2: Adjacent Categories
Adjacent categories are divided into left and right either, respectively refer to the number of elements in LNS and RNS.

Definition 3: Pair of Adjacent Set (abbreviated as **PNS**)
Each occurrence of left and right context word of the string S constitutes an adjacent pair $<L_i, R_i>$, all adjacent pairs of the string S in corpus form PNS. Pair of adjacent set can indicate the complete pragmatic environment of a string.

Definition 4: Categories of Adjacent Pair
It denotes the number of elements in the set PNS.

Definition 5: Adjacent Entropy
We name entropy of the adjacent pair of string S as Adjacent Entropy; Entropy is the basic unit of information measure, represents the overall statistical characteristics of the uncertainty. Frequency n_i denotes occurrence of each pair of adjacent $<L_i, R_i>$ in Tibetan corpus; the sum of frequencies denoted as N, the entropy of adjacent pair can be formulated by the following:

$$E_L = -\sum_{i=1}^{|V_L|} \frac{n_i}{n} \log(\frac{n_i}{n}) \tag{1}$$

The greater adjacent entropy is, the more flexible pragmatic environment of string S is; so that it is more likely to be a meaningful string. When the corpus smaller, types of adjacent is relatively small, entropy's ability to distinguish become poor.

4.2   Two-Word Coupling Degree

For each adjacent pair of words (w_1, w_2), the Coupling Degree (short for CD) is measured by the following formula:

$$CD(w1, w2) = \frac{VMI(w1, w2)}{H(w1) + H(w2)} \tag{2}$$

where VMI is a variant of average mutual information; w_1, w_2 represent occurrence of words. VMI is defined as follows:

$$\begin{aligned}
VMI(w1, w2) = {} & P(w1, w2) \log \frac{P(w1, w2)}{P(w1)P(w2)} + P(\overline{w1}, \overline{w2}) \log \frac{P(\overline{w1}, \overline{w2})}{P(\overline{w1})P(\overline{w2})} \\
& -P(w1, \overline{w2}) \log \frac{P(w1, \overline{w2})}{P(w1)P(\overline{w2})} - P(\overline{w1}, w2) \log \frac{P(\overline{w1}, w2)}{P(\overline{w1})P(w2)}
\end{aligned} \tag{3}$$

In this formula, $P(w1, w2)$ is the probability of sentences where both w_1 and w_2 adjacently occur. $P(\overline{w1}, \overline{w2})$ is the probability of sentences where both w_1 and w_2 won't occur. $P(w1, \overline{w2})$ is the probability of sentences where w_1 occur with other right-hand adjacent word but not w_2. $P(\overline{w1}, w2)$ is the probability of sentences where w_2 occur with other left-hand adjacent word but not w_1.

The denominator in $CD(w_1, w_2)$ is a smoothing factor. A high $VMI(w_1, w_2)$ value shows that w_1 and w_2 have strong tendency to appear together. It is possible that one or both of them are highly frequency words, where $H(w_1)$ and/or $H(w_2)$ have high values. Divided by this denominator, coupling degree of word pairs is decreased.

H refers to the entropy of a Tibetan syllable, defined as following formula:

$$H(s) = -[P(s)\lg P(s) + P(\overline{s})\lg P(\overline{s})] \tag{4}$$

4.3 Tibetan Syllable Inside Word Probability

Tibetan each syllable has its own unique word-formation usage; certain syllables are often in one or a few specific location (word-initial, word-medial, word-final) on compound words. This paper focuses on word-initial and word-final syllable and their probabilities to be a word.

Definition 6: inside word probability (short for IWP)
IWP is the probability of a sequence of two or more Tibetan syllables being a sequence of independent MWE. IWP is defined as follows:

$$P_{word}(c, pos) = \frac{N(c, pos)}{N(c, word)} \tag{5}$$

where value range of pos is 0 and 1; 0 indicates word-initial and 1 indicates word-final.

Makes statistics for N, N_1, N_2 of each syllable on word segmented corpus. N, N_1, N_2 denotes the total number, the number of occurrence in the word-initial and word-final position respectively; then word-initial IWP is the ratio of N_1 and N, word-final IWP is the ratio of N_2 and N.

Generally, a MWE begins with word-initial syllable of one word and must ends with word-final syllable of another word. When too low word-initial IWP is detected for the first syllable of a string, it might be noise. Similarly, when too low word-final IWP is detected for the last syllable of a string, we can regard it as a noise. This rule can effectively filter out disturbance term.

This comprehensive statistical filtering measure for n-gram syllable string is able to extract more correct MWE. The performance of different measures, including context analysis and language model-based analysis, on Tibetan MWE identification is given in experimental parts.

5 Experiments

5.1 Experimental Data

We conduct following experiments, on one hand, to validate effectiveness and feasibility of context analysis and the language model-based analysis; on the other hand, to test the ability of the framework on large-scale corpus. We have built 326,062,576-bytes Tibetan news corpus over the internet via an automatic crawler. They are from three web sites, that are, *Tibet Daily*, *People's Daily* and *Qinghai Daily*. We will utilize this Tibetan News Corpus to evaluate extracted Tibetan MWEs in Sect. 5.2.3. Part of this News Corpus is used in Sect. 5.2.1 and 5.2.2, which is randomly selected and has MWE manual checking results. The two-word coupling degree dictionary and Tibetan syllables inside word probability dictionary are trained from annotated training corpus (58 MB). Parameters (i.e. Thresholds) used in the experiment are listed in Table 1.

Table 1. Value of parameters in following experiment.

Parameter names	Function	Value
C_{max}	Two-word integration threshold	0.9
C_{min}	Two-word separation threshold	0.3
P_{inital}	Tibetan syllable word-initial estimation	0.4
P_{final}	Tibetan syllable word-final estimation	0.5

5.2 Evaluation

We will evaluate the precision (P), recall (R), f-score (F) of Tibetan MWE identification in experimental part.

$$P = N_1/N_2 \tag{6}$$

$$R = N_1/N_3 \tag{7}$$

$$F = 2PR/(P+R) \tag{8}$$

where N_1 denotes the number of correctly segmented Tibetan MWEs; N_2 denotes total number of segmented Tibetan MWEs; N_3 denotes the total number of Tibetan MWEs in testing texts.

5.2.1 Evaluation for Different Strategies in Identifying Framework

Context analysis, two-word Coupling Degree and Tibetan syllable inside word probability are three strategies in Tibetan MWE identification framework. In this subsection, we will measure the different combination of these three strategies without segmentation for pre-processing. In Table 2, CNG indicates candidate n-grams, CA indicates context analysis, CD indicates Coupling Degree, IWP indicate inside word probability.

Table 2. Results for different combination of three strategies.

Different combination	P	R	F
CNG	0.03	1.0	5.83%
CNG + CA	0.09	0.70	15.95%
CNG + CD	0.04	0.94	7.67%
CNG + IWP	0.05	0.89	9.47%
CNG + CA + CD	0.13	0.70	21.93%
CNG + CA + IWP	0.20	0.68	30.91%
CNG + CD + IWP	0.05	0.87	9.46%
CNG + CA + CD + IWP	0.41	0.67	50.87%

Table 2 illustrates the comparison results for various combinations of three strategies. CNG is the baseline, the f-score of CA is the best when these strategies independently used. It means CA is most effective. IWP is better than CD; the recall of CD is the best. In pair-wise testing, combination with CA is better than without CA. It shows that context analysis prior to language model-based analysis is reasonable. CA can eliminate many noises, while language model-based analysis works as a supplement filter.

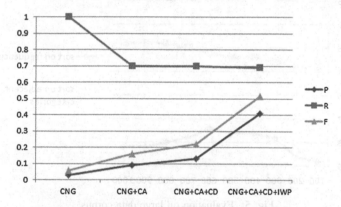

Fig. 4. Results of ascending series of the strategies

As we see from Fig. 4, each step of filtering operations greatly improved the precision, while reduced the recall smoothly. It means each filtering strategies works well. CA missed correct candidate MWE more due to the small size of test corpus, it leads to the reduction of the recall. On a large scale corpus, the problem can weaken.

5.2.2 Evaluation for the Effect of Context Analysis Granularity

Context analysis granularity is syllable or word. In this subsection, we will evaluate the different granularity of CA. In pre-processing step, sentences in test corpus are segmented or unsegmented will produce n-gram words or n-gram syllables respectively. Results are in Table 3.

Table 3. Comparison of different granularity.

Context analysis granularity	P	R	F
Syllable (unsegmented)	0.41	0.67	50.87%
Word (segmented)	0.74	0.78	75.95%

Table 3 shows that, both precision and recall significantly improved when word-segmented in pre-processing. The reason is word-segmentation can avoid the "semi-meaningless word".

5.2.3   Evaluation on Large Corpus

Preliminary experimental results, on small scale of corpus, illustrate the effectiveness of the combination of context analysis and language model-based analysis. The following test will be made on the whole corpus. The size of whole corpus is too large, manually check all extracted MWEs is impractical. In order to quantify the result, sort the results by the frequency or adjacent categories, and then P@N measure is used.

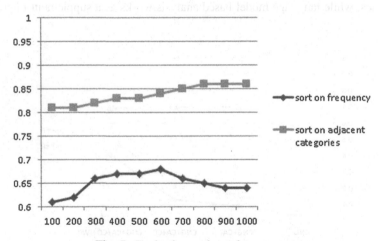

Fig. 5. Evaluation on large data corpus

Figure 5 shows the P@N results in two different sort order, the frequency and adjacent categories respectively. Comparative analysis of results found that sorting by adjacent categories is effective than the frequency. When N changes from 100 to 1000, results of adjacent-categories-based sorting keep steady above 80%. In terms of one curve, the P@N first increase and then decline. It is because of some high frequency stop-word list are in the identification results in 300 best.

The experimental results demonstrate that three strategies in framework can improve the precision of MWEs identification; the context analysis is indeed helpful to promote the accuracy and recall rates of Tibetan MWEs on large scale corpus.

6 Conclusion

We are in the initial stage of identification of Tibetan MWEs. On the basis of the existing resources of our group, we propose Tibetan MWE identification framework and implement all its components. As a result, it works on different scale of corpus. On small test corpus, the best F-score achieves 75.95%. On larger corpus, the P@N (N is 800) overcomes 85%. With only minor adjustment, it can be ported to other languages. Due to the lack of resources and previous technology, the result is acceptable. Further improvement is needed to become practically applicable for MT system.

Acknowledgements. We thank the reviewers for their critical and constructive comments and suggestions that helped us improve the quality of the paper. The research is partially supported by National Science Foundation (No. 61303165) and Informatization Project of the Chinese Academy of Sciences (No. XXH12504-1-10).

References

1. Smadja, F.: Retrieving collocations from text: Xtract. Comput. Linguist. **19**(1), 143–177 (1993)
2. Dagan, I., Church, K.: Termight: identifying and translating technical terminology. In: Proceedings of 4th Conference on Applied Natural Language Processing, Stuttgart, German, pp. 34–40 (1994)
3. Daille, B.: Combined approach for terminology extraction: lexical statistics and linguistic filtering. Technical paper 5, UCREL, Lancaster University (1995)
4. McEnery, T., Langé, J.-M., Oakes, M., Véronis, J.: The exploitation of multilingual annotated corpora for term extraction. In: Garside, R., Leech, G., McEnery, A. (eds.) Corpus Annotation – Linguistic Information from Computer Text Corpora, pp. 220–230. Longman, London (1997)
5. Michiels, A., Dufour, N.: DEFI, a tool for automatic multi-word unit recognition, meaning assignment and translation selection. In: Proceedings of 1st International Conference on Language Resources & Evaluation, Granada, Spain, pp. 1179–1186 (1998)
6. Diana, M., Sophia, A.: Trucks: a model for automatic multiword term recognition. J. Nat. Lang. Process. **8**(1), 101–126 (2000)
7. Merkel, M., Andersson, M.: Knowledge-lite extraction of multi-word units with language filters and entropy thresholds. In: Proceedings of 2000 Conference User-Oriented Content-Based Text and Image Handling (RIAO 2000), Paris, France, pp. 737–746 (2000)
8. Piao, S.S., McEnery, T.: Multi-word unit alignment in English-Chinese parallel corpora. In: Proceedings of Corpus Linguistics 2001, Lancaster, UK, pp. 466–475 (2001)
9. Sag, I.A., Baldwin, T., Bond, F., Flickinger, D.: Multiword expressions: a pain in the neck for NLP. In: LinGO Working Paper No. 2001-03, Stanford University, CA (2001)
10. Baldwin, T., Bannard, C., Tanaka, T., Widdows, D.: An empirical model of multiword expression decomposability. In: Proceedings of ACL-2003 Workshop on Multiword Expressions: Analysis, Acquisition and Treatment, Sapporo, Japan, pp. 89–96 (2003)
11. Dias, G.: Multiword unit hybrid extraction. In: Proceedings of Workshop on Multiword Expressions: Analysis, Acquisition and Treatment, at ACL 2003, Sapporo, Japan, pp. 41–48 (2003)

12. Nivre, J., Nilsson, J.: Multiword units in syntactic parsing. In: Proceedings of LREC-2004 Workshop on Methodologies & Evaluation of Multiword Units in Real-world Applications, Lisbon, Portugal, pp. 37–46 (2004)
13. Pereira, R., Crocker, P., Dias, G.: A parallel multikey quicksort algorithm for mining multiword units. In: Proceedings of LREC-2004 Workshop on Methodologies & Evaluation of Multiword Units in Real-world Applications, Lisbon, Portugal, pp. 17–23 (2004)
14. Piao, S.S., Rayson, P., Archer, D., Wilson, A., McEnery, T.: Extracting multiword expressions with a semantic tagger. In: Proceedings of Workshop on Multiword Expressions: Analysis, Acquisition and Treatment, at ACL 2003, Sapporo, Japan, pp. 49–56 (2003)
15. Piao, S.S., Rayson, P., Archer, D., McEnery, T.: Comparing and combining a semantic tagger and a statistical tool for MWE extraction. Comput. Speech Lang. **19**(4), 378–397 (2005)
16. Rayson, P., Archer, D., Piao, S.S., McEnery, T.: The UCREL semantic analysis system. In: Proceedings of Workshop on Beyond Named Entity Recognition Semantic Labelling for NLP Tasks in Association with LREC 2004, Lisbon, Portugal, pp. 7–12 (2004)
17. Piao, S.S., Sun, G., Rayson, P., Yuan, Q.: Automatic extraction of Chinese multiword expressions with a statistical tool. In: Proceedings of 44th Annual Meeting of the Association for Computational Linguistics (2006)
18. Jiang, D.: On syntactic chunks and formal markers of Tibetan. Minor. Lang. China (3), 30–39 (2003a)
19. Jiang, D., Long, C.: The markers of non-finite VP of Tibetan and its automatic recognizing strategies. In: Proceedings of 20th International Conference on Computer Processing of Oriental Languages (ICCPOL 2003) (2003b)
20. Huang, X., Sun, H., Jiang, D., Zhang, J., Tang, L.: The types and formal markers of nominal chunks in contemporary Tibetan. In: proceedings of 8th Joint Conference on Computational Linguistics (JSCL 2005) (2005)
21. Nuo, M., Liu, H., Ma, L., Wu, J., Ding, Z.: Construction of Chinese-Tibetan multi-word equivalence pair dictionary. J. Chin. Inf. Process. **26**(3), 98–103 (2012)
22. Nuo, M., Liu, H., Zhao, W., Ma, L., Wu, J., Ding, Z.: Tibetan base noun phrase identification framework based on Chinese-Tibetan sentence aligned corpus. In: Proceedings of 26th International Conference on Computational Linguistics Conference, pp. 2141–2157 (2012)
23. Lü, X., Zhang, L., Hu, J.: Statistical substring reduction in linear time. In: Su, K.-Y., Tsujii, J., Lee, J.-H., Kwong, O.Y. (eds.) IJCNLP 2004. LNCS (LNAI), vol. 3248, pp. 320–327. Springer, Heidelberg (2005). doi:10.1007/978-3-540-30211-7_34
24. Nagao, M., Mori, S.: A new method of N-gram statistics for large number of n and automatic extraction of words and phrases from large text data of Japanese. In: COLING-1994 (1994)

Building Powerful Dependency Parsers
for Resource-Poor Languages

Junjie Yu, Wenliang Chen(✉), Zhenghua Li, and Min Zhang

School of Computer Science and Technology,
Soochow University, Suzhou 215006, Jiangsu, China
jjyu@stu.suda.edu.cn, {wlchen,zhli13,minzhang}@suda.edu.cn

Abstract. In this paper, we present an approach to building dependency parsers for the resource-poor languages without any annotated resources on the target side. Compared with the previous studies, our approach requires less human annotated resources. In our approach, we first train a POS tagger and a parser on the source treebank. Then, they are used to parse the source sentences in bilingual data. We obtain auto-parsed sentences (with POS tags and dependencies) on the target side by projection techniques. Based on the fully projected sentences, we can train a base POS tagger and a base parser on the target side. But most of sentence pairs are not fully projected, so we get lots of partially projected sentences. To make full use of partially projected sentences, we implement a learning algorithm to train POS taggers, which leads to better parsing performance. We further exploit a set of features from the large-scale monolingual data to help parsing. Finally, we evaluate our proposed approach on Google Universal Treebank (v2.0, standard). The experimental results show that the proposed approach can significantly improve parsing performance.

Keywords: Dependency parsing · POS tagging · Resource-poor languages · Bilingual data

1 Introduction

Since the contribution of Penn Treebank [17], statistical parsing has attracted a lot of researchers. Many supervised algorithms have been proposed on phrase-structure parsing, dependency parsing and other formalisms [6,12,19,23,24,32]. The experimental results in recent studies show that these supervised methods have achieved high levels of accuracies on treebanks of several languages [20].

However, there are many languages lack human annotated resources which are available for the major languages, such as English. One solution is to manually create treebanks for the resource-poor languages which requires high cost. Thus, there are a vast amount of researchers working on unsupervised grammar induction on unannotated data [5,8,9]. Unfortunately, the performance of the unsupervised grammar induction is significantly lower than the supervised methods.

© Springer International Publishing AG 2016
C.-Y. Lin et al. (Eds.): NLPCC-ICCPOL 2016, LNAI 10102, pp. 27–38, 2016.
DOI: 10.1007/978-3-319-50496-4_3

In recent years, many researchers work on transferring linguistic structures across languages to build high performance dependency parsers for the resource-poor languages. McDonald et al. [22] propose directly transferring delexicalized models which based on universal POS tags. The performance of delexicalized parsers significantly outperform state-of-the-art unsupervised grammar induction models. Ma and Xia [15] and Rasooli and Collins [27] both use bilingual data as a bridge between a source resource-rich language and a target resource-poor language. They obtain state-of-the-art performance on Google Universal Treebank (v2.0, standard)[1]. However, the main problem in their methods is that they assume the target language has annotated data for training a POS tagger.

In this paper, we present an approach to building a dependency parser for the target language without any annotated resources on the target side. In our approach, the input resources include the treebank of source side, bilingual data and the large-scale monolingual data of target side. We first train a POS tagger and a parser on the source treebank. Then, they are used to parse the source sentences in bilingual data. The information of POS tags and dependencies are transferred by projection techniques via word alignment. After transferring, we obtain the auto-annotated sentences on the target side. Based on the fully projected sentences, we can train a base POS tagger and a base parser on the target side. But most of sentence pairs are partially projected. To make full use of the partially projected sentences, we implement a learning algorithm to train a POS tagger which leads to better parsing performance. We further exploit a set of features from the large-scale monolingual data including word-cluster based features and subtree based features to help parsing. Finally, we evaluate our proposed approach on six languages of Google Universal Treebank (v2, standard). The experimental results show that the proposed approach can significantly improve parsing performance.

In summary, our contributions are as follows:

1. We propose an approach to building dependency parsers for the target languages without any annotated resources on the target side. Compared with the previous studies, our work requires less human annotated resources.
2. We implement a learning algorithm to train a POS tagger on partially annotated data which can improve parsing performance. We further improve the systems by exploiting a set of features extracted from monolingual data.

2   Our Approach

In this section, we describe our approach of building dependency parsers for target languages. The framework of our approach is shown in Fig. 1. The approach includes three parts: (1) Projecting dependencies and POS tags: the information of POS tags and dependencies are transferred via projection. (2) Building POS taggers and parsers: the models are trained on the auto-annotated data. (3) Enhancing the parsers: a set of features are exploited from large-scale monolingual data.

---

[1] https://code.google.com/p/uni-dep-tb/.

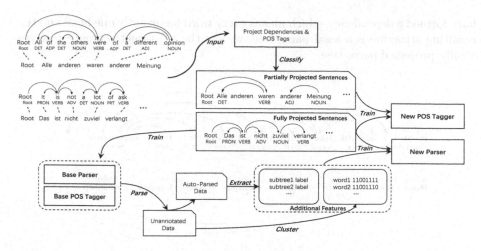

Fig. 1. The framework of our approach. Processing of English (source) and German (target) as an example.

2.1 Data Preprocessing

We first preprocess source sentences in bilingual data. In order to get syntactic information on source side, a source POS tagger and parser are trained on human annotated treebank. The tagger and parser are used to process the source sentences. Finally, to get correlations between two languages, we create alignments on bilingual data by word alignment tools.

2.2 Projecting Dependencies and POS Tags

Following Rasooli and Collins [27], we now give a brief description of transferring knowledge on bilingual data.

For kth parallel sentence pair $S^k = S_1^k \ldots S_{s_k}^k$ and $T^k = T_1^k \ldots T_{t_k}^k$, where S_i^k and T_j^k are i^{th} and j^{th} word in source and target sentence respectively, s_k and t_k are the length of S^k and T^k. $A_{k,j}$ is an integer representing which word in k^{th} source sentence is aligned to the target j^{th} word.

The source sentences in bilingual data are parsed and each can provide a dependency set $D_{k,l} = \{(h, d)\}$, where $l \in \{s, t\}$ means a source or target language sentence, k is k^{th} parallel pair, h and d represent head index and dependent index in sentence which can form a dependency relation.

$$D_{k,t} = \{(i,j)|(A_{k,i}, A_{k,j}) \in D_{k,s}, i, j = 0 \ldots t_k, \ i \neq j\} \tag{1}$$

$$T_{full} = \{D_{k,t}|(*, i) \in D_{k,t}, \forall i = 1 \ldots t_k \ \wedge \ D_{k,t} \in \mathbf{P}\} \tag{2}$$

For k^{th} target sentence, if $A_{k,i}$ and $A_{k,j}$ belong to the dependency Set $D_{k,s}$, then we say the two words in target sentence can build a dependency and (i,j) will be added to the target dependency set $D_{k,t}$. If all words in target sentence have formed a dependency, which means every word has exactly one head and the resulting structure is a legal parse tree, we say the kth target sentence receives a fully projected parse tree.

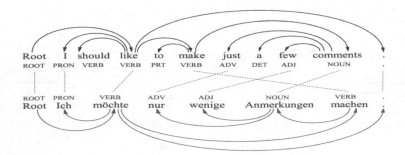

Fig. 2. An example of projecting dependencies and POS tags. If two aligned words of two target words exist a dependency relation in source parsed sentence, this dependency relation is transferred to the target words. In this example, target words "*Ich*" and "*möchte*" have aligned words "*I*" and "*like*", meanwhile there is a dependency relation in source sentence: "*I* ← *like*". So we can get a dependency relation: "*Ich* ← *möchte*". POS tags are also transferred when a dependency relation is generated.

During projecting, the POS tags are also transferred from the source side to the target side. Ma and Xia [15] and Rasooli and Collins [27] both train a supervised POS tagger for each target language on the human annotated training data. As an alternative solution, we also transfer the POS tags.

In our solution, the POS tags of target words are directly copied from the aligned words in the source sentences. Figure 2 shows an example of projecting dependency and POS tag from parallel sentences between English and German.

Since some words on the target side are not aligned during projection, they remain unannotated. Therefore, we obtain some fully projected sentences and lots of partially projected sentences.

2.3   CRF-Based POS Tagging Model

This section describes how to build base POS taggers and how to use partially projected sentences to improve the accuracy of POS taggers.

Before parsing we need to tag the input sentences with POS tags. We use the fully projected sentences as training data since each word has projected with a POS tag. Then a base POS tagger is trained by a CRF-based model.

However, we find that about 95% of the sentences (German for example) in bilingual data are partially projected. In order to fully exploit the projected data, the key challenge is how to let our CRF-based POS tagger learn from partially annotated data. Marcheggiani and Artières [16] show that a CRF-based POS tagger can naturally and effectively learn from partially annotated data by converting a partially tagged sequence into an exponential-size set of POS tag sequences and using all POS tags as the gold-standard reference during training, also known as ambiguous labeling [28,30].

We directly use the basic CRF-based tagger implemented in Li et al. [13] to learn from partially projected sentences.

2.4 Graph-Based Dependency Parsing Model

After projecting dependencies in bilingual data, we select fully projected sentences of target side to train a base parser.

We use a graph-based model described in Chen et al. [4] to build dependency parsers. The algorithm proposed by Carreras [2] is used for decoding and the Margin Infused Relaxed Algorithm (MIRA) [7,18] is used to train feature weights. We use the feature templates of Chen et al. [4] as our feature templates, which produces state-of-the-art accuracies.

3 Enhancing the Parsers

In the above section, we build dependency parsers for resource-poor languages with the help of bilingual data. However, the performance is still not good since the auto-generated training data on the target side contains noise. In this section, we further enhance the parsers by exploiting additional features from large-scale monolingual data.

3.1 Subtree Based Features

Firstly, we use base POS tagger and base parser to process sentences in monolingual data. Then, we extract subtrees in a similar way used in Chen et al. [3]. Finally, the subtrees are classified into several sets based on frequency of subtree. Before describing the details about subtrees, we will discuss the differences between Chen et al. [3] and this paper. First, the work in Chen et al. [3] only focus on two languages: English and Chinese, while we work on six languages. Second, the parsers they used to obtain auto-parsed data achieve higher performance than ours since their models are trained on treebanks. It is very interesting to see whether the subtree-based method can work under our settings.

We extract two types of subtrees: bigram-subtree and trigram-subtree. If a subtree contains two nodes, it is a bigram-subtree. If a subtree contains three nodes, we call it a trigram-subtree. For extracting trigram-subtrees, we focus on two common structures: sibling-type and parent-child-grandchild type (grandchild-type, for short).

After finished subtree extraction, we classify the subtrees into four types based on the frequency. The top 10% most frequent subtrees are added a high-frequency (HF) label, the top 20% most frequent subtrees are added a middle-frequent (MF) label, and left are added a low-frequency (LF) label. If a subtree is unseen in subtree list, we add a ZERO label. Table 1 shows the subtree based

Table 1. Subtree based features.

$T1 : label(h, d)$
$T2 : label(h, d_{-1})$
$T3 : label(h, d_{+1})$
$T4 : label(h_{-1}, d)$
$T5 : label(h_{+1}, d)$
$T6 : label(h, c_h, d)$
$T7 : label(h, d, c_d)$

Table 2. Word-cluster based features.

$c4_h$	$c4_d$	$c6_h$	$c6_d$	$c*_h$	$c*_d$	$c4_h$ $c4_d$	$c4_{c_h}$
$c4_h$	p_d	$c6_h$	p_d	$c*_h$	$c4_d$	$c6_h$ $c6_d$	$c6_{c_h}$
p_h	$c4_d$	p_h	$c6_d$	$c4_h$	$c*_d$	hp $dc4$	$c4_{c_h}$
$c4_h$	w_d	$c6_h$	w_d	$c*_h$	$c6_d$	$c4_h$ $c4_d$	$c4_{c_d}$
w_h	$c4_d$	hw	$c6_d$	$c6_h$	$c*_d$	$c6_h$ $c6_d$	$c6_{c_d}$
$\dots$		$\dots$		$\dots$		$\dots$	

features, where h refers to the head word, d refers to the dependent word, c_h refers to the child word of the head, c_d refers to the child word of the dependent, -1 refers to the word to the left of the target word, $+1$ refers to the word to the right of the target word, $label(h, d)$ is a label of subtree (h, d) and $T[1-7]$ refer to the type of the corresponding feature template.

3.2 Word-Cluster Based Features

The word-cluster based method can reduce the need for supervised data [11], we use them as additional features to relieve sparse problem on target languages. Besides, word-cluster information only relies on unannotated data, so it is feasible in our task.

We use the implementation [14] of Brown algorithm [1] to provide word-clusters. The word-clusters are represented as a bit string. For example, the word "apple" and the word "pear" are represented as "00110000" and "00110001", respectively. The length of the bit string means the degree of the clusters. We use the same feature set as used in Koo et al. [11]. Both short bit string prefix and full bit string clusters are used in first and second order parsing models. Table 2 shows some examples of word-cluster based features, where h, d, c_h, c_d represent head, dependent, sibling and grandchild, respectively. 4, 6, $*$ means the 4, 6, full bit length of word-cluster. c, p, w means word-cluster, POS tag and word.

4 Experiments

In the experiments, we use English as source language, the target languages are German (de), Spanish (es), French (fr), Italian (it), Portuguess (pt) and Swedish (sv). Unlabeled accuracy score (UAS) is used to measure the performance on all sentence length, excluding punctuation.

4.1 Data Sets

We use six languages in version 2.0 of Google Universal Treebanks [21] as our test data. And the English portion is used to train a supervised source language parser and POS tagger. We use EruoParl data [10] as bilingual data. Sentences in bilingual data are tokenized[2] before parsing and performing alignments with Giza++ toolkit [25]. The Giza++ toolkit will generate results from both aligned directions, we combined them to get intersection results. In order to fast our system, we removed the sentences with length greater than 80. The large-scale monolingual data for target languages are obtained from wikipedia[3]. We randomly select 2 millions sentences for each language after tokenization.

4.2 Results on POS Tagging

In this section, we conduct the experiments to evaluate the performance of POS tagging. The POS tag set we used in this paper is the universal POS tag set defined by Petrov et al. [26]. There are 12 tags in total: NOUN (nouns), VERB (verbs), ADJ (adjectives), ADV (adverbs), PRON (pronouns), DET (determiners and articles), ADP (prepositions and postpositions), NUM (numerals), CONJ (conjunctions), PRT (particles), '.' (punctuation marks) and X (others).

Table 3. POS tagging accuracies on different languages of (1) the POS tagger only trained on fully projected sentences and (2) the POS tagger trained on sentences that at least 80% words have POS tags.

Lang	de	es	fr	it	pt	sv	avg
#sent w/ 100% proj	23k	24k	17k	15k	16k	47k	24k
accuracy	87.58	85.24	85.51	87.18	88.55	87.32	86.90
#sent w/ above 80% proj	57k	187k	112k	114k	120k	240k	138k
accuracy	88.25	84.80	86.91	88.44	89.06	87.78	$87.54_{+0.64}$

Table 3 shows the statistics on POS tagged training data that we obtained for target languages. We first use fully projected sentences as training data to train POS taggers. Then, we add the partially projected sentences in which at least 80% words have the POS tags to train new POS taggers. The results are evaluated on test data from treebanks. From the table, we find that the average accuracy of our POS taggers is about 86.90% when training on fully projected sentences. After adding partially projected sentences, the POS tagging accuracy has a 0.64 average absolute improvement which achieves 87.54%. As reported in Ma and Xia [15], the average accuracy of POS taggers which trained from hand-annotated data is around 95%. Although there is a big gap between our accuracy and the supervised accuracy, it is reasonable since our method only depend on alignment information and source resources.

---

[2] https://github.com/moses-smt/mosesdecoder/blob/master/scripts/tokenizer/tokenizer.perl.

[3] https://dumps.wikimedia.org/.

4.3 Results on Parsing

In this section, we evaluate the parsing performance on six target languages. Table 4 lists all results of first-order and second-order systems.

Table 4. Parsing results on Google Universal Treebank (v2.0, standard). We use first and second order models respectively. "base" is the baseline model that parsers POS taggers are trained by fully projected sentences. "+p" means adding the partially projected sentences to train POS taggers. "+st" represents adding subtree based features and "+cl" is adding word-cluster based features.

First order					
Lang	Base	+p	+p+st	+p+cl	+p+st+cl
de	61.62	$62.09_{+0.47}$	$63.66_{+2.04}$	$65.61_{+3.99}$	$64.85_{+3.23}$
es	68.63	$69.06_{+0.43}$	$70.58_{+1.95}$	$71.40_{+2.77}$	$71.75_{+3.12}$
fr	67.51	$68.11_{+0.60}$	$68.65_{+1.14}$	$68.42_{+0.91}$	$69.05_{+1.54}$
it	69.43	$71.05_{+1.62}$	$70.62_{+1.19}$	$71.85_{+2.42}$	$71.89_{+2.46}$
pt	66.70	$68.86_{+2.16}$	$69.70_{+3.00}$	$71.21_{+4.51}$	$71.49_{+4.79}$
sv	72.56	$72.38_{-0.18}$	$73.01_{+0.45}$	$72.74_{+0.18}$	$73.13_{+0.57}$
avg	67.74	$68.59_{+0.85}$	$69.37_{+1.63}$	$70.21_{+2.47}$	$70.36_{+2.62}$

Second order					
Lang	Base	+p	+p+st	+p+cl	+p+st+cl
de	64.67	$65.06_{+0.39}$	$65.71_{+1.04}$	$67.04_{+2.37}$	$67.62_{+2.95}$
es	70.29	$71.04_{+0.75}$	$71.66_{+1.37}$	$73.23_{+2.94}$	$73.62_{+3.33}$
fr	68.62	$69.71_{+1.09}$	$70.97_{+2.35}$	$70.74_{+2.12}$	$70.79_{+2.17}$
it	70.00	$71.69_{+1.69}$	$72.10_{+2.10}$	$72.66_{+2.66}$	$72.82_{+2.82}$
pt	68.12	$70.34_{+2.22}$	$71.30_{+3.18}$	$72.54_{+4.42}$	$72.94_{+4.82}$
sv	73.88	$73.70_{-0.18}$	$73.84_{-0.04}$	$73.87_{-0.01}$	$74.42_{+0.54}$
avg	69.26	$70.26_{+1.00}$	$70.93_{+1.67}$	$71.68_{+2.42}$	$72.05_{+2.79}$

Parsing with Base POS Taggers. The base parser is trained by fully projected sentences. From the "base" column, it has a performance of 67.74% in first order and 69.26% in second order. The "base" model in second order model has a 1.52 absolute improvement than in first order model. As mentioned before, our approach is totaly an automatic system that can provide POS taggers and dependency parsers for target languages. There is no previous work can be compared directly, so we use these results as our Baseline.

Parsing with New POS Taggers. Meanwhile, when we add partially projected sentences to train new POS taggers for giving POS tags, the parsing performance has an obvious improvement due to the improvement on POS tagging accuracy. It achieves 68.59% and 70.26% in first and second order models, respectively.

Parsing with Subtree Based Method. From Table 4, we can see that the subtree based method also has an improvement on baseline. Both first order and second order models, it gives about a 1.6 average absolute improvement.

Parsing with Word-Cluster Based Method. Following Täckström et al. [31], the number of word-clusters is set to be 256. As shown in "+p+cl" column, a 2.47 and 2.42 absolute improvement have got for both first and second order models. When we directly minus the improvement caused by "+p", the improvement is still impressive.

Parsing with Hybrid Method. Our training algorithm can combine subtree and word-cluster features to train a new model. When adding these features at the same time, both first order and second order models can get the best results. Especially the second order model reaches an average UAS of 72.05% for six languages which is also the best performance in this paper.

Compared with Ma and Xia [15] (76.67%) and Rasooli and Collins [27] (78.89%)[4], our parsers perform a little worse. However, our approach does not require any annotated resources on the target side while theirs need human-annotated POS tags for target sentences. This indicates that there still has much room to improve our parser. In future work, we will consider to combine the techniques in their approaches with ours.

5   Related Work

Some work focus on unsupervised grammar induction methods. Based on shared logistic normal distribution, Cohen and Smith [5] modify the EM algorithm for learning a probabilistic grammar. Spitkovsky et al. [29] combine several simple algorithms to build organized networks. Unfortunately, the unsupervised methods significantly lag behind supervised methods.

Some work focus on syntactic information transferring from resource-rich languages. Based on a universal POS tag set for different languages, McDonald et al. [22] train delexicalized parsers which can directly parse target languages. Täckström et al. [30] apply typological and language-family features to a discriminative parser.

Recently, work based on parallel data get a high accuracy. Ma and Xia [15] use unannotated data as entropy regularization and parallel guidance to train probabilistic parsing models for resource-poor languages. Based on alignment information and the dependency relations in source sentences, Rasooli and Collins [27] propose a density-driven method which get state-of-the-art performance.

Based on parallel data, dependencies transfer is a useful method to deal with the dependency parsing problem on languages which lack manually annotated resources. Our approach is inspired by Rasooli and Collins [27], we use the similar way to obtain dependency projected sentences in bilingual data. However, they add soft POS tag constraints since they assume the target words have POS tags. The main difference in this paper is that the POS tags for target sentence

---

[4] When using multiple source languages, they get an average accuracy of 82.18%.

is generated by projected sentences instead of tagging by a POS tagger trained on treebank. In this way, our approach is more practical to apply on resource-poor languages. Meanwhile, we demonstrate the utility of subtree based and word-cluster based methods on six languages.

6 Conclusions

We present a simple yet effective approach for parsing resource-poor languages without any supervised direction. In our approach, we use partially projected sentences to improve the accuracy of POS taggers that later results in better parsing performance. Subtrees from auto-parsed data and word-clusters from unannotated data are used to further improve the performance of parsing models. We first obtain projected parse trees from bilingual data, and the POS tags are directly copied from source word in projected word pair. Second, base parsers are trained by these fully projected sentences. We train POS taggers using fully projected and partially projected sentences. Finally, we add subtree based and word-cluster based features to enhance the parsers. In this approach, bilingual data and monolingual data are raw resources that the target language can easily provide, which makes our approach more practical than the previous studies. Future work we will consider more on the accuracy of POS tags and enlarge the train data for dependency parser.

Acknowledgement. This project is supported by National Natural Science Foundation of China (Grant No. 61373095, 61572338, 61502325). This work is also partially supported by Collaborative Innovation Center of Novel Software Technology and Industrialization.

References

1. Brown, P.F., Desouza, P.V., Mercer, R.L., Pietra, V.J.D., Lai, J.C.: Class-based n-gram models of natural language. Comput. Linguist. **18**(4), 467–479 (1997)
2. Carreras, X.: Experiments with a higher-order projective dependency parser. In: Proceedings of the CoNLL Shared Task Session of EMNLP-CoNLL 2007, pp. 957–961. Association for Computational Linguistics, Prague, June 2007
3. Chen, W., Kazama, J., Uchimoto, K., Torisawa, K.: Exploiting subtrees in auto-parsed data to improve dependency parsing. Comput. Intell. **28**(28), 426451 (2012)
4. Chen, W., Zhang, Y., Zhang, M.: Feature embedding for dependency parsing. In: Proceedings of the COLING 2014, the 25th International Conference on Computational Linguistics: Technical Papers, pp. 816–826. Dublin City University and Association for Computational Linguistics, Dublin, August 2014
5. Cohen, S., Smith, N.A.: Shared logistic normal distributions for soft parameter tying in unsupervised grammar induction. In: Proceedings of Human Language Technologies: The 2009 Annual Conference of the North American Chapter of the Association for Computational Linguistics, pp. 74–82. Association for Computational Linguistics, Boulder, June 2009

6. Collins, M.: Three generative, lexicalised models for statistical parsing. In: Proceedings of the 35th Annual Meeting of the Association for Computational Linguistics, pp. 16–23. Association for Computational Linguistics, Madrid, July 1997

7. Crammer, K., Singer, Y.: Ultraconservative online algorithms for multiclass problems. J. Mach. Learn. Res. **3**, 951–991 (2003)

8. Grave, E., Elhadad, N.: A convex and feature-rich discriminative approach to dependency grammar induction. In: Proceedings of the 53rd Annual Meeting of the Association for Computational Linguistics and the 7th International Joint Conference on Natural Language Processing, vol. 1(Long Papers), pp. 1375–1384. Association for Computational Linguistics, Beijing, July 2015

9. Klein, D., Manning, C.: Corpus-based induction of syntactic structure: models of dependency and constituency. In: Proceedings of the 42nd Meeting of the Association for Computational Linguistics (ACL 2004). Main Volume, pp. 478–485. Barcelona, Spain, July 2004

10. Koehn, P.: Europarl: a parallel corpus for statistical machine translation. In: Mt Summit, vol. 5 (2004)

11. Koo, T., Carreras, X., Collins, M.: Simple semi-supervised dependency parsing. In: Proceedings of ACL 2008: HLT, pp. 595–603. Association for Computational Linguistics, Columbus, June 2008

12. Koo, T., Collins, M.: Efficient third-order dependency parsers. In: Proceedings of the 48th Annual Meeting of the Association for Computational Linguistics, pp. 1–11. Association for Computational Linguistics, Uppsala, July 2010

13. Li, Z., Chao, J., Zhang, M., Chen, W.: Coupled sequence labeling on heterogeneous annotations: POS tagging as a case study. In: Proceedings of the 53rd Annual Meeting of the Association for Computational Linguistics and the 7th International Joint Conference on Natural Language Processing, vol. 1(Long Papers), pp. 1783–1792. Association for Computational Linguistics, Beijing, July 2015

14. Liang, P.: Semi-supervised learning for natural language. Masters thesis Mit (2005)

15. Ma, X., Xia, F.: Unsupervised dependency parsing with transferring distribution via parallel guidance and entropy regularization. In: Proceedings of the 52nd Annual Meeting of the Association for Computational Linguistics, vol. 1(Long Papers), pp. 1337–1348. Association for Computational Linguistics, Baltimore, June 2014

16. Marcheggiani, D., Artières, T.: An experimental comparison of active learning strategies for partially labeled sequences. In: Proceedings of the 2014 Conference on Empirical Methods in Natural Language Processing (EMNLP), pp. 898–906. Association for Computational Linguistics, Doha, October 2014

17. Marcus, M.P., Marcinkiewicz, M.A., Santorini, B.: Building a large annotated corpus of english: the Penn treebank. Comput. Linguist. **19**(2), 313–330 (1993)

18. McDonald, R., Crammer, K., Pereira, F.: Flexible text segmentation with structured multilabel classification. In: Proceedings of Human Language Technology Conference and Conference on Empirical Methods in Natural Language Processing, pp. 987–994. Association for Computational Linguistics, Vancouver, October 2005

19. McDonald, R., Crammer, K., Pereira, F.: Online large-margin training of dependency parsers. In: Proceedings of the 43rd Annual Meeting of the Association for Computational Linguistics (ACL 2005), pp. 91–98. Association for Computational Linguistics, Ann Arbor, June 2005

20. McDonald, R., Nivre, J.: Tutorial: Recent advances in dependency parsing (2014). http://eacl2014.org/tutorial-dependency-parsing

21. McDonald, R., Nivre, J., Quirmbach-Brundage, Y., Goldberg, Y., Das, D., Ganchev, K., Hall, K., Petrov, S., Zhang, H., Täckström, O., Bedini, C., Bertomeu Castelló, N., Lee, J.: Universal dependency annotation for multilingual parsing. In: Proceedings of the 51st Annual Meeting of the Association for Computational Linguistics, vol. 2(Short Papers), pp. 92–97. Association for Computational Linguistics, Sofia, August 2013
22. McDonald, R., Petrov, S., Hall, K.: Multi-source transfer of delexicalized dependency parsers. In: Proceedings of the 2011 Conference on Empirical Methods in Natural Language Processing, pp. 62–72. Association for Computational Linguistics, Edinburgh, July 2011
23. Mcdonald, R.T., Pereira, F.C.N.: Online learning of approximate dependency parsing algorithms. In: Eacl 2006, Conference of the European Chapter of the Association for Computational Linguistics, Proceedings of the Conference, April 3–7, 2006, Trento, Italy, pp. 81–88 (2006)
24. Nivre, J., Scholz, M.: Deterministic dependency parsing of english text. In: Proceedings of Coling 2004, pp. 64–70. COLING, Geneva, 23–27 August 2004
25. Och, F.J., Ney, H.: A systematic comparison of various statistical alignment models. Comput. Linguist. **29**(1), 19–51 (2003)
26. Petrov, S., Das, D., Mcdonald, R.: A universal part-of-speech tagset. Comput. Sci. **1**(3), 2089–2096 (2011)
27. Rasooli, M.S., Collins, M.: Density-driven cross-lingual transfer of dependency parsers. In: Proceedings of the 2015 Conference on Empirical Methods in Natural Language Processing, pp. 328–338. Association for Computational Linguistics, Lisbon, September 2015
28. Riezler, S., King, T.H., Kaplan, R.M., Crouch, R., Maxwell, J.T.I., Johnson, M.: Parsing the wall street journal using a lexical-functional grammar and discriminative estimation techniques. In: Proceedings of 40th Annual Meeting of the Association for Computational Linguistics, pp. 271–278. Association for Computational Linguistics, Philadelphia, Pennsylvania, USA, July 2002
29. Spitkovsky, V.I., Alshawi, H., Jurafsky, D.: Breaking out of local optima with count transforms and model recombination: a study in grammar induction. In: Proceedings of the 2013 Conference on Empirical Methods in Natural Language Processing, pp. 1983–1995. Association for Computational Linguistics, Seattle, October 2013
30. Täckström, O., McDonald, R., Nivre, J.: Target language adaptation of discriminative transfer parsers. In: Proceedings of the 2013 Conference of the North American Chapter of the Association for Computational Linguistics: Human Language Technologies, pp. 1061–1071. Association for Computational Linguistics, Atlanta, June 2013
31. Täckström, O., McDonald, R., Uszkoreit, J.: Cross-lingual word clusters for direct transfer of linguistic structure. In: Proceedings of the 2012 Conference of the North American Chapter of the Association for Computational Linguistics: Human Language Technologies, pp. 477–487. Association for Computational Linguistics, Montréal, June 2012
32. Zhang, H., Huang, L., Zhao, K., McDonald, R.: Online learning for inexact hypergraph search. In: Proceedings of the 2013 Conference on Empirical Methods in Natural Language Processing, pp. 908–913. Association for Computational Linguistics, Seattle, October 2013

Bidirectional Long Short-Term Memory with Gated Relevance Network for Paraphrase Identification

Yatian Shen$^{(\boxtimes)}$, Jifan Chen$^{(\boxtimes)}$, and Xuanjing Huang$^{(\boxtimes)}$

School of Computer Science, Fudan University,
825 Zhangheng Road, Shanghai, China
{10110240031,jfchen14,xjhuang}@fudan.edu.cn

Abstract. Semantic interaction between text segments, which has been proven to be very useful for detecting the paraphrase relations, is often ignored in the study of paraphrase identification. In this paper, we adopt a neural network model for paraphrase identification, called as bidirectional Long Short-Term Memory-Gated Relevance Network (Bi-LSTM+GRN). According to this model, a gated relevance network is used to capture the semantic interaction between text segments, and then aggregated using a pooling layer to select the most informative interactions. Experiments on the Microsoft Research Paraphrase Corpus (MSRP) benchmark dataset show that this model achieves better performances than hand-crafted feature based approaches as well as previous neural network models.

Keywords: Gated relevance network · Paraphrase identification · LSTM

1 Introduction

Paraphrase Identification is usually formalized as a binary classification task, which determines whether two text segments of arbitrary length and form contain the same meaning. Identifying paraphrases plays an important role in question answering [1], text similarity measures [2], natural language inference [4] and plagiarism detection [3]. For instance, one would like to detect that the following two sentences are paraphrases:

S1. *The settlement includes $4.1 million in attorneys' fees and expenses.*
S2. *Plaintiffs' attorneys would get $4.1 million of the settlement.*

Recently, neural network models have been increasingly focused on for their ability to minimize the effort in feature engineering of NLP tasks [5–7]. Deep feature learning has also been explored in paraphrase identification. [8] uses unsupervised recursive autoencoders to compute representations on all levels of a parse tree. These features are used to measure the word- and phrase-wise similarity between two sentences. [9] adopts convolutional neural network models

© Springer International Publishing AG 2016
C.-Y. Lin et al. (Eds.): NLPCC-ICCPOL 2016, LNAI 10102, pp. 39–50, 2016.
DOI: 10.1007/978-3-319-50496-4_4

for paraphrase identification. [11] learns multigranular sentence representations using convolutional neural network (CNN) and models interaction features at each level. These features are then fed to a logistic classifier for paraphrase identification. [12] first models each sentence using a convolutional neural network that extracts features at multiple levels of granularity and then uses multiple types of pooling to find the most informative features.

Until now, most works on paraphrase identification focus only on feature extraction. On the other hand, in paraphrase identification, a proper modeling of the feature-feature interaction is also very important. For instance, consider the example inputs:

S1. *Other changes in the plan refine his original vision, Libeskind said.*
S2. *Many of the changes are improvements to the original plan, Libeskind said.*

In the above examples, although S1 and S2 have different syntactic structures, S1 is a paraphrase of S2 since both of them express the same meaning, and "refine" and "improvements" are synonyms. S1 and S2 own intensive semantic correlations, which determine the paraphrase relationships between two sentence. Therefore, how to acquire the semantic correlation or interaction between sentence pairs is of great value for paraphrase identification.

In this paper, based on our previous work, we leverage a neural network model for paraphrase identification, called as bidirectional Long Short-Term Memory-Gated Relevance Network (Bi-LSTM+GRN), which is originally proposed to detect implicit discourse relation [13]. In order to preserve the contextual information around the word, we encode the text segment to its positional representation via a recurrent neural network, specifically, a bidirectional LSTM. Then, to capture the interaction between text segments, we adopt a gated relevance network to capture the semantic interaction between those positional representations. Finally, all the interaction scores generated by the relevance network are fed to a max pooling layer to find the strongest interactions. We then aggregate them to predict the paraphrase relation through a multi-layer perceptron (MLP). Our model is trained end to end by back-propagation. The main contribution of this paper can be summarized as follows:

(1) A gated relevance network is adopted to capture the semantic interaction between text segments, and then aggregated using a pooling layer to select the most informative interactions.
(2) In order to preserve the contextual information, we encode the text segment to its positional representation through a bidirectional LSTM.
(3) We conduct experiments on the Microsoft Research Paraphrase Corpus (MSRP). Extensive experimental results demonstrate that the neural network is effective for paraphrase identification.

2   Related Works

Prior works on paraphrase identification have mainly focused on feature engineering. Several types of features have been found useful, including: (1) string similarity metrics such as n-gram overlap and BLEU score [14,15], as well as string kernels [16]; (2) syntactic operations on the parse structure [17,18]; and (3) distributional features obtained by latent semantic analysis [19,20].

Recent work has moved away from handcrafted features to modeling with distributed representations and neural network architectures. [8] computes the representations of constituents in a binarized constituent parse using recursive neural network. [21] first uses matrix factorization techniques to obtain sentence representations, and combines them with fine-tuned sparse features using an SVM classifier for paraphrase identification. [9] proposes convolutional neural network models for matching two sentences. They perform comparisons directly over sentence representations without considering the positional information. [22] proposes a tree-based LSTM neural network architecture for sentence modeling. [11] also develops a convolutional neural network architecture for paraphrase identification. [12] first models each sentence using a convolutional neural network that extracts features at multiple levels of granularity and then uses multiple types of pooling to find valuable features. [10] is very similar to our work. The tensor layer is used for modeling the interactions between two text segments in semantic matching task.

Our method is different to these research in several ways. First, we do not use syntactic parsers, yet our method still outperforms [22] on the paraphrase identification task. This result is appealing because high-quality parsers are difficult to obtain for low-resource languages or in specialized domains. Second, we encode the text segment to its positional representation through a bidirectional LSTM, which is able to capture some latent linguistic structures. Third, we use a gated relevance network to capture the semantic interaction between the intermediate representations of the text segments, which is shown to be very effective for paraphrase identification.

3   Methodology

The architecture of our method is shown in Fig. 1, which is composed of such components as word representation, Bi-LSTM based sentence modeling, gated relevance network, max-pooling and MLP. In the following sections, we will illustrate the details of the proposed framework.

3.1   Embedding Layer

In the word representation component, each input word token is transformed into a vector by looking up word embeddings. It is reported in [5] that word embeddings learned from large amounts of unlabeled data are far more satisfactory than the randomly initialized embeddings. Currently, there are many pre-trained word embeddings that are freely available [25]. A comparison of the available word embeddings is beyond the scope of this paper. Our experiments directly utilize the publicly available word embeddings trained on 100 billion words of Google News by [25].

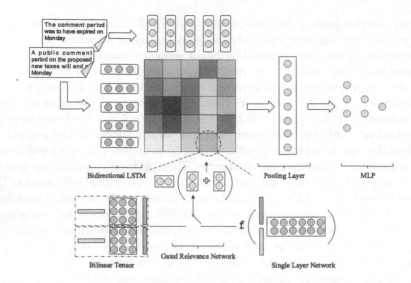

Fig. 1. A illustration of bidirectional LSTM-GRN for paraphrase identification.

3.2 Sentence Modeling with Bi-LSTM

The recurrent neural network is suitable for modeling sequential data by nature, as it keeps a hidden state vector h, which changes with input data at each step accordingly [26–28].

One problem of the recurrent neural network is known as gradient vanishing or exploding. This leads to the difficulty of training. Long short term memory (LSTM) units are proposed in [29] to overcome this problem. The main idea is to introduce an adaptive gating mechanism, which decides the degree to which LSTM units keep the previous state and memorize the extracted features of the current data input.

Concretely, the LSTM-based recurrent neural network comprises four components: an input gate i_t, a forget gate f_t, an output gate o_t, and a memory cell c_t.

$$i_t = \sigma(W_i.x_t + U_i.h_{t-1} + b_i) \tag{1}$$

$$f_t = \sigma(W_f.x_t + U_f.h_{t-1} + b_f) \tag{2}$$

$$o_t = \sigma(W_o.x_t + U_o.h_{t-1} + b_o) \tag{3}$$

$$g_t = \tanh(W_g.x_t + U_g.h_{t-1} + b_g) \tag{4}$$

The three adaptive gates i_t, f_t, and o_t depend on the previous state h_{t-1} and the current input x_t. An extracted feature vector g_t is also computed by Eq. 4, serving as the candidate content.

The current memory cell c_t is a combination of the previous cell content c_{t-1} and the candidate content g_t, weighted by the input gate i_t and forget gate f_t, respectively.

$$c_t = i_t \otimes g_t + f_t \otimes c_{t-1} \tag{5}$$

The output of LSTM units is the recurrent networks hidden state, which is computed as follows.

$$h_t = o_t \otimes \tanh c_t \tag{6}$$

In the above equations, σ denotes a sigmoid function; $\otimes$ denotes element-wise multiplication.

We use the bidirectional LSTM to capture the context from both the past and the future [31]. Two separate LSTMs are used to preserved the previous and future context information in the bidirectional LSTM model, one encodes the sentence from the start to the end, and the other encodes the sentence from the end to the start. Therefore, we can gain two representations $\overrightarrow{h_t}$ and $\overleftarrow{h_t}$ at each position t of the sentence. Then we concatenate them to get the intermediate representation at position t, i.e. $h_t = [\overrightarrow{h_t}, \overleftarrow{h_t}]$. h_t is interpreted as a representation summarizing the word at position t and its contextual information. A illustration for the bidirectional LSTM are shown in Fig. 2.

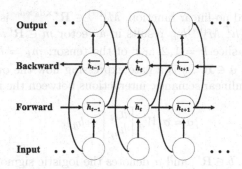

Fig. 2. A illustration of bidirectional LSTM.

3.3 Gated Relevance Network

$X = x_1, x_2, ..., x_n$ and $Y = y_1, y_2, ..., y_n$ are two text segments, and we use a bidirectional LSTM to get their positional encoding $X_h = x_{h_1}, x_{h_2}, ..., x_{h_n}$ and $Y_h = y_{h_1}, y_{h_2}, ..., y_{h_n}$ respectively. Then the relevance score is computed between every intermediate representation pair x_{h_i} and y_{h_j}. Generally, the main methods to measure their relevance include cosine distance, bilinear model [32,33], single layer neural network [34], etc.

Bilinear Model is defined as follows:

$$s(h_{x_i}, h_{y_j}) = h_{x_i}^T M h_{y_j} \tag{7}$$

$M \in \mathbf{R}^{d_h \times d_h}$. The bilinear model is a simple but efficient way to incorporate the strong linear interactions between two vectors. But this model has a weakness, which is the lack of ability to deal with nonlinear interaction.

Single Layer Network is defined as:

$$s(h_{x_i}, h_{y_j}) = u^T f(V \begin{bmatrix} h_{x_i} \\ h_{y_j} \end{bmatrix} + b), \tag{8}$$

where f represent a standard no-linear function, $V \in \mathbf{R}^{k \times 2d_h}$, $b \in \mathbf{R}^k$, and $u \in \mathbf{R}^k$. The single layer network could capture nonlinear interaction, while at the expense of a weak interaction between two vectors.

Each of the two models have its own advantages, and they can not take the place of each other. In our work, we adopt gated relevance network to incorporate the two models through the gate mechanism, which can capture more complex semantic interactions more powerfully. The incorporated model, namely **gated relevance network** (GRN), is defined as:

$$\begin{aligned} s(h_{x_i}, h_{y_j}) &= u^T (g \odot h_{x_i}^T M^{[1:r]} h_{y_j} \\ &\quad + (1 - g) \odot f(V \begin{bmatrix} h_{x_i} \\ h_{y_j} \end{bmatrix}) + b), \end{aligned} \tag{9}$$

where f is a standard no-linear function, $M^{[1:r]} \in \mathbf{R}^{r \times d_h \times d_h}$ is a bilinear tensor. The tensor product $h_{x_i}^T M^{[1:r]} h_{y_j}$ results in a vector $m \in \mathbf{R}^r$, where each entry is computed by one slice $k = 1, 2, ..., r$ of the tensor: $m_k = h_{x_i}^T M^{[1:r]} h_{y_j}$. $V \in \mathbf{R}^{r \times 2d_h}$, $b \in \mathbf{R}^r$ and $u \in \mathbf{R}^r$. g is a gate expressing how the output is produced by the linear and nonlinear semantic interactions between the inputs, defined as:

$$g = \sigma(W_g \begin{bmatrix} h_{x_i} \\ h_{y_j} \end{bmatrix} + b_g), \tag{10}$$

where $W_g \in \mathbf{R}^{r \times 2d_h}$, $b \in \mathbf{R}^r$, and σ denotes the logistic sigmoid function.

The gated relevance network will produce a semantic interaction score for the intermediate representation of two text segments between them. Thus the output of the gated relevance network for two text segments is an interaction score matrix.

3.4 Max-Pooling Layer and MLP

The paraphrase relation between two text segments is often dominated by some strong semantic interactions, therefore, we adopt the max-pooling strategy which partitions the score matrix as shown in Fig. 1 into a set of non-overlapping sub-regions, and for each such sub-region, outputs the maximum value. The pooling scores are further reshaped to a vector and fed to a multi-layer perceptron (MLP). For the task of paraphrase identification, the outputs of the whole network are the probabilities of two different classes, which is computed by a softmax function after the fully-connected layer. We name the full architecture of our model **Bi-LSTM+GRN**.

3.5   Model Training

Deep architecture with gated relevance network for paraphrase identification could be stated as a parameter vector θ. Given a text segment pair (X, Y) and its label l, the training objective is to minimize the cross-entropy of the predicted and the true label distributions, defined as:

$$L(X, Y; l, \hat{l}) = -\sum_{j=1}^{C} l_j \log(\hat{l}_j), \tag{11}$$

where l is the one-hot representation of the ground-truth label l; $\hat{l}$ is the predicted probabilities of labels; C is the class number.

To minimize the objective, we use stochastic gradient descent with the diagonal variant of AdaGrad [30] with minibatches. The parameter update for the i-th parameter $\theta_{t,i}$ at time step t is as follows:

$$\theta_{t,i} = \theta_{t-1,i} - \frac{\alpha}{\sqrt{\sum_{\tau=1}^{t} g_{\tau,i}^2}} g_{t,i}, \tag{12}$$

where α is the initial learning rate and $g_\tau \in \mathbf{R}^{|\theta_{\tau,i}|}$ is the gradient at time step τ for parameter $\theta_{\tau,i}$.

4   Experiments

4.1   Dataset and Evaluation Metrics

To evaluate the performance of our method, we use the Microsoft Research Paraphrase Corpus (MSRP)[35]. The dataset consists of 5,801 sentence pairs, which contains 4,076 instances for training and 1,725 for test, respectively. The average sentence length is 21, the shortest sentence has 7 words and the longest has 36. Each sentence pair is annotated with a binary label indicating whether the two sentences are paraphrases, so the task here is a kind of binary classification. The training set contains 2753 true and 1323 false paraphrase pairs; the test set contains 1147 true and 578 false pairs. Systems are evaluated by the accuracy and macro-averaged F1 score.

4.2   Parameter Settings

In this section, we experimentally study the effects of different kinds of parameters in our proposed method: word embedding size, pooling size, number of tensor slices, learning rate, and minibatch size. For the initialization of the word embeddings used in our model, we use the publicly available word2vec vectors that were trained on 100 billion words from Google News. The vectors have the dimensionality of 300 and were trained using the continuous bag-of-words architecture [25]. Words not presented in the set of pre-trained words are initialized randomly. All the text segments are padded to have the same length of

30, and the intermediate representations of LSTM are also set to 50. The other parameters are initialized by randomly sampling from the uniform distribution in $[-0.1, 0.1]$.

For other hyper-parameters of our proposed model, we take those hyper-parameters that achieved best performance on the development set. The final hyper-parameters are show in Table 1.

Table 1. Hyper-parameters of our model

Minibatch size	$m = 64$
Word embedding size	$d = 300$
Pooling size	$(p, q) = (3, 3)$
Number of tensor slices	$r = 2$
Learning rate	$\alpha = 0.01$

4.3   Baselines

Several variants of our method of Bi-LSTM+GRN are selected as the baselines for comparison, which are listed as below:

- LSTM: We use two single LSTMs to encode the two text segments, then concatenate them and feed to a MLP for paraphrase identification.
- Bi-LSTM: We use two single bidirectional LSTMs to encode the two text segments, then concatenate them and feed to a MLP for paraphrase identification.
- LSTM+GRN: We use the gated relevance network to calculate the semantic interaction scores between every intermediate representation pair in the two text segments generated by LSTM. The rest of the method is the same as our full model.

The results on Microsoft Research Paraphrase Corpus (MSRP) are shown in Table 2. From the experimental results, we have several findings.

Table 2. The performances of different variants on the MSRP Corpus.

Variants	F_1
LSTM	69.76%
Bi-LSTM	72.53%
LSTM+GRN	83.13%
Bi-LSTM+GRN	**86.5%**

It is easy to notice that LSTM and Bi-LSTM achieve lower performance than all of the methods using gated relevance network to capture the semantic interactions between the intermediate representation pairs. It helps to show that the main disadvantage of using LSTM or Bi-LSTM to encode a text segment into a single representation is that some important semantic interactions can not be fully preserved when compressing a long sentence into a single representation.

Our model and its closest variant, namely, Bi-LSTM+GRN and LSTM+GRN achieve better performance than LSTM and Bi-LSTM. It helps to show that the interaction between intermediate representation pairs is useful. The main disadvantage of using LSTM or Bi-LSTM to encode a text segment into a single representation is that some important semantic interactions can not be fully preserved when compressing a long sentence into a single representation. The Bi-LSTM+GRN approach can further improve the performance of LSTM+GRN, which also demonstrates that Bi-LSTM is more powerful in modeling the paraphrase identification.

4.4   Results of Comparison Experiments

To evaluate the performance of our method, we select six approaches as competitors. Table 3 summarizes the performances of [8,9,11,12,18,21] and our model. The accuracy and macro-averaged F1 measure results are presented for these methods. Based on the experimental results, we make the following observations:

Table 3. Comparison of the proposed method with existing methods in the MSRP dataset.

Model	Acc.	F_1
[18]	76.1%	82.7%
[8]	76.8%	83.6%
[21]	80.41%	85.96%
[9]	69.9%	80.9%
[11]	78.4%	84.6%
[12]	78.6%	84.73%
Adopted	**80.92%**	**86.5%**

Most models adopt word embedding as representation except [18,21]. [18,21] are both traditional hand-crafted feature based methods, which do not use neural networks for feature learning. Of the two, [21] makes use of unsupervised learning on the MSRP test set and rich sparse features, so it can obtain higher F1.

Our method, Bi-LSTM+GRN, obtains the highest F1 of 86.5% without extra artificial features. It outperforms previously reported best system of [21] with the F1 of 85.96%, although it has taken extra hand-crafted features into account. It shows that our method can learn a robust and effective representation by using Bi-LSTM.

[8] use feature learning procedures to avoid intensive feature engineering, and can capture the meaning combination to a certain extent and achieve a higher performance. However, the recursive procedures depends on the syntactic tree. Errors in syntactic parsing inhibit the ability of it to learn higher quality features.

[9,11,12] all apply convolution neural network to the extraction of sentence features and lead to satisfactory results, which shows CNN is able to learn valuable features for paraphrase identification.

Compared with CNN based methods, our models yield a better performance. One of the reason is that the way of sentence representation are different. Our model uses LSTM as the encoder. We take word positional representation into account through a bidirectional LSTM, which is beneficial to select the most informative interaction in later stage. Since [9,11,12] leverage CNN to learn representation of the entire sentence, it helps to show that the bi-LSTM is valuable for sentence modeling in paraphrase identification. Another reason should be due to that we adopt a gated relevance network to capture the semantic interaction between text segments, which can model interactions between text segments precisely.

5   Conclusion

In this paper, we adopted bidirectional Long Short-Term Memory-Gated Relevance Network (Bi-LSTM+GRN) for paraphrase identification, which uses a gated relevance network to capture the semantic interaction between text segments, and then aggregate those semantic interactions using a pooling layer to select the most informative interactions. Experiments on the Microsoft Research Paraphrase Corpus (MSRP) benchmark dataset show that our model achieves better performances than previous neural network models with the F1 of 86.5%.

In the future work, we will extend this model to related tasks including question answering and information retrieval.

References

1. Marsi, E., Krahmer, E.: Explorations in sentence fusion. In: Proceedings of the European Workshop on Natural Language Generation, pp. 109–117. Citeseer (2005)
2. Gomaa, W.H., Fahmy, A.A.: A survey of text similarity approaches. Int. J. Comput. Appl. **68**, 13 (2013). Foundation of Computer Science
3. Clough, P., Gaizauskas, R., Piao, S.S., Wilks, Y.: Meter: measuring text reuse. In: Proceedings of the 40th Annual Meeting on Association for Computational Linguistics, pp. 152–159. Association for Computational Linguistics (2002)
4. Parikh, A.P., Täckström, O., Das, D., Uszkoreit, J.: A Decomposable Attention Model for Natural Language Inference. arXiv preprint arXiv:1606.01933 (2016)
5. Collobert, R., Weston, J., Bottou, L., Karlen, M., Kavukcuoglu, K., Kuksa, P.: Natural language processing (almost) from scratch. J. Mach. Learn. Res. **12**, 2493–2537 (2011). JMLR.org

6. Zheng, X., Chen, H., Xu, T.: Deep learning for Chinese word segmentation and POS tagging. In: EMNLP, pp. 647–657 (2013)
7. Pei, W., Ge, T., Baobao, C.: Max margin tensor neural network for Chinese word segmentation. In: Proceedings of ACL (2014)
8. Socher, R., Huang, E.H., Pennin, J., Manning, C.D., Ng, A.Y.: Dynamic pooling and unfolding recursive autoencoders for paraphrase detection. In: Advances in Neural Information Processing Systems, pp. 801–809 (2011)
9. Hu, B., Lu, Z., Li, H., Chen, Q.: Convolutional neural network architectures for matching natural language sentences. In: Advances in Neural Information Processing Systems, pp. 2042–2050 (2014)
10. Wan, S., Lan, Y., Guo, J., Xu, J., Pang, L., Cheng, X.: A Deep Architecture for Semantic Matching with Multiple Positional Sentence Representations. arXiv preprint arXiv:1511.08277 (2015)
11. Yin, W., Schütze, H.: Convolutional neural network for paraphrase identification. In: Proceedings of the 2015 Conference of the North American Chapter of the Association for Computational Linguistics: Human Language Technologies, pp. 901–911 (2015)
12. He, H., Gimpel, K., Lin, J.: Multi-perspective sentence similarity modeling with convolutional neural networks. In: Proceedings of the 2015 Conference on Empirical Methods in Natural Language Processing, pp. 1576–1586 (2015)
13. Chen, J., Zhang, Q., Liu, P., Qiu, X., Huang, X.: Implicit discourse relation detection via a deep architecture with gated relevance network. In: Proceedings of ACL (2016)
14. Wan, S., Dras, M., Dale, R., Paris, C.: Using dependency-based features to take the "para-farce" out of paraphrase. In: Proceedings of the Australasian Language Technology Workshop, vol. 2006 (2006)
15. Madnani, N., Tetreault, J., Chodorow, M.: Re-examining machine translation metrics for paraphrase identification. In: Proceedings of the 2012 Conference of the North American Chapter of the Association for Computational Linguistics: Human Language Technologies, pp. 182–190. Association for Computational Linguistics (2012)
16. Bu, F., Li, H., Zhu, X.: String re-writing kernel. In: Proceedings of the 50th Annual Meeting of the Association for Computational Linguistics: Long Papers, vol. 1, pp. 449–458. Association for Computational Linguistics (2012)
17. Wu, D.: Recognizing paraphrases and textual entailment using inversion transduction grammars. In: Proceedings of the Joint Conference of the 47th Annual Meeting of the ACL and the 4th International Joint Conference on Natural Language Processing of the AFNLP, vol. 1, pp. 25–30. Association for Computational Linguistics (2005)
18. Das, D., Smith, N.A.: Paraphrase identification as probabilistic quasi-synchronous recognition. In: Proceedings of the ACL Workshop on Empirical Modeling of Semantic Equivalence and Entailment, pp. 468–476. Association for Computational Linguistics (2009)
19. Hassan, S.: Measuring semantic relatedness using salient encyclopedic concepts. University of North Texas (2011)
20. Guo, W., Diab, M.: Modeling sentences in the latent space. In: Proceedings of the 50th Annual Meeting of the Association for Computational Linguistics: Long Papers, vol. 1, pp. 864–872. Association for Computational Linguistics (2012)
21. Ji, Y., Eisenstein, J.: Discriminative improvements to distributional sentence similarity. In: EMNLP, pp. 891–896 (2013)

22. Tai, K.S., Socher, R., Manning, C.D.: Improved semantic representations from tree-structured long short-term memory networks. arXiv preprint arXiv:1503.00075 (2015)
23. Hochreiter, S., Schmidhuber, J.: Long short-term memory. Neural Computation, vol. 9, pp. 1735–1780. MIT Press (1997)
24. Turian, J., Ratinov, L., Bengio, Y.: Word representations: a simple and general method for semi-supervised learning. In: Proceedings of the 48th Annual Meeting of the Association for Computational Linguistics, title=Word Representations: A Simple and General Method for Semi-supervised Learning, pp. 384–394. Association for Computational Linguistics (2010)
25. Mikolov, T., Sutskever, I., Chen, K., Corrado, G.S., Dean, J.: Distributed representations of words and phrases and their compositionality. In: Advances in Neural Information Processing Systems, pp. 3111–3119 (2013)
26. Rumelhart, D.E., Hinton, G.E., Williams, R.J.: Learning representations by back-propagating errors. Cogn. Model. 5, 1 (1988)
27. Elman, J.L.: Finding structure in time. Cogn. Sci. 14, 179–211 (1990). Elsevier
28. Werbos, P.J.: Generalization of backpropagation with application to a recurrent gas market model. Neural Netw. 1, 339–356 (1998). Elsevier
29. Hochreiter, S.: The vanishing gradient problem during learning recurrent neural nets and problem solutions. Int. J. Uncertainty Fuzziness Knowl.-Based Syst. 6, 107–116 (1998). World Scientific
30. Duchi, J., Hazan, E., Singer, Y.: Adaptive subgradient methods for online learning and stochastic optimization. J. Mach. Learn. Res. 12, 2121–2159 (2011)
31. Schuster, M., Paliwal, K.K.: Bidirectional recurrent neural networks. IEEE Trans. Sig. Process. 45, 2673–2681 (1997). IEEE
32. Sutskever, I., Tenenbaum, J.B., Salakhutdinov, R.R.: Modelling relational data using bayesian clustered tensor factorization. Advances in Neural Information Processing Systems, pp. 1821–1828 (2009)
33. Jenatton, R., Roux, N.L., Bordes, A., Obozinski, G.R.: A latent factor model for highly multi-relational data. Advances in Neural Information Processing Systems, pp. 3167–3175 (2012)
34. Collobert, R., Weston, J.: A unified architecture for natural language processing: deep neural networks with multitask learning. In: Proceedings of the 25th International Conference on Machine Learning, pp. 160–167. ACM (2008)
35. Dolan, B., Quirk, C., Brockett, C.: Unsupervised construction of large paraphrase corpora: exploiting massively parallel news sources. In: Proceedings of the 20th International Conference on Computational Linguistics, p. 350. Association for Computational Linguistics (2004)

Syntactic Categorization and Semantic Interpretation of Chinese Nominal Compounds

Taizhong Wu[1], Jian Liu[2], Xuri Tang[3], Min Gu[1], Yanhui Gu[1,2], Junsheng Zhou[1,2], and Weiguang Qu[1,2(✉)]

[1] School of Computer Science and Technology, Nanjing Normal University, No. 1 Wenyuan Road, Nanjing 210023, Jiangsu, People's Republic of China
wgqu@njnu.edu.cn
[2] Jiangsu Research Center of Information Security and Privacy Technology, No. 122 Ninghai Road, Nanjing 210097, Jiangsu, People's Republic of China
[3] School of Foreign Languages, Huazhong University of Science and Technology, No. 1037 Luoyu Road, Wuhan 410074, Hubei, People's Republic of China

Abstract. The development in society and technology generates more Nominal Compounds to represent new concepts in various domains. Earlier literature in linguistic studies has gathered and established several syntactic categories of Nominal Compounds, which can be used for automatic syntactic categorization of these compounds. This paper is focused on Nominal Compounds of head-modifier construction because experiments show that most Nominal Compounds are head-modifier constructions. Based on the combination of templates and word similarity, this paper proposes an algorithm for automatic semantic interpretation which improves the recall ratio while maintaining the precision ratio. The results of syntactic categorization and automatic semantic interpretation of the Nominal Compounds are also applied in dependency parsing and machine translation.

Keywords: Nominal Compound in Chinese · Syntactic category · Automatic semantic interpretation · Dependency parsing · Machine translation

1 Introduction

N + N Compounds are important in language. A large number of new concepts are generated by combining two nouns, such as "jishu jingji, 技术 经济(Technology Economics)" and "xinxi jishu, 信息 技术(Information Technology)". The N + N Compounds are also called Nominal Compounds. Leonard [1] showed that the number of Nominal Compounds are increasing in an explosive speed. Statistics in Zhu [2] showed that there are about 14,249 Nominal Compounds in every 10,000 sentences.

Several Natural Language Processing tasks such as Machine Translation, Information Retrieval require the syntactic categorization and automatic semantic interpretation of Nominal Compounds. Nominal Compounds are formed by adjoining two nouns. However, the relationships between the two nouns are hard to detect. For instance, the "zhuozi yizi, 桌子椅子(desk and chair)" is a coordination, while the

© Springer International Publishing AG 2016
C.-Y. Lin et al. (Eds.): NLPCC-ICCPOL 2016, LNAI 10102, pp. 51–62, 2016.
DOI: 10.1007/978-3-319-50496-4_5

"mutou zhuozi, 木头桌子(wooden table)" is a head-modifier construction. How to identify the syntactic structure of a Nominal Compound and interpret its semantics is a challenging research topic.

2 Related Literature

Different from many other languages, Chinese grammar is more flexible and is not characterized by morphological inflections. As a result, the syntactic categorization and the automatic semantic interpretation are more difficult. Wu [3] initially analyzed the combination modes of Nominal Compounds on the basis of syntactic structure, semantic structure and rhetorics. Yang and Feng [4] and Li [5] and some others discussed the issue of classification of Nominal Compounds from the linguistic perspective. However, there is few research conducted on the automatic syntactic categorization of Nominal Compounds.

In regard of the automatic semantic interpretation of Nominal Compounds, Zhao et al. [6] used a top-down approach to annotate the semantic roles of the Nominal Compounds beginning with nominalized verbs. Wang et al. [7] used the bottom-up approach to search for "implicit predicates" [8] in Nominal Compounds and used searching engines for semantic interpretation. Liu [9] discussed the automatic syntactic categorization of Nominal Compounds and proposed an improved method for automatic semantic interpretation based on Wang's research. Pasca [10, 11] models the semantic interpretation template of Nominal Compounds as expression query.

Wei [12] combined the bottom-up and top-down approaches and proposed a new approach to automatic semantic interpretation based on Nominal Compound templates. The implicit predicates proposed in Wei are mostly their functional roles or agents [13]. The experiments in the research showed that the automatic semantic interpretation achieved a precision of 94.2% for 245 Nominal Compounds, but the recall is about 60.0%. In addition, Wei's study is weakened for its limited knowledge base of the nouns, limited number of function roles and agents, insufficient generalization of semantic interpretation templates, and lack of in-depth exploration of the template ambiguity. The research above assumes that Nominal Compounds are head-modifier constructions, which is not the case in language. Thus it is necessary to conduct syntactic categorization first.

3 Syntactic Categorization of Nominal Compounds in Chinese

3.1 Basic Rules

Linguists have already collected several rules for the detection of syntactic relations in Nominal Compounds. These rules requires SKCC [14] and HowNet [15] for implementation, as shown in Table 1.

The rules for the coordination construction, the subject-predicate construction, the appositive construction and the head-modifier construction are used in sequence.

Table 1. Rules for syntactic categorization of Nominal Compounds

Syntactic relation	Rule	Instance
Coordination relation	The semantic class of N1 is the same as that of N2	小麦 玉米 (wheat and corn)
	The DEFs in HowNet of the two nouns are identical	男生 女生 (boys and girls)
	The corresponding IDs of N1 and N2 are identical or their first 4 digits are identical and both end with "01"	
Subject-predicate relation	The semantic class of N1 is TIME or HUMAN	今天 星期天 (today is Sunday)
	The semantic class of N2 is TIME its DEF in HowNet is "time|时间"	
	The semantic class of N1 is BODY COMPONENT	浑身 冷汗 (covered with cold sweat)
	The semantic class of N2 is BODY COMPONENT, ARTIFACT, WASTE, COLOR or NATURAL-STUFF	
Apposition	The semantic class of N1 is PROFESSION	警察 叔叔 (policeman)
	The semantic class of N2 is RELATION	
	The semantic class of N1 is PROFESSION	东道主 学校 (host school)
	The semantic class of N2 is ORGANIZATION or INDIVIDUAL	
	N1 is the hypernym of N2	妖怪 白骨精 (Monster Baigujing)
	N2 is the hyponym of N1	
Head-modifier relation	The semantic classes of N1 and N2 are different and the compound is not subject-predicate or apposition relation	专家 小组 (expert group)
	N1 is the hyponym of N2, N2 is the hypernym of N1	书法 艺术 (art of calligraphy)
	N1 and N2 are part-whole relation	飞机 机舱 (aircraft nacelle)
	The DEFs in HowNet of the two nouns are identical	高血压 病 (hypertensive)
	N1 and N2 share the same ID in TongYiCiCiLin except for the last two digits and the ID of the second noun ends with "01"	

3.2 Context-Based Rules

The syntactic relation of Nominal Compounds can also be identified according to the phrases constructed from N1 and N2. For instance, if the construction "N1的N2(N2 of N1)" is legal, the N1 N2 construction is identified as head-modifier construction. If the construction "N1和/及/与/以及N2(N1 and N2)" is legal, the N1 N2 construction is identified as coordination construction. Based on the above observation, we established the following rules:

If only the construction "N1的N2(N2 of N1)" is found in corpora, "N1N2" is a head-modifier construction; if only the constructions "N1和/与/及/以及N2(N1 and N2)" are found in the corpora, "N1N2" is a coordination construction; If all the above constructions are found in corpora and the occurrences of "N1和/与/及/以及N2 (N1 and N2)" are more frequent than "N1的N2 (N2 of N1)", the construction is a coordination construction, otherwise it is a head-modifier relation. For instance the compound "游客和导游(tourist and guide)" occurs more frequent than "游客的导游(the guide of tourist)", thus "youke, 游客(tourist) daoyou, 导游(guide)" is a coordination construction.

3.3   Rules of Named Entities

This section explains the rules for Nominal Compounds with named entities. Named entities include name of person, name of place and name of organization etc. Both "NT + NS" and "NR + NS" are illegal compounds. "NS + NT", "NR + NT", "NT + NR", "NS + NR", "NT + N" and "NS + N" are head-modifier constructions. The "N + NR" compound is an apposition. The "NR + NR" is not discussed in the present research.

In regard of NS1 + NS2, if NS1 and NS2 are of the same ID in TongYiCiCiLin, the compound is a coordination construction, otherwise it is a head-modifier construction. For instance, "aomen, 澳门(Macao) taiwan, 台湾(Taiwan)" is a coordination construction, while "jiangsu, 江苏(Jiangsu) nanjing, 南京(Nanjing)" is a head-modifier construction.

As for N + NS compound, if N is of the semantic class SPACE, LOCATION, RELATION, IDENTITY or GEOGRAPHIC-ENTITY, the compound is an apposition. Otherwise if N contains the character "ji, 籍(ancestral home)", it is a subject-predicate construction, otherwise it is a head-modifier construction. For instance, the compound "shoudu, 首都(capital) beijing, 北京(Beijing)" is an apposition, and the compound "zuji, 祖籍(ancestral home) zhejiang, 浙江(Zhejiang)" is a subject-predicate construction.

In regard of NT1 + NT2, if NT1 and NT2 share the same affix, the compound is a coordination construction, otherwise it is a head-modifier construction. For instance, the "minzhengbu, 民政部(ministry of civil affairs) caizhengbu, 财政部(ministry of finance)" is a coordination construction.

In regard of N + NT, if N is of the semantic class ORGANIZATION, IDENTITY, PEOPLE and HUMAN, the compound is an apposition, otherwise it is a head-modifier construction. For instance, the compound "zhongzi, 种子(seed) zhongguodui, 中国队 (Chinese team)" is a apposition.

As for NR + N compound, if N is of the semantic class IDENTITY, PROFESSION, PERSON AND RELATION, the compound is an apposition. Otherwise if N is of the semantic class ORIGIN, APPEARANCE, or PHYSIOLOGY, the compound is a subject-predicate construction, otherwise it is a head-modifier construction. For instance, the compound "jinyong, 金庸(Louis Cha) xiansheng, 先生(mister)" is an apposition and the compound "luxun, 鲁迅(Lu Xun) shaoxingren, 绍兴人(native of Shaoxing)" is a subject-predicate construction.

3.4   Rules for Syntactic Categorization

We summarize the above rules and propose the following rules for Nominal Compounds:

(1) If the compound N + N contains a named entity, the rules of named entities applies for syntactic categorization;
(2) Otherwise, the DEFs for N1 and N2 are obtained from HowNet and the basic rules applies (if the noun is not found in HowNet, it is replaced by a synonym in TongYiCiCiLin);
(3) If the above rules cannot deal with the situation (for instance, the noun is not found in HowNet), the context-based rules apply.

3.5   Syntactic Categorization Experiments

The data for syntactic categorization are selected from the corpora compiled from the texts of the first half of 1998 People's Daily and the texts from 1991 and 2004 Xinhua News. A total number of 770,456 Nominal Compounds is retrieved for the experiment.

After the test, 688,247 compounds are categorized, among them are 224 appositions, 28 subject-predicate constructions, 3,413 coordination constructions and 684,582 head-modifier constructions. The other 82, 209 compounds are not categorized. Manual check is performed on all the subject-predicate constructions, coordination constructions, appositions and a sampling of 3,000 head-modifier constructions. Because the numbers of appositions, subject-predicate constructions, and coordination constructions are small, the computation of precision, recall and F-measure is conducted on head-modifier constructions.

Table 2 shows that the head-modifier constructions take a large share in Nominal Compounds. We have therefore proceed to conduct automatic semantic interpretation on those head-modifier constructions which are automatically acquired and manually checked in the above process.

Table 2. Classification results of modifier-head construction

Syntactic relation	Precision	Recall	F-measure
Head-modifier relation	96.12%	96.68%	96.40%

4   Automatic Semantic Interpretation of Head-Modifier Nominal Compounds

4.1   Description of the System

The discussion above shows that the head-modifier constructions take a large share in Nominal Compounds. We have therefore proceed to conduct automatic semantic interpretation on those head-modifier constructions. Figure 1 illustrates the structure of the system. We have modified Wei's algorithm by introducing TongYiCiCiLin and adding new semantic interpretation templates and template-based acquisition of similar

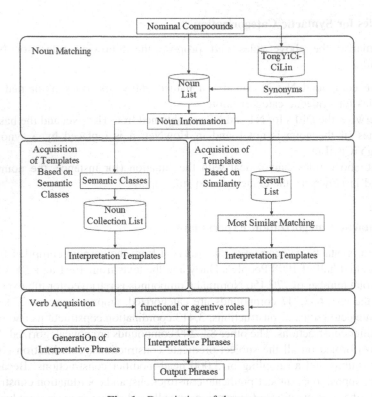

Fig. 1. Description of the system

words. The algorithm consists of the following components: noun matching, acquisition of interpretation templates, verb acquisition and generation of interpretative phrases.

4.2 Resources and Similarity Computation

The following resources are used for similarity computation: TongYiCiCiLin, a noun list, a noun collocation list and a result list. TongYiCiCiLin is used to extend the dictionary and to compute similarity. The noun list contains information about the semantic class, semantic roles of the nouns. The noun collocation list contains different combinations of semantic classes and their corresponding semantic interpretation templates. The Nominal Compounds and the semantic interpretation templates that obtain correct interpretations are chosen to form the result list.

Based on TongYiCiCiLin, we propose an algorithm to compute the similarity between Nominal Compounds that contain the same number of nouns. Before computing the similarity between Nominal Compounds, the similarity between the nouns are first computed. In TongYiCiCiLin, the nouns are stored in the data structure of trees. The method to compute the similarity between noun A and noun B is give in Eq. 1.

$$S(A, B) = \begin{cases} \lambda_0 & A, B \text{ is not in the same tree} \\ \lambda_i \times \frac{n-k+1}{n} & A, B \text{ is in the i-th branch} \\ 1 & A, B \text{ is in the same leaf node} \end{cases} \quad (1)$$

where $\lambda_0 = 0.1$, $\lambda_1 = 0.65$, $\lambda_2 = 0.8$, $\lambda_3 = 0.9$, $\lambda_4 = 0.96$.

Last, the similarity between two Nominal Compounds NC1 and NC2 that have the same number of nouns is computed with Eq. 2.

$$Sim(\text{NC1}, \text{NC2}) = (\prod_{i=1}^{n} S(A_i, B_i))^{\frac{1}{n}} \quad (2)$$

where A_i is the ith noun in NC1, B_i is the ith noun in NC2, n is the number of nouns in NC1 or NC2.

4.3 Noun Matching

When we are searching for a noun, if it is in the Noun List, information can be retrieved directly. Otherwise, we switch to TongYiCiCiLin to search for all the synonyms and then search for the synonyms in the Name List. All the information obtained in the above search is stored as the information for the noun. For instance, if "quanguo, 全国 (whole country)" is not found in the Name List, we use the information of "juguo, 举国 (whole country)" for the purpose.

4.4 Acquisition of Semantic Interpretation Templates

Template Acquisition Based on Semantic Class Combination. In Wei's method, semantic interpretation templates are acquired via semantic class combination in Nominal Compounds. We have adopted Wei's method in this paper. To interpret a Nominal Compound, we retrieve the information of semantic classes of S1 and S2 for the nouns N1 and N2. If the combination of S1 and S2 is found in Noun Collocation List, the template can be used straight forwardly. Otherwise, the higher semantic classes of S1 and S2 are obtained and searched for in Noun Collocation List. This process is repeated until a template is obtained or the top semantic class is reached. Algorithm 1 illustrates the above process.

Template Acquisition Based on Word Similarity. Although the semantic interpretation templates for the majority of Nominal Compounds can be directly obtained from Noun Collocation List, it is difficult to obtain semantic interpretation templates for some Nominal Compounds. To solve this issue, we acquire the templates on the basis of word similarity. The Nominal Compound in the Result List that is the most similar to the one in question is named as the "maximum match". When the similarity of the "maximum match" is above 0.8, the filter value, the correct semantic interpretation template is used as the template for the Nominal Compound in question. Algorithm 2 illustrates the process of acquire templates based on word similarity.

Algorithm 1. Template Matching by Semantic Class

```
Require: N1's and N2's semantic class set S1 and S2
Ensure: interpretation template set Template
GetTemplate(S1, S2)
{
  if S1 is null or S2 is null
    then return null
  foreach S in S1
    foreach S' in S2
  if S+S' in the Noun Collection List
  then {
      Get the templates T
      Template.Add(T)
  }
  else {
      GetTemplate(S1.HigherSemanticClass, S2)
      GetTemplate(S1, S2.HigherSemanticClass)
  }
}
```

Algorithm 2. Template Matching by Similarity

```
Require: N1 and N2
Ensure: interpretation template set Template
if Template = null
then {
  Calculate all the similarity with NCs in the Result
List
  Get the most similar NC's templates T and its similari-
ty S
  if S > 0.8
  then Template.Add(T)
}
```

Verb Acquisition and Generation of Interpretative Phrases. When a semantic interpretation template requires a functional role or a thematic role for a noun, it can be obtained by looking up the word for its information.

Finally the nouns and the functional roles or thematic roles (if needed) acquired are inserted into corresponding places to generate interpretative phrases.

For instance, the compound "shiyou shichang 石油 市场(Oil Market)" possesses the interpretative template "V2 + N1 + 的 + N2" where V2 is the functional role of N2. Thus the function role of "shichang 市场(market)" (N2) is "maimai 买卖(trade)", and the interpretative phrase is "买卖石油的市场(the market of trading oil)".

4.5 Experiments of Automatic Semantic Interpretation

The test set is randomly selected from the head-modifier constructions acquired from the experiments of Nominal Compound syntactic classification that also occur frequently in the corpora. We have used Wei's algorithm as the base line and introduced the semantic interpretation template, synonym matching and templates acquired on the basis of word similarity. The experiments for both the base line algorithm and the algorithm proposed in this paper are given in Table 3. It can be seen in the Table that the algorithm proposed in this paper achieved an increase of 15.07% in recall while maintaining the precision ratio. The F-measure has increased 7.86%. This shows that the methods proposed in the paper has achieved its goal.

The analysis on those Nominal Compounds that are not correctly interpreted in both the base line and the proposed algorithm is given in Fig. 2. The nouns for which no information can be obtained are themselves compound words, such as "gaoxinjishu 高新技术(high and new technology)" and "huodezhe 获得者(gainer)".

Table 3. Experimental result.

The improved process	Token sum	Number of nominal compounds for interpretation	Number of correct interpretation	Precision	Recall	F-measure
Base line	1,069	825	715	86.67%	66.88%	76.25%
+Template	1,069	932	810	86.91%	75.77%	80.96%
+Synonyms	1,069	950	828	87.16%	77.46%	81.31%
+Similarity	1,069	1,014	876	86.39%	81.95%	84.11%

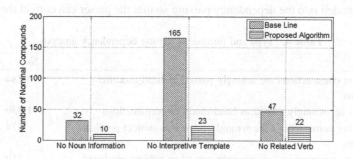

Fig. 2. Statistics of failure interpretation

5 Application in Syntactic Parsing and Machine Translation

5.1 Correction in Syntactic Parsing

Nominal Compounds are common in Chinese. In written Chinese, the ratio is even higher. In dependency parsing, Nominal Compounds form an important part which have to be dealt with in the process of parsing sentences. We analyzed the retrieval and analysis in dependency parsing and identified the weakness in its process so that the proposed method can be used to improve the analysis of Nominal Compounds in dependency parsing.

4,036 Nominal Compounds are selected from the automatic syntactic classification and manual checking. For each Nominal Compound, sentences are retrieved from the corpora. In total 66,698 non-repetitive sentences are collected. The sentences are parsed using HIT Dependency Parser. For instance, the parsing result for the sentence "这是一次展示国威军威的远航(This is a voyage to display national and military prestige)" is given in Fig. 3. In the parsing result, the compound "guowei 国威(national prestige) junwei 军威(military prestige)" is identified as head-modifier construction, but it is in fact a coordination construction.

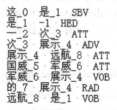

Fig. 3. Example of syntactic analysis

Manual check shows that 25,628 sentences are correct and 41,070 are wrong. The reasons that cause the above errors in parsing are summarized in Table 4. As shown in the table, the major factors that cause errors are coordination constructions and appositions. In other words, if these two types of constructions are correctly parsed, the parser shall perform better. We hope that the automatic syntactic categorization system can be integrated into the dependency parsing so that the parser can correct these errors.

Table 4. Type and number of wrong dependency analysis

Error type	No.	%
Coordination constructions are wrongly parsed as head-modifier constructions	38,784	94.43
Appositions are wrongly parsed as head-modifier constructions	1,739	4.23
Head-modifier constructions are wrongly parsed as subject-predicate constructions	274	0.67
Coordination constructions are wrongly parsed as subject-predicate constructions	119	0.29
Other error	154	0.38

5.2   Application in Machine Translation

We randomly select 100 Nominal Compounds that are correctly interpreted. For each Nominal Compound, a sentence that contains the compound is selected from the corpora. The sentence is then modified by replacing the original compound with its interpretation.

Both the original sentence and new sentence are fed into Google translator and Baidu translator. The translation results are assessed manually. The score is distributed within [−5, +5], where −5 denotes a completely incorrect translation and +5 a fully correct translation. The assessment of the translation results are given in Table 5. In the figure, the second line is the Google translation, and the third is the Baidu translation.

Table 6 gives the experiment results. It shows that the Chinese-English of Google on-line translation system yields poorer translation when the replacement is performed while the Baidu translation system gives better overall translation results. We hope that the research result can be integrated into Machine Translation systems.

Table 5. Translation results and scores

Phrase/sentence	Translation by Google/score		Translation by Baidu/score	
材料硬度	Hardness	1	Material hardness	4
材料的硬度	Hardness of the material	5	Hardness of materials	5
PBO材料硬度很高不易加工。	PBO high hardness of the material difficult to process	3	PBO material hardness is not easy to process	4
PBO材料的硬度很高不易加工。	PBO high hardness materials difficult to process	2	The hardness of PBO material is very difficult to be processed	5

Table 6. Mean score of machine translation test

Phrase/sentence	Score for Google	Score for Baidu
Nominal Compounds	1.0400	1.2800
Interpretation of Nominal Compounds	0.7366	2.0700
Sentence Instance where Nominal Compounds are found	0.1233	0.4267
Sentences with Nominal Compounds replaced	0.1167	0.4900

6 Conclusions

This paper proposed a rule-based method of syntactic categorization of Nominal Compounds, improved the automatic semantic interpretation based on TongYiCiCiLin and Nominal Compound similarity, and added to the semantic interpretation templates. The obtained experiment results are applied in dependency parsing and machine translation with satisfactory results.

We plan to further explore the syntactic categorization of Nominal Compounds and their automatic semantic interpretation and apply the obtained knowledge in other tasks.

Acknowledgement. This work is partially supported by Chinese National Fund of Natural Science under Grant 61272221 and 61472191, Jiangsu Province Fund of Social Science under Grant 12YYA002, and Natural Science Research of Jiangsu Higher Education Institutions of China under Grant 14KJB520022, 15KJA420001.

References

1. Leonard, R.: The interpretation of English noun sequences on the computer. J. Immunol. **111** (4), 1176–1182 (1984)
2. Zhu, H.: Research on the Methods of Chinese Noun Compounds Identification and Classification. Harbin Institute of Technology (2007). (in Chinese)
3. Wu, J.: Schema Theory and Interpretation of Compound Words in Contemporary Chinese. Shanghai International Studies University (2006). (in Chinese)
4. Yang, Q., Feng, Z.: Research on the structural ambiguity of noun-noun in modern Chinese. Stud. Lang. Linguist. **25**(04), 105–111 (2005). (in Chinese)
5. Li, S.: How to distinguish the type of structure of noun-noun in modern Chinese by computer. Acad. Forum **194**(03), 177–180 (2007). (in Chinese)
6. Zhao, J., Liu, H., Lu, R.: Semantic labeling of compound nominalization in Chinese. In: Proceedings of Workshop on a Broader Perspective on Multiword Expressions, pp. 73–80. ACL, Prague (2007)
7. Wang, M., Huang, J., Yu, S., et al.: Chinese noun compound interpretation based on paraphrasing verbs. J. Chin. Inf. Process. **24**(06), 3–9 (2010). (in Chinese)
8. Yuan, Y.: Predicate implicit and syntactic consequences. Chin. Lang. **1995**(4), 241–255 (1995). (in Chinese)
9. Liu, J.: Research on the Syntactic Classification and Automatic Interpretation of Chinese N + N Compound. Nanjing Normal University (2016). (in Chinese)
10. Pasca, M.: Interpreting compound noun phrases using web search queries. In: Proceedings of North American Chapter of the Association for Computational Linguistics: Human Language Technologies, pp. 335–344. NAACL, Denver (2015)
11. Pasca, M.: The role of query sessions in interpreting compound noun phrases In: Proceedings of 24th ACM International on Conference on Information and Knowledge Management, pp. 1121–1129. CIKM, Melbourne (2015)
12. Wei, X.: Research on Chinese Noun Compound Interpretation for Semantic-Query. Peking University (2012). (in Chinese)
13. Pustejovsky, J.: The generative lexicon. Comput. Linguist. **17**(4), 409–441 (1991)
14. Wang, H., Zhan, W., Yu, S.: The semantic knowledge-base of contemporary Chinese and its applications in MT. Lang. Appl. **2006**(01), 134–141 (2006). (in Chinese)
15. Dong, Z.: The expression of semantic relation and the construction of knowledge system. Lang. Appl. **1998**(3), 79–85 (1998). (in Chinese)

TDSS: A New Word Sense Representation Framework for Information Retrieval

Liwei Chen[1,2]($\boxtimes$), Yansong Feng[1], and Dongyan Zhao[1]

[1] Institute of Computer Science and Technology, Peking University, Beijing, China
chenliwei@baidu.com, {fengyansong,zhaodongyan}@pku.edu.cn
[2] Baidu Inc., Beijing, China

Abstract. Word sense representation is important in the tasks of information retrieval (IR). Existing lexical databases, e.g., WordNet, and automated word sense representing approaches often use only one view to represent a word, and may not work well in the tasks which are sensitive to the contexts, e.g., query rewriting. In this paper, we propose a new framework to represent a word sense simultaneously in two views, explanation view and context view. We further propose an novel method to automatically learn such representations from large scale of query logs. Experimental results show that our new sense representations can better handle word substitutions in a query rewriting task.

Keywords: Word sense induction · Graph clustering · Query rewriting

1 Introduction

As the amount of the information on the Internet increasing exponentially, there are growing demands in the information retrieval (IR) industry to understand the queries better, so as to provide the users with more accurate and diverse results. Such query understanding tasks require fine modeling of word meanings to capture subtle semantic differences of words. For example, query rewriting, an important IR task in many realistic search engines, should rewrite a query with synonymous or similar words with the ones in the query, so as to obtain more retrieval results. In practice, in order to avoid semantic drift of query meanings, we mainly use synonyms to rewrite the query. Take the query "五道口附近哪里吃早点(Where can I have breakfast in Wudaokou)" as an example, we would like to use "早餐(breakfast)" to substitute "早点(breakfast)" as a rewriting of the query. However, many words in queries are ambiguous, and we need to use the context to determine which sense a word would use, and the synonymous words of this sense will be used to rewrite the query. This means that the task should exploit two views of a word sense: the explanation view, containing synonyms of the sense, and the context view, representing in what contexts this sense is used. Unfortunately, most existing works on word sense representations are not suitable for the task.

© Springer International Publishing AG 2016
C.-Y. Lin et al. (Eds.): NLPCC-ICCPOL 2016, LNAI 10102, pp. 63–75, 2016.
DOI: 10.1007/978-3-319-50496-4_6

Traditional lexical databases, such as WordNet [10,11], groups words into sets of synonyms called synsets, providing short definitions and usage examples. It only uses the explanation view to represent the word senses, while the context in the usage examples is rather limited. Furthermore, it requires lots of human efforts to construct and update, thus is difficult to adapt to other domains or languages.

On the other hand, automated word sense induction (WSI) has attracted more and more attention. Previous works on WSI mainly focus on characterizing word meanings by modeling the contexts or descriptions of the ambiguous word, including unsupervised clustering [5,14,15], or topic models [2]. Recent research efforts also attempt to build a continuous vector to represent a word or a sense of a word [3,4,6,7,9,12,16], and the models are usually trained on the contexts and/or the textual descriptions of the words. Those approaches often use only one view to represent a word, which makes the two aspects of word sense interact with each other, and may confuse the query rewriting model.

In this paper, we propose a novel framework, two-dimensional semantic space (TDSS), which jointly use two vectors, the explanation vector and the context vector, to represent a word sense. The explanation vector is generated using synonyms, serving as a description of this sense. For convenience, we also call those words as its *explanation words*. The context vector is constructed based on the corresponding context of the sense. We further propose an approach to obtain such TDSS representations for word senses from large scale query logs. The explanation words and context words are extracted from the query paraphrases, and further grouped into multiple senses. Experimental results on 33 Chinese words and a query rewriting case study show that our approach can output reasonable word senses, which can be further used in the task of query rewriting.

2   Related Work

In this section, we briefly review previous studies on traditional context-oriented WSI methods.

Previous studies in WSI are often context-oriented. Those approaches can be divided into three categories: unsupervised clustering approaches, generative approaches and word embedding approaches.

In cluster-based approaches, WSI is treated as a clustering problem. The mentions of a target word are grouped into several clusters according to the similarity of their contexts. Many different clustering algorithms have been used so far, e.g., k-means [14], agglomerative clustering [15], information bottleneck [13].

The graph-based cluster methods can also be used in the task of WSI [8], where words are the nodes and the co-occurrence between words are the edges. Community detection algorithms can be employed to discover word communities in the graph, which is used to represent word senses.

Generative approaches assume that different senses have different lexical distributions. For example, [2] utilizes a parametric Bayesian model, i.e., LDA, to solve the WSI task. The word senses are characterized as distributions over words and an ambiguous word is then drawn from a distribution of senses. In order to automatically decide the number of senses, instead of LDA, [17] propose to use a nonparametric Bayesian model, called Hierarchical Dirichlet Process (HDP).

Recently word embedding approaches have attracted more and more attention In those approaches, a word or the sense of a word is often represented by a continuous vector which is built by neural network algorithms [3,4,6,7,9,12,16]. Most approaches use the contexts and/or the textual descriptions of the words to train those models.

3   A New Word Sense Representation Framework

In TDSS, we represent the sense of a word in two views, explanation view and context view. We use synonyms of a word to generate its explanation view. Take the word "看(see, look)" as an example, the explanation view of one of its senses may consist words such as "阅读(read)" and "浏览(browse)".

For the context view, we extract words from the contexts where this meaning is used. In the example of the word "看(see, look)" we can use the words which often exist in its contexts, such as "书(book)", "报纸(newspaper)", etc., to generate the context view.

Formally, given a word w with k senses, its ith sense can be represented as a tuple $S_i = < E_i, C_i >$, where E_i is a vector representing the explanation of this sense, and C_i is a vector representing the context of this sense. We also assign a popularity for E_i, which indicates how popular E_i is among all sense explanations of the target word. We restrict that the popularity of all sense explanations of a word should sum up to 1:

$$\sum_{i=1}^{k} Pop(E_i) = 1 \qquad (1)$$

Generally speaking, the senses used in more common and diverse contexts are often more popular. We calculate the popularity of a sense based on the probability of the sense's contexts:

$$Pop(S_i) = \frac{P(C_i)}{\sum_{j=1}^{k} P(C_j)} \qquad (2)$$

In this paper we construct the vectors as a simple bag of words (BoW) model, where each dimension of the vector is a word in the sense explanations or contexts. It is possible to use more sophisticated models such as topic models or word embedding, which will be our future work.

4   TDSS Sense Extraction

In order to automatically obtain the TDSS representations of word senses, we first extracting paraphrases from the query logs, and detect word alignments between those paraphrase pairs. Then we extract substitution pairs as well as the corresponding contexts based on the alignments. The substitutions of a word will be considered as its explanation words. Finally, for a given word, we collect all its substitutions as well as the corresponding contexts, adopt a clustering algorithm to group the substitutions into different senses and further obtain the TDSS representation from each sense.

4.1   Explanation Words and Context Extraction

Generating Paraphrases. Given the query logs, we adopt the approach in [18] to generate sentential paraphrases from them, which will be further used as the sources of mining explanation words and contexts of word meanings.

Word Alignment. For each pair of sentential paraphrases, we align the words in one paraphrase to their corresponding substitution words in the other. We adopt a rule-based aligning strategy for the word alignment. Two words are aligned if they are the same, synonyms (according to an existing thesaurus), or the words inside a window around them (window size is set to 1) are the same or synonyms.

Substitution and Context Extraction. Generally speaking, two aligned words a and b in a paraphrase pair can be synonyms, co-hyponyms or hypernyms, etc. Thus, we can use a word's substitutions to form the explanation views of its senses. For each sense, we also need a context vector C. The words inside a fixed window size (set to 3 empirically) of the query paraphrases are extracted to generate the context vectors.

Now for each substitution pair, we will compute the substitution probability approximately based on all paraphrases. Given a word a and its substitution b, the probability of a is substituted by b can be calculated as:

$$p(a \rightarrow b) = \frac{freq(a \rightarrow b)}{\sum_{b_i \in B} freq(a \rightarrow b_i)} \tag{3}$$

where $freq(a \rightarrow b)$ is the times a is substituted by b in total, B is all words which can substitute a.

It is also important to estimate the probability of the target word w substituted by the explanation word e given the context word c. Formally, $p(w \rightarrow e|c)$ can be calculated as:

$$p(w \rightarrow e|c) = \frac{freq(w \rightarrow e|c)}{\sum_{e_i \in E_c} freq(w \rightarrow e_i|c)} \tag{4}$$

where $freq(w \rightarrow e|c)$ is the times that w is substituted by e given the context word c, E_c is the set of all words that can substitute w under the context word c.

4.2   Sense Graph Construction

In our approach, the senses of a word are captured from the sense graph of this word. The graph is constructed based on the substitution pairs and the context words extracted in the previous subsection. For a given word, we collect all its substitution words, which can be seen as its explanation words. Then we connect the obtained explanation words by their pairwise relatedness estimated based on the substitution probabilities and context words obtained in the previous subsection.

Graph Pruning. Since there are lots of noises in the generated substitution pairs, we need to prune the sense graph to reduce the noises. The following strategies are used to prune the graph.

The first strategy is simple: we prune any explanation words with low substitution probabilities or low substitution frequencies. The pruning thresholds are set empirically for this strategy.

The second strategy utilizes triangle-like substitutions to prune unreliable graph nodes and edges. The assumption is that a triangle-like substitution structure are more stable and reliable, and can help us to prune the noises from the graph. Suppose we have a node a in the sense graph of a word w, which means w can be substituted by a. If we can find another node b in the graph satisfying a can be replaced by b, then we reserve both a and b. Otherwise, a will be pruned from the graph. Figure 1 illustrates a triangle-like substitution structure, where 去(go on a trip) is the word w, 游览(travel) is the word a and 旅行(take a trip) is the word b.

Edge Weighting. The weights of the edges in the sense graph indicate the relatedness between the explanation words. Given the sense graph of a word w, and two nodes a and b in this graph, the edge e_{ab} between the two nodes is weighted as:

$$weight(e_{ab}) = \alpha sub(a, b) + (1 - \alpha)sim(a, b) \tag{5}$$

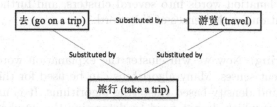

Fig. 1. Illustration of the triangle-like substitution structure.

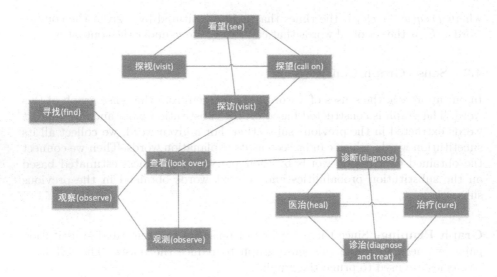

Fig. 2. An abridged example of the semantic graph. The weights of the edges are also omitted for the sake of brevity.

$sub(a, b)$ is the substitution relatedness between a and b, which is calculated as the average value of $p(a \to b)$ and $p(b \to a)$. $sim(a, b)$ is the context similarity (cosine similarity) between a and b, calculated based on the contexts in which w is substituted by a and b respectively. The context word c is weighted by the conditional probability $p(a \to b|c)$. α is a parameter used to adjust the importance of the two components. It will be optimized on a held out set.

After the pruning and edge weighting step, for each target word, we obtain a sense graph from all remaining substitutions as well as their pairwise weightings. Figure 2 illustrates an abridged version of a sense graph for the word 看. The meanings of 看 in Chinese includes 看望(visit), 治疗(cure) and 观察(observe), etc.

4.3   Sense Generation and Weighting

After we construct the sense graph for a word, we adopt a clustering method to group the explanation words into several clusters, and further generate the TDSS representation for the senses of this word.

Graph Clustering. Now we will cluster the explanation words and context words into different senses. Many algorithms can be used for this task, such as KMeans, HAC, and density-based clustering algorithms. It is more suitable to use the algorithms which do not need to determine the number of clusters in advance, since it is difficult for us to know the exact numbers of the senses of each word.

We choose a label propagation algorithm to cluster the graph. All nodes of the graph will be initialized with a different sense. In each iteration, for each node of the graph, we collect all its neighbors, and the score of each sense is calculated by summing the weights of all neighbors which support it. The senses whose scores are higher than a threshold will be the senses of this node. If the senses of less than 10% nodes are modified in an iteration, the procedure will stop.

Sense Generation. After the clustering, we can obtain the TDSS representations for senses of the target word w. Each cluster can be used to construct the explanation vector of one sense. The value of each dimension in an explanation vector E is the substitution probability of the corresponding explanation word:

$$E = (p(w \rightarrow e_1), p(w \rightarrow e_2), ..., p(w \rightarrow e_m)) \tag{6}$$

where e_i is the explanation words in the cluster. For each sense, we aggregate all its sense words' contexts together, and filter the ones whose frequencies are too low. The remaining words form the C vector of this sense. The value of the elements in C is the conditional probability that the target word w is substituted by the explanation words of the current sense given the corresponding context word c. Thus, C is computed as:

$$C = (p(w \rightarrow E|c_1), p(w \rightarrow E|c_2), ..., p(w \rightarrow E|c_n)) \tag{7}$$

where E is the set of the explanation words of the corresponding sense, and $p(w \rightarrow E|c_i)$ is calculated as:

$$p(w \rightarrow E|c_i) = \sum_{e_j \in E} p(w \rightarrow e_j|c_i) \tag{8}$$

According to the definition of the sense popularity in Sect. 3, given a word w which has k senses, the popularity of S_i can be computed as:

$$Pop(S_i) = \frac{\sum_{c \in C_i} freq(c)}{\sum_{j=1}^{k} \sum_{c \in C_j} freq(c)} \tag{9}$$

where $freq(c)$ is the frequency of the context word c, C_i is the set of context words of S_i. Since the popular senses are usually more important for the users, we collect the senses with the top n popularity as our results. Table 1 shows some samples of the generated senses for the word 打(beat).

5   Experiments

We construct a dataset with 33 ambiguous Chinese words to evaluate the performance of our model. Those words are manually selected from the ambiguous

Table 1. Samples for induced word senses

Word	Sense word cluster S_i and context cluster C_i
打(beat)	$Sense_1$: 打针(injection), 注射(injection)
	$Context_1$:美白(whitening), 乙肝 (hepatitis B), 麻药(Anesthetic)
	$Sense_2$: 打仗(to war), 攻略(strategy), 过关(pass game level), 进攻(attack)
	$Context_2$:剑灵(Blade Soul), 装备 (equipment), 外挂(plug-in), 技能(skills)
	$Sense_3$: 标出(mark), 写成(written), 键入(keyboard input), 打出(show)
	$Context_3$:WPS, 括号(parentheses), 平方(square), 文档(document)
	$Sense_4$: 毒打(beat cruelly), 挨打(be beaten), 掌掴(Slap), 殴打(beat up)
	$Context_4$:苏醒(wake up), 婴儿(baby), 老公(husband), 保安(guard)

words in the Chinese query logs, and the dataset is designed to be representative for different kinds of words, including nouns, verbs, adjectives, adverbs, words with only one character, and words with multiple POS tags. Resolving the ambiguity of those words is highly important for the task of query understanding in the industry. The words we use are listed in Table 2: Each word's explanation words are collected and clustered into senses manually by three volunteers. We integrate their annotations by majority vote. This dataset will be our gold standard for evaluating the explanation view. We do not manually generate the context views because they usually contain too many words. The context views will be evaluated implicitly in the case study.

Table 2. The words used in our evaluation. The English words afterwards illustrate two representative meanings of the Chinese words.

戒(ring, give up, etc.)	完(whole, finish, etc.)
淡薄(weak, thin, etc.)	新鲜(fresh, novel, etc.)
黄色(yellow, adult, etc.)	信(letter, trust, etc.)
门槛(sill, threshold, etc.)	包(wrap, bag, etc.)
加油(fuel charging, cheer up, etc.)	直(straight, directly, etc.)
去(leave, remove, etc.)	放(put, release, etc.)
热(hot, popular, etc.)	代表(represent, representative, etc.)
光(light, smooth, etc.)	好(good, like, etc.)
透(through, completely, etc.)	便宜(cheap, interest, etc.)
挂钩(hook, link up with, etc.)	算账(reckoning, get even with, etc.)
水分(humidity, exaggeration, etc.)	同志(comrade, gay, etc.)
看(look, read, etc.)	口(mouth, opening, etc.)
宽(wide, relieve, etc.)	结实(solid, strong, etc.)
打(hit, from, etc.)	分(branch, divide, etc.)
赶(rush for, catch up with, etc.)	花(flower, spend, etc.)
早点(breakfast, a bit earlier, etc.)	疙瘩(pimple, knot, etc.)
负(negative, burden, etc.)	

The query logs we use are from one popular Chinese search engine. We collect the queries from the year 2012 and 2013, producing about 230,000,000 paraphrase pairs.

5.1 Evaluating Explanation Word Extraction

It is almost impossible to compute the exact recall of explanation words extraction because we can only collect the ones which are common. Thus, we only consider the precision as well as the recall with respect to common explanation words against human annotations. The results show that our explanation word extraction can achieve *a precision of 62.9%, and a recall of 79.1%*. In order to study how the incorrect extractions are generated, we randomly select 200 incorrect substitutions, and manually investigate the paraphrases from which they are extracted. We summarize the major reasons with the top 3 proportion are: incorrect paraphrase mappings, incorrect word segmentations and typos or grammatical errors in the queries. The proportion of each reason is listed in Table 3.

Table 3. The major reasons of incorrect substitution extraction.

Reasons	Percentage(%)
Incorrect paraphrase mappings	37.0
Incorrect word segmentations	32.0
Typos or grammatical errors	35.0

The top 1 reason is incorrect paraphrase mappings. Since the paraphrases are automatically generated from query logs, they inevitably contain some noises and incorrect mappings. Sometimes a user may click a title which is highly related but not the same as the query. For example, the query is "如何看qq空间照片"(How to see the pictures in the QZone), but the title which the user actually clicked is "如何上传qq空间照片"(How to upload the pictures to the QZone). This will make "看"(see) be aligned to "上传"(upload), and afterwards an incorrect substitution is extracted.

Second, incorrect word segmentation results may also invite incorrect substitutions. In Chinese natural language processing, word segmentation is an important and necessary preprocessing step. The errors in word segmentations would certainly effect the task of word alignments, and further bring noises to substitution extraction. For instance, in the paraphrases "有一个人让我好想念"(There is a person I miss so much) and "有一个女孩让我好想念"(There is a girl I miss so much), the correct segmentation of the last three characters should be "好(so much) 想念(miss)", but the second sentence is wrongly segmented as "好想(miss so much) 念(miss)". It makes "好(so much)" be aligned to "好想(miss so much)", which does not make sense.

Finally, the queries input by the users, and the titles of the clicked webpages, are often not well normalized. Some of them may contain wrongly written or mispronounced characters, some of them may even contain serious grammatical errors. Under these circumstances, a word may be aligned to another word which is fully unrelated with it. Take the paraphrases "怎么在战网上完魔兽"(How to complete Warcraft on Battle.net) and "怎么在战网上打魔兽"(How to play Warcraft on Battle.net) as an example, the word " 完"(complete) in the first sentence should actually be the word "玩"(play), which is a synonym of the word "打"(play) in this context. Because "完"(complete) and "玩"(play) pronounce the same in Chinese, sometimes the users may use the first word by mistake. This will generate an incorrect substitution between "完"(complete) to "打"(play).

We can observe from Table 3 that the sum of the proportions of the three reasons is larger than 100%. This is because some incorrect substitutions are extracted for multiple reasons.

5.2   Evaluating Word Sense Generation

We use the B-cubed criterion [1] to evaluate the performance of the explanation word clustering. We also manually evaluate the performance of generated word senses according to the explanation view. The results of the top 20 senses are listed in Table 4.

Table 4. The performance of explanation words clustering.

	P(%)	R(%)	FMeasure(%)
Clustering	89.4	49.3	60.1
Word sense	67.0	59.7	63.1

We can observe that the senses we generated achieve a precision of 67%. The correct explanation views can represent the sense of a word well. For example, one sense of the word " 看(see)" consists of explanation words " 治疗(treat a disease)"," 治(cure)" and " 医治(heal)". We can also see that the clustering precision is much higher than the recall. This is because we tune the parameters to make the clusters smaller but more accurate, so as to decrease the effect of the noises in the explanation words. Furthermore, in most tasks of query understanding, a smaller but more accurate cluster would be better than a larger cluster with noises.

5.3   Case Study: Query Rewriting

Now we will evaluate how the TDSS representations of word senses perform in the query rewriting task compared with two strong continuous word representation approaches, CBOW and skip-gram [9]. We randomly collect 921 queries containing the 33 Chinese words, and manually labeled the words which can substitute the target word.

For CBOW and skip-gram baselines, we first selected the top 100 similar words from the vocabulary as candidates. Then we compute the similarity between the candidates and the contexts of the target words in the queries, and the ones above a threshold will be collected as the rewriting words. We use the extracted query paraphrases which contain the 33 words to train the CBOW and skip-gram model.

For our TDSS word senses, we select the best sense for the target word based on the similarities between the query and the context views, and the explanation words of the selected sense will be used as the rewriting words. As for the evaluate criterion, we use the precision of the generated rewriting words. Since it is difficult to obtain the exact recall of the results, we use the average number of correct rewriting words of all the queries in the dataset instead. The results are listed in Table 5.

Table 5. The performance of TDSS and the baselines in query rewriting.

Approach	Precision(%)	Average number of correct rewriting words
CBOW	19.0	1.8
Skip-Gram	6.4	**3.2**
TDSS	**51.2**	2.9

From the results we can observe that our TDSS representations can obtain the best precision. This is mainly because that it separates the essentials of a word sense, explanations and contexts, into two views, while the existing approaches, i.e., CBOW and skip-gram, combines them into one view, which may blur the differences of the two types of information. Skip-Gram can obtain a little more correct rewriting words than TDSS, but in practice the precision of the words are more important for us since a incorrect substitution would invite incorrect retrieval results, which may decrease the user experience. The results also imply that the context view works well in query rewriting, which implicitly proves that our approach can generate reliable context view for word senses.

6 Conclusions

In this paper, we describe a novel word sense representation framework, which captures the sense of a word in two separate views, explanation and context, and further propose an approach to extract such representations from large scale of query logs, without replying on much human involvement. Experimental results on a Chinese dataset show that our new word sense representation framework can help better handle information retrieval tasks, such as query rewriting, where fine modelling of word meanings is desired. For further work, we will look for more robust representations for word meanings to better represent the two views, and will also attempt to apply the obtained word senses to more retrieval applications.

Acknowledgement. We would like to thank Ben Xu, Wensong He, Shuaixiang Dai, Xiaozhao Zhao, Qiannan Lv, and the anonymous reviewers for their helpful feedback. This work is supported by National High Technology R&D Program of China (Grant No. 2015AA015403, 2014AA015102) and Natural Science Foundation of China (Grant No. 61202233, 61272344, 61370055). For any correspondence, please contact Liwei Chen.

References

1. Bagga, A., Baldwin, B.: Entity-based cross-document coreferencing using the vector space model. In: International Conference on Computational Linguistics, vol. 1, pp. 79–85 (1998)
2. Brody, S., Lapata, M.: Bayesian word sense induction. In: Proceedings of the 12th Conference of the European Chapter of the Association for Computational Linguistics, pp. 103–111. Association for Computational Linguistics (2009)
3. Chen, T., Xu, R., He, Y., Wang, X.: Improving distributed representation of word sense via wordnet gloss composition and context clustering. In: Proceedings of the 53rd Annual Meeting of the Association for Computational Linguistics and the 7th International Joint Conference on Natural Language Processing, vol. 2 (Short Papers), pp. 15–20. Association for Computational Linguistics, Beijing, July 2015. http://www.aclweb.org/anthology/P15-2003
4. Chen, X., Liu, Z., Sun, M.: A unified model for word sense representation and disambiguation. In: Proceedings of the 2014 Conference on Empirical Methods in Natural Language Processing (EMNLP), pp. 1025–1035. Association for Computational Linguistics, Doha, October 2014. http://www.aclweb.org/anthology/D14-1110
5. Dorow, B., Widdows, D.: Discovering corpus-specific word senses. In: Proceedings of the Tenth Conference on European Chapter of the Association for Computational Linguistics, vol. 2, pp. 79–82. Association for Computational Linguistics (2003)
6. Guo, J., Che, W., Wang, H., Liu, T.: Learning sense-specific word embeddings by exploiting bilingual resources. In: Proceedings of COLING 2014, the 25th International Conference on Computational Linguistics: Technical Papers, pp. 497–507. Dublin City University and Association for Computational Linguistics, Dublin, August 2014. http://www.aclweb.org/anthology/C14-1048
7. Huang, E., Socher, R., Manning, C., Ng, A.: Improving word representations via global context and multiple word prototypes. In: Proceedings of the 50th Annual Meeting of the Association for Computational Linguistics, vol. 1 (Long Papers), pp. 873–882. Association for Computational Linguistics, Jeju Island, July 2012. http://www.aclweb.org/anthology/P12-1092
8. Jurgens, D.: Word sense induction by community detection. In: Proceedings of TextGraphs-6: Graph-based Methods for Natural Language Processing, pp. 24–28. Association for Computational Linguistics (2011)
9. Mikolov, T., Chen, K., Corrado, G., Dean, J.: Efficient estimation of word representations in vector space. CoRR abs/1301.3781 (2013). http://dblp.uni-trier.de/db/journals/corr/corr1301.html#abs-1301-3781
10. Miller, G.A.: Wordnet: a lexical database for English. Commun. ACM **38**(11), 39–41 (1995)

11. Miller, G.A., Beckwith, R., Fellbaum, C., Gross, D., Miller, K.J.: Introduction to wordnet: an on-line lexical database*. Int. J. Lexicogr. **3**(4), 235–244 (1990)

12. Neelakantan, A., Shankar, J., Passos, A., McCallum, A.: Efficient non-parametric estimation of multiple embeddings per word in vector space. In: Proceedings of the 2014 Conference on Empirical Methods in Natural Language Processing (EMNLP), pp. 1059–1069. Association for Computational Linguistics, Doha, October 2014. http://www.aclweb.org/anthology/D14-1113

13. Niu, Z.Y., Ji, D.H., Tan, C.L.: I2r: three systems for word sense discrimination, Chinese word sense disambiguation, and English word sense disambiguation. In: Proceedings of the 4th International Workshop on Semantic Evaluations, pp. 177–182. Association for Computational Linguistics (2007)

14. Purandare, A., Pedersen, T.: Word sense discrimination by clustering contexts in vector and similarity spaces. In: Proceedings of the Conference on Computational Natural Language Learning, Boston, vol. 72 (2004)

15. Schütze, H.: Automatic word sense discrimination. Comput. Linguist. **24**(1), 97–123 (1998)

16. Tian, F., Dai, H., Bian, J., Gao, B., Zhang, R., Chen, E., Liu, T.Y.: A probabilistic model for learning multi-prototype word embeddings. In: Proceedings of COLING 2014, the 25th International Conference on Computational Linguistics: Technical Papers, pp. 151–160. Dublin City University and Association for Computational Linguistics, Dublin, August 2014. http://www.aclweb.org/anthology/C14-1016

17. Yao, X., Van Durme, B.: Nonparametric Bayesian word sense induction. In: Proceedings of TextGraphs-6: Graph-based Methods for Natural Language Processing, pp. 10–14. Association for Computational Linguistics (2011)

18. Zhao, S., Wang, H., Liu, T.: Paraphrasing with search engine query logs. In: Proceedings of the 23rd International Conference on Computational Linguistics, pp. 1317–1325. Association for Computational Linguistics (2010)

A Word Vector Representation Based Method for New Words Discovery in Massive Text

Yang Du, Hua Yuan, and Yu Qian[✉]

School of Management and Economics, University of Electronic Science
and Technology of China, Chengdu 611731, China
qiany@uestc.edu.cn

Abstract. The discovery of new words is of great significance to natural language processing for the Chinese language. In recent years, training words in a corpus into a new word vector representation with neural network model has shown a good performance in representing the original semantic relationship among words. Accordingly, the word vector representation is then introduced into the discovery of new word in Chinese text. In this work, we propose a new unsupervised method for discovering new word based on n-gram method. To that end, we first trains the words in corpus into a word vector space, and then combine some elements in the corpus as candidates for new words. Finally, the noise candidates are dropped based on the similarity between two elements in the new word vector space. By comparing to some classical unsupervised methods such as mutual Information and adjacent entropy, the experiment results show that the propose method has great advantage on performance in discovering new words.

Keywords: Word embedding · New words discovery · Semantic relationship · n-gram

New word discovery is a very important research topic in Chinese natural language processing. As we know that Chinese is not like the language of English, in which there are fixed separators between words in text, thus word segmentation is usually a necessary step at the beginning of information processing with massive text in Chinese. Since the performance of the best word segmentation is not so perfect that the new word in a corpus may be divided into smaller word elements, obviously, which may cause a wrong results of information retrieval. Therefore, the task of new word discovery is closely related to word segmentation [1]. Sproat and Emerson pointed out that the emergence of new words greatly influenced the segmentation accuracy of word segmentation tools, and 60% of word segmentation errors were caused by new words [2]. However, the concept of "new word" are not well-defined in literature. In the field of Chinese textual information processing, there are two concepts: new words and unlisted words. New words refer to words that appear with the development of the times, whereas, unlisted words refer to words that do not appear in the dictionary of current word-segmentation tools. In literature, the new words and unlisted words did not be distinguished [3], so do in this study.

© Springer International Publishing AG 2016
C.-Y. Lin et al. (Eds.): NLPCC-ICCPOL 2016, LNAI 10102, pp. 76–88, 2016.
DOI: 10.1007/978-3-319-50496-4_7

At present, the methods for new words discovery methods are divided into two types of supervised and unsupervised. The supervised method is mainly based on statistical learning. This method requires a large amount of labeled data and a large number of feature selection work. However, obtaining a large amount of labeled data is often costly, and feature selection requires a wealth of experience for textual semantics recognition. The unsupervised method is mainly based on a set of rules, or calculating some statistical measurements. Rule-based approach requires the development of a large number of language rules, and thus their reusability is poor. The methods based on some simple statistical indicators are also with poor performance in new words discovery because of their high computational complexity.

With the great development of research on neural network training and deep learning in recent years, some word vector representation models can characterize the implication of words very well as well as the semantic relationship between words. Especially, we notice that if a new word is wrongly separated by the software, the separated parts should be semantically similar in the new word vector space. For example, word 'Zhang Yong' (张勇) is used as a name of Chinese people, but it had always been separated by software into the wrong form of two smaller word elements as 'Zhang/Yong/' (张/勇/). Now, with an appropriate trained neural network model, we can find that the corresponding word vectors of the two words of 'Zhang' (张) and 'Yong' (勇) are very similar. Based on this interesting semantic relationship, we propose a new algorithm to identify new words from massive Chinese text based on the well trained word vectors. Along this line, the n-gram (n > 2) word string whose term frequency is greater than 2 in the corpus is extracted as the candidates of word. Then, based on the similarity of two word vectors, the wrong combined new words are pruned. Finally, a set of new words are obtained.

1 Related Work

As an important step in the field of Chinese textual information processing, new word discovery can also be regarded as a form of multi-word expression. In recent years, there are lots of researchers have been devoted into this area. The methods for new word discovery are mainly of two categories, the one is the supervision method, mainly based on the statistical method. This type of methods usually uses the new word discovery task to transform the sequence label task, using the machine learning method to train the model on the artificial labeled data, and then use the trained model to mark the unlabeled data automatically. Fu and Luke regarded the recognition of new words as a sequence labeling process. Some of the data are first hand-marked to train the Hidden Markov Model (HHM), which marks the contextual characteristics of the words, the connection and the word-formation patterns. And then use the trained model to predict the word segmentation and get the marked sequence. Finally, a new word is obtained according to the marking pattern. Their experiments have achieved a good result [4]. However, the process of this method is relative complicated, and the large corpus is another limitation. Goh et al. [5] used the HHM model for coarse word segmentation and pre-labeling. In the method, the SVM model was trained to obtain the character-based annotation, and then the new words were detected using the tag of word sequence to obtain the final segmentation. However, the initial error of word segmentation in this method would be a big inducement of the big errors generated in the follow-up processing work. By using initial word segmentation and part of speech tagging, Xu and Gu [6] presents a method based on SVM, which is trained for a new word space vector. The candidate words in their work are predicted by combining the related constraints and relaxation variables on a test corpus. The candidate of new words is vectorized and then put into the SVM classifier. The classification results would be introduced into judging the candidates were new words or not. Chen et al. [7] used the conditional random field to transform the new word detection task into a problem of evaluating whether a word segmentation boundary is a new boundary. Along this line, they proposed a series of statistical features to distinguish the new word boundary. And then use the conditional random field method to synthesize these features to achieve the new words in an open field. Although good results had been achieved in their experiments, their method still need a large number of data labeling and complex features building.

The other kind of method is the unsupervised methods, including the rule-based and some statistical indicators based method. The rule-based methods use the language rules to match the new words in the text. The methods based on statistical indicators usually find the repeated n-gram word strings in the corpus as candidate word strings, and use some statistical indicators to check whether the candidate word string can be recognized as a new word. In the method presented by Wang et al. [8], they first make word segmentation, then sort out the 2- to 8-gram word strings, and finally use some matching and statistical information to identify new words. Zheng et al. [1] proposed a new word discovery method based on users' behavior in a specific area. First, they select representative words in a field, then use these words, as well as some of user input dictionary to find experts in the field, and they do the new word discovery by analyzing the input dictionary of the experts. Pecina and Schlesinger [9] used 55 different statistics to carry out 2-gram lexical recognition experiments. The results show that mutual information (MI) algorithm is one of the best methods to measure lexical relevance. In [10], the PMI algorithm is combined with a small number of basic rules to automatically identify 2- and n-gram new words from large-scale corpus. In [11], the authors argue that if the candidate word string can be recognized as a new word, the word string should also be appeared in a different sentence environment. Based on this idea, the new word can be discovered by evaluating the information entropy around the candidate word string.

It can be seen that the methods based on machine learning, such as HMM and conditional random fields, can achieve good results, but still need a large amount of pre-labeled data. Usually these data are difficult to obtain and need to carefully features selection and optimization. Methods based on rules or some indicators do not need lots of labeled data, but the calculation of these indicators is usually costly. Another feasible way is to integrate rules and a variety of indicators together, or embedded these indicators into a machine learning model [7]. In this work, we propose an unsupervised method for new word recognition based on word vectors representation, which is simple and efficient.

2 The New Word Discovery Method Based on Word Vector Pruning

In textual information processing, the word vectors trained by neural network or deep learning, can be a good representation of words and a feasible token of the se-mantic relationship between words and words. In this paper, we will leverage the se-mantic relationship to recognize the new words in a Chinese corpus. Firstly, the text is seg-mented, and then the n-gram word string whose frequency is greater than the threshold is extracted as candidate new words. Finally, the similarity or distance of the word vectors between the words in different parts of n-gram is used to prune. The n-gram (n > 2) obtained after pruning is used as a new word.

The new word recognition process is shown in Fig. 1. The corpus used in exper-iment consists of two part, one is the mass of external text data, mainly used to train word vector, the other is used to discover the new words.

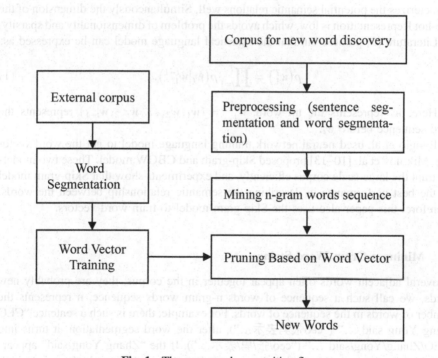

Fig. 1. The new words recognition flow

2.1 Data Preprocessing

This method mainly uses two parts of corpus, one part is external corpus, and the other part is the corpus used for new word discovery task. The external corpus does not need special data preprocessing, but word segmentation. This method also can use the other trained word vectors by some institutions, such as Google. However, pre-trained

Chinese word vector is relatively lacking, but [10] pointed out that an optimized model of single-machine multi-threading can train billions of words per hour, and these trained words can be saved for other natural language processing tasks. The corpus of the new word discovery task is divided by Chinese sentences or question marks, and then the word segmentation is performed by word segmentation software.

2.2   Word Vector Representation and Training

If we want to use machine learning method to solve the Natural language processing problem, we need to mathematical characteristics of some symbols, change the word into the word vector is one of the ways. There are two kinds of word vectors. One is the One-hot Representation, that is, to build a lexicon, the dimension of the vector is equal to the size of the lexicon, the corresponding dimension is 1; the other is the word vector, which is the Distributed Representation. It is the word vector got when training language model by neural network or deep learning. Distributed Representation word vector characterizes the potential semantic relations well. Simultaneously the dimension of the One-hot Representation is low, which avoids the problem of dimensionality and sparsity.

Literature [9] pointed out that the statistical language model can be expressed as:

$$p\left(w_1^T\right) = \prod_{t=1}^{T} p\left(w_t | w_1^{t-1}\right), \tag{1}$$

Here, w_t represents the tth word, $w_1^{t-1} = (w_1, w_2, \ldots, w_{t-2}, w_{t-1})$ represents the word sequence before w_t.

Bengio et al. used neural network training language model to get the word vector [10], Mikolov et al. [10–13] proposed Skip-gram and CBOW model. These two models can train the large-scale corpus efficiently, and experiments show that Skip-gram model get the best performance in describing the semantic relationship between the words. Therefore, this paper also uses the Skip-gram model to train word vectors.

2.3   Mining n-Gram Word String

If several adjacent words often appear together in the corpus, they are probably new words, we call such a sequence of words n-gram words sequence, n represents the number of words in the sequence of words. For example, there is such a sentence "CEO Zhang Yong said …" ("ceo张勇表示…"), after the word segmentation, it turns into "CEO/Zhang/Yong/said …" ("ceo/张/勇/表示…"). If the "Zhang Yong said" appears in multiple sentences, we can find 3-gram words sequence {'Zhang', 'Yong', 'said'}. Our goal is to find all n-grams whose frequency of occurrence is greater than the threshold, while n in each n-word string is as large as possible. In this paper, an efficient algorithm is designed to mining the n-word string whose n is the maximum.

Firstly, construct the data set T: The text data set D is crawled from the target website by the crawling software in the beginning; and then a standard text prepro-cessing mentioned above is performed on the data set D; For each document $D_i \in D$, use the segmentation software to segment the content and label the punctuation marks and stop words, thus D_i is divided into n_i terms d_j (j = 1, ..., n_i). Scan the word segmentation results, replace all the punctuation marks and stop words with line breaks, complete the text segmentation, and form the final text data set T. In fact, the i th segmented text in the data set T can be regarded as a word vector t_i composed of a series of ordered semantic words. Where t_i is consist of m_i ordered semantic word units t_{ij} (j = 1, ..., m_i). The element t_{ij} is the j th semantic word in the i th segmented text in the data set T.

$$T = \{t_1, \ldots, t_i, \ldots, t_{|T|}\}, \tag{2}$$

Here, |T| indicates the number of text after the division.

Next, we scan the dataset T to find all 2-gram words whose frequency is greater than the threshold, and record the location index of all these 2-gram words. These 2-gram strings are then incremented left and right to increase N according to their position index until the stop condition is reached. Stop conditions is that the string frequency is less than the threshold or encountering stop words when left and right expansion. Through this algorithm we can find a large number of candidate word strings, but these candidate words cannot be directly seen as a new word, because this error rate is high. The candidate words sequence forms we found by the frequent sequence mining algorithm are shown in Table 1.

Table 1. Sample for candidate word sequence

T	Candidate word string
T1	{"Zhang", "Yong", "Said"} ({"张", "勇", "表示"})
T2	{"alibaba", "declared"} ({"阿里巴巴", "宣布"})
T3	{"integrity", "department"}({"廉正", "部"})
T4	{"propose", "privatization", "offer"} ({"提出", "私有化", "要约"})

It can be seen from Table 1 that the extracted n-gram candidate words sequence can not be directly used as a new word, for example, in the candidate word series of {'Zhang', 'Yong', 'Said'}({'张', '勇', '表示'}), "Zhang Yong" is a new word, but "Zhang Yong said" cannot serve as a new word. Therefore, we need to introduce pruning at this time, remove the word "said", the remaining "Zhang Yong" as a new word.

2.4 Pruning Based on Word Vector

If a new word is mistakenly separated, the different parts of the misclassified semantics should be very similar, and the word vector is a good representation of this semantics, that is, their word vector should be very similar. For example, in our experiments we can find in the 3-gram words sequence of {'Zhang', 'Yong', 'Said'}, the cosine similarity between word vectors corresponding to "Zhang" and "Yong" is 0.38, while the cosine similarity between the word vector of "Yong" and "Said" is 0.01. Based on this feature, we prune the candidate words sequence, that is, pruning the distance of the corresponding word vector in the candidate words sequence. If the similarity between words and words is less than a certain threshold, we prune them:

$$f(vec1, vec2) > threshold, \tag{3}$$

Where f is a function of the vector similarity or distance metric, depending on the specific form of more than f or less than f. Table 2 lists the word vector pruning algorithm. Here, all candidate word strings are denoted by C, and C is a two-dimensional array form. Each item represents a candidate word string, and Vec represents the training word vector.

Table 2. Word vector pruning algorithm

Algorithm 1 Word vector pruning algorithm
Input: C, Vec, *threshold*
Output: new words sets NW
1: NW = ∅
2: for item in C do
3:   flag=0
4:   for i = 1 to |item| do
5:     if *f*(Vec[item[i]],Vec[item[i+1]])>*threshold*:
6:       if len(item[flag:i])>1:
7:         NW ← item[FLAG: i]
8:         FLAG=I+1
9:     end if
10:   end for
11: end for
12: return NW

After the pruning of the word vector, we find that the "Said" in candidate word strings of ["Zhang", "Yong", "Said"] can be removed, so as to correctly identify the new word such as 'Zhang Yong'.

3 Experiment Results

3.1 Data Sets and Experimental Settings

In this paper, we collected a total of 53.9 M corpus of company news from SINA finance network (http://finance.sina.com.cn/chanjing/). In the experiments, the first 5,000 sentences in the 53.9 M news corpus are selected as the corpus of the new word discovery task. The data preprocessing is carried out on the selected 5000 sentences, including sentence segmentation with Chinese full stops and question marks and the word segmentation with Jieba, and a total of 143765 words are obtained after the process.

We use the Google's open-source tool word2vec (https://code.google.com/p/word2vec/) to generate word vectors. The selected model is Skip-gram model with window size 6. In word2vec, the word vector dimension is adjustable. The experimental results in literature [10] demonstrate that the higher the word vector dimension, the better the effect, while more data is required. In this paper, the dimension of word vector after training is 200 dimensions.

3.2 The Result of New Word Detection

In the corpus of new word discovery task, 278 new words are marked in this paper. We get 604 candidate word strings by mining the n-gram word strings, and compute the frequency distribution of n-gram word strings and the frequency distribution of n in n-gram, as shown in Figs. 2 and 3. Finally, we get 216 new words after pruning algorithm. Many of these new words are named entities such as "Mogujie" ("蘑菇街"), "Qiongyouwang" ("穷游网"), "Hedge Fund" ("对冲基金"), "Shareholding Ratio" ("持股比例"), "Lin Han" ("林翰"), "Shao Xiaofeng" ("邵晓锋"), "Jiang Peng" ("姜鹏") and so on.

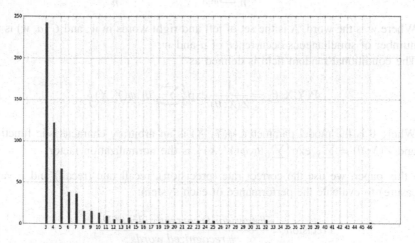

Fig. 2. The frequency of n-gram

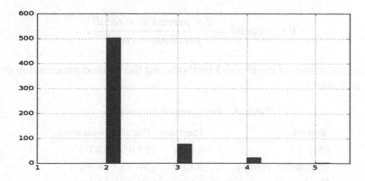

Fig. 3. The frequency of n

3.3 Comparative Analysis

In order to better illustrate the effectiveness of the new word discovery method proposed in this paper, we conduct a comparative analysis of existing methods under the same data set, mainly with unsupervised methods of mutual information and left-right information entropy, and supervised method based on conditional random field.

(1) Mutual information is defined as

$$PMI(x, y) = log \frac{p(x, y)}{p(x) . p(y)},\qquad(4)$$

Where $p(x)$ is the probability that x occurs.

(2) The entropy of information entropy is defined as

$$LE(w) = -\frac{1}{n} \sum_{a \in A} C(a, w) \, log \frac{C(a, w)}{n},\qquad(5)$$

Where w is the word, A is the set of left and right words in w, and $C(a, w)$ is the number of simultaneous occurrence of a and w.

(3) The conditional random field is defined as

$$P(Y|X; \theta) = \frac{1}{Z(X; \theta)} exp\left\{\sum_k \theta_k . \varphi(Y, X)\right\},\qquad(6)$$

Where θ is the model parameter, $\varphi(Y, X)$ is an arbitrary characteristic function, and $Z(X; \theta) = \sum_{Y'} exp\left\{\sum_k \theta_k . \varphi(Y', X)\right\}$ is the normalization factor.

In this paper, we use the correct rate (precision), recall rate (recall) and F value (F-measure) to evaluate the performance of each system:

$$Precision = \frac{\#new\,words\,correctly\,identified}{\#recognized\,words},\qquad(7)$$

$$recall = \frac{\#\,new\,words\,correctly\,identified}{\#new\,words\,in\,corpus},\qquad(8)$$

$$F - measure = \frac{2 \times precision \times recall}{precision + recall},\qquad(9)$$

The experimental results of the above 3 methods and the method presented in this paper are shown in Table 3.

Table 3. The comparison results

Method	Precision	Recall	F–measure
PMI	61.8%	55.9%	58.7%
Information entropy	59.1%	51.3%	54.9%
Conditional random field	72.2%	50.6%	61.1%
Word vector pruning	**81.2%**	**60.1%**	**69.1%**

From the results in Table 3, it can be seen that the new word discovery method based on word vector pruning proposed in this paper is much better than other methods. This method can make full use of the word vector by external corpus training, which has already depicted the semantic relations, but mutual information and left-right information entropy can not use these external information, which is one reasonable reason why our method can get better performance than other two indicators. Worthy of note is, due to the lack of training datasets and special feature selection optimization, the conditional random field method cannot reach a good performance.

3.4 Different Vector Similarity Measure Pruning Comparison

The metric of similarity or distance between two vectors is mainly Cosine similarity, Euclidean distance, Manhattan distance, etc. We use these three indicators to prune the word vector, and conduct a comparative analysis of the performance of these indicators. The three indicators are calculated as follows:

Cosine similarity:

$$\cos \theta = \left(\frac{\sum_{i=1}^{n} x_i \cdot y_i}{\sqrt{\sum_{i=1}^{n} x_i^2} \cdot \sqrt{\sum_{i=1}^{n} y_i^2}} \right), \tag{10}$$

Euclidean distance:

$$\mathrm{dist}(X, Y) = \sqrt{\sum_{i=1}^{n} (x_i - y_i)^2}, \tag{11}$$

Manhattan distance:

$$\mathrm{dist}(X, Y) = \sum_{i=1}^{n} |x_i - y_i|, \tag{12}$$

When the cosine similarity indicator is selected, the candidate word string is scanned, if the cosine similarity between the adjacent two word words is smaller than a certain threshold value, the pruning is carried out; If Euclidean distance or Manhattan distance is selected, the similarity of distance between adjacent word words is larger than the threshold value, and the pruning is carried out. Figure 4 is the experimental results of the pruning with different indicators, in each plot the abscissa represents the threshold, the red solid line represents the corresponding accuracy, the blue dashed line represents the recall rate.

As we can see from Fig. 4, the intersection of accuracy rate and recall rate is located in the vertical coordinates of 0.7 when Cosine similarity is selected, and those rates are less than 0.6 when Euclidean or Manhattan distance is selected. For a more intuitive comparison, Fig. 5 shows the accuracy-recall curve at different distance methods, and we also add the accuracy-recall curve based on n-gram word frequency pruning. The results show that the best performance reached by using the cosine similarity, while Euclidean distance and Manhattan distance are significantly worse than the cosine similarity. The worst is based on N-word string frequency pruning, but

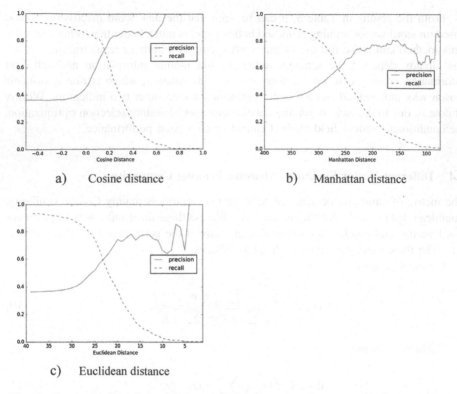

a)   Cosine distance   b)   Manhattan distance

c)   Euclidean distance

Fig. 4. Comparing the effect of different pruning by vector distance (Color figure online)

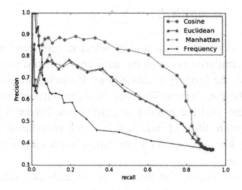

Fig. 5. Precision-Recall rate curve

its accuracy rate is very high when the recall rate is low. Therefore, we choose the cosine similarity to measure word vector distance. Meanwhile, the high frequency N-gram word string is directly selected as a new word, which can correct some errors of the words vector pruning, as to improve the algorithm accuracy and recall rate.

4 Conclusions and Future Work

New words will be continuously emerged along with the development of society, these new words will be used to delivery more and more new information in communication with text. Simultaneously, people rely much on word segmentation for textual information processing, especially, under the situation of massive data. However, the dictionaries used in current tool for word segmentation can not include all the new words. The new word is not only a key point but difficulty in Chinese natural language processing.

In recent years, the word vector representation obtained by neural network model can maintain the semantic relationship between words well. We can see that, if a new word is misclassified into smaller parts by a word segmentation software, the different parts of the misclassification should be similar in the new vector space. Based on this consideration, this paper proposes a new unsupervised method for word discovery. The method is mainly contributed to drop noise candidates based on the similarity between two elements with their new word representation. Moreover, it is a combination of word vector representation with the traditional n-gram method. Experiments show that the proposed method is superior to the existing unsupervised method.

In the future, we will further increase volume of the corpus for training better word vector representation, and improve the accuracy of the algorithm of word discovery by introducing some other methods, such as mutual information index.

Acknowledgments. The work was partly supported by the National Natural Science Foundation of China (No. 71271044/71572029/71671027).

References

1. Zheng, Y., Liu, Z., Sun, M., et al.: Incorporating user behaviors in new word detection. In: IJCAI, vol. 9, pp. 2101–2106 (2009)
2. Sproat, R., Emerson, T.: The first international Chinese word segmentation bakeoff. In: Proceedings of 2nd SIGHAN Workshop on Chinese Language Processing, vol. 17. Association for Computational Linguistics, pp. 133–143 (2003)
3. Li, H., Huang, C.-N., Gao, J., Fan, X.: The use of SVM for Chinese new word identification. In: Su, K.-Y., Tsujii, J., Lee, J.-H., Kwong, O.Y. (eds.) IJCNLP 2004. LNCS (LNAI), vol. 3248, pp. 723–732. Springer, Heidelberg (2005). doi:10.1007/978-3-540-30211-7_76
4. Fu, G., Luke, K.-K.: Chinese unknown word identification using class-based LM. In: Su, K.-Y., Tsujii, J., Lee, J.-H., Kwong, O.Y. (eds.) IJCNLP 2004. LNCS (LNAI), vol. 3248, pp. 704–713. Springer, Heidelberg (2005). doi:10.1007/978-3-540-30211-7_74
5. Goh, C.L., Asahara, M., Matsumoto, Y.: Machine learning-based methods to Chinese unknown word detection and POS tag guessing. J. Chin. Lang. Comput. **16**(4), 185–206 (2006)
6. Xu, Y., Gu, H.: New word recognition based on support vector machines and constraints. In: 2015 2nd International Conference on Information Science and Control Engineering (ICISCE), pp. 341–344. IEEE (2015)

7. 陈飞，刘奕群，魏超，等.: 基于条件随机场方法的开放领域新词发现. J. Softw. 24(5) (2013). Chen, F., Liu, Y.Q., Wei, C., Zhang, Y.L., Zhang, M., Ma, S.P.: Open domain new word detection using condition random field method. Ruan Jian Xue Bao/J. Softw. 24(5):1051–1060 (2013). (in Chinese)
8. Wang, M.C., Huang, C.R., Chen, K.J.: The identification and classification of unknown words in Chinese: an n-grams-based approach. Festschrift for Professor Akira Ikeya, pp. 113–123 (1995)
9. Pecina, P., Schlesinger, P.: Combining association measures for collocation extraction. In: Proceedings of COLING/ACL on Main Conference Poster Sessions. Association for Computational Linguistics, pp. 651–658 (2006)
10. 杜丽萍, 李晓戈, 于根, 等.: 基于互信息改进算法的新词发现对中文分词系统改进. 北京大学学报 (自然科学版) 52(1), 35–40 (2016). Liping, D.U., Xiaoge, L.I., Gen, Y.U., et al.: New word detection based on an improved PMI algorithm for enhancing segmentation system. Acta Scientiarum Naturalium Universitatis Pekinensis (2016)
11. Huang, J.H., Powers, D.: Chinese word segmentation based on contextual entropy. In: Proceedings of 17th Asian Pacific conference on Language, Information and Computation, pp. 152–158 (2003). Bengio, Y., Ducharme, R., Vincent, P., et al.: A neural probabilistic language model. J. Mach. Learn. Res. 3(Feb): 1137–1155 (2003)
12. Bengio, Y., Ducharme, R., Vincent, P., et al.: A neural probabilistic language model. J. Mach. Learn. Res. 3(Feb), 1137–1155 (2003)
13. Mikolov, T., Chen, K., Corrado, G., et al.: Efficient estimation of word representations in vector space. Comput. Sci. (2013)

Machine Translation and Multi-lingual Information Access

Better Addressing Word Deletion for Statistical Machine Translation

Qiang Li[1]([✉]), Dongdong Zhang[2], Mu Li[2], Tong Xiao[1], and Jingbo Zhu[1]

[1] Northeastern University, Shenyang, China
liqiangneu@gmail.com, {xiaotong,zhujingbo}@mail.neu.edu.cn
[2] Microsoft Research Asia, Beijing, China
{dongdong.zhang,muli}@microsoft.com

Abstract. Word deletion (WD) problems have a critical impact on the adequacy of translation and can lead to poor comprehension of lexical meaning in the translation result. This paper studies how the word deletion problem can be handled in statistical machine translation (SMT) in detail. We classify this problem into *desired* and *undesired word deletion* based on *spurious* and *meaningful* words. Consequently, we propose four effective models to handle undesired word deletion. To evaluate word deletion problems, we develop an automatic evaluation metric that highly correlates with human judgement. Translation systems are simultaneously tuned for the proposed evaluation metric and BLEU using minimum error rate training (MERT). The experimental results demonstrate that our methods achieve significant improvements in word deletion problems on Chinese-to-English translation tasks.

Keywords: Machine translation · Word deletion · Automatic evaluation

1 Introduction

Machine translation (MT) has been applied to many applications. The evaluation of MT system quality often considers both adequacy and fluency [1]. For poor translation results with low adequacy, the problem is mainly caused by word deletion problems, word insertion problems, and incorrect word choices. Word insertion problems are not common during translation [2]. Incorrect word choices are eliminated by improving translation model [3,4] or using domain adaptation [5]. So far, the word deletion (WD) problem has not gotten enough attention in statistical machine translation (SMT) systems and research community.

Every language has some *spurious* words that do not need to be translated, referred to as *desired WD*. See Fig. 1 for an example. The Chinese word '就/jiu' and the English word 'the' have no counterparts in the other language and will be translated to empty word ϵ during translation. It is possible to learn phrase pairs '就/jiu, ϵ' and 'the, ϵ' for desired WD from a word aligned bilingual training corpus. Consequently, SMT systems realize the function of desired WD. For

© Springer International Publishing AG 2016
C.-Y. Lin et al. (Eds.): NLPCC-ICCPOL 2016, LNAI 10102, pp. 91–102, 2016.
DOI: 10.1007/978-3-319-50496-4_8

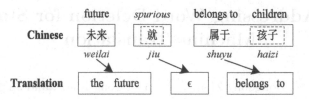

Fig. 1. Example of desired and undesired word deletion. Words in dashed rectangle do not have counterparts in the target language. Letters under Chinese words are Chinese Pinyin.

desired WD, Li et al. in [6] proposed three models to handle spurious words and utilized different methods to calculate the translation probability that the source words would be translated into empty word ϵ. However, *undesired WD* appears along with desired WD during phrase extraction. For example, the phrase pair '属于/shuyu 孩子/haizi, belongs to' in Fig. 1 is an undesired WD as the source *meaningful* word '孩子/haizi' has no counterparts in the target language and results in a translation error.

In this paper, we focus on WD problems for SMT systems. First of all, to identify desired and undesired WD, we use frequency to identify spurious and meaningful words in the source language. Second, as undesired WD is directly caused by incorrect phrase pairs, we categorize undesired WD into four classes at the level of phrase pairs. For each class, we introduce a model that is used as a feature and integrated into a log-linear model [7] for SMT to improve translation performance. In addition, WD problems are more about the adequacy needed for evaluation. But the most commonly used evaluation metrics, like BLEU [1] and METEOR [8], are more about precision and fluency and do not take WD into account. However, the human evaluation approach is quite expensive that it can take weeks or longer to finish the evaluation. Therefore, we develop an automatic evaluation metric that highly correlates with human judgement to evaluate the translation performance in terms of adequacy. Finally, translation systems are simultaneously tuned for our proposed evaluation metric and BLEU using MERT [9]. The experimental results demonstrate that our proposed methods achieve promising improvements on Chinese-to-English translation tasks.

2   The Proposed Approach

This section presents a number of solutions for the problem of WD. As desired WD is about source spurious words and undesired WD is about source meaning-ful words. To identify desired and undesired WD, we use frequency to distinguish between spurious and meaningful words. As spurious words always have high frequencies in one language, we refer to the words with high frequencies as spurious words, and the others as meaningful words. Despite the obvious need for handling undesired WD, it is surprising that most current SMT approaches do not consider undesired WD explicitly and undesired WD problems frequently appear in the output of SMT systems [3,4,10]. Therefore, as undesired WD is directly caused by incorrect phrase pairs selected by the decoder, then we categorize it into four classes at the level of phrase pairs. As a result, we introduce four models that can easily be integrated into the standard log-linear model to tackle undesired WD issues.

2.1   Undesired WD Classification

Previous work demonstrated that improving the quality of phrase pairs was more effective than improving word alignment for tackling WD issues [11]. Meanwhile, undesired WD is directly caused by incorrect phrase pairs selected by the decoder. So, first of all, we categorize the direct causes of undesired WD problems into four classes at the level of phrase pairs.

1. *Empty Translation*: A source phrase with only one word that is meaningful is translated to empty word ϵ. See Fig. 2(1).
2. *Unaligned Words*: Undesired WD occurs with the unaligned source meaningful words that have no counterparts in the target language. Figure 2(2) shows an example.
3. *N-to-1 Alignment Error*: Multi-words of a source phrase are aligned to the same target word, and some of the alignments are incorrect. It reads as if some of source words are not translated at all. See Fig. 2(3).
4. *Meaningful-to-Spurious Phrase*: A source phrase having meaningful words is translated into a target phrase having no meaningful words. Undesired WD occurs with the source meaningful words. See Fig. 2(4).

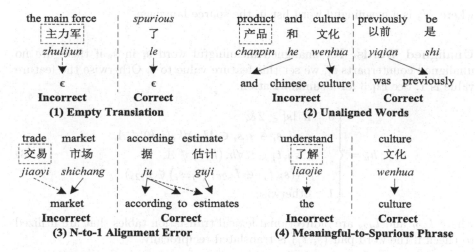

Fig. 2. Categorization of undesired WD problems. Words in dashed rectangle do not have counterparts in the target language. The dashed arrows between source and target phrases are incorrect alignments.

Figure 2 shows the four classes of undesired WD. In Fig. 2, cases on the left side are incorrect and cases on the right side are correct. The first three classes have no overlap, but the forth class may include the first three classes.

2.2   Undesired WD Model

For each class of undesired WD problems, we use an effective model to handle it. This model is summarized in Eq. 1.

$$h = F(s, t, M, L, A) \tag{1}$$

where s is the source phrase, t is the target phrase, M is the meaningful word list, L is the lexical translation tables for which only top-n items that are sorted according to the maximum likelihood probability will be reserved, and A is the word alignment between s and t.

Based on Eq. 1, we design four new features that can easily be integrated into the log-linear model for SMT.

Empty Translation. If a source phrase s, having only one word that is meaningful that is translated to empty symbol ϵ on the target side, we set this feature value to 0. Otherwise the feature value is 1. The empty translation model is summarized in Eq. 2.

$$h_e = \begin{cases} 0 & \text{if } |s| = 1 \,\&\, s \in M_s \,\&\, t = \epsilon \\ 1 & \text{otherwise} \end{cases} \tag{2}$$

where M_s is a meaningful word list in the source language.

Unaligned Words. For unaligned meaningful word s_i in s, if there are no unaligned counterparts t_j, we set this feature value to 0. Otherwise the feature value is 1. See Eq. 3 for a summarization.

$$h_u = \begin{cases} 0 & \text{if } |s| \geq 2 \,\&\, \\ & \exists i, s_i \in s, s_i \in M_s, \forall k, (i, k) \notin A, \\ & \forall j, t_j \in t, \forall h, (h, j) \notin A, \\ & ((s_i, t_j) \notin L_{s2t} \mid (t_j, s_i) \notin L_{t2s}) \\ 1 & \text{otherwise} \end{cases} \tag{3}$$

where L_{s2t} and L_{t2s} are bidirectional lexical translation tables that are utilized to check if the word pair (s_i, t_j) is translated reciprocally.

N-to-1 Alignment Error. For a phrase pair (s, t), a source word s_i in s has just one aligned target word t_j in t, and t_j has more than one aligned source words, if (s_i, t_j) is not translated reciprocally, an undesired WD occurs. Also, we use L_{s2t} and L_{t2s} to check if the word pair (s_i, t_j) is translated reciprocally. This model is summarized in Eq. 4.

$$
h_a = \begin{cases}
0 & \text{if } |s| \geq 2 \, \& \\
& \exists i, s_i \in s, s_i \in M_s, \\
& \exists j, (i, j) \in A, \forall h, h \neq j, (i, h) \notin A, \\
& \exists k, k \neq i, (k, j) \in A, \\
& ((s_i, t_j) \notin L_{s2t} \mid (t_j, s_i) \notin L_{t2s}) \\
1 & \text{otherwise}
\end{cases} \tag{4}
$$

Meaningful-to-Spurious Phrase. If a source phrase s with meaningful words is translated into a target phrase t having only spurious words, a new feature with value 0 will be added to indicate this. Otherwise the feature value is 1. This model is summarized in Eq. 5.

$$
h_p = \begin{cases}
0 & \text{if } \exists i, s_i \in s, s_i \in M_s \, \& \\
& \forall j, t_j \in t, t_j \notin M_t \\
1 & \text{otherwise}
\end{cases} \tag{5}
$$

where M_t is a meaningful word list of the target language side.

2.3   Integration into SMT Decoder

An undesired WD model can easily be integrated into the standard log-linear model for SMT. In Eq. 6, four new features are added to the log-linear model:

$$
\begin{aligned}
\hat{e}_1^I &= \operatorname*{argmax}_{e_1^I} \{ Pr\left(e_1^I | f_1^J\right) \} \\
&= \operatorname*{argmax}_{e_1^I} \{ \sum_{m=1}^{M} \lambda_m h_m \left(e_1^I, f_1^J\right) \} \\
&= \operatorname*{argmax}_{e_1^I} \{ \sum_{m=1}^{N} \lambda_m h_m \left(e_1^I, f_1^J\right) \\
&\quad + \lambda_e h_e + \lambda_u h_u + \lambda_a h_a + \lambda_p h_p \}
\end{aligned} \tag{6}
$$

where the first N features come from the baseline SMT model, and h_e, h_u, h_a, and h_p are the proposed four new features for undesired WD problems, λ_e, λ_u, λ_a, and λ_p are the corresponding feature weights.

3   Evaluation Metric - Recall of WD

The human evaluation approach for WD problems is quite expensive. This is a big problem because MT researchers want to see daily quality improvement for their MT systems. This is our motivation to develop an automatic evaluation metric.

Generally speaking, undesired WD is about the source language in which meaningful words are not translated. But from another point of view, reference translations produced by human beings in the development set contain complete lexical meaning for each corresponding source sentence. Therefore, the higher the recall of meaningful words between the machine-produced translation and human-produced reference translations, the less undesired WD occurs.

In this section, we describe the recall of WD, an automatic evaluation metric that is based on unigram recall between the machine-produced translation and human-produced reference translations of SMT. Unlike BLEU and METEOR, not all words are useful to calculate the recall of WD. First of all, we use the meaningful word list M_t of the target language to weed out spurious words from meaningful words of machine-produced translations and human-produced reference translations. Second, we use the reserved meaningful words to calculate this score.

More importantly, we will simultaneously use the proposed recall of WD and BLEU to define an error function through interpolation and learn optimized feature weights using MERT.

3.1   Unigram Recall

At the sentence-level, the unigram recall is represented by R_1 in Eq. 7.

$$R_1 = \frac{\sum_{unigram \in C} c}{\sum_{unigram' \in R} r}$$

$$c = C_{clip}(unigram)$$

$$r = \sum_{n=1}^{N} w_n \cdot C_n\left(unigram'\right) \tag{7}$$

to compute c, first, we must count the maximum number of times a word occurs in any single reference translation. Second, we clip the total count of each candidate word by its maximum reference count, and the clipped counts are the values of c for each candidate word. The definition of c shows here is the same as the one used by Papineni et al. in [1]. r is the average number of times a word occurs in all reference translations. N is the number of reference translations and w_n is the uniform weights. In our baseline, we use $N = 4$ and uniform weights $w_n = 1/N$.

From Eq. 7 we can see that the sentence is our basic unit of evaluation, but one usually evaluates SMT systems on a corpus of entire documents. In Eq. 8, r_1 is the unigram recall score on a corpus of entire documents.

$$r_1 = \frac{\displaystyle\sum_{C \in \{candidates\}} \sum_{unigram \in C} c}{\displaystyle\sum_{R \in \{references\}} \sum_{unigram' \in R} r} \tag{8}$$

First of all, we compute the unigram matches sentence by sentences. Second, we add the clipped unigram counts for all the candidate sentences and divide by the average value of the total number of words in all reference translations in the test corpus to compute the recall score. As defined, the r_1 ranges from 0 to 1, if r_1 is more than 1, we set r_1 to 1. Few translation will attain a score of 1 unless they are identical to one of the several reference translations. To verify that r_1 distinguishes between very good translations and bad translations on undesired WD problems, we will give the verification of r_1 in Sect. 4.4.

Finally, the evaluation score for MERT is summarized in Eq. 9.

$$Score = \alpha * BLEU + (1 - \alpha) * Recall \tag{9}$$

we set α to 0.7 in our experiment by default because it seemed work best on our data sets.

4 Evaluation

In this section, we applied the proposed methods to a state-of-the-art phrase-based SMT system [12] and carried out experiments on two Chinese-to-English translation tasks.

4.1 Experiment Setup

Our SMT system followed the general framework of phrase-based translation [10], including bidirectional phrase translation probabilities, bidirectional lexical weights, an n-gram language model, target word penalty, and phrase penalty. In addition, the ME-based lexicalized reordering model proposed by Xiong et al. in [13] was employed in our system. We used a decoder with beam search and cube pruning [14] to decode new sentences. By default, the reordering limit was set to 10 and the beam size was set to 30. The maximum length of the source and target phrases were limited to 5 words. A specific empty symbol ϵ on the target language side was posited and any source words were allowed to translate into ϵ [6].

4.2 Corpus

Our experiments were conducted on two Chinese-to-English translation tasks: news and web domains. In both domains, our bilingual data consisted of 2.43 million sentence pairs selected from the NIST portion of the bilingual data of NIST MT 2008 Evaluation. The 5-gram language model for both translation tasks was trained on the Xinhua portion of English Gigaword corpus (16.28 M) in

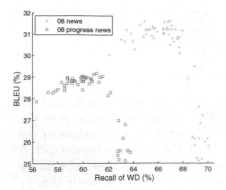
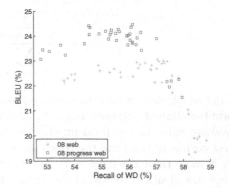

Fig. 3. A relationship between recall of WD and BLEU4 on newswire translation.

Fig. 4. A relationship between recall of WD and BLEU4 on web translation.

addition to the target side of the bilingual data. For the news domain, we used the NIST 2006 Newswire MT evaluation set as our development set (616 sentences) and the NIST 2008 Newswire and 2008 progress Newswire MT evaluation sets as our test sets (691 and 688 sentences). For the web domain, we used the NIST 2006 Webdata MT evaluation set as our development set (483 sentences) and the NIST 2008 Webdata and 2008 progress Webdata MT evaluation sets as our test sets (666 and 682 sentences).

The GIZA++ [15] tool was used to perform the bidirectional word alignment between the source and target sentences. After running GIZA++ in both directions, we applied the *grow-diag-final* refinement rule on the intersection alignments for each sentence pair. More importantly, our comparison systems were simultaneously tuned for recall of WD and BLEU through interpolation using MERT.

4.3   Results

Tables 1 and 2 depict the recall of WD and BLEU score of different systems for the Chinese-to-English translation. In all tables, * indicates a score significantly better than baseline at $p < 0.05$.

On the Chinese-to-English Newswire translation in Table 1, all of our proposed models improved the recall score on the test sets (Row *+Empty, +Unaln, +N-to-1*, and *+Content*). When the four new features were used together for tackling undesired WD issues, our proposed method achieved a recall of WD score increase of 4.66 and 3.79 for the NIST 2008 newswire and 2008 progress newswire test sets (Row *+All*), respectively. More interesting, our method yielded a gain of 0.90 BLEU score increase on the NIST 2008 progress newswire test set. Figure 3 explains this phenomenon, if recall of WD increases in a reasonable range and the BLEU score will remain stable at the same time. But when the score exceeds a reasonable range, the BLEU score will decreased obviously.

Table 1. BLEU4 and recall of WD for various methods on newswire translation.

Method	NIST 2008 nw		NIST 2008 pro nw	
	BLEU%	Recall%	BLEU%	Recall%
Baseline	30.76	63.03	28.28	57.26
+ Empty	31.17	65.66*	28.73	59.23*
+ Unaln	30.85	66.09*	28.75	59.58*
+ N-to-1	31.15	65.84*	28.90*	59.43*
+ Content	31.13	65.85*	28.69	59.22*
+ All	30.88	67.69*	29.18*	61.05*

Table 2. BLEU4 and recall of WD for various methods on web translation.

Method	NIST 2008 wb		NIST 2008 pro wb	
	BLEU%	Recall%	BLEU%	Recall%
Baseline	22.22	53.62	23.07	52.77
+ Empty	22.55	55.40*	24.09*	54.74*
+ Unaln	22.37	56.35*	24.14*	55.74*
+ N-to-1	22.49	56.11*	23.97*	55.24*
+ Content	22.67	56.64*	23.89*	55.69*
+ All	22.31	57.82 *	23.90*	57.01*

From Fig. 3 we can see that the reasonable range for the NIST 2008 progress newswire test set was from 58.2 to 61.4. A recall score that is less than 58.2 or more than 61.4 can result in a decrease for the BLEU score. As the recall of WD for baseline system is 57.26 which is less than 58.2, it is reasonable that the BLEU score of baseline system is less than the BLEU score of the proposed system.

When we switch to Chinese-to-English Web translation in Table 2, the results are similar to those in Table 1. E.g., the achievements are 4.20 and 4.24 points on the recall of WD for the NIST 2008 web and 2008 progress web test sets, respectively. On the NIST 2008 progress web test set our method yields a gain of 0.83 BLEU score increase, which is the same for Newswire translation task, Fig. 4 can explain this phenomenon and shows the reasonable ranges for different test sets on the Chinese-to-English Web translation task.

4.4 Recall of WD vs Human Evaluation

To verify that the proposed recall of WD distinguishes between translations with more or less undesired WD, we computed the recall of WD on the output of a human translator, a good SMT system with the four proposed models, and a baseline SMT system. Our experiments were conducted on the Chinese-to-English Newswire domain. The test set was the NIST 2008 newswire. The

Table 3. Distinguishing translations of different quality for undesired WD in the Chinese-to-English newswire translation task.

Method	2008 newswire		
	BLEU%	Recall%	# Delete
Baseline	27.73	60.78	450
Proposed	27.89	64.94	330
Human	46.74	79.48	0

human translation was made by extracted one of the four reference translations, and the other three reference translations were used to evaluate the translation performance.

The results are shown in Table 3. Column '# Delete' in Table 3 is the number of undesired WD determined by human evaluators from 200 randomly selected translation results. For the human translation, we regard the value of '# Delete' as 0. The recall score of a human translation with 0 deleted meaningful words in row *Human* is 79.48, while the recall score of baseline system with 450 deletion errors in row *Baseline* is 60.78. From this we can see that recall of WD can distinguish between a good translation (human translation) and a bad translation (SMT). To be useful, this metric must also reliably distinguish between translations that do not differ so greatly in terms of BLEU score. Table 3 shows that the recall score of the proposed system with 330 deleted meaningful words in row *Proposed* is 64.94, which is higher than 60.78 for the baseline system with 450 deleted meaningful words. From the results we can see that the proposed recall of WD have a high correlation with human judgement for WD issues. The less undesired WD occurs, the higher the value of recall score is, and vice versa.

5 Related Work

Li et al. in [6] proposed three models to handle spurious source words. They utilized different methods to calculate the translation probability that the source words to be translated into empty word ϵ. Menezes and Quirk in [16] presented an extension of the treelet translation method to include order templates with structural insertion and deletion. The above studies focus only on desired WD problems caused by spurious words. Zhang et al. in [11] focused on unaligned words only and applied hard deletion and optional deletion of the unaligned words on the source side before phrase extraction. Though easy to implement, this method introduced more noise into the phrase table. Zhang et al. in [11] showed that reducing the noise in phrase extraction is more effective than improving word alignment [17–20]. Parton et al. in [21] presented a hybrid approach, APES, to target adequacy errors. Huck and Ney in [22] investigated an insertion and deletion model that was implemented as phrase-level feature functions that counted the number of inserted or deleted word.

In contrast to previous studies, we handle this problem in detail. We first categorize WD problems into desired and undesired WD. Second, we categorize the undesired WD problems into four sub-categories and develop four effective models to tackle this issue. Consequently, we have proposed an automatic evaluation metric for WD problems that allows MT researchers to see quality improvement for an SMT system every day. Finally, our comparison systems were simultaneously tuned for the proposed metric and BLEU using MERT.

6   Conclusion and Future Work

In this paper, we tackle the WD issue for SMT systems. First of all, we use frequency to classify WD problems into two categories, desired and undesired WD. Second, we categorize the direct causes of undesired WD into four classes. For all classes, we have developed effective models that are used as features and integrated into an SMT log-linear model to address the undesired WD problem. Finally, we propose an automatic evaluation metric, recall of WD, that is based on a generalized concept of unigram recall between the machine-produced translation and human-produced reference translations to evaluate the translation performance for WD problems. Meanwhile, our translation systems were simultaneously tuned for recall of WD and BLEU through interpolation using MERT. The experimental results demonstrate that our proposed methods achieve significant improvements in the Chinese-to-English translation tasks.

In the future, we plan to continue our research on the automatic evaluation metric for WD problems. In addition, we will study sophisticated models to tackle the WD issue.

Acknowledgements. This work was done while the first author was visiting the machine translation group at Microsoft Research Asia, and was mainly supported by the Fundamental Research Funds for the Central Universities under Grant No. N140406003, the China Scholarship Council, and the National Natural Science Foundation of China under Grant No. 61272376, No. 61300097 and No. 61432013.

References

1. Papineni, K., Roukos, S., Ward, T., Zhu, W.J.: BLEU: a method for automatic evaluation of machine translation. In: Proceedings of ACL, pp. 311–318 (2002)
2. Vilar, D., Xu, J., d'Haro, L.F., Ney, H.: Error analysis of statistical machine translation output. In: Proceedings of LREC, pp. 697–702 (2006)
3. Chiang, D.: Hierarchical phrase-based translation. Comput. Linguist. **33**(2), 201–228 (2007)
4. Galley, M., Hopkins, M., Knight, K., Marcu, D.: What's in a translation rule? In: Proceedings of HLT-NAACL, pp. 273–280 (2004)
5. Koehn, P., Schroeder, J.: Experiments in domain adaptation for statistical machine translation. In: Proceedings of the Second Workshop on Statistical Machine Translation, pp. 224–227 (2007)

6. Li, C.H., Zhang, D., Li, M., Zhou, M., Zhang, H.: An empirical study in source word deletion for phrase-based statistical machine translation. In: Proceedings of the Third Workshop on Statistical Machine Translation, pp. 1–8 (2008)

7. Och, F.J., Ney, H.: Discriminative training and maximum entropy models for statistical machine translation. In: Proceedings of ACL, pp. 295–302 (2002)

8. Banerjee, S., Lavie, A.: METEOR: an automatic metric for MT evaluation with improved correlation with human judgments. In: Proceedings of the ACL Workshop on Intrinsic and Extrinsic Evaluation Measures for Machine Translation and/or Summarization, pp. 65–72 (2005)

9. Och, F.J.: Minimum error rate training in statistical machine translation. In: Proceedings of ACL, pp. 160–167 (2003)

10. Koehn, P., Och, F.J., Marcu, D.: Statistical phrase-based translation. In: Proceedings of HLT-NAACL, pp. 48–54 (2003)

11. Zhang, Y., Matusov, E., Ney, H.: Are unaligned words important for machine translation? In: Proceedings of EAMT, pp. 226–233 (2009)

12. Xiao, T., Zhu, J., Zhang, H., Li, Q.: NiuTrans: an open source toolkit for phrase-based and syntax-based machine translation. In: Proceedings of ACL 2012 System Demostrations, pp. 19–24 (2012)

13. Xiong, D., Liu, Q., Lin, S.: Maximum entropy based phrase reordering model for statistical machine translation. In: Proceedings of ACL, pp. 521–528 (2006)

14. Huang, L., Chiang, D.: Forest rescoring: faster decoding with integrated language models. In: Proceedings of ACL, pp. 144–151 (2007)

15. Och, F.J., Ney, H.: Improved statistical alignment models. In: Proceedings of ACL, pp. 440–447 (2000)

16. Menezes, A., Quirk, C.: Syntactic models for structural word insertion and deletion. In: Proceedings of EMNLP, pp. 735–744 (2008)

17. Hermjakob, U.: Improved word alignment with statistics and linguistic heuristics. In: Proceedings of EMNLP, pp. 229–237 (2009)

18. Zhu, J., Li, Q., Xiao, T.: Improving syntactic rule extraction through deleting spurious links with translation span alignment. Nat. Lang. Eng. 21(2), 227–249 (2015)

19. Liu, Y., Liu, Q., Lin, S.: Discriminative word alignment by linear modeling. Comput. Linguist. 36(3), 303–339 (2010)

20. Deng, Y., Zhou, B.: Optimizing word alignment combination for phrase table training. In: Proceedings of ACL-IJCNLP, pp. 229–232 (2009)

21. Parton, K., Habash, N., McKeown, K., Iglesias, G., de Gispert, A.: Can automatic post-editing make MT more meaningful? In: Proceedings of EAMT, pp. 111–118 (2012)

22. Huck, M., Ney, H.: Insertion and deletion models for statistical machine translation. In: Proceedings of HLT-NAACL, pp. 347–351 (2012)

A Simple, Straightforward and Effective Model for Joint Bilingual Terms Detection and Word Alignment in SMT

Guoping Huang[1,2], Jiajun Zhang[1], Yu Zhou[1], and Chengqing Zong[1](✉)

[1] National Laboratory of Pattern Recognition, Institute of Automation,
Chinese Academy of Sciences, Beijing, China
{guoping.huang,jjzhang,yzhou,cqzong}@nlpr.ia.ac.cn
[2] University of Chinese Academy of Sciences, Beijing, China

Abstract. Terms extensively exist in specific domains, and term translation plays a critical role in domain-specific statistical machine translation (SMT) tasks. However, it's a challenging task to extract term translation knowledge from parallel sentences because of the error propagation in the SMT training pipeline. In this paper, we propose a simple, straightforward and effective model to mitigate the error propagation and improve the quality of term translation. The proposed model goes from initial weak monolingual detection of terms based on naturally annotated resources (e.g. Wikipedia) to a stronger bilingual joint detection of terms, and allows the word alignment to interact. The extensive experiments show that our method substantially boosts the performance of bilingual term detection by more than 8 points absolute F-score. And the term translation quality is substantially improved by more than 3.66% accuracy, as well as the sentence translation quality is significantly improved by 0.38 absolute BLEU points, compared with the strong baseline, i.e. the well tuned Moses.

1 Introduction

Terms, defined by specialists, a noun or compound word used in a specific context, deliver essential context and meaning in human languages [25], such as technical terms "header text" and "summary"[1]. Terms extensively exist in specific domains. For example, in Microsoft Translation Memory, there are 8 terms out of every 100 words, whereas named entities are nearly nonexistent. What's more, new terms are being created all the time, such as in areas of computer science and medicine. Thus, term translation plays a critical role in domain-specific statistical machine translation (SMT) tasks.

However, unlike person names or other named entities having obvious characteristics and boundary clues, it's a challenging task to extract term translation knowledge from parallel sentences in the SMT training pipeline. A typical SMT training pipeline consists of monolingual term recognition, word alignment and

---

[1] In this paper, we do not consider named entities (e.g., person names, location names, organization names, time and numbers) and treat named entities non-terms.

© Springer International Publishing AG 2016
C.-Y. Lin et al. (Eds.): NLPCC-ICCPOL 2016, LNAI 10102, pp. 103–115, 2016.
DOI: 10.1007/978-3-319-50496-4_9

translation rule extraction. So, the term recognization errors will propagate into the next stages. To make matters worse, it is expensive to annotate training data, in practice, to obtain high-quality term recognizers for various specific domains.

As a result, the poor performance of term recognition further decreases the quality of word alignment and translation rule extraction. Thus, it is a challenging task to extract term translation knowledge from parallel sentences. Thus, frequent term translation errors make users hard to follow MT results in specific areas. For example, in the case of Microsoft Translation Memory, more than 10% of high-frequency terms are incorrectly translated by our baseline system, although the BLEU-score is up to 63%.

In order to mitigate the error propagation and improve the quality of term translation, we propose in this paper a simple, straightforward and effective model for jointing bilingual term detection and word alignment. The proposed model goes from the initial weak monolingual detection of terms based on naturally annotated resources, e.g., Wikipedia, to a stronger bilingual joint detection of terms, and allows the word alignment to interact. A brief overview of the proposed model is shown in Fig. 1.

In Fig. 1(a), the starting point is the weak English term recognizer, the weak Chinese term recognizer and the HMM-based word alignment model. Obviously, there are some critical errors denoted by red color (the italics words and the dotted lines).

Fortunately, based on Fig. 1(a), we have the following observations: (1) The initially recognized monolingual terms can act as anchors for further detecting terms. (2) The source terms and target terms in parallel sentences come in pair, and it provides mutual constraints for bilingual term detection. (3) The detected bilingual term pairs can further improve the performance of word alignment, in turn, word alignment can contribute to term recognition.

Based on the above observations and inspired by [2,27], the proposed model adopts the initial results as anchors, then enlarges or shrinks the boundaries of the anchors to generate new term candidates, and allows the word alignment to interact, as shown in Fig. 1(b). Finally, we get a stronger bilingual joint detection of terms and the promoted word alignment as seen in Fig. 1(c).

In the experiments, our proposed joint model has achieved remarkable results on bilingual term detection, word alignment, term translation and sentence translation. In summary, this paper makes the following contributions:

1. The proposed simple and straightforward model jointly performs bilingual term detection and word alignment for the first time.
2. The proposed joint model starts with low-quality naturally annotated monolingual resources rather than expensive human annotated data to perform initial term recognition, and allows the word alignment to interact with bilingual term detection, finally gets a stronger bilingual detection of terms.
3. The proposed model substantially boosts the performance of bilingual term detection and word alignment, and finally significantly improves the performance of term translation in the specific domain compared to a strong baseline.

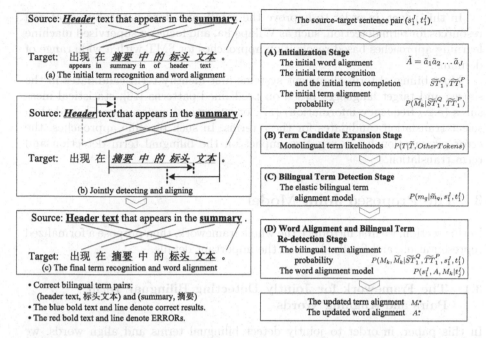

Fig. 1. A brief work flow overview of the proposed model. (Color figure online)

Fig. 2. The four-stage framework for joint bilingual term detection and word alignment.

2 Related Work

To automatically recognize terms, researchers have proposed many approaches, which can be divided into two types. One aims at using linguistic tools (e.g. POS tagger, phrase chunker) to filter out stop words and restrict candidate terms to noun phrases [1]. The other focuses on employing statistical measures to rank the candidate terms (n-gram sequences), such as mutual information [4], log likelihood [17], t-test [6], TF-IDF [20], C-value/NC-value [9], and many others [14,30]. More recent term recognition systems use hybrid approaches that combine both linguistic and statistical information.

However, seldom is the full range of the problem dealt with by any one method. First, most works rely on the simplifying assumption [11,15] that the majority of terms consist of multi-word, In fact, [21] claims that 85% of domain-specific terms are multi-word units, while [15] claims that only a small percentage of gene names are multi-word units. Such an assumption leads to very low recall for some domains. Second, some approaches apply frequency thresholds to reduce the algorithm's search space by filtering out low frequency term candidates. Such methods have not taken into account Zipf's law, again leading to reduced recall.

In this paper, in order to improve the recall, we adopt naturally annotated resources for term detection, such as Wikipedia, and focus on supervised machine learning approaches based recognition approaches for SMT with a wide range of domains.

Most bilingual term alignment systems first identify term candidates in the source and target languages based on predefined patterns [16], statistical measures (e.g., frequency information) [17], or supervised approaches [7], and then select translation candidates for these terms. In such pipeline approaches, the error propagation has a negative impact on the bilingual term detection and term translation.

3   The Proposed Joint Model

In this section, we first introduce the whole framework, then propose a formalized representation, and finally describe the important details.

3.1   The Framework for Jointly Detecting Bilingual Term Pairs and Aligning Words

In this paper, in order to jointly detect bilingual terms and align words, we propose a four-stage framework as shown in Fig. 2: (A) Initialization stage goes from initial weak monolingual detection of terms based on naturally annotated resources. (B) Term candidate expansion stage, expanding the associated term candidate set to remedy the errors occurred in the previous stage. (C) Bilingual term detection stage. The framework obtains a stronger bilingual joint detection of terms. (D) Word alignment and bilingual term re-detection stage. The framework allows the word alignment to interact with the bilingual term detection results. In Fig. 2, only the key points are showed.

(A) Initialization Stage

The first stage includes the following steps: initial word alignment, initial term recognition, initial term completion and initial term alignment. Let $s_1^J = s_1 s_2 \ldots s_J$ denote the source sentence, and $t_1^I = t_1 t_2 \ldots t_I$ denote the target sentence, where J and I are the numbers of words in source sentence and target sentence, respectively.

Initial Word Alignment and Initial Term Recognition: Given the source-target sentence pair (s_1^J, t_j^I), we can get the initial word alignment $\widetilde{A} = \tilde{a}_1 \tilde{a}_2 \ldots \tilde{a}_J$, the initial recognized source terms $\widetilde{ST}_1^Q$, and the initial recognized target terms $\widetilde{TT}_1^P$, where Q and P are the numbers of initially recognized terms of the source and the target sentence, respectively. In word alignment, $\tilde{a}_j = \{i | a(j) = i\}$, and the expression $a(j) = i$ denotes that the target word t_i is connected to the source word s_j.

For this work, the word alignment refers to the HMM-based word alignment model by default. The term recognition tool is based on the Stanford

Classifier [19], which is trained by naturally annotated Wikipedia monolingual sentences, e.g., hyperlinks, boldfaces and quotes. And a beam search style decoding algorithm is employed to convert the classification results to appropriate term recognition results. As a result, we can get initial weak monolingual term detectors.

Initial Term Completion: In order to prevent the incorrect term alignment caused by the initial term recognition errors, $\widetilde{ST}_1^Q$ and $\widetilde{TT}_1^P$ will be fixed by the following operation: if none of aligned target words of the source term $\widetilde{ST}_q$ is recognized as the term, then the one, which is most likely to be a term, of them will be added into $\widetilde{TT}_1^P$; the same operation will be applied to the target terms.

Initial Term Alignment: We construct the initial term alignment set $\widetilde{M} = \widetilde{M}_1^{(P^Q)}$ by generating a Cartesian product of the source term set $\widetilde{ST}_1^Q$ and the target term set $\widetilde{TT}_1^P$. We rank each candidate $\widetilde{M}_k$ of the initial term alignment set in descending order with the score calculated by the Viterbi algorithm [8] using the pre-trained term alignment model. The k-th initial term alignment is denoted by $\widetilde{M}_k = \widetilde{m}_1\widetilde{m}_2\ldots\widetilde{m}_Q$, where $\widetilde{m}_q = (\widetilde{ST}_q, \widetilde{TT}_p)$.

In the first stage, the initial term alignment is based on the pre-trained term alignment model, which is implemented according to the HMM-based word alignment model. And the training data is the bilingual term dictionary consisting of Wikipedia titles and the domain-specific term database.

Example: For the example in Fig. 1, the input of the first stage is the following:

---

(1) The English (source) tagged sentence "<Header> text that appears in the <summary> ." and the Chinese (target) tagged sentence "出现 在 <摘要 中 的 标头 文本> 。".
(2) The initial English terms ([header], [summary]) and the initial Chinese terms ([摘要 中 的 标头 文本]).
(3) The initial word alignment "NULL{3} 出现{1,4} 在{5,6} 摘要{7} 中{} 的{} 标头{} 文本{2} 。{8}".

And the output is the following result:

---

(1) The fixed initial English terms ([header], [summary]) and the fixed initial Chinese term ([出现], [摘要中的标头文本]).
(2) The initial term-alignment set ({[header]::[出现], [summary]::摘要 中 的 标头 文本]}; {[header]::[摘要 中 的 标头 文本], [summary]::[出现]}; {[header]::[摘要 中 的 标头 文本], [summary]::[摘要 中 的 标头 文本]}; {[header]::[出现], [summary]::[出现]}).

(B) Term Candidate Expansion Stage

In order to mitigate the error occurred in the previous stage, we generate another two term candidate sets $ST_1^{Q'}$ and $TT_1^{P'}$ sets by allowing the initial term to enlarge/shrink its boundaries up to four words on each side. Each time, when the one of the boundaries is enlarging/shrinking, the another one should be fixed. And finally we get a series of term candidates. The limitation "four words" is an empirical value. In addition, the regenerated terms in this stage are not allowed to overlap different initial terms, but they can share the same base initial term.

Example: For the example in Fig. 1, the input of the second stage is the initial term-alignment set, and the output is the following result:

> (1) The regenerated English term set ([header] → {[header text], [header text that], [header text that appears], [header text that appears in]}; [summary] → {[summary], [the summary], [in the summary], [appears in the summary], [that appears in the summary]}).
>
> (2) The regenerated Chinese term set([出现] → {[出现 在]}, [摘要 中 的 标头 文本] → {[在 摘要 中 的 标头 文本], [摘要 中 的 标头 文本 。], [摘要 中 的 标头], [摘要 中 的], [摘要], [中 的 标头 文本], [的 标头 文本], [标头 文本], [文本]}).

(C) Bilingual Term Detection Stage

The third stage is to jointly perform monolingual term detection and bilingual term alignment. We conduct a beam search process to select the top K updated term alignment set $M = M_1^K$ based on the initial term alignment set $\widetilde{M}$, the re-generated source terms $ST_1^{Q'}$ and the re-generated target terms $TT_1^{P'}$. The searching process will keep removing those overlapping terms from the candidate list. The k-th updated term alignment is denoted as $M_k = m_1 m_2 \ldots m_Q$ where $m_q = (TT_p, ST_q)$. We can get the probability of each updated term alignment $P(M_k | ST_1^{Q'}, TT_1^{P'})$ for each k. As a result, the proposed framework obtains a stronger bilingual term detection.

Example: For the example in Fig. 1, the input of the third stage includes the regenerated English term set and the regenerated Chinese term set, and the output is the following result:

> The updated-term-alignment set ({[header text]::[标头文本], [summary]::[摘要中]}; {[header text]::[的标头文本], [summary]::[摘要]}; ⋯Total 132 (11 × 12) term pairs will be generated).

(D) Word Alignment and Bilingual Term Re-detection Stage

In the last stage, the framework allows the word alignment to interact with the bilingual term detection results through jointly executing bilingual term re-detection and word alignment via a generative model. The joint word alignment tool in this stage is the extension for the initial word alignment tool in the first stage. As a result, we can get the final word alignment $A^* = a_1^* a_2^* \ldots a_J^*$ and the final term alignment $M^* = m_1^* m_2^* \ldots m_Q^*$ using the generative word alignment model based on the constraint of the updated term alignment M.

Example: For the example in Fig. 1, the input of the last stage is the updated-term-alignment set, and the output is the following result:

> (1) The re-ranked updated-term-pair set({[header text]::[标头 文本], [summary]::[摘要]}; {[header text]::[的 标头 文本], [summary]::[摘要]}; ⋯).
>
> (2) The top 1 word alignment "NULL{6} 出现{4} 在{5} 摘要{7} 中{3} 的{} 标头{1} 文本{2} 。{8}".
>
> (3) The top 1 term alignment in updated-term-pair set({[header text]::[标头 文本], [summary]::[摘要]}).

3.2 The Joint Model

We put all the four stages together, and the proposed joint model can be formulated as:

$$(A^*, M^*) = \operatorname*{argmax}_{(M_k, A)} \left[\max_{\widetilde{M_k}} P(M_k, \widetilde{M_k} | \widetilde{ST}_1^Q, \widetilde{TT}_1^P, s_1^J, t_1^I) \times P(s_1^J, A, M_k | t_1^I) \right] \quad (1)$$

where $P(M_k, \widetilde{M_k}|\widetilde{ST}_1^Q, \widetilde{TT}_1^P, s_1^J, t_1^I)$ refers to the bilingual term alignment probability, and $P(s_1^J, A, M_k|t_j^I)$ refers to the the word alignment model based on the constraint of the updated term alignment M_k.

The following steps are executed jointly with respect to $\widetilde{ST}_1^Q$, $\widetilde{TT}_1^P$, s_1^J and t_1^I: monolingual term recognition, bilingual term alignment and word alignment. And there is no independence assumption among those term pairs including in the associated term-pair sequence.

Next, we will introduce the important derivation details. The derivation looks like a somewhat complicated framework, but it's not so hard to comprehend and implemented.

3.3   Derivation Details

In Eq. (1), the bilingual term alignment probability, in the fourth stage as shown in Fig. 2, is computationally infeasible and will be simplified and derived as follows:

$$P(M_k, \widetilde{M_k}|\widetilde{ST}_1^Q, \widetilde{TT}_1^P, s_1^J, t_1^I) \approx P(\widetilde{M_k}|\widetilde{ST}_1^Q, \widetilde{TT}_1^P) \times \prod_{m_q \in M_k} \prod_{\widetilde{m}_q \in \widetilde{M}_k} P(m_q|\widetilde{m}_q, s_1^J, t_1^I)$$

(2)

It implies that monolingual term recognition and bilingual term alignment are executed jointly. In Eq. 2, $P(\widetilde{M_k}|\widetilde{ST}_1^Q, \widetilde{TT}_1^P)$ denotes the initial term alignment probability in the first stage, and $P(m_q|\widetilde{m}_q, s_1^J, t_1^I)$ denotes the elastic bilingual term alignment model in the third stage.

In the next subsections, we will introduce how to compute the important submodels embedded in the four stages as shown in Fig. 2.

(1) The Initial Term Alignment Probability

The initial term alignment probability, in the first stage, is based on the maximum entropy model [3]. In this paper, we design a set of feature functions $h_f(\widetilde{M}_k, \widetilde{ST}_1^Q, \widetilde{TT}_1^P)$, where $f = 1, 2, \ldots, F$. Let λ_f be the weight corresponding to the feature function. We adopt GIS algorithm [5] to train the weight λ_f. According to [22], we have the following initial term alignment model:

$$P(\widetilde{M_k}|\widetilde{ST}_1^Q, \widetilde{TT}_1^P) = \frac{\exp\left[\sum_{f=1}^F \lambda_f h_f(\widetilde{M}_k, \widetilde{ST}_1^Q, \widetilde{TT}_1^P)\right]}{\sum_{\widetilde{M}_k'} \exp\left[\sum_{f=1}^F \lambda_f h_f(\widetilde{M}_k', \widetilde{ST}_q, \widetilde{TT}_p)\right]}$$

(3)

In order to calculate the initial term alignment model, we employ the following three feature functions in this paper: phrase translation probability (denoted as h_1), lexical translation probability (h_2) and co-occurrence feature (h_3).

The phrase translation probability h_1 is calculated by the pre-trained term word alignment model as follows:

$$h_1(\widetilde{M}_k, \widetilde{ST}_1^Q, \widetilde{TT}_1^P) = \log P(\widetilde{ST}_1^Q|\widetilde{TT}_1^P, \widetilde{M}_k) + \log P(\widetilde{TT}_1^P|\widetilde{ST}_1^Q, \widetilde{M}_k)$$

(4)

The lexical translation probability h_2 is calculated by the pre-trained term word alignment:

$$h_2(\widetilde{M}_k, \widetilde{ST}_1^Q, \widetilde{TT}_1^P) = \log lex(\widetilde{ST}_q^Q | \widetilde{TT}_1^P, \widetilde{M}_k) + \log lex(\widetilde{TT}_1^P | \widetilde{ST}_1^Q, \widetilde{M}_k) \quad (5)$$

The co-occurrence feature h_3 is calculated based the current parallel corpus:

$$h_3(\widetilde{M}_k, \widetilde{ST}_1^Q, \widetilde{TT}_1^P) = \log \prod_{q=1}^{Q} \left(\frac{count(\widetilde{ST}_q, \widetilde{TT}_{\tilde{m}(q)})}{count(*, \widetilde{TT}_{\tilde{m}(q)})} + \frac{count(\widetilde{TT}_{\tilde{m}(q)}, \widetilde{ST}_q)}{count(*, \widetilde{ST}_q)} \right) \quad (6)$$

(2) The Monolingual Term Likelihoods

This is the key step of the third stage as well as the whole joint model. Given the initial term $\widetilde{T} = \widetilde{T}_1^{\widetilde{H}} = \widetilde{w}_1 \widetilde{w}_2 \ldots \widetilde{w}_{\widetilde{H}}$, where $\widetilde{w}_i$ refers to the i-th word, and $\widetilde{H}$ is the number of words. Then, the re-generated term T can be formulated as $T = T_1^H = w_1 w_2 \ldots w_H = \widetilde{w}_{-d_L} \ldots \widetilde{w}_{-1} \widetilde{w}_1 \widetilde{w}_2 \ldots \widetilde{w}_{\widetilde{H}} \widetilde{w}_{+1} \ldots \widetilde{w}_{+d_R}$, where d_L refers to the left distance, namely numbers of words enlarged ($d_L \geq 1$) or shrunk ($d_L \leq -1$) from the left boundary; similarly, d_R refers to the right distance. In fact, $\tilde{t}_1$ and $\tilde{t}_{\widetilde{H}}$ are the anchor points that we can enlarge or shrink the initial recognized term. Then, the monolingual term likelihoods can be derived as:

$$P(T|\widetilde{T}, OtherTokens) \approx P(T)^{\beta_1} \times (1 - P(\widetilde{w}_{-d_L} \ldots \widetilde{w}_{-1}))^{\beta_2} \times$$
$$(1 - P(\widetilde{w}_{+1} \ldots \widetilde{w}_{+d_R}))^{\beta_3} \times P(\widetilde{T})^{\beta_4} \quad (7)$$

where $P(*)$ refers to the probability that $*$ is a term given by the initial monolingual term recognition model; $1 - P(*)$ refers to the probability that the enlarged/shrunk part $*$ is not a term; β refers to the corresponding weight (the optional value is 0.25).

(3) The Elastic Bilingual Term Alignment Model

The elastic bilingual term alignment model, in the third stage, can be further decomposed:

$$P(m_q|\tilde{m}_q, s_1^J, t_1^I) = \sum_{L_k} P(L_k | ST_q, TT_p) \times P'(m_q|\tilde{m}_q, s_1^J, t_1^I) \quad (8)$$

where L_k denotes internal component alignment, $P'(m_q|\tilde{m}_q, s_1^J, t_1^I)$ denotes the elastic bilingual term model, and the word alignment probability $P(L_k|ST_q, TT_p)$ is determined by the pre-trained term alignment model. The elastic bilingual term model can be derived based on the monolingual term likelihoods as follows:

$$P'(m_q|\tilde{m}_q, s_1^J, t_1^I) \approx P(ST_q|\widetilde{ST}_q, OtherTokens) \times P(TT_p|\widetilde{TT}_p, OtherTokens) \quad (9)$$

(4) The Word Alignment Model

The word aligned model, in the last stage, is calculated according to the HMM word alignment model [26]:

$$P(s_1^J, A, M_k | t_j^I) = \prod_{j=1}^{J} p(a_j, M_k | a_{j-1}, I) \times P(s_j | t_{a_j}) \quad (10)$$

where $P(s_j | t_{a_j})$ denotes the word translation probability.

Let $p(a_j|a_{(j-1)}, I)$ be the HMM alignment probability according to [26], and $conflict(j, M_k)$ be the indicator which indicates whether the current word alignment a_j has a conflict with the term alignment M_k, then:

$$p(a_j, M_k|a_{(j-1)}, I) = \begin{cases} 0 & if\ conflict(j, M_k) = true \\ p(a_j|a_{(j-1)}, I) & if\ conflict(j, M_k) = false \end{cases} \quad (11)$$

At last, about the computational cost of our implementation, the time tends to increase 3–4 times more than the baseline HMM-based word alignment, and the memory requirement rises at nearly 2–3 times.

4 Experiments

We conduct the experiments to test the performance of our four-stage joint model in improving the performance of bilingual term detection and word alignment. In addition, we will check how much improvement the proposed model can achieve on the final SMT result. The performance of recognition and alignment is evaluated by precision (P), recall (R) and F-score (F); the quality of term translation and sentence translation is evaluated by precision (P) and BLEU, respectively.

Table 1. The performance of term recognition.

	P/%	R/%	F/%
En-Baseline	62.94	65.61	64.25
Ch-Baseline	57.21	66.67	61.58
En-Joint-C-Stage	67.35	71.47	69.34
Ch-Joint-C-Stage	65.13	74.86	69.65
En-Joint-D-Stage	71.20**	76.84**	**73.91****
Ch-Joint-D-Stage	67.89**	75.03**	**71.28****

Table 3. The performance of word alignment

	P/%	R/%	F/%
GIZA++	69.28	75.83	72.41
Baseline-1	67.06	73.18	69.99
Baseline-2	64.47	70.62	67.41
Joint-C-Stage	69.45	76.49	72.80
Joint-D-Stage	71.19**	78.51**	**74.67****

Table 2. The performance of bilingual term alignment

	P/%	R/%	F/%
Baseline	49.38	56.41	52.66
Joint-C-Stage	53.47	59.44	56.29
Joint-D-Stage	58.29**	63.78**	**60.91****

Table 4. The performance of translation

	Term/P/%	Sent/BLEU/%
Moses	87.30	63.58
Baseline-1	86.53	63.09
Baseline-2	78.43	62.68
Joint-C-Stage	87.73	63.54
Joint-D-Stage	**91.04****	**63.96****

"**" means the scores are significantly better than the corresponding previous line with $p < 0.01$.

4.1   Experimental Setup

All the experiments are conducted on our in-house developed SMT toolkit including a typical phrase-based decoder [28] and a series of tools, including term recognition, term alignment, word alignment and phrase table extraction.

We test our method on English-to-Chinese translation in the field of software localization. The training data (1,199,589 sentences) and annotated test data (1,100 sentences) are taken from Microsoft Translation Memory, which is a domain-specific dataset. And additional data employed by this paper includes Wikipedia terms (1,133,913) and Microsoft Terminology Collection (24,094 terms). The gold standard of term recognition and word alignment are human annotated. What's more, all data have been submitted for public. The statistical significance test is performed by the re-sampling approach [12].

4.2   Results and Analysis

(1) The Term Recognition Tests

First, we compare the performances of term recognition in the different joint stages with the baseline system, e.g., the pipeline approach. The corresponding systems are denoted as "En-baseline", "Ch-Baseline", "En-Joint-C-Stage", "Ch-Joint-C-Stage", "En-Joint-D-Stage" and "Ch-Joint-D-Stage", respectively. "*-Baseline" refers to that term recognition and bilingual term alignment are executed individually. "*-C-Stage" means that only term recognition and term alignment are executed jointly. "*-D-Stage" refers the proposed four-stage framework. We report all the term recognition results in Table 1.

In contrast to the pipeline approach, the figures in Table 1 show that the initially detected terms can act as quite useful anchors for further detection, and the performance of monolingual term recognition has been increased by at least 9.66 points absolute F-score through the proposed four-stage framework. According to the bold figures in Table 1, we can draw a conclusion that word alignment can substantially increase the performance of monolingual term recognition.

(2) The Bilingual Term Alignment Tests

Second, we compare the performances of bilingual term alignment in different stages. We report all the bilingual term alignment results in Table 2. The bold figures in Table 2 indicate that the performance of bilingual term alignment has been increased by 8.25 points absolute F-score, with the feedback of word alignment and the constraint of source terms and target terms being pairing off.

(3) The Word alignment Tests

Third, we evaluate the performance of proposed joint model on word alignment. Both GIZA++ [23] and the HMM-based approach "Baseline-1" take no account of terms. Then, the term pipeline approach is implemented as our "Baseline-2". The term pipeline approach means that the following steps will be accomplished sequentially without feedback: term recognition, bilingual term alignment and word alignment. "Joint-C-Stage" means that word alignment is executed individually in the fourth stage. And "*-D-Stage" refers the proposed four-stage framework. In this paper, we adopted the balanced F-measure [10,18] as our evaluation metric for word alignment. All results are reported in Table 3.

In Table 3, "Baseline-1" is the pure HMM-based word alignment, while GIZA++ enables IBM model 1–5, HMM and other alignment improvements. Thus, the word alignment result of "Baseline-1" is worse than that of GIZA++. And the pipeline approach ("Baseline-2") cannot improve the performance of word alignment, because the performance of monolingual term recognition is too weak for the scarcity of specialized annotated data. The bold figures in Table 3 show that our proposed joint model has increased the performance of word alignment by 4.68 and 2.26 points absolute F-score, compared to the HMM-based method and GIZA++, respectively.

(4) The SMT Translation Tests

Finally, we test whether the proposed joint model can further improve the performance of term and sentence translation. The Moses (GIZA++) and the HMM-based approach "Baseline-1" take no account of terms. Then, the term pipeline approach is implemented as our "Baseline-2". The word alignment was conducted bidirectionally and then symmetrized for extracting phrases as Moses [13] does. All the MT systems are trained by the same training set and tuned by the development set (1,100 sentences) using ZMERT [29] with the objective to optimize BLEU [24]. The test set includes 1,100 sentences with 1,208 bilingual term pairs altogether. In order to highlight the performance of term translation, we count the number of terms that is translated exactly correctly, and the term translation results are denoted as "Term/P" (exact match). The sentence translation results are labeled "Sent/BLEU". We report all the translation results in Table 4.

In Table 4, GIZA++ makes the SMT result of "Baseline-1" are worse than Moses. However, with the help of the proposed joint model, the term translation quality is significantly improved by more than 3.66% accuracy. Non-term words are also strongly improved by the joint model, because the accuracy rating of term words alignment has been much improved and fewer non-term words are aligned incorrectly to term words. In sentence translation, the bold figures in Table 4 demonstrate that it improves the translation quality by 0.38 absolute BLEU points, compared with the strong baseline system, i.e., well tuned Moses. Considering one term on average in a single sentence in the test set, the BLEU scores are very promising actually, and our goals on term translation have been achieved.

For the example in Fig. 1, with the aid of the joint model, the SMT system acquired more reliable term translation knowledge from training sentences, such as "header text ||| 标头文本". For the source sentences "header text is not included", the result of the baseline systems is "不包含头部文本, head text is not included". Fortunately, we can achieve the correct term translation result "不包含标头文本" from the system "Joint-D-Stage".

In summary, we can draw the conclusion that the proposed four-stage joint model significantly improves the performance of monolingual term recognition, bilingual term alignment and word alignment, and further significantly improves the performance of SMT in term translation and sentence translation.

5   Conclusion

In this paper, we have presented a simple, straightforward and effective joint model for bilingual term detection and word alignment. The proposed model starts with weak monolingual term detection based on naturally annotated monolingual resources, then jointly performs bilingual term detection and word alignment, finally substantially boosts bilingual term detection and word alignment, and significantly improves the quality of term translation and sentence translation. The experimental results are promising.

Acknowledgments. The research work has been funded by the Natural Science Foundation of China under Grant No. 61403379.

References

1. Ananiadou, S.: A methodology for automatic term recognition. In: Proceedings of COLING 1994 (1994)
2. Chen, Y., Zong, C., Su, K.Y.: A joint model to identify and align bilingual named entities. Comput. Linguist. **39**(2), 1–64 (2012)
3. Chieu, H.L., Ng, H.T.: Named entity recognition: a maximum entropy approach using global information. In: Proceedings of the 19th International Conference on Computational Linguistics (2002)
4. Daille, B.: Study and implementation of combined techniques for automatic extraction of terminology. Balanc. Act: Comb. Symb. Stat. Approaches Lang. **1**, 49–66 (2002)
5. Darroch, J.N., Ratcliff, D.: Generalized iterative scaling for log-linear models. Ann. Math. Stat. **43**(5), 1470–1480 (1972)
6. Fahmi, B.I., Bouma, G., Plas, L.V.D.: Improving statistical method using known terms for automatic term extraction. In: Computational Linguistics in the Netherlands-CLIN 2007 (2007)
7. Fan, X., Shimizu, N., Nakagawa, H.: Automatic extraction of bilingual terms from a Chinese-Japanese parallel corpus. In: International Universal Communication Symposium 2009 (2009)
8. Forney, G.D.: The viterbi algorithm. Proc. IEEE **61**(3), 268–278 (1973)
9. Frantzi, K., Ananiadou, S., Mima, H.: Automatic recognition of multi-word terms: the c-value/nc-value method. Int. J. Digit. Libr. **3**(2), 115–130 (2000)
10. Fraser, A., Marcu, D.: Measuring word alignment quality for statistical machine translation. Fraser Alexander Daniel Marcu **33**(3), 293–303 (2007)
11. Kageura, K., Umino, B.: Methods of automatic term recognition: a review. Terminology **3**(2), 259–289 (1996)
12. Koehn, P.: Statistical significance tests for machine translation evaluation. In: Proceedings of the EMNLP 2004 (2004)

13. Koehn, P., Hoang, H., Birch, A., Callison-Burch, C., Federico, M., Bertoldi, N., Cowan, B., Shen, W., Moran, C., Zens, R.: Moses: open source toolkit for statistical machine translation. In: Proceedings of ACL 2007 (2007)
14. Kostoff, R.N., Block, J.A., Solka, J.L., Briggs, M.B., Rushenberg, R.L., Stump, J.A., Johnson, D., Lyons, T.J., Wyatt, J.R.: Literature-related discovery. Ann. Rev. Inf. Sci. Technol. **43**(1), 171 (2009)
15. Krauthammer, M., Nenadic, G.: Term identification in the biomedical literature. J. Biomed. Inform. **37**(6), 512–526 (2004)
16. Kupiec, J.: An algorithm for finding noun phrase correspondences in bilingual corpora. In: Proceedings of ACL 1993 (1993)
17. Lefever, E., Macken, L., Hoste, V.: Language-independent bilingual terminology extraction from a multilingual parallel corpus. In: Proceedings of EACL 2009 (2009)
18. Liu, Y., Liu, Q., Lin, S.: Discriminative word alignment by linear modeling. Comput. Linguist. **36**(3), 303–339 (2010)
19. Manning, C., Dan, K.: Optimization, maxent models, and conditional estimation without magic. In: Proceedings of the NAACL 2003 (2003)
20. Medelyan, O., Witten, I.H.: Thesaurus based automatic keyphrase indexing. In: Proceedings of the ACM/IEEE-CS Joint Conference on Digital Libraries (2006)
21. Nakagawa, H., Mori, T.: Nested collocation and noun for term extraction. In: Proceedings of the First Workshop on Comutational Terminology (COMPUTERM 1998) (1998)
22. Och, F.J., Ney, H.: Discriminative training and maximum entropy models for statistical machine translation. In: Proceedings of ACL 2002 (2002)
23. Och, F.J., Ney, H.: A systematic comparison of various statistical alignment models. Comput. Linguist. **29**(1), 19–51 (2003)
24. Papineni, K., Roukos, S., Ward, T., Zhu, W.: BLEU: a method for automatic evaluation of machine translation. In: Proceedings of the ACL 2002 (2002)
25. Sager, J.C., Dungworth, D., McDonald, P.F.: English Special Languages: Principles and Practice in Science and Technology. John Benjamins Publishing Company, Amsterdam (1980)
26. Vogel, S., Ney, H., Tillmann, C.: HMM-based word alignment in statistical translation. In: Proceedings of the 16th Conference on Computational Linguistics, vol. 2, pp. 836–841 (1996)
27. Wang, M., Che, W., Manning, C.D.: Joint word alignment and bilingual named entity recognition using dual decomposition. In: Proceedings of ACL 2013 (2013)
28. Xiong, D., Liu, Q., Lin, S.: Maximum entropy based phrase reordering model for statistical machine translation. In: proceedings of COLING-ACL 2006 (2006)
29. Zaidan, O.F.: Z-MERT: a fully configurable open source tool for minimum error rate training of machine translation systems. Prague Bull. Math. Linguist. **91**, 79–88 (2009)
30. Zhang, Z., Iria, J., Brewster, C.: A comparative evaluation of term recognition algorithms. In: LREC 2008 (2008)

Bilingual Parallel Active Learning Between Chinese and English

Longhua Qian[1,2(⊠)], JiaXin Liu[1,2], Guodong Zhou[1,2],
and Qiaoming Zhu[1,2]

[1] Natural Language Processing Lab, Soochow University,
Suzhou 215006, Jiangsu, China
{qianlonghua, gdzhou, qmzhu}@suda.edu.cn,
1060907970@qq.com
[2] School of Computer Science and Technology, Soochow University,
Suzhou 215006, Jiangsu, China

Abstract. Active learning is an effective machine learning paradigm which can significantly reduce the amount of labor for manually annotating NLP corpora while achieving competitive performance. Previous studies on active learning are focused on corpora in one single language or two languages translated from each other. This paper proposes a Bilingual Parallel Active Learning paradigm (BPAL), where an instance-level parallel Chinese and English corpus adapted from OntoNotes is augmented for relation extraction and both the seeds and jointly selected unlabeled instances at each iteration are parallel between two languages in order to enhance active learning. Experimental results on the task of relation classification on the corpus demonstrate that BPAL can significantly outperform monolingual active learning. Moreover, the success of BPAL suggests a new way of annotating parallel corpora for NLP tasks in order to induce two high-performance classifiers in two languages respectively.

Keywords: Active learning · Parallel corpus · Relation classification

1 Introduction

Supervised learning, particularly statistical supervised learning, has amassed a huge success in natural language processing during the past decades, from fundamental tasks such as POS tagging, chunking and parsing etc. to a wide range of high-level applications such as information extraction, question answering, sentiment analysis and machine translation etc. Nevertheless, it is based on many high-quality and high-volume manually annotated corpora, whose construction is both expensive and time-consuming.

Active learning (Settles 2009) is an effective way to significantly reduce the amount of labeled training data while preserving the comparable performance with supervised learning, avoiding the disadvantages caused by semi-supervised learning (Zhu 2005) or distant learning (Mintz et al. 2009). Current studies on active learning focus on annotating corpora for a specific NLP task or multiple related tasks in the same language (Reichart et al. 2008). With the emergence of large amount of parallel corpora, e.g. in machine translation, one may ask the question: can active learning benefit from these parallel corpora?

© Springer International Publishing AG 2016
C.-Y. Lin et al. (Eds.): NLPCC-ICCPOL 2016, LNAI 10102, pp. 116–128, 2016.
DOI: 10.1007/978-3-319-50496-4_10

However, there are few instance-level parallel corpora for NLP tasks except machine translation where only sentence-level parallel corpora are available. In order to investigate bilingual active learning on NLP tasks in a broad sense, e.g. relation extraction, we first construct an instance-level (e.g. semantic relation instances between entities) parallel corpus from the Chinese/English bilingual corpora of OntoNotes, then based on the corpus we propose a BPAL paradigm where all instances for training and testing are parallel.

The effectiveness of our BPAL paradigm suggests that a new bilingual annotation scheme can work in this way. Given a small number of labeled instances for seeds, two classifiers in Chinese and English are induced respectively, which are in turn used to predict the unlabeled instances. The most informative unlabeled instances are jointly selected and presented to an oracle for annotation and further added to the training dataset. This annotation process is repeated until two classifiers achieve competitive performance. Thus our contributions lie in three aspects:

(1) Construct an instance-level parallel Chinese/English corpus for relation extraction
(2) Propose a bilingual parallel active learning paradigm
(3) Induce a new way of bilingual annotation for NLP tasks

The paper is organized as follows. Section 2 reviews the related work, particularly in multi-task active learning. Section 3 details the construction process of a parallel corpus while Sect. 4 presents our Bilingual Parallel Active Learning paradigm. Finally Sect. 5 reports the experimental results and Sect. 6 concludes the paper.

2 Related Work

Active Learning in NLP

Active learning (AL) has been successfully applied to a lot of NLP tasks, such as POS tagging (Engelson and Dagan 1996; Ringger et al. 2007), word sense disambiguation (Chan and Ng 2007; Zhu and Hovy 2007), syntactical parsing (Hwa 2004; Osborne and Baldridge 2004), named entity recognition (Shen et al. 2004; Tomanek et al. 2007; Tomanek and Hahn 2009) and sentiment detection (Brew et al. 2010; Li et al. 2012) etc.

Multi-task Active Learning in NLP

Different from the aforementioned AL studies on a single task, Reichart et al. (2008) introduce a multi-task active learning (MTAL) paradigm, where unlabeled instances are selected using rank combination for two annotation tasks (i.e. named entity and syntactic parse tree). They demonstrate that MTAL in the same language outperforms both random selection and one-sided example selection AL strategies.

Zhang (2010) propose an MTAL framework exploiting output (label) constraints (e.g., inconsistent predictions) among related tasks. They formalize this idea as a cross-task value of information criteria, in which the reward of a labeling assignment is propagated and measured over all tasks. Experiments on Named Entity Recognition demonstrate its effectiveness in actively collecting labeled examples for multiple related tasks.

Machine translation is an important NLP application inherently involving bilingual parallel corpora. Haffari and Sarkar (2009) utilize active learning for multilingual machine translation, where highly informative sentences for a newly added language in multilingual parallel corpora are jointly selected in order to enhance the overall performance for multiple language pairs. Different from their method involving multiple language pairs, we actively and jointly select parallel relation instances used for relation classification in two languages respectively.

Our work is most similar to Qian et al. (2014), where comparable Chinese and English corpora are used in bilingual active learning. Two pseudo-parallel corpora are generated by first translating from one language to the other, then aligning entity mentions and relation instances between two languages. However, the pseudo-parallel corpora contain much noise caused by automatic translation and imperfect entity alignment. Moreover, their training and test datasets are not parallel. Instead, we build our active learning paradigm on manually annotated parallel corpora. All the training and test datasets are parallel, making them an ideal and fair platform to test the bilingual active learning paradigm, we call this learning paradigm Bilingual Parallel Active Learning (BPAL).

3   Corpus Annotation

Acquisition of instance-level parallel corpora is a great challenge to bilingual parallel active learning, considering the prohibitive labor amount to label entities and relations in two languages and then align them with instances in a traditional way. We address this issue by selecting a parallel corpus containing entity annotation in one language, augmenting it with relationship annotation, then mapping these annotations into the other language, and finally review them manually to ensure the annotation quality.

3.1   Corpus Selection

There are many parallel corpora for machine translation, but there are few with entity annotation. Although the ACE RDC2005 (ACE 2002–2007) corpora containing entity and relationship annotations do have both English and Chinese versions, they are at most comparable in some degree. Turning one of them into a instance-level parallel corpus is both labor-intensive and time-consuming. Fortunately, the OntoNotes corpus has 325 Chinese/English parallel articles from Xinhua News Agency where the English articles are manually translated from Chinese. Therefore, they have high rate of sentence alignment, furthermore, entity and coreference information has already been annotated. Nevertheless, only named entities are annotated in the corpus, i.e., entities with "NAM" mention level. All the "Nominal" and "Pronoun" entity mentions are left out. Another issue with the corpus is the partial coreference chains, i.e., many broken coreference chains exist in OntoNotes. This does not fully satisfy the requirement of relation extraction in a broad sense.

3.2 Annotation of Chinese Corpus

In order to take full advantage of the annotation information in the OntoNotes corpus, we first extract annotated entities and coreference chains from the Chinese corpus. However, due to the problem of partial entity mention and the broken coreference chain, in the second step we manually adjust entity annotation, either add new entity mentions with nominal or pronoun expressions, or combine two separate coreference chains into a unified one, finally the relationships between two entities are annotated. A specific annotation tool in Java is developed for this purpose.

In order to reflect the common characteristics in Chinese and English, we make some modifications to the ACE annotation scheme. The first is related to entity nesting. While it is common in both languages, it is ignored in the ACE annotation for technicality purpose. We argue that the inclusion of entity nesting will greatly increase the number of entity mentions and relationships because there usually exists a relationships between an entity mention and its nested one. Another issue is related to entity role. Some entities may assume different roles in different contexts, e.g., a GPE entity can represent an area, its organization or its people. This difference can be realized by various roles assigned to a GPE entity mention depending on its context. In a similar way, we find that another type of entity (ORG) also has this characteristic yet not addressed in the ACE scheme, therefore we introduce the roles of "ORG" and "FAC" to the ORG entity type to better discern between different contexts.

3.3 Mapping to English Corpus

Mapping the entity and relationship annotations from Chinese to English includes four steps, i.e., sentence alignment, word alignment, entity and relation mapping.

Sentence Alignment: Due to the high translation quality of news text from Xinhua News Agency, a simple yet effective similarity-based unsupervised method is adopted to automatically map Chinese and English sentences. The similarity score between Chinese and English sentence pair is based on the location and length of the sentences, the number of entity mentions in the sentences and the pairwise word similarity between two sentences. Sentence alignment can be performed based on the pairwise similarity scores between Chinese and English sentences. The basic idea is first to find the maximally matching sentence pair as the parallel pair, then split the sentence ranges using this pair, and continue the process in the respective sentence sub-ranges.

Word Alignment: GIZA++ is applied to word alignment between Chinese and English. The small scale of the OntoNotes parallel corpus will decrease the performance of word alignment, so the corpus is first incorporated into the FBIS corpus and then they as a whole are fed into GIZA++.

Entity Mapping: A simple heuristic strategy is adopted to entity mapping other than more complex methods, such as Maximum Entropy (Feng et al. 2004). In order to further simplify the mapping process, two constraints are applied. The first is that an entity mention in Chinese is a string of contiguous words, so is its counterpart in English; the second is that at most one Chinese entity mention can be mapped into an

English entity mention. The basic idea for entity mapping is that first find all the English words that are aligned with the Chinese words in a Chinese entity mention and conjoin those English words into an English entity mention if they are closely positioned and do not intertwine with other English entity mentions.

Relation Mapping: Given entity mapping has been finished, relation mapping is quite intuitive. If two entity mentions involved in a relationship in Chinese are both mapping to their counterparts in English, then their counterparts in English also have a relationship with the same relation type. However, two issues should be considered in the mapping process. The first is that two English entity mentions involved in a relationship must be in the same sentence, which is not always the case when a Chinese sentence is translated to English. The second is that if two entities in English exchange their order, the direction of their relationship should be reversed.

3.4   Manual Adjustment

Due to the high quality of the corpus, no significant manual adjustment is needed after mapping. The only exception is about syntactic class for relation instances in English since it is likely to change from Chinese to English and it can not be predicted reliably. In order to facilitate the analysis afterwards, all the relation instances in English should be examined and modified accordingly to ensure that their syntactic classes are correct.

3.5   Alignment Statistics

In order to examine how much of the annotated information in Chinese is retained after they are aligned with those in English, Table 1 reports the number of original annotations in Chinese, the number of aligned annotations in English and their alignment rate (AR) for different levels of annotated information such as entities, entity mentions and relationships.

Table 1. Annotation alignment statistics

Annotation types	Chinese	English	AR (%)
Entity mentions	14,982	14,738	98.4
Entities	6,917	6,864	99.2
Relationships	4,905	4,732	96.5

The table shows that the AR scores for all annotated information are well above 95%, suggesting that no significant information loss occurs during the mapping from Chinese to English. Furthermore, the AR score for entities is the highest while that for relationships is the lowest. The reason is intuitive, that if any one of entity mentions is aligned, the entity is aligned, and only if two entity mentions involved in a relationship are aligned, can the relationship between them be aligned.

4 Bilingual Parallel Active Learning

4.1 Problem Definition

With an instance-level Chinese and English (designated as c and e) parallel corpus at hand, this paper intends to examine the effect of bilingual active learning using relation classification as an example. Assume we have labeled and aligned a small number of labeled instances in two languages, denoted as Lc and Le respectively, and a large number of unlabeled, but aligned instances in both languages, denoted as Uc and Ue. The test instances in both languages are also aligned (denoted as Tc and Te.) in order to ensure that the test instances for both languages are the same for fair comparison. Generally, we have the following parallel data sets:

$$L_c \leftrightarrow L_e$$
$$U_c \leftrightarrow U_e$$
$$T_c \leftrightarrow T_e$$

The objective is to actively induce SVM classifiers in both languages which assign relation labels to candidate instances that have semantic relationships, denoted as SVM_c and SVM_e respectively, to improve their classification performance. We call this task as Bilingual Parallel Active Learning since there are not only two languages involved, but the instances are parallel anywhere, any time during learning process.

4.2 BPAL Algorithm

The basic idea of BPAL is that given instance-level parallel seed set at hand, unlabeled instances are jointly selected in two languages are the most informative to both classifiers and therefore they can boost the classification performance in greater degree than two individual classifiers do. Figure 1 shows the algorithm for BPAL, where the batch size n denotes the number of unlabeled instances augmented to the training set at each iteration.

Note that at Step 5 the unlabeled instances are jointly selected according to their uncertainty scores, which is the combination of two uncertainty scores from two individual classifiers. Similar to Qian et al. (2014), the individual score is gauged using least confidence (LC) metric (Settles and Craven 2008), denoted as H_c and H_e for Chinese and English instances respectively. That is, the least confidence a classifier has for an instance, the most informative it is to the classifier. Specifically, the geometric mean is adopted as the joint uncertainty score as follows:

$$H_g = \sqrt{H_c * H_e} \tag{1}$$

Where H_g is the joint uncertainty score for the parallel instance.

Algorithm Bilingual Parallel Active Learning

Input:
  - L_c and L_e, labeled parallel instances in Chinese and English respectively
  - U_c and U_e, unlabeled parallel instances in Chinese and English respectively
  - n, batch size
Output:
  - SVM_c and SVM_e, two classifiers for Chinese and English respectively
Repeat:
  1. Learn the Chinese classifier SVM_c from L_c
  2. Use SVM_c to classify instances in U_c
  3. Learn the English classifier SVM_e from L_e
  4. Use SVM_e to classify instances in U_e
  5. Jointly choose the n most uncertain instance pairs $\{E_c|E_e\}$ from $\{U_c|U_e\}$, and have them labeled by an oracle
  6. Remove E_c from U_c and add them to L_c with their manual labels
  7. Remove E_e from U_e and add them to L_e with their manual labels
Until certain number of instances are labeled or certain performance is reached

---

Fig. 1. Bilingual parallel active leaning algorithm

5 Experiments

5.1 Corpora

The above corpus is used as the experimental dataset, which contains 6,864 entities and 4,732 positive relation instances aligned between Chinese and English. Relation instances are generated pairwise between entity mentions in a sentence which has a relationship. Evaluation is done in a five-fold cross-validation strategy. For the purpose of fair comparison, the partition of training and test sets is exactly the same between Chinese and English. The SVMLIB package[1] is adopted as our multi-class classifier with default linear kernel and parameters. The standard Precision (P), Recall (R) and F1-score (F1) are used to evaluate the classification performance.

5.2 Experimental Methods

In order to evaluate the advantage of bilingual parallel active learning, we performed five different methods as follows. For fair comparison, it is worth to note that the total number of labeled instances in Chinese and English remain the same across different methods.

SL-MO (Supervised Learning with monolingual labeled instances): only the monolingual labeled instances are fed to the SVM classifiers for both Chinese and English respectively. In each iteration step, n randomly selected Chinese or English instances

---

[1] https://www.csie.ntu.edu.tw/~cjlin/libsvm/.

are augmented to the training data L_c and L_e respectively. Therefore, the total number of added instances in each iteration is $2n$.

AL-MO (Active Learning with monolingual instances): this is the normal active learning method applied to a single language. That is, in each iteration, n Chinese instances as well as n English instances are selected based on uncertainty score. The total number remains $2n$.

AL-CR-MO (Monolingual Active Learning with cross-lingual instances): normal active learning is performed in a source language, however, in each iteration, $2n$ least confidently predicted instances are additionally mapped to the target language and fed to that classifier, so the target classifier is solely dependent on the source language. For example, if Chinese is the source language, $2n$ Chinese instances are mapped to English and thus augmented to the English training data L_e. Another experiment should be performed when English is the source language.

AL-CR-BI (Bilingual Active Learning with cross-lingual instances): the same as AL-MO, normal active learning is applied to both Chinese and English respectively. However, in each iteration, n selected Chinese instances are mapped to English and fed to the English training data L_e. Likewise, n selected English instances are mapped to Chinese and fed to the Chinese training data L_c. The total number remains $2n$.

AL-BI (Active Learning with bilingual instances, i.e. **BPAL**): the two actively learning classifiers are independently trained and used to predicted the unlabeled instances, however, they share the same labeled and unlabeled data with Chinese and English views. That is, $2n$ unlabeled instances are chosen by the joint uncertainty score predicted by two classifiers in two languages. (cf. Sect. 4.2).

5.3 Features for Relation Classification

We follow a feature-based approach for the underlying relation classifiers other than kernel-based one since the latter performs much slow and thus is inappropriate for active learning. The features adopted are similar to those in Zhou et al. (2005) and Qian et al. (2014), including four major categories related to lexical and entity features as follows:

(a) Lexical features for entities and their contexts: WM1, HM1, WM2, HM2, HM12, WBNULL, WBFL, WBF, WBL, WBO
(b) Entity types and classes: ET12, EST12, EC12
(c) Mention levels: ML12, MT12
(d) Overlap: #WB, #MB, M1 > M2 or M1 < M2

5.4 Evaluation Metrics

Standard metrics such as Precision/Recall/F1-score are often used to evaluate the performance for supervised learning relation extraction. However, it is better to quantitatively compare various active learning methods using a statistical metric called deficiency (*DEF*) (Schein and Ungar 2007):

$$DEF_n(AL, REF) = \frac{\sum_{i=1}^{n} (F_n(REF) - F_i(AL))}{\sum_{i=1}^{n} (F_n(REF) - F_i(REF))} \qquad (2)$$

Where n is the number of iterations involved in active learning and F_i is the F1-score of relation classification at the ith iteration. *REF* is the baseline method like **SL-MO** and *AL* is an improved variant of *REF*, such as **AL-CR-MO, AL-CR-BI** or **AL-BI** etc. This metric actually measures the extent to which *REF* outperforms *AL*.

5.5   Experimental Results

Comparison of Various Active Learning Methods

Table 2 reports the performance of *DEF* for various active learning methods where **SL-MO** is used as a baseline for *DEF* calculation. The *DEF* scores are averaged for 10 runs. Each run has five disjoint test data sets and its *DEF* scores are averaged across these sets. All the following experiments adopt this setting except explained otherwise.

Table 2. Comparison of different active learning methods

Languages	AL-MO	AL-CR-MO	AL-CR-BI	AL-BI
Chinese	0.349	0.271	0.274	**0.233**
English	0.378	0.362	0.291	**0.277**

The table shows that **AL-BI** performs best among these active learning methods while **AL-MO** performs worst. This demonstrates that BPAL can achieve the best performance due to the fact that the unlabeled instances are selected based on the joint uncertainty score in both languages, thus these instances are informative for both classifiers. However, there are mixed results for the other two methods. While **AL-CR-BI** outperforms **AL-CR-MO** in English, the former underperforms the latter in Chinese. It implies that the Chinese instances mapped from the English instances which are selected by the English classifier are as informative as those selected by its own classifier while this is not true vice versa.

Learning Curves for Active Learning

In order to gain some insight into the learning process, Fig. 2 illustrates the F1-scores during iterations for five learning methods in Chinese and English respectively. The performance scores for a particular method are sampled from one of 10 runs in one specific data set. Note that for **AL-CR-MO** and **AL-BI**, the iteration number is only 19 because their batch size is twice that of other three learning methods.

The figure shows that during all iterations generally **AL-BI** performs best among all learning methods while **SL-MO** performs worst. This advantage is more obvious during initial steps. **AL-BI** and **AL-CR-MO** perform comparably better during the first

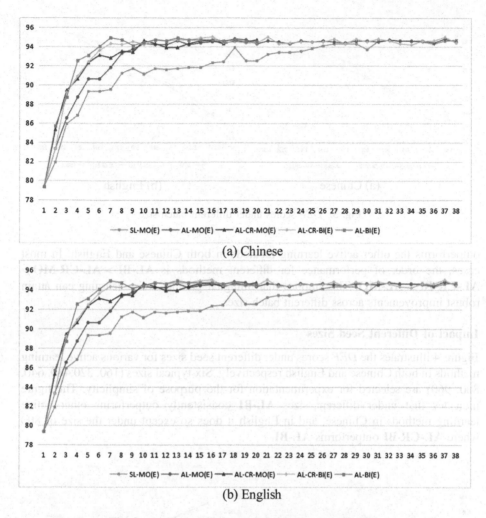

(a) Chinese

(b) English

Fig. 2. Active learning curves for Chinese and English

three iterations, but ever since **AL-BI** outperforms **AL-CR-MO** and reaches the apex at the 7th iteration. It implies that two languages interplay to a great degree during that period. After the 10th iteration, all active learning methods show similar behavior because the most informative instances have already been added to the training set.

Impact of Different Batch Size

Figure 3 depicts the *DEF* scores under different batch sizes for various active learning methods in Chinese and English respectively. The horizontal axis represents the batch size with variable steps while the vertical axis represents the *DEF* score. For meaningful comparison, the batch size for **AL-CR-MO** and **AL-BI** is twice that of the other methods. The figure shows that under different batch sizes **AL-BI** consistently

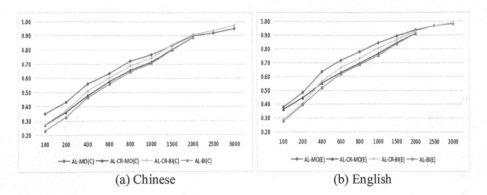

(a) Chinese   (b) English

Fig. 3. *DEF* scores under different batch size

outperforms the other active learning methods in both Chinese and English. In most cases, the order of performance for different methods is **AL-BI** > **AL-CR-MO** > **AL-CR-BI** > **AL-MO**. This implies that bilingual parallel active learning can attain robust improvements across different batch sizes.

Impact of Different Seed Sizes

Figure 4 illustrates the *DEF* scores under different seed sizes for various active learning methods in both Chinese and English respectively. Six typical sizes (160, 320,480, 640, 800, 960) are selected for experimentation for the purpose of simplicity. The figure indicates that under different sizes **AL-BI** consistently outperforms other active learning methods in Chinese, and in English it does so except under the size of 800 where **AL-CR-BI** outperforms **AL-BI**.

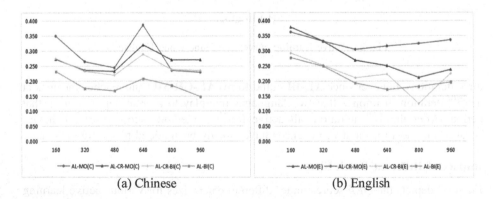

(a) Chinese   (b) English

Fig. 4. *DEF* scores under different seed size

6 Conclusion

In order to investigate the effectiveness of active learning in two languages, this paper first manually builds an instance-level Chinese/English parallel corpus based on the parallel part of OntoNotes. Then a Bilingual Parallel Active Learning paradigm is proposed to make full use of bilingual corpora to reduce the amount of labeled instances for relation classifiers in two languages while obtaining the comparable performance with supervised learning. Experimental results show that the BPAL paradigm outperforms active learning in one single language and also performs robustly across various settings. This implies a potential annotation scheme can be induced from the effectiveness of BPAL for other NLP tasks.

We will publish the instance-level Chinese/English corpus in the future for other bilingual research on the corpus. We will also combine co-training with active learning to further reduce the amount of manual labor for annotation.

Acknowledgement. This work is funded by the National Natural Science Foundation of China [Grant Nos. K111817913, 61373096, 61305088, and 90920004] and the Research and Innovation Project for College Graduates of Jiangsu Province (Grant No. SJLX16_0536).

References

ACE: Automatic Content Extraction (2002–2007). http://www.ldc.upenn.edu/Projects/ACE/

Brew, A., Greene, D., Cunningham, P.: Using crowdsourcing and active learning to track sentiment in online media. In: ECAI 2010, pp. 145–150 (2010)

Chan, Y.S., Ng, H.T.: Domain adaptation with active learning for word sense disambiguation. In: ACL 2007 (2007)

Engelson, S.P., Dagan, I.: Minimizing manual annotation cost in supervised training from corpora. IN: ACL 1996, pp. 319–326 (1996)

Feng, D., Lü, Y., Zhou, M.: A new approach for English-Chinese named entity alignment. In: EMNLP 2004, pp. 372–379 (2004)

Haffari, G., Sarkar, A.: Active learning for multilingual statistical machine translation. In: ACL-IJCNLP 2009, pp. 181–189 (2009)

Hwa, R.: Sample selection for statistical parsing. Comput. Linguist. **30**(3), 253–276 (2004)

Li, S.S., Ju, S.F., Zhou, G.D., Li, X.J.: Active learning for imbalanced sentiment classification. In: EMNLP-CoNLL 2012, pp. 139–148 (2012)

Mintz, M., Bills, S., Snow, R., Jurafsky, D.: Distant supervision for relation extraction without labeled data. In: ACL-IJCNLP 2009, pp. 1003–1011 (2009)

Osborne, M., Baldridge, J.: Ensemble based active learning for parse selection. IN: HLT-NAACL 2004, pp. 89–96 (2004)

Qian, L.H., Hui, H.T., Hu, Y.N., Zhou, G.D., Zhu, Q.M.: Bilingual active learning for relation classification via pseudo parallel corpora. In: ACL 2014, 582–592 (2014)

Reichart, R., Tomanek, K., Hahn, U., Rappoport, A.: Multi-task active learning for linguistic annotations. In: ACL 2008, pp. 861–869 (2008)

Ringger, E., McClanahan, P., Haertel, R., Busby, G., Carmen, M., Carroll, J., Seppi, K., Lonsdale, D.: Active learning for part-of-speech tagging: accelerating corpus annotation. In: Proceedings of Linguistic Annotation Workshop at ACL 2007, pp. 101–108 (2007)

Schein, A.I., Ungar, L.H.: Active learning for logistic regression: an evaluation. Mach. Learn. **68**(3), 235–265 (2007)

Settles, B.: Active learning literature survey. Computer Sciences Technical report 1648, University of Wisconsin, Madison (2009)

Shen, D., Zhang, J., Su, J., Zhou, G.D., Tan, C.L.: Multi-criteria-based active learning for named entity recognition. IN: ACL 2004 (2004)

Tomanek, K., Hahn, U.: Semi-supervised active learning for sequence labeling. In: ACL-IJCNLP 2009, pp. 1039–1047 (2009)

Tomanek, K., Wermter, J., Hahn, U.: An approach to text corpus construction which cuts annotation costs and maintains reusability of annotated data. In: EMNLP-CoNLL 2007, pp. 486–495 (2007)

Zhang, Y.: Multi-task active learning with output constraints. In: AAAI 2010 (2010)

Zhou, G.D., Su, J., Zhang, J., Zhang, M.: Exploring various knowledge in relation extraction. In: ACL 2005, pp. 427–434 (2005)

Zhu, J.B., Hovy, E.: Active learning for word sense disambiguation with methods for addressing the class imbalance problem. In: EMNLP-CoNLL 2007, pp. 783–790 (2007)

Zhu, X.: Semi-supervised learning literature survey. Technical report 1530, Department of Computer Sciences, University of Wisconsin, Madison (2005)

Study on the English Corresponding Unit of Chinese Clause

Wenhe Feng[1,2(✉)], Yi Yang[3], Yancui Li[4], Xia Li[2], and Han Ren[2(✉)]

[1] Wuhan University, Wuhan 430073, Hubei, China
wenhefeng@gmail.com
[2] Guangdong University of Foreign Studies,
Guangzhou 510006, Guangdong, China
200211025@oamail.gdufs.edu.cn, softrl@126.com
[3] Ural Federal University, Yekaterinburg 620000, Russia
xwyang@mail.ru
[4] Henan Institute of Science and Technology, Xinxiang 453003, Henan, China
yancuili@gmail.com

Abstract. This paper annotates the English corresponding units of Chinese clauses in Chinese-English translation and statistically analyzes them. Firstly, based on Chinese clause segmentation, we segment English target text into corresponding units (clause) to get a Chinese-to-English clause-aligned parallel corpus. Then, we annotate the grammatical properties of the English corresponding clauses in the corpus. Finally, we find the distribution characteristics of grammatical properties of English corresponding clauses by statistically analyzing the annotated corpus: there are more clauses (1631,74.41%) than sentences (561,25.59%); there are more major clauses (1719,78.42%) than subordinate clauses (473,21.58%); there are more adverbial clauses (392,82.88%) than attributive clauses (81,17.12%) and more non-defining clauses (358,75.69%) than restrictive relative clauses (115,24.31%) in subordinate clauses; and there are more simple clauses (1142,52.1%) than coordinate clauses (1050,47.9%).

Keywords: Clauses · Parallel corpus · Clause-based · Clause alignment · Discourse-based translation · Chinese-to-English translation

Clause is the basic unit of discourse translation. Previous research has shown that in Machine Translation Systems, the acceptance rate of clause-based translation is 45% higher than the sentence-based translation [1]. Thus, clause-based translation model has become an important subject for discourse-based machine translation studies [2]. Nowadays, statistical translation is grounded on the large scale bilingual aligned samples and bilingual grammatical knowledge. Therefore, one of the most important issues for discourse-based machine translation studies appears to be building clause-aligned and -annotated parallel corpora.

In Chinese-to-English translation, English corresponding units of Chinese clauses (ECUCC) in the translation are complex and diverse. One key issue of translation is to select the proper form of ECUCC for translation. For example, in (1), Chinese clauses C1 and C2 are translated to English corresponding units E1 and E2. Functionally, E1 is the major clause and E2 is the subordinate clause (the adverbial clause); structurally, E1 is the restrictive relative clause and E2 is the non-defining clause (the present participle).

© Springer International Publishing AG 2016
C.-Y. Lin et al. (Eds.): NLPCC-ICCPOL 2016, LNAI 10102, pp. 129–140, 2016.
DOI: 10.1007/978-3-319-50496-4_11

(1)   ^{C1}上海浦东近年来颁布实行了涉及经济、贸易、建设、规划、科技、文教等领域的七十一件法规性文件，^{C2}确保了浦东开发的有序进行。

^{E1}In recent years Shanghai's Pudong has promulgated and implemented 71 regulatory documents relating to areas such as economics, trade, construction, planning, science and technology, culture and education, etc., ^{E2}ensuring the orderly advancement of Pudong's development.

As shown in (1), if we can provide bilingual clause-aligned samples and add grammatical annotations for clauses, it will not only provide an effective guide for the translation of parallel clauses, but will also lay a foundation for discourse-based Machine Translation Studies. At present, several Chinese-English parallel corpora have been built on the sentence- (usually marked with period) or paragraph-alignment [3, 4]. Studies on clause-aligned parallel corpus at a preliminary stage [2] that there are few annotated resources of grammatical knowledge for segmenting parallel texts into clauses.

In this paper, we recount our experience in annotating ECUCC and statistically analyze them. Firstly, based on Chinese clause segmentation we segment English texts into corresponding units for parallel text to get a Chinese-to-English clause-aligned parallel corpus (Sect. 1). Then, we annotate the grammatical s of the ECUCC in the corpus to get a grammatical annotated corpus (Sect. 2). Finally, based on the annotated corpus we find the distribution characteristics of grammatical properties of ECUCC by statistically analyzing the annotated corpus (Sect. 3).

1   Chinese-to-English Clause-Aligned Parallel Corpus

Building a Chinese-to-English clause-aligned parallel corpus is based on the following principles: (1) define the rules for Chinese clause segmentation in Chinese-English parallel texts; (2) based on the results of Chinese clause segmentation, divide English translated texts into units, and get the best English corresponding units in a linear sequence, which are ECUCC.

The rules for Chinese clause segmentation in our study applies the definition of clause by Li [6, 7]: "Clause is the basic unit of discourse analysis, including the traditional simple sentences and clauses in compound sentences. Structurally, an independent clause contains at least one predicate and at least one proposition; functionally, an independent clause is not used as any grammatical component to other clauses, and there is only propositional relationship between two independent clauses; formally, there must be punctuation (comma, semicolon, or period) between two independent clauses. Besides, some traditional phrases, which are similar to typical clauses in structure, function and forms are treated as clauses." Studies [5, 6] have shown that such definition of Chinese clause provides operability to create and automatic analyze large-scale annotated corpus.

The "based on the results of Chinese clause segmentation divide English translated texts into units" means that we divide English translated texts based on the results of segmentation Chinese clauses. In example (2), Chinese text is divided into three clauses which are marked as C1, C2 and C3 and accordingly, English corresponding unit are divided as E1, E2 and E3. Grammatically, E1 is a typical clause, E2 and E3 are not. E2 is a clause group, and E3 is an infinitive phrase. According to the nature of English, E2 would be divided into two English clauses ("...expand..." and "use..."). But we analyze E2 which is the corresponding unit to Chinese clause C2 as the final unit, based on the rules for Chinese clause segmentation. Therefore, we call E1, E2 and E3 as English corresponding unit of C1, C2 and C3. However, sometimes we also call these corresponding units of Chinese clause as "English clause".

(2) ^{C1}浙江省今后将进一步提高对外开放水平，//^{C2}努力扩大对外贸易、利用外资和国际经济技术合作，/^{C3}并逐步完善对外经贸营销网络。

^{E1}Zhejiang Province will further raise the level of opening up to the outside world, //^{E2}diligently expand its foreign trade, and use foreign funds and international economic and technical co-operation, /^{E3}to progressively perfect its marketing network of foreign economic and trade business.

(3) ^{C1}这一数字比上年末增加二百零三亿元，/^{C2}增长百分之二十七。

^{E1}This number was an increase of 20.3 billion yuan, /^{E2}a growth of 27% compared to the end of the previous year.

The "best English corresponding units in a linear sequence" means that the English corresponding unit segmentation should correspond to the Chinese clauses in a linear sequence, but not necessary in semantics. For example, in (3), E1 and E2 semantically are not equal to the C1 and C2 because of the position of the adverb (compared to the end of the previous year). In this case, E1 and E2 are the best English corresponding units in a linear sequence of C1 and C2.

Based on the above principles, we select 100 Chinese-English parallel texts (news) to build a Chinese-to-English clause-aligned parallel corpus, in which Chinese clauses and their English corresponding units are aligned.

2 ECUCC Grammatically Annotated Corpus

In the ECUCC grammatically-annotated corpus, 2192 ECUCC taken from the Chinese-to-English Clause-Aligned Corpus are analyzed and annotated. Grammatical properties of ECUCC are analyzed and annotated under certain principles and systems.

2.1 Grammatical Analytic Principles of ECUCC

To deal with problems of grammatical analysis of English corresponding units, we formulated the analytic principles through analysis and verification.

First, in the process of identification of the grammatical properties of ECUCC, both their inner structure and external function should be considered. As shown in Example (1), structurally, the core verbs in E1 and E2 are different between restrictive relative and non-defining; functionally, general structures are different between the major and subordinate in the global structure.

Second, for identifying the major object of ECUCC, the global function takes priority over the local function. Sometimes ECUCC is complicated in the inner structure, and it is difficult to identify its grammatical properties. In this case, the identification of the structure and function is based on the major object of the unit, while the identification of the major object is based on the global function of its global structure. For example, in (4), E1 is complicated by its inner structure (it consists of major clause and adverbial clause, while adverbial clause is composed of coordinate attributive clauses). The whole sentence is a complex sentence: E1 is the major clause, E2 is a subordinate clause. Thus, E1 can be identified as "major clause + finite structure" according to the function of major object ("recently there were…").

(4)   C1据浦东新区经贸局对浦东开发七年来引进投资一千万美元以上的一百五十七个工业大项目跟踪调查，目前建成投产的有一百一十六个，/C2投产率高达百分之七十三点九。

E1According to the Pudong New Region's Economy and Trade Bureau follow - up investigation into 157 large industrial projects that were introduced in the seven years of Pudong's development, and that have more than 10 million US dollars invested, recently there were 116 that finished construction and went into operation, /E2 with the percentage of going into operation reaching up to 73.9%.

Third, sometimes omissions in ECUCC influence the identification of their grammatical properties. In this case, the analysis should be based on the completed sentence. For example, in (5), there is an ellipsis of preposition "with" in clause E3 and E4. It is required to complete E3 and E4 before the analysis. Thus, E3 and E4 are identified as "coordinate" "prepositional phrase" and "adverbial".

(5) C1去年一至十一月，内地在香港新签对外承包工程、劳务合作和设计咨询合同一千四百七十四份，/C2合同金额二十点九四亿美元，//C3完成营业额十五点八亿美元，//C4输港派出劳务二万一千一百五十三人次。

E1From January to November of last year, the inland signed 1,474 new contracts for foreign contracted projects and cooperation of labor service and design consultation in Hong Kong, /E2with a contracted value of 2.094 billion US dollars, //E3a completed turnover of 1.58 billion US dollars //E4and 21,153 man - times of labor service sent to Hong Kong.

2.2   Grammatical Analytic System of ECUCC

Based on the studies of the corpus, the grammatical analytic system has been functionally and structurally formed [7] (Further details follow in Sect. 3).

Functionally: firstly, according to the grammatical properties of a whole sentence (simple sentence, coordinate sentence, complex sentence) and the position of a clause, English clauses can be divided into independent clauses, coordinate clause, major clauses and subordinate clauses; secondly, according to the function, clauses can be divided into adverbial clauses, attributive clauses and so on; finally, according to quantity of clauses with the same function in a sentence, clauses can be divided into simple clauses and coordinate clauses.

Structurally: firstly, according to the properties of predicate verbs, clauses can be divided into restrictive relative clauses and non-defining clauses; secondly, depending on particular conditions, non-defining clauses can be divided into infinitive, present participle, past participle, non-verb, preposition structure and other subcategories.

3   Classification and Statistical Analysis of ECUCC

3.1   Sentences and Clauses

ECUCC may be a sentence, or a clause. Separate sentence as example (6) and clause group as example (7) can independently performed an utterance function. Clauses which include coordinate clauses and various types of major or subordinate clauses (see Sect. 3.2) cannot performed an utterance function. It should be combined with other clauses to form a complete sentence.

(6) ^{C1}建筑是开发浦东的一项主要经济活动，/^{C2}这些年有数百家建筑公司、四千余个建筑工地遍布在这片热土上。

^{E1} Construction is a principal economic activity in developing Pudong. /^{E2}These years there have been several hundred construction companies and over four thousand construction sites that have spread out all over this stretch of hot turf.

(7) ^{C1}在世界经济一体化与日俱增的环境下，各国面对全球化带来的挑战，应通过持续推行健全的经济政策以及深化结构改革来从全球化进程中最大限度地受益并把负面影响减少到最小程度。

^{E1}The unification of the world economy is intensifying with each passing day. Facing the Challenges brought by globalization, each country should continuously implement sound economic policies and deepen structural reform so as to enjoy the most benefits from the process of globalization and to minimize the negative effects.

The statistical distribution of sentences and clauses of ECUCC is given in Fig. 1. The results show that clauses are more than sentences by three times which indicates that Chinese clauses are more likely to be translated as English clauses rather than English sentences.

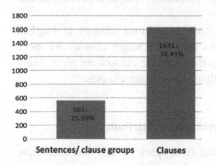

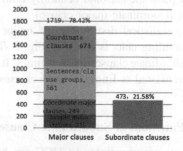

Fig. 1. Statistical distribution of sentences and clauses in English corresponding units

Fig. 2. Statistical distribution of major clauses and subordinate clauses in English corresponding units

3.2 Major Clauses and Subordinate Clauses

ECUCC may be characterized by major clauses or subordinate clauses. English major clause units include simple major clauses (example 9) and coordinate major clauses (example 10) (details of simple/coordinate clauses follow in Sect. 3.5 below), coordinate clauses (example 8), sentences (example 6) and clause groups (example 7). The major clause units are generally finite structures and can be independently used as sentences. Subordinate clause units include 20 kinds of clauses such as attributive clauses, adverbial clauses, infinitive, and present participle clauses (see Sects. 3.3, 3.4 and Table 1). Subordinate clause units are barely used as independent sentences.

(8) ^{C1}去年十月，中国进出口银行聘请日本野村证券公司作顾问，^{C2}向日本著名的评级机构日本公社债研究所提出正式评级申请。

^{E1}LastOctober, the Import and Export Bank of China invited Nomura Securities of Japan to be advisors, ^{E2}and submitted a formal assessment application to the Commune Bond Research Institute of Japan, a famous assessment institution in Japan (Coordinate clause).

(9) …… ^{C1}而是借鉴发达国家和深圳等特区的经验教训，^{C2}聘请国内外有关专家学者，$//^{C3}$积极、及时地制定和推出法规性文件，$//^{C4}$使这些经济活动一出现就被纳入法制轨道。

……. ^{E1}Instead, Pudong is taking advantage of the lessons from experience of developed countries and special regions such as Shenzhen ^{E2}by hiring appropriate domestic and foreign specialists and scholars, $//^{E3}$by actively and promptly formulating and issuing regulatory documents, $//^{E4}$and by ensuring that these economic activities are incorporated into the sphere of influence of the legal system as soon as they appear (Simple major clause).

(10) ^{C1}当前经济的关键不是争取更高的增长速度 $//^{C2}$而是调整结构,提高效益, ^{C3}以使一九九三年下半年以来实行的宏观调控取得更大成果，$//^{C4}$把国民经济推上一条持续、快速、健康发展之路。

^{E1}The key of the current economy is not striving for a higher growth rate, $//^{E2}$but is adjusting structures and increasing benefits, ^{E3}so as to make macro controls which were implemented from the second half year of 1993 obtain greater achievements $//^{E4}$and push the national economy onto a road of constant, rapid and healthy development (Coordinate major clause).

The statistical distribution of major clauses and subordinate clauses in English corresponding units is given in Fig. 2. The results show that major clauses are more than subordinate clauses by four times. It indicates that Chinese clauses are more likely to be translated as English major clauses rather than subordinate clauses.

3.3 Functions of Subordinate Clauses: Adverbial and Attributive

Functions of subordinate ECUCC can be adverbial (examples 11–12) and attributive (examples 13–14).

(11) ^{C1}如果亚洲的经济形势恶化或者金融危机对外界的影响增大，^{C2}全球原油需求量的增长幅度可能会进一步缩小。

^{E1}If the Asian economic situation deteriorates or the outside influence of the financial crisis becomes larger, ^{E2}the growth rate of worldwide demand for crude oil may possibly further decrease (Simple adverbial clause).

(12) ^{C1}由于茅台酒制作工艺复杂，^{C2}生产周期长，^{C3}因而其产量十分有限。

^{E1}Because the art of manufacturing Mao - tai is complicated //^{E2}and its production cycle is long, ^{E3}the output of Mao - tai is extremely limited (Coordinate attributive clause).

(13) ^{C1}中国进出口银行最近在日本取得债券信用等级AA –, ^{C2}这是日本金融市场当前对中国银行的最高债券评级。

^{E1}Recently, the Import and Export Bank of China won a bond credit rating of AA - in Japan, ^{E2}which is currently the highest bond rating given to a Chinese bank by the Japanese financial market (Simple attributive clause).

(14) ^{C1}据统计，在目前已投产外资大企业的主要产品中，有一百零二个品牌，^{C2}其中国外品牌五十二个，//^{C3}国内品牌五十个。

^{E1}According to statistics, among the main products of large foreign funded enterprises that have currently been put into production, there are 102 brands, ^{E2}of which 52 are foreign brands //^{E3}and 50 are domestic brands (Coordinate attributive clause).

The statistical distribution of adverbial clauses and attributive clauses in English corresponding subordinate clauses is given in Fig. 3. The results show that adverbial clauses are more than attributive clauses by five times. It indicates that English corresponding subordinate clauses are translated as adverbial clauses in most situations.

3.4   Structures of Subordinate Clauses: Restrictive Relative and Non-defining

Depending on core verbs, English subordinate clauses can be divided into restrictive relative clauses and non-defining clauses. Core verbs in restrictive relative clauses vary in terms of tense (for examples 11–14), core verbs in non-defining clauses not vary in terms of tense or omitted. Non-defining verbs can be divided into infinitive (example 15), present participle (example 16), past participle (example 17), non-verb (example 18), nominative absolute structure (example 19), prepositional phrase (example 20) and other structural forms.

(15) ^{C1}进出口银行决定先在日本取得信用评级是为进入国际资本市场融资创造作准备，^{C2}以便扩大资金来源。

^{E1}The reason behind the decision by the Import and Export Bank of China to obtain a credit rating in Japan first is to prepare for entry into the international capital market for financing, ^{E2}so as to expand sources of funds (Infinitive).

(16) ^{C1}据统计，目前在纽约证交所上市的外国企业已达 340 多家，^{C2}为5年前的三倍。

[E1]According to statistics, currently, foreign enterprises listed on the New York Stock Exchange have reached more than 340, /[E2]tripling the Fig. 5 years ago (Present participle).

(17) [C1]在经营方面，[C2]该行加强了存款工作，/[C3]使人民币存款的增幅回升，/[C4]同时通过签订银企合作协议和加强对大客户服务等方式，发展有潜力的优质客户。

[E1]Regarding operations, this bank strengthened deposit work, /[E2]made RMB deposit growth rate come back, /[E3]at the same time, through methods such as signing bank - enterprise cooperation agreements and strengthening services to major clients, etc., [E4]developed potential high grade clients (Past participle).

(18) [C1]东亚首脑非正式会晤在历史上尚属首次，[C2]这是一个良好的开端。

[E1]This informal meeting of heads of Eastern Asian countries, the first time in history, [E2]is a good start (Non-verb).

(19) [C1]报告说，1997年是经济转轨国家自停止实行中央计划经济以来的第一个经济增长年份，/[C2]增长率达百分之一点七，/[C3]1998年预计增长百分之三点二五。

[E1]The report said that 1997 was the first year of economic growth for those countries with transitioning economies since they had stopped implementing centrally planned economies, [E2]the rate reaching 1.7%, [E3] and estimated to grow by 3.25% for 1998 (Nominative absolute structure).

(20) [C1]镍被称作"现代工业的维生素"，/[C2]其合金有三千多种，/[C3]是发展航天、航空、军事和现代科技的特需材料。

[E1]Nickel, called the "vitamin of modern industry", [E2]and with more than 3,000 varieties of alloy, [E3] it is the material specially required to develop space - flight, aviation, military and modern science and technology (Prepositional phrase).

The statistical distribution of restrictive relative clauses and non-defining clauses in English corresponding subordinate clauses is given in Fig. 4. The results show that:

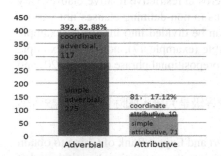

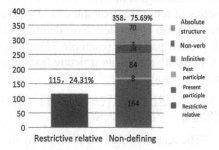

Fig. 3. Statistical distribution of adverbial clauses and attributive clauses in English corresponding subordinate clauses

Fig. 4. Statistical distribution of restrictive relative clauses and non-defining clauses in English corresponding subordinate clauses

(1) There are more non-defining clauses (358, 75.69%) than restrictive relative clauses (115, 24.31%). It indicates that English corresponding subordinate clauses are translated as non-defining clauses in most cases.

(2) In the non-defining clauses, the above three categories (present participle structure, infinitive and prepositional phrase) account for nearly 90% of the total. The other three structures (non-verb, past participle, nominative absolute structure) account for 11% of the total. It indicates that English non-defining clauses are more likely to be translated as present participle structures, infinitive structures and prepositional phrase structures than others.

3.5   Simple Clauses and Coordinate Clauses

English clauses are divided into simple clauses and coordinate clauses according to their function. In coordinate clauses, two or two more English clauses perform the same function. Simple clauses can be divided into sentences (example 8), simple major clauses (example 9), simple adverbial subordinate clauses (example 11) and simple attributive subordinate clauses (example 13). Coordinate clauses can be divided into coordinate clauses (example 8), coordinate major clauses (example 10), coordinate adverbial subordinate clauses (example 12) and coordinate attributive subordinate clauses (example 14).

The statistical results show that: (1) simple clauses (1142, 52.1%) are slightly more than coordinate clauses (1050, 47.9%) (Fig. 5); (2) coordinate major clauses (923, 53.69%) are more than simple major clauses (796, 46.31%) (Fig. 6); (3) simple subordinate clauses (346, 73.15%) are much more than coordinate subordinate clauses (127, 26.85%) (Fig. 7).

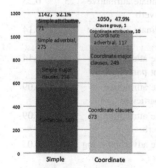 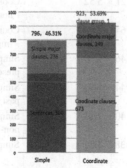 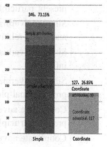

Fig. 5. Distribution of sim ple/coordinate clauses

Fig. 6. Distribution of sim ple/coordinate major clauses

Fig. 7. Distribution of sim ple/coordinate subordinate clauses

3.6 General Analysis

1. Distribution of Types of ECUCC

The Table 1 summarizes the distribution of types of ECUCC. ECUCC are grouped in the table by frequency range (high-frequency, intermediate frequency and low-frequency). The table shows that: (1) There are 4 types of ECUCC of high-frequency ($X > 10\%$) in the corpus which account for 78.38% of the total distribution. Compared with other grammatical types (except clause group) these four types clauses are major clause units (see Table 2). (2) In the corpus 8 types of ECUCC of intermediate frequency ($1\% < X < 10\%$) account for 18.93% of the total distribution, which including 7 adverbial subordinate clauses (16.01%) and 1 attributive subordinate clause 2.92%. (3) 13 types of ECUCC of low-frequency ($X < 1\%$) account for 2.69% in the corpus. In addition to clause group, the remaining 12 categories are subordinate clause units.

Table 1. Distribution of types of ECUCC

Frequency range	Types	No.	%	Frequency range	Types	No.	%
X > 10%	Coordinate clause	673	30.70	X < 1%	Simple adverbial - non-verb	21	0.96
	Independent clauses	560	25.55		Coordinate attributive - restrictive relative	8	0.36
	Coordinate major clause	249	11.36		Coordinate attributive - restrictive relative	6	0.27
	Simple major clause	236	10.77		Simple adverbial - past participle	5	0.23
1% < X < 10%	Simple adverbial - present participle	121	5.52		Coordinate attributive - non-verb	5	0.23
	Simple adverbial - restrictive relative	64	2.92		Coordinate attributive - -ing	3	0.14
	Simple adverbial - infinitive	46	2.10		Simple attributive - present participle	3	0.14
	Simple adverbial - prepositional phrase	44	2.01		Simple attributive - past participle	2	0.09
	Coordinate adverbial - present participle	40	1.82		Simple attributive - non-verb	2	0.09
	Coordinate adverbial - infinitive	38	1.73		Simple adverbial - -ing	1	0.05
	Simple adverbial - restrictive relative	37	1.69		Coordinate attributive - past participle	1	0.05
	Coordinate adverbial - prepositional phrase	25	1.14		Coordinate attributive - prepositional phrase	1	0.05
					Clause group	1	0.05
Total					2192		100.00

2.   Distribution of Grammatical Functions of English Corresponding Units

The distribution of grammatical functions of English corresponding units is given in Table 2. In general, there are two features: (1) In terms of quantity, there are 1719 major clause units (78%) and 473 subordinate clause units (22%). The former is about 4 times of the latter. Thus the major clause units are more important in Chinese-to-English translation. (2) In terms of structure and function, the major clause units are more complex than subordinate clause units. Structurally, the core verbs in the major clause units are usually finite verbs, but in subordinate clause units there are different forms of core verb such as: infinitive, present participle and so on; functionally, all types of major clause units can be independently used as sentences. Subordinate clauses are different between adverbial, attributive and others. Therefore, the difficulty of Chinese-to-English translation is the translation of the subordinate clause units.

Table 2. Distribution of grammatical functions of English corresponding units

Functional structure	Major clause units				Subordinate clause units				Total
	Independent clauses	Coordinate	In complex clauses		Adverbial		Attributive		
	Simple	Coordinate	Simple	Coordinate	Simple	Coordinate	Simple	Coordinate	
Restrictive relative	560	673	236	249	37	6	64	8	1833
Present participle					121	40	3		164
Infinitive					46	38			84
Prepositional phrase					44	25		1	70
Non-verb					21	5	2		28
Past participle					5		2	1	8
Independent structure					1	3			4
Clause group	1								1
Total	561	673	236	249	275	117	71	10	2192
	1719				473				

4   Conclusion and Further Research

In this paper, we annotate and present the grammatical properties of ECUCC in the Chinese-to-English clause-aligned parallel corpus. It is of a great significance to Chinese-to-English translation. However, it should be noted here that:

(1)   Chinese-to-English translation is different from English-to-Chinese translation. It is necessary to distinguish the two translation directions during the analyzing process. The next step of our work is to build an English-to-Chinese clauses-aligned corpus. The basic idea is the same as building the Chinese-to-English clause-aligned and -annotated parallel corpus.

(2) It is still unknown the grammatical properties of Chinese clauses in the source texts due to the lack of annotations. Therefore, in the future work, grammatical properties of the Chinese clauses also will be annotated. Another paper illustrating the problem of Chinese clauses will be written.

(3) Building the Chinese-to-English clause-aligned and -annotated parallel corpus is grounded in the theoretical framework of Chinese-English discourse structure parallel corpus [8]. The grammatical annotation of ECUCC is one of the important problems under the perspective of discourse structure. In the following works, our studies will improve and expand the scale of both corpora.

Acknowledgments. This paper was supported by Program of humanities and Social Sciences of Ministry of Education (13YJC740022, 15YJC740021), Major projects of basic researches of Philosophy and Sociology in colleges, Henan (2015-JCZD-022), China Postdoctoral Fund (2013M540594), National Natural Science Foundation of China (61273320, 61502149, 61402119), China Scholarship Council (201508090048) and Programs to Improve Competitiveness, Russia (02.A03.21.0006).

References

1. Wang, J.: Computer-Oriented Chinese Translation Studies of English Clauses. Beijing Language and Culture University Press, Beijing (2009)
2. Song, R., Ge, S.: English-Chinese translation unit and translation model for discourse-based machine translation. J. Chin. Inf. Process. **29**(15), 125–135 (2013)
3. Bai, X., Chang, B., Zhan, W., Wu, Y.: The construction of a large-scale Chinese-English parallel corpus. In: Proceeding of 2002 National Machine Translation Conference on Advances in Machine Translation Studies (2002)
4. Wang, K.: Bilingual Corpus: Development and Application. Foreign Language Teaching and Research Press, Beijing (2004)
5. Li, Y., Feng, W., Zhou, G., Zhu, K.: Research of Chinese clause identification based on comma. Acta Sci. Nat. Univ. Pekin. **49**(1), 7–14 (2013)
6. Li, Y., Feng, W., Sun, J., Kong, F., Zhou, G.: Building Chinese discourse corpus with connective-driven dependency tree structure. In: Proceedings of EMNLP, pp. 2105–2114 (2014)
7. Zhang, Z.: A New English Grammar Coursebook. Shanghai Foreign Language Education Press, Shanghai (2013)
8. Feng, W.: Alignment and annotation of Chinese-English discourse structure. J. Chin. Inf. Process. **27**(6), 158–164 (2013)

Research for Uyghur-Chinese Neural Machine Translation

Jinying Kong[1,2,3], Yating Yang[1,2,4(✉)], Xi Zhou[1,2], Lei Wang[1,2],
and Xiao Li[1,2]

[1] Xinjiang Technical Institute of Physics and Chemistry,
Chinese Academy of Sciences, Urumqi 830011, China
yangyt@ms.xjb.ac.cn
[2] Xinjiang Laboratory of Minority Speech and Language Information
Processing, Urumqi 830011, China
[3] University of Chinese Academy of Sciences, Beijing 100049, China
[4] Institute of Acoustics Chinese Academy of Sciences, Beijing, China

Abstract. The problem of rare and unknown words is an important issue in Uyghur-Chinese machine translation, especially using neural machine translation model. We propose a novel way to deal with the rare and unknown words. Based on neural machine translation of using pointers over input sequence, our approach which consists of preprocess and post-process can be used in all neural machine translation model. Pre-process modify the Uyghur-Chinese corpus to extend the ability of pointer network, and the post- process retranslating the raw translation by a phrase-based machine translation model or a wordlist. Experiment show that neural machine translation model used the approach proposed by this paper get a higher BLEU score than the phrase-based model in Uyghur-Chinese MT.

1 Introduction

Deep neural networks, representative of deep learning technology, have shown great breakout in many areas such as images recognition and speech recognition. Furthermore, numbers of tasks in natural language processing (NLP) have been resolved by neural network such as recurrent neural network (RNN). Neural machine translation (NMT) is one of the application of sequence-to-sequence consisting of two RNNs. The sequence-to-sequence model can cope with so many NLP tasks that it is very widely used nowadays. In sequence-to-sequence model, one builds two RNNs that one named encoder reads a source sentence and the other named decoder generates its relevant target sentence. If the model used for question answering (QA) system, then the relevant target sentence should be answer to the question. Or if the model used for machine translation (MT), the relevant target sentence is translation. By far, NMTs have achieved promising performance comparing with the state-of-the-art phrase based MT.

Uyghur-Chinese MT is one of the branches in MT. The research of Uyghur-Chinese MT always focus on conventional translation systems such as phrase based model, example based model, etc. This paper aims at solving Uyghur-Chinese MT by using a new approach of NMT. NMT has some significant advantages over the existing

C.-Y. Lin et al. (Eds.): NLPCC-ICCPOL 2016, LNAI 10102, pp. 141–152, 2016.
DOI: 10.1007/978-3-319-50496-4_12

statistical MT. First of all, NMT needs less domain knowledge. Second, NMT is jointly tuned to maximize the translation performance, unlike the phrase based MT consisting of so many feature functions tuned separately. Last but not the least, NMT often requires much smaller memory size than the existing MT system relying on large scale of phrase table. As Uyghur is a raw language lacking of corpus, especially relevant domain knowledge and Uyghur tool, NMT seems fit for Uyghur-Chinese MT.

But Uyghur-Chinese Neural Machine Translation also has some fundamental challenges. The first problem is parallel corpus of Uyghur-Chinese full with wrong knowledge. And the performance of approaches based statistical is really rely on the quality and scale of parallel corpus. Second, as Uyghur is a kind of adhesive language, the number of Uyghur words is very large. Third, there are so many UNK in Uyghur-Chinese NMT as the number of Chinese word is really big but the scale of target vocabulary of NMT is restricted.

To solve the above problems, we present a new NMT model consisting of pre-process, pointer-NMT model, and post-process. Pre-process firstly segment the Uyghur words, then check the wrong information in corpus and correct it. Pointer-NMT model which is a sequence-to-sequence model with attention-based pointing mechanism translate the Uyghur sentence into raw Chinese sentence included some Uyghur words. Post-process translate the Uyghur words in raw Chinese sentence to Chinese words by a trained phrased-based MT model or the wordlist. Figure 1 shows how our model works.

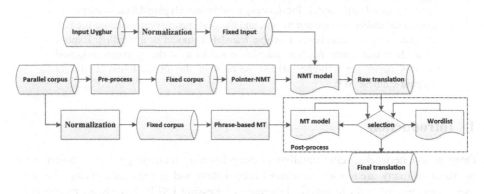

Fig. 1. Operational flow of Uyghur-Chinese NMT

2   Related Work

Due to the academic value and application value, Uyghur-Chinese Machine Translation is one of the test program in China Workshop of Machine Translation (CWMT) [1]. Uyghur-Chinese MT model based phrase is one of the best performance model, so phrase-based MT model is the main stream in Uyghur-Chinese MT and many research works have been done in it, Li et al. pointed these in a nice review of Uyghur-Chinese MT in 2016 [2]. The specific research of Uyghur-Chinese MT includes: reordering model of Uyghur-Chinese MT [3], filtering of Uyghur-Chinese parallel corpus for Uyghur-Chinese MT [4], embedding syntactic information of Uyghur on Uyghur-Chinese MT [5], and so on [6, 7]. These works mostly based on phrase based MT, none research work have been done in Uyghur-Chinese NMT.

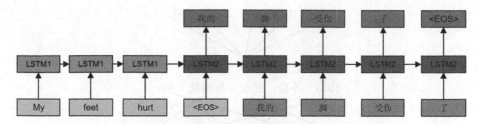

Fig. 2. The process of NMT

NMT, one of the sequence-to-sequence model, consists of an encoder and a decoder. An encoder reads source sentence in word order and records the useful information. A decoder produces target sentence by utilize the information of encoder and prior word. This process is illustrated as Fig. 2. With different structure of neural network in encoder or decoder, the performance of NMT can be vary wildly. Devlin et al. use a feed forward neural network to model a translation model by predicting one word at a time in 2014 [8]. Zou et al. do not take the order of words in source and target phrases into account [9], but Cho et al. done in a novel RNN Encoder-Decoder [10]. Based these researches, Bahdanau et al. proposed an attention-based NMT [11]. The model of Bahdanau have archive good performance, but huge numbers of OOVs handicap it to get a better result. It is worth mentioning that the question is what this paper aims to work out.

3 Model

In this paper, we propose a novel Neural Machine Translation approach that smoothly translates Uyghur including noise to Chinese. In pre-process, we firstly figure out the wrong information in Uyghur sentence and normalize it. Then we train a new NMT model by utilizing a fixed corpus which we will explicitly explain later. With the trained NMT model, we can translate Uyghur sentence into raw Chinese. At last, we get our final translation by retranslating the Uyghur words to Chinese words in raw Chinese in post-process.

Our approach can be applied in all neural machine translation and effectively enhance its performance. We describe our approach in detail as follows: we explicate pre-process in Sect. 3.1, new Neural Machine Translation in Sect. 3.2, and post-process in Sect. 3.3.

3.1 Pre-process

In this section, we introduce our method in pre-process which consist of two units: normalization and modification. Normalization include segmentation of Uyghur word and correction of wrong expression. And modification is just replacing some Chinese words with by Uyghur word.

Normalization
Using proposed method by Yang Yating 2014, the identification of stems and affixes is treated as a sequence labeling problem which can be achieved by conditional random

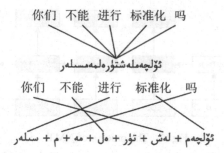

Fig. 3. An example of segmentation of Uyghur word

field model. Effectively stems and affixes segmentation can significantly reduce the data sparseness problem of Uyghur-Chinese MT, furthermore, can improve the quality of translation model. For example, in Fig. 3, "nimen buneng jinxing biaozhunhua ma". If there is no segmentation, the knowledge of this bilingual sentence will be difficult to use in the process of translation. Appling stems and affixes segmentation to the corpus for machine translation benefit us much, including smaller granularity alignment and more accurate translation knowledge.

On the other hand, misspelling is very common in Uyghur. As Uyghur word consists of many similar letters, it is hard to avoid spelling mistakes. Because the object of this study is Machine Translation from Uyghur to Chinese, so we check the spelling of Uyghur.

```
Alogrithm 1. To normalize by Levenshtein Distance
Input: sentence={word₁,word₂,word₃,...,word_i} ,
       dic={word₁,word₂,...,word_k}
Output: sentence
1:Wordlist=Map[10]
2:for word in sentence :
3:  if dic.has(word) :
4:      continue;
5:  else :
6:    for comparison in dic :
7:        distance=
8:        Levenshtein.distance(compasison,word)
9:        if Wordlist.notFull():
10:           Wordlist[compasison]=distance
11:        else:
12:           key = findMaxValue(Wordlist)
13:        if Wordlist.getValue(key)> distance :
14:           delete(Wordlist[key])
15:           Wordlist[comparison]=distance
16:    for checker in Wordlist:
17:        word=maxNgramCount(checker,sentence)
18:return sentence
```

In this paper, we use a simple Levenshtein distance and standard Uyghur dictionary method to check the Uyghur word. Levenshtein distance is very effective for the language whose word is formed by letters. Algorithm 1 is the specific ideas of using Levenshtein distance to spell check, the input standard dictionary is extracted from other corpus (such as domain of news) of the standard language. The algorithm retains 10 nearest words with the wrong word, and finally uses the N-gram model to score the best selection of the correct spelling of the word.

Modification

Our work makes an extension on Caglar et al. in 2016 [13]. In order to reduce the OOVs of output sentence, we strengthen the ability of pointer network. Unlike Caglar, we train our pointer network on a fixed Uyghur-Chinese parallel corpus with some Uyghur words in Chinese sentence.

Before training the Pointer-model, we do not only the pre-processing but also this modification to the parallel corpus. Our modification is finding the Chinese words of target sentence which is inside wordlist and replacing it with corresponding Uyghur words. This change is very simple but effective as it expands the scope of applicable of Pointer-NMT.

A wordlist must fellow these points: (1) Wordlist consist of Chinese words and its corresponding Uyghur words. (2) A word in wordlist always is a name entity. (3) A word in wordlist should not so frequency. (4) A word in wordlist must have only one-to-one translation word, and this point is very important. For instance, the English word 'England' and the Chinese word 'ying ge lan' can be as one record of the in wordlist.

Besides, there is still some OOVs when training the Pointer-NMT with pre-process and modify done on the corpus. If the word is OOV, we mark it to UNK. Although this work is common in NMT, but it has different significance as the Point-NMT can record the useful information of location. And this work can help us restore the right Chinese word in later step.

3.2 Pointer-NMT Model

A pointer-NMT model trained on a processed corpus can reduce the number of OOVs. Pointer-NMT is a new model of attention based neural machine translation with pointer network. Pointer-NMT use a MLP to decide the source of output word. If the decision of MLP is shortlist, then translation of this word is a process of NMT. On the other hand, the translation of this word is a process of pointing.

Attention Based NMT

Attention based NMT consisting of an encoder and a decoder is a novel model for machine translation. Inputting to the layer in Encoder is word vectors in accordance with the source language sentences in the order of the input source language in each of the word through the Embedding. When read to the end of the sentence, the hidden layer in the decoder generates output in accordance with the state of the source language sentence and the encoder's hidden layer, and the hidden layer state is recorded for the next time step usage. The output layer of the decoder generates the probability of each target word according to the output of the hidden layer state and the relevant information of the source language. Finally, based on the probability of the target word generated from each time series, the maximum probability score of the target word is found by using the beam search algorithm.

The encoder works as follows:

a. Encoder sequentially read word vector to calculate and record the hidden layer state of moment T by using formula 1.
b. Encoder reversely read word vector to calculate and record the hidden layer state of moment T by using formula 1.

$$\overrightarrow{h_t} = f(x^{(t)}, \overrightarrow{h_{(t-1)}})$$ (1)

c. To calculate the state of the BiRNN encoder of the moment T. The calculation method of the hidden layer state of BiRNN at the moment T is shown in formula 2.

$$h_t = \begin{bmatrix} \overrightarrow{h_t} \\ \overleftarrow{h_t} \end{bmatrix}$$ (2)

d. Followed by an iterative execution of a, b, and c steps until the input is finished, h_t is saved at each moment.

After reading all the source language sentences, we can get a series of encoder hidden states. The attention based neural network translation will save all the states of hidden layer, and use a soft alignment model to select useful information between the source sentence and output word.

The alignment model in the neural Machine Translation is different from the traditional statistical alignment model, and it is a kind of soft alignment model. Formula 3 represents the definition of the alignment model.

$$e_{ij} = a(s_{i-1}, h_j)$$ (3)

e_{ij} represents the matching digress of a word i in the target language with the word j in the source language. $a()$ represents a nonlinear function (also can be a feed forward neural network). $a()$ can be produced by s_{i-1} (the hidden layer state of RNN of moment $i-1$) together with h_j (the j word vector in the source sentence), and can also trained with other part of Machine Translation system (The problem can be seen as find the probability of h_j given s_{i-1}).

With the alignment model, we can get context dependent vector c_i. The calculation method can be calculated by the formula 4 and the formula 5.

$$c_i = \sum_{j=1}^{T_X} a_{ij} h_j$$ (4)

$$a_{ij} = \frac{\exp(e_{ij})}{\sum_{k=1}^{T_x} \exp(e_{ik})} \tag{5}$$

Except the big difference on the calculation of context vector between attention-based and the other neural network, the method for calculating the probability score of the target word vector is similar.

$$s_i = f(s_{i-1}, y_{i-1}, c_i) \tag{6}$$

According to the formula 6, we can calculate the hidden layer state of i time by the hidden layer state of the $i-1$ time, the previous target word vector and the context dependent vector. $f()$ is a nonlinear function.

Finally, we can get the probability score of the word by the hidden layer state of the $i-1$ time, the previous target word vector and context dependent vector.

$$p(y_i \mid y_1, \ldots, y_{i-1}, x) = g(y_{i-1}, s_i, c_i) \tag{7}$$

$g()$ in formula 7 in the general is a nonlinear function, but also can be a multi-layer neural network. It is important to note that the initial value of the hidden state in the general NMT decoder is the final value of the hidden state in the encoder.

Directly visible, the introduction of soft alignment model as the attention greatly reduced burden of compressing all source sentence in a fixed vector. The experiment of Bahdanau also show that this approach can effectively improve the final translation results.

Pointer-NMT

Pointer network proposed by Oriol et al. in 2015 [14] is one of neural attention, it can handle the problems such as sorting variable sized sequences and other optimization problems belong to this class. Pointer network differs from the common neural attention attempts in that, instead of using attention to blend hidden units of an encoder to a context vector at each time step, it uses attention as a pointer to select a unit of the input sentence as the output.

Pointer-NMT not only predict whether it is required to use the pointing or not at each time step, but also point any location of the context sequence whose length can vary widely over examples. To achieve this, Point-NMT consists of the shortlist softmax layer and location softmax layer.

More specifically, goal of the last softmax layer of Point-NMT is to maximize the probability of output word sequence $y = \{y_1, y_2, \ldots, y_t\}$ and the sequence of binary variable Z_t which indicates whether to use shortlist softmax(when z = 1) or the location softmax(when z = 0). Formula 8 simply describe the goal, $x = \{x_1, x_2, \ldots, x_t\}$ is input context sequence.

$$p_\theta(y, z \mid x) = \prod_{t=1}^{T_y} p_\theta(y_t, z_t \mid y < t, z < t, x) \tag{8}$$

In formula 8, t means time, y < t means all previous value of y, and the others as well.

Formula 9 factorize the formula 8 further. In formula 9, the first factor means the probability of shortlist, and the second factor means the probability of location list.

$$p(y,z \mid x) = \prod_{t \in T_w} p(w_t, z_t \mid (y,z) < t, x) \times \prod_{t' \in T_l} p(l_{t'}, z_{t'} \mid (y,z) < t', x) \qquad (9)$$

The switch probability is modeled as a multilayer perceptron with binary output.

$$p(w_t, z_t \mid (y,z) < t) = \sigma(f(x, h_{t-1}; \theta)) * p(w_t \mid z_t = 1, (y,z) < t) \qquad (10)$$

$$p(l_t, z_t \mid (y,z) < t) = (1 - \sigma(f(x, h_{t-1}; \theta))) * p(l_t \mid z_t = 0, (y,z) < t) \qquad (11)$$

$p(w_t \mid z_t = 1, (y,z) < t)$ is the shortlist softmax, $p(l_t \mid z_t = 0, (y,z) < t)$ is location softmax which can be a pointer network. What we should notice is that we omitted x which is conditioned on all probabilities in the above. $\sigma(f(x, h_{t-1}; \theta))$ is a sigmoid function as common. With formula 10 and formula 11, we can get the final result.

3.3   Post-process

In decoding step, we create an array to store the Uyghur words and its location when translation meets OOVs. At the same time, we mark the OOVs to UNK for translation and call this translation raw translation. Considering above processes, we may get an output sentence with Uyghur words or UNK after translating the input Uyghur sentence. As illustrated in Fig. 4, there is an output sentence with UNK. If we want to get the final translation, we must do post-process on the raw translation.

We may find UNK or Uyghur words in output sentence because the pointer model point the source of output word to location list. Obviously, we should translate the UNK or Uyghur to Chinese in step of post-process. Luckily, the Uyghur words in raw translation are contained in wordlist. So we can translate the Uyghur word by searching the wordlist. A wordlist consists of words with single translation. When we meet UNK in raw translation, we should consider how to translate the words in its relative array.

Fig. 4. A raw Chinese sentence of pointer-NMT

All in all, post-process of raw translation can be illustrated as the flow chat in Fig. 1. The details are as follows:

a. Training a phrase based Machine translation model with Uyghur-Chinese parallel corpus with normalized.
b. Input a raw translation.

c. Replacing the UNK to Uyghur words according to its relative array.
d. Finding the Uyghur words which contained in wordlist and replace it to its corresponding Chinese word according to wordlist.
e. Translating the remaining Uyghur words by phrase-based Machine translation model.
f. Get the final translation.

4 Experiment

In experiment, we use the Uyghur-Chinese parallel corpus with 140,000 sentences which published in CWMT2016 to evaluate our approach. To prove the efficiency of our approach, we divide our corpus as illustrate in Table 1. In Table 1, 'train' means size of training set, 'dev' means size of development set, 'test' means size of test set.

Table 1. The details of Uyghur-Chinese parallel corpus

Group number	train	dev	test
Group1	30,000	1,000	1,000
Group2	70,000	1,000	1,000
Group3	100,000	1,000	1,000
Group4	140,000	1,000	1,000

4.1 Experiment Set

We compare our approach with three state-of-art Machine Translation system: a phrase-based SMT and an attention-based NMT, a pointer-NMT. In experiment, we tried the following combinations: phrase-based MT and phrase-based MT with post-process, attention-based NMT and attention-based NMT with post-process, pointer-NMT and pointer-NMT of modification.

The OS we used is Ubuntu 14.04, and we use Moses3.0 to train the phrase-based MT model. Our experiment use GIZA++ open source toolkit for word alignment tools with the "grow-diag-the-final-and" strategy for word alignment. Except these, we limit the extraction of phrase length to 7. In the tune process, we select the minimum error training methods to optimize model parameters. In addition, we use SRILM tools on the Chinese sentence in the training set to train a 5-gram language model with Kneser-Ney smooth estimated parameter. We modified the phrased-based MT model by adding a post-process of replacing or retranslating the OOVs after decoding.

In attention-based NMT model, we use GROUNDHOG on the parallel corpus to train the NMT model. And our approach modified NMT by adding a pre-process of replacing Chinese words and a post-process of replacing or retranslating the OOVs after decoding. We set the vocabulary size to 30 K for each language, the beam size for reaching is 10. And the other sets are the default of RNN-RNN model in Bahana et al.

In our pointer-NMT model, we have an existing code provided in https://github.com/kyunghyuncho/dl4mt-material. In our experiments, we changed the last softmax layer like Caglar. And the other sets also like Caglar. We have create a word-level dictionary from Uyghur to Chinese which contains 1103 words that neither in shortlist vocabulary nor dictionary of common words. We modified pointer-NMT model by training the corpus adding a pre-process and a post-process of replacing or retranslating the OOVs after decoding.

These above combinations are respectively test on the corpus illustrated in Table 1. The evaluation metric is BLEU as calculated by the muli-bleu.perl script which is part of moses3.0.

4.2   Results of Experiment

Table 2 shows the BLEU scores on Uyghur-Chinese datasets illustrated in Table 1. We find our model leads to surprisingly substantial improvement on neural machine translation.

First of all, our method of machine translation archived the best translation. Obviously, the better BLEU score the system get, the better performance the system archive. From Table 2, we can draw conclusion that the Pointer-NMT with modification which proposed by this paper is the best system among those six systems. It seems that our approach substantially expand the ability of pointer neural network and effectively reduce the problem of OOVs in machine translation. In test of each group, the system of Pointer-NMT with modification get the best result.

Secondly, the modification which proposed by this paper not only worked in attention-based NMT, but also worked in Pointer-NMT. From Table 2, we can find significant increase between NMT and NMT with modification. What is more, Pointer-NMT increase more than attention-based NMT when adding modification. This because pointer neural network can point the location of OOVs in output sentence.

Thirdly, phrased-based MT with modification can get increase BLEU score, but not clearly. The reason leading to this is just the efficiency of wordlist. In other words, wordlist help extend its word table, but the effect of the operation in traditional way is limited.

Last but not the least, the modification which proposed by this paper is more efficiency in NMT when the corpus become lager. That because the numbers of vocabulary is become more and more lager when the corpus become lager in Uyghur-Chinese, but the size of vocabulary in NMT is fixed as usual. With the effective post-process, NMT can reduce the OOVs by retranslating them.

Table 2. The result of Uyghur-Chinese machine translation

System	Modifying	Group1	Group2	Group3	Group4
Phrase-based MT	No	14.12	20.56	24.13	28.15
	Yes	15.34	20.76	24.34	28.45
Attention-based NMT	No	15.23	22.23	23.14	25.97
	Yes	15.57	23.88	24.15	26.14
Pointer-NMT	No	16.12	22.48	24.07	26.12
	Yes	17.87	23.34	24.25	29.10

5 Conclusion

In this paper, we propose a simple extension to neural machine translation model. In order to reduce the OOVs in Uyghur-Chinese NMT, we try to add a modification consisting of a pre-process and a pro-process in a NMT using pointers over the input sequence. We show that the modification is really worked in Uyghur-Chinese NMT, especially in NMT which have pointer network.

Nowadays, many research works treat neural machine translation model as a feature function on phrase-based machine translation. And many of them did great job. While in this paper, we simply use the phrase-based machine translation model to translate the OOVs of NMT. Our next step is treating phrase-based MT model as an input in the last softmax layer of NMT.

Acknowledgements. This work is supported by the Young Creative Sci-Tech Talents Cultivation Project of Xinjiang Uyghur Autonomous Region (2014711006, 2014721032), the Natural Science Foundation of Xinjiang (2015211B034), the Xinjiang Key Laboratory Fund under Grant No. 2015KL031 and the Strategic Priority Research Program of the Chinese Academy of Sciences under Grant No. XDA06030400.

References

1. Wang, Y., Wong, D.F., Chao, L,S,, et al.: The report of NLP 2 CT for CWMT 2015 evaluation task. In: The China Workshop on Machine Translation (2015)
2. Xiao, L., Tonghai, J., Xi, Z., et al.: An overview of research on the key technology of Uyghur-Chinese machine translation. Netw. New Media Technol. **5**(01), 19–25 (2016)
3. Chen, K.: Research on the key technology of reordering model in Uyghur-Chinese machine translation. University of Chinese Academy of Sciences (2013)
4. Kong, J., Yang, Y., Wang, L., et al.: Research in corpus filtering technique for Uyghur Chinese Machine Translation. Appl. Res. Comput. 33 (2016)
5. Aisha, B., Sun, M.: Uyghur-Chinese statistical machine translation by incorporating morphological information. J. Comput. Inf. Syst. **6**, 3137–3145 (2010)
6. Mi, C., Yang, Y., Zhou, X., et al.: A phrase table filtering model based on binary classification for Uyghur-Chinese machine translation. J. Comput. **9**(12), 2780–2786 (2014)
7. Murat, A., Yusup, A., Abaydulla, Y.: Research and implementation of the Uyghur-Chinese personal name transliteration based on syllabification. In: International Conference on Asian Language Processing, pp. 71–74. IEEE (2013)
8. Devlin, J., Zbib, R., Huang, Z., et al.: Fast and robust neural network joint models for statistical machine translation. In: Meeting of the Association for Computational Linguistics, pp. 1370–1380 (2014)
9. Zou, W.Y., Socher, R., Cer, D., et al.: Bilingual word embeddings for phrase-based machine translation. In: Empirical Methods in Natural Language Processing (2013)
10. Cho, K., Van Merrienboer, B., Gulcehre, C., et al.: Learning phrase representations using RNN encoder-decoder for statistical machine translation. In: Empirical Methods in Natural Language Processing (2014)
11. Bahdanau, D., Cho, K., Bengio, Y.: Neural machine translation by jointly learning to align and translate. Computer Science (2014)

12. Yang, Y., Mi, C., Ma, B., Dong, R., Wang, L., Li, X.: Character tagging-based word segmentation for Uyghur. In: Shi, X., Chen, Y. (eds.) CWMT 2014. CCIS, vol. 493, pp. 61–69. Springer, Heidelberg (2014). doi:10.1007/978-3-662-45701-6_6
13. Gulcehre, C., Ahn, S., Nallapati, R., et al.: Pointing the unknown words. Computer Science (2016)
14. Vinyals, O., Fortunato, M., Jaitly, N.: Pointer networks. Computer Science (2015)

MaxSD: A Neural Machine Translation Evaluation Metric Optimized by Maximizing Similarity Distance

Qingsong Ma[1,2]([⊠]), Fandong Meng[1,2], Daqi Zheng[1,2], Mingxuan Wang[1,2], Yvette Graham[3], Wenbin Jiang[1,2], and Qun Liu[1,3]

[1] Key Laboratory of Intelligent Information Processing,
Institute of Computing Technology, Chinese Academy of Sciences, Beijing, China
{maqingsong,mengfandong,zhengdaqi,wangmingxuan,jiangwenbin}@ict.ac.cn,
qun.liu@dcu.ie
[2] University of Chinese Academy of Sciences, Beijing, China
[3] ADAPT Centre, School of Computing, Dublin City University, Dublin, Ireland
graham.yvette@gmail.com

Abstract. We propose a novel metric for machine translation evaluation based on neural networks. In the training phrase, we maximize the distance between the similarity scores of high and low-quality hypotheses. Then, the trained neural network is used to evaluate the new hypotheses in the testing phase. The proposed metric can efficiently incorporate lexical and syntactic metrics as features in the network and thus is able to capture different levels of linguistic information. Experiments on WMT-14 show state-of-the-art performance is achieved in two out of five language pairs on the system-level and one on the segment-level. Comparative results are also achieved in the remaining language pairs.

Keywords: Machine translation evaluation · Neural networks · Similarity distance · Maximization

1 Introduction

With the development of machine translation (MT), MT evaluation (MTE) has received increasing attention. Traditional lexical-based metrics such as BLEU [8], Meteor [3], and TERp [11] take n-grams, synonyms, stems, word order, and phrases into account. However, metrics based on lexical and syntactic information are insufficient to evaluate the quality of the hypotheses, due to mismatch errors caused by limited synonyms and references.

Recently, semantic-based metrics have become more feasible with the help of deep learning. This paper presents an effective metric based on neural networks, i.e. Bidirectional Long Short Term Memory (Bi-LSTM) network [7,10] for MTE. To capture the inner connection between hypotheses and references, we also explore the effect of an enhanced Bidirectional Combined LSTM (BiC-LSTM)

© Springer International Publishing AG 2016
C.-Y. Lin et al. (Eds.): NLPCC-ICCPOL 2016, LNAI 10102, pp. 153–161, 2016.
DOI: 10.1007/978-3-319-50496-4_13

network, which takes the concatenation of the hypothesis and the reference as the input, rather than feeding them separately into the network as Bi-LSTM does.

Generally, the goal of the framework is to predict quality scores of hypotheses, which requires references and hypotheses together with quality scores as training examples. However, the difficulty of obtaining hypotheses with quality scores leads to the insufficiency of training examples. For instance, ReVal [6] devotes extra effort to compute quality scores of hypotheses, producing less than 15 thousand training examples from the human judgement file of WMT-13 [1], and subsequently requires extra resources to enlarge the training set. As the amount of training examples is crucial to network performance, we design a new objective during the training process, which maximizes the distance between two similarity scores: one between the reference ref and a high-quality hypothesis $posh$, and the other one between ref and a low-quality one $negh$. Thus, two hypotheses, as well as the reference comprise a training example, which allows us to extract adequate training examples from WMT human judgements. Furthermore, for testing, the network takes only one hypothesis and one reference as an input, then outputs an evaluation score of the hypothesis. Compared with Guzmán et al. (2015), our metric significantly reduces complexity in this respect, as we can evaluate with a single hypothesis, while they require a pairwise setting. Experiments on WMT-14 show that state-of-the-art performance is achieved in two out of five language pairs on the system-level and one on the segment-level, comparative results are obtained for remaining language pairs.

2   Learning Task

The goal of the training process in our neural network is to maximize the distance of the similarity score between ref and $posh$, and the other one between ref and $negh$. In the testing process, we evaluate the quality of hyp given ref by computing the similarity score between them.

Thus, the input of our neural network is a tuple, marked as $(ref, posh, negh)$. The loss function of the neural network is formulated as follows:

$$J_\theta = - \sum_n max(0, simP - simN) \tag{1}$$

where $simP$ is the similarity score between ref and $posh$, and $simN$ is that between ref and $negh$. A more detailed computation is illustrated below.

3   MaxSD Model: Maximizing Similarity Distance Model

3.1   MaxSD Model

In order to learn the similarity scores, $simP$ and $simN$, we build a maxSD model. We explore two versions of MaxSD model, the performance of two LSMT networks, namely Bi-LSTM and BiC-LSTM. As showed in Fig. 1, we first obtain

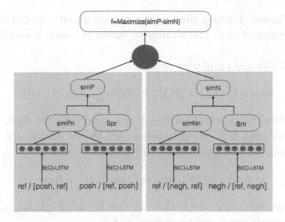

Fig. 1. The overall architecture of the maxSD model. Bi(C)-LSTM means either Bi-LSTM or BiC-LSTM network. Bi-LSTM network takes the left side of '/' as input, while BiC-LSTM the right one. The Bi-LSTM or BiC-LSTM network produces the representation of each input, which then are used to compute $simPn$ and $simNn$. $simP$ and $simN$ are computed by incorporating 5 metric scores, namely s_{pr} and s_{nr} respectively. The objective of the architecture is to maximize the distance between $simP$ and $simN$ are.

the continuous space representations of ref, $posh$, and $negh$ through the Bi-LSTM and BiC-LSTM networks, respectively. Then, the representations are fed into a feed-forward neural network as inputs to obtain neural network(NN)-based similarity scores, which are computed as below:

$$simPn = \sigma(\mathbf{V} \cdot \sigma(\mathbf{W}[ref_r, posh_r] + \mathbf{b})) \qquad (2)$$

$$simNn = \sigma(\mathbf{V} \cdot \sigma(\mathbf{W}[ref_r, negh_r] + \mathbf{b})) \qquad (3)$$

where $posh_r$ denotes the representation of $posh$, and $negh_r$ of $negh$. $simPn$ refers to the NN-based similarity score of $posh$, while $simNn$ of $negh$ given ref_r. $simPn$ and $simNn$ share the same parameter weights $\mathbf{W}$, $\mathbf{V}$ and the bias term $\mathbf{b}$.

Incorporating Other Metrics. Next, we further optimize our model by incorporating lexical and syntactic metrics as features (in terms of metric scores), namely BLEU, NIST, METEOR, TERp and DPMF [13]. The concateanation of these 5 metric scores and the NN-based similarity scores are fed into a feed-forward layer, whose output shows the final similarity scores, $simP$ and $simN$ (mentioned in formula (1)).

$$simP = \sigma(\mathbf{W_s}[simPn, s_{pr}] + \mathbf{b_s}) \qquad (4)$$

$$simN = \sigma(\mathbf{W_s}[simNn, s_{nr}] + \mathbf{b_s}) \qquad (5)$$

where $\mathbf{W_s}$ is the parameter weight and $\mathbf{b_s}$ is a bias term. s_{nr} refers to the concatenated 5 metric scores of neg, while s_{pr} that of pos.

The Testing Phase. During the testing phase, given a hypothesis *hyp* and a corresponding reference *ref*, the similarity score between them is computed as follows.

Firstly, the NN-based similarity score:

$$sim(ref, hyp) = \sigma(\mathbf{V} \cdot \sigma(\mathbf{W}[ref_r, hyp_r] + \mathbf{b})) \tag{6}$$

where ref_r denotes the representation of *ref*, and hyp_r of *hyp*. $\mathbf{W}$ and $\mathbf{V}$ are parameter weights, and $\mathbf{b}$ is the bias term. All $\mathbf{W}$, $\mathbf{V}$ and $\mathbf{b}$ are the same with that in the training phase. Then, the final similarity score

$$sim = \sigma(\mathbf{W_s}[sim(ref, hyp), s_r] + \mathbf{b_s}) \tag{7}$$

where $\mathbf{W_s}$, $\mathbf{b_s}$ are the same with that in the training phase. s_r refers to the concatenated 5 metric scores of *hyp* given *ref*.

3.2   Bi-LSTM and BiC-LSTM Networks

We use Bi-LSTM and BiC-LSTM networks separately to produce the continuous space representations of *ref*, *posh* and *negh*, which are denoted as ref_r, $posh_r$ and $negh_r$.

Bi-LSTM Network. Bi-LSTM networks have been employed to substantially improve performance in several NLP tasks. As illustrated in Fig. 1, Bi-LSTM network consists of two parallel layers, a forward and a backward layer, propagating in two directions. These two layers enable the network to capture both past and future features for a given timestep. The two representation sequences produced by each layer are concatenated at each timestep, followed by mean pooling which outputs the representation of the sentence.

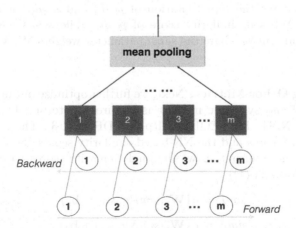

Fig. 2. The Bi-LSTM network. The circles marked from 1 to m consist of a sentence, whose representation is trained by the Bi-LSTM network.

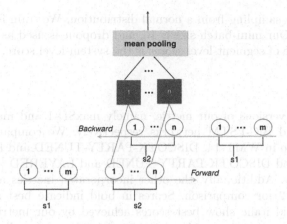

Fig. 3. The BiC-LSTM network. $s1$ denotes a sentence with length of m, while $s2$ the other with that of n. $s1$ and $s2$ are concatenated to go through the BiC-LSTM network, producing the representation of the second sentence $s2$, which contains the inner connection between $s1$ and $s2$.

BiC-LSTM Network. In order to capture inner connection between two sentences, we further propose an enhanced BiC-LSTM network (as illustrated in Fig. 2), which takes the concatenation of the two sentences as input. The output is the representation of the second sentence. For instance, if the input of the forward layer is the concatenation of hyp and ref, denoted by $[hyp, ref]$, and that of the backward layer is the concatenation of reversals of both hyp and ref, then the network produces the representation of ref (Fig. 3).

4 Experiments and Results

4.1 Datasets

Experiments are conducted on the WMT metric shared task. Each training example is a tuple $(ref, posh, negh)$, extracted from the human judgement file of WMT-13, of which each line contains 5 human ranks of 5 randomly chosen hypotheses of a specific segment.

For duplicated tuples, we only retain one of them. There are also two tuples with opposite positions of $posh$ and $negh$ due to the inconsistent ranks between two annotators [2], in which case we remove the tuple appearing less often. Hence, we clean the training with respect to inconsistency and redundancy. In all, we obtain 285908 tuples for training. Evaluation is conducted on WMT-14 for other languages into English.

4.2 Setups

Sentences with lengths exceeding 100 words are filtered out. The 300-dimensional *glove* word vectors [9] are used as the word embedding. The parameter weights are initialized by sampling from a normal distribution. We train for 10 epoches using adadelta. Our mini-batch size is 16, and dropout is used as suggested by [14]. The average of segment-level scores is the system-level score.

4.3 Results

We present two versions of our metric, namely maxSD-1 and maxSD-2 based on Bi-LSTM and BiC-LSTM networks respectively. We compare our metric with the best two in WMT-14, DISCOTK-PARTY-TUNED and BEER [12] on segment-level, and DISCOTK-PARTY-TUNED and LAYERED [4] on system-level respectively. Additionally, the other incorporated metrics are also listed in Tables 1 and 2 for comparison. Scores in bold indicate best scores overall and those in bold italic show best scores achieved by our metric. Results in Tables 1 and 2 show that two versions of our metric outperform all other metrics, except DISCOTK-PARTY-TUNED, in all five directions both at the segment- and system-level. And our metrics are slightly behind the top-performing metric DISCOTK-PARTY-TUNED, which combines 17 different metrics requiring external resources and tuning efforts. However, for 'hi-en', we yield better results than DISCOTK-PARTY-TUNED, achieving the state-of-the-art results, with Kendall tau of 0.444 on the segment level and Pearson correlation of 0.979 on the system level. It is also worthy noting that maxSD-2 achieves the best performance in two ('hi-en' and 'fr-en') out of five directions at the system-level, and maxSD-1 the best in one direction at the segment-level. One interesting finding is that the enhanced maxSD-2 does not outperform maxSD-1. We suspect that the long length of the concatenated sentence affects the performance of BiC-LSTM network. As recommended by [5], significance tests for differences in dependent correlation with human assessment were carried out for all competing metrics. Results of significance tests are shown in Fig. 4.

Table 1. Segment-level Kendall's tau correlations on WMT-14.

Metrics	cs-en	de-en	fr-en	ru-en	hi-en	PAvg
BLEU	.218	.266	.376	.263	.299	.285
NIST	.231	.295	.392	.285	.342	.309
TERp-A	.293	.335	.389	.307	.407	.346
METEOR	.282	.334	.406	.333	.407	.355
DPMF	.283	.332	.404	.324	.426	.354
maxSD-1	*.312*	*.353*	.429	*.342*	**.444**	*.376*
maxSD-2	.310	*.353*	*.431*	*.342*	.440	.375
DISCOTK-PARTY-TUNED	**.328**	**.380**	**.433**	**.355**	.434	**.386**
BEER	.284	.337	.417	.333	.438	.362

Table 2. System-level correlations on WMT-14.

Metrics	cs-en	de-en	fr-en	ru-en	hi-en	Average
BLEU	.963	.830	.961	.784	.928	.893
NIST	.949	.803	.964	.796	.667	.836
TERp-A	.863	.909	.976	.815	.438	.800
METEOR	.980	.927	.975	.807	.457	.829
DPMF	**.999**	.920	.967	.832	.882	.920
maxSD-1	.945	*.920*	*.977*	*.827*	.978	*.930*
maxSD-2	*.948*	.919	*.977*	.825	*.979*	*.930*
DISCOTK-PARTY-TUNED	.975	**.943**	*.977*	**.870**	.956	**.944**
LAYERED	.941	.893	.973	.854	.976	.927

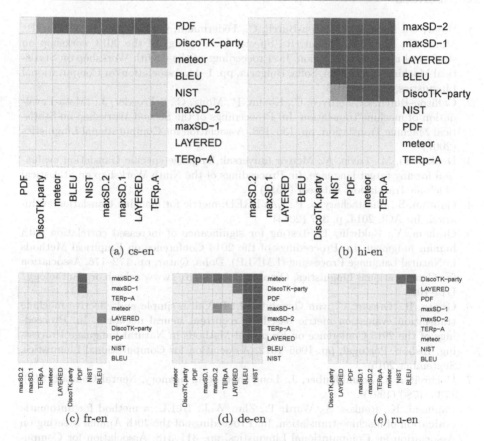

(a) cs-en   (b) hi-en

(c) fr-en   (d) de-en   (e) ru-en

Fig. 4. Significance test results for differences in dependent correlation with human judgement (Williams test) for all competing pairs of metrics. A green cell denotes a significant win for the metric in a given row over the metric in a given column at $p < 0.05$. "PDF" in the figure corresponds to "DPMF" mentioned above. (Color figure online)

5   Conclusion

Our proposed metric based on neural networks effectively achieves the state-of-the-art performance in two out of five language pairs on system-level and one on segment-level, and achieve comparative results for the remaining language pairs.

Acknowledgements. This work is supported by National Natural Science Foundation of P. R. China under Grant No. 61379086, European Union Horizon 2020 research and innovation programme under grant agreement 645452 (QT21), and the ADAPT Centre for Digital Content Technology (www.adaptcentre.ie) at Dublin City University funded under the SFI Research Centres Programme (Grant 13/RC/2106) co-funded under the European Regional Development Fund.

References

1. Bojar, O., Buck, C., Callison-Burch, C., Federmann, C., Haddow, B., Koehn, P., Monz, C., Post, M., Soricut, R., Specia, L.: Findings of the 2013 workshop on statistical machine translation. In: Proceedings of the Eighth Workshop on Statistical Machine Translation, Sofia, Bulgaria, pp. 1–44. Association for Computational Linguistics, August 2013
2. Callison-Burch, C., Fordyce, C., Koehn, P., Monz, C., Schroeder, J.: (Meta-) evaluation of machine translation. In: Proceedings of the Second Workshop on Statistical Machine Translation, pp. 136–158. Association for Computational Linguistics (2007)
3. Denkowski, M., Lavie, A.: Meteor universal: language specific translation evaluation for any target language. In: Proceedings of the Ninth Workshop on Statistical Machine Translation. Citeseer (2014)
4. Gautam, S., Bhattacharyya, P.: LAYERED: metric for machine translation evaluation. In: ACL 2014, p. 387 (2014)
5. Graham, Y., Baldwin, T.: Testing for significance of increased correlation with human judgment. In: Proceedings of the 2014 Conference on Empirical Methods in Natural Language Processing (EMNLP), Doha, Qatar, pp. 172–176. Association for Computational Linguistics, October 2014. http://www.aclweb.org/anthology/D14-1020
6. Gupta, R., Orasan, C., van Genabith, J.: ReVal: a simple and effective machine translation evaluation metric based on recurrent neural networks. In: Proceedings of the 2015 Conference on Empirical Methods in Natural Language Processing, Lisbon, Portugal, pp. 1066–1072. Association for Computational Linguistics, September 2015
7. Hochreiter, S., Schmidhuber, J.: Long short-term memory. Neural Comput. **9**(8), 1735–1780 (1997)
8. Papineni, K., Roukos, S., Ward, T., Zhu, W.J.: BLEU: a method for automatic evaluation of machine translation. In: Proceedings of the 40th Annual Meeting on Association for Computational Linguistics, pp. 311–318. Association for Computational Linguistics (2002)
9. Pennington, J., Socher, R., Manning, C.D.: GloVe: global vectors for word representation. EMNLP **14**, 1532–1543 (2014)
10. Schuster, M., Paliwal, K.K.: Bidirectional recurrent neural networks. IEEE Trans. Signal Process. **45**(11), 2673–2681 (1997)

11. Snover, M., Madnani, N., Dorr, B., Schwartz, R.: Fluency, adequacy, or HTER? Exploring different human judgments with a tunable MT metric. In: Proceedings of the Fourth Workshop on Statistical Machine Translation, Athens, Greece, pp. 259–268. Association for Computational Linguistics, March 2009

12. Stanojevic, M., Sima'an, K.: BEER: better evaluation as ranking. In: Proceedings of the Ninth Workshop on Statistical Machine Translation, Baltimore, Maryland, USA, pp. 414–419. Association for Computational Linguistics, June 2014

13. Yu, H., Wu, X., Jiang, W., Liu, Q., Lin, S.: An automatic machine translation evaluation metric based on dependency parsing model. arXiv preprint arXiv:1508.01996 (2015)

14. Zaremba, W., Sutskever, I., Vinyals, O.: Recurrent neural network regularization. arXiv preprint arXiv:1409.2329 (2014)

Automatic Long Sentence Segmentation for Neural Machine Translation

Shaohui Kuang and Deyi Xiong[✉]

Soochow University, Suzhou, China
shaohuikuang@foxmail.com, dyxiong@suda.edu.cn

Abstract. Neural machine translation (NMT) is an emerging machine translation paradigm that translates texts with an encoder-decoder neural architecture. Very recent studies find that translation quality drops significantly when NMT translates long sentences. In this paper, we propose a novel method to deal with this issue by segmenting long sentences into several clauses. We introduce a split and reordering model to collectively detect the optimal sequence of segmentation points for a long source sentence. Each segmented clause is translated by the NMT system independently into a target clause. The translated target clauses are then concatenated without reordering to form the final translation for the long sentence. On NIST Chinese-English translation tasks, our segmentation method achieves a substantial improvement of 2.94 BLEU points over the NMT baseline on translating long sentences with more than 30 words, and 5.43 BLEU points on sentences of over 40 words.

1 Introduction

Neural machine translation [1,17], as a newly emerging machine translation approach, quickly achieves state-of-the-art performance on some language pairs, e.g., English-to-French [5,8,13]. It establishes a neural translation architecture with an encoder and decoder, which is very different than that of traditional statistical machine translation. The encoder reads variable-length source sentences and encodes them into a fixed-length vector while the decoder generates a target translation from this fixed-length vector. The entire encoder-decoder model is jointly trained to optimize the likelihood of a target translation given a source sentence.

Pioneering studies on NMT [3,16] show that the performance of NMT is getting worse as source sentences get longer. The primary cause of translation quality loss on long sentences, not difficult to understand, is that fixed-size vector representations produced by the encoder for source sentences are not capable of encoding all cues for the decoder to generate translations.

In order to address this issue, attentional mechanisms [1,12] have been proposed to enhance the ability of the decoder to selectively focus on parts of a source sentence that are relevant to predicting the next target word, instead of only relying on fixed-size vectors. Yet another strand of approaches to dealing with this issue is to segment long sentences into a sequence of phrases.

© Springer International Publishing AG 2016
C.-Y. Lin et al. (Eds.): NLPCC-ICCPOL 2016, LNAI 10102, pp. 162–174, 2016.
DOI: 10.1007/978-3-319-50496-4_14

For example, Pouget-Abadie et al. [16] propose a segmentation method that use the same encoder-decoder network to find an optimal segmentation by measuring confidence scores of segmented phrases. Their method, unfortunately, cannot handle long-distance reordering.

In this paper, we propose a simple yet effective approach to long sentence segmentation for NMT based on traditional word alignments. Our goal is to segment long sentences into short clauses, each of which can be not only translated into target language as a whole unit, but also concatenated to form the final translation without reordering. In order to achieve this goal, we incorporate two sub-models into our method: a split and a reordering model. The split model finds segmentation points on long sentences to ensure that each segmented clause can be translated as a whole unit. The reordering model measures the probability that translations of two neighboring segmented clauses can be concatenated in a straight order. The two models are used to collectively detect the optimal sequence of segmentation points for long source sentences.

Our contributions lie in three aspects. First, we are the first to add a reordering model to the segmentation method so as to avoid reorderings across segmented clauses. Second, the proposed method uses word alignments generated by traditional SMT methods to guide segmenting for NMT, which combines the merits of both SMT and NMT. Third, our method can substantially improve NMT on long sentence translation by more than 5 BLEU points on a Chinese-to-English translation task.

2   Related Work

A variety of long sentence segmentation methods have been proposed for conventional statistical machine translation. In early work, Brown et al. [2] propose a method to divide a long source sentence into a series of segments in order to increase translation speed. Doi and Sumita [7] generate segment sequence candidates based on an N-gram model, and select the best segment sequence according to the measure of sentence similarity. Xu et al. [20] present an alignment-based segmentation method that segment clauses recursively until the length of a segmented clause is smaller than a given threshold. In spoken language translation, Matusov et al. [14] introduce an approach to long sentence segmentation that determines segment boundaries with a log-linear combination of a language model, prosodic features as well as a segment length model. Xiong et al. [19] present a framework to learn segments of sentences that can be translated as a unit into the target language.

With regard to neural machine translation, the performance drop on long sentence translations is much more bigger than that of traditional statistical machine translation due to fixed-size representations used for variable-length source sentences in NMT. Attentional mechanisms [1,12] have been introduced for robust long sentence translation by accompanying fixed-size representations with additional cues of source words that are going to be translated. Segmentation methods that are specifically designed for NMT have also been explored.

Pouget-Abadie et al. [16] propose a segmentation method that finds optimal segmentations with maximal confidence scores computed by an RNN encoder-decoder network. Our method can be considered as a combination of segmentation and attention philosophies as we split long sentences into a sequence of clauses that are then translated with an attention-based NMT system. Additionally, the advantage of our method over that of Pouget-Abadie et al.'s is the ability of handeling reorderings across segmented clauses. We will empirically show that this ability contributes a lot to improvements in Sect. 5.

3   Neural Machine Translation

Typically, neural machine translation builds on a recurrent neural network based encoder-decoder framework [4,17]. Without loss of generality, we take the NMT architecture proposed by Cho et al. [4] in this paper. In their framework, the encoder encodes a source sentence x and repeatedly generates a hidden vector over each word of the source sentence as follows:

$$h_t = f(x_t, h_{t-1}) \tag{1}$$

where x_t is the word embedding of the tth word in the input sentence, h_t is a hidden state at time t (Note that h_0 is an all-zero vector), and f is a non-linear activation function. Normally the function is defined as a gated recurrent unit (GRU) [6], which is computed as follows:

$$
\begin{aligned}
h_t &= (1 - z_t) \circ h_{t-1} + z_t \circ \tilde{h}_t, \\
z_t &= \sigma(W_z x_t + U_z h_{t-1}), \\
\tilde{h}_t &= tanh(W x_t + U(r_t \circ h_{t-1})), \\
r_t &= \sigma(W_r x_t + U_r h_{t-1}).
\end{aligned}
\tag{2}
$$

where $\circ$ is an element-wise multiplication, σ is a logistic sigmoid function. z_t and r_t are the update and reset gate, respectively.

The decoder is also an RNN that predicts the next word y_t given the context vector c (i.e., the fixed-size vector of the source sentence, normally the last hidden state of the encoder computed in Eq. (1)) and hidden state s_t. The hidden state of the decoder s_t at time t is computed as follows:

$$s_t = f(s_{t-1}, y_{t-1}, c), \tag{3}$$

where f is the activation function, the same as that used in the encoder. The conditional probability of the next word is calculated as follows:

$$p(y_t | y_{t-1}, y_{t-2}, \ldots, y_1, c) = g(s_t, y_{t-1}, c). \tag{4}$$

where g is a softmax activation function.

Bahdanau et al. [1] introduce an attention network into NMT to cope with the issue of long sentence translation. The conditional probability is therefore reformulated as:

$$p(y_t|y_{t-1}, y_{t-2}, \ldots, y_1, c) = g(s_t, y_{t-1}, c_t), \tag{5}$$

$$s_t = f(s_{t-1}, y_{t-1}, c_t), \tag{6}$$

where the context vector c_t computed as a weighted sum of all hidden states of the encoder as follows:

$$c_t = \sum_{i=1}^{T_x} \alpha_{tj} h_j, \tag{7}$$

$$\alpha_{tj} = \frac{exp(e_{tj})}{\sum_{k=1}^{T_x} exp(e_{tk})}, \tag{8}$$

$$e_{tj} = a(s_{t-1}, h_j), \tag{9}$$

where α_{tj} is the weight of each hidden state h_j, e_{tj} is a matching score of the input around position j and the output at position t obtained by an alignment model a.

The encoder-decoder NMT framework can be trained to optimize the likelihood of the target given the source on a parallel corpus, for instance, using a minibatch stochastic gradient descent algorithm with Adadelta. In our experiments, we use the RNNsearch model [1] with the attentional mechanism as our NMT baseline.

4 The Segmentation Method

In this section, we describe the proposed segmentation model, including the split and reordering sub-models.

4.1 The Split Model

The split model is used to find the optimal sequence of split positions so that each segmented clause can be translated as a whole unit. In other words, the translations of these segments are still continuous in the target language. Satisfying this requirement, each clause can be translated by the NMT system independently.

So how can we find these split positions? We use word alignments, which can be obtained from either a traditional SMT system or an attention-based NMT system. As we want to combine the strengths of the two machine translation paradigms, we use a traditional word aligner (e.g., GIZA++) to produce word alignments in this paper. Given a source sentence $c = \{c_1, c_2, \ldots, c_n\}$, its counterpart target sentence $e = \{e_1, e_2, \ldots, e_m\}$ and their word alignments A. we can find a consecutive source sequence c_i^j that is mapped to a consecutive target segquence e_h^k using the phrase extraction algorithm [15] except for that we do not impose any length constraints. We refer to the source sequence c_i^j as a splittable segment. For a position k, if we can find a splittable segment c_k^j ($j > k$) or c_i^k ($k > i$), k is regarded as a split position, otherwise it is not. Through this method, we can collect a set of split and non-split positions. The split model is similar to the bracketing model proposed by Xiong et al. [19]. The difference is that we use it for segmenting instead of bracketing.

Using these positions as positive and negative training instances, we can train a maximum entropy classifier (MaxEnt) to automatically detect split positions on new source sentences. In particular, the classifier predicts whether a source word w is a split position as follows:

$$p(y|x(w)) = \frac{exp(\sum_i \theta_i f_i(y, x(w)))}{\sum_{y'} exp(\sum_i \theta_i f_i(y', x(w)))} \tag{10}$$

where $y \in \{true, false\}$ (split, non-split), the function $f_i \in (0, 1)$ are features, θ_i are the weights of these features, and $x(w)$ is the context of word w.

We define the features as binary indicator functions $f(x(w), y)$, which can be formulated in the following way:

$$f_1(x(w), y) = \begin{cases} 1, & y = true \ and \ w_1 = \text{``ren''} \\ 0, & otherwise \end{cases} \tag{11}$$

The context $x(w)$ is defined as a 7-word window centered at the current word w: $x(w) = \{w_{-3}, w_{-2}, w_{-1}, w, w_1, w_2, w_3\}$. In Table 1, we show feature templates that we use in our experiments. $\beta \in \{true, false\}$, γ is a word from the context $x(w)$.

Table 1. Teature templates for the split model

Template	$f(x(w), y) = 1$ if and only if
1	$y = \beta$ and $w_{-3} = \gamma$
2	$y = \beta$ and $w_{-2} = \gamma$
3	$y = \beta$ and $w_{-1} = \gamma$
4	$y = \beta$ and $w = \gamma$
5	$y = \beta$ and $w_1 = \gamma$
6	$y = \beta$ and $w_2 = \gamma$
7	$y = \beta$ and $w_3 = \gamma$

We can compute the probability that a word w_i is a split position using the split classifier. For a source sentence, we can find the optimal sequence of split positions $s = \{s_1, s_2, \ldots, s_k\}$ as follows:

$$s = argmax \prod_{i=1}^k q_{s_i} \tag{12}$$

where q_{s_i} denotes the probability of the split position s_i, computed according to Eq. (10).

4.2   The Reordering Model

The proposed split model does not solve the reordering problem of segmented clauses. We therefore further propose a reordering model to address this issue. As we mentioned before, we do not want to reorder segmented clauses after translation. Instead, we want to concatenate the translations of segmented clauses monotonically (i.e., in a straight order). The reordering model is to ensure that the found sequence of split positions has the highest probability that any two neighboring clauses are in a straight order.

Given a sequence of segmented positions $s = \{s_1, s_2, \ldots, s_k\}$, the reordering model is formulated as follows:

$$r = \prod_{i=1}^{k} p(straight|C_{s_i}^p, C_{s_i}^n) \tag{13}$$

where $C_{s_i}^p$ is the segmented clause before the split position s_i, $C_{s_i}^n$ is after the split the position. $p(straight|C_{s_i}^p, C_{s_i}^n)$ is the probability that the two clauses are in a straight order after translation.

In order to calculate the probability of a straight order, we again resort to the MaxEnt model. The probability is computed as follows:

$$p(straight|C_{s_i}^p, C_{s_i}^n)) = \frac{exp(\sum_h \theta_h f_h(straight, C_{s_i}^p, C_{s_i}^n))}{\sum_o exp(\sum_h \theta_h f_h(o, C_{s_i}^p, C_{s_i}^n))} \tag{14}$$

where $o \in \{straight, inverted\}$. Similar to Xiong et al. [18], we use boundary words of clauses as features f_h. Taking the two neighboring clauses w_i^j and w_{j+1}^k as an example, we will extract boundary words w_i, w_j, w_{j+1}, w_k to construct the feature functions.

4.3   Joint Model: Combining the Two Submodels

We combine the split and reordering model together to form the joint model. Given a segment position sequence s_1^k, the joint model is defined as follows:

$$JM = \prod_{i=1}^{k} p_{s_i} * r_{s_i} \tag{15}$$

where, p_{s_i} is the split probability computed according to Eq. (10), r_{s_i} is the straight probability estimated according to Eq. (14).

We use a beam search algorithm to find the optimal sequence of segmentation positions s:

$$s = argmax \prod_{i=1}^{k} p_{s_i} * r_{s_i} \tag{16}$$

5   Experiment

We conducted a series of experiments on Chinese-English translation to examine the effectiveness of the proposed long sentence segmentation method. Particularly, we investigate:

- Whether the split and reordering model can improve NMT on long sentence translation.
- Whether our model is able to outperform other segmentation methods, such as random segmentation, segmentation according to punctuation or clause length.
- How the proposed model changes the way that NMT translates long sentences.

5.1   Setup

We used Chinese-English bilingual corpora that contain 2.9 M sentence pairs with 80.9 M Chinese words and 86.4 M English words as our training data. All corpora are from LDC data.[1]

For the NMT system, we used the GoundHog[2], a Theano-based implementation of RNNsearch-50 [1]. In the RNNsearch model, the attentional mechanism was added. The encoder of RNNsearch consists of a forward (1000 hidden unit) and backward (1000 hidden unit) recurrent neural network. The maximum length of sentences that we used to train GroundHog in our experiments was set to 50 for both the Chinese and English side. Sentences with more then 30 words account for 37.92% in the training data. We used the most frequent 30 K words and replaced rare words with a special token "UNK". We used the stochastic descent algorithm with mini-batch and Adadelta to train the model. Once the RNNsearch model was tranied, we adopted a beam search to find possible translations with high probabilities. We set the beam width of RNNsearch to 10. The BLEU scores of RNNsearch model on NIST test set are shown in Table 4.

We also trained Moses [11] on our data as yet another baseline. Word alignments were produced by GIZA++. We ran GIZA++ on the corpus in both directions, and merged alignments in two directions with "grow-diag-final" refinement rule [10]. We trained a 5-gram language model on the Xinhua portion of the GIGA-WORD corpus using SRILM Toolkit with modified Kneser-Ney Smoothing.

The beam width that we used to search the optimal sequence of segmentation positions was set to 5. And the minimum length of segmented clauses was set to 18 words.

In order to validate the effectiveness of the proposed segmentation method, we concatenated NIST02 and NIST03 and selected sentences of length >30 words from the combined set to form our dev-set. Similarly, we concatenated NIST04/05/06/08 into one corpus, from which we extracted sentences with more than 30 words to form our test set. We used case-insensitive BLEU to evaluate

---

[1] The corpora include LDC2003E14, LDC2004T07, LDC2005T06, LDC2005T10 and LDC2004T08 (Hong Kong Hansards/Laws/News).

[2] https://github.com/lisa-groundhog/GroundHog.

translation quality. We tested statistical significance in BLEU score differences with the paired bootstrap re-sampling [9].

5.2   The Split Model

In order to examine the effectiveness of the proposed split model, we use this model alone to segment long sentences through a beam search. The segmented clauses are then translated by the baseline NMT system and concatenated monotonically to form final translations for long sentences. In order to study the performance change of NMT translating longer sentences, we extract sentences with more than 40 words from our test set to construct a new test set Test-40.

The results are shown in Table 2. From the table, we can clearly observe a large drop of translation quality in terms of BLEU when the NMT baseline (RNNsearch) translates sentences of over 40 words vs. sentences of over 30 words (23.55 vs. 27). Although RNNsearch is equipped with an attention network that alleviates the issue of fixed-size representations by allowing the decoder to pay attention to relevant parts of source sentences, translating long sentences remains a big challenge for NMT. In contrast, we do not observe performance drop on the traditional SMT system Moses.

Table 2. BLEU scores of our split and reordering model against the two baselines (RNNsearch and Moses) on the test set. Test-30/Test-40: the test set that consists of sentences with more than 30/40 words. +: statistically significantly better than RNNsearch (p < 0.01). *: statistically significantly better than Moses.

System	Test-30	Test-40
RNNsearch	27.00	23.55
Moses	29.53	29.74
RNNsearch + split	27.77^{+}	25.00^{+}
RNNsearch + split + reordering	$29.94^{+,*}$	28.89^{+}

Although the performance is lower than that of Moses, the split model achieves a gain of 0.77 BLEU points on Test-30 and 1.45 BLEU points on Test-40. These improvements suggest that the split model is able to improve NMT, especially when sentences are very long (e.g., >40 words).

5.3   The Reordering Model

Pouget-Abadie et al. [16] introduce a segmentation method that does not deal with reordering issue. Since they have carried out experiments on translations between English and French that follow a very similar word order, this is not a big problem. However, for Chinese and English, the word order difference cannot

Table 3. BLEU scores of different segmentation methods on Test-30. Rand.: random segmentation. Leng.: segmentation according to the length of clauses. Punct.: segmentation according to punctuations.

System	Test-30
RNNsearch	27.00
Moses	29.53
RNNsearch + Rand.	26.26
RNNsearch + Leng.	26.73
RNNsearch + Punct.	27.67
RNNsearch + Joint.	29.94

Table 4. The BLEU scores of the GroundHog on the NIST test set. We select the NIST03 as our development set and NIST04, NIST05, NIST06, NIST08 as our test set.

NIST	BLEU
NIST03	32.71
NIST04	35.52
NIST05	30.92
NIST06	29.32
NIST08	22.51

be neglected. Our strategy to address this problem is to keep reorderings inside clauses so that we do not need to reorder clauses. In doing so we can focus on long sentence segmentation while avoiding inter-clause reorderings. Intra-clause reorderings are still handled by the NMT system.

We further conducted experiments to investigate the impact of the proposed reordering strategy on long sentence translation. The last row of Table 2 shows the results. The incorporation of the reordering model can further achieve an improvement of 2.17 BLEU points on Test-30 and 3.89 on Test-40. Comparing with the improvements obtained by the split model, we find that the longer sentences get, the larger improvement the reordering model can obtain. This is reasonable. On the one hand, the NMT baseline suffers from a larger loss when sentences get longer. On the other hand, there are more long-distance reorderings when sentences get longer. Therefore the reordering model will be more beneficial.

We also observe that the joint model achieves an improvement of 2.94 BLEU points over RNNsearch on Test-30. The performance is even higher than the state-of-the-art SMT system Moses by 0.41 BLEU points.

5.4 Comparison

We further compared our segmentation model with three different segmentation methods: random segmentation, segmentation by length, and segmentation by punctuations. The first randomly segments long sentences into clauses without using any constraints. The second segments long sentences into clauses the length of which is in the range of [avg−12, avg+12] where avg is the average number of words per sentence of the entire test set. The last method segments long sentences according to Chinese punctuations, e.g., comma, question mark and so on. We segment sentences on every punctuation marks regardless of segment length.

The comparison results are shown in Table 3. Only the segmentation by punctuation is better than RNNsearch. The other two methods (random segmentation

Table 5. Average length of target translations generated by different systems on Test-40.

System	Avg-length
RNNsearch	43.71
RNNsearch + joint model	54.87
Moses	56.91

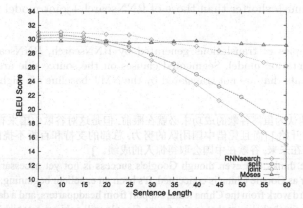

Fig. 1. Performance curves of RNNsearch, the split model, joint model and Moses in terms of the length of source sentences.

and segmentation by length) undermines translation quality of long sentences. All these three segmentation methods significantly underperform the joint model.

5.5 Analysis

We want to further study how the proposed segmentation method changes the way that NMT translates long sentences. In order to answer this question, we first investigated the performance curves of the NMT baseline, the split model, Moses and the joint model in terms of the length of source sentences. We plot these curves in Fig. 1, from which we can observe that

- Attention-based NMT still suffers from an increasing loss when sentences get longer on Chinese-English translation. This indicates that long sentence translation remains an unsolved challenge for attention-based NMT.
- The curves of both the split and joint model always appear to be on top of the curve of the NMT baseline. Surprisingly, the joint model is able to strongly prevent from performance drop when sentences get long. Comparing the performance of translating sentences of over 60 words against that on short sentences, we find that the joint model suffers from an absolute drop of less than 5 BLEU points while the attention-based NMT loses more than 15 BLEU points.

- Regarding the conventional SMT system Moses, we do not observe a significant drop of performance on long sentences. This is consistent with prvevious findings on traditional SMT.

Second, we took a deep look into target translations generated by RNNsearch and RNNsearch enhanced with the proposed segmentation model. Particularly, we analyzed the average length of these translations. Table 5 provides this statistical information. The average length of translations generated by RNNsearch is 43.7 words, much shorter than those of RNNsearch+joint model (54.9 words)

Table 6. Examples of translations generated by RNNsearch, RNNsearch with the proposed segmentation model. Segmented clauses on the source side are indicated in "[]". The fragments that are not translated by the NMT baseline are highlighted in red color.

Source	[他认为虽然谷歌的成功未必就在眼前, 但是这对谷歌中国来有了一个很好的开始,] [而且凭借中国团队的努力, 总部的支持和百折不挠的精神, 他坚信在未来, 谷歌在中国会取得惊人的成绩。]
Reference	He thinks that even though Google's success is not yet necessarily visible, as far as Google China is concerned, it's been an excellent beginning, and that with hard work from the China team, support from headquarters, and a dauntless spirit, he firmly believes that in the future Google will achieve astonishing success in China.
RNNsearch	he said that although the success of the valley was not enough in front, it was a very good start in china. he firmly believes that in the future, the south african valley will make an unprecedented achievement in the future.
RNNsearch + Joint Model	[he thinks that although the success of the valley songs may not necessarily lie ahead, this is a good beginning .] [in addition, by relying on the efforts of the chinese team, he firmly believes that in the future, the song of valley songs will attain astonishing results.]
Source	[在马沙勒重申拒绝承认以色列的之前呢, 哈马斯另外一位政治领导人马尔祖克在接受埃及电视采访时表示:] [哈马斯决不会承认以色列的合法地位, 但新政府将会继续同以色列在各个领域进行接触。因为是否承认以色列和与否同他打交道是两码事。]
Reference	Prior to Mashal's reiteration of refusing to recognize Israel, Marzouk, another Hamas political leader, said in an interview with Egyptian TV that Hamas will absolutely not recognize the legitimate status of Israel, but the new government will continue to keep contact with Israel in various areas, because recognizing Israel or not is a totally different thing from whether to have contact with it.
RNNsearch	when UNK reiterated that he refused to acknowledge israel's legitimate status, the new administration would continue to engage in contact with israel in various fields, because whether or not israel and UNK have dealings with him.
RNNsearch + Joint Model	[when UNK reiterated that he refused to acknowledge israel, another political leader, a political leader of the united states, stated:] [UNK will not recognize the legitimate status of israel. but the new administration will continue to hold contact with israel in various fields, for whether or not israel will deal with each other.]

and Moses (56.9 words). This indicates that some information of source sentences may be lost and not translated by RNNsearch.

Table 6 displays two examples that exactly verify this. In the first example, the beginning part of the second segmented clause on the source side '而且凭借……百折不 挠的精神' is not translated at all by RNNsearch. Similar cases are also found in other translation examples (highlighted in red color). In contrast, our segmentation method is able to help the NMT system convey the missing information from the source side to the target side.

6   Conclusion and Future Work

In this paper, we have presented a new segmentation method for neural machine translation to deal with long sentence translation. The method consists of a split and reordering model. The split model segments long sentences into clauses that can be translated as a whole unit while the reordering model is able to avoid inter-clause reorderings. The two models collectively find the optimal sequence of clauses that can be translated independently by NMT system and monotonically concatenated to form final translations for long sentences. It achieves an improvement of up to 5 BLEU points over the baseline on long sentence translation.

As we train the split and reordering model based on word alignments, we would like to investigate how big the impact of word alignment quality imposes on our model. We are also interested in exploring linguistic information in our split and reordering model, such as source-side parse trees.

Acknowledgements. The authors were supported by National Natural Science Foundation of China (Grant No. 61403269) and Natural Science Foundation of Jiangsu Province (Grant No. BK20140355). We also thank the anonymous reviewers for their insightful comments.

References

1. Bahdanau, D., Cho, K., Bengio, Y.: Neural machine translation by jointly learning to align and translate. arXiv preprint arXiv:1409.0473 (2014)
2. Brown, P.F., Della Pietra, S.A., Della Pietra, V.J., Mercer, R.L., Mohanty, S.: Dividing and conquering long sentences in a translation system. In: Proceedings of the Workshop on Speech and Natural Language, pp. 267–271. Association for Computational Linguistics (1992)
3. Cho, K., van Merriënboer, B., Bahdanau, D., Bengio, Y.: On the properties of neural machine translation: encoder-decoder approaches. In: Syntax, Semantics and Structure in Statistical Translation, p. 103 (2014)
4. Cho, K., Van Merriënboer, B., Gulcehre, C., Bahdanau, D., Bougares, F., Schwenk, H., Bengio, Y.: Learning phrase representations using RNN encoder-decoder for statistical machine translation. arXiv preprint arXiv:1406.1078 (2014)
5. Jean, S., Cho, K., Memisevic, R., Bengio, Y.: On using very large target vocabulary for neural machine translation. Computer Science (2014)
6. Chung, J., Gulcehre, C., Cho, K., Bengio, Y.: Empirical evaluation of gated recurrent neural networks on sequence modeling. arXiv preprint arXiv:1412.3555 (2014)

7. Doi, T., Sumita, E.: Splitting input sentence for machine translation using language model with sentence similarity. In: COLING (2004)
8. Firat, O., Cho, K., Bengio, Y.: Multi-way, multilingual neural machine translation with a shared attention mechanism. arXiv preprint arXiv:1601.01073 (2016)
9. Koehn, P.: Pharaoh: a beam search decoder for phrase-based statistical machine translation models. In: Frederking, R.E., Taylor, K.B. (eds.) AMTA 2004. LNCS (LNAI), vol. 3265, pp. 115–124. Springer, Heidelberg (2004). doi:10.1007/978-3-540-30194-3_13
10. Koehn, P., Axelrod, A., Birch, A., Callison-Burch, C., Osborne, M., Talbot, D., White, M.: Edinburgh system description for the 2005 IWSLT speech translation evaluation. In: IWSLT, pp. 68–75 (2005)
11. Koehn, P., Hoang, H., Birch, A., Callison-Burch, C., Federico, M., Bertoldi, N., Cowan, B., Shen, W., Moran, C., Zens, R., et al.: Moses: open source toolkit for statistical machine translation. In: Proceedings of the 45th Annual Meeting of the ACL on Interactive Poster and Demonstration Sessions, pp. 177–180. Association for Computational Linguistics (2007)
12. Luong, M.T., Pham, H., Manning, C.D.: Effective approaches to attention-based neural machine translation (2015)
13. Luong, M.T., Sutskever, I., Le, Q.V., Vinyals, O., Zaremba, W.: Addressing the rare word problem in neural machine translation. arXiv preprint arXiv:1410.8206 (2014)
14. Matusov, E., Mauser, A., Ney, H.: Automatic sentence segmentation and punctuation prediction for spoken language translation. In: IWSLT, pp. 158–165. Citeseer (2006)
15. Och, F.J.: Statistical machine translation: from single-word models to alignment templates. Ph.D. thesis, Bibliothek der RWTH Aachen (2002)
16. Pouget-Abadie, J., Bahdanau, D., van Merriënboer, B., Cho, K., Bengio, Y.: Overcoming the curse of sentence length for neural machine translation using automatic segmentation. In: Syntax, Semantics and Structure in Statistical Translation, p. 78 (2014)
17. Sutskever, I., Vinyals, O., Le, Q.V.: Sequence to sequence learning with neural networks. In: Advances in Neural Information Processing Systems, pp. 3104–3112 (2014)
18. Xiong, D., Liu, Q., Lin, S.: Maximum entropy based phrase reordering model for statistical machine translation. In: Proceedings of the 21st International Conference on Computational Linguistics and the 44th annual meeting of the Association for Computational Linguistics, pp. 521–528. Association for Computational Linguistics (2006)
19. Xiong, D., Zhang, M., Li, H.: Learning translation boundaries for phrase-based decoding. In: Human Language Technologies: The 2010 Annual Conference of the North American Chapter of the Association for Computational Linguistics, pp. 136–144. Association for Computational Linguistics (2010)
20. Xu, J., Zens, R., Ney, H.: Sentence segmentation using IBM word alignment model 1. In: Proceedings of EAMT 2005 (10th Annual Conference of the European Association for Machine Translation), pp. 280–287 (2005)

Machine Learning for NLP

Topic Segmentation of Web Documents with Automatic Cue Phrase Identification and BLSTM-CNN

Liang Wang[1], Sujian Li[1,3(✉)], Xinyan Xiao[2], and Yajuan Lyu[2]

[1] Key Laboratory of Computational Linguistics,
Peking University, MOE, Beijing, China
{intfloat,lisujian}@pku.edu.cn
[2] Baidu Inc., Beijing, China
{xiaoxinyan,lvyajuan}@baidu.com
[3] Collaborative Innovation Center for Language Ability, Xuzhou, Jiangsu, China

Abstract. Topic segmentation plays an important role for discourse analysis and document understanding. Previous work mainly focus on unsupervised method for topic segmentation. In this paper, we propose to use bidirectional long short-term memory (BLSTM) model, along with convolutional neural network (CNN) for learning paragraph representation. Besides, we present a novel algorithm based on frequent subsequence mining to automatically discover high-quality cue phrases from documents. Experiments show that our proposed model is able to achieve much better performance than strong baselines, and our mined cue phrases are reasonable and effective. Also, this is the first work that investigates the task of topic segmentation for web documents.

Keywords: Topic segmentation · Neural network · Web documents · Sequence mining

1 Introduction

Topic segmentation is a natural language processing (NLP) task, which aims to segment a document into topically similar parts, it is also called text segmentation or discourse segmentation in various scenarios. This level of analysis provides a better understanding about document structure and topic shift, which are helpful information for many NLP tasks such as discourse parsing, dialogue generation etc.

There have been decades of research about topic segmentation, previous work mainly focus on unsupervised approach. TextTiling [12] is one of the most famous and earliest algorithms for topic segmentation. It is based on one simple intuition: lexical cohesion within each topic segment is high, while lexical cohesion between different topic segments is low. Therefore, the core part of TextTiling algorithm is to calculate lexical similarity of adjacent segments and then choose

© Springer International Publishing AG 2016
C.-Y. Lin et al. (Eds.): NLPCC-ICCPOL 2016, LNAI 10102, pp. 177–188, 2016.
DOI: 10.1007/978-3-319-50496-4_15

an appropriate threshold to determine topic boundaries. This algorithm is simple and computationally efficient, however, when annotated corpus is available, it fails to utilize training data and unable to learn an accurate model. Other unsupervised variants of TextTiling algorithm such as C99 [6] and TopicTiling [18] also suffer from this issue.

On the contrary, supervised approach is able to learn more complex and accurate model. As long as training data is sufficient and feature set is good enough, its performance is much better than unsupervised approaches. In this paper, we conduct experiments with conditional random field (CRF) and LSTM, both of them significantly outperform TextTiling algorithm.

For sequence modeling task such as topic segmentation, capturing long distance information is a key issue. Thanks to the gating mechanism in LSTM, it preserves useful information for a long time period. Bidirectional LSTM is a combination of forward LSTM and backward LSTM, therefore it is able to exploit useful features from both sides. Our experiments show that BLSTM consistently beats CRF and LSTM, and achieves best f1-score.

Different from previous work which focus on news or scientific documents, in our work, we conduct text segmentation for web documents. According to our observation, cue phrase is a strong indicator for topic boundary. For example, "第一", "第二" are frequently used to start a new topic. [9] presented a bayesian framework to identify cue phrases automatically. Different from their work, we treat cue phrase identification as a frequent subsequence mining problem, and come up with a variant of *Apriori* algorithm to mine cue phrases from annotated corpus. It turns out that our proposed algorithm is able to precisely locate those cue phrases and therefore boost system performance.

This paper makes three major contributions: 1. To the best of our knowledge, this is the first work that successfully applies neural network model for supervised topic segmentation and achieves promising results; 2. We present a novel algorithm based on frequent subsequence mining to identify cue phrases; 3. For the first time, the possibility of topic segmentation for web documents is examined.

2 Related Work

Due to the lack of large scale high-quality topic segmentation datasets, unsupervised approach is most widely adopted. Two of the early algorithms are TextTiling [12] and C99 [6], both of which are based on the intuition that word distributions differ significantly if there is a transition in topic. TextTiling is more computationally efficient while C99 algorithm shows better performance. Vector space model is used to compute cosine similarity of sentences, but it fails to capture semantic similarity of different words. Later work used Latent Semantic Analysis (LSA) [7] and Latent Dirichlet Allocation (LDA) [16,18] to compute sentence similarity more accurately.

Generative models were also presented to improve performance of topic segmentaion system. Similar to LDA, topics are seen as latent variables and words are seen as visible variables. Hidden Markov Model (HMM) [20] and several variants of LDA [8,14,17] were proposed. Carefully designed generative models outperform lexical similarity based models, however they are usually much more complicated and require efficient inference algorithms.

Supervised approach is also examined when large amount of training data is available. Therein, topic segmentation is formulated as a binary classification task. [10] trained decision tree classifier on a rich set of features such as cue phrases and lexical cohesion. Support Vector Machine (SVM) [11] was also tried on datasets from different domains. Experiment results showed its superiority over unsupervised models.

Evaluation of topic segmentation systems is non-trivial. Classification-based metrics such as precision, recall and f1-score are useful but sometimes too strict. P_k metric was proposed by [2] to alleviate this problem. To calculate P_k, we need a sliding window of fixed length, and check whether the predicted segmentation is consistent with ground truth within this window. Now P_k is the most widely used metric within the literature of topic segmentation. However, P_k metric also has its own problems, WindowDiff (WD) [15] and word error rate based [3] metrics were proposed in later research.

LSTM [13] is a variant of vanilla recurrent neural network (RNN), which aims to solve gradient vanishing/exploding issue during training and allow useful information to flow over a long distance. It has been widely used for sequence modeling tasks such as word segmentation [4], named entity recognition [5] and Part-of-Speech tagging [19] etc.

3 Models

3.1 BLSTM (Bidirectional Long Short Term Memory)

LSTM is a recurrent network with gating mechanism. There are many variants of LSTM unit, here we adopt one widely used architecture with three types of gates: input gate $\mathbf{i}^t$, forget gate $\mathbf{f}^t$ and output gate $\mathbf{o}^t$, t denotes time step. The formula for calculating each gate and memory cell unit are as follows:

$$\mathbf{i}^t = tanh(\mathbf{W}_i\mathbf{x}^t + \mathbf{R}_i\mathbf{y}^{t-1} + \mathbf{b}_i) \tag{1}$$

$$\mathbf{f}^t = tanh(\mathbf{W}_f\mathbf{x}^t + \mathbf{R}_f\mathbf{y}^{t-1} + \mathbf{b}_f) \tag{2}$$

$$\mathbf{o}^t = tanh(\mathbf{W}_o\mathbf{x}^t + \mathbf{R}_o\mathbf{y}^{t-1} + \mathbf{b}_o) \tag{3}$$

$$\mathbf{z}^t = tanh(\mathbf{W}_z\mathbf{x}^t + \mathbf{R}_z\mathbf{y}^{t-1} + \mathbf{b}_z) \tag{4}$$

$$\mathbf{c}^t = \mathbf{i}^t \odot \mathbf{z}^t + \mathbf{f}^t \odot \mathbf{c}^{t-1} \tag{5}$$

$$\mathbf{y}^t = \mathbf{o}^t \odot tanh(\mathbf{c}^t) \tag{6}$$

Here $\mathbf{x}^t \in \mathbb{R}^d$, $\mathbf{y}^t \in \mathbb{R}^d$ are d dimensional input vectors and output vectors. $\mathbf{c}^t$ is the memory cell vector at time step t. $\mathbf{W}_z$, $\mathbf{W}_i$, $\mathbf{W}_f$, $\mathbf{W}_o$ are weight matrices for input. $\mathbf{R}_z$, $\mathbf{R}_i$, $\mathbf{R}_f$, $\mathbf{R}_o$ are weight matrices for output. $\mathbf{b}_z$, $\mathbf{b}_i$, $\mathbf{b}_f$, $\mathbf{b}_o$ are corresponding bias. $tanh$ is used as non-linear activation function.

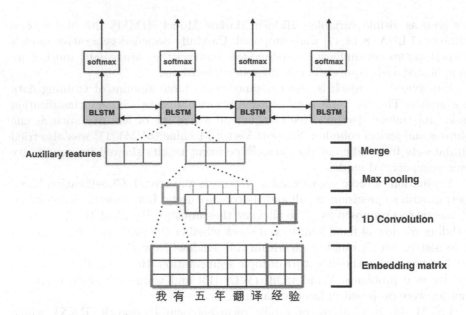

Fig. 1. BLSTM-CNN for topic segmentation. Example text: 我有五年翻译经验 (I have five years of experience as a translator.)

Compared to LSTM, bidirectional LSTM captures information from both directions of a sequence. It is a combination of two independent LSTM with opposite directions: forward LSTM and backward LSTM. The final output vector $\mathbf{y}^t$ is concatenation of these two LSTM.

Below shows BLSTM's updating formula for memory cell $\mathbf{c}^t$, output gate $\mathbf{o}^t$, we omit other gates for simplicity as they are similar.

$$\mathbf{c}_k^t = \mathbf{i}_k^t \odot \mathbf{z}_k^t + \mathbf{f}_k^t \odot \mathbf{c}_k^{t-1}, \ k \in \{f, b\} \tag{7}$$

$$\mathbf{o}_k^t = tanh(\mathbf{W}_o^k \mathbf{x}^t + \mathbf{R}_o^k \mathbf{y}_k^{t-1} + \mathbf{b}_o^k), \ k \in \{f, b\} \tag{8}$$

$$\mathbf{y}_k^t = \mathbf{o}_k^t \odot tanh(\mathbf{c}_k^t), \ k \in \{f, b\} \tag{9}$$

$$\mathbf{y}^t = [\mathbf{y}_f^t, \ \mathbf{y}_b^t] \tag{10}$$

Among those equations, f denotes forward pass layer, b denotes backward pass layer, $\mathbf{y}^t$ is a concatenation of $\mathbf{y}_f^t$, $\mathbf{y}_b^t \in \mathbb{R}^d$ and therefore $\mathbf{y}^t \in \mathbb{R}^{2d}$.

For our classification task, there is a softmax layer over output vectors:

$$\mathbf{P}_t(y|x) = softmax(\mathbf{W}_h \mathbf{y}^t + \mathbf{b}_h) \tag{11}$$

$$\mathbf{Y}_{pred} = argmax \ \mathbf{P}_t(y|x) \tag{12}$$

The final prediction is the label with highest probability $argmax \ \mathbf{P}_t(y|x)$.

3.2 CNN for Paragraph Representation

There are many ways to represent paragraph text, one-hot encoding representation would result extremely sparse feature vector. In this paper, we adopt a popular CNN architecture to represent entire paragraph as a low dimensional dense vector. In other words, CNN serves as a text feature extractor for BLSTM model.

The input to CNN is a word sequence, each word w is mapped to an embedding vector $\mathbf{x}_w$ by matrix-vector product:

$$\mathbf{x}_w = \mathbf{W}^{d \times |V|} \mathbf{v}^w \tag{13}$$

$\mathbf{W}^{d \times |V|}$ is a d dimensional word embedding matrix for entire vocabulary V, $\mathbf{v}^w$ is one-hot vector representation of word w.

The output of embedding layer is a word embedding sequence $\mathbf{x}_{1:n}$.

$$\mathbf{x}_{1:n} = [\mathbf{x}_1, \mathbf{x}_2, \dots, \mathbf{x}_n] \tag{14}$$

Every convolution operation involves applying a filter $\mathbf{v} \in \mathbb{R}^{hd}$ to a window of h words to produce a new feature. For example, a feature f_i is generated from a window of words $\mathbf{x}_{i:i+h-1}$ by

$$f_i = h(\mathbf{v} \cdot \mathbf{x}_{i:i+h-1} + b). \tag{15}$$

$b \in \mathbb{R}$ is a bias term, h is a non-linear transformation function such as $tanh$. This operation is applied to every possible window $\{\mathbf{x}_{1:h}, \mathbf{x}_{2:h+1}, \dots, \mathbf{x}_{n-h+1:n}\}$ to produce a feature map:

$$\mathbf{f} = [f_1, f_2, \dots, f_{n-h+1}], \tag{16}$$

with $\mathbf{f} \in \mathbb{R}^{n-h+1}$. Max-pooling operation applies to the entire feature map and chooses the maximum value as the feature.

$$\hat{f} = \max\{\mathbf{f}\} \tag{17}$$

The overall network architecture is shown in Fig. 1. Parameters of CNN and BLSTM are jointly learned. The final output of CNN is a vector representation of given paragraph.

3.3 Model Learning

We formulate topic segmentation as a binary classification task, and use cross entropy loss function:

$$J = -\frac{1}{N} \sum_{i=1}^{N} (y^* \log y + (1 - y^*) \log(1 - y)) \tag{18}$$

where N represents the size of training set; y^* is the ground truth label, y is model's probability output.

To train our network, we use mini-batch stochastic gradient descent (SGD) with adaptive learning rate computed by *Adadelta* [21], which shows better performance and convergence property.

4   Features

4.1   Frequent Subsequence Mining Based Cue Phrase Identification

When writing articles, people often use cue phrase to start a new topic, such as "首先", "然后", "最后". They are strong indicators for detecting topic boundary. Collecting those cue phrases by hand would be time-consuming. Moreover, cue phrases are often dependent on corpus domain and language. If we transplant our system to a new domain, we have to manually summarize cue phrases all over again.

In this paper, we propose a novel algorithm to automatically discover cue phrases base on frequent subsequence mining. It is a variant of the famous *Apriori* algorithm [1] for frequent itemset mining, with one key difference that itemset is unordered while cue phrase sequence is ordered. The intuition behind our algorithm is that cue phrase sequence usually appear more often at topic boundary than other words.

Algorithm 1. Cue Phrase Sequence Mining Algorithm
Input: Corpus $D = \{$d | d is a document$\}$,
minsup: minimum support to become a frequent subsequence,
maxlen: maximum length of cue phrase sequence
Output: a list of cue phrase sequence $S = \{$ p | p is a cue phrase sequence$\}$

```
 1: function MINE(D, minsup, maxlen)
 2:     C₁ ← count each word w ∈ D
 3:     P₁ ← {w | w.count ≥ minsup}
 4:     S ← {}
 5:     for i ← 2 to maxlen do
 6:         Cᵢ ← CANDIDATE-GEN(Pᵢ₋₁, i - 1)
 7:         for candidate in Cᵢ do
 8:             for each document d ∈ D do
 9:                 if IS-SUBSEQUENCE(d, candidate) then
10:                     candidate.count++
11:         Pᵢ ← {candidate | candidate.count ≥ minsup }
12:     S ← ∪ {P₁, P₂ ... P_maxlen}
13:     return S
 1: function CANDIDATE-GEN(Cᵢ, len)
 2:     candidates ← {}
 3:     for tₐ in Cᵢ do
 4:         for t_b in Cᵢ do
 5:             if tₐ[1:len] == t_b[0:(len - 1)] and CO-OCCURRENCE(tₐ, t_b) ≥ minsup
                then
 6:                 candidates ← candidates ∪ (tₐ[1:len] + t_b[len - 1])
 7:     return candidates
```

Our proposed algorithm is summarized above.

We omit the implementation details of two functions: *IS-SUBSEQUENCE(d, candidate)* and *CO-OCCURRENCE(t_a, t_b)*. *IS-SUBSEQUENCE(d, candidate)* checks whether given *candidate* is a subsequence of given document *d*. We adopt two sequence matching strategies: prefix matching and suffix matching. In prefix matching strategy, a candidate cue phrase *w* matches a paragraph *p* when *w* is a prefix of *p*; Similarly, in suffix matching strategy, a candidate cue phrase *w* matches a paragraph *p* when *w* is a suffix of *p*. *CO-OCCURRENCE(t_a, t_b)* calculates the number of document *d* that both *IS-SUBSEQUENCE(d, t_a)* and *IS-SUBSEQUENCE(d, t_b)* evaluate to *true*.

This is an iterative algorithm, which involves two key steps at each iteration: candidate generation and candidate validation. In candidate generation step, for each pair of length *len* cue phrase sequence t_a and t_b, if the $(len - 1)$-suffix of t_a is equal to $(len - 1)$-prefix of t_b, and their co-occurrence count is no less than *minsup*, then t_a and t_b can be combined into a length $len + 1$ candidate. The co-occurrence constraint is not necessary, but it can greatly reduce the number of candidates. In our experiments, it reduces the number of length-2 candidates from over 20,000 down to less than 300. In candidate validation step, for each *candidate*, the algorithm calculates in how many documents this *candidate* sequence appears, then candidates whose frequency is no less than *minsup* get into the final result set *S*.

The worst time complexity of our proposed algorithm is exponential, however, the number of cue phrases in real dataset is often limited. Our python implementation without any further optimization finishes within 10 s.

Table 1. Examples of cue phrase sequence, "xxx" denotes some other irrelevant words

	1.xxx	一、xxx	工具xxx	xxx介绍
Cue Phrase Sequence	2.xxx	二、xxx	方法xxx	xxx介绍
	3.xxx	三、xxx	注意事项xxx	xxx介绍
	first.xxx	first.xxx	tools xxx	xxx introduction
English Explanation	second.xxx	second.xxx	method xxx	xxx introduction
	third.xxx	third.xxx	precautions xxx	xxx introduction

Some of the cue phrase sequences are listed in Table 1. It is clear that our algorithm is able to find out high quality cue phrases. As expected, people often use number sequence to start a new topic. The last two are due to the large number of tutorial documents on web, and they are much less common in other domains. Handcrafted cue phrase set may very likely miss them. Compared to time-consuming and possibly incomplete manual cue phrase selection process, our algorithm is more accurate, efficient and can be easily adapted to other domains.

4.2   Other Features

Besides cue phrase, here is a list of other features we used in experiments.

1. **Lexical feature.** Paragraph text is encoded as a dense feature vector via CNN model described above.
2. **Part-of-Speech (POS) feature.** The POS tags of words in current paragraph. We perform word segmentation and POS tagging with open source library *jieba*[1], the same is true for other features related to word segmentation.
3. **Length feature.** The number of characters and words in current paragraph, previous paragraph and next paragraph. It also includes the number of paragraph in current document.
4. **Position feature.** Whether current paragraph is the document's first paragraph or last paragraph.
5. **Hyperlink feature.** Whether current paragraph contains text with embedded hyperlink.
6. **Text font feature.** Whether current paragraph contains text with bold or italic font. For web documents, the first paragraph of a new topic often contains such text, they can be useful information.

Many other types of features are also examined, including LDA features and syntactic features, but they show no performance gain, therefore we choose to not list them here.

5   Experiments

5.1   Data and Setup

Our dataset is provided by Baidu[2] and consists of 2951 web documents with human annotated ground truth labels. To the best of our knowledge, this is the largest human annotated topic segmentation dataset. Dataset used in previous research are either much smaller or constructed automatically with the help of some heuristics. Table 2 shows some statistics for our datasets.

Table 2. Statistics for our topic segmentation dataset.

Number of documents	Average number of paragraphs	Average number of topics
2951	15.75	2.33

Dataset is randomly split into training set (70%), validation set (10%), test set (20%). Hyperparameters are chosen via grid search by maximizing f1-score on validation set. Once hyperparameters are fixed, we train on both training set and validation set, then report model's performance on test set.

---

[1] https://github.com/fxsjy/jieba.
[2] Not publicly available for now.

Our implementation of BLSTM is based on open source library *keras*[3]. We use *Adadelta* [21] to compute learning rate. The dimension of memory cell is set to 50, mini-batch size is 16. To combat overfit, we add one dropout layer above BLSTM output, dropout probability is set to 0.5. For CNN, the number of filters is set to 150, the window size is set to 4 for 1D convolution, and the size of word embedding d is set to 32, word embedding matrix $\mathbf{W}^{d \times |V|}$ is initialized with uniform random values from $[-0.5, 0.5]$.

As comparison, we also implemented some other algorithms such as TextTiling, CRF[4]. Similar to BLSTM, hyperparameters are chosen according to validation set.

To have a comprehensive comparison of model's effectiveness, we evaluate on multiple metrics: precision, recall, f1-score and P_k.

5.2 Results

Table 3 shows model's performance with all features, except TextTiling algorithm is unsupervised and doesn't need any feature. Notice that for P_k metric, smaller value means better performance.

Table 3. Performance comparison of different models.

Model	Precision	Recall	F1-score	P_k
TextTiling	0.762	0.448	0.565	0.146
CRF	**0.859**	0.624	0.723	0.133
LSTM-CNN	0.786	0.716	0.750	0.092
BLSTM-CNN	0.829	**0.730**	**0.776**	**0.075**

We can clearly see that supervised models significantly outperform unsupervised TextTiling algorithm on every metric. CRF is a widely used model for sequence labeling, it gets highest precision, while performs much worse than our neural network models on other metrics. LSTM-CNN is a forward LSTM stacking with CNN, all other parameters are same with BLSTM-CNN. Its f1-score is 2.6% lower than BLSTM-CNN, and P_k metric 0.017 higher than BLSTM-CNN. This performance gap implies that being able to capture information from both left and right is helpful to do topic segmentation. BLSTM-CNN achieves the best overall performance, highest recall, highest f1-score and lowest P_k.

To examine the effects of different features, we conduct a series of experiments with BLSTM-CNN model. The results are shown in Table 4. For the mapping relations between arab number and feature name, please refer to Sect. 4.2.

Feature 1 to 4 are called basic features, in the sense that they are shared across documents in all domains, not just web documents. Experiments show

---

[3] https://github.com/fchollet/keras.
[4] https://github.com/tpeng/python-crfsuite.

Table 4. Comparison of BLSTM-CNN performance on different feature set.

Feature set	Precision	Recall	F1-score	P_k
1 + 2 + 3 + 4	0.831	0.666	0.739	0.095
1 + 2 + 3 + 4 + 5	**0.850**	0.669	0.749	0.085
1 + 2 + 3 + 4 + 5 + 6	0.835	0.708	0.767	0.079
1 + 2 + 3 + 4 + 5 + 6 + Cue phrase	0.829	**0.730**	**0.776**	**0.075**

that basic features are already enough to deliver a competitive result. Hyperlink (feature 5), bold and italic text (feature 6) are unique characteristics for web documents. Incorporating these two features results in better performance, f1-score goes up by 2.8% and P_k value goes down by 0.016. Table 4 also shows that our frequent subsequence mining based cue phrase identification algorithm is crucial to further boost system performance.

5.3   Error Analysis

By analyzing bad cases, we find there are two major types of document structure that our model performs poorly: the document with hierarchical topic structure or implicit topic structure.

– **Hierarchical topic structure.** When we formulate topic segmentation as binary classification task, we actually make an implicit assumption that document topics have a linear structure. However, some documents have hierarchical topic structure. Such document contains several major topics, and each major topic contains many subtopics. For example, one document describes how to properly configure a computer, it involves hardware configuration topic and software installation topic. Within software installation topic, it contains many subtopics about how to install different softwares. Our model has trouble with determining the granularity of topics.
– **Implicit topic structure.** Cue phrase is a useful feature to identify topic boundary. However, sometimes people starts a new topic without using any cue phrase, and the lexical distribution between topics has no obvious difference. For example, one document contains two topics: one topic is about positive effects of NATO[5], the other one is about negative effects of NATO. There is a significant lexical overlap between these two topics, and our model fails to recognize the transition of underlying topic.

To handle document with hierarchical topic structure, our model need to have a better understanding of document's global structure, rather than merely focus on local structure; for document with implicit topic structure, more accurate semantic analysis algorithms are needed to detect topic boundary.

---

[5] North Atlantic Treaty Organization.

6   Conclusion and Future Work

In this paper, we propose to use BLSTM stacking with CNN to do topic segmentation of web documents. CNN enables efficient and effective paragraph representation learning, while BLSTM manages to capture and preserve useful information from both directions. Based on the characteristics of web documents, a frequent subsequence mining based cue phrase identification algorithm is presented to identify cue phrases automatically. Experiments show that our BLSTM-CNN model combined with cue phrase feature is able to achieve much better performance than strong baseline models.

For future work, we would like to verify our model's effectiveness on other domains and other languages. Also, other network architectures will be examined to further improve the performance of our topic segmentation system.

Acknowledgements. We thank all the anonymous reviewers for their insightful comments on this paper. This work was partially supported by Baidu-Peking University joint project, and National Natural Science Foundation of China (61273278 and 61572049).

References

1. Agrawal, R., Srikant, R., et al.: Fast algorithms for mining association rules. In: Proceedings of 20th International Conference Very Large Data Bases, VLDB, vol. 1215, pp. 487–499 (1994)
2. Beeferman, D., Berger, A., Lafferty, J.: Statistical models for text segmentation. Mach. Learn. **34**(1–3), 177–210 (1999)
3. Carroll, L.: Evaluating hierarchical discourse segmentation. In: Human Language Technologies: The 2010 Annual Conference of the North American Chapter of the Association for Computational Linguistics, pp. 993–1001. Association for Computational Linguistics (2010)
4. Chen, X., Qiu, X., Zhu, C., Liu, P., Huang, X.: Long short-term memory neural networks for Chinese word segmentation. In: Proceedings of the Conference on Empirical Methods in Natural Language Processing (2015)
5. Chiu, J.P., Nichols, E.: Named entity recognition with bidirectional LSTM-CNNs (2015). arXiv preprint: arXiv:1511.08308
6. Choi, F.Y.: Advances in domain independent linear text segmentation. In: Proceedings of the 1st North American Chapter of the Association for Computational Linguistics Conference, pp. 26–33. Association for Computational Linguistics (2000)
7. Choi, F.Y., Wiemer-Hastings, P., Moore, J.: Latent semantic analysis for text segmentation. In: Proceedings of EMNLP. Citeseer (2001)
8. Du, L., Buntine, W.L., Johnson, M.: Topic segmentation with a structured topic model. In: HLT-NAACL, pp. 190–200 (2013)
9. Eisenstein, J., Barzilay, R.: Bayesian unsupervised topic segmentation. In: Proceedings of the Conference on Empirical Methods in Natural Language Processing, pp. 334–343. Association for Computational Linguistics (2008)
10. Galley, M., McKeown, K., Fosler-Lussier, E., Jing, H.: Discourse segmentation of multi-party conversation. In: Proceedings of the 41st Annual Meeting on Association for Computational Linguistics, vol. 1, pp. 562–569. Association for Computational Linguistics (2003)

11. Georgescul, M., Clark, A., Armstrong, S.: Word distributions for thematic segmentation in a support vector machine approach. In: Proceedings of the Tenth Conference on Computational Natural Language Learning, pp. 101–108. Association for Computational Linguistics (2006)
12. Hearst, M.A.: TextTiling: segmenting text into multi-paragraph subtopic passages. Comput. Linguist. **23**(1), 33–64 (1997)
13. Hochreiter, S., Schmidhuber, J.: Long short-term memory. Neural Comput. **9**(8), 1735–1780 (1997)
14. Jameel, S., Lam, W.: An unsupervised topic segmentation model incorporating word order. In: Proceedings of the 36th International ACM SIGIR Conference on Research and Development in Information Retrieval, pp. 203–212. ACM (2013)
15. Pevzner, L., Hearst, M.A.: A critique and improvement of an evaluation metric for text segmentation. Comput. Linguist. **28**(1), 19–36 (2002)
16. Riedl, M., Biemann, C.: How text segmentation algorithms gain from topic models. In: Proceedings of the 2012 Conference of the North American Chapter of the Association for Computational Linguistics: Human Language Technologies, pp. 553–557. Association for Computational Linguistics (2012)
17. Riedl, M., Biemann, C.: Text segmentation with topic models. J. Lang. Technol. Comput. Linguist. **27**(1), 47–69 (2012)
18. Riedl, M., Biemann, C.: TopicTiling: a text segmentation algorithm based on LDA. In: Proceedings of ACL 2012 Student Research Workshop, pp. 37–42. Association for Computational Linguistics (2012)
19. Wang, P., Qian, Y., Soong, F.K., He, L., Zhao, H.: Part-of-speech tagging with bidirectional long short-term memory recurrent neural network (2015). arXiv preprint: arXiv:1510.06168
20. Yamron, J.P., Carp, I., Gillick, L., Lowe, S., van Mulbregt, P.: A hidden Markov model approach to text segmentation and event tracking. In: Proceedings of the 1998 IEEE International Conference on Acoustics, Speech and Signal Processing, vol. 1, pp. 333–336. IEEE (1998)
21. Zeiler, M.D.: ADADELTA: an adaptive learning rate method (2012). arXiv preprint: arXiv:1212.5701

Multi-task Learning for Gender and Age Prediction on Chinese Microblog

Liang Wang[1], Qi Li[1], Xuan Chen[2], and Sujian Li[1,3(✉)]

[1] Key Laboratory of Computational Linguistics,
Peking University, MOE, Beijing, China
[2] School of Information, Shandong University of Political Science and Law,
Jinan, China
{intfloat,qi.li,lisujian}@pku.edu.cn
[3] Collaborative Innovation Center for Language Ability, Xuzhou, Jiangsu, China
chenx@sdupsl.edu.cn

Abstract. The demographic attributes gender and age play an important role for social media applications. Previous studies on gender and age prediction mostly explore efficient features which are labor intensive. In this paper, we propose to use the multi-task convolutional neural network (MTCNN) model for predicting gender and age simultaneously on Chinese microblog. With MTCNN, we can effectively reduce the burden of feature engineering and explore common and unique representations for both tasks. Experimental results show that our method can significantly outperform the state-of-the-art baselines.

Keywords: Multi-task learning · Social media · Neural network

1 Introduction

Chinese microblog (Weibo), which owns large number of users, has drawn great research interests in recent years. In many cases, some users are unwilling to share their personal information including gender, age, name and profession etc. However, these user attributes are valuable for many applications such as e-commerce, recommendation and burst event detection. Thus, how to recover the missing attributes is a challenging and hot topic in social media research. In this paper, we focus on predicting two important user attributes: gender and age.

Many previous studies have conducted wide investigation on gender prediction and age prediction using textual information on social media. Therein, feature selection is the research focus and some important findings have been concluded. For example, females tend to use more pronouns and emotion words, while males tend to use more technology words and links. Younger people use more alphabetical lengthening, more capitalization of words, more slang words and more Internet acronyms, compared to elders.

As we know, previous work is mainly confined to bag-of-words text representation and feature engineering, a large amount of language processing work is

© Springer International Publishing AG 2016
C.-Y. Lin et al. (Eds.): NLPCC-ICCPOL 2016, LNAI 10102, pp. 189–200, 2016.
DOI: 10.1007/978-3-319-50496-4_16

required, especially when those systems are transplanted to another language. In our work, we aim to predict user gender and age on Weibo and can not completely draw on the experience of prior research due to the immature Chinese language processing tools such as word segmentation and emotion word identification. In such case, we hope to seek a new text representation which is relatively independent of language and appropriate for predicting user gender and age.

The second limitation of previous studies is that they usually treat each attribute prediction task independently. For example, [16] employed a logistic regression model to predict gender, and a linear regression model to predict age. The two regression models were essentially independent and are susceptible to different sets of features. However, in our opinion, with the same text as input, there must exist some underlying connections between two different prediction tasks.

In recent years, convolutional neural network (CNN) has shown great success over simple bag-of-words method for modeling text data [10, 22]. With the considerations above, we adopt CNN to learn word embeddings and useful task-specific features, and further design the multi-task convolutional neural network (MTCNN) to predict user gender and age simultaneously on Weibo, inspired by the work of [7] which achieves success in several NLP tasks. On one hand, the neural network techniques exhibit more expressive power and have shown promising performance, compared to the widely used model such as SVM. On the other hand, the multi-task learning framework can learn several tasks at the same time with the aim of mutual benefit. With the neural networks embedded in the multi-task learning framework, the lower layer implicitly learns the general representation shared by gender prediction and age prediction, and the last layers generate unique efficient features that are task-specific. In addition, to the best of our knowledge, we are the first to jointly predict user gender and age on Chinese social media.

To adapt to the characteristics of Chinese language, we directly make use of Chinese words and characters as input of the MTCNN model, avoiding complex language analysis. Finally, experiments show that our neural network model outperforms the SVM baseline, and multi-task learning further improves performance on both tasks.

2 Multi-task Convolutional Neural Network (MTCNN)

If multiple tasks share the same input or have some underlying connections, it makes sense that the multi-task learning model has the capability to exploit useful information from multiple data sources, and leads to better generalization performance. Within the framework of multi-task learning, there are a whole bunch of different algorithms along with various application scenarios. In this paper, we choose NN-based model, whose key idea is to share lower representation layers and have independent task-specific output layers.

Referring to [7], under the MTCNN model, we define two prediction tasks:

Task 1: Gender Classification
Task 2: Age Regression

The output of task 1 is a probability distribution, while the output of task 2 is a single real value.

2.1   Model Description

Our MTCNN model is designed to consist of one input layer, one embedding layer which maps input word sequence to a word embedding matrix, followed by one convolution layer and one max-pooling layer, finally two independent output layers, as shown in Fig. 1. For gender classification, we use softmax output layer; for age regression, linear output layer is used. Here, we do not use deeper structure, as it requires longer training time and does not show much performance gain in our experiments. The MTCNN model can also be seen as the combination of several independent CNNs with shared parameters.

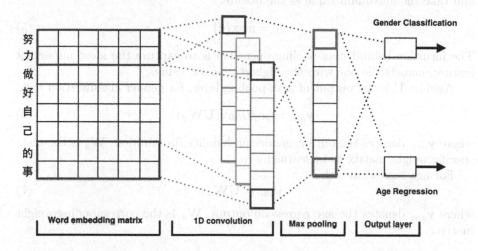

Fig. 1. Multi-task Convolutional Neural Network (MTCNN). Example sentence: 努力做好自己的事(Focus to finish my own business.)

Words are represented by column vectors in an embedding matrix $\mathbf{W}^{d \times |V|}$, where d is a hyperparameter denoting the size of word embedding, $|V|$ is the size of vocabulary. Each column in $\mathbf{W}_i^{d \times |V|} \in \mathbf{R}^d$ corresponds to the embedding of the i-th word in the vocabulary V. A word w is mapped into its embedding $\mathbf{x}_w$ by matrix-vector product:

$$\mathbf{x}_w = \mathbf{W}^{d \times |V|} \mathbf{v}^w \tag{1}$$

where $\mathbf{v}^w$ is a one-hot vector of size $|V|$ which has value 1 at index w and zero in all other positions. The word embedding matrix $\mathbf{W}^{d \times |V|}$ is a parameter to be learned.

The output of embedding layer is a word embedding sequence $\mathbf{x}_{1:n}$, where each row $\mathbf{x}_i$ corresponds to one word.

$$\mathbf{x}_{1:n} = [\mathbf{x}_1, \mathbf{x}_2, \ldots, \mathbf{x}_n] \tag{2}$$

Then comes one convolution layer and one max-pooling layer. A convolution operation involves a filter $\mathbf{v} \in \mathbb{R}^{hd}$, which is applied to a window of h words to produce a new feature. For example, a feature c_i is generated from a window of words $\mathbf{x}_{i:i+h-1}$ by

$$c_i = f(\mathbf{v} \cdot \mathbf{x}_{i:i+h-1} + b). \tag{3}$$

Where $b \in \mathbb{R}$ is a bias term and f is a non-linear transformation function such as $tanh$. This operation is applied to every possible window of words in the sentence $\{\mathbf{x}_{1:h}, \mathbf{x}_{2:h+1}, \ldots, \mathbf{x}_{n-h+1:n}\}$ to produce a feature map:

$$\mathbf{c} = [c_1, c_2, \ldots, c_{n-h+1}], \tag{4}$$

with $\mathbf{c} \in \mathbb{R}^{n-h+1}$. We then apply a max-pooling operation over the feature map and take the maximum value as the feature.

$$\hat{c} = \max\{\mathbf{c}\} \tag{5}$$

The intuition behind max-pooling operation is to capture the most important feature, namely the one with the highest numeric value.

Assume $\mathbf{U}$ is the output of max-pooling layer, for gender classification task,

$$\mathbf{y}_{gen} = softmax(\mathbf{U}\mathbf{W}_g) \tag{6}$$

where $\mathbf{y}_{gen}$ denotes the output gender probability distribution, $\mathbf{W}_g$ is the task-specific weight matrix to be learned.

For age regression task,

$$\mathbf{y}_{age} = \mathbf{U}\mathbf{W}_a \tag{7}$$

where $\mathbf{y}_{age}$ denotes the age regression output, $\mathbf{W}_a$ is the corresponding weight matrix.

2.2   Model Learning

To train MTCNN, we need to define the loss function first. For gender classification task, we use cross entropy error function:

$$J_{gen} = -\frac{1}{N} \sum_{i=1}^{N} \sum_{j}^{n_c} (\mathbf{g}_i^j \log \mathbf{y}_i^j) \tag{8}$$

where N represents the size of training set; n_c is the number of possible classes, which is 2 in this task, male or female; $\mathbf{g}_i^j$ is an indicator function, which evaluates to 1 if ith instance's label is class j, and 0 otherwise; $\mathbf{y}_i^j$ is the output probability distribution.

For age regression task, we use mean square error (MSE) function:

$$J_{age} = -\frac{1}{N} \sum_{i=1}^{N} (\mathbf{y}_i - \mathbf{y}_i^*)^2 \tag{9}$$

where $\mathbf{y}_i$ is a real value provided by model output, $\mathbf{y}_i^*$ is the groundtruth value of user's age.

The overall loss function is a linear combination of above two loss functions:

$$J(\mathbf{W}, \mathbf{W}_{gen}, \mathbf{W}_{age}) = J_{gen} + C J_{age} \tag{10}$$

where C is a hyperparameter to be chosen to balance two loss functions and make sure two tasks achieve best performance at roughly the same time.

We use similar learning procedure with [7]. Instead of using stochastic gradient descent (SGD), we use mini-batch SGD with adaptive learning rate computed by *Adam* algorithm [11], which shows better performance empirically.

More details about our model's learning procedure are shown below:

1. Select the next task.
2. Select next mini-batch of training examples for current task.
3. Update network parameters by backpropagation.
4. Go to step 1, unless validation error no longer decreases.

3 Weibo Data

Weibo[1] is a Chinese social network and microblogging service with more than 300 million monthly active users. The main language that users publish is Chinese, but sometimes they may use some English words. For the purpose of this study, we implement a spider[2] to collect data from Weibo. We remove those users with less than 40 followers as they are likely to be spam users. Verified organizations are also excluded.

Finally, our dataset consists of 263,460 entries of weibo text. 20% is randomly chosen as test set, 10% as validation set, and 70% as training data. All users have public gender information as it's mandatory. The age information is deduced from birthday. Birthdays earlier than 1950-01-01 or equal to 1970-01-01 are filtered. In our dataset, 136,072 entries of weibo have valid birthday information.

Table 1 shows some statistics about our dataset, 53% of users with valid gender and birthday information are female, which is slightly more than male users. Majority of users are young people ranging from 16 to 25 years old.

To gain an intuitive insight about our dataset, we exhibit several most representative words for different groups. We use an open source Chinese word segmentation tool *Jieba*[3] to process the Weibo text and compute the ratio of the

---

[1] http://weibo.com.
[2] https://github.com/intfloat/sina-weibo-crawler.
[3] https://github.com/fxsjy/jieba.

Table 1. Statistics of our dataset with both valid gender and birthday information

	Gender		Age				
	Male	Female	0–15	16–25	26–35	36–45	46+
Count	63069	73003	10760	78417	33052	10832	3011
Percentage	46.3%	53.6%	7.9%	57.6%	24.3%	7.9%	2.2%

segmented words occurring in each group. Table 2 shows the highest-frequency words in each group. The results are consistent with previous studies: females focus more on emotion and entertainment, and males are more interested in technology; Young people love to express their feelings, and elders talk more about serious topics such as finance.

Table 2. Words with highest frequency ratio. (corresponding English explanation in parenthesis)

Age				Gender			
young(≤ 25)	ratio	elder(> 25)	ratio	male	ratio	female	ratio
少女(young girls)	8.92	股市(stock market)	0.47	哥们(brother)	6.71	!!	0.14
cry	8.85	公开(public)	0.76	LIVE	6.29	飞吻(kiss)	0.19
眼泪(tears)	8.22	指数(index)	0.86	乐视(company name)	5.68	公举(princess alias)	0.23
萌(cute)	8.0	博客(blog)	0.93	杀手(killer)	5.58	杨幂(actress name)	0.25

4 Experiments

4.1 Experimental Setup

In our experiment, we configure the hyperparameters of the MTCNN model through grid search by maximizing performance on validation data. Finally, the size of word embedding d is set to 50, the number of filters is 250. We use *Adam* algorithm to compute adaptive learning rate [11], and mini-batch size is fixed to 32. The hyperparameter C is set to 120 to balance two loss functions. Word embedding matrix **W** is initialized with uniform random values from $[-0.5, 0.5]$.

Unlike English, Chinese text has no space to explicitly separate word from characters, word segmentation alone is a difficult task, especially for social media text. It is generally agreed that character-level model suffers less from data sparseness problem, while word-level model can better capture the underlying meaning of text. Therefore, it would be interesting to compare those two different settings. In our experiments, we examine both character-level models and word-level models.

4.2   Baselines

To evaluate our method, three models are used for comparison.

- **Baseline.** For gender classification, baseline model always predicts the majority class, which is female. For age regression, baseline model always outputs the average age of training dataset to minimize MSE.
- **SVM.** We extract unigram features and then train two support vector machine models. One is for gender classification and the other one for age regression.
- **Convolutional Neural Network (CNN).** We build two separate CNN models with same network structure as our proposed MTCNN model, except they don't share any parameters.

The SVM model is implemented using the machine learning tool *sklearn* [17]. The implementation of the neural networks is based on the widely used *theano* library [3]. For the NN-based models CNN and MTCNN, we adopt the same network configuration and hyperparameters.

Text preprocessing is same for all models, we remove characters and words whose frequency is no more than 3, replace consecutive number sequence and url with special symbols. English characters are all converted to lowercase.

4.3   Results

We compare the three baseline models with MTCNN, considering segmented words or characters as the text features. Accuracy and MSE are used as the evaluation metrics. The experimental results are shown in Table 3. From this table, it is clear that segmented words are more appropriate to be features of social media text than Chinese characters. Once the size of available dataset is large enough, the data sparseness is no longer a serious problem.

Table 3. Model comparison

		Gender (Accuracy)	Age (MSE)
Baseline		0.536	80.86
Char-Level	SVM	0.643	71.71
	CNN	0.665	68.63
	MTCNN	**0.687**	**68.17**
Word-Level	SVM	0.670	67.57
	CNN	0.710	61.86
	MTCNN	**0.714**	**59.07**

On the whole, the two neural network models MTCNN and CNN both significantly outperform SVM, as they have the capability of learning useful combination and transformation of raw text features. SVM is elegant, intuitive and often used as state-of-the-art model for user attributes prediction in previous work. However, SVM is basically a linear model, which makes it fail to learn more abstract features. We also tried kernel SVM, however, it shows worse performance and requires longer training time.

Another interesting phenomenon is that our best model's performance is far from perfect. To figure out the reasons, we carried out some preliminary experiments to examine how well human can do in these prediction tasks, results show human can only do slightly better than our best model, if not worse. One reason is the existence of spam users, who just keep publishing ads, and make it almost impossible to discriminate their gender or age, even though we have already applied some rules to exclude spam users when collecting data. Meanwhile, due to the informal expression of Weibo text and some disguise of users, even human fail to precisely locate some strong indicators and know the user's real interests. Similar results on Twitter were given in [16], concluding that gender and age prediction on social media is a difficult task even for human.

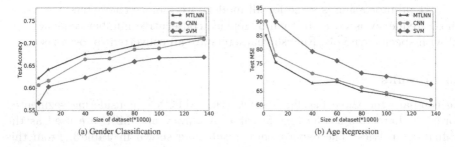

(a) Gender Classification   (b) Age Regression

Fig. 2. Model performance comparison with respect to various size of dataset

To further examine why we adopt the multi-task learning framework, we compare MTCNN and CNN, as they both adopt the NN technique and CNN also achieves comparable performance. Figure 2 shows the performance comparison of the models on gender and age prediction respectively. The curves describe the changing of the test accuracy/MSE with respect to the size of dataset. We can clearly see from those two groups of curves: as more data come in, the accuracy of gender classification steadily increases, and the MSE of age regression steadily decreases. Meanwhile, the MTCNN model consistently beats CNN regardless of dataset size, especially when the dataset is relatively small, and their performances are pretty close when dataset is large enough. As all configurations are exactly the same for them except MTCNN has shared layers, multi-task learning mechanism becomes the only factor that can explain the difference between MTCNN and CNN. That means multi-task learning is able to get better generalization performance and learn more robust features.

4.4 Error Analysis

To have a deeper understanding about our model's behavior and the major difficulty of this task, we choose some representative examples from our dataset, as listed in Table 4. There are two groups: Gender Group and Age Group. Each group consists of three cases.

Table 4. Positive and negative cases by SVM and MTCNN

	Weibo text	Truth	SVM	MTCNN
Gender Cases	绝对，绝对不能再胖了！！ (Can not be fatter any more!!)	Female	Female	Female
	人生最可怕的事，是一边后悔一边生活…… (Most horrible thing in life is to live while regretting)	Female	Male	Female
	脚又扭了心累 (I twisted my ankle again, sad)	Male	Female	Female
Age Cases	保持最近的距离，形成最远的遐想。[位置]西安·西安翻译学院 (Make the distance small, make the dream big, at Xi'an Fanyi University)	19	20.0	20.5
	转发了每日经济新闻的微博...(too long to show) (Retweet from Daily Economic News...)	34	20.0	27.6
	这个炒饭的精髓在于辣白菜，其他的全是次要的 (The key of this fried rice is spicy cabbage, all other stuff are secondary.)	17	39.0	29.8

For the first case in both groups, there are some strong indicators such as "胖(fat)", "！！" and "学院(university)", hence both models easily predict the correct value. For the second case, MTCNN model manages to get better results than SVM, there is no obvious evidence for these two cases, but it is quite likely to infer the correct result. "人生(life)" "后悔 (regret)" are about introspection, female users are usually more likely to do that. "经济(economic)" "新闻(news)" are serious topics, elder businessman are generally more interested to economic news than young students. For the third case, both of our models perform poorly, "脚又扭(twisted my ankle again)" is simply a fact and has very little to do with user's gender or age. It seems that our models think females get their ankles twisted more often. "炒饭(fried rice)" "辣白菜(spicy cabbage)" are all about cooking, it is even surprising to me that a 17-year-old would be interested to cooking.

In conclusion, to get cases like second one correct, our model needs to have a good understanding of given text's semantics, which might need complex language inference process. Cases like third one partly explains the inherent difficulty of this task, it is impossible to get the right answer if there is contradictory information or no relevant information at all.

5 Related Work

Relationship between gender and language has been studied for a long time. One major aspect is to apply machine learning algorithms to automatically classify gender in various context, including twitter [1,4,8,9], email, blog [14], formal document [12] etc. Studies show that significant difference does exist between male and female, for example, female tend to use more emoticons, while male tend to use more technology and political words. Another aspect is to model gender as a social variable rather than biological variable [2], study reveals that social gender and biological gender are not always consistent, which actually sets an upper bound for performance of machine learning system.

Age prediction is formulated as classification or regression problem in different scenarios. Different datasets choose different threshold to convert age into discrete variables, then classifiers including SVM [20], maximum entropy model [21] and decision tree [18] are trained to do age classification. Common scenarios include twitter [13,20], blog [15], conversation [15,19]. There are also some work that treat age as continuous variable [15], and formulate age prediction as a regression problem.

[16] conducted an experiment showing gender and age prediction are hard tasks for English text. No similar experiment has been done for Chinese. For user attributes prediction in non-English context, [6] examined French, Indonesian, Turkish and Japanese text. Results showed that accuracy for Japanese is much lower than other languages. Note that Japanese and Chinese are very similar languages, therefore we expect this is a challenging task for Chinese, too.

Multi-task learning framework includes a large set of algorithms in machine learning literature. In this paper, we only focus on one specific form of multi-task learning by sharing lower layers in neural network [5]. Multi-task learning neural network can be used to learn robust features and help to deal with limited training data problem. It has shown promising performance in many NLP tasks such as part of speech tagging, semantic role labeling [7] and chunking. CNN is a widely used model in computer vision, most state-of-the-art image recognition models involve some variants of CNN. Recently, CNN has been successfully applied to NLP tasks, such as sentence classification [10], sentiment analysis [22] etc.

6   Conclusion and Future Work

In this paper, we propose to use the MTCNN model for joint gender and age prediction on Chinese microblogs. With Chinese word sequence as input, our method is free from complex text analysis and able to seek the common and unique representations useful for both tasks. Experiments show that our method achieves much better performance than SVM and beats CNN by large margin when the size of dataset is relatively small. Compared to similar work on English tweets, it also shows that user attributes prediction task is harder for Chinese text.

There has been growing interests in NLP community to do text representation via recurrent neural network (RNN), our preliminary attempts show relatively poor performance if we replace CNN with RNN. In the future work, we would like to examine the feasibility of RNN for social media user attributes prediction. Also, we will further verify the MTCNN model on other languages and test our model on predicting more user attributes.

Acknowledgements. We thank all the anonymous reviewers for their insightful comments on this paper. This work was partially supported by National Natural Science Foundation of China (61273278 and 61572049).

References

1. Alowibdi, J.S., Buy, U.A., Yu, P.: Language independent gender classification on Twitter. In: 2013 IEEE/ACM International Conference on Advances in Social Networks Analysis and Mining (ASONAM), pp. 739–743. IEEE (2013)
2. Bamman, D., Eisenstein, J., Schnoebelen, T.: Gender identity and lexical variation in social media. J. Sociolinguist. **18**(2), 135–160 (2014)
3. Bergstra, J., Breuleux, O., Bastien, F., Lamblin, P., Pascanu, R., Desjardins, G., Turian, J., Warde-Farley, D., Bengio, Y.: Theano: a CPU and GPU math expression compiler. In: Proceedings of the Python for scientific computing conference (SciPy), Austin, TX, vol. 4, p. 3 (2010)
4. Burger, J.D., Henderson, J., Kim, G., Zarrella, G.: Discriminating gender on Twitter. In: Proceedings of the Conference on Empirical Methods in Natural Language Processing, pp. 1301–1309. Association for Computational Linguistics (2011)
5. Caruana, R.: Multitask learning. Mach. Learn. **28**(1), 41–75 (1997)
6. Ciot, M., Sonderegger, M., Ruths, D.: Gender inference of Twitter users in Non-English contexts. In: EMNLP, pp. 1136–1145 (2013)
7. Collobert, R., Weston, J.: A unified architecture for natural language processing: deep neural networks with multitask learning. In: Proceedings of the 25th International Conference on Machine Learning, pp. 160–167. ACM (2008)
8. Culotta, A., Kumar, N.R., Cutler, J.: Predicting the demographics of Twitter users from website traffic data. In: AAAI, pp. 72–78 (2015)
9. Jaech, A., Ostendorf, M.: What your username says about you (2015). arXiv preprint: arXiv:1507.02045
10. Kim, Y.: Convolutional neural networks for sentence classification (2014). arXiv preprint: arXiv:1408.5882
11. Kingma, D., Ba, J.: Adam: a method for stochastic optimization (2014). arXiv preprint: arXiv:1412.6980
12. Koppel, M., Argamon, S., Shimoni, A.R.: Automatically categorizing written texts by author gender. Lit. Linguist. Comput. **17**(4), 401–412 (2002)
13. Mislove, A., Lehmann, S., Ahn, Y.Y., Onnela, J.P., Rosenquist, J.N.: Understanding the demographics of Twitter users. In: 5th ICWSM 2011 (2011)
14. Mukherjee, A., Liu, B.: Improving gender classification of blog authors. In: Proceedings of the 2010 Conference on Empirical Methods in Natural Language Processing, pp. 207–217. Association for Computational Linguistics (2010)
15. Nguyen, D., Smith, N.A., Rosé, C.P.: Author age prediction from text using linear regression. In: Proceedings of the 5th ACL-HLT Workshop on Language Technology for Cultural Heritage, Social Sciences, and Humanities, pp. 115–123. Association for Computational Linguistics (2011)
16. Nguyen, D.P., Trieschnigg, R., Doğruöz, A., Gravel, R., Theune, M., Meder, T., de Jong, F.: Why gender and age prediction from tweets is hard: lessons from a crowdsourcing experiment. Association for Computational Linguistics (2014)
17. Pedregosa, F., Varoquaux, G., Gramfort, A., Michel, V., Thirion, B., Grisel, O., Blondel, M., Prettenhofer, P., Weiss, R., Dubourg, V., et al.: Scikit-learn: machine learning in python. J. Mach. Learn. Res. **12**, 2825–2830 (2011)

18. Pennacchiotti, M., Popescu, A.M.: A machine learning approach to Twitter user classification. ICWSM **11**(1), 281–288 (2011)
19. Pennebaker, J.W., Stone, L.D.: Words of wisdom: language use over the life span. J. Pers. Soc. Psychol. **85**(2), 291 (2003)
20. Rao, D., Yarowsky, D., Shreevats, A., Gupta, M.: Classifying latent user attributes in Twitter. In: Proceedings of the 2nd International Workshop on Search and Mining User-Generated Contents, pp. 37–44. ACM (2010)
21. Sarawgi, R., Gajulapalli, K., Choi, Y.: Gender attribution: tracing stylometric evidence beyond topic and genre. In: Proceedings of the Fifteenth Conference on Computational Natural Language Learning, pp. 78–86. Association for Computational Linguistics (2011)
22. Zhang, X., LeCun, Y.: Text understanding from scratch (2015). arXiv preprint: arXiv:1502.01710

Dropout Non-negative Matrix Factorization for Independent Feature Learning

Zhicheng He[1,2], Jie Liu[1,2](✉), Caihua Liu[1,2], Yuan Wang[1,2], Airu Yin[1,2], and Yalou Huang[1,2]

[1] College of Computer and Control Engineering,
Nankai University, Tianjin, China
{hezhicheng,liucaihua,yayaniuzi23}@mail.nankai.edu.cn,
{jliu,yinar,ylhuang}@nankai.edu.cn
[2] College of Software, Nankai University, Tianjin, China

Abstract. Non-negative Matrix Factorization (NMF) can learn interpretable parts-based representations of natural data, and is widely applied in data mining and machine learning area. However, NMF does not always achieve good performances as the non-negative constraint leads learned features to be non-orthogonal and overlap in semantics. How to improve the semantic independence of latent features without decreasing the interpretability of NMF is still an open research problem. In this paper, we put forward dropout NMF and its extension sequential NMF to enhance the semantic independence of NMF. Dropout NMF prevents the co-adaption of latent features to reduce ambiguity while sequential NMF can further promote the independence of individual latent features. The proposed algorithms are different from traditional regularized and weighted methods, because they require no prior knowledge and bring in no extra constraints or transformations. Extensive experiments on document clustering show that our algorithms outperform baseline methods and can be seamlessly applied to NMF based models.

Keywords: Non-negative Matrix Factorization · Dropout NMF · Sequential NMF · Independent feature learning

1 Introduction

Non-negative Matrix Factorization (NMF) is a widely employed multivariate analysis and latent feature learning method in machine learning. NMF use non-negative constraint to take the place of conventional orthogonal constraint in matrix factorization models, and is more flexible and easier to implement in practice [1, 2].

Suppose the input sample size is N and each observation consists of M variables, a data matrix $\mathbf{X} \in R_+^{M \times N}$ is built and decomposed as $\mathbf{X} = \mathbf{UV}$, where $\mathbf{U} \in R_+^{M \times K}$ and $\mathbf{V} \in R_+^{K \times N}$ are base and coefficient matrix respectively and K is the number of latent features. Usually, we have $K \ll \min(M, N)$ for rank reduction and the compact representation $\mathbf{v}_i \in R_+^K$ gives original data vector $\mathbf{x}_i \in R_+^M$ a parts-based representation by allowing additive combination of base vectors.

© Springer International Publishing AG 2016
C.-Y. Lin et al. (Eds.): NLPCC-ICCPOL 2016, LNAI 10102, pp. 201–212, 2016.
DOI: 10.1007/978-3-319-50496-4_17

However, latent features learned in NMF often overlap in semantics as orthogonality is not required. Besides, the local optimum problem is unsolved since existing optimization algorithms are all incapable of finding a global optimum [3–5]. Many researchers have worked out various improved methods to pick out a better-to-fit solution to NMF, which can be roughly divided into regularized NMF, weighted NMF and others. Regularized NMF use task specific regularization terms to construct loss functions [6–11]. While weighted NMF assigns weights to individual observations in loss functions according to prior knowledge [12, 13]. Or in other occasions, multiple matrix factorization [14], matrix tri-factorization [15], and tensor factorization [16] are adopted for multiple kinds of interconnected data sources. However, all methods mentioned above require prior knowledge or task specific information for those additional terms. While those supplementary information is not always available in practice.

In this paper, we formulize NMF from a linear reconstruction perspective and propose dropout to improve the independent feature learning ability of NMF by breaking the correlations between latent features. Thus the semantic information in latent features are more definite and the representations in latent space are more discriminative. Based on dropout NMF, we further propose sequential NMF that enforces independent learning of individual features and reduces ambiguity in semantics. We compare our methods to several baseline NMF models on document clustering and use a real-world case to demonstrate how our methods distinguish semantically related topics. The main contributions of our work can be summarized as follows:

- Novel dropout NMF and sequential NMF that can improve NMF by preventing feature co-adaption without additional terms or transformations are proposed.
- The proposed methods have good extensibility and applicability to existing NMF based frameworks as detailed in experiments.
- The proposed methods show a comparable computational complexity to standard NMF algorithm.

The rest of this paper is organized as follows. In Sect. 2, we discuss related work. Section 3 introduces our algorithms. Experimental results on clustering lay in Sect. 4. Finally, Sect. 5 concludes our work.

2 Related Work

NMF is an active research topic in machine learning and data mining community for its innate interpretability. Research efforts have been made to improve NMF from various perspectives, like regularized NMF [6–11] and weighted NMF [12, 13]. Regularization terms in NMF are usually based on task specific assumptions and prior knowledge. The most common regularized NMF is sparse NMF that assumes sparse representations to be more clear and appropriate, which is typically measured via L_1 norm [6, 7], and a new sparseness measure based on the mixture of L_1 and L_2 norms is put forward in [8]. Graph and relation regularized NMFs achieve good performances by preserving local structures and relationships with low rank approximation of data [9–11]. While weighted NMFs are popular in collaborative filtering and clustering tasks as they incorporate prior knowledge into loss function according to connections of instances [12, 13]. Other than regularized and weighted NMF, multiple matrix factorization [14], matrix tri-factorization [15], and tensor factorization [16] are proposed for tasks with complicated and heterogeneous information sources.

First proposed in deep neural networks, dropout prevents the co-adaption of hidden units by randomly omitting hidden units in training [17, 18] and can be considered as a regularization method. Since the stationary co-occurrence is broken, hidden units can still learn from others but with less dependence. Another dropout strategy is omitting the connections between hidden units, which can also help improve the performance [19]. A nested dropout algorithm is put forward in [20] to learn ordered representations of data, in which the information contained in latent features decays along with the index. Fast dropout training [21] is conducted by integrating a Gaussian approximation of the objective function. Wager S et al. justified the equivalence of dropout and L_2 regularization in generalized linear models [22]. And an adaptive dropout method is proposed in an expectation perspective of after-dropout feature detectors [23]. Inspired by these, we propose a novel dropout for NMF based models that works by changing the update process of latent features instead of omitting them.

In the following section, we find that NMF can be analogized to linear neural networks and improved with dropout strategy naturally. Hence we incorporate dropout into NMF and NMF based methods. Moreover, sequential algorithm is proposed as extension to dropout NMF to further improve feature independence.

3 Methodology

NMF focuses on decomposing the input non-negative data matrix into non-negative base and coefficient matrices. Formula description of NMF is shown in Eq. (1):

$$L = D(\mathbf{X} \,|\, \mathbf{UV}), \ s.t. \ \mathbf{U} \in R_+^{M \times K}, \ \mathbf{V} \in R_+^{K \times N}, \tag{1}$$

$D(\cdot|\cdot)$ measures the loss of information between $\mathbf{X}$ and its reconstruction $\mathbf{UV}$. Squared Euclidean distance and generalized Kullback-Leibler divergence are the most common $D(\cdot|\cdot)$ function in practice [2]. The former gives a quadratic loss function and the latter yields a good probabilistic explanation. In this paper, we adopt the squared Euclidean distance loss function:

$$L = ||\mathbf{X} - \mathbf{UV}||_2^2 = tr(\mathbf{X}^T\mathbf{X}) - 2tr(\mathbf{X}^T\mathbf{UV}) + tr(\mathbf{V}^T\mathbf{U}^T\mathbf{UV}), \tag{2}$$

$|| \cdot ||_2^2$ is the squared L_2 norm and $tr(\cdot)$ represents the trace of matrix. The multiplicative update rules of gradient descent algorithm are shown as follows:

$$u_{mk} \leftarrow u_{mk} \frac{(\mathbf{XV}^T)_{mk}}{(\mathbf{UVV}^T)_{mk}}, \ v_{kn} \leftarrow v_{kn} \frac{(\mathbf{U}^T\mathbf{X})_{kn}}{(\mathbf{U}^T\mathbf{UV})_{kn}}. \tag{3}$$

3.1   NMF as a Linear Neural Network

NMF can be formulated as a linear neural network as the input $\mathbf{x}_i$ is represented by a linear combination of base vectors in $\mathbf{U}$:

$$\mathbf{x}_i = \mathbf{U}\mathbf{v}_i = \sum_k v_{ki}\mathbf{u}_k. \qquad (4)$$

For intuitive understanding, we visualize the reconstruction process in Fig. 1. The left half of Fig. 1 is the conventional notation of NMF and matrices are disassembled into vectors to figure out how data vectors are rebuilt with linear combinations in the right half. This is similar to a linear neural network, where matrix $\mathbf{V}$ serves as full-connect coefficients between layers and $\{\mathbf{u}_k\}_{k=1:K}$ are feature detectors. Overfitting happens when the feature detectors strike a balance at a saddle point during optimization process.

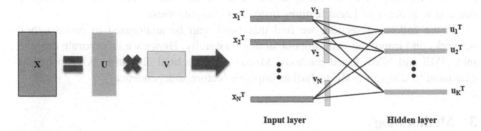

Input layer   **Hidden layer**

Fig. 1.   NMF from the reconstruction perspective.

3.2   Dropout and Sequential NMF

The gradient of loss function L in Eq. (2) to the k-th latent feature is a function of all K latent features:

$$\partial L/\partial \mathbf{u}_k = -2(\mathbf{X}\mathbf{V}^T)_k - 2\sum_{k'}(\mathbf{V}\mathbf{V}^T)_{k'k}\mathbf{u}_{k'} = g_k(\mathbf{u}_1,\ldots,\mathbf{u}_k). \qquad (5)$$

In other words, when we update $\mathbf{u}_k$ in any gradient descent based algorithm, $\mathbf{u}_k$ is learnt from all other latent features:

$$\mathbf{u}_k \leftarrow \mathbf{u}_k - \mathbf{\Pi}_k g_k(\mathbf{u}_1,\ldots,\mathbf{u}_k), \qquad (6)$$

$\mathbf{\Pi}_k$ is the diagonal learning rate matrix for $\mathbf{u}_k$. This innate correlation between latent features influences the optimization process and increases the difficulty of minimizing L, unfortunately it cannot be eliminated. Traditional NMF variants, like sparse NMF [6, 7] and weighted NMF [12, 13], try to find a better-to-fit solution with additional constraints and transformations, as Fig. 2 shows. Sparse NMF acquires sparseness in $\mathbf{u}_k$ or $\mathbf{v}_i$ and weighted NMF transfers $\mathbf{x}_i$ into $w(\mathbf{x}_i)$. However, the proposed dropout NMF tries to reduce the influence of correlations between latent features.

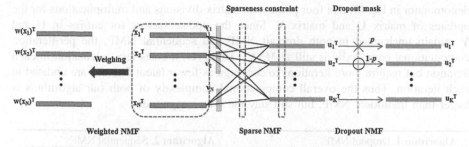

Fig. 2. Illustration and comparison of different NMF based algorithms.

Since latent features are correlated in NMF, co-adaption is a state that the updates of $\{\mathbf{u}_k\}_{k=1:K}$ stop at a saddle point, where L can still be further optimized until it reaches the max iteration. This happens because $\{\mathbf{u}_k\}_{k=1:K}$ have achieved a balance according to their correlations during the past iterations. Researchers tried to avoid co-adaption by conducting many separate NMFs on the same dataset with different initializations or initialization strategies, which are computationally expensive [4]. Therefore, we propose dropout NMF to randomly conduct a huge number of different NMFs in a reasonable time. In each iteration, latent features will be randomly dropped out with constant drop probability $p \in [0, 1]$, and $(1 - p) \times K$ latent features are expected to be held. However, if $\mathbf{u}_k$ is completely removed in an iteration, the reconstruction of all observations will lack a corresponding component and gradients of $\mathbf{u}_{k' \neq k}$ will be incorrect. To avoid such a situation, dropout takes place after the calculation of gradients but before the updates of latent features by setting the learning rate $\mathbf{\Pi}_k$ to $\mathbf{0}$:

$$\mathbf{u}_k \xleftarrow{p} \begin{cases} \mathbf{u}_k - \mathbf{\Pi}_k g_k(\mathbf{u}_1, \ldots, \mathbf{u}_k) & \textit{dropped} \text{ out} \\ \mathbf{u}_k & \textit{undropped} \text{ out} \end{cases} \tag{7}$$

The after-dropout feature set, *undroppedSet* in Algorithm 1 is required to have at least one latent feature to avoid void iterations.

When $p \to 0$, dropout NMF will degenerate to original NMF. However, there is a high probability only one latent feature will be updated if $p \to 1$. In such an extreme case, $\mathbf{u}_k$ will be independently updated and the influence of correlations will be reduced to the least extent. However, the update process will be rather randomized, since few latent features are kept through dropout. In order to achieve a controllable and stable optimization process, we rearrange the update order of latent features and propose sequential NMF in Algorithm 2. Thus latent features are sequentially updated until convergence, just like a special case when $p \to 1$ in dropout NMF but with more deterministic orders.

3.3 Complexity Analysis

The multiplicative update algorithm has a per-iteration computational complexity of $O(MNK)$ [2], which consists of six matrix multiplications for those numerators and denominator in Eq. (3) and four point-wise matrix divisions and multiplications for the updates of matrix $\mathbf{U}$ and matrix $\mathbf{V}$. Since the update factors for entries in $\mathbf{U}$ and $\mathbf{V}$ remain unchanged in both dropout NMF and sequential NMF, the per-iteration computational complexity is still $O(MNK)$. However, it costs less calculation in each iteration but require more iterations to converge as fewer latent features are updated in each iteration. Thus the overall computational complexity of both our algorithms is larger than traditional NMF, but still stay the same magnitude.

Algorithm 1. Dropout NMF	**Algorithm 2**. Sequential NMF
Input: $\mathbf{X}$, #feature K, dropout probability p	Input: $\mathbf{X}$, #feature K
Output: $\mathbf{U}$, $\mathbf{V}$	Output: $\mathbf{U}$, $\mathbf{V}$
1: Random Initialization of $\mathbf{U}$ and $\mathbf{V}$	1: Random Initialization of $\mathbf{U}$ and $\mathbf{V}$
2: **for** t = 1 → *maxIteration* **do**	2: **for** k = 1 → K **do**
3: *undroppedSet* = *dropout*(K, p)	3: **for** t = 1 → *maxIteration* **do**
4: **for** $k \in$ *undroppedSet* **do**	4: Update $\mathbf{u}_k$ as in Equation (3)
5: Update $\mathbf{u}_k$ as in Equation (3)	5: Update $\mathbf{V}$ as in Equation (3)
6: **end for**	6: **if** Converge **then**
7: Update $\mathbf{V}$ as in Equation (3)	7: **break**
8: **if** Converge **then**	8: **end if**
9: **break**	9: **end for**
10: **end if**	10: **end for**
11: **end for**	

4   Experimental Results

Document clustering is the typical scenario for latent semantic representation of a document corpus, where NMF is a classical solution [9, 10]. Since latent features extracted from a document corpus can be understood as semantic topics, clustering is conducted according to the vector-based representations in latent space.

4.1   Datasets

Two corpora are applied to evaluate the proposed methods. The first one is NIST Topic Detection and Tracking (TDT2) corpus [24] from 6 news sources published in 1998. It consists of 11,201 pieces of news from 96 topics, and each topic is a publicly concerned event. We remove documents about multiple topics and preserve only the largest thirty topics. The processed dataset contains 9,394 documents and 36,093 different words.

The second corpus is 20 Newsgroups [25], which is a collection of about 20,000 news documents, partitioned into 20 different groups. It was originally collected by Lang Ken and contains 18,662 documents and only 1,359 high frequent words after preprocess. Unlike TDT2, the news groups are not specific issues but semantically related subjects and are further classified into 6 general categories. Detailed statistics about these 2 datasets are in Table 1.

Table 1. Statistics of datasets.

Statistics	TDT2	20 Newsgroups
# documents	9394	19662
# words	36093	1359
# topics	30	20
Max. #documents in topic	1844	4817
Min. #documents in topic	52	950
Med. #documents in topic	131	3923
Avg. #documents in topic	313	3100

4.2 Experimental Settings

Compared Algorithms. We compare dropout NMF and sequential NMF to traditional NMF [2], sparse NMF (SNMF) [6] and normalized cut weighted NMF (NCWNMF) [13]. L_1 norm of V is used in SNMF to get sparse representations of the input documents. While relations among input documents are used to conduct a transform on X in NCWNMF. To verify the universality and extensibility of our algorithms, we also implement the dropout and sequential versions of SNMF and NCWNMF.

Evaluation Metrics. As document x_i is represented by v_i in latent space, we set $l_i = \arg_k \max(v_{ki})$ to be the cluster label of x_i. Accuracy (AC) and normalized mutual information (NMI) are used to evaluate the clustering performance. Suppose a_i is the original topic label of x_i, AC is calculated as:

$$AC = \sum_{i=1}^{N} \delta(a_i, map(l_i))/N, \ map(l) = \arg_k \max(|\{x_i \mid l_i = l, a_i = k\}|), \quad (8)$$

where $map(\cdot)$ maps cluster label to corresponding topic label as described above, and $\delta(\cdot, \cdot)$ checks the equivalence. Mutual information (MI) measures how clusters are divided:

$$MI(C, C') = \sum_{c_i \in C, c_j \in C'} p(c_i, c_j)(\log_2 p(c_i, c_j) - \log_2 p(c_i) - \log_2 p(c_j)), \quad (9)$$

C and C' are two different clustering of the same sample set, $p(c_i)$ and $p(c_j)$ denote the probability that an arbitrarily selected document belongs to the i-th cluster in C and the j-th cluster in C' respectively, and $p(c_i, c_j)$ is the joint probability. Since $MI(C, C')$ is less than the entropy of C and C' we normalize $MI(C, C')$ for intuitive understanding: $NMI(C, C') = MI(C, C')/\max(H(C), H(C'))$, $H(\cdot)$ denotes entropy of a division.

Parameter Settings. After grid search on TDT2, the parameter p for dropout NMF is set to 0.5, and the balance parameter of regularization term for SNMF is set to 10. To verify the performances on different data sizes, K is set to {5, 10, 15, 20, 25, 30} respectively. To eliminate noise, we randomly select 20 different subsets of documents with K topics from corpus when $K < 30$. Clustering is evaluated by the average performance on those subsets. As to 20 Newsgroups dataset, we use the whole dataset for clustering. K is set to 200 for a fine grained understanding of the overlapping topics,

208   Z. He et al.

and documents are mapped into the 6 general topics as in Eq. (8). Other parameters of 20 Newsgroups dataset are the same as those in TDT2.

4.3   Clustering Results

Tables 2 and 3 show the comparisons of three baseline methods with their dropout and sequential versions on TDT2 evaluated by AC and NMI respectively. We use seq to denote sequential for short. The best performances in three versions of methods are boldfaced, and the global optimums are underlined. It shows that dropout and sequential version methods perform better than conventional methods regardless of K. it demonstrates the effectiveness of preventing the co-adaption of latent features. Dropout NMF and sequential NMF achieve better results than SNMF, while only sequential NMF performs better than NCWNMF. However, the best results of different K are achieved by sequential NCWNMF, and it indicates the extensibility and universal applicability of the proposed sequential technique. Besides, the overall performances decrease with K because a larger dataset with more topics are more difficult for clustering.

The results on 20 Newsgroups are listed in Table 4. Similar to TDT2, performances of both dropout and sequential algorithms are better than original algorithms, and the best results are achieved by sequential NCWNMF. NCWNMF performs worst on 20 Newsgroups. This leads to the suspicion that the weighing procedure is influenced by the roughly processed vocabulary, but sequential NCWNMF overcomes this obstacle.

Table 2. The AC of clustering on TDT2.

K	NMF	Dropout NMF	Seq NMF	SNMF	Dropout SNMF	Seq SNMF	NCW NMF	Dropout NCWNMF	Seq NCWNMF
5	0.895	0.924	**0.954**	0.865	**0.929**	0.870	<u>**0.971**</u>	0.969	**0.971**
10	0.842	0.849	**0.924**	0.844	0.868	**0.915**	0.914	0.921	<u>**0.951**</u>
15	0.803	0.815	**0.892**	0.804	0.809	**0.885**	0.879	0.884	<u>**0.931**</u>
20	0.783	0.805	**0.855**	0.784	0.795	**0.859**	0.848	0.867	<u>**0.906**</u>
25	0.762	0.786	**0.834**	0.768	0.771	**0.826**	0.821	0.838	<u>**0.879**</u>
30	0.733	0.750	**0.810**	0.755	0.760	**0.789**	0.812	0.816	<u>**0.869**</u>
Avg.	0.803	0.822	**0.878**	0.803	0.822	**0.857**	0.874	0.883	<u>**0.918**</u>

Table 3. The NMI of clustering on TDT2.

K	NMF	Dropout NMF	Seq NMF	SNMF	Dropout SNMF	Seq SNMF	NCW NMF	Dropout NCWNMF	Seq NCWNMF
5	0.763	0.804	**0.877**	0.699	**0.822**	0.742	0.914	0.903	<u>**0.921**</u>
10	0.718	0.729	**0.855**	0.717	0.757	**0.826**	0.839	0.845	<u>**0.903**</u>
15	0.673	0.679	**0.818**	0.671	0.676	**0.797**	0.797	0.805	<u>**0.881**</u>
20	0.655	0.666	**0.773**	0.647	0.650	**0.761**	0.760	0.789	<u>**0.848**</u>
25	0.657	0.673	**0.762**	0.649	0.669	**0.731**	0.749	0.767	<u>**0.830**</u>
30	0.608	0.617	**0.747**	0.645	0.643	**0.699**	0.741	0.754	<u>**0.832**</u>
Avg.	0.679	0.695	**0.805**	0.671	0.703	**0.759**	0.800	0.811	<u>**0.869**</u>

Table 4. Clustering performances on 20 Newsgroups.

	NMF	Dropout NMF	Seq NMF	SNMF	Dropout SNMF	Seq SNMF	NCW NMF	Dropout NCWNMF	Seq NCWNMF
AC	0.628	0.631	**0.633**	0.614	**0.629**	0.628	0.589	0.621	**0.635**
NMI	0.288	0.291	**0.294**	0.273	**0.288**	**0.288**	0.249	0.290	**0.297**

4.4 Parameter Selection and Convergence Analysis

Figure 3(a) shows the convergence curves of dropout NMF on TDT2 dataset with $K = 30$, when p is set to $\{0.1, 0.3, 0.5, 0.7, 0.9\}$ respectively. Curves are drawn according to clustering AC along with the increase of iteration number. It can be seen that smaller p achieves better performances when iteration number is fewer than 100. This is because that more latent features are updated in each iteration, and the accumulated effect leads to a better performance. The AC curves grow gradually after iteration number exceeds 100, especially when $p \geq 0.5$. Considering both clustering performance and time consumption, we set p to 0.5 as mentioned above.

We also compare the convergence curves of our algorithms with baselines on TDT2 in Fig. 3(b), and K is also set to 30. The overall trend is similar to Fig. 3(a), and all methods tend to converge within 100 iterations. The AC curve of sequential NMF does not constantly grow with the iteration number. We can see a sharp vibrate when iteration number is around 50. This is partially because that the iteration of sequential NMF is set for each latent feature respectively. Thus a small change in the update of each latent feature will accumulate to a vibrate. We also find that the performance of sequential NMF is much better than dropout NMF with $p = 0.9$, for that sequential NMF has a more deterministic update process.

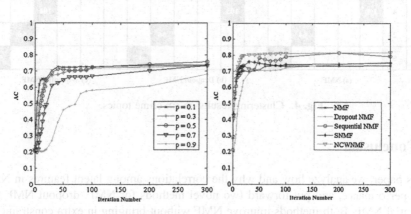

Fig. 3. Convergence curves on TDT2.

4.5 Case Study

To a better understanding of how different algorithms distinguish semantically related topics, we pick out six publicly concerned crime topics from TDT2, and compare the clustering results with original topics on NMF, dropout NMF and sequential NMF. Since legal terminologies and words about crimes are frequent in all six topics, algorithms must detect out the core differences of these topics. The six criminal topics are, (1) Middle school shooting near Jonesboro, (2) Sergeant Major Gene McKinney is court martialed, (3) Theodore John "Ted" Kaczynski, the "Unabomber", (4) Eric Rudolph, the Olympic Park Bomber, (5) James Earl Ray, assassin of Martin Luther King, died of disease in prison, and (6) The first woman, Karla Faye Tucker, to be executed in America since 1984.

Results are shown in Fig. 4, the rows and columns of confusion matrices correspond to the original topics and predicted cluster I.D.s respectively, and an entry tells how many documents from row-indicated topic are divided into the column-indicated cluster. Dropout NMF performs slightly better than NMF, and sequential NMF shows significant improvements that only 19 out of 633 documents are mistakenly clustered. Notice that both NMF and dropout NMF fail to distinguish topic 4 from topic 2, because both crimes are motivated by gender issues and reporters are likely to discuss both of them in the same news report: Gene McKinney (topic (2)) is convicted of sexual harassment and Eric Rudolph (topic (4)) is responsible for a series of anti-abortion and anti-gay-motivated bombings.

Topic	Cluster						Cluster						Cluster					
	1	2	3	4	5	6	1	2	3	4	5	6	1	2	3	4	5	6
1	159					1	159					1	149		9			2
2		131							131				125	6				
3	6	1	109			4	2	1	115			2			120			
4	4	100					1	103								104		
5	2			64							66						66	
6	5					47	5					47	2					50

| (a) NMF | (b) Dropout NMF | (c) Sequential NMF |

Fig. 4. Clustering results on six crime topics.

5 Conclusion

In this paper, we analyze how and why the correlations among latent features in NMF affect performance, and put forward two novel methods for NMF, dropout NMF and sequential NMF. Both methods improve NMF without bringing in extra constraints or transformations. In dropout NMF, only a random subset of latent features is updated in each iteration, and latent features are sequentially updated until convergence in sequential NMF. Co-adaption is effectively prevented in the proposed algorithms, so latent features are more definite and discriminative. Experimental studies on document clustering demonstrate that our algorithms not only achieve improvements on NMF, but also further improve existing variants of NMF. In the future, we will explore dropout and sequential techniques for NMF with other loss functions and variations. The new dropout strategies will also be put forward to deal with other latent representation based applications in different fields such as computer vision and bioinformatics.

Acknowledgement. This research is supported by the Natural Science Foundation of China (No. 61105049), the Natural Science Foundation of Tianjin (No. 14JCQNJC00600), the Science and Technology Planning Project of Tianjin (No. 13ZCZDGX01098), and the Open Project Foundation of Information Technology Research Base of Civil Aviation Administration of China (No. CAAC-ITRB-201502).

References

1. Lee, D.D., Seung, H.S.: Learning the parts of objects by non-negative matrix factorization. Nature **401**(6755), 788–791 (1999)
2. Lee, D.D., Seung, H.S.: Algorithms for non-negative matrix factorization. In: Advances in Neural Information Processing Systems, pp. 556–562 (2001)
3. Berrya, M.W., Browne, M., Langville, A.N., Paucac, V.P., Plemmons, R.J.: Algorithms and applications for approximate nonnegative matrix factorization. Comput. Stat. Data Anal. **52** (1), 155–173 (2007)
4. Langville, A.N., Meyer, C.D., Albright, R., Cox, J., Duling, D.: Algorithms, initializations, and convergence for the nonnegative matrix factorization. arXiv preprint arXiv:1407.7299 (2014)
5. Lin, C.-J.: Projected gradient methods for nonnegative matrix factorization. Neural Comput. **19**(10), 2756–2779 (2007)
6. Kim, J., Park, H.: Sparse nonnegative matrix factorization for clustering. Georgia Institute of Technology, Technical report GT-CSE-08-01 (2008)
7. Kim, J., Park, H.: Sparse non-negative matrix factorizations via alternating non-negativity-constrained least squares for microarray data analysis. Bioinformatics **23** (12), 1495–1502 (2007)
8. Hoyer, P.O.: Non-negative matrix factorization with sparseness constraints. J. Mach. Learn. Res. **5**, 1457–1469 (2004)
9. Cai, D., He, X., Han, J.: Graph regularized nonnegative matrix factorization for data representation. IEEE Trans. Pattern Anal. Mach. Intell. **33**(8), 1548–1560 (2011)
10. Cai, D., He, X., Wu, X., Han, J.: Non-negative matrix factorization on manifold. In: Proceedings of the 8th IEEE International Conference on Data Mining (ICDM 2008), pp. 63–72 (2008)
11. Li, W.-J., Yeung, D.-Y.: Relation regularized matrix factorization. In: Proceedings of the 21st International Joint Conference on Artificial Intelligence (IJCAI 2009), pp. 1126–1131 (2009)
12. Gu, Q., Zhou, J., Ding, C.: Collaborative filtering: weighted nonnegative matrix factorization incorporating user and item graphs. In: Proceedings of the 2010 SIAM International Conference on Data Mining (SDM 2010), pp. 199–210 (2010)
13. Xu, W., Liu, X., Gong, Y.: Document clustering based on non-negative matrix factorization. In: Proceedings of the 26th Annual International ACM SIGIR Conference on Research and Development in Information Retrieval, pp. 267–273 (2003)

14. Takeuchi, K., Ishiguro, K., Kimura, A., Sawada, H.: Non-negative multiple matrix factorization. In: Proceedings of the 23rd International Joint Conference on Artificial Intelligence (IJCAI 2013), pp. 1713–1720 (2013)
15. Li, T., Sindhwani, V., Ding, C., Zhang, Y.: Bridging domains with words: opinion analysis with matrix tri-factorizations. In: Proceedings of the 2010 SIAM International Conference on Data Mining (SDM 2010), pp. 293–302 (2010)
16. Zhang, Z.-Y., Li, T., Ding, C.: Non-negative tri-factor tensor decomposition with applications. Knowl. Inf. Syst. **34**(2), 243–265 (2013)
17. Hinton, G., Srivastava, N., Krizhevsky, A., Sutskever, I., Salakhutdinov, R.: Improving neural networks by preventing co-adaptation of feature detectors (2012). arXiv:1207.0580
18. Srivastava, N., Hinton, G., Krizhevsky, A., Sutskever, I., Salakhutdinov, R.: Dropout: a simple way to prevent neural networks from overfitting. J. Mach. Learn. Res. **15**(1), 1929–1958 (2014)
19. Wan, L., Zeiler, M., Zhang, S., LeCun, Y., Fergus, R.: Regularization of neural networks using dropconnect. In: Proceedings of the 30th International Conference on Machine Learning (ICML 2013), pp. 1058–1066 (2013)
20. Rippel, O., Gelbart, M.A., Adams, R.P.: Learning ordered representations with nested dropout. In: Proceedings of the 31st International Conference on Machine Learning (ICML 2014), pp. 1746–1754 (2014)
21. Wang, S.I., Manning, C.D.: Fast dropout training. In: Proceedings of the 30th International Conference on Machine Learning (ICML 2013), pp. 118–126 (2013)
22. Wager, S., Wang, S., Liang, P.S.: Dropout training as adaptive regularization. In: Advances in Neural Information Processing Systems (NIPS 2013), pp. 351–359 (2013)
23. Ba, J., Frey, B.: Adaptive dropout for training deep neural networks. In: Advances in Neural Information Processing Systems (NIPS 2013), pp. 3084–3092 (2013)
24. Cieri, C., Graff, D., Liberman, M., Martey, N., Strassel, S.: The TDT-2 text and speech corpus. In: Proceedings of the DARPA Broadcast News Workshop, pp. 57–60 (1999)
25. Ken, L.: NewsWeeder: learning to filter netnews. In: Proceedings of the 12th International Conference on Machine Learning (ICML 1995), pp. 331–339 (1995)

Analysing the Semantic Change Based on Word Embedding

Xuanyi Liao[✉] and Guang Cheng

Beijing University of Post and Telecommunication, Beijing 100876, China
hgfi199146@126.com, chenguang@bupt.edu.cn

Abstract. This paper intend to present an approach to analyse the change of word meaning based on word embedding, which is a more general method to quantize words than before. Through analysing the similar words and clustering in different period, semantic change could be detected. We analysed the trend of semantic change through density clustering method called DBSCAN. Statics and data visualization is also included to make the result more clear. Some words like 'gay', 'mouse' are traced as case to prove this approach works. At last, we also compared the context words and similar words on semantic presentation and proved the context words worked better.

Keywords: Semantic change · Word embedding · Google books N-gram corpus · Word similarity

1 Introduction

With the promotion of computer power and development of machine learning, an increasing number of people studied in semantic analysis. Besides Word Semantic Disambiguation (WSD) and Word Semantic Induction (WSI), semantic change analysis is a more novel task in semantic analysis. It is defined as a change of one or more meanings of the word in time [2], and is closely related to the task of word sense detection [5]. The phenomenon of semantic change is widely existed, such as the word 'gay' which changed the meaning from joy to male homosexuality [19]. It has become more and more common today especially through the Internet.

Analysis on semantic change has quantities of applications in natural language process. For example, the hot spot in social media and news report often occurs with high frequency of key word, which usually gains new meaning in current context. So the detection of semantic change could apply to the hot spot detection and event tracking. As we known, word meaning is closely related to its context. When the semantic change occurs, words in its context also change. For polysemant, some context words occur more frequently along with one meaning widely used and new context words might mean a new meaning arising. The past approaches to analyse the semantic change, no matter LSA method [18] or LDA method [19] are both based on the context. As the most popular word

© Springer International Publishing AG 2016
C.-Y. Lin et al. (Eds.): NLPCC-ICCPOL 2016, LNAI 10102, pp. 213–223, 2016.
DOI: 10.1007/978-3-319-50496-4_18

representation approach, word embedding [16] which vectoring a word abstractly by its context should be valuable in this task.

This paper intends to analyse semantic change by using word embedding to present the word. Due to its excellent ability in semantic expression, word embedding could reflect on the semantic change more accurately. This paper intended to detect the change occurred. We trained the word embedding on Google-N-gram corpus, which include the publication with 500 billion words distributed in n-gram form over centuries and analyse the change by statics and data visualization. This approach does better in semantic change detection and express the tendency more directly.

2   Related Work

Word semantic modelling is based on the assumption that its meaning could be inferred from the context. Word semantic analysis mainly concentrates on the Word Semantic Disambiguation (WSD) and Word Semantic Induction (WSI) before. Closely related to these tasks, semantic change analysis could use the same approach called Latent Semantic Analysis (LSA) too. Varieties of approach have been applied to accomplish the Latent Semantic Analysis. Sagi [18] used the TF-IDF to build a word-context matrix and obtain word vector by Singular Value Decomposition (SVD). Then he clustered the context word and judge the meaning of word broader or narrower by the density of cluster. The density is defined as the average cosine similarity between words in the cluster. Gulordava and Baroni [7] computed local mutual information (LMI) score between the centre word and the context word and transited the word to vector by the bag of context words. The he compared the vector of the same words from 60s and 90s corpus. Low similarity means the semantic changes has occurred.

After LDA gained improvement in natural language processing tasks, it also has been applied to detect semantic change. Rohrdantz et al. [17] modeled context by LDA in New York Times corpus. He regarded one topic as one meaning and clustered the context into different semantics. Then he traced the context by data visualization and detected the semantic change by the proportion of context belong to one meaning. However Wijaya and Yeniterzi [19] treated context in the whole year as a document and trained LDA on them. He traced the change of topic rates over year to detect the semantic change and analyse the change tendency by the topic words. He constructed a network linking words to its context, and observes the change of the network structure.

In Jatowt's [11] and Davies' [3] works, semantic change were directly analyzed through the change of context words during decades. Especially in Jatowt's [11] work, he proposed a framework for analyzing semantic change, which is capturing semantic change of a single word and then finding evolution of similarities between contrasting pairs of words. This framework was applied in many works on analysing semantic change. After Mikolov et al. [16] proposed word embedding, There were also some works applied word embedding on analysing semantic change, both Kulkarni et al. [12] and Hamilton et al. [8] trained embedding and a transfer matrix to map vectors from different decades into the same vector space, which make the semantic change more obvious.

3 Approaches

This section mainly introduces the approaches we applied during analysing the semantic change phenomenon and explain the reason we chose these methods.

3.1 Word Embedding

It has been a long time to represent word as continuous vectors [4,9,10]. After Bengio et al. [1] proposed the popular model for estimating neural network language model (NNLM), word vector was first learned with a single hidden layer of neural network [14,15]. Then in 2013, Mikolov et al. [16] proposed a new model architecture to obtain the word vector directly using the CBoW and Skip-gram model. The optimization is to maximize the joint probability between word and its context word with a log-linear model. In this paper, we choose the skip-gram architecture with negative sampling; its optimization is as following:

$$p(c_i|w_i) \propto exp(c_i * w_i) \tag{1}$$

This vector, we also called word embedding, was performed excellent in semantic presentation with lower dimension than before. Recently, it is widely used in neural network as input to deal with the natural language processing tasks.

3.2 Random Project Forest

Computation on similarity among the whole corpus for each pair was time wasted, this paper apply the popular approximate nearest neighbour method called Random Project Forest [13]. This method chose a point randomly and divided the whole corpus into two parts by the vector dot product. This operation tended to project the other vectors into the direction of the vector we picked. Recursively dividing the part until reaching the minimum leaf node size, we got a search tree. Constructing several search trees in this way, we got random Project Forest. In fact, each search tree is a hash function to map the vector into a low dimension space according to the cosine distance and the forest consists of several search tree is to improve the accuracy of mapping. To find the nearest neighbourhoods of one vector, we just searched in each tree and got the union set of each leaf nodes.

3.3 DBSCAN

This paper tends to cluster the vectors of words to analyse the polysemy. The similarity of word embedding is often computed by the cosine distance, which is hard to be applied to the prototype-based clustering method such as k-means.

And we also wanted to cluster the vectors without defining the cluster number. So we applied a density-based clustering method called DBSCAN (Density-Based Spatial Clustering of Applications with Noise) [6] to deal with the problem. It defined the ϵ neighbourhood of one sample as an area in which all the distance with other samples is no more than ϵ. And it defined the core object as the sample which holds more than N samples in its ϵ neighbourhood. N is the minimum batch size. To cluster the samples, we traced the core object to search its density-reachable samples. Repeating this process until all the samples were assigned to a cluster, we got the clustering result.

4   Experiments

In this section, we introduce the experiment we applied to analyse the semantic change. We could see the word embedding give a good performance in this task. Then we compared the similar word with the context in the semantic change analysis.

4.1   Preparations

Before the experiments, we should pre-process the corpus and train the word embedding. We used Google Books N-gram corpus in this experiment. This corpus includes publications with over 500 billion words in 7 different languages over centuries. For the reason of copyright limitations, it is distributed in n-gram format. The corpus provides data in five gram format with the frequency of each n-gram in one year, the count of pages and volume it occurred. During pre-processing, we replace the blank space with the mark /ss and remove the five gram which has more than three continuous blank space in order to avoid repeated train. Then we abstract the five grams in certain years and treated five gram in a whole year as a corpus.

When training the embedding, we use the word2vec tools by Google and make some modifications. As we trained vectors by the five gram corpus, the windows length had to be fixed on two. During training each five gram, we regarded the third word as target word and others as context. Each five gram record was attached with its frequency as format (word1, word2, ..., word5, frequency). We apply skip-gram architecture and set negative sampling to 25. To make the training more closely to the natural language, we apply sampling in the training to avoid training one block repeatedly. The sampling formula is showed as following:

$$probabilty = min(\frac{frequency}{samplingbase}) \tag{2}$$

Sampling could also prevent training bias on frequent words through adjust the value of sampling base. For frequent word, the value of sampling base is less than its frequency, so the sampling probability was set to 1. In fact, this step reduced the occurrence of the frequent word and increased the sampling probability of infrequent word than before.

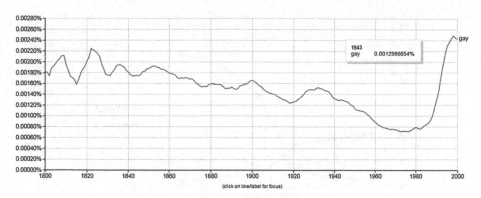

Fig. 1. Frequency change of the word 'gay' in Google Books N-gram Viewer

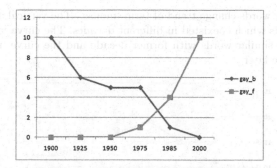

Fig. 2. The similar words change trend of term 'gay'. The vertical axis is the number of similar words which coexisted in different decades. The curve 'gay_b' means comparing current similar words with former decade and the curve 'gay_f' means comparing with the later.

4.2 Detecting the Semantic Change Based on Word Embedding

After we got the vector presentation of a word, we could detect the semantic change trough comparing word with its similar words. The idea is that the most similar words are not always fixed in each different year. The word which holds the same meaning has stable contexts and similar words, while the polysemous one has shifty contexts and similar words. So the changes of most similar words reflect the semantic change. We use cosine similarity to show the correlation in this paper.

In order to get the similar words, we compute the cosine similarity between each word and extract the top N words. In order to reduce the complexity of similarity computation, we use the Random Project Forest [13], an approximate nearest neighbourhood algorithm based on cosine distance, to find the top N similar words. In this paper, we filtered the top 50 similar words for each term. Then we compared the similar words with the past decades and the next decades to get the number of duplication. It is obvious that the semantic change has occurred (Figs. 3 and 4).

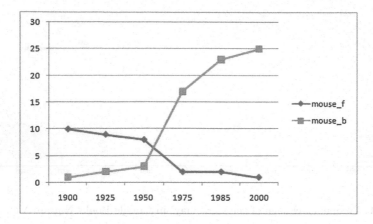

Fig. 3. The similar words change trend of term 'mouse'. The vertical axis is the number of similar words which coexisted in different decades. The curve 'mouse_b' means comparing current similar words with former decade and the curve 'mouse_f' means comparing with the later.

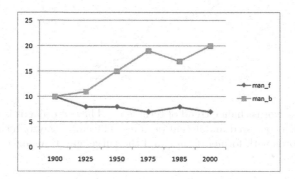

Fig. 4. The similar words change trend of term 'man'. The vertical axis is the number of similar words which coexisted in different decades. The curve 'man_b' means comparing current similar words with former decade and the curve 'man_f' means comparing with the later.

We firstly apply our approach on the words which the meaning is changing over time. After a word got a new meaning, the original one may get suppressed and even disappeared. For instance, the word 'gay' was used as the meaning of 'joy' originally. As shown in the Fig. 1, its frequency decreased sustainably before 1970s. After 1970s, the frequency increased as long as the meaning of 'male homosexuality' occurred and gradually became the main meaning. We compared the vectors from the corpus during 1900 to 2000, curve '_b' (backward) means comparing the current decade similar words to the 1900 and curve '_f' (forward) means comparing to the 2000. Each point shows the concurrent number of the similar words between two years. We can see the backward curve decreased while the forward curve increased over years. The cross point between two curves means the sense of the word going to change. In Fig. 2, it was in the 1970s which met the historical materials.

As we consider the case 'mouse', it shows similar phenomenon. Before 1950s, most similar words of 'mouse' were both other animals. After 1950s, with the development of biology, it tends to behave the meaning in clone technology. Then in 1990s, personal computer became popular, it tends to represent the device of computer. As for the stable word 'man', we can see the backward curve is steady, which means comparing to the 1900s, the similar words was stable over years. Although the forward curve increased, it was caused by the increase of the vocabulary. Corpus in recent years has varieties of new words that not occurred before, which depress the similarity between past words and modern ones. Through the above observation, semantic change occurred when one curved decrease and the other increased.

Compared to the works of Jatowt and Duh [11] and Davies [3], we replaced the context vectors with the word embedding. According to Jatowts [11] works, we chose the candidate words. He also computed the similarity of example words in different stage to represent the semantic change and the similarity curve ascended with the change. Compared to Jatowts [11] works, our approach represented the change more obviously with the steep curve. And with the two cross curve, our approach represent whether the change happened more clearly too. As for Kulkarni's [12] and Hamilton's [8] works, it transfer the vectors into the same vector space and present the semantic but consumed more computation source and didn't reveal that the change occurred.

4.3   Analysing the Semantic Trend with Word Embedding

Besides tracking the quantity of the similar words, this paper also analyse the variation of similar words. In Fig. 5, we can see not only relevance between words and its similar words but also similar words inside. In this experiment, we extract the top 10 similar word. To show the relevance between the similar words, we observe whether the word was top 20 similar of others.

In Fig. 5 the word 'gay', its similar words originally aggregate on the meaning of joy. In 1900, it was divided into two part represent 'joyous' and 'charming', then in 2000, this word changed to present the meaning of 'male homosexuality', its similar word became 'lesbian' and 'homosexual'. We could see little overlap between top ten similar words in 1900 and 2000. The reason is that the semantic change of words 'gay' was one-way, which means single meaning to single meaning. New meaning occurred and gradually depressed the original one. Another case is the word 'mouse' in Fig. 6. After it gained the new meaning, the original one didn't disappear. So we can see the word finally fixed on two meanings. This kind of change could be called one-to-many, which means the new meaning coexisted with the original one.

This phenomenon also revealed that the similar words mainly reflected a word's major meaning in current context. If term meaning changed one-to-one,

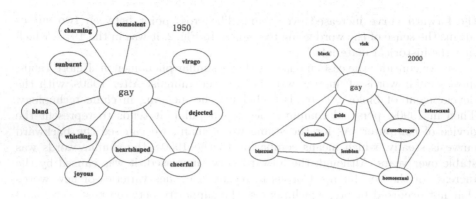

Fig. 5. The similar words network change trend of term 'gay'

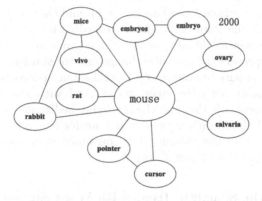

Fig. 6. The similar words network change trend of term 'mouse'

the similar word always concentrated on the same meaning. If it is changed one-to-many, the similar word may cluster into several parts. Well do more analysis in the next section.

4.4   Clustering on the Similar Words and Context Words

In the last section, we have proved the semantic change of a word could be expressed by its similar word. Gulordava [6,7] showed the context word has a similar effect on this problem. This section, we tried to compare the similar words and context words on the presentation ability through clustering them.

We apply DBSCAN [6,14], a density clustering method, to cluster the words. There are two parameters in this method: Epsilon to limit the maximum distance in the neighbourhood and Minimum size to limit the minimum number of neighbourhood for a core object. The cosine distance ranged from -1 to 1 and 1 means two samples were the equal. During the clustering, we define the distance as follow:

$$distance = 1 - cos(vec1, vec2) \qquad (3)$$

In this paper, we set ϵ to 0.5 and Minimum size to 3, we can compare the clustering difference between two word lists (Tables 1 and 2).

Table 1. The context words clusters of term 'mouse'

Clusters	Words
1	the, of, to, a, in, and, that, I, It
2	is, be, was, not, have, are, been, had
3	over, around, across
4	all, between, both
5	cell, cells, brain, skin, rat, embryo
6	move, moved, moving, passes
7	Am, Proc, Dev
8	use, click, button, select, drag, Place
9	transfer, release, releasing, targeting
10	pointer, keyboard, cursor

Table 2. The similar words clusters of term 'mouse'

Clusters	Words
1	rat, embryo, rabbit, mice, ovary, embryos, vivo, mast, mammary, monkey, hippocampus, H19, vitro, liver pancreas, retina
2	pointer, cursor

As no matter whether TF-IDFS or LDA approaches both used the context words to represent the meaning of one word, we firstly clustered context words to attained the division of semantic. In the case of 'mouse', we could find that the top 200 context words were divided into ten parts, including signs and stop words. The part 5 tends to express the 'creature' meaning of 'mouse' while the part 8 and part 10 tends to express the 'computer device'. Observing the words in different clusters, each cluster tends to hold the same characteristic or usage, which makes it hard to ensure the meaning of a cluster. And Quantities of stop words often holds high frequency, which leads more context words being computed and make it even hard to distinguish the cluster with each other.

On the contrary, the similar words were clearly divided into two clusters; each cluster corresponded to the meaning of 'mouse'. With the similar words, we could easily distinguish the meaning the two clusters expressed. And according to the size of the clusters, we could also judge which meaning played a leading role in the corpus decade.

5   Conclusion and Future Work

This paper provided a new analysis method on semantic change task based on the word embedding. This paper verified that the similar word computed through the word embedding could reflect the semantic change. Tracing the variation of similar words, we could find the period change occurred and the variation trend of the meaning. Compared to the context words used before, it reflected the trend more clearly and the clusters are much more meaningful.

The experiment showed that Google books N-gram corpus adapted to the semantic change task. It holds abundant data in regular format and long time span. In the whole corpus, the semantic changes happened frequently make it convenient to analyse this phenomenon. To compute the similarity of the words in less cost, we applied approximate nearest neighbour algorithm and gain equal effect. Different from the past method which fixed the cluster quantity, we used the density clustering method to recognize the polysemy automatically.

During the experiments, we could see that the similar words of a term reflect its semantic change excellently. The doublication between former and later present the semantic stability of the word and the variation of the similar words clusters present the trend of the semantic change. The clusters of the similar word present the polysemy of the word more accurately than the context words and more directly than the LDA methods, so the change of clusters density might also be a signal for the semantic change.

In the future, we would try to quantize the semantic change based on the word embedding. This paper proved the word embedding has good stability with its context and similar words. A word with no semantic change holds the stable context and similar words. We plan to find the stable relationship and transform the vectors into the same vector space by the stable part. Then we could model the semantic change process and analyse whether there are other factors influence the semantic change. And the time cost is still a shortcoming of this approach, we also intended to optimize the training time.

References

1. Bengio, Y., Schwenk, H., Senécal, J.S., Morin, F., Gauvain, J.L.: Neural probabilistic language models. In: Holmes, D.E., Jain, L.C. (eds.) Innovations in Machine Learning, vol. 194, pp. 137–186. Springer, Heidelberg (2006). doi:10.1007/3-540-33486-6_6
2. Campbell, L.: Historical linguistics: an introduction. Diachronica: Int. J. Hist. Linguist. (1), 159–160 (1998)
3. Davies, M.: Making Google Books n-grams useful for a wide range of research on language change. Int. J. Corpus Linguist. **19**(3), 401–416 (2014)
4. Elman, J.L.: Finding structure in time. Cogn. Sci. **14**(2), 179–211 (1990)
5. Erk, K.: Unknown word sense detection as outlier detection. In: Proceedings of the Human Language Technology Conference of the North American Chapter of the Association of Computational Linguistics, New York, USA, 4–9 June 2006 (2006)

6. Ester, M., Kriegel, H.P., Sander, J., Xu, X.: A density-based algorithm for discovering clusters in large spatial databases with noise. In: KDD, vol. 96, pp. 226–231 (1996)
7. Gulordava, K., Baroni, M.: A distributional similarity approach to the detection of semantic change in the Google Books Ngram corpus. In: GEMS 2011 Workshop on GEometrical MODELS of Natural Language Semantics, pp. 67–71 (2011)
8. Hamilton, W.L., Leskovec, J., Dan, J.: Diachronic word embeddings reveal statistical laws of semantic change (2016)
9. Hinton, G., Rumelhart, D., Williams, R.: Learning internal representations by back-propagating errors. Parallel Distrib. Process. Explor. Microstruct. Cogn. **5**, 1 (1985)
10. Hinton, G.E., Mcclelland, J.L., Rumelhart, D.E.: Distributed representations. In: Parallel Distributed Processing: Explorations in the Microstructure of Cognition, vol. 1: Foundations (1986)
11. Jatowt, A., Duh, K.: A framework for analyzing semantic change of words across time. In: Digital Libraries, pp. 229–238 (2014)
12. Kulkarni, V., Alrfou, R., Perozzi, B., Skiena, S.: Statistically significant detection of linguistic change. In: Computer Science (2014)
13. McFee, B., Lanckriet, G.R.: Large-scale music similarity search with spatial trees. In: ISMIR, pp. 55–60 (2011)
14. Mikolov, T.: Language models for automatic speech recognition of Czech lectures. In: Proceedings of STUDENT EEICT (2008)
15. Mikolov, T., Kopecký, J., Burget, L., Glembek, O., Černocký, J.H.: Neural network based language models for highly inflective languages. In: IEEE International Conference on Acoustics, Speech and Signal Processing, ICASSP 2009, pp. 4725–4728. IEEE (2009)
16. Mikolov, T., Sutskever, I., Chen, K., Corrado, G., Dean, J.: Distributed representations of words and phrases and their compositionality. Adv. Neural Inf. Process. Syst. **26**, 3111–3119 (2013)
17. Rohrdantz, C., Hautli, A., Mayer, T., Butt, M., Keim, D.A., Plank, F.: Towards tracking semantic change by visual analytics. In: Proceedings of the 49th Annual Meeting of the Association for Computational Linguistics: Human Language Technologies: Short Papers, vol. 2, pp. 305–310. Association for Computational Linguistics (2011)
18. Sagi, E., Kaufmann, S., Clark, B.: Semantic density analysis: comparing word meaning across time and phonetic space. In: The Workshop on Geometrical MODELS of Natural Language Semantics, pp. 104–111 (2010)
19. Wijaya, D.T., Yeniterzi, R.: Understanding semantic change of words over centuries. In: International Workshop on Detecting and Exploiting Cultural Diversity on the Social Web, pp. 35–40 (2011)

Learning Word Sense Embeddings from Word Sense Definitions

Qi Li[1,2], Tianshi Li[1,2], and Baobao Chang[1,2(✉)]

[1] Key Laboratory of Computational Linguistics,
Ministry of Education School of Electronics Engineering and Computer Science,
Peking University, No. 5 Yiheyuan Road, Haidian District, Beijing 100871, China
{qi.li,chbb}@pku.edu.cn, lts_417@hotmail.com
[2] Collaborative Innovation Center for Language Ability, Xuzhou 221009, China

Abstract. Word embeddings play a significant role in many modern NLP systems. Since learning one representation per word is problematic for polysemous words and homonymous words, researchers propose to use one embedding per word sense. Their approaches mainly train word sense embeddings on a corpus. In this paper, we propose to use word sense definitions to learn one embedding per word sense. Experimental results on word similarity tasks and a word sense disambiguation task show that word sense embeddings produced by our approach are of high quality.

Keywords: Word sense embedding · RNN · WordNet

1 Introduction

With the development of the Internet and computational efficiency of processors, gigantic unannotated corpora can be obtained and utilized for natural language processing (NLP) tasks. Those corpora can be used to train distributed word representations (i.e. word embeddings) which play an important role in most state-of-the-art NLP neural network models. The word embeddings capture syntactic and semantic properties which can be exposed directly in tasks such as analogical reasoning [14], word similarity [8] etc. Prevalent word embedding learning models include Skip-gram [14], Glove [20] and variants of them.

Basic Skip-gram [14] and Glove [20] output one vector for each word. However, multi-sense words (including polysemous words and homonymous words) should inherently have different embeddings for different senses. Therefore researchers propose to use one embedding per word sense [2,8,9,11,12,19,21,23,24]. Previous work tends to perform word sense induction (WSI) or word sense disambiguation (WSD) on the corpus to determine the senses of words. Then they train the word sense embeddings on it using variants of Skip-gram or other approaches. However, the result of WSI or WSD on the corpus is not reliable and the errors from WSI or WSD will have bad effect on the quality of word sense embeddings. Besides, these approaches normally produce bad embeddings for rare word senses.

© Springer International Publishing AG 2016
C.-Y. Lin et al. (Eds.): NLPCC-ICCPOL 2016, LNAI 10102, pp. 224–235, 2016.
DOI: 10.1007/978-3-319-50496-4_19

Lexical ontologies such as WordNet [15] and BabelNet [18] are built by specialists in linguistics and they provide semantic information of word senses including their definitions. Different from determining word senses by WSI or WSD models, semantic information provided by lexical ontologies is normally accurate and reliable. To utilize the accurate information of word senses provided by lexical ontologies, we propose an approach based on recurrent neural networks (RNN) to learn word sense embeddings from word sense definitions. Our approach learns both word sense embeddings and a definition understanding model. Since the collection of definitions is much smaller in scale than a corpus for embedding training, our approach is less time-consuming comparing with corpus-based learning approaches. Experimental results show that the word sense embeddings are of high quality for both common and rare words and the definition understanding model can understand other natural language text besides word sense definitions.

Our contributions can be summarized as follows:

- We propose to learn word sense embeddings from word sense definitions using RNN-based models.
- Different from previous embedding learning approaches, our learning is conducted in a supervised paradigm.
- Our approach is less time-consuming comparing with corpus-based learning approaches.
- Our approach treats senses of rare words and of common words equally since definitions have no tendency to common words and this is hard to achieve for corpus-based learning approaches.

The rest of this paper is organized as follows: Sect. 2 presents details of our approach. Section 3 reports experimental results. Section 4 introduces the related work. Section 5 concludes our work.

2 Methodology

While a corpus presents distributional properties of words, definitions provide semantic information of word senses in a compositional way. Therefore, we believe that we can compute word sense embeddings from definitions. We choose to use recurrent neural networks to model semantic compositionality because RNN-based models have been shown to be able to model semantic compositionality in many tasks, such as neural machine translation [1,6,10], text entailment recognition [22] etc.

2.1 Definition Understanding Model

A word sense definition is a word sequence: $\{x_1, x_2, \ldots, x_n\}$. As Fig. 1 shows, RNN models take word embeddings of the words in definitions one by one and update the internal memory according to its computation unit. The output of

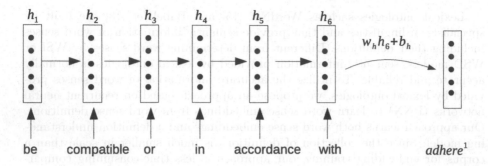

Fig. 1. Mapping definitions to word sense embeddings with RNN-based model.

the RNN at the last word of the definition, i.e., h_n is assumed to contain the semantic meaning of the definition. Hence we map h_n to sense embedding space with a transformation matrix:

$$e_{\widetilde{ws}} = W_h h_n + b_h \tag{1}$$

where W_h is the transformation matrix, b_n is the bias term and $e_{\widetilde{ws}}$ is the sense embedding computed by the definition understanding model.

The specific RNN model can be a vanilla RNN model, Gated Recurrent Unit (GRU) [3] or Long Short Term Memory (LSTM) [7]. Comparing with vanilla RNNs, LSTMs and GRUs can hold long-term information, i.e., they can alleviate the gradient vanishing and information-forgetting problem associated with the vanilla RNN for long sequences [3,7].

2.2 Training Definition Understanding Model with Definitions of Monosemous Words

Having determined the model structure, the challenge is how to train the RNN-based definition understanding model. Since the contexts of a monosemous word are associated with its only word sense, we assume its word sense embedding is similar to its word embedding. So we initialize sense embeddings of monosemous words with their word embeddings trained with Skip-gram [14] on a corpus and thus we can train the RNN-based model parameters with sense embeddings of monosemous words as target and their definitions as inputs. The words in definitions are represented by their word embeddings. Word embeddings are kept fixed during the whole training process. As word embeddings trained on a corpus provide distributional properties of the words, our approach provides a supervised training for model parameters by combining distributional and compositional properties of word senses. The objective function of this training step is

$$J_1 = - \sum_{w \in V_{mono}} cos(e_{ws}, e_{\widetilde{ws}}) \tag{2}$$

where V_{mono} is the set of monosemous words and e_{ws} is the initialized sense embedding of the monosemous word w and $e_{\tilde{w}s}$ is the word sense embedding produced by our RNN-based definition understanding model. With this objective function, we train $e_{\tilde{w}s}$ to be similar to e_{ws}. Both the sense embeddings and word embeddings used in definitions are fixed in this step, i.e., we only train model parameters in this step.

2.3   Word Sense Embedding Learning

We have trained RNN-based definition understanding model with sense embeddings of monosemous words and their definitions in the previous step. However, we still haven't use definitions of senses of multi-sense words. Since the word embeddings are trained according to the co-occurrences from a corpus, the word embedding of a multi-sense word usually represent the most common sense better and this is shown by our nearest neighbor evaluation in Sect. 3.2. So it is not appropriate to initialize all sense embeddings of a multi-sense word with its word embedding. Since WordNet provides a set of synonyms for each word sense, we initialize the embedding of a word sense using the word embedding of a synonym which contains only one sense. If there is no synonym conforms to this condition, we initialize the sense embedding with the word embedding of a word in its definition which has the largest cosine similarity with the original word. Besides, the similarity should exceed a threshold δ which we set to be 0.2 or we will use the word embedding of the target word sense to initialize its sense embedding. Although these sense embeddings are simply initialized, they still contain meaningful semantic information for training the definition understanding model and reversely they will also be tuned by our model. Comparing with the last step, we still optimize the cosine similarities between embeddings produced by the RNN-based definition understanding model and the initialized word sense embeddings. The difference is that in this step we use definitions of both monosemous words and multi-sense words and update all sense embeddings jointly including sense embeddings of monosemous words because some of them are of low quality if the words are of low frequency in the corpus their word embeddings are trained. The objective function is as follows:

$$J_2 = -\sum_{w \in V} \sum_{s \in S_w} cos(e_{ws}, e_{\tilde{w}s}) \qquad (3)$$

where V is the whole word set and S_w is the set of word senses of word w. To sum up, we make word sense embeddings and RNN-based definition understanding model tune each other in this step.

2.4   Training with Word Sense Embeddings to Represent Words in Definitions

In the previous two steps, we train the definition understanding model and learn sense embeddings jointly using word embeddings to represent words in definitions. However, some words in definitions are multi-sense words and therefore to use sense embeddings to represent those words is assumed to be more appropriate. Besides, it can also be seen as an application of the word sense embeddings trained in the last step.

To this end, we perform WSD for the words in definitions. We apply S2C (simple to complex) strategy described in [2] to implement WSD. Specifically, we identify the senses for words with less senses first and then for words with more senses. We compute the cosine similarity between each sense embedding of a word with its context embedding and choose the sense with greatest cosine similarity with the context embedding as the sense of the word. The context embedding is the average embedding of some other words in definitions. These words include nouns, verbs, adjectives and adverbs. We use the sense embeddings of those words whose senses have been identified and use the word embeddings of the rest words.

The objective function is the same as the previous step, but we use sense embeddings to represent words in definitions in this step and their sense embeddings are updated for the optimization of the objective function.

3   Experiments

We present qualitative evaluations and quantitative evaluations in this section. To show our word sense embeddings capture the semantics of word senses, we present the nearest neighbors of a word sense based on cosine similarity between the embedding of the center word sense and embeddings of other word senses. Besides, to show our model can actually understand a definition or any description, we present the most matched word senses for a given description according to our RNN-based definition understanding model. In our quantitative evaluations, we evaluate the sense embeddings on word similarity tasks and a word sense disambiguation task.

3.1   Setup

We use WordNet 3.0[1] as the lexical ontology to acquire the definitions of word senses. We choose the publicly released 300 dimensional vectors[2] trained with Skip-gram [14] on part of Google News dataset (about 100B words) as word embeddings used in our approach. We also take the word embeddings as our baseline. We randomly initialize model parameters within $(-0.012, 0.012)$ except that bias terms are initialized as zero vectors. We adopt Adadelta [25] with mini-batch to minimize our objective functions and set the initial learning rate to be 0.12.

3.2   Qualitative Evaluations

To illustrate the quality of our word sense embeddings, we show the nearest neighbors of words and of their senses in Table 1. The nearest neighbors of words are

---

[1] http://wordnet.princeton.edu/.

[2] https://code.google.com/archive/p/word2vec/.

Table 1. Nearest neighbors based on cosine similarity between word embeddings or sense embeddings.

Center word/sense	Nearest neighbors
Bank	ATM machines, Iberiabank, automated teller machines
*bank*1	financial, deposit, ATMs
*bank*2	riverbank, water, slope
Star	matinee idol, singer, superstar
*star*1	asteroid, celestial, supernova
*star*2	legend, standout, footballer
Pretty	wonderfully, unbelievably, nice
*pretty*1	remarkably, extremely, obviously
*pretty*2	beauteous, dainty, lovely

computed using word embeddings. The nearest neighbors of word senses are computed using word sense embeddings trained with our definition understanding model which uses GRU as its specific RNN. We leave out the sense numbers of nearest senses because the numbers are meaningless to be presented here. As can be seen, the nearest neighbors of the center words are normally associated with the most common sense of the word. Whereas, the nearest neighbors of word senses are associated with the corresponding sense of the word. Besides, some nearest neighbours (e.g., "supernova", "dainty") are rare to be seen in a corpus. Therefore it indicates even the sense embeddings of rare words are meaningful.

Although we train RNN-based definition understanding model to map a definition to its sense embedding, we will show the RNN-based definition understanding model can also understand descriptions we made up. We compute the cosine similarities between the embedding produced by our model according to the description and all word sense embeddings to find those most matched word senses. We still choose GRU as the specific RNN. Table 2 shows the most matched word senses to the given descriptions. The descriptions in the upper subfield are

Table 2. Using our definition understanding model to find the most matched word senses for descriptions.

Description	Most matched words
Free of deceit	Aboveboard, gullible, genuine
Causing one to believe the truth of something	Prove, convince, falsifiable
Make (someone) agree, understand, or realize the truth or validity of something	Convince, inform, acknowledge
The place where people live in	Home, dwellings, inhabited
A machine we use every day	Counter, computer, dishwasher
The animal which lives in the sea	Clam, nautilus, stonefish

definitions from WordNet and those in the under subfield are casual descriptions made up by us. Most of the predicted words match the meaning the descriptions convey and those that don't exactly match (e.g., "gullible", "falsifiable") are semantically relevant. The predicted words of the descriptions we make up are coincident with the descriptions. That illustrates our definition understanding model is effective to understand natural language.

3.3   Quantitative Evaluations

Word Similarity Evaluation on WordSim-353. WordSim-353 dataset [4] consists of 353 pairs of nouns which are associated with human judgments on their similarities without context information. The evaluation metrics on this dataset is the Spearman's rank correlation coefficient ρ between the average human score and the cosine similarity scores predicted by the system.

Following [8,9,21], we use weighted average of cosine similarities between each possible word sense pair as the similarity of the two words. Since there is no context provided, the weights can be uniformly distributed which is adopted by [8,21] or be determined by word sense frequency in the training set which is adopted by [9]. We choose to take the weights uniformly distributed. The following equation describe the weighted strategy:

$$WeiSim(w, w') = \sum_i^{n_1} \sum_j^{n_2} p(s_i|w)p(s_j|w')cos(e_{w_{si}}, e_{w'_{sj}}) \qquad (4)$$

where w and w' are the two given words, n_1 and n_2 are the number of senses of the two words and $p(s_i|w)$ and $p(s_j|w')$ are the normalized weights to use s_i and s_j to compute similarity, $e_{w_{si}}$ and $e_{w'_{sj}}$ are sense embeddings.

Table 3 shows our results compared with previous approaches. Reisinger and Mooney [21] propose to cluster the contexts of each word into groups and make each cluster a distinct prototype vector. Huang et al. [8] also use contexts to determine the number of senses of a word and use global context to improve word representations. Neelakantan et al. [19] extend Skip-gram [14] to learn multiple embeddings per word. Wu and Giles [24] cluster word senses and learn word sense embeddings from related Wikipedia concepts. Iacobacci et al. [9] use BabelNet [18] as the word sense inventory and apply WSD to a corpus before they train word sense embeddings with Continuous Bag of Words (CBOW) archi-tecture [13].

As can be seen, our approach achieves significant improvement over the orig-inal word embeddings we use. Most improvements come from the step we train word sense embeddings with our RNN-based models when the definitions are still represented by word embeddings. We achieve further significant improve-ments when we continue to jointly train the model and learn sense embeddings using sense embeddings trained in the previous step to represent words in defini-tions. It can be seen as an application of sense embeddings in a natural language understanding task, so it also illustrates our sense embeddings are better than

Table 3. Performances on WordSim-353. The bottom subfield shows the performance of different settings of our system. SG represents just using word embeddings we acquired. Def (Word) represents the step in which we use word embeddings to represent words in definitions to train model and sense embeddings. Def (Sense) represents the step in which we use sense embeddings to represent words in definitions to train model and sense embeddings. * indicates statistical significant differences in t-test between performances of SG(100B) and SG (100B) + Def (Word). ** indicates statistical significant differences in t-test between performances of SG (100B) + Def (Word) and SG (100B) + Def (Word) + Def (Sense) with the same RNN model.

System	$\rho \times 100$
Reisinger and Mooney [21] tf-idf (Wiki2.05B)	76.0
Huang et al. [8] (0.99B)	71.3
Neelakantan et al. [19] (0.99B)	71.2
Wu and Giles [24]	73.9
Iacobacci et al. [9]	**77.9**
SG (100B)	66.5
SG (100B) + Def (Word) (vanilla RNN)	67.4(+0.9)*
SG (100B) + Def (Word) + Def (Sense) (vanilla RNN)	68.2(+0.7)**
SG (100B) + Def (Word) (LSTM)	74.1(+7.6)*
SG (100B) + Def (Word) + Def (Sense) (LSTM)	**75.0**(+0.9)**
SG (100B) + Def (Word) (GRU)	73.7(+7.2)*
SG (100B) + Def (Word) + Def (Sense) (GRU)	74.7(+1.0)**

word embeddings for natural language understanding from the perspective of real-world natural language understanding tasks. The LSTM version and GRU version present comparable performances to be used as the specific RNN in definition understanding model and vanilla RNN performs much worse than the other two models. This is in accordance with what previous work illustrated about the superiority of GRUs and LSTMs over vanilla RNNs [3,7].

Word Similarity Evaluation on Stanford's Contextual Word Similarities. Since we need a context to determine the sense of a word when we use the sense embeddings in real-world tasks and evaluation on context-free word similarity datasets does not allow us to determine the sense, it cannot fully reveal the quality of our sense embeddings. Stanford's Contextual Word Similarities (SCWS) [8] is a data set which provides the contexts of the target words. The way we determine the sense of the target words is the same S2C strategy we described in Sect. 2.4. Having determined the senses of the target words, we compute cosine similarity of their sense embeddings as their similarity. The evaluation metrics is also the Spearman's rank correlation coefficient ρ between the average human rating and the cosine similarity scores given by our approach.

Table 4. Performances for our system and other proposed approaches on SCWS dataset.

System	$\rho \times 100$
Huang et al. [8] (0.99B)	65.7
Chen et al. [2] (1B) + WordNet	68.9
Tian et al. [23] (0.99B)	65.4
Neelakantan et al. [19] (0.99B)	69.3
Li et al. [11] (120B)	**69.7**
Liu et al. [12] (0.99B)	68.1
Wu and Giles [24]	66.4
Iacobacci et al. [9]	62.4
SG (100B)	64.4
SG (100B) + Def (Word) (vanilla RNN)	66.2(+1.8)*
SG (100B) + Def (Word) + Def (Sense) (vanilla RNN)	66.8(+0.6)**
SG (100B) + Def (Word) (LSTM)	68.9(+4.5)*
SG (100B) + Def (Word) + Def (Sense) (LSTM)	69.5(+0.6)**
SG (100B) + Def (Word) (GRU)	69.1(+4.7)*
SG (100B) + Def (Word) + Def (Sense) (GRU)	**69.5**(+0.4)**

Table 4 shows our results compared to previous approaches. Besides the models we have mentioned, Chen et al. [2] use WordNet to acquire number of senses of words and use definitions just to initialize sense embeddings and then train sense embeddings on a corpus processed with WSD model. Tian et al. [23] model word polysemy from a probabilistic perspective and combine it with Skip-Gram [14] model. Liu et al. [12] incorporate topic models into word sense embedding learning. Li and Jurafsky [11] use Chinese Restaurant Processes to determine the sense of a word and learn the sense embeddings jointly.

As can be seen, the improvements from each training step of our approach are in accordance with the results in WordSim-353 evaluation. LSTM and GRU also present much more improvements than vanilla RNN. Our proposed approach present high overall performance on both word similarity tasks. That illustrates the word sense embeddings indeed capture the semantics of word senses. Strictly speaking, the comparison between different approaches are not totally fair because the resources different approaches use are different.

Word Sense Disambiguation Evaluation. We also apply our word sense embeddings in a word sense disambiguation task to show the word sense embeddings capture the differences between senses of a word. In Semeval-2007 coarse-grained all-words WSD task [17], WordNet is used as the word sense inventory. But the evaluation of word sense disambiguation result is on a coarser-grained version of the WordNet sense inventory and those word senses which are hard to disambiguate even for human are clustered into one class. The version of WordNet used in this task is 2.1, but we learn our word sense embeddings with WordNet 3.0. So we use the sense map[3] between the two versions provided by the developers to address this issue. To compare the effectiveness of our word sense embedding on this task with previous work, following Chen et al. [2], we still adopt the S2C strategy we described in Sect. 2.4 to disambiguate word sense. We also show the result produced by randomly choosing the sense of words according to [2].

Table 5. Performances on Semeval-2007 coarse-grained all-words WSD task.

System	F1
Random	62.7
Chen et al. [2] (1B) + WordNet	75.8
SG (100B) + Def (Word) (vanilla RNN)	69.5
SG (100B) + Def (Word) + Def (Sense) (vanilla RNN)	70.3(+0.8)**
SG (100B) + Def (Word) (LSTM)	75.6
SG (100B) + Def (Word) + Def (Sense) (LSTM)	**76.4(+0.8)**
SG (100B) + Def (Word) (GRU)	75.7
SG (100B) + Def (Word) + Def (Sense) (GRU)	**76.3(+0.6)**

The results are shown in Table 5. After we train our model and word sense embeddings using sense embeddings to represent words in definitions, our approach outperforms Chen et al. [2] on this task. It illustrates that our sense embeddings can actually distinguish different senses of a word and our approach can actually learn the semantics of senses from definitions.

4   Related Work

Early word embedding learning approaches learn one embedding per word. Skipgram [14] and Glove [20] are the most prevalent models of this kind. Both of them use context information extracted from an unannotated corpus to learn word embeddings.

Since one embedding for each word sense are suggested to be better than a single embedding for a word, many word sense embedding learning approaches have been proposed [2,8,9,11,12,19,21,23,24]. Researchers tend to extend Skipgram and Glove models to learn sense embeddings with WSI or WSD as a preliminary. Reisinger and Mooney [21] propose to cluster the contexts of each word into groups and make each cluster a distinct prototype vector. Huang et al. [8] determine the sense of a word by clustering the contexts and then apply it to neural language model with global context. Guo et al. [5] propose to use parallel

---

[3] https://wordnet.princeton.edu/man/sensemap.5WN.html.

data for WSI and learning word sense embeddings. Neelakantan et al. [19] extend Skip-gram [14] to a model which jointly performs word sense discrimination and embedding learning. Liu et al. [12] associate words with topics and then extend Skip-gram [14] to learn sense and topic embeddings. Wu and Giles [24] propose to use Wikipedia concepts to cluster word senses and to learn sense-specific embeddings of words. Li and Jurafsky [11] use Chinese Restaurant Processes to determine the sense of a word and learn the sense embedding jointly. Iacobacci et al. [9] use BabelNet [18] as the word sense inventory and opt for Babelfy [16] to perform WSD on Wikipedia[4]. Then they train word sense embeddings using CBOW architecture [13] on the processed corpus. Chen et al. [2] use WordNet as its lexical ontology to acquire numbers of word senses and use the average word embedding of words chosen from definitions as the initialization of sense embeddings. And then they do WSD on a corpus and train sense embeddings with a variant of Skip-gram on the corpus. Both of our approaches use words in definitions to initialize word sense embeddings, but after that their training still concentrates on the corpus while we train our model and word sense embeddings with definitions. The disadvantage to use a corpus processed by WSD or WSI may come from the unreliability of the processing results and since a corpus for embedding training is usually much larger in scale than the summation of all the definitions to get satisfied result, their approach inevitably consumes much more time on WSD and training.

5   Conclusion

In this paper, we propose to use RNN-based models to learn word sense embeddings from sense definitions. Our approach produces an effective natural language understanding model and word sense embeddings of high quality. Comparing with previous work training word sense embeddings on a corpus, our approach is less time-consuming and better for rare word senses. Experimental results show our word sense embeddings are of high quality.

Acknowledgments. This work is supported by National Key Basic Research Program of China under Grant No. 2014CB340504 and National Natural Science Foundation of China under Grant No. 61273318. The Corresponding author of this paper is Baobao Chang.

References

1. Bahdanau, D., Cho, K., Bengio, Y.: Neural machine translation by jointly learning to align and translate (2014). CoRR arXiv:1409.0473
2. Chen, X., Liu, Z., Sun, M.: A unified model for word sense representation and disambiguation. In: EMNLP (2014)
3. Chung, J., Gülehre, C., Cho, K., Bengio, Y.: Empirical evaluation of gated recurrent neural networks on sequence modeling (2014). CoRR arXiv:1412.3555

---

[4] http://dumps.wikimedia.org/enwiki/.

4. Finkelstein, L., Gabrilovich, E., Matias, Y., Rivlin, E., Solan, Z., Wolfman, G., Ruppin, E.: Placing search in context: the concept revisited. ACM Trans. Inf. Syst. **20**, 116–131 (2001)
5. Guo, J., Che, W., Wang, H., Liu, T.: Learning sense-specific word embeddings by exploiting bilingual resources. In: COLING (2014)
6. Hermann, K.M., Kociský, T., Grefenstette, E., Espeholt, L., Kay, W., Suleyman, M., Blunsom, P.: Teaching machines to read and comprehend (2015). CoRR arXiv:1506.03340
7. Hochreiter, S., Schmidhuber, J.: Long short-term memory. Neural Comput. **9**, 1735–1780 (1997)
8. Huang, E.H., Socher, R., Manning, C.D., Ng, A.Y.: Improving word representations via global context and multiple word prototypes. In: Annual Meeting of the Association for Computational Linguistics (ACL) (2012)
9. Iacobacci, I., Pilehvar, M.T., Navigli, R.: SensEmbed: learning sense embeddings for word and relational similarity. In: ACL (2015)
10. Kalchbrenner, N., Blunsom, P.: Recurrent continuous translation models. In: EMNLP (2013)
11. Li, J., Jurafsky, D.: Do multi-sense embeddings improve natural language understanding? In: EMNLP (2015)
12. Liu, Y., Liu, Z., Chua, T.S., Sun, M.: Topical word embeddings. In: AAAI (2015)
13. Mikolov, T., Chen, K., Corrado, G., Dean, J.: Efficient estimation of word representations in vector space (2013). CoRR arXiv:1301.3781
14. Mikolov, T., Sutskever, I., Chen, K., Corrado, G., Dean, J.: Distributed representations of words and phrases and their compositionality (2013). CoRR arXiv:1310.4546
15. Miller, G.A.: Wordnet: a lexical database for English. Commun. ACM **38**, 39–41 (1992)
16. Moro, A., Raganato, A., Navigli, R.: Entity linking meets word sense disambiguation: a unified approach. TACL **2**, 231–244 (2014)
17. Navigli, R., Litkowski, K.C., Hargraves, O.: SemEval-2007 task 07: Coarse-grained English all-words task (2007)
18. Navigli, R., Ponzetto, S.P.: Babelnet: The automatic construction, evaluation and application of a wide-coverage multilingual semantic network. Artif. Intell. **193**, 217–250 (2012)
19. Neelakantan, A., Shankar, J., Passos, A., McCallum, A.: Efficient non-parametric estimation of multiple embeddings per word in vector space. In: EMNLP (2014)
20. Pennington, J., Socher, R., Manning, C.D.: Glove: global vectors for word representation. In: EMNLP (2014)
21. Reisinger, J., Mooney, R.J.: Multi-prototype vector-space models of word meaning. In: NAACL (2010)
22. Rocktäschel, T., Grefenstette, E., Hermann, K.M., Kociský, T., Blunsom, P.: Reasoning about entailment with neural attention (2015). CoRR arXiv:1509.06664
23. Tian, F., Dai, H., Bian, J., Gao, B., Zhang, R., Chen, E., Liu, T.Y.: A probabilistic model for learning multi-prototype word embeddings. In: COLING (2014)
24. Wu, Z., Giles, C.L.: Sense-aware semantic analysis: a multi-prototype word representation model using Wikipedia (2015)
25. Zeiler, M.D.: ADADELTA: an adaptive learning rate method (2012). CoRR arXiv:1212.5701

Information Extraction, Question Answering and Knowledge Acquisition

Character-Based LSTM-CRF with Radical-Level Features for Chinese Named Entity Recognition

Chuanhai Dong[1], Jiajun Zhang[1], Chengqing Zong[1(✉)], Masanori Hattori[2], and Hui Di[2]

[1] National Laboratory of Pattern Recognition, Institute of Automation, Chinese Academy of Sciences, Beijing, China
{chuanhai.dong,jjzhang,cqzong}@nlpr.ia.ac.cn
[2] Toshiba (China) R&D Center, Beijing, China
masanori.hattori@toshiba.co.jp, dihui@toshiba.com.cn

Abstract. State-of-the-art systems of Chinese Named Entity Recognition (CNER) require large amounts of hand-crafted features and domain-specific knowledge to achieve high performance. In this paper, we apply a bidirectional LSTM-CRF neural network that utilizes both character-level and radical-level representations. We are the first to use character-based BLSTM-CRF neural architecture for CNER. By contrasting the results of different variants of LSTM blocks, we find the most suitable LSTM block for CNER. We are also the first to investigate Chinese radical-level representations in BLSTM-CRF architecture and get better performance without carefully designed features. We evaluate our system on the third SIGHAN Bakeoff MSRA data set for simplfied CNER task and achieve state-of-the-art performance 90.95% F1.

Keywords: BLSTM-CRF · Radical features · Named Entity Recognition

1 Introduction

Named Entity Recognition (NER) is a fundamental technique for many natural language processing applications, such as information extraction, question answering and so on. Carefully hand-crafted features and domain-specific knowledge resources, such as gazetteers, are widely used to solve the problem. As to Chinese Named Entity Recognition (CNER), there are more complicated properties in Chinese, for example, the lack of word boundary, the complex composition forms, the uncertain length, NE nesting definition and so on [7].

Many related research regards NER as a sequence labelling task. The applied methods on CNER include Maximum Entropy (ME) [3,20], Hidden Markov Model (HMM) [8], Support Vector Machine (SVM) [19] and Conditional Random Field (CRF) algorithms [7,10]. Character-based tagging strategy achieves comparable performance without results of Chinese Word Segmentation (CWS) [2,31], which means Chinese character can be the minimum unit to identify NEs

© Springer International Publishing AG 2016
C.-Y. Lin et al. (Eds.): NLPCC-ICCPOL 2016, LNAI 10102, pp. 239–250, 2016.
DOI: 10.1007/978-3-319-50496-4_20

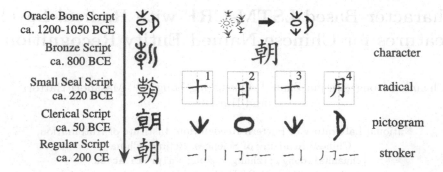

Fig. 1. Decomposition of Chinese character

instead of words. Character-based tagging simplifies the task without reducing performance, so we apply character-based tagging strategy in this paper. With the rapid development of deep learning, neural networks start to show its great capability in NLP tasks and outperform popular statistical algorithms like CRF [16]. Recurrent Neural Network (RNN) learns long distance dependencies better than CRF which utilizes features found in a certain context window. As a special kind of RNN, Long Short-term Memory (LSTM) neural network [13] is proved to be efficient in modeling sequential text [14]. LSTM is designed to cope with the gradient varnishing/exploding problems [1]. Char-LSTM [17] is introduced to learn character-level sequences, such as prefix and suffix in English. As to Chinese, each character is semantically meanful, thanks to its pictographic root from ancient Chinese as depicted in Fig. 1 [26]. The left part of Fig. 1 illustrates the evolution process of Chinese character "朝". The right part of Fig. 1 demonstrates the decomposition. This character "朝", which means "morning", is decomposed into 4 radicals[1] that consists of 12 strokes. As depicted by the pictograms in the right part of Fig. 1, the 1st radical (and the 3rd that happens to be the same) means "grass", and the 2nd and the 4th mean the "sun" and the "moon", respectively. These four radicals altogether convey the meaning that "the moment when sun arises from the grass while the moon wanes away", which is exactly "morning". On the other hand, it is hard to decipher the semantics of strokes, and radicals are the minimum semantic unit for Chinese.

In this paper, we use a character-based bidirectional LSTM-CRF (BLSTM-CRF) neural network for CNER task. By contrasting results of LSTM varients, we find a suitable LSTM block for CNER. Inspired by char-LSTM [17], we propose a radical-level LSTM for Chinese to capture its pictographic root features and get better performance on CNER task.

2   Related Work

In the third SIGHAN Bakeoff [18] CNER shared task, there are three kinds of NEs, namely locations, persons, organizations. Although other statistical models,

---

[1] https://en.wikipedia.org/wiki/Radical_(Chinese_characters).

such as HMM and ME, once achieved good results [3,8,20], nearly all leading performance are achieved using CRF model on this bakeoff. Many following work emphasizes on feature-engineering of character-based CRF model [7,10].

Several neural architectures have previously been proposed for English NER. Our model basically follows the idea of [17]. [17] presented a LSTM-CRF architecture with a char-LSTM layer learning spelling features from supervised corpus and didn't use any additional resources or gazetteers except a massive unlabelled corpus for unsupervised learning of pretrained word embeddings. Instead of char-LSTM for phonogram languages in [17], we propose a radical-level LSTM designed for Chinese characters. [6] uses a Convolutional Neural Network (CNN) over a sequence of word embeddings with a CRF layer on top. [14] presented a model similar to [17]'s LSTM-CRF, but used hand-crafted spelling features. [4] proposed a hybrid of BLSTM and CNNs to model both character-level and word-level representations in English. They utilized external knowledge such as lexicon features and character-type. [22] proposed a BLSTM-CNNs-CRF architecture using CNNs to model character-level information. [28] proposed a hierarchical GRU neural network for sequence tagging using multi-task and cross-lingual joint training.

Only a few work focused on Chinese radical information. [27] proposed a feed-forward neural network similar to [6], but used Chinese radical information as supervised tag to train character embeddings. [21] trained their character embeddings in a holistic unsupervised and bottom-up way based on [23,24], using both radical and radical-like components. [26] used radical embeddings as input like ours and utilized word2vec [23] package to pretrain radical vectors, but they used CNNs, while we use LSTM to obtain radical-level information.

3   Neural Network Architecture

3.1   LSTM

RNNs are a family of neural networks designed for sequential data. RNNs take as input a sequence of vectors $(\mathbf{x}_1, \mathbf{x}_2, \ldots, \mathbf{x}_n)$ and return another sequence $(\mathbf{h}_1, \mathbf{h}_2, \ldots, \mathbf{h}_n)$ that represents state layer information about the sequence at each step in the input. In theory, RNNs can learn long dependencies but in practice they tend to be biased towards their most recent inputs in the sequence [1]. Long Short-term Memory Networks (LSTMs) incorporate a memory-cell to combat this issue and have shown great capabilities to capture long-range dependencies. Our LSTM has input gate, output gate, forget gate and peephole connection. The update of cell state use both input gate and forget gate results. The implementation is:

$$\mathbf{i}_t = \sigma(\mathbf{W}_{xi}\mathbf{x}_t + \mathbf{W}_{hi}\mathbf{h}_{t-1} + \mathbf{W}_{ci}\mathbf{c}_{t-1} + \mathbf{b}_i) \qquad (input\ gate)$$

$$\mathbf{f}_t = \sigma(\mathbf{W}_{xf}\mathbf{x}_t + \mathbf{W}_{hf}\mathbf{h}_{t-1} + \mathbf{W}_{cf}\mathbf{c}_{t-1} + \mathbf{b}_f) \qquad (forget\ gate)$$

$$\mathbf{c}_t = \mathbf{f}_t \odot \mathbf{c}_{t-1} + \mathbf{i}_t \odot tanh(\mathbf{W}_{xc}\mathbf{x}_t + \mathbf{W}_{hc}\mathbf{h}_{t-1} + \mathbf{b}_c) \qquad (cell\ state)$$

$$\mathbf{o}_t = \sigma(\mathbf{W}_{xo}\mathbf{x}_t + \mathbf{W}_{ho}\mathbf{h}_{t-1} + \mathbf{W}_{co}\mathbf{c}_t + \mathbf{b}_o) \qquad (output\ gate)$$

$$\mathbf{h}_t = \mathbf{o}_t \odot tanh(\mathbf{c}_t) \qquad (output)$$

where σ is the element-wise sigmoid function, $\odot$ is the element-wise product, $\mathbf{W}$'s are weight matrices, and $\mathbf{b}$'s are biases.

We get the context vector of a character using a bidirectional LSTM. For a given sentence $(\mathbf{x}_1, \mathbf{x}_2, \ldots, \mathbf{x}_n)$ containing n characters, each character represented as a d-dimensional vector, a LSTM computes a representation $\overrightarrow{\mathbf{h}_t}$ of the left context of the sentence at every character t. Similarly, the right context $\overleftarrow{\mathbf{h}_t}$ starting from the end of the sentence should provide useful information. By reading the same sentence in reverse, we can get another LSTM which achieves the right context information. We refer to the former as the forward LSTM and the latter as the backward LSTM. The context vector of a character is obtained by concatenating its left and right context representations, $\mathbf{h}_t = \left[\overrightarrow{\mathbf{h}_t}; \overleftarrow{\mathbf{h}_t} \right]$.

3.2   CRF

The hidden context vector $\mathbf{h}_t$ can be used directly as features to make independent tagging decisions for each output y_t. But in CNER, there are strong dependencies across output labels. For example, I-PER cannot follow B-ORG, which constraints the possible output tags after B-ORG. Thus, we use CRF to model the outputs of the whole sentence jointly. For an input sentence,

$$\mathbf{X} = (\mathbf{x}_1, \mathbf{x}_2, \ldots, \mathbf{x}_n)$$

we regard $\mathbf{P}$ as the matrix of scores outputted by BLSTM network. $\mathbf{P}$ is of size $n \times k$, where k is the number of distinct tags, and $P_{i,j}$ is the score of the jth tag of the ith character in a sentence. For a sequence of predictions,

$$\mathbf{y} = (y_1, y_2, \ldots, y_n)$$

we define its score as

$$s(\mathbf{X}, \mathbf{y}) = \sum_{i=0}^{n} A_{y_i, y_{i+1}} + \sum_{i=1}^{n} P_{i, y_i} \tag{1}$$

where $\mathbf{A}$ is a matrix of transition scores which models the transition from tag i to tag j. We add *start* and *end* tag to the set of possible tags and they are the tags of y_0 and y_n that separately means the start and the end symbol of a sentence. Therefor, $\mathbf{A}$ is a square matrix of size $k + 2$. After applying a softmax layer over all possible tag sequences, the probability of the sequence $\mathbf{y}$:

$$p(\mathbf{y}|\mathbf{X}) = \frac{e^{s(\mathbf{X}, \mathbf{y})}}{\sum_{\tilde{\mathbf{y}} \in \mathbf{Y}_\mathbf{X}} e^{s(\mathbf{X}, \tilde{\mathbf{y}})}} \tag{2}$$

We maximize the log-probability of the correct tag sequence during training:

$$\log(p(\mathbf{y}|\mathbf{X})) = s(\mathbf{X}, \mathbf{y}) - \log(\sum_{\tilde{\mathbf{y}} \in \mathbf{Y}_\mathbf{X}} e^{s(\mathbf{X}, \tilde{\mathbf{y}})}) \tag{3}$$

$$= s(\mathbf{X}, \mathbf{y}) - \operatorname*{logadd}_{\tilde{\mathbf{y}} \in \mathbf{Y}_\mathbf{X}} s(\mathbf{X}, \tilde{\mathbf{y}}) \tag{4}$$

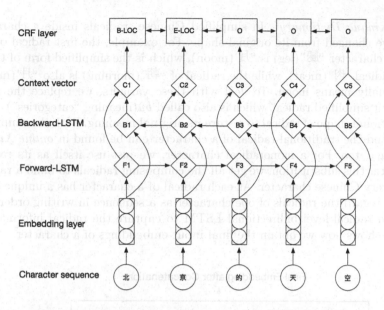

Fig. 2. Main architecture of character-based BLSTM-CRF.

where $\mathbf{Y_X}$ represents all possible tag sequences including those that do not obey the IOB format constraints. It's evident that invalid output label sequences will be discouraged. While decoding, we predict the output sequence that gets the maximum score given by:

$$\mathbf{y}^* = \underset{\tilde{\mathbf{y}} \in \mathbf{Y_X}}{\arg\max}\, s(\mathbf{X}, \tilde{\mathbf{y}}) \tag{5}$$

We just consider bigram constraints between outputs and use dynamic programming during decoding (Fig. 2).

3.3 Radical-Level LSTM

Chinese characters are often composed of smaller and primitive radicals, which serve as the most basic unit for building character meanings [21]. These radicals are inherent features inside Chinese characters and bring additional information that has semantic meaning. For example, the characters "你"(you), "他"(he), and "们"(people) all have the meanings related to human because of their shared radical "亻"(human), a variant of Chinese character "人"(human) [21]. Intrinsically, this kind of radical semantic information is useful to make characters with similar radical sequences close to each other in vector space. It motivates us to focus on the radicals of Chinese characters.

In modern Chinese, character usually contains several radicals. In MSRA data set, including training set and test set, 75.6% characters have more than one radical. We get radical compositions of Chinese characters from *online Xinhua Dictionary*[2]. In simplified Chinese, radicals inside a character may have changed from its original shape. For example, the first radical of the Chinese character "腿"(leg) is "月"(moon), which is the simplified form of traditional radical "肉"(meat), while the radical of "朝"(morning) is also "月"(moon) and actually means moon. To deal with these variants, we replace the most important simplified radical, which is also called *bù*(meaning "categories"), with its traditional shape of radical to restore its original meaning. Both the simplified radical and the traditional radical of a character can be found in *online Xinhua Dictionary*, too. For a monoradical character, we just use itself as its radical part. After this substitution, we get all the composing radicals to build a radical list of every Chinese character. As each radical of a character has a unique position, we regard the radicals of one character as a sequence in writing order. We employ a radical-level bidirectional LSTM to capture the radical information. Figure 3 shows how we obtain the final input embeddings of a character.

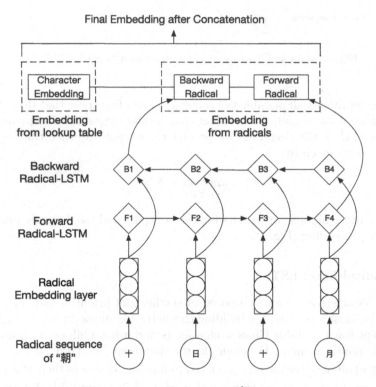

Fig. 3. The final embeddings of Chinese character "朝". We concatenate the final outputs of the radical-level BLSTM to the character embedding from a lookup table as the final representation for the character "朝".

---

[2] http://tool.httpcn.com/Zi/.

3.4 Tagging Scheme

As we use a character-based tagging strategy, we need to assign a named entity label to every character in a sentence. Many NEs span multiple characters in a sentence. Sentences are usually represented the IOB format(Inside, Outside, Beginning). In this paper, we use IOBES tagging scheme. Using this scheme, more information about the following tag is considered.

4 Network Training

4.1 LSTM Variants

We compare results of LSTM variants on CNER to find a better variant of LSTM. The initial version of LSTM block [13] included cells, input and output gates to solve the gradient varnishing/exploding problem. So we keep input and output gate in most of the variants. The derived variants of LSTM mentioned in Sect. 3.1 are the following:

1. No Peepholes, No Forget Gate, Coupled only Input Gate (NP, NFG, CIG)
2. Peepholes, No Forget Gate, Coupled only Input Gate (P, NFG, CIG)
3. No Peepholes, Forget Gate, Coupled only Forput Gate (NP, FG, CFG)
4. No Peepholes, Forget Gate, Coupled Input and Forget Gate (NP, FG, CIFG)
5. No Peepholes, Forget Gate(1), Coupled Input and Forget Gate (NP, FG(1), CIFG)
6. Gated Recurrent Unit (GRU)

Considering formule *cell state* in Sect. 3.1, if we use CIG to update cell state, there will be only one gate for both the input and the cell state, so forget gate will be omitted. This is equivalent to setting $f_t = 1 - i_t$ instead of using the forget gate independently. GRU [5] is a variant of LSTM without having separate memory cells and exposes the whole state each time. (5) means bias of forget gate are initialized to 1 instead 0. Results of different variants are reported in Sect. 5.2.

4.2 Pretrained Embeddings

There are usually too many parameters to learn from only a limited training data in deep learning. To solve this problem, unsupervised learning method to pretrain embeddings emerged, which only used large unlabelled corpus. Instead of randomly initialized embeddings, well pretrained embeddings have been proved important for performance of neural network architectures [11,17]. We observe significant improvements using pretrained character embeddings over randomly initialized embeddings. Here we use gensim[3] [25], which contains a python version implementation of word2vec. These embeddings are fine-tuned during training. We use Chinese Wikipedia backup dump of 20151201. After transforming traditional Chinese to simplified Chinese, removing non-utf8 chars and unifying

---

[3] https://radimrehurek.com/gensim/index.html.

different styles of punctuations, we get 1.02 GB unlabelled corpus. Character embeddings are pretrained using CBOW model because it's faster than skip-gram model. Results using different character embedding dimension are shown in Sect. 5.2. Radical embeddings are randomly initialized with dimension of 50.

4.3 Training

We use dropout training [12] before the input to LSTM layer with a probability of 0.5 in order to avoid overfitting and observe a significant improvement in CNER performance. According to [17], we train our network using the back-propagation algorithm updating our parameters on every training example, one at a time. We use stochastic gradient decent (SGD) algorithm with a learning rate of 0.05 for 50 epochs on training set. Dimension of LSTM is the same as its input dimension.

5   Experiments

5.1   Data Sets

We test our model on MSRA data set of the third SIGHAN Bakeoff Chinese named entity recognition task. This dataset contains three types of named entities: locations, persons, organizations. Chinese word segmentation is not available in test set. We just replace every digit with a zero and unify the styles of punctuations appeared in MSRA and pretrained embeddings.

5.2   Results

Table 1 presents our comparisons with different variants of LSTM block. (1) achieves best performance among all the variants. We observe that peephole connections do not improve performance in CNER, but they increase training time because of more connections. Different from conclusions of [9,15], performance decreases after adding the forget gate no matter how to update cell state.

Table 1. Results with LSTM variants.

Table 2. Results with different character embedding dimensions.

ID	Variants of LSTM	F1
(1)	NP, NFG, CIG	90.75
(2)	P, NFG, CIG	90.37
(3)	NP, FG, CFG	89.85
(4)	NP, FG, CIFG	89.90
(5)	NP, FG(1), CIFG	90.45
(6)	GRU	90.43

Dimension	F1
50	88.92
100	90.75
200	90.44

But performance is prompted after setting bias of the forget gate to 1, which make the forget gate to tend to remember long distance dependencies. The way to couple the input and forget gates does not have significantly impact on performance, which is the same as [9]. GRU needs less training time due to the simplification of inner structure without hurting performance badly. Finally, we choose (1) as the LSTM block in the following experiments.

Table 2 shows results with different character embedding dimensions. We use pretrained character embeddings, dropout training, BLSTM-CRF architecture on all three experiments. Different from results reported by [17] in English, 50 dims is not enough to represent Chinese character. 100 dims achieve 1.83% better than 50 dims in CNER, but no more improvement is observed using 200 dims. We use 100 dims in the following experiments.

Our architecture have several components that have different impact on the overall performance. Without CRF layer on top, the model does not converge to a stable state in even 100 epochs using the same learning rate 0.05. We explore the impact that dropout, radical-level representations, pretraining of character emebeddings have on our LSTM-CRF architecture. Results with different architectures are given in Table 3. We find that radical-level LSTM gives us an improvement of +0.53 in F_1 with random initialized character embeddings. It is evident that radical-level information is effective for Chinese. Pretrained character embeddings, which is trained using unlabelled Chinese Wikipedia corpus by unsupervised learning, increase result by +1.84 based on dropout training. Dropout is important and gives the biggest improvement of +3.88. Radical-level LSTM makes out-of-vocabulary characters, which are initialized with random embeddings, close to known characters that have similar radical components. Only 3 characters in the training and test set can not be found in Wikipedia corpus. In other words, there are few characters initialized with random embeddings. So we do not find further improvement using both radical-level LSTM and well pretrained character embeddings. Radical-level LSTM is obviously effective when there is no large corpus for character pretrainings.

Table 3. Results with different components.

Variant	F1
random + dropout	88.91
random + radical + dropout	89.44
pretrain + dropout	90.75
pretrain	86.87

Table 4 shows our results compared with other models for Chinese named entity recognition. To show the capability of our model, we train our model for 100 epochs instead of 50 epochs in the previous experiments. Zhou [31] got first place using word-based CRF model with delicated hand-crafted features in the

Table 4. Results with different methods. We train our models for 100 epochs in this experiment. [a]Indicates results in the open track.

Model	PER-F	LOC-F	ORG-F	P	R	F
Zhou [31]	90.09	85.45	83.10	88.94	84.20	86.51
Chen [2]	82.57	90.53	81.96	91.22	81.71	86.20
Zhou [32]	90.69	91.90	86.19	91.86	88.75	90.28
Zhang [29][a]	96.04	90.34	85.90	92.20	90.18	**91.18**
BLSTM-CRF + radical	89.62	91.76	85.79	91.39	88.22	89.78
BLSTM-CRF + pretrain	91.77	**92.10**	**87.30**	91.28	**90.62**	**90.95**

closed track on MSRA data set with F1 86.51%. Chen [2] achieved F1 86.20% using character-base CRF model. Zhou [32] used a global linear model to identify and categorize CNER jointly with 10 carefully designed feature templates for CNER and 31 context feature templates from [30]. Zhou [32] adopted a more granular labelling schemes for example changing PER tags that are shorter than 4 characters and begin with a Chinese surname to Chinese-PER. In the open track, Zhang [29] got first place using ME model combining knowledge from various sources with 91.18%, such as person name list, organization name dictionary, location keyword list and so on. Our BLSTM-CRF with radical embeddings outperforms previous best CRF model by +3.27 in overall. Our BLSTM-CRF with pretrained character embeddings outperforms all the previous models except for results of Zhang [29] in the open track and achieves state-of-the-art performance with F1 90.95%. Especially for ORG entities, which is the most difficult category to recognize, our approach utilizes the capability of LSTM to learn long-distance dependencies and achieves a remarkable performance. The main reason that Zhang [29] obtained better performance than ours by +0.23 in overall F_1 is that they used additional name dictionaries to achieve very high PER-F while we do not use those dictionaries. Our neural network architecture does not need any hand-crafted features which are important in Zhou [32].

6   Conclusion

This paper presents our neural network model, which incorporates Chinese radical-level information to character-based BLSTM-CRF and achieves state-of-the-art results. We utilize LSTM block to learn long distance dependencies which are useful to recognize ORG entities. Different from research focused on feature engineering, our model does not use any hand-crafted features or domain-specific knowledge and thus, it can be transferred to other domains easily. In the future, we would like to transfer our model to Chinese social media domain.

Acknowledgements. This research work has been partially funded by the Natural Science Foundation of China under Grant No. 91520204 and No. 61303181.

References

1. Bengio, Y., Simard, P., Frasconi, P.: Learning long-term dependencies with gradient descent is difficult. IEEE Trans. Neural Netw. **5**, 157–166 (1994)
2. Chen, A., Peng, F., Shan, R., Sun, G.: Chinese named entity recognition with conditional probabilistic models. In: Proceedings of 5th SIGHAN Workshop on Chinese Language Processing, pp. 173–176 (2006)
3. Chieu, H.L., Ng, H.T.: Named entity recognition: a maximum entropy approach using global information. In: Proceedings of 19th International Conference on Computational Linguistics, vol. 1, pp. 1–7. Association for Computational Linguistics, Morristown (2002)
4. Chiu, J.P.C., Nichols, E.: Named entity recognition with bidirectional LSTM-CNNs. In: Transactions of the ACL, pp. 1–9 (2015)
5. Cho, K., van Merrienboer, B., Bahdanau, D., Bengio, Y.: On the properties of neural machine translation: encoder-decoder approaches. In: SSST-8, pp. 103–111 (2014)
6. Collobert, R., Weston, J., Bottou, L., Karlen, M., Kavukcuoglu, K., Kuksa, P.: Natural language processing (almost) from scratch. J. Mach. Learn. Res. **12**, 2493–2537 (2011)
7. Duan, H., Zheng, Y.: A study on features of the CRFs-based Chinese. Int. J. Adv. Intell. **3**, 287–294 (2011)
8. Fu, G., Luke, K.K.: Chinese named entity recognition using lexicalized HMMs. ACM SIGKDD Explor. Newsl. **7**, 19–25 (2005)
9. Greff, K., Srivastava, R.K., Koutník, J., Steunebrink, B.R., Schmidhuber, J.: LSTM: a search space odyssey. p. 10 (2015). arXiv
10. Han, A.L.-F., Wong, D.F., Chao, L.S.: Chinese named entity recognition with conditional random fields in the light of Chinese characteristics. In: Kłopotek, M.A., Koronacki, J., Marciniak, M., Mykowiecka, A., Wierzchoń, S.T. (eds.) IIS 2013. LNCS, vol. 7912, pp. 57–68. Springer, Heidelberg (2013). doi:10.1007/978-3-642-38634-3_8
11. Hinton, G.E., Salakhutdinov, R.R.: Reducing the dimensionality of data with neural networks. Science **313**, 504–507 (2006)
12. Hinton, G.E., Srivastava, N., Krizhevsky, A., Sutskever, I., Salakhutdinov, R.R.: Improving neural networks by preventing co-adaptation of feature detectors. pp. 1–18 (2012). arXiv e-prints
13. Hochreiter, S., Schmidhuber, J.: Long short-term memory. Neural Comput. **9**, 1735–1780 (1997)
14. Huang, Z., Xu, W., Yu, K.: Bidirectional LSTM-CRF models for sequence tagging (2015). arXiv
15. Jozefowicz, R., Zaremba, W., Sutskever, I.: An empirical exploration of recurrent network architectures. In: Proceedings of 32nd International Conference on Machine Learning, pp. 2342–2350 (2015)
16. Lafferty, J., McCallum, A., Pereira, F.: Conditional random fields: probabilistic models for segmenting and labeling sequence data. In: Proceedings of 18th International Conference on Machine Learning, ICML 2001, pp. 282–289 (2001)
17. Lample, G., Ballesteros, M., Subramanian, S., Kawakami, K., Dyer, C.: Neural architectures for named entity recognition. pp. 1–10 (2016). arXiv
18. Levow, G.A.: The third international Chinese language processing bakeoff: word segmentation and named entity recognition. In: Computational Linguistics, pp. 108–117 (2006)

19. Li, L., Mao, T., Huang, D., Yang, Y.: Hybrid models for Chinese named entity recognition. In: Proceedings of 5th SIGHAN Workshop on Chinese Language Processing, pp. 72–78 (2006)
20. Li, W., Li, J., Tian, Y., Sui, Z.: Fine-grained classification of named entities by fusing multi-features. pp. 693–702 (2012)
21. Li, Y., Li, W., Sun, F., Li, S.: Component-enhanced Chinese character embeddings. In: EMNLP, pp. 829–834 (2015)
22. Ma, X., Hovy, E.: End-to-end sequence labeling via bi-directional LSTM-CNNs-CRF (2016). arXiv:1603.01354v4 [cs.LG]
23. Mikolov, T., Corrado, G., Chen, K., Dean, J.: Efficient estimation of word representations in vector space. In: Proceedings of International Conference on Learning Representations (ICLR 2013), pp. 1–12 (2013)
24. Mikolov, T., Sutskever, I., Chen, K., Corrado, G., Dean, J.: Distributed representations of words and phrases and their compositionality. In: NIPS, pp. 1–9 (2013)
25. Řehůřek, R., Sojka, P.: Software framework for topic modelling with large corpora. In: Proceedings of LREC 2010 Workshop on New Challenges for NLP Frameworks, pp. 45–50. ELRA, Valletta, Malta (2010). http://is.muni.cz/publication/884893/en
26. Shi, X., Zhai, J., Yang, X., Xie, Z., Liu, C.: Radical embedding: delving deeper to Chinese radicals. In: Proceedings of 53rd Annual Meeting of the Association for Computational Linguistics and the 7th International Joint Conference on Natural Language Processing (vol. 1: Long Papers), pp. 594–598 (2015)
27. Sun, Y., Lin, L., Yang, N., Ji, Z., Wang, X.: Radical-enhanced chinese character embedding. In: Loo, C.K., Yap, K.S., Wong, K.W., Teoh, A., Huang, K. (eds.) ICONIP 2014. LNCS, vol. 8835, pp. 279–286. Springer, Heidelberg (2014). doi:10.1007/978-3-319-12640-1_34
28. Yang, Z., Salakhutdinov, R., Cohen, W.: Multi-task cross-lingual sequence tagging from scratch (2016). arXiv preprint arXiv:1603.06270
29. Zhang, S., Qin, Y., Wen, J., Wang, X.: Word segmentation and named entity recognition for SIGHAN Bakeoff3. In: Proceedings of 5th SIGHAN Workshop on Chinese Language Processing, pp. 158–161 (2006)
30. Zhang, Y., Clark, S.: A fast decoder for joint word segmentation and POS-tagging using a single discriminative model. In: Proceedings of 2010 Conference on Empirical Methods in Natural Language Processing, pp. 843–852 (2010)
31. Zhou, J., He, L., Dai, X., Chen, J.: Chinese named entity recognition with a multi-phase model. In: Proceedings of 5th SIGHAN Workshop on Chinese Language Processing, pp. 213–216 (2006)
32. Zhou, J., Qu, W., Zhang, F.: Chinese named entity recognition via joint identification and categorization. Chin. J. Electron. **22**, 225–230 (2013)

Improving First Order Temporal Fact Extraction with Unreliable Data

Bingfeng Luo[1], Yansong Feng[1(✉)], Zheng Wang[2], and Dongyan Zhao[1]

[1] Institute of Computer Science and Technology,
Peking University, Beijing, People's Republic of China
{bingfeng_luo,fengyansong,zhaody}@pku.edu.cn
[2] School of Computing and Communications, Lancaster University, Bailrigg, UK
z.wang@lancaster.ac.uk

Abstract. In this paper, we deal with the task of extracting first order temporal facts from free text. This task is a subtask of relation extraction and it aims at extracting relations between entity and time. Currently, the field of relation extraction mainly focuses on extracting relations between entities. However, we observe that the multi-granular nature of time expressions can help us divide the dataset constructed by distant supervision into reliable and less reliable subsets, which can help to improve the extraction results on relations between entity and time. We accordingly contribute the first dataset focusing on the first order temporal fact extraction task using distant supervision. To fully utilize both the reliable and the less reliable data, we propose to use curriculum learning to rearrange the training procedure, label dropout to make the model be more conservative about less reliable data, and instance attention to help the model distinguish important instances from unimportant ones. Experiments show that these methods help the model outperform the model trained purely on the reliable dataset as well as the model trained on the dataset where all subsets are mixed together.

Keywords: Temporal fact extraction · Distant supervision · Knowledge base

1 Introduction

Knowledge base population aims at automatically extracting facts about entities from text to extend knowledge bases. These facts are often organized as (*subject, relation, object*) triples. Among these relations, the relations that require time expressions as objects play an important role in the completeness of knowledge base. For example, every person should have *date_of_birth* and almost all asteroid should have *date_of_discovery*. However, we find that in Wikidata[1], 19.3% people do not have *date_of_birth*, and 39.3% asteroids do

---

[1] www.wikidata.org. It is a rapid-growing knowledge base and Freebase (www.freebase.com) is migrating its data to it.

© Springer International Publishing AG 2016
C.-Y. Lin et al. (Eds.): NLPCC-ICCPOL 2016, LNAI 10102, pp. 251–262, 2016.
DOI: 10.1007/978-3-319-50496-4_21

not have *date_of_discovery*. Therefore, extracting relations between entity and time is an important task.

As suggested by T-YAGO [20], which extends YAGO [6] with temporal aspects, there are two types of facts that we need to extract: *First order facts* are triples like (*Barack_Obama*, spouse, *Michelle_Obama*), whose subjects are entities. *Higher order facts* take other facts as subjects. For example, ((*Barack_Obama*, *spouse*, *Michelle_Obama*), *start_time*, 3_October_1992) is a higher order fact indicating the start time of the marriage of Barack Obama and Michelle Obama. In this paper, we will focus on first order temporal fact extraction, which is a subtask of first order fact extraction (often referred to as *relation extraction*) that focuses on extracting facts that take time expressions as objects.

Previous work of relation extraction mainly focuses on extracting relations between entities, and the task of extracting first order temporal facts receives only limited attention. Some researchers try to extract first order temporal facts from semi-structured documents like Wikipedia[2] [9], but how to extract first order temporal facts from free text is seldom investigated specifically.

Indeed, most of the existing methods developed to extract relations between entities can be used directly to extract first order temporal facts, which to some extent explains the sparsity of researches in first order temporal fact extraction. However, there are still interesting properties in first order temporal fact extraction that the entity-entity relation extraction task does not have.

When extracting first order facts from free text, distant supervision is often used to build noisy datasets [12]. Given a (subject s, relation r, object o) triple in a knowledge base, it uses s and o to retrieve text corpora like Wikipedia articles, and collects sentences containing both s and o as supports for this triple. The noisy nature of distant supervision has long been bothering researchers, and various techniques have been introduced to deal with the noise [16,17].

However, it is different when applying distant supervision to first order temporal fact extraction. We find that the more fine-grained the time expression is, the more likely the retrieved sentence is a true support for this triple. For example, sentences containing both *Oct. 5, 2011* and *Steve Jobs* are highly likely to indicate Steve Jobs' death date, while sentences containing only *2011* and *Steve Jobs* may only talk about his resignation. The intuition is that, there is usually only one important thing that relates to an entity in a single day. As the time granularity becomes coarser, more important things are likely to happen in the same time period, and hence the data quality goes down.

We find that sentences containing full date (day, month and year) are highly reliable and we can train a relation extractor as if we are using human labeled data. However, there is still useful knowledge remaining in sentences containing only coarser granularities. Therefore, how to use the less reliable data to improve the model becomes another problem.

Following this observation, we construct the first order temporal fact extraction dataset with distant supervision. The dataset is grouped into 4 smaller

---

[2] www.wikipedia.org.

dataset with decreasing reliability. To fully utilize both the reliable and less reliable data, we propose to use curriculum learning to rearrange the training procedure, label dropout to make the model more conservative about less reliable data, and instance attention to help the model distinguish important instances from unimportant ones. Experiments show that these methods help the model outperform the model trained purely on the reliable dataset as well as the model trained on the dataset where all subsets are mixed together.

2 Related Work

Relation Extraction. The most related thread of work to us is relation extraction. Most of the methods in this field can be applied directly to first order temporal fact extraction, which possibly explains why there are seldom researches that focus specifically on extracting first order temporal facts from free text. The commonly used paradigm in relation extraction is distant supervision [12], which tries to construct a noisy dataset using triples in a knowledge base as guidance. Feature based [12], graphic model based [7,16] and neural network based [23] methods have been applied under this paradigm. To cope with the noisy nature of distant supervision, there are also some researches aim at reducing the noise introduced by distant supervision [17], or put this task in the multi-instance paradigm [7,16,23]. In first order temporal facts extraction, we find that the multi-granular nature of time expressions can help us distinguish reliable distant supervision data from less reliable ones, and we can use this property to improve the model performance.

Higher Order Temporal Fact Extraction. Higher order temporal fact extraction mainly aims at identifying the valid time scope of a (subject, relation, object) triple. Therefore, it is also referred to as temporal scoping. The commonly used dataset is introduced by the 2011 and 2013 temporal slot filling (TSF) shared tasks hosted by Text Analysis Conference (TAC) [5,8]. Regular expression based methods [20], graph based methods [19] and distant supervision based methods [2,15] have been used in this task. While our task focuses on first order temporal facts which contain a variety of relations (see Table 1), this thread of work only tries to find the start time and end time of a triple, which makes this task seems easier. However, since this task takes a triple as subject, people need to come up with different methods to handle this property, and thus makes this task harder.

Event Temporal Relation Identification. Event temporal relation identification is a related task introduced by TempEval [14,18]. This task aims at identifying event-time and event-event temporal relations like *before*, *after* and *overlap*. Feature based methods [11] and Markov Logic Network based methods [22] have been applied to this task. Apart from ordering events, TIE system [10] also uses probabilistic inference to bound the start and the ending time of events. This task differs from our task in that it deals with the relations between event and time rather than entity and time, and it mainly focuses on ordering events while we focuses on extracting triples that take time expressions as objects.

3   Dataset Construction

We use Wikidata as the knowledge base and Wikipedia articles as the corpus. There are about 29 relations that require time as object in Wikidata. To ensure sufficient training instances for each relation, 12 relations are used (see Table 1).

Distant Supervision. For each (entity e, relation r, time t) triple, we use the official name and the aliases in Wikidata of entity e as its surface forms. As for time t, we generate its surface forms in 4 granularities: *Full Date* (like 12 Jan. 2011), *Month Year* (like Jan. 2011), *Year Only* (like 2011), and *Month Day* (like 12 Jan.).

Negative Data. The negative data come from two sources. First, for every entity mention $\tilde{e}$ in a retrieved sentence, each $(\tilde{e}, t)$ pair except (e, t) is considered to have no relation. Entity mentions are identified by finding strings that matches the canonical names or aliases of entities in Wikidata using Aho-Coraisake algorithm [1]. Second, we retrieve all the sentences containing the surface forms of entity e and detect time mentions $\tilde{t}$ with SUTime [4]. For each entity surface form, we find at most 5 corresponding entities using Wikidata API[3]. If $\tilde{t}$ does not appear in any triples that take entity e as subject in Wikidata, the entity mention and the time mention are considered to have no relation.

Dataset Validation. We manually examined 20 randomly selected sentences for each relation in each granularity (see Table 1). We find that full-date data have high quality and the data quality goes down as the granularity becomes coarser. Since sentences containing only day and month are limited, some relations do not have 20 instances in month-day data. Considering the limited number and low quality, month-day data will not be used in the experiment. Note that *point_in_time* and *end_time* data in full-date granularity are not very reliable. This is because that these two relations often take battles as subjects. However, descriptions about battles are often very detailed, and many retrieved sentences actually describe specific events in the battle rather than the battle itself.

4   Model

The inputs to our first order temporal fact extraction model are sentences labeled with an entity mention e and a time mention t. The task is to identify the relation between the given time and entity. We will first briefly introduce the baseline model. Then we will discuss several methods to utilize both the reliable and the unreliable data to achieve better performance.

---

[3] www.wikidata.org/w/api.php.

Table 1. Statistics of extracted temporal relation mention. Left side of the slash is the number of correct relation mentions, right side is the number of mentions examined.

Relation	Full Date	Month Year	Year Only	Month Day
date_of_birth	**20/20**	**19/20**	**19/20**	11/20
date_of_death	**20/20**	13/20	13/20	9/20
time_of_discovery	**20/20**	15/20	12/20	5/20
inception	**17/20**	15/20	7/20	4/20
dissolved_or_abolished	15/20	8/20	10/20	1/5
time_of_spacecraft_launch	**19/20**	**17/20**	13/20	1/1
time_of_spacecraft_landing	**18/20**	5/20	7/20	4/5
first_performance	**18/20**	**16/20**	15/20	1/2
publication_date	**19/20**	15/20	**16/20**	5/12
point_in_time	13/20	13/20	**19/20**	8/19
start_time	**18/20**	**18/20**	14/20	14/18
end_time	10/20	13/20	9/20	11/20

4.1 PCNN Model

Our basic model is the Piecewise Convolutional Neural Network (PCNN) [23], which achieves the state-of-art results in entity-entity relation extraction task. Following the PCNN work, we also concatenate position embeddings to the original word embedding as input. To be concrete, for each word in the sentence, we calculate its distance to the entity mention and the time mention. Each distance (e.g. -2, -1, 1, 2, etc.) is associated with a randomly initialized embedding vector, which will be updated during training.

As shown in Fig. 1, the input sentence is divided into three parts by the entity mention e and the time mention t. The convolution and max-pooling operation are applied to the three parts separately to obtain the embeddings of each part.

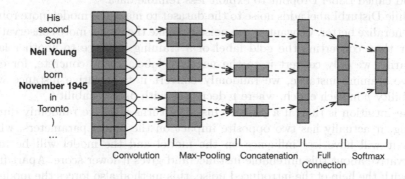

Fig. 1. The architecture of the PCNN model. In this example, *Neil Young* is the entity mention and *November 1945* is the time mention.

After that, these three embeddings are concatenated and fed to a full connection layer. Finally, the softmax classifier is used to generate the relation distribution, and cross entropy is used as loss function.

Due to the noise in the less reliable data, we find that the model trained on the dataset where all the subsets (except the month-day data) mixed together performs significantly worse than the model trained only on the full-date data. Therefore, we consider the latter one as our baseline model. Due to the high reliability of full-date data, we use multi-class classification paradigm rather than the multi-instance classification paradigm used in the original PCNN paper.

4.2 Curriculum Learning

Instead of adding less reliable data directly to the training set, an alternative way to incorporate these data is to use the idea of curriculum learning [3]: start with easier aspect of the task and then increase the difficulty level gradually.

To be concrete, we first train our model on the reliable full-date data for c_1 epochs. Since the data are highly reliable, the task is relatively easy for the model and can give the model the basic classification ability. After that, we add the less reliable month-year data to the training set to increase the difficulty and train for another c_2 epochs. Finally, the most unreliable year-only data are added, and the model is trained for the last c_3 epochs.

The intuition behind this is that, after training on the reliable data for several epochs, the model has already been positioned near the optimal point in the space of model parameters, and therefore it is less likely to be misled by less reliable data. Also note that since the reliable data are used throughout the entire training procedure and is fitted more times than less reliable data, the reliable data actually lead the entire training procedure.

4.3 Label Dropout

Inspired by the DisturbLabel method [21], which randomly convert the gold label of a training instance to another label arbitrarily, we propose a more conservative method called Label Dropout to exploit less reliable data.

While DisturbLabel adds noise to the dataset to make the model more robust and generalize better, we want to use noise to make the model more conservative. Rather than converting the gold label of a training instance to another label arbitrarily, we only convert it to the negative label. To be concrete, for each positive training instance, we randomly convert it to negative instance with probability p in each epoch, where p decreases with data reliability.

The intuition is that, if a positive instance turns negative randomly during training, it actually has two opposite impact on the model parameters, which means it will have less influence on the model and the model will be more conservative about this unreliable instance and gives it lower score. Apart from that, with the help of the introduced noise, this method also forces the model to learn the most essential features in less reliable data, and thus avoids the model from learning unreliable features.

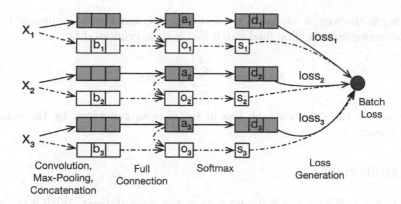

Fig. 2. Instance attention model. The part with solid squares and solid lines is the vanilla PCNN for relation extraction. The part with hollow squares and dashed lines is the W-PCNN used to obtain weights for each training instance x_i. a_i is the output of the full connection layer of PCNN, b_i is the output of the connection layer of W-PCNN, o_i is the output of the full connection layer of W-PCNN, s_i is the instance weight and d_i is the relation distribution.

4.4 Instance Attention

To make the training procedure more robust, we further introduce a novel instance attention method. The intuition is that we want the model to be able to distinguish important instances from unimportant ones. This is achieved by applying attention mechanism to the instance level. In each batch, we generate a weight for each instance to indicate its importance. On the one hand, under the framework of curriculum learning, the model can learn the pattern of noisy data and give them lower weights. On the other hand, the model can learn to give up very hard instances or concentrate on promising instances that is not well-learned.

To be more specific, we train a parallel PCNN model containing both the original PCNN and a smaller PCNN (referred to as W-PCNN) with fewer convolution kernels designed to produce the weight for each instance x_i. As shown in Fig. 2, the part with solid squares and solid lines is the original PCNN model, and the part with hollow squares and dashed lines is the W-PCNN. To consider both the information of the input instance and the PCNN prediction, we concatenate the output vector a_i of the full connection layer in the original PCNN and the output vector b_i of the concatenation layer in W-PCNN. The concatenated vector $c_i = [a_i^T, b_i^T]^T$ is fed to a full connection layer, generating an output vector o_i:

$$o_i = W_o \times c_i \tag{1}$$

where W_o is the weight matrix. The weight of the input instance x_i is generated by instance level softmax:

$$s_i = \frac{e^{w_s^T o_i}}{\sum_{i=1}^{k} e^{w_s^T o_i}} \tag{2}$$

where $\mathbf{w_s}$ is the weight vector, k is the batch size and the denominator is the used for normalization. The final batch loss is then generated by:

$$batch\_loss = \sum_{i=1}^{k} s_i \times loss_i \qquad (3)$$

where $loss_i$ is the cross entropy loss of instance $\mathbf{x_i}$ generated by the original PCNN model.

5   Experiments

Dataset Detail. We use the full-date data as our basic dataset. With 8:1:1 split, we get 22,214 positive instances for training, 2,776 for validation and 2,771 for testing[4]. Since *date_of_birth* and *date_of_death* (*big relations*) take a large portion of the data, we only use relations other than them in month-year and year-only data as additional unreliable data, which contains 2,094 and 53,469 positive instances separately. We generate 2 negative instances for every positive instance using the first strategy. As for the second strategy, we generate 40,000 negative instances for training, 3,576 for validation, and 3,493 for testing.

Hyperparameters. We use 100-dimension word embedding pre-trained using GloVe [13] and 20 dimensional randomly initialized position embedding. We use SGD for optimization with batch size 20, learning rate 0.1, dropout probability 0.5. The PCNN model has 200 convolution kernels followed by a full connection layer with 200 output units. W-PCNN has 50 convolution kernels and the full connection layer has 200 output units. The settings of curriculum learning parameters are $c_1 = c_2 = c_3 = 15$, which means the month-year data are added in the 16th epoch, and the year-only data are added in the 31th epoch. The label dropout method drops month-year data with probability 0.5, and year-only data with probability 0.7 (we do not conduct label dropout for full-date data).

5.1   Main Results

Following previous work on relation extraction, we report the precision recall curve (PR curve) of our model. The overall PR curve on test set is shown in Fig. 3(a). We can see that if we do not distinguish the subsets with different reliability and mix them together (see the *mixed* line), we will get significant worse results than the model trained with only reliable subset. Therefore, we consider the latter model as our baseline. After adding curriculum learning, the model gains a significant boost over the baseline PCNN. Label dropout improves the performance in the low recall region (corresponding to high precision). Instance attention further improves the results in both high and low recall region. This shows that all of the three proposed methods help the model make better use of the less unreliable data.

---

[4] The dataset can be downloaded from: github.com/pfllo/TemporalFactExtraction.

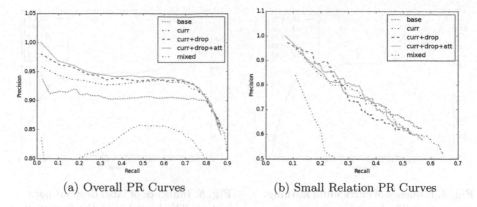

(a) Overall PR Curves   (b) Small Relation PR Curves

Fig. 3. Precision recall curves on test data. The label *base* refers to the basic PCNN model trained only on the full-date data, *curr* refers to curriculum learning, *drop* refers to label dropout, *att* refers to instance attention, *mixed* refers to the model trained with these three types of data mixed together. The figure is truncated to better display the main results. Therefore, some parts of the *mixed* line are invisible.

To further investigate where these improvements come from, we also report PR curves of *small relations* (relations other than *date_of_birth* and *date_of_death*) in Fig. 3(b). As we can see, the small-relation curve of curriculum learning is close to the baseline, showing that the additional noisy instances does not contribute much useful information to small relations and the overall boost comes mainly from the improvement of big relations. Recall that we do not use big relations in less reliable data, therefore the reason for the improved performance of big relations should come mainly from the reduced false positive rate.

When label dropout is added, the noisy positive data become useful and make the model be more conservative about its prediction. When the model assigns a positive label to an instance that it is not very confident about, it will produce a lower score than before, and thus makes the scores of confident predictions and less confident predictions more separable from each other, which is reflected by the better performance of low recall region. However, the lowered scores of less confident predictions make them less separable from those instances that the model is very unconfident about. Therefore, the performance decreases in the high recall region.

Finally, instance attention enables the model to avoid the influence of noise and very hard instances by giving them lower weights and concentrate on promising instances that are not well learned. This mechanism makes the training procedure more self-adaptive and thus smoothes the small relation curve of label dropout, which leads to good performance in both high and low recall regions.

5.2 Influence of Curriculum Learning Parameters

Since the curriculum learning method contributes the major boost, it is worth further investigating how its parameters influence the result. We report the PR

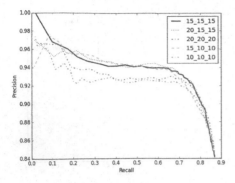
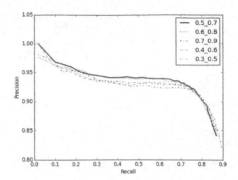

Fig. 4. Influence of curriculum learning parameters. The legend is c_1_c_2_c_3, corresponding to the epochs trained with only full-date data, the epochs trained with full-date and month-year data, and the epochs trained with all data.

Fig. 5. Influence of label dropout parameters. The legend is in the format of p_1_p_2, which corresponds to the label dropout rate of month-year data and the label dropout rate of the year-only data respectively.

curves of our full model with different settings of c_i. As we can see from Fig. 4, $c_1 = c_2 = c_3 = 15$ achieves the best overall performance. Slightly increasing c_1 or slightly decreasing c_2 and c_3 does not significantly influence the overall performance, which shows the robustness of the model.

However, when we decrease the epochs trained only with full-date data (c_2 and c_3 are also decreased to reduce their influence), the performance significantly drops. This indicates that we should train the model with only reliable data for enough epochs so that it is tuned near the optimal position in parameter space before exposed to less reliable data. Otherwise, the model will be easily misled to suboptimal positions by the noise. We can also see that increasing the epochs for less reliable data impairs the overall performance as well. This indicates that although our model has some resistance to the noise in less reliable data, it still tend to overfit the less reliable data given enough training epochs.

To conclude, when tuning the model, it is safer to use larger c for reliable data and smaller c for less reliable data. Note that 15 is the number of epochs that the baseline model needs to roughly converge, which to some extent explains why the model underfits the reliable data when c_1 is smaller than 15, and why the model overfits the less reliable data when c_2 and c_3 is bigger than 15.

5.3   Influence of Label Dropout Parameters

To see how the label dropout parameters influence the model performance, we report the PR curves of our full model with different settings of label dropout parameters in Fig. 5. As we can see, the best performance is achieved when $p_1 = 0.5$ (label dropout rate of month-year data) and $p_2 = 0.7$ (label dropout rate of year-only data). Slightly increase the label dropout rate does not produce significant difference, which to some extent shows the model robustness. Further increasing the label dropout rate will produce the results that are consistently worse, indicating that high label dropout rate will decrease the amount the information that the model can learn from the less reliable data. However, the performance drops immediately when the label dropout rate decreases. This indicates that the increased influence of unreliable positive data causes more harm to the model than the loss of learnable information.

6 Conclusion

In this paper, we contribute the first dataset that focuses specifically on first order temporal fact extraction using distant supervision. We observe that, by grouping the data with different time granularities, we can naturally obtain data groups with different levels of reliability. Although we can train our model directly on the reliable full-date data, methods like curriculum learning, label dropout and instance attention can further exploit the less reliable data and produce better results than the model trained with only reliable ones.

Acknowledgement. This work was supported by National High Technology R&D Program of China (Grant Nos. 2015AA015403, 2014AA015102), Natural Science Foundation of China (Grant Nos. 61202233, 61272344, 61370055) and the joint project with IBM Research. Any correspondence please refer to Yansong Feng.

References

1. Aho, A.V., Corasick, M.J.: Efficient string matching: an aid to bibliographic search. Commun. ACM **18**(6), 333–340 (1975)
2. Artiles, J., Li, Q., Cassidy, T., Tamang, S., Ji, H.: CUNY BLENDER TACKBP 2011 temporal slot filling system description. In: Proceedings of Text Analysis Conference (TAC) (2011)
3. Bengio, Y., Louradour, J., Collobert, R., Weston, J.: Curriculum learning. In: Proceedings of 26th Annual International Conference on Machine Learning, pp. 41–48. ACM (2009)
4. Chang, A.X., Manning, C.D.: SUTime: a library for recognizing and normalizing time expressions. In: LREC, pp. 3735–3740 (2012)
5. Dang, H.T., Surdeanu, M.: Task description for knowledge-base population at TAC 2013 (2013)
6. Fabian, M., Gjergji, K., Gerhard, W.: YAGO: a core of semantic knowledge unifying WordNet and Wikipedia. In: 16th International World Wide Web Conference, WWW, pp. 697–706 (2007)
7. Hoffmann, R., Zhang, C., Ling, X., Zettlemoyer, L., Weld, D.S.: Knowledge-based weak supervision for information extraction of overlapping relations. In: Proceedings of ACL (2011)
8. Ji, H., Grishman, R., Dang, H.: Overview of the TAC 2011 knowledge base population track. In: Text Analysis Conference (2011)
9. Kuzey, E., Weikum, G.: Extraction of temporal facts and events from wikipedia. In: Proceedings of 2nd Temporal Web Analytics Workshop, pp. 25–32. ACM (2012)

10. Ling, X., Weld, D.S.: Temporal information extraction. In: AAAI, vol. 10, 1385–1390 (2010)
11. Mani, I., Verhagen, M., Wellner, B., Lee, C.M., Pustejovsky, J.: Machine learning of temporal relations. In: Proceedings of 21st International Conference on Computational Linguistics and the 44th Annual Meeting of the Association for Computational Linguistics (2006)
12. Mintz, M., Bills, S., Snow, R., Jurafsky, D.: Distant supervision for relation extraction without labeled data. In: Proceedings of 47th Annual Meeting of the Association for Computational Linguistics (2009)
13. Pennington, J., Socher, R., Manning, C.D.: Glove: global vectors for word representation. In: EMNLP, vol. 14, pp. 1532–1543 (2014)
14. Pustejovsky, J., Verhagen, M.: SemEval-2010 task 13: evaluating events, time expressions, and temporal relations (TempEval-2). In: Proceedings of Workshop on Semantic Evaluations: Recent Achievements and Future Directions, pp. 112–116. Association for Computational Linguistics (2009)
15. Sil, A., Cucerzan, S.: Temporal scoping of relational facts based on Wikipedia data. In: CoNLL-2014, p. 109 (2014)
16. Surdeanu, M., Tibshirani, J., Nallapati, R., Manning, C.D.: Multi-instance multi-label learning for relation extraction. In: Proceedings of 2012 Joint Conference on Empirical Methods in Natural Language Processing and Computational Natural Language Learning, pp. 455–465. Association for Computational Linguistics (2012)
17. Takamatsu, S., Sato, I., Nakagawa, H.: Reducing wrong labels in distant supervision for relation extraction. In: Proceedings of 50th Annual Meeting of the Association for Computational Linguistics (2012)
18. Verhagen, M., Gaizauskas, R., Schilder, F., Hepple, M., Katz, G., Pustejovsky, J.: SemEval-2007 task 15: TempEval temporal relation identification. In: Proceedings of 4th International Workshop on Semantic Evaluations, pp. 75–80. Association for Computational Linguistics (2007)
19. Wang, Y., Yang, B., Qu, L., Spaniol, M., Weikum, G.: Harvesting facts from textual web sources by constrained label propagation. In: Proceedings of 20th ACM International Conference on Information and Knowledge Management (2011)
20. Wang, Y., Zhu, M., Qu, L., Spaniol, M., Weikum, G.: Timely YAGO: harvesting, querying, and visualizing temporal knowledge from Wikipedia. In: Proceedings of 13th International Conference on Extending Database Technology (2010)
21. Xie, L., Wang, J., Wei, Z., Wang, M., Tian, Q.: DisturbLabel: regularizing CNN on the loss layer (2016). arXiv preprint arXiv:1605.00055
22. Yoshikawa, K., Riedel, S., Asahara, M., Matsumoto, Y.: Jointly identifying temporal relations with Markov logic. In: Proceedings of ACL-IJCNLP (2009)
23. Zeng, D., Liu, K., Chen, Y., Zhao, J.: Distant supervision for relation extraction via piecewise convolutional neural networks. In: EMNLP (2015)

Reducing Human Effort in Named Entity Corpus Construction Based on Ensemble Learning and Annotation Categorization

Tingming Lu[1,2], Man Zhu[3], and Zhiqiang Gao[1,2]([✉])

[1] Key Lab of Computer Network and Information Integration,
(Southeast University), Ministry of Education, Nanjing, China
lutingming@163.com, zqgao@seu.edu.cn
[2] School of Computer Science and Engineering, Southeast University, Nanjing, China
[3] School of Computer Science and Technology,
Nanjing University of Posts and Telecommunications, Nanjing, China
mzhu@njupt.edu.cn

Abstract. Annotated named entity corpora play a significant role in many natural language processing applications. However, annotation by humans is time-consuming and costly. In this paper, we propose a high recall pre-annotator which combines multiple existing named entity taggers based on ensemble learning, to reduce the number of annotations that humans have to add. In addition, annotations are categorized into normal annotations and candidate annotations based on their estimated confidence, to reduce the number of human corrective actions as well as the total annotation time. The experiment results show that our approach outperforms the baseline methods in reduction of annotation time without loss in annotation performance (in terms of F-measure).

Keywords: Corpus construction · Named Entity Recognition · Assisted annotation · Ensemble learning

1 Introduction

Named Entity Recognition (NER), one of the fundamental tasks for building Natural Language Processing (NLP) systems, is a task that detects Named Entity (NE) mentions in a given text and classifies these mentions to a pre-defined list of types. Machine learning (ML) based approaches can achieve good performance in NER, but they often require large amounts of annotated samples, which are time-consuming and costly to build. One usual way to improve this situation is to automatically pre-annotate the corpora, so that human annotators need merely to correct errors rather than annotate from scratch.

Resulted from more than two decades of research, many named entity taggers are publicly available now, so a question to ask is how to utilize these existing taggers to assist named entity annotation. It is well known that multiple taggers can be combined using ensemble learning techniques to create a system that

© Springer International Publishing AG 2016
C.-Y. Lin et al. (Eds.): NLPCC-ICCPOL 2016, LNAI 10102, pp. 263–274, 2016.
DOI: 10.1007/978-3-319-50496-4_22

outperforms the best individual taggers within the system [1,2]. Therefore a natural solution is to create a pre-annotator combining multiple taggers based on ensemble learning. However, as far as we know, no previous study leverage ensemble learning to combine multiple existing taggers to assist named entity annotation.

On the other hand, when served as a pre-annotator, a system is expected to have high recall [3,4], because in general, adding a new annotation takes more time than modifying an existing pre-annoteated one for an annotator. Most NE taggers are tuned to a trade-off between recall and precision, and not all taggers support setting parameters to increase the recall. A high recall pre-annotator may introduces some low confidence annotations, which are more likely to be spurious than those with high confidence. In extremes, too many spurious annotations may mislead annotators and therefore hurt precision of the result corpus. Our intuition is that low confidence annotations play a different role with those with high confidence. But in previous work, annotations are all treated in the same way regardless of their confidence.

In order to address these issues, we propose an approach which combines multiple existing NE taggers based on ensemble learning to create a high recall pre-annotator. Annotations produced by this pre-annotator are categorized into *normal annotations* with high confidence and *candidate annotations* with low confidence.

Take Fig. 1 as an example. Background color indicates the NE type (person, location, or organization) of the annotation. A general pre-annotator may produce annotations like Fig. 1(a). Then annotators need to delete the spurious annotation 'Washington/LOC', and add the missed annotation 'MaliVai Washington/PER'. In Fig. 1(b), annotators do not need to add 'MaliVai Washington/PER' due to high recall of the pre-annotator, although they still need to delete 'Washington/LOC', and in addition, they have to delete the new introduced spurious annotation 'Alami/LOC'. Our approach is illustrated in Fig. 1(c), where *normal annotations* are rendered with black font and underline, while *candidate annotations* with gray font. Annotators do not need to delete the *candidate annotation* 'Alami/LOC', since *candidate annotations* will not be counted as valid annotations when annotators submit the results. All that annotators have to do is approving 'MaliVai Washington/PER' by a simple click on it, and the annotation 'Washington/LOC' will be deleted automaticly because it has a overlapping token 'Washington' with the approved annotation 'MaliVai Washington/PER'. As shown in the above example, *candidate annotations* improve the recall, so annotators need to add less annotations. Spurious ones among the *candidate annotations* do not need to be deleted by annotators, so the number of human corrective actions will not increase significantly.

In summary, we make the following contributions in this paper. (1) We propose an approach which combines multiple existing named entity taggers based on ensemble learning to create a high recall pre-annotator. Our approach does not require annotators to annotate additional training data. (2) Annotations are categorized into *normal annotations* with high confidence and *candidate*

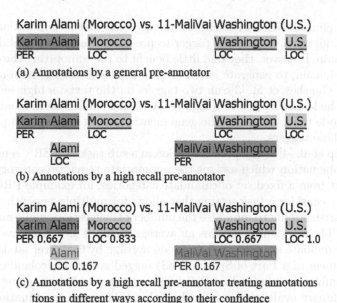

Fig. 1. Illustration of annotations by various pre-annotators.

annotations with low confidence, and treated in different ways to reduce the annotation time. (3) We empirically show that our approach outperforms several baseline approaches in terms of annotation time on a test dataset collected from three publicly available datasets. The related resources are freely available[1] for research purposes.

The remaining part of this paper is organized as follows: In Sect. 2, we mention related work. Section 3 introduces definitions and system architecture, and Sect. 4 details our method. Section 5 describes the experimental setup, followed by analysis on the obtained results. Finally, we conclude and discuss future directions in Sect. 7.

2   Related Work

The goal of pre-annotation is to reduce the time required to annotate a text by reducing the number of annotations an annotator must add or modify. Pre-annotation has been studied widely in NLP tasks such as NER [3,5,6], semantic category disambiguation [4], and part of speech tagging [7].

Many applications for different domains have been built in order to assist named entity annotation, using a single tagger [5,6], or multiple taggers [3]. Lingren et al. [5] pre-annotate disease and symptom entities for clinical trial announcements using either an automatically extracted or a manually generated dictionary. They conclude that dictionary-based pre-annotation can reduce

---

[1] http://58.192.114.226/assistedNER.

the cost of clinical NER without introducing bias in the annotation process. Ogren et al. [6] use a third party tagger to pre-annotate disease and disorder in clinical domain. However, they find little benefit to pre-annotating the corpus. In biomedical domain, to generate potential gene mentions for the semi-automated annotation, Ganchev et al. [3] run two taggers on the texts: a high recall tagger trained on the local corpus and a high recall tagger trained on a standalone corpus. At decode time, they take the gene mentions from the top two predictions of each of these taggers.

Stenetorp et al. [4] study pre-annotation in a sub task of NER – semantic category disambiguation which assigns the appropriate semantic category to given spans of text from a fixed set of candidate categories, for example PROTEIN to Fibrin. They consider a task setting that allows for multiple semantic categories to be suggested, aiming to minimize the number of suggestions while maintaining high recall. Their system maintains an average recall of 99% while reducing the number of candidate semantic categories on average by 65% over all datasets. In the development of a Part of Speech (PoS) tagged corpus of Icelandic, Loftsson et al. [7] combine five individual PoS taggers to improve the tagging accuracy. Their preliminary evaluation results show that this tagger combination method is crucial with regard to the amount of hand-correction that must be carried out in future work.

Our approach combining multiple taggers is different from [5,6] which use a single tagger. And it differs from [3] which uses the union of the outputs by two taggers and requires additional training data. In addition, our study is unique in the sense that we categorize annotations into *normal annotations* and *candidate annotations* to reduce the number of corrective actions. Unlike NER, either semantic category disambiguation and part of speech tagging does not deal with mention detection, so methods in [4,7] can not be applied directly to assisted named entity annotation.

3   Preliminaries

3.1   Definitions

NER task can be splitted into the identification phase, where NE mentions are identified in text; and the classification phase, where the identified NE mentions are classified into the predefined types. Only three types are considered in this paper, namely person (PER), location (LOC), and organization (ORG). To construct a NE corpus, texts in the corpus are often pre-annotated with annotations so that human do not have to manually annotate the texts from scratch. Further, we categorize the annotations into *normal annotations* and *candidate annotations* based on their estimated confidence. In the following, formal definitions for annotation, *normal annotation*, and *candidate annotation* are presented.

Definition 1 (Annotation). *An annotation is a tuple* $A = \langle B, T \rangle$, *where B is the boundary which consists of a start position and an end position indicating a sequence of words that makes up the mention of A, and T is the type of A, $T \in$*

$T = \{PER, ORG, LOC\}$. We say $B = B'$ if they have identical start positions and identical end positions, and $B \neq B'$ otherwise.

Definition 2 (Normal Annotation). *A normal annotation is an annotation with relative high confidence. If a normal annotation is spurious, annotators shall delete it.*

Definition 3 (Candidate Annotation). *A candidate annotation is an annotation with relative low confidence. If a candidate annotation is correct, annotators shall approve it. If a candidate annotation is spurious, annotators do not need to delete it.*

After the texts in a corpus have been pre-annotated, texts and annotations are displayed to annotators in an user interface (UI). In our task setting, annotators shall add missed annotations, re-select type for annotations with incorrect types, delete spurious *normal annotations*, and approve correct *candidate annotations*. Notice that annotators do not need to delete spurious *candidate annotations*, and they also do not need to approve correct *normal annotations*. Since re-selecting, deleting and approving are all actions performed on pre-annotated annotations, they are collectively referred to as *modifying actions*. The definitions of *adding action* and *modifying action* are given below.

Definition 4 (Adding Action). *An adding action is an action of selecting a span of text and selecting a type for it to create an annotation.*

Definition 5 (Modifying Action). *An modifying action is an action of re-selecting type of an annotation, deleting a normal annotation, or approving a candidate annotation.*

3.2   System Architecture

The system architecture is presented in Fig. 2. Input text is annotated by several individual taggers firstly. Then the outputs of the taggers are fed to a combiner which produces *normal annotations* and *candidate annotations* based on ensemble learning techniques. Via a Web-based UI, annotators can add new annotations and modify pre-annotated annotations, while statistical informations including total time, number of *adding actions*, and number of *modifying actions*, are recorded automaticly by a background program. Finally, annotations and statistical informations are submitted and stored in a database.

In the beginning of the annotation process, Majority Voting (MV) is used as the combination strategy. After some texts have been manually annotated, these data can be utilized to train a classifier, so the combination strategy is switched to stacking. During the whole annotation process, newly annotated data is added to the training data continually to retrain the classifier, and annotators do not need to annotate additional training instances.

Annotators can add new annotations by mouse drags. When the mouse is over an annotation, a menu will pop up, and annotators can re-select NE type

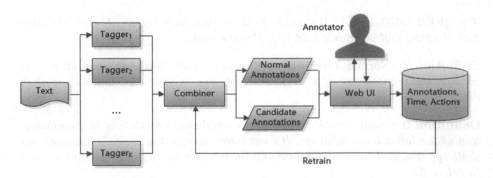

Fig. 2. Overview of our approach.

for the annotation. If annotators need to delete a *normal annotation* or approve a *candidate annotation*, a simple mouse click on the annotation will be enough.

The UI is implemented in Java Server Page (JSP) and JavaScript, and all of the data is stored in a MySQL database. The UI runs in annotator's browser, and no additional software or plug-ins are required.

4 Method

Suppose there are K taggers. Given a text, the kth tagger outputs M^k annotations $A_1^k, \ldots, A_{M^k}^k$, $A_m^k = \langle B_m^k, T_m^k \rangle$. We note the set of M^k boundaries produced by the kth tagger as $\boldsymbol{B}^k$. Then the set of distinct boundaries by K taggers is

$$\boldsymbol{B} = \bigcap_{k=1}^{K} \boldsymbol{B}^k \tag{1}$$

For each boundary B in $\boldsymbol{B}$, we create a vector

$$\boldsymbol{x} = (L^1, \ldots, L^K) \tag{2}$$

where

$$L^k = \begin{cases} T_m^k & \text{if } \exists B_m^k, B_m^k = B, \\ \text{NONE} & \text{otherwise.} \end{cases} \tag{3}$$

$L \in \boldsymbol{L} = \boldsymbol{T} \cup \{\text{NONE}\} = \{\text{PER, ORG, LOC, NONE}\}$. Now, we can utilize $\boldsymbol{x}$ to estimate the confidence score S of B to be labeled with a label L, based on a voter or a classifier f,

$$S(B, L) = f(\boldsymbol{x}) \tag{4}$$

For an annotation $A = \langle B, T \rangle$, if $S(B, T) = \arg\max_{L \in L} S(B, L)$, then it is a *normal annotation*, otherwise it is a *candidate annotation*. In this way, the produced annotations are categorized into *normal annotations* with relatively high confidence and *candidate annotations* with relatively low confidence.

5   Experimental Setup

5.1   Datasets

All the datasets in our experiments are public available. From these datasets, 64 sentences are collected as the test set to perform the actual assisted annotation experiments, and 22 sentences to train the annotators. An overview of the datasets is shown in Table 1. The last two columns are the average number of tokens and the average number of annotations per sentence in the test set.

The three datasets are detailed below. The AKSW-News dataset consists of 325 newspaper articles as described in [2]. Most articles in the dataset are reports in aerospace domain. The CoNLL-2003 shared task [8] data is widely used in NER task. Since one of our tagger (Stanford Named Entity Recognizer) is trained on the training part of CoNLL-2003, we only use the testing part (CoNLL'03-Test). The average number of entities per sentence of CoNLL'03-Test is much larger than the other two datasets, because many articles in this dataset are about sports events, and therefore there are many players, teams, cities or countries. Different with the previous two datasets, NEs identified in the Reuters-128 dataset [9] are manually disambiguated to knowledge bases, while the entity types are not given. So we manually annotated the types of the entities in this dataset.

Table 1. Datasets used in the experiments.

Dataset	Total articles	Testing sentences	Avg. tokens	Avg. annotations
AKSW-News	325	28	34.0	2.1
CoNLL'03-Test	447	28	86.1	13.6
Reuters-128	128	8	37.9	3.1

5.2   Taggers

Six named entity taggers are involved so far: the Stanford Named Entity Recognizer[2] (Stanford) [10], the Illinois Named Entity Tagger[3] (Illinois) [11], the Ottawa Baseline Information Extraction[4] (Balie) [12], the Apache OpenNLP Name Finder[5] (OpenNLP) [13], the General Architecture for Text Engineering[6] (GATE) [14] and the Line Pipe[7] (LingPipe). For outputs of these taggers, only three classes were considered in our experiment, namely person, location, and organization. Performance of these taggers on our test set are listed in Table 2.

---

[2] http://nlp.stanford.edu/software/CRF-NER.shtml (version 3.6.0).
[3] http://cogcomp.cs.illinois.edu/page/software_view/NETagger (version 2.8.8).
[4] http://balie.sourceforge.net (version 1.8.1).
[5] http://opennlp.apache.org/index.html (version 1.6.0).
[6] http://gate.ac.uk/ (version 8.1).
[7] http://alias-i.com/lingpipe/ (version 4.1.0).

Table 2. Performance of the taggers on the testing sentences.

Tagger	Precision	Recall	F_1
Stanford	0.931	0.901	0.916
Illinois	0.880	0.825	0.852
OpenNLP	0.817	0.806	0.811
LinePipe	0.724	0.672	0.697
Gate	0.759	0.616	0.680
Balie	0.511	0.416	0.458

5.3 Pre-annotators

The pre-annotator Ensemble+Categorization_6 which combines the six taggers based on ensemble learning and produces *normal* and *candidate annotations* is used to evaluate our approach. In order to measure the impact of *candidate annotations*, a baseline pre-annotator Ensemble_6 which combines the same six taggers but produces only *normal annotations* is tested. Another baseline pre-annotator Union_6 produces annotations which are union of the outputs of the six taggers. No ensemble learning technique is applied on Union_6.

To test the case where less taggers are available, a group of pre-annotators combining two taggers are tested, which are denoted as Ensemble+Categorization_2, Ensemble_2, and Union_2. For fair comparison, we choose Stanford and Illinois – the best two taggers in terms of F_1 on the test dataset (Table 2).

We also create two other baseline pre-annotators. The first one None do not use any tagger, so annotators have to annotate sentences from scratch. The second one Stanford uses a single tagger (Stanford) to produce annotations.

For the pre-annotators based on ensemble learning, to simulate the annotation process, four strategies are used, including Majority Voting which do not need training data, and Support Vector Machine (SVM) [15] which is trained using 10%, 50%, 90% portion of articles in each dataset. The SVM implementation is provided by LIBSVM [16].

5.4 Assisted Annotation Experiments

Eight annotators (H_1 to H_8) participate in our annotation experiments. They are graduate students in our school, and major in NLP study. Each annotator has to annotate all of the 64 sentences, after he/she has annotated 22 sentences to get familiar with the Web-based UI.

The 64 testing sentences are splitted into 8 subsets (S_1 to S_8), each of which contains 8 sentences. Annotators are presented with the sentences in the same order (Table 3), but each sentence is pre-annotated by different pre-annotators (P_1 to P_8) for different annotators (H_1 to H_8). We carefully design the experiments, to ensure that each sentence will be pre-annotated by all the pre-annotators, and will be manually annotated by all the annotators.

Table 3. Assisted annotation experiments. Annotators are assigned to annotate sentences with various pre-annotations. P_1, ..., P_8 stand for the pre-annotators None, Stanford, Union_2, Ensemble_2, Ensemble+Categorization_2, Union_6, Ensemble_6, and Ensemble+Categorization_6, respectively.

Subset	H_1	H_2	H_3	H_4	H_5	H_6	H_7	H_8
S_1	P_1	P_8	P_3	P_6	P_5	P_4	P_7	P_2
S_2	P_2	P_7	P_4	P_5	P_6	P_3	P_8	P_1
S_3	P_3	P_6	P_5	P_4	P_7	P_2	P_1	P_8
S_4	P_4	P_5	P_6	P_3	P_8	P_1	P_2	P_7
S_5	P_5	P_4	P_7	P_2	P_1	P_8	P_3	P_6
S_6	P_6	P_3	P_8	P_1	P_2	P_7	P_4	P_5
S_7	P_7	P_2	P_1	P_8	P_3	P_6	P_5	P_4
S_8	P_8	P_1	P_2	P_7	P_4	P_5	P_6	P_3

6   Results and Analysis

6.1   Performance of Pre-annotated Annotations

In Table 4, we present performance of pre-annotated annotations. The pre-annotator Ensemble+Categorization_6 achieves highest recall of 0.981, and only 0.14 annotations per sentence need to be added by annotators. Annotators do not need to modify spurious *candidate annotations*, and only 0.58 *normal annotations* need to be modified per sentence, although the precision of Ensemble+Categorization_6 is very poor.

Table 4. Performance of pre-annotated annotations. 'Spurious' stands for the average number of spurious annotations per sentence, which annotators have to modify, either delete or re-select the entity type. 'Missed' stands for the average number of missed annotations per sentence, which annotators need to add.

Pre-annotator	Precision	Recall	Spurious	Missed
None	N/A	N/A	**0.00**	7.25
Stanford	**0.931**	0.901	0.48	0.72
Union_2	0.854	0.948	1.17	0.38
Ensemble_2	0.908	0.871	0.64	0.94
Ensemble+Categorization_2	0.326	0.950	0.69	0.36
Union_6	0.528	0.976	6.33	0.17
Ensemble_6	0.928	0.922	0.52	0.56
Ensemble+Categorization_6	0.256	**0.981**	0.58	**0.14**

6.2 Performance of Annotators

The performance of annotators are presented in Table 5. The pre-annotator Ensemble+Categorization_6 which combines six taggers and produces *normal* and *candidate annotations* assists human to take the least time per sentence.

Table 5. Experimental results. The second column Time is the average time in seconds taken per sentence, N_{add} is the average number of *adding actions* per sentence, and N_{modify} is the average number of *modifying actions*.

Pre-annotator	Time	N_{add}	N_{modify}	Precision	Recall	F_1
None	38.05	7.39	**0.00**	0.920	0.916	0.918
Stanford	19.25	0.56	0.34	0.959	0.951	0.955
Union_2	19.58	0.38	1.08	**0.970**	**0.959**	**0.965**
Ensemble_2	20.80	0.72	0.61	0.961	0.953	0.957
Ensemble+Categorization_2	19.23	0.34	0.81	0.959	0.949	0.954
Union_6	26.97	0.16	6.23	0.963	0.953	0.958
Ensemble_6	18.80	0.48	0.44	0.961	0.951	0.956
Ensemble+Categorization_6	**18.27**	**0.14**	0.75	**0.970**	**0.959**	**0.965**

6.3 Analysis

There are 64 sentences in the test dataset, and each of them is pre-annotated by 8 pre-annotators, and then annotated by 8 annotators. Finally we get 512 instances. The time model computed on these instances by means of linear regression is as follows:

$$Time = 0.14 \cdot N_{Token} + 2.83 \cdot N_{Add} + 1.84 \cdot N_{Modify} + 8.60 \qquad (5)$$

where $Time$ is the total time in seconds spent on a sentence, N_{Token} is the number of tokens in the sentence, N_{add} is the number of *adding actions*, and N_{modify} is the number of *modifying actions*. The model has an intuitive interpretation: the annotator read each token (0.14 sec per token); adding an annotation takes 2.83 sec, and modifying an annotation takes 1.84 sec. Additionally, there is 8.60 sec of overhead per sentence. For this model, the Relative Absolute Error (RAE) is 33.2%.

As we expected, adding an new annotation takes more time than modifying an existing annotation. The estimated time taken by adding and modifying annotations per sentence is listed in Table 6. Ensemble+Categorization_6 outperforms Ensemble_6 because *candidate annotations* improve recall. Union_6 does not achieve good performance due to too much spurious annotations which need to be deleted. Since two taggers does not bring as many annotations as six taggers do, Ensemble+Categorization_2 does not perform as well as Ensemble+Categorization_6.

Table 6. Estimated time taken by *adding actions* and *modifying actions* per sentence.

Pre-annotator	$\hat{T}_{add}$	$\hat{T}_{modify}$	$\hat{T}_{add+modify}$
None	20.92	**0.00**	20.92
Stanford	1.59	0.63	2.22
Union_2	1.06	1.98	3.04
Ensemble_2	2.03	1.12	3.16
Ensemble+Categorization_2	0.97	1.50	2.47
Union_6	0.44	11.47	11.91
Ensemble_6	1.37	0.81	2.18
Ensemble+Categorization_6	**0.40**	1.38	**1.78**

7 Conclusion

In this paper, we employ ensemble learning techniques including voting and stacking to combine multiple existing named entity taggers. The proposed pre-annotator achieves high recall, and therefore the number of *adding actions* is reduced. Based on their estimated confidence, annotations are categorized into *normal annotations* and *candidate annotations* to reduce the number of *modifying actions*. In addition, our approach does not require human to annotate additional training data. We conduct experiments under various pre-annotation conditions. The experiment results show that our approach outperforms the baseline methods in reduction of the number of corrective actions as well as the annotation time, without loss of performance (in terms of F-measure). In future work, we will increase the amount of testing data, evaluate on Chinese datasets, and apply our approach to other NLP tasks.

Acknowledgement. This work is partially funded by the National Science Foundation of China under Grant 61170165, 61602260, 61502095. We would like to thank all the anonymous reviewers for their helpful comments.

References

1. Wu, D., Ngai, G., Carpuat, M.: A stacked, voted, stacked model for named entity recognition. In: Proceedings of the Seventh Conference on Natural Language Learning at HLT-NAACL 2003, CONLL 2003, vol. 4, pp. 200–203. Association for Computational Linguistics, Stroudsburg (2003)
2. Speck, R., Ngonga Ngomo, A.-C.: Ensemble learning for named entity recognition. In: Mika, P., Tudorache, T., Bernstein, A., Welty, C., Knoblock, C., Vrandečić, D., Groth, P., Noy, N., Janowicz, K., Goble, C. (eds.) ISWC 2014. LNCS, vol. 8796, pp. 519–534. Springer, Heidelberg (2014). doi:10.1007/978-3-319-11964-9_33
3. Ganchev, K., Pereira, F., Mandel, M., Carroll, S., White, P.: Semi-automated named entity annotation. In: Proceedings of the Linguistic Annotation Workshop, pp. 53–56. Association for Computational Linguistics (2007)

4. Stenetorp, P., Pyysalo, S., Ananiadou, S., Jun'ichi, T.: Generalising semantic category disambiguation with large lexical resources for fun and profit. J. Biomed. Semant. **5**, 26 (2014)
5. Lingren, T., Deleger, L., Molnar, K., Zhai, H., Meinzen-Derr, J., Kaiser, M., Stoutenborough, L., Li, Q., Solti, I.: Evaluating the impact of pre-annotation on annotation speed and potential bias: natural language processing gold standard development for clinical named entity recognition in clinical trial announcements. J. Am. Med. Inform. Assoc. **21**(3), 406–413 (2014)
6. Ogren, P.V., Savova, G.K., Chute, C.G.: Constructing evaluation corpora for automated clinical named entity recognition. In: Proceedings of the Language Resources and Evaluation Conference (LREC), pp. 28–30 (2008)
7. Loftsson, H., Yngvason, J.H., Helgadóttir, S., Rögnvaldsson, E.: Developing a PoS-tagged corpus using existing tools. In: Proceedings of "Creation and use of basic lexical resources for less-resourced languages", workshop at the 7th International Conference on Language Resources and Evaluation (2010)
8. Tjong Kim Sang, E. F., De Meulder, F.: Introduction to the CoNLL-2003 shared task: language-independent named entity recognition. In: Proceedings of the Seventh Conference on Natural Language Learning at HLT-NAACL 2003, vol. 4, pp. 142–147. Association for Computational Linguistics (2003)
9. Röder, M., Usbeck, R., Hellmann, S., Gerber, D., Both, A.: N3-a collection of datasets for named entity recognition and disambiguation in the NLP interchange format. In: Proceeding of the Ninth International Conference on Language Resources and Evaluation (2014)
10. Finkel, J.R., Grenager, T., Manning, C.: Incorporating non-local information into information extraction systems by gibbs sampling. In: ACL, pp. 363–370 (2005)
11. Ratinov, L., Roth, D.: Design challenges and misconceptions in named entity recognition. In: Proceedings of the Thirteenth Conference on Computational Natural Language Learning, CoNLL 2009, pp. 147–155. Association for Computational Linguistics, Stroudsburg (2009)
12. Nadeau, D.: Balie-baseline information extraction: multilingual information extraction from text with machine learning and natural language techniques. Technical report, University of Ottawa (2005)
13. Baldridge, J.: The OpenNLP Project (2005)
14. Cunningham, H.: GATE: a general architecture for text engineering. Comput. Humanit. **36**(2), 223–254 (2001)
15. Boser, B.E., Guyon, I.M., Vapnik, V.N.: A training algorithm for optimal margin classifiers. In: Proceedings of the Fifth Annual Workshop on Computational Learning Theory, pp. 144–152. ACM (1992)
16. Chang, C.C., Lin, C.J.: LIBSVM: a library for support vector machines. ACM Trans. Intell. Syst. Technol. (TIST) **2**(3), 27 (2011)

A Convolution BiLSTM Neural Network Model for Chinese Event Extraction

Ying Zeng[1], Honghui Yang[1], Yansong Feng[1(✉)],
Zheng Wang[2], and Dongyan Zhao[1]

[1] Institute of Computer Science and Technology,
Peking University, Beijing, People's Republic of China
{ying.zeng,yanghonghui,fengyansong,zhaody}@pku.edu.cn
[2] School of Computing and Communications, Lancaster University, Lancaster, UK
z.wang@lancaster.ac.uk

Abstract. Chinese event extraction is a challenging task in information extraction. Previous approaches highly depend on sophisticated feature engineering and complicated natural language processing (NLP) tools. In this paper, we first come up with the language specific issue in Chinese event extraction, and then propose a convolution bidirectional LSTM neural network that combines LSTM and CNN to capture both sentence-level and lexical information without any hand-craft features. Experiments on ACE 2005 dataset show that our approaches can achieve competitive performances in both trigger labeling and argument role labeling.

Keywords: Event extraction · Neural network · Chinese language processing

1 Introduction

Event extraction aims to extract events with specific types and their participants and attributes from unstructured data, which is an important and challenging task in information extraction. In this paper, we focus on the Chinese event extraction task proposed by the Automatic Content Extraction (ACE) program [7], which defines the following terminology for event extraction:

Trigger: the main word that most clearly expresses the occurrence of an event.

Argument: an entity, temporal expression or value that plays a certain role in the event.

There are two primary subtasks of an ACE event extraction system, namely *trigger labeling* and *argument labeling*. For example, consider the following Chinese sentence:

S1: Intel 在 中国 成立 了 研究中心。
Intel **founds** a research center in China.

C.-Y. Lin et al. (Eds.): NLPCC-ICCPOL 2016, LNAI 10102, pp. 275–287, 2016.
DOI: 10.1007/978-3-319-50496-4_23

In the trigger labeling task, "成立" (founds) should be labeled as the trigger of event type *Business*. Then in the argument labeling task, "Intel", "中国" (China), and "研究中心" (research center) should be labeled as the roles of Agent, Place and Time respectively in this event.

Current state-of-the-art approaches [4,5,14] usually rely on a variety of elaborately features. In general, we can divide them into two categories: **lexical features** and **sentence-level features**. Take trigger labeling on the following sentences for example: the word "成立" (found) indicates a *Business* event in S1 but not in S2 or S3.

S2: 它 成立 于 1994 年 ， 现在 是 一支 深受 欢迎 的 乐队。
It was **founded** in 1994, and now is a very popular band.
S3: 医院 已 成立 救援中心。
The hospital has **founded** rescue centers.

Sentence-level features maintain important clues of the whole sentence. We can summarize S2 as "它 是 一支 乐队" (it is a band) and encode it into a sentence-level feature, which indicates that the verb "成立" (founded) is not a trigger.

Lexical features contain semantic information of words and their surrounding context. In S3, given the next word "救援中心" (rescue centers) as a lexical feature, we can infer that "成立" (founded) is not a trigger of type *Business*.

Traditional approaches [2,4,6,13] usually rely on a series of NLP tools to extract lexical features (e.g., part-of-speech tagging, named entity recognition) and sentence-level features (e.g., dependency parsing). Although they achieve high performance, they often suffer from hard feature engineering and error propagation from those external tools.

Recently, neural network models have been employed to produce competitive performance against traditional models for many NLP tasks. Chen et al. [5] propose a convolutional neural network to capture lexical-level clues, with a dynamic multi-pooling layer to capture sentence-level features, which yields state-of-art on English event extraction.

Inspired by the effectiveness of neural networks, in Sect. 2, we present a convolution bidirectional LSTM neural network that can learn both lexical and sentence-level features without any hand-engineered features in Chinese event extraction task. Specifically, we first use a bidirectional LSTM to encode the semantics of words in the entire sentence into **sentence-level features** without any parsing. Then, we can take advantage of a convolutional neural network to capture salient local **lexical features** for trigger disambiguation without any help from POS tags or NER.

We are also enlightened by the work of Chen and Ji [6], who are the first to report the language specific issue in Chinese trigger labeling. So we propose a character-based method committed to the problem in Sect. 2.3. Section 3 presents the model applied to argument labeling, and Sect. 4 discusses the experimental results. Section 5 concludes this paper.

2 Trigger Labeling

Trigger labeling, also called event detection, aims to discover the event triggers and assign them a predefined event type.

Unlike previous work [2,6], which divide event detection into two subtasks: (1) trigger identification: to recognize the event trigger; (2) trigger classification: to assign an event type for an identified trigger. We jointly learn trigger identification and type classification by one network to reduce the error propagation problem of a pipeline model. Before we present our solution, we first come up with the language specific issue in Chinese trigger labeling.

2.1 Language Specific Issues

Unlike English, Chinese do not have delimiters between words. That makes word segmentation a fundamental step in Chinese event detection. However, we find that segmentation granularity does have an impact on the prediction. As shown in Table 1, these triggers cannot be recognized accurately if we simply predict whether a word is an event trigger or not. We summarize them as the following two types.

Table 1. Examples of inconsistency problem between words and triggers. Words are segmented by spaces.

#	Sentence	Triggers
S4	犯罪 嫌疑人 都 落入 法网。 The suspects were **arrested**.	落入法网 (arrested)
S5	警察 击毙 了 一名 歹徒。 Polices **shoot** and **kill** a criminal.	击 (shoot) 毙 (kill)
S6	这 是 一件 预谋 的 凶杀案。 It is a premeditated **murder** case.	凶杀 (murder)

Cross-word Triggers: While many events anchor on a single word, multiple words could reasonably be called a trigger. In S4, the *arrest_jail* event should be triggered by neither "落入" nor "法网", but "落入法网" (arrested).

Inside-word Triggers: Almost all Chinese characters have their own meanings, and some of which can be triggers themselves. There may be greater than one trigger in a word like "击毙" (shoot and kill). Continuous characters of a word can also form a trigger such as "凶杀" (murder) in "凶杀案" (murder case).

Table 2 summarizes the number of problematic triggers we found in ACE 2005 Chinese corpus using different Chinese word segmentation tools. Even the minimum inconsistency rate is as high as 14%.

To address the language specific issues, we treat event detection as a sequence labeling task rather than classification. Sentences are tagged in the *BIO* scheme, where each token is labeled as *B-type* if it is the beginning of an event trigger with type *type*, or *I-type* if it is inside a trigger, or *O* otherwise. Our first labelling model is a word-based BiLSTM model with a CNN layer as shown in Fig. 1.

Table 2. Number of triggers inconsistent with the words.

NLP tools	Cross-word	Inside-word	Total
Stanford NLP[a]	487	166	653
Jieba[b]	554	85	639
NLPIR[c]	314	172	486

[a] http://nlp.stanford.edu/software/segmenter.shtml.
[b] https://github.com/fxsjy/jieba.
[c] https://github.com/NLPIR-team/NLPIR

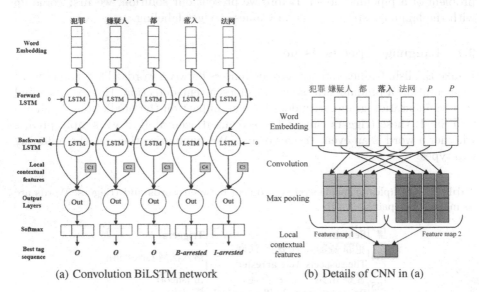

(a) Convolution BiLSTM network   (b) Details of CNN in (a)

Fig. 1. The main architecture of our word-based model. The local contextual feature c_t (grey rectangle) in (a) for each word w_t is computed by the CNN as (b) illustrated. Our convolutional neural network learns a representation of local context information about the center word "落入". Here the context size is 7 (3 words to the left and to the right of a center word), and we use a kernel of size 4 with two feature maps. The symbol P in sentence of (b) represents a padding word.

2.2 Word-Based Method

LSTM Network. Recurrent neural networks (RNNs) maintain a memory based on historical contextual information, which makes them a natural choice for processing sequential data. Unfortunately, it is difficult for standard RNNs to capture long range dependencies due to vanishing/exploding gradients [3]. Long Short-Term Memory [10] is explicitly designed to solve the long-term dependency problem through purpose-built memory cells. They consist of three multiplicative gates that control the proportion of information to forget and to store in the cell states.

For the event extraction task, if we access to both past and future contexts for a given time, we can make use of more sentence-level information and make better prediction. This can be done by bidirectional LSTM networks [8,9]. Figure 1(a) shows the layers of a BiLSTM trigger identification model.

A forward LSTM network computes the hidden state $\overrightarrow{h_t}$ of the past (left) context of the sentence at word w_t, while a backward LSTM network reads the same sentence in reverse and outputs $\overleftarrow{h_t}$ given the future (right) context. In our implementation, we concatenate these two vectors to form the hidden state of a BiLSTM network, i.e. $h_t = [\overrightarrow{h_t}; \overleftarrow{h_t}]$.

Convolutional Neural Network. Convolutional neural networks are originally applied to computer vision to capture local features [12]. CNN architectures have gradually shown effectiveness in various NLP tasks, and have been used for event extraction in preceding studies [5]. We employ a convolutional neural network as illustrated in Fig. 1(b) to extract local contextual information for each word in a sentence.

Given a sentence containing n words $\{w_1, w_2, \ldots, w_n\}$, and the current center word w_t, a convolution operation involves a kernel, which is applied to words surrounding w_t in a window to generate the feature map. We can utilize multiple kernels with different widths to extract local features of various granularities. Then max pooling is performed over each map so that only the largest number of each feature map is recorded. One property of pooling is that it produces a fixed size output vector, which enables us to apply variable kernel sizes. And by performing the max operation, we are keeping the most salient information. Finally, we take the fixed length output vector c_{w_t} as a representation of local contextual information about center word w_t.

In our implementation, the sliding window size is 7 (3 words to the left and to the right of a center word), and we use several sizes of kernels to capture context information of various granularities.

The Output Layer. We concatenate the hidden state h_t of BiLSTM with contextual feature c_{w_t} extracted by CNN at each time step t. Then $[h_t; c_{w_t}]$ is fed into a softmax layer to produce the log-probabilities of each label for w_t.

However, word-base method still cannot solve the inconsistency problem caused by inside-word triggers. Like Chen and Ji [6], we construct a global errata table to record the most frequent triggers in the training set. During testing, if a word has an entry in the errata table, we replace its label with its corresponding trigger type directly.

2.3 Character-Based Method

Despite of the effectiveness of the errata table, word-based method is not a flawless solution because it only recognizes triggers across words or frequent inside-word triggers appearing in training data.

Ideally, character-based method may solve both inconsistency problem. It uses the same tagging scheme as word-based method to label each character. As shown in Fig. 2, the only difference between them is the input layers of their networks: a character-based method uses character embedding while a word-base method uses word embedding.

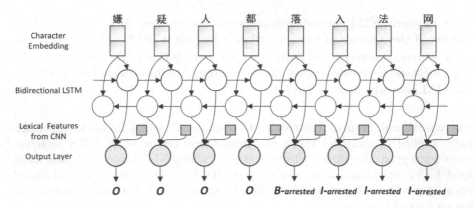

Fig. 2. Character-based Convolution BiLSTM network.

3 Argument Labeling

In the above section, we present our convolution BiLSTM model for trigger label-ing. The idea of this neural network architecture is also suitable for argument labeling: we use a bidirectional LSTM to encode its sentence-level information, concatenated with a CNN-extracted local lexical feature, to predict whether an entity serves as an argument in a sentence. Next, we will present the main differences between the models used in trigger labeling and argument labeling.

3.1 Input Layer

As a pipeline system, besides word embeddings, we can use information extracted from upstream trigger labeling task. Therefore, we propose four additional types of feature embeddings to form the input layer of BiLSTM and CNN.

- Trigger position feature: whether a word is in a trigger
- Trigger type feature: classified trigger type of a word, and *NONE* type for non-trigger words
- Entity position feature: whether a word is in an entity
- Entity type feature: entity type of a word, and *NONE* type for non-entity word. The ACE dataset provides ground truth of entity recognition, so we can generate entity features directly without external NLP tools.

We then transform these features into vectors by their lookup tables, and concatenate them with the original word embeddings, as the final input layer of BiLSTM and CNN.

3.2 Output Layer

It is worth mentioning that argument labeling is no longer a sequence tagging task, but a classification task. ACE dataset provides ground truth of entity recognition, and it guarantees that arguments can only be labeled from those entities. As a result, we only need to predict the role of a tagged entity instead of every word in the entire sentence. For instance, there are three triggers (bold words), and three entities (italic words) in S7, which together makes up nine pairs of trigger and argument candidate to be classified.

S7: 六起 **谋杀案** 发生 在 *法国*，包括 *Bob* 的 **暗杀** 和 *Joe* 的 **杀害**。

Six **murders** occurred in *France*, including the **assassination** of *Bob* and the **killing** of *Joe*.

We modify the output layers of both CNN and BiLSTM network to adapt to the the new task. For BiLSTM, we still try to make use of its ability to memory long sequences, so we regard the hidden state of the last word h_N as sentence-level information. And for CNN, we take all words of the entire sentence as the context, rather than a shallow window for each center word. Finally, we feed the concatenation of output vectors from two networks into a softmax classifier just like trigger labeling.

4   Experiments

4.1   Experimental Setup

We used the standard ACE 2005 corpus for our experiments, which contains 633 Chinese documents. Following the setup of Chen and Ji [6], we also randomly selected 509 documents for training and 64 documents as test set, and the reserved 60 documents for validation.

Evaluation Metric: Similar to previous work, we evaluated our models in terms of *precision* (P), *recall* (R), and *F-measure* (F) for each subtask. These performance metrics are computed following the standards of correctness for these subtasks:

- A trigger is correctly *identified* if its offsets exactly match a reference trigger;
- A trigger is correctly *classified* if its trigger type and offsets exactly match a reference trigger;
- An argument is correctly *identified* if its offset, related trigger type and trigger's offsets exactly match a reference argument;
- An argument is correctly *classified* if its offsets, role, related trigger type and trigger's offsets exactly match a reference argument.

4.2   Network Training

We implement the neural network using the Tensorflow library [1]. During training, we keep checking performance on the validation set and pick the highest F-score parameters for final evaluation.

Parameter Initialization: Weight matrix parameters are randomly initialized with uniform samples from $[-0.01, 0.01]$. Bias vectors are initialized to zero.

Pre-trained Embeddings: Word and character embeddings are pre-trained on over 261 thousand articles crawled from Chinese news website. All embeddings are fine-tuned during training.

Optimization Algorithm: For all models presented, parameter optimization is performed using Adam [11] with gradient clipping [15]. We also apply the dropout method [16] on both the input and output vectors of all models to mitigate overfitting.

Hyper-parameters: In different stages of event extraction, we adopted different parameters. Table 3 summarizes the chosen hyper-parameters for all experiments.

Table 3. Hyper-parameters for all experiments.

Layer	Hyper-parameter	Trigger identification and classification	Argument identification and classification
Input	Word embedding	100	100
	Character embedding	50	100
	Entity feature embedding	–	32
	Trigger feature embedding	–	32
LSTM	State size	100	120
CNN	Context size	7	Sentence length
	Kernel size	[3, 5, 7]	[2, 3, 4, 5]
	Number of filters	[32, 32, 32]	[64, 64, 64, 64]
Dropout	Dropout rate	0.5	0.5
	Batch size	32	20
	Gradient clipping	1.0	2.0

4.3   Trigger Labeling

Table 4 lists the results of previous work [4,6] and our models. The performances of *Char-MEMM* and *Rich-L* are reported in their paper.

- *Char-MEMM* [6] is the first character-based method to handle the language specific issue, which trains a Maximum Entropy Markov Model to label each character with BIO tagging scheme.
- *Rich-L* [4] is a joint-learning, knowledge-rich approach that extends the union of the features employed by *Char-MEMM* and Li et al. [13] with six groups of linguistic features, including character-based features and discourse consistency features, which is the feature-based state-of-art system.

Compared with the feature-based approaches, all neural network based models outperform *Char-MEMM*, because they can capture semantic and syntactic information in the absence of feature engineering and avoid the errors propagated from other NLP tasks like NER and POS tagging.

Rich-L performs 10-fold cross-validation experiments, so that the results reported by them obtain more accurate estimation of system performance. Therefore, it is unfair to directly compare our results with them. But we can still see the models evaluated in the bucket achieve competitive F-score on event identification without any human-designed features and discourse level knowledge.

Table 4. Comparison of different models on Chinese event detection (trigger identification and classification) (%).

Model	Trigger identification			Trigger classification		
	P	R	F	P	R	F
Char-MEMM [6]	**82.4**	50.6	62.7	**78.8**	48.3	59.9
Rich-L [4]	62.2	71.9	**66.7**	58.9	68.1	**63.2**
Word-based CNN	71.7	58.3	64.3	67.7	55.1	60.7
Word-based BiLSTM	68.4	61.2	64.6	63.9	57.4	60.5
Word-based C-BiLSTM	75.8	59.0	66.4	**69.8**	54.2	61.0
+ Errata table	**76.0**	63.8	**69.3**	**69.8**	59.9	**64.5**
Character-based C-BiLSTM	65.6	66.7	66.1	60.0	60.9	60.4
+ Errata table	68.1	**69.2**	68.7	61.6	**64.7**	63.1

Word-Based Models vs. Character-Based Models. As we can summarize from Table 4, when applying the same network architecture, word-based methods always have higher precisions while character-based methods always have higher recalls.

We then take a further step to see their impacts on different kinds of triggers. Table 5 shows that: (1) Word-based methods can not label inside-word triggers, while character-based methods can handle this issue nicely, which brings them higher overall recall; (2) Two methods achieve similar F-measure in regular trigger identification; (3) It is harder for character-based method to correctly identify cross-word triggers. As there are more cross-word triggers than inside-word triggers in dataset, the overall F-measure of word-based method is slightly higher.

There are several reasons causing the low precision of character-based method:

(1) Character-based method has to learn the extra word segmentation by themselves. 7.3% of triggers identified by it are partially mislabeled, like triggers in S8 and S9.

(2) Word embedding brings richer semantic information than character embedding. Take S10 as an example, characters "胡" and "同" do not have any meaning related to the formed word "胡同" (the end of a road). But this word strongly

Table 5. Results of different types of triggers with different models on trigger identification. Regular triggers mean triggers composed of exactly one word.

Model	Regular triggers			Inside-word triggers			Cross-word triggers		
	P	R	F	P	R	F	P	R	F
Word-based C-BiLSTM	0.78	0.65	0.71	–	0	–	0.64	0.39	0.48
Character-based C-BiLSTM	0.72	0.70	0.71	0.30	0.69	0.41	0.57	0.22	0.32

suggests that "死" (dead) is not a trigger. Given the more accurate embedding of surrounding context, word-based networks can understand the meaning of the center word better and do better disambiguation.
(3) RNN in character-based method needs to maintain information for longer sequence, as 1.7 times longer than the average length of word sequences. Evaluating on sentences containing more than 150 characters, F-measure of character-based method is 70%, while word-based method can achieve 72.8% (Table 6).

Table 6. Error analysis: examples of triggers mislabeled by character-based C-BiLSTM, but can be identified correctly by word-based C-BiLSTM.

#	Sentence	Correct Labels	Wrong Labels
S8	走访 相关 人员 以后，... After **visiting** to relevant staff, ...	走访 (visiting) BI	 BO
S9	贺电 全文 如下： There is the full **congratulatory message**	贺 (congratulatory) 电 (message) BI	 OB
S10	小偷 被 逼 进 死 胡同。 The thief was chased into a **dead end**.	死 (dead) 胡同 (end) O OO	 B OO

Neural Network Architectures. Our convolution BiLSTM model has two main components that we could take them apart to understand their impacts on the overall performance. As Table 4 shows, BiLSTM is slightly more efficient than CNN, and the convolution BiLSTM model outperforms other models. Constructing an errata table is an effective method that increases both precisions and recalls.

We also evaluate the capacity of each network on trigger disambiguation. Table 7 provides suggestive evidence that CNN-extracted local features, together with LSTM-extracted sentence-level information can help reduce some errors caused by ambiguous triggers as we expected.

4.4   Argument Labeling

Table 8 shows results for argument labeling after trigger labeling. As we can observe from our evaluation standards that once a trigger has not been labeled correctly, neither of its arguments will be labeled correctly. In the stage of trigger

Table 7. Percentages of ambiguous words whose all occurrences in the test set are classified correctly. Ambiguous words can have different labels according to their meaning and context, like the word "成立" (found) in S1 ∼ S3. All networks listed in this table are word-based.

	BiLSTM	CNN	C-BiLSTM
Ambiguous word classification (%)	58.4	60.0	62.5

Table 8. Comparison of different models on Chinese argument labeling (%). +e means that the input (result of trigger labeling) has been modified by an errata table.

Model	Argument identification			Argument classification		
	P	R	F	P	R	F
Char-MEMM	**64.4**	36.4	46.5	**60.6**	34.3	43.8
Rich-L	43.6	**57.3**	**49.5**	39.2	**51.6**	**44.6**
Word-based C-BiLSTM	56.6	43.6	49.3	49.7	38.3	43.2
Word-based C-BiLSTM + (e)	56.5	47.0	51.3	49.6	41.3	45.0
Character-based C-BiLSTM	53.2	51.6	52.4	47.0	45.6	46.3
Character-based C-BiLSTM + (e)	53.0	52.2	**52.6**	47.3	46.6	**46.9**

labeling, the character-based methods have higher recalls and can extract more golden triggers. As a result, character-based methods perform much better than word-based methods in argument labeling. And we can draw the same conclusion that word-based methods have higher precision while character-based methods achieve higher recalls, as trigger labeling.

Errata table is not such effective as in trigger labeling, especially for character-based C-BiLSTM. Adding an errata table even drops a little precision in argument identification.

Char-MEMM concludes that *neighbor word* features are fairly applicable. They utilize the left word and right word of an entity to reduce spurious argument, which is a similar objective with our CNN-extracted lexical features. Nonetheless, we can achieve much better results in argument identification and classification.

It is worth noting that some of the arguments are not in the same sentence with their triggers. It is a bottleneck of our C-BiLSTM model, while *Rich-L* uses discourse-level features to deal with this problem. Under this unfavorable circumstance, our C-BiLSTM can still achieve a comparable result against sophisticated human designed features.

5   Conclusion

In this paper, we propose a novel convolution bidirectional LSTM model on Chinese event extraction task. Our model departs from the inherent characteristic of Chinese, formulates the event detection task as a sequence labeling fashion, and features both bidirectional LSTM and CNN to capture both sentence-level and lexical features from raw text. Experimental results show that without human-designed features and external resources, our neural network method can achieve comparable performances on ACE 2005 datasets with traditional feature based methods.

Acknowledgement. This work was supported by National High Technology R&D Program of China (Grant Nos. 2015AA015403, 2014AA015102), Natural Science Foundation of China (Grant Nos. 61202233, 61272344, 61370055) and the joint project with IBM Research. Any correspondence please refer to Yansong Feng.

References

1. Abadi, M., Agarwal, A., Barham, P., Brevdo, E., Chen, Z., Citro, C., Corrado, G.S., Davis, A., Dean, J., Devin, M., et al.: Tensorflow: Large-scale machine learning on heterogeneous distributed systems. arXiv preprint arXiv:1603.04467 (2016)
2. Ahn, D.: The stages of event extraction. In: Proceedings of the Workshop on Annotating and Reasoning about Time and Events, pp. 1–8. Association for Computational Linguistics (2006)
3. Bengio, Y., Simard, P., Frasconi, P.: Learning long-term dependencies with gradient descent is difficult. IEEE Trans. Neural Netw. **5**(2), 157–166 (1994)
4. Chen, C., Ng, V.: Joint modeling for Chinese event extraction with rich linguistic features. In: COLING, pp. 529–544. Citeseer (2012)
5. Chen, Y., Xu, L., Liu, K., Zeng, D., Zhao, J.: Event extraction via dynamic multi-pooling convolutional neural networks. In: Proceedings of the 53rd Annual Meeting of the Association for Computational Linguistics and the 7th International Joint Conference on Natural Language Processing, vol. 1, pp. 167–176 (2015)
6. Chen, Z., Ji, H.: Language specific issue and feature exploration in chinese event extraction. In: Proceedings of Human Language Technologies: The 2009 Annual Conference of the North American Chapter of the Association for Computational Linguistics, Companion Volume: Short Papers, pp. 209–212. Association for Computational Linguistics (2009)
7. Doddington, G.R., Mitchell, A., Przybocki, M.A., Ramshaw, L.A., Strassel, S., Weischedel, R.M.: The automatic content extraction (ACE) program-tasks, data, and evaluation. In: LREC, vol. 2, p. 1 (2004)
8. Graves, A., Schmidhuber, J.: Framewise phoneme classification with bidirectional LSTM and other neural network architectures. Neural Netw. **18**(5), 602–610 (2005)
9. Graves, A., Mohamed, A.R., Hinton, G.: Speech recognition with deep recurrent neural networks. In: 2013 IEEE International Conference on Acoustics, Speech and Signal Processing (ICASSP), pp. 6645–6649. IEEE (2013)
10. Hochreiter, S., Schmidhuber, J.: Long short-term memory. Neural Comput. **9**(8), 1735–1780 (1997)
11. Kingma, D., Ba, J.: Adam: A method for stochastic optimization. arXiv preprint arXiv:1412.6980 (2014)
12. LeCun, Y., Bottou, L., Bengio, Y., Haffner, P.: Gradient-based learning applied to document recognition. Proc. IEEE **86**(11), 2278–2324 (1998)

13. Li, P., Zhou, G., Zhu, Q., Hou, L.: Employing compositional semantics and discourse consistency in Chinese event extraction. In: Proceedings of the 2012 Joint Conference on Empirical Methods in Natural Language Processing and Computational Natural Language Learning, pp. 1006–1016. Association for Computational Linguistics (2012)
14. Li, Q., Ji, H., Huang, L.: Joint event extraction via structured prediction with global features. In: ACL (1), pp. 73–82 (2013)
15. Pascanu, R., Mikolov, T., Bengio, Y.: On the difficulty of training recurrent neural networks. ICML **3**(28), 1310–1318 (2013)
16. Srivastava, N., Hinton, G., Krizhevsky, A., Sutskever, I., Salakhutdinov, R.: Dropout: a simple way to prevent neural networks from overfitting. J. Mach. Learn. Res. **15**(1), 1929–1958 (2014)

Detection of Entity Mixture in Knowledge Bases Using Hierarchical Clustering

Haihua Xie[1,2,3(✉)], Xiaoqing Lu[1], Zhi Tang[1], and Xiaojun Huang[4]

[1] Institute of Computer Science and Technology,
Peking University, Beijing 100871, China
haihuaxie@foxmail.com,
{lvxiaoqing, tangzhi}@pku.edu.cn
[2] State Key Laboratory of Digital Publishing Technology,
Peking University Founder Group Co. LTD., Beijing, China
[3] Postdoctoral Workstation of the Zhongguancun Haidian Science Park,
Beijing, China
[4] Department of Knowledge Service Technology,
Beijing Founder Apabi Technology Limited, Beijing 100097, China
hxj@founder.com.cn

Abstract. Entity mixture in a knowledge base refers to the situation that some attributes of an entity are mistaken for another entity's, and it often occurs among homonymous entities which have the same value of the attribute "Name". Elimination of entity mixture is critical to ensure data accuracy and validity for knowledge based services. However, current researches on entity disambiguation mainly focuses on determining the identity of entities mentioned in text during information extraction for building a knowledge base, while little work has been done to verify the information in a built knowledge base. In this paper, we propose a generic method to detect mixed homonymous entities in a knowledge base using hierarchical clustering. The principle of our methodology to differentiate entities is detecting the inconsistence of their attributes based on analysis of the appearance distribution of their attribute values in documents of a common corpus. Experiments on a data set of industry applications have been conducted to demonstrate the workflow of performing the clustering and detecting mixed entities in a knowledge base using our methodology.

Keywords: Entity · Entity mixture · Hierarchical clustering · Knowledge base · Knowledge graph · Homonymous entities · Triple

1 Introduction

With integration of Artificial Intelligence and Database System, knowledge based system is a prevailing framework of knowledge storage, organization and application in academia and industry [1]. The fundamental part of knowledge based systems, a knowledge base, contains information of entities, in the form of triples <Entity, Predicate, Attribute Value/Entity>. Each triple describes an attribute of an entity (when the third element is Attribute Value) or the relation between two entities (when the third element is Entity). With the structured representation of knowledge by using triples,

© Springer International Publishing AG 2016
C.-Y. Lin et al. (Eds.): NLPCC-ICCPOL 2016, LNAI 10102, pp. 288–299, 2016.
DOI: 10.1007/978-3-319-50496-4_24

knowledge base enables effective knowledge representation, verification and reasoning [2]. Nowadays knowledge bases are used as the underlying database in a wide range of applications such as question-answer systems and big data analysis of a specific industry [3].

Data accuracy of the knowledge base is an essential requirement for knowledge based systems to provide high quality services [4]. Because triples are the major part of a knowledge base, data accuracy can be measured based on evaluation of the correctness of each triple. The primary step to evaluate the correctness of a triple <Entity, Predicate, Attribute Value/Entity> is to determine the ontology of each entity involved in the triple. For example, in a triple <Plato, BirthYear, BC427> which indicates that the birth year of Plato is B.C. 427. To determine the correctness of the information in such triple, the first step is to determine the entity Plato is the famous Greek philosopher, not the comic poet Plato or other Plato, and then check if the birth year of Plato is B.C. 427.

In the process of building a knowledge base, homonymous entities may be mixed to be one entity, *i.e.*, the attributes of an entity are mistakenly labeled to be another entity's. Sometimes, the inconsistence between attributes of an entity can be easily detected, such as <LiBai, BirthYear, 1910> and <LiBai, Dynasty, Tang> are conflicting because the year 1910 is not in the duration of the Tang Dynasty, so that the entities LiBai in these two triples actually represent different persons. However, in many cases the inconsistence between attributes cannot be straightforwardly discovered, particularly for those attributes without direct correlations. For example, the triples <LiBai, BirthPlace, Hunan> and <LiBai, Dynasty, Tang> are actually about two different persons named LiBai, but the inconsistence between them can only be detected using multistep reasoning based on adequate background knowledge. Meanwhile, the selection of reasoning methods depends on the predicates and attributes in the triples. As a result, there is currently a lack of generic methodologies to distinguish mixed entities in a knowledge base by using reasoning approaches.

This paper proposes a generic method to distinguish homonymous entities in a knowledge base. Our methodology tries to classify entities into different classes using hierarchical clustering based on analysis of their attributes. The set of documents that describe an entity is supposed to be distinguishable from that of another entity. Thus, the criterion of classifying entities is the appearance distribution of the attribute values of each entity in documents of a common corpus. Experiments on a data set of industry applications was conducted to demonstrate the workflow of detecting mixed entities in a knowledge base by using our methodology.

This paper is organized as follows: Sect. 2 briefly reviews the literatures on knowledge base, knowledge service and entity disambiguation. Section 3 presents the basic concepts and the workflow of detecting entity mixture and the procedure of hierarchical clustering. Section 4 explains our experiments and the experimental results. Section 5 discusses the limitations of our methodology and potential speculations of our works.

2 Background and Related Work

2.1 Knowledge Base and Knowledge Service

Knowledge bases store information and facts about the world in the form of structured data [5]. Various knowledge bases have been developed to describe different aspects of the world, such as YAGO, Freebase and WordNet [6]. Knowledge based systems can be built on top of a knowledge base and an inference engine that represents logical assertions and conditions about the world [7]. Because of the integration of Artificial Intelligence and Database System, knowledge based systems provide effective supports for the development of intelligence information service applications such as personalized recommendation and intelligent searching [8]. In the internet search industry, a lot of companies have launched knowledge based products to improve their searching results, such as Google Knowledge Graph, Microsoft Bing Satori, Baidu Zhixin and Sogou Knowledge Cube. Knowledge base also finds its applications in question-answering systems such as IBM Watson, and big data analytics in light of specific industries such as finance and entertainment, etc. [9].

Besides the generic and large-scale knowledge bases that aims at providing comprehensive description about the world, there are domain-specific knowledge bases that store information about a particular field. For example, a textile press may need a knowledge base about the material and design of textile commodities of East Asia. Because the expertise of such fields is mostly presented in electric books and publications in the form of unstructured data, the information for building the domain-specific knowledge bases is usually obtained from textual data using approaches of unstructured information extraction or summarized by domain experts. In the process of building a knowledge base, errors are inevitable in the data sources or the procedure of information extraction and summarization [10], while checking the contents by manual is not economical for enterprises. Therefore, it is necessary to design a generic and efficient approach to verify the contents in a knowledge base to ensure its effectiveness for supporting knowledge services.

2.2 Entity Disambiguation and Entity Linking

Entity disambiguation (or entity linking) is the task of mapping ambiguous terms in natural-language text to its entities in a knowledge base [11]. Entity disambiguation is often conducted in the process of Knowledge Base (KB) Population [12], while it is called coreference resolution when performed without a KB [13]. Most works of entity disambiguation make use of context-aware features derived from the reference knowledge base, and the features heavily rely on the cross-document hyperlinks within the knowledge base [14]. For example, Mann and Yarowsky disambiguate person names using biographic facts, such as birth year, occupation and affiliation [15]. [16] uses convolutional neural networks to capture semantic correspondence between a mention's context and a proposed target entity. In [17], authors propose an approach to tackle Named Entity Disambiguation with Linkless Knowledge Bases (LNED) to expand the application of Entity Disambiguation to closed domain knowledge bases.

Entity disambiguation finds its applications in improving the accuracy of information extraction on unstructured data set. For example, Wikification [18] supports entity linking in relation extraction with Wikipedia as the target knowledge base.

Entity disambiguation is different from the problem discussed in this paper in two aspects: (1) Entity disambiguation utilizes the knowledge in knowledge bases to identify entities in texts, while the detection of entity mixture uses knowledge in texts to identify entities in knowledge bases; (2) The purpose of entity disambiguation is to map a mention in texts to an entity in a knowledge base, while detection of entity mixture aims at eliminating mixed entities in a knowledge base.

3   Detection of Homonymous Entities Mixture

3.1   Definition of Homonymous Entities Mixture

In this section, we give the definitions and descriptions of related concepts that are involved in our methodology of entity mixture detection.

1. Entity: an entity is a physical or an abstract concept in the application domain. For example, a person, a place, or a digital number can be defined as an entity. Normally, each entity in a knowledge base is represented using a unique identification (ID) number. For each entity, there is a set of triples to describe its attributes or relations between it and other entities. For example, there are a set of triples related to entity ent_1 as follows:

   $<ent_1$, Name, Michael Jordan$>$
   $<ent_1$, BirthYear, 1963$>$
   $<ent_1$, Teammate, $ent_2>$
   $<ent_2$, Name, Scottie Pippen$>$

   In the above example triples, ent_1 is an entity refers to the famous basketball player Michael Jordan. The first two triples describe the attributes of ent_1; the third triple specifies the relation between ent_1 and ent_2; the last one specifies the attribute "Name" of entity ent_2.
2. Knowledge base: a database that stores the information of entities, including the attributes of entities and relations among entities, in the form of triples. With an inference engine, triple-based reasoning enables information mutual verification to be performed internally in a knowledge base. For example, the triples $<ent_1$, Teammate, $ent_2>$ and $<ent_2$, Teammate, $ent_1>$ can be used to mutually verify each other. Meanwhile, triples $<ent_1$, Teammate, $ent_2>$ and $<ent_1$, Team, $ent_3>$ can be used together to prove that $<ent_2$, Team, $ent_3>$ is correct. For those triples that cannot be verified through internally mutual verification, their correctness can only be evaluated based on information outside the knowledge base.
3. Homonymous Entities: entities with the same value of the attribute "Name". For example, there can be two entities named Michael Jordan, and one refers to the famous basketball player and the other refers to an expert in machine learning. The homonymous entities should have different IDs in the knowledge base.

4. Entity Mixture: the information of different entities, usually homonymous entities, are mixed, *i.e.*, the ID of different entities are the same in the knowledge base. In the process of building a knowledge base, it is possible to mistakenly label an attribute of an entity to be that of a homonymous entity, because the collection of an entity's information is often based on the entity's name. For example, when constructing the knowledge graph of Michael Jordan (the basketball player), people might misuse the residence of another Michael Jordan (the machine learning expert). Entity mixture often occurs among information that cannot be verified through mutual verification inside the knowledge base, but can only be detected based on external data.

3.2   Workflow of Entity Mixture Detection

Our study proposes a methodology to distinguish different entities in a knowledge base, and it can be used to detect homonymous entities mixture. An example of homonymous entities mixture is showing below:

$<ent_1$, Name, Michael Jordan$>$
$<ent_1$, BirthPlace, Brooklyn New York$>$
$<ent_1$, BirthYear, 1963$>$
$<ent_1$, Residence, Berkeley California$>$
$<ent_1$, Expertise, Machine Learning$>$

In the above example, the second and the third triples specify the information of a basketball player and the last two triples specify that of a professor at Berkeley. However, the ID of the entities in these triples are the same, *i.e.*, ent_1.

Our methodology of distinguishing different entities is built based on the following assumption: the set of documents that describe an entity is distinguishable from those describe another entity. Thus, to distinguish two entities with a same name, the sets of documents that involve each triple of the entities are obtained, and then clustering is performed on the sets of documents to classify entities. For example, in the result of differentiating the two Michael Jordan, the sets of documents of the second and the third triples (showing at the beginning of this section) will be classified to be one group (a basketball player), and those of the fourth and fifth triples will be classified to be another group (a machine learning expert). Meanwhile, if all triples specify a same entity, the documents of them will be classified into one group. The number of classes is uncertain before the classification is performed.

The detailed steps of our methodology to determine if there is entity mixture for entity *ent* are as follows:

1. Obtain Triples: Obtain all the triples with *ent* as the subject element in the knowledge base, *i.e.*, all triples with the form $<ent$, Predicate, $val/ent_1>$, in which the third element can be the value of an attribute (*val*) or the ID of an entity (ent_1);
2. Transfer Triples using Name of Entities: Replace the ID of entities in each triple with the name of entities, *i.e.*, $<ent$, Predicate, $ent_1>$ will be changed to be $<name\_of\_ent$, Predicate, $val/name\_of\_ent_1>$, in which *name_of_ent* is the value of the attribute Name of *ent*;

3. Find Co-appearance Documents: For each triple *<name_of_ent*, Predicate, *val/name_of_ent₁>*, check each document in the corpus to see if it contains *name_of_ent* and *val* (or *name_of_ent₁*) in a same sentence. A document can be a webpage, a chapter of a book, an article in a newspaper, etc.

4. Build Appearance Vectors: For each triple *tr*: *<name_of_ent*, Predicate, *val/name_of_ent₁>*, build an appearance vector *<f(tr, doc₁), f(tr, doc₂), ..., f(tr, docₙ)>*, *n* is the number of documents in the corpus. There is:

$$f(tr, doc_i) = \begin{cases} 1, & \text{if a sentence in } doc_i \text{ contains both} \\ & name\_of\_ent \text{ and } val \text{ (or } name\_of\_ent_1) \\ 0, & \text{otherwise} \end{cases}$$

That is, the value of each element in the vector represents the appearance of *name_of_ent* and *val/name_of_ent₁* in the sentences of the corresponding document. For example, if there is a sentence in the first document of the corpus contains "Michael Jordan" and "Scottie Pippen", the first element in the appearance vector of <Michael Jordan, Teammate, Scottie Pippen> is 1, otherwise it is 0.

5. Hierarchical Clustering of Appearance Vectors: Based on the appearance vectors of each triple, hierarchical clustering is applied to classify the triples and further decide if there is entity mixture for *ent*.

In the result of classification in Step 5, if all the triples are classified to be one group, there is no entity mixture for *ent*. Otherwise, it is supposed to have multiple homonymous entities mixed in triples of *ent*.

According to the above description, each step of our methodology is conducted using statistical or machine learning techniques. Thus, our methodology requires few manual work or knowledge of domain experts, so it is supposed to be generally applicable, flexible, and adaptive in a wide range of applications. The detailed steps are depicted in Fig. 1. The following section discusses the core steps of the workflow in detail.

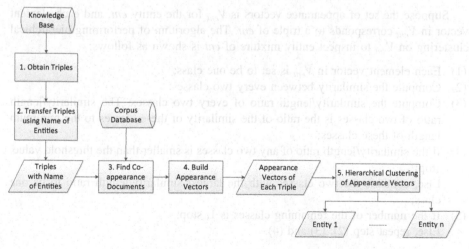

Fig. 1. Workflow of entity mixture detection for entity *ent*

3.3 Hierarchical Clustering for Detection of Entity Mixture

The critical step of our methodology for detection of entity mixture is applying hierarchical clustering on the set of appearance vectors to classify triples of the entity. Since the number of mixed entities is uncertain, we choose hierarchical clustering because it does not require a targeted number of classes before performing the classification. To give an intuitive explanation of our methodology, the following graph shows the outcome of each step during inspection of possibly mixed entities named Michael Jordan (Fig. 2).

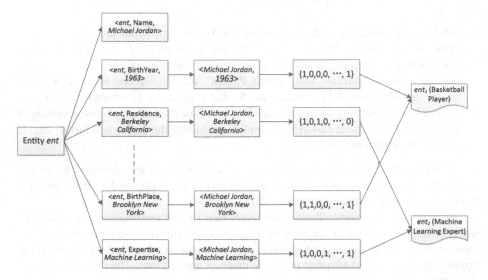

Fig. 2. Outcome of steps during inspection of possibly mixed entities named Michael Jordan

Suppose the set of appearance vectors is V_{ent} for the entity *ent*, and each element vector in V_{ent} corresponds to a triple of *ent*. The algorithm of performing hierarchical clustering on V_{ent} to inspect entity mixture of *ent* is shown as follows:

(1) Each element vector in V_{ent} is set to be one class;
(2) Compute the similarity between every two classes;
(3) Compute the similarity/length ratio of every two classes. The similarity/length ratio of two classes is the ratio of the similarity of these classes to the minimum length of these classes;
(4) If the similarity/length ratio of any two classes is smaller than the threshold value, stop;
    Else, combine the two classes with the largest similarity/length ratio to be one class;
(5) If the number of the remaining classes is 1, stop;
    Else, repeat step (2), (3) and (4).

The number of classes in the result of the above process indicates the number of entities mixed in triples of *ent*. If the number is 1, no mixture happens.

The algorithm to compute the similarity of two classes in step (2) is:

$$Similartity(C_1, C_2) = |C_1 \& C_2| \tag{1}$$

Where C_1 and C_2 are classes, and they are also appearance vectors. Suppose $C_1 = \{c_{11}, c_{12}, \ldots, c_{1n}\}$, $C_2 = \{c_{21}, c_{22}, \ldots, c_{2n}\}$, there are:

$$C_1 \& C_2 = \{c_{11} \& c_{21}, c_{12} \& c_{22}, \ldots, c_{1n} \& c_{2n}\} \tag{2}$$

$$c_{1i} \& c_{2i} = \begin{cases} 1 & \text{if } c_{1i} = 1 \text{ and } c_{2i} = 1 \\ 0 & \text{otherwise} \end{cases}$$

According to the above formulas, the similarity value of two classes is the number of bits that equals 1 in both of the two classes.

In step (3), the similarity/length ratio of two classes that used to select classes to combine is computed using the following formula:

$$SimilarityLengthRatio(C_i, C_j) = \frac{Similarity(C_i, C_j)}{\min(length(C_i), length(C_j))} \tag{3}$$

The length of a class C_i, $length(C_i)$, is the number of 1 in the vector C_i.

In step (4), the criterion of halting the clustering is:

$$\forall C_i, C_j \in V_{ent}, Similarity(C_i, C_j) < \eta * \min(length(C_i), length(C_j))$$

η is the threshold value that decides whether to halt the clustering or combine the pair of classes with the largest similarity/length ratio to be one class. The value of η may vary in different applications and it is determined according to domain experts' experience or trials. For example, in our experiments, the value of η is set to be 1/4.

The algorithm to combine two classes into one class is as follows:

$$C_{12} = Combine(C_1, C_2) = \{c_{11} \,|\, c_{21}, c_{12} \,|\, c_{22}, \ldots, c_{1n} \,|\, c_{2n}\} \tag{4}$$

$$c_{1i} \,|\, c_{2i} = \begin{cases} 1 & \text{if } c_{1i} = 1 \text{ or } c_{2i} = 1 \\ 0 & \text{otherwise} \end{cases}$$

Where C_1 and C_2 are classes, and C_{12} is the result class of combining C_1 and C_2. Suppose C_1 is the appearance vector of triple *<ent, val_1>* and C_2 is the appearance vector of triple *<ent, val_2>*. According to the above formula, the combination of C_1 and C_2 represents the set of documents that either *<ent, val_1>* or *<ent, val_2>* co-appears in at least one sentence. That is, the documents that describe *<ent, val_1>* or *<ent, val_2>* are combined together, since *val_1* and *val_2* are supposed to the attributes of a same entity.

4 Experiments of Entity Mixture Detection

This chapter presents experiments on data sets of industrial applications and the experimental results of entity mixture detection using hierarchical clustering.

4.1 Experiment Environments and Settings

The experiments were conducted on two data sets, one of which is a knowledge base (*i.e.*, KB) and the other is an e-book library (*i.e.*, EB). KB contains 1,382,056 triples of 90,412 entities, and EB contains 80,552 e-books in various categories. Most of the data and articles in KB and EB are in Chinese. Each e-book in EB is separated to be several documents (*e.g.*, chapters or sections) with an average 3000 characters. In sum, there are about 700 thousand documents in EB.

There are 100 pairs of homonymous entities and 100 individual entities randomly selected as the test cases in our experiments. Each entity in a pair of homonymous entities has a unique ID and different attribute values in the knowledge base. For example, two entities with the name Chen Deng are selected, and one is an official in the Song Dynasty (ID: YNNNZk8F) and the other is a scholar in the Ming Dynasty (ID: YNNNZmR2).

Based on the selected entities, 200 sets of triples are obtained from the knowledge base. The first 100 sets are those mixed triples of the homonymous entities. For example, the triples of the two entities named Chen Deng are mixed to be one set. The first 100 sets are called the sets of mixed triples. Another 100 sets are those triples without entity mixture, and they are called the sets of pure triples.

The purpose of the experiments is to evaluate the performance of our methodology for detecting entity mixture from two aspects: the ratio of correct detection of entity mixture in the sets of mixed triples, and the ratio of false detection of entity mixture in the sets of pure triples.

4.2 Analysis of Experimental Results

An appearance vector was built for each triple in the test sets based on documents in EB, then hierarchical clustering was performed on the sets of appearance vectors to classify the homonymous entities and individual entities. The results of the experiment showed that each set of mixed triples were divided into multiple groups, *i.e.*, entity mixture was detected for each set of mixed triples. However, 6 sets of mixed triples were divided into 3 or more groups. Meanwhile, 7 sets of pure triples were divided into two or more groups, *i.e.*, entity mixture was mistakenly detected for 7 entities.

In sum, the accuracy rate of our methodology in the experiment is 93.5% (187 of 200 sets are correctly divided), and the recall rate is 94% (94 of 100 sets of mixed triples are correctly divided). In the point of view of mixture detection, the accuracy rate is 96.5% (entity mixture was detected for all the sets of mixed triples, and no entity mixture was correctly labeled for 93 sets of pure triples), and the recall rate is 100% (all entities with entity mixture are detected).

Since there is currently no similar work on detection of entity mixture for our methodology to compare, it is not able to show the improvements of our methodology over other people's work. Thus, we demonstrate the performance of our methodology through comparing the experimental results with those of other alternative methods. A critical factor that influences the accuracy rate of entity mixture detection is the value of η which decides the classes to combine or to halt the clustering process (see Sect. 3.3). In our experiments we choose 1/4 as the value of η based on our experience. The following table shows the comparison of experimental results of entity mixture detection based on different values of η.

As shown in Table 1, 1/4 is currently the best choice of the value of η.

Table 1. Results of entity mixture detection based on different values of η

Halting threshold	Accuracy%	Recall%	F Value
1/2	83.5% (92.5%[a])	82% (100%[a])	82.74% (96.1%[a])
1/4	93.5% (96.5%[a])	94% (100%[a])	93.75% (98.22%[a])
1/6	94% (95.5%[a])	93% (96%[a])	93.5% (95.75%[a])
1/8	93% (94%[a])	87% (89%[a])	89.9% (91.43%[a])

[a]In the point view of entity mixture detection.

5 Conclusion

This paper presents a methodology to detect entity mixture in knowledge bases using hierarchical clustering. The main contribution of our methodology is to propose a generic and automated approach to distinguish entities based on the appearance distribution of their triples in documents of a common corpus. The results of experiments conducted on data sets of industrial applications show that the accuracy rate and recall rate of entity mixture detection are both high (>90%) by using our methodology. Furthermore, a comparison of detection performance based on different values of the threshold to combine classes or halt the clustering shows that our methodology is currently optimal for detecting entity mixture.

There are two advantages of our methodology in detection of entity mixture. First, our methodology is able to distinguish entities regardless of the types of mixed attributes, i.e., the types of attributes (e.g., "BirthPlace", "BirthDate", etc.) or the relations between entities (e.g., "Friend", "Teammate", etc.) do not have difference in detection of entity mixture by using our methodology. Secondly, few manual work is required for detection of entity mixture by using our methodology. Since our methodology is designed based on statistical and machine learning techniques, it is believed to have a great advantage in the era of big data.

However, there are some limitations exist in our work:

(1) Though our methodology is supposed to be generic in different applications, it has not been tested on data sets of various languages. Our experiments were only conducted on Chinese data set.
(2) In our methodology, the difference of entities is determined based on the appearance distribution of their attribute values in documents. To extend the application scope of our methodology, more parameters should be considered for distinguishing entities and building the classifier, such as the number of appearance of an attribute value in one document.

According to the above limitations, we propose the future directions of our work for us to continue and improve our methodology as follows:

(1) Our methodology should be applied in data sets of different languages to verify its validity in detecting entity mixture.
(2) More parameters should be considered to determine the difference between entities.
(3) Our methodology should be integrated into the process of knowledge base construction and population to improve the data accuracy of knowledge bases and the quality of knowledge services.

Acknowledgments. This work is supported by the projects of National Natural Science Foundation of China (No. 61472014, No. 61573028 and No. 61432020), the Natural Science Foundation of Beijing (No. 4142023) and the Beijing Nova Program (XX2015B010). We also thank all the anonymous reviewers for their valuable comments.

References

1. Weichselbraun, A., Gindl, S., Scharl, A.: Enriching semantic knowledge bases for opinion mining in big data applications. Know. Based Syst. **69**(1), 78–85 (2014)
2. Bengio, Y., Courville, A., Vincent, P.: Representation learning: a review and new perspectives. IEEE Trans. Softw. Eng. **35**(8), 1798–1828 (2014)
3. Sondhi, P., Zhai, C.: Mining semi-structured online knowledge bases to answer natural language questions on community QA websites. In: Proceedings of the 23rd ACM International Conference on Information and Knowledge Management (CIKM 2014), pp. 341–350 (2014)
4. West, R., Gabrilovich, E., Murphy, K., Sun, S., Gupta, R., Lin, D.: Knowledge base completion via search-based question answering. In: Proceedings of the 23rd International Conference on World Wide Web (WWW 2014), pp. 515–526 (2014)
5. Chen, M., Pavalanathan, U., Jensen, S., Plale, B.: Modeling heterogeneous data resources for social-ecological research: a data-centric perspective. In: Proceedings of the 13th ACM/IEEE-CS Joint Conference on Digital Libraries (JCDL 2013), pp. 309–312 (2013)
6. Gassler, W., Zangerle, E., Specht, G.: Guided curation of semi-structured data in collaboratively built knowledge bases. Future Gener. Comput. Syst. **31**(31), 111–119 (2014)
7. Cobo, M.J., Martínez, M.A., Salcedo, M.G., Fujita, H., Viedma, E.H.: Twenty-five years at knowledge-based systems: a bibliometric analysis. Knowl. Based Syst. **80**, 3–13 (2015)

8. Singhal, A.: Introducing the knowledge graph: things, not strings. http://googleblog. blogspot.co.uk/2012/05/introducing-knowledge-graph-things-not.html. Accessed July 2016
9. Yahya, M., Berberich, K., Elbassuoni, S., Weikum, G.: Robust question answering over the web of linked data. In: Proceedings of the 22nd ACM International Conference on Information & Knowledge Management (CIKM 2013), pp. 1107–1116 (2013)
10. Xie, H., Lu, X., Tang, Z., Ye, M.: A methodology to evaluate triple confidence and detect incorrect triples in knowledge bases. In: Proceedings of the 16th ACM/IEEE-CS on Joint Conference on Digital Libraries, pp. 251–252 (2016)
11. Han, X., Sun, L.: An entity-topic model for entity linking. In: Proceedings of the 2012 Joint Conference on Empirical Methods in Natural Language Processing & Computational Natural Language Learning, pp. 105–115 (2012)
12. Dredze, M., Mcnamee, P., Rao, D., Gerber, A., Finin, T.: Entity disambiguation for knowledge base population. In: Proceedings of the 23rd International Conference on Computational Linguistics, no. 3, pp. 277–285 (2010)
13. Gooi, C.H., Allan, J.: Cross-document coreference on a large scale corpus. In: Human Language Technology Conference of the North American Chapter of the Association for Computational Linguistics, pp. 9–16 (2004)
14. Chisholm, A., Hachey, B.: Entity disambiguation with web links. Trans. Assoc. Comput. Linguist. 3, 145–156 (2015)
15. Mann, G.S., Yarowsky, D.: Unsupervised personal name disambiguation. In: Proceedings of the Seventh Conference on Natural Language Learning (2003)
16. Cao, C., Liu, X., Yang, Y., Yu, Y., Wang, J.: Look and think twice: capturing top-down visual attention with feedback convolutional neural networks. In: IEEE International Conference on Computer Vision, pp. 2956–2964 (2015)
17. Li, Y., Tan, S., Sun, H., Han, J., Roth, D., Yan, X.: Entity disambiguation with linkless knowledge bases. In: Proceedings of the 23rd International Conference on World Wide Web (2016)
18. Blanco, R., Boldi, P., Marino, A.: Entity-linking via graph-distance minimization. In: Proceedings of GRAPHITE, pp. 30–43 (2014)

Knowledge Base Question Answering
Based on Deep Learning Models

Zhiwen Xie, Zhao Zeng, Guangyou Zhou$^{(\boxtimes)}$, and Tingting He

School of Computer, Central China Normal University, Wuhan 430079, China
{xiezhiwen,zhaozeng}@mails.ccnu.edu.cn, {gyzhou,tthe}@mail.ccnu.edu.cn

Abstract. This paper focuses on the task of knowledge-based question answering (KBQA). KBQA aims to match the questions with the structured semantics in knowledge base. In this paper, we propose a two-stage method. Firstly, we propose a topic entity extraction model (TEEM) to extract topic entities in questions, which does not rely on hand-crafted features or linguistic tools. We extract topic entities in questions with the TEEM and then search the knowledge triples which are related to the topic entities from the knowledge base as the candidate knowledge triples. Then, we apply Deep Structured Semantic Models based on convolutional neural network and bidirectional long short-term memory to match questions and predicates in the candidate knowledge triples. To obtain better training dataset, we use an iterative approach to retrieve the knowledge triples from the knowledge base. The evaluation result shows that our system achieves an AverageF_1 measure of 79.57% on test dataset.

1 Introduction

Automatic question answering systems are aimed at returning the direct and exact answers to natural language questions. Recently, with the development of large-scale knowledge bases, such as Freebase [1] and DBPedia [2], knowledge bases become very important resources for open domain question answering. Recently, most research studies focus on the task of knowledge based QA (KBQA). In this paper, we focus on the task of NLPCC-ICCPOL 2016 KBQA for Chinese language.

The major challenge of KBQA is how to understand natural language questions and match the questions with structured semantics of knowledge bases. To address this challenge, previous work in the literature uses semantic parsing, which map the natural language question into a formal representation, such as logical form or SPARQL. However, most of the semantic parsers need to annotate logical forms of questions as supervision and rely on predefined rules and linguistic tools. The annotated logical forms always can't coverage all the predicates in the knowledge base. In addition, parsing the questions needs to recognize the topic entity which is the main entity referring to the subject of the corresponding knowledge triple in knowledge base. However, most word segmentation and named entity recognition tools are not very good and can't recognize some

© Springer International Publishing AG 2016
C.-Y. Lin et al. (Eds.): NLPCC-ICCPOL 2016, LNAI 10102, pp. 300–311, 2016.
DOI: 10.1007/978-3-319-50496-4_25

complicated topic entities in questions. This problem can be solved by using an advanced entity linking system, but it still rely on quality of linguistic tools and always introduce many noise entities. In this paper, we use a topic entity extraction model based on deep learning to solve this problem.

Recently, deep learning models have achieved remarkable results in natural language processing, such as word vector representations [3–5], deep structured semantic models (DSSM) [6–8], machine translation [9] and text summarization [10].

In this paper, we use two deep learning strategies to address the KBQA task in two stages. Firstly, we propose a topic entity extraction model (TEEM) with deep learning, which is used to extract the topic entities in questions. Our entity extraction model does not rely on hand-draft features or linguistic tools and can extract topic entities in the questions accurately. This model is based on convolutional neural network. The results of TEEM is used to retrieve candidate knowledge triples which is related to the topic entities in the questions. Thus, we can prune the space for semantic matching and make the matching more efficient by focusing on the most related part of the knowledge base. Then, instead of pure lexical matching we apply deep structured semantic models (DSSM) to match questions with the predicates of the candidate knowledge triples in a semantic space. In this study, we develop the DSSM by using a bidirectional long short term memory neural network (BiLSTM-DSSM). To obtain more composite representation, we add an convolutional layer on the top of the BiLSTM Layer. We also leverage a recently developed structured semantic model based on convolutional neural network (C-DSSM) and we combine the scores of the DSSMs as the final semantic relevance score. The words in questions and knowledge base are represented by word vectors, which can represent words in a dense and semantic space. In this paper, we train all the models on top of word vectors obtained from an unsupervised neural language model.

To obtain better training dataset, we use an iterative approach to retrieve the knowledge triples from the knowledge base for training. Firstly, the question-answer pairs are used to search the corresponding knowledge triples from the knowledge base. The results are used as the initial training data to train the topic entity extraction model. Since the initial training data is always inaccurate, to better the training data, we use the entities extracted by the trained TEEM as additional information and retrieve the knowledge triples again. Thus, the training data will be better with less noise and the accuracy of models will improve.

The rest of this paper is structured as follows: Sect. 2 describes the related work. Section 3 introduces the details of the proposed methods; Experimental results are presented in Sect. 4. Finally, we conclude the paper in Sect. 5.

2   Related Work

Automatic question answering aims at returning a direct and exact answer for a natural language question. Recently, with the rise of structured and large-scale knowledge base, KBQA has attached much attention. Most of the KBQA systems are based on semantic parsing, where a question is converted into logical form and then transformed into structured query to be executed on knowledge base. Traditional semantic parsers require annotated logical forms as supervisions to train [11,12], which is very expensive. To reduce the costs, recently works focus on using question-answer pairs as weak training signals [13,14]. With the progress of deep learning in natural language processing, deep learning models are used by more and more KBQA systems and achieve a significant success. Yih et al. [15,16] developed semantic parsing frameworks based on semantic similarity by using Staged Query Graph Generation and convolutional neural network semantic models. Dong et al. [17] proposed multi-column convolutional neural networks to understand questions from three different aspects (namely, answer path, answer context, and answer type) and learn their distributed representations. Zhang [18] proposed a neural attention-based model to represent the questions dynamically according to the different aspects of various candidate answer aspects. Meanwhile, they also integrated the rich KB information into the representation of the answer.

3 Methods

The overview of our KBQA system framework is shown in Fig. 1. As is shown in Fig. 1, our system is mainly composed of four modules: TEEM module, DSSM module, IR module and Answer Extraction module. The TEEM module is used to extract topic entities from natural language questions. The DSSM module is used to transform the natural language questions and predicates into semantic vectors in the same semantic space, so that the semantic similarities between questions and predicates can be measured by cosine similarities of the semantic vectors. The KB index is an index of knowledge base. The results of TEEM module are fed into the IR module and we retrieve the candidate knowledge triples from the KB index. Then, in the Answer Extraction module, we calculate the semantic matching scores of the candidate knowledge triples and select triples with the highest score as the final answers.

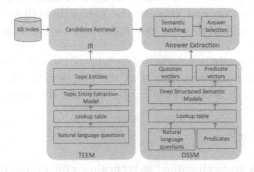

Fig. 1. The overview of the KBQA system framework.

3.1 Topic Entity Extraction Models

Topic entity for a question is the main entity which the question asks for. There may be many entities in a question. However we need extract the topic entity to retrieve the most relevant candidate triples. Topic entity extraction is an important step in the KBQA system, which can directly impact the results of candidate retrieval. Traditional QA systems extract topic entities by using linguistic tools, such as name entity recognition tools. These methods strongly rely on the quality of the linguistic tools, which are not always work well especially with Chinese. To extract high-quality topic entities in questions, we develop a Topic Entity Extraction Model (TEEM). The architecture of our TEEM model which is based on convolutional neutral network (CNN) is illustrated in Fig. 2.
Each word in a question first is transformed into a word vector with k dimensions. Then a question of length n can be represented as a sequence of word vectors. In our experiment, the question length n is set to 20 (any tokens less than this range will be padded and out of this range will be discarded). We define the question as $q = (x_1, x_2, \cdots, x_n)$, where $x_i \in R^k$ is corresponding to the i-th word in the question. The convolution operation can be view as a sliding window which can extract local features in a question sentence. Whether a word is part of a topic entity is depended on the contextual information of the word. In the convolutional layer, we use multiple filters to obtain multiple local contextual features for each of the words in the questions. The word vectors of words within a sliding window of 3 words are mapped into a new local contextual feature, as shown in Fig. 2. A max-pooling layer is followed to select the most important feature in a max-pooling window and filter out undesirable features. The convolutions and max-pooling in deeper layers are defined in a similar way. In the final max-pooling layer, it can reach a fixed length vector. A full connection layer is followed to obtain the final output vector of the model.

For each word in a question, if the word is part of the topic entity, we set 1 as the tag of this word, otherwise we set 0 as the tag. Thus, we can obtain the supervise label vector of each question which is described as $y = (y_1, y_2, \cdots, y_n)$, where y_i is the label of the i-th word in the question. For instance, for the question "命运石之门是哪一种类型的游戏" , the label of each word in the question is "命运/1 石/1 之门/1 是/0 哪/0 一/0 种/0 类型/0 的/0 游戏/0" and the label vector is (1,1,1,0,0,0,0,0,0,0).

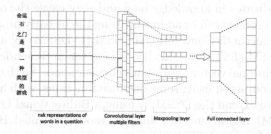

Fig. 2. TEEM architecture for an example question.

The output vector of our model is fixed length vector of n dimensions (n is the length of the input sequences). We denote the output vector as $z = (z_1, z_2, \cdots, z_n)$, where z_i is corresponding to the tag of the i-th word in the input question. The goal of TEEM is to minimize the difference between the output vector z and corresponding label vector. We use the mean squared error as the loss function of the TEEM, which is defined as

$$MSE(w, b) = \frac{1}{n} \sum_{i=1}^{n} (z_i - y_i)^2 + \lambda \|w\|_2^2 \tag{1}$$

where w is the weight parameters of the model, and b is the bias parameters of the model. $\|w\|_2^2$ is the L2-regularization of the weight vectors which is added to combat overfitting. λ is a hyper-parameter which controls the relative importance of the regularization parameter.

Table 1. Topic entities extracted by TEEM

Question	Topic Entity
3|-| 溴 | 化 | 苯甲 | 酮 | 的 | 熔点 | 是 | 多少 | 摄氏度 |?	3-溴化苯甲酮
金鱼 | 素 | 馅 | 包 | 的 | 辅料 | 都 | 有 | 什么 |?	金鱼素馅包
上海 | 逸 | 凡 | 居 | 旅店 | 有 | 哪些 | 休闲 | 设施 |?	上海逸凡居旅店
中 | 虹 | 花园 | 新都 | 苑 | 何时 | 竣工 | 的 |?	中虹花园新都苑
中国 | 电子 |m|5| 支持 | 电子书 | 功能 | 吗 |?	中国电子 m5

Through the TEEM module, we can extract topic entities in most questions. These topic entities can be used to retrieve the candidate knowledge triples and can significantly improve the quality of the retrieval results. Some topic entities extracted by the TEEM are shown in Table 1. The words in questions are separated by "|".

3.2 Deep Structured Semantic Models

The Deep Structured Semantic Model (DSSM) is used to measure the semantic similarity between the questions and the predicates in knowledge base. The predicate words mentioned in questions are always different from those defined in the knowledge base, which makes it very difficult to calculate the similarity between questions and predicates in knowledge base and may cause the ontology matching problem. This problem can be addressed using the recently proposed DSSM [6] and the improved methods Convolutional DSSM (C-DSSM) [8] and Long-Short-Term Memory DSSM (LSTM-DSSM) [19]. These semantic models map the sentences into k-dimensional vectors in a latent semantic space. So that their semantic similarity can be computed using some distance functions, such as cosine.

In this work, we extend the DSSM by using a Bidirectional Long Short-Term Memory (BiLSTM) neural network and the model is called BiLSTM-DSSM. Long short-Term Memory (LSTM) [20] is one of the popular variations of Recurrent Neural Networks (RNN) which is widely used to deal with variable-length

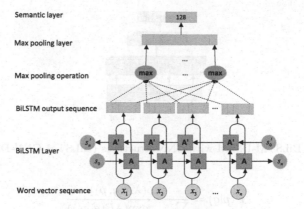

Fig. 3. Architecture of BiLSTM-DSSM.

sequence input. LSTMs are capable of learning long-term dependencies and remembering information for long periods of time. However, single directional LSTMs still suffer a weakness of not utilizing the contextual information from the future tokens. To handle this problem, we use the bidirectional LSTM, which can utilize both the previous and future context by processing the sequence on two directions. The architecture of the BiLSTM-DSSM is illustrated in Fig. 3. Unlike the previous semantic model, we use word vectors to represent the questions instead of the word hashing technique proposed in [6]. At the BiLSTM layer, A and A' are chunks of neural network which can look at an input vector and output a value. The input sequence is processed in the forward direction and the reverse direction. At each time step, we concatenate the two output vectors from both directions to obtain the final output vector of the BiLSTM Layer. Followed the BiLSTM Layer, we apply a max pooling layer to extract the most salient features and form a global feature vector with a fixed length. Then a feed-forward semantic layer is used to extract a high-level semantic feature vector for the input word sequence.

In order to obtain more composite representation of questions and predicates, we also develop a variant of the BiLSTM-DSSM model by integrate the CNN structures on the top of BiLSTM layer, which is called BiLSTM-CNN-DSSM, as shown in Fig. 4. The architecture the BiLSTM layer is similar to that in Fig. 3.

We use the cosine similarity to measure the semantic relevance score between question and each predicate in knowledge base. Formally, the semantic relevance score between a question q and a predicate p is measured as:

$$R(q,p) = cosine(y_q, y_p) = \frac{y_q^T y_p}{\|y_q\|\|y_p\|} \qquad (2)$$

where y_q and y_p are the semantic vectors of the question and the predicate, respectively.

Following [6], we first compute the posterior probability of a predicate given a question from the semantic relevance score between them through a softmax function:

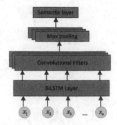

Fig. 4. BiLSTM-DSSM with CNN structures (BiLSTM-CNN-DSSM).

$$P(p|q) = \frac{\exp(\lambda R(q, p))}{\sum_{p' \in \mathbf{P}} \exp(\lambda R(q, p'))} \tag{3}$$

where λ is a smoothing factor in the softmax function. $\mathbf{P}$ denotes the set of candidate predicates to be ranked, including a positive predicate and several negative predicates. The goal is to maximize the likelihood of the positive predicate of the given question. Therefore, we need to minimize the following loss function:

$$L(\Lambda) = -\log \prod_{r}^{R} P(p_r^+ | q_r) \tag{4}$$

where Λ is the parameters of the neural networks, p_r^+ is the positive predicate of the r-th question out of R questions and $P(p_r^+ | q_r)$ is the probability of the positive predicate given the r-th question.

3.3   Candidates Retrieval

Given a question, the main goal of the retrieval model is to find the most relevant knowledge triples in the knowledge base. First of all, we use the trained TEEM to extract the topic entity in the question. Then the topic entity is used to retrieve the relevant knowledge triples from the knowledge base as candidates. For example, for the question "上海逸凡居旅店有哪些休闲设施？", the topic entity extracted by TEEM is "上海逸凡居旅店" and we can get the candidate knowledge triples by retrieve the knowledge base as shown in Table 2.

Table 2. The candidate knowledge triples for topic entity "上海逸凡居旅店"

Subject	Predicate	Object
上海逸凡居旅店	休闲设施	咖啡厅、理发美容室、棋牌麻将
上海逸凡居旅店	餐饮设施	中餐厅
上海逸凡居旅店	地址	上海市虹口区场中路 787 号
上海逸凡居旅店	别名	上海逸凡居旅店

3.4   Answer Selection

Once we obtain the candidate knowledge triples, the DSSM models can be used to map the question and candidate predicates into semantic vectors and then we can calculate the semantic relevant score between them. We use a question DSSM to encode questions and a predicate DSSM to encode predicates. To get better semantic matching score, we combine the semantic relevant scores of BiLSTM-DSSM, BiLSTM-CNN-DSSM and C-DSSM. And the final semantic relevant score is denoted as:

$$S(q,p) = \alpha R_b(q,p) + \beta R_{bc}(q,p) + \lambda R_c(q,p) \tag{5}$$

where $R_b(q,p)$, $R_{bc}(q,p)$ and $R_c(q,p)$ are the semantic relevance scores of the BiLSTM-DSSM, BiLSTM-CNN-DSSM and C-DSSM, respectively. And α, β, λ are the coefficient parameters of the three scores.

In order to select the best matching answers for a question, we also consider the lexical similarity between a question and a predicate at the character level. For each question-predicate pair, we segment the question and predicate into characters. The question vector c_q and the predicate vector c_p are constructed based on the characters. Each character is a dimension of the vector. If the character is appeared in the string the corresponding dimension is set to 1, otherwise set to 0. We use the cosine similarity to measure the lexical matching score:

$$LS(q,p) = \cos(c_q, c_p) = \frac{c_q^T c_p}{\|c_q\|\|c_p\|} \tag{6}$$

The final matching score can be defined as following:

$$score = \mu S(q,p) + \omega LS(q,p) \tag{7}$$

where $S(q,p)$ is the semantic relevant score, $LS(q,p)$ is the lexical matching score, and μ, ω are the coefficient parameters of $S(q,p)$ and $LS(q,p)$ respectively.

In this paper, we rank the candidates according to the score defined in Eq. (7) and select the most relevant candidates as the final answer.

4   Experiment

4.1   Data Set

In this paper, we use the data set released by NLPCC-ICCPOL 2016 KBQA task. The data set includes 14,609 question-answer pairs and a knowledge base called nlpcc-iccpol-2016.kbqa.kb which contains 43M knowledge triples. The format of the triples in knowledge base nlpcc-iccpol-2016.kbqa.kb is: Subject ||| Predicate ||| Object.

In this paper, we need the question-entity pairs to train the TEEM and question-predicate pairs to train DSSMs. However, the given data set only contains question-answer pairs. To obtain better training dataset, we use an iterative approach to retrieve the knowledge triples from the knowledge base for training. Firstly, the question-answer pairs are used to search the corresponding knowledge triples from the knowledge base. The results are used as the initial training data to train the topic entity extraction model. Since there are plenty of noise entities in a question, the initial training data is always inaccurate. In order to get more high-quality training data, we use the entities extracted by the trained TEEM as additional information and retrieve the knowledge triples again. At last, we obtain 14165 question-entity pairs and 14165 question-predicate pairs. The negative examples for the DSSMs are randomly sampled from the training data.

4.2   Setup

The word vectors in this work is trained by word2vec [4], and the word vector size is 200. We use a zero vector to represent the word which is out of vocabulary. We use Stochastic Gradient Descent (SGD) to optimize the objective functions. The window size of the CNN layer in TEEM is 3. The dimension of the DSSMs output vector is set to 128. The smoothing factor λ in Eq. (3) is set to 5. We train our models in mini-batches and the batch size is set to 10. We randomly sampled 5 negative samples for each question-predicate pair. The maximum length of word sequence for questions and predicates are set to 20 and 5 respectively. Any tokens less than this range will be padded and out of this range will be discarded, so that the length of the samples within a mini-batch can have the same length.

4.3   Evaluation Metric

The quality of the KBQA system is evaluated by AverageF_1, which is defined as:

$$\text{Average}F_1 = \frac{1}{|Q|} \sum_{i=1}^{|Q|} F_i \tag{8}$$

F_i denotes the F_1 score for question Q_i computed based on C_i and A_i. F_i is set to 0 if the generated answer set C_i for Q_i is empty or doesn't overlap with the golden answers A_i for Q_i. Otherwise, F_i is computed as follows:

$$F_i = \frac{2 \cdot \frac{\#(C_i, A_i)}{|C_i|} \cdot \frac{\#(C_i, A_i)}{|A_i|}}{\frac{\#(C_i, A_i)}{|C_i|} + \frac{\#(C_i, A_i)}{|A_i|}} \tag{9}$$

where $\#(C_i, A_i)$ denotes the number of answers occur in both C_i and A_i. $|C_i|$ and $|A_i|$ denote the number of answers in C_i and A_i respectively.

4.4   Experimental Results

In this section, we analyze the experimental results of our experiments. As introduced in Sect. 3, there are many parameters to be adjusted in the answer selection module. We can adjust the coefficient parameters in Eqs. (5) and (7) to get better results. Table 3 summarizes some results of different semantic matching methods in the case that the ω parameter in Eq. (7) is set to 0.5 and μ is set to 5. The Combined-DSSM uses Eq. (5) to combine the semantic relevant scores of C-DSSM, BiLSTM-DSSM and BiLSTM-CNN-DSSM. And the parameters in Eq. (5) are $\alpha = 0.4$, $\beta = 0.1$ and $\lambda = 0.5$. Some of the results of our experiment are shown in Table 3. The baseline system which is released by NLPCC-ICCPOL 2016 KBQA task is based on C-DSSM without using TEEM. As is shown in Table 3, the result of the Combined-DSSM, which is the submitted result for NLPCC-ICCPOL 2016 KBQA task, is much better than other methods. And all the models proposed in this paper substantially outperform the baseline system, which indicate that the proposed TEEM can significantly improve the results.

Table 3. The experimental results of different semantic matching methods

Models	AverageF_1
Baseline system(C-DSSM)	0.5247
TEEM+C-DSSM	0.7808
TEEM+BiLSTM-DSSM	0.7529
TEEM+BiLSTM-CNN-DSSM	0.7815
TEEM+Combined-DSSM	**0.7957**

Figure 5 shows the AverageF_1-ω curves of the four sematic matching methods in the paper, which indicate the impact of the lexical matching score on the results. Here, ω is the parameter in Eq. (7). As is illustrated in Fig. 5, the AverageF_1 can be improved by adjusting the parameter ω appropriately. The best result of our proposed methods can achieve an AverageF_1 of 81.77% when the ω is set to 5.

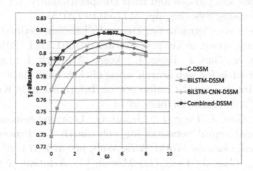

Fig. 5. The AverageF_1-ω curves of the four sematic matching methods in the paper.

5   Conclusion

In this paper, we present a KBQA system framework to address the question answering problem. In our KBQA system, we propose a topic entity extraction model to extract the topic entities in questions at the candidate retrieval stage. And we apply deep structured semantic models to calculate the semantic similarity between questions and predicates at the answer selection stage. We extend the DSSM by using bidirectional long short-term memory and integrate a CNN structure on the top of the BiLSTM layer. The experimental results demonstrate that our system achieve good performances and substantially outperform the baseline system.

Acknowledgments. This work was supported by the National Natural Science Foundation of China (No. 61303180 and No. 61573163), the Fundamental Research Funds for the Central Universities (No. CCNU15ZD003 and No. CCNU16A02024), and also supported by Wuhan Youth Science and technology plan. We thank the anonymous reviewers for their insightful comments.

References

1. Bollacker, K., Evans, C., Paritosh, P., Sturge, T., Taylor, J.: Freebase: a collaboratively created graph database for structuring human knowledge. In: Proceedings of the SIGMOD 2008, pp. 1247–1250 (2008)
2. Auer, S., Bizer, C., Kobilarov, G., Lehmann, J., Cyganiak, R., Ives, Z.: DBpedia: a nucleus for a web of open data. In: Aberer, K., et al. (eds.) ASWC/ISWC - 2007. LNCS, vol. 4825, pp. 722–735. Springer, Heidelberg (2007). doi:10.1007/978-3-540-76298-0_52
3. Pennington, J., Socher, R., Manning, C.D.: Glove: global vectors for word representation. In: EMNLP, vol. 14, pp. 1532–43 (2014)
4. Mikolov, T., Sutskever, I., Chen, K., Corrado, G.S., Dean, J.: Distributed representations of words and phrases and their compositionality. In: Advances in Neural Information Processing Systems, pp. 3111–3119 (2013)
5. Mikolov, T., Chen, K., Corrado, G., Dean, J.: Efficient estimation of word representations in vector space. arXiv preprint arXiv:1301.3781 (2013)
6. Huang, P. S., He, X., Gao, J., Deng, L., Acero, A., Heck, L.: Learning deep structured semantic models for web search using clickthrough data. In: Proceedings of the 22nd ACM International Conference on Information & Knowledge Management, pp. 2333–2338. ACM, October 2013
7. Shen, Y., He, X., Gao, J., Deng, L., Mesnil, G.: Learning semantic representations using convolutional neural networks for web search. In: Proceedings of the 23rd International Conference on World Wide Web, pp. 373–374. ACM, April 2014
8. Shen, Y., He, X., Gao, J., Deng, L., Mesnil, G.: A latent semantic model with convolutional-pooling structure for information retrieval. In: Proceedings of the 23rd ACM International Conference on Information and Knowledge Management, pp. 101–110. ACM, November 2014
9. Bahdanau, D., Cho, K., Bengio, Y.: Neural machine translation by jointly learning to align and translate. arXiv preprint arXiv:1409.0473 (2014)

10. Rush, A.M., Chopra, S., Weston, J.: A neural attention model for abstractive sentence summarization. arXiv preprint arXiv:1509.00685 (2015)
11. Zettlemoyer, L.S., Collins, M.: Learning to map sentences to logical form: structured classification with probabilistic categorial grammars. arXiv preprint arXiv:1207.1420 (2012)
12. Kwiatkowski, T., Zettlemoyer, L., Goldwater, S., Steedman, M.: Inducing probabilistic CCG grammars from logical form with higher-order unification. In: Proceedings of the 2010 Conference on Empirical Methods in Natural Language Processing, pp. 1223–1233, October 2010
13. Krishnamurthy, J., Mitchell, T.M.: Weakly supervised training of semantic parsers. In: Proceedings of the 2012 Joint Conference on Empirical Methods in Natural Language Processing and Computational Natural Language Learning, pp. 754–765, July 2012
14. Berant, J., Chou, A., Frostig, R., Liang, P.: Semantic parsing on freebase from question-answer pairs. In: EMNLP, vol. 2, no. 5, p. 6, October 2013
15. Yih, W.T., Chang, M.W., He, X., Gao, J.: Semantic parsing via staged query graph generation question answering with knowledge base. In: Association for Computational Linguistics (ACL)
16. Yih, W.T., He, X., Meek, C.: Semantic parsing for single-relation question answering. In: ACL, vol. 2, pp. 643–648, June 2014
17. Dong, L., Wei, F., Zhou, M., Xu, K.: Question answering over freebase with multi-column convolutional neural networks. In: Proceedings of Association for Computational Linguistics, pp. 260–269 (2015)
18. Zhang, Y., Liu, K., He, S., Ji, G., Liu, Z., Wu, H., Zhao, J.: Question answering over knowledge base with neural attention combining global knowledge information. arXiv preprint arXiv:1606.00979 (2016)
19. Palangi, H., Deng, L., Shen, Y., Gao, J., He, X., Chen, J., Ward, R.: Semantic modelling with long-short-term memory for information retrieval. arXiv preprint arXiv:1412.6629 (2014)
20. Hochreiter, S., Schmidhuber, J.: Long short-term memory. Neural Comput. 9(8), 1735–1780 (1997)

An Open Domain Topic Prediction Model for Answer Selection

Zhao Yan[1(✉)], Nan Duan[2], Ming Zhou[2], Zhoujun Li[1], and Jianshe Zhou[3]

[1] Beihang University, No.37 Xueyuan Road, Beijing 100191, China
{yanzhao,lizj}@buaa.edu.cn
[2] Microsoft Research Asia, Beijing, China
{nanduan,mingzhou}@microsoft.com
[3] BAICIT, Capital Normal University, Beijing, China
zhoujs@cnu.edu.cn

Abstract. We present an open domain topic prediction model for the answer selection task. Different from previous unsupervised topic modeling methods, we automatically extract high quality and large scale ⟨sentence, topic⟩ pairs from Wikipedia as labeled data, and train an open domain topic prediction model based on convolutional neural network, which can predict the most possible topics for each given input sentence. To verify the usefulness of our proposed approach, we add the topic prediction model into an end-to-end open domain question answering system and evaluate it on the answer selection task, and improvements are obtained on both WikiQA and QASent datasets.

Keywords: Answer selection · Question answering · Topic prediction

1 Introduction

Answer selection (AS) is a subtask of the open-domain question answering (QA) problem has received considerable attention in past few years [4,12,16,17]. The goal of this task is to select answer sentences of a given question from a set of pre-selected answer candidates. Previous solutions to this task either use the surface form overlaps between questions and answer sentences, or try to learn the matching of different surface forms with similar meanings between questions and answer sentences based on labeled data. The former ones cannot handle questions who don't share any content word with their answer sentences; while the latter ones depend heavily on the limited training data, and are lack of scalability to other unseen open domain questions.

Motivated by the issues mentioned above, we propose an open domain topic prediction model for the answer selection task, which aims to measure the relevance between questions and answer sentences on the topic-level semantic space. The contributes of this paper are two-fold:

© Springer International Publishing AG 2016
C.-Y. Lin et al. (Eds.): NLPCC-ICCPOL 2016, LNAI 10102, pp. 312–323, 2016.
DOI: 10.1007/978-3-319-50496-4_26

- We show how to automatically acquire high-quality and large scale ⟨sentence, topic⟩ pairs based on Wikipedia as labeled data for the topic prediction model training[1];
- We show how to train the topic prediction model based on Convolutional Neural Network (CNN), and how to use it to enhance an existing answer selection baseline with state-of-the-art results on the WikiQA and QASent dataset.

2 Topic Prediction Model

Formally, given an input sentence $\mathcal{S}$ (either a question or an answer sentence), the goal of topic prediction is to predict the most possible N topics that $\mathcal{S}$ is talking about $\mathcal{T} = [\langle t_1, p_1 \rangle, ..., \langle t_N, p_N \rangle]$, where t_i denotes the ith predicted topic, with its corresponding prediction probability p_i.

In this section, we first illustrate how to acquire training data from Wikipedia, and then describe how to train topic prediction model based on CNN.

2.1 Training Data Acquisition

To ensure the usefulness of our proposed topic prediction model, the training data should cover most of common topics. Instead of letting human annotators to label training data, which is very expensive and time-consuming, we propose a simple but effective method to extract large scale and open domain labeled data automatically from Wikipedia.

Each Wikipedia page is an entity-centered document, which follows the following format illustrated in Fig. 1, where **Entity** denotes the central entity that the current Wikipedia page is talking about, **Topic** denotes an entry existed in the Content table[2], **Topic Sentence** denotes a sentence that introduces the given topic of the current entity.

Based on this format, we extract ⟨sentence, topic⟩ pairs by the following three steps:

Topic Selection. We first extract all content tables from the Wikipedia dump[3]. Entries in content tables are considered as topic candidates. As we can see in Fig. 1, topics in content tables are organized in a tree-like structure. In this work, we only consider topics in the first level, as topics in other levels are more specific to entities. As the total number of topic candidates (741,060 topics in the first level) is very large, we filter the topic candidates based on the following two rules: (1) each topic should be covered by at least 20 Wikipedia pages; (2) each topic should not be contained by a general keyword list, such as "abstract", "reference" and "others", as these kind of keywords are too general to be useful in downstream tasks. After applying these two filter rules, there are 7,218 topics left.

---

[1] The dataset is available now and can be downloaded at https://github.com/helloQA/WikiTopicPredictionData.
[2] Each content table is the outline of the current page.
[3] https://dumps.wikimedia.org/.

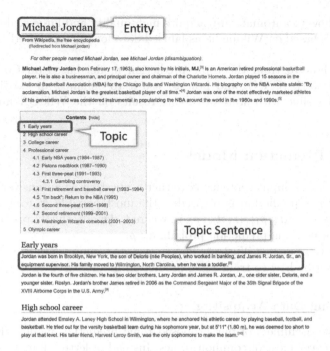

Fig. 1. The typical format of a Wikipedia page.

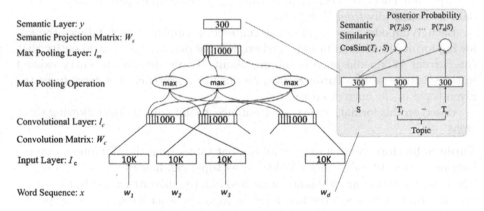

Fig. 2. Illustration of the architecture for the topic prediction model.

⟨Setence, Topic⟩ **Pair Extraction.** For each topic, we then extract its corresponding topic sentences from Wikipedia pages. In Wikipedia, each topic in the content table will be introduced by one or multiple paragraphs. In this work, we only select the first sentence in the first paragraph of a given topic as its topic sentence, as we find that the first sentence has the largest possibility to introduce the topic. More than 4.3 M ⟨Setence, Topic⟩ pairs are left after this step.

⟨Setence, Topic⟩ **Pair Balance.** The number of ⟨Setence, Topic⟩ pairs for different topics are extremely unbalanced. It will lead huge bias for training topic prediction model. In this step, we sample 300 ⟨Setence, Topic⟩ pairs for each topic and ignore those topics that contains ⟨Setence, Topic⟩ pairs less than 300. Consequently, 1,287 topics and 384,965 ⟨Setence, Topic⟩ pairs are left in the final dataset[4].

2.2 Model Training

A convolutional neural network based model, which resembles [5] and [11], is used to train the topic prediction model, by (1) encoding each sentence and its corresponding topic into two topic-level semantic representations; and (2) making sure at the same time that the distance between the representations of each sentence and its correct topic is closest. We show the architecture of this model in Fig. 2.

- **Input Layer.** As the size of English words is large, it is expensive to learn model parameters. So we obtain representation of the tth word-n-gram in a sentence S by concatenating the tri-letter vectors of each word as: $l_t = [w_{t-d}^T, ..., w_t^T, ..., w_{t+d}^T]^T$, where w_t denotes the tth word representation, and $n = 2d + 1$ denotes the contextual window size, which is set to 3.
- **Convolution Layer.** The convolution layer performs sliding window-based feature extraction to project the vector representation l_t of each word-n-gram to a contextual feature vector h_t:

$$h_t = tanh(W_c \cdot l_t)$$

where W_c is the convolution matrix, $tanh(x) = \frac{1-e^{-2x}}{1+e^{-2x}}$ is the activation function.
- **Pooling Layer.** The pooling layer aggregates local features extracted by the convolution layer to form a sentence-level global feature vector with a fixed size independent of the length of the input utterance. *Max pooling* is used to force the network to retain the most useful local features by $l_p = [v_1, ..., v_K]^K$, where

$$v_i = \max_{t=1,...,T} \{h_t(i)\}$$

- **Semantic Layer.** For the global representation l_p of S, one more non-linear transformation is applied as:

$$y(S) = tanh(W_s \cdot l_p)$$

where W_s is the semantic projection matrix, $y(S)$ is the final topic-level semantic vector representation of S.

---

[4] 1,135 sentences are removed by some rules, such as minimum length, which are too detailed to introduce in this paper.

We first compute semantic vectors for sentence $\mathcal{S}$ and all topic candidates using CNN. We then compute a cosine similarity score between $\mathcal{S}$ and each topic candidate t_i. The posterior probability of a topic given a sentence is computed based on this cosine similarity score through a softmax function, and the model is trained by maximizing the likelihood of the correctly associated topic given training $\langle$sentence, topic$\rangle$ pairs, using the mini-batch stochastic gradient descent (SGD) algorithm.

3 Topic Prediction Model for Answer Selection

Given a question $\mathcal{Q}$ and an answer sentence $\mathcal{A}$, we design two types of features to use our proposed topic prediction model in the answer selection task.

3.1 Implicit Topic Matching Feature

The 1st feature is called the *Implicit Topic Matching* (or **ITM**) feature. Implicit topic matching feature computes the relevance between $\mathcal{Q}$ and $\mathcal{A}$ directly as:

$$ITM(\mathcal{Q}, \mathcal{A}) = Cosine(y(\mathcal{Q}), y(\mathcal{A}))$$

where $y(\mathcal{Q})$ and $y(\mathcal{A})$ are topic-level vector representations for $\mathcal{Q}$ and $\mathcal{A}$ respectively, which are generated based on the CNN model described in Sect. 2.2.

3.2 Explicit Topic Matching Feature

The 2nd feature is called the *Explicit Topic Matching* (or **ETM**) feature. Aiming to compute this feature for each $\langle \mathcal{Q}, \mathcal{A} \rangle$ pair, we first predict the most possible M^5 topics for $\mathcal{Q}$ and $\mathcal{A}$ respectively. The prediction score of a topic $t_i^{\mathcal{S}}$ given a sentence $\mathcal{S}$ (either a question or an answer sentence) is computed as:

$$Score(\mathcal{S}, t_i^{\mathcal{S}}) = Cosine(y(\mathcal{S}), y(t_i^{\mathcal{S}}))$$

$y(\mathcal{S})$ and $y(t_i^{\mathcal{S}})$ denote the topic-level embedding vectors for $\mathcal{S}$ and $t_i^{\mathcal{S}}$ respectively, which are generated based on the model described in Sect. 2.2. Then, we concatenate the predicted topics of $\mathcal{Q}$ and $\mathcal{A}$ respectively, and generate two topic strings:

$$Str_{\mathcal{Q}} = t_1^{\mathcal{Q}} t_2^{\mathcal{Q}} ... t_M^{\mathcal{Q}}$$
$$Str_{\mathcal{A}} = t_1^{\mathcal{A}} t_2^{\mathcal{A}} ... t_M^{\mathcal{A}}$$

Based on which, we define three methods, $ETM_{MT}(\mathcal{Q}, \mathcal{A})$, $ETM_{WE}(\mathcal{Q}, \mathcal{A})$ and $ETM_{PP}(\mathcal{Q}, \mathcal{A})$, to measure the explicit topic semantic similarity between $\mathcal{Q}$ and $\mathcal{A}$:

---

[5] In this work, M is set to 10 empirically.

– $ETM_{MT}(\mathcal{Q}, \mathcal{A})$ is a word-based translation model score:

$$ETM_{MT}(\mathcal{Q}, \mathcal{A}) = \frac{\sum_{i=1}^{|Str_{\mathcal{Q}}|} \ln(\frac{\sum_{j=1}^{|Str_{\mathcal{A}}|} p(w_{Aj}|w_{Qi})}{|Str_{\mathcal{A}}|})}{|Str_{\mathcal{Q}}|}$$

where $p(w_{Aj}|w_{Qi})$ denotes the probability that the ith word w_{Qi} in $Str_{\mathcal{Q}}$ can be translated into the jth word w_{Aj} in $Str_{\mathcal{A}}$. In this paper, we run GIZA++ [9] to train word alignments based on $10M$ ⟨question, related question⟩ pairs crawled from the community QA website (i.e., YahooAnswers[6]).

– $ETM_{WE}(\mathcal{Q}, \mathcal{A})$ represent the word embedding-based feature to measure the topic semantic similarity between $\mathcal{Q}$ and $\mathcal{A}$:

$$ETM_{WE}(\mathcal{Q}, \mathcal{A}) = \frac{\sum_{i=1}^{|Str_{\mathcal{Q}}|} \ln(\frac{\sum_{j=1}^{|Str_{\mathcal{A}}|} cosine(v_{w_{Qi}}, v_{w_{Aj}})}{|Str_{\mathcal{A}}|})}{|Str_{\mathcal{Q}}|}$$

where $v_{w_{Qi}}$ (or $v_{w_{Aj}}$) denotes the word embedding learnt for the word w_{Qi} (or w_{Aj}). We generate word embeddings using word2vec [8] base on the sentences from GoogleNews[7]. The dimension of each word embedding vector is set to 300.

– $ETM_{PP}(\mathcal{S}, \mathcal{Q})$ is defined as a paraphrase-based feature. Given a phrase table PT extracted from a bilingual corpus[8], we follow [1] to extract a paraphrase table PP, which has the following form:

$$PP = \{\langle s_i, s_j, score(s_j; s_i) \rangle\}$$

where s_i and s_j denote two phrases in source language, $score(s_j; s_i)$ denotes a confidence score that s_i can be paraphrased to s_j, which is computed based on the phrase table PT as:

$$score(s_j; s_i) = \sum_{t} \{p(t|s_i) \cdot p(s_j|t)\}$$

The underlying idea of this approach is that, two source phrases that are aligned to the same target phrase trend to be paraphrased.

Based on PP, we define a paraphrase-based feature to measure the semantic similarity between $\mathcal{S}$ and $\mathcal{Q}$:

$$ETM_{PP}(\mathcal{Q}, \mathcal{A}) = \frac{\sum_{n=1}^{N} \frac{\sum_{j=1}^{M} Count_{PP}(t_A^j, Str_{\mathcal{Q}})}{M}}{N}$$

where t_A^j denotes the jth topic phrase in A and N denotes the maximum n-gram order (here is 3). $Count_{PP}(t_A^j, Str_{\mathcal{Q}})$ is computed based on the following rules:

---

[6] https://answers.yahoo.com/.

[7] The embedding file is available at https://code.google.com/archive/p/word2vec/.

[8] We use 0.5M Chinese-English bilingual sentences in phrase table extraction, i.e., LDC2003E07, LDC2003E14, LDC2005T06, LDC2005T10, LDC2005E83, LDC2006E26, LDC2006E34, LDC2006E85 and LDC2006E92.

- If $t_A^j \in Str_Q$, then $Count_{PP}(t^j, Str_Q) = 1$;
- Else, if $\langle t_A^j, s, score(s; t_A^j) \rangle \in PP$ and t_A^j's paraphrase s occurs in Q, then $Count_{PP}(t_A^j, Q) = score(s; t_A^j)$
- Else, $Count_{PP}(t_A^j, Q) = 0$.

There are other ways to compute the similarity between two sentences as well, such as bi-LSTM (Long Short Term Memory), GRU (Gated Recurrent Unit), and etc. Due to space limitation, we leave more experiments as our future work.

4 Related Work

The lexical gap between semantically correlative sentences is one of the biggest challenges for modeling the relationship between question-answer pairs. Some works use machine translation approach to representing words or phrases in discrete space [6,7]. [2] proposed to use a topic modeling method with the assumption that Q-A pairs should share similar topic distributions. Other works considering the relevance between questions and answers in the syntactic level instead of word level, by matching parse trees [4,12,15]. Representation learning by neural network has become a hot method as well, to learn sentence-level representations for the answer selection task [3,10,17].

Uniquely, our method proposes a simple but effective way to extract labeled data for the supervised topic prediction model training, demonstrate the effective of such semantic-level feature in QA task.

5 Experiment

5.1 Evaluation on Topic Prediction

We first evaluate our proposed model in a topic prediction task.

Based on the training data extraction method described in Sect. 2.1, we collect 1,287 most-frequent topics and 384,965 ⟨sentence, topic⟩ pairs from 5,028,106 English Wikipedia pages. We further divide all ⟨sentence, topic⟩ pairs into two datasets: 346,480 ⟨sentence, topic⟩ pairs as **training set**, 38,485 ⟨sentence, topic⟩ pairs as **testing set**.

We train the topic prediction model on training set, and use it to predict the most possible topics for each sentence in testing set. Accuracy@N (ACC@N) is used as evaluation metric. We use **Naive Bayes (NB)** and **TFIDF** as baselines, where

$$NB(t_k, S) = \log P(t_k) + \sum_{i=1}^{|S|} \log P(w_i|t_k)$$

$$TFIDF(t_k, S) = \sum_{i=1}^{|S|} TF(w_i, t_k) \cdot \log(IDF(w_i, T))$$

Table 1. Evaluation on topic prediction task.

Model	ACC@1	ACC@3	ACC@5	ACC@10
NB	10.3%	18.1%	22.7%	30.6%
TFIDF	31.2%	49.0%	56.9%	67.3%
Our model	**33.9%**	**51.2%**	**58.7%**	**68.8%**

Table 2. Example of topic prediction.

Sentence	Top 10 predicted topics
Question: How much is 1 tablespoon of water	Measurement, features, usage, uses, comparison, water, size, physical characteristics, characteristics, outline
Answer candidate 1 (Correct): This tablespoon has a capacity of about 15 ml	Size, features, statistics, ports, infrastructure, elements, specifications, measurement, sources, facilities
Answer candidate 2 (Incorrect): It is abbreviated as t, tb, tbs, tbsp, tblsp, or tblspn	Occurrence, nomenclature, branches, general information, name, terminology, list, grammar, concept, availability

Evaluation results are shown in Table 1, where ours topic prediction model achieves better results than the baselines.

The meaning between some topics are very similar, such as "usage" and "uses" in Table 2, which makes getting higher ACC@1 difficult. The model with 58.7% ACC@5 and 68.8% ACC@10 is acceptable and can provide enough semantic info to enhance the answer selection task.

5.2 Experiment on Answer Selection

For answer selection task, we select two benchmarks WikiQA[9] [14] and QASent [13] as the evaluation datasets.

Dataset. The same triple format $< Q_i, A_{i,j}, label >$ is used to represent the data in both WikiQA and QASent dataset. Given question Q_i, each candidate answer sentences $A_{i,1}...A_{i,k}$ are labeled as 1 or 0, where 1 denotes the current sentence is a correct answer sentence, and 0 denotes the opposite meaning.

The WikiQA dataset is precisely constructed based on natural language questions and Wikipedia documents. The questions are collected from question-like Bing search queries and have clicks to Wikipedia. WikiQA dataset contains 2,118

---

[9] http://aka.ms/WikiQA.

questions and 20,360 'question-answer' (Q-A) pairs in the training set, 296 questions and 1,130 'Q-A' pairs in development set, and 633 questions and 2,352 'Q-A' pairs in testing set.

The QASent dataset select questions in TREC 8-13 QA tracks and chose sentences share one or more non-stopwords from questions. QASent dataset contains 94 questions and 5,919 'Q-A' pairs in the training set, 65 questions and 1,117 'Q-A' pairs in development set, and 68 questions and 1,442 'Q-A' pairs in testing set.

Metrics. The performance of answer selection is evaluated by Mean Average Precision (MAP) and Mean Reciprocal Rank (MRR). Among all 'Q-A' pairs in WikiQA, only one-third of questions contain at least one correct answer. Similar to previous work, questions without correct answers in the candidate sentences are not taken into account.

Results and Discussion. We re-implement bi-CNN [14] as our baseline, which uses a bi-gram CNN model combining with a word overlap feature that counts the number of non-stopwords in the question that also occur in the answer. **LDA** represent a cosine of topic distributions of a Q-A pair. The topic distribution is estimated by LightLDA [18] on sentences from English wikipedia, where the topic number is set to 1,000. In our experiment, features are combined by a logistic regression function.

We first run evaluation on **all questions** in WikiQA. Table 3 shows that different topic matching features can achieve comparable results with baselines. This is due to the fact that only 20.3% answer sentences share no content word with corresponding questions in WikiQA dataset. Therefore, the word overlap feature plays an important role in all settings.

Table 3. Evaluation result on **all questions** of WikiQA.

	Model	MAP	MRR	ACC@1
Baselines	bi-CNN$_{cnt}$	65.27%	66.61%	51.35%
	bi-CNN$_{cnt}$+LDA	65.74%	67.71%	52.24%
Single features	ITM	47.24%	45.57%	26.58%
	ETM$_{TM}$	53.42%	53.73%	33.74%
	ETM$_{WE}$	49.28%	48.68%	28.40%
	ETM$_{PP}$	53.28%	53.54%	33.33%
Merged methods	bi-CNN$_{cnt}$+ITM	65.72%	67.73%	51.90%
	bi-CNN$_{cnt}$+ETM$_{TM}$	66.81%	68.27%	52.32%
	bi-CNN$_{cnt}$+ETM$_{WE}$	65.92%	67.17%	51.64%
	bi-CNN$_{cnt}$+ETM$_{PP}$	66.51%	68.29%	52.74%
	bi-CNN$_{cnt}$+ALL	**67.50%**	**69.19%**	**54.43%**

In order to illustrate the effectiveness of our model, we then run evaluation on **hard questions**, each of which shares no content word with its corresponding answer sentences. Table 4 shows that using the two topic-level semantic features (ITM and ETM) brings significant and the biggest improvements, comparing to bi-CNN$_{cnt}$ and bi-CNN$_{cnt}$+LDA settings.

Table 4. Evaluation result on **hard questions** of WikiQA.

	Model	MAP	MRR	ACC@1
Baselines	bi-CNN$_{cnt}$	42.40%	43.02%	23.08%
	bi-CNN$_{cnt}$+LDA	42.45%	43.22%	23.15%
Merged methods	bi-CNN$_{cnt}$+ITM	42.34%	42.96%	23.08%
	bi-CNN$_{cnt}$+ETM$_{TM}$	46.48%	47.87%	29.77%
	bi-CNN$_{cnt}$+ETM$_{WE}$	42.47%	43.09%	24.26%
	bi-CNN$_{cnt}$+ETM$_{PP}$	42.35%	42.92%	22.84%
	bi-CNN$_{cnt}$+ALL	**47.36%**	**48.10%**	**30.77%**

The results in Table 5 shows that our model can also achieve better results on QASent dataset. The QASent data set is independent with Wikipedia articles which both WikiQA and our topic prediction model are related to.

Table 5. Evaluation result on QASent.

	Model	MAP	MRR	ACC@1
Baselines	bi-CNN$_{cnt}$	69.52%	76.33%	61.76%
	bi-CNN$_{cnt}$+LDA	69.75%	76.85%	63.23%
Merged methods	bi-CNN$_{cnt}$+ITM	70.12%	78.62%	64.03%
	bi-CNN$_{cnt}$+ETM$_{TM}$	70.62%	78.62%	65.63%
	bi-CNN$_{cnt}$+ETM$_{WE}$	69.64%	76.55%	62.79%
	bi-CNN$_{cnt}$+ETM$_{PP}$	70.36%	77.87%	64.71%
	bi-CNN$_{cnt}$+ALL	**71.09%**	**78.97%**	**66.17%**

To compare with implicit topic modeling methods, such as LDA and ITM, our ETM method have good interpretability to explain why question-answer pair have good (or bad) semantic relationship in topic level.

6   Conclusion

This paper introduces a method to obtain large scale open domain labeled data, and propose a topic prediction model for the answer selection task. The result shows our topic prediction model achieves promising results on WikiQA dataset, especially on the hard questions. We also release our ⟨sentence, topic⟩ labeled pairs, to support researchers to use it in more NLP tasks, such as answer selection.

Acknowledgments. This work was supported by Beijing Advanced Innovation Center for Imaging Technology (No. BAICIT-2016001), the National Natural Science Foundation of China (Grand Nos. 61370126, 61672081), National High Technology Research and Development Program of China (No. 2015AA016004), the Fund of the State Key Laboratory of Software Development Environment (No. SKLSDE-2015ZX-16).

References

1. Bannard, C., Callison-Burch, C.: Paraphrasing with bilingual parallel corpora. In: Proceedings of Annual Meeting of the Association for Computational Linguistics (ACL), pp. 597–604 (2005)
2. Duan, H., Cao, Y., Lin, C.Y., Yu, Y.: Searching questions by identifying question topic and question focus. In: Proceedings of Annual Meeting of the Association for Computational Linguistics (ACL), pp. 156–164 (2008)
3. Feng, M., Xiang, B., Glass, M.R., Wang, L., Zhou, B.: Applying deep learning to answer selection: a study and an open task. In: Automatic Speech Recognition and Understanding Workshop (ASRU) (2015)
4. Heilman, M., Smith, N.A.: Tree edit models for recognizing textual entailments, paraphrases, and answers to questions. In: Proceedings of Annual Conference of the North American Chapter of the Association for Computational Linguistics: Human Language Technologies (NAACL-HLT), pp. 1011–1019 (2010)
5. Huang, P.S., He, X., Gao, J., Deng, L., Acero, A., Heck, L.: Learning deep structured semantic models for web search using clickthrough data. In: Proceedings of the Conference on Information and Knowledge Management (CIKM), pp. 2333–2338 (2013)
6. Jeon, J., Croft, W.B., Lee, J.H.: Finding similar questions in large question and answer archives. In: Proceedings of the International Conference on Information and Knowledge Management (CIKM), pp. 84–90 (2005)
7. Li, S., Manandhar, S.: Improving question recommendation by exploiting information need. In: Proceedings of Annual Meeting of the Association for Computational Linguistics (ACL), pp. 1425–1434 (2011)
8. Mikolov, T., Sutskever, I., Chen, K., Corrado, G.S., Dean, J.: Distributed representations of words and phrases and their compositionality. In: Advances in Neural Information Processing Systems (NIPS), pp. 3111–3119 (2013)
9. Och, F.J., Ney, H.: A systematic comparison of various statistical alignment models. Comput. Linguist. **29**(1), 19–51 (2003)
10. Severyn, A., Moschitti, A.: Learning to rank short text pairs with convolutional deep neural networks. In: Proceedings of ACM SIGIR Conference on Research and Development in Information Retrieval, pp. 373–382 (2015)
11. Shen, Y., He, X., Gao, J., Deng, L., Mesnil, G.: A latent semantic model with convolutional-pooling structure for information retrieval. In: Proceedings of the Conference on Information and Knowledge Management (CIKM), pp. 101–110 (2014)

12. Wang, M., Manning, C.D.: Probabilistic tree-edit models with structured latent variables for textual entailment and question answering. In: Proceedings of the International Conference on Computational Linguistics (COLING), pp. 1164–1172 (2010)
13. Wang, M., Smith, N.A., Mitamura, T.: What is the jeopardy model? A quasi-synchronous grammar for QA. In: Proceedings of the Conference on Empirical Methods in Natural Language Processing (EMNLP), vol. 7, pp. 22–32 (2007)
14. Yang, Y., Yih, W.T., Meek, C.: WikiQA: a challenge dataset for open-domain question answering. In: Proceedings of the Conference on Empirical Methods in Natural Language Processing (EMNLP), pp. 2013–2018 (2015)
15. Yao, X., Van Durme, B., Callison-Burch, C., Clark, P.: Answer extraction as sequence tagging with tree edit distance. In: Proceedings of Annual Conference of the North American Chapter of the Association for Computational Linguistics: Human Language Technologies (NAACL-HLT), pp. 858–867 (2013)
16. Yih, W.t., Chang, M.W., Meek, C., Pastusiak, A.: Question answering using enhanced lexical semantic models. In: Proceedings of Annual Meeting of the Association for Computational Linguistics (ACL), pp. 1744–1753 (2013)
17. Yu, L., Hermann, K.M., Blunsom, P., Pulman, S.: Deep learning for answer sentence selection. In: NIPS Deep Learning and Representation Learning Workshop (2014)
18. Yuan, J., Gao, F., Ho, Q., Dai, W., Wei, J., Zheng, X., Xing, E.P., Liu, T.Y., Ma, W.Y.: Lightlda: big topic models on modest computer clusters. In: Proceedings of the Annual International Conference on World Wide Web, pp. 1351–1361 (2015)

Joint Event Extraction Based on Skip-Window Convolutional Neural Networks

Zhengkuan Zhang[1], Weiran Xu[2(✉)], and Qianqian Chen[3]

[1] Automation School of Beijing University of Posts and Telecommunications,
No. 10 Xitucheng Road, Haidian District, Beijing 100876, China
zhangzhengkuan.jacky@gmail.com
[2] Beijing University of Posts and Telecommunications, Beijing, China
xuweiran@bupt.edu.cn
[3] Emory University, Apt 2, 1535 N. Decatur Rd NE, Atlanta, GA 30307, USA

Abstract. Traditional approaches to the task of ACE event extraction are either the joint model with elaborately designed features which may lead to generalization and data-sparsity problems, or the word-embedding model based on a two-stage, multi-class classification architecture, which suffers from error propagation since event triggers and arguments are predicted in isolation. This paper proposes a novel event-extraction method that not only extracts triggers and arguments simultaneously, but also adopts a framework based on convolutional neural networks (CNNs) to extract features automatically. However, CNNs can only capture sentence-level features, so we propose the skip-window convolution neural networks (S-CNNs) to extract global structured features, which effectively capture the global dependencies of every token in the sentence. The experimental results show that our approach outperforms other state-of-the-art methods.

1 Introduction

Event extraction is an important and challenging task in Information Extraction (IE), which aims to discover event triggers with specific types and their arguments. Traditional methods [1, 8, 9, 14] usually break down the whole task into separate subtasks, such as trigger identification/classification and argument identification/classification, and use sequential pipelines architecture as a two-stage, multi-class classification framework. One common drawback to this approach is that the errors in upstream component are often compounded and propagated to the downstream classifiers. The downstream components, however, cannot impact earlier decisions [12].

Li [12] formulates the ACE event extraction task as a structured learning problem, and presents a joint framework based on structured perceptron with beam search [4, 17, 18], which predicts the triggers and arguments simultaneously and solves the error propagation problem. However, all of the approaches above use a set of elaborately designed features relying on human ingenuity which takes a large amount of human effort and are prone to generalization and data-sparsity problems.

Recent improvements of convolutional neural networks (CNNs) have been proven efficient for capturing syntactic and semantics between words within a sentence

© Springer International Publishing AG 2016
C.-Y. Lin et al. (Eds.): NLPCC-ICCPOL 2016, LNAI 10102, pp. 324–334, 2016.
DOI: 10.1007/978-3-319-50496-4_27

[5, 10, 11, 24] for NLP tasks. Chen [2] presents a novel framework for event extraction, which can automatically induce lexical-level and sentence-level features from plain texts via a dynamic multi-pooling convolutional neural network. Problematically, it also uses a two-stage pipelines framework, so it may suffer from the same drawback as the staged architecture's.

Therefore, we intend to use convolutional neural networks (CNNs) in joint model to automatically extract features. However, the types of features used in joint model are usually **global structured features** in the token-level, indicating the global dependencies between a single token and every other token in the sentence. These dependencies play an irreplaceable role in operating structured learning. However, CNNs typically use a fixed-size window sliding along the sentence, and operate the convolution and max-pooling at the same time, which can only extract sentence-level features. It is thus intractable to capture the **global structured features**.

Furthermore, Li's joint model is based on structured perceptron with beam search [17, 18], which heavily relies on the quality of the human-designed features and may lack generalization. Recent studies [19, 20] have proved that recurrent neural networks (RNNs) are able to effectively deal with variable-length input sequences and discover long-term dependencies, and we find that it is a perfect model to operate structured learning.

In this paper, we propose a novel joint event extraction framework which not only uses skip-window convolutional neural networks (S-CNNs) to automatically extract global structured features, but also predicts the triggers and arguments simultaneously via RNNs.

In summary, the contributions of this paper are as follows:

- We present a novel framework that combines both deep learning and structured learning methods.
- We propose a skip-window convolution neural network which is able to capture the global structured features automatically.
- We propose to use RNNs to operate structured learning, and use beam search to find the best configuration for the input sentence.

2 Event Extraction Task

In this paper, we focus on the event extraction task defined in Automatic Content Extraction (ACE) evaluation where an event is defined as a specific incident involving participants. The task defines 8 event types and 33 subtypes such as Elect, Transfer, etc. We introduce the terminology of the ACE event extraction that we use in this paper:

- **Event mention:** a phrase or sentence within which an event is described, including a trigger and arguments.
- **Event trigger:** the word that most clearly expresses the event mention.
- **Event argument:** an entity mention, temporal expression or value (e.g. Job-Title) that serves as a participant or attribute with a specific role in an event mention.
- **Argument role:** the relationship between an argument to the event in which it participates.

Given an English text document, an event extraction system should predict event triggers with specific subtypes and their arguments from each sentence.

For example:

S1: In Baghdad, a cameraman **died** when an American tank **fired** on the Palestine Hotel.

Sentence S1 contains two events:

(1) The **Die** event triggered by "died", its arguments are Baghdad, cameraman, and American tank, and the roles of these arguments are Place, Victim, and Instrument;

(2) The **Attack** event triggered by "fired", its arguments are Baghdad, cameraman, American tank and Palestine Hotel, and the roles of these arguments are Place, Target, Instrument and Target.

In this work, we assume that argument candidates such as entities are part of the input to the event extraction following most previous works [8, 9, 14].

3 Methodology

In this paper, event extraction is also formulated as a structured learning problem. We propose to use S-CNNs and RNNs to jointly extract triggers and arguments that co-occur in the same sentence. In this section, we will describe the training and decoding algorithms for this model.

Our model is also based on structured perceptron which is proposed in [17]. Given a sentence instance $\chi \in X$, which in our case is a sentence with argument candidates, the decoding process is to find the best configuration $z \in \Upsilon$, which in our case is the expected labels of all the tokens in the sentence, according to the current model:

$$z = argmax_{y' \in \Upsilon_{(x)}} F(x, y')$$ (1)

where $F(x, y')$ is a score function, we'll explain in Sect. 3.4.

A typical dynamic programming algorithm can be employed to perform exact inference, but to improve the search efficiency, we use beam search in our model.

The whole architecture of joint event extraction model primarily involves the following four components: (i) word-embedding learning, which reveals the embedding vectors of words in an unsupervised manner; (ii) global structured feature extraction via S-CNNs, which turn every embedding vector into a global structured feature vector, as the input of the final ranker; (iii) label vector learning, which turn the label of every word into a embedding vector, as the other input of the ranker; (iv) the ranker, search for the best configuration under the current parameters, in dynamic programming way (Fig. 1).

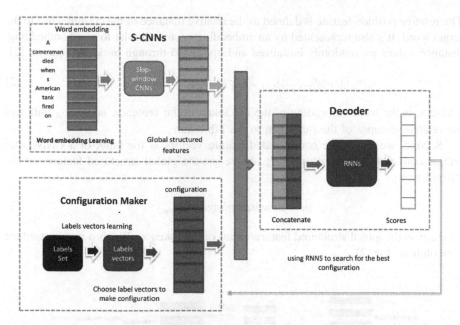

Fig. 1. Illustrates the processing of the decoding. The S-CNNs step will turn every token in the sentence into their global structured feature vector. The Configuration Maker step will turn every label into label vector and make them into configuration. The Final score step will provide feedback to the Configuration Maker to search for the best configuration.

3.1 Word Embedding Learning

In this paper, we use word embedding [3, 22, 26, 27] as base features, which are proved to be powerful for capturing the meaningful semantic regularities of words [6]. More concretely, we use the Skip-gram model [16] to pre-train the word embedding. This model is the state-of-the-art model in many natural language processing (NLP) tasks [25]. We use these base features to extract global structured features via S-CNNs.

3.2 Skip-Window Convolutional Neural Networks

CNNs typically use a max-pooling layer, which aims to capture the most useful information and extract sentence-level features. But these features cannot capture the global dependencies between a single token and every other token in the sentence, however, those dependencies are irreplaceable in operating structured learning. What we need are **global structured features** in the token-level, which are usually elaborately designed and extracted by complicated NLP tools.

In this paper, we proposed the skip-window convolution neural networks (S-CNNs) which is able to capture the global structured features automatically.

To be more specific, the algorithm takes two steps:

First, we concatenate the word embedding of current word and every other word's word embedding along with their relative position feature (*pf*) in the sentence.

The relative position feature is defined as the relative distance of the current word to the target word. It's also represented by an embedding vector. Similar to word embedding, distance values are randomly initialized and optimized through back propagation [2].

$$v_i = [[x_i, pf_{|i-s|}, x_s], \ldots, [x_i, pf_{|i-j|}, x_j], \ldots, [x_i, pf_{|i-n|}, x_n]] \qquad (2)$$

where x_i is the word embedding of the i-th token in the sentence, and $pf_{|i-j|}$ indicates the relative distance of the i-th token to the j-th token.

Second, we take these concatenated feature vectors as the input of a CNN, after simple convolution and max-pooling, we've got the global structured features of the current word.

$$p_i = downsampling(v_i \cdot W_{sw}) \qquad (3)$$

where p_i is the global structured feature vector of the token x_i, W_{sw} is a matrix used for convolution (Fig. 2).

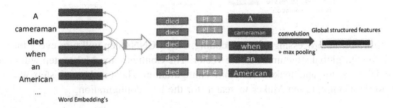

Fig. 2. Describes the specific process of the S-CNNs on word "**died**" in sentence S1

After the S-CNNs step, each word in the sentence is represented as global structured features.

3.3   Label Vectors Learning

Unlike classification frameworks, we need a score function to evaluate which label make the best configuration, so we need to encode each label value into an embedding vector. ACE defines 33 event subtypes and 28 role types, so include the no-trigger and no-role, we need 34 trigger label vectors and 29 role labels vectors. And we use the same way as position features to get these trigger and role vectors.

Actually, there are lots of ways to train these label vectors. To be more specific, every token in the sentence has these two properties. Like the relative position feature, just take the event label value and role label value as features and use these features in any other NLP tasks, of course, these feature vectors should also be randomly initialized and optimized through back propagation. We pre-train these label vectors in a classification task, which is not the focus of this paper.

We use these label vectors to make configuration, and leverage the feedback of the score function to find the best configuration of the input sentence.

3.4   Use RNNs to Operate Sequence Labeling

As we described in formula (1), we use a score function to search for the best configuration for the sentence instance, to be more specific, the detailed functions are showed below:

$$l_i = \sigma\left(W_{in} \cdot \left[p_i, y'\right] + b_{in}\right) \tag{4}$$

$$h_i = \sigma(W_h \cdot h_{i-1} + l_i + b_h) \tag{5}$$

$$F\left(x, y'\right) = \sigma'(W_{out} \cdot h_i) \tag{6}$$

where p_i is the output of the S-CNNs, h means the hidden state, and σ is a relu activation function [28], σ' is a sigmoid activation function, $F(x, y')$ is the score of the current partial configuration.

With the ability of explicitly modeling time-series data, RNNs are being increasingly applied to sentence modeling [19, 20]. But unlike the normal uses of RNNs, we found it is also a perfect model to operate structured learning, because the output of RNN is both decided by the input value and the former hidden states. For example, if we take the output as the score, and we aim to find the configuration with the highest score, then this is typical dynamic programming problem. In our model, we use beam search to improve search efficiency, to be more specific, we store the K-best hidden states in the beams.

Since every score is corresponding to a given input and a given hidden state, so we can easily use these scores to get the K-best inputs, and of course, the corresponding K-best hidden states, assuming the beam size is K. And we keep track of the source of each score, which means we know the corresponding input and corresponding beam of every calculated score. With the process of labeling, we use the scores to rank all the partial configurations and store the K-best beams, then we can easily get the best configuration in the end.

Just like Li's work [12], we use the same decoding order:

Let $x = \langle(x_1, x_2, \ldots, x_s), \varepsilon\rangle$ denote the sentence instance, where x_i represents the i-th token in the sentence and $\varepsilon = \{e_k\}$ is the set of argument candidates. During each step with token i, there are two sub-steps:

- Trigger labeling: We enumerate all possible trigger labels for the current token under the given score function. Then the K-best partial configurations are selected to the beam, assuming the beam size is K.
- Argument Labeling: After the trigger labeling step, we traverse all configurations in the beam, once a trigger label is found, then the decoder search through the argument candidates to label the possible role (Fig. 3).

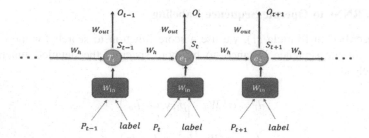

Fig. 3. Describes the architecture of the decoder of the model, after labeling the i-th token, the decoder turns to the role labeling step.

3.5   Training

We define all of the parameters for the model as $\theta = (E, L, PF, W_{sw}, W_{in}, W_h, W_{out}, b_{in}, b_h)$. Specifically, E is the word embedding, L is the label embedding, PF is the position embedding, W_{sw} is the parameter of the S-CNNs, W_{in} and b_{in} is the parameters of the input layer of the RNNs, W_h and b_h is the parameters of the hidden layer of the RNNs, W_{out} is the parameters of the output layer of the RNNs. We use a typical back-propagation algorithm to train the model.

$$\text{cost} = \frac{1}{n}\sum_i (O_i - \text{flag})^2 \tag{7}$$

$$\text{flag} = \begin{cases} 1 & \textit{label is right} \\ 0 & \textit{label is wrong} \end{cases} \tag{8}$$

where O_i is the score of the i-th token in the decoded configuration.

4   Experiment

4.1   Dataset and Evaluation Metric

We utilize the ACE 2005 corpus as our dataset. For comparison, as the same as [2, 8, 9, 12, 14], we use the same test set with 40 newswire articles and the same development set with 30 other documents randomly selected from different genres and the remaining 529 documents are used for training. Similar to previous work, we use the following criteria to judge the correctness of each predicted event mention:

- A trigger is correct if its event subtype and offsets match those of a reference trigger.
- An argument is correctly identified if its event subtype and offsets match those of any of the reference argument mentions.
- An argument is correctly classified if its event subtype, offsets and argument role match those of any of the reference argument mentions.

4.2 Baselines

We select the following state-of-the-art methods for comparison.

(1) Li's baseline is the feature-based system proposed by Li et al. [12], which only employs human-designed lexical features, basic features and syntactic features.

(2) Liao's cross-event is the method proposed by Liao and Grishman [14], which uses document level information to improve the performance of ACE event extraction.

(3) Hong's cross-entity is the method proposed by Hong et al. [8], which extracts event by using cross-entity inference. To the best of our knowledge, it is the best-reported feature-based system in the literature based on gold standards argument candidates.

(4) Li's structure is the method proposed by Li et al. [12], which extracts events based on structure prediction. It is the best-reported structure based system.

(5) Chen's DMCNN is the method proposed by Chen et al. [2], which proposed a word-representation model to capture meaningful semantic regularities for words and adopt a framework based on a dynamic multi-pooling convolutional neural networks. It is the best-reported word-embedding based system.

4.3 Overall Performance

Following Li et al. [12], we tune the model parameters on the development through grid search [21]. Specifically, we set the dimension of label as 100, the dimension of PF as 20, the numbers of the feature maps in S-CNNs as 100, and the beam size as 5. Following previous work, we also train the word embedding using the Skip-gram algorithm on the NYT corpus (Table 1).

From the results, we can see that our model can improve the best F1 [2] in the state-of-the-arts for the trigger identification task by 1.3%, and achieves comparable performance for the trigger classification task. This demonstrates the effectiveness of the proposed method. Moreover, we can see our model gain higher recall rates in the trigger identification/classification task. we believe it is the arguments' contributions

Table 1. Shows the overall performance on the blind test dataset.

Methods	Trigger identification (%)			Trigger identification + classification (%)			Argument identification (%)			Argument role (%)		
	P	R	F	P	R	F	P	R	F	P	R	F
Li's baseline	76.2	60.5	67.4	74.5	59.1	65.9	74.1	37.4	49.7	65.4	33.1	43.9
Liao's cross-event	N/A			68.7	68.9	68.8	50.9	49.7	50.3	45.1	44.1	44.6
Hong's cross-entity	N/A			72.9	64.3	68.3	53.4	52.9	53.1	51.6	45.5	48.3
Li's joint model	76.9	65.0	70.4	73.7	62.3	67.5	69.8	47.9	56.8	64.7	44.4	52.7
DMCNN model	80.4	67.7	73.5	75.6	63.6	69.1	68.8	51.9	59.1	62.2	46.9	53.5
S-CNNs model	78.1	71.8	**74.8**	74.1	64.8	69.1	69.2	50.8	58.6	63.3	45.8	53.1

that are driving this change, since they were extracted jointly. Furthermore, some comparisons of Li's joint model with Hong's cross-entity, Liao's cross-event, and Li's baseline illustrate that richer feature sets often lead to better performance when using traditional human-designed features. However, our model could obtain better results without using any complicated NLP tools. Specifically, compared to Hong's cross-entity, it gains 0.8% improvement on trigger classification F1 and 4.8% improvement on argument classification F1. We believe the reason is that our model can automatically capture global structured features, which efficiently represent the global dependencies of every token in the sentence.

4.4 The Effectiveness of S-CNNs

Compared to Li's joint model, also as a structured learning framework, our model is proved to be efficient. To be more specific, our model gains 1.6% improvement in the trigger classification task, and 0.4% improvement in the role classification task. But Li's joint model uses a large set of human-designed features to operate structured learning, however, our model simply use the S-CNNs to automatically extract global structured features, and also obtain remarkable results. This demonstrates the effectiveness of our S-CNNs framework.

5 Related Work

Since event extraction plays an important role in NLP, many approaches have been explored for the task. Nearly all of the ACE event extraction use supervised paradigm, which can be divided into feature-based methods and structure-based methods [2].

Furthermore, we think feature-based methods can also be divided into two categories: elaborately human designed features and embedding features which automatically extracted by neural networks.

In former methods, a diverse set of strategies has been exploited to convert classification clues (such as sequences and parse trees) into feature vectors. Ahn [1] uses the lexical features (e.g., full word, pos tag), syntactic features (e.g., dependency features) and external knowledge features (WordNet) to extract the event. Inspired by the hypothesis of "One Sense Per Discourse" [23], Ji and Grishman [9] combined global evidence from related documents with local decisions for the event extraction. To capture more clues from the texts, Gupta and Ji [7], Liao and Grishman [14] and Hong et al. [9] proposed the cross-event and cross-entity inference for the ACE event task [2].

In latter methods, Chen [2] proposed a framework called dynamic multi-pooling CNNs to extract features from lexical-level and sentence-level.

In structure-based methods, researchers treat event extraction as the task of predicting the structure of the event in a sentence. McClosky et al. [15] casted the problem of biomedical event extraction as a dependency parsing problem. Li et al. [12] presented a joint framework for ACE event extraction based on structured perceptron with beam search. To use more information from the sentence, Li et al. [13] proposed to extract entity mentions, relations and events in ACE task based on the unified structure [2].

Although all of these approaches achieve high performance, they either depend strongly on the quality of the designed features and endure the errors in the existing NLP tools, or suffer from error propagation problem as a common drawback of the staged framework.

6 Conclusion

This paper proposes a novel joint event extraction framework that not only uses skip-window convolutional neural networks (S-CNNs) to automatically extract global structured features from plain texts, but also predicts the triggers and arguments simultaneously via RNNs. The experimental results prove the effectiveness of the proposed method.

Acknowledgments. This work was supported by the 111 Project of China under Grant No. B08004, the key project of ministry of science and technology of China under Grant No. 2011ZX03002-005-01, the National Natural Science Foundation of China under Grant No. 61273217, the Natural Science Foundation of China under Grant No. 61300080 and the Ph.D. Programs Foundation of Ministry of Education of China under Grant No. 20130005110004.

References

1. Ahn, D.: The stages of event extraction. In: Proceedings of the Workshop on Annotating and Reasoning about Time and Events. Association for Computational Linguistics, pp. 1–8 (2006)
2. Chen, Y., Xu, L., Liu, K., et al.: Event extraction via dynamic multi-pooling convolutional neural networks. In: Proceedings of the 53rd Annual Meeting of the Association for Computational Linguistics and the 7th International Joint Conference on Natural Language Processing, vol. 1, pp. 167–176 (2015)
3. Bengio, Y., Ducharme, R., Vincent, P., et al.: A neural probabilistic language model. J. Mach. Learn. Res. 3(Feb), 1137–1155 (2003)
4. Chen, C., Ng, V.: Joint modeling for Chinese event extraction with rich linguistic features. In: COLING (2012)
5. Collobert, R., Weston, J., Bottou, L., et al.: Natural language processing (almost) from scratch. J. Mach. Learn. Res. 12(Aug), 2493–2537 (2011)
6. Erhan, D., Bengio, Y., Courville, A., et al.: Why does unsupervised pre-training help deep learning? J. Mach. Learn. Res. 11(1), 625–660 (2010)
7. Gupta, P., Ji, H.: Predicting unknown time arguments based on cross-event propagation. In: Proceedings of the ACL-IJCNLP 2009 Conference Short Papers, pp. 369–372. Association for Computational Linguistics (2009)
8. Hong, Y., Zhang, J., Ma, B., et al.: Using cross-entity inference to improve event extraction. In: Proceedings of the 49th Annual Meeting of the Association for Computational Linguistics: Human Language Technologies, -vol. 1, pp. 1127–1136. Association for Computational Linguistics (2011)
9. Ji, H., Grishman, R.: Refining event extraction through cross-document inference. In: ACL, pp. 254–262 (2008)
10. Kalchbrenner, N., Grefenstette, E., Blunsom, P.: A convolutional neural network for modelling sentences (2014). arXiv preprint: arXiv:1404.2188

11. Kim, Y.: Convolutional neural networks for sentence classification (2014). arXiv preprint: arXiv:1408.5882
12. Li, Q., Ji, H., Huang, L.: Joint event extraction via structured prediction with global features. In: ACL (1), pp. 73–82 (2013)
13. Li, Q., Ji, H., Hong, Y., et al.: Constructing information networks using one single model. In: EMNLP, pp. 1846–1851 (2014)
14. Liao, S., Grishman, R.: Using document level cross-event inference to improve event extraction. In: Proceedings of the 48th Annual Meeting of the Association for Computational Linguistics, pp. 789–797. Association for Computational Linguistics (2010)
15. McClosky, D., Surdeanu, M., Manning, C.D.: Event extraction as dependency parsing. In: Proceedings of the 49th Annual Meeting of the Association for Computational Linguistics: Human Language Technologies, vol. 1, pp. 1626–1635. Association for Computational Linguistics (2011)
16. Morin, F., Bengio, Y.: Hierarchical probabilistic neural network language model. In: AISTATS, vol. 5, pp. 246–252 (2005)
17. Collins, M.: Discriminative training methods for hidden markov models: theory and experiments with perceptron algorithms. In: Proceedings of the ACL-2002 Conference on Empirical Methods in Natural Language Processing, vol. 10, pp. 1–8. Association for Computational Linguistics (2002)
18. Huang, L., Fayong, S., Guo, Y.: Structured perceptron with inexact search. In: Proceedings of the 2012 Conference of the North American Chapter of the Association for Computational Linguistics: Human Language Technologies, pp. 142–151. Association for Computational Linguistics (2012)
19. Hochreiter, S., Schmidhuber, J.: Long short-term memory. Neural Comput. 9(8), 1735–1780 (1997)
20. Cho, K., Van Merriënboer, B., Gulcehre, C., et al.: Learning phrase representations using RNN encoder-decoder for statistical machine translation (2014). arXiv preprint: arXiv:1406.1078
21. Zeiler, M.D.: ADADELTA: an adaptive learning rate method (2012). arXiv preprint: arXiv:1212.5701
22. Turian, J., Ratinov, L., Bengio, Y.: Word representations: a simple and general method for semi-supervised learning. In: Proceedings of the 48th Annual Meeting of the Association for Computational Linguistics, pp. 384–394. Association for Computational Linguistics (2010)
23. Yarowsky, D.: Unsupervised word sense disambiguation rivaling supervised methods. In: Proceedings of the 33rd Annual Meeting on Association for Computational Linguistics, pp. 189–196. Association for Computational Linguistics (1995)
24. Zeng, D., Liu, K., Lai, S., et al.: Relation classification via convolutional deep neural network. In: COLING, pp. 2335–2344 (2014)
25. Baroni, M., Dinu, G., Kruszewski, G.: Don't count, predict! A systematic comparison of context-counting vs. context-predicting semantic vectors. In: ACL (1), pp. 238–247 (2014)
26. Mikolov, T., Chen, K., Corrado, G., et al.: Efficient estimation of word representations in vector space (2013). arXiv preprint: arXiv:1301.3781
27. Mikolov, T., Sutskever, I., Chen, K., et al.: Distributed representations of words and phrases and their compositionality. In: Advances in Neural Information Processing Systems, pp. 3111–3119 (2013)
28. Krizhevsky, A., Sutskever, I., Hinton, G.E.: ImageNet classification with deep convolutional neural networks. In: Advances in Neural Information Processing Systems, pp. 1097–1105 (2012)

Improving Collaborative Filtering with Long-Short Interest Model

Chao Lv, Lili Yao, Yansong Feng$^{(\boxtimes)}$, and Dongyan Zhao

Institute of Computer Science and Technology,
Peking University, Beijing 100871, China
{lvchao,yaolili,fengyansong,zhaodongyan}@pku.edu.cn

Abstract. Collaborative filtering (CF) has been widely employed within recommender systems in many real-world situations. The basic assumption of CF is that items liked by the same user would be similar and users like the same items would share a similar interest. But it is not always true since the user's interest changes over time. It should be more reasonable to assume that if these items are liked by the same user in the same time period, there is a strong possibility that they are similar, but the possibility will shrink if the user likes them in a different time period. In this paper, we propose a long-short interest model (LSIM) based on the new assumption to improve collaborative filtering. In special, we introduce a neural network based language model to extract the sequential features on user's preference over time. Then, we integrate the sequential features to solve the rating prediction task in a feature based collaborative filtering framework. Experimental results on three MovieLens datasets demonstrate that our approach can achieve the state-of-the-art performance.

Keywords: Recommender system · Collaborative filtering · Long-short interest model

1 Introduction

In the modern era of information overload, recommender system (RS) has become more and more popular in many real-world situations. Lots of websites (e.g. Amazon, Netflix, Alibaba and Hulu) use recommender system to target customers and provide them with useful information. An excellent recommendation system can effectively increase the amount of sales. For instance, 80% of movies watched on Netflix come from their recommender system [3].

Lots of classical recommendation methods have been proposed during the last decade, and they can be categorized into two classes: content based methods and collaborative filtering based methods. Content based methods [11] take advantage of user profiles and item properties for recommendation. While collaborative filtering based approaches [15] utilize the past interactions or preferences, such as users' ratings on items, without using user or product content information for recommendation. Collaborative filtering based approaches have attracted more

© Springer International Publishing AG 2016
C.-Y. Lin et al. (Eds.): NLPCC-ICCPOL 2016, LNAI 10102, pp. 335–346, 2016.
DOI: 10.1007/978-3-319-50496-4_28

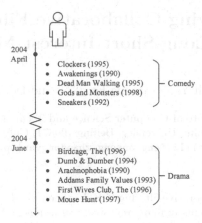

Fig. 1. The preference records of user whose id is 5988 in MovieLens-1 M dataset, which are sorted by their rated time.

attention due to their impressive performance, hence they develop for many years and keep to be a hot area in both academia and industry.

Collaborative filtering assumes that items liked by the same user would be similar and users like the same items would share a similar interest. However, it is not always true because the user's interest changes over time. For example, given a user in MovieLens-1 M dataset whose id is 5988, Fig. 1 shows the movies he watched sorted by the rating time. We can find that this user liked watching comedy movies in April 2004 and changed to love watching drama movies in June 2004. These movies are going to be treated similarly in conventional collaborative filtering, but they are not in fact. A more reasonable assumption, aka long-short interest assumption, should be that items liked by the same user in the same time period have a higher possibility to be similar than items liked by the same user in different time period.

Inspired by paragraph2vec algorithm [6] for learning vector representations of words which take advantage of a word order observed in a sentence, we introduce a long-short interest model (LSIM) to extract sequential features of users and items based on the new assumption. As illustrated in Fig. 2, user is similar with

Fig. 2. Paragraph2vec learns vector representations of sentences and words based on the word order while LSIM extracts sequential features of users and items based on the rating order.

the sentence, both of them contains a sequence following some order, and items are similar with words because both of them follow the law that the closer they are, the more similar they are. To verify the effectiveness of the learned sequential features of users and items, we integrate them as side information to solve the rating prediction task in a feature based collaborative filtering framework.

The main contributions of this paper include: (1) We introduce a long-short interest model (LSIM) to extract sequential features of users and items based on the long-short interest assumption. (2) We demonstrate the effectiveness of the sequential features via integrating them as side information to solve the rating prediction task. (3) Experiments on three public MovieLens show that LSIM can achieve the state-of-the-art performance.

The rest of the paper is organized as follows. Section 2 gives an overview of the related work. Then, we describe our long-short interest model and the feature based collaborative filtering framework in Sect. 3. The experimental results, as well as the comparisons with baseline system, are shown in Sect. 4. Finally, we conclude the paper and outline our future work in Sect. 5.

2 Related Work

Our work is closely related to collaborative filtering and neural network language model. We will discuss them in the following subsections.

2.1 Collaborative Filtering

Matrix factorization (MF) is the most popular collaborative filtering methods, their success at the Netflix competition [4] have demonstrated their amazing strength, and lots of variants of it have been proposed in the following works. Basically, the given ratings matrix $\mathbf{R} \in \mathbb{R}^{N*M}$ consisting of the item preferences of the users can be decomposed as a product of two low dimensional matrices $\mathbf{U} \in \mathbb{R}^{N*K}$ and $\mathbf{V} \in \mathbb{R}^{K*M}$. $\mathbf{U}$ could be treated as a user-interest matrix while $\mathbf{V}$ could be treated as an item-interest matrix. K is the amount of interest. The decomposition can be carried out by a variety of methods such as singular value decomposition (SVD) based approaches [9], non-negative matrix factorization approach [7] and regularized alternative least square (ALS) algorithm [16]. Meanwhile, non-linear algorithms are proposed to catch subtle factors, such as Non Linear Probabilistic Matrix Factorization [5], Factorization Machines [12] and Local Low Rank Matrix Approximation [8]. However, these methods group users and treat items they rated equally, which will lose the sequential features to describe the long-short interest.

2.2 Neural Network Language Model

Traditional language model uses a one-hot representation to represent each word as a feature vector, where these feature vectors have the same length as the size of vocabulary, and the position that corresponds to the observed word is equal to

1, and 0 otherwise. However, this approach often exhibits significant limitations in practical tasks, suffering from high dimensionality and severe data sparsity. Mikolov *et al.* [10] proposed the word2vec algorithm to address these issues. They take advantage of the word order in text documents, explicitly modeling the assumption that closer words in the word sequence are statistically more dependent, and have generalized the classic n-gram language models by using continuous variables to represent words in a vector space. The continuous bag-of-words (CBOW) and skip-gram (SG) language models are highly scalable for learning word representations from large-scale corpora. The word2vec algorithm breaks the semantic gap between words. For example, "trade" and "deal" are totally different words in the one-hot representation, but they are similar in word2vec distribution representation.

3   Our Approach

3.1   Problem Definition

Given N users and M items, the rating r_{ij} is the rating given by the ith user for the jth item. In the common real-world situations, users usually rate on a fraction of items, not on the whole items. Therefore, those ratings entail a big and sparse matrix $\mathbf{R} \in \mathbb{R}^{N \times M}$. The goal of recommender system is to make a prediction on the missing ratings. Based on that, we will know the preference of a user on the items he never rates, and recommend high score items to him. Table 1 summarizes the symbols used in our approach.

Table 1. Summary of notations.

Notation	Description
N	Number of users
M	Number of items
K	Dimension of latent factors
D	Dimension of sequential features
$\mathbf{R} \in \mathbb{R}^{N \times M}$	Rating matrix
$\mathbf{U} \in \mathbb{R}^{N \times K}$	Latent factors of users
$\mathbf{V} \in \mathbb{R}^{M \times K}$	Latent factors of items
$\mathbf{X} \in \mathbb{R}^{N \times D}$	sequential features of users
$\mathbf{Y} \in \mathbb{R}^{M \times D}$	sequential features of items

3.2   Long-Short Interest Model

The basic assumption of collaborative filtering is that items liked by the same user would be similar or users like the same items would share a similar interest. However, in real-world situations, it is not always true because users' interest may change over a long time period. Meanwhile, the interest distribution of a user in a fixed time period are stable and don't change too much. To describe this phenomenon, we propose the definition of **long interest** and **short interest**.

- **long interest** reflects the interest distribution of a user in a long time period, and it is reflected in the whole items list of the user's preference.
- **short interest** reflects the interest distribution of a user in a short time period, and it is reflected in a fraction of the whole items list of the user's preference in a fixed length sliding window.

Under this definition, two assumptions are proposed as below.

1. items liked in the same short interest of the same long interest have a higher possibility to be similar than ones liked in different short interest of the same long interest.
2. the more times items show in the same short interest of different long interest, the higher possibility they are similar.

For example, as illustrated in the top of Fig. 3, **item2** should be more similar with **item1** than **item5** in the low dimensional embedding space.

Inspired by paragraph2vec algorithm [6] for learning vector representations of words which take advantage of a word order observed in a sentence, we introduce a neural network based language model to carry out the embedding of sequential features. The embedding model simultaneously learns vector representations of users and items by considering the user as a global context, and the architecture of the embedding model is illustrated in Fig. 4.

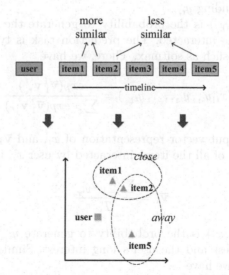

Fig. 3. A example for short interest and long interest

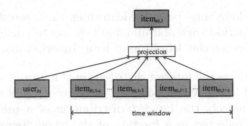

Fig. 4. Embedding model for extracting interest similarity from users and items

The training data set was derived from users' interaction timeline T, which comprises users $x_i (i = 1, 2, \ldots, N)$ and their interacted items ordered by the interacted time, $y_{i_1}, y_{i_2}, \ldots, y_{i_{L_i}}$[1], where L_i denotes number of items interacted by user x_i, which is much less than the amount of items M. To characterize the *long interest*, we consider the whole items list as the context and generate the long interest of the current user. To characterize the *short interest*, we consider items in the same local interest as the context and generate items in it one by one with the help of long interest. More formally, objective of the embedding model is to maximize the log-likelihood over the set of T of all the interaction timeline,

$$\sum_{i=1}^{N} \left(p(x_i | y_{i_1}, y_{i_2}, \ldots, y_{i_{L_i}}) + \sum_{j=1}^{L_i} p(y_{i_j} | y_{i_{j-c}} : y_{i_{j+c}}, x_i) \right) \tag{1}$$

where c is the time window size, $y_{i_{j-c}} : y_{i_{j+c}}$ denotes the sequence $y_{i_{j-c}}$, $y_{i_{j-c+1}}, \ldots, y_{i_{j+c}}$ excluding y_{i_j}.

$p(x_i | y_{i_1}, y_{i_2}, \ldots, y_{i_{L_i}})$ is the probability to generate the long interest of u_i based on all items he interacted. The prediction task is typically done via a multi-class classifier, such as softmax. There, we have

$$p(x_i | y_{i_1}, y_{i_2}, \ldots, y_{i_{L_i}}) = \frac{exp(\overline{\mathbf{v}}_1^T \mathbf{v}'_{x_i})}{\sum_{x'} exp(\overline{\mathbf{v}}_1^T \mathbf{v}'_{x'})} \tag{2}$$

where $\mathbf{v}'_{x_i}$ is the output vector representation of x_i, and $\overline{\mathbf{v}}_1$ is averaged input vector representation of all the items interacted by user x_i, i.e.

$$\overline{\mathbf{v}}_1 = \frac{\sum_{j=1}^{T_i} \mathbf{v}_{y_{i_j}}}{T_i} \tag{3}$$

$p(y_{i_j} | y_{i_{j-c}} : y_{i_{j+c}}, x_i)$ is the probability to generate y_{i_j} based on items in the same short interest and the user's long interest. Similarly, using softmax multi-class classifier we have

---

[1] we use symbol x and y instead of classic u and v to avoid confusion between v and vector symbol $\mathbf{v}$ in neural network language model.

$$p(y_{i_j}|y_{i_{j-c}} : y_{i_{j+c}}, x_i) = \frac{exp(\overline{\mathbf{v}}_2^{\mathrm{T}} \mathbf{v}'_{y_{i_j}})}{\sum_{y'} exp(\overline{\mathbf{v}}_2^{\mathrm{T}} \mathbf{v}'_{y'})} \qquad (4)$$

where $\mathbf{v}'_{y_{i_j}}$ is the output vector representation of y_{i_j}, and $\overline{\mathbf{v}}_2$ is averaged input vector representation of items int the same short interest and corresponding long interest x_i.

$$\overline{\mathbf{v}}_2 = \frac{\mathbf{v}_{x_i} + \sum_{-c \leq k \leq c, k \neq 0} \mathbf{v}_{y_{i_{j+k}}}}{2c + 1} \qquad (5)$$

Stochastic Gradient Descent (SGD) are used as the training method, hierarchical softmax and negative sampling are two main approaches to accelerate the computation, and we use negative sampling approach in this paper.

3.3 Feature Based Collaborative Filtering

Feature based collaborative filtering [1] is a variety of collaborative filtering, it allows us to build factorization models incorporating side information such as temporal dynamics, neighborhood relationship, and hierarchical information compared with conventional collaborative filtering.

There are two kinds of side information in collaborative filtering: user side information and item side information. Feature based collaborative filtering summarizes the two factors as feature vectors (denoted by $\mathbf{u}_i \in \mathbb{R}^n$ and $\mathbf{v}_j \in \mathbb{R}^m$) and predicts the preference score $\hat{r}$ as

$$\hat{r}_{ij} - \sum_{k=1}^{n} \alpha_k \mathbf{u}_{ik} + \sum_{k=1}^{m} \beta_k \mathbf{v}_{jk} + \left(\sum_{k=1}^{n} \mathbf{u}_{ik} \mathbf{p}_k\right)^{\mathrm{T}} \left(\sum_{k=1}^{m} \mathbf{v}_{jk} \mathbf{q}_k\right) \qquad (6)$$

where α and β controls the influence of each feature, $\mathbf{p}_k \in \mathbb{R}^K$ and $\mathbf{q}_k \in \mathbb{R}^K$ are K dimensional latent factors associated with each feature. If we represent one-hot representation of users and items like

$$\mathbf{u}_{ik} = \begin{cases} 1, k = i \\ 0, k \neq i \end{cases}, \mathbf{v}_{jk} = \begin{cases} 1, k = j \\ 0, k \neq j \end{cases} \qquad (7)$$

the equation for rating prediction will reduce to the basic matrix factorization

$$\hat{r}_{ij} = \alpha_i + \beta_j + \mathbf{p}_i^{\mathrm{T}} \mathbf{q}_j \qquad (8)$$

where α, β are the biases and $\mathbf{p}_i$, $\mathbf{q}_j$ are the latent factors for user $\mathbf{u}_i$ and item $\mathbf{v}_j$.

In our work, the representation of users and items learned from long-short interest model can be treated as a kind of side information. Hence, we define $\tilde{\mathbf{u}}_i$ as the learned vector representation of users and $\tilde{\mathbf{v}}_j$ as the learned vector representation of items. Then, we get new features of users and items by add the learned vector representation to original one-hot representation.

$$\mathbf{u}_i = \{\mathbf{u}_i, \tilde{\mathbf{u}}_i\}, \mathbf{v}_j = \{\mathbf{v}_j, \tilde{\mathbf{v}}_j\} \qquad (9)$$

There, the equation for rating prediction will change to

$$\hat{r}_{ij} = \sum_{k=1}^{N+D} \alpha_k \{\mathbf{u}_i, \tilde{\mathbf{u}}_i\}_k + \sum_{k=1}^{M+D} \beta_k \{\mathbf{v}_j, \tilde{\mathbf{v}}_j\}_k + \left(\sum_{k=1}^{N+D} \{\mathbf{u}_i, \tilde{\mathbf{u}}_i\}_k \mathbf{p}_k \right)^{\mathrm{T}} \left(\sum_{k=1}^{M+D} \{\mathbf{v}_j, \tilde{\mathbf{v}}_j\}_k \mathbf{q}_k \right) \tag{10}$$

where N is the number of users, M is the number of items, D is the dimension of sequential features of users and items learned from our long-short interest model, $\mathbf{p}_k \in \mathbb{R}^K$ and $\mathbf{q}_k \in \mathbb{R}^K$ are K dimensional latent factors associated with each feature.

4   Experiment

In this section, we conduct several experiments to evaluate the effectiveness of our proposed long-short interest model on three public MovieLens[2] datasets. In these experiments, we also conduct corresponding analysis to investigate: (1) the rating prediction performance of our long-short interest model compare with other benchmark models; (2) the effect of our long-short interest model on users own different interaction number.

4.1   Experimental Setup

Dataset. We conduct experiments on three MovieLens datasets, i.e. MovieLens-1 M, MovieLens-10 M and MovieLens-20 M, which are commonly used for evaluating collaborative filtering algorithms. Table 2 summarizes the statistics of three datasets. These datasets also provide some side information about users and items, such as gender, age and occupation of users and movies' genres, but we don't use the side information in all our experiments.

Table 2. Statistics of three MovieLens datasets and Netflix dataset.

Dataset	#users	#items	#ratings	Sparsity
ML-1M	6,040	3,706	1,000,209	95.53%
ML-10M	69,878	10,677	10,000,054	98.66%
ML-20M	138,493	26,744	20,000,263	99.46%

Metrics. We employ the Root Mean Square Error (RMSE) to measure the rating prediction quality. The metric RMSE is defined as:

$$RSME = \sqrt{\frac{1}{N} \sum_{i,j} I_{ij}(R_{ij} - \hat{R}_{ij})^2} \tag{11}$$

---

[2] http://grouplens.org/datasets/movielens/.

where R_{ij} denotes the ground-truth rating the user i gives to the item j, $\hat{R}_{ij}$ denotes the corresponding predicted rating, I_{ij} is a binary matrix that indicates the ratings in the test set, and N is the total number of ratings in the test set.

4.2   Benchmark Models

we use two popular toolkits, LibMF and LibFM, that are widely used in both academia and industry as our benchmark models.

LibMF is an open source tool for approximating an incomplete matrix using the product of two matrices in a latent space. It provides solvers for real-valued matrix factorization, binary matrix factorization, and one-class matrix factorization, and also supports parallel computation in a multi-core machine using CPU instructions (e.g., SSE) to accelerate vector operations. Its paper [2] won the best paper award in RecSys 2013.

Factorization machines (FM) are a generic approach that allows to mimic most factorization models by feature engineering. This way, factorization machines combine the generality of feature engineering with the superiority of factorization models in estimating interactions between categorical variables of a large domain. LibFM [13] is a software implementation for factorization machines that features Stochastic Gradient Descent (SGD) and Alternating Least Squares (ALS) optimization as well as Bayesian inference using Markov Chain Monte Carlo (MCMC).

4.3   Overall Results

In this section, we report the experimental results to demonstrate the effectiveness of our long-short interest model. The model proposed in LibMF toolkit is denoted as **LibFM**, the dimension of latent factors is set to 100 and the number of iterations is set to 1000. For the model proposed in LibFM, we denote the LibFM model optimized by SGD as **LibFM-SGD**, the learn rate is set to 0.01, the regular parameter is set to $(0,0,0.01)$ and the stdev for initialization of 2-way factors is set to 0.1. Then we denote the LibFM model optimized by ALS as **LibFM-ALS**, the regular parameter is set to $(0,0,10)$ and the stdev for initialization of 2-way factors is set to 0.1. Lastly, the LibFM model optimized by MCMC is denoted as **LibFM-MCMC**, the stdev for initialization of 2-way factors is set to 0.1. Meanwhile, we denote our long-short interest model as **LSIM**, the slide window size is set to 10, the dimension of latent factors is set to 256 and the dimension of sequential features is set to 100. For feature based collaborative filtering framework, the learn rate is set to 0.005 and the regular parameter is set to 0.024 for both users and items.

We split the rating data in each dataset into random 90%–10% training-test datasets, the training dataset are used for building our proposed model and benchmark models, the remaining data are used for testing. This process is repeated five times, and we report the mean value and standard deviation of the RMSE scores on Table 3. From this table, we can clearly observe:

Table 3. RMSE Performance comparison of our proposed model and benchmark models with a training ratio of 90%/10% on three MovieLens datasets.

Algorithms	MovieLens-1 M	MovieLens-10 M	MovieLens-20 M
LibMF	0.8554 ± 0.0013	0.8090 ± 0.0004	0.8023 ± 0.0004
LibFM-SGD	0.8641 ± 0.0015	0.8022 ± 0.0013	0.7945 ± 0.0023
LibFM-ALS	0.8453 ± 0.0015	0.7936 ± 0.0004	0.7860 ± 0.0004
LibFM-MCMC	0.8460 ± 0.0011	0.7866 ± 0.0004	0.7787 ± 0.0005
LSIM	**0.8355 ± 0.0014**	**0.7740 ± 0.0013**	**0.7656 ± 0.0019**

1. The rating prediction performance of **LibMF** is worst among all the models, the reason should be that it focuses on accelerating the training speed of matrix factorization by parallelization, and doesn't pay enough attention on optimizing the prediction precision.
2. In three **LibFM** models, MCMC optimization **LibFM-MCMC** shows a better performance in large datasets (MovieLens-10 M and MovieLens-20 M) while ALS optimization **LibFM-ALS** shows a better performance in small datasets (MovieLens-1 M). The performance of SGD optimization **LibFM-SGD** is the worst.
3. Our **LSIM** has the best performance between among all models in RMSE performance on all three MovieLens datasets, which shows the effectiveness of the long-short interest model. To the best of our knowledge, the best results published regarding MovieLens-1 M and MovieLens-10 M are reported by both [8,14] with a final RMSE of 0.831 ± 0.003 and 0.782 ± 0.003. These scores are obtained with a training ratio of 90%/10% and without side information. That means our proposed model can achieve the start-of-the-art performance.

4.4 Effects on Different Users

In our long-short interest model, the change of users' interest over time has been embedding into the sequential features. For these users with a lot of interactions, their long interest and short interest will be detailedly extracted via LSIM. But for the others with few interactions, LSIM only can extract marginal sequential features because their interest keeps stable. This phenomenon means that our LSIM will show a better performance on users with lots of interactions than ones with few interactions.

In order to exhibit this character of LSIM, we carry on some experiments on the MovieLens-1M dataset. First, we sort the users on MovieLens-1M according to their respective number of ratings, those users are grouped by their ranking order into 5 clusters (i.e. 0–20%, 20–40%, 40–60%, 60–80% and 80–100%), and RMSE is computed by cluster respectively with a training ratio of 90%/10%. For instance, the first cluster contains the 20% of users with the least number of ratings and the last cluster contains the 20% of users with the highest number of ratings. The provided results are the mean reported through 5-cross validation.

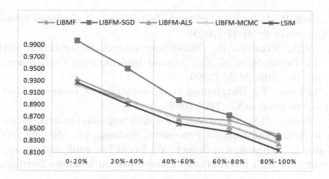

Fig. 5. RMSE computed by cluster of users sorted by their respective number of ratings on MovieLens-10 M with a training ratio of 90%/10%.

It can be clearly observed from Fig. 5 that all these recommendation models benefit from the increase of the count of items the user interact with on RSME metric. Our proposed **LSIM** don't perform well at the first "0%–20%" user cluster, its RMSE score is 0.9275 which is less than **LibFM-MCMC**. But when the interactions become more, its performance rapidly increases, and beats the baseline methods obviously, which shows the effectiveness of our long-short interest model.

5   Conclusions

In this study, we propose to use long-short interest model to utilize the rich sequential information on users' interaction history to solve the rating prediction task in recommender system. By incorporating the sequential features into feature based collaborative filtering framework, better prediction performance can be obtained. Our thorough evaluation, using three standard MovieLens datasets, demonstrates the effectiveness of the proposed method.

Acknowledgement. This work was supported by National High Technology R&D Program of China (Grant Nos. 2015AA015403, 2014AA015102), Natural Science Foundation of China (Grant Nos. 61202233, 61272344, 61370055) and the joint project with IBM Research. Any correspondence please refer to Yansong Feng.

References

1. Chen, T., Zheng, Z., Lu, Q., Zhang, W., Yu, Y.: Feature-based matrix factorization (2011). arXiv preprint arXiv:1109.2271
2. Chin, W.S., Zhuang, Y., Juan, Y.C., Lin, C.J.: A fast parallel stochastic gradient method for matrix factorization in shared memory systems. ACM Trans. Intell. Syst. Technol. (TIST) **6**(1), 2 (2015)
3. Gomez-Uribe, C.A., Hunt, N.: The Netflix recommender system: algorithms, business value, and innovation. ACM Trans. Manag. Inf. Syst. (TMIS) **6**(4), 13 (2015)

4. Koren, Y., Bell, R., Volinsky, C.: Matrix factorization techniques for recommender systems. Computer **8**, 30–37 (2009)
5. Lawrence, N.D., Urtasun, R.: Non-linear matrix factorization with Gaussian processes. In: Proceedings of 26th Annual International Conference on Machine Learning, pp. 601–608. ACM (2009)
6. Le, Q.V., Mikolov, T.: Distributed representations of sentences and documents (2014). arXiv preprint arXiv:1405.4053
7. Lee, D.D., Seung, H.S.: Algorithms for non-negative matrix factorization. In: Advances in Neural Information Processing Systems, pp. 556–562 (2001)
8. Lee, J., Kim, S., Lebanon, G., Singer, Y.: Local low-rank matrix approximation. In: Proceedings of 30th International Conference on Machine Learning, pp. 82–90 (2013)
9. Mazumder, R., Hastie, T., Tibshirani, R.: Spectral regularization algorithms for learning large incomplete matrices. J. Mach. Learn. Res. **11**, 2287–2322 (2010)
10. Mikolov, T., Chen, K., Corrado, G., Dean, J.: Efficient estimation of word representations in vector space (2013). arXiv preprint arXiv:1301.3781
11. Pazzani, M.J., Billsus, D.: Content-based recommendation systems. In: Brusilovsky, P., Kobsa, A., Nejdl, W. (eds.) The Adaptive Web. LNCS, vol. 4321, pp. 325–341. Springer, Heidelberg (2007). doi:10.1007/978-3-540-72079-9_10
12. Rendle, S.: Factorization machines. In: 2010 IEEE 10th International Conference on Data Mining (ICDM), pp. 995–1000. IEEE (2010)
13. Rendle, S.: Factorization machines with libFM. ACM Trans. Intell. Syst. Technol. (TIST) **3**(3), 57 (2012)
14. Sedhain, S., Menon, A.K., Sanner, S., Xie, L.: AutoRec: autoencoders meet collaborative filtering. In: Proceedings of 24th International Conference on World Wide Web Companion, pp. 111–112. International World Wide Web Conferences Steering Committee (2015)
15. Su, X., Khoshgoftaar, T.M.: A survey of collaborative filtering techniques. Adv. Artif. Intell. **2009**, 4 (2009)
16. Zhou, Y., Wilkinson, D., Schreiber, R., Pan, R.: Large-scale parallel collaborative filtering for the Netflix prize. In: Fleischer, R., Xu, J. (eds.) AAIM 2008. LNCS, vol. 5034, pp. 337–348. Springer, Heidelberg (2008). doi:10.1007/978-3-540-68880-8_32

Discourse Analysis

Leveraging Hierarchical Deep Semantics to Classify Implicit Discourse Relations via Mutual Learning Method

Xiaohan She[1], Ping Jian[1,2(✉)], Pengcheng Zhang[1],
and Heyan Huang[1,2]

[1] School of Computer Science and Technology, Beijing Institute of Technology,
5 South Zhongguancun Street, Beijing 100081, China
{xhshe,pjian,pengchengzhang,hhy63}@bit.edu.cn
[2] Beijing Engineering Research Center of High Volume Language Information
Processing and Cloud Computing Application, 5 South Zhongguancun Street,
Beijing 100081, China

Abstract. This paper presents a mutual learning method using hierarchical deep semantics for the classification of implicit discourse relations in English. With the absence of explicit discourse markers, traditional discourse techniques mainly concentrate on discrete linguistic features in this task, which always leads to data sparse problem. To relieve this problem, we propose a mutual learning neural model which makes use of multilevel semantic information together, including the distribution of implicit discourse relations, the semantics of arguments and the co-occurrence of words. During the training process, the predicted target of the model which is the probability of the discourse relation type, and the distributed representation of semantic components are learnt jointly and optimized mutually. The results of both binary and multiclass identification show that this method outperforms previous works since the mutual learning strategy can distinguish Expansion type from the others efficiently.

Keywords: Implicit discourse relation classification · Hierarchical deep semantics · Mutual learning neural network

1 Introduction

As a member task in natural language processing (NLP), discourse relation classification is always a significant procedure of automatic discourse understanding. The bottleneck of this task is how to efficiently and effectively identify the sense of implicit discourse relations that are not marked by explicit discourse connectives [1, 2]. Things get challenging as discourse connective is a kind of surface and strong cue for discourse relation classification, and we're finally forced to capture the deep sense held between two adjacent text spans (arguments) without the help of discourse connectives.

When dealing with implicit discourse relations, transforming the two arguments into a cluster of features sounds like a feasible alternative. Traditional methods focus on extracting words from each argument, and set the corresponding pair of words as triggers of certain relation types. Here is an implicit instance:

© Springer International Publishing AG 2016
C.-Y. Lin et al. (Eds.): NLPCC-ICCPOL 2016, LNAI 10102, pp. 349–359, 2016.
DOI: 10.1007/978-3-319-50496-4_29

(a) *The recent explosion of country funds mirrors the "closed-end fund mania" of the 1920s, Mr. Foot says, when narrowly focused funds grew wildly* **popular**.

(b) *They fell into* **oblivion** *after the 1929 crash.*

In (a), the term "popular" conveys positive emotion of people towards funds, whereas in (b), the head word "oblivion" means time changes. The pair of (popular, oblivion), as the function of discourse connective "but" or "however", is likely to show that there may be a contrast relation between (a) and (b).

Features like word pairs have been proved to be effective to predict the implicit discourse relation in a way, while some corresponding problems follow. On the one hand, the one-hot representation of word pairs is so sparse that this kind of discrete feature cannot reach to an acceptable convergence by common classifiers. In addition, the composition for different types of word pairs seems to be a difficult problem. On the other hand, the mainstream annotated corpus of discourse analysis is Penn Discourse Treebank (PDTB) [3], which contains only 16,053 implicit samples. As we can see, the lack of natural implicit discourse relations with convincing labels which always aggravates the situation of data sparseness will lead to serious under-fitting during training process.

In this paper, we propose a method to alleviate these problems mentioned above. Illuminated by the neural probabilistic language model (NPLM) [4, 5], we employ the distributed representation of word pairs, argument pairs and relations as classification triggers instead of discrete features. In our model, embeddings of these hierarchical semantic components are learnt to optimize the probability of corresponding discourse relation type. As the prior distribution of the implicit discourse relations, the semantic senses of the argument pairs and word pairs are jointly learnt and the relation type is more likely to be inferred correctly. When facing the data sparsity problem, the employment of distributed representation can effectively relieve this situation by aggregating features together, which has been proved to be feasible in many previous works, *e.g.*, [6]. The result of experiment shows that our method enhances the semantically expressing power than the discrete one or the simple addition method.

The organization of this paper is as follows. Section 2 discusses relevant works towards implicit discourse relation classification. Section 3 presents the main framework and detail description of our mutual learning neural model. Section 4 shows the specific natural and artificial implicit data we using and the experimental results of our method and the compared baselines. And the conclusions are concluded in Sect. 5.

2   Related Works

In recent years, many works have studied the implicit discourse relation classification problem in different ways. Marcu and Echihabi [7] presents a pattern matching approach considering the lack of implicit data. They extract sentence pairs matching the pattern like [Arg1, but Arg2] from raw corpus and remove their connectives as implicit one, which means explicit and implicit discourse relations are similar to each other.

Afterwards, more and more implicit discourse relation corpus are manually labelled and released, so does relevant supervised works. Soricut and Marcu [8] use the RST corpus [9] to analyze this task restricted within a sentence. Wellner et al. [10] employ an alternative corpora GraphBank [11] and propose that the head word and the first or last words of each argument are distinctive in implicit discourse analysis. More works are conducted on PDTB, the largest manually labelled corpus of discourse structures so far. Pitler et al. [12] has conducted a variety of experiments about different linguistic features, and concluded that word pairs feature is of great importance in implicit discourse relation classification. Meanwhile, Lin et al. [13] and Wang et al. [14] pay more attention to syntactic structures, which prove to be helpful to infer the corresponding relation type. Zhou et al. [15], in other way, use language model, which helps the implicit relation recognition via an additional feature, to predict implicit discourse connectives rather than the relation type.

Things change as the lack of annotated training data becomes new bottleneck of implicit discourse relation analysis, and semi-supervised methods become popular and popular. Biran and McKeown [6] present aggregated word pair features which are generated from the Gigaword corpus to replace the original discrete ones. They combine text classification techniques, for example, TF-IDF and mutual information, etc., with discourse analysis and achieve close to the state of the art performance compared to [12]. Lan et al. [16] innovatively combine implicit discourse relation recognition and multi-task learning together. The automatically labelled data and manually labelled explicit data are both auxiliary for implicit one. Fisher and Simmons [17] propose a spectral method based on Hidden Markov Model (HMM) which regards discourse relations in the same document effected with each other by a latent variable. Braud and Denis [18], on the other hand, analyze the distribution of different relation types between natural and synthetic implicit data in French, and achieve a proper balance using domain adaption.

More recently, deep learning is widely used in NLP, since distributed representation brings much more semantic information rather than traditional one-hot representation. As we can see, the NPLM proposed by Bengio et al. [4] is a proper entry point for semantic tasks. Based on that, Mikolov et al. [5] use word co-occurence and shallow syntactic information to automatically generate the semantics of words as word embeddings, which definitely enhances the performance of many semantic tasks, *e.g.*, sentiment analysis [19] and topic model [20]. As another semantic task in NLP, it's intuitional to combine implicit discourse relation classification and distributed representation together.

3 Method

In this section, we mainly demonstrate our proposed model for implicit discourse relation classification. Unlike the literature methods above, we choose distributed representation of semantic components instead of discrete linguistic features such as polarity and verbs. Furthermore, we composite multilevel embeddings together in order to express the meaning of relations in different ways. Since the classification task aims to capture the deep sense between two arguments, introducing argument embedding is obviously contributed to the classification, so is the distribution of implicit discourse relations.

The primary training process pays more attention to optimize the probability of each discourse relation type, while the embeddings of different semantic component are learnt simultaneously. Besides that, all kinds of embeddings are also learnt jointly and have effect on each other mutually. In a word, the proposed model is a mutual learning neural model aiming to automatically label implicit discourse relations and generate task-specific embeddings of relations, arguments and word pairs mutually.

3.1 Mutual Learning Neural Model

This model computes the probability towards different type of implicit discourse relations when dealing with a pair of arguments holding implicit discourse relation. The mutuality in our method is reflected in the following two respects: (1) the probabilities towards different relation types and the distributed representation of semantic components are optimized mutually; and (2) the embeddings of hierarchical semantic components are learnt jointly and affected by each other during the training process. Figure 1 shows the system framework and the data stream of each semantic unit.

Concerning the specific feature selection about implicit discourse relation classification, some works like Pitler et al. [12] prefer word pairs while others rely much more on sentence structure. In our method, we choose embeddings of both word pairs and arguments to represent implicit discourse relations in different ways. Since the border of arguments is determined by annotation manually or punctuation automatically, the word pairs are always selected by statistics such as information gain or Gini

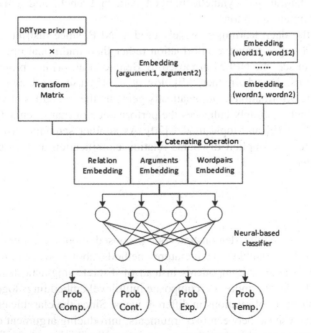

Fig. 1. The framework of our mutual learning neural method and the arrows illustrate the main data stream of each semantic components

coefficient. Moreover, Yang et al. [20] regard topic model as a kind of Gaussian mixture model (GMM) and introduce the distribution of topics to conduct clustering. This work tells us to utilize the prior probability of implicit discourse relations which is also treated as relation embeddings to conduct classification. The usage of multilevel embeddings expresses the implicit sense held between the two arguments detailedly and accurately, since the single one always contains bias.

When talking about the architecture of the neural network classifier, previous works like [5] prefer to add embeddings of input layer together as hidden layer, while we prefer different semantic levels to be catenated one by one. We assume that all kinds of embeddings are unique compared with each other and equally important in semantics. On one hand, uniqueness means that the simple addition of different kinds of embeddings hurts the presentation of the entire sense of the relation, but catenation performs better. On the other hand, the usage of transform matrix is to ensure that the vector length of prior probability for implicit discourse relations is same as the other semantic unit, which reveals they have the equal weight in semantics.

The output of classification is four kinds of probabilities, each of which is mapped to the top level of the sense annotations in PDTB: Comparison, Contingency, Expansion and Temporal. Each word and argument embedding is in d-dimension and is initialized using the PV method introduced by Le and Mikolov [21]. They add the argument embedding to the sum of word embedding together and optimize these embeddings simultaneously. All of word embeddings are stored in the word embedding matrix $V \in \mathbb{R}^{d \times |V|}$ where $|V|$ is the size of vocabulary in training data, so are argument embeddings whose embedding matrix is $A \in \mathbb{R}^{d \times |S|}$. The prior probability $p \in \mathbb{R}^{1 \times 4}$ of implicit discourse relation type is calculated by the corresponding distribution in PDTB. The transform matrix is $T \in \mathbb{R}^{4 \times 2d}$, as the number of discourse relation type is 4 and the dimensions of word and argument pair are both 2d. The product of p and T is seen as implicit discourse relation embedding matrix $D \in \mathbb{R}^{1 \times 2d}$ below.

3.2 Learning Model Parameters and Semantic Embeddings

Since all levels of embeddings are initialized well, we set the four probabilities towards corresponding discourse relation type as training target. When dealing with an actual implicit discourse relation with the type r, there're probably more than one pair of words that's useful in classification. So we optimize just one word pair during each iteration. Let $C \in \mathbb{R}^{1 \times 6d}$ as the catenation of all embeddings. Formally, the score towards each specific type is defined by:

$$P = f(W^{T}C) = f \left(W^{T} \cdot \begin{bmatrix} v_1, v_2 \\ a_1, a_2 \\ pT \end{bmatrix} \right) \tag{1}$$

where $f(\cdot)$ = sigmoid$(\cdot)$ is a standard nonlinear function, $W \in \mathbb{R}^{6d \times 4}$ is the parameter matrix needed to be learnt, $v_1, v_2 \in V$ and $a_1, a_2 \in A$ are corresponding semantic embeddings. Matrix P represents the probabilities of the four kinds of relation types.

We put the embeddings of word pairs, argument pairs and relations in an equal position, and allocate corresponding parameters to each of them. The cross product of those embeddings and their parameters is treated as the scores of relation types, and nonlinear function f is the softmax layer.

As we optimize both the probability of corresponding discourse relation type and the distributed representation of semantic components mutually, parameter matrix W and these embeddings are about to be learnt by maximizing the log-likelihood of the probability. The probability log-likelihood for each type is equal to:

$$
\begin{aligned}
l_i &= \log \left(f(W_i^T C)^{\text{label}} \left(1 - f(W_i^T C) \right)^{1-\text{label}} \right) \\
&= \text{label} \cdot \log f(W_i^T C) + (1 - \text{label}) \cdot \log \left(1 - f(W_i^T C) \right)
\end{aligned}
\tag{2}
$$

where label is a value determined by the equality situation between real type r and predicted type i. If r is equal to i, label = 1; otherwise, label = 0. This means that we'll use gradient ascent strategy towards the r-type and descent strategy towards the non-r-type, which makes the score of r-type become distinctly higher than others.

Steps following are iteratively optimization using alternating gradient ascent and descent strategy, i.e., fix parameter matrix W, to find catenated semantic embeddings C that minimizes the value of loss function in (2), and repeat it reversely. The gradient of catenated semantic embeddings C is in the following form:

$$
\partial l_i / \partial C = \left[\text{label} - f(W_i^T C) \right] \cdot W_i^T
\tag{3}
$$

In (3), the catenated embedding C is learnt by both the type of the implicit discourse relation (the label) and the cross product of multilevel embeddings and their parameters. In other words, the embeddings of each semantic component is optimized by not only themselves but also the others. The usage of those hierarchical semantic embeddings is to optimize themselves from each other via this mutual learning strategy.

For the symmetry between C and W in the loss function (2), the gradient of parameter matrix W is shown as follows, which is highly similar to (3):

$$
\partial l_i / \partial W_i^T = \left[\text{label} - f(W_i^T C) \right] \cdot C
\tag{4}
$$

Besides C and W, there's also another parameter matrix T which is the transform matrix of implicit discourse relation distribution. As the derivatives of relation embedding D and catenated embedding C are in equal, the gradient of transform matrix T can be computed as following:

$$
\partial l_i / \partial T = \partial l_i / \partial D \cdot p^T = \left[\text{label} - f(W_i^T C) \right] \cdot W_i^T \cdot p^T
\tag{5}
$$

In summary, the training process has two key stage: (1) training to get the embeddings of relations, arguments and word pairs by the relation type and mutual influence among themselves; and (2) training to get the parameters matrix W to ensure that the probability of relation type and the cross product of C and W is highly consistent.

4 Experiment

In this section, we use a semi-supervised learning strategy to train our model since the size of annotated resource for discourse relations does not match this problem in scale. Followed the corresponding evaluations in [12, 22, 23], we compare our model with their best results in F1-score and provide the relevant explanations about difference in result.

4.1 Datasets

For our experiments, on one hand, we use the Penn Discourse Treebank as natural discourse relations, which are done on 2,312 Wall Street Journal articles aligned with the Penn Treebank (PTB) [24]. According to the statistics in [3], there're 16,053 tokens of manually labelled implicit discourse relations divided into 25 Sections, and they're all annotated in the form of hierarchical sense tags. The top level of these tags, such as Comparison, Contingency, Expansion and Temporal, is set as the target of prediction. Conventionally, we use Sections of 2–20 of the PDTB as training set and Sections 21–22 as testing set. Sections 0–1 are used as development set for parameter tuning.

On the other hand, the proposed neural model contains so many parameters needed to be learnt that it's not enough to use only natural implicit data, thus synthetic data is introduced into this work. We utilize two large scale corpus Central News Agency of Taiwan, English Service (CNA) and Xinhua News Agency, English Service (XIN) that are both extracted from English Gigaword Fifth Edition[1] to train our model.

Since the raw corpora is prepared, we use the pattern matching approach presented in [7] to extract explicit discourse relations from CNA and XIN. In respect of differences between explicit and implicit discourse data, Prasad et al. [3] mainly describe the breakdown of relative position of arguments and discourse markers. The situation that Arg1 is located within the same sentence as the discourse marker is called SS, PS means Arg1 is in the previous sentence of the connective, and following sentence is named FS. The majority explicit discourse relations in PDTB are SS, however, implicit discourse relations cannot be held in only one sentence, which implies that explicit discourse relations in SS type do not match implicit data well by removing discourse markers. As the percentage of FS type is less than 0.1% in extracted discourse relations, we transform those explicit data in PS type into implicit ones.

Besides, the rest synthetic implicit relations are not similar enough to natural ones in distribution of relation type, which is shown in Table 1. The majority type of both natural and synthetic implicit relations are Expansion, while the percentage of Comparison in synthetic data is obviously higher than the natural one, but the Contingency is on the contrary. As a result, we balance the distribution of relation type between different implicit data by discarding redundant synthetic discourse relations.

Last but not least, the match of useful word pairs needs the help of other annotated corpora. Pitler et al. [12] introduce the Multi-perspective Question Answering Opinion

---

[1] https://catalog.ldc.upenn.edu/LDC2011T07.

Table 1. The distribution of senses of natural and artificial implicit discourse relations

Relation type	Training dataset					Test dataset
	Natural dataset	Synthetic dataset				
	PDTB	CNA	CNA clean	XIN	XIN clean	
Comparison	1551	9895	1218	100835	13717	79
Contingency	2994	2351	2351	26478	26478	177
Expansion	5971	17189	4689	145922	52806	298
Temporal	492	2870	386	21333	4351	40
All	11008	32305	8644	294568	97352	594

Corpus [25] and the General Inquirer lexicon [26], which are also utilized in our experiment, to extract word pairs. The extracted word pairs are made up of sentiment or semantically relevant words. Moreover, we count all of word pairs in training set and remove these items appeared less than five times. We rank the rest by information gain and include the top as the set of useful word pairs.

4.2 Classification Results

Since we aim to achieve implicit discourse relation classification, we respectively run four binary classifiers to distinguish the top level of sense from the others. We compare our result with ones of [12, 22, 23], which have built a set of classifiers using the PDTB. The performance measured by F1-score is shown in Table 2.

Table 2. Binary implicit discourse relation classification on the top-level PDTB annotations

Relation type	Pitler et al. (2009)	R&X (2014)	R&X (2015)	R&X + extra data (2015)	Our work
Comparison	22.0	39.7	38.0	41.0	35.9
Contingency	47.1	54.4	53.9	53.8	52.5
Expansion	76.4	70.2	67.9	69.4	**77.0**
Temporal	16.8	28.7	24.6	33.3	18.2

As we can see, our results is better than the ones of Pitler et al. [12] in all respects. The main reason is that we use both semantic embeddings and synthetic training data to reach a higher accuracy. Our mutual learning method, in other words, is capable to integrate the advantages of those resource and classify the implicit discourse relations in different ways.

When compared with the works of Rutherford and Xue [22, 23], the classification result of Comparison and Temporal type in our work is weaker than the baseline, while Expansion type is on the contrary. We consider that the proportion of implicit discourse relations in Comparison and Temporal type is not more than twenty percent in training data, which may have side effects on training process in condition of suffering from the imbalanced distribution. Moreover, the word pairs selected by information gain are not efficient due to the lack of the Comparison and Temporal samples. These word pairs disappeared in training data cannot get a relevant score about whether they're chosen as an implicit discourse relation trigger.

Things change since the number of Contingency and Expansion type is sufficient for our mutual learning process. While the result of Contingency type is as the same level as the baseline, our method achieves significant improvement in Expansion classifier.

In order to verify the performance of our method when dealing with multiclass identification problem, we report the result in both accuracy and F1-score in Table 3. We do not add the results of Pitler et al. [12] and Rutherford and Xue [22] because they do experiments only on binary classification.

Table 3. Multiclass implicit discourse relation classification on the top-level PDTB annotations

Model	Accuracy	Macro F_1
R&X (2015)	55.0	38.4
R&X + extra data (2015)	57.1	40.5
Our work	**60.3**	**42.9**

Though we do not provide distinct advantages in each binary classification shown in Table 2, we still outperform all alternatives on both metrics. It's obviously that the Expansion type is so important in the implicit discourse relation classification that we'll get positive results if our method can distinguish the Expansion ones from the other types. In a word, we conclude that word pairs embedding plays an important role in binary classification while multiclass classification rely more on implicit discourse relation distribution.

5 Conclusion

In this paper, we have presented a probabilistic neural model via mutual learning method over implicit discourse relation classification between two adjacent arguments. This model combines deep sense of hierarchical semantic components together, and mutually promote the prediction of corresponding discourse type and the embeddings optimization of those semantic components. Besides, we utilize both natural and synthetic implicit discourse relations during training process to ensure that parameters of the whole neural network will not be under-fitted. The results show that our model has obviously positive effect on multiclass prediction and the binary prediction between Expansion and the others.

Implicit discourse relation classification is still the most challenging task in discourse analysis. Deep learning and distributed representation provide an effective way to deal with data sparse and scarcity problem. However, the more complicated model is still remained to be proposed since the semantic sense is not captured perfectly in existing methods.

Acknowledgment. The authors would like to thank the organizers of NLPCC-ICCPOL 2016 and the reviewers for their helpful suggestions. This research is supported by the National Natural Science Foundation of China (61202244, 61502259) and the National Basic Research Program of China (973 Program, 2013CB329303).

References

1. Pitler, E., et al.: Easily identifiable discourse relations. In: International Conference on Computational Linguistics, Posters Proceedings, COLING 2008, 18–22 August 2008, Manchester, UK (2008)
2. Park, J., Cardie, C.: Improving implicit discourse relation recognition through feature set optimization. In: International Conference on Computational Science and Engineering (2009)
3. Prasad, R., Miltsakaki, E., Dinesh, N., Lee, A., Joshi, A.: The Penn discourse treebank 2.0 annotation manual. In: Proceedings of LREC, vol. 24, p. 2961 (2008)
4. Bengio, Y., Schwenk, H., Senécal, J.S., Morin, F., Gauvain, J.L.: A neural probabilistic language model. J. Mach. Learn. Res. **3**, 1137 (2003)
5. Mikolov, T., Sutskever, I., Chen, K., Corrado, G., Dean, J.: Distributed representations of words and phrases and their compositionality. In: Advances in Neural Information Processing Systems, vol. 26, p. 3111 (2013)
6. Biran, O., Mckeown, K.: Aggregated word pair features for implicit discourse relation disambiguation. In: Meeting of the Association for Computational Linguistics, vol. 69 (2013)
7. Marcu, D., Echihabi, A.: An unsupervised approach to recognizing discourse relations, Philadelphia, Pennsylvania, USA, 368 p. (2002)
8. Soricut, R., Marcu, D.: Sentence level discourse parsing using syntactic and lexical information. In: Conference of the North American Chapter of the Association for Computational Linguistics on Human Language Technology, vol. 149 (2003)
9. Carlson, L., Marcu, D., Okurowski, M.E.: Building a Discourse-Tagged Corpus in the Framework of Rhetorical Structure Theory. Springer, Netherlands (2003)
10. Wellner, B., Pustejovsky, J., Havasi, C., Rumshisky, A., Saurí, R.: Classification of discourse coherence relations: an exploratory study using multiple knowledge sources. In: Proceedings of 7th SIGDIAL Workshop on Discourse and Dialogue, vol. 117 (2006)
11. Wolf, F., Gibson, E.: Representing discourse coherence: a corpus-based study. Comput. Linguist. **32**, 249 (2005)
12. Pitler E., Louis A., Nenkova A.: Automatic sense prediction for implicit discourse relations in text. In: ACL 2009, Proceedings of the Meeting of the Association for Computational Linguistics and the International Joint Conference on Natural Language Processing of the AFNLP, 2–7 August 2009, Singapore, vol. 683 (2009)
13. Lin, Z., Kan, M.Y., Ng, H.T.: Recognizing implicit discourse relations in the Penn Discourse Treebank. In: Conference on Empirical Methods in Natural Language Processing, vol. 343 (2009)
14. Wang, W.T., Su, J., Tan, C.L.: Kernel based discourse relation recognition with temporal ordering information. In: ACL 2010, Proceedings of the Meeting of the Association for Computational Linguistics, 11–16 July 2010, Uppsala, Sweden, vol. 710 (2010)
15. Zhou, Z.M., Xu, Y., Niu, Z.Y., Lan, M., Su, J., Tan, C.L.: Predicting discourse connectives for implicit discourse relation recognition. In: International Conference on Computational Linguistics: Posters (2010)

16. Lan, M., Xu, Y., Niu, Z.: Leveraging synthetic discourse data via multi-task learning for implicit discourse relation recognition. In: Meeting of the Association for Computational Linguistics (2013)
17. Fisher, R., Simmons, R.: Spectral semi-supervised discourse relation classification, Beijing, China, 89 p. (2015)
18. Braud, C.E., Denis, P.: Combining natural and artificial examples to improve implicit discourse relation identification, Dublin, Ireland, 1694 p. (2014)
19. Socher, R., Perelygin, A., Wu, J.Y., Chuang, J., Manning, C.D., Ng, A.Y., Potts, C.: Recursive deep models for semantic compositionality over a sentiment treebank (2013)
20. Yang, M., Cui, T., Tu, W.: Ordering-sensitive and semantic-aware topic modeling. In: Computer Science (2015)
21. Le, Q.V., Mikolov, T.: Distributed representations of sentences and documents. In: Computer Science, vol. 4, p. 1188 (2014)
22. Rutherford, A.T., Xue, N.: Discovering implicit discourse relations through Brown cluster pair representation and conference patterns, vol. 645 (2014)
23. Rutherford, A., Xue, N.: Improving the inference of implicit discourse relations via classifying explicit discourse connectives. In: Conference of the North American Chapter of the Association for Computational Linguistics: Human Language Technologies (2015)
24. Marcus, M.P., Marcinkiewicz, M.A., Santorini, B.: Building a large annotated corpus of English: the Penn treebank. Comput. Linguist. 19, 313 (1993)
25. Wilson, T., Wiebe, J., Hoffmann, P.: Recognizing contextual polarity in phrase-level sentiment analysis. Int. J. Comput. Appl. 7, 347 (2005)
26. Stone, P.J.: The General Inquirer: A Computer Approach to Content Analysis. M.I.T. Press, Cambridge (1966)

Transition-Based Discourse Parsing with Multilayer Stack Long Short Term Memory

Yanyan Jia, Yansong Feng[(⊠)], Bingfeng Luo, Yuan Ye, Tianyang Liu, and Dongyan Zhao

Institute of Computer Science & Technology, Peking University, Beijing, China
{jiayanyan,fengyansong,bingfeng_luo,pkuyeyuan,
ltyang,zhaodongyan}@pku.edu.cn

Abstract. Discourse parsing aims to identify the relationship between different discourse units, where most previous works focus on recovering the constituency structure among discourse units with carefully designed features. In this paper, we propose to exploit Long Short Term Memory (LSTM) to properly represent discourse units, while using as few feature engineering as possible. Our transition based parsing model features a multilayer stack LSTM framework to discover the dependency structures among different units. Experiments on RST Discourse Treebank show that our model can outperform traditional feature based systems in terms of dependency structures, without complicated feature design. When evaluated in discourse constituency, our parser can also achieve promising performance compared to the state-of-the-art constituency discourse parsers.

1 Introduction

The task of discourse parsing is to identify the coherence relationship between discourse units which is important for many NLP tasks such as sentiment analysis [31], text summarization [24], question-answering [11] and so on.

Previously, constituency based discoursing parsing method [10,18,22] acts as the dominant parsing approach, though suffering from the high complexity and local maximum problem. One noteworthy work is [23]. They first apply dependency parsing to discourse since dependency trees contain much fewer nodes and with Rhetorical Structure Theory (RST) [25] analyzing the relations between element discourse unites (EDUs) is feasible and straightforward. In RST framework, text spans or EDUs are marked with nucleus or satellite according to their importance. The nucleus span is core of the discourse with essential information and the satellite span gives supporting evidence to the nucleus. However, [23] used Eisner Algorithm [8] and Maximum Spanning Tree Algorithm [26] which are both graph-based approaches. They suffer from two main problems. Firstly, they need sophisticated features to represent EDUs, as no grammatical or morphology information could help; Secondly, they suffer from Graph-based parsing method's $O(n^3)$ time complexity.

© Springer International Publishing AG 2016
C.-Y. Lin et al. (Eds.): NLPCC-ICCPOL 2016, LNAI 10102, pp. 360–373, 2016.
DOI: 10.1007/978-3-319-50496-4_30

Since deep learning methods have been booming recently and various models have been proposed such as Long Short Term Memory (LSTM) [17], Gated Recurrent Unit (GRU) [5], attention-based models [4] and enormous varieties. These models have gained significant results in many areas like sequence labeling, question answering and speech recognition. Hence, to address the first inefficient and complex feature engineering problem, we resort to neural network model to gain better performance with fewer features. To be specific, we propose to use LSTM to encode the long term parsing state with the memory-gate architecture using as few features as possible.

Furthermore, inspired by [2], they do sentence-level parsing by modeling characters instead of words and gain good performance in morphologically rich languages. We propose a new multilayer stack LSTM discourse parsing model with novel word based and word/pos based EDU representation methods which give each EDU a unique surface form or portray. However, intra-sentence character modeling for words and inter-sentence word modeling for EDUs are absolutely different tasks and the later is more difficult. Firstly, words have surface form, part of speech tag and the morphology spelling includes only 26 characters. But what do EDUs have? EDUs could contain diverse number of words from the over six hundred thousand words vocabulary taking English for example. There are out of vocabulary words and massive low term frequency words making EDU representation more difficult. Secondly, the number of words in EDUs could be more than the number of letters in the words and the order of the words arranged in the EDUs could be more diverse.

To solve the second problem, we adopt a transition-based dependency parsing model. Though time complexity decline to $O(n)$ with the transition-based parsing approach, most generally the overall accuracy will be worse than the graph-based parsing method, since the transition-based parsing works in a greedy way using the local optimization to gain the global optimization along with an error propagation problem. Hence this is a great challenge to our model and EDU representation method. However, encouragingly, our method gains a better result than the graph-based model with the same or even less features. Besides, this better result to some extent shows LSTM model's high capacity in discourse parsing.

The contribution of this paper is threefold. First, with our novel EDU representation method, each EDU obtains a unique "face" and this surface form helps saving human effort in designing various features. Second, we propose a novel multilayer LSTM model for dependency discourse parsing with encouraging results both in dependency structure and discourse constituency. Third, we initially propose to use LSTM to do dependency discourse parsing.

2   Related Work

Recently, LSTMs have been widely used in multiple NLP tasks with various structures. [30] proposed the tree structure LSTM and used it to predict semantic relevance. [13] investigated the use of Deep Bidirectional LSTM (DBLSTM) in a standard neural network-HMM hybrid system. [7] used a multilayer LSTM to parse the intra-sentence relation. All these tasks take advantage of LSTM's memory-gate mechanism which makes it easier to capture useful information both local and global. So, following [7], we adopt a stack LSTM to do the discourse parsing.

However, many previous works make great efforts in designing multiple features to represent EDUs. [23] used 6 sets of sophisticated features including 15 kinds of features and resources such as WordNet to gain a state-of-art accuracy. [16] used SVM with a greedy bottom-up way to do discourse segmentation and relation labeling. For encoding textual organization they listed 13 kinds of features along with dominance set as defined in [29]. [19] separated discourse parsing into two stages and used two Conditional Random Fields (CRFs) to do the intra-sentential parsing and multi-sentential parsing. They organized the features used in their parsing model into several sets including 8 organizational features, 4 text structural features, 8 n-gram features, 5 dominance set features, 8 lexical chain features, 2 contextual features and 2 substructure features.

Hence, we try to use as few feature engineering as possible to save human effort. With our stack LSTM model we gain an encouraging improvement compared with graph-based model when we use the same or even less features. Furthermore, our multilayer LSTM model with the novel EDU embedding method gives a new direction in modeling EDUs and could be improved in many ways. With this potential method people do not need to rack brains to design features elaborately.

3   Long Short Term Memory Theory

LSTM is designed to cope with the problem of vanishing or exponentially growing gradient over long sequence inherent in recurrent neural networks (RNNs). The typical LSTM cell contains an extra memory "cell" (c) and three kinds of multiplicative gates, the input gate (i), output gate (o) and forget gate (f). The memory cell collects inputs from the input gate and then pass them to the forget gate and finally to the output gate. This mechanism makes the useless information "forgotten" and only the helpful proportion of the current input remained. The computation functions are given below:

$$i_t = \sigma(W_{xi} \times x_t + W_{hi} \times h_{t-1} + W_{ci} \times c_{t-1} + b_i)$$

$$f_t = \sigma(W_{xf} \times x_t + W_{hf} \times h_{t-1} + W_{cf} \times c_{t-1} + b_f)$$

$$c_t = f_t \odot c_{t-1} + i_t \odot tanh(W_{xc} \times x_t + W_{hc} \times h_{t-1} + b_c)$$

$$o_t = \sigma(W_{xo} \times x_t + W_{ho} \times h_{t-1} + W_{co} \times c_t + b_o)$$

$$h_t = o_t \odot tanh(c_t)$$

Here σ is the logistic sigmoid function, $\odot$ denotes the element-wise multiplication operator; b is the bias and t is the time step, W is the weight matrices and h is the hidden state vector. See details in [9]. In this paper we use the multilayer stack LSTM to encode the parsing state. Details will be discussed in Sect. 5.

4 Transition-Based Parsing

Our parser is based on the arc-standard transition inventory [27]. There are four kinds of actions: SHIFT, SWAP, REDUCE-RIGHT and REDUCE-LEFT as shown in Table 1. We use three stacks: Buffer(B), Stack(S), Action(A) to load the input sequence, the dependency tree fragment and the history parsing actions. During decision making stage, when SHIFT operation is selected, the top element in B is popped and then pushed into S. Reduce action pop off two tree fragments from S (represented with m and n) and combine them into a new tree fragment represented with $g_r(M,N)$ or $g_r(N,M)$ depending on the direction of attachment (REDUCE-RIGHT or REDUCE-LEFT), which is then pushed back into S waiting to be processed next. Here m and n denote the tree fragments, M and N denotes the corresponding embeddings. With relation r, we use a recursive neural network g to compose the representations of the two subtrees. The resulting vector embeds the tree fragment in the same space as EDUs. The composition detail was thoroughly explored in prior work [28].

Table 1. Transition actions of the parser

$Stack_t$	$Buffer_t$	Action	$Stack_{t+1}$	$Buffer_{t+1}$	Dep
S	(M,m), B	SHIFT	(M,m), S	B	-
(M,m), (N,n), S	B	SWAP	(M,m), S	(N,n), B	-
(M,m), (N,n), S	B	REDUCE-RIGHT(r)	$(g_r(M,N),m)$, S	B	$m \xrightarrow{r} n$
(M,m), (N,n), S	B	REDUCE-LEFT(r)	$(g_r(N,M),n)$, S	B	$n \xrightarrow{r} m$

5 Method

5.1 EDU Representation

Features used in this paper are listed below:

(a) First, second and last word of the EDU;
(b) First, second and last word's POS tag of the EDU;
(c) Paragraph ID, inter paragraph order, sentence ID, inter sentence order (two form);
(d) 61 frequently used Conjunctions (not listed for space limitation);
(e) Whether the two top EDUs in S and B belong to the same sentence or paragraph;

5.1.1 Standard EDU Embedding Method

To represent the surface form of the input EDUs, we use the features listed in Sect. 5.1 to encode their property. Here we concatenate two kinds of vectors. Firstly, learned vector representations for each feature extracted from the EDU.

Secondly, a fixed vector representation(t) from other language models as pre-trained embedding. Here, we use Paragraph Vector [20] to provide the pre-trained embeddings of the EDUs and these vectors will not change in our model. In the Paragraph Vector framework the fixed length feature representations could encode variable length texts with an unsupervised algorithm. Hence we use it to encode the variable length EDUs. In this Framework, our model do not has a feature number limitation. However, since in this work we fight for using as fewer features as possible to gain high performance and saving human effort, we do not use too many sophisticated features as other works listed in Sect. 2.

We apply a linear map (F) to the resulting vector and passed through a component-wise ReLU as Eq. 1. Here, take first word of the EDU(w_1), POS tag of the first word(p_1) as example and fea_1 to fea_n could be any feature, b is the bias and t is the pre-trained embedding (optional).

$$x = max\{0, F(w_1, p_1, fea_1...fea_n, t) + b\} \tag{1}$$

5.1.2   Word Based and Word/POS Based EDU Embedding Method

We compute the continuous space vector embeddings of EDUs using bidirectional LSTMs [14] in the EDU embedding layer, multilayer LSTM details will be discussed in Sect. 5.3. Here, we discuss the word based embedding method of EDUs. This process is shown in Fig. 1. For example, when parsing the EDU: "He works in a small company named "OPOG".", the bidirectional LSTM reads the EDU twice, once in forward order and the other in reverse. Each word element is represented with an LSTM cell and we concatenate the two EDU vectors with the opposite directions to represent the EDU. Then the bidirectional LSTM embedding of the EDU is concatenated with other extracted feature representations. The equation is represented with Eq. 2. Here, $\vec{e}$ means the forward order EDU representation and $\overleftarrow{e}$ is the reverse order EDU representation, b is the bias, fea_1 and fea_n mean the standard features extracted from the EDU. However we do not use many sophisticated features and the experiment detail will be discussed in Sect. 6.

Additionally, we propose a word/pos based embedding method of EDUs. Words with low term frequency will be replaced with the pos tag of the corresponding word as shown in Fig. 1. We view words appear once in the corpus as low term frequency words. For example in "He works in a small company named "OPOG".", here, OPOG is a low term frequency word and we replace it with it's pos tag "NN". The computation is also done in EDU embedding layer as the word based EDU embedding method.

$$x = max\{0, F(\vec{e}, \overleftarrow{e}, fea_1...fea_n) + b\} \tag{2}$$

5.2   Stack LSTM

Following [7] we use stack LSTM to encode the states. There is a "stack pointer" (marked with "top" in Fig. 2) with each LSTM and it determines which cell in

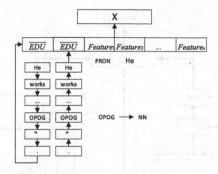

Fig. 1. Word based and word/POS based EDU embedding method

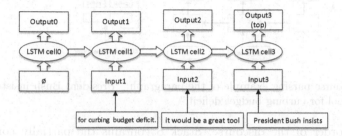

Fig. 2. Stack LSTM

the LSTM provides c_t and h_t when computing $t + 1$ time step memory cell contents. The stack LSTM provides PUSH and POP operations. POP operation moves the stack pointer to the previous element that could be placed in any location in the stack. PUSH operation adds a new element to the stack pointed by the previous top element (In Fig. 2 the "output3" element marked with "top" is pointed by the stack pointer). The output vector of the top element could be viewed as the "summary" of the contents with the current stack configuration and in this paper only the output vector of the top element is processed. For example, when parsing the paragraph shown in Fig. 2, the three golden divided EDUs (1. "President Bush insists"; 2. "it would be a great tool"; 3. "for curbing budget deficit.") serve as the input to the LSTM represented with the rectangle in the lowest row. Memory cells and gates illustrated with the oval are located in the middle row. The upper row gives the output of the LSTM represented with rectangle.

5.3 Multilayer Stack LSTM Discourse Parsing Model

Our arc-standard transition-based parsing model is equipped with three stacks (A, B, S) and takes the EDUs, actions and their intermediate embeddings as inputs. Each stack is a stack LSTM that provides embedding of their current contents. As Fig. 3, stack B contains the embedding of the input EDUs

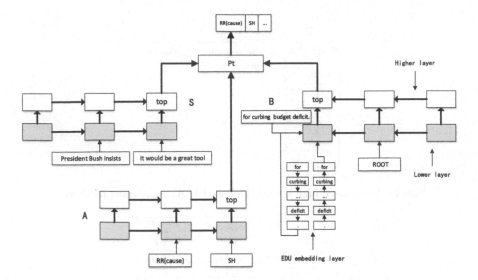

Fig. 3. Discourse parsing example of the paragraph: "President Bush insists it would be a great tool for curbing budget deficit."

in reverse order of the discourse. Stack S contains the partially constructed dependency subtrees with their embeddings. Stack A is used to preserve the history actions along with the corresponding relations taken by the parser. Actions used here include REDUCE-LEFT (RL), REDUCE-RIGHT (RR), SHIFT (SH) and SWAP (SW). Hence, in Fig. 3, "RR(cause)" means the action is REDUCE-RIGHT and the relation is "cause".

Notably, our model is a multilayer LSTM composed of three layers, EDU embedding layer, the lower layer and the higher layer. As illustrated in Fig. 3, we encode the EDU: "for curbing budget deficit." in EDU embedding layer and details are discussed in Sect. 5.1.2. Besides word based and word/POS based EDU embedding method, there can be many potential pre-processing method to encode EDUs.

Besides, based on the equations in Sect. 3, here, x_t is the input to the lower layer (gray rectangle) and h_t of the lower layer acts as the input to the higher layer (white rectangle). Output is produced from h_t at the top layer.

5.4   Parsing with Multilayer Stack LSTM Model

Initially, stack S and stack A only contain the empty symbol ($\emptyset$). The discourse to be parsed is located in B with reading order from top to the bottom (the "ROOT" symbol). The parsing unit is EDU. At each time step, based on the configurations of B, S and A, the parser computes the representation of the current stack state, predicts the action to take and updates the stacks. Until S contains the full parse tree rooted with the "ROOT" symbol and an empty symbol, B only contains the empty symbol and A filled with all the shift-reduce actions and relations taken by the parser, the parsing process completes.

The action predicting formulas are listed below. In Eq. 3, s_t, b_t and a_t are the LSTM embedding of the three stacks; W is a parameter matrix to be learned and c is the bias. These parameters pass through a rectified linear unit (ReLU) nonlinearity [12] to compute the parser state representation at time t represented by p_t.

$$p_t = max\{0, W(s_t, b_t, a_t) + c\} \qquad (3)$$

Then we apply an affine transform to the embedding of p_t and transfer it to the softmax layer to produce a distribution over parsing decisions (actions and relations) as shown in Eq. 4. The parsing actions could be the four kinds of actions listed in Table 1. Here, g_z is a row vector representing the output embedding of the parser action z. b_z is the bias of action z and $A(S, B)$ is the set of the feasible actions that could be taken given the current state of the stacks. According to the chain rule, the probability of the parsing actions z conditioned on the input could be represented as Eq. 5.

$$p(z_t | p_t) = \frac{exp(g_{z_t} \times p_t + b_{z_t})}{\sum_{z' \in A(S,B)} exp(g_{z'} \times p_t + b_{z'})} \qquad (4)$$

$$p(z|w) = \prod_{t=1}^{|z|} p(z_t | p_t) \qquad (5)$$

5.5 Composition Functions

As discussed in Sect. 4, we use recursive neural network as our composition function to encode the dependency tree fragment in stack S in the same vector space as EDU embeddings. We apply the composition function to the <head(h), modifier(d), relation(r)> triples. We concatenate the vectors of the head, modifier and relation, then apply a linear operator and a component-wise nonlinearity. See Eq. 6, we use the parser action (such as syntactic relation and direction of attachment) to encode the relation vector.

$$c = tanh(0, V(h, d, r) + b) \qquad (6)$$

6 Experiment

6.1 Data

RST Discourse Treebank [3] is a corpus annotated in the framework of RST theory which contains 385 documents from the Wall Street Journal. To make fair comparison with [23], we follow them to use 380 documents to do the experiments, 342 for training and 38 for testing. Totally, there are 21111 EDUs and 8272 sentences in detail. Every document contains 55 EDUs in average and every sentence contains 2.55 EDUs in average. In this paper we use the 111 fine-grained relations and gain the POS tags using NLTK maxent_treebank_pos_tagger.

6.2 Results and Discussion

6.2.1 Results with Standard EDU Embedding Method

With the standard EDU embedding method in Sect. 5.1.1, we list results in Table 2. Here we cite results of [23] with their feature sets 1 and 2[1] including 8 features. We listed the methods for comparison, "Eisner" and "MST" are algorithms in [23]. "EDUVEC" means paragraph vector of the EDU and used only in this sub-section, all the experiments in other sub-sections exclude the EDUVEC. "FW" means first word of the EDU, "FP" means the first word's POS tag, "LW" means the last word of the EDU and "Feature only" means we exclude EDUVEC and only use features in the standard EDU embedding way. Here LAS means labeled accuracy, with relation and head. UAS means unlabeled accuracy, with head only.

We can see in Table 2 with only the EDUVEC and no features, the UAS rises encouragingly to 38.79%. This is a good proof for the high power of LSTM model to do discourse parsing. Compared with [23] we use only two features, first word of the EDU(FW), first word's POS of the EDU(FP) in their large feature set 1 and set 2, the UAS rises to 50.04% and both the UAS and LAS are higher than their better Eisner method by 12.61% and 2.39%. When we include the last word(LW) the UAS and LAS are higher than Eisner by 16.91% and 4.87%.

This means our stack LSTM model could gain much higher result than [23], even when we use much fewer features. LSTM discourse parsing model with standard EDU embedding method could gain a much higher result with fewer features over graph-based parsing method even with transition-based framework. That is a solid proof to LSTM model's suitability for discourse parsing task especially when people want to save efforts in designing sophisticated features.

6.2.2 Results with Word Based and Word/POS Based EDU Embedding Method

With the method in Sect. 5.1, the results are listed in Table 3. We use feature sets: a, b, c, d listed in Sect. 5.1 and "Feature only" means we use the standard EDU embedding method in Sect. 5.1.1, here it is the baseline. "WME" means the word based EDU embedding method discussed in Sect. 5.1.2. Though this is a good direction in embedding EDUs, but there are 19262 tokens in the vocabulary, including upper or lower case of the same words, numbers, special symbols and low term frequency words. These will inevitably give bad effect on the accuracy. So we replace various numbers in the vocabulary with the same token and only use the lower case of the word, hence 15696 tokens remain and

---

[1] In Table 2 row ID 1 and row ID 2, we use results of [23] when they do experiment with their whole feature set 1 and feature set 2. We list their two feature sets below:
(1) WORD: The first one word, the last one word, and the first bigrams in each EDU, the pair of the two first words and the pair of the two last words in the two EDUs are extracted as features.
(2) POS: The first one and two POS tags in each EDU, and the pair of the two first POS tags in the two EDUs are extracted as features.

Table 2. Comparison with graph-based discourse parsing method

ID	Method	Features	UAS	LAS
1	Eisner	8 features (set 1 + set 2)	0.3743	0.2421
2	MST	8 features (set 1 + set 2)	0.2080	0.1300
3	EDUVEC	NONE	**0.3879**	0.0356
4	EDUVEC + FW	FW	**0.5029**	**0.2467**
5	EDUVEC + FP	FP	**0.3968**	0.1745
6	Feature only	FW + FP	**0.5004**	**0.2660**
7	EDUVEC + FW + FP	FW + FP	**0.5141**	0.2523
8	Feature only	FW + FP + LW	**0.5434**	**0.2908**

the UAS raises to 57.78 %. Both the UAS and LAS are higher than the baseline by 1.05% and 2.09%. These give a potential on other EDU pre-processing method. "WPE" means the word/POS based EDU embedding method discussed in Sect. 5.1.2. When we replace words with low term frequency (tokens appear once in vocabulary) with their POS tags, the vocabulary size decline to 8256 tokens. The UAS rises to 58.61% and 1.88% higher than the baseline.

These results show our new multilayer stack LSTM discourse parsing model with novel EDU embedding method is stronger than the baseline (two layer stack LSTM model without the EDU embedding layer). Our novel EDU embedding method is a potential improvement direction in discourse parsing since this method gives each EDU an portray and could be improved in many ways because besides words' surface form and POS tag, other information could be used in the same way and encode the EDUs into our multilayer stack LSTM discourse parsing model. And this method is useful especially when people do not want to or can not design complex features.

Table 3. Parsing results with word based and word/Pos based EDU embedding method

ID	Method	Features	UAS	LAS
1	Feature only	a + b + c + d	0.5673	0.3065
2	Feature + WME	a + b + c + d	**0.5778**	**0.3274**
3	Feature + WPE	a + b + c + d	**0.5861**	**0.3214**

6.2.3 Comparison with Structured Perceptron Based Dependency Discourse Parsing

In order to verify the ability of our multilayer LSTM discourse parser, we implement a dependency discourse parser in perceptron based shift-reduce framework with early update strategy [6] as our baseline. The input EDUs are initially sent to a queue and the algorithm removes the EDUs and pushes them into a stack which stores the temporary dependency structures of the processed part of EDUs according to the transition rules. The algorithm terminates when the queue is empty. With an arc-eager style, the perceptron based parser have four actions: Left-ARC, Right-Arc, Reduce and Shift, details could resort to [1]. Further, We use four perceptrons to predict the score for each transition action and train them in a greedy way. Before each transition, the perceptron predicts the best action instead of the LSTM. We use the features listed in Sect. 5.1 (set a, b, c, d) and use 72 feature templates including the first, second and third element's fea_i of the 12 features both in the queue and the stack. This is the method "Perceptron" in Table 4. "LSTM" means the stack LSTM with standard EDU embedding method in Sect. 5.1.1, and "WME" and "WPE" have the same meaning as Table 3.

As seen in Table 4, with the standard EDU embedding method, the two layer LSTM discourse parser has an UAS of 56.73%, about 3.62% higher than the baseline but the LAS is lower for 0.55%. But with our word/POS based EDU embedding method in Sect. 5.1.2, our multilayer LSTM parser wins both in UAS and LAS when we use the same feature sets a, b, c, d. In order to test the performance with complex features we add the pairwise features as [23], so we add feature set e, this time both the WME and WPE raise. Finally, after tuning the dimensions of the LSTM parameters, "LSTMT + WME" gains the higher results.

Though, with few simple features our results have gap with the state-of-art, but [23] use many complex features such as bigrams, pairwise words, pairwise POS tags and pairwise intra sentence/paragraph position, length of EDU, dominate nodes, semantic similarity from WordNet that we all exclude. Our focus is to verify the LSTM like deep learning method's ability in saving human feature design effort especially with the EDU's given "face" (word based and word/POS based EDU embedding method in Sect. 5.1.2). And our WPE and WME have already win the perceptron based parser (with 72 feature template) using the same four feature sets.

Table 4. Comparison with perceptron based dependency discourse parser

ID	Method	Features	UAS	LAS
1	Perceptron	72 feature templates	0.5311	0.3120
2	LSTM	a + b + c + d	**0.5673**	0.3065
3	LSTM + WME	a + b + c + d	**0.5778**	**0.3274**
4	LSTM + WPE	a + b + c + d	**0.5861**	**0.3214**
5	LSTM + WME	a + b + c + d + e	**0.5968**	**0.3453**
6	LSTM + WPE	a + b + c + d + e	**0.5929**	**0.3316**
7	LSTMT + WME	a + b + c + d + e	**0.6142**	**0.3410**

6.2.4 Performance in Discourse Constituency

We also evaluate our parser in term of discourse constituency where we evaluate the parsing performance with F measure [15] of the blank tree structure (S), the tree structure with nuclearity indication (N) and the tree structure with rhetorical relation indication but no nuclearity indication (R). To compare our dependency parsing results with constituency works, we convert the dependency trees to constituency trees. In Table 5, other discourse parsing methods include: (1) "Eisner": the state-of-art dependency parser with their full 6 sets features. (2) "Perceptron": our perceptron based dependency parser as discussed in Sect. 6.2.3 with 72 feature templates designed from feature sets a,b,c,d. (3) "HILDA": SVM based constituency discourse parser [16]. (4) "LeThanh": multi-level rule based constituency parser [21]. (5) "Marcu": decision tree based constituency parser [15]. "LSTM + WPE(abcd)" is our multilayer stack LSTM dependency parser with word/POS based embedding method and feature set a, b, c, d. "LSTM + WME(abcde)" is our word based embedding method with feature set a, b, c, d, e. With few features, "LSTM + WME(abcde)" wins all the other parsers except Eisner (Eisner uses their full 6 sets more complex features, we only use our smaller five simple feature sets) although we are not designed specially for constituency parsing.

Table 5. Comparison in discourse constituency

ID	Method	S	N	R
1	Eisner	83.4	73.8	57.8
2	LSTM + WME(abcde)	**80.90**	**66.07**	**51.37**
3	LSTM + WPE(abcd)	**79.89**	**63.66**	**49.56**
4	Perceptron	76.22	59.98	44.99
5	HILDA	72.3	59.1	47.8
6	LeThanh	53.7	47.1	39.9
7	Marcu	44.8	30.9	18.8

7 Conclusion

In this paper, we first propose to use LSTM for discourse parsing, with this method people could use as few feature engineering as possible to gain high performance. Then we propose a novel multilayer stack LSTM dependency discourse parsing model with word based and word/POS based EDU representation which are potential improvement direction in discourse parsing. With this multilayer LSTM discourse parsing model, we gain better performance than perceptron based discourse parser and graph-based model under the same or even worse feature condition. Even when evaluated in discourse constituency, our results are still encouraging compared to the state-of-the-art constituency discourse parsers.

Acknowledgments. We would like to thank Sujian Li, Liang Wang, and the anonymous reviewers for their helpful feedback. This work is supported by National High Technology R&D Program of China (Grant Nos. 2015AA015403, 2014AA015102), Natural Science Foundation of China (Grant Nos. 61202233, 61272344, 61370055) and the joint project with IBM Research. For any correspondence, please contact Yansong Feng.

References

1. Abney, S.P., Johnson, M.: Memory requirements and local ambiguities of parsing strategies. J. Psycholinguist. Res. **20**, 233–250 (1991)
2. Ballesteros, M., Dyer, C., Smith, N.A.: Improved transition-based parsing by modeling characters instead of words with LSTMs. In: EMNLP 2015, Lisbon, Portugal, pp. 349–359 (2015)
3. Carlson, L., Marcu, D., Okurowski, M.E.: Building a discourse-tagged corpus in the framework of rhetorical structure theory. In: SIGdial Workshop, pp. 1–10 (2001)
4. Chorowski, J., Bahdanau, D., Serdyuk, D., Cho, K., Bengio, Y.: Attention-based models for speech recognition (2015). CoRR arXiv:1506.07503
5. Chung, J., Gülçehre, Ç., Cho, K., Bengio, Y.: Empirical evaluation of gated recurrent neural networks on sequence modeling (2014). CoRR arXiv:1412.3555
6. Collins, M., Roark, B.: Incremental parsing with the perceptron algorithm. In: Proceedings of 42nd Annual Meeting of the Association for Computational Linguistics, Barcelona, Spain, 21–26 July 2004, pp. 111–118 (2004)
7. Dyer, C., Ballesteros, M., Ling, W., Matthews, A., Smith, N.A.: Transition-based dependency parsing with stack long short-term memory. In: ACL 2015, Beijing, vol. 1, pp. 334–343 (2015)
8. Eisner, J.: Three new probabilistic models for dependency parsing: an exploration. In: COLING 1996, 5–9 August 1996, pp. 340–345 (1996)
9. Eyben, F., Böck, S., Schuller, B.W., Graves, A.: Universal onset detection with bidirectional long short-term memory neural networks. In: ISMIR 2010, Utrecht, Netherlands, 9–13 August 2010, pp. 589–594 (2010)
10. Feng, V.W., Hirst, G.: A linear-time bottom-up discourse parser with constraints and post-editing. In: ACL 2014, Baltimore, MD, USA, vol. 1, pp. 511–521 (2014)
11. Ferrucci, D.A., Brown, E.W., Chu-Carroll, J., Fan, J., Gondek, D., Kalyanpur, A., Lally, A., Murdock, J.W., Nyberg, E., Prager, J.M., Schlaefer, N., Welty, C.A.: Building Watson: an overview of the DeepQA project. AI Mag. **31**(3), 59–79 (2010)
12. Glorot, X., Bordes, A., Bengio, Y.: Deep sparse rectifier neural networks. In: AISTATS 2011, Fort Lauderdale, USA, 11–13 April 2011, pp. 315–323 (2011)
13. Graves, A., Jaitly, N., Mohamed, A.: Hybrid speech recognition with deep bidirectional LSTM. In: 2013 IEEE Workshop on Automatic Speech Recognition and Understanding, Olomouc, Czech Republic, 8–12 December 2013, pp. 273–278 (2013)
14. Graves, A., Schmidhuber, J.: Framewise phoneme classification with bidirectional LSTM and other neural network architectures. Neural Netw. **18**(5–6), 602–610 (2005)
15. Hahn, U.: The theory and practice of discourse parsing and summarization by Daniel Marcu. Comput. Linguist. **28**(1), 81–83 (2002)
16. Hernault, H., Prendinger, H., duVerle, D.A., Ishizuka, M.: HILDA: a discourse parser using support vector machine classification. D&D **1**(3), 1–33 (2010)
17. Hochreiter, S., Schmidhuber, J.: Long short-term memory. Neural Comput. **9**(8), 1735–1780 (1997)

18. Ji, Y., Eisenstein, J.: One vector is not enough: entity-augmented distributed semantics for discourse relations. TACL **3**, 329–344 (2015)
19. Joty, S.R., Carenini, G., Ng, R.T., Mehdad, Y.: Combining intra- and multi-sentential rhetorical parsing for document-level discourse analysis. In: ACL 2013, Sofia, Bulgaria, vol. 1, pp. 486–496 (2013)
20. Le, Q.V., Mikolov, T.: Distributed representations of sentences and documents. In: ICML 2014, Beijing, China, 21–26 June 2014, pp. 1188–1196 (2014)
21. LeThanh, H.: Generating discourse structures for written texts. In: Proceedings of 20th International Conference on Computational Linguistics, pp. 329–335 (2004)
22. Li, J., Li, R., Hovy, E.H.: Recursive deep models for discourse parsing. In: EMNLP 2014, Doha, Qatar, 25–29 October 2014, pp. 2061–2069 (2014)
23. Li, S., Wang, L., Cao, Z., Li, W.: Text-level discourse dependency parsing. In: ACL 2014, Baltimore (vol. 1: Long Papers), pp. 25–35 (2014)
24. Louis, A., Joshi, A.K., Nenkova, A.: Discourse indicators for content selection in summarization. In: SIGDIAL 2010 Conference, Tokyo, Japan, pp. 147–156 (2010)
25. Mann, W., Thompson, S.: Rhetorical structure theory: toward a functional theory of text organization. Text-Interdiscip. J. Study Discourse **8**, 243–281 (1988)
26. McDonald, R.T., Crammer, K., Pereira, F.C.N.: Online large-margin training of dependency parsers. In: ACL 2005, University of Michigan, USA (2005)
27. Nivre, J., Scholz, M.: Deterministic dependency parsing of english text. In: COLING 2004, Geneva, Switzerland, 23–27 August 2004 (2004)
28. Socher, R., Karpathy, A., Le, Q.V., Manning, C.D., Ng, A.Y.: Grounded compositional semantics for finding and describing images with sentences. TACL **2**, 207–218 (2014)
29. Soricut, R., Marcu, D.: Sentence level discourse parsing using syntactic and lexical information. In: HLT-NAACL (2003)
30. Tai, K.S., Socher, R., Manning, C.D.: Improved semantic representations from tree-structured long short-term memory networks. In: ACL 2015, Beijing, pp. 1556–1566 (2015)
31. Voll, K., Taboada, M.: Not all words are created equal: extracting semantic orientation as a function of adjective relevance. In: Orgun, M.A., Thornton, J. (eds.) AI 2007. LNCS (LNAI), vol. 4830, pp. 337–346. Springer, Heidelberg (2007). doi:10.1007/978-3-540-76928-6_35

Predicting Implicit Discourse Relation with Multi-view Modeling and Effective Representation Learning

Haoran Li[1,2], Jiajun Zhang[1,2], Yu Zhou[1,2], and Chengqing Zong[1,2(✉)]

[1] National Laboratory of Pattern Recognition,
Institute of Automation Chinese Academy of Sciences, Beijing, China
{haoran.li,jjzhang,yzhou,cqzong}@nlpr.ia.ac.cn
[2] University of Chinese Academy of Sciences, Beijing, China

Abstract. Discourse relations between two text segments play an important role in many natural language processing (NLP) tasks. The connectives strongly indicate the sense of discourse relations, while in fact, there are no connectives in a large proportion of discourse relations, i.e., implicit discourse relations. The key for implicit relation prediction is to correctly model the semantics of the two discourse arguments as well as the contextual interaction between them. To achieve this goal, we propose a multi-view framework that consists of two hierarchies. The first one is the model hierarchy and we propose a neural network based method considering different views. The second one is the feature hierarchy and we learn multi-level distributed representations. We have conducted experiments on the standard benchmark dataset and the results show that compared with several methods our proposed method can achieve the best performance in most cases.

1 Introduction

Discourse relation inference is a pivotal task for discourse analysis. According to whether there are connectives or not, discourse relations can be categorized into explicit and implicit relations. The goal of our task is to recognize implicit discourse relations existing between two given discourse arguments. Most of the existing work regards this task as a classification problem and typical classifier such as SVM are leveraged to perform this task. Recently, neural networks are employed to boost the recognition performance.

Besides the model, the features are also important. The previous work usually resorts to discrete features [1,8,10,11,13,15] which strongly depend on the linguistic lexicons and lead to data sparsity. Recently, many studies [3,5,18,24] demonstrate that the distributed representations can improve implicit relation prediction. However, the distributed representations focus only on certain aspects, such as surface words or arguments, which lack modeling multi-level features.

In this paper, we propose a multi-view framework to tackle implicit relation recognition and the architecture of our model is shown in Fig. 1. Our framework

© Springer International Publishing AG 2016
C.-Y. Lin et al. (Eds.): NLPCC-ICCPOL 2016, LNAI 10102, pp. 374–386, 2016.
DOI: 10.1007/978-3-319-50496-4_31

consists of two hierarchies. One is the model hierarchy (Fig. 1(b)) which is based on neural network modeling discourse relations from the relation classification view and the relation transformation view. The other is the feature hierarchy (Fig. 1(a)) which learns distributed representations from different levels, namely from words, arguments, syntactic structures to sentences.

We make the following contributions in this paper.

- We design a multi-view neural network model to recognize implicit discourse relations considering the interactions between two discourse arguments and the relation transformation property.
- We propose to represent discourse arguments by multi-level distributed features, from words, arguments, syntactic structures to sentences.

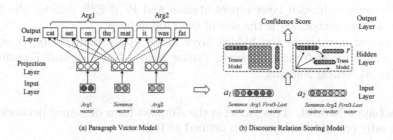

(a) Paragraph Vector Model   (b) Discourse Relation Scoring Model

Fig. 1. The architecture of our model. To simplify the figure we neglect the word vectors of the input layer in the Paragraph Vector Model.

Table 1. Implicit discourse relation examples in PDTB

1	Sense	Comparison.Contrast
	Arg1	The common view is that there will be mild economic growth, modest profit expansion, and things are going to be hunky-dory
	Arg2	Our view is that we may see a profit decline
2	Sense	Expansion.Instantiation
	Arg1	Futures prices declined
	Arg2	One below 50 indicates a contraction may be ahead

2 Overview of the Penn Discourse Treebank

The PDTB [16] is the largest available English discourse corpus. The senses of discourse relations are organized into a hierarchical structure in which the top level contains four major classes: Comparison, Contingency, Expansion and Temporal. The next two levels consist of more fine-grained relation types. A discourse relation instance consists of two arguments denoted by *Arg1* and *Arg2*. We give two examples in PDTB in Table 1.

3   Model

3.1   Discourse Relation Scoring Model

As shown in Fig. 1(b), each discourse relation argument pair is represented as two dense embeddings a_1 and $a_2 \in \mathbb{R}^{H_1}$ where H_1 is the size of the embeddings. The representation learning of a_1 and a_2 will be introduced in Sect. 4. Then a_1 and a_2 serve as input of the neural network model in which we design multiple kinds of hidden layers. Above the hidden layer, the model outputs a confidence score for specific relations using a linear transformation of the following function:

$$f(a_1, a_2) = W^T h$$

$h \in \mathbb{R}^{H_2}$ denotes hidden layer representation and $W \in \mathbb{R}^{H_2}$ denotes the linear transformation vector. H_2 is the size of the hidden layer.

To better investigate the hidden layer h, we apply multiple types of networks: Single-Layer Neural Network, Tensor Neural Network and Transformation (Trans) Neural Network.

Single-Layer Model. This model is the simplest form of neural network containing only one hidden layer. It is defined as follows:

$$h = tanh(W_s[a_1; a_2] + b_s)$$

where $W_s \in \mathbb{R}^{H_2 \times 2H_1}$ and $b_s \in \mathbb{R}^{H_2}$. $[a_1; a_2] \in \mathbb{R}^{2H_1}$ denotes concatenation of a_1 and a_2.

Tensor Model. A tensor is a multi-dimensional array that can connect two input vectors in every dimension. Tensor model has been widely used in many NLP tasks [14,20]. It can be defined as follows:

$$h = tanh(a_1^T W_t^{[1:H_2]} a_2 + W_s[a_1; a_2] + b_s)$$

where $W_t^{[1:H_2]} \in \mathbb{R}^{H_1 \times H_1 \times H_2}$ is a H_2-way tensor.

Tensor model can be regarded as an extreme form of feature combination as the input embedding pair can be multiplicatively related element by element. Intuitively, different explicit interactions among argument pair can be modeled by each slice of tensor independently.

Trans Model. This model intends to explicitly explore relations between arguments by modeling the relative position information of arguments in the vector space, which can be defined as follows:

$$h = tanh(W_e(a_1 + r - a_2) + W_s[a_1; a_2] + b_s)$$

where $W_e \in \mathbb{R}^{H_2 \times H_1}$ and $r \in \mathbb{R}^{H_1}$.

The transformation operation can be explained as follows: if $Arg1$ and $Arg2$ hold a relation rel, there should be a specific spatial relationship measure that captures the relation between these two arguments. To be straightforward, we expect a transformation embedding r representing relation rel, such that a_1 can correlate to a_2 after adding r. The motivation comes from the work of Mikolov et al. [12], in which the authors state that semantic relations between two words could be found in the embeddings space such as $Paris$ - $France$ = $Rome$ - $Italy$. The work most related to our Trans model is the study of Bordes et al. [2], in which the authors propose a TransE model to learn the entity relations.

TTNN Model. We integrate **T**ensor and **T**rans **N**eural **N**etwork to create a new model called **TTNN** model which is defined as follows:

$$h = tanh(a_1^T W_t^{[1:H_2]} a_2 + W_e(a_1 + r - a_2) + W_s[a_1; a_2] + b_s)$$

Tensor model focuses on the view of interaction between arguments. Trans model intends to explore the view of relative position information of two arguments in the embedding space. Therefore our combined multi-view model should have much more expressive power than each single model.

3.2 Max-Margin Learning

After we obtain the relation score of discourse argument pair, we apply max-margin learning framework to optimize the neural network. We define different objective functions for two implicit discourse relation recognition tasks, i.e., binary classification for first-level discourse relations and multiclass classification for second-level discourse relations.

For binary classification, given a training set R of all the (a_1, a_2) pairs with the specific discourse relations, we minimize an objective function defined as follows:

$$L_1(\theta) = \sum_{(a_1,a_2) \in R} \sum_{(a_1',a_2') \notin R} \max\{0, 1 - f(a_1, a_2) + f(a_1', a_2')\} + \lambda \|\theta\|_2^2$$

For each positive discourse argument pair (a_1, a_2), we randomly sample a certain number of negative pairs (a_1', a_2') that do not hold the same discourse relation as (a_1, a_2). L_2 regularization is used to penalize the size of all the parameters to prevent overfitting, which is weighted by λ. The objective function L_1 favors higher score for positive training pairs than for negative pairs.

In the testing phase, for each one of the four binary classification sub-tasks, we first use the development set to obtain a threshold T_{rel} for relation rel so that for each argument pair in testing set if $f(a_1, a_2) \geqslant T_{rel}$, then (a_1, a_2) holds the relation rel.

For multiclass classification, we minimize an objective function defined as follows:

$$L_2(\theta) = \sum_{(a_1,a_2)\in R} \sum_{f':f'\neq f} \max\{0, 1 - f^+(a_1,a_2) + f^-(a_1,a_2)\} + \lambda \|\theta\|_2^2$$

For each discourse argument pair (a_1, a_2) holding the specific discourse relation rel_i, we score it with $\theta_{rel} = \{W^{rel}, W_s^{rel}, W_t^{rel}, W_e^{rel}, b^{rel}\}_{rel=rel_i}$ as $f^+(a_1, a_2)$, and with $\theta_{rel'} = \{W^{rel'}, W_s^{rel'}, W_t^{rel'}, W_e^{rel'}, b^{rel'}\}_{rel'\neq rel_i}$ as $f^-(a_1, a_2)$. The objective function L_2 favors higher score for training pairs (a_1, a_2) with series of parameters corresponding to their classes rel_i than with any other series of parameters corresponding to the classes rel' which is not rel_i.

In the testing phase, for each argument pair (a_1, a_2), we score it with the series of parameters for all relations, among which the relation rel with the highest score is held.

4   Multi-level Representations for the Arguments

It is crucial to effectively represent the arguments. Previous work mostly explore various surface features, which cannot capture the features at the segment level. Neural network models can learn segment level information, but the word level information is ignored. Furthermore, syntactic features have been proven to be effective. This motivates us to seek a novel approach that covers not only the multi-level features from token to segments, but also both lexical and syntactic features.

Token Level Lexical Features. Pitler et al. [15] proposes to use the first three and the last words of the argument as features, where connective-like expressions often appear. Thus, we introduce embeddings of tokens that are located at the first three and the last positions of the arguments, which is called **First3-Last** embedding. To obtain the First3-Last embedding, we can simply concatenate or average the embeddings of the first three and the last tokens. The token-level representations can be fine-tuned during training. The token level embeddings are obtained by Word2Vec[1] and we train the model with random initializations.

Segment Level Lexical Features. In addition to token level embeddings, segment embeddings are also indispensable. Segment embeddings learned using a small corpus PDTB[2] through supervised methods [5, 24] cannot beat the surface features, which is in accord with the conclusions of Braud et al. [3]. Paragraph Vector Model, as the augmentation of Word2Vec model, can learn segment level representations in an unsupervised way. In this way, we can obtain the **Sentence embeddings**. Specifically, in order to obtain the **Arguments embeddings**, we

---

[1] https://code.google.com/p/word2vec/.

[2] PDTB contains only 16,053 implicit discourse relation instances.

assign to them vectors that participate in predicting the target word as sentence vectors do. An example is shown in Fig. 1(a). Note that "Sentence" here means an argument pair.

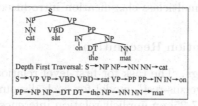

Fig. 2. Linearizations of a parse tree by depth first traversal.

Syntactic Features. To infer the implicit relation between two arguments, the structure difference between them may provide some clues. Lin et al. [8] propose to employ the production rules extracted from constituent parse trees as features and since then these features have been widely used in implicit discourse relation recognition. Some production rule examples in Fig. 2 are: S → NP VP, NN → "cat". Li and Nenkova [7] propose a "stick" version of production rules by splitting all the children of a (parent, children) production rule into several sticks where each one only contains one child. For instance, S → NP VP is converted to S → NP and S → VP. Through depth-first traversal, we linearize a constituent parser tree to a production stick sequence which is shown in Fig. 2. Then, we can learn multi-level distributed representations of syntactic features (in the form of production stick sequences) in the same way as lexical features. The syntactic embeddings are obtained by Word2Vec. For example, the token level syntactic embedding is a representation for each production stick and segment level syntactic embedding is a representation for a production stick sequence.

5 Implementation Details

The optimization is carried out by L-BFGS-B [21] with batch normalization [4] in which we update the model parameters $\{W, W_s, W_t, W_e, b\}$ and word embeddings. We also try AdaGrad but find that it does not work well. We apply norm clipping with a threshold of 5 to overcome the gradient exploding problem and early stop with the development set to avoid overfitting. We select the dimensions of sentences, arguments and word embeddings d among $\{25, 50, 100\}$, learning rate η among $\{0.01, 0.001, 0.0001\}$, regularization parameter λ among $\{0.01, 0.001, 0.0001\}$, number of negative samples for binary classification N among $\{10, 30, 50, 100\}$, and size of the hidden layer as well as number of slices in tensor H_2 among $\{3, 5, 10, 15\}$. The optimal configurations are determined according to the performance on the development set. The chosen configurations are $d = 25$, $\eta = 0.001$, $\lambda = 0.0001$, $N = 50$. For binary classification, $H_2 = 10$, while for multiclass classification, $H_2 = 3$.

6   Experiments

We test our method on PDTB dataset in two tasks including first-level discourse relation binary classification which attracts more attention recently and second-level discourse relation multiclass classification introduced by Lin et al. [8].

6.1   First-Level Relation Recognition

Experimental Settings. The task for first-level relation binary classification is to construct a "one-versus-rest" model for each discourse relation. Following the previous work [15,17,25] on implicit relation inference, we use sections 2–20 of PDTB as the training set, sections 0–1 as the development set and sections 21–22 as the test set. Note that the data preparation for Expansion relation follows the work of Zhou et al. [25] and Rutherford and Xue [17]. It is different from the work of Pitler et al. [15] and Ji and Eisenstein [5] in which they regard EntRel relation as a part of Expansion.

To evaluate the effect of syntactic feature on real world data, we do not use the gold standard parse results provided by the Penn Treebank. Our constituent parse results are obtained by using the Stanford Parser [6]. We also employ lowercasing and tokenization. To enlarge the data scale for Paragraph Vector training, we employ a large-scale unlabeled monolingual data from Reuters. From the raw Reuters data, we choose only the sentences in which all the words should appear in PDTB so as to avoid noise. The selected Reuters corpus contains 1.7 billion tokens and 67.2 million sentences. We obtain First3-Last embeddings via an averaging operation and keep them fixed during training. A detailed comparison of different First3-Last embedding compositions will be given on the second-level classification task.

With different lexical and syntactic features, i.e., production rules, we test Single-Layer (SL), Tensor, Trans models and the hybrid TTNN model respectively. The results are reported in Table 2. Finally, we integrate multi-level lexical and syntactic information by summing up the confidence scores obtained by the models with these two features for each instance. Table 3 presents the final performance of our model compared with that of other competitive methods.

Experimental Results. In this section, we try to answer three questions: (1) which model for discourse relation scoring performs better; (2) which kinds of distributed features are more effective.

The detailed experimental results listed in Table 2 can answer the first two questions. Overall, among all four models, the hybrid TTNN is superior to others, and among the three single models, Tensor model has similar performance to Trans model, which is obviously better than Single-Layer model. Regarding the features, the syntactic features perform better and achieve the best performance in most cases over the four relations.

The results shown in Table 3 can answer the last question. The experimental results in Table 3 tell us that our method can achieve the best performance in

Table 2. The performance (F1-score/%) on recognizing first-level implicit discourse relation with different features and models on PDTB test set.

	SL	Tensor	Trans	TTNN
Comparison				
Lexical	36.31	40.01	38.29	**41.82**
Syntactic	36.75	39.69	39.34	41.39
Contingency				
Lexical	48.49	51.30	50.10	52.31
Syntactic	48.53	52.35	51.29	**54.17**
Expansion				
Lexical	65.69	70.11	71.07	71.03
Syntactic	66.83	70.90	70.91	**71.08**
Temporal				
Lexical	28.81	31.64	30.09	32.75
Syntactic	29.12	31.81	31.57	**34.04**

Table 3. The performance (F1-score/%) for first-level discourse relation classification using multi-level lexical and syntactic features on PDTB test set.

	COM.	CON.	EXP.	TEM.
Pitler et al. (2009)	21.96	47.13	–	16.76
Zhou et al. (2010)	31.79	47.16	65.95	20.30
Rutherford et al. (2014)	39.70	54.42	70.23	28.69
Ji and Eisenstein (2015)	35.93	52.78	–	27.63
Braud and Denis (2015)	36.36	**55.76**	67.42	29.30
Zhang et al. (2015)	34.22	52.04	69.59	30.54
Liu et al. (2016)	37.91	55.88	69.97	**37.17**
TTNN (ours)	**41.91**	54.72	**71.54**	34.78

Comparison and Expansion relation recognition tasks when compared to the state-of-the-art approaches (significantly better, McNemar's Chisquared test, $p < 0.05$). We obtain a competitive result for the Contingency and Temporal relation. These results demonstrate that our method is promising for implicit discourse relation inference.

6.2 Second-Level Relation Recognition

Experimental Settings. This task belongs to a multiclass classification. Following the work of Ji and Eisenstein [5] in which sections 2–20 of PDTB are used as the training set, sections 0–1 as the development set and sections 21–22 as the test set. There are totally 16 second-level relations while five of them only contains nine samples, and we exclude them as previous work does. For this task, we only implement our TTNN model because it performs best with respect to binary classification. To our knowledge, this is the first work to use the first three and the last one token embeddings to infer discourse relations. Thus, in this task, we conduct extra experiments to evaluate the validity of these token-level embedding features of lexical and syntactic.

We represent First3-Last by concatenating or averaging its token embeddings, and compare First3-Last embedding with sentence and argument embeddings respectively, and then we concatenate First3-Last embedding with sentence and argument embeddings. Moreover, we evaluate whether it is necessary to update the token-level embeddings in training process.

Finally, to compare our model more precisely with other neural network based methods, we choose the best model with distributed representations and add standard surface features as they did. Following Lin et al. [8], we apply feature selection to obtain 500 word pair features, 100 production rule features, 100 dependency rule features and 600 Brown cluster features. The difference lies in the fact that we use information gain (IG) instead of mutual information (MI) as selection criteria because of its better performance [23]. The hidden layer with surface features is defined as follows:

$$h = tanh(a_1{}^T W_t{}^{[1:H_2]} a_2 + W_e(a_1 + r - a_2) + W_s[a_1; a_2] + W_{sur} v + b_s)$$

where $W_{sur} \in \mathbb{R}^{H_2 \times d}$ and $v \in \mathbb{R}^d$ is the surface feature vector.

Experimental Results. Table 4 can answer three questions about the embedding layer: (1) what type of embeddings are more effective; (2) what type of

Table 4. The accuracy (%) for second-level discourse relation classification using TTNN with different embeddings on PDTB test set. "Sen", "Arg" and "FL" denote sentence, argument and First3-Last embeddings. "Con." and "ave." denote the concatenating and averaging. "Static" denotes keeping the token embeddings during training while "Dynamic" denotes updating them.

		Lexical	Syntactic
Static	Sen	31.85	32.76
	Arg	37.38	38.09
	Sen + Arg	38.19	38.59
	FL(con.)	32.76	29.44
	FL(ave.)	34.57	31.15
	Sen + Arg + FL(con.)	38.09	39.20
	Sen + Arg + FL(ave.)	**40.90**	39.89
Dynamic	Sen + Arg + FL(con.)	35.97	36.20
	Sen + Arg + FL(ave.)	40.70	39.49

First3-Last representation is better; and (3) do we need to update the token embeddings. As shown in the first five lines of Table 4, argument embeddings are the most effective while sentence embeddings are the worst. From the remaining lines in Table 4, we can conclude that averaging is better than concatenation for First3-Last embedding composition. Although concatenation can introduce the word order information, it may lead to the sparsity problem due to separate treatments being used for each word located at the first three and last position of the arguments. Updating the token-level embeddings does not contribute to the classification accuracy perhaps because of the overfitting problem in this model.

Table 5. Performance (accuracy/%) comparison for second-level implicit discourse relation classification on PDTB test set.

	Models	Accuracy
Surface features based models	Lin et al. (2009)	40.20
	Ji and Eisenstein (2015)	**40.66**
	TTNN (ours)	40.52
Neural networks based models	Ji and Eisenstein (2015)	36.98
	Rutherford et al. (2016)	39.56
	TTNN with lexical features	40.90
	TTNN with syntactical features	39.94
	TTNN with lexical and syntactical features	**41.39**
Neural networks based models + surface features	Ji and Eisenstein (2015)	44.59
	TTNN	**44.75**

Table 5 shows the final results of our model compared with other competitive systems. For surface features, our model achieves the performance similar to that of the other two systems. When excluding surface features, the classification accuracy of our model is the best, with a 4.41% and 1.83% improvement over the system of Ji and Eisenstein [5] and Rutherford et al. [18]. Note that their models do not beat Lin's purely surface feature model. In contrast, our model outperforms the surface features based model (statistically significant, $p < 0.01$; t-test). Finally, when surface features are further added to our model, we can achieve the best accuracy of 44.75%. Note that the bilinear model of Ji and Eisenstein [5] can be regarded as a special case of the one-way Tensor model without a hidden layer and the transformation property is out of their consideration, so that our model has much more expressive power.

7   Discussion

To better understand the strength of our multi-level distributed representations, some discourse relation instances which are extracted from the test set of PDTB are given in Table 1. The recognition results of these instances are incorrect by the model using discrete surface features while correct using the distributed representations. We first explain the necessity of our distributed First3-Last embeddings and then we explore the deeper reasons at the sentence level.

Pitler et al. [15] proposes that connective-like expressions appear at the first three and the last words of the arguments and we find that our distributed First3-Last embeddings have advantage over their discrete features. We demonstrate this using the first example in Table 1. In Example (1) of Table 1, the first three words of $Arg1$ - "The common view" and the first two words of $Arg2$ - "Our view" indicate that it will pose opposite opinions for the two arguments, thus, the Contrast relation exists between the argument pair. However, this rule does not appear in the training set of PDTB. In other words, it is impossible to detect the discourse relation by using the discrete First3-Last features. In contrast, our distributed First3-Last representation can capture these connective-like expressions and recognize the discourse relation successfully.

Next, we show the effectiveness of segment-level distributed representations. Lin et al. [8] explains that implicit discourse relation recognition needs a deeper semantic representation and a more robust model. Distributed representation of word or segment and neural network model may meet these requirements. Regarding example (2) in Table 1, $Arg2$ is an instantiation of $Arg1$. Word pair "declined, off" provides a strong indication for this discourse relation, but we find that such a case does not occur in the training set, thus it is not surprising that using surface features including word pairs fails to detect the relation.

For our distributed representation based model, the recognition result is correct. We seek the most similar argument in the PDTB training set of $Arg1$ and $Arg2$ using cosine similarity in vector space, yielding "For the first nine months, the trade deficit was 14.933 trillion lire, compared with 10.485 trillion lire in the year-earlier period" (denoted as $Arg1'$) for $Arg1$ and "The stock fell 75 cents" (denoted as $Arg2'$) for $Arg2$. We find that there is a few words overlap between $Arg1'$ and $Arg1$ as well as between $Arg2'$ and $Arg2$, but there is a relatively high semantic similarity between of $Arg1'$ and $Arg1$, and also between $Arg2'$ and $Arg2$: $Arg1'$ and $Arg1$ both express the meaning of slowdown in terms of the economy; $Arg2'$ and $Arg2$ express that the price of something decreases by a specific number of cents.

According to the analyses above, we can conclude that our model has the ability to capture deeper semantic meaning while the discrete surface feature model fails.

8   Related Work

Most of the previous work [8,15,22,25] regards implicit discourse relation recognition as a classification task that focuses on feature engineering. Subsequent work [1,7,17,19] focuses on addressing the data sparsity problem. Recently, deep learning methods [5,9,18,24] have been applied to this task. Ji and Eisenstein [5] employs a recursive neural network and achieves state-of-the-art performance for second-level relations. However, without the surface features, the performance of Ji and Eisenstein [5] model is about 3% lower than surface features based model of Lin et al. [8]. Part of the reason may be that it is difficult to learn satisfying representations of sentence with small-sized PDTB corpus.

9 Conclusion

In this paper, we proposed a novel method for implicit discourse relation recognition based on neural network in which the model hierarchy and the feature hierarchy are proposed. Regarding the model hierarchy, we propose a max-margin neural network that considers two views, including the relation classification view and the relation transformation view. Regarding the feature hierarchy, we learn and leverage distributed representations from multi-levels, namely from words, arguments and syntactic structures to sentences.

We test our method in implicit discourse relation binary classification and multi-class prediction. The experimental results demonstrate that our method can achieve new state-of-the-art performance in most cases. Furthermore, we find for the first time that the distributed features can perform better than surface discrete features for second-level implicit discourse relation recognition.

Acknowledgments. The research work has been funded by the Natural Science Foundation of China under Grant No. 61403379.

References

1. Biran, O., McKeown, K.: Aggregated word pair features for implicit discourse relation disambiguation. In: Proceedings of ACL Conference, p. 69 (2013)
2. Bordes, A., Usunier, N., Garcia-Duran, A., Weston, J., Yakhnenko, O.: Translating embeddings for modeling multi-relational data. In: Advances in Neural Information Processing Systems, pp. 2787–2795 (2013)
3. Braud, C., Denis, P.: Comparing word representations for implicit discourse relation classification. In: EMNLP 2015 (2015)
4. Ioffe, S., Szegedy, C.: Batch normalization: accelerating deep network training by reducing internal covariate shift (2015). arXiv preprint arXiv:1502.03167
5. Ji, Y., Eisenstein, J.: One vector is not enough: entity-augmented distributed semantics for discourse relations. Trans. Assoc. Comput. Linguist. **3**(1), 329–344 (2015). http://aclweb.org/anthology/Q15-1024
6. Klein, D., Manning, C.D.: Accurate unlexicalized parsing. In: Proceedings of ACL 2003, pp. 423–430 (2003)
7. Li, J.J., Nenkova, A.: Reducing sparsity improves the recognition of implicit discourse relations. In: 15th Annual Meeting of the Special Interest Group on Discourse and Dialogue, p. 199 (2014)
8. Lin, Z., Kan, M.Y., Ng, H.T.: Recognizing implicit discourse relations in the Penn Discourse Treebank. In: Proceedings of EMNLP 2009 (2009)
9. Liu, Y., Li, S., Zhang, X., Sui, Z.: Implicit discourse relation classification via multi-task neural networks (2016). arXiv preprint arXiv:1603.02776

10. Louis, A., Joshi, A., Prasad, R., Nenkova, A.: Using entity features to classify implicit discourse relations. In: Proceedings of 11th Annual Meeting of the Special Interest Group on Discourse and Dialogue, pp. 59–62 (2010)
11. Marcu, D., Echihabi, A.: An unsupervised approach to recognizing discourse relations. In: Proceedings of ACL 2002, pp. 368–375. Association for Computational Linguistics (2002)
12. Mikolov, T., Chen, K., Corrado, G., Dean, J.: Efficient estimation of word representations in vector space (2013). arXiv preprint arXiv:1301.3781
13. Park, J., Cardie, C.: Improving implicit discourse relation recognition through feature set optimization. In: Proceedings of 13th Annual Meeting of the Special Interest Group on Discourse and Dialogue (2012)
14. Pei, W., Ge, T., Baobao, C.: Maxmargin tensor neural network for Chinese word segmentation. In: Proceedings of ACL (2014)
15. Pitler, E., Louis, A., Nenkova, A.: Automatic sense prediction for implicit discourse relations in text. In: Proceedings of ACL 2009 (2009)
16. Prasad, R., Lee, A., Miltsakaki, E., Robaldo, L., Joshi, A.K., Webber, B.L., Dinesh, N.: The Penn Discourse Treebank 2.0. In: LREC 2008, pp. 2961–2968 (2008)
17. Rutherford, A., Xue, N.: Improving the inference of implicit discourse relations via classifying explicit discourse connectives. In: Proceedings of NAACL 2015, pp. 799–808. Association for Computational Linguistics (2015). http://aclweb.org/anthology/N15-1081
18. Rutherford, A.T., Demberg, V., Xue, N.: Neural network models for implicit discourse relation classification in English and Chinese without surface features (2016)
19. Rutherford, A.T., Xue, N.: Discovering implicit discourse relations through brown cluster pair representation and coreference patterns. In: EACL 2014, p. 645 (2014)
20. Socher, R., Chen, D., Manning, C.D., Ng, A.: Reasoning with neural tensor networks for knowledge base completion. In: Advances in Neural Information Processing Systems, pp. 926–934 (2013)
21. Tang, W., Zhang, L., Linninger, A.A., Tranter, R.S., Brezinsky, K.: Solving kinetic inversion problems via a physically bounded Gauss-Newton (PGN) method. Ind. Eng. Chem. Res. 44(10), 3626–3637 (2005)
22. Xu, Y., Lan, M., Lu, Y., Niu, Z.Y., Tan, C.L.: Connective prediction using machine learning for implicit discourse relation classification. In: The 2012 International Joint Conference on Neural Networks (IJCNN), pp. 1–8. IEEE (2012)
23. Yang, Y., Pedersen, J.O.: A comparative study on feature selection in text categorization. In: ICML, vol. 97, pp. 412–420 (1997)
24. Zhang, B., Su, J., Xiong, D., Lu, Y., Duan, H., Yao, J.: Shallow convolutional neural network for implicit discourse relation recognition. In: Proceedings of EMNLP 2015 (2015)
25. Zhou, Z.M., Xu, Y., Niu, Z.Y., Lan, M., Su, J., Tan, C.L.: Predicting discourse connectives for implicit discourse relation recognition. In: Proceedings of 23rd International Conference on Computational Linguistics: Posters, pp. 1507–1514. Association for Computational Linguistics (2010)

A CDT-Styled End-to-End Chinese Discourse Parser

Fang Kong[✉], Hongling Wang, and Guodong Zhou

School of Computer Science and Technology, Soochow University, Suzhou, China
{kongfang,hlwang,gdzhou}@suda.edu.cn

Abstract. Discourse parsing is a challenging task and plays a critical role in discourse analysis. Since the release of the Rhetorical Structure Theory Discourse Treebank (RST-DT) and the Penn Discourse Treebank (PDTB), the research on English discourse parsing has attracted increasing attention and achieved considerable success in recent years. At the same time, some preliminary research on certain subtasks about discourse parsing for other languages, such as Chinese, has been conducted. In this paper, the Connective-driven Dependency Treebank (CDTB) corpus is introduced. Then an end-to-end Chinese discourse parser to parse free texts into the Connective-driven Dependency Tree (CDT) style is presented. The parser consists of multiple components including elementary discourse unit detector, discourse relation recognizer, discourse parse tree generator and attribution labeler. In particular, attribution labeler determines two attributions (sense and centering) for every non-terminal node in the discourse parse trees. Effective feature sets are proposed for every component respectively. Comprehensive experiments are conducted on the Connective-driven Dependency Treebank (CDTB) corpus with an overall F1 score of 20.0%.

Keywords: Chinese discourse parser · Connective-driven Dependency Tree · Elementary discourse unit · Discourse relation

1 Introduction

Discourse parsing determines the internal structure of a text via identifying the discourse relations between its text units and benefits a wide range of downstream natural language tasks, such as coherence modeling [8], statistical machine translation [10].

Since the release of the Rhetorical Structure Theory Discourse Treebank (RST-DT) [1] and the Penn Discourse Treebank (PDTB) [12], the research on English discourse parsing has attracted increasing attention in recent years [6,9,11]. At the same time, the discourse-level annotation for other languages, such as Chinese, has been carried out and achieved considerable success [3,7,13,16–18]. Using these discourse corpora, some preliminary research has been conducted [4,5,15]. In this paper, using the Connective-driven Dependency Treebank (CDTB) [7], we propose an end-to-end Chinese discourse parser.

© Springer International Publishing AG 2016
C.-Y. Lin et al. (Eds.): NLPCC-ICCPOL 2016, LNAI 10102, pp. 387–398, 2016.
DOI: 10.1007/978-3-319-50496-4_32

The complete parser consists of four components, i.e., elementary discourse unit detector, discourse relation recognizer, discourse parse tree generator and attribution labeler. For every component, a set of effective features are presented. We also show a serial of experiments to evaluate our discourse parser comprehensively.

2   The Chinese Discourse Tree Bank

The CDTB corpus follows the CDT scheme [7]. It regards elementary discourse units (EDUs) as leaf nodes and connectives as non-leaf nodes. In particular, connectives are employed to directly represent the hierarchy of the tree structure and convey the rhetorical relation of a discourse, while the nuclei of discourse units (i.e., centering) are globally determined with reference to the dependency theory. A three-level set of discourse relations are recommended by the CDTB corpus. First level contains four relations: causality, coordination, transition and explanation, which are further clustered into 17 sub-relations in the second level. In the third level, the connectives are under each sub-relation. In this paper, the 4 top-level relations are considered.

This corpus chooses 500 Xinhua newswire articles from the Chinese Treebank (CTB) [14] to add a layer of discourse annotations. In particular, each paragraph generates a corresponding discourse tree. For more details, please refer to Li et al. [7]. In this paper, we give an example to show the CDT scheme and introduce the task of our CDT-styled discourse parser.

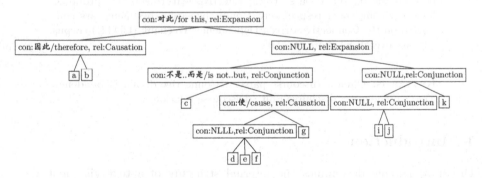

Fig. 1. The gold-standard discourse tree corresponding to Example (1)

(1) (a)浦东开发开放是一项振兴上海，建设现代化经济、贸易、金融中心的跨世纪工程，　**(b)**因此大量出现的是以前不曾遇到过的新情况、新问题。**(c)**对此，浦东不是简单的采取"干一段时间，等积累了经验以后再制定法规条例"的做法，　**(d)**而是借鉴发达国家和深圳等特区的经验教训，　**(e)**聘请国内外有关专家学者，　**(f)**积极、及时地制定和推出法规性文件，　**(g)**使这些经济活动一出现就被纳入法制轨道。**(h)**去年初浦东新区诞生的中国第一家医疗机构药品采购服务中心，正因为一开始就比较规范，　**(i)**运转至今，**(j)**成交药品一亿多元，　**(k)**没有发现一例回扣。

Example (1) shows a paragraph consisting of 3 sentences from chtb_0001. From the discourse perspective, this paragraph contains 11 EDUs with its corresponding CDT representation shown in Fig. 1.

In CDT scheme, the combination of different EDUs can be considered in a higher level and new discourse units can thus be combined into higher-level units from bottom to up. For example, in Example (1), the units (a) and (b) are combined as a new EDU participating the higher level discourse relation driven by the connective "对此(for this)". In this way, the discourse structure can be expressed as a tree structure via bottom-up combination of EDUs.

3   End-to-End Chinese Discourse Parser

In this section, we first briefly browse the framework of our end-to-end Chinese discourse parser and then introduce all the components in detail.

3.1   System Overview

In order to simplify our parsing algorithm, instead of following the top-down approach employed in annotation procedure, our parsing algorithm first detects the EDUs, and then generates the discourse parse tree in the bottom-up way. Upon this, the discourse tree is traversed and the sense and centering attributions are determined for every non-terminal nodes. Figure 2 shows the framework of our end-to-end Chinese discourse parser, which consists of EDU detector, discourse relation recognizer, discourse tree generator and attribution labeler. In particular, attribution labeler contains four components, i.e., connective identifier, explicit classifier, non-explicit classifier and centering labeler.

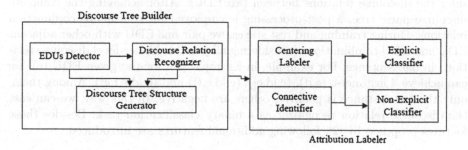

Fig. 2. Framework of our end-to-end Chinese discourse parser.

Our system takes a fully data-driven, supervised learning approach. In following descriptions, we refine this overview by detailing the component designs as well as the derived feature sets.

3.2 Elementary Discourse Unit Detector

As the first step of Chinese discourse parsing, the performance of EDU detector is crucial for other downstream components. Referring to the CDTB [7], an EDU should be segmented by some punctuation and contain at least one predicate and express at least one proposition. Since sentence end punctuations (i.e., period, question mark and exclamatory mark) are certainly EDU boundaries, we cast the EDU detection task as comma disambiguation motivated by Yang and Xue [15] by classifying the commas into two categories, boundary of EDU and non-boundary of EDU with two types of feature employed in this component,

- Lexical: the string and POS of 5 words before or after the given comma, the string and POS of the word just following the given comma, the words of all the connective candidates in the later text span, all punctuation marks in current sentence.
- Syntactic: the context of the given commander[1], whether the POS of the leftmost sibling of the comma's parent node is a PP construction, whether the siblings of the comma's parent node have and only have an IP construction, whether the first leaf node's POS of the comma's parent node is CS or AD construction, whether the first child of the comma's left sibling is the PP construction, whether the current and next text spans contain VC, VA, VE,VV construction.

3.3 Discourse Relation Recognizer

After detecting all the EDUs in a paragraph, discourse relation recognizer is adopted to determine whether a discourse relation occurs between two EDUs.

In order to simplify the discourse parsing algorithm, we firstly only consider the discourse relations between two EDUs. After achieving the complete discourse parse tree, a post-processing is employed for continuous conjunction relations. During training and test stages, we pair one EDU with other adjacent EDU and EDU combinations (considering all possible higher-level discourse relation) in one sentence. For example, in Example (1), for the given EDU (c), we can achieve 4 instances: (c,d), (c,[d,e]), (c,[d,e,f]) and (c,[d,e,f,g]). Among them, only the last instance is positive, others are negative. In this way, we can cast the discourse relation recognizer as a binary classification task. Besides those features proposed by [2], following additional features are introduced:

- Semantic similarity: the string and POS of word pairs from two EDUs with the same semantic class in HIT-CIR Tongyici Cilin.
- Context of the connective of the given two EDUs if having.

---

[1] We use POS combination of the parent, left sibling and right sibling of the given comma to present the context.

3.4 Discourse Parse Tree Generator

After determining all EDUs in a paragraph, based on the relation existence probability returned by the discourse relation recognizer, we can generate a discourse tree for the paragraph. Algorithm 1 shows the detailed steps in discourse tree generation. Obviously, this is a bottom-up merging procedure with the final EDU as the root of the discourse tree.

Input: P a given paragraph
Output: A discourse tree t

Initialization: Set $t = null$
$E \leftarrow$ EDUDetector(P)
while Len$(E) > 1$ **do**
    init$(score)$
    for E_i in E **do**
        $score[i] \leftarrow$ DRRecognizer(E_i, E_{i+1})
    end
    $i \leftarrow$ Max$(Score)$
    $newST \leftarrow$ CreateTree(E_i, E_{i+1})
    Replace$([E_i, E_{i+1}], newST)$
end
$t \leftarrow E_0$

Algorithm 1. Algorithm for discourse tree generation. Here *EDU Detector* is the EDU detector, *DRRecognizer* achieves the relation existence probability between two given EDUs, and *CreateTree* generates a new EDU based two given EDUs.

3.5 Attribution Labeler

After constructing the complete discourse tree for every paragraph, we label the sense and centering attributions for every non-terminal nodes, i.e. discourse relations. For sense classification, we classify the discourse relations into explicit and implicit relations referring to whether relation is explicitly signaled by a discourse connective. So for every discourse relation, the parser starts by identifying whether a connective occurs. If a connective is identified, the explicit classifier is employed to determine the sense of the given discourse relation. Otherwise, the non-explicit classifier is employed. Additionally, centering of the discourse relation is labeled at the same time.

Connective Identifier. Our connective identifier works in two steps. First, the connective candidates are extracted from the given EDUs referring to the CDTB, where 282 types of discourse connectives are annotated. Then, every connective candidate is checked whether it functions as a discourse connective or not. For simplicity, we only find the most likely connective for every given discourse relation. Features employed in our classification approach include:

- Lexical: connective itself, POS of the connective, combinations of connective with its previous word, its next word, the location of the connective in the sentence, i.e., start, middle and end of the sentence.
- Syntactic: the syntactic category of the given connective (i.e., subordinating, coordinating, or discourse adverbial), the highest node in the parse tree that covers the connective words (dominating node), the context of the dominating node[2], the path from the parent node of the connective to the root of the parse tree.
- Bilingual knowledge: While Chinese has similar types of discourse connectives as English, they are different in syntactic, statistical distributions and lexical realizations. In comparison with English, Chinese has a wider range of forms of connectives [18]. Commonly occurring in Chinese discourse, there are many paired Chinese connectives, e.g. "不是..而是(is not..but)", "因为..所以(because..so)", "虽然..但是 (although..but)", and so on. Even in some paired connectives, such as "由于..所以(because..so)", a word (i.e., "由于(because)", "所以(so)") in a paired connective can appear independently as a connective. Furthermore, many different connectives in Chinese convey the same meaning and can substitute for each other in the same context. Observing this, we firstly introduce two headwords corresponding to the given connective. One is the English translated phrase (E-head), the other is the Chinese translated phrase corresponding to the E-head (C-head). After achieving E-head and C-head, we extract their context from their parse trees and also include them in our connective identifier.

Explicit Classifier. After a discourse connective is identified, the explicit sense classifier is provided to decide the sense that the relation conveys. Similar to the case in English, although the same connective may carry different semantics under different contexts, only a few connectives are ambiguous in Chinese [18]. Following the work of Lin et al. [9] in English, we introduce three features to train a sense classifier: the connective itself, its POS and the previous word.

Non-explicit Classifier. If the given discourse relation hasn't overt discourse connective, the non-explicit classifier is employed to identify the sense. Our non-explicit sense classifier includes four types of features:

- Verbs: Following the work of Pitler and Nenkova [11], we extract the pairs of verbs from the given EDUs. Besides, the average length of verb phrases in each EDU, and the POS of main verbs are included.
- Modality: We include a set of features to record the presence or absence of specific modal words (i.e., can, may, will, shall, must, need) in EDUs, and their cross-product.

---

[2] We use POS combination of the parent, left sibling and right sibling of the dominating node to represent the context. When no parent or siblings, it is marked NULL.

- Production rules: Since the syntactic structure of one argument may constrain the relation type and the syntactic structure of the other argument, three features are introduced to denote the presence of syntactic productions in EDUs. Here, the production rules are extracted from the training data and the rules with frequency less than 5 are ignored.
- Dependency rules: Similar to production rules, three features denoting the presence of dependency in other EDUs or both are introduced in our system.

Besides, we introduce two features which describe the automatically determined connective list contained by the two EDUs respectively, to capture the co-occurrence relationship between non-explicit and explicit discourse relations.

Centering Labeler. Discourse relations may be either mononuclear or multinuclear. A mononuclear relation holds between a nucleus and a satellite unit. Normally, the nucleus usually reflects the intention focus of the discourse and is thus more salient in the discourse structure, while the satellite usually represents supportive information for the nucleus. In comparison, a multi-nuclear relation usually holds two or more discourse units of equal weight in the discourse structure. Since CDT for nucleus determination adopts the dependency grammar and selects the unit standing for the relationship with other discourse units in a discourse, we name the nucleus as the centering of the discourse relation.

We cast the centering labeling as a three categories classification task. That is to say, centering labeler need to determine whether the front EDU, the later EDU or both EDUs of the given discourse relation act as the centering. In this paper, four types of features are employed in this task:

- Verbs: pairs of verbs and POS in the given EDUs.
- Word pairs: pairs of words in the given EDUs.
- Dependency rules: features denoting the presence of dependency productions in other EDUs or both.
- Semantic pairs: the string and POS of word pairs from two EDUs with the same semantic class in HIT-CIR Tongyici Cilin.

4 Experiments

In this section, we systematically evaluate our CDT-styled end-to-end Chinese discourse parser on the CDTB corpus.

4.1 Experimental Setting

All our classifiers are trained using the OpenNLP maximum entropy package[3] with the default parameters (i.e. without smoothing and with 100 iterations). The automatic parse trees of the CDTB are achieved using the Berkeley parser. Table 1 shows the training and testing data split, and Table 2 shows the distribution of discourse relations over different sense categories.

---

[3] http://maxent.sourceforge.net/.

Table 1. Training and testing data split.

	Training	Testing
#Doc	450	50
#File list	0001–0090, 0101–0190,0201–0290, 0301–0325,0400–0454, 0500–0509, 0520–0544, 0590–0596,0600–0647	0091–0100, 0191–0200,0291–0300, 0510–0519,0648–0657
#Tree	2125	217
#EDU	9630	1013

Table 2. Distribution of discourse relations over different categories.

	Training		Test	
Discourse relation type	Explicit	Non-explicit	Explicit	Non-explicit
Expansion	188	1276	12	140
Adversative	163	38	10	1
Causation	426	786	40	79
Conjunction	880	2859	95	317

4.2 Experimental Results and Analysis

Firstly, we evaluate the performance of the elementary discourse unit detector under automatic parse trees and achieve 95.7%, 91.9% and 93.8% in precision, recall and F1-measure respectively. The accurate of EDU detector under automatic parse trees also reaches 91.2%. Obviously, it is a satisfied performance.

Secondly, we evaluate the performance of our discourse relation recognizer. Table 3 shows the performance under the gold standard EDUs. We also list the intra- and inter-sentential results. From the results, we can find that, inter-sentential discourse relation recognizer achieves better performance than intra-sentential cases. In fact, in Chinese, there are much more long complex sentences than in English. Thus, it is more difficult to analyze the intra-sentential structure. Besides, frequently occurring ellipses much increase the difficulty of intra-sentential discourse analysis.

Table 3. Performance of our discourse relation recognizer using gold EDUs.

	Setting	P (%)	R (%)	F1 (%)
With relation	Intra	80.0	95.7	87.2
	Inter	85.6	96.4	90.0
	Overall	81.2	95.7	87.9

In order to focus on the performance of our discourse parse tree generator, we evaluate the performance of the discourse tree structure under gold standard

EDUs. Using automatic parse trees, our discourse parse tree generator achieves 51.7%, 53.0%, and 52.3% in precision, recall and F1-measure, respectively.

After constructing the discourse parse trees, we traverse the discourse tree and determine the sense and centering attributions for every non-terminal nodes. We firstly focus on the performance of every component of attribution labeler under gold standard discourse tree structure.

For connective classifier, we achieve 79.8%, 62.9% and 70.4% in precision, recall and F1-measure respectively. We can find that, in comparison with English connective identification, the performance of Chinese connective identification is much lower. In fact, just noted as Xue [13], there are much more challenge in Chinese due to a large number of paired-connectives.

Table 4 shows the results of explicit classifier under both gold and automatic connectives. We can find that, using gold standard connectives, (1) explicit classifier achieves satisfied performance, (2) in comparison with using gold standard connectives, the errors propagated from connective identification largely reduce the performance of explicit classifier by about 15% in F-measure.

Table 4. Performance of our explicit classifier using gold discourse tree structure.

Types	Gold connective			Auto connective		
	R (%)	P (%)	F (%)	R (%)	P (%)	F (%)
Causation	91.8	91.8	91.8	72.9	81.4	76.9
Adversative	95.4	77.6	85.6	73.7	72.8	73.2
Conjunction	92.0	96.7	94.3	64.7	95.8	77.2
Expansion	94.8	92.4	93.6	82.7	87.0	84.8

Due to the unbalanced distribution of the training and testing data, we neglect the *Adversative* discourse relations and cast the non-explicit classifier as a three-category classification task. Table 5 shows the results of non-explicit classifier under both gold and automatic connectives. We can find that:

Table 5. Performance of our non-explicit classifier using gold discourse tree structure.

Types	Gold connective			Auto connective		
	R (%)	P (%)	F (%)	R (%)	P (%)	F (%)
Causation	84.2	43.2	57.1	40.6	27.7	32.4
Conjunction	77.5	96.0	85.8	73.7	82.3	77.3
Expansion	55.9	49.1	51.8	54.3	31.9	40.2

- Similar to the case in English, in comparison with the performance of explicit classifier, the performance of non-explicit classifier is much lower. In fact, just as noted in previous work, in the PDTB, non-explicit discourse relations occupies about 54.4% in English [11], while this ratio rises up to about 82% in Chinese [13]. The majority of non-explicit discourse relations makes the Chinese discourse parsing task much more difficult than English.
- Errors propagated from connectives also reduces the performance of non-explicit classifier about 15% in F-measure.

Similar to sense classifiers, we firstly evaluate the performance of centering labeler, without considering the influence of the errors propagated from discourse tree generation. Table 6 shows the performance of our centering labeler. We can find that, for multi-nuclear case, our centering labeler achieves the best performance. This is due to that most of multi-nuclear cases are Conjunction discourse relations. On the other hand, for mononuclear cases, the performance of backward centering identifier is much better than forward centering.

Table 6. Performance of our centering labeler using gold discourse tree structure.

Types	P (%)	R (%)	F1 (%)
Forward-mononuclear	62.2	33.5	43.6
Backward-mononuclear	67.2	41.7	51.5
Multi-nuclear	70.4	90.8	79.3

After evaluating all the components independently, we evaluate our end-to-end Chinese discourse parser under fully automatic setting. That is to say, using automatic parse trees, our discourse parser starts from parsing a free text. Table 7 shows the results. The first line of the Table 7 lists the performance of our tree structure after automatic EDU detection and discourse relation recognizer. In comparison with the results under gold standard EDUs, we can find that the errors propagated from EDU detector reduce the performance of discourse tree generation by about 6% in F-measure. Considering the sense attribution (containing both explicit and non-explicit discourse relations), the performance of tree structure reduces by about 18% in F-measure. In fact, referring to the non-explicit sense classification results as shown in Table 5 and considering the proportion of non-explicit discourse relations in Chinese, this reduction is inevitable. Considering the results of both discourse tree structure and centering labeling, our discourse parser achieves about 23.1% in F-measure. In comparison with only considering the tree structure results, the performance also reduces about 23.3%. Considering both sense and centering attributions, our discourse parser achieves 20.0% in F-measure. Obviously, there are much room to improve.

Table 7. Performance of our discourse parser under full automation.

Setting	P (%)	R (%)	F1 (%)
Tree structure	44.0	49.1	46.4
+sense	27.3	30.5	28.8
+centering	21.5	24.8	23.1
+sense & centering	19.0	21.2	20.0

5 Related Work

In comparison with English, due to the lack of corpora, there are much less studies of work on Chinese discourse parsing. To address this problem, most of current studies on the building of discourse corpora. As a pioneer, Xue [13] discussed the range, distribution and sense discrimination of Chinese discourse connectives. Motivated by the work of Xue [13], Zhou and Xue [17] used the PDTB annotation guidelines to annotate Chinese discourse corpus with 98 files from Chinese Treebank of Xinhua newswire. Zhou and Xue [18] further scaled the corpus up to 164 files. In the meantime, Li et al. [7] proposed the Connective-driven Dependency Tree (CDT) scheme and annotated 500 Xinhua newswire articles from the CTB by adding a layer of discourse annotations.

With the release of the discourse-level corpora, Huang and Chen [4] proposed a supervised statistical classifier to identify explicit discourse relations.

6 Conclusion

In this paper, a CDT-styled end-to-end Chinese discourse parser is proposed. The parser consists of four components, i.e., elementary discourse unit detector, discourse relation recognizer, discourse parse tree generator and attribution labeler. In particular, attribution labeler need to determine two attributions (sense and centering) for every discourse relation and consist of four classifiers, connective identifier, explicit classifier, non-explicit classifier and centering labeler. For every component, we propose a set of effective features. Comprehensive experiments are conducted on the CDTB corpus and the parser achieves an overall system F1 score of 20.0% under full automation. To the best of our knowledge, this is the first research in building an end-to-end Chinese discourse parser, particularly of a tree structure.

Acknowledgements. This research is supported by Key project 61333018 under the National Natural Science Foundation of China, Project 61472264 and 61402314 under the National Natural Science Foundation of China.

References

1. Carlson, L., Marcu, D., Okurowski, M.E.: Building a discourse-tagged corpus in the framework of rhetorical structure theory. In: Proceedings of 2001 SIGdial Workshop on Discourse and Dialogue (2001)
2. Feng, V.W., Hirst, G.: Text-level discourse parsing with rich linguistic features. In: Proceedings of ACL 2012 (2012)
3. Huang, H.H., Chen, H.H.: An annotation system for development of Chinese discourse corpus. In: Proceedings of COLING 2012 Demonstration Papers (2012)
4. Huang, H.H., Chen, H.H.: Chinese discourse relation recognition. In: Proceedings of IJCNLP 2011 (2011)
5. Huang, H.H., Chen, H.H.: Contingency and comparison relation labeling and structure prediction in Chinese sentences. In: Proceedings of 2012 Special Interest Group on Discourse and Dialogue (2012)
6. Kong, F., Ng, H.T., Zhou, G.: A constituent-based approach to argument labeling with joint inference in discourse parsing. In: Proceedings of EMNLP 2014 (2014)
7. Li, Y., Feng, W., Sun, J., Kong, F., Zhou, G.: Building Chinese discourse corpus with connective-driven dependency tree structure. In: Proceedings of EMNLP 2014 (2014)
8. Lin, Z., Ng, H.T., Kan, M.Y.: Automatically evaluating text coherence using discourse relations. In: Proceedings of ACL 2011 (2011)
9. Lin, Z., Ng, H.T., Kan, M.Y.: A PDTB-styled end-to-end discourse parser. Nat. Lang. Eng. **20**(2), 151–184 (2014)
10. Meyer, T., Webber, B.: Implicitation of discourse connectives in (machine) translation. In: Proceedings of 2013 Workshop on Discourse in Machine Translation (2013)
11. Pitler, E., Nenkova, A.: Using syntax to disambiguate explicit discourse connectives in text. In: Proceedings of ACL-IJCNLP 2009 Short Papers (2009)
12. Prasad, R., Dinesh, N., Lee, A., Miltsakaki, E., Robaldo, L., Joshi, A., Webber, B.: The Penn Discourse TreeBank 2.0. In: Proceedings of LREC 2008 (2008)
13. Xue, N.: Annotating discourse connectives in the Chinese Treebank. In: Proceedings of 2005 Workshop on Frontiers in Corpus Annotations (2005)
14. Xue, N., Xia, F., Chiou, F.D., Palmer, M.: The Penn Chinese Treebank: phrase structure annotation of a large corpus. Nat. Lang. Eng. **11**, 207–238 (2005)
15. Yang, Y., Xue, N.: Chinese comma disambiguation for discourse analysis. In: Proceedings of ACL 2012 (2012)
16. Zhou, L., Li, B., Wei, Z., Wong, K.F.: The CUHK Discourse Treebank for Chinese: annotating explicit discourse connectives for the Chinese Treebank. In: Proceedings of LREC 2014 (2014)
17. Zhou, Y., Xue, N.: PDTB-style discourse annotation of Chinese text. In: Proceedings of ACL 2012 (2012)
18. Zhou, Y., Xue, N.: The Chinese Discourse Treebank: a Chinese corpus annotated with discourse relations. Lang. Resour. Eval. **49**(2), 397–431 (2015)

NLP for Social Media

Events Detection and Temporal Analysis in Social Media

Yawei Jia$^{(\boxtimes)}$, Jing Xu, Zhonghu Xu, and Kai Xing

University of Science and Technology of China, No. 443, Huangshan Road,
Shushan District, Hefei 230027, Anhui, China
{ywjia,jxu125,xzhh}@mail.ustc.edu.cn, kxing@ustc.edu.cn

Abstract. In the past few years, event detection has drawn a lot of attention. We proposed an efficient method to detect event in this paper. An event is defined as a set of descriptive, collocated keywords in this paper. Intuitively, documents that describe the same event will contain similar sets of keywords. Individual events will form clusters in the graph of keywords for a document collection. We built a network of keywords based on their co-occurrence in documents. We proposed an efficient method which create a keywords weight directed graph named KeyGraph and use community detection method to discover events. Clump of keywords describing an event can be used to analyse the trend of the event. The accuracy of detecting events is over eighty percents with our method.

Keywords: Event detection · KeyGraph · Co-occurrence · Temporal analysis

1 Introduction

With fast development of social media, such as micro-blog, which becomes the most popular platfom to communicate and express their views. A large amount of data is produced each day, which contains large amount of valuable information. In fact the communication and interactions in social media reflect events and dynamics in real world. We propose a method to mine social media to discover events happened in reality and an algorithm to identify hot events in this paper.

Generally, an event can be described by a set of descriptive, collocated keywords or terms. The mission of event detection is to cluster these topological meaningful keywords into groups. There are several ways to extract and cluster keywords from documents. We might take the document-pivot clustering methods which firstly cluster documents into several groups and then select keywords from the clusters of documents based on some feature selection approaches. However, the association relationship of keywords and the influence of one keyword on another are missed in these methods. In fact, the co-occurrence of terms is very important in event detection. For example, it is meaningless if the terms *Trump, Hillary* and *President* appear in three distinguish documents. If they co-occur in documents and we know the conditional probability one term occur

© Springer International Publishing AG 2016
C.-Y. Lin et al. (Eds.): NLPCC-ICCPOL 2016, LNAI 10102, pp. 401–412, 2016.
DOI: 10.1007/978-3-319-50496-4_33

on another, we know more from the constellations of keywords. We build, therefore, a weighted directed graph named KeyGraph to capture the topological information existing among keywords.

In consideration of the importance of source of documents, we innovatively focused the authority of author of documents when keywords are extracted from documents. We try to create a graph of keywords, nodes of which are the keywords, and there exists an edge between keywords if they co-occur in a document. The weight of edge is computed by a probabilistic feedback mechanism. We adopt community detection algorithm adapted from social network analysis algorithm on the graph to discover events. Constellations of terms describing events may be used to track the trend of events.

2   Related Work

The target of event detection is to find a minimal set of keywords that can indicate an event. Kumaran et al. showed how performance on new event detection can be improved with using text classification technique [4], and Yang et al. adopted several supervised text categorization methods specifically some variants of K Nearest Neighbour algorithm to track events [10]. All of the methods mentioned above are based on document-pivot clustering. In general, all documents are clustered into several groups at first. Then, They select features or terms from the clusters of documents with some feature selection approaches to represent an event. It is worth noting that in the document-pivot clustering approach, keywords as a whole need to be considered to measure the similarity between two documents. Fung et al. reported that the most similar documents often belong to different categories, therefore this approach can be biased to the noisy keyword [3].

Li et al. [5] proposed a probabilistic model for news event detection, they use a mixture of unigram models to model contents and Gaussian Mixture Model (GMM) to model timestamps, and the parameters are estimated by Expectation Maximization (EM) algorithm. Those algorithms require the number of events. [9] propose a novel sketch-based topic model together with a set of techniques to achieve real-time detection and [11] proposed a novel solution to detect both stable and temporal topics simultaneously from social media data.

3   Keywords Extraction

Let us denote $D = \{d_1, d_2, \ldots, d_n\}$ be the collections of documents and $U = \{u_1, u_2, \ldots, u_i\}$ be the users set of these documents (user refers to the author of documents in this paper). And $W = \{w_{11}, w_{12}, \ldots, w_{ij}, \ldots\}$ is the words set. w_{ij} means the jth word in the ith document. Each word w_{ij} is from a document d_i in documents collection D. This section focus on how to extract keywords from words set. Considering the importance of source of documents, we innovatively take user's authority into consideration. Specifically, we estimate users' authority with an algorithm adapted from the classical PageRank Algorithm, and compute the keywords tf-idf value. With users' authority and keywords, we can compute a score of candidate keywords. Then, the keywords could be selected from the words set W according to the scores.

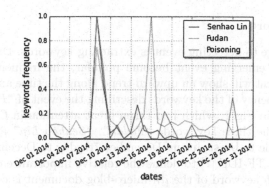

Fig. 1. An example for frequency of keywords associating with hot event.

3.1   User Authority Estimation

Considering that our experiment is conducted on the social network documents dataset, we use the user of social network to introduce user's authority estimation. Social network such as tweeter allow all the registered people to post and share short messages. Since every user has different influence on the public, the contents whose generator has higher authority are easier to be disseminated among social community, and the contents are more likely to be a hot event.

In social network community, if user u_i is interested in the contents which user u_j posts or shares, u_i may follow user u_j and u_i is called a follower of u_j. And u_j does not have to reciprocate by following user u_i. We can model the relationship of users in the social community using a directed graph $G = <U, E>$ where U is the set of users and E is the set of edges between users. There is a directed edge from user u_i to u_j, if user u_i is a follower of u_j. As the directed graph is similar to the web page network in topology, the authority of users can be estimated by the following formula adapted from PageRank algorithm:

$$auth(u_i) = (1 - \alpha) + \alpha \cdot \sum_{u_j \in follower(u_i)} \frac{auth(u_j)}{following(u_j)} \quad (1)$$

In the formula (1), α is a dumping parameter which is introduced by the author in [6]. Its value is usually set to 0.85, which represents the probability that a random surfer of the graph G moves from a user to another. $follower(u_i)$ is the set of users who follow the user u_i. Then we can compute each user's authority with an iterate algorithm based on the Page-Rank Algorithm [6] with an initial value:

$$auth(u_i) = \frac{1}{|following(u_i)|}$$

3.2 Words Score

The first challenge to detecting event is extracting keywords. During the period within which an emerging event become popular, the frequency of keywords indicating the event will show an upward trend along the time axis. For example, we show the frequency of the keywords describing the event of "*Fudan University Poisoning case*" in Fig. 1, which had taken great attention in China in 2014. It is obvious that the three key words "*Fudan*", "*Senhao Lin*" and "*Poisoning*" happen to coincide to burst during December 7th day to December 11th day in 2014. We use the TF-IDF [7] to define the relative importance of keyword. The tf value of the *jth* keyword of the *ith* micro-blog document is computed by:

$$tf_{i,j} = 0.5 + 0.5 \cdot \frac{tf_{i,j}}{tf_{i,j}^{max}} \tag{2}$$

then the idf value of the *jth* keyword of the *ith* document is shown as follows:

$$idf_{i,j} = log(\frac{|D|}{1 + |i \in D : j \in i|}) \tag{3}$$

where $|D|$ is the total number of documents. Given tf and idf, the tf-idf value is given by:

$$tfidf_{i,j} = tf_{i,j} \cdot idf_{i,j} \tag{4}$$

With tf-idf value of keyword and users' authority, the score of words w_{ij} is computed by the following equation:

$$score_{i,j} = \sum_{d_i \in D} tfidf_{i,j} \cdot auth(user(d_i)) \tag{5}$$

where $user(d_i)$ here is the author of document d_i.

3.3 Keywords Selection

With the score list of all words, we can select words with higher score as keywords. Intuitively the words describing a hot event will have a high score because the hot event usually could catch the user's attention who has a high authority and have a high tf-idf value for the wide spread. We use the following method based on [1] to compute the cut-off point to identify keywords:

1. First rank the words in descending order of score computed.
2. Compute the *maximum drop* in match and identifies the corresponding drop point.

3. Compute the *average drop* (between consecutive keywords) for all those key-words that are ranked before the identified maximum drop point.
4. The first drop which is higher than the average drop is called the *critical drop*. We returned keywords ranked better than the point of critical drop as candidate keywords.

4   Events Detection

We adopt a community detection algorithm on a keywords graph named Key-Graph to discover events. We build a KeyGraph whose nodes are the keywords and edges are formed between nodes when keywords co-occurs in a document. Generally, keywords co-occur when there is some meaningful topological rela-tionship between them. We can regard the KeyGraph as a social network of relationship between keywords. As is shown in Fig. 2, it is clear that community of keywords are densely linked and there are few links between keywords from different communities.

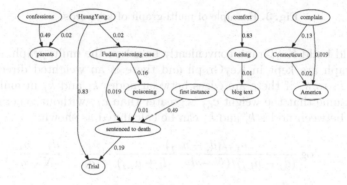

Fig. 2. An example for KeyGraph.

4.1   Building KeyGraph

We build KeyGraph through a multigraph of keywords. Nodes are the keywords and there are n edges between the nodes if keywords co-occur n times in docu-ments. As in Fig. 3, if there is some meaningful topological relationship between keywords, there are many edges between them. We can take advantage of this property to remove some noise in data. Specifically, we repeat the following two steps on each node and edge of the multigraph until nothing can be done.

(a) The number of edges between the two keywords must be larger than some minimum threshold. Otherwise, all of the edges between the two keywords are removed.

(b) The degree of each node in the multi-graph must be equal or larger than the threshold that is set in the rule (a). Or the node will be eliminated from multi-graph.

In short, edges are removed if the keywords associated with nodes co-occur below a minimum threshold and the resulted isolated keywords are removed.

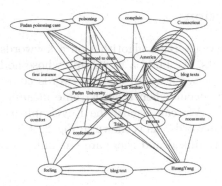

Fig. 3. Example of multi-graph of keywords.

We could build KeyGraph conveniently based on the multi-graph. All nodes in multi-graph are kept in KeyGraph and there is an weighted directed edge from node k_i to k_j if there are edges between nodes k_i and k_j in multi-graph. Here we assume that the weight $c_{i,j}$ is greater than $c_{j,i}$ without generality. The weight $c_{i,j}$ between nodes k_i and k_j can be calculated as shown:

$$c_{i,j} = \log \frac{n_{i,j}/(d_i - n_{i,j})}{(d_j - n_{i,j})/(N - d_j - d_i + n_{i,j})} \cdot |\frac{n_{i,j}}{d_i} - \frac{d_j - n_{i,j}}{N - d_i}| \qquad (6)$$

where:

- $n_{i,j}$ is the number of edges between the nodes k_i and k_j in the multi-graph.
- d_i is the degree of node k_i in the multi-graph.
- d_j is the degree of node k_j in the multi-graph.
- N is the total number of nodes.

It is noticed that the first term in the formula will increase as the times of co-occurrences between keywords i and j increase and the second term will decrease as the number of occurrences of a single keyword reduce. Actually, the $c_{i,j}$ is similar to conditional probability $p(k_i|k_j)$ of seeing keywords k_i in a document if k_j exists in the document which reflects the influence one keyword on another. Figure 2 shows an example for KeyGraph.

4.2   Community Detection

We apply community detection techniques adapted from network analysis method to discover events from the KeyGraph. Because the KeyGraph is a weighted directed graph, we adopt the method proposed in [2]. We first find all fixed size k of clique, for example k-clique ($k = 3$). Only when the intensity of clique is larger than a threshold value, will the clique be included. Two cliques are defined adjacent if they share $k-1$ nodes. A community is the union of cliques, in which we can reach any k-clique from any other clique through a series of k-clique adjacencies. Finally the communities of describing, collocated keywords are the discovered events we want.

5   Temporal Analysis

Event always has a temporal characteristics. The events detected by the algorithm should have a trend along the time axis. Basically, hot event would be spread widely and many documents will report the event. Considering the fact that the collocated keywords describing the event would cumulatively increase, we define a binary-valued function:

$$f(k|d) = \begin{cases} 1, k \in d \\ 0, k \notin d \end{cases} \tag{7}$$

where k is a keyword and d is a piece of document. For the detected event e_i, its trend in time internal $[t_0, t_0 + t]$ is shown as follows:

$$tr^{(t)}(e_i) = \sum_{k \in e_i} \sum_{d \in D^{(t)}} f(k|d) \tag{8}$$

where e_i is the ith event discovered by the algorithm, $D^{(t)}$ is the collection documents in time internal $[t_0, t_0 + t]$ and t_0 is a point time.

For each event e, we could compute its $tr^{(t_j)}(e), j = 1, \ldots, n$ in n series time unit. In order to detect the burst point of $tr(e)$, we compute the cumsum of the series $tr(e)$ as follows:

First, we compute the mean value of $tr^{(t_j)}(e), j = 1, \ldots n$:

$$\overline{X} = \frac{\sum_{i=1}^{n} tr^{(t_i)}(e)}{n} \tag{9}$$

Then, the cumsum is denoted as S_j:

$$\begin{aligned} S_1 &= tr_{(t_1)} \\ S_j &= S_{j-1} + tr_{(t_j)}(e) - \overline{X} \end{aligned} \tag{10}$$

In general, $tr(e)$ added to S_j is positive and the S_j will steadily increase. And if the event occurs at a certain time, the sum value will rapidly increase. A segment of the cumsum chart with an upward slop appears before the burst point, which indicates a period of time where the values tend to be larger than the average. A change in direction of cumsum chart shows that the event bursts after the change point in the cumsum chart. We introduce an algorithm to detect the change point. The estimator of magnitude of the change is defined as follows:

$$S_{diff} = S_{max} - S_{min} \tag{11}$$

Where $S_{max} = \max_{j=1,...,n} S_j$ and $S_{min} = \min_{j=1,...,n} S_j$.

For an event e and its $tr^{(t_j)}(e)$ values in n time units, we perform a bootstrap analysis [8] as follows:

1. Generate a bootstrap sample by randomly reordering the $tr^{(t_j)}(e)$.
2. Based on the bootstrap sample, compute the bootstrap cumsum as shown in the formula (10) denoted as $S_1^{(b)}, \ldots, S_n^{(b)}$.
3. Compute the maximum, minimum and the difference of bootstrap cumsum which are denoted as $S_{min}^{(b)}, S_{max}^{(b)}$ and $S_{diff}^{(b)}$.
4. Compare the original S_{diff} to the bootstrap $S_{diff}^{(b)}$. If S_{diff} is larger than $S_{diff}^{(b)}$, the event e is labelled as a hot event.

The idea behind the bootstrap analysis is that we can estimate how much $S_{diff}^{(b)}$ would vary if no change took place by performing a large number of bootstrap sample. Then We compare the bootstrap $S_{diff}^{(b)}$ value with the S_{diff} of original data so as to assure whether there are change point in the original data.

6   Experiment Analysis

In order to evaluate the performance of the method proposed in this paper, we conduct the experiment on sinaweibo micro-blog documents that we have collected during the twelve month from January to December in 2014. In this section we give a description of dataset on which experiment conducted and then provide the experiment result with analysis.

6.1   Dataset

We crawled the micro-blog documents from the internet. The total dataset has over 70 millions records and each record consists of micro-blog document texts, the generator of a piece of micro-blog document and the timestamp when the micro-blog document was created. Considering the volume of datasets and the nature of events distribution, we partitioned the datasets into twelve timeslots from Jan 2014 to Dec 2014. Each timeslot contains the micro-blog document data posed in one month.

6.2   Experiment Result and Analysis

Compared with English, Chinese must be segmented into words first. We choose to use NLPIR[1] to segment micro-document texts into words. After removing stopwords and non-characters such as emotion symbols, we applied the proposed

---

[1] A Chinese word segmentation system. http://ictclas.nlpir.org/.

Table 1. The events detected during January through December in 2014.

Date	Keywords	Events description
Jan 2014	{Open,Champion,Final,Won, Women's Single,Dominika Cibulkova,Eugenie Bouchard,Li Na,Australian Open,Azarenka } { Indonesia,volcano,burst}	{Li Na won Australian Open Women's Singles } {Indoesia volcano burst }
Feb 2014	{Portugal,legend super-star,Eusebio,died,Panthers} {President,Ukraine,Viktor Yanukovich,lift, parliamentary,duties }	{The death of Eusebio } {Ukrainian Parliament Deprives Yanukovych Of Presidential }
Mar 2014	{hospital,blood cen-ter,Kunming,reinforcement} {taking the virus,Kindergarten, children,investigation}	{Need to reinforce the blood center of Kunming hospital} {Children of a Kindergarten in Jilin were taken the "spiritual virus"}
Apr 2014	{Star Wars,death,funeral, boy,British,wishes} {wreck,South Korea,staff,escape}	{4-Year-Old Receives Star Wars-Themed Funeral As His Final.} {South Korean ferry disaster}
May 2014	{Gutman,won,the European cham-pionship,UEFA Europa League Cup }	{Gutman won championship in UEFA Europa League Cup}
Jun 2014	{Nanjing,Yangzi,refinery, explosion,fire,apparatus} {Abe,Tokyo,protest,lifted, collective,self-defense right,self-immolation}	{Petrochemical explosion in Nanjing China} {A Japanese committed self-immolation to protest Japan's push to expand defense role}
Jul 2014	{Temporary shelters,period ex-pired,license,Snowden,asylum}	{The period of temporary asylum of Snowden expire.}
Aug 2014	{Earthquake,disaster, emergency,rescue, soldiers,marching,army} {Accident,Investigation, intervention,Kunshan, explosion}	{Troops rush to quake to rescue refugees} {Investigate the accident of Jiangsu Kunshan plant explosion}
Sep 2014	{Entrance Examination,reform,cancel, division,arts,science.} {rural,homestead, occupied,Zhangquan Liu,Chuanming Zhou,rogue}	{the Entrance Examination reform cancel the division of arts and science.} {rural homestead was occupied by rouge Zhangquan Liu and Chuanming Zhou}
Oct 2014	{ Artist, misdeeds, drug, ban, prostitu-tion }	{SARFT of China claims to ban misdeeds artists }
Nov 2014	{The Navy, Colonel, trickster, posing, cheat}	{Laid-off workers posing Navy Colonel cheat two women.}
Dec 2014	{Fudan University, Senhao Lin, poison-ing, sentenced to death}	{Senhao Lin, student in Fudan Univer-sity, was sentenced to death for poisoning his roommate.}

method and algorithm to the dataset. Experiment result showed that is quite efficient with our algorithm as listed in Table 1.

In Table 1, the second column are the collocated keywords that belong to one community and the third column is the description of corresponding event. For each detected event we checked the mainstream media so as to determine whether it really happened in the real world. The accuracy was computed as follows:

$$Accuracy = \frac{\#true\_events}{\#true\_events + \#false\_events} \tag{12}$$

where

- #true_events is the number of events that really happened in real world.
- #false_events is the number of mistaken events by our algorithm.

The experiment result showed that the accuracy is around 80% as is seen in Fig. 4.

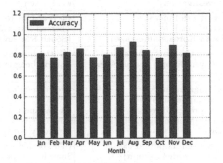

Fig. 4. Accuracy.

For identifying hot events, we compute the cumsum of $tr(e)$ to detect the burst of events. If an event won't become hot, its $tr(e)$ would not burst suddenly. What's reflected in the cumsum chart is that the cumsum chart will be a smooth line. In other words, there won't be change points in cumsum chart. With that we design a bootstrap sample analysis based algorithm to detect the hot events. In the algorithm, for an event, we determine whether it is a hot event by detecting the change point in the cumsum chart. Like the events in the left side of Fig. 5 the cumsum line increase sharply where there is a change point. The change points are detected by our algorithm, the events *Australian Open Women's Champion(Na Li from China won the Champion)* and *Mo Zhang detained for taking drugs* are identified as hot events. On the contrary, the events in the right side of Fig. 5 would not be identitied as hot events because no change points are detected. The experiment results demonstrate that the algorithm is very efficient.

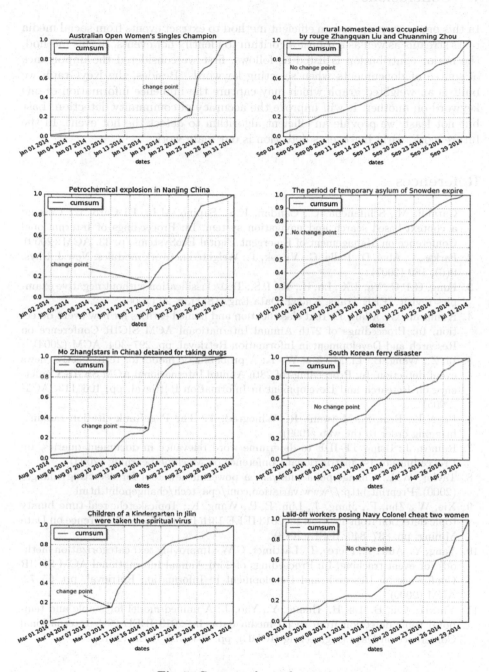

Fig. 5. Cumsum chart of events.

7 Conclusions

In this paper we proposed an efficient method to extract events from social media texts streams as well as a robust algorithm to identify hot events. In this method, the major contribution is listed as follows, first we considered the importance of source of doucuments when selecting keywords. Besides, the KeyGraph we built is an weighted graph which may capture the influence information of one keyword on another. It will improve the accuracy of community detection. Last but not least, we provide an efficient algorithm to detect the hot event. In the future work, early hot events detection is our main work.

References

1. Cataldi, M., Schifanella, C., Candan, K.S., Sapino, M.L., Di Caro, L.: Cosena: a context-based search and navigation system. In: Proceedings of International Conference on Management of Emergent Digital EcoSystems, p. 33. ACM (2009)
2. Farkas, I., Ábel, D., Palla, G., Vicsek, T.: Weighted network modules. New J. Phys. 9(6), 180 (2007)
3. Fung, G.P.C., Yu, J.X., Lu, H., Yu, P.S.: Text classification without negative examples revisit. IEEE Trans. Knowl. Data Eng. 18(1), 6–20 (2006)
4. Kumaran, G., Allan, J.: Text classification and named entities for new event detection. In: Proceedings of 27th Annual International ACM SIGIR Conference on Research and Development in Information Retrieval, pp. 297–304. ACM (2004)
5. Li, Z., Wang, B., Li, M., Ma, W.-Y.: A probabilistic model for retrospective news event detection. In: Proceedings of 28th Annual International ACM SIGIR Conference on Research and Development in Information Retrieval, pp. 106–113. ACM (2005)
6. Page, L., Brin, S., Motwani, R., Winograd, T.: The PageRank citation ranking: bringing order to the web (1999)
7. Ramos, J.: Using TF-IDF to determine word relevance in document queries. In: Proceedings of 1st Instructional Conference on Machine Learning (2003)
8. Taylor, W.A.: Change-point analysis: a powerful new tool for detecting changes (2000). Preprint http://www.variation.com/cpa/tech/changepoint.html
9. Xie, W., Zhu, F., Jiang, J., Lim, E.-P., Wang, K.: Topicsketch: real-time bursty topic detection from Twitter. In: 2013 IEEE 13th International Conference on Data Mining, pp. 837–846. IEEE (2013)
10. Yang, Y., Ault, T., Pierce, T., Lattimer, C.W.: Improving text categorization methods for event tracking. In: Proceedings of 23rd Annual International ACM SIGIR Conference on Research and Development in Information Retrieval, pp. 65–72. ACM (2000)
11. Yin, H., Cui, B., Lu, H., Huang, Y., Yao, J.: A unified model for stable and temporal topic detection from social media data. In: 2013 IEEE 29th International Conference on Data Engineering (ICDE), pp. 661–672. IEEE (2013)

Discovering Concept-Level Event Associations from a Text Stream

Tao Ge[1,2], Lei Cui[3], Heng Ji[4], Baobao Chang[1,2], and Zhifang Sui[1,2(✉)]

[1] Key Laboratory of Computational Linguistics, Ministry of Education,
School of EECS, Peking University, Beijing, China
{getao,chbb,szf}@pku.edu.cn
[2] Collaborative Innovation Center for Language Ability, Xuzhou, China
[3] Microsoft Research, Beijing, China
lecu@microsoft.com
[4] Rensselaer Polytechnic Institute, Troy, NY, USA
jih@rpi.edu

Abstract. We study an open text mining problem – discovering concept-level event associations from a text stream. We investigate the importance and challenge of this task and propose a novel solution by using event sequential patterns. The proposed approach can discover important event associations implicitly expressed. The discovered event associations are general and useful as knowledge for applications such as event prediction.

1 Introduction

People often seek event associations because such knowledge enables them to predict the future, take certain precautions, or make wise decisions under a specific circumstance. For example, if one knows landslides often occur after earthquakes, the risk of damages can be reduced.

Due to the importance of event associations, this paper studies concept-level event association discovery. In contrast to the previous work studying specific and context-dependent events (e.g., *Jim hit John yesterday*), concept-level events (e.g., *earthquake*) are context-independent and thus their associations (e.g., (*earthquake-landslide*)) are general and useful as knowledge, which has attracted so much attention that some semantic networks and knowledge bases (e.g., ConceptNet[1]) have started to incorporate concept-level event association knowledge due to its potential ability in knowledge inference and decision making. Formally, given two concept-level events e_i and e_j, we define e_i and e_j are associated if e_j tends to to be triggered, caused or affected by e_i, and e_j is not a part of e_i.

Despite extensive studies on event relations [1–5,13,16–19,22] in NLP field, the task of concept-level event association discovery has not been much explored. Most work [9–12,20,21,23] related to concept-level event association discovery

---

[1] http://conceptnet5.media.mit.edu/.

© Springer International Publishing AG 2016
C.-Y. Lin et al. (Eds.): NLPCC-ICCPOL 2016, LNAI 10102, pp. 413–424, 2016.
DOI: 10.1007/978-3-319-50496-4_34

mainly focused on causality extraction based on text clues (e.g., causal verbs and connectives), which is usually insufficient because event associations are not limited to causality explicitly expressed. For many associations that are implicitly expressed, it is difficult for text-based approaches to discover. Although the implicit event associations might be discovered by the methods based on word co-occurrence (e.g., Point-wise Mutual Information (PMI)), these methods do not work well for our goal for two reasons. First, computing PMI of arbitrary event pairs is time-consuming and will introduce many trivial and uninformative event pairs like (*say, sit*). Second, event pairs with high PMI may not be truly associated since events in some pairs are minor events (e.g., *donation* and *evacuate* in Fig. 1) triggered by a major event (e.g., *earthquake*) and they are not associated though they always co-occur.

To solve this problem, we study this task from a novel viewpoint – exploiting Burst Sequential Patterns (BSPs[2]) of events in a text stream to discover event associations. Intuitively, if a word describing an event always bursts after or co-bursts with another event word throughout a text stream, these two events are probably associated (e.g., the word *donation* usually bursts after *earthquake*). By analyzing such BSPs in a text stream, it is possible to discover event associations even if they are implicitly expressed. For this goal, we propose to use *Burst Information Networks (BINets)* [6–8] as a representation of a text stream, which can overcome the limitations of traditional PMI-based methods.

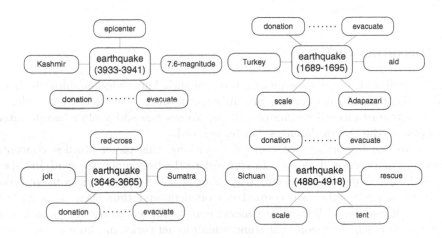

Fig. 1. A BINet example. The numbers in the round brackets denote the burst period of the node. Due to space limitation, we only show *earthquake*'s burst period (days after Jan 1, 1995). Dash lines denote false associations.

In a BINet (Fig. 1), a node is a burst word (including entities and events) with the time span of one of its burst periods, and an edge between two nodes indicates how strongly they are related. Since only burst words are in a BINet,

---

[2] We treat co-burst as a special case of BSPs.

trivial events are naturally excluded. In a BINet, event BSPs (e.g., *donation* and *earthquake*) can be clearly observed. Moreover, nodes in a community in a BINet are not only topically but also temporally coherent; thus, we can say a community describes an event's topic. Based on a community's structure, it is easy to distinguish major events and minor events for removing false association pairs like (*donation, evacuate*) in Fig. 1.

Experiments show the BINet-based approach can not only discover concept-level event associations with comparable precision to text clue based approaches but also discover many important event associations that are not explicitly expressed, and that the BINet and the text clue based approach can nicely complement each other, yielding significant improvement of performance.

2   Burst Information Networks

2.1   Burst Detection

To build a Burst Information Network mentioned in the above section, we first need to detect bursts of words. In general, a word's burst might indicate important events or trending topics. For example, as shown in Fig. 1, the word *earthquake* has a burst from the 4880th to the 4918th days because of a strong earthquake occuring in China on May 12, 2008. For a timestamped document collection $C = \{D_1, D_2, ..., D_t, ..., D_T\}$, we define a word w's burst sequence $s = (s_1, s_2, ..., s_t, ..., s_T)$ in which s_t is either 1 or 0 to indicate whether the word w bursts or not at time t. Based on the idea of [14,24], this burst sequence can be simply found by searching for the optimal sequence s^* to minimize the cost function defined as follows:

$$Cost(s, p, q^{(0)}, q^{(1)}) =$$
$$\sum_{t=1}^{T} |\log p_t - \log q^{(s_t)}| + \sum_{t=1}^{T-1} \beta * \mathbf{1}(s_t \neq s_{t+1}) \quad (1)$$

where $p = (p_1, ..., p_t, ..., p_T)$ in which p_t is the probability of the word at t, $q^{(0)}$ is the base probability of the word and it is often defined as the probability of the word on the whole data/corpus, $q^{(1)}$ is the probability of the word in the burst state and it is often defined as $q^{(1)} = \alpha q^{(0)}$ ($\alpha > 1$).

The first term of Eq. (1) measures the difference between p_t and $q^{(s_t)}$. If a word bursts (i.e., p_t is high), $|log p_t - log q^{(1)}|$ will be smaller than $|log p_t - log q^{(0)}|$ and thus in the optimal sequence s^*, s_t tends to be 1; otherwise, s_t tends to be 0. The last term of Eq. (1) is for penalizing transition of burst states through the time to avoid too frequent transition of burst states for smoothing and β is the parameter controlling this part's weight.

Specifically, if a word w is in a burst state at every time t during a period, we call this period as a burst period of w, and w has a burst during this period. In Fig. 1, *earthquake* has 3 burst periods (i.e., (3646–3665), (3933–3941), and (4880–4918)).

Formally, we define $\mathcal{P}_i(w)$ as the ith burst period of the word w. It is a consecutive time sequence (i.e., time interval) during which w bursts at every time epoch t:

$$\mathcal{P}_i(w) = [t_i^s(w), t_i^e(w)]$$
$$\forall t \in \mathcal{P}_i(w) \quad s_t(w) = 1$$

where $t_i^s(w)$ and $t_i^e(w)$ denote the starting and ending time of the ith burst period of w, and $s_t(w)$ denotes the burst state of w at time t.

2.2   BINet Construction

A *"Burst Information Network (BINet)"* represents associations between key facts in a text stream, which has been proven to be effective in multiple knowledge mining tasks [6–8]. The basic component of a BINet is burst elements which are nodes of the information network:

A **Burst Element** is a burst of a word. It can be represented by a tuple: $\langle w, \mathcal{P}_i(w) \rangle$ where w denotes the word and $\mathcal{P}_i(w)$ denotes one burst period of w.

A BINet is defined as $G = \langle V, E \rangle$. Each node $v \in V$ is a burst element and each edge $e \in E$ denotes the association between burst elements. Intuitively, if two burst elements frequently co-occur, then they should be highly weighted. We define $\omega_{i,j}$ as the global weight of an edge between v_i and v_j, which is equal to the number of documents where v_i and v_j co-occur, and $\pi_{i,j}$ as the local weight, which equals to the number of documents in which v_i and v_j form a bigram (i.e., v_i and v_j are adjacent in context). Since a node in BINet contains both semantic and temporal information, nodes in a community are topically and temporally coherent.

3   Event Association Discovery

We first extract events (Sect. 3.1), identify major events for removing false associations (Sect. 3.2) from the BINet, and then rank event associations (Sect. 3.3).

3.1   Event Extraction

Since there is no available open-domain event extraction systems despite some event extractors for limited types of events (e.g., 33 event types in ACE evaluation), we use words in the following list as event trigger words to identify nodes describing events in the BINet, and call the nodes whose word is in the following list **event nodes**:

- Nouns and verbs in frames with *time* attribute in FrameNet[3].
- Trigger word list in ACE evaluation.
- Natural hazards in Wikipedia.

---

[3] https://framenet.icsi.berkeley.edu/fndrupal/.

Since one node is a unigram[4] (with its burst period), an event node sometimes may not describe an event well (e.g., "test" is too general to describe an event). Hence, for an event node v_i, we try to find its adjacent node to form a bigram to represent the event (e.g., for a node whose word is "test", we may use its adjacent node "nuclear" to represent the event as "nuclear test"). Specifically, we first find the set of nodes locally strongly related to v_i:

$$C(v_i) = \{v_j | \pi_{i,j} > \pi_t\}$$

where π_t is a threshold. Then, we find v_i's most globally related node v_k from $C(v_i)$:

$$v_k = arg \max_{v_j \in C(v_i)} \omega_{i,j}$$

Table 1. Designed POS pattern for event bigram phrase extraction. The bold means it is the head word of the bigram which should be an event node.

Bigram	POS pattern
v_i, v_k	JJ,**NN** | NN,**NN** | NN,**VB** | **VB**,NN

If part-of-speech (POS) tags of v_i and v_k match the patterns in Table 1, then v_i and v_k form a valid event bigram. If we cannot find a v_k making v_i and v_k form an event bigram, v_i is considered as an independent event unigram. Note that if a bigram contains a named entity, we use the type of the entity to replace the entity string for generalization. For example, *Tohoku earthquake* will be replaced with *LOCATION earthquake*.

3.2 Major Event Identification

To identify major events, we first need to detect topics in the text stream and then identify the major event of every topic. As mentioned before, nodes in a community in a BINet describe an event's topic. Therefore, we model topic detection as a community discovery problem.

We first compute PageRank value of nodes in a BINet and rank them by their PageRank values. Note that the weights for PageRank computation are the global weights (ω) of the BINet. Then, we repeatedly choose the node that has the highest PageRank value but does not belong to any community, with its closely related nodes to form a new community $\mathcal{E}$. The algorithm is summarized in Algorithm 1 where $\mathcal{L}$ is the ranking list of nodes by their PageRank values, $V' \subset V$ is the set of nodes that does not belong to any communities, $\hat{\omega}_{v,u}$ is the normalized weight of the edge between v and u, and σ is the threshold for selecting closely related nodes. The algorithm discovers communities greedily and thus is fast.

After topics in a text stream are detected, we identify major events for each topic. Intuitively, a major event must be most frequently mentioned and it should

---

[4] Here, a named entity is considered as a unigram even if it is composed of multiple words such as *Hong Kong*.

418   T. Ge et al.

be strongly related to other nodes in its community; thus, its PageRank value
should be at the top in the community. Hence, we select the event phrase (unigram or bigram) whose PageRank value is the highest among all event phrases
in a community as the major event, as shown in Table 2. Note that a bigram's
PageRank value is the average of its words.

Table 2. An example of communities (topics) discovered by our approach. Major
events (the bold words) usually have the top PageRank value.

Topic	Key phrases
1	**Iraq war**, Iraqi, US-led, Baghdad
2	**Attack**, terrorist, New York, Washington, Afghanistan
3	**Earthquake**, quake, Wenchuan, Sichuan, quake-hit
4	**Hong Kong return**, motherland, handover, hk
5	Deng Xiaoping, Deng, **death**, condolence, mourn

Algorithm 1. Topic detection

1: **Input:** $\mathcal{L}$, $G = \langle V, E \rangle$;
2: **Output:** A list of communities: $\mathcal{C} = [\mathcal{E}_1, \mathcal{E}_2, ..., \mathcal{E}_k]$
3: $V' \leftarrow V$
4: **while** $\|\mathcal{L}\| > 0$ **do**
5:    $v \leftarrow \mathcal{L}[0]$ (the first element in $\mathcal{L}$)
6:    $\mathcal{E} \leftarrow \{v\} \cup \{u | u \in V' \wedge \hat{w}_{v,u} > \sigma\}$
7:    $\mathcal{C}.add(\mathcal{E})$; $\mathcal{L} \leftarrow \mathcal{L} - \mathcal{E}$; $V' \leftarrow V' - \mathcal{E}$
8: **end while**

3.3 Event Association Pair Ranking

We select all event pairs in which two events are adjacent in the BINet as candidates and remove (minor event, minor event) pairs which account for most false
association cases.

Moreover, we exclude the pairs in which the semantic similarity[5] of two events
is higher than a threshold τ because they usually refer to the same event (e.g.,
quake and *earthquake*).

For the remaining pairs, we rank event association pairs (e_1, e_2) using the
following metric inspired by Pointwise Mutual Information (PMI):

$$M(e_1, e_2) = \frac{n_{e_1,e_2}}{n_{e_1} \times n_{e_2}} (\log n_{e_1,e_2} + \alpha) \tag{2}$$

where e is an event uni- or bi-gram in Sect. 3.1, n_e is the count of e, n_{e_1,e_2} is
the count of cases where e_1 is adjacent to e_2 in a BINet (e.g., $n_{earthquake} =$

---
[5] Cosine similarity computed based on word embeddings trained on English Gigaword
corpus.

$n_{earthquake,donation} = 4$ for the BINet in Fig. 1), and the factor $(\log n_{e_1,e_2} + \alpha)$ is for promoting event pairs with high support where α is a smoothing parameter for avoiding (2) being 0 if $n_{e_1,e_2} = 1$.

4   Experiments and Evaluations

4.1   Data

We evaluate our approach on 1995–2010 Xinhua news in English Gigaword[6] which contains 1,482,560 news articles.

We used Stanford CoreNLP toolkit to perform POS tagging, lemmatization, named entity recognition, and apply our Burst Information Network (BINet) construction algorithm on this dataset. We remove edges whose global weights are less than a threshold ω_t for reducing noise. The resulting BINet includes 414,944 nodes and 3,699,537 edges.

4.2   End-to-end Evaluation

We discover event associations in an end-to-end fashion. Hyper-parameters ($\sigma = 0.0005$, $\tau = 0.7$, $\pi_t = 5$, $\omega_t = 5$, $\alpha = 0.01$) are tuned on a development set. Totally, we mined 6,084 event association pairs.

We compare the following approaches:

PMI-E: Ranking association pairs by PMI computed over all event words based on their co-occurrence in documents.

PMI-S: PMI of event words are computed based on co-occurrence in sentences.

BINet-E: BINet-based approach without removing false association pairs.

BINet-E+: BINet-based approach where false association are removed.

Text-E: This model extracts causality of event trigger words based on the most commonly used unambiguous causal verbs and connectives, as [20] did, and ranks by frequency. The details of the implementation of this baseline is introduced in the Appendix Section.

Combine: we re-rank the results of BINET-E+ by combining the results of TEXT-E:

$$\hat{M}(e_1, e_2) = M(e_1, e_2) + \log n_t(e_1, e_2)$$

where $n_t(e_1, e_2)$ is the count of cases where causality of e_1 and e_2 is explicitly expressed by causal verbs and connectives.

In baseline methods, event words include the event bigrams in Sect. 3.1 for fair comparison. We do not compare to [11,12] because their supervised approaches require annotated data that is not publicly available, and do not make a comparison to [23] due to their limited focus on deverbal nouns. [9,10,21] are not compared either because their focus is not mining event associations.

Event association discovery is an open text mining problem and there is no closed gold standard for this task though some knowledge resources (e.g., ConceptNet) can be used as references but they are far from complete. Alternatively,

---

[6] https://catalog.ldc.upenn.edu/LDC2011T07.

Table 3. Precision of top 500 discovered event association pairs in end-to-end evaluation.

Model	Precision@500
Pmi-E	1.6%
Pmi-S	4.4%
BINet-E	17.2%
BINet-E+	35.6%
Text-E	36.2%
Combine	**43.0%**

we manually evaluate the quality of discovered event associations and use Precision of top K (500) pairs to measure the performance. We do not evaluate recall since it is impractical to find all event associations. We pooled the top K pairs outputted by each system evaluated in this paper for annotation. The annotation[7] is done by 2 annotators who are asked to tell if words/phrases in a pair are associated events by considering whether a word/phrase pair satisfy the event association definition and the association is informative and self-interpretable.

The annotations have fairly good agreement (84.4% overlapping). The difference in the annotators' background knowledge accounts for most annotation disagreement cases. During evaluation, we consider an event association pair as correct if both of the annotators annotate it as correct.

As shown in Table 3, Pmi-E and Pmi-S yield poor performance because many event pairs are either about trivial events or are not associated. Introducing BINets improves PMI-based methods because large numbers of trivial events are excluded. When we remove false association pairs based on the network structure, the performance (BINet-E+) gets significant boost (18.4% gain) and achieves comparable performance to Text-E. When we re-rank the results of BINet-E+ with text clue information, the performance is markedly improved (7.4% and 6.8% gain over BINet-E+ and Text-E respectively), demonstrating these two approaches can well complement each other.

Moreover, we show the performance of models with various Ks in Fig. 2. Text-clue based approach can accurately mine event associations if K is small while its performance drops drastically with K increasing because the number of explicitly expressed event associations is limited. In contrast, the BINet-based approach is more stable, which outperforms the text-based model when K is large. As the results in Table 3, the combination of these approaches improves both of them.

We analyze error cases of the discovered event pairs. The event extraction mistakes are the main source of errors because event extraction is a challenging task, especially for open domains, which affects event association discovery

---

[7] The annotators mainly used ConceptNet and Wikipedia as references to help with the annotation.

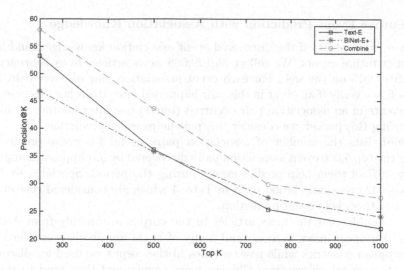

Fig. 2. Precision curves of various models.

results. Another type of errors is that some events are over-generalized because unigram and bigram event representations sometimes are insufficient to describe a complicated event. For example, in the association pair (*financial crisis, impact*), the event *impact* is too general to be informative. In addition, events in some pairs do not satisfy the definition of association (e.g., one event is a part of the other event in a pair like (*match,goal*)).

Table 4. Examples of discovered event association pairs. Of these 32 event association pairs, only 14 (bold) are explicitly expressed by textual clues.

Earthquake	Flood	Financial crisis	Protest
Donation	Divert floodwater	**Shrink**	Election
Landslide	Mine accident	**Financial reform**	Declaration
Humanitarian aid	**Dike breach**	Stimulate economic	**Violence**
Mourn	Remain trapped	**Loan**	Nuclear test
Search	**Evacuation**	Rate cut	War
Death	Rehabilitation	**Slump**	**Conflict**
Evacuation	Flood control	**Plunge**	Invasion
Medical treatment	**Damage**	**Unemployment**	**Arrest**

As a qualitative evaluation, we present examples of event associations discovered by BINET-E+ in Table 4. The event associations are general and useful as knowledge. Moreover, we analyze these 32 event pairs and find only 14 (43.75%) of them are explicitly expressed by the textual clues used in TEXT-E, showing the limitation of the textual clue based approach and the importance of studying BSP-based approaches for this task.

4.3   Future Event Prediction with Association Knowledge

Moreover, we evaluate if the discovered event association knowledge could help us predict future events. We collect 36,129,066 news articles from February to December 2015 on the web. For each event association pair discovered by our approach, we verify if an event in this pair happened after the other. Specifically, if the events in an association pair occurred (burst) one after another within 7 days during this period, we consider this pair helps event prediction.

Table 5 lists the number of association pairs useful for event prediction. Among the top 5,000 event association pairs discovered by our approach, approximately 20% of them help predict events during the period. Specially, we also test those 32 event association pairs in Table 4 which are considered correct. 15 (46.9%) of them help event prediction.

It is notable that the news articles in the corpus are mainly from American and European news agencies and many of them are about events in USA and European countries while news articles in the corpus we used for discovering event associations are from Chinese news agency and they tend to report Chinese local events. Even so, the discovered event associations are still successfully used for prediction, showing that the event association knowledge is general and location-independent.

Table 5. The number of association pairs helpful for future event prediction

Top	500	1000	2000	5000
Predicted	111	197	382	848

5   Related Work

Most work [9 12,20,21,23] related to concept-level event association discovery mainly study extracting causality based on text clues (e.g., causal verbs and connectives). Among them, [9,10] studied mining textual patterns that describe causal relations, [23] derived event associations by focusing on deverbal nouns within a discourse, [20] proposed to extract event causality and use it to predict future events based on explicit discourse connectives, [21] focused on estimation of the probability that an event occurring after the other given a query event pair, [11,12] used supervised models to extract event causality, and [15] utilized hierarchical topic structure to capture event associations. In contrast, our approach is unsupervised, efficient, and does not rely on explicit discourse connectives but can nicely complement the textual-based approach. The discovered association knowledge is general and related to important events and thus useful for applications like event prediction and event-centric knowledge base construction.

Another research branch related to this paper is event relation extraction [3–5,22]. Different from our task that discovers concept-level event associations that can be used as general knowledge, these studies focus on extracting relations between events in a local context (a sentence or a document).

6 Conclusion

We study an open text mining problem – concept-level event association discovery based on burst sequential pattern mining by using a novel graph-based text stream representation, which makes it possible to discover massive implicit event associations and presents chances for event knowledge discovery and event prediction from big data.

Acknowledgements. We appreciate the helpful comments of the reviewers. This work is supported by the National Key Basic Research Program of China (No. 2014CB340504), the Research Fund for the Doctoral Program of Higher Education (20130001110027) and the National Natural Science Foundation of China (No. 61375074, 61273318). The contact author is Zhifang Sui.

Appendix

We introduce how we implement the TEXT-E approach mentioned in Sect. 4. As [20] did, we use the most commonly used unambiguous causal verbs and connectives in Table 6 to extract causality as event associations. We did not use *as* and *after* because *as* is ambiguous, and *after* cannot guarantee that events connected by it are associated according to definition in our paper.

Table 6. Patterns for extracting causality. Note that for *because, because of* and *due to*, both of *a* and *b* should have a direct path to the causal markers.

Causal marker	Dependency pattern	Instance(a,b)
Because	advcl(a,b)	They **killed** him because he **divulged** the secret
Because of	prep_because_of(a,b)	The election is **postponed** because of the **outbreak** of plague
Due to	prep_due_to(a,b)	The province has **suffered** heavy losses of arable land due to water **erosion** for the past several years
Cause	nsubj(cause,a); dobj(cause,b)	The **earthquake** caused severe **damages** in Japan
	vmod(a, cause); agent(cause, b)	The move is aimed at increasing investment in key sectors and reducing the **burden** caused by inefficient public **enterprises** on the economy
Affect	nsubj(affect,a); dobj(affect,b)	Same with cause
	vmod(a, affect); agent(affect, b)	Same with cause
Lead to	nsubj(lead, a); prep_to(lead, b)	In fact, such **activities** not only harm reforms, national economic development and social stability but lead to high production and construction **costs** for the local economies

References

1. Abe, S., Inui, K., Matsumoto, Y.: Two-phased event relation acquisition: coupling the relation-oriented and argument-oriented approaches. In: COLING (2008)
2. Bethard, S., Martin, J.H.: Learning semantic links from a corpus of parallel temporal and causal relations. In: ACL (2008)
3. Chambers, N., Jurafsky, D.: Unsupervised learning of narrative schemas and their participants. In: ACL (2009)
4. Chambers, N., Jurafsky, D.: Unsupervised learning of narrative event chains. In: ACL (2008)
5. Do, Q.X., Chan, Y.S., Roth, D.: Minimally supervised event causality identification. In: EMNLP (2011)
6. Ge, T., Cui, L., Chang, B., Li, S., Zhou, M., Sui, Z.: News stream summarization using burst information networks. In: EMNLP (2016)
7. Ge, T., Cui, L., Chang, B., Sui, Z., Zhou, M.: Event detection with burst information network. In: COLING (2016)
8. Ge, T., Dou, Q., Pan, X., Ji, H., Cui, L., Chang, B., Sui, Z., Zhou, M.: Aligning coordinated text streams through burst information network construction and decipherment. arXiv preprint. arXiv:1609.08237 (2016)
9. Girju, R.: Automatic detection of causal relations for question answering. In: Workshop on Multilingual Summarization and Question Answering (2003)
10. Girju, R., Moldovan, D.I., et al.: Text mining for causal relations. In: FLAIRS Conference (2002)
11. Hashimoto, C., Torisawa, K., Kloetzer, J., Oh, J.H.: Generating event causality hypotheses through semantic relations. In: AAAI (2015)
12. Hashimoto, C., Torisawa, K., Kloetzer, J., Sano, M., Varga, I., Oh, J.H., Kidawara, Y.: Toward future scenario generation: extracting event causality exploiting semantic relation, context, and association features. In: ACL (2014)
13. Hashimoto, C., Torisawa, K., Kuroda, K., De Saeger, S., Murata, M., Kazama, J.: Large-scale verb entailment acquisition from the web. In: EMNLP (2009)
14. Kleinberg, J.: Bursty and hierarchical structure in streams. Data Min. Knowl. Disc. **7**(4), 373–397 (2003)
15. Li, R., Wang, T., Wang, X.: Tracking events using time-dependent hierarchical dirichlet tree model. In: SDM (2015)
16. Mirza, P., Tonelli, S.: An analysis of causality between events and its relation to temporal information. In: COLING (2014)
17. Mulkar-Mehta, R., Welty, C., Hoobs, J.R., Hovy, E.: Using granularity concepts for discovering causal relations. In: FLAIRS (2011)
18. Oh, J.H., Torisawa, K., Hashimoto, C., Sano, M., De Saeger, S., Ohtake, K.: Why-question answering using intra- and inter-sentential causal relations. In: ACL (2013)
19. Pantel, P., Bhagat, R., Coppola, B., Chklovski, T., Hovy, E.H.: ISP: learning inferential selectional preferences. In: HLT-NAACL (2007)
20. Radinsky, K., Davidovich, S., Markovitch, S.: Learning causality for news events prediction. In: WWW (2012)
21. Radinsky, K., Horvitz, E.: Mining the web to predict future events. In: WSDM (2013)
22. Riaz, M., Girju, R.: Another look at causality: discovering scenario-specific contingency relationships with no supervision. In: ICSC (2010)
23. Tanaka, S., Okazaki, N., Ishizuka, M.: Acquiring and generalizing causal inference rules from deverbal noun constructions. In: COLING (2012)
24. Zhao, W.X., Chen, R., Fan, K., Yan, H., Li, X.: A novel burst-based text representation model for scalable event detection. In: ACL (2012)

A User Adaptive Model for Followee Recommendation on Twitter

Yang Liu[1], Xuan Chen[2], Sujian Li[1,3(✉)], and Liang Wang[1]

[1] Key Laboratory of Computational Linguistics,
Peking University, MOE, Beijing, China
{cs-ly,lisujian,intfloat}@pku.edu.cn
[2] School of Information, Shandong University of Political Science and Law,
Jinan, China
chenx@sdupsl.edu.cn
[3] Collaborative Innovation Center for Language Ability, Xuzhou, Jiangsu, China

Abstract. On the Twitter platform, an effective followee recommendation system is helpful to connecting users in a satisfactory manner. Topological relations and tweets content are two main factors considered in a followee recommendation system. However, how to combine these two kinds of information in a uniform framework is still an open problem. In this paper, we propose to combine deep learning techniques and collaborative information to explore the user representations latent behind the topology and content. Over two kinds of user representations (i.e., topology representation and content representation), we design an adaptive layer to dynamically leverage the contribution of topology and content to recommending followees, which changes the situation where the contribution weights are usually predefined. Experiments on a real-world Twitter dataset show that our proposed model provides more satisfying recommendation results than state-of-the-art methods.

1 Introduction

Twitter is a popular microblogging platform with over 200 million active users all over the world. Different from other social networks, such as Facebook or MySpace, Twitter is mainly composed of asymmetric *following* relations from followers to followees. Users (followers) follow other users (followees) with no need of being accepted or reciprocated, and receive the updated tweets from their followees. At the same time, most users hope to avoid the disturbance from uninterested users and may not follow their followers. Developing an effective followee recommendation system (RS) can assist users to connect with other users in a satisfactory manner and share information in time.

Existing followee recommendation schemes mainly follow the homophily effect [20] that users tend to follow those users of similar characteristics. The key issue here is to precisely represent a user using the available information. Two kinds of information are commonly used: topology of social relations and content of posted tweets. One line of research only considers the user itself and

© Springer International Publishing AG 2016
C.-Y. Lin et al. (Eds.): NLPCC-ICCPOL 2016, LNAI 10102, pp. 425–436, 2016.
DOI: 10.1007/978-3-319-50496-4_35

explores some shallow features from the two information sources [1,10,12]. These kinds of features are not so precise to represent users though they have made some progress in followee recommendation.

The other line of research applies collaborative filtering (CF) techniques in user profiling by virtue of many users with similar tastes. The state-of-the-art CF models based on matrix factorization explore various latent feature vectors to represent users [6,14,19,24]. Therein, [6] propose a variant of latent factor model (LFM) which can learn two latent vectors to represent topology and content respectively. In their work, a linear combination of these two vectors is regarded as the deep representation of a user. On one hand, this work inspires us to explore the low-dimensional user representations with respect to both topology and content. On the other hand, we raise the following question: Is it appropriate to combine topology-based and content-based feature vectors in a linear manner for followee recommendation?

To obtain a better latent representation for users, we survey deep learning techniques which can successfully encode the semantic representations of things [2,3,22]. Bordes *et al.* [3] model both relations and entities in knowledge bases (KB), and build structural embeddings for relation prediction and entity resolution. In our opinion, a user on Twitter is just analogous to an entity in a knowledge base, while the topological connections (i.e., existing *following* relations) between users analogous to entity relations in KB. Thus, inspired from [3], we model users and their connections and design two kinds of neural networks in terms of topology and content respectively. To cater for the followee recommendation task, we incorporate the collaborative information of users by modeling followers of followees and followees of followers. In the topology-based neural network, we represent each user with a continuous vector and utilize the *following* relations between users to learn the user vectors. In the content-based neural network, stacked denoising autoencoders are designed to pretrain the content-based user representations based on the posted tweets, as an alternative to the bag-of-words representation of content. Two kinds of representations, namely topology-based vector and content-based vector, are then learned.

Next, we have to face the question above: how to apply the topology-based representation and content-based representation in followee recommendation? A direct summation of these two representations is based on the assumption that they belong to the same feature space, which can not be ensured. In our implementation, we can get two relevance scores: the topological relevance between two users is computed based on topology-based vectors while the content relevance relies on content-based vectors. To combine these two relevance scores, the usual practice is to get a weighted average of them, where the weights are fixed once they are learned. However, for followee recommendation on Twitter, the contribution of topological information and content information does not always keep consistent. Following the adaptive idea of [8] which selects different functions based on input components and [23] which uses the "attention mechanism" to focus on different objects during decoding, we design an adaptive layer to dynamically tune the weights imposed on topology relevance and content relevance.

2   Approach Overview

The basic idea of our recommendation algorithm is to compute a score to signify the possibility of forming a *following* relation between two users. Formally, given two users u and v, the relevance score $score_{rel}(u, v)$ represents the possibility of u following v. The higher the score is, the more likely u follows v.

To calculate the relevance score, we design a neural network framework to take advantage of the two kinds of resources: the topology of the existing *following* relations and the content of posted tweets, as illustrated in Fig. 1. Two subnetworks, namely topology-based neural network and content-based neural network, are constructed to model users and their connections. Specifically, given two users u and v, the topology-based neural network can calculate the topology relevance score $(score_{topo}(u, v))$ of u following v. Likewise, the content-based neural network calculates the content relevance score $(score_{con}(u, v))$ of u following v. Different from [3], We utilize the collaborative information in our model. That means, when predicting the relation between two users, we not only consider their own information, but also their observed followees and followers. This will give our model much more information and boost its performance.

Next, we linearly combine the topology and content relevance scores, and adaptively tune their weights to get the final relevance score $(score_{rel})$. To this end, an adaptive layer is designed to generate the parameter α, which leverages the topology and content information in followee recommendation. As the profile attributes (e.g., number of followers, number of tweets) are important to determining the contribution of topology and content, we consider the attributes as a kind of input to control the generation of α by representing them with a vector $A_{u,v}$. Then, three kinds of factors: the topology-based user representation (E_u and E_v), content-based user representation (C_u and C_v) and a feature vector of the explicit attributes ($A_{u,v}$), serve as the input to the adaptive layer.

The goal of a followee recommendation system is to predict the potential *following* relations between two users, given the observed *following* relations. Let us notate the set of users as U and the set of observed *following* relations as $D = \{(u, v) | u, v \in U\}$. Intuitively, the observed (follower, followee) pairs should have a higher relevance score than the remaining pairs. For this reason,

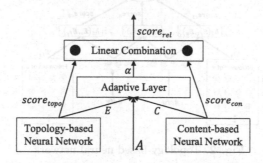

Fig. 1. User adaptive model for followee recommendation

for each training pair $t = (u, v) \in D$ we construct a set of negative examples $\{t' = (((u', v)|(u, v')) \notin D)\}$ where u' or v' is randomly selected from U. With the criterion that the score difference between positive and negative pairs is larger than the predefined margin Ω, we minimize the following formula:

$$\sum_{t} \sum_{t'} max(0, \Omega - score_{rel}(t) + score_{rel}(t')) \tag{1}$$

3   User Modeling

To model users, we exploit the topology and content information and design two neural networks, i.e. topology-based neural network and content-based neural network. Further, we construct an adaptive layer to leverage topology and content in followee recommendation.

3.1   Topology-Based Neural Network

The topology-based neural network (TBNN) encodes each user with a semantic representation, referring to the method proposed by [4]. Formally, each user u is represented with a d_t-dimensional vector (topology-based user embedding) $E_u \in \mathbb{R}^{d_t}$ stored in a lookup table $LT \in \mathbb{R}^{d_t * |U|}$. For any two users u and v, we assign a score $score_{topo}(u, v)$ to signify their topology relevance of u being a follower and v being a followee. The higher the score is, the more likely u may follow v. That is, the TBNN takes embeddings as input and the topology relevance score as output, as shown in Fig. 2.

The main improvement of our model is the incorporation of collaborative information hidden among users, which has been proven effective in people recommendation [5]. In our work, we take into account followees of followers and followers of followees. That is u's followees and v's followers, when we model the topology relevance of u following v. This makes sense, because u may share some common characteristics with v's other followers and v may have common

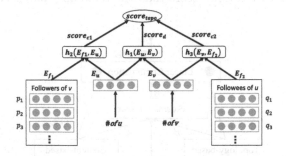

Fig. 2. Topology-based neural network

characteristics with u's other followees, if u follows v. Here, we use the averaged embeddings to represent the collaborative information.

$$E_{f_1} = \frac{1}{m} \sum_{p_i \in follower(v)} E_{p_i}, \ E_{f_2} = \frac{1}{n} \sum_{q_j \in follower(u)} E_{q_j} \quad (2)$$

where $follower(v) = \{p_1, p_2, \cdots, p_m\}$ represents a set of $v's$ followers, and $followee(u) = \{q_1, q_2, \cdots, q_n\}$ represents $u's$ followees. TBNN regards the topology relevance $score_{topo}$ as the sum of a direct relevance score ($score_d$) and two collaborative scores ($score_{c_1}$ and $score_{c_2}$). That is,

$$score_{topo} = score_d + score_{c_1} + score_{c_2} \quad (3)$$

To compute $score_d$, we use a bilinear function $h_1(.)$ which calculates the dot product of two linearly transformed embeddings, referring to [4].

$$
\begin{aligned}
score_d = h_1(E_u, E_v) &= (W_{tl}E_u{}^T + b_{tl})^T (W_{tr}E_v{}^T + b_{tr}) \\
&= E_u W_{tl}{}^T W_{tr} E_v^T + b_{tl}{}^T W_{tr} E_v{}^T + E_u W_{tl}{}^T b_{tr} + b_{tl}{}^T b_{tr}
\end{aligned} \quad (4)
$$

where $W_{tl}, W_{tr} \in \mathbb{R}^{d_t \times d_t}$ and $b_{tl}, b_{tr} \in \mathbb{R}^{d_t}$ are the weight matrices and biases. Then, two collaborative scores are computed in a similar manner:

$$score_{c_1} = h_2(E_u, E_{f_1}) = (W_{tl}E_u^T + b_{tl})^T (W_{tl}E_{f_1}^T + b_{tl}) \quad (5)$$

$$score_{c_2} = h_3(E_v, E_{f_2}) = (W_{tr}E_v^T + b_{tr})^T (W_{tr}E_{f_2}^T + b_{tr}) \quad (6)$$

3.2 Content-Based Neural Network

The design of the content-based neural network (CBNN) is similar to that of the TBNN, as shown in Fig. 3. We also take the collaborative information into consideration. The difference is that we take the binary bag-of-words vectors as input to represent users' tweets and construct two hidden layers (i.e., hid_1 and hid_2) to generate the low-dimensional representations which can encode general concepts in user content. First, the stacked denoising autoencoders (SDAs) are

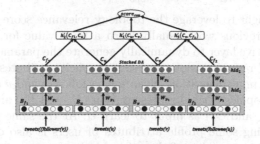

Fig. 3. Content-based neural network

applied to pre-train these two hidden layers, since SDAs have been proven useful in training deep neural models [11]. Then, the whole network is tuned by the final supervised objective, and the representations in the upper hidden layer are input to calculate the content relevance between users.

Formally, to measure the content relevance of u following v, we collect all the tweets posted by u, v, u's followees, and v's followers, and represent them respectively with binary BOW vectors B_u, B_v, B_{f_1}, $B_{f_2} \in \mathbb{R}^{|V|}$ where $|V|$ is the size of our vocabulary. Assuming C_u, C_v, C_{f_1} and C_{f_2} are d_c-dimensional encodings generated in the upper hidden layer (hid_2) , we transform them linearly and use the dot product calculation to get the content relevance $score_{con}$.

$$score_{con} = h_1'(C_u, C_v) + h_2'(C_u, C_{f_1}) + h_3'(C_v, C_{f_2}) \tag{7}$$

$$h_1'(C_u, C_v) = (W_{cl}C_u^T + b_{cl})^T (W_{cr}C_v^T + b_{cr}) \tag{8}$$

$$h_2'(C_u, C_{f_1}) = (W_{cl}C_u^T + b_{cl})^T (W_{cl}C_{f_1}^T + b_{cl}) \tag{9}$$

$$h_3'(C_v, C_{f_2}) = (W_{cr}C_v^T + b_{cr})^T (W_{cr}C_{f_2}^T + b_{cr}) \tag{10}$$

where $W_{cl}, W_{cr} \in \mathbb{R}^{d_c \times d_c}$ and $b_{cl}, b_{cr} \in \mathbb{R}^{d_c}$ are the weight matrices and biases.

Unsupervised Pre-training. In the pre-training stage, stacked denoising auto-encoders are built in an unsupervised layer-wise fashion to initialize the weights and hidden representations. Two hidden layers are designed with the same d_c dimensions, as illustrated in the dotted frame of Fig. 3. The weights and biases between the input layer and the first hidden layer (hid_1) are notated as $W_{p_1} \in \mathbb{R}^{V \times d_c}$ and $b_{p_1} \in \mathbb{R}^{d_c}$, and the weights and biases between two hidden layers $W_{p_2} \in \mathbb{R}^{d_c \times d_c}$ and $b_{p_2} \in \mathbb{R}^{d_c}$.

Referring [9], the rectifier activation function $max(0, x)$ is used for encoding the hidden layers. In the reconstruction stage, we use $sigmoid$ activation function along with a cross-entropy cost for the first layer, and the $softplus$ activation function along with the squared loss function for the second layer.

3.3   Adaptive Layer

An intuitive way to measure the final relevance of two users is to learn a linear combination of $score_{topo}$ and $score_{con}$. That is,

$$score_{rel} = \alpha * score_{topo} + (1 - \alpha) * score_{con} \tag{11}$$

where α is the weight to leverage the topology relevance score and the content relevance score. Previous work usually learn a fixed value for α. In our work, we design an adaptive layer to dynamically generate the parameter according to two kinds of users' representations and some explicit attributes.

In the detailed implementation, given u as a follower and v as a followee, we use their learned topology-based representation (E_u and E_v) and content-based representation (C_u and C_v) as input to learn α. At the same time, the profile vector $A_{u,v}$ denoting some profile attributes of users is also considered as an input. With the concatenation of these five kinds of vectors, we get α using a $sigmoid$ function as follows:

$$\alpha = sigmoid\left(W_{ada}\left[E_u, E_v, C_u, C_v, A_{u,v}\right]\right) \tag{12}$$

where W_{ada} is the weight matrix.

4 Learning

We use Θ to denote all the parameters, which include W_{tl}, W_{tr}, W_{cl}, W_{cr}, W_{p_1}, W_{p_2}, LT, and W_{ada}. For simplicity, we ignore all the biases. To learn these parameters, we first pre-train W_{p_1} and W_{p_2} using the stacked denoising auto-encoders and initialize the other parameters randomly. Then, we use the stochastic gradient descent (SGD) algorithm to fine-tune all the parameters through looping over all the training data with the objective of minimizing Formula (1). Each update of the model parameters is carried out by backpropagation.

We implement our model using the Theano library. The learning rate λ is set to 0.01. Learning is carried out using mini-batches and the mini-batch size is set to 200. All hyperparameter values are set using the validation set. The dimension (d_t) of the topology-based user representation is set to 50. In the content-based neural network, the dimensions (d_c) of the two hidden layers are both set to 600 by experience. The training process stops after 3000 epochs.

5 Experiments

5.1 Experiment Setup

In our experiments, we use a real world Twitter dataset provided by UIUC [15], which contains about 3.9 million users, 50 million tweets and 284 million *following* relations crawled in May 2011. From this dataset, we randomly select 20 users as seeds and follow their social relations to expand to 8,000 users (denoted as U) with at least one followee (or follower) and one tweet, since our work does not focus on cold-start recommendation. Finally, we get a dataset composed of 8,000 users, 3,114,925 tweets and 598,091 *following* relations. For each user in U, we record three kinds of information: the *ids* of her/his followers and followees, her/his posted tweets, and her/his profile attributes such as the number of tweets and the number of followers or followees.

To pre-train W_{p_1} and W_{p_2} using the SDAs, we select 30,000 users including U with at least one tweet and collect 7,153,129 tweets in total. We preprocess these tweets by removing stop words and stemming. Then for each user, all of her/his posted tweets as a whole are converted into a binary BOW vector, where the dimensions are determined by the top frequent 60,000 ($|V|$) words.

To evaluate the recommendation performance of our proposed model, we randomly select 800 users ($U_{test} \subset U$) as test users. For each user in U_{test}, we put a percentage (p) of her/his followees in the gold standard recommendation lists and remove the corresponding *following* relations from our data. From the remaining *following* relations, 10% is taken as the validation set to define the hyperparameters and the rest 90% as the training set to fine tune our model.

After our proposed model is learned, we input each test user as a follower and compute the score $score_{rel}$ that s/he follows each of the other users. The k users who get the highest scores are set as a system-generated recommendation list. To evaluate recommendation performance, we adopt the metric of the average precision $P@k$ which measures the overlap between the system-generated recommendation list and the gold-standard recommendation list.

5.2   Comparison with Recommendation Methods

We compare our models (named Our) with several existing user recommendation methods including Adamic/Adar, Twittomender, SVD++, LDA, Factorization machine (FM) and Propflow. The implementations of these baseline methods are briefly described below.

(1) **Adamic/Adar**: The Adamic/Adar [16] measures the common friends of two users to predict whether users should be recommended. Here, we implement this metric using the LPmade [17] package.

(2) **Twittomender**: We follow the work of [10] and implement two versions of Twittomender. One named **TM-con** uses the posted tweets to represent users. The other one named **TM-id** represents a user with the ids of his followers and followees. Then the followees are acquired using the indexing and retrieval modules of the Lucene platform.

(3) **SVD++**: SVD++ is a matrix factorization model which takes the implicit feedback information into consideration [14]. In the followee recommendation task, we regard the implicit feedback as the existent followees of one user.

(4) **Latent Dirichlet Allocation (LDA)**: LDA has been widely used in modeling objects with latent topics. In our work, we regard all the posted tweets of one user as one document, and each user is viewed as a mixture of topics. Then, we compute the Kullback-Leibler divergence score between the topic distribution of two users to measure the possibility of forming a *following* relation.

(5) **Factorization Machine (FM)**: The factorization machines (FM) proposed by [21] combines the advantages of Support Vector Machines with factorization models. With a FM, we incorporate various information including topology and content of users, and factorize the relationship between a follower and a followee. In our work, the minimal least square error with $L2$ regularization is used as the optimization objective.

(6) **Propflow**: Propflow [18] calculates the probability of a restricted random walk from one node to another in finite steps based on link weights and a modified breadth-first search strategy. The probability serves as the likelihood of forming a new *following* relation.

In our experiments, we remove a percentage (p) of the *following* relations from the test users and set $p = 0.2, 0.5, 0.75, 0.875$ respectively. Four sets of experiments are conducted to compare our model Our with all the baselines.

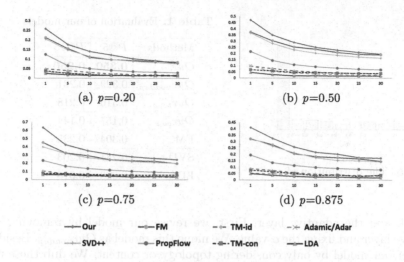

(a) p=0.20

(b) p=0.50

(c) p=0.75

(d) p=0.875

Fig. 4. Performance comparison

The recommendation performance $P@k$ is shown in Fig. 4. Overall, the average precision of all the methods decline with k increasing, since the higher ranked users are more likely to be followees.

From Fig. 4 we can see that our proposed model *Our* beats all the baseline methods. *LDA* performs unexpectedly worst of all the baselines, though this method has been successfully used in topic detection. *SVD++* achieves a relatively high performance, almost comparable to the *FM* method and much better than *TM-con* and *LDA*. *Adamic/Adar*, *TM-con* and *TM-id* denoted by the dotted lines all adopt shallow features such as *id*s of followees(or followers) or bag-of-words to represent users, with a relatively low performance. *TM-id* is slightly better than *Adamic/Adar*, indicating the TF-IDF representation used in *TM-id* is better than a simple set operation in *Adamic/Adar*. *Propflow* adopts the well-known graph-based strategy to seek the possibility of forming a *following* relation and performs mediocre in all the experiments.

5.3 Analysis of Our Model

In this subsection, we look into the design of our model. First, we observe the distribution of the α values to analyze the adaptive layer of our proposed model. Here, we set p as 0.5 to train our model, and then output all the final α values on the training data. Figure 5 shows the percentage of α distributing in different intervals such as 0.0 to 0.1, 0.1 to 0.2, and so on. From this figure, we can see that α scatters on two ends more than in the middle and distributes more on the right end than the left end. 50.2% of the α values distribute in the interval of $[0.9, 1]$ and 14.9% in the interval of $[0, 0.1]$.

Next, we design a set of experiments to evaluate the performance of different components including the topology-based neural network, content-based neural

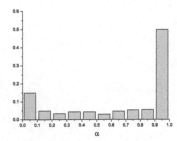

Fig. 5. The distribution of α.

Table 1. Evaluation of our models

Methods	$P@5$	$P@15$
Our	**0.350**	**0.250**
Our_{noadap}	0.329	0.231
Our_{topo}	0.316	0.218
Our_{con}	0.157	0.144
FM	0.304	0.235
SVD++	0.281	0.203
LDA	0.028	0.018

network and the adaptive layer. First, we revise our model by removing the adaptive layer and fixing the α value. We name this model as Our_{noadap}. Besides, we alter our model by only considering topology or content. We dub these two models Our_{topo} and Our_{con} respectively.

We set k as 5 and 15, and compare our models with LDA, $SVD++$ and FM, which all explore the latent representations of users. Table 1 shows the average precision scores. We can see that Our performs the best by dynamically tuning the contribution of topology and content. Through observing more experiments beyond $P@5$ and $P@15$, we find Our outperforms consistently better than Our_{noadap}, though this predominance is not significant. Without the adaptive layer, Our_{noadap} performs better than Our_{topo} and Our_{con}. We can also see that Our_{topo} is slightly worse than Our_{noadap} and much better than Our_{con}.

We compare Our_{noadap} with FM which models both topology and content, and Our_{topo} with $SVD++$ which only considers topology. We find that Our_{noadap} is slightly better than FM and Our_{topo} slightly better than $SVD++$. We can see that the adatpive model Our performs much better than FM.

6 Related Work

To develop a user recommendation system, the existing research mainly follows the homophily effect [20] and selects similar users as followees or friends. How to precisely represent users and measure their similarity is the main issue.

Two kinds of information resources, namely the content of posted tweets and the topology of the existing user relations, are normally considered in a user recommendation system. TWITTOMENDER proposed by [10] is a system developed based on Lucence and can model a user by his tweets, friends, followers, friends' tweets and followers' tweets. Kim and Shim et al. [12] proposed a probabilistic model to conduct top-K followee recommendation with consideration of both tweet content and relationship between users.

Recently, due to the efficiency in dealing with traditional user-item recommendation, some collaborative filtering techniques have been proposed for followee recommendation. Matrix factorization models are the most commonly-used model-based collaborative filtering techniques [7,14,19,24]. They explore the latent representation of users, based on which they predict the potential *following* relations. To the best of our knowledge, the matrix factorization models used in current followee recommendation systems are always designed in a similar way to those in traditional item recommendation systems. Kim and Shim [13] proposed a graphical model that defines the generative process of user following each other and publishing tweets. It combined the topic model and collaborative filtering with matrix factorization. Smith *et al.* [22] designed a recommendation system based on the latent neural network. It modeled both the correlations and descriptions of the rated items.

7 Conclusions

Topology and content are two kinds of important information available for modeling users in followee recommendation. In our work, we first design two neural networks: one is to explore the topology-based latent representation of users and calculate the topology relevance scores between users, and the other one is to mine users' content-based representations and produce the content-based relevance scores. The improvement of these two neural networks is that the collaborative information including followers of followees and followees of followers is naturally modeled. We further design an adaptive layer to tune the contribution of topology and content in followee recommendation and dynamically predict the *following* relation between any two users. Experiments verify that our methods can efficiently model users and are competitive in recommending followees compared to the state-of-the-art recommendation methods.

Acknowledgement. We thank all the anonymous reviewers for their insightful comments on this paper. This work was partially supported by National Natural Science Foundation of China (61273278 and 61572049). The correspondence author of this paper is Sujian Li.

References

1. Armentano, G.M., Godoy, L.D., Analia, A.A.: A topology-based approach for followees recommendation in Twitter. In: 9th Workshop on Intelligent Techniques for Web Personalization and Recommender Systems (2011)
2. Bengio, Y., Schwenk, H., Senécal, J.S., Morin, F., Gauvain, J.L.: Neural probabilistic language models. In: Holmes, D.E., Jain, L.C. (eds.) Innovations in Machine Learning, vol. 194, pp. 137–186. Springer, Heidelberg (2006)
3. Bordes, A., Glorot, X., Weston, J., Bengio, Y.: A semantic matching energy function for learning with multi-relational data. Mach. Learn. **94**(2), 233–259 (2014)
4. Bordes, A., Weston, J., Collobert, R., Bengio, Y., et al.: Learning structured embeddings of knowledge bases. In: Proceedings AAAI (2011)
5. Cai, X., Bain, M., Krzywicki, A., Wobcke, W., Kim, Y.S., Compton, P., Mahidadia, A.: Collaborative filtering for people to people recommendation in social networks. In: Li, J. (ed.) AI 2010. LNCS (LNAI), vol. 6464, pp. 476–485. Springer, Heidelberg (2010). doi:10.1007/978-3-642-17432-2_48

6. Chen, H., Cui, X., Hai, J.: Top-k followee recommendation over microblogging systems by exploiting diverse information sources. Future Comput. Syst. (2014)
7. Chen, T., Tang, L., Liu, Q., Yang, D., Xie, S., Cao, X., et al.: Combining factorization model and additive forest for collaborative followee recommendation. In: KDD-Cup Workshop (2012)
8. Dong, L., Wei, F., Zhou, M., Xu, K.: Adaptive multi-compositionality for recursive neural models with applications to sentiment analysis. In: Proceedings of AAAI, pp. 1537–1543 (2014)
9. Glorot, X., Bordes, A., Bengio, Y.: Domain adaptation for large-scale sentiment classification: a deep learning approach. In: Proceedings of ICML, pp. 513–520 (2011)
10. Hannon, J., Bennett, M., Smyth, B.: Recommending Twitter users to follow using content and collaborative filtering approaches. In: Proceedings of the Fourth ACM Conference on Recommender Systems, pp. 199–206. ACM (2010)
11. He, Z., Liu, S., Li, M., Zhou, M., Zhang, L., Wang, H.: Learning entity representation for entity disambiguation. In: Proceedings of ACL, pp. 30–34 (2013)
12. Kim, Y., Shim, K.: TWITOBI: a recommendation system for Twitter using probabilistic modeling. In: Proceedings of ICDM, pp. 340–349. IEEE (2011)
13. Kim, Y., Shim, K.: TWILITE: a recommendation system for twitter using a probabilistic model based on latent dirichlet allocation. Inf. Syst. **42**, 59–77 (2014)
14. Koren, Y.: Factorization meets the neighborhood: a multifaceted collaborative filtering model. In: Proceedings of ACM SIGKDD, pp. 426–434 (2008)
15. Li, R., Wang, S., Chang, K.C.C.: Multiple location profiling for users and relationships from social network and content. Proc. VLDB Endow. **5**(11), 1603–1614 (2012)
16. Liben-Nowell, D., Kleinberg, J.: The link-prediction problem for social networks. J. Am. Soc. Inform. Sci. Technol. **58**(7), 1019–1031 (2007)
17. Lichtenwalter, R.N., Chawla, N.V.: LPmade: link prediction made easy. J. Mach. Learn. Res. **12**, 2489–2492 (2011)
18. Lichtenwalter, R.N., Lussier, J.T., Chawla, N.V.: New perspectives and methods in link prediction. In: Proceedings of ACM SIGKDD, pp. 243–252. ACM (2010)
19. Ma, T., Yang, Y., Liangwei, W., Yuan, B.: Recommending people to follow using asymmetric factor models with social graphs. In: KDD-Cup Workshop (2012)
20. McPherson, M., Smith-Lovin, L., Cook, J.: Birds of a feather: homophily in social networks. Annu. Rev. Sociol. **27**, 415–444 (2001)
21. Rendle, S.: Factorization machines. In: Proceedings of ICDM, pp. 995–1000 (2010)
22. Smith, M.R., Gashler, M.S., Martinez, T.: A hybrid latent variable neural network model for item recommendation. In: Proceedings of IJCNN, pp. 1–7 (2015)
23. Sutskever, I., Vinyals, O., Le, Q.V.: Sequence to sequence learning with neural networks. In: Proceedings of NIPS, pp. 3104–3112 (2014)
24. Yu, Y., Qiu, G.R.: Followee recommendation in microblog using matrix factorization model with structural regularization. Sci. World J. (2014)

Who Will Tweet More? Finding Information Feeders in Twitter

Beibei Gu, Zhunchen Luo[✉], and Xin Wang

China Defense Science and Technology Information Center, Beijing, China
gubeiguying@sina.com, zhunchenluo@gmail.com, 20150101xl@sina.cn

Abstract. Twitter is an important source of information to users for its giant user group and rapid information diffusion but also made it hard to track topics in oceans of tweets. Such situation points the way to consider the task of finding **information feeders**, a finer-grained user group than domain experts. Information feeders refer to a crowd of topic tracers that share interests in a certain topic and provide related and follow-up information. In this study, we explore a wide range of features to find Twitter users who will tweet more about the topic after a time-point within a machine learning framework. The features are mainly extracted from the user's history tweets for that we believe user's tweet decision depends most on his history activities. We considered four feature families: **activeness, timeliness, interaction** and **user profile**. From our results, activeness in user's history data is most useful. Besides that, we concluded people who gain social influence and make quick response to the topic are more likely to post more topic-related tweets.

1 Introduction

Twitter, one of the most successful social media platforms with giant user groups and a cornucopia of information, has already become a major channel for content distribution where gathers first-hand information of most influential events and topics worldwide. In the meanwhile, information environment in Twitter is complex, where messages are in form of tweets within 140 characters, usually brief, massive and highly distributed, leading to data sparseness and redundancy for traditional information retrieval for a given topic. How to efficiently capture useful messages in an ocean of data is a hard question left to researchers. Here, we consider to find informing users to avoid some disadvantages.

Users are thought to be the center of releasing and distributing multi-sources information with the backup of their social networks. Out of interest or duty, some people will pay continuous attention to some certain topic and keep tweeting subsequent information as the topic continues and evolves. This kind of people usually have long term interests in topic-related fields. They probably have accumulated a certain amount of relevant knowledge and collected some reliable information sources, making themselves potential information providers of the topic.

© Springer International Publishing AG 2016
C.-Y. Lin et al. (Eds.): NLPCC-ICCPOL 2016, LNAI 10102, pp. 437–448, 2016.
DOI: 10.1007/978-3-319-50496-4_36

We aim to identify people with the potential to keep releasing information about a topic. We call them *information feeders*. Obviously, rapidly identifying information feeders offers a new approach to keep track of topics directly from information sources and may avoid situations such as unpredictable subject terms caused by topic floating by means of keyword searching [9].

It is noteworthy that, different from **domain experts**, which usually means people with some expertise or experience about a certain subject, the concept of "information feeder" refers to a finer-grained user group, namely topic tracers, and especially emphasizes those who have a relatively high probability to give out further information on a specific topic. Online information explosion is simply too much for experts to allocate their finite attention for each and every topic within the domain, as a result, an expert does not necessarily keep track of a topic all the way, but an information feeder does. Information feeders around a topic unit are usually highly dynamic during the topic evolution, while domain experts are rather static. Instant recognition of the aforementioned type of users is of interest to information seekers like journalists and companies. This is a challenging task in face of various user characteristics and unpredictable changes over time.

In this paper, we explore the way to identify information feeders within the huge amount of Twitter users in conjunction with given topics. We formulate the task as a binary classification problem and apply a machine learning framework for predicting whether a user will tweet more about the topic, which relies on four feature families: activeness, timeliness, interaction and user profile. From our results, activeness in user's history data is thought to be most useful and that users with some social influence and quick response to the topic are more likely to continue to post topic-related tweets.

The main contributions of this paper can be summarized as follows. Firstly, to the best of our knowledge, this paper is the first to predict whether a user will continue to tweet more on certain topics and such users are so-called "information feeders" in this work. Moreover, this paper has presented a novel set of features and approaches for predicting information feeders. Finally, we build our own annotated data for the attributes concerned. All of the manually-annotated Twitter data sets developed in this work will be made available as a new shared resource to the research community.

2   Related Work

The public nature of Twitter and the cornucopia of users as well as information sources have made it a hot topic focused and lasted during recent years. Related work can be divided into following parts:

User Behaviour Analysis and Prediction. Efforts on users' behavior prediction mainly focus on retweeting, which is regarded as an important pattern in information propagates. Suh *et al.* [16] provided with a detailed and large-scale analysis of factors that have an impact on retweeting. The number of followers and friends showed much impact in their results. Boyd *et al.* [2] treated retweeting as a means of participating in a diffuse conversation, and presented a very in-depth study about retweeting in diverse ways through actually interviewing Twitter users on the reasons why and what they retweet most. Zaman *et al.* [20] trained a probabilistic collaborative filter model for predicting the spread of information via retweet in Twitter network. They found that the identity of the source of the tweet and retweeter were most important features for prediction. Artzi *et al.* [1] predicted the likelihood of a retweet through a discriminative model. Luo *et al.* [10] firstly brought up with a learning-to-rank framework to find out retweeters to a certain tweet, showing that the retweet history and the similarity between the content of the tweet and the posting times of followers are most effective for the task. In this paper, we make prediction on whether a user will continue to post messages related to a certain topic, including retweets.

Demographics in Twitter. User feature analysis is an important part in our method. A lot of achievements on latent attribute inference of Twitter users have been made, with recent work focusing on age [11], gender [15], user profile extraction [4,8], location [3,6], occupational class [13], political tendency [17], voting intention [7] and brand preferences [18], among which various research angles have been applied for different purposes. Our work builds on these findings to predict users that will tweet more on certain topics.

User Identification in Twitter. Twitter has collected all kinds of user types together, of which the defined information feeders can also be viewed as one. Diakopoulos *et al.* [5] is a related work for identifying credible sources. However, they aimed at getting access to information sources for journalists' reporting mission, while we intended to predict how many topic-related messages an information feeder will continue to provide for topic tracking. Zafarani *et al.* [19] developed a methodology that identifies malicious users with limited information. They made a detailed analysis of five general characteristics of malicious users and demonstrated that 10 bits of information can help a lot in the task.

3 Method

3.1 Task Description

In this paper, we present the task on automatically predicting whether a user will post more topic-related tweets. Given a topic T, we retrieve tweets and obtain initial user set U who have posted topic-related tweets from retrieval results. Our goal is to train a classification model R that predicts whether user u from U will continue to tweet about T.

The set of features we explore below is used in conjunction with a supervised machine learning framework providing models for binary classification. From the user information and their tweet data, we extracted features related to the prediction of information feeders. In the following, we describe our feature sets in more detail.

3.2 User Features

It is observed that decisions of a user can be explained better by his activity in the recent past, i.e., temporally local history [14]. A user's decision of tweeting more about topic T depends significantly on his temporal behavior. Thus the recent topic-related data of the user is considered to contain important information about his tweeting decision on topic T. **Activeness, timeliness** and **interaction** are three main aspects of the user's recent behavior characteristics that we analysis. We also believe that a user's basic **profile** indicates his general image on Twitter. Hence, we explore user features from these four dimensions. A summary of features shows in Table 1.

Table 1. Summary of features for information feeders

Feature family	Feature name	Description
Activeness	Count_Tw	Number of all tweets during the *period* (from the first topic-related tweet's posting time to the time t)
	Count_RelaledTw	Number of topic-related tweets posted by time t
	Ratio_RelatedTw	Ratio of topic-related tweets to all tweets during the *period*
	Ratio_RelatedOr	Ratio of original topic-related tweets to topic-related tweets
Timeliness	TD_Related	Time difference between the latest two topic-related tweets by time t, in seconds
	Response_Time	Time difference between the initial time of topic and the first topic-related tweet's posting time in seconds
Interaction	Ratio_Mt	Ratio of tweets with @username in topic-related tweets
	Ratio_Rt	Ratio of retweets in topic-related tweets
	Ratio_Fav	Ratio of favorites in topic-related tweets
Profile	Count_Fol	Number of user u's followers
	Count_Fri	Number of user u's friends
	Topic_Similarity	Similarity of user u's history tweets and the topic description

Activeness. Instinctively, an active user usually receives more information from all aspects and creates more tweets. The number of tweets posted in his recent past (i.e., the period from the beginning of topic T to the time when we collected the user data) indicates user u's recent activeness. We include the count of all tweets (**Count_Tw**) as well as topic-related tweets posted

(**Count_RelaledTw**) during that period as two features to measure user u's activeness on Twitter, especially on topic T. We also think the ratio of topic-related tweets (**Ratio_RelatedTw**) during the recent history describes the user's concentration on topic T.

Original tweets refer to those whose contents are edited by the user himself. Editing original tweets usually means new information, which requires to learn enough knowledge about topic T and form his own understanding. The ratio of original topic-related tweets (**Ratio_RelatedOr**) describes the user's tweet originality to some degree and can be regarded as an indicator of the user's activeness to T.

Timeliness. Information feeders are those who are willing to pay plenty of attention to topic T and keenly aware of the topic update. They are usually quick to keep up with a new topic with interest and provide fresh information about it whenever it has new evolution. So we regard user u's timeliness towards topic T as a measurement of u's interest in T.

Two features are selected to reflect user timeliness: **TD_Related** and **Response_Time**. The former describes the time difference between the latest two topic-related tweets, an expression of u's recent update frequency of information about T. **Response_Time** denotes how long it took u to post his first topic-related tweet from the start time of T. However, the initial time of a topic is usually hard to capture, so we replace it with the time of the earliest topic-related tweet in our dataset. Both the features are measured in seconds.

Interaction. Interaction in Twitter is a great motivation for users to get involved in information creation and diffusion. Mentions, giving likes and retweeting are three major mechanisms for user interaction. Posting tweets with mentions are meant to send information specifically to somebody which may possibly bring about a tweet stream between the users. Moreover, people usually give likes or retweet to show their agreement to the user's opinion or information. This can be seen as an encouragement for the user to post related tweets.

An information feeder is more likely to be encouraged by interaction with others. Thus we calculate the ratio of u's topic-related tweets with mention (**Ratio_Mt**) and the ratio of tweets got favorites (**Ratio_Rt**) or retweeted (**Ratio_Fav**) by others.

Profile. This feature family contains three features that can give an overview of the user's general image on Twitter, which are the numbers of the user's followers (**Count_Fol**) and friends (**Count_Fri**), and the similarity of the topic description and users' previous tweets (**Topic_Similarity**).

Count_Fol is a major factor of his influence and also a reflection of the quality of tweets. A regular information feeder may have gained his reputation and attracts a number of followers for his tweets. We include the feature **Count_Fri** for similar reason.

User's interest is another part of user's profile. If something has ever drawn one's attention, he is likely to be attracted for a second time when a new topic about it shows up. Take the topic *"Diesel gate of Volkswagen"* for example, if a user once tweeted about news about vehicles, which indicates he used to have interests in it, he is far more likely to be attracted by Volkswagen's emission cheating case and to post some messages about that than those who showed no interest in automotive news. It inspires us to calculate the similarity of the topic description and users' previous tweets (**Topic_Similarity**). When calculating the value of similarity, we filtered the top 100 high frequent words and the words which appear less than 5 times in our collected data [10].

4   Experiments

4.1   Data Preparation

To the best of our knowledge, there is no annotated dataset available, so we created labeled data required for this task. We document in detail our analytical method and the way we collected our data set. We randomly chose five topics of interest, including a live topic of the moment *#AlphaGo*, a gusty topic *#Turkey Ankara explosion*, a long-term topic *#American 2016 Presidential Election*, and two cooling topics *#NASA astronaut return to Earth* and *#Gravitational Waves*).

We searched for the hash tags of the topics and collected a significant number of topic-related tweets through the Twitter API for a whole day on March 17th, 2016. Hence, we got initial user set U. Then we filtered those who tweeted less than 500 tweets in total and whose tweeting frequency was beyond 30 and below 0.3 posts per day on average in order to reject inactive users and robots. About 200 users were randomly selected respectively for each topic from the filtered user set. 3200 recent tweets[1] posted by each user was crawled on March 27th, 2016. Our limitation to users' tweeting frequency makes sure that the crawled data covers all tweets posted from the beginning of our topics.

Two people involved in the manually annotating topic-related tweet process. The annotation process is applied with elicitation methods and take the starting time of each topic as well as their keywords as assistance. For each topic, any tweet with information related to the topic is labeled as "Related", and unwanted users such non-English users were rejected through judging by human experience. Final number of valid users in our dataset is 438, and 8,297 topic-related tweets were annotated. Table 2 displays the statistics of our data.

4.2   Data Description

The temporal distribution of the topic-related tweets for each topic is displayed in Fig. 1. In the pictures, we can see that the distributions of related tweets for the five topics respectively have different trending features. Although most topics follow the power law distribution with a peak near the beginning of the

---

[1] The maximum limitation of Twitter REST API is 3200 recent tweets per user.

Table 2. Data statistics of each topic

Number of valid users	438
Total number of tweets[a]	976,532
Number of topic-related tweets	8,297
Average number of topic-related tweets per user	18.90

[a]This number refers to the summation of tweets of all valid users
we obtained from Twitter API.

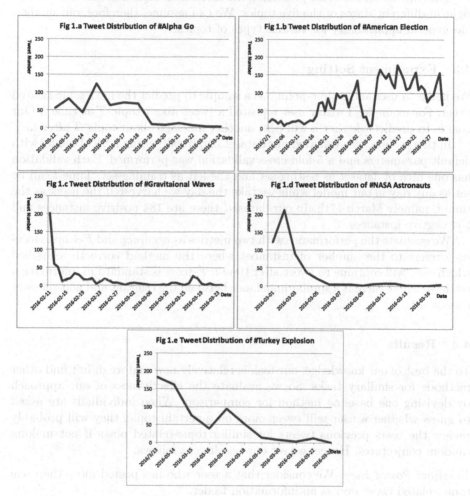

Fig. 1. From Fig. 1.a to 1.e, there are *(1) #AlphaGo, (2) #American 2016 Presidential Election, (3) #Gravitational Waves, (4) #NASA Astronauts Return to Earth* and *(5) #Turkey Ankara Explosion* related tweet distribution in sequence.

topic discussion time and then following a decrement, the duration and strength of each peak and the decay rate of each decrement have nothing in common with each other.

The long-term topic *American 2016 Presidential Election* shows a rather special distribution of topic-related tweets. From the distribution graph, tweets posted at the beginning of the preparation period of the elections are steady and rather sparse while a series of small peaks show up in sequence. It is totally different from the rest topics. The reason may be that there are plenty of movements during the elections, which make the subtopics and motivates bursts of tweeting.

The time we seleceted for predicting the user's next topic-related tweet stands right in different states of the five topics. We can assume, therefore, our method has general applicability for various types of topics.

4.3 Experiment Setting

We make "a user and a time-point" as a sample to predict the next topic-related tweet. For example, Twitter user u posted a tweet about topic T at time t. Our goal is to predict whether a will post another message about topic T after t.

In this section, we evaluated our dataset empirically using a SVM model with default parameters and a 5-fold cross validation was performed. Each validation has one fifth of dataset as testing set and the left as training set. Time t can be set as any day in our model while we take the day we harvested the users as the time t, namely March 17th. In our dataset, there are 184 positive instances and 254 negtive instances.

We evaluate the performance with two metrics as *accuracy* and *F-score*. *Accuracy* refers to the number of instances where the method correctly classified which user will continue to tweet after time t. *F-score* is standard in information retrieval where there is a similar imbalance between the relevant and non-relevant classes [12].

4.4 Results

To the best of our knowledge, our task is relatively new and we didn't find other methods for similary tasks. So we evaluate the effectiveness of our approach by devising one baseline method for comparison. When individuals are asked to guess whether a user will tweet more on a certain topic, they will probably review the users previous tweets for similar topic-related posts if not making random conjectures. Hence, we set our baseline as follows:

Baseline: Posted Ever. We consider that a user who has posted more than one topic-related tweet ever is an information feeder.

From our annotated data, we labeled the users by whether they posted topic-related data before March 17th as ground truth.

Comparison of Feature Families. In this part, we display our feature effectiveness by testing feature families along with the baseline method using SVM. As a baseline, we use a feature **PostedEver** indicating whether a user has

Table 3. Results for different feature families with SVM (Bold numbers denote the best).

Feature set	Accuracy	F-Score
PostedEver	0.5321	0.5655
Activeness	0.6134	**0.7434**
Timeliness	0.5878	0.6669
Interaction	0.5991	0.7215
Profile	0.5907	0.7315
PostedEver + Activeness	0.6179	0.7399
PostedEver + Timeliness	0.5920	0.6698
PostedEver + Interaction	0.5951	0.7112
PostedEver + Profile	0.5865	0.7251
Full	**0.6551**	0.7372

posted topic-related tweets ever with boolean value for modeling. Results are summarized in Table 3.

We can see that experiments with full feature set gained best performance, giving us a huge improvement in both accuracy and F-score over the baseline. *Activeness* features provided the highest F-score and a relatively good accuracy 0.6134. *Interaction* and *Profile* features showed an average level in all the metrics while *Timeliness* features had very poor F-score. Each feature family and their combination showed relatively great effectiveness for our task and overrode the baseline method.

Besides, all of our feature families improve the classification performance over the baseline method. The combinations of baseline and each feature family significantly improve the results when used with the baseline method in isolation.

Feature Analysis. We investigate whether our features can improve tweet prediction and are also interested in which features in particular are highly valued by our model. We combine each feature with baseline feature within our framework.

Table 4 shows the performance of each classification model. The features are ranked by F-score. We can see that all of our features improve the results with statistically significance.

All the four features of *Activeness* provide pretty good performance in testing models, ranking within the topic five, revealing that users' history information is helpful in our task, especially user activeness during the recent past. The result of **Ratio_RelatedOr** also proves that tweet originality is a strong indicator to user's interest in topic T which drives him to continue to tweet.

We also find that social features of a user perform well. **Count_Fol** brought about pretty good scores of accuracy and F-score, which means that user's influence may motivate him to tweet more.

Table 4. Performance of each classification model.

Feature set	Accuracy	F-Score
PostedEver	0.5321	0.5655
PostedEver + Ratio_RelatedTw	0.6218	0.7459
PostedEver + Count_RelatedTw	0.5942	0.7440
PostedEver + Count_Tw	0.5962	0.7428
PostedEver + Count_Fol	0.5907	0.7418
PostedEver + Ratio_RelatedOr	0.5872	0.7396
PostedEver + Response_Time	0.5869	0.7396
PostedEver + Ratio_Mt	0.5897	0.7352
PostedEver + Topic_Similarity	0.5865	0.7272
PostedEver + Ratio_Fav	0.5849	0.7252
PostedEver + Count_Fri	0.5820	0.7251
PostedEver + Ratio_Rt	0.5734	0.6749
PostedEver + TD_Related	0.5891	0.6659

Response_Time is another useful feature with a substantial improvement of about 5 points in accuracy and 17 points in F-score over the baseline. **Response_Time** stands for user's timeliness to topic T by measuring time it took the user to make response to a new topic. To a large extent, a user with little time's delay to keep up with a new topic is usually engaged in it and willing to tweet more.

The significant effectiveness of **Count_Fol** and **Response_Time** illustrates that user influence and timeliness on a certain topic are important indicators to whether a user will become an information feeder. Users with a range of followers and quick response to a topic are more likely to continue to pay attention to topic T and post more topic-related tweets.

5   Examples

Here are some examples showing the usefulness of our features.

ScottyFinch, a frequent Twitter user who provided a live report about the matches between AlphaGo and Lee Sedol from the staring time of the topic. 38 tweets related to Alphago were posted by March 17th (the time we collected our data), making up more than 30% in his tweet timeline. He shows a high possibility to keep tweeting on the AlphaGo topic. Our method predicted that *ScottyFinch* is an information feeder and actually he did tweeted a lot more after March 17th.

A counter-example is *wildhare*, who posted 1,523 tweets in total during the topic *Gravitational Waves*'s discussion time, but only 10 retweets were about the topic. His first topic-related tweet was 4.5 hours later when the bursting news came out. *wildhare* showed no concentration or strong interest in the topic with low update rate. He posted no more tweets about *Gravitational Waves* and our method predicted so.

6   Conclusion and Future Work

In this paper, we studied the task of finding information feeders by predicting whether a user will tweet more about certain topics. This is a new task and our results benefit information seekers for acquiring topic-related information more efficiently and effectively via information feeders in Twitter, and also broaden ways to make better use of social media information.

We focus on users history tweet features for our predictive models, including users' activeness, timeliness and interaction features in the temporally local history, as well as user profile features. From the results, we find people who show plenty of concentration on information about T and active in the topic discussion are more likely to be information feeders.

Our approach is very flexible and allows for improvements on our current models by incorporating information such as users neighborhood status in Twitter as well as on other social media platforms. In the future we plan to apply new features to improve the performance of our predictive model and explore futher into topic specific tasks.

References

1. Artzi, Y., Pantel, P., Gamon, M.: Predicting responses to microblog posts. In: Proceedings of the 2012 Conference of the North American Chapter of the Association for Computational Linguistics: Human Language Technologies, pp. 602–606. Association for Computational Linguistics (2012)
2. Boyd, D., Golder, S., Lotan, G.: Tweet, tweet, retweet: conversational aspects of retweeting on Twitter. In: 2010 43rd Hawaii International Conference on System Sciences (HICSS), pp. 1–10. Institute of Electrical and Electronics Engineers (2010)
3. Cheng, Z., Caverlee, J., Lee, K.: You are where you tweet: a content-based approach to geo-locating Twitter users. In: Proceedings of the 19th Association for Computing Machinery International Conference on Information and Knowledge Management, pp. 759–768. Association for Computing Machinery (2010)
4. Culotta, A., Ravi, N.K., Cutler, J.: Predicting the demographics of Twitter users from website traffic data. In: Proceedings of the International Conference on Web and Social Media (ICWSM). AAAI Press, Menlo Park (2015, in press)
5. Diakopoulos, N., De Choudhury, M., Naaman, M.: Finding and assessing social media information sources in the context of journalism. In: Proceedings of the SIGCHI Conference on Human Factors in Computing Systems, pp. 2451–2460. Association for Computing Machinery (2012)
6. Jurgens, D.: That's what friends are for: inferring location in online social media platforms based on social relationships. ICWSM **13**, 273–282 (2013)
7. Lampos, V., Preotiuc-Pietro, D., Cohn, T.: A user-centric model of voting intention from social media. In: Association for Computational Linguistics, vol. 1, pp. 993–1003 (2013)

8. Li, J., Ritter, A., Hovy, E.: Weakly supervised user profile extraction from Twitter. In: Association for Computational Linguistics, Baltimore (2014)
9. Lin, J., Efron, M., Wang, Y., Sherman, G.: Overview of the TREC-2014 microblog track. Technical report, DTIC Document (2014)
10. Luo, Z., Osborne, M., Tang, J., Wang, T.: Who will retweet me?: finding retweeters in Twitter. In: Proceedings of the 36th International ACM SIGIR Conference on Research and Development in Information Retrieval, pp. 869–872. Association for Computing Machinery (2013)
11. Nguyen, D., Gravel, R., Trieschnigg, D., Meder, T.: How old do you think i am?; a study of language and age in Twitter. In: Proceedings of the Seventh International AAAI Conference on Weblogs and Social Media. AAAI Press (2013)
12. Petrovic, S., Osborne, M., Lavrenko, V.: RT to win! Predicting message propagation in Twitter. In: International Conference on Weblogs Social Media (2011)
13. Preoţiuc-Pietro, D., Lampos, V., Aletras, N.: An analysis of the user occupational class through Twitter content. In: Association for Computational Linguistics (2015)
14. Rangnani, S., Devi, V.S., Murty, M.N.: Autoregressive model for users retweeting profiles. In: Liu, T.Y., Scollon, C.N., Zhu, W. (eds.) SocInfo 2015. LNCS, vol. 9471, pp. 178–193. Springer International Publishing, Heidelberg (2015)
15. Rao, D., Yarowsky, D., Shreevats, A., Gupta, M.: Classifying latent user attributes in Twitter. In: Proceedings of the 2nd International Workshop on Search and Mining User-generated Contents, pp. 37–44. Association for Computing Machinery (2010)
16. Suh, B., Hong, L., Pirolli, P., Chi, E.H.: Want to be retweeted? Large scale analytics on factors impacting retweet in Twitter network. In: 2010 IEEE Second International Conference on Social Computing (SocialCom), pp. 177–184. Institute of Electrical and Electronics Engineers (2010)
17. Volkova, S., Coppersmith, G., Van Durme, B.: Inferring user political preferences from streaming communications. In: Proceedings of Association for Computational Linguistics, pp. 186–196 (2014)
18. Yang, C., Pan, S., Mahmud, J., Yang, H., Srinivasan, P.: Using personal traits for brand preference prediction (2015)
19. Zafarani, R., Liu, H.: 10 bits of surprise: detecting malicious users with minimum information. In: Proceedings of the 24th Association for Computing Machinery International Conference on Information and Knowledge Management, pp. 423–431. Association for Computing Machinery (2015)
20. Zaman, T.R., Herbrich, R., Van Gael, J., Stern, D.: Predicting information spreading in Twitter. In: Workshop on Computational Social Science and the Wisdom of Crowds, NIPS, vol. 104, pp. 17599–601. Citeseer (2010)

Short Papers

Short Papers

Discrete and Neural Models for Chinese POS Tagging: Comparison and Combination

Meishan Zhang[✉], Nan Yu, and Guohong Fu

School of Computer Science and Technology, Heilongjiang University, Harbin, China
mason.zms@gmail.com, yunan2012@foxmail.com, ghfu@hotmail.com

Abstract. Discrete and Neural models are two mainstream methods for Chinese POS tagging nowadays. Both have achieved state-of-the-art performances. In this paper, we compare the two kinds of models empirically, and further investigate the combination methods of them. In particular, as the pre-trained word embeddings are exploited under the neural setting, one can regard neural models as semi-supervised setting. To make a fairer comparison of the discrete and the neural models, we incorporate word clusters for both models as well as their combination, since it has been generally accepted that word clusters can encode similar information as pre-trained word embeddings.

Keywords: Neural networks · Combination model · POS tagging

1 Introduction

POS tagging, which labels each word in a sentence according to its syntactic function (for example, noun, verb or adjective), has received long term research interests in the natural language processing (NLP) community [3,8,9,19]. We focus on Chinese language, which is more difficult than English. [13] reported that POS tagging can have an accuracy over 97% on a standard benchmark of WSJ corpus, which can be regarded as a resolved problem. While for the Chinese POS tagging, we can obtain an accuracy only around 94% on a dataset based on a similar genre, nearly having twice number of errors as the English language.

State-of-the-art POS taggers usually treat the task as a typical sequence labeling problem, exploiting structural learning methods such as conditional random field (CRF) [7] or structural perceptron [2]. Traditionally, discrete one-hot features are used, and then are fed into a linear model based on the above frameworks. These features are designed sophisticatedly, by first collecting several useful atomic features including the current/previous/next word, prefixes/suffixes of the current word, cluster of the current word and etc., and then manually combining these features into the final features.

Recently, neural networks have been intensively studied for a number of NLP tasks, because they have achieved competitive performances for several tasks [12,25], thanks to the work of word embeddings [14]. For Chinese POS tagging, neural models can also achieve better performances than discrete models as we

© Springer International Publishing AG 2016
C.-Y. Lin et al. (Eds.): NLPCC-ICCPOL 2016, LNAI 10102, pp. 451–460, 2016.
DOI: 10.1007/978-3-319-50496-4_37

will show. The main idea of neural networks is to model atomic features by low-dimensional dense vectors, which is totally different with traditional one-hot representation. Using this way, feature combination can be conducted automatically by neural layers, from simple non-linear feed-forward neural networks to complicated long-short-term-memory (LSTM) neural networks.

Discrete and neural Chinese POS tagging models are highly different, which can be attributed to their different feature representations. One natural question arises that could we benefit by a combination of the two different models. This is one key point of this work. There are several feature combination methods, and representative frameworks include directly feature combination and model combination. The former can be achieved by direct feature addition, while the later can be achieved by stacking [21]. In this paper, we investigate both the two frameworks to find which one is better, or do they have large influences of the final combination performances for Chinese POS tagging.

While neural-based POS tagging models always require pre-trained word embeddings as input, which are learnt from large-scale unlabeled corpus and can encode certain syntactic and semantic information, thus several researchers argue that these models are actually semi-supervised models. In order to compare with discrete models more fairly, we incorporate word clusters into both discrete and neural models as well as their combination.

In this paper, we build two Chinese POS tagging models, one being a discrete model and the other being a neural model, to study the above mentioned two issues. First we introduce the two baseline models, describing their differences theatrically. Second we combine the two models, by both the feature combination and the stacking methods. Third we enhance the baseline models as well as their combinations by word clusters. Experimental results on the Chinese Treebank (CTB) 5.1 dataset show that: (1) the feature combination method is more effective than stacking, (2) even with word clusters, the discrete model could not beat the neural model, and (3) the neural model can be further enhanced by word cluster features while we could get the same observation for the combination model.

2   Baseline Models

In this section, we present our baseline discrete and neural models, which are both CRF models. The main differences between the two models are the output features at the penultimate layer, as shown in Fig. 1. For the discrete model, they are sparse one-hot features that are designed manually, while for the neural model, they are low-dimensional real-valued features abstracted by neural layers.

2.1   The Discrete Model

CRF model is highly suitable for Chinese POS tagging, and has achieved state-of-the-art performances for this task. The overall architecture is shown in Fig. 1(a),

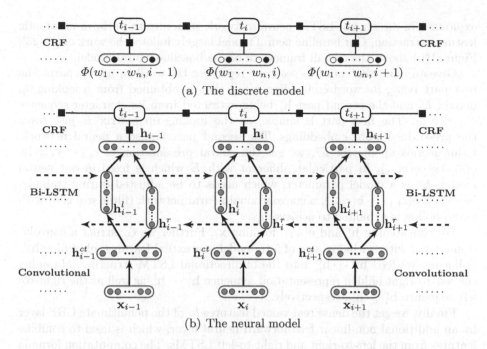

(a) The discrete model

(b) The neural model

Fig. 1. The frameworks of the baseline discrete and neural models.

where $w_1 \cdots w_n$ denotes the input sentence, and $\Phi(\cdot)$ denotes the feature extraction function, which is actually conducted manually. For a certain output tagging sequence $t_1 \cdots t_n$, its score is defined by

$$Score(t_1 \cdots t_n) = \sum_{i \in [1,n]} \theta[t_i] \cdot \Phi(w_1 \cdots w_n, i) + A[t_{i-1}][t_i], \quad (1)$$

where θ and A are both model parameters. The decoding procedure aims to find a max-score tagging sequence for each input sentence, which can be accomplished by viterbi algorithm. Actually, we can formulate Eq. 1 as a CRF layer, in order to align with the definition of neural layers in neural models.

We follow [8] to define the feature templates of Chinese POS tagging, where we have three kinds of atomic features, including contextual words, word characters, and word length. Based these features, we combine them manually, forming the final features for CRF.

2.2 The Neural Model

Consistent with the baseline discrete model, our baseline neural model also exploits the CRF layer as the penultimate layer. However, the inputs of the CRF layer are different. While the discrete model uses the manually designed feature function $\Phi(\cdot)$ to extract the features for the CRF layer, the neural model exploits a bi-directional LSTM neural network structure to perform automatic feature extraction. Our baseline neural model largely follows the work of [12,23]. Figure 1(b) shows the overall framework of the baseline neural model.

Give an input sentence $w_1 \cdots w_n$, we represent the word w_i by two parts, the first part being its word embedding $\mathbf{e}(w_i)$ that is obtained from a looking-up matrix E, and the second part $\mathbf{h}_i^c$ being extracted from its character sequence $c_{i,1} \cdots c_{i,m}$. The first part is simple, as the looking-up matrix E just saves the pre-trained word embeddings. The second part is also a neural network. Using a look-up matrix E^c, we get the neural presentation of $c_{i,1} \cdots c_{i,m}$ by $\mathbf{e}(c_{i,1}) \cdots \mathbf{e}(c_{i,m})$. In particular, different with E which is fixed in our neural model, E^c is a model parameter, which needs to be adjusted during training. Based on $\mathbf{e}(c_{i,1}) \cdots \mathbf{e}(c_{i,m})$, a convolutional neural network (filter size is 5) with max-pooling is exploited to achieve $\mathbf{h}_i^c$.

We concatenate $\mathbf{h}_i^c$ and $\mathbf{e}(w_i)$, forming $\mathbf{x}_i$. Further we construct a convolutional layer with a window size of 5 to model contextual features, obtaining $\mathbf{h}_i^{ct}$. Following we feed $\mathbf{h}_1^{ct} \cdots \mathbf{h}_n^{ct}$ into the bi-directional LSTM structure, obtaining the left-to-right hidden representation sequence $\mathbf{h}_1^l \cdots \mathbf{h}_n^l$ as well as the right-to-left sequence $\mathbf{h}_1^r \cdots \mathbf{h}_n^r$, respectively.

Finally, we get the dense real-valued features h_i of the penultimate CRF layer by an additional non-linear feed-forward neural layer, which is used to combine features from the left-to-right and right-to-left LSTMs. The computation formula is defined as follows:

$$\mathbf{h}_i = \tanh(W_{fe}[\mathbf{h}_i^l; \mathbf{h}_i^r] + \mathbf{b}_{fe}).$$

The obtained hidden sequence $h_1 \cdots h_n$ plays the same role in the neural model as $\Phi(\cdot)$ in the discrete model.

2.3 Training Method

We exploit the online learning to train both the discrete and neural models, based on the max-margin strategy plus with a l2 regularization, whose loss function is defined as:

$$L(\Theta) = \max_{t_i \in T} \left(Score(t_1 \cdots t_n) + \eta \delta(t_1 \cdots t_n, t_1^g \cdots t_n^g) \right) - Score(t_1^g \cdots t_n^g) + \frac{\lambda}{2} \parallel \Theta \parallel^2,$$

where Θ is the set of all model parameters, $t_1^g \cdots t_n^g$ is the gold-standard POS tagging sequence, $\delta(\cdot)$ is the Hamming distance function, η and λ are two hyper-parameters. We use the AdaGrad algorithm [4] to update the model parameters, with an additional hyper-parameter α to control update setps. Especially, our objective function is not differentiable, and we use sub-gradients instead.

3   Combination

The baseline discrete and neural models exploit the same CRF framework for the final prediction, but they have very different feature representations. We expect that a combination of the two models can bring better Chinese POS tagging accuracies. In this work, we exploit two combination methods. The first one is feature combination as the two models have the same penultimate layer. Second, we use the widely-exploited stacked learning to combine the two models.

3.1 Feature Combination

The feature combination method is very simple. One requirement of this combination method is that the baseline models should have a same output layer, which is satisfied in our case.

As introduced, the output layers of the discrete and neural models are both CRF layers, and the only difference is the features. Given a sentence $w_1 \cdots w_n$, after several steps, we obtain the features $\Phi(w_1 \cdots w_n, 1), \cdots, \Phi(w_1 \cdots w_n, n)$ and $h_1 \cdots h_n$ for the CRF layers of the discrete and neural models, respectively. The simple thing for feature combination is to concatenate the two kinds features at each position, achieving a new feature sequence $h'_1 \cdots h'_n$, where $h'_i = \Phi(w_1 \cdots w_n, i) \oplus h_i$. This new feature sequence is fed into the output CRF layer to predict the final Chinese POS tagging sequence.

3.2 Stacked Learning

Stacked learning, also named as stacking or guided learning, is a typical method to integrate different models [21]. The key idea of this method is feature guiding. It is a two-level framework, where one baseline model is chosen as the level-2 model, and the other baseline models are level-1 models, whose outputs are fed into the level-2 model as atomic features. In our case, there are two baseline models, thus we have two choices to perform stacked learning, one using the baseline discrete model as the layer-2 model and the other using the baseline neural model as the layer-2 model.

When the baseline discrete model is exploited as the layer-2 model, we simply add some new discrete features from the outputs of the baseline neural model. While When the baseline neural model is exploited as the layer-2 model, we simply extend the word representation at each position i by an additional embedding of the output label from the baseline discrete model.

4   Incorporating Cluster Features

In the baseline neural model, the word representation exploits the pre-trained word embeddings learnt from large-scale unlabeled corpus, thus it can encode certain latent syntactic and semantic information [14]. While for the baseline discrete model, no extra information is exploited except the bare training corpus, thus direct comparisons may be unfair.

In this work, we exploit word clusters, which can also include latent syntactic and semantic information to certain extend, to make the comparison fairer.

For the discrete model, we incorporate the information of word clusters simply by adding some new features that encode the word clusters. Assuming the input word sequence is $w_1 \cdots w_n$ and the corresponding cluster label sequence is $l_1 \cdots l_n$, we add four different features for each position i, respectively l_i, $l_{i-1}l_i$, l_il_{i+1} and $l_{i-1}l_il_{i+1}$.

For the neural model, we incorporate the word clusters by extending the word representation with cluster embedding. Based on the same above sentence $w_1 \cdots w_n$, we append the embedding of $\mathbf{e}(l_i)$ to the baseline word representation of word w_i, thus $\mathbf{x}_i = \mathbf{h}_i^c \oplus \mathbf{e}(w_i) \oplus \mathbf{e}(l_i)$, where the embedding is obtained by a look-up matrix E^l, which is a model parameter.

For the combinations, no matter the feature combination or the stacked learning, there are no big changes after incorporating cluster features.

5 Experiments

5.1 Experimental Settings

Data and Evaluation. We follow [8], exploiting the CTB 5.1 to conduct experiments. We adopt the same dividing method as theirs to split the data into training, development and test corpus. Totally, there are 16,091 training sentences, 803 development sentences and 1,910 test corpus, respectively. We use the standard tagging accuracy as the main metric to evaluate different models.

Table 1. The hyper-parameter values in our proposed discrete and neural models, where $d(\cdot)$ denotes the dimension size of a vector.

Type	Hyper-parameters
Network structure	$d(\mathbf{e}(w)) = d(\mathbf{e}(c)) = d(\mathbf{e}(t)) = d(\mathbf{e}(l)) = 50$, $d(\mathbf{h}^c) = 50$, $d(\mathbf{h}^{ct}) = 200$, $d(\mathbf{h}^r) = d(\mathbf{h}^l) = 100$, $d(\mathbf{h}) = 100$
Training	$\lambda = 10^{-8}$, $\alpha = 0.01$, $\eta = 0.2$

Hyper-Parameters. There are a number of hyper-parameters in our models, especially for the neural network models we need to define the dimension size of all neural layers. We show all the hyper-parameter values in Table 1. These value are tuned according to the developmental performances.

Word Embeddings. The pre-trained word embeddings used in the neural models are trained on Chinese Gigaword corpus (LDC2011T13). We use ZPar[1] to segment the raw corpus, in order to obtain the segmented corpus, and further we exploit the tool word2vec[2] to train word embeddings. Different with other embeddings such as E^c, E^l and E^t, word embeddings are kept fixed during neural network training.

---

[1] https://sourceforge.net/projects/zpar, version 0.7.
[2] http://word2vec.googlecode.com/.

5.2   Development Results

In this section, we conduct several experiments based on the development corpus, to comprehensively understand the baseline models and their combinations, as well as the effectiveness of word clusters.

Baseline Results. Table 2 shows the performances of our baseline discrete ad neural models. We find that the baseline neural model can get significantly better accuracies than the baseline discrete model. The result is reasonable, just as some researchers argue that, the neural models with pre-trained word embeddings should be categorized into a semi-supervised setting, because their word representations encode latent semantic and syntactic information, similar to the condition that word cluster features are used in the discrete models.

Besides, we compare the error distributions of the two models to look into their differences in detail. We achieve this goal by a scatter graph, observing their tagging accuracies with respect to sentences. Figure 2 shows the comparison results, where each point in the graph denotes an accuracy contrast of the two models, with the x-axis value being the accuracy of the discrete model, and the y-axis value being the accuracy of the neural model. We can see that all points are distributed without any obvious rules between the two models, demonstrating their different error distributions.

Combination. Our first motivation is to verify whether a combination of the baseline discrete and neural models could result in better Chinese POS tagging accuracies, and further we compare two different combination methods. Table 2 shows the combination results as well as the comparisons of the two combination methods. The results show that the combination of the two models does bring better accuracies for Chinese POS tagging. In addition, we find that the simple feature combination method can obtain the best improvements, resulting increases of over 0.5%. Stacked learning with the neural model as the layer-2 model is better than the discrete as the layer-2 model. According to the results, we exploit feature combination as the final combination method. All the later experiments of combination exploit the feature combination mechanism.

Cluster Enhanced Models. In order to make a fair comparison of the discrete and neural models, we incorporate word clusters into the baseline discrete model. The word clusters are trained by brown cluster[3] with the predefined cluster number being 1,000, according to [17,20]. As shown in Table 2, the results demonstrate that with the clustering features, the discrete model is still a little worse than the neural model. In particular, we incorporate the word clusters into the neural model and the feature combination model as well. Table 2 shows the results. We find that small improvements can be achieved by word clusters in the neural model, while for the combination model the improvements is insignificant.

---

[3] We use the tool available at https://github.com/percyliang/brown-cluster to produce word clusters, using the same corpus as the training of word embeddings.

Table 2. Development results.

Model	Discrete	Neural
Baseline	94.04	94.79
Stacked learning	94.94	94.98
Feature combination	**95.33**	
+ Word clusters		
Baseline	94.69	95.16
Feature combination	**95.44**	

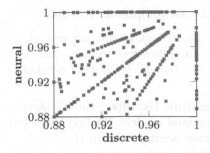

Fig. 2. Comparisons by error distributions.

5.3   Final Results

Table 3 shows our final results on the test dataset. We list the results of the baseline discrete and neural models and their combination. In addition, we show the performances when the three models are enhanced with word clusters as well. Overall, the performances are in consistent with developmental results. The baseline neural model is better than the baseline discrete model, and also slightly better than the discrete model with clustering features. The combination of discrete and neural model can bring significant improvements, reaching 95.12%. When word clusters are exploited, both the baseline discrete and neural models can have improvements, while the neural models is relatively small. For the combination model, there is no change by adding word cluster features.

We compare our results with other state-of-the-art models as well, as shown in Table 4, where [8] uses the additional heterogonous POS tagging annotations for Chinese POS tagging, and [6,11,22] are joint models for Chinese POS tagging and dependency parsing. The results show that our combination method gives the top performance on Chinese POS tagging.

Table 3. Final results on the test dataset.

Model	Without word clusters			With word clusters		
	Discrete	Neural	Combination	Discrete	Neural	Combination
Acc	93.89	94.52	**95.12**	94.43	94.70	**95.12**

Table 4. Comparisons with other work.

Model	Our best	[8]	[22]	[11]	[6]
Acc	**95.12**	95.00	94.95	94.60	94.01

6   Related Work

POS tagging has been a fundamental task of NLP. A number of work has been proposed for this task [2,19], which can be applied for both Chinese and English languages. Early studies focus on the traditional discrete models, which are based on the manually-designed one-hot features. State-of-the-art methods exploit whether a classification framework [1,5] or a sequence labeling framework [2,7]. In this work, we choose the latter based on CRF to perform Chinese POS tagging.

Recently, neural models for POS tagging have received much attention as well, due to the competitive performances achieved by neural networks. [3] proposed a simple feed-forward neural network. [15] incorporated character representation to improve neural POS tagging. [12,23] suggested bidirectional LSTMs to enhance neural feature representations for POS tagging. All above methods exploit the CRF framework similar with our baselines.

Combination of different models has also been a hot research topic, because it can always bring better performances in general. Stacked learning has been studied for model combinations in several other NLP tasks. For example, [10] have exploited this method for dependency parsing. Besides stacked learning, there exists several work using other methods such as bagging and voting [16, 18]. For combination of discrete and neural models, the majority work exploits feature combination [24,26].

7 Conclusion

We built a discrete model and a neural model for Chinese POS tagging, and compared them in detail. We interpreted their differences in feature engineering, and showed their different error distributions. Further, we combined the two kinds models, finding that improved accuracies can achieved. We also incorporated word clusters as one semi-supervised feature source, which is similar to pre-trained word embeddings, in order to make a fair comparison between discrete and neural models. Our experimental results show that even with word clusters, the discrete model cannot outperform the neural model without word clusters, and the performance of the neural model can be boosted a little by word clusters. We make our codes together with the pre-trained word embeddings and clusters publicly available at https://github.com/zhangmeishan/NNPOSTagging.

Acknowledgments. This work is supported by National Natural Science Foundation of China (NSFC) under grant 61602160 and 61672211, Natural Science Foundation of Heilongjiang Province (China) under grant No. F2016036.

References

1. Brants, T.: TnT: a statistical part-of-speech tagger. In: Proceedings of the Sixth Conference on Applied Natural Language Processing, pp. 224–231 (2000)
2. Collins, M.: Discriminative training methods for hidden Markov models: theory and experiments with perceptron algorithms. In: EMNLP (2002)
3. Collobert, R., Weston, J., Bottou, L., Karlen, M., Kavukcuoglu, K., Kuksa, P.: Natural language processing (almost) from scratch. JMLR **12**, 2493–2537 (2011)
4. Duchi, J., Hazan, E., Singer, Y.: Adaptive subgradient methods for online learning and stochastic optimization. JMLR **12**, 2121–2159 (2011)

5. Giménez, J., Marquez, L.: SVMTool: a general POS tagger generator based on support vector machines. In: Proceedings of the 4th LREC (2004)
6. Hatori, J., Matsuzaki, T., Miyao, Y., Tsujii, J.: Incremental joint POS tagging and dependency parsing in Chinese. In: IJCNLP, pp. 1216–1224 (2011)
7. Lafferty, J.D., McCallum, A., Pereira, F.C.N.: Conditional random fields: probabilistic models for segmenting and labeling sequence data. In: ICML, pp. 282–289 (2001)
8. Li, Z., Chao, J., Zhang, M., Chen, W.: Coupled sequence labeling on heterogeneous annotations: POS tagging as a case study. In: ACL, pp. 1783–1792 (2015)
9. Li, Z., Che, W., Liu, T.: Improving Chinese POS tagging with dependency parsing. In: IJCNLP, pp. 1447–1451 (2011)
10. Li, Z., Liu, T., Che, W.: Exploiting multiple treebanks for parsing with quasi-synchronous grammars. In: Proceedings of the 50th ACL, pp. 675–684 (2012)
11. Li, Z., Zhang, M., Che, W., Liu, T.: A separately passive-aggressive training algorithm for joint POS tagging and dependency parsing. In: COLING 2012, pp. 1681–1698 (2012)
12. Ma, X., Hovy, E.: End-to-end sequence labeling via bi-directional LSTM-CNNS-CRF. In: ACL (2016)
13. Manning, C.D.: Part-of-speech tagging from 97% to 100%: is it time for some linguistics? In: Gelbukh, A.F. (ed.) CICLing 2011. LNCS, vol. 6608, pp. 171–189. Springer, Heidelberg (2011). doi:10.1007/978-3-642-19400-9_14
14. Mikolov, T., Chen, K., Corrado, G., Dean, J.: Efficient estimation of word representations in vector space. arXiv preprint arXiv:1301.3781 (2013)
15. dos Santos, C.N., Zadrozny, B.: Learning character-level representations for part-of-speech tagging. In: ICML, pp. 1818–1826 (2014)
16. Sun, W.: Word-based and character-based word segmentation models: comparison and combination. In: COLING 2010: Posters, pp. 1211–1219 (2010)
17. Sun, W., Uszkoreit, H.: Capturing paradigmatic and syntagmatic lexical relations: towards accurate Chinese part-of-speech tagging. In: ACL 2012, pp. 242–252 (2012)
18. Sun, W., Wan, X.: Data-driven, PCFG-based and pseudo-PCFG-based models for Chinese dependency parsing. TACL 1(1), 301–314 (2013)
19. Toutanova, K., Klein, D., Manning, C., Singer, Y.: Feature-rich part-of-speech tagging with a cyclic dependency network. In: HLT-NAACL 2003 (2003)
20. Wang, Y., Kazama, J., Tsuruoka, Y., Chen, W., Zhang, Y., Torisawa, K.: Improving Chinese word segmentation and POS tagging with semi-supervised methods using large auto-analyzed data. In: IJCNLP, pp. 309–317 (2011)
21. Wolpert, D.H.: Stacked generalization. Neural Netw. 5, 241–259 (1992)
22. Zhang, M., Che, W., Liu, T., Li, Z.: Stacking heterogeneous joint models of Chinese POS tagging and dependency parsing. In: COLING 2012, pp. 3071–3088 (2012)
23. Zhang, M., Yang, J., Teng, Z., Zhang, Y.: LibN3L: a lightweight package for neural NLP. In: LREC (2016)
24. Zhang, M., Zhang, Y.: Combining discrete and continuous features for deterministic transition-based dependency parsing. In: EMNLP, pp. 1316–1321 (2015)
25. Zhang, M., Zhang, Y., Fu, G.: Transition-based neural word segmentation. In: Proceedings of the 54nd ACL (2016)
26. Zhang, M., Zhang, Y., Vo, D.T.: Neural networks for open domain targeted sentiment. In: Proceedings of the EMNLP, pp. 612–621 (2015)

Improving Word Vector with Prior Knowledge in Semantic Dictionary

Wei Li[1], Yunfang Wu[1($\boxtimes$)], and Xueqiang Lv[2]

[1] Key Laboratory of Computational Linguistics,
Peking University, Beijing, China
{liweitj47,wuyf}@pku.edu.cn
[2] Beijing Key Laboratory of Internet Culture and Digital Dissemination
Research, Beijing, China
lxq@bistu.edu.cn

Abstract. Using low dimensional vector space to represent words has been very effective in many NLP tasks. However, it doesn't work well when faced with the problem of rare and unseen words. In this paper, we propose to leverage the knowledge in semantic dictionary in combination with some morphological information to build an enhanced vector space. We get an improvement of 2.3% over the state-of-the-art Heidel Time system in temporal expression recognition, and obtain a large gain in other name entity recognition (NER) tasks. The semantic dictionary Hownet alone also shows promising results in computing lexical similarity.

Keywords: Rare words · Semantic dictionary · Morphological information · Word embedding

1 Introduction

To get a good representation of words has been a fundamental task for many natural language processing (NLP) tasks. The bag of words model (BOW) has been a practical and handy way. However, it cannot encode any information within the representation itself. With the help of neural networks, researchers are now able to represent words with distributed low dimensional vectors. Mikolov et al. (2013) proposed continuous bag of words model (CBOW) and continuous skip gram model to learn the word vectors, which have been very successful. However, it still suffers from the sparsity problem, because this kind of model learns word embeddings entirely on the basis of contexts, leading to unreliable representations for rare words.

To deal with the sparsity problem, Luong et al. (2013) and Qiu et al. (2014) proposed to consider the words and their morphemes together when building the vector space. Cui et al. (2015) tried to seek morphological information to revise the vectors of rare words in English. Chen et al. (2015) proposed Character-enhanced word embedding model (CWE) to combine words and multiple prototype character embedding together. Sun et al. (2014) and Li et al. (2015) proposed to leverage the component (or radical) information to learn Chinese character embedding. Peng and Dredze (2015) proposed a joint training objective for NER tasks in social media corpus with character

© Springer International Publishing AG 2016
C.-Y. Lin et al. (Eds.): NLPCC-ICCPOL 2016, LNAI 10102, pp. 461–469, 2016.
DOI: 10.1007/978-3-319-50496-4_38

embedding. These kinds of models all try to introduce the information of inner structure of a word to supplement the word level embedding.

In this paper, we propose to apply the sememes in Hownet (Dong and Dong 2006) together with morphological information to deal with the sparsity problem. In our opinion, sematic dictionaries like Hownet are very valuable resources. To utilize the knowledge of the dictionary, we calculate the embedding of each sememe whose target words appear in training corpus and then for each word, we sum the sememes of the word according to the semantic dictionary to form an approximate embedding of the word. Experiments show that this produces a highly correlated description with human judgment. As far as we know, this is the first time that the knowledge from a semantic dictionary like Hownet sememes been introduced to word vector space.

We apply our new word embeddings to tackle the problem of recognizing temporal expressions, person names and locations. Compared with the state-of-the-art F value of 87.3 from Heidel Time (Li et al. 2014), We got an F value of 89.6 on temeval-2 data concerning temporal expression recognition, improving the F value by 2.3 without any hand crafted feature. We also achieve competitive results on recognizing person names and locations.

2   Our Approach

Our approach is shown in Fig. 1. First, we get the *original word vector space* produced by word2vec. Then, we use the morphological information to find the similar words for a target word, the rare and unseen words. After that, we get the *similar word vector space* based on the word embeddings of the similar words. Then we update the vector space by combining the original vector and the similar words' vectors with weights tuned by term frequency. We concatenate this new vector with a context window of 2, along with *Hownet vector* and *Character vector* which we will come to later, and get the final *complete vector space*. The complete vectors are then used as real-number features to predict the tag of the word with multi-class logistic regression.

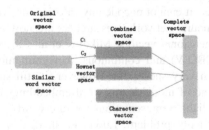

Fig. 1. Word embedding for rare words

2.1   Hownet Semantic Knowledge

Hownet is an influential semantic dictionary in Chinese. It describes the meaning of a word by a series of concepts. The concepts are further explained by a finite set of 1,500 sememes from ten classes and the relationship between them. An example is shown in Table 1.

Table 1. Example of Hownet description

Chinese	POS	English	Description
房租	N	House rent	Expenditure |费用,*borrow |借入, # house |房屋

In this example, "房租" (House rent) is the target word, "费用 (expenditure), 借入 (borrow), 房屋 (house)" are the corresponding sememes. The symbols "*,#" indicate the relations between the sememes, which we omit for now. On one hand this type of representation loses some details and can only give a rough description, on the other hand we believe it brings generality to the space.

1. Ideally, we want to use existing embeddings of sememes trained from real corpus. However, many of the sememes are rare or unseen. For instance, the second sememe in our example, "借入". Though its meaning is very clear, it can be rarely seen in real life corpus as it is too formal. So we need to get a good sememe embedding first.

2. To learn sensible sememe embeddings, we replace the words with their first sememe into the training corpus, and train the embedding using word2vec. For instance in our example, all occurrences of "房租" in the corpus would all be replaced by "费用", and thus we can get the embedding of the sememe "费用", $\theta("费用")$. In the dictionary, the sememe "费用" appears not only in "房租", but also in a lot of other words like "安家费" (settlement allowance), so $\theta("费用") \neq \theta("房租")$. The first sememes are all basic sememes, containing most of the meaning.

3. We do the same thing for the second and the third sememes of each word. For instance, "借入", "房屋" will be put back to the corpus and replace the original word "房租" separately and get their according embeddings $\theta("借入")$ and $\theta("房屋")$. Because these sememes appear in different words, they would have different word embeddings, that is to say, $\theta("费用")$, $\theta("借入")$ and $\theta("房屋")$ are different. By getting the Hownet embeddings this way, we only hold the basic sememes of each word. This trick is handy and pragmatic, but it also makes the Hownet embedding lose some detail, which can cause ambiguity.

4. Inspired by the attribute of word vectors observed in Mikolov et al. (2013) that simple algebraic addition can lead to very interesting results, for example, $\theta("Germany") + \theta("capital") \approx \theta("Berlin")$. We sum the embeddings of all sememes of a word to get a new embedding, and we call it the Hownet embedding. Concretely, in our example, we use $\theta("费用") + \theta("借入") + \theta("房屋")$ as an approximation to $\theta("房租")$.

With the method above, we can produce word embeddings out of the sememe embeddings and we call this the *Hownet vector space* in Fig. 1.

2.2 Similar Words

In Chinese, the vocabulary size of characters is much smaller than that of words, which means it is much rarer to meet new characters than new words. Apart from that, most of the words consist of only two to three characters, especially in nouns. Based on these observations and the assumption that morphologically similar words tend to be semantically similar, we want to find the morphologically similar words of rare and unseen words to help learn or revise their embeddings.

We applied longest common substring (LCS), edit distance, cosine similarity to measure the morphological similarity between words. After we get the similarity scores from these three measurements, we use a simple perceptron to tune their weights.

1. We use another semantic dictionary in Chinese called "*tong yi ci ci lin*" to build the training set. This dictionary contains the categorical information about the synonymous sets of words. The pairs of words in the training set are selected either from the same category or randomly from different categories. If two words belong to the same category, which means they are synonyms, we set the similarity to be *1*. If they belong to different categories, we set the similarity score to be *0*.
2. We use the method aforementioned to find the similarity scores between the rare or unseen words in the new coming corpus and the words in the existing vocabulary (words from the training set). We put the top five words that have the highest similarity scores into the candidate set.
3. We use term frequency of words in the training set as weights to calculate a weighted average of these candidate word embeddings. We then set this new embedding to be the embedding of the rare or unseen words.

As the frequency of some words can be very large, giving them too much significance, we use a function f consists of five buckets to separate these words with different weights rather than use their term frequency (tf) directly as is shown below.

$$f(tf) = \begin{cases} 4 \text{ if } tf > 100 \\ 3 \text{ if } tf > 20 \text{ and } tf < = 100 \\ 2 \text{ if } tf > 5 \text{ and } tf < = 20 \\ 1 \text{ if } tf > 2 \text{ and } tf < = 5 \\ 0 \text{ if } tf < = 2 \end{cases}$$

After the revision, we get a new version of the embedding space of rare and unseen words which is the *Similar word vector space* in Fig. 1. We can then combine this space with the *original vector space* produced by word2vec as a complement to form a new *combined vector space* (Fig. 1). When we combine these two vector spaces, we also use two weights C_1 and C_2 in Fig. 1 to weighted sum the two embeddings. The weights here also depend on term frequency.

2.3   Character Embedding

Besides the fact that similar words should have similar meanings and similar embeddings, the inner structure of a word also provides valuable information. It is observed that the last character of a word holds most part of the meaning for most of nouns. This characteristic is very useful in the problem of recognizing temporal expressions and name entity words. For instance, in the temporal expression "4月5日", "日" is a very clear sign indicating that the word should be a date. To get the character level embedding, we feed the separate characters instead of the original words in the same training corpus to word2vec. We call this space of character level embedding the *character vector space*.

3 Experiment

3.1 Correlation with Human Judgement

Word embedding has been proven to be successful in measuring the similarity or relatedness between words. In this experiment, we show that the cosine similarity calculated with the Hownet embedding show a good correlation with human judgement. We design a questionnaire of forty pairs of words. The words are all selected from Hownet, and at least one of the words in each pair is not observed in our training data. We use the corpus of three-month People Daily to be the training data.

In the experiment, we ask ten students to mark the similarity between words, ranging from 1 to 10. We average the ten scores, and set the mean as the human judgement. Then we calculate the cosine similarity within the word pairs based on *Hownet embedding* we get, and use **Spearman** to measure the correlation between Hownet embedding similarity and human judgement, obtaining a Spearman of 56.6. We also implement the similarity computing method of Liu and Li (2002) (also based on Hownet) with all default settings in the same data, and get a Spearman of only 38.0. Some examples are shown in Table 2, where Word 1 is the rare word.

This result shows that the embedding learnt from Hownet has a fairly strong correlation with human judgement. While most of the cosine similarity between our Hownet embedding and human judgement result correlate with each other, some of the words failed. We think this is partly due to the fact that we dropped the last sememes of the words, and this way of representing words loses the details of the words.

One point should be stated is that although Hownet contains only a limited number of words, our main purpose is not using any specific dictionary, but to introduce this new way of constructing embeddings or to bring the information into the vector space.

Table 2. Examples of Hownet experiment

Word 1	Word 2	Human	Hownet	Liu and Li (2002)
殃及	到达	2.3	0.021	0.138
伤残人	敌人	2.6	0.02	0.722
六月份	时间	5.6	0.451	0.6
薪水	工资	9.2	1	1
活该	应该	3.2	0.332	0.074
次序	秩序	4.7	1	1
衣料	材料	5.3	0.143	1
阿拉伯人	阿拉伯	7.2	0.106	0.149
妥当	合适	7.8	0.168	1
找出	发现	7.4	0.268	0.55

3.2   Temporal Tagging

We focus on the recognition part of Chinese temporal expressions in Tempeval-2 (Verhagen et al. 2010). This part of the data consists of 931 sentences in the train set, 345 sentences in the test set, which were all newspaper texts and correctly segmented. There are four tags, namely, Time, Date, Duration, Set, following the timex3 standard. There are 936 temporal expressions in total. In our experiment, we tag the words with "BI" system. Because of the shortage of data, the distribution of the tags in the data is highly skewed and can be seen in Fig. 2.

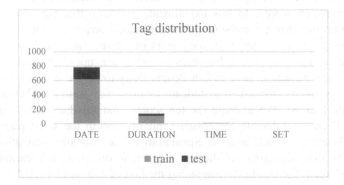

Fig. 2.   Tag distribution in Tempeval2 task

For a long time, researchers have been in favor of rule-based methods to do the job, and got a fairly good result. Li et al. (2014) created a rule-based Heidel Time system adapted from English and got the art-of-the-art F value of 87.3. We train the embedding with word2vec on the corpus of three-month People Daily News together with the train data provided in Temevel-2, revise it to get an enhanced embedding with the method aforementioned.

Considering the fact that the training data in temeval-2 is rather small, we feed the vectors into a log-linear classifier (Fan et al. 2008) with L2 regularization to do the work to avoid overfitting. We deal with the problem as a multi-class classification (logistic regression) problem, and the vectors learnt from our models can be put forward to the log-linear classifier directly as real number features. We choose a context window of 2 concatenated with our modified vector.

The settings of our baselines are listed below.

- **Word2vec**: This method feeds the embedding learnt with word2vec (*original vector space*) with a context window of 2 directly to the log-linear classifier.
- **Character**: This method concatenates the embedding from the *original vector space* in a window of 2 and the embedding of the last character of the word (*character vector space*), then feeds this new embedding to the classifier.
- **Morphological**: This method feeds the embedding from *combined vector space* with a context window of 2 to the classifier.

- **Hownet**: This method concatenates the embedding from the *original vector space* in a window of 2 with the embedding from *Hownet vector space*, and feeds this new embedding to the classifier.
- **Final model**: This method feeds the embedding from the *complete vector space*, which is the concatenation of embeddings from *combined vector space*, *character vector space* and *Hownet vector space*, to the classifier.

The results are shown in Table 3. It shows that our proposed Hownet embedding brings a big improvement compared to the original word2vec space in F value (**79.8** to **83.1**). And with the help of other methods, the overall result beats the Heidel Time baseline. It can also be seen that the overall method gives a big improvement to the original word2vec method, which indicates that the revised vector space captures the information better than the original one. Still, the lack of tagged data and the skewness of the tags strongly hold the performance back.

Table 3. Temp2eval results

Method	P	R	F
Heidel time	93.4	82	87.3
Word2vec	86.5	74.1	79.8
Character	85.0	81.4	83.2
Morphological	86.6	74.7	80.2
Hownet	87.0	79.6	83.1
Final model	93.7	86.0	89.6

3.3 People Daily NER

Person names and locations have been a central part in name entity recognition problem. In this paper, we use an open corpus of 10 days of People Daily (1998) as our train and test data, and test data is extracted with five-fold fashion. This data was segmented and tagged with part of speech information by the institute of Computational Linguistics of Peking University, and can be freely downloaded. We build the test set using the POS tags of "ns" and "nr", and so when training the classifier, POS tags are omitted. We predict ns and nr tags with our enhanced embedding, based only on the segmented words. The results are shown in Table 4. We also treat this NER problem as a multi-class logistic regression problem with the vectors as real-number features. The settings of the baselines are the same as in tempeval2 task.

Table 4. NER results on people daily news

Method	NR			NS		
	P	R	F	P	R	F
Word2vec	92.6	83.4	87.8	82.6	65.3	72.9
Character	92.0	86.1	88.9	83.6	73.3	78.1
Similar words	90.9	85.8	88.3	80.4	67.3	73.3
Hownet	93.4	86.3	89.8	85.1	71.7	77.8
Final model	93.5	89.6	91.5	85.8	78.9	82.2

In both these two tasks, our enhanced embedding performs much better than the original version of word2vec. And Hownet embedding gives big improvement over the original word2vec vector space by an F score of almost 5%. We think this improvement comes not only from the Hownet and character embedding for the rare and unseen words, but also from the generality these two embeddings bring to the original embeddings. This phenomenon is true especially when one cannot get a big enough training data.

4   Conclusion

Although the deep neural network alone seems very promising in capturing the semantics of words, we believe that the prior knowledge that experts have been working on for decades should not be ignored. In this paper, we propose a method of introducing the knowledge of semantic dictionary Hownet together with some morphological information into the vector space. Experiments show that this method is very effective in capturing semantic information, especially when we don't have the access to big training data. As should be pointed out, our way of using semantic dictionary Hownet aims to provide a new perspective of utilizing semantic dictionary information, which should not be limited to this particular dictionary. In the future, we hope to find more efficient and suitable ways to automatically construct these sememe embeddings, and combine them with more sophisticated neural networks.

Acknowledgement. This work is supported by National Natural Science Foundation of China (61371129), National Key Basic Research Program of China (2014CB340504), Key Program of Social Science foundation of China (12&ZD227), and the Opening Project of Beijing Key Laboratory of Internet Culture and Digital Dissemination Research (ICDD201402).

References

Chen, X., Xu, L., Liu, Z., Sun, M., Luan, H.: Joint learning of character and word embeddings. In: Proceedings of IJCAI, pp. 1236–1242 (2015)

Cui, Q., Gao, B., Bian, J., Qiu, S., Dai, H., Liu, T.-Y.: KNET: a general framework for learning word embedding using morphological knowledge. ACM Trans. Inf. Syst. (TOIS) 34(1), 4 (2015)

Dong, Z., Dong, Q.: HowNet and the Computation of Meaning. World Scientific, Beijing (2006)

Fan, R.-E., Chang, K.-W., Hsieh, C.-J., Wang, X.-R., Lin, C.-J.: LIBLINEAR: a library for large linear classification. J. Mach. Learn. Res. 9, 1871–1874 (2008)

Li, H., Strötgen, J., Zell, J., Gertz, M.: Chinese temporal tagging with heideltime. In: EACL, pp. 133–137 (2014)

Li, Y., Li, W., Sun, F., Li, S.: Component-enhanced chinese character embeddings (2015). arXiv preprint: arXiv:1508.06669

Liu, Q., Li, S.: Word similarity computing based on How-net. Comput. Linguist. Chin. Lang. Process. 7(2), 59–76 (2002)

Luong, T., Socher, R., Manning, C.D.: Better word representations with recursive neural networks for morphology. In: CoNLL, pp. 104–113. Citeseer (2013)

Mikolov, T., Sutskever, I., Chen, K., Corrado, G.S., Dean, J.: Distributed representations of words and phrases and their compositionality. In: Advances in Neural Information Processing Systems, pp. 3111–3119 (2013)

Peng, N., Dredze, M.: Named entity recognition for Chinese social media with jointly trained embeddings (2015)

Qiu, S., Cui, Q., Bian, J., Gao, B., Liu, T.-Y.: Co-learning of word representations and morpheme representations. In: COLING, pp. 141–150 (2014)

Sun, Y., Lin, L., Yang, N., Ji, Z., Wang, X.: Radical-enhanced Chinese character embedding. In: Loo, C.K., Yap, K.S., Wong, K.W., Teoh, A., Huang, K. (eds.) ICONIP 2014. LNCS, vol. 8835, pp. 279–286. Springer, Heidelberg (2014). doi:10.1007/978-3-319-12640-1_34

Verhagen, M., Sauri, R., Caselli, T., Pustejovsky, J.: SemEval-2010 task 13: TempEval-2. In: Proceedings of the 5th International Workshop on Semantic Evaluation, pp. 57–62. Association for Computational Linguistics (2010)

Adapting Attention-Based Neural Network to Low-Resource Mongolian-Chinese Machine Translation

Jing Wu, Hongxu Hou[✉], Zhipeng Shen, Jian Du, and Jinting Li

College of Computer Science, Inner Mongolia University, Hohhot, China
cshhx@imu.edu.cn

Abstract. Neural machine translation (NMT) has shown very promising results for some resourceful languages like En-Fr and En-De. The success partly relies on the availability of large scale and high quality parallel corpora. We research on how to adapt NMT to very low-resource Mongolian-Chinese machine translation by introducing attention mechanism, sub-words translation, monolingual data and a NMT correction model. We proposed a sub-words model to address the out-of-vocabulary (OOV) problem in attention-based NMT model. Monolingual data help alleviate the low-resource problem. Besides, we explore a Chinese NMT correction model to enhance the translation performance. The experiments show that the adapted Mongolian-Chinese attention-based NMT machine translation obtains an improvement of 1.70 BLEU points over the phrased-based statistical machine translation baseline and 3.86 BLEU points over normal NMT baseline on an open training set.

Keywords: Low-resource · Mongolian-Chinese · Machine translation · SMT · NMT

1 Introduction

NMT has been proposed in recent years and shows promising results [1–4]. Many NMT models follow the encoder and decoder framework proposed by [3] which consists of one encoder RNN (Recurrent Neural Network) and one decoder RNN. The encoder converts source sentences into vectors and the decoder generates target sentences based on the vectors of source sentence representation. Attention mechanism was first introduced in NMT by [4] to learn a soft alignment between the source and target words. We apply an attention-based NMT [3, 4] to adapt the Mongolian-Chinese machine translation.

Mongolian language has been used by millions of people in different countries and regions in the world. The translation between Mongolian and Chinese is important and necessary. However, the small scale of Mongolian-Chinese parallel corpus is not sufficient to build a decent translation model. We have accumulated some experiences of tackling with these problems in the SMT training. However, how to adapt the new approach of NMT to the low-resource Mongolian-Chinese task is still a challenge. Based on the attention-based NMT, we apply three methods of sub-words training,

C.-Y. Lin et al. (Eds.): NLPCC-ICCPOL 2016, LNAI 10102, pp. 470–480, 2016.
DOI: 10.1007/978-3-319-50496-4_39

monolingual data and a NMT correction model to boost the low-resource Mongolian-Chinese NMT model to a better performance. The methods mainly focus on the low-resource of the parallel corpus, the out-of-vocabulary (OOV) words, the complex Mongolian morphology and the better utilizing of the attention mechanism.

Sub-words are used in NMT model and show potential advantages [5]. A significant weakness in conventional NMT systems is their inability to successfully translate OOV words. The target vocabulary size must be limited for the complexity of NMT training increases as the number of target words increases. Any words not included in the target vocabulary is mapped to a special token of unknown word (UNK) [6, 7]. Chinese words are in a huge number while the commonly used Chinese characters are no more than 5000. Hence, using Chinese characters rather than words as basic units can basically solve the OOV problem. Mongolian vocabulary is often filled with many similar words that share the same lexeme but have different morphology [8]. Therefore, we also use Mongolian sub-words as stem+case suffix to address this problem. One of the major factors behind the success of neural network for machine translation is the capable of high quality and large scale parallel corpora [9]. We believe it is important to utilize monolingual corpora in low-resource Mongolian-Chinese NMT task because the parallel corpora are in very small scale and insufficient to train a decent NMT model. We also train a Chinese NMT correction model to act as a re-translation correction system.

Rests of the paper are organized as follows: Sect. 2 describes the model of attention-based NMT; Sect. 3 describes the sub-words Mongolian-Chinese NMT model; Sect. 4 introduces the monolingual data and Sect. 5 applies correction model to attention-based NMT; Sect. 6 is the evaluation while Sect. 7 is the conclusion and future work.

2 Attention-Based Neural Network Machine Translation

This syntax difference between Chinese and Mongolian leads to bad word order. The soft-alignment can capture more partly relations and be good at the big constituent order difference. The attention-based Neural Network model we followed is [3, 4] which is a bidirectional recurrent neural network (BiRNN) [12] and consists of one encoder RNN with attention mechanism and one decoder RNN. The usual encoder RNN, described as Eq. (1),

$$h_t = f(x_t, h_{t-1}) \tag{1}$$

where $h_t \in R^n$ is a hidden state at time t, f is a kind of nonlinear functions. This RNN encoder model reads input sentences $X = (x_1, \cdots, x_{T_x})$ in order from x_1 to x_{T_x} and stops at the ending symbol (<eos>). The forward network of BiRNN $\overrightarrow{f}$ reads the input sentences in order to the hidden states $\left(\overrightarrow{h_1}, \cdots, \overrightarrow{h_{T_x}} \right)$ and the backward RNN $\overleftarrow{f}$ reads the input sentences in the reverse order (from x_1 to x_{T_x}) to the backward hidden states $\left(\overleftarrow{h_1}, \cdots, \overleftarrow{h_{T_x}} \right)$. At each location in the input sentence, we concatenate the hidden states from the forward and reverse RNNs together to summarize the whole input sentence in c (Eq. (2)),

$$z_i = \emptyset_\theta(u_{i-1}, z_{i-1}, c) \tag{2}$$

where z_i is the hidden state of the decoder RNN, $\emptyset_\theta$ is a recurrent active function. c is the summary vector of the source sentence which is a fixed-length vector, u_{i-1} is the previous word and z_{i-1} is the previous internal state. Then the decoder computes the conditional distribution as Eq. (3) displays over all possible translations by assigning a probability p_i on each word.

$$p(y) = \prod_{t=1}^{T} p(y_t|\{y_1, \cdots, y_{t-1}\}, c) = g(y_{t-1}, s_t, c) \tag{3}$$

The normal RNN model we described above attempts to encode a whole input sentence into a single fixed-length vector c, which is unnecessary and increases the computation complexity. The attention mechanism frees the decoder from the fixed-length vector and makes neural machine translation system more robust to long relations. The attention mechanism is implemented as a neural network with a single hidden layer and a single scalar output $e_j \in R$. The weight of each annotation h_j is computed through an alignment model a_{ij} is in Eq. (4), which models the probability that y_i is aligned to x_j. c in Eq. (2) is replaced by $c = \{c_1, c_2, \cdots, c_M\}$ in Eq. (5). Then the conditional probability in Eq. (3) is redefined as Eq. (6).

$$a_{ij} = \frac{\exp(e_j)}{\sum_{j'} \exp(e_{j'})} \tag{4}$$

$$c_i = \sum_{j=1}^{T} a_j h_j \tag{5}$$

$$p(y) = \prod_{t=1}^{T} p(y_t|\{y_1, \cdots, y_{t-1}\}, c_i) = g(y_{t-1}, s_t, c_i) \tag{6}$$

The whole model, consisting of the encoder, decoder and soft-alignment mechanism, is then tuned to minimize the negative log-likelihood using stochastic gradient descent. The attention mechanism provides a soft alignment a_{ij} to make the RNN model focus more attention on different parts of the source sentences. More detail description can be found in [2–4].

3   Sub-words Mongolian-Chinese NMT

Many previous researches on machine translation have considered Chinese words as basic units. However, using Chinese character can significantly reduce the OOV words in NMT. Hence, Chinese characters allow the NMT model to provide a sufficient training with a very small target vocabulary.

Mongolian is an agglutinative language where words are made by concatenating morphemes. An example of stem concatenating morphemes to become different words has been shown in Table 1. The kinds of suffixes are countless and suffixes can be added to either stems or normal words multiply. Mongolian word UILED (Latin alphabet) theoretically has at least 1710 deformations by adding suffixes constantly [14]. Case suffix normally is the last suffix adding to the stem. They play important roles to the sentence structure but have minimum influence to the lexeme of Mongolian words which makes different Mongolian words share the same lexeme.

Table 1. Example of Mongolian morphology

Mongolian words	ᠲᠣᠰᠤ	ᠲᠣᠰᠤᠳᠠ	ᠲᠣᠰᠤᠲᠠᠢ
Mongolian stem + suffix	ᠲᠣᠰᠤ	ᠲᠣᠰᠤ + ᠳᠠ	ᠲᠣᠰᠤ + ᠲᠠᠢ
Part of speech	stem	verb	adjective
Lexeme	oil	cover with oil	oily

Lemmatization by cutting off the suffixes and removing them from the sentences can alleviate the data sparsity and improves the translation in SMT, leads to bad performance in NMT. The reason we believe is that one of the strength of NMT lies in that the semantic and structure information of the sentences are learned by taking the global or local context into consideration, which is quite different from SMT to provide translation by count-based estimator of probabilities [15, 16]. Simply removing the suffixes may lose many features and broke the reasonable sentence structure that might be useful for the NMT model to learn the features. So in our work, we cut the case suffix off but leave the stems and case suffixes as sub-words in the sentences. The algorithm we use to do lemmatization is rule-based as the work of [17].

Because of the low-resource of parallel corpora, the information represented by the small amount of Chinese words is very limited while Chinese characters can represent much more by different combination. Hence, sub-words sequences allow the NMT model to obtain more various manifestation of the source language and provide more possible translations for the decoder to generate translations.

4 Applying Monolingual Data to NMT

One of the major factors behind the success of neural network for machine translation is the capable of high quality and large scale parallel corpora. For the low-resource Mongolian-Chinese machine translation task, the parallel corpora are in very small scale and limits the NMT performance. [11, 18] introduce monolingual corpora into attention-based encoder-decoder NMT and achieve improvements both in high resource and low resource language. In SMT, Monolingual data in target side can help boost fluency of the target language [18]. However, Mongolian-Chinese parallel data (around 65 K pairs of sentences) is even smaller than the other low-resource data like

Turkish-English in [11, 18] and insufficient for training a decent SMT or NMT translation system. How to use the monolingual data properly in the attention-based NMT but not introduce too much noises is important.

Hence, we directly add monolingual data in the target side of the encoder-decoder training process. We apply 200 K Chinese monolingual language sentences getting from Chinese-English multilingual corpora (from Computational Linguistics Institute of Peking University) to the target training set. To fill the absence in the source side, we translate the Chinese sentences to Monolingual by a SMT system and add the translations to the source training set. We also use a NMT correct system which we will describe in Sect. 5 to correct the translated Mongolian sentences to improve its quality. After mixing the monolingual data and the filled data with the training set, we get a new training set of 265 k parallel training corpora to conduct the attention-based NMT training.

5 Applying Correction Model to NMT

Different from the work of [19, 20] who added correction patterns and rules to correct the grammars, we simply build this correction system by regarding the process of correction as a translation task from the "wrong" target language to "right" target language. We expect the system to learn how to translate a bad representation to its correct representation in a translation mode. It acts as a re-translation. The correction system is built as Fig. 1 shows, we use the 65 K pairs of Mongolian-Chinese parallel corpora to train a NMT system and translate the very 65 K Mongolian sentences to Chinese. We use the Chinese translation results as source language and the true Chinese sentences of Mongolian-Chinese parallel as target sentences to train the correction

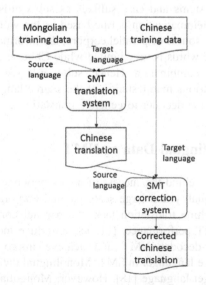

Fig. 1. The framework of the SMT-based correction

system. The built correction system can improve the translation results produced by normal SMT and NMT translation systems. We use the SMT-based correction to further improve our attention-based NMT.

6 Evaluation

6.1 Setting

A public Mongolian-Chinese parallel corpora CWMT'2009 [21] is used for the training. The CWMT corpus is the only public Mongolian-Chinese training set as well as a very small training set which remains 65 K sentences after we limit the length of sentences to 50. The develop set and test set selected from the training set are both 1000 pairs of sentences.

We build a PBSMT system which is a re-implementation of state-of-the-art work like [22] with Moses toolkits [23] as Baseline 1. The alignment is performed by GIZA++ toolkit [24]. A phrase-based MT decoder similar to [22] is implemented with the decoding weights optimized by MERT [25]. We use the open-source NMT system GroundHog [4] with default settings as Baseline 2. We train Baseline 1 and Baseline 2 several times and apply the best BLEU scores, which is character-level, as the baselines as Table 2 shows.

Table 2. Baseline of PBSMT and GroundHog

System	Chinese & Mongolian	BLEU
PBSMT (baseline 1)	Words	29.48
GroundHog (baseline 2)	Words	27.32

6.2 Evaluation of Attention-Based NMT

We train the attention-based NMT with 1024 dimensional for word embedding and 1024 hidden units per layer for both encoder and decoder. We limit the source vocabulary to 50 K and target vocabulary to 10 K. A mini-batch stochastic gradient decent (SGD) together with Adadelta is used to train the network. In the training, we also use early stopping to prevent overfitting. A beam search of 10 is used to find the most likely translation. We also randomly shuffle the training set and develop set during the training. We ran the model on GPU of NVIDIA Tesla K80. All the experiments on attention-based NMT in the following share the same settings.

As Table 3 shows, the word-level attention-based based NMT is 28.04 which is 0.72 points higher than the normal NMT GroundHog but lower than the best PBSMT.

Table 3. BLEU of the attention-based NMT and baselines

System	Chinese & Mongolian	BLEU
Attention-based NMT	Words	28.04

6.3   Evaluation of Sub-words NMT

We evaluate a words to sub-words model and a sub-words model as shown in Table 4. The words to sub-words model applies Chinese character in target language while the sub-words model applies character to Chinses and stem+case suffix to source language of Mongolian.

Table 4. BLEU of the sub-words attention-based NMT

System	Chinese/Mongolian	BLEU
Attention-based NMT	Words/words	28.04
Sub-words to words attention-based NMT	Characters/words	29.42 (+1.38)
Sub-words attention-based NMT	Characters/stem+case	30.52 (+2.48)

The sub-words of Chinese character improves the attention-based NMT to 29.42, which is 1.38 point higher than the word-based model. We believe that the improvement mainly due to the significantly decrease of OOV words. Observing from the training process, we find that there are almost no UNK words in target language while there are 4.5% in the translation results of words level attention-based NMT.

When we use sub-words for both ends, the BLEU score reaches to 30.52 which is higher than the words level attention-based NMT for 2.48 BLEU points. During the training of the sub-words model, very few UNK in source language are found for the source vocabulary.

The sub-words model exceeds two baselines for 1.04 and 3.20 points respectively. The experiments show that using sub-words to conduct the NMT model can improve the translation performance significantly. Besides, we can see that compared with words level translation result, the structure and translation options of the sub-words model are more flexible.

6.4   Evaluation of Monolingual

We evaluate the Monolingual data based on the sub-words attention-based NMT model as Sect. 6.3 implemented. A Chinese-Mongolian PBSMT system as Sect. 6.1 described trained by CWMT'9 was used to translate the Chinese monolingual data to Mongolian. The BLEU score of the Chinese-Mongolian PBSMT system is 29.96. Then we fill the translation in the source side of the sub-words attention-based NMT.

From the experiment result as Table 5 shows, the BLEU score increase to 31.00. The improvements of 0.48 BLEU points show that reasonable use of monolingual can enhance the low-resource Mongolian-Chinese translation.

Table 5. BLEU of the sub-level attention-based NMT + monolingual system

System	BLEU
Sub-level attention-based NMT + monolingual	31.00

6.5   Evaluation of NMT Correction

We apply the NMT correction system to several different SMT and NMT translation tasks to test its effectiveness. These experiments show that the correction can enhance the BLEU score for 0.21 points in average. We do correction to the result of sub-words attention-based NMT+monolingual model and enhance the BLEU score for 0.18 points as Table 6 shows. From the comparison between the results before and after the correction, we find that the model learns the inappropriate representations and the corresponding appropriate representations from the Chinese to Chinese training and uses them to correct the input translation. As some examples shown in Table 7, some unnecessary words are eliminated like row 1 and row 2 while some words are added to the sentences like rows 3, 4 and 5 show. Some inappropriate representations are corrected such as unit or article words in 5 and 6.

Table 6. BLEU of the sub-words attention-based NMT + monolingual + correction system

System	BLEU
Sub-level attention-based NMT + monolingual + NMT correction	31.18

Table 7. Examples of the results in NMT correction model

	Before correction	After correction	Reference
1	做什么时间*的*？	做什么时间？	订什么时间？ What time will you book to?
2	哪*种种*类型号比较好。	哪*种*类型号比较好。	哪*种*车的性能好。 Which car is better?
3	你钢笔是什么颜色的？	你*的*钢笔是什么颜色的？	你的钢笔什么颜色？ What colour is your pen?
4	你结婚吗？	你结婚*了*吗？	你结婚了吗？ Have you got married?
5	你可以用一张千日的钞票从这个机器里买张票。	你可以用一张千日*元*的钞票从这个机器里买张票。	你可以用一千日元的钞票从这个机器里买张票。 You can buy a ticket from the machine by 1000 yuan.
6	这*个*裤子会适应吗？	这*条*裤子会适应吗？	这条裤子是尼龙的吗？ Is this a nylon pants?

6.6   Comparison

We compare all the experiments of our methods with baselines in Table 8. Our four methods in total enhance 1.69 BLEU points over the PBSMT system and 3.86 points over the normal RNN system. Sub-words method individually contributes 2.48 BLEU points, monolingual individually contributes 0.48 and NMT correction contributes 0.18 BLEU points. At last, we enhance the Mongolian-Chinese attention-based NMT to 31.18 BLEU score.

Table 8. Comparison of the experiments.

System	BLEU
PBSMT (baseline 1)	29.48
GroundHog (baseline 2)	27.32
Attention-based NMT	28.04
Attention-based NMT + sub-words to sub-words	30.52
Attention-based NMT + sub-words to sub-words + monolingual	31.00
Attention-based NMT + sub-words+monolingual + NMT correction	31.18

7   Conclusion

We utilize attention mechanism, sub-words method, monolingual data and a NMT correction model to adapt NMT model to low-resource Mongolian-Chinese translation task. The experiments show that the four methods are effective to improve the Mongolian-Chinese NMT model. The attention mechanism implements a soft-alignment between the source and the target language and performs better in the long-term distance contributes to cope with the structure difference and the length increase for using sub-words. Based on this attention-based NMT model, we proposed sub-words as basic units for translation. The attention-based NMT model provides a good conditions for the sub-words to play a role in the translation task. We introduce monolingual data to the target side and fill the source side with its SMT translation. At last, we utilize a NMT correction model to further correct and enhance the BLEU of the attention-based NMT system for BLEU points. As adapting attention-based NMT for low-resource task, we believe the methods are instructive and might be effective for other low-resource translation tasks.

As a new approach, the NMT still has more potential. How to improve low-resource translation task of NMT model to a leapfrog program is still a big challenge. In the future, we plan to do more work at combing the different NMT models and SMT models to capture better translation ability. We believe that the SMT model and the NMT model are both powerful translation models, so to boost them to their best works is a very interesting and promising work. Moreover, the improvement of using monolingual is not very significant as we expected, so we will try other ways to adding the source and target monolingual data to NMT model.

Acknowledgements. This work is supported by the National Natural Science Foundation of China (No. 61362028).

References

1. Kalchbrenner, N., Kalchbrenner, N.: Recurrent convolutional neural networks for discourse compositionality. In: Proceedings of ACL 2013 (2013)
2. Sutskever, I., Vinyals, O., Le, Q.V.: Sequence to sequence learning with neural networks. In: NIPS 2014 (2014)

3. Cho, K., van Merriënboer, B., Gulcehre, C., Bahdanau, D., Bougares, F., Schwenk, H., Bengio, Y.: Learning phrase representations using RNN encoder-decoder for statistical machine translation. In: Proceedings of EMNLP 2014 (2014)
4. Bahdanau, D., Cho, K., Bengio, Y.: Neural machine translation by jointly learning to align and translate. In: Proceedings of ACL – IJCNLP 2015, vol. 1 (2015). Long Papers
5. Sennrich, R., Haddow, B., Birch, A.: Neural machine translation of rare words with sub-word units. In: Proceeding of CoRR 2015 (2015)
6. Jean, S., Cho, K., Memisevic, R., Bengio, Y.: On using very large target vocabulary for neural machine translation. In: Proceedings of the 53rd Annual Meeting of the Association for Computational Linguistics, vol. 2 (2015). Short Papers
7. Sutskever, I., Le, Q.V., Vinyals, O., Zaremba, W.: Addressing the rare word problem in neural machine translation. In: Proceedings of ACL – IJCNLP 2015, vol. 1, 11–19, 127–133 pages (2015). Long Papers
8. Wu, J., Hou, H., Monghjaya, F.B., Xie, C.: Introduction of traditional Mongolian-Chinese machine translation. In: Proceeding of International Conference on Electrical, Automation and Mechanical Engineering, EAME 2015, Phuket, pp. 357–360 (2015)
9. Gülçehre, Ç., Firat, O., Xu, K., Cho, K., Barrault, L., Lin, H., Bougares, F., Schwenk, H., Bengio, Y.: On using monolingual corpora in neural machine translation. In: Proceedings of CoRR 2015 (2015)
10. Koehn, P., Och, F.J., Marcu, D.: Statistical phrase-based translation. In: Proceedings of HLT-NAACL (2003)
11. Sennrich, R., Haddow, B., Birch, A.: Improving neural machine translation models with monolingual data. In: Proceeding of ACL 2016 (2016)
12. Schuster, M., Paliwal, K.K.: Bidirectional recurrent neural networks. Sig. Process. IEEE Trans. 45(11), 2673–2681 (1997)
13. Huang, C., Zhao, H.: Chinese word segmentation: a decade review. J. Chin. Inf. Process. 21 (3), 8–20 (2007)
14. Wu, J., Hou, H., Bao, F., Jiang, Y.: Template-based model for BiRNN Mongolian – Chinese machine translation. In: Proceedings of TAAI 2015 (2015)
15. Chung, J., Cho, K., Bengio, Y.: A character-level decoder without explicit segmentation for neural machine translation. In: Proceedings of ACL 2016 (2016)
16. Costajussà, M.R., Fonollosa, J.A.R.: Character-based neural machine translation. In: Proceedings of ACL 2016 (2016)
17. Yu, M., Hou, H.: Researching of mongolian word segmentation system based on dictionary, rules and language model. Inner Mongolian University (2011)
18. Lambert, P., Schwenk, H., Servan, C., Abdul-Rauf, S.: Investigations on translation model adaptation using monolingual data. In: Proceedings of the Sixth Workshop on Statistical Machine Translation, Edinburgh, Scotland, pp. 284–293 (2011)
19. Yuan, Z., Felice, M.: Constrained grammatical error correction using statistical machine translation. In: Proceeding of CoNLL 2013 (2013)
20. Wang, Y., Wang, L., Wong, D.F., Chao, L.S., Zeng, X., Lu, Y.: Factored statistical machine translation for grammatical error correction. In: Proceedings of the Eighteenth Conference on Computational Natural Language Learning 2014 (2014)
21. Zhao, H., Lv, Y., Ben, G., Huang, Y., Liu, Q.: Summary on CWMT2011 MT translation evaluation. J. Chin. Inf. Process. 26(1), 22–30 (2011)
22. Koehn, P., Och, F.J., Marcu, D.: Statistical phrase-based translation. In: Proceeding of NAACL 2003 (2003)

23. Koehn, P., Hoang, H., Birch, A., Callison-Burch, C., Federico, M., Bertoldi, N., Cowan, B., Shen, W., Moran, C., Zens, R., Dyer, C., Bojar, O., Constantin, A., Herbst, E.: Moses: open source toolkit for statistical machine translation. In: ACL 2007 Demonstration Session (2007)
24. Och, F.J., Ney, H.: A systematic comparison of various statistical alignment models. Comput. Linguist. **29**(1), 19–51 (2003)
25. Och, F.J.: Minimum error rate training in statistical machine translation. In: Proceedings of ACL 2003, pp. 440–447 (2003)

Sentence Similarity on Structural Representations

Meng Yang[1,2], Peifeng Li[1,2(✉)], and Qiaoming Zhu[1,2]

[1] Natural Language Processing Lab, Soochow University, Suzhou 215006, China
pfli@suda.edu.cn
[2] School of Computer Science and Technology, Soochow University,
Suzhou 215006, China

Abstract. Most previous approaches used various kinds of plain similarity features to represent the similarity of a sentence pair, and one of its limitations is its weak representation ability. This paper introduces the relational structures representation (shallow syntactic tree, dependency tree) to compute sentence similarity. Experimental results manifest that our approach achieves higher performance than that only uses plain features.

Keywords: Sentence similarity · Structural representations · Shallow syntactic tree · Dependency tree

1 Introduction

Most of the sentence similarity approaches treat the input sentences as feature vectors. But these approaches usually have their limitations due to the fact that the plain feature vector is weak to represent the sentences and their relation. Since the kernel method can make full use of structured features to get more information, many researchers used kernel method currently (e.g., Culotta [1], Bunescu [2] and Zhang [3]). In this paper, we use structural features to represent the syntax, semantic and dependency relation information of a sentence or a sentence pair. And apply the tree kernel to compute sentence similarity.

We first process these sentences into a variety of basic structural representations, and then optimize each basic structure to make it more suitable for this task. Finally, we combine the structural features and plain features to unify a feature vector, and use the kernel function of a support vector regression (SVR) model to compute sentence similarity.

The rest of this paper is organized as follows: Sect. 2 reviews the related work of sentence similarity computation. Section 3 describes the structural features used in this paper. Section 4 introduces the baseline, experimental results and performance analysis. Finally, Sect. 5 concludes our work.

2 Related Work

In general, there are four kinds of sentence similarity computation approaches: (1) word overlap based method, (2) corpus statistics based method, (3) linguistics based method, and (4) hybrid method which combine the above methods.

C.-Y. Lin et al. (Eds.): NLPCC-ICCPOL 2016, LNAI 10102, pp. 481–488, 2016.
DOI: 10.1007/978-3-319-50496-4_40

The word overlap-based method use words which appear in both sentences to compute sentence similarity. Jacob [4] computed similarity by the ratio of the size of the intersection of words and union of words in two sentences. Metzler [5] used inverse document frequency (IDF) as the weight of words appeared in both sentences to improve performance of similarity computation.

The corpus-based method uses words in sentences pair as the feature set, and then compute the similarity by using the cosine value of vectors. Based on the analysis on a large text corpus, Landauer [6] computed the TF-IDF values of the keywords to get similarity. Lund [7] extracted the contextual-usage meaning of words by statistical computations applied to a large corpus of text to compute sentence similarity.

The linguistic method took use of the semantic relations between words and their grammatical components. Kashyap [8] used word semantic similarity, Malik [9] got the maximum of the sum of the similarity as the sentence similarity.

Mix method tried to integrate two or more methods above. For example, Chukfong [10] combined several methods to compute sentence similarity.

In recent years, only a few works focus on using structural representation to compute sentence similarity. For example, Aliaksei [11] put forward a method based on simple structured representation.

3   Structural Representations

In this paper, we use shallow syntactic tree and dependency tree as basic structural representation. And then we modify these two kinds of structures respectively to make the structural features to represent sentence syntax, semantics better.

3.1   Motivation

Some of the latest similarity computation methods dependent on collocation of words and gaining knowledge from large data (such as wikipedia) for similarity computation, regardless of the sentence syntactic structured information, etc.

Suppose there are two sentences S1 and S2, these methods tend to do the following processing: As a first step, each word in s1 will match the most similar word in s2. In the second step, similar scores of all the match words are summed. And the similarity of sentences S1 to S2 is obtained.

Given a pair of sentences: S1: Tigers hit lions S2: Lions hit tigers. By using the method mentioned above, each word in S1 will find the most similar word in S2(in this case, the two words are same) to match. Thus similarity computation result will show that the meanings of these two sentences are same. As showed in Fig. 1, agent and

Fig. 1. Dependency trees of "Tigers hit lions" and "Lions hit tigers"

patient of the sentence pair are swapped. Even though these two sentences consist of the same words, their meanings are different.

Syntactic and other structural information is very important in the application of Natural Language Processing. However, how to use structural information in various tasks is a common problem. When a plain feature is used to represent a structural feature, some useful information might be lost. By using the tree kernel, we direct calculate the same substructure number of two structural features to determine the similarity. The method based on tree kernel function does not need to construct high dimension feature vector space. The method based on tree kernel can explore high dimensional feature space implicitly, which can utilize the structural information such as syntactic tree effectively.

3.2   Shallow Syntactic Tree

Shallow syntactic tree is a simple structural representation. The basic form of the shallow syntactic tree is a tree with a depth of 3, the bottom (leaf node) is the word itself, the middle layer is the part of speech of the word, upper layer (root node) is a combination of these words.

Firstly, this paper adds a layer of syntactic information to the shallow syntactic tree. The word nodes and their part of speech nodes which share the same syntactic constituent are organized into the same node (chunker) and then the chunker nodes are organized by the root node. Chunker nodes organize the words in a sentence into a number of syntactic components, and ignore their internal syntactic structure.

Secondly, we add semantic information, i.e., named entity recognition (NER) and WordNet (WNSS) label, to the shallow syntactic tree. NER can detect whether the

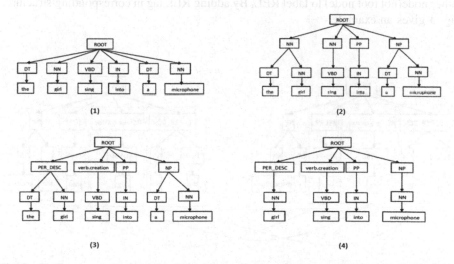

Fig. 2. Shallow tree of a sentence "the girl sing into a microphone" (1) the original shallow syntactic tree (2) + chunker nodes (3) + semantic information (4) – unimportant information from tee

phrase belongs to a predefined category and WNSS can make words to be assigned into 41 broad semantic categories WordNet. If a word has NER or WNSS information, we change the syntactic information of the chunker node into NER or WNSS information. Figure 2 shows an example of a modified shallow tree.

Finally, we delete all definite article nodes, conjunctions nodes and their father nodes (POS node) since they cannot impact the computation results.

3.3 Dependency Tree

Dependency tree is a tree structure that can represent the relationship between words in a sentence. We use the dependency analysis tool to get the relations between the words in the sentence, and then organize these relations into a tree structure. The node in tree either is word node or dependent relation node. Related words in the dependency tree are connected by the dependency relation node, so the related words have shorter distance in tree that tree kernel can extract effective subtree structure.

Dependency tree and constituency tree have their own advantages: First of all, compared to constituency tree, dependency tree gives more information about the relations between words. From the theoretical analysis, the syntactic and semantic information given by a dependency tree is more intuitive, simple and direct. Secondly, constituency tree contains more syntactic and lexical information (such as words, part of speech). To combine the advantages of dependency tree and constituency tree, Wu [22] proposed a phrase-based dependency tree, the dependency relation belongs to the same phrase will be compressed into a node. Different from Wu, the compressed nodes are stored as a shallow subtree rooted at the unified node in this paper.

We tag related structures with label REL and use the following method: for the word appear in both sentences, we get their father nodes (part of speech) and grand-father node(not root node) to label REL. By adding REL tag in corresponding structure, Fig. 3 gives an example.

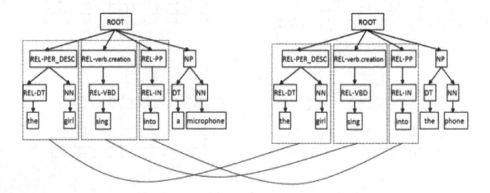

Fig. 3. Related tree fragments linked with a REL tag

4 Experiment

4.1 Baseline

In this paper, the baseline uses features in UKP [12] and Takelab [13], which are two best systems in the SemEval conference 2012 text semantic similarity (STS) task.

UKP provides a total of 18 features, such as matching of character, word n-grams and common subsequences, Explicit Semantic Analysis (Gabrilovich [14]) feature and aggregation of word similarity (such as WordNet) based on lexical-semantic resources.

Takelab provides a total of 21 features, including n-gram matching of varying size, weighted word matching, length difference, WordNet similarity and vector space similarity where pairs of input sentences are mapped into Latent Semantic Analysis (LSA) space.

Therefore, our baseline consists of these 39 features from the above systems.

4.2 Experimental Setup

To compare with the baseline system, this paper uses the training and test sets provided in STS-2012, including SMTeuroparl (1500 sentences which do not conform to the rules of grammar, Training vs Test: 750 vs 750), MSRvid (1500 short sentences, training vs Test: 750 vs 750), and MSRpar (1183 long sentences, Training vs Test: 734 vs 459). The performance of the experiment is evaluated by the Pearson correlation coefficient following STS-2012. Besides, Stanford syntactic analysis tools are used to obtain complete syntax and dependent relationship.

To combine the plain feature vector with the structural feature, a pair of sentences is defined as a set of trees t and a vector v, i.e., $<t, v>$ and the kernel function is as follows:

$$K\left(x^{(1)}, x^{(2)}\right) = K_{TK}\left(t^{(1)}, t^{(2)}\right) + K_{fvec}\left(v^{(1)}, v^{(2)}\right) \tag{1}$$

Where K_{TK} is a kernel function to compute structural feature, while K_{fvec} is a kernel function of plain features. This paper uses the support vector regression (SVR) framework in the SVM-Light-TK1 toolkit. We use the following parameter settings: -t 5 -F 1 -W A –C +, where (–C +) specifies a combination of trees and feature vectors, (-F 1) specifies the tree kernel function, (-W A) specifies all-vs-all mode and polynomial kernel of degree 3 for the feature vector (active by default).

4.3 Experimental Results and Analysis

Table 1 lists the experimental results of UKP, TakeLab, the baseline, ST and DT. DT is our system to combine the baseline and our shallow tree, while ST is our system to combine the baseline and our dependency tree. The result in Table 1 shows that the performance of UKP is slightly worse than Takelab on two data sets (MSRvid and MSRpar), and the performance of TakeLab is much better than UKP on the rest data set

(SMTeuroparl). The experimental result also shows that the performance of our baseline is more stable with the combination of the two systems.

Table 1 shows, the performance of our ST and DT is much better than the baseline, except DT on SMTeuroparl. Besides, it also illustrates that the performances of our ST and DT on short sentence (MSRvid) are better than that on long sentence (MSRpar, SMTeuroparl).

Table 1. Performance of shallow tree and phrase-dependency tree

	MSRvid	MSRpar	SMTeuroparl
UKP	0.853	0.667	0.542
Takelab	0.887	0.742	0.337
Baseline	0.853	0.697	0.538
ST(Baseline + our shallow tree)	0.908	0.732	0.571
DT(Baseline + our dependency tree)	0.886	0.776	0.528

Table 2 shows the experimental performance of our shallow tree. '+' means add additional information on the basis of the last structural feature. Table 2 shows that the unmodified shallow tree can improve the performance of the three data sets significantly. The chunker node also improves the performance both of MSRpar and SMTeuroparl. This results show that the deeper layer in the syntactic structure of long sentences is beneficial to sentence similarity. Syntactic structures of short sentences are similar to those adding the chunker node, so the deeper syntactic structure cannot provide syntactic information effectively. For example, sentences "A man is dancing." and "A man is drinking." have the same syntactic structures, but their meanings are different.

Table 2. Performance of shallow tree

	MSRvid	MSRpar	SMTeuroparl	Mean
Baseline	0.853	0.697	0.538	0.719
+Shallow tree	0.888(+0.035)	0.712(+0.015)	0.570(+0.032)	0.743(+0.024)
+Chunker	0.887 (−0.001)	0.746(+0.034)	0.581(+0.011)	0.761(+0.018)
+NER	0.887 (+0.000)	0.745(−0.001)	0.566 (−0.015)	0.757(−0.004)
+WNSS	0.897(+0.010)	0.745(+0.000)	0.557(−0.009)	0.759(+0.002)
− Unimportant information	0.908(+0.011)	0.732(−0.013)	0.571(+0.014)	0.761(+0.002)

Table 2 also shows that WNSS, NER information can improve the performance on MSRvid, while harm the performance both on MSRpar and SMTeuroparl. It shows that in short sentences sometimes only semantics of a word will affect the similarity. Finally, we delete the definite articles and conjunctions and other unimportant information, which make the performance to be improved.

Table 3 presents the experimental performance of the dependency tree and phrase based dependency tree. The result in Table 3 shows the dependency tree can improve the performance on the three data sets. As for the phrase based dependency tree, the performance can be improved both on MSRvid and MSRpar while it is decreased on SMTeuroparl. Since the dependency structures of long sentences are complex, the phrase based syntactic structures will lead to less similar structure and then harm the performance. For example, a pair of sentences which contain time adverbial "recently" and "a period of time", which have the same meaning. Due to their different syntactic structures, their similarity score is low.

Table 3. Performance of phrase-dependency tree

	MSRvid	MSRpar	SMTeuroparl	Mean
Baseline	0.853	0.697	0.538	0.719
+Dependency tree	0.876 (+0.022)	0.725(+0.028)	0.559(+0.021)	0.743(+0.023)
+Phrase based dependency tree.	0.886(+0.010)	0.736(+0.011)	0.528(–0.030)	0.745(+0.002)

5 Summary

In this paper, we use shallow syntactic tree and dependency tree as basic structural representation. And then we modify these two kinds of structures respectively to make the structural features to represent sentence syntax, semantics better. The experimental result shows that the system performance can be improved by structural representations. Further research will be made on structural features. We will consider make semantic information of a sentence as a structural feature.

References

1. Culotta, A., Sorensen, J.: Dependency tree kernels for relation extraction. In: ACL, pp. 423–429 (2004)
2. Banko, M., Cafarella, M.J., Soderland, S., Broadhead, M., Etzioni, O.: Open information extraction from the web. Commun. ACM **51**(12), 68–74 (2008)
3. Zhang, M., Zhang, J., Su, J., Zhou, G.: A composite kernel to extract relations between entities with both flat and structured features. In: ACL (2006)
4. Bank, J., Cole, B.: Calculating the jaccard similarity coefficient with map reduce for entity pairs in wikipedia. Wikipedia Similarity Team (2008)
5. Metzler, D., Bernstein, Y., Croft, W.B., Moffat, A., Zobel, J.: Similarity measures for tracking information flow. In: ACM CIKM International Conference on Information and Knowledge Management, pp. 517–524 (2005)
6. Landauer, T.K., Foltz, P.W., Laham, D.: An introduction to latent semantic analysis. Discourse Proc. **25**(2), 259–284 (1998)

7. Lund, K., Burgess, C.: Producing high-dimensional semantic spaces from lexical co-occurrence. Behav. Res. Meth. **28**(2), 203–208 (1996)
8. Kashyap, A., Han, L., Yus, R., Sleeman, J., Satyapanich, T.: Robust semantic text similarity using LSA, machine learning, and linguistic resources. Lang. Resour. Eval. **50**(1), 125–161 (2016)
9. Malik, R., Subramaniam, L.V., Kaushik, S.: Automatically selecting answer templates to respond to customer emails. In: International Joint Conference on Artifical Intelligence, pp. 1659–1664. Morgan Kaufmann Publishers Inc. (2007)
10. Jaffe, E., et al.: AZMAT: Sentence similarity using associative matrices. In: International Workshop on Semantic Evaluation (2015)
11. Severyn, A., Nicosia, M., Moschitti, A.: Learning semantic textual similarity with structural representations. In: ACL (2013)
12. Daniel, R., Biemann, C., Gurevych, I., Zesch, T.: UKP: computing semantic textual similarity by combining multiple content similarity measures. In: Joint Conference on Lexical and Computational Semantics. Association for Computational Linguistics, pp. 435–440 (2012)
13. Saric, F., Glavas, G., Karan, M., Snajder, J., Basic, B.D.: Takelab: Systems for measuring semantic text similarity. In: SemEval (2012)
14. Gabrilovich, E., Markovitch, S.: Wikipedia-based semantic interpretation for natural language processing. J. Artif. Intell. Res. **34**(4), 443–498 (2009)
15. Severyn, A., Moschitti, A.: Structural relationships for large-scale learning of answer re-ranking. In: International ACM SIGIR Conference on Research and Development in Information Retrieval, pp. 741–750 (2012)

Word Sense Disambiguation Using Context Translation

Zhizhuo Yang[⊠], Hu Zhang, Qian Chen, and Hongye Tan

School of Computer and Information Technology, Shanxi University, Taiyuan, Shanxi, China
Yangzhizhuo_662@163.com, {zhanghu, chenqian}@sxu.edu.cn, hytan_2006@126.com

Abstract. Word Sense Disambiguation (WSD) is one of the key issues in natural language processing. Currently, supervised WSD methods are effective ways to solve the ambiguity problem. However, due to lacking of large-scale training data, they cannot achieve satisfactory results. In this paper, we present a WSD method based on context translation. The method is based on the assumption that translation under the same context expresses similar meanings. The method treats context words consisting of translation as the pseudo training data, and then derives the meaning of ambiguous words by utilizing the knowledge from both training and pseudo training data. Experimental results show that the proposed method can significantly improve traditional WSD accuracy by 3.17%, and outperformed the best participating system in the SemEval-2007: task #5 evaluation.

Keywords: Data sparseness · Context translation · Bayesian model · Translation · Parameter estimation

1 Introduction

Word Sense Disambiguation (WSD), the task of identifying the intended meaning (sense) of words in a given context is one of the most important problem in natural language processing. Various approaches have been proposed to deal with the WSD problem. Hwee et al. [1], found that the supervised machine learning methods are the most successful approach to WSD when contextual features have been used to distinguish ambiguous words in these methods. However, word occurrences in the context are too diverse to capture the correct pattern, which means that the dimension of contextual words will be very large when all words are used in robust WSD system. It has been proved that expanding context window size around the target ambiguous word can help to enhance the WSD performance. However, expanding window size unboundedly will bring not only useful information but also some noise which may deteriorate the WSD performance. Can we find another way to expand context words without bringing too much noise?

In this paper, we propose to conduct WSD based on context translation, which acquires WSD knowledge by using machine translation system. The assumption of our approach is that contextual words around ambiguous word can be substituted by

© Springer International Publishing AG 2016
C.-Y. Lin et al. (Eds.): NLPCC-ICCPOL 2016, LNAI 10102, pp. 489–496, 2016.
DOI: 10.1007/978-3-319-50496-4_41

translation, and the new context represented by translation expresses the same meaning, thus the sense of the ambiguous word in new context remains unchanged. Therefore, the new context can provide more knowledge for us to improving WSD performance. Under this assumption, we propose two methods to integrate the contribution of translation into supervised WSD model. The first method directly considers translation as contextual feature, and exploit translation feature to train supervised WSD model. The second method treats the new context represented by translation as pseudo training data. In the method, the pseudo and authentic training data are both utilized to train supervised model. Consequently, the sense of ambiguous word is not only determined by authentic training data, but also pseudo training data. Experiments are carried out on dataset and the results confirm the effectiveness of our approach. The translation for context word can significantly improve the performance of WSD.

The rest of paper is organized as follows: The proposed method is described in detail in Sect. 2, and experimental results are presented in Sect. 3. Lastly we conclude this paper.

2   Proposed Approach

2.1   The Bayesian Classifier

Naïve Bayesian model have been widely used in most classification task, and was first used in WSD by Gale et al. [9]. The classifier works under the assumption that all the feature variables are conditionally independent given the classes. For word sense disambiguation, the context in which an ambiguous word occurs is represented by a vector of feature variables $F = \{f_1, f_2, \ldots, f_n\}$. The sense of ambiguous word is represented by variables $S = \{s_1, s_2, \ldots, s_n\}$. Finding the right sense of the ambiguous word equal to choosing the sense s' that maximizes the conditional probability as follow:

$$s' = \arg\max_{s_i \in S} \prod_{f_j \in F} P(f_j|s_i)P(s_i) \tag{1}$$

The probability of sense $P(s_i)$ and the conditional probability of feature f_j with observation of sense $P(f_j|s_i)$ are computed via Maximum-Likelihood Estimation:

$$P(s_i) = \frac{C(s_i)}{\sum_{s_i \in S} C(s_i)} \tag{2}$$

$$P(f_j|s_i) = \frac{C(f_j, s_i)}{C(s_i)} \tag{3}$$

where $C(s_i)$ is the number of sense s_i that appears in training corpus. $C(f_j, s_i)$ is the number of occurrences of feature f_j in context with sense s_i in the training corpus. We use "add one" data smooth strategies to avoid data sparse problem when estimating the conditional probabilities of the model.

2.2 WSD Methods Based on Context Translation

Machine translation is the automatic translation process from one natural language into anther using computers. In recent years, with the continuous development of statistical machine translation technology, translation quality has also gradually improved. At present, several well-known machine translation systems around the world include Google, Baidu, Bing and YouDao Translation[1], etc.

In this paper, we expand the context around ambiguous words into a larger dimension using translation output by machine translation system, which could provide more knowledge and clues for WSD task. In the previous study of WSD, the most widely used assumption is that words of the same meaning usually play the same role in the language. The assumption can be further extended as words of the same meaning often occur in similar context.

Base on the above assumptions, we propose basic assumption in this study, translation of context express similar meaning to that of original context, thus the sense of ambiguous word appear in the two similar contexts remains unchanged. For example, in Chinese sentence "稳妥地推进中医医疗体制改革" (steadily push forward the reform of traditional Chinese medicine system), the target ambiguous word is"中医", it has two meanings as a noun in HowNet[2] which are "medical science" and "doctor". We can easily infer the meaning of ambiguous word as "medical science" based on the context. After word segmentation, the context around ambiguous word can be expanded into translation set as Fig. 1. Since the context nearby ambiguous word has the largest impact to the sense of ambiguous word, only four contextual word "稳妥地, 推进, 医疗体制, 改革" are listed and expanded with translations in the figure. We simply expand each contextual word with four translation output by Google,

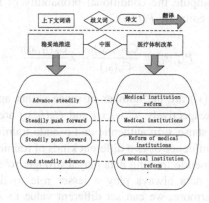

Fig. 1. WSD method base on context translation

---

[1] http://translate.google.cn/, http://fanyi.baidu.com/, http://www.bing.com/translator/, http://fanyi.youdao.com/.

[2] http://www.keenage.com/.

Baidu, Bing and YouDao system, actually more translation could be added into the translation set. Given ambiguous word and translation set for each contextual word, some reliable training data could be generated. For example, "Steadily push forward Medical institution reform", "Advance steadily Medical institution reform", "And steadily push forward Reform of medical institutions", etc. The ambiguous word "中 医" express the same meaning "medical science" in all of these training examples. It is obvious that translations provide additional knowledge for training model, and the knowledge can be exploited to improve the WSD performance.

The first method we proposed is that treating these expanded translations as topic feature. Then, we use these features together with other features to train the classifier. The method is quite straightforward. If contextual words near ambiguous word appear once in training data, translations of these contextual words are supposed to appear once in the corpus at the same time. Trained WSD model first translate the new instance into another language, then if the new instance contains context of the translation, the meaning of ambiguous word could be decided according to the training corpus. For example, in the previous example, if the testing instance contain contextual word "Medical institution reform" or "Steadily push forward", it is likely that the sense of ambiguous word "中医" could be inferred as "medical science" by Bayesian classifier. But it should be noted that the method has its own shortcomings. The authentic training data is labeled by human while the training data which consists of translations is generated automatically by machine. Thus the latter training data contain some noise compared to former training data, and should not play the same role when deducing the sense of the ambiguous word.

In order to overcome the disadvantage of method 1, we proposed method 2. The data which consist of translation are regarded as pseudo training data in method 2. The pseudo and authentic training data are both utilized to train the classifier. Instead of using formula (3) to compute the conditional probability of feature with sense, we apply follow formula to compute $P(f_j|s_i)$:

$$P(f_j|s_i) = \frac{C_a(f_j, s_i)}{C_a(s_i)} + \lambda \frac{C_p(f_j, s_i)}{C_p(s_i)} \tag{4}$$

Here, $C_a(s_i)$ and $C_p(s_i)$ are the number of sense s_i that appears in authentic and pseudo training corpus respectively. $C_a(f_j, s_i)$ and $C_p(f_j, s_i)$ are the number of occurrences of feature f_j with sense s_i in authentic and pseudo training corpus respectively. Parameter λ adjusts the influence of two different kinds of training data. We can set λ to a larger value to let the pseudo training data play a stronger role, and vice versa. In the model, pseudo training data always play a lesser role to determine the sense of ambiguous word. Furthermore, we can set different value to λ for different kinds of ambiguous word.

We encounter one problem when expanding the contextual word with translations. The problem is that not all translations are suitable for generating training data. For example, translation in Fig. 1 contains some noises such as 'A', 'And', etc. It is obvious that these noises should not be added into the expanded translation set. In order to solve the problem, we exploit voting method to remove the noise of the machine translation system. Specifically, the context is translated by multiple translation systems simultaneously. Then count the number of occurrences of co-occurrence, only the frequency of translation which exceeds a certain number will be trained to classifier. This strategy can solve the problem of noise greatly caused by translation system. The collocation parameter threshold *threshold_cooc* will be adjusted in the experiment.

3 Experiment

3.1 Experimental Setup

Training and testing data: In SemEval-2007, the 4th international workshop on semantic evaluations under conference of ACL-2007 [10], we used task#5 multilingual Chinese English lexical sample to test our methods. Macro-average precision (Liu et al. 2007) was used to evaluate word sense disambiguation performance.

Since we aim to evaluate discriminating power of translation feature, in the experiment, only some basic features such as topic words, collocations, and words assigned with their positions were used. We compare two baseline methods with our methods, the two baseline methods are as follows:

(1) Original: WSD method based on traditional Bayesian Classifier.
(2) SRCP_WSD [11]: The system participated in semeval-2007 and won the first place in multilingual Chinese English lexical sample task. ($p_{mar} = 74.9\%$)

Our methods:

(1) Method_1: The first method we proposed. This method was based on traditional Bayesian classifiers, which use translation feature and basic features to train model.
(2) Method_2: The second method we proposed. This method was also based on Bayesian classifiers, which use Basic features to train model. But this method computed the conditional probability using formula (4).

3.2 Evaluation Results

Because not all words in the sentence are useful for WSD, the contextual words are restricted by syntactic filters, i.e., only the words with a certain part of speech are added.

(1) In order to compare the performances of various methods, Table 1 gives the average precision of four methods. It can be seen that method_1 and method_2

Table 1. Experimental result of 4 methods

	Original	Method_1	SRCP_WSD	Method_2
Average precision (p_{mar})	0.7336	0.7447	0.7490	0.7597
Improving performance (%)	3.17	1.50	1.07	0

obtain improvement over original method, which shows that the methods we propose are effective. Moreover, method_2 also outperforms the best system participated in SemEval-2007.

(2) In order to investigate how the window sizes around the ambiguous word influences WSD performance, we conduct experiment with different window size for 3 methods. Figure 2 shows the curves for 3 methods with different window sizes. In both figures, window size ranges from 1 to 5. It can be seen from both figures that almost all curves decline as the window size increasing which means that the context words near ambiguous word have the best disambiguation capacity and enlarging window size will bring noisy information. The best WSD performance was achieved when window sizes are fixed at 1.

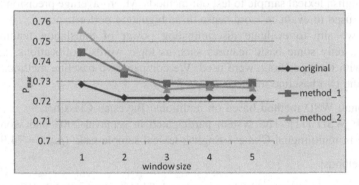

Fig. 2. Comparison result of different window size

(3) In order to investigate how the threshold of co-occurrences number influence the performance, experiment on different *threshold_cooc* was conducted, and the results are shown in Fig. 3. The figure shows the curves for two methods when *threshold_cooc* ranges from 0 to 4. We can see that the performance of the two methods first increases and then decreases with the increase of *threshold_cooc*.

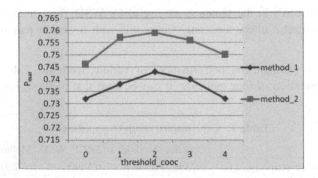

Fig. 3. Comparison result of different *threshold_cooc*

The trend demonstrates that extremely small or large co-occurrences number will deteriorate the results. Because a small number means that too many translations are used to train the classifier, which introduce noisy knowledge. On the other hand, a large number means very few translations are used to train the classifier and cannot provide sufficient knowledge. The best performance was achieved when set *threshold_cooc* to 2.

(4) In order to investigate how the λ parameter in formula (4) influences the performance, we conduct experiment with different value of λ as shown in Fig. 4. In this experiment, we set λ from 0.1 to 1. We can see from the Fig. 4 that the value of λ cannot achieve the best effect of disambiguation when λ set to 0 or 1 (means pseudo training corpus does not play a role or play a larger role respectively). On one hand, it proves that the pseudo training instance can provide some disambiguation knowledge; on the other hand, pseudo training instance also has a certain amount of noise. The pseudo training instance should not play the same role as authentic training corpus when conduct WSD task. The best experimental result is achieved when λ is set to 0.7.

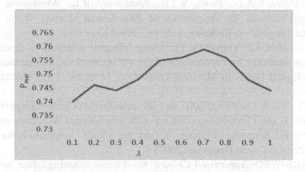

Fig. 4. Comparison result of different value of λ

Conclusion and perspectives. In this paper, we proposed two novel methods for supervised word sense disambiguation by leveraging translation for context around ambiguous word. The experimental results on dataset demonstrate the effectiveness of our methods. In current study, we obtain English translation by machine translation system. In future work, we will retrieve other languages from machine translation system to expand context nearby ambiguous word, attempting to further improve the performance of WSD.

Acknowledgments. This work is supported by the National Natural Science Foundation of China (61502287, 61673248, 61403238, 61502288), National High Technology Research and Development Program of China (863 Program) (No. 2015AA015407) and Shanxi Province scientific and technological innovation projects (2015105, 201504).

References

1. Ng, H.T., Wang, B., Chan, Y.S.: Exploiting parallel texts for word sense disambiguation. In: Proceedings of the 41st Annual Meeting of the Association for Computational Linguistics, pp. 455–462 (2003)
2. Navigli, R.: Word sense disambiguation: a survey. ACM Comput. Surv. **41**(2), 1–69 (2009)
3. Mihalcea, R., Moldovan, I.: A method for word sense disambiguation of unrestricted text. In: Proceedings of the 37th Annual Meeting of the Association for Computational Linguistics, pp. 152–158 (1999)
4. Agirre, E., Martínez, D.: Unsupervised WSD based on automatically retrieved examples: the importance of bias. In: Proceedings of the International Conference on Empirical Methods in Natural Language Processing, pp. 25–32 (2004)
5. Brody, S., Lapata, M.: Good neighbors make good senses: exploiting distributional similarity for unsupervised WSD. In: Proceedings of COLING, pp. 65–72 (2008)
6. Lu, Z., Wang, H., Yao, J.: An equivalent pseudoword solution to chinese word sense disambiguation. In: Proceedings of the 44th Annual Meeting of the Association for Computational Linguistics, pp. 457–464 (2006)
7. Yarowsky, D.: Unsupervised word sense disambiguation rivaling supervised methods. In: Proceedings (1995)
8. Brown, P.F., Pietra, S.A.D., Pietra, V.J.D., Andmercer, R.L.: Word-sense disambiguation using statistical methods. In: Proceedings of 29th Annual Meeting of the Association for Computational Linguistics, Berkeley, CA, pp. 264–270 (1991)
9. Gale, W.A., Church, K., Yarowsky, D.: Using bilingual materials to develop word sense disambiguation methods. In: Proceedings of the 4th International Conference on Theoretical and Methodological Issues in Machine Translation, Montreal, P.Q., Canada, pp. 101–112 (1992)
10. Jin, P., Wu, Y., Yu, S.: SemEval-2007 task 05: multilingual Chinese-English lexical sample task. In: Agirre, E. (ed.) Proceedings of the Fourth International Workshop on the Evaluation of Systems for the Semantic Analysis of Text, pp. 19–23. Association for Computational Linguistics, Prague, Czech Republic (2007)
11. Xing, Y.: SRCB-WSD: Supervised Chinese word sense disambiguation with key features. In: Proceedings of the 4th International Workshop on Semantic Evaluations (SemEval-2007), pp. 300–303 (2007)

Cyrillic Mongolian Named Entity Recognition with Rich Features

Weihua Wang, Feilong Bao[✉], and Guanglai Gao

College of Computer Science, Inner Mongolia University,
Hohhot 010021, China
wangweihuacs@163.com, {csfeilong, csggl}@imu.edu.cn

Abstract. In this paper, we first create a Cyrillic Mongolian named entity manually annotated corpus. The annotation types contain person names, location names, organization names and other proper names. Then, we use Condition Random Field as classifier and design few categories features of Mongolian, including orthographic feature, morphological feature, gazetteer feature, syllable feature, word clusters feature etc. Experimental results show that all the proposed features improve the overall system performance and stem features improve the most among them. Finally, with a combination of all the features our model obtains the optimal performance.

Keywords: Cyrillic Mongolian · Named entity recognition · Morphological features · Conditional random field

1 Introduction

Named entity recognition (NER) is a challenging problem in natural language processing (NLP) community. It defined as identifying and classifying names in an open domain text. The predefined categories include person, organization and location [1]. It is an important tool for developing almost all NLP applications, such as question answering, machine translation, social media analysis, semantic search and automatic summarization.

NER system in many languages have been developed as the basic tools, such as, English and Arabic. The methods for NER categorize into rule based [1] and machine learning based. The rule based approaches always heavily rely on the knowledge of linguist and can not apply across different language. Due to these weaknesses, many systems tend to choose machine learning methods. The machine learning methods include Hidden Markov Model [2], Maximum Entropy Model [3], Support Vector Machine [4] and Conditional Random Field (CRF) [5]. Among all these classifiers, CRF can use features more efficiently and reach the global optimum.

However, the Cyrillic Mongolian NER has not been explored. There is no public corpus available and no related linguistic resource for Cyrillic Mongolian NER. Cyrillic Mongolian, its user mainly spear over Mongolia and Russia. Its script different from the Classical Mongolian which uses in China.

In this paper, we build a Cyrillic Mongolian corpus that annotated by Mongolian native person. By analyzing the characteristics of Cyrillic Mongolian, we proposed

© Springer International Publishing AG 2016
C.-Y. Lin et al. (Eds.): NLPCC-ICCPOL 2016, LNAI 10102, pp. 497–505, 2016.
DOI: 10.1007/978-3-319-50496-4_42

several kinds of features. These features include capitalization feature, abbreviation feature, Mongolian person name spelling feature, stem feature, suffix features, gazetteer feature, mix vowel polarity feature and word clusters feature. These features effects are compared in experiment and stem feature improves most. Through the combination of feature, the system obtains $F_1 = 78.29$.

2   Construction of Cyrillic Mongolian

2.1   Characteristics of Mongolian

A Mongolian word can be decomposed into one stem and several inflectional suffixes. Among all inflectional suffixes, case suffixes, reflexive suffix and mood suffixes always place in the end of words and occur only once in a word [6]. In this work, we will split these suffixes to get the stems. As shown in Table 1, the same stems can add different inflectional suffixes to change the word.

Table 1. Example of Cyrillic Mongolian stems when adding different suffixes

Stems	Suffixes	Word	English translation
Парис	аас	Парисаас	from Paris
	ын	Парисын	Paris'
	т	Парист	in Paris
Яв	х	явах	go
	жаа	явжаа	went
	на	явна	going

According to spelling rules of Mongolian, there might occur syllable insert, drop and replace when suffix coupling the stem. We establish a database for Cyrillic Mongolian stems, suffixes and connection rules. For example, "a" will be inserted when suffix "x" adds to the stem "Яв".

In addition, Mongolian vowels are divided into three groups: strong vowel, weak vowel and neutral vowel. In compliance with the rules of vowel harmony, only strong vowels or only weak vowels can appear in one Mongolian word. The vowel "и" can occur with either set of vowels.

2.2   Collection of Corpus

The raw corpus mainly gathered from Cyrillic Mongolian news web site, including www.montsame.mn, www.assa.mn, www.gonews.mn etc. The content of this corpus cover politics, economy, culture, entertainment etc. After analyzing the HTML tags of each web page, we extract the key information about content, title, date, author to form the raw data. These information will be stored as XML format to use easily. The raw data shows in Fig. 1.

```
<Id>1</Id>
<Title> ОХУ, БНХАУ-ыг холбосон хамгийн дөт замыг тавьж болно</Title>
<Date>2014 оны 06 сарын 27</Date>
<Content>
З.Энхболд: Монголын зүүн хэсгээр ОХУ, БНХАУ-ыг холбосон хамгийн дөт
Холбооны Зөвлөлийн дарга В.И.Матвиенкогийн Монгол Улсад хийсэн айлчл
өгч, ОХУ, БНХАУ-ын хооронд шинэ "Талын зам"-ыг байгуулахад Монгол Ул
-Сергей Романович: Ноён Энхболд, Та ОХУ, Монгол Улсын парламент хоор
хэрхэн нөлөөлөх вэ?
```

Fig. 1. Raw data fragment of Cyrillic Mongolian in XML format

2.3 Annotation of Corpus

After cleaning useless tags and splitting sentences, we extract 15000 sentences from the raw corpus. The length of sentences will be restricted to between 15 and 25. Then, we make rules about the named entity annotation range and rules referring to CoNLL [7] and MUC [8].

The annotation scope has four groups: person name, location name, organization name and other proper name. The person entities contain names of Mongolian nation, names of Chinese and names of foreigner. The location entities contains natural locations, public places, commercial places, assorted buildings etc. The organization entities mainly contain bank, school, publication, companies etc. The other type entities contain events, songs, movies, games etc.

The annotation guidelines are as follows: (1) title of people will be not annotate. (2) each type can not be nest in other named entity. (3) a named entity engaging with other names will be annotated separately.

The annotation task carries out under the open source platform BRAT [9], show in Fig. 2. The annotation takes about half a year with a Mongolian native person. As the annotation carries on, the accuracy is improved.

During training, the annotated corpus will convert into the BIO format, which "B" denote the begin of current named entity, "I" represent inside of named entity and "O" means outside the named entity. In this setting, there will be night tags to classify. These night tags are: "B" of each type have 4 tags, "I" of each type have 4 tags and one tag "O".

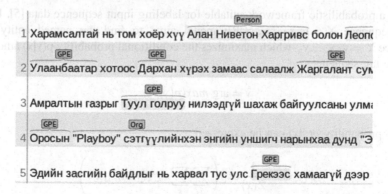

Fig. 2. The annotation platform for Cyrillic Mongolian named entity

Table 2 indicates the statistics of entity number and entity average length. As shown in Table 2, location entities account for 41.91% of total entities, while other type has the least number. The average length of both organization names and other type names are greater than 2, while the average length of person names is shortest. The longer named entities are, the harder recognize them.

Table 2. Statistics of our named entity annotated corpus

Type	Number	Ratio (%)	Average length
Person	7509	30.78	1.29
Location	10224	41.91	1.40
Organization	5661	23.21	2.06
Other	1000	4.10	2.24

Table 3 suggests the occurrence of our corpus. As shown in Table 3, more than half named entities occur only once. That because of the agglutinative structure of Mongolian, that is, the same stems adding different suffixes can build different named entities.

Table 3. Occurrence frequency of our named entity corpus

Frequency	Vocabulary	Ratio (%)
1	8296	74.50
2	2109	18.60
3	378	3.33
Over 3	552	4.87

3   The Model

3.1   CRF Framework

CRF is a probabilistic framework suitable for labeling input sequence data [5]. For an input sequence $X = x_1, x_2 \ldots x_n$, CRF model aims to find the named entity label sequence $Y = y_1, y_2 \ldots y_n$, which maximizes the conditional probability $p(y|x)$ among all possible tag sequences.

$$\tilde{y} = \arg \max_{\tilde{y} \in Y}(p(y|x))$$

The probability $p(y|x)$ can be expressed as:

$$p(y|x) = \frac{1}{Z(x)} \exp\left(\sum_t \sum_k \lambda_k f_k(y_t, y_{t-i}, x_t)\right)$$

where λ_k represent the weight assigned to different features. $Z(x)$ is the normalizing function, it can be defined as:

$$Z(x) = \sum_{y \in Y} \exp(\lambda_k f_k(y_t, y_{t-1}, x_t))$$

$f_k(y_t, y_{t-1}, x_t)$ is the binary feature function, it can be expressed as:

$$f_k(y_t, y_{t-1}, x_t) = \begin{cases} 1, & \text{if } y_{t-1} = u \text{ and } y_t = v \\ 0, & \text{other} \end{cases}$$

3.2 Features

By analyzing the characteristic and grammar of Cyrillic Mongolian, we design several features for NER system.

1. Capitalization feature (CAP): proper names write in Cyrillic script will be capitalized. If a word is capitalized, this feature will be "1", otherwise "0". For example, the feature of "Монгол", means "Mongolia", will be "1".
2. Abbreviation feature (ABB): if the current word is an abbreviation, this feature will be "1" otherwise "0". For example, "НУБ", means "UN", its abbreviation feature will be "1".
3. Mongolian person name spell feature (MPN): the Mongolian person name will be often inserted "." between last name and first name. Moreover, the first name and last name will be also capitalized. For example, "Б.Батмөнх" is a Mongolian person name, its MPH will be "1".
4. Stem feature and Suffix feature: this two features are obtained from the Mongolian morphological analyzing. We summarize 35452 noun class stems, 29838 verb stems, 335 noun class suffixes and 495 verb suffixes. We split the stems and suffixes by maximum match with reverse order.
5. Mix vowel polarity feature (MVP): some loan word do not obey vowel harmony rule. For example, "Чавестай", is a foreigner name, the vowel "a" is strong, but the vowel "e" is weak, so the MVP feature of "Чавестай" is "0".
6. Gazetteer feature (GAZ): we extract location manually from Mongolian-Chinese dictionary. This gazetteer contains 1309 world and Mongolian location names. This feature define by the position in the gazetteer entry. For example, "Баян Хонгор аймаг" is a Mongolian location name in this gazetteer, the tag of each word in search dictionary will be "Баян": "BG", "Хонгор": "IG", "аймаг": "EG", other word outside gazetteer will assign "OG".
7. Language type feature (LAT): for some loan word from English, Cyrillic Mongolian often use them directly without transliterating. If the word compose with English stem and Mongolian suffix, this feature will define by the English stem. For example, "Apple-ийн", means "Apple's", its language type feature will be "En".
8. Word cluster IDs: this feature learn from massive unlabeled corpus through LDA and word2vec [10]. LDA cluster IDs are obtained from tools describing in [11].

Word2vec cluster id obtain from skip-gram with minimum count 3, context window 10 and embedding dimension 200, This cluster ID train corpus also crawled from web sites in a wider range. It contains 2451403 sentences, 38273452 tokens and 263555 vocabularies.

4 Experiment

4.1 Setting up

We divided the whole corpus into train and test with the proportion 80% and 20%, respectively. We conduct our experiment under 5-fold cross validation. The feature window of all our experiment fix at 3, that is, put the previous feature, current feature and next feature into consideration. We also convert all digit expression into "<num>". The average sentences number and vocabulary in train and test set show in Table 4.

Table 4. Statistics of train and test data in experiment

	Sentence number	Vocabulary	Out-of-vocabulary
Train set	12000	41264	–
Test set	3000	17186	6485

We evaluated the results by the metrics of precision, recall and F_1. Precision, means the percentage of corrected named entities (NEs) found by the classifier. It can be expressed as:

$$precsion = \frac{Num(correct\,NEs\,predicted)}{Num(NEs\,predicted)}$$

Recall is the percentage of NEs existing in the corpus and which were found by the system. It can be expressed as:

$$recall = \frac{Num(correct\,NEs\,predicted)}{Num(all\,NEs)}$$

F_1 is the harmonic mean of precision and recall. It can be express as:

$$F_1 = \frac{2 * precision * recall}{precision + recall}$$

4.2 Results and Analysis

Firstly, in order to assess the effect of each feature, we add only one feature to the baseline system. The baseline system uses context feature under CRF framework. Results show in Table 5.

Table 5. System performance with different features

Features	P	R	F
Baseline	77.51	53.75	63.45
Baseline + CAP	73.00	63.88	68.10
Baseline + ABB	77.64	55.32	64.57
Baseline + MPN	**83.34**	59.84	69.29
Baseline + Stem	78.58	**67.62**	**72.66**
Baseline + Suffix	74.72	59.27	66.08
Baseline + MVP	77.10	54.74	64.00
Baseline + GAZ	77.58	54.66	64.11
Baseline + LAT	78.18	54.14	63.95

Among all features, the stem features improve performance the most. It indicates that the stems can decrease the rate of unseen word. The decreased rate benefits the classifier. The suffixes improve the F_1 mainly due to improving the recall.

Other features play their unique role to the whole system. The CAP features improve the recall distinctly, and the MPN features improve the precision a lot. The effect of MPN suggests that a large proportion of Mongolian person names. However, the abbreviation words are often labelled as other type, so the improvement is small for the whole system. Since the scale of gazetteer is small, the effect of GAZ is limited. The MVP and LAT feature improve overall performance in some degree.

Secondly, we compare different impact on cluster method and cluster number. We will only add word cluster id feature with baseline system. The results show in Table 6. The more cluster dimension the better performance. When dimension fixed at 200, the performance reach best with both two methods. In addition, the performance of "word2vec" is higher than "LDA" in all condition.

Table 6. System performance (in F1) with word cluster id feature

Cluster ID number	LDA	Word2Vec
50	66.79	66.71
100	66.74	67.20
200	**66.82**	**68.03**
500	66.78	67.99

Finally, in order to reach best performance, we select LDA200, LDA500, W2V200 and W2V500 to combine other features respectively. We also add the "stem/cluster id" into the feature set because the significant influence of stem. "TFC" means all feature except word cluster feature. As shown in Table 7, the combination with word2vec perform better than LDA. With all proposed features the system reach best performance.

Among the four type of named entity, the other type perform the lowest, while the person names perform best. It is because that there are many English phrase that unseen word in other type named entities. Mongolian person names spell with obvious feature

Table 7. System perform with different feature combination

Feature combination	F	R	F
TFC	78.26	72.29	75.12
TFC + LDA200	79.44	74.36	76.79
TFC + LDA500	79.08	74.18	76.52
TFC + W2V200	79.62	74.78	77.09
TFC + W2V500	79.76	75.10	77.33
TFC + LDA200 + W2V500	80.14	75.14	77.69
All features	80.60	76.16	**78.29**

and account for a large proportion of person names, so the F_1 highest among all the four types. The performance of Cyrillic Mongolian NER can not compare with other language, because the supported resource is relative lack, such as part-of-speech tagger, large scale gazetteer and so on.

5 Conclusion

In this paper, we propose Cyrillic Mongolian named entity corpus and compare with different features on this corpus. All features paly their important role on the whole system. We implement the NER system based on features combination under CRF, and the result achieves $F_1 = 78.29$. This work provides the benchmark result for future Cyrillic Mongolian NER research.

In the future, we will extend our work on annotating this corpus and building related resources. In addition, we will try to use deep learning to solve the NER for agglutinative language [12].

Acknowledgements. This research is partially supported by the China National Nature Science Foundation (No. 61263037, No. 61303165 and No. 61563040), Inner Mongolia Nature Science Foundation (No. 2014BS0604 and No. 2016ZD06) and the program of high-level talents of Inner Mongolia University. Finally, we thank the anonymous reviews for their many helpful comments.

References

1. Yan, D., Bi, Y.: Rule-based recognition of vietnamese named entities. J. Chin. Inf. Process. **28**(5), 198–206 (2014)
2. Zhou, G., Su, J.: Named entity recognition using an hmm-based chunk tagger. In: Proceedings of the 40th Annual Meeting of the Association for Computational Linguistics, July 6–12, 2002, Philadelphia, PA, USA, pp. 473–480 (2002)
3. Bender, O., Och, F.J., Ney, H.: Maximum entropy models for named entity recognition. In: Proceedings of the Seventh Conference on Natural Language Learning, CoNLL 2003, Held in cooperation with HLT-NAACL 2003, Edmonton, Canada, 31 May–1 June 2003, pp. 148–151 (2003)

4. Kravalová, J, Žabokrtský, Z.: Czech named entity corpus and SVM-based recognizer. In: Proceedings of the 2009 Named Entities Workshop: Shared Task on Transliteration. Association for Computational Linguistics, pp. 194–201 (2009)
5. Lafferty, J., McCallum, A., Pereira, F.C.N.: Conditional random fields: probabilistic models for segmenting and labeling sequence data (2001)
6. Tserenpil, D., Kullmann, R.: Mongolian grammar. Dandii-Yadamyn Tserenpil (2008)
7. Tjong, E.F., Sang, K., De Meulder, F.: Introduction to the CoNLL-2003 shared task: language-independent named entity recognition. In: Proceedings of CoNLL, pp. 142–147 (2003)
8. Nancy, C.: MUC-7 Named Entity Task Definition (Version 3.5). MUC-7. Fairfax, Virginia (1998)
9. Stenetorp, P., Pyysalo, S., Topic, G., et al.: Brat: a web-based tool for NLP-assisted text annotation. In: Proceedings of the Demonstrations at the 13th Conference of the European Chapter of the Association for Computational Linguistics, pp. 102–107 (2012)
10. Mikolov, T., Chen, K., Corrado, G., et al.: Efficient estimation of word representations in vector space. In: ICLR Workshop (2013)
11. Chrupala, G.: Efficient induction of probabilistic word classes with LDA. In: Proceedings International Joint Conference on Natural Language Processing (2011)
12. Lample, G., Ballesteros, M., Subramanian, S., Kawakami, K., Dyer, C.: Neural architectures for named entity recognition. In: Proceedings of the 2016 Conference of the North American Chapter of the Association for Computational Linguistics: Human Language Technologies, pp. 260–270 (2016)

Purchase Prediction via Machine Learning in Mobile Commerce

Chao Lv, Yansong Feng(✉), and Dongyan Zhao

Institute of Computer Science and Technology,
Peking University, Beijing 100871, China
{lvchao,fengyansong,zhaodongyan}@pku.edu.cn

Abstract. In this paper, we propose a machine learning approach to solve the purchase prediction task launched by the Alibaba Group. In detail, we treat this task as a binary classification problem and explore five kinds of features to learn potential model of the influence of historical behaviors. These features include user quality, item quality, category quality, user-item interaction and user-category interaction. Due to the nature of mobile platform, time factor and spacial factor are considered specially. Our approach ranks the 26th place among 7186 teams in this task.

Keywords: Purchase prediction · Machine learning

1 Introduction

Recently, the Alibaba Group launched a purchase prediction task known as Ali Mobile Recommendation Algorithm[1]. This purchase prediction task provides the historical behaviors data of users in the mobile platform during a period of one month to help predict purchase behaviors will happen in the following one day. The historical behaviors include click, collect, add-to-cart and payment. Conventional methods in recommender system [6], such as collaborative filtering and matrix factorization, don't obtain a good performance in this task.

In this paper, we propose a machine learning approach to solve this purchase prediction task, instead of CF-based methods. This task is treated as a binary classification problem, and five kinds of features are explored from different aspects to learn potential model of the historical browsing behaviors, including user quality, item quality, category quality, user-item interaction and user-category interaction. Those features could reflect the willingness of users to buy items. In particular, we concentrate on the time and spacial factor. The time factor is incorporated into the feature families and features are extracted in different time dimension. The spacial factor is employed in the filtering module. For any purchase behaviors we predict, if the location of item is far away from the user, we will remove it from our prediction results.

---

[1] http://tianchi.aliyun.com.

© Springer International Publishing AG 2016
C.-Y. Lin et al. (Eds.): NLPCC-ICCPOL 2016, LNAI 10102, pp. 506–513, 2016.
DOI: 10.1007/978-3-319-50496-4_43

2   Related Work

The most prominent technique in recommender system is Collaborative Filtering (CF) [8]. The basic insight for this technique is a sort of continuity in the realm of taste. If users Alice and Bob have the same utility for items 1 through k, then the chances are good that they will have the same utility for item $k + 1$. Usually, these utilities are based on ratings that users have applied for items with which they are already familiar. CF is roughly classified into two categories, i.e. memory-based approachs [5, 9] and model-based approachs [1, 3].

The Netflix million-dollar challenge boosted interest in CF and yielded the publication of a number of new methods. Several matrix factorization techniques have been successfully applied to CF, including Singular Value Decomposition (SVD) [7] and Non-negative Matrix Factorization (NMF) [4]. A joint non-nagative matrix factorization method proposed in [2] trys to solve the purchase prediction task launched by the Alibaba Group in 2014. The goal of that task in 2014 is to predict purchase behaviors in the following one month based on historical behaviors data in a period of four months.

3   Problem Definition

Notations: U stands for the set of users, I stands for the whole set of items, P stands for the subset of items, $P \subseteq I$, D stands for the user behaviors data set in all the set of all items. Our objective is to develop a recommendation model for users in U on the business domain P using the data D. In detail, our goal is to predict purchase behaviors over P in the following one day based on the behaviors data during one month in D.

4   Method

We treat the target problem as a binary classification problem, i.e. any (*user, item*) pairs will be divided into two classes: "buy" and "not buy". The framework of which is showed in Fig. 1.

First, we would like to learn a model from the behaviors data over the whole set of items in the **training module**, which can reflect why users will buy items in the following one day and how their historical behaviors influence their future purchase behaviors. In detail, if a *user* is going to buy an *item* in the following one day, this (*user, item*) pair will be labeled as a positive instance while other pairs that doesn't be bought are going to be labeled as a negative instance. In addition, this trained model is applied to the behaviors data over the subset of items in the **prediction module** and positive instances in the prediction results will be seen as purchase behaviors will happen in the following one day. Then, we take spacial factor into consideration and remove pairs with too long distance in those positive instances via the **filtering module**. In the last, the filtered predicted purchase behaviors are compared with the real purchase behaviors to evaluate the performance of our approach in the **evaluation module**.

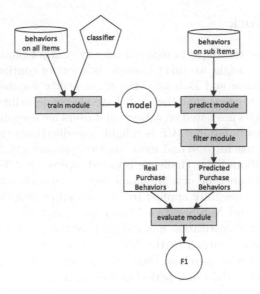

Fig. 1. The machine learning diagram for purchase prediction

4.1 Training Module and Prediction Module

Training set is a basic component in the training module just like test set in the prediction module, but there is little difference between the generation of them. Because we can't use the future infomation, i.e. we don't know purchase behaviors on the whole set of items in the following one day, we split bahaviors data in the last day of the month and use them to label (*user*, *item*) pairs that appear in the remainder of the month. This process is illustrated in Fig. 2.

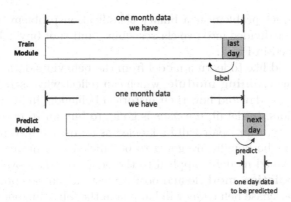

Fig. 2. Training set and test set

4.2 Feature Project

Feature project is an important component in our machine learning approach and we will discuss feature families detailly in this section.

For a certain (*user*, *item*) pair, the *item* belongs to a *category*, we consider the following five feature families, i.e. user quality, item quality, category quality, user-item interaction and user-category interaction.

User Quality estimates the purchasing power and vitality of users. In the mobile commerce, some users are active and have strong purchase desire while others are inactive and not willing to buy items frequently.

- *Last Login Day* represents the last login day of a user.
- *Conversion Ratio* represents the ratio of purchase behaviors of a user in his total behaviors.
- *Behaviors Statistics* stands for the count of a user's behaviors. The more this user browses, the higher possibility he will buy. There is an example in the left of Fig. 3 to explain the definition. In this example, a user click for 3 times in the first day, 1 time in the second day and 2 times in the fourth day, so the count of his total behaviors in the last four days equals $3 + 1 + 0 + 2 = 6$.
- *Active Days* means the count of active days of a user. This feature could represent the positivity of a user directly. There is an example in the right of Fig. 3 to explain the definition. In this example, a user login in the first day, the second day and the fourth day, so the count of his active days in the last four days equals $1 + 1 + 0 + 1 = 3$.

Item Quality reflects the popularity of an item. Obviously, more popular items have bigger tendency to be sold.

- *Last Browsed Day* represents the last day an item is browsed.
- *Conversion Ratio* represents the ratio of purchase behaviors of an item in its total browsed behaviors.
- *Behaviors Statistics* stands for the count of an item's browsed behaviors. The more this item is browsed, the higher possibility it will be sold.
- *Active Days* means the count of days an item is browsed. This feature could represent the popularity of an item.

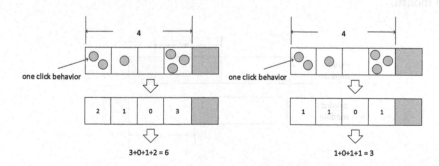

Fig. 3. An example of behaviors statistics

Category Quality describes the popularity of a category. The definition of *Last Browsed Day, Conversion Ratio, Behaviors Statistics* and *Active Days* in it is similar with those in **Item Quality**.

User-Item Interaction describes the interaction between the user and item. it is a direct aspect to reflect the willing that the user want to buy the item.

- *Behaviors Statistics* represents the count of a user's browsing behaviors on one item.
- *Active Days* means the count of days in which the user browses the item.

User-Category Interaction represents the interaction between the user and the category. It is similar with **User-Item Interaction**, and *behaviors Statistics* and *Active Days* will be generated in the same way.

4.3 Filtering Module

This purchase prediction task is based on a typical O2O business model, in which users pay online and consume offline. This means that users are not willing to buy items which are far away from them because they have to go there to consume. Based on the fact, we propose Filter Module to remove those pairs with too long distance. In detail, in a $(user, item)$ pair, if the distance between the location of the *item* and the *user* is bigger than L, any purchase behaviors will happen on this pair. We set $L = 100$ km from experience in this paper.

4.4 Reduced Data

Because the volume of our data set is too large, it will spend unacceptable time for training process in the machine learning approach. Hence, we use a reduced data set to solve this problem and keep prediction performance at the same time, which is showed in Fig. 4.

Instead of using all the $(user, item)$ pairs happened in the one month, we use pairs show up in the last N days to train and predict. $N = 1$ means that we use data in the last day while $N = 30$ means that we use all data over the whole one month.

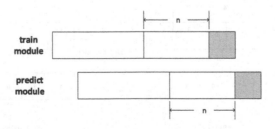

Fig. 4. Definition of the reduced data set

5 Experiments

5.1 Data Description

The data contains two parts. The first part is the dataset D, the mobile behaviors data of users in the set of all items, with the following columns: $user\_id$, $item\_id$, $behaviors\_type$, $user\_geohash$, $item\_category$ and $time$. The second part is the dataset P, the subset of items data, with the following columns: $item\_id$, $item\_geohash$ and $item\_category$. The training data contains the mobile behaviors data of certain quantity of sampled users (D) from November 18, 2014 to December 18, 2014. The evaluation data is the purchase data of these same users of the items in P in December 19, 2014. Summary statistics of the data are listed in Table 1.

Table 1. The statistics of the data set

#table D	#table P	#user set	#total item set	#sub item set	#category set
5,822,532,780	14,397,493	5,000,000	156,226,243	13,435,163	13,128

5.2 Two Rule-Based Baselines

CartRule is the first strategy of most participants, and we select it as our first baseline. In detail, *CartRule* thinks that if a user adds an item into his cart and doesn't buy it in that day, it's likely that he will buy it in the next day. In addition, we propose *CartRuleTime* which adds time factor into consideration based on *CartRule*. *CartRuleTime* thinks that if a user adds an item into his cart and doesn't buy it after m o'clock ($m \in \{0, 1, ..., 23\}$) in that day, it's likely that he will buy it in the next day. When m is set to 15, the performance is the best according to our experiments.

5.3 Result

We set $N \in \{1, 2, 3, 4\}$ in the reduced data in this paper and apply three classifiers: LR (Linear Regression), RF (Random Forest) and GBDT (Gradient Boosting Decision Tree). Table 2 shows the prediction performance of different approachs in this purchase prediction task. *N1_LR* means that $N = 1$ and $classifier = LR$, *N4_GBDT* means that $N = 4$ and $classifier = GBDT$, others could be explained in the same way. *CartRuleTime* has little improvement compared to *CartRule* because *CartRuleTime* takes the time factor into consideration. Those machine learning approachs we proposed have a much better performance than two rule-based methods, which could proves the effectiveness of our approachs to some extent. Compare the performance of different classifiers, we could see easily that *GBDT* is the best choice. With the increase of N, the F1 score changes littlely. This phenomenon proves that reduced data could accelerate the process of machine learning and keeps the performance at the same time (Table 3).

Table 2. Performance of different approachs

Approach	F1(%)	Precision(%)	Recall(%)
CartRule	5.5480	4.1824	8.2377
CartRuleTime	5.8007	5.3018	6.4033
N1_LR	6.8985	7.8298	6.1652
N1_RF	8.0064	8.3249	7.7114
N1_GBDT	**8.3841**	**8.2591**	**8.5129**
N2_LR	6.3266	6.5820	6.0902
N2_RF	7.9830	8.5378	7.4959
N2_GBDT	**8.4264**	**8.2036**	**8.6617**
N3_LR	6.5542	7.4360	5.8593
N3_RF	7.9152	8.9481	7.0960
N3_GBDT	**8.4719**	**8.6591**	**8.2926**
N4_LR	6.5015	7.1628	5.9520
N4_RF	7.9152	8.8237	7.1764
N4_GBDT	**8.4410**	**8.4336**	**8.4485**

Table 3. Performance of different features

Approach	F1(%)	Precision(%)	Recall(%)
U+I+C	2.8068	7.3183	1.7364
UI+UC	7.4938	8.2366	6.8740
All	8.4719	8.6591	8.2926

To prove the effectiveness and robustness of feature families explored, we test a series of combination of feature families on *N3_GBDT*, which is the best result mentioned above. *U+I+C* means we use quality features only and *UI+UC* means we use interaction features only. The performance of *U+I+C* is poorer than *UI+UC*, which explains the importance of interaction features. The performance of *All* is better than *UI+UC*, which reflects the supporting role of the quality features.

6   Conclusion

We present a machine learning approach to solve the purchase prediction task launched by the Alibaba Group. Five kinds of features are explored to describe the willingness of users' purchase desires on items. In particular, we take the time and spacial factor into consideration. Experimental results prove the effectiveness of our proposed approach.

Acknowledgement. The work reported in this paper was supported by the National Natural Science Foundation of China Grant 61272344 and 61370116.

References

1. Adomavicius, G., Tuzhilin, A.: Toward the next generation of recommender systems: a survey of the state-of-the-art and possible extensions. IEEE Trans. Knowl. Data Eng. **17**(6), 734–749 (2005)
2. Ju, B., Ye, M., Qian, Y., Ni, R., Zhu, C.: Modeling behaviors of browsing and buying for alidata discovery using joint non-negative matrix factorization. In: 2014 Tenth International Conference on Computational Intelligence and Security (CIS), pp. 114–118. IEEE (2014)
3. Koren, Y., Bell, R., Volinsky, C., et al.: Matrix factorization techniques for recommender systems. Computer **42**(8), 30–37 (2009)
4. Lee, D.D., Seung, H.S.: Learning the parts of objects by non-negative matrix factorization. Nature **401**(6755), 788–791 (1999)
5. Linden, G., Smith, B., York, J.: Amazon.com recommendations: item-to-item collaborative filtering. IEEE Internet Comput. **7**(1), 76–80 (2003)
6. Lü, L., Medo, M., Yeung, C.H., Zhang, Y.C., Zhang, Z.K., Zhou, T.: Recommender systems. Phys. Rep. **519**(1), 1–49 (2012)
7. Paterek, A.: Improving regularized singular value decomposition for collaborative filtering. In: Proceedings of KDD Cup and Workshop, vol. 2007, pp. 5–8 (2007)
8. Su, X., Khoshgoftaar, T.M.: A survey of collaborative filtering techniques. Adv. Artif. Intell. **2009**, 4 (2009)
9. Wang, J., De Vries, A.P., Reinders, M.J.: Unifying user-based and item-based collaborative filtering approaches by similarity fusion. In: Proceedings of the 29th Annual International ACM SIGIR Conference on Research and Development in Information Retrieval, pp. 501–508. ACM (2006)

Exploring Long Tail Data in Distantly Supervised Relation Extraction

Yaocheng Gui[1,2], Qian Liu[3], Man Zhu[3], and Zhiqiang Gao[1,2(✉)]

[1] Key Lab of Computer Network and Information Integration (Southeast University),
Ministry of Education, Nanjing, China
{yaochgui,zqgao}@seu.edu.cn
[2] School of Computer Science and Engineering, Southeast University, Nanjing, China
[3] School of Computer Science and Technology,
Nanjing University of Posts and Telecommunications, Nanjing, China
{qianliu,mzhu}@njupt.edu.cn

Abstract. Distant supervision is an efficient approach for various tasks, such as relation extraction. Most of the recent literature on distantly supervised relation extraction generates labeled data by heuristically aligning knowledge bases with text corpora and then trains supervised relation classification models based on statistical learning. However, extracting long tail relations from the automatically labeled data is still a challenging problem even in big data. Inspired by explanation-based learning (EBL), this paper proposes an EBL-based approach to tackle this problem. The proposed approach can learn relation extraction rules effectively using unlabeled data. Experiments on the New York Times corpus demonstrate that our approach outperforms the baseline approach especially on long tail data.

Keywords: Distant supervision · Explanation-based learning · Relation extraction

1 Introduction

Relation extraction aims to extract relational facts in unstructured text to populate knowledge bases. Various supervised machine learning approaches have been developed to explore this task, however, these approaches have limitations due to lack of labeled data. One of the most promising approaches to address this problem is based on distant supervision, which employs existing knowledge bases as the source of supervision. A sentence is heuristically labeled with a relation if it contains the same entity pair as in a relation instance. Then the heuristically labeled sentences are employed to train supervised relation classification models based on statistical learning [4,12,18,20].

Most of the previous work in distant supervision mainly focused on reducing noise in training data by modeling entity pairs in the text and their relation labels in graphical models with latent variables [6,15,18]. Upon that, researchers further improved the performance by adding preprocessing steps [17,19,21] or

© Springer International Publishing AG 2016
C.-Y. Lin et al. (Eds.): NLPCC-ICCPOL 2016, LNAI 10102, pp. 514–522, 2016.
DOI: 10.1007/978-3-319-50496-4_44

additional information [8,11,16]. These approaches are effective for data-rich relations, however, they did not seriously study data-scarce long tail relations.

In fact, long tail relations are important and cannot be ignored. Riedel et al. [15] observed that there are only a small number of cases in which two related Freebase entities are mentioned in the same sentence of the New York Times corpus. By analyzing 480 Freebase relations we find that only 87 relations have at least one instance whose entities are mentioned in the New York Times corpus.

One of the challenges in dealing with long tails is that very few training examples can be used to build an effective extractor. To tackle this problem, we propose an approach to explore long tail data in distantly supervised relation extraction, which can learn relation extraction rules effectively using unlabeled data and produce interpretable results. It is inspired by explanation-based learning (EBL) [13]. Unlike statistical learning, EBL does not limited in the theoretical bounds of training examples and does well on limited data.

We propose to combine EBL with distant supervision to make EBL workable with unlabeled data, and improve the quality of distant supervision with the guidance of the domain theory. Our work makes the following contributions:

- To explore long tail relations, we combine EBL with distant supervision, which can learn relation extraction rules effectively from unlabeled data under the supervision of existing knowledge bases.
- Our approach can produce accurate and interpretable results. Experiments on both long tail and standard data show that our approach outperforms the baseline approach especially in dealing with long tail relations.

2 Related Work

Distant supervision, also known as knowledge-based weak supervision, was first introduced by Craven and Kumlien [3] and Mintz et al. [12]. Most of the previous work focused on the issue of noise in training data generated by distant supervision. Riedel et al. [15], Hoffmann et al. [6] and Surdeanu et al. [18] proposed a series of graphical models to solve the problem. A variety of strategies have been proposed for correcting wrong labels, e.g., Takamatsu et al. [19], Intxaurrondo et al. [7], Xu et al. [21], Augenstein et al. [1], and Roller et al. [17].

Recent work has begun to explore additional information to augment the distantly supervised relation extraction, such as the prior of positive bags [11], the side information about rare entities [16], the fine-grained entity types [8,10], the human labeled data [14], the indirect supervision knowledge [5], and the document structure [2].

Our work is most related to Krause et al. [9]. They proposed a rule-based relation extraction system to tackle the long tail problem, which learned large scale grammar-based rules (about 40 k rules per relation) from the Web using distant supervision. Then they used the information from parallel learning of multiple relations to filter out invalid rules.

The proposed approach is different from Krause et al. [9] in two-fold. (1) We can learn generalized rules from unlabeled data based on domain theory, and the number of learnt rules for each relation can be greatly reduced (about 400 rules per relation). (2) We can leverage domain theory to avoid invalid rules.

3   Problem Definition

The definition of the EBL-based distantly supervised relation extraction problem involves specifying three kinds of information.

The *text corpus* S contains a set of sentences that each sentence contains at least two entities. S is divided into training set and testing set.

The *relation instances* I are initially extracted from the given knowledge bases. In this paper, we restrict our attention to binary relations, i.e., relations that involve two entities.

The *domain theory* T includes two parts. One is a set of pre-defined relation extraction rules that explain why sentences are members of the relations. The rules are mainly entity type constraints of the relations which can be obtained from the schema of the knowledge bases. The other is a set of *relation keywords*, denoted as K, which is a set of words that semantically represent the relations, and defines the multiple-to-multiple correspondence from words to relations.

Our task is to first build an extractor based on the training data, and then apply the extractor to the testing data to output a set of relation instances.

4   Rule Learning Using EBL-Based Distant Supervision

We first detail the algorithm DistantEBL, short for EBL-based distantly supervised relation extraction. Then introduce the extraction of relation keywords.

4.1   Algorithm DistantEBL

As shown in Algorithm 1, DistantEBL consists of four main steps, i.e., *extract uncovered relation instances, explain, verify* and *analyze.*

Step 1 (extract uncovered relation instances, lines 3–6): This step obtains relation instances that cannot be covered by current rules for the given sentence. For each sentence s in S^{train}, we first employ function EXTRACTRELATIONS(s, T, R) to extract all relation instances that can be deduced from s, denoted as A_s (lines 3–4). Then for each relation instance $r(e_1, e_2)$ in I, $r(e_1, e_2)$ is inserted into I_s if the entities e_1 and e_2 appear in s (line 5). All the relation instances in A_s are covered by current rules in R. We learn new rules from the remaining uncovered relation instance set, i.e., $I'_s = I_s - A_s$ (line 6).

Step 2 (explain, line 7–8): This step generates candidate explanations based on the supervision of the uncovered relation instances. Let $G = (N, E)$ be the dependency graph of a sentence, where N is the node set containing words and named entities, E is the edge set containing dependency relations between nodes.

Algorithm 1. DistantEBL($\mathcal{S}^{train}, \mathcal{T}, \mathcal{I}$)

input: $\mathcal{S}^{train}$, a set of sentences for training; $\mathcal{T}$, domain theory, i.e., pre-defined rules and relation keywords for each relation; $\mathcal{I}$, a set of relation instances in the given knowledge base.

output: $\mathcal{R}$, a set of syntactic extraction rules learned from the training data.

1: $\mathcal{R} \leftarrow \{\}$ // initialize an empty rule set $\mathcal{R}$
2: **for** each sentence $s \in \mathcal{S}^{train}$ **do**
3:      $\mathcal{A}_s \leftarrow$ EXTRACTRELATIONS$(s, \mathcal{T}, \mathcal{R})$
4:      $\mathcal{I}_s \leftarrow \{r(e_1, e_2) | r(e_1, e_2) \in \mathcal{I},$ and sentence s mentions the entities $e_1, e_2\}$
5:      $\mathcal{I}'_s \leftarrow \mathcal{I}_s - \mathcal{A}_s$
6:      **if** $\mathcal{I}'_s \neq \emptyset$ **then**
7:          $\mathcal{L}^+_s \leftarrow$ EXPLAIN$(s, \mathcal{I}'_s)$
8:          $\mathcal{L}_s \leftarrow$ VERIFY$(\mathcal{L}^+_s, \mathcal{T})$
9:          $\mathcal{R}_s \leftarrow$ ANALYZE$(\mathcal{L}_s)$
10:         $\mathcal{R} \leftarrow \mathcal{R} \cup \mathcal{R}_s$
11:     **end if**
12: **end for**
13: **return** $\mathcal{R}$

Let $\mathcal{N}^e$ be the entity set and $\mathcal{N}^k$ be the relation keyword set, an *explanation* is an induced subgraph $\mathcal{G}[\mathcal{N}^e \cup \mathcal{N}^k]$ of $\mathcal{G}$, which contains the nodes in $\mathcal{N}^e \cup \mathcal{N}^k$ and the edges connecting them. By choosing different sets of entities and keywords, we can generate a set of candidate explanations. If there is at least one instance in $\mathcal{I}'_s$, i.e., $\mathcal{I}'_s \neq \emptyset$ (line 7), the function EXPLAIN$(s, \mathcal{I}'_s)$ generates a set $\mathcal{E}^+_s$ of candidate explanations from s and $\mathcal{I}'_s$ (line 8).

Step 3 (verify, line 9): This step verifies the candidate explanations. Given a set $\mathcal{L}^+_s$ of candidate explanations and domain theory $\mathcal{T}$, the function VERIFY$(\mathcal{L}^+_s, \mathcal{T})$ selects a set $\mathcal{L}_s$ of explanations from $\mathcal{L}^+_s$ that can satisfy $\mathcal{T}$. An explanation l is said to satisfy $\mathcal{T}$ if it satisfies the following constraints: (1) entity types in l agree with those defined in $\mathcal{T}$, (2) POS tags of keywords in l agree with those defined in $\mathcal{T}$, (3) keywords in l correspond to at least one relation in $\mathcal{T}$.

Step 4 (analyze, lines 10–14): This step analyzes the verified explanations to construct syntactic extraction rules. Given the set $\mathcal{L}_s$ of verified explanations, the function ANALYZE$(\mathcal{L}_s)$ first generalizes the explanations in $\mathcal{L}_s$, then constructs a set $\mathcal{R}_s$ of syntactic extraction rules from the generalized explanations (line 10). An explanation can be generalized by substituting the nodes and edges in its induced subgraph with more general categories when necessary. The new rules are then added into $\mathcal{R}$, i.e., $\mathcal{R} = \mathcal{R} \cup \mathcal{R}_s$ (line 11). The algorithm continues until all the sentences in $\mathcal{S}^{train}$ are processed, the set $\mathcal{R}$ contains all syntactic extraction rules learnt from $\mathcal{S}^{train}$ (lines 12–14).

4.2 Relation Keyword Extraction

We first collect a small set of seed keywords for each relation, and each keyword is assigned to at least one relation manually. The quantity of seed relation keywords is expanded after rule-based keyword extraction. However, there may be errors in the expanded set. We propose to filter the expanded keywords using pre-trained word vectors based on cosine similarities. In this work, word vectors are trained on New York Times corpus using word2vec[1], a threshold is used to filter unlikely relation keywords.

5   Experiments

We evaluate the proposed approach on both long tail data and standard data using two tasks. (1) *Sentential extraction* is the task to label each sentence by the relation it expresses, or by a None label if it does not express any. (2) *Aggregate extraction* is the task to extract a set of relation instances from text corpus, such that each extracted relation instance is expressed at least once in the corpus.

We compare the proposed approach with **MultiR**, which was introduced by Hoffmann et al. [6]. It uses the perceptron algorithm for learning and a greedy search algorithm for inference. We implemented this model using the publicly available code provided by the authors[2].

5.1   Data Generation

We use the same approach as Riedel et al. [15] to generate data for distant supervision. The New York Times corpus and Freebase are used in our experiments. Stanford CoreNLP[3] is used for POS tagging, NER and dependency parsing.

Standard Data. Ten most frequent relations of four domains (i.e., People, Organization, Location and Business) from the latest version of Freebase[4] are studied, they are also used in [6]. Relation instances are divided into two parts, the set $\mathcal{I}^{train}$ is for training, and the set $\mathcal{I}^{test}$ is for testing. The New York Times corpus is also divided into two parts, the set $\mathcal{S}^{train}$ is for training, which is extracted from the years 2005–2006, the set $\mathcal{S}^{test}$ is for testing, which is extracted from the year 2007. There are 7,731,008 relation instances in $\mathcal{I}^{test}$ and 1,446,367 sentences in $\mathcal{S}^{test}$. These datasets are regarded as standard data.

Long Tail Data. Long tail training sets are constructed based on $\mathcal{S}^{train}$ and ten most frequent relations in Freebase. We restrict that the training set uses at most n instances for each of the ten relations and n sentences for each instance. In our experiments, we choose two small numbers, i.e., $n = 10$ and $n = 50$ to generate two simulated long tail training sets $\mathcal{S}_{10}^{train}$ and $\mathcal{S}_{50}^{train}$.

---

[1] https://code.google.com/archive/p/word2vec/.

[2] www.cs.washington.edu/ai/raphaelh/mr/.

[3] http://stanfordnlp.github.io/CoreNLP/.

[4] The selected domains are not the same as in [15] due to different versions of Freebase.

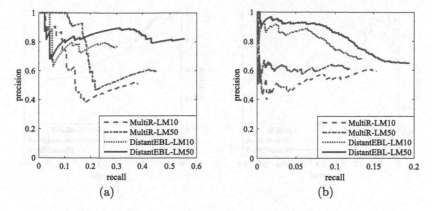

Fig. 1. Precision and recall curves of MultiR and DistantEBL on the simulated long tail data in the (a) sentential extraction task, and (b) aggregate extraction task. LM_{10} (LM_{50}) means that the approach uses $\mathcal{S}_{10}^{train}$ ($\mathcal{S}_{50}^{train}$) for training.

5.2 Evaluation on Long Tail Data

We evaluate both sentential extraction task and aggregate extraction task on the on long tail data. For sentential extraction task, we first learn relation extraction rules from $\mathcal{S}_{10}^{train}$ ($\mathcal{S}_{50}^{train}$) under the supervision of $\mathcal{I}^{train}$, and then evaluate the learnt rules on the set $\mathcal{S}_{1000}^{test}$, which contains about 1000 sentences that were manually annotated by Hoffmann et al. [6]. For aggregate extraction task, we learn relation extraction rules on the same setting as in the sentential extraction task, and evaluate on the set $\mathcal{I}^{test}$.

Figure 1 shows the precision and recall curves of MultiR and DistantEBL on the simulated long tail data. We can see that our approach significantly outperforms MultiR in both sentential and aggregate extraction tasks. Specifically, in sub-figures (a) and (b), DistantEBL-LM_{10} (DistantEBL-LM_{50}) achieves higher precision over most ranges of recall than MultiR-LM_{10} (MultiR-LM_{50}), and DistantEBL-LM_{50} is also better than DistantEBL-LM_{10}. LM_n means that the approach uses $\mathcal{S}_n^{train}$ for training. The results further prove that DistantEBL is promising in tackling the long tail relations in Freebase.

5.3 Evaluation on Standard Data

For both sentential and aggregate extraction tasks, we learn relation extraction rules from $\mathcal{S}^{train}$ under the supervision of $\mathcal{I}^{train}$. For sentential extraction task, we evaluate using S_{1000}^{test}. For aggregate extraction task, we evaluate using $\mathcal{I}^{test}$. Two sets of relation keywords are used in DistantEBL to train the rule learner, i.e., DistantEBL-E used the expanded keywords obtained using keyword extraction rules, and DistantEBL-S used the keywords selected from the expanded set based on word vector similarities (see Sect. 4.2).

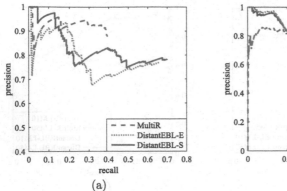 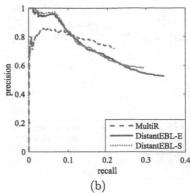

(a)   (b)

Fig. 2. Precision and recall curves of MultiR and DistantEBL on standard data in the (a) sentential extraction task, and (b) aggregate extraction task. DistantEBL-E (DistantEBL-S) means that DistantEBL uses expanded (selected) relation keywords for training.

We observe from Fig. 2 that our approach extends the highest recall, thus reaches better final F_1-score than the baseline approach. Figure 2(a) shows the precision and recall curves in the sentential extraction task on the standard data. DistantEBL models (i.e., DistantEBL-E and DistantEBL-S) achieve competitive overall results compared with MultiR. The precisions of DistantEBL are higher than MultiR before the recalls reach 0.12. According to the overall curves, DistantEBL models achieve higher recall than MultiR. DistantEBL-S reaches higher precision than DistantEBL-E. Figure 2(b) shows the precision and recall curves in the aggregate extraction task on the standard data. DistantEBL models achieve better performance than MultiR. When the recalls are lower than 0.08, the precisions of two DistantEBL models are higher than 0.9 and also higher than MultiR. However, the precisions of DistantEBL models are lower than MultiR when the recalls are higher than 0.11. According to the overall curves, DistantEBL models achieve higher recalls than MultiR. DistantEBL achieves higher precision when using selected keywords and higher recall when using expanded keywords.

6   Conclusion

In this paper, we proposed the algorithm DistantEBL to explore the long tail problem in distantly supervised relation extraction. DistantEBL combines EBL with distant supervision, which enables the algorithm to learn relation extraction rules effectively from long tail data. DistantEBL can produce accurate and interpretable predictions on two tasks of relation extraction. Experiments on the New York Times corpus demonstrate that our approach outperforms the baseline approach especially on long tail data. In future work, we plan to explore other approaches to generate relation keywords and approaches to select accurate extraction rules from the learnt rule set.

Acknowledgement. This work is partially funded by the National Science Foundation of China under Grant 61170165, 61602260, 61502095.

References

1. Augenstein, I.: Seed selection for distantly supervised web-based relation extraction. In: Proceedings of SWAIE (2014)
2. Bing, L., Ling, M., Wang, R.C., Cohen, W.W.: Distant IE by bootstrapping using lists and document structure. In: AAAI (2016)
3. Craven, M., Kumlien, J.: Constructing biological knowledge bases by extracting information from text sources. ISMB **1999**, 77–86 (1999)
4. Grave, E.: A convex relaxation for weakly supervised relation extraction. In: Conference on Empirical Methods in Natural Language Processing (EMNLP) (2014)
5. Han, X., Sun, L.: Global distant supervision for relation extraction. In: Thirtieth AAAI Conference on Artificial Intelligence (2016)
6. Hoffmann, R., Zhang, C., Ling, X., Zettlemoyer, L., Weld, D.S.: Knowledge-based weak supervision for information extraction of overlapping relations. In: Proceedings of the 49th Annual Meeting of the Association for Computational Linguistics: Human Language Technologies, vol. 1, pp. 541–550. ACL (2011)
7. Intxaurrondo, A., Surdeanu, M., de Lacalle, O.L., Agirre, E.: Removing noisy mentions for distant supervision. Procesamiento del lenguaje natural **51**, 41–48 (2013)
8. Koch, M., Gilmer, J., Soderland, S., Weld, D.S.: Type-aware distantly supervised relation extraction with linked arguments. In: Proceedings of EMNLP. ACL (2014)
9. Krause, S., Li, H., Uszkoreit, H., Xu, F.: Large-scale learning of relation-extraction rules with distant supervision from the web. In: Cudré-Mauroux, P., et al. (eds.) ISWC 2012. LNCS, vol. 7649, pp. 263–278. Springer, Heidelberg (2012). doi:10.1007/978-3-642-35176-1_17
10. Liu, Y., Liu, K., Xu, L., Zhao, J.: Exploring fine-grained entity type constraints for distantly supervised relation extraction. In: Proceedings of the 25th International Conference on Computational Linguistics, COLING 2014, Dublin, Ireland, pp. 2107–2166, August 2014. Technical Papers
11. Min, B., Grishman, R., Wan, L., Wang, C., Gondek, D.: Distant supervision for relation extraction with an incomplete knowledge base. In: HLT-NAACL, pp. 777–782 (2013)
12. Mintz, M., Bills, S., Snow, R., Jurafsky, D.: Distant supervision for relation extraction without labeled data. In: Proceedings of ACL-IJCNLP, vol. 2, pp. 1003–1011. ACL (2009)
13. Mitchell, T.M., Keller, R.M., Kedar-Cabelli, S.T.: Explanation-based generalization: a unifying view. Mach. Learn. **1**(1), 47–80 (1986)
14. Pershina, M., Min, B., Xu, W., Grishman, R.: Infusion of labeled data into distant supervision for relation extraction. In: Proceedings of ACL (2014)
15. Riedel, S., Yao, L., McCallum, A.: Modeling relations and their mentions without labeled text. In: Balcázar, J.L., Bonchi, F., Gionis, A., Sebag, M. (eds.) ECML PKDD 2010. LNCS (LNAI), vol. 6323, pp. 148–163. Springer, Heidelberg (2010). doi:10.1007/978-3-642-15939-8_10

16. Ritter, A., Zettlemoyer, L., Etzioni, O., et al.: Modeling missing data in distant supervision for information extraction. Trans. Assoc. Comput. Linguist. 1, 367–378 (2013)
17. Roller, R., Agirre, E., Soroa, A., Stevenson, M.: Improving distant supervision using inference learning. In: Proceedings of the ACL-IJCNLP, vol. 2, pp. 273–278. ACL, Beijing, July 2015. Short Papers
18. Surdeanu, M., Tibshirani, J., Nallapati, R., Manning, C.D.: Multi-instance multi-label learning for relation extraction. In: Proceedings of the 2012 Joint Conference on Empirical Methods in Natural Language Processing and Computational Natural Language Learning, pp. 455–465. ACL (2012)
19. Takamatsu, S., Sato, I., Nakagawa, H.: Reducing wrong labels in distant supervision for relation extraction. In: Proceedings of ACL, pp. 721–729. ACL (2012)
20. Wu, F., Weld, D.S.: Autonomously semantifying wikipedia. In: Proceedings of the Sixteenth ACM Conference on Conference on Information and Knowledge Management, pp. 41–50. ACM (2007)
21. Xu, W., Hoffmann, R., Zhao, L., Grishman, R.: Filling knowledge base gaps for distant supervision of relation extraction. In: ACL (2), pp. 665–670 (2013)

Detecting Potential Adverse Drug Reactions from Health-Related Social Networks

Bo Xu, Hongfei Lin$^{(\boxtimes)}$, Mingzhen Zhao, Zhihao Yang, Jian Wang, and Shaowu Zhang

School of Computer Science and Technology, Dalian University of Technology,
Dalian 116024, Liaoning, China
hflin@dlut.edu.cn

Abstract. In recent years, adverse drug reactions have drawn more and more attention from the public, which may lead to great damage to the public health and cause massive economic losses to our society. As a result, it becomes a great challenge to detect the potential adverse drug reactions before and after putting drugs into the market. With the development of the Internet, health-related social networks have accumulated large amounts of users' comments on drugs, which may contribute to detect the adverse drug reactions. To this end, we propose a novel framework to detect potential adverse drug reactions based on health-related social networks. In our framework, we first extract mentions of diseases and adverse drug reactions from users' comments using conditional random fields with different levels of features, and then filter the indications of drugs and known adverse drug reactions by external biomedical resources to obtain the potential adverse drug reactions. On the basis, we propose a modified Skip-gram model to discover associated proteins of potential adverse drug reactions, which will facilitate the biomedical experts to determine the authenticity of the potential adverse reactions. Extensive experiments based on DailyStrength show that our framework is effective for detecting potential adverse drug reactions from users' comments.

Keywords: Adverse drug reactions · Health-related social network · ADRs

1 Introduction

Adverse drug reactions (ADRs) have drawn more and more attention from the public, which may not only lead to serious physical injuries, but also cause great economic losses. It is estimated that each year about 2 million patients in the United States experience serious ADRs by using marketed drugs, resulting in more than 100,000 deaths. ADRs are considered to be the fourth leading cause of death [1], and about $136 billion is spent on treating ADRs in the United State every year [2]. Therefore, research on detecting adverse drug reactions has been studies for years. For example, Rahmani et al. [3] proposed a novel network-based approach to predict the ADRs by modeling the interactions among different drugs. Casillas et al. [4] present a hybrid system utilizing a self-developed morpho-syntactic and semantic analyzer for medical texts in Spanish. These studies detect ADRs mainly based on extracting drug-drug

© Springer International Publishing AG 2016
C.-Y. Lin et al. (Eds.): NLPCC-ICCPOL 2016, LNAI 10102, pp. 523–530, 2016.
DOI: 10.1007/978-3-319-50496-4_45

interactions or drug reaction events from existing literatures. However, it remains a great challenge to automatically detect potential ADRs, which have not been verified.

In recent years, health-related social networks have attracted much attention from the public, which accumulate large amounts of users' comments about drugs. These comments contain a great deal of information related to potential ADRs. To capture the information, Leaman et al. [2] use dictionary-based method to recognize the mentions of ADRs, and achieve promising results, which is one of the earliest researches to mine the relationships between drugs and adverse reactions from health-related social networks. Dai et al. [5] focus on the recognition of ADRs from twitter in terms of feature engineering by extracting various features and examining the performance of different combinations of features. Since tweets are short texts and contain many colloquial expressions, there exist lots of noises in the corpus, producing negative impact on their results. To deal with the problem, Yates and Goharian [6] annotate 2500 pieces of users' comments on five drugs on breast cancer to find the patterns of the mentions of ADRs in social networks. These studies show that comments on social networks are potentially useful for detecting ADRs.

In this paper, we propose a novel framework to detect potential ADRs from health-related social networks. In the framework, we adopt the conditional random fields with different combinations of features to recognize the mentions of diseases and ADRs. After that, we filter the indications of drugs and known ADRs to obtain the potential ADRs. On the basis, we also seek to find the associated proteins for the potential ADRs, which can link the drugs to the potential adverse reactions, and give adequate evidence for ADR verifications.

2   Detecting Potential ADRs on Health-Related Social Networks

Our framework is designed to detect potential adverse drug reactions from health-related social networks, and discover the associated proteins on ADRs to provide the most likely evidence chains for practitioners to verify the ADRs. Overall, there are three modules in our framework, including the data acquisition module, potential ADRs detecting module and the associated protein recognition modules. We will introduce each module in details in the following subsections.

2.1   Data Acquisition Module

To obtain the data from the DailyStrength, we use Scrapy (http://scrapy.org/) program to crawl the comments of drug takers. Scrapy, implemented in Python, is an open source and collaborative framework for acquiring the data from the Internet. We obtain the comments mainly on the boards of drugs with most posts for further processing. After obtaining the drug posts, we preprocess the data by removing special characters and noisy posts with only a few words. It should be noted that since our method is general, it can also be applied for other health-related social networks, such as MedHelp or Ask a Patient.

2.2   Potential ADRs Detecting Module

There are three steps in detecting potential ADRs based on the users' comments, including named entity recognition for disease and ADRs, filtering the indications and filtering the known ADRs. We introduce the steps in details as follows.

As the first step, we recognize named entities for diseases and ADRs. Users' comments from health-related social network contain both ADR names and disease names, we recognize both names in the phase of named entity recognition.

We take the problem of extracting the names from users' comments as a sequence labeling problem, solved using conditional random field (CRF) model. To apply the CRF model for extracting names of diseases and ADRs, we first define some features to discriminate the mentions of drugs and diseases from other elements. Overall, we define two kinds of features, word-level features and dictionary-based features.

For word-level features, we define three features, the original word feature (OW), the stemmed word feature (SW) and part-of-speech word feature (POS). We use Stanford POS Tagger [7] to generate the POS for words. For dictionary-based features, we extract domain-specific features to improve the performance of CRF by selecting the indications and ADRs to generate a disease and ADR name dictionary from SIDER [8], which is a standard drug adverse reactions database. We define four features in this set, namely SIDER-based feature (SF), first-word feature (FF), last-word feature (LF) and single-word feature (SinF). SIDER-based feature can be extracted based on whether a word exists in the disease and ADR name dictionary SIDER. First-word feature measures whether a word is at the first position of some disease names or ADR names in the dictionary. Last-word feature measures whether a word is at the last position of names in the dictionary. Single-word feature is determined by considering whether a word is a disease name or ADR name. We train CRF model with all the defined features to extract the mentions of disease names and ADR names.

As the second step, we filter drug indications. In users' comments, there exists a mixture of adverse reactions and drug indications. Indications refer to the corresponding symptoms of disease a drug treats, which would be of less use for detecting the potential ADRs. Therefore, we seek to filter indications of drugs. Since the users' comments are organized by drug names from DailyStrength, we can easily learn which drug some users' comments belong to, and use external resources to filter the indications.

To find the indications of drugs, we resort to the DrugBank [9] database and the Semantic MEDLINE database (SemMedDB) [10] to filter the indications. We first adopt DrugBank to obtain indications with respect to certain drugs, and then use SemMedDB to filter other indications. SemMedDB contains a large amounts of triples in the style of (*subject, predicate, object*) extracted from MEDLINE by SemRep [11], a semantic interpreter of biomedical text. If a triple <*drug_i, TREATS, symptom_j*> exists in the SemMedDB, we know *symptom_j* is one indication of *drug_i*.

As the third step, we filter known ADRs. After filtering the indications, we obtain the mentions of ADRs, some of which have been recorded in official instructions. We take the recorded ADRs as known ADRs. We filter the known ADRs using SIDER database, which is an official released adverse drug reaction database.

2.3 Associated Protein Recognition Modules

In the field of clinical medicine, verifying ADRs require much time and efforts by large amounts of clinical trials and observations. Therefore, to facilitate the verifications, we adopt text mining techniques to discover the associated proteins, which refer to the effected proteins by taking a certain drug, and may cause some adverse reactions. Generally, associated protein can be taken as an evidence of adverse drug reactions, and provide much help for medical experts to verify the potential ADRs.

To recognize associated proteins, we propose a modified Skip-gram model to generate distributed representations of drugs, proteins and potential ADRs, and measuring the similarity degrees among them. The Skip-gram model is proposed by Google [12, 13], which generates distributed representations for words in the training corpus, capturing the syntactic and semantic relationships among them [13].

We use citations in MEDLINE with annotated Medical Subject Headings (MeSH) terms to train the distributed representations. The MeSH terms can reflect the topics of each article, and the co-occurrences of the MeSH terms in one article indicate the correlations among the entities. Therefore, we train the Skip-gram model based on the MeSH term sets of the articles about certain drugs. Since the original Skip-gram model is trained on corpus using slide windows and the MeSH term sets are out-of-order, we modify the Skip-gram model by transforming the sliding window to document window, taking every MeSH term as a single word.

After generating distributed vectors for every MeSH term, we define the association function for each triple of the drug, one associated protein and one potential ADR (d, p, a) as follow.

$$f(d,p,a) = \frac{sim(d,p) + sim(p,a)}{1 + |sim(d,p) - sim(p,a)|} \qquad (1)$$

where d is the drug, a is one potential adverse reaction, p is associated protein. $sim(x, y)$ measures the similarity between entity x and entity y. intuitively, if $sim(d, p) + sim(p, a)$ is larger, the protein p is more likely to be the associated protein between drug d and the potential ADR a. To avoid that $sim(d, p)$ or $sim(p, a)$ is too large to impact the result, we normalize the function using the smoothing factor as the denominator of Eq. (1). The function f can be used to measure the association degree among the items in the triple (d, p, a). For all the potential ADRs of the drug d, we sort the associated proteins based on the association function $f(d, p, a)$ and take the top-k proteins as the final associated proteins.

3 Experiments and Result Analysis

3.1 Datasets

In our experiments, we crawl users' comments before June 2, 2014 from health-related social network DailyStrength with respect to 50 most focused drugs. There are totally 600,237 pieces of comments in 1075 health-related topics. We also use the annotated MeSH sets of article citations on certain drugs, containing more than 22 million

MEDLINE citations before the year of 2013 and extract the MeSH sets from them as the train data for training the modified Skip-gram model. We set the dimension of the vectors to be 100 for relatively good performance. We conduct three groups of experiments to evaluate the performance of our framework. The first experiment is conducted to examine the performance of CRF based named entity recognition with different subsets of features. The second experiment is designed to verify the detected ADRs based on the literatures. The third experiment is to find the associated proteins with respect the potential ADRs.

3.2   Performance on Recognizing Mentions of Diseases and ADRs

To train the CRF model for recognizing names of diseases and ADRs, we annotated 2000 pieces of users' comments in our experiments. For every combination of features, we evaluate the performance of the CRF model on accuracy, recall and F1 scores using 10-fold cross evaluation. Table 1 shows the results for CRF with different feature combinations. Compared with the original word features, the set with all of the defined features achieves the best performance, which achieves the best F1 score 83%, while the F1 score is 82% when using only the word-level feature set. The performance is improved by adding the dictionary-based feature set.

Table 1. Performance on recognizing mentions by the CRF model

Feature combinations	Recall	Accuracy	F1
SW + POS	0.76	0.87	0.81
OW + POS	0.74	0.88	0.80
OW + POS + SW	0.76	0.88	0.82
OW + POS + SW + SF	0.77	0.88	0.82
OW + POS + SW + SF + FF	0.77	0.87	0.82
OW + POS + SW + SF + FF + LF	0.77	0.87	0.82
ALL	0.78	0.87	0.83

3.3   Performance on Potential ADRs Detection

In this section, we take three drugs as examples to compare the detected top-10 ADRs by our method with those by Leaman's Method [2] in Table 2. In the table, "-" stands for the indication of drugs, "+" stands for the known ADRs and "*" stands for the potential ADRs. The Sim. scores measure the confidence degree to verify the potential ADRs with respect to the corresponding drug by each method. From the table, we can find that the detected ADRs by these two methods are highly correlated, which indicates our method is as effective as the state-of-the-art work.

On this basis, we filter the indications and ADRs using some domain-specific resources. We totally extract 993 item mentions, 231 of which can be verified as indications using semantic MEDLINE and 34 of which can be verified as indications using DrugBank. For the recognized potential ADRs, 240 of which can be verified using the SIDER database and 488 of which can be taken as potential ADRs. From the

Table 2. Comparison with Leaman's results

Drug names	Leaman's results [2]		Our results	
	Mentions	Sim.	Mentions	Sim.
Carbamazepine	somnolence or fatigue	12.3%	seizures-	29.6%
	allergy	5.2%	not as effective*	23.8%
	weight gain	4.1%	pain-	17.0%
	rash	3.5%	rash-	10.2%
	depression	3.2%	sleepy*	4.4%
	dizziness	2.4%	effect increased*	3.9%
	tremor/spasm	1.7%	weight gain abnormal*	3.2%
	headache	1.7%	dizziness+	2.7%
	appetite increased	1.5%	headache-	2.7%
	nausea	1.5%	nausea+	2.7%
Trazodone	somnolence or fatigue	48.2%	insomnia-	18.1%
	nightmares	4.6%	anxiety*	12.8%
	insomnia	2.7%	not as effective*	10.9%
	addiction	1.7%	wakefulness*	10.4%
	headache	1.6%	sleepy*	7.6%
	depression	1.3%	nightmare-	7.3%
	hangover	1.2%	hangover effect*	4.8%
	anxiety attack	1.2%	feeling high*	4.4%
	panic reaction	1.1%	drowsiness-	3.9%
	dizziness	0.9%	headache+	3.4%
Ziprasidone	somnolence or fatigue	20.3%	not as effective*	33.7%
	dyskinesia	6.0%	sleepy*	15.2%
	mania	3.7%	anxiety+	9.6%
	anxiety attack	3.5%	mania-	6.3%
	weight gain	3.2%	weight gain abnormal*	4.5%
	depression	2.4%	hallucination*	4.3%
	allergic reaction	1.9%	suicide*	3.9%
	dizziness	1.2%	feeling high*	2.9%
	panic reaction	1.2%	effect increased*	2.5%

table, we also find that drug takers are likely to comment on the ADRs not presented in the instructions. That is to say, if the drug instruction already tells that the drug may cause some kinds of ADRs, the takers would consider the presented ADRs as normal reactions before taking the drug. Otherwise, the drug takers tend to resort to the health-related social network for help.

After the extraction, we filter the indications and known ADRs. In the known ADRs, 71 of them can be verified by Semantic MEDLINE, which have not been recorded in SIDER.

3.4 Associated Proteins for Potential ADRs

We consider ADRs not existed in the SIDER and without evidences from semantic MEDLINE as potential ADRs, and attempt to find associated proteins using the distributed entity representations. We list the associated proteins between *trazodone* and *anxiety* in Table 3, and try to verify their association from existing literatures. From Gingrich's work [14], we can find that serotonin receptors are related to anxiety. Goldman et al. [15] indicate serotonin transporter is related to anxiety. As a special serotonin transporter, we can infer that serotonin plasma membrane transport proteins are related to anxiety. Shishkina et al. [16] indicate that adrenergic receptors are related to anxiety. On the other hand, trazodone is an antidepressant of the serotonin antagonist and reuptake inhibitor class and it has the alpha-adrenergic blocking property. So in the five detected associated proteins, we can obtain three triples, *<trazodone, serotonin receptors, anxiety>*, *<trazodone, serotonin plasma membrane transport proteins, anxiety>* and *<trazodone, adrenergic receptors, anxiety>*, which will help the biomedical experts determine the relationships between trazodone and anxiety.

Table 3. The associated proteins of trazodone and anxiety

Associated proteins	$f(d,p,a)$
receptors, serotonin	0.83
5-hydroxytryptophan	0.76
serotonin plasma membrane transport proteins	0.75
receptors, adrenergic	0.75
receptor, serotonin, 5-ht1a	0.74

4   Conclusion and Future Work

In this paper, we propose a novel framework to detect potential adverse drug reactions from health-related social networks. In the framework, we first extract mentions of diseases and ADRs using CRF with different features. Then, we filter indications of drugs and known ADRs with the help of biomedical databases, including SIDER, DrugBank and Semantic MEDLINE, to obtain the potential ADRs. Finally, to facilitate verifications of potential ADRs, we propose a modified Skip-gram model to discover the associated proteins between a certain drug and its corresponding potential ADRs by generating distributed representations of biomedical entities. Experimental results show the effectiveness of our framework to detect the potential ADRs from social network DailyStrength. In our future work, we will attempt to generate representations for other biomedical entities, not limited to MeSH, and develop other effective method to find associations for potential ADRs beyond associated proteins.

Acknowledgements. This work is partially supported by grant from the Natural Science Foundation of China (Nos. 61277370, 61402075, 61572102, 61632011, 61602078, 61572098), Natural Science Foundation of Liaoning Province, China (Nos. 201202031, 2014020003), State Education Ministry and The Research Fund for the Doctoral Program of Higher Education (No. 20090041110002), the Fundamental Research Funds for the Central Universities. The 12th five year national science and technology supporting programs of China under Grant No. 2015BAF20B02.

References

1. Giacomini, K.M., Krauss, R.M., Roden, D.M., Eichelbaum, M., Hayden, M.R., Nakamura, Y.: When good drugs go bad. Nature **446**(7139), 975–977 (2007)
2. Leaman, R., Wojtulewicz, L., Sullivan, R., Skariah, A., Yang, J., Gonzalez, G.: Towards internet-age pharmacovigilance: extracting adverse drug reactions from user posts to health-related social networks. In: Paper Presented at the Proceedings of the 2010 Workshop on Biomedical Natural Language Processing (2010)
3. Rahmani, H., Weiss, G., Méndez-Lucio, O., Bender, A.: ARWAR: a network approach for predicting adverse drug reactions. Comput. Biol. Med. **68**, 101–108 (2016)
4. Casillas, A., Pérez, A., Oronoz, M., Gojenola, K., Santiso, S.: Learning to extract adverse drug reaction events from electronic health records in Spanish. Expert Syst. Appl. **61**, 235–245 (2016)
5. Dai, H.J., Touray, M., Jonnagaddala, J., Syed-Abdul, S.: Feature engineering for recognizing adverse drug reactions from Twitter posts. Information **7**(2), 27 (2016)
6. Yates, A., Goharian, N.: ADRTrace: detecting expected and unexpected adverse drug reactions from user reviews on social media sites. In: Serdyukov, P., Braslavski, P., Kuznetsov, S.O., Kamps, J., Rüger, S., Agichtein, E., Segalovich, I., Yilmaz, E. (eds.) ECIR 2013. LNCS, vol. 7814, pp. 816–819. Springer, Heidelberg (2013). doi:10.1007/978-3-642-36973-5_92
7. Toutanova, K., Klein, D., Manning, C.D., Singer, Y.: Feature-rich part-of-speech tagging with a cyclic dependency network. In: Paper presented at the Proceedings of the 2003 Conference of the North American Chapter of the Association for Computational Linguistics on Human Language Technology-Volume 1 (2003)
8. Kuhn, M., Campillos, M., Letunic, I., Jensen, L.J., Bork, P.: A side effect resource to capture phenotypic effects of drugs. Mol. Syst. Biol. **6**(1), 343 (2010)
9. Wishart, D.S., Knox, C., Guo, A.C., Shrivastava, S., Hassanali, M., Stothard, P., Woolsey, J.: DrugBank: a comprehensive resource for in silico drug discovery and exploration. Nucleic Acids Res. **34**(suppl 1), D668–D672 (2006)
10. Wishart, D.S., Knox, C., Guo, A.C., Cheng, D., Shrivastava, S., Tzur, D., Hassanali, M.: DrugBank: a knowledgebase for drugs, drug reactions and drug targets. Nucleic Acids Res. **36**(suppl 1), D901–D906 (2008)
11. Rindflesch, T.C., Fiszman, M.: The interaction of domain knowledge and linguistic structure in natural language processing: interpreting hypernymic propositions in biomedical text. J. Biomed. Inf. **36**(6), 462–477 (2003)
12. Mikolov, T., Chen, K., Corrado, G., Dean, J.: Efficient estimation of word representations in vector space. arXiv preprint arXiv:1301.3781 (2013)
13. Mikolov, T., Sutskever, I., Chen, K., Corrado, G.S., Dean, J.: Distributed representations of words and phrases and their compositionality. In: Paper presented at the Advances in Neural Information Processing Systems (2013)
14. Gingrich, J.A.: Mutational analysis of the serotonergic system: recent findings using knockout mice. Curr. Drug Targets-CNS Neurol. Dis. **1**(5), 449–465 (2002)
15. Goldman, D., Oroszi, G., Omalley, S., et al.: COMBINE genetics study: the pharmacogenetics of alcoholism treatment response: genes and mechanisms. J. Stud. Alcohol Suppl. **66** (15), 56–64 (2005). discussion 33
16. Shishkina, G., Kalinina, T., Dygalo, N.: Attenuation of α 2A-adrenergic receptor expression in neonatal rat brain by RNA interference or antisense oligonucleotide reduced anxiety in adulthood. Neuroscience **129**(3), 521–528 (2004)

Iterative Integration of Unsupervised Features for Chinese Dependency Parsing

Te Luo, Yujie Zhang[✉], Jinan Xu, and Yufeng Chen

School of Computer and Information Technology,
Beijing Jiaotong University, Beijing, China
{14120472,yjzhang}@bjtu.edu.cn

Abstract. Since Chinese dependency parsing is lack of a large amount of manually annotated dependency treebank. Some unsupervised methods of using large-scale unannotated data are proposed and inevitably introduce too much noise from automatic annotation. In order to solve this problem, this paper proposes an approach of iteratively integrating unsupervised features for training Chinese dependency parsing model. Considering that more errors occurred in parsing longer sentences, this paper divide raw data according to sentence length and then iteratively train model. The model trained on shorter sentences will be used in the next iteration to analyze longer sentences. This paper adopts a character-based dependency model for joint word segmentation, POS tagging and dependency parsing in Chinese. The advantage of the joint model is that one task can be promoted by other tasks during processing by exploring the available internal results from the other tasks. The higher accuracy of the three tasks on shorter sentences can bring about higher accuracy of the whole model. This paper verified the proposed approach on the Penn Chinese Treebank and two raw corpora. The experimental results show that F1-scores of the three tasks were improved at each iteration, and F1-score of the dependency parsing was increased by 0.33%, compared with the conventional method.

Keywords: Chinese dependency parsing · Iteration · Unsupervised learning · Joint model

1 Introduction

Dependency parsing, which attempts to build dependency arcs between words in a sentence, is widely used in Machine Translation and automatic question answering system. Many methods of Chinese dependency parsing are proposed recently. Whether graph-based method [1, 2] or transition-based method [3, 4] are belong to supervised learning method, therefore, the model accuracy is limited by the scale and quality of the manual annotated treebank. Due to the difficulty of manual annotation of dependency treebank, there are almost no large-scale Chinese dependency treebank, and most of the dependency treebank used in research are automatically converted from the phrase treebank. On the other hand, large-scale raw corpus are relatively easy to obtain, and many researchers have proposed some unsupervised learning methods [5–9] using raw corpus to improve the accuracy of dependency parsing.

C.-Y. Lin et al. (Eds.): NLPCC-ICCPOL 2016, LNAI 10102, pp. 531–540, 2016.
DOI: 10.1007/978-3-319-50496-4_46

Unsupervised learning methods usually extract the feature from the results of automatic annotation [8, 10]. The main problem is that the errors in automatic annotation resulted in a large amount of noise in the feature extraction. There are less errors in the short sentences than the long sentences owning to the simple structure. Conventional methods do not pay attention to this difference and use the raw corpus without any discrimination on sentence length. Considering the less errors in automatic annotation for short sentences, we propose an approach of iteratively exploring unsupervised features for training Chinese dependency parsing model. We prefer to use shorter sentences of raw data to train model firstly, and then the trained model will be used in the next iteration to analyze longer sentences. Particularly, we adopt a character-based dependency model for joint word segmentation, POS tagging and dependency parsing in Chinese. The advantage of the joint model is that one task can be promoted by other tasks during processing by exploring the available internal results from the other tasks. The higher accuracy of each task on short sentences can bring about higher accuracy of the whole model.

2   Previous Work

There are usually two ways using raw corpus in unsupervised learning method. The one is to directly use the automatic annotation as training data. Zhu [5] applied a high-accuracy parser (such as the Berkeley parser) to automatically analyze raw corpus, and then the new annotated treebank was applied as additional training data to build a shift-reduce parser.

Another one is to extract statistical features from raw corpus. Zhou exploited the feature of web-data to improve the supervised statistical dependency parsing [6]. Chen extracted the short dependency relations from the results of automatic annotation, and then map to different categories based on their frequency. Finally, they train the dependency parser by using the information as features [7]. Chen calculated the scores of dependency language model from the results of automatic annotation, and then map the scores to different categories, and integrate them in the decoding algorithm directly using beam-search [9].

Although the two ways improved the accuracy of the dependency parsing by large-scale raw corpus, lots of noise from automatic annotation remained because of long sentences. In this paper, we focus on the more effective unsupervised learning method by preferring the short sentences.

3   Joint Word Segmentation, POS Tagging and Dependency Parsing Model

In this paper, we adopt the shift-reduce frame, combine the three task, word segmentation, POS tagging and dependency parsing, into a joint model [10–13]. We use the online perceptron algorithm with early-update [14] for global learning and beam search algorithm for decoding [15]. The advantage of the joint model is that one task can be promoted by other tasks during processing by exploring the available internal results from the other tasks.

3.1   Character-Based Joint Model

Word-based dependency tree is for build dependency arcs between words in a sentence. Because a sentence can be divided into different numbers of words in word segmentation, the number of dependency arc is also different. Character-based dependency tree is for build dependency arcs between characters in a sentence. For a sentence with L characters, the number of dependency arcs is N-1 for character-based dependency tree.

The analysis of a sentence is divided into several transition actions in shift-reduce joint model. In order to improve the search efficiency, for candidate results with the same number of transition actions, we only keep the top N results. Therefore, the model requires the candidate with the same number of transition actions is comparable, which requires all candidate results just experience the same number of transition actions from the initial state to the ending state. Thus, character-based dependency tree meets the requirements. Zhang [10] manually annotate the structures of words that occur in CTB5. We transform the word-based dependency tree into the character-based dependency tree by this way.

In a shift-reduce parser, an input sentence is processed in a linear left-to-right pass, and the output is constructed by a state-transition process. Every transition state includes a stack and a queue, where stack contains a sequence of partially-parsed dependency trees, and the queue consists of unprocessed input characters. There are two transition actions, shift and reduce, in word-based joint model. In this paper, we adjust the two transition actions in character-based joint model. The shift action is divided into four types, which are shift_S (the character is a single word), shift_B (the character is the first character of a word), shift_M (the character is the middle character of a word) and shirt_E (the character is the tail character of a word). The reduce action is divided into two types, which are the construction of inter-word dependency arc and intra-word dependency arc. Based on the above transfer strategy, a sentence with L characters requires 2L-1 transition actions from the initial state to the terminal state. In this paper, we use the same feature template with Guo [12] and Zhang [13].

3.2   Unsupervised Feature Using in Joint Model

In this paper, we extract two kinds of unsupervised feature, 2-gram string feature [16] and 2-gram dependency subtree feature [8], from large-scale raw corpus.

2-gram string feature is added to the joint model in the following way. In a sentence, each character c_i is labeled with a tag t_i after automatically word segmentation. In other word, the output of automatically word segmentation is a sequence $\{(c_i, t_i)\}_{i=1}^{L}$, L is the length of the sentence. Then, we can extract all two consecutive characters and its label (g, seg) from the segmented data, g is $c_i c_{i+1}$, and seg is $t_i t_{i+1}$. Next, we can extract a list of $\{g, seg, f(g, seg)\}$ from the segmented data. Here, f(g, seg) is the frequency of the cases where 2-gram g is segmented with the segmentation profile seg. In order to alleviate the sparseness of the data, we group all the (g, seg) into three sets: high-frequency(HF), middle-frequency(MF), and low-frequency(LF). The grouping way are defined as follows: if the f(g, seg) is one of the top 10% of all the f(g, seg), the label of (g, seg) is represented as HF; if it is between top 10% and 30%, it is represented as MF, otherwise it is represented as LF. Finally 2-gram $\{g, seg, label\}$ lists are produced. When transition actions for word segmentation and POS tagging are being formed, we extract the 2-gram string about the character and get label from the $\{g, seg, label\}$ lists. We combine the 2-gram string and the label as the 2-gram string feature of the character.

2-gram dependency subtree feature is added to the joint model in the following way. We extract subtrees containing two words from the automatically parsed dependency trees express as $st = w1\_w2\_R/L$. Here, w1 and w2 are words, and the order of w1 and w2 corresponds to the sequence of them in the original sentence, R and L is right dependency arc and left dependency arc respectively. Then, we can extract a list of $\{(st, f(st))\}$ from the parsed data. Here, $f(st)$ is the frequency of st appeared in the whole corpus. Next, we group all the $f(st)$ into three sets: high-frequency(HF), middle-frequency(MF), and low-frequency(LF). The grouping way is same with the previous paragraph. Finally we get the subtree lists $\{st, label\}$. When we judge whether the top two nodes S1 and S0 on stack have dependency relationship, we get labels for all kinds of subtree between S1 and S0 as features using the subtree lists.

4   Iterative Exploring of Unsupervised Features for Chinese Dependency Parsing

In word segmentation, POS tagging and dependency parsing joint model, we propose a more effective unsupervised learning method in which the shorter sentences of raw corpus are preferred and iterative training is conducted. In this way, less noise will be introduced in the feature extraction. At first, we investigate the relationship between the accuracy of the dependency parsing and the length of sentences.

4.1   Preliminary Investigation

Given the sentence of length L, the number of possible dependency tree can be calculated by the following formula (1) [17].

$$\frac{1}{L} 2^{(L-1)} C_{(L-1)} \tag{1}$$

The number of possible dependency trees grows rapidly as the length becomes larger. The longer the sentence, the higher the complexity of the dependency parsing. The accuracy will be decreased unavoidably.

We conducted the following preliminary experiment related to the sentence length. First, we trained a joint model using CTB5 and then conducted a closed test. We calculated the average F1-score on different sentence length for word segmentation, POS tagging and dependency parsing. The average numbers of sentences of different length are about 200. The longest sentence consists of 418 characters and 240 words. The relationship between the length of sentence and F1-score of the three tasks on the sentences is shown in Fig. 1. From Fig. 1, we can see that with the increase of the

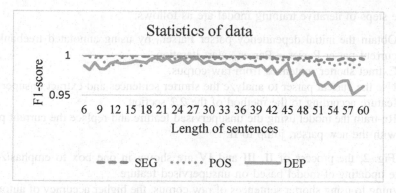

Fig. 1. The relationship between the sentence length and F1-score on the three tasks

length of sentence, the F1-score of the three tasks got decreased. Particularly, the decrease on the accuracy of dependency parsing is obvious. In POS tagging, F1-score at sentence length of 11 and 17 have greatly decreased. This is because that the word "新华社" appears several times, but is annotated POS with "NN" here and "NR" there.

The investigation result further prove the above expectation we obtained based on the formula (1) and provide the support for our proposed method.

4.2 Iterative Exploring of Unsupervised Feature

We propose an approach of iterative exploring of unsupervised features for training Chinese dependency parsing model. The framework is shown in Fig. 2.

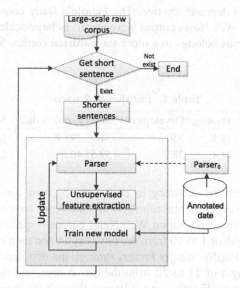

Fig. 2. Framework of iterative training of dependency parsing

The steps of iterative training model are as follows:

I. Obtain the initial dependency parser $Parser_0$ by using annotated treebank, set current parser Parser = $Parser_0$, start iteration.
II. Extract shorter sentences from raw corpus.
III. Use the current parser to analyze the shorter sentences and extract unsupervised feature according to the method of the 2.2 section.
IV. Re-train the model using the unsupervised feature and replace the current parser with the new parser, jump to II.

In Fig. 2, the process of II, III and IV are shown in one box to emphasize the iterative updating of model based on unsupervised feature.

Owning to using shorter sentences of raw corpus, the higher accuracy of automatic annotation of three tasks, word segmentation, POS tagging and dependency parsing, are expected to obtain. Since in the adopted joint model, one task can be promoted by exploring the available internal results from the other tasks during processing, the higher accuracy of three tasks on short sentences can bring about higher accuracy to the whole model. As a result, the higher accuracy of automatic annotation will be achieved.

5   Experiments

5.1   Experimental Settings

We use Chinese Tree Bank (CTB5) as annotated corpus, and it was separated into several parts: Training data set (chapter: 1–270, 400–931 and 1001–1151), development data set (chapter: 301–325) and test data set (chapter 271–300) [10]. As the names described, training data used for training joint model, development data was used for tuning parameters, and test data used for evaluation. We adopted Penn2Malt to transfer phrase structure tree to dependency tree. The People's Daily corpus (the first half of 1998 year) and Sogou Web News corpus were regard as large-scale raw corpus, which the People's Daily corpus belongs to a more standardized corpus. Statistics of datasets are shown in Table 1.

Table 1. Statistics of datasets

	Training	Development	Test	People's daily	Sogou web news
Number of sentences	18 K	350	348	295 K	18 M
Average length	44.4	38.2	39.5	40.5	51.3

In order to compare the accuracy in each iteration, and compare with the conventional method. The experimental setting is as follow, we have four experiments on The People's Daily corpus and Sogou Web News corpus respectively. (1) We extract the sentences with length of 1 to 10 from the raw corpus, and then extract unsupervised feature using $Parser_0$. Finally, we get $Parser_1$ through the first iteration. (2) We extract the sentences with length of 11 to 20 from the raw corpus, and then extract unsupervised feature using $Parser_1$. Finally, we get $Parser_2$ through the second iteration. (3) We extract the sentences with length of 21 to 30 from the raw corpus, and then extract unsupervised feature using $Parser_2$. Finally, we get $Parser_3$ through the third iteration. (4) We merge the raw corpus extracted in (1), (2) and (3), and we get $Parser_{mix}$ by using the mix raw corpus to train with conventional method. The beam size of joint model is set as 64 in this paper.

In this paper, we used F1-score as the accuracy metric to measure the performance of word segmentation, POS tagging and dependency parsing. Note that a dependency relationship is correct only when the two related words are all recalled in word segmentation and the head direction is correct. Following conventions, the relationships containing and punctuation are ignored.

5.2 Experimental Result and Analyses

The F1-score of four models' evaluation results on The People's Daily corpus are shown in Table 2. From Table 2, we can see that $Parser_3$ achieved higher F1-score than $Parser_2$ and $Parser_2$ achieved higher F1-score than $Parser_1$ in word segmentation, POS tagging and dependency parsing respectively, demonstrating the effectiveness of iterative training the model. We speculate that with the increase of the number of iterations, the accuracy of the three tasks will continue to improve. $Parser_{mix}$ achieved higher F1-score than $Parser_1$ in the three tasks, demonstrating the increase of the scale of raw corpus will increase the accuracy of the model. $Parser_{mix}$ achieved the same F1-score with $Parser_2$ in word segmentation, slightly lower F1-score than $Parser_2$ in POS tagging, and slightly higher F1-score than $Parser_2$ in dependency parsing. However, the corpus' scale of $Parser_2$ is smaller than $Parser_{mix}$, which indicates that the iterative method is significant in the three tasks. With the same scale of raw corpus, $Parser_3$ achieved higher F1-score than $Parser_{mix}$, demonstrating iteratively using raw corpus is better than conventional method. The F1-score of four models' evaluation results on Sogou Web News corpus are shown in Table 2. The difference in accuracy between the three models is similar to Table 3, which further proves the effectiveness of our method.

Table 2. The people's daily corpus

Model	SEG	POS	DEP
$Parser_1$	97.71	94.19	80.10
$Parser_2$	97.80	94.40	80.36
$Parser_3$	**97.95**	**94.53**	**80.71**
$Parser_{mix}$	97.80	94.36	80.38

Table 3. Sogou web news corpus

Model	SEG	POS	DEP
$Parser_1$	97.87	94.26	80.05
$Parser_2$	97.90	94.40	80.21
$Parser_3$	**97.98**	**94.49**	**80.51**
$Parser_{mix}$	97.92	94.38	80.25

The accuracy of iterative exploring of unsupervised feature in three tasks is better than the conventional method. By comparing the results of the two methods, we find some errors in conventional method is correct in our method. This situation includes the following three types:

The first one is the dependency error caused by the word segmentation error. For example: (1) 在会见乌拉圭客人时, 钱其琛对加米奥副外长来访和进行政治磋商表示欢迎。

The partial result of conventional method and our method are shown in Fig. 3(a) and 3(b). Figure 3(a) incorrectly divided the "来访(visit)" into two words "来(come)" and "访(visit)", shown by the underline. "来(come)" become a verb, resulting in "钱其琛(Qian Qichen)" and "对(treat)" modified "访(visit)". As our method get the less noise of 2-gram string feature from the shorter sentences, it correct the word segmentation of "来访(visit)", and the three tasks is promoted by each other, and the dependency error is also corrected.

Fig. 3. Dependency results of example (1)

The second one is the dependency error caused by the POS tagging error. For example: (2) 中方主张应通过有关各方的协商和对话解决朝鲜半岛的有关问题。

The partial result of conventional method and our method are shown in Fig. 4(a) and 4(b) (Because the sentence is too long to display all, the incomplete part of line indicates that the modified word is not in the figure). Figure 4(a) incorrectly labeled the POS tagging of "有关(concerned)" as preposition (P), leading the dependency relationship error of "有关(concerned)", "方(parties)" and "的(of)". As our method get the less noise of 2-gram subtree feature from the short sentences, it correct the POS tagging error, and the three tasks is promoted by each other, the dependency error is also corrected.

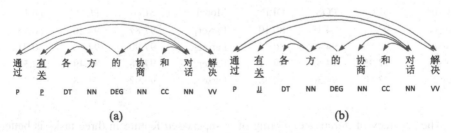

Fig. 4. Dependency results of example (2)

The third one is the dependency error with the correct word segmentation and POS tagging. For example: (3) 尼克松先生是一位具有战略远见和政治勇气的政治家。

The partial result of conventional method and our method are shown in Fig. 5(a) and 5(b). Figure 5(a) shows "战略(strategic)", "远见(vision)" and "和(and)" all incorrectly modified "政治(political)". As our method get the less noise 2-gram subtree feature from the short sentences, it correct the dependency error directly.

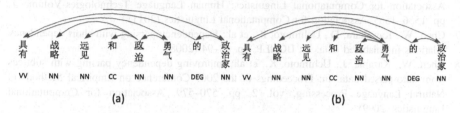

Fig. 5. Dependency results of example (3)

6 Conclusions

This paper proposes an approach of iterative exploring of unsupervised features for training Chinese dependency parsing model. Considering more errors are resulted in long sentence, we prefer to use shorter sentences as raw data first. The model trained on short sentences will be used in the next iteration to analyze longer sentences, and so on. We use a character-based dependency model for joint word segmentation, POS tagging and dependency parsing in Chinese. The advantage of the joint model is that one task can be promoted by other tasks during processing by exploring the available internal results from the other tasks. The higher accuracy of three task on short sentences can bring about higher accuracy of the whole model. We verified the approach on the Penn Chinese Treebank. The experimental results show that F1-scores of three tasks were improved at each iteration, and F1-score of dependency parsing was increased by 0.33%, compared with the conventional method.

Acknowledgments. The authors are supported by National Nature Science Foundation of China (Contract 61370130 and 61473294), and the Fundamental Research Funds of the Central Universities (2014RC040).

References

1. Koo, T., Collins, M.: Efficient third-order dependency parsers. In: Proceedings of the 48th Annual Meeting of the Association for Computational Linguistics. Association for Computational Linguistics, pp. 1–11 (2010)
2. McDonald, R., Crammer, K., Pereira, F.: Online large-margin training of dependency parsers. In: Proceedings of the 43rd Annual Meeting on Association for Computational Linguistics, pp. 91–98. Association for Computational Linguistics (2005)

3. Yamada, H., Matsumoto, Y.: Statistical dependency analysis with support vector machines. In: Proceedings of IWPT, vol. 3 (2003)
4. Nivre, J.: Algorithms for deterministic incremental dependency parsing. Comput. Linguist. **34**(4), 513–553 (2008)
5. 朱慕华, 王会珍, 朱靖波, 等. 向上学习方法改进移进-归约中文句法分析. 中文信息学报 29(2), 33–39 (2015)
6. Zhou, G., Zhao, J., Liu, K., et al.: Exploiting web-derived selectional preference to improve statistical dependency parsing. In: Proceedings of the 49th Annual Meeting of the Association for Computational Linguistics: Human Language Technologies-Volume 1, pp. 1556–1565. Association for Computational Linguistics (2011)
7. Chen, W., Kawahara, D., Uchimoto, K., et al.: Dependency parsing with short dependency relations in unlabeled data. In: IJCNLP, pp. 88–94 (2008)
8. Chen, W., Kazama, J., Uchimoto, K., et al.: Improving dependency parsing with subtrees from auto-parsed data. In: Proceedings of the 2009 Conference on Empirical Methods in Natural Language Processing, vol. 2, pp. 570–579. Association for Computational Linguistics (2009)
9. Chen, W., Zhang, M., Li, H.: Utilizing dependency language models for graph-based dependency parsing models. In: Proceedings of the 50th Annual Meeting of the Association for Computational Linguistics, Long Papers-Volume 1, pp. 213–222. Association for Computational Linguistics (2012)
10. Zhang, M., Zhang, Y., Che, W., et al.: Chinese Parsing Exploiting Characters. Proceedings of the 51st Annual meeting of the Association for Computational Linguistics, Long Papers-volume 1. Association for Computational Linguistics, pp. 125–134 (2013)
11. Hatori, J., Matsuzaki, T., Miyao, Y., et al.: Incremental joint approach to word segmentation, pos tagging, and dependency parsing in Chinese. In: Proceedings of the 50th Annual Meeting of the Association for Computational Linguistics, Long Papers-Volume 1. Association for Computational Linguistics, pp. 1045–1053 (2012)
12. Guo, Z., Zhang, Y., et al.: Character-level dependency model for joint word segmentation, POS tagging, and dependency parsing in Chinese. IEICE TRANS. Inf. Syst. **99**, 257–264 (2016)
13. Zhang, M., Zhang, Y., Che, W., et al.: Character-level chinese dependency parsing. In: Proceedings of the 52nd Annual Meeting of the Association for Computational Linguistics, pp. 1326–1336 (2014)
14. Collins, M., Roark, B.: Incremental parsing with the perceptron algorithm. In: Proceedings of the 42nd Annual Meeting on Association for Computational Linguistics, p. 111. Association for Computational Linguistics (2004)
15. Zhang, Y., Nivre, J.: Analyzing the effect of global learning and beam-search on transition-based dependency parsing. In: Proceedings of the COLING (Posters), pp. 1391–1400 (2012)
16. Wang, Y., Jun'ichi Kazama Y.T., Tsuruoka Y., et al.: Improving Chinese word segmentation and POS tagging with semi-supervised methods using large auto-analyzed data. In: IJCNLP, pp. 309–317 (2011)
17. Ozeki, K.: A multi-stage decision algorithm to select optimum bunsetsu sequences based on degree of Kakariuke-dependency. IEICE Trans. Inf. Syst. **70**, 601–609 (1987)

Can We Neglect Function Words in Word Embedding?

Gongbo Tang[1,2], Gaoqi Rao[3], Dong Yu[1,2(✉)], and Endong Xun[1,2]

[1] Institute of Big Data and Language Education, Beijing Language and Culture
University, Beijing 100083, China
tanggongbo@126.com, yudong_blcu@126.com, edxun@126.com

[2] College of Information Science, Beijing Language and Culture University,
Beijing 100083, China

[3] The Center for Studies of Chinese as a Second Language, Beijing Language
and Culture University, Beijing 100083, China
raogaoqi-fj@163.com

Abstract. Distributed representation is the most popular way to capture
semantic and syntactic features recently, and it has been widely used in various
natural language processing tasks. Function words express a grammatical or
structural relationship with other words in a sentence. However, previous works
merely considered that function words are equal to content words or neglected
function words, there is no experimental analyses about function words. In this
paper, we explored the effect of function words on word embedding with a word
analogy reasoning task and a paraphrase identification task. The results show
that neglecting function words has different effects on syntactic and semantic
related tasks, with an increase or a decrease in accuracy, moreover, the model of
training word embeddings does also matter.

Keywords: Word embedding · Function words

1 Introduction

Word embedding is the most popular representation for various natural language processing (NLP) tasks recently, which can capture both syntactic and semantic features of
words from a large unlabeled corpus. Most word embedding models are based on
Harris's distributional hypothesis that words occur in similar contexts tend to have
similar meanings [1]. These vectors are used as an end in itself or a representational basis
for NLP tasks, such as computing the similarity of terms [2], text classification [3], text
clustering [4], named entity recognition [5], paraphrase identification [6], word sense
disambiguation [7], POS tagging [8], parsing [9], sentiment analysis [10], machine
translation [11], and information retrieval [12], etc. Obviously, word embedding is not
only used in semantic related tasks, but also in syntactic related tasks, and even in
sentiment related tasks.

Many different models and training skills are proposed to generate a better word
embedding, which are used to improve the results of various NLP tasks, such as
exploring the best training corpus (domain and size) [13] and training parameters

© Springer International Publishing AG 2016
C.-Y. Lin et al. (Eds.): NLPCC-ICCPOL 2016, LNAI 10102, pp. 541–548, 2016.
DOI: 10.1007/978-3-319-50496-4_47

(including vector dimension, context window size, iterations, etc.) [13, 14], training several vectors for a polysemy word [7, 15], giving different attentions to context words and function words [16], using external relations [17], etc.

Function words are words that express a grammatical or structural relationship with other words in a sentence [18]. Some most common words, or words useless to a specific task are always filtered out when we process natural language data, and these words are called stop words. Stop words are always removed to improve the performance of information retrieval. In contrast to content words, a function word has little or no meaningful content, therefore, most NLP tasks view function words as stop words, and neglect them when processing a specific task.

Although we have mentioned that function words are removed in many tasks, many scholars still insist that function words are important in linguistic structure, and these words should be reserved. In addition, previous works on word embedding do not take account of the effect of neglecting function words. To explore whether neglecting function words has an effect on word embedding, this paper focuses on comparing the performance of word embeddings trained by different models with or without function words. We used predict-based and count-based models, which are including continuous bag-of-word (CBOW), Skip-gram and GloVe models [2, 14, 19], to train word embeddings on two corpora, one is pre-processed English Wikipedia, and the other is Wikipedia without function words. In addition, we used these word embeddings to do a paraphrase identification task to explore effects on sentence representation. To the best of our knowledge, no such study has previously been performed.

The rest of this paper is organized as follows: Sect. 2 describes function words and three models for word embedding training; then Sect. 3 gives the experiment details, results and discussions; Sect. 4 reviews related works; and finally, Sect. 5 concludes this paper.

2 Word Embedding Models

Word embedding models can be classified into two categories, predict-based models and count-based models. The key idea of predict-based models is to predict target words with context words with the help of conditional probability. While count-based models use a matrix which is relevant to the co-occurrence times of the corresponding word and context. The most popular word embedding training models are CBOW and Skip-gram (predict-based), and GloVe (count-based), they are simple but effective.

CBOW. It is a simplification of neural net language model, which the hidden layer is removed and the projection layer is shared for all words. It use the representations of context words $w_{t-c} ..., w_{t-1}, w_{t+1} ..., w_{t+c}$ to predict the current word w_t.

Skip-Gram. This model is similar to CBOW model, while its objective function is to maximize the likelihood of the prediction of context words given the center word.

GloVe. The author shows that ratios of word co-occurrence probabilities have the potential for encoding some forms of the meaning. The training objective is to learn word embeddings that their dot product equals the logarithm of the words' probability of co-occurrence.

As mentioned before, function words are related to grammar and structure parts of a sentence. Even though researchers usually neglect function words empirically, no one has made an experiment to verify the validity. Therefore, we want to explore whether function words have an effect on the performance of word embedding, so, we need a vector space that without function words which can compared with a normal vector space. The function words are words with POS tags in Table 1, and the POS tags are from Penn Treebank Project[1].

Fortunately, it is easy to train such vector spaces by those three models, what we just need is to replace all function words in training corpus with a special token. Hence, we choose these three models to train word embeddings for our experiment.

Table 1. POS tags of processed function words

CC (Coordinating conjunction)	CD (Cardinal number)
DT (Determiner)	EX (Existential there)
IN (Preposition or subordinating conjunction)	MD (Modal)
PRP (Personal pronoun)	PRP$ (Possessive pronoun)
RP (Particle)	TO (to)
WDT (Wh-determiner)	WP (Wh-pronoun)
WP$ (Possessive wh-pronoun)	WRB (Wh-adverb)

3 Experiments

3.1 Dataset and Settings

In this experiment, we download the training corpus for word embedding from the latest English Wikipedia dump[2], and the size is about 12.3 G after pre-processing (removed all punctuations, and lowercased all letters). Then we used Stanford POS-tagger[3] to tag the corpus, to generate another corpus that function words are replaced by a specific token. There are about 2.1 billion tokens in each corpus and the vocabulary size is about 1.9 million.

We used the word2vec[4] and GloVe[5] tools (including CBOW, Skip-gram and GloVe models) to train word embeddings with these two corpora. And the dimension is set to 50, 100, 200, 300 and 500. For CBOW and Skip-gram, we use Hierarchical Softmax method. To compare the results between predict-based and count-based models, both window size are set to 5 and 15 in CBOW, Skip-gram and GloVe models.

---

[1] https://www.ling.upenn.edu/courses/Fall_2003/ling001/penn_treebank_pos.html.

[2] https://dumps.wikimedia.org/enwiki/.

[3] http://nlp.stanford.edu/software/tagger.html.

[4] https://code.google.com/archive/p/word2vec/.

[5] http://nlp.stanford.edu/projects/glove/.

3.2   Tasks

To explore whether neglecting function words has any effects on word embedding, we evaluated our word embeddings on a word analogy reasoning task [2]. And the word analogy task was divided into a syntactic subset and a semantic subset. In addition, we did a semantic related paraphrase identification task to explore further effect on sentence representation. Since function words cannot be neglected in some syntactic tasks, such as POS tagging and dependency parsing, we do not do syntactic related experiments further.

Word Analogy. There are about 10.5 K syntactic analogy questions, like "eat is to eats as go is to (goes)", and 9 K semantic analogy questions, like "Moscow is to Russia as Beijing is to (China)" in this task. We answered the question "a is to b as c is to _?" by finding the word whose vector v_d is closest to $v_b - v_a + v_c$ according to the cosine similarity.

Paraphrase Identification. In this experiment, we did a classification on Microsoft Research Paraphrase Corpus [20], with 4076 sentence pairs in training set and 1725 sentence pairs in testing set.

We used the cosine similarity between two sentence vectors, which are accumulated by word vectors in corresponding sentence, to represent each sentence pair [21], in addition, words out of vocabulary will not be considered. If the cosine similarity exceeds a certain threshold, the sentence pair will be classified as a paraphrase, otherwise as not a paraphrase. Then we use LIBSVM [22] to fulfill this classification.

3.3   Results and Discussion

We present results of word analogy and paraphrase identification tasks in Table 2. It is obvious to see that neglecting function words has different effects on different types of tasks, moreover, the model of training word embeddings also matters.

Word Analogy. Firstly, let us have a look at the predict-based models. For semantic subset, the performances of all vector spaces trained by CBOW and Skip-gram models have an obvious increase after neglecting function words with only one exception. Since function words which have a lot syntactic features in sentences have been replaced, and the vocabulary reduces in size, the model can focus on capturing more semantic features in a smaller vector space. For syntactic subset, the result is just on the contrary to the semantic analogy task. There is an evident decrease of accuracy for all the vector spaces trained by CBOW and Skip-gram models, it can be explained by the loss of function words, which means that sentence structures and grammatical knowledge are losing because of replacing function words. The less function words, the less syntactic features are captured. Secondly, the result of count-based models seems different from that of predict-based models. We can see that neglecting function words has little effect on both semantic and syntactic analogy, all the scores have a change less than 1% after replacing function words.

Table 2. The results of word analogy and paraphrase identification tasks, given as percent accuracy. With-FW means training corpus with function words, while Non-FW means training corpus with no function words. Bold scores mean that there is an increase over 1% after neglecting function words, while underlined scores present a decrease over 1%, and the rest italic scores show changes under 1%. SG is short for Skip-gram, and the window size of these three models are all set to 5.

Model	Dim.	Analogy				Paraphrase	
		Sem.		Syn.			
		FW	Non-FW	FW	Non-FW	FW	Non-FW
CBOW	50	35.38	**38.45**	29.26	<u>27.24</u>	68.52	*68.88*
	100	44.33	**48.8**	38.2	<u>37.49</u>	69.57	*69.57*
	200	49.59	**56.21**	48.08	*47.63*	70.2	**71.19**
	300	53.84	**56.31**	51.69	<u>49.62</u>	70.71	**71.42**
	500	53.68	**55.28**	53.11	<u>51.52</u>	71.03	**71.75**
SG	50	40.87	**42.09**	27.01	<u>25.14</u>	67.88	*68.17*
	100	53.03	**56.68**	38.65	<u>36.22</u>	68.23	**69.86**
	200	64.67	**65.78**	45.69	<u>43.31</u>	69.04	**70.55**
	300	67.81	**68.54**	49.84	<u>47.23</u>	69.33	**72**
	500	69.75	*69.31*	52.06	<u>50.04</u>	69.86	**72.06**
GloVe	50	49.2	*49.61*	35.97	*35.62*	66.49	*66.49*
	100	64.21	*64.02*	47.82	*47.43*	66.49	*66.49*
	200	72.87	*72.24*	55.64	*55.09*	66.49	*66.55*
	300	76.07	*75.36*	56.91	*56.38*	66.49	*66.96*
	500	77.74	*76.97*	56.44	*55.91*	66.55	*67.13*

Figure 1 shows the effects on accuracy after neglecting function words. It tells us that neglecting function words has an obvious influence on predict-based models compared with count-based model. In addition, as for predict-based models, neglecting function words make a greater change in semantic sub-task for CBOW model, and a more evident change in syntactic sub-task for Skip-gram model.

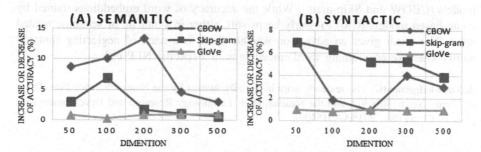

Fig. 1. Changes caused by neglecting function words in word analogy task

Paraphrase Identification. This task is a semantic related classification at sentence level, and sentences are represented by word vectors. Even though a sentence contains some structural and grammatical information, semantic section dominates in paraphrase identification tasks. Nearly all the vector spaces trained by predict-based models have a growth, which confirms that neglecting function words can improve embedding quality trained by predict-based models in semantic vector space once again. While the scores of models trained by GloVe nearly have no change, similar to the results in word analogy task.

4   Related Work

Function words are always neglected in some NLP tasks. Huang used the sentences around target word to disambiguate, which sentences are represented by verbs and nouns, without any function words [23]. Tang used content words in an entity description for candidate entity re-ranking [24]. However, some people insist that content words and function words work as a whole and they should treated equally. All the words in a sentence, including content words and functions words, are used to represent the corresponding sentence [6]. Let alone tasks like POS tagging and dependency parsing, function words are not negligible obviously. Moreover, some researchers do not process function words so absolutely. Since function words has generally less predictive power in the CBOW model, they are tend to be attributed very low attention, and they are given lower weights, while content words are attributed higher weights [15]. Although there are various processing ways for function words, no one has designed an experiment about function words. Therefore we want to explore what is the role of function words played in distributed representation.

5   Conclusion

In this paper, we did a word analogy reasoning task and a paraphrase identification task to explore the effect on word embeddings when we neglect function words. The result shows that the accuracy has an obvious decrease and an evident increase in syntactic tasks and semantic tasks respectively after replacing function words for predict-based models (CBOW and Skip-gram). While the accuracy of word embeddings trained by count-based models (GloVe) nearly keeps still, either in syntactic or semantic related tasks. The result gives an advice on whether there is a need of neglecting function words when we are training word embeddings in a specific NLP task.

Acknowledgements. The research work is partially funded by the Natural Science Foundation of China (No. 61300081), and the National High Technology Research and Development Program of China (No. 2015AA015409).

References

1. Harris, Z.S.: Distributional structure. Word **10**(2–3), 146–162 (1954)
2. Mikolov, T., Chen, K., Corrado, G., Dean, J.: Efficient estimation of word representations in vector space. arXiv preprint arXiv:1301.3781 (2013)
3. Lai, S., Xu, L., Liu, K., Zhao, J.: Recurrent convolutional neural networks for text classification. In: AAAI, pp. 2267–2273 (2015)
4. Nasir, J.A., Varlamis, I., Karim, A., Tsatsaronis, G.: Semantic smoothing for text clustering. Knowl.-Based Syst. **54**, 216–229 (2013)
5. Zirikly, A., Diab, M.: Named entity recognition for arabic social media. In: Proceedings of NAACL-HLT, pp. 176–185 (2015)
6. Milajevs, D., Kartsaklis, D., Sadrzadeh, M., Purver, M.: Evaluating neural word representations in tensor-based compositional settings. arXiv preprint arXiv:1408.6179 (2014)
7. Chen, X., Liu, Z., Sun, M.: A unified model for word sense representation and disambiguation. In: EMNLP, pp. 1025–1035 (2014)
8. Santos, C.D., Zadrozny, B.: Learning character-level representations for part-of-speech tagging. In: Proceedings of the 31st International Conference on Machine Learning (ICML 2014), pp 1818–1826 (2014)
9. Chen, W., Zhang, Y., Zhang, M.: Feature embedding for dependency parsing. In: COLING, pp. 816–826 (2014)
10. Tang, D., Wei, F., Yang, N., Zhou, M., Liu, T., Qin, B.: Learning sentiment-specific word embedding for twitter sentiment classification. In: ACL (1), pp. 1555–1565 (2014)
11. Zhang, J., Liu, S., Li, M., Zhou, M., Zong, C.: Bilingually-constrained phrase embeddings for machine translation. In: ACL (1), pp. 111–121 (2014)
12. Clinchant, C.S., Perronnin, F.: Aggregating continuous word embeddings for information retrieval. In: Proceedings of the Workshop on Continuous Vector Space Models and their Compositionality, pp. 100–109 (2013)
13. Lai, S., Liu, K., Xu, L., Zhao, J.: How to generate a good word embedding? ArXiv preprint arXiv:1507.05523 (2015)
14. Pennington, J., Socher, R., Manning, C.D.: Glove: Global vectors for word representation. In EMNLP **14**, 1532–1543 (2014)
15. Tang, G., YU, D., Xun, E.: An unsupervised word sense disambiguation method based on sememe vector in HowNet. J. Chin. Inf. Process. **29**(6), 23–29 (2015). (In Chinese)
16. Ling, W., Tsvetkov, Y., Amir, S., Fermandez, R., Dyer, C., Black, A.W., Trancoso, I., Chu-Cheng, L.: Not all contexts are created equal: better word representations with variable attention. In: Proceedings of the 2015 Conference on Empirical Methods in Natural Language Processing, Lisbon, Portugal, pp. 1367–1372. Association for Computational Linguistics, September 2015
17. Faruqui, M., Dodge, J., Jauhar, S.K., Dyer, C., Hovy, E., Smith, N.A.: Retrofitting word vectors to semantic lexicons. ArXiv preprint arXiv:1411.4166 (2014)
18. Fries, C.C.: The structure of english: an introduction to the construction of English sentences. Language **31**(2), 312–345 (1952)
19. Mikolov, T., Sutskever, I., Chen, K., Corrado, G.S., Dean, J.: Distributed representations of words and phrases and their compositionality. In: Advances in neural information processing systems, pp. 3111–3119 (2013)
20. Dolan, B., Brockett, C., Quirk, C.: Microsoft research paraphrase corpus (2005). Retrieved 29 Mar 2008

21. Mitchell, J., Lapata, M.: Vector-based models of semantic composition. In: ACL, pp. 236–244 (2008)
22. Chang, C.-C., Lin, C.-J.: LIBSVM: a library for support vector machines. ACM Trans. Intell. Syst. Technol. (TIST) 2(3), 27 (2011)
23. Huang, H., Zhizhuo, Y.: Unsupervised word sense disambiguation using neighborhood knowledge. In: 25th Pacific Asia Conference on Language, Information and Computation, pp. 333–342 (2011)
24. Tang, G., Guo, Y., Yu, D., Xun, E.: A hybrid re-ranking method for entity recognition and linking in search queries. In: Li, J., Ji, H., Zhao, D., Feng, Y. (eds.) NLPCC 2015. LNCS (LNAI), vol. 9362, pp. 598–605. Springer, Heidelberg (2015). doi:10.1007/978-3-319-25207-0_57

A Similarity Algorithm Based on the Generality and Individuality of Words

Yinfeng Zou, Chunping Ouyang[✉], Yongbin Liu,
Xiaohua Yang, and Ying Yu

School of Computer Science and Technology,
University of South China, Hengyang 421001, China
ouyangcp@126.com

Abstract. "HowNet" is a popular platform of Chinese text similarity calculation. The study has found that there is still some short-comings about the effect of "HowNet" architecture, the organization of vocabulary, concept description on word similarity measurement. In hence, on the basis of analyzing the generality and individuality of words in "HowNet", a similarity algorithm based on the generality and individuality of words is proposed. Furthermore, experimental data is from NLPCC-ICCPOL 2016 Chinese words similarity evaluation task data set. Experimental results show that the algorithm is more feasible and stable, and better than some of the other classic algorithms. Moreover, the size of experimental data sets has a little influence on experimental results. In all experiments, the Pearson correlation coefficient and the Spearman's coefficient have stably reached 0.460 and 0.440.

Keywords: Words similarity · HowNet · Pearson correlation coefficient · Spearman's coefficient

1 Introduction

Word similarity calculation is a basic research in the field of natural language processing, which is widely used in information extraction, text classification, word sense disambiguation, automatic question answering and other fields. These studies focus on quantitative analysis of the complicated semantic similarity between words, which used a simple numerical value to measure the semantic similarity [1].

Recently, word similarity algorithm can be divided into two categories. The one is based on statistical word similarity calculation which is represented by the method based on traditional corpus and the method based on Web corpus. Both these methods have characters of simple calculation and higher performance, and they also can reflect objectively the differences and similarities of words in semantic and pragmatic aspects. However, most of these methods ignore lexical semantic information so that the accuracy of the experimental results is reduced. In addition, these methods depend on the corpus too much, which lead to unstable experimental results. Another type of method is the similarity calculation based on the semantic of words, including similarity calculation based on traditional semantic dictionary or the online encyclopedia dictionary. These methods are more stable, and close to the subjective judgment of the human. But the words of the traditional semantic dictionaries are finite and updated

© Springer International Publishing AG 2016
C.-Y. Lin et al. (Eds.): NLPCC-ICCPOL 2016, LNAI 10102, pp. 549–558, 2016.
DOI: 10.1007/978-3-319-50496-4_48

slowly, which causes difficult to the similarity calculation of unknown words. What's more, the online encyclopedia dictionary is mainly finished by non-experts. As a result, the content of dictionary lacks of professional and is not fixed. In addition, some researchers have studied on word similarity calculation based on the fusion of the above methods. Although the fusion method can adopt both advantages of different methods, the technology of fusion is worthy to make further studies.

According to the above analysis, word similarity calculation methods based on the traditional semantic dictionaries have certain advantages both in the completeness and the stability of calculation. However, these existing methods have shortcomings in considering and analyzing the semantic dictionaries, such as the architecture of the traditional semantic dictionary, the organization mode and the form of concept description, so this paper proposes a similarity algorithm based on the generality and individuality of words.

2 Related Works

"HowNet" has become a typical platform of Chinese words similarity calculation, because of the rich semantic knowledge and scientific form of knowledge description. The semantic description of concepts in "HowNet" has been summarized into several abstract data structures (basic sememe description, relational sememe description, symbol sememe description and specific words) [2]. The similarity of concept is composed of the summation of each abstract data structure similarity. Currently, most of word similarity calculation research based on 'HowNet' tends to improve the algorithm of word similarity calculation on the basis of understanding in the literature [2]. The research focus on two ways: proposing new algorithm of sememes similarity or improving the concept similarity calculation. Some researchers analyze the effect of sememes' tree structure on word similarity calculation from different perspectives and provide a new kind of algorithm of sememes similarity calculation [3, 4]. The research of improving the algorithm of concept similarity calculation focuses on the function of the first independent sememes on the concept similarity calculation [4, 5] and the adjustment of weight parameters in the process of calculating the similarity of words [6, 7]. SunJing proposed a method about dynamic weighted reverse word similarity calculation using TDIDF algorithm [7]. Moreover, some studies have used the new version of "HowNet" for words similarity calculation [8, 9].

Most of the above solutions about word similarity calculation mainly focus on the analysis and discussion of a single concept description item of words in "HowNet", and they have no consideration about the design that a single word is described by multiple concepts in "HowNet".

3 Word Similarity Calculation

The solution of word similarity calculation based on "HowNet" can be divided into three steps: sememes similarity calculation, concepts similarity calculation, and words similarity calculation. An improved word similarity calculation is proposed only computing the words included in "HowNet". Considering the effect of 'specific words' on the concept similarity calculation is the major improvements.

3.1 Sememe Similarity Calculation

The sememes similarity computation method based on the "HowNet" mainly depends on the "tree structure" of sememe. Calculating and analyzing the distance of two nodes in the tree structure gets the solution of sememes similarity calculation. This similarity calculation method is mature, and many scholars have given their own calculation formula [2, 4]. This paper adopts three formula (1), (2) and (3) from [2, 4, 5].

$$Sim(S_1, S_2) = \frac{\alpha}{\alpha + dist(S_1, S_2)} \tag{1}$$

Here, S1, S2 is two sememes, dist(S1, S2) is the path length between S1 and S2, α is an adjustment parameter which suggests path length when the similarity is 0.5

$$\begin{aligned} Sim(S_1, S_2) &= \kappa \times [depth(S_1) + depth(S_2)] / [\kappa \times (depth(S_1) + depth(S_2)) \\ &+ dist(S_1, S_2) + |depth(S_1) - depth(S_2)|] \end{aligned} \tag{2}$$

The depth (S1) represents the depth of sememe S1, κ is an adjustment parameter which suggests the effect of depth on similarity

$$\begin{aligned} Sim(S_1, S_2) &= 2 \times Spd(S_1, S_2) / [Dsd(S_1, S_2) + Spd(S_1, S_2)] \\ &= 2 \times Spd(S_1, S_2) / [depth(S_1) + depth(S_2)] \end{aligned} \tag{3}$$

The Spd(S1, S2) is the path length of the same parent node between S1 and S2 in the hierarchy of sememes, Dsd(S1, S2) is the shortest path summation of S1 and S2 reaching the nearest same parent node.

As the sememes in "HowNet" are not all in the same tree, so the paper set a smaller parameter η as the sememe similarity while the two sememes are in the difference sememe trees.

3.2 Concepts Similarity Calculation

The words in "HowNet" are composed of content words and function words. There is a great difference between content words and function words, so the similarity of content words and function words could be ignored and set to 0. The concept description item of content words in "HowNet" is complex. It is divided into four abstract data structures, including "basic sememe description", "symbol sememe description", "relational sememe description" and "specific word", to calculate concepts similarity. The calculation method of function words similarity is same as the content words.

Existing researches overlook the function of the distribution of the specific words on the process of concept similarity calculation. In most rules, the specific word similarity is stipulated to 1 when they are the same, and otherwise it is set to 0. This operation simplifies the complexity of concept similarity calculation, but enlarges the effect of the same specific words. This operation also ignores effect of the difference between the specific words. Hence, this paper argues that when the specific words are the same, the influence on generality of words could be ignored; when the specific words are different, the differences of words represent individuality of words, so the concept similarity calculation is modified as follows:

Rule 1: when the specific words are same, ignore its impact on the concept similarity calculation and set the value of similarity to 0;

Rule 2: when specific words are different, the specific words are looked as common words that could be restored the knowledge expression of concept of "HowNet", then restore the specific words, calculate the basic sememe similarity of the new word and take it the negative as the final specific words similarity, which suggests the individuality difference of concepts. For example, the expression of word "毛泽东" is "human|人, official|官, politics|政, ProperName|专, (China|中国)", such as the structure "human|人, official|官, politics|政, ProperName|专" is the "basic sememe description" and "(China|中国)" is "specific word". When calculating the similarity of the specific words "中国", we need to deal with the word "中国" as the same as "毛泽东", and recalculate the similarity after querying the expression of "中国".

Rule 3: the similarity calculation of concepts pair (C1, C2) is divided into four parts: basis sememe description $Sim1(C1, C2)$, relational sememe description $Sim2(C1, C2)$, symbol sememe description $Sim3(C1, C2)$, specific word $Sim4(C1, C2)$. When relational sememe description or symbol sememe description is null, $Sim2(C1, C2)$ or $Sim3(C1, C2)$ takes a smaller value λ. Assuming concept similarity is $Sim(C1, C2)$:

if $Sim_4(C_1, C_2) \geq 0$:

$$Sim(C_1, C_2) = \beta_1[Sim_1(C_1, C_2) + Sim_4(C_1, C_2)] + \beta_2 Sim(C_1, C_2) + \beta_3 Sim(C_1, C_2) \tag{4}$$

else

$$Sim(C_1, C_2) = \beta_1 Sim_1(C_1, C_2) + \beta_2 Sim_2(C_1, C_2) + \beta_3 Sim(C_1, C_2) + \beta_4 Sim(C_1, C_2) \tag{5}$$

Here $\beta_i (1 \leq i \leq 4)$ is adjustment parameter, and meets $\beta_1 + \beta_2 + \beta_3 = 1, \beta_1 \geq \beta_2 \geq \beta_3 > 0, 0 < \beta_4 < 1$

According to the above rules, the specific calculation process is as follows:

Step1: Similarity calculation of base sememe description. The similarity of all sememe and null takes a smaller parameter δ. Assuming the basic sememe sets of concept C1 and C2 are as follows:

$Set_1 = \{p_1, p_2, \dots p_n\}$
$Set_2 = \{p_1, p_2, \dots p_m\}$

```
Set /Set₁/ represents the amount of set Set₁
maxSize=max{| Set₁|,| Set₂|},
minSize=min{| Set₁|,| Set₂|},
score=0.0;
while(| Set₁|>0 or | Set₂|>0){
Find the set of sememes that their similarity is biggest
in all sememes combination.
Pᵢ ∈ Set₁ and Pⱼ ∈ Set₂;
score=score+Sim(pᵢ,pⱼ)
Set₁= Set₁-{ pᵢ }
Set₂= Set₂-{ pⱼ }
}
Sim(C₁,C₂)=[score+(maxSize-minSize)*δ]/max
```

Step 2: Similarity calculation of relational sememes description. The matching of relational sememes is very simple. The relational sememes that has same type of relation are divided into a set to calculate sememe similarity. The similarity of relational sememe and null takes a smaller parameter λ and the sememes similarity calculation that has same relation is same as Step 1.

Step 3: Similarity calculation of symbol sememes description. It is similar to Step 2.

Step 4: Similarity calculation of specific word. When sememes are same, their similarity is 0. Otherwise, the specific words will be restored as its semantic expression in "HowNet", then the base sememes similarity of the semantic expression is calculated as similarity of the specific words. The similarity of specific word and null takes a smaller parameter λ.

3.3   Word Similarity Calculation

At present, most of word similarity calculation research based on the "HowNet" focus on the aspect of the DEF description of the concept considered as the main research object. During word similarity calculation, the effect of the difference of words is rarely considered. Therefore, Alignment of the generality and individuality of the words in "HowNet", the word similarity calculation rules are defined as follows:

Rule 3: The similarity of words is expressed by the partial similarity and the whole similarity;

Rule 4: The whole similarity of words is equal to 1 - "the whole difference";

Rule 5: When the similarity is less than 0, it suggests the difference between words.

A new formula for word similarity calculation is defined:

$$Sim(W_i, W_j) = \frac{partSim(W_i, W_j) + allSim(W_i, W_j)}{2} \tag{6}$$

Here, the Wi and Wj are two words, the partSim(Wi, Wj) is the partial similarity of Wi and Wj. allSim(Wi, Wj) is the whole similarity of Wi and Wj. Assuming the CSet1 and CSet2 represent the concepts sets of W1 and W2, |CSet1| and |CSet2| represent the size of concepts set of W1 and W2, DiffRate represents the whole difference of W1 and W2, count(def) represents the total number of the specific concept description item included in "HowNet". The $\beta_4 (0 < \beta_4 < 1)$ is a weight adjustment parameter

$$partSim(W_1, W_2) = Max\{Sim(C_i, C_j)|C_i \in W_1, C_j \in W_2\} \tag{7}$$

$$allSim(W_i, W_j) = 1 - DiffRate(W_i, W_j) \tag{8}$$

If the two words contain only one concept and the concepts description item is the same

$$DiffRate(Wi, Wj) = \frac{1}{count} \tag{9}$$

else,

$$DiffRate(Wi, Wj) = \frac{||CSet_i| - |CSet_j||}{Max\{|CSet_i|, |CSet_j|\}} \tag{10}$$

The improved algorithm has taken the generality and individuality of the words into account, and it highlights the importance of individuality in the process of word similarity calculation. It also promotes the objectivity and accuracy of word similarity calculation. The shortcoming of this algorithm is that it needs to restore the specific words as the word semantic expression in "HowNet" and calculate the basic sememe description similarity again, which increases extra computational cost, but it has little effect on the overall performance.

4   Experiment and Result

4.1   Experimental Data

The experimental data set is composed of the NLPCC-ICCPOL 2016 Chinese word similarity computing task evaluation data set and sample data set, excluding the duplicate words and unknown words in "HowNet". The final data set includes a total of 427 word pairs, and each word pair has an artificial judgment value which is from the average value of artificial judgment gave by twenty post-graduate students mayor in linguistics. The experimental parameters are set as shown in Table 1.

Table 1. Experimental parameter settings

α	δ	κ	η	λ	β1	β2	β3	β4
0.5	0.05	0.5	0.5	0.3	0.55	0.25	0.20	0.3

4.2   Evaluation Standard

In this experiment, the Pearson correlation coefficient and Spearman's rank correlation coefficient are used to evaluate the similarity between the target words and the results of the artificial judgment. R represents the correlation coefficient, which suggests the degree of linear correlation between the two variables and whose value is between -1 and $+1$. The greater the absolute value of R, the stronger the correlation. Pearson correlation coefficient formula is formula (11) and Spearman's rank correlation coefficient formula is formula (12)

$$r = \frac{1}{n-1} \sum_{i=1}^{n} \left(\frac{X_i - \overline{X}}{S_X} \right) \left(\frac{Y_i - \overline{Y}}{S_Y} \right) \tag{11}$$

Here S_X and S_X is the variance of X and Y, $\overline{X}$ and $\overline{Y}$ is the mean value of X and Y, n is size of sample

$$r = 1 - \frac{6 \sum_{i=1}^{n} (R_{Xi} - R_{Yi})^2}{n(n^2 - 1)} \tag{12}$$

Here, RX is the rating parameters of X, RY is the rating parameters of Y.

4.3   Experimental Results and Analysis

In this experiment, three similarity calculation methods are designed except for the method of Liu [2] and Xia [3]. There is only the algorithm of sememe similarity calculation is different among the three methods. The Method One uses the formula (1), the Method Two uses the formula (2) and the Method Three uses the formula (3).

Due to the imbalance of the distribution of words pair similarity in the experimental data, a different number of word pairs set, such as 100, 150, 200, 250, 300, 350, 400, are extracted from the experimental data set. This process is repeated 10 times to obtain 10 groups of experimental result set from each class of word pair set. The average value of the Pearson coefficient and Spearman's coefficient of each kind of words pair set is used as final evaluation data. Figures 1 and 2 show the comparison of the methods proposed by this paper and two classical methods about the Pearson coefficient and Spearman's coefficient.

It is shown in Figs. 1 and 2 that, the Pearson correlation coefficient and Spearman's rank correlation coefficient of our three methods are larger than both of LiuQun's Method and XiaTian's Method. The Pearson correlation coefficient was improved by 6% and Spearman's rank correlation coefficient increases by 3%. In addition, among the three methods, Method Three gets the best result while the two correlation coefficients of Method Three are largest and most stable. The main reason is that the Method One and Method Two focus on the breadth or depth of sememes similarity calculation respectively, but Method Three emphasize both of the two aspects of sememes. In this paper, Method One and LiuQun's Method take the same algorithms to

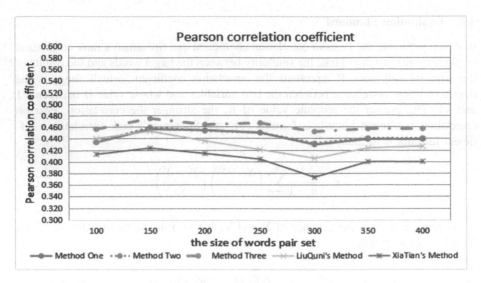

Fig. 1. Comparison chart about Pearson correlation coefficient of the five methods

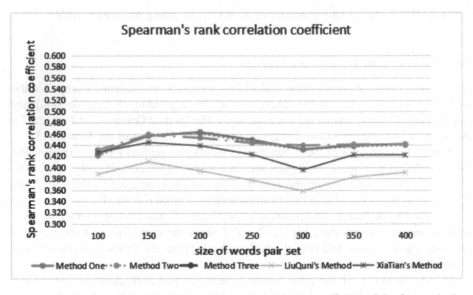

Fig. 2. Comparison chart about Spearman's rank correlation coefficient of the five methods

calculate the sememe similarity, meanwhile, Method Three and XiaTian's Method take the another same algorithms to calculate the sememe similarity. It can be seen from Figs. 1 and 2 that the experimental results of Method One and Method Three are better than LiuQun's and XiaTian's method. The results have shown the high accuracy of the improved word similarity algorithm in this paper.

According to NLPCC-ICCPOL 2016 final evaluation results of Chinese word similarity task, compared with the result of the team that got the first prize in the evaluation contest (Pearson correlation coefficient is 0.519, Spearman's rank coefficient is 0.518), our results are close to the best result (Pearson correlation coefficient is 0.450, Spearman's rank coefficient is 0.450) and the algorithm is stable, so the method proposed by this paper still can be improved deeply.

5 Conclusion

"HowNet" is a popular platform of Chinese words similarity calculation and has been widely applied and studied in the relevant fields. While the existing solutions have shortcomings in the aspect of the traditional semantic dictionary research, such as the architecture of the traditional semantic dictionary, the organization mode and the form of concept description, so a similarity algorithm based on the generality and individuality of words is proposed. The method not only promotes the accuracy of word similarity calculation, but also is stable. The results show our method keep a strong consistency and correlation with people's subjective judgment. In the following work, we will do further researches on the other characteristics of concept description of words in "HowNet". We plan to take advantage of the existing words in "HowNet" to calculate the semantic similarity of unknown words in "HowNet". Furthermore, using the new version of "HowNet" to perfect our method is the main work of next step.

Acknowledgement. This research work is supported by National Science Foundation of China (No. 61402220, No. 61502221), the Scientific Research Fund of Hunan Provincial Education Department (No. 14B153, No. 16C1378, No. 15C1186), the Philosophy and Social Science Foundation of Hunan Province (No. 14YBA335).

References

1. Guo, Y.: The Research of HowNet Based Word Similarity Computation and its Application: The Master's Degree Thesis of Hunan University in China, pp. 8–16 (2012)
2. Liu, Q., Li, S.J.: Lexical semantic similarity calculation based on HowNet. In: Proceedings of the Third Symposium on Chinese Lexical Semantics, Taibei (2002)
3. Hua, X.L., Zhu, Q.M.: Chinese text similarity method research by combining semantic analysis with statistics. Appl. Res. Comput. **29**(3), 833–836 (2012)
4. Xia, T.: Study on Chinese words semantic similarity computation. Appl. Res. Comput. **33**(6), 191–194 (2007)
5. Jiang, M., Xiao, S.B., Wang, H.W., et al.: An improved word similarity computing method based on HowNet. J. Chin. Inf. Process. **22**(3), 84–89 (2008)
6. Wang, X.L., Wang, Y.: Improved word similarity algorithm based on HowNet. Appl. Res. Comput. **31**(11), 3075–3077 (2011)

7. Sun, J., Zhang, D.Z.: Word similarity calculation based on inverse concept frequency. J. Xiamen Univ. (Nat. Sci.) **54**(2), 257–262 (2015)
8. Zhang, L., Yin, C.Y., et al.: Chinese word similarity computing based on semantic tree. J. Chin. Inf. Process. **24**(6), 23–30 (2010)
9. Liu, J., Guo, Y., et al.: Word similarity computation based on the HowNet 2008. J. Chin. **36** (8), 1728–1733 (2015)

An Improved Information Gain Algorithm Based on Relative Document Frequency Distribution

Jian Peng, Xiao-Hua Yang[✉], Chun-Ping Ouyang,
and Yong-Bin Liu

School of Computer Science and Technology, University of South China,
Hengyang 421001, China
xiaohua1963@yahoo.com.cn

Abstract. Feature selection algorithm plays an important role in text categorization. Considering some drawbacks proposed from traditional and recently improved information gain (IG) approach, an improved IG feature selection method based on relative document frequency distribution is proposed, which combines reducing the impact of unbalanced data sets and low-frequency characteristics, the frequency distribution of features within category and the relative frequency document distribution of features among different categories. The experimental results of NLPCC-ICCPOL 2016 stance detection in Chinese microblogs show that the performance of the improved method is better than traditional IG approach and another improved method in feature selection.

Keywords: Feature selection · Information gain · Relative document frequency distribution · Low-frequency characteristic

1 Introduction

Texts are typically represented by the vector space model (VSM) in text categorization systems. However the high dimensionality and scarcity of the vector space reduce the performance of the classifier [1]. Therefore, it is necessary to use feature selection to reduce the feature space in text categorization.

In the text categorization, there are several common feature selection methods like document frequency thresholding (DF), mutual information (MI), expected cross entropy (ECE), information gain (IG) and so on. Yang et al. [2] proposed that IG is one of the most effective feature selection algorithms. Currently IG has become a commonly used algorithm, so it is significant to improve the efficiency of feature selection by finding the deficiencies of IG method and making effective improvements.

In recent years, some research works have been finished to improve the efficiency of the IG algorithms. Based on term frequency, the traditional IG method was improved from three aspects: word frequency, within-class item distribution and between-class item distribution [3]. However, the unbalanced data set was not considered. Guo et al. [4] introduced the dispersion within the class, the concentration among categories and

C.-Y. Lin et al. (Eds.): NLPCC-ICCPOL 2016, LNAI 10102, pp. 559–567, 2016.
DOI: 10.1007/978-3-319-50496-4_49

scale factor into the traditional IG method to improve the classification effect. However impacts that different corpus set have on classification results were ignored. Xu et al. [5] improved the conventional IG algorithm was by taking reducing the impact of unbalanced data sets and low-frequency characteristics, the frequency distribution of features within category and the frequency distribution of document with features among different categories into account. However, the frequency distribution of document with features among different categories reduced classification accuracy when categories of the data set were unbalanced. Therefore, this paper proposed an improved IG method based on relative document frequency distribution, which replaced the frequency distribution of document with features among different categories with the relative frequency distribution of document.

2 Information Gain

Information Gain (IG) is a text feature selection algorithm based on information entropy, which refers to the difference between the information entropy produced by a feature item in the text or not [6]. The greater the difference is, the stronger the classification ability of the feature item is. Some significant words whose IG value is greater are selected from every characteristic in training set [7]:

$$
\begin{aligned}
IG(w) = &- \sum_i P(C_i) \log P(C_i) + P(w) \sum_i P(C_i|w) \log P(C_i|w) \\
&+ P(\bar{w}) \sum_i P(C_i|\bar{w}) \log P(C_i|\bar{w})
\end{aligned}
\tag{1}
$$

Where $P(w)$ is the probability that word w occurs in formula (1), $\bar{w}$ means that word w does not occur, $P(C_i)$ is the probability of the ith class value, $P(C_i|w)$ is the conditional probability of the ith class value given that w occurs, while $P(C_i|\bar{w})$) is the conditional probability of the ith class value given that word w does not occur.

3 An Improved Information Gain Algorithm Based on Relative Document Frequency Distribution

Selecting suitable feature set will be able to increase the performance of the text classifier [8]. According to the analysis of the first formula, the main problem of the traditional IG is that it emphasizes on the contribution to the features on the classification of the whole system rather than being specific to a certain category. This issue forces all the categories to use the same "global" collection of characteristics. The frequency distribution of document with features among different categories proposed by Xu et al. [5] reduced classification accuracy when categories of the data set were unbalanced. To address the above problem, this paper tries to provide a better solution.

3.1 Feature Selection by Categories

According to the above analysis, the IG algorithm tends to select the feature of the whole data set. In particular, the problem becomes more serious when the data set category distribution is unbalanced. In order to solve this problem, first IG value of each feature in each category is calculated. Then IG value of each category is sorted in descending order and top-n words are selected. Finally top-n words of each category are selected and combined to make the final feature vector.

In the merge feature, redundant features may appear in more than one class. In order to solve this problem, an optimization method was put forward that the highest threshold ratio of categories containing repeat feature was set [5]. In this paper the ratio is set to be 100%. That is to say, there are three categories in a data set, if a feature appears repeatedly in more than three categories, it should be deleted. This optimized method makes feature vector have a high discrimination in the process of text classification.

3.2 Reducing the Impact of Unbalanced Data Sets

According to the traditional IG method, when the data set is seriously unbalanced, the IG value of the feature words will be significantly reduced, which has a negative impact on the feature selection. Based on this issue, Professor Yang et al. [2] conducted deep studies about feature selection algorithms of English text categorization. The improved IG feature selection proposed by him is as follow:

$$IG(w) = P(w) \sum_i P(C_i|w) \log \frac{P(C_i|w)}{P(C_i)} + P(\bar{w}) \sum_i P(C_i|\bar{w}) \log \frac{P(C_i|\bar{w})}{P(C_i)} \quad (2)$$

3.3 Reducing the Impact of the Low-Frequency Characteristics

Information gain feature selection method considers the presence or absence of a term in a document, so the effect is significant in the removal of "useless words". When the feature does not appear, the contribution to text categorization is much less than backdrop. Especially in the case of highly unequal distribution of categories and features, the probability that the low-frequency words do not appear is much larger than the that of emergence, that is to say $P(w) \gg P(\bar{w})$. So it is very necessary to reduce the proportion of the non appearance of the characteristic words. The improved formula is as follow [9]:

$$IG(w) = P(w)(\sum_i P(C_i|w) \log \frac{P(C_i|w)}{P(C_i)} + \sum_i P(C_i|\bar{w}) \log \frac{P(C_i|\bar{w})}{P(C_i)}) \quad (3)$$

3.4   Within-Class Word Frequency Distribution

In the same category, the more uniform distribution of the feature of each text is, the stronger the classification ability of the feature becomes. Therefore, the concept of sample variance is introduced, and the essence of sample variance in statistics is to reflect the degree of dispersion among samples. It is supposed that the frequency that feature $w_j(1 \leq j \leq m)$ appears in the document $d_{ik}(1 \leq k \leq N_i)$ of category $C_i(1 \leq i \leq n)$ is $f_{ik}(w_j)$. So that the variance of word frequency that a feature w_j appears in all the texts of the same category C_i is as follow:

$$\alpha_j = \sqrt{\frac{1}{N_i - 1} \sum_{K=1}^{N_i} \left[f_{ik}(w_j) - \frac{1}{N_i - 1} \sum_{K=1}^{N_i} f_{ik}(w_j) \right]^2} \tag{4}$$

As the variance of word frequency in every document has an inverse relationship with the feature's ability of classification. Normalization process and necessary correction is applied to the parameter α_j:

$$\alpha = 1 - \frac{a_j}{\sqrt{\sum_{j=1}^{m} \alpha_j^2}} \tag{5}$$

3.5   Between-Class Features Selection Based on Relative Document Frequency Distribution

3.5.1   Limitations of Features Selection Based on Absolute Document Frequency Distribution

Xu et al. [5] pointed out that the difference of between-class document frequency distribution of the feature also reflects the ability to classify categories. The bigger the sample variance of the number of the documents that the word appears, the better classification results of the word is. Assume the number of texts of all categories $C_i(1 \leq i \leq n)$ in which word $w_j(1 \leq j \leq m)$ appears to be $f_{C_i}(w_j)$, so that the variance of document frequency of each category C_i that feature w_j appears is as follow:

$$\beta_j = \sqrt{\frac{1}{n - 1} \sum_{i=1}^{n} [f_{C_i}(w_j) - \frac{1}{n - 1} \sum_{i=1}^{n} f_{C_i}(w_j)]^2} \tag{6}$$

Then, normalization process is applied to the parameter β_j:

$$\beta = \frac{\beta_j}{\sqrt{\sum_{j=1}^{m} \beta_j^2}} \tag{7}$$

Assuming that there are, 4 categories. Feature, document and category information distribution is shown in Table 1:

Table 1. Features and documents information

Category	Number of document in C_i	Number of document with w_1 in C_i	Number of document with w_2 in C_i
C_1	100	50	95
C_2	200	100	100
C_3	400	200	150
C_4	800	400	200

The formula (6) is used to calculate the sample variance of the document frequency of w_1 or w_2 each category. The result is that $\beta_1 = 154.78 > \beta_2 = 49.22$. It is concluded that the classification ability of w_1 is stronger than that of w_2.

However, as is shown in the Table 1, distribution of the 4 categories is seriously unbalanced. Although the document frequency of w_1 in C_4 is more than other three categories, all the 4 categories contains the documents with w_1 accounting for 50%, that is to say, documents containing w_1 are evenly distributed in 4 categories with the same proportion, so the classification ability of w_1 is not strong. However, in the 4 categories, documents containing w_2 accounted for respectively 95%, 50%, 37.5%, 25%. Apparently, proportion of the document containing w_2 in C_1 is the highest, accordingly, the classification ability of w_2 is stronger. Therefore, the classification ability of w_2 is stronger than that of w_1, that is to say, the conclusion drawn by Xu et al. [5] is not very accurate in the case of uneven distribution of the data set, and even cause serious disturbance to the classification. When the category distribution of data set is seriously unbalanced, We tend to choose these features contained by documents whose quantity instead of proportion is lager in a class. As a result, a text that does not belong to a class is divided into the class by mistake.

3.5.2 Advantages of Features Selection Based on Relative Document Frequency Distribution

In order to eliminate negative effects brought by between-class absolute document frequency distribution of features, this paper proposed a method that the frequency distribution of document with features among different categories is replaced with the relative frequency distribution of document. Assume the proportion of texts of all categories $C_i(1 \leq i \leq n)$ in which word $w_j(1 \leq j \leq m)$ appears to be $rdff_{C_i}(w_j)$. The relative document frequency is as follow [10]:

$$rdff_{C_i}(w_j) = \frac{f_{C_i}(w_j)}{N_i} \bigg/ \sum_{i=1}^{n} \frac{f_{C_i}(w_j)}{N_i} \qquad (8)$$

So that the variance of relative document frequency of each category C_i that feature w_j appears is as follow:

$$RDF\beta_j = \sqrt{\frac{1}{n-1} \sum_{i=1}^{n} \left[rdff_{C_i}(w_j) - \frac{1}{n-1} \sum_{i=1}^{n} rdff_{C_i}(w_j) \right]^2} \qquad (9)$$

Then, normalization process is applied to the parameter $RDF\beta_j$:

$$RDF\beta = \frac{RDF\beta_j}{\sqrt{\sum_{j=1}^{m} RDF\beta_j^2}} \qquad (10)$$

For Table 1, the formula (9) is used to calculate the sample variance of the relative document frequency of w_1 or w_2 each category. The result is that $RDF\beta_1 = 0 < RDF\beta_2 = 0.15$. It is concluded that the classification ability of w_2 is stronger than that of w_1. Thus, while the absolute document frequency distribution of the class is replaced, the limitation of the absolute document frequency distribution of the characteristic words is overcome.

In summary, on the basis of the improved formula (3), within-class word frequency distribution and between-class relative document frequency distribution of features are both joined to get the following improvements:

$$rdfnewIG(w) = \alpha \times RDF\beta \times P(w)(\sum_i P(C_i|w)\log\frac{P(C_i|w)}{P(C_i)}$$

$$+ \sum_i P(C_i|\bar{w})\log\frac{P(C_i|\bar{w})}{P(C_i)}) \qquad (11)$$

4 Experiment Results and Analysis

Three feature selection methods are verified and analyzed, including the traditional information gain feature selection method, an improved methods in [5] and an improved algorithm proposed in this paper. Java platform is used to implement the comparison of three methods. The experimental data come from NLPCC-ICCPOL 2016 Chinese Microblogs stance detection corpus, which includes three categories: Against (C1), Favor (C2) and None (C3).

4.1 Experimental Procedure

Firstly, 1200 Microblogs of C1, 800 Microblogs of C2, 600 Microblogs of C3 are extracted from NLPCC-ICCPOL 2016 Chinese Microblogs stance detection Task_A corpus being an unbalanced training set and 1000 Microblogs of Task_A_gold in test_data_gold being the testing set. Secondly, ICTCLAS is used to do segmentation of words [11]. After word segmentation, stop words will be removed and bag of words model can be built. Thirdly, three methods are used respectively to calculate every feature of the training set. Fourthly, top 2000 features respectively from four algorithms are chosen to build 2000-dimensional feature vector space. Fifthly, map all the documents in the unbalanced training set and the testing set to the 2000-dimensional feature vector space. Sixthly, TFIDF algorithm [12] is used to calculate the weight value of each characteristic of vector space, and the calculation results are converted into libsvm corpus format [13]. In the end, support vector machine (SVM) is used to perform classification experiments, where radial basis kernel function of libsvm is adopted.

4.2 Evaluation Criterion

In this paper, the F_{avg} (macro-average F value) of $F_{against}$ and F_{favor} is used as the bottom-line evaluation metric. The calculation is as follow:

$$F_{against} = \frac{2 \times P_{against} \times R_{against}}{P_{against} + R_{against}} \qquad (12)$$

$$F_{favor} = \frac{2 \times P_{favor} \times R_{favor}}{P_{favor} + R_{favor}} \qquad (13)$$

$$F_{avg} = \frac{F_{against} + F_{favor}}{2} \qquad (14)$$

Where $R_{against}$ and $P_{against}$, are recall and precision of stance detection of category Against, R_{favor} and P_{favor}, are recall and precision of stance detection of category Favor.

4.3 Experiments Results Analysis and Comparison

The experimental results of traditional IG algorithm, improved IG algorithm of [5] and improved IG algorithm of this paper are shown in Table 2, and F_{AVG} of these three algorithms as shown in Fig. 1:

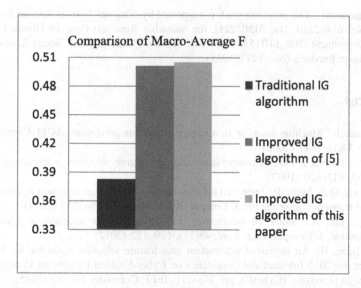

Fig. 1. Macro-average F value of three IG feature selection algorithms

Table 2. The experiment results of traditional IG

Feature selection algorithm	$F_{against}$	F_{favor}	F_{avg}
Traditional IG algorithm	0.63971	0.12579	0.38275
Improved IG algorithm of [5]	0.64298	0.35932	0.50115
Improved IG algorithm of this paper	0.64039	0.36949	0.50494

As is shown in Table 2, comparing with traditional IG, F_{avg} of Improved IG algorithm of [5] improves 0.11840, and F_{avg} of Improved IG algorithm of this paper improves 0.12219.

As the training set is unbalanced, it can be seen from Fig. 1 that for each category, macro-average F value of our method is higher than the value of the other two algorithms.

5   Conclusions and Future Work

Based on the analysis of the improved IG algorithm in recent years, this paper has overcome the shortcomings of the traditional IG algorithm. What is more, considering side effects brought by between-class absolute document frequency distribution of features in [5], between-class relative document frequency distribution of features put forward by this paper further reduce the disturbance caused by the unbalanced training set and improve the performance of classification. It can be seen from the experimental results, compared with the traditional algorithm and another improved algorithm, our method has better performance on macro-average F value in the unbalanced training set. The further work is to combine information gain algorithm and semantic understanding to get better classification results.

Acknowledgements. This research work is supported by National Natural Science Foundation of China (No. 61402220, No. 61502221), the Scientific Research Fund of Hunan Provincial Education Department (No. 14B153, No. 16C1378), the Philosophy and Social Science Foundation of Hunan Province (No. 14YBA335).

References

1. Sebastiani, F.: Machine learning in automated text categorization. ACM Comput. Surv. (CSUR) **34**(1), 1–47 (2002)
2. Yang, Y., Pedersen, J.O.: A comparative study on feature selection in text categorization. ICML **97**, 412–420 (1997)
3. Shi, H., Jia, D.P., Miao, P.: Improved information gain text feature selection algorithm based on word frequency information. J. Comput. Appl. **34**(11), 3279–3282 (2014)
4. Guo, Y., Liu, X.: Study on information gain-based feature selection in Chinese text categorization. J. Comput. Eng. Appl. **48**(27), 119–122 (2012)
5. Xu, J., Jiang, H.: An improved information gain feature selection algorithm for SVM text classifier. In: 2015 International Conference on Cyber-Enabled Distributed Computing and Knowledge Discovery (CyberC), pp. 273–276. IEEE Computer Society (2015)

6. Xu, Y., Chen, L.: Term-frequency based feature selection methods for text categorization. In: Proceedings of the 2010 Fourth International Conference on Genetic and Evolutionary Computing, pp. 280–283. IEEE Press, Piscataway (2010)
7. Mladenic, D., Grobelnk, M.: Feature selection for unbalanced class distribution and naive Bayes. In: Proceedings of the Sixteenth International Conference on Machine Learning, ICML 1999, pp. 258–267. ACM Press, New York (1999)
8. Forman, G., Guyon, I., Elisseeff, A.: An extensive empirical study of feature selection metrics for text classification. J. Mach. Learn. Res. 3, 1289–1305 (2003)
9. Ren, Y.G.: Information-gain-based text feature selection method. J. Comput. Sci. 39(11), 127–130 (2012)
10. Ren, K.Q.: Feature reduction based on relative document frequency balance information gain. J. Jiangxi Univ. Sci. Technol. 29(5), 68–71 (2008)
11. Zhang, H.P., Yu, H.K., Xiong, D.Y., Liu, Q.: HHMM-based Chinese lexical analyzer ICTCLAS. In: Proceedings of the Second SIGHAN Workshop on Chinese Language Processing, vol. 17, pp. 184–187. Association for Computational Linguistics (2003)
12. Shi, C., Xu, C., Yang, X.: Study of TFIDF algorithm. J. Comput. Appl. 6(29), 167–170 (2009)
13. Chang, G.C.C., Lin, C.J.: LIBSVM: a library for support vector machines. ACM Trans. Intell. Syst. Technol. (TIST) 2(3), 27 (2011)

Finding the True Crowds: User Filtering in Microblogs

Bin Hao[1(✉)], Min Zhang[1], Weizhi Ma[1], Jiashen Sun[2], Yiqun Liu[1], Shaoping Ma[1], Xuan Zhu[2], and Hengliang Luo[2]

[1] Tsinghua National Laboratory for Information Science and Technology, Department of Computer Science and Technology, Tsinghua University, Beijing, China {haob15,mawz14}@mails.tsinghua.edu.cn, {z-m,yiqunliu,msp}@tsinghua.edu.cn
[2] Samsung R&D Institute, Beijing, China {jiashens.sun,xuan.zhu,hl.luo}@samsung.com

Abstract. Nowadays users like to share their opinions towards a product/service or policy in social media, which is important to the manufacturers and governments to collect feedbacks from the crowds. While in microblogs, information is highly unbalanced that lots of posts are published and spread by ghost-writers/spammers, sellers, official accounts, etc., but information provided by the true crowds is overwhelmed frequently. Previous studies mostly concern on how to find one specific type of users; but do not investigate how to filter multiple types of specific users so as to keep only the true crowds, which is the main topic of this work. In this paper, we first show the categorization on four different types of users, namely *ghost-writers*, *sellers*, *official accounts* and *end-users* (the former three are noted as a broad sense *advertisers* in the paper), and study their characteristics. Then we propose a Topic-Specific Divergence based model to filter out *advertisers* so that *end-users* can be kept. Meta-information, content are investigated in comparative analysis. Encouraging experimental results on real dataset clearly verify that the proposed approach outperforms the state-of-art methods significantly.

Keywords: User filtering · Topic-Specific Divergence

1 Introduction

Nowadays users like to share their opinions towards a product/service or policy in social media, which is important to the manufacturers and governments to collect feedbacks from the crowds. While in most work of finding users' opinion via microblog platform for market research or government policy feedback, voices from opinion leaders, who have millions of followers, have been paid much attention to due to their influences. But we believe that at any time, voices from the true crowds (leaders and ordinary people) should be concerned carefully. Their feedback is definitely important for business intelligence, for example, as real end-users.

It is not an easy task to capture the ordinary users' information because in social media platforms, information is greatly unbalanced in different aspects, such as the

© Springer International Publishing AG 2016
C.-Y. Lin et al. (Eds.): NLPCC-ICCPOL 2016, LNAI 10102, pp. 568–574, 2016.
DOI: 10.1007/978-3-319-50496-4_50

number of followers, counts of published posts, etc. There are lots of ghost-writers, spammers, advertisers, and official accounts, who are more active compared with common end-users, especially in business related topics. In previous work, researchers focused on detecting spammers, finding experts, identifying lurkers, or discovering hot spots in breaking events. While to the best of our knowledge, this is the first attempt to filter out the multiple types of special users so as to find the true crowds.

In this paper, we first give a categorization on different users and study their characteristics, based on which useful features and proper algorithms are possibly designed. Then a Topic-Specific Divergence based approach is proposed to filter out non-end-users. To verify the effectiveness of the approach, comparative experiments have been made with the state-of-arts user filtering and classification algorithms on a real microblog dataset. Another contribution of this work is that we show it possible to filter multiple types of special users by taking subtopic-level content information into consideration.

2 Related Work

Spammer detection in social network has been widely studied in recent years. Despite of using single type features such as network attributes [2] and content information [8], current major trend is to combine multiple features [5]. In [9], user behavior information is also introduced. Furthermore, motivated by psychological findings, sentiments are also incorporated [4]. The findings inspire us to find effective feature to preprocess our dataset.

On another point of view, some researchers try to find domain experts in social networks. Link-based approaches such as PageRank-like algorithm achieves encouraging results. Community detection and topical authorities are also helpful on such tasks. Interestingly Meta-information is put in, such as user tags [10], twitter list names and descriptions [3], etc. Topic-specific notion is emphasized in some researches [6]. Another noticeable point is that many features used in expert finding are different with those in spammer detection.

Research on finding lurkers has been made during these years. The reason Why lurkers lurk is expounded [7]. Classification and link-based approach have been applied to find lurkers in social network.

Microblog Hot Spot Mining is also partially related to our work. Keywords frequency, patterns and topic models are the popular factors taken into account [1]. Context-sensitive information and sentiment information are also proposed to be integrated.

3 Categorization of Users in Microblogs

3.1 Categorization of Microblog Users

We propose a four-type category for Microblog users as follows:

- *Ghost-writer*: the user whose purpose is to put forward some specific information, such as product promotion, rubbishing the competitor, and in most cases, is paid for the designated information sharing behavior. Spammer is also included in this class.

- **Seller**: the user who takes social media as an advertising platform to attract others for further purchase.
- **Official account**: the account that is maintained by an organization/institute/ company, etc.
- **End-user**: the common user of a given topic, who is a part of the true crowds, no matter whether he/she is an expert on the domain, a big fan or abominator to a product/company, or just a man in the street. In real scenarios, an end-user is easily confused with skilled ghost-writer or seller.

The key idea of this paper is to identify and filter out the former three types of specific users, so that only the true crowds will be retained for consequent analysis. To simplify the representation, we would like to call the former three types of users in a broad sense **"advertisers"** according to their different advertisement intention to a specific topic. Sometimes they are also named as **"non-end-users"** for diverse representation purpose in the paper.

4 Unified Filtering Model for Advertisers

4.1 Study on Non-content Features

To construct an effective unified model that can filtering all types of *advertisers*, a set of useful features should be designed, which are able to separate *end-users* to the others. Firstly, the characteristics of different features for the four types of users are studied. Figure 1 shows the comparative analyses in terms of Meta information including verification and years since registration, number of followers and followees respectively, and average number of daily posts.

According to the figures, *end-users* act differently with part of *advertisers* in varies conditions. For example, *end-users* and *ghost-writers* have significant difference in terms of **verification info** and **years since registration**; on **average number of daily**

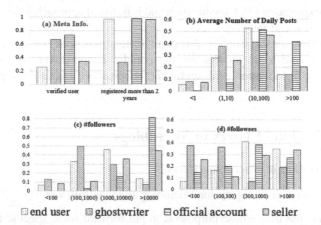

Fig. 1. Characteristics of different types of users on: (a) Meta info. (b) Avg. #dailyPosts (c) #followers (d) #followees

posts, *end-users* are not distinct from *ghost-writers* and *sellers*, but varies to *official accounts*; according to features of **#followers**, official accounts can be clearly separated from the others; while **#followees** helps detect *ghost-writers*. Generally speaking, *ghost-writers* and *official accounts* are relatively easier to be detect by various features.

We also find that **keywords in user name** contains very important information, especially for *official accounts* and *sellers*. For example, some sellers use "海淘", "代购" in their name, or the entities like "报", "公司" give strong signals on the official account of institute.

4.2 Topic-Specific Divergence (TSD)

Further, borrowing idea of how human beings identify *end-users* from others, **content information** should also be taken into consideration. The basic intuition is that *end-users* generally like to share diverse topics, while *advertisers* are more focused due to specific intentions. While directly use content similarity within a user's posts may derive problems, because *ghost-writers* and *official accounts* likewise publish different content with similar meanings. Therefore, identification based on posts-similarity in user-level is not effective. We solve the problem on another viewpoint: the extension of topic-level similarity, shown as follows:

1. Posts are organized as subtopics based on content similarity. Bag of words based Cosine similarity is a good and fundamental choice. Hierarchical clustering is performed to generate subtopics.
2. Then **Subtopic entropy** is calculated by:

$$Entropy_i = \sum_{u \in i} -p_{ui} \log p_{ui}, \quad p_{ui} = N_{ui} \bigg/ \sum_{u \in i} N_{ui} \tag{1}$$

Where u is a user whose post(s) have been assigned into the subtopic i. Note that one user's posts may belong to different subtopics. p_{ui} is calculated by maximum likelihood estimation, and N_{ui} is the number of posts in subtopic i that is published by the user u. Lower $Entropy_i$ implies higher possibility of advertisements.

3. Furthermore, the value of subtopic entropy is naturally sensitive to the number of users involved in the subtopic. Given two subtopics i and j, related users numbers M_i and M_j, and numbers of posts in two subtopics N_i and N_j, respectively. If each post is published by a different user in both subtopics (i.e. $M_i = N_i$ and $M_j = N_j$), both $Entropy_i$ and $Entropy_j$ will achieve their maximum values. However the two scores would be totally different if M_i and M_j varies greatly. To reduce such sensitivity, normalized subtopic entropy is proposed.

We define **Topic-Specific Divergence (TSD)** by normalized subtopic entropy, shown as:

$$TSD_i = \begin{cases} Entropy_i \ (= 0) & \text{if } N_i = 1 \\ Entropy_i/IdealEntropy_i & otherwise \end{cases} \tag{2}$$

Where **IdealEntropy$_i$** is the ideal subtopic entropy that assume each post in the sub-topic i is published by a different user, namely no matter whatever original N_{ui} is, let $N_{ui}' = 1$ and $M_i' = N_i$, and then use the new N_{ui}' and M_i' to calculate the subtopic entropy.

According to the definition of *IdealEntropy$_i$*:

$$IdealEntropy_i = \sum -\frac{1}{N_i}\log\frac{1}{N_i} \tag{3}$$

Adding Eqs. (1) and (3) into Eq. (2), we have

$$TSD_i = \begin{cases} 0 & \text{if } N_i = 1 \\ -\dfrac{1}{N_i \log N_i}\sum_{u\in i} N_{ui}\log\dfrac{N_{ui}}{\sum\limits_{u\in i} N_{ui}} & otherwise \end{cases} \tag{4}$$

Since $\sum\limits_{u\in i} N_{ui} = N_i$, Finally the TSD is given by:

$$TSD_i = \begin{cases} 0 & \text{if } N_i = 1 \\ 1 - \sum\limits_{u\in i} N_{ui}\log N_{ui} \Big/ N_i \log N_i & otherwise \end{cases} \tag{5}$$

After normalization, *TSD$_i$* ranges from 0 to 1. Then different subtopics can be fairly compared. Lower *TSD* implies higher possibility of the subtopic being generated by advertisers in the viewpoint of content information.

4.3   Advertisers Filtering Model

As shown in Sect. 4.2, Topic-Specific Divergence (TSD) is calculated in topic-level. Since different users can be connected to multiple topics according to their published posts, it is nature to generate a topic-related advertiser score S_{ui} for each user u in the subtopic i, and then combine all the scores collected from different subtopics to generate a final advertising score of the user, S_u.

A heuristic formulation is leveraged in this work, taking the impact factors into consideration, based on their relationship of the advertising possibility, including inverted *TSD$_i$* score (the higher divergence for the subtopic, the less possible to be advertisement/promotions), inner-subtopic similarity *ITS$_i$* as weighting factor for the subtopic, and the number of a users' posts within a subtopic, N_{ui}, as the weighting factor for the user inside the subtopic. Hence final advertiser scoring equation is represented as:

$$S_u = \begin{cases} \sum_{topic\ i} ITS_i * \quad (1 - \frac{TSD_i}{\alpha}) * \log(N_i * N_{ui}), & if\ TSD_i < \alpha \\ 0, & otherwise \end{cases} \quad (6)$$

where α is the threshold which is set to **0.85** in our experiments. Then users can be ranked by their advertiser scores and top ranked ones could be filtered to keep the true crowds.

5 Comparative Experimental Analysis

We random selected and labeled 4,554 users from the dataset crawled from Weibo (30,389 users and). The post number of these users is 18,731. There are 2,522 *end-users* and 2,032 *non-end-users* in this dataset.

In our experiment, we apply 5-fold cross validation to derive the average Precision, Recall and F-score.

Then experiments are made on the dataset with different classification algorithms, such as SVM, Decision Tree, Bayes Net, Native Bayes and Random Forest. Results that only use the features in Sect. 4.1 (say, using non-TSD features) are taken as baselines. Comparative analyses are made on these baselines and the corresponding algorithms + TSD. The classification result for identify non-end-users is shown in Table 1.

Table 1. Classification results for identify *non-end-users*

Methods	Precision	Recall	F-score
J48	0.860	0.785	0.821
BayesNet	0.836	0.783	0.809
NativeBayes	0.947	0.552	0.697
SVM	0.965	0.545	0.697
RandomForest	0.860	0.795	0.826
J48 + TSD	0.875	0.790	0.830
BayesNet + TSD	0.865	0.783	0.822
NativeBayes + TSD	0.951	0.596	0.733
SVM + TSD	**0.971**	0.591	0.735
RandomForest + TSD	0.936	**0.798**	**0.862**

It is shown that TSD filtering method can effectively improve the performance on the total sample dataset. It is because that TSD filtering method can effectively identify Weibo users who published low quality Weibo posts.

6 Conclusions and Future Work

In this paper we propose the problem of finding the true crowds in microblogs, investigate the categorization and characteristics of different user types, and provide an effective solution based on the novel Topic-Specific Divergence based unified model. It is the first time to filter out mixed types of microblog users, including ghost-writers, sellers and official accounts. In the future, more theoretical analyses will be made on finding stronger models. Furthermore, the consequent common user profiling is also a reasonable and interesting research direction.

References

1. Chen, Y., Xu, B., Hao, H., Zhou, S., Cao, J.: User-defined hot topic detection in microblogging. In: Proceedings of the Fifth International Conference on Internet Multimedia Computing and Service, pp. 183–186. ACM (2013)
2. Danezis, G., Mittal, P.: Sybilinfer: detecting sybil nodes using social networks. In: NDSS the Internet Society (2009)
3. Ghosh, S., Sharma, N., Benevenuto, F., Ganguly, N., Gummadi, K.: Cognos: crowdsourcing search for topic experts in microblogs. In: Proceedings of the 35th International ACM SIGIR Conference on Research and Development in Information Retrieval, pp. 575–590. ACM (2012)
4. Hu, X., Tang, J., Gao, H., Liu, H.: Social spammer detection with sentiment information. In: 2014 IEEE International Conference on Data Mining (ICDM), pp. 180–189. IEEE (2014)
5. Hu, X., Tang, J., Liu, H.: Online social spammer detection. In: AAAI, pp. 59–65 (2014)
6. Li, Y., Li, W., Li, S.: A hierarchical knowledge representation for expert finding on social media. In: Proceedings of the 53rd Annual Meeting of the Association for Computational Linguistics and the 7th International Joint Conference on Natural Language Processing (Short Papers), pp. 616–622 (2015)
7. Nonnecke, B., Preece, J.: Why lurkers lurk. In: Paper presented at the Americas Conference on Information Systems, Boston (2001)
8. Liu, L., Jia, K.: Detecting spam in chinese microblogs-a study on Sina Weibo. In: 2012 Eighth International Conference on Computational Intelligence and Security (CIS), pp. 578–581. IEEE (2012)
9. Liu, Y., Wu, B., Wang, B., Li, G.: SDHM: a hybrid model for spammer detection in Weibo. In: 2014 IEEE/ACM International Conference on Advances in Social Networks Analysis and Mining (ASONAM), pp. 942–947 (2014)
10. Tagarelli, A., Interdonato, R.: "Who's out there?" Identifying and ranking lurkers in social networks. 2013 IEEE/ACM International Conference on Advances in Social Networks Analysis and Mining (ASONAM), pp. 215–222. IEEE (2013)

Learning to Recognize Protected Health Information in Electronic Health Records with Recurrent Neural Network

Kun Li[1(✉)], Yumei Chai[1], Hongling Zhao[2], Xiaofei Nan[1], and Yueshu Zhao[2,3]

[1] Information Engineering School, Zhengzhou University, Zhengzhou, China
likun@stu.zzu.edu.cn, {ieymchai,iexfnan}@zzu.edu.cn
[2] Collaborative Innovation Center for Internet Healthcare,
Zhengzhou University, Zhengzhou, China
hlzhaozzu@163.com, zyswr@163.com
[3] Hospital of Zhengzhou University, Zhengzhou, China

Abstract. De-identification in electronic health records is a prerequisite to distribute medical records for further clinical data processing or mining. In this paper, we introduce a framework based on recurrent neural network to solve the de-identification problem, and compare state-of-the-art methods with our framework. It is integrated, which includes records skeleton generation, chunk representation and protected information labeling. We evaluate our framework on three datasets involving two English datasets from i2b2 de-identification challenge and a Chinese dataset we created. To the best of our knowledge, we are the first to apply RNN model to the Chinese de-identification problem. The experimental results indicate that our framework not only achieves high performance but also has strong generalization ability.

Keywords: De-identification · Electronic Health Record · Recurrent Neural Network

1 Introduction

Electronic Health Records (EHRs) are generated in hospitals every day. These records are valuable research resources because of the abundant information they contain. However, these data cannot be easily accessed by researchers or organizations for a large amount of protected health information existed in EHRs. Therefore de-identification of such data is a prerequisite for using EHRs out of hospitals.

Early in 1996, Sweeney proposed the first de-identification system by a rule-based approach [1]. In the same year in United States, the Health Insurance Portability and Accountability Act (HIPAA) was passed. The HIPAA defines 18 categories of protected health information (PHI), which must be removed from clinical data before it can be considered safely de-identified. These categories include patients' names, ID numbers, dates, locations, etc. Since then, many pattern-matching-based and data-driven systems have been introduced [2]. These systems used complex heuristic rules and domain-specific dictionaries to perform de-identification.

© Springer International Publishing AG 2016
C.-Y. Lin et al. (Eds.): NLPCC-ICCPOL 2016, LNAI 10102, pp. 575–582, 2016.
DOI: 10.1007/978-3-319-50496-4_51

To accelerate EHRs de-identification research, the 2006 i2b2 de-identification challenge firstly provided a unified platform to evaluate different systems [3]. Eight PHI categories were defined in this challenge to annotate the data from Partner Healthcare. The competing systems include rule-based [4] and statistic-based methods. Some of the submissions viewed the challenge as a problem of classification of tokens. Others viewed it as a sequence labeling problem. These methods include Hidden Markov Models, Conditional Random Fields [5], Support Vector Machines [6], and Decision Trees [7]. The results showed that machine learning-based systems performed the best [3].

Along with some recent studies [8], researchers reached an agreement that it is necessary to build a stricter standard than HIPAA. To achieve the goal, the 2014 i2b2 de-identification challenge for longitudinal clinical narratives focused on 25 PHI types, inclusive of 12 types as defined by HIPAA [9, 10]. Some well performed systems which are submitted to 2014 i2b2 de-identification track, employed Conditional Random Fields mixed with dictionaries and regular expressions [11, 12]. Dernoncourt et al. [13] introduced the first de-identification based on ANN and achieved state-of-the-art results on two English datasets.

In this paper, we propose a new framework to solve the de-identification challenge. The framework uses Recurrent Neural Network (RNN) [14] to recognize protected information in EHRs. Without any structure change, the framework works well on 2006 i2b2 de-identification dataset, 2014 i2b2 de-identification dataset and a Chinese EHR dataset we annotated ourselves. Especially on the Chinese dataset, our framework achieved a micro-averaged F1-score of 0.98.

2   De-Identification with Recurrent Neural Network

Our de-identification framework mainly consists of three parts—skeleton generation, chunk representation and sequence labeling. Each part has strong generalization ability as no dictionaries or hand-made rules are used.

2.1   Records Preprocessing and Skeleton Generation

Compared with common articles, EHRs have more short sentences and abbreviations. Moreover, in some categories of EHRs, there are a great number of table-like texts and special writing formats. Figure 1 presents a snippet of an EHR, the PHIs are mainly in the first three lines of the snippet with short sentences. "BCH" is a location, "HESS, CLARENCE" is a patient's name, "643-65-59-5" is an ID, "2060-10-11" and "10/11/60" are simulative dates.

In many traditional named entity recognition tasks, a named entity is recognized by sentence. If we still use sentence scale context in EHRs de-identification, many sentences will just consist of one or two words. Especially in some extreme cases, the whole sentence is a PHI instance. To address this insufficient context problem, we concatenate all sentences of a record to a long sentence, adding a "#RETURN" symbol between each two sentences. After concatenation, the snippet in Fig. 1 is processed to

---

Record date: 2060-10-11
BCH EMERGENCY DEPT VISIT
HESS,CLARENCE   643-65-59-5   VISIT DATE: 10/11/60

HISTORY OF PRESENTING COMPLAINT: The patient is a 46 year old male with complaints of chest pain and throat tightness.

Fig. 1. A snippet of an EHR

"Record date: 2060-10-11 #RETURN BCH EMERGENCY DEPT VISIT #RETURN HESS,CLARENCE 643-65-59-5 VISIT DATE: 10/11/60…". Thus, the local structure is presented in single line, which the line is sequentially scanned by context windows.

As the formats in EHRs are more special than traditional text, the skeleton of a record, which is beneficial to protect information recognition, is extracted to help RNNs learn. We propose a statistical approach to extract the skeletons of records, which the skeletons reveal the different format and punctuation usage between corpuses. Specifically, only words occurring in training set over t times retain and the others are marked as <UNK>. Different skeletons, that contain various amount of information, can be obtained by tuning t. However, in practice, the range of t is imponderable, thus we propose a way to establish the value of t as Eq. (1). Here *vocabSize* is the size of vocabulary of the dataset, f_i is the number of words which have the frequency equal to i, *maxFreq* is the maximum frequency. r is a factor between 0 and 1, it determines the dictionary size of the skeleton approximately. Thus appropriate value of t can be obtained by tuning r.

$$t = \operatorname*{argmin}_{n} | \sum_{i=1}^{n} f_i - r * vocabSize |$$
$$s.t. \quad 0 < n < \max Freq$$
$$0 < r < 1$$
(1)

It avoid searching t in a large range by adopting Eq. (1) as the appropriate r often falls in a small range. In different datasets, the best t could be smaller than 15 or larger than 100 but the corresponding r frequently fall in between 0.05 to 0.2.

2.2   Chunk Representation Schemes

De-identification challenge is viewed as a sequence labeling task in this work, therefore, transforming the original tags to another appropriate representation scheme is an indispensable step. Five schemes are focused—multi-BIO, uni-BIO, multi-BILOU, multi-PO and uni-PO (the latter two are proposed in the paper). The "multi" prefix means that this type of token consists of multiple subtypes which correspond to multiple categories. For example, multi-BIO has several B labels like B-hospital, B-date, while the uni-BIO has only one B label. The PO scheme we introduce in this paper is similar to BIO. Without distinguishing **B**egin and **I**nside tokens, our PO

BIO scheme:

Mr.	HESS	was	seen	by	me	in	BCH	with	Dr.	Whittaker
B	I	O	O	O	O	O	B	O	B	I

PO scheme:

Mr.	HESS	was	seen	by	me	in	BCH	with	Dr.	Whittaker
P	P	O	O	O	O	O	P	O	P	P

Fig. 2. Comparison between BIO and PO

scheme annotates all PHI words with Protected tokens. Figure 2 shows the comparison of BIO and PO. This idea follows an intuition that in most cases the PHI will be removed after being recognized, thus, the details are inconsequential.

2.3 Sequence Labeling Using RNNs

RNNs are the central portion of our framework and the model we propose in this paper is summarized in Fig. 3. x' is the skeleton of record we have extracted, x is the text after it is preprocessed. Note that x and x' have the same length, but they are input into different branch of the network. The difference between forward RNN layer and backward RNN layer lies in whether the input is received by RNN in forward direction or backward direction. Finally, after the Softmax regression, each word in the sentence yields a corresponding label y_i in the output layer.

Once the word embeddings have been learned in an unsupervised fashion, fine-tuning them during supervised training on the task of interest is possible and have some advantages [17]. A dictionary, which is prepared for tuning embedding, should be built automatically based on the training data. All words embeddings are initialized

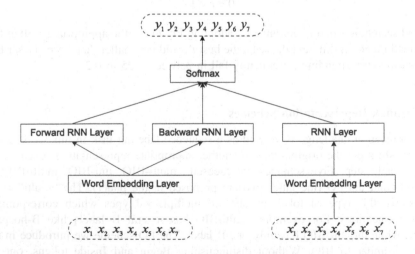

Fig. 3. Sequence labeling with RNNs

randomly before being tuned. As some previous works [18], all words with only one single occurrence in training set as well as unseen words in the test set are marked as <UNK>. Numbers both in training data and in test data are converted into the string DIGIT. For instance, the date "2060-10-11" we mentioned above will be converted to "DIGITDIGITDIGITDIGIT-DIGITDIGIT-DIGITDIGIT". This trick is adopted to reduce the size of the dictionary for a mass of numbers exist in EHRs.

The RNN layers (include forward RNN and backward RNN) can be viewed as any RNN architectures. We used standard RNN, LSTM [15] and GRU [16]. Finally, the reason why the Softmax regression is stacked upon the RNN layer is that the output labels are mutually exclusive. A label dictionary, which generative process can be combined with the automatic generation of word dictionary, is also indispensable to decide the output dimension of Softmax.

3 Experiments and Discussion

We evaluate the results at token-level and entity-level, which is the same as the evaluation method in i2b2 de-identification challenge [3, 10]. We also evaluate at binary token-level (PHI token versus non-PHI token) which is meaningful because it can show the integrity of EHRs distinctly after de-identification. Retaining the non-PHI is our primary target, and only integrated de-identified EHRs can be used for further research.

3.1 Datasets

We evaluate our framework on three datasets, which two English datasets are 2006 i2b2 de-identification challenge dataset [3] and 2014 i2b2 de-identification dataset [10], another one is a Chinese dataset we annotate ourselves. The Chinese EHRs come from a maternal and child health-care hospital consisting of 9700 medical records of 485 gravidas. The sizes of the datasets and the distributions of primary PHI categories are presented in Table 1.

3.2 Parameters of the Framework

Under subsets of i2b2 datasets, we obtained optimized parameters of the framework. Each kind of RNN layers can be applied to the sequence labeling stage presented in Fig. 3. Early-stopping is used to tune the parameters of RNNs on validation set (20% of the training data). Here is the overview of optimized parameters:

- r: 0.1 (corresponding t of i2b2-2006, i2b2-2014 and Chinese dataset are 20, 14 and 101)
- Tagging scheme: multi-BIO
- RNN architecture: LSTM
- Hidden dimension and Embedding dimension: 128
- Early-stopping: 5 epochs

Table 1. Overview of the datasets

	i2b2-2006	i2b2-2014	Chinese
Number of records	669	1304	9700
Number of tokens	560852	1005582	3026944
Number of PHIs	19498	28862	48072
Number of PHI tokens	29917	38435	137496
Vocabulary Size	20254	41879	32265
Percentage of ID	24.6%	3.6%	8.8%
Percentage of DATE	36.4%	43.2%	38.9%
Percentage of HOSPITAL	12.3%	8.0%	2.2%
Percentage of DOCTOR	19.2%	16.6%	14.7%
Percentage of PATIENT	4.7%	7.6%	17.3%
Percentage of AGE	0.1%	6.9%	16.1%

3.3   Performance on i2b2 Datasets

We compare our framework with state-of-the-art frameworks and models, Table 2 presents the binary token-based precisions, recalls and F1-scores. Wellner et al. [5] was the best system from the i2b2 2006 de-identification challenge. The Nottingham system [12], which was the winner of i2b2 2014 de-identification challenge, has no results on 2006 i2b2 dataset as it is not publicly available. MIST [19] is an off-the-shelf program for de-identification and CRF+ANN was proposed by Dernoncourt et al. [13]. CRF is the model based on Conditional Random Field, Uni-RNN and Bi-RNN are classic RNN-based models. RNN + Skeleton is the model we proposed in this work.

Table 2. Comparison of state-of-the-art methods and our framework

Model	2006 i2b2			2014 i2b2		
	P	R	F1	P	R	F1
Wellner	**0.9870**	0.9750	0.9810	-	-	-
Nottingham	-	-	-	0.9900	0.9640	0.9768
MIST	-	-	-	0.9529	0.7569	0.84367
CRF	0.9640	0.9371	0.9504	0.9842	0.9663	0.9752
CRF + ANN	-	-	-	0.9792	**0.9784**	0.9788
Uni-RNN	0.9207	0.9145	0.9175	0.9529	0.9336	0.9432
Bi-RNN	0.9723	0.9656	0.9689	0.9878	0.9389	0.9627
RNN + Skeleton	**0.9870**	**0.9862**	**0.9866**	**0.9931**	0.9676	**0.9802**

3.4   Performance on Chinese Dataset

We use 80% of the Chinese dataset for training and the other 20% are for testing. Our framework achieves a micro-averaged F1-score of 0.98 at token-level and 0.96 at entity-level. Table 3 compares classic models and frameworks with models introduced in this work. The rule-based model was built by regular expressions and dictionaries in

Table 3. Performance on the Chinese dataset

Model	Precision	Recall	F1-score
Rule-based	0.8747	0.9276	0.9003
CRF	**0.9815**	0.8972	0.9375
Uni-RNN	0.9539	0.8866	0.9190
Bi-RNN	0.9701	0.9235	0.9462
RNN + Skeleton	0.9796	**0.9431**	**0.9610**

the early stage of our de-identification work. The precisions, recalls and F1-values are entity-level results, as the rule-based model has no token-level results.

Figure 4 shows the entity-level F1-scores for each PHI category on the Chinese dataset. The recall of the PATIENT category is clear lower than other recalls. This is due to many patient names appear in uncertain locations without much context in our Chinese medical records. Moreover, almost all names occurred once in the dataset, thus they were marked as <UNK> for reducing the size of the dictionary. The performance of the LOCATION category is also lower than the average. The reason behind the result is that the number of LOCATION (the percentage of LOCATION is about 2%) is relatively small.

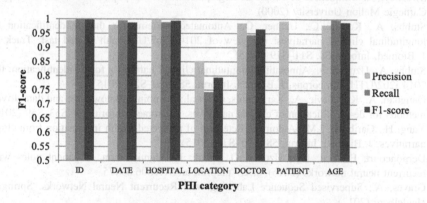

Fig. 4. Entity-level F1-scores for each PHI category

4 Conclusion

In order to solve the de-identification challenge, we proposed a universal framework with generalization ability which is based on recurrent neural network. We evaluated our framework on three datasets at entity-level, token-level and binary-token-level respectively. The experimental results illustrate that the RNN framework performs well in de-identification task. In Chinese dataset our framework achieved a micro-averaged F1-score of 0.98 at token-level and 0.96 at entity-level. Further analysis shows that the special context in EHR makes de-identification challenge different from traditional NER task, therefore further research base on RNN can focus on the usage of context and the architecture of RNN.

References

1. Sweeney, L.: Replacing personally-identifying information in medical records, the Scrub system. In: Proceedings of AMIA Annual Fall Symposium, p. 333. American Medical Informatics Association (1996)
2. Ruch, P., Baud, R.H., Rassinoux, A.M., et al.: Medical document anonymization with a semantic lexicon. In: Proceedings of AMIA Symposium, p. 729. American Medical Informatics Association (2000)
3. Uzuner, Ö., Luo, Y., Szolovits, P.: Evaluating the state-of-the-art in automatic de-identification. J. Am. Med. Inform. Assoc. **14**(5), 550–563 (2007)
4. Guillen, R.: Automated de-identification and categorization of medical records. In: i2b2 Workshop on Challenges in Natural Language Processing for Clinical Data, p. 116 (2006)
5. Wellner, B., Huyck, M., Mardis, S., et al.: Rapidly retargetable approaches to de-identification in medical records. J. Am. Med. Inform. Assoc. **14**(5), 564–573 (2007)
6. Hara, K.: Applying a SVM based Chunker and a text classifier to the deid challenge. In: i2b2 Workshop on Challenges in Natural Language Processing for Clinical Data, pp. 10–11. (2006)
7. Szarvas, G., Farkas, R., Busa-Fekete, R.: State-of-the-art anonymization of medical records using an iterative machine learning framework. J. Am. Med. Inform. Assoc. **14**(5), 574–580 (2007)
8. Sweeney, L.: Uniqueness of simple demographics in the US population. Technical report, Carnegie Mellon University (2000)
9. Stubbs, A., Kotfila, C., Uzuner, Ö.: Automated systems for the de-identification of longitudinal clinical narratives: overview of 2014 i2b2/UTHealth shared task Track 1. J. Biomed. Inform. **58**, S11–S19 (2015)
10. Stubbs, A., Uzuner, Ö.: Annotating longitudinal clinical narratives for de-identification: the 2014 i2b2/UTHealth corpus. J. Biomed. Inform. **58**, S20–S29 (2015)
11. Dehghan, A., Kovacevic, A., Karystianis, G., et al.: Combining knowledge-and data-driven methods for de-identification of clinical narratives. J. Biomed. Inform. **58**, S53–S59 (2015)
12. Yang, H., Garibaldi, J.M.: Automatic detection of protected health information from clinic narratives. J. Biomed. Inform. **58**, S30–S38 (2015)
13. Dernoncourt, F., Lee, J.Y., Uzuner, O., et al.: De-identification of patient notes with recurrent neural networks (2016). arXiv preprint arXiv:1606.03475
14. Graves, A.: Supervised Sequence Labelling with Recurrent Neural Networks. Springer, Heidelberg (2012)
15. Hochreiter, S., Schmidhuber, J.: Long short-term memory. Neural Comput. **9**(8), 1735–1780 (1997)
16. Cho, K., Van Merriënboer, B., Gulcehre, C., et al.: Learning phrase representations using RNN encoder-decoder for statistical machine translation (2014). arXiv preprint arXiv:1406. 1078
17. Mesnil, G., He, X., et al.: Investigation of recurrent-neural-network architectures and learning methods for spoken language understanding. In: INTERSPEECH, pp. 3771–3775 (2013)
18. Yao, K., Zweig, G., Hwang, M.Y., et al.: Recurrent neural networks for language understanding. In: INTERSPEECH, pp. 2524–2528 (2013)
19. Aberdeen, J., Bayer, S., Yeniterzi, R., et al.: The MITRE identification scrubber toolkit: design, training, and assessment. Int. J. Med. Inform. **79**(12), 849–859 (2010)

Sentiment Classification of Social Media Text Considering User Attributes

Junjie Li[1,3], Haitong Yang[2], and Chengqing Zong[1,3(✉)]

[1] National Laboratory of Pattern Recognition, Institute of Automation,
Chinese Academy of Sciences, Beijing, China
{junjie.li,cqzong}@nlpr.ia.ac.cn
[2] University of Chinese Academy of Sciences, Beijing, China
htyang@mail.ccnu.edu.cn
[3] School of Computer, Central China Normal University, Wuhan 430079, China

Abstract. Social media texts pose a great challenge to sentiment classification. Existing classification methods focus on exploiting sophisticated features or incorporating user interactions, such as following and retweeting. Nevertheless, these methods ignore user attributes such as age, gender and location, which is proved to be a very important prior in determining sentiment polarity according to our analysis. In this paper, we propose two algorithms to make full use of user attributes: (1) incorporate them as simple features, (2) design a graph-based method to model relationship between tweets posted by users with similar attributes. The extensive experiments on seven movie datasets in Sina Weibo show the superior performance of our methods in handling these short and informal texts.

1 Introduction

With the rapid development of social media, more and more people express their opinions in the web, such as Twitter, Sina Weibo, etc. To automatically mine public opinions for business marketing or social studies, sentiment classification has attracted much attention [7,11].

Following [12], lots of researches use machine learning algorithms to build sentiment classifier and their approaches work well on formal texts. However, these methods usually perform poorly when handling social media text. Because these texts are often short and contain many informal words (like 'coooool'). To alleviate this problem, researchers focus on two kinds of methods. On one hand, they try to employ sophisticated features, such as emoticons [8] and character ngrams [9]. On the other hand, some studies [3,4,15] explore the effects of user interactions (such as following and retweeting) on sentiment classification.

Despite the success of these approaches, they typically only consider user interactions and ignore demographics information such as age, gender, location, etc. (also called user attributes). After considering user attributes, we can not only improve sentiment classification accuracy of these informal texts, but also mine opinions about products by different attribute groups (such as male or age:

© Springer International Publishing AG 2016
C.-Y. Lin et al. (Eds.): NLPCC-ICCPOL 2016, LNAI 10102, pp. 583–594, 2016.
DOI: 10.1007/978-3-319-50496-4_52

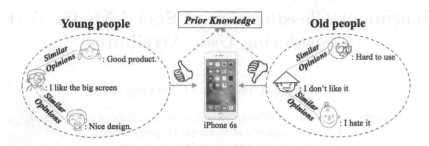

Fig. 1. An illustration to explain *Prior Knowledge* and *Similar Opinions*.

'19–30') of consumers. Specifically, we find these attributes can provide lots of information to determine the polarity of social media text, which contains:

- *Prior Knowledge*: User attributes can provide some prior knowledge about the polarity. For the same product, like iPhone 6s in Fig. 1, people with different attributes may hold different opinions. Young people may like the product since it is beautiful and runs smoothly, while old people may give negative comments to it because it is hard to operate.
- *Similar Opinions*: People with similar attributes may have similar backgrounds and possess similar opinions to the same product. Two young people may give similar (positive) comments to iPhone 6s, while two old people may both dislike it.

Therefore, it is feasible to leverage these attributes to build a smarter sentiment classifier and achieve better performance. To take *Prior Knowledge* and *Similar Opinions* into consideration, we propose two strategies: (1) take them as simple features, (2) design a graph-based model to encode relations between tweets posted by users with similar attributes.

We evaluate our methods on seven movie datasets from Sina Weibo[1], which is the largest Chinese microblogging service. Compared with existing content-based methods, the two strategies we proposed can improve average classification accuracy by 1.9 percent and 1.0 percent respectively. When we combine them together, we can get the best results which outperform the baseline by 2.2 percent on average.

In sum, our contributions in this paper are twofold. First, we propose two strategies to effectively capture *Prior Knowledge* and *Similar Opinions* and integrate them into a graph-based model (Sect. 3). Second, in order to stimulate further research on this direction, we make our datasets (Sect. 2) consisting of 6,498 movie reviews with reviewers' attribute information publicly available.

---

[1] http://weibo.com/.

2 Datasets

2.1 Data

Our datasets are made up of tweets from the movie special column[2] of Sina Weibo, in which users can post comments about movies. The statistics about our datasets are given in Table 1. Not only we crawl tweets from Sina Weibo, we have also crawled all available information about users who post the tweets, including their following relationships and public profiles like age and gender. Each tweet is rated by the users from Star-1 to Star-5. The tweets with Star-1 and Star-2 are labeled as *Negative*, and those with Star-4 and Star-5 are labeled as *Positive*. From Table 1, we can find the average length of tweets is very short (around 28 words), which accords with the characteristics of social media text. *All the data used in our experiments will be made available.*

Table 1. Dataset statistics. Movie name: movie name of the dataset. (N_+, N_-): number of positive and negative tweets. l: average number of words per tweet. Movie type: different types of movie.

Dataset	Movie name	(N_+, N_-)	l	Movie type
MH	Monster Hunt	(292, 292)	28.94	Comedy, fantasy
TT4	Tiny Times 4.0	(397, 397)	31.95	Love
SS	Silent Separation	(596, 596)	22.82	Love
FY	Forever Young	(611, 611)	31.13	Love
FOT	Fleet Of Time	(479, 479)	25.48	Love
MCDTM	Monk Comes Down The Mountain	(505, 505)	29.27	Comedy, love
AHON	A Hero Or Not	(369, 369)	25.70	Comedy, fantasy

2.2 User Attributes

We collected four kinds of user information in Sina Weibo: *gender, age, location* and *fan*, in which *fan* indicates whether the user is fan of the main actors or actresses and can be obtained easily from users' follow list. To quantitatively measure these attributes, we have further discretized them into different bins and the details of user attributes are shown in Table 2. Since we have four dimensions in user attributes, we utilize a quadruple to represent attribute information of a user and call it attribute quadruple. If we don't collect any value in a dimension, we use 'NULL' to represent it. For example, we can use a quadruple (male, 1–18, abroad, true) to represent a 16 years old boy, who is the fan of the main actress and lives abroad.

---

[2] http://movie.weibo.com.

Table 2. List of user attributes and the overall percentage of each attribute-value in all datasets.

Attribute	Values (percentage)
Gender	Male (29.75%), Female (70.25%)
Age	1–18 (19.26%), 19–30 (37.34%), 31–45 (3.09%), 45+ (0.27%), NULL (40.04%)
Location	Abroad (3.28%), first-tier city[a] (13.75%), second-tier city (24.25%), third-tier city (27.73%), fourth-tier (17.82%), NULL (13.17%)
Fan	True (40.58%), false (59.42%)

[a]We divide all cities in China into different grades according to their economic level. For example, the first-tier city contains Beijing, Shanghai, etc.

From Table 2, we can find that users always keep their age privacy and don't fill in age(the filling rate in age is about only 60%), while 100% users write gender and about 87% users provide location. Among all users, female and young account for a significant proportion (70.25% and 56.6%).

3   The Proposed Method

In this section, we propose two methods to model *Prior Knowledge* and *Similar Opinions* and a combination strategy to merge them together. In the following, we introduce these methods respectively.

3.1   Some Notations

For clear illustration, some notations are given. Suppose our dataset D has n tweets. For each tweet t_i, we collect its content d_i, attribute quadruple of its owner u_i and its sentiment label y_i. So the dataset D can be formalized: $D = \{(t_i, d_i, u_i, y_i)\}_{i=1}^n \cdot c \in \{pos, neg\}$ denotes the sentiment label that is to be predicted by classification methods.

3.2   Content-Based Method

The content-based method only uses tweet content and it computes the probability of a label c being assigned to a tweet t_i as follows:

$$p(c|t_i) = p(c|d_i) \tag{1}$$

in which $p(c|d_i)$ can be computed by any generative or discriminative model with content features.

3.3 Feature-Based Method

In this subsection, we propose a feature-based method to consider *Prior Knowledge*.

When computing the probability of c to t_i, we not only consider tweet content d_i, but also incorporate attribute quadruple of its owner u_i. Its formulation is as follows:

$$p(c|t_i) = p(c|d_i, u_i) \qquad (2)$$

in which $p(c|d_i, u_i)$ can also be computed by any generative or discriminative model with the combination of content features and user attributes features. We take all attribute-values in Table 2 as binary features and treat these features as User Attributes Features (UAF).

Algorithm 1. Pruning

Input: old UAG(oUAG), pruning parameter λ, train dataset D;
Output: new UAG(nUAG)
1: allAGList = ConstructAllAttrGroups()
2: hcAGList ← ∅
3: **for** each group $g \in$ allAGList **do**
4:     posPer ← ComputePosPerForGroup(D, g)
5:     negPer ← 1 - posPer
6:     **if** |posPer - negPer| $\geq \lambda$ **then**
7:         hcAGList ← hcAGList ∪ g
8:     **end if**
9: **end for**
10: nUAG ← oUAG
11: **for** each edge $e \in$ nUAG **do**
12:     d1, d2 = getNodeAttributeInfo(e)
13:     **if** d1 ∉ hcAGList **or** d2 ∉ hcAGList **then**
14:         delete e from nUAG
15:     **end if**
16: **end for**

3.4 Graph-Based Method

We design a graph-based method to incorporate *Similar Opinions*. First, a graph called User Attributes Graph(UAG) is constructed according to user similarity, in which we connected tweets posted by similar users. Then, we use an iterative method to infer the graph.

Now, we present the details on constructing UAG:

1. **Connecting tweets posted by similar users:** The idea of constructing UAG is to connect tweets posted by similar users, because similar users may have similar opinions. We use a similarity score to measure the similarity of any two users, which can be obtained by computing the number of same value (except for 'NULL') in their attribute quadruple. If the similarity score of two

users is higher than half of the number of all dimensions in user attributes (the value is 2 since we collect 4 dimensions in Table 2), we call they are similar users and connect tweets posted by them. For example, the similarity score of two users, whose attribute quadruples are (male, 1–18, abroad, true) and (female, 1–18, abroad, true), is 3. Because their *age*, *location* and *fan* are same and are not 'NULL'. Thus, we connect their tweets.

2. **Pruning**: In the construction of UAG, we connect all tweets posted by similar users. However, this may bring some noises into our graph because similar users don't have to hold the same sentiment exactly. Therefore, to improve sentiment consistency of all edges in UAG, we propose a simple pruning strategy. The detailed pruning process is shown in Algorithm 1. Firstly we build all attribute groups by traversing any combinations of attribute-value in Table 2 (line:1). Attribute groups can contain one dimension such as (Gender:male) or the combination of different dimensions such as (Fan:true ∩ Gender:female ∩ Age: 1–18). Secondly, we need to mine some high consistency attribute groups through pruning parameter λ, where users in these groups tend to express the same opinions with high probability (line: 2–9). Thirdly, we remove the edge in UAG, whose nodes' owner (users) are not in these high consistency attribute groups (line: 10–16). We also test the influences of different λ for our method in Sect. 4.3, and we set λ to 0.7.

After UAG being constructed, we design a graph-based method for sentiment classification of tweets. In our model, G means UAG, $N(t_i)$ represents the neighborhood of t_i in G and $l(t_i)$ denotes the label of tweet t_i. When computing the probability of c to t_i in G, we make the Markov assumption that the determination of sentiment polarity can only be influenced by either the content of the tweet d_i or sentiment assignments of neighbor tweets $t_k \in N(t_i)$. Thus we get Eq. 3.

$$p(c|t_i, G) = p(c|d_i, N(t_i))$$ (3)

After applying the additional independence assumption that there is no direct coupling between the content of a document and the labels of its neighbors and using $l(N(t_i))$ to represent a specific assignment of sentiment labels to all immediate neighbors of the review t_i, we get Eq. 4.

$$p(c|d_i, N(t_i)) = p(c|d_i) \times \sum_{l(N(t_i))} p(c|l(N(t_i)))p(l(N(t_i)))$$ (4)

We can convert the output scores of a review by the content-based method into probabilistic form and use them to approximate $p(c|d_i)$, which is a base classifier to the graph-based method. Then a relaxation labeling algorithm described in [2] can be used on the graph to iteratively estimate $p(c|t_i, G)$ for all reviews. After the iteration ends, for any review in the graph, the sentiment label that has the maximum $p(c|t_i, G)$ is considered the final label.

3.5   Combination Strategy

To merge *Prior Knowledge* and *Similar Opinions* together, we improve the graph-based method by adding u_i when computing c to t_i:

$$p(c|d_i, N(t_i)) = p(c|d_i, u_i) \times \sum_{l(N(t_i))} p(c|l(N(t_i)))p(l(N(t_i))) \qquad (5)$$

The only difference between Eqs. 4 and 5 is the base classifier. In Eq. 4, the base classifier is computed by $p(c|d_i)$ and only takes content information to decide the label. However in Eq. 5, we can add user demographics u_i into the content-based method and utilize $p(c|d_i, u_i)$ to build the base classifier.

4   Experiments

4.1   Experimental Settings

We evaluate the proposed methods on seven datasets introduced in Sect. 2. In our experiments, tweets in each dataset are randomly split up into five folds (with four folds serving as training data and the remaining one fold serving as test data). All of the following results are reported in terms of an averaged accuracy of five-fold cross validation. We compare our model with content-based sentiment classification methods:

(1) NB: We implement the Naïve Bayes Classifier based on a multinomial event model.
(2) ME: Maxent Entropy[3] is a classic discriminative model and widely used in sentiment classification.
(3) SVM: Support Vector Machine is a also widely used baseline method to build sentiment classifier. LibSVM[4] toolkit is chosen as the SVM classifier. The penalty parameter is set as 0.1.

Following the standard experimental settings in sentiment classification, we use term presence as the weight of feature, and evaluate two kinds of features, (1) *ui*: unigrams, (2) *bi*: both unigrams and bigrams. The paired t-test [20] is performed for significant testing with a default significant level of 0.05.

4.2   Performance Comparison

Table 3 reports the classification accuracy of baseline systems. On one hand, we can find that NB gets the best results in our datasets. Some researchers [10,17] showed that NB is better than SVM when the training set is small or texts are short. Our datasets satisfy the two conditions, thus, it is not surprising that NB

---

[3] http://homepages.inf.ed.ac.uk/lzhang10/maxent_toolkit.html.
[4] http://www.csie.ntu.edu.tw/~cjlin/libsvm.

Table 3. Classification accuracy of baseline systems. The best results are in **bold**.

Methods	MH	TT4	SS	FY	FOT	MCDTM	AHON	Average
NB-ui	0.8750	**0.8387**	0.7961	0.8740	0.8507	**0.7941**	0.8495	0.8397
NB-bi	**0.8904**	0.8236	**0.8071**	**0.8765**	**0.8508**	0.7733	**0.8617**	**0.8405**
SVM-ui	0.8444	0.7682	0.7777	0.8265	0.8319	0.7495	0.8102	0.8012
SVM-bi	0.8410	0.7657	0.7819	0.8331	0.8246	0.7366	0.8129	0.7994
ME-ui	0.8358	0.7796	0.7819	0.8314	0.8319	0.7554	0.7899	0.8008
ME-bi	0.8409	0.7745	0.7802	0.8405	0.8226	0.7386	0.8130	0.8015

Table 4. Classification accuracy of our methods. *Base*: the baseline system (NB-*bi* in Table 3). *Base+UAF*: Adding user attribute features into the baseline. *Base+UAG*: Using *Base* as the base classifier to construct graph-based model. *Base+UAF+UAG*: Using *Baseline+UAF* as the base classifier to construct graph-based model. The best results are in **bold**.

Methods	MH	TT4	SS	FY	FOT	MCDTM	AHON	Average
Base	0.8904	0.8236	0.8071	0.8765	0.8508	0.7733	0.8617	0.8405
Base+UAG	0.8990	0.8488	0.8138	0.8822	0.8601	0.7792	0.8699	0.8504
Base+UAF	0.9008	0.8690	0.8246	0.8854	0.8633	0.7921	0.8820	0.8596
Base+UAF+UAG	**0.9059**	**0.8753**	**0.8255**	**0.8887**	**0.8664**	**0.7931**	**0.8848**	**0.8628**

obtains better performance. On the other hand, adding bigram features always improve the performance. Thus, we choose NB-*bi* as our baseline system.

The results of our methods are shown in Table 4. From the results, we can get the following observations. Firstly, after user attribute as feature added into the baseline system, we get 1.9 percent improvements on average, which indicates that user attributes are very useful for sentiment classification and taking user attribute as features can be a good supplement to content features. Secondly, after encoding relations between tweets in our graph-based method, we can outperform the baseline system by 1.0 percent on average, which shows the effectiveness of our graph-based method. Lastly, after the two strategies is integrated, we achieve the best performance, which surpasses the baseline system by 2.2 percent on average and is significant according to the paired t-test.

4.3   Effects of Pruning

In the process of building UAG, we propose a pruning strategy and set pruning parameter λ to 0.7. To further investigate the need of the pruning strategy and the sensitivity of graph-based method to the pruning parameter λ, we give the experiment results in Table 5 and plot the sentiment classification accuracy with pruning parameter λ from 0.0 to 1.0 on our datasets in Fig. 2.

Table 5. *edgeNum*, *conProb* and classification accuracy in UAG before and after pruning.

UAG		MH	TT4	SS	FY	FOT	MCDTM	AHON	Average
Before pruning	edgeNum	31,636	65,926	136,141	171,950	102,513	85,506	45,151	91,260
	conProb	0.8281	0.8728	0.7772	0.8173	0.7825	0.7623	0.7818	0.8031
	accuracy	0.8871	0.8438	0.8121	0.8707	0.8528	0.7644	0.8780	0.8441
After pruning	edgeNum	13,037	31,340	4,477	7,408	11,427	1,327	5,309	10,618
	conProb	0.9558	0.9588	0.8635	0.9856	0.9985	0.9726	0.9849	0.9600
	accuracy	0.8990	0.8488	0.8138	0.8822	0.8601	0.7792	0.8699	0.8504

Before Pruning vs. After Pruning

In theory, our graph-based method is influenced by two important factors: edge number of the graph (*edgeNum*) and the probability of sentiment consistency (*conProb*) of all edges in the graph. More *edgeNum*, and higher *conProb* will result in better performance. Thus, we give statistics about the two factors of graph before pruning and graph after pruning in Table 5.

From Table 5, we can find before pruning, the UAG graph contains 91,260 edges average and the average *conProb* is only 0.8031. After pruning, although *edgeNum* drops to 10,618, *conProb* rises greatly to 0.96. Just as stated before, the two factors (*edgeNum* and *conProb*) have great effects on the graph-based model. But we think compared with *edgeNum*, *conProb* is more important because a lot of inconsistent edges may cause many noises. Finally, after the pruning strategy, our model improve the average accuracy by 0.6 percent.

Sensitivity to Different Pruning Parameter

From Fig. 2, we can find when λ equals to 0.0 (it means there is no pruning in constructing UAG), *edgeNum* reaches the maximum, *conProb* gets the minimum and the accuracy is worst, which means many inconsistent edges in UAG hurt the performance. As λ increases, we add pruning in building UAG and delete many

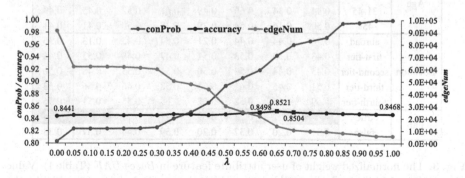

Fig. 2. Average *conProb*, average *edgeNum* and average accuracy in our datasets when varing λ.

noisy edges in UAG, get higher *conProb* and better performance. The curves of accuracy always reach the peak when λ is around 0.65. When we continue to increase λ, the performance begin to decrease. In this case, *conProb* is at a high value (average *conProb* is higher than 0.94) and can insure edges in UAG are mostly consistent. As λ increases, we can get higher *conProb*. Meanwhile we also lose too many consistent edges which results in the bad performance. Especially, when λ equals to 1.0, *edgeNum* drops to less than 10,000 and the accuracy drops to 0.8468.

4.4   Attribute Group Preference Analysis

Through considering user attributes, our model can not only boost sentiment classification accuracy, but also learn which attribute group is more or less likely to like a given movie, which is called attribute group preference analysis. Figure 3 shows the normalized weight of user attribute feature in *Base+UAF*.

For *gender*, we find that the average feature weight of male users is only 0.29 (less than 0.3), which shows male users always give negative comments. The reason is that compared with plain movies, such as love movies, male users may like adventure and excitement ones, while from Table 1 we can find this kind of movies take up a large of proportion in our datasets. Female users may like love movies, therefore the average feature weight of female users is about 0.6, which shows they always write positive comments.

With increasing age (1–18, 19–30, 31–45, 45+), the average feature weight (0.69, 0.49, 0.49, 0.41) decreases, which shows young users often give positive comments and middle-aged ones always write negative comments. We think the reason is that with increasing age, users are increasingly demanding.

Attribute		MH	TT4	SS	FY	FOT	MCDTM	AHON	Average
Gender	female	0.64	0.61	0.55	0.59	0.57	0.61	0.56	0.59
	male	0.06	0.06	0.49	0.13	0.49	0.38	0.42	0.29
Age	1-18	0.62	0.70	0.73	0.65		0.73	0.49	0.69
	19-30	0.51	0.37	0.53	0.46	0.48	0.48	0.58	0.49
	31-45	0.44	0.34	0.60	0.49	0.61	0.52	0.45	0.49
	45+	0.50	0.16	0.54	0.29	0.38	0.59	0.41	0.41
Location	abroad	0.34	0.44	0.44	0.21	0.54	0.45	0.13	0.36
	first-tier	0.43	0.39	0.53	0.51	0.47	0.48	0.53	0.48
	second-tier	0.45	0.44	0.54	0.50	0.51	0.55	0.48	0.50
	third-tier	0.51	0.45	0.61	0.53	0.58	0.46	0.56	0.53
	fourth-tier	0.59	0.55	0.52	0.52	0.65	0.55	0.51	0.56
Fan	true		0.72	0.73	0.69	0.71	0.71		
	false	0.31	0.20	0.37	0.20	0.39	0.44	0.37	0.33

Fig. 3. The normalized weight of user attribute feature in *Base+UAF* (Table 4). Value (from 0.0 to 1.0) shows how possible a user with the attribute feature might like the specific movie. We use different colors to fill in the box. High value with dark color and low value with light color.

For *fan*, we can find users following the main actor or actress of a movie will get high average feature weight about 0.76 and always like the movie, while users being not the fan always give negative comments, which is broadly in line with what we expected.

5 Related Work

Sentiment classification has been studied for years. Lots of researches follow [12] and use machine learning algorithms to build sentiment classifier from reviews with sentiment labels [5,6,13,18,19].

[3,4,15] make use of user interactions (such as following, retweeting etc.) to improve the performance. Their main idea is that sentiments of two messages posted by friends are more likely to be similar than those of two randomly selected messages. Incorporating this information into a graph-based model [4] or a supervised method [3] gets good results in the task. Other studies [1,14,16] also incorporate the user itself to improve sentiment classification accuracy.

6 Conclusion and Future Work

In this paper, we exploit user attributes to help sentiment classification on social media text. We propose two methods to incorporate user attributes: (1) take them as features; (2) use them to construct user attribute graph and design a graph-based model to handle it. We conduct experiments on seven datasets from Sina Weibo. Experimental results show that incorporating user attributes can significantly boost sentiment classification accuracy.

Since many researchers have proven the effectiveness of user interactions in social media on the sentiment classification task and we have also demonstrated user attributes can be useful for the task. In the future, we would like to investigate how to combine these two kinds of information together.

Acknowledgments. We thank the three anonymous reviewers for their helpful comments and suggestions. The research work has been funded by the Natural Science Foundation of China under Grant No. 61333018.

References

1. Al Boni, M., Zhou, K.Q., Wang, H., Gerber, M.S.: Model adaptation for personalized opinion analysis. In: Proceedings of Annual Meeting of the Association for Computational Linguistics, pp. 769–774 (2015)
2. Angelova, R., Weikum, G.: Graph-based text classification: learn from your neighbors. In: Proceedings of the Annual International ACM SIGIR Conference on Research and Development in Information Retrieval, pp. 485–492 (2006)
3. Hu, X., Tang, L., Tang, J., Liu, H.: Exploiting social relations for sentiment analysis in microblogging. In: Proceedings of the International Conference on Web Search and Data Mining, pp. 537–546 (2013)

4. Jiang, L., Yu, M., Zhou, M., Liu, X., Zhao, T.: Target-dependent Twitter sentiment classification. In: Proceedings of Annual Meeting of the Association for Computational Linguistics, pp. 151–160 (2011)
5. Li, S., Xia, R., Zong, C., Huang, C.R.: A framework of feature selection methods for text categorization. In: Proceedings of Annual Meeting of the Association for Computational Linguistics, pp. 692–700 (2009)
6. Li, S., Xue, Y., Wang, Z., Zhou, G.: Active learning for cross-domain sentiment classification. In: Proceedings of the International Joint Conference on Artificial Intelligence, pp. 2127–2133 (2013)
7. Liu, B.: Sentiment analysis and opinion mining. Synth. Lect. Hum. Lang. Technol. 5(1), 1–167 (2012)
8. Liu, K.L., Li, W.J., Guo, M.: Emoticon smoothed language models for Twitter sentiment analysis. In: Proceedings of the International Joint Conference on Artificial Intelligence, pp. 1678–1684 (2012)
9. Mohammad, S.M., Kiritchenko, S., Zhu, X.: NRC-canada: building the state-of-the-art in sentiment analysis of tweets. In: Proceedings of the International Workshop on Semantic Evaluation SemEval, pp. 321–327 (2013)
10. Ng, A.Y., Jordan, M.I.: On discriminative vs. generative classifiers: a comparison of logistic regression and naive Bayes. Proc. Adv. Neural Inf. Process. Syst. 28(3), 169–187 (2001)
11. Pang, B., Lee, L.: Opinion mining and sentiment analysis. Found. Trends Inf. Retrieval 2(1–2), 1–135 (2008)
12. Pang, B., Lee, L., Vaithyanathan, S.: Thumbs up?: sentiment classification using machine learning techniques. In: Proceedings of the International Conference on Empirical Methods in Natural Language Processing, pp. 79–86 (2002)
13. Socher, R., Perelygin, A., Wu, J.Y., Chuang, J., Manning, C.D., Ng, A.Y., Potts, C.: Recursive deep models for semantic compositionality over a sentiment treebank. In: Proceedings of the Conference on Empirical Methods in Natural Language Processing, pp. 1631–1642 (2013)
14. Song, K., Feng, S., Gao, W., Wang, D., Yu, G., Wong, K.F.: Personalized sentiment classification based on latent individuality of microblog users. In: Proceedings of the International Joint Conference on Artificial Intelligence, pp. 2277–2283 (2015)
15. Tan, C., Lee, L., Tang, J., Jiang, L., Zhou, M., Li, P.: User-level sentiment analysis incorporating social networks. In: Proceedings of the International Conference on Knowledge Discovery and Data mining, pp. 1397–1405. ACM (2011)
16. Tang, D., Qin, B., Liu, T.: Learning semantic representations of users and products for document level sentiment classification. In: Proceedings of the International Conference on Annual Meeting of the Association for Computational Linguistics, pp. 1014–1023, July 2015. http://www.aclweb.org/anthology/P15-1098
17. Wang, S., Manning, C.D.: Baselines and bigrams: simple, good sentiment and topic classification. In: Proceedings of the International Conference on Annual Meeting of the Association for Computational Linguistics, pp. 90–94. Association for Computational Linguistics (2012)
18. Xia, R., Zong, C., Hu, X., Cambria, E.: Feature ensemble plus sample selection: domain adaptation for sentiment classification. IEEE Intell. Syst. 28(3), 10–18 (2013)
19. Xia, R., Zong, C., Li, S.: Ensemble of feature sets and classification algorithms for sentiment classification. Inf. Sci. 181(6), 1138–1152 (2011)
20. Yang, Y., Liu, X.: A re-examination of text categorization methods. In: Proceedings of the International Conference on Research and Development in Information Retrieval, pp. 42–49. ACM (1999)

Learning from User Feedback for Machine Translation in Real-Time

Guoping Huang[1,2], Jiajun Zhang[1], Yu Zhou[1], and Chengqing Zong[1(✉)]

[1] National Laboratory of Pattern Recognition, Institute of Automation,
Chinese Academy of Sciences, Beijing, China
{guoping.huang,jjzhang,yzhou,cqzong}@nlpr.ia.ac.cn
[2] University of Chinese Academy of Sciences, Beijing, China

Abstract. Post-editing is the most popular approach to improve accuracy and speed of human translators by applying the machine translation (MT) technology. During the translation process, human translators generate the translation by correcting MT outputs in the post-editing scenario. To avoid repeating the same MT errors, in this paper, we propose an efficient framework to update MT in real-time by learning from user feedback. This framework includes: (1) an anchor-based word alignment model, being specially designed to get correct alignments for unknown words and new translations of known words, for extracting the latest translation knowledge from user feedback; (2) an online translation model, being based on random forests (RFs), updating translation knowledge in real-time for later predictions and having a strong adaptability with temporal noise as well as context changes. The extensive experiments demonstrate that our proposed framework significantly improves translation quality as the number of feedback sentences increasing, and the translation quality is comparable to that of the off-line baseline system with all training data.

1 Introduction

Computer-aided translation (CAT) is a form of language translation in which a human translator uses a software to perform and facilitate the translation process. To further improve the translation efficiency, incorporating the technology of machine translation (MT), especially statistical machine translation (SMT), into the CAT tools has drawn more and more attention. In practice, post-editing is the most popular approach to apply the MT technology to upgrade the CAT system.

In the post-editing scenario, translators generate the translation by correcting the MT results during the translation process. If the raw MT output is good enough, it will take translators little time to achieve the final acceptable translation. Considerable evidence has shown that human translators are more productive and the translation results are more accurate when post-editing is adopted [6,13,15,36]. In the real world, there are a number of CAT tools supporting post-editing, such as SDL Trados and MemoQ.

© Springer International Publishing AG 2016
C.-Y. Lin et al. (Eds.): NLPCC-ICCPOL 2016, LNAI 10102, pp. 595–607, 2016.
DOI: 10.1007/978-3-319-50496-4_53

However, post-editing is far from perfect in fact. So far, MT has focused on providing rough translations for having a glance, rather than outputs that minimize the effort of a translator. As a result, the biggest problem is that the low-quality of MT results often makes a translator disheartened to edit. What's worse, the underlying MT system will repeat the same errors in the following tasks, in spite of the fact that the translator has corrected them in many times. Therefore, the promotion of machine translation and post-editing is not easy in the human translation community.

Fortunately, the post-editing scenario fits well into an online learning protocol [7], where a stream of human translations is revealed to the MT system one by one as shown in Fig. 1. For each source sentence, the system will make an MT output. And then, the automatic translation will be corrected by the translator. As a result, before translating the next sentence, there is a learning loop can be enhanced for the underlying MT system. In the learning loop, the system can use the perfect human translation to upgrade itself to avoid repeating the same translation errors in the following tasks. As we can see, this is an important and challenging problem in the post-editing scenario.

In this paper, to avoid repeating the same MT errors, we present an efficient framework to upgrade the MT system in real-time by learning from user feedback. This proposed framework includes: (1) an anchor-based word alignment model based on Hidden Markov Model (HMM), being specially designed to get correct alignments for unknown words and new translations of known words, for extracting the latest translation knowledge from feedback sentences; (2) an online translation model based on random forests (RFs), updating translation knowledge in real-time for later predictions and having a strong adaptability with temporal noise as well as context changes during translating.

For example, during the English-to-Chinese translation task as shown in Fig. 1, the MT results of "publication chair" and "Hitoshi Isahara" are

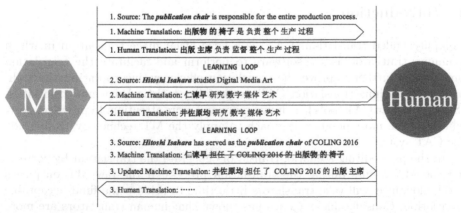

The correct key phrase pairs: "publication chair" ||| "出版 主席"; "Hitoshi Isahara" ||| "井佐原均".

Fig. 1. An overview of learning from users for machine translation in real-time.

completely wrong. With the help of user feedback, the first step in the learning loop is to successfully grasp the known word "chair" to its new correct translation "主席(chairman)", and align the unknown words "Hitoshi Isahara" (person name) to the proper Chinese translation "佐原均". The key to the solution is integrating phrase segmentation into word alignment under the guidance of alignment anchors, e.g., "responsible ||| 负责" and "studies ||| 研究". In this paper, we employ mutual information (MI) to find correct alignment anchors with a much higher accuracy rate. As a result, we can get the correct phrase pair candidates: "publication chair ||| ||| 出版主席" and "Hitoshi Isahara ||| ||| 井佐原均". The next step is to update the RFs-based online translation model in real-time using the extracted phrase pair candidates with context information. As we can see, the quality of the third sentence has been substantially improved by the updated translation model.

In the experiments, our proposed novel framework significantly improves translation quality with the number feedback sentences increasing, and the translation quality is comparable to that of the off-line baseline system with all training data. So far as we know, it is the first RFs-based translation model.

In summary, this paper makes the following contributions:

(1) The novel anchor-based HMM word alignment model gets more reliable and accurate alignments for unknown words, new translations of known words, and translation knowledge embedded in long sentences. It substantially improves the extraction of the latest translation knowledge from user feedback sentences.
(2) The well designed RFs-based online translation model continuously learns extracted new translation knowledge in real-time. The proposed model significantly outperforms the traditional translation model in terms of online learning.
(3) The proposed online translation model has a strong adaptability with temporal noise and context changes during translating. The algorithm discards trees from forests and continuously grows new trees based on estimated translation errors to promote the translation quality.

2   Related Work

To update SMT systems in a post-editing scenario where corrected MT output is constantly being returned, previous works can be divided into four types: (1) adapting word alignment model [2,9,11,19,35], (2) adding new rules to the translation model from the post-edited content [1,8,11,20,23,26], (3) updating the target language model [1,8], and (4) renewing the MT system's discriminative parameters [1,8].

In this paper, we focus on incremental learning for word alignment model, and online learning for translation model. We first pay attention to alignment problems of unknown words, new translations of known words and long sentences in the post-editing scenario. Second, differing from their work, in this paper, in order to guarantee the comparable performance to the off-line mode, we design the RFs-based translation model, differing from the rule selection model in [12,18], to implement online learning. What's more, our model can discard old translation knowledge based on estimated translation errors.

3 Online Learning Framework

In this work, we distinguish "online" from "incremental" learning. Online learning has to discard a sample after learning without memorization, and unlike incremental learning allowing to store it. Another related concept is batch learning. If the training data grows, batch learning requires retraining with all previous data and the new data [17]. Our proposed online learning framework includes an anchor-based incremental word alignment model and an online translation model. We will give a detailed description of this framework in next subsections.

3.1 Anchor-Based Word Alignment Method

Let $S = s_1^J = s_1 s_2 \ldots s_J$ denote the source sentence, and $T = t_1^I = t_1 t_2 \ldots t_I$ denote the target sentence, where J and I are the numbers of words in source sentence and target sentence, respectively. Word alignment can be defined as a task to find the optimal sequence $A = a_1 a_2 \ldots a_J$, where the expression $a(j) = i$ denotes that the target word t_i is connected to the source word s_j. The standard approach to word alignment makes use of various combinations of five generative models "Model 1–5" [5], HMM-based model [30], and "Model 6" [22]. In machine translation, word alignment plays a crucial role as the precondition.

However, in the learning loop of the post-editing scenario, there are two main challenges for aligning words. The bigger one is the unexpected unknown words and new low frequency translations of known words. That makes it hard for correctly aligning words and further extracting the latest translation knowledge based on only one sentence. For another challenge, long sentences greatly decrease the performance of word alignment. But in the post-editing scenario, we cannot simply filter them as preprocessing in the traditional MT pipeline because of the data sparsity and the long tail theory.

In this paper, we propose a novel anchor-based word alignment method to reduce the scope of alignments of unknown words and new low frequency translations, and meanwhile improve the alignment performance of long sentences. The core idea of the proposed word alignment model is to segment the bilingual sentence pair into bilingual phrases based on alignment anchors before searching the best alignment sequence. In this paper, we employ mutual information (MI) to find alignment anchors with a much higher accuracy rate (over 90%), being similar to [34]:

$$MI[s,t] = \log_2 \frac{P(s,t)}{P(s)P(t)}. \tag{1}$$

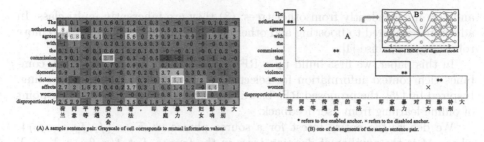

Fig. 2. The anchor-based word alignment model.

This model includes the following three steps as shown in Fig. 2:

(1) Find enough anchors based on MI scores as shown in Fig. 2(A). (a) For each word pair, compute the corresponding MI score according to Eq. 1. (b) Find the maximum score $MI[s', t']$, and label the cell $[s', t']$ as an anchor. Meanwhile, set $MI[s', \cdot]$ and $MI[\cdot, t']$ to the minimum MI score. (c) If the current maximum distance d between adjacent anchors is bigger than the limitation $\mathcal{D}$, repeat Step **b**. We set $\mathcal{D} = 7$ to cooperate the maximum phrase length in translation model.

(2) Segment the sentence pair into bilingual phrases according to the anchors as Zone A of Fig. 2(B). Generate *anchor*-centered bilingual phrase set $\{h\}$ with the **restriction**: $\forall \, \overline{d} \in \{h.s.end-anchor.s, h.t.end-anchor.t, anchor. s-h.s.start, anchor.t-h.t.start\}, \overline{d} < \mathcal{D}$. To prevent the anchor error to propagate into next steps, each anchor can be disabled with the restriction.

(3) Search the best word alignment using dynamic programming as shown in Zone B of Fig. 2(B). In this paper, we employ the modified HMM word alignment model with the anchor constant to align the words of the generated bilingual segments. It should be noted that the initial position of the modified HMM word alignment model is the anchor cell $[anchor.s, anchor.t]$, rather than the random position $[1, \cdot]$ for the original HMM word alignment model. The correct alignment result in Fig. 2 is: "The Netherlands {{荷兰}} agrees {{同意}} with the commission {{委员会}} that {{, 即}} domestic {{家庭}} violence {{暴力}} affect {{影响}} women {{妇女}} disproportionately {{特别 大}}".

In this paper, the step of incremental word alignment is set to 100 sentences.

3.2 Online Translation Model

3.2.1 RFs-Based Translation Model

There has been a recent interest in using random forests (RFs) [4] for natural language processing problems [32]. It has been demonstrated that RFs are better than or at least comparable to other state-of-the-art methods in classification [3,4]. For MT, RFs provide the following advantages that make them suitable for translation model: (1) decision trees are very fast in both training and classification; (2) they can be easily parallelized, because each tree in a forest is built and test independently from other trees; (3) they are inherently multi-class. In addition, compared to boosting and other ensemble methods, RFs are also more robust against noise [4].

In this paper, we first build up a RFs-based translation model, which combines rich context information for selecting translation rules during decoding. Inspired by [25], the proposed RFs-based translation model is the starting point of online learning from user feedback.

We denote the entire forest for a source phrase as $\mathcal{F} = \{f_1, f_2, \ldots, f_M\}$, where M is the number of decision trees in the forests. Let $f(x, \theta_m) : \mathcal{X} \to \mathcal{Y}$ denote the mth tree of the forest, where θ_m is a random vector capturing the various stochastic elements of the tree, e.g., the randomly sub-sampled training set and selected random tests at its decision nodes. As a result, given the source phrase $\bar{s}$, the estimated translation probability for the target phrase $\bar{t}$ can be derived as:

$$p(\bar{t}|\bar{s}) = \frac{1}{M} \sum_{m=1}^{M} p_m(\bar{t}|\bar{s}). \tag{2}$$

Each decision tree in a forest is built and tested independently from other trees. During the training, each tree receives a new bootstrapped training set generated by sub-sampling with replacement of the original training set. We refer to those samples which are not included during the training of a tree as the out-of-bag (OOB) samples, which can be used to compute the out-of-bag-error (OOBE) of the tree. The tests, in form of $g(x) > \theta$, at each decision node of the tree usually contain two parts: (1) a randomly generated test function; (2) a threshold θ which based on the random feature which decides the left/right propagation of samples. The tests are selected by first creating a set of random tests and then picking the best among them according to the entropy:

$$L(\mathcal{R}_j) = -\sum_{\bar{t}=1}^{\bar{T}} p_{\bar{t}}^j \log(p_{\bar{t}}^j) \tag{3}$$

where $p_{\bar{t}}^j$ is the probability of target phrase $\bar{t}$ in node j, and $\bar{T}$ is the number of target phrases.

More specifically, a set of N random tests $\mathcal{S} = \{(g_1(x), \theta_1), \ldots, (g_N(x), \theta_N)\}$ will be created when the node j is created. This node then starts to collect the statistics $p_j = [p_1^j, \ldots, p_{\bar{T}}^j]$ of the samples falling in it. For a random test $d \in \mathcal{D}$, two sets of statistics are also collected: $p_{jld} = [p_1^{jld}, \ldots, p_{\bar{T}}^{jld}]$ and $p_{jrd} = [p_1^{jrd}, \ldots, p_{\bar{T}}^{jrd}]$ corresponding to the statistics of samples falling into left(l) and right(r) partitions according to test d.

The information gain with respect to a test d can be measured as:

$$\Delta L(\mathcal{R}_j, d) = L(\mathcal{R}_j) - \frac{|\mathcal{R}_{jld}|}{|\mathcal{R}_j|} L(\mathcal{R}_{jld}) - \frac{|\mathcal{R}_{jrd}|}{|\mathcal{R}_j|} L(\mathcal{R}_{jrd}) \tag{4}$$

where $\mathcal{R}_{jld}$ and $\mathcal{R}_{jrd}$ are the left and right partitions made by the test s and $|\cdot|$ denotes the number of samples in a partition. A test with higher gain, produces better splits of the data with respect to reducing the impurity of a node. Therefore, when splitting a node, the test with the highest gain will be chosen as the main decision test of that node.

Draw on the experience of the translation rule selection model introduced by [12,18], we design the following kinds of features for an extracted phrase pair $\langle s = $"domestic violence" $t = $ "家庭暴力"$\rangle$ from Fig. 2 according to [16]:

- **Lexical features**: the 6 words immediately to the left of the source phrase $WS_{s-6} = $ "Netherlands" $, \ldots, WS_{s-1} = $ "that" ; the 6 words immediately to the right of the source phrase $WS_{s+1} = $ "affect" $, \ldots, WS_{s+6} = $ "EOS"; the first word of the source phrase $WSL_s = $ "domestic"; the last word of the target phrase $WSR_s = $ "violence"; the first word immediately to the left of the target phrase $WTL_{t-1} = $ "即"; the last word immediately to the right of the target phrase $WTL_{t+1} = $ "对"; the current lexical weights $P_w(t|s)$ and $P_w(s|t)$; post-editing support $PS = 1$.
- **Length features**: the length of the source phrase $Len_s = 2$ and the length of the target phrase $Len_t = 2$.

We integrate the RFs-based translation model into the log-linear model used by the SMT decoder during the translation of each source sentence. The log-linear model combines features: the translation probabilities $p(t|s)$ and $p(s|t)$ computed by the RFs-based translation model, the lexical weights $p_w(t|s)$ and $p_w(s|t)$, the language model, the reordering model, the word penalty, and the phrase penalty.

3.2.2 Online Learning for Translation Model

The original RFs-based translation model is designed to learn in batch or off-line model, i.e., each tree is trained a full sub-set of bilingual phrase pairs. There exist incremental methods for single decision trees but they are either memory intensive, because every node sees and stores all the data [29], or have to discard important information if parent nodes change.

To make the algorithm operate in online learning for translation model, there are two main problems: (1) How to perform bagging in online translation model? (2) How to grow random trees on-the-fly? RFs are ensembles of randomized decision trees combined using bagging. Accordingly, the online version has to combine online bagging [24] and online decision trees with random feature-selection.

(1) Online Bagging

For the bagging part, in this paper, the sequential arrival of the bilingual phrase pairs is modeled by a Poisson distribution. Each tree $f_t(x)$ is updated on each sample k times in a row where k is a random number generated by Poisson(λ) [24].

(2) Online Random Decision Trees

For the growing part, we employ extremely randomized forests [10]: the threshold θ and the test function $g(x)$ of the test $g(x) < \theta$ are chosen *randomly*. During growing of an extremely randomized tree, each decision node randomly creates

---

Algorithm 1. ORFs-based online translation model

Input: Sequential bilingual phrase pair $\langle s, t \rangle$, the size of the forest T.
Input: The minimum number of samples α, the minimum gain β, the knowledge wighting rate γ.
Output: The forest $\mathcal{F}$.
1: //For all trees
2: **for** $t = 1 \rightarrow T$ **do**
3:     $k \leftarrow$ POISSON(λ)
4:     **if** $k > 0$ **then**
5:         //Update k times.
6:         **for** $u = 1 \rightarrow k$ **do**
7:             $j =$ FINDLEAF(s)
8:             UPDATENODE($j, \langle s, t \rangle$)
9:             **if** $|\mathcal{R}_j| > \alpha$ and $\exists s \in \mathcal{S}: \Delta L(\mathcal{R}_j, s) > \beta$ **then**
10:                 //Find the best test.
11:                 $s_j = \arg\max_{s \in \mathcal{S}} \Delta L(\mathcal{R}_j, s)$
12:                 CREATELEFTCHILD(p_{jls})
13:                 CREATERIGHTCHILD(P_{jrs})
14:             **end if**
15:         **end for**
16:     **else**
17:         $OOBE_t \leftarrow$ UPDATEOOBE($\langle s, t \rangle$)
18:         WEIGHTINGTREE($f_t, OOBE_t, \gamma$)
19:     **end if**
20: **end for**
21:
22: **function** WEIGHTINGTREE($f_t, OOBE_t, \gamma$)
23:     $age_t \leftarrow$ NUMBEROFSAMPLES(f_t)
24:     **if** $age_t > \frac{1}{\gamma}$ and $OOBE_t >$ RAND( ) **then**
25:         //Discard the tree.
26:         $f_t =$ NEWTREE( )
27:     **end if**
28: **end function**

---

a set of tests and picks the best according to the test functions and thresholds. When operating in the off-line mode, the decision node has access to all the data falling to that node, and therefore has a more robust estimate of these statistics, compared to node operating. However, in the online mode, the statistics are gathered over time. Therefore, the decision when to split depends on: (1) if there has been enough samples in a node to have a robust statistics; (2) whether the splits are good enough for the classification purpose. Here, we introduce two hyper-parameters: (1) the minimum number of samples α that a node has to see before splitting; (2) the minimum gain a split β that has to achieve before splitting. Thus a node splits if and only if $\mathcal{R}_j > \alpha$ and $\exists d \in \mathcal{D}: \Delta L(\mathcal{R}_j, d) > \beta$.

(3) Temporal Weighting

In post-editing scenario, it requires of the underlying translation model a strong adaptability since the context changes during translating as time goes on. Therefore, we allow our forest to discard the entire tree. To achieve the goal, we can estimate the $OOBE_m$ of the mth tree online. Based on this estimate, we propose to discard trees randomly depending on its OOBE and its age, namely, the number of phrase pairs it has seen so far. By doing this, we can continuously ensure adaptivity throughout time.

In summary, the entire online translation model is depicted in Algorithm 1, where we set $\alpha = 30$, $\beta = 0.1$ and $\gamma = 0.02$.

4 Experiments

We conduct the experiments to test the performance of our proposed framework on improving translation quality with the number of training sentences increasing in the post-editing scenario.

4.1 Experimental Setup

All the experiments are conducted on our in-house developed SMT toolkit including a typical phrase-based decoder and a series of tools, including word alignment and phrase table extraction. All the MT systems are tuned by the development set using ZMERT [33] with the objective to optimize TER [27]. The lower the TER score, the better the translation. And the statistical significance test is performed by the re-sampling approach [14].

We test our method on English-to-Chinese news translation. The training set (1,997,900 sentences, 29,672,190 source words, 27,280,438 target words), development set (1,000 sentences, 27,965 source words, 25,638 target words) and test set (1,100 sentences, 29,570 source words, 26,985 target words) are taken from bilingual news in time order. The histogram for the length of sentences is shown in Fig. 3.

Compared to traditional SMT experiments, one big difference is that we preserve the original order of the sentences to simulate post-editing scenario. And additional data employed by this paper includes 10,000,000 Chinese news sentences for training the language model using SRILM toolkit [28]. The maximal entropy based reordering model [31] is trained by the whole training set. As our goal is to test the performance of translation model and word alignment model, we employ the same language model and reordering model for all experiments.

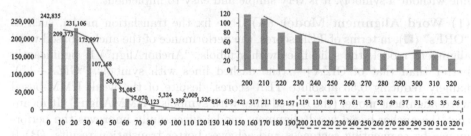

The horizontal coordinate refers to the sentence length, and the vertical coordinate refers to the number of sentences. For example, the second column (10, 209373) means that there are 209,373 sentences each of which contains 10-19 words.

Fig. 3. A histogram for the length of sentences.

4.2   Results and Analysis

Firstly, we will evaluate the performance of the anchor-based word alignment model and HMM word alignment model on improving the translation quality in the online learning scenario, being denoted as "AnchorAlign" and "HMMAlign", respectively.

Secondly, we evaluate the performance of our RFs- and ORFs-based translation model on improving the translation quality. The baseline system uses precomputed phrase translation probabilities, independent of any other context information. To train the translation model of the baseline system, we run GIZA++ [21] to obtain word alignment in both translation directions, and the word alignment is refined by performing "grow-diag-final" method [16]. The maximum initial phrase length is set to 7. The baseline system, being denoted as "Baseline", contains a traditional off-line translation model. The full training process will be operated each time, including word alignment, phrase extraction, tuning with the development set, and testing with the test set.

Meanwhile, we gather context features based on the word alignment results for training the RFs- and ORFs-based translation models, denoted as "RFs" and "ORFs" respectively. In addition, we have re-implemented two other translation online adaptation methods introduced by [1], i.e., translation adaptation with an external cache, being denoted as "ExternalCache", and an internal cache, being denoted as "InternalCache". Because the principal topic is online learning in this paper, we do not compare among various discriminative translation models or rule selection models.

To improve the clarity, we report all experimental results with respect to the ratio of training sentences in Fig. 4. In Fig. 4, "RFs" refers to off-line training with respect to the ratio of training sentences. And "ORFs" refers to the online training sentence by sentence, but we reports the results on the test set corresponding to the above ratio.

As shown in Fig. 4, all methods will get better results as the training data increasing. Though the cache-based online adaption methods (the dotted lines without a symbol) cannot compare with the off-line baseline system (black solid line without a symbol), it is very simple and easy to implement.

(1) Word Alignment Model: **(A)** If we fix the translation model, such as "ORFs" (■), in terms of TER scores, the performance of the anchor-based word alignment model (the solid lines with symbols, "AnchorAlign") is significantly better than that of GIZA++ (the dashed lines with symbols, "GIZA++"), namely reducing 0.55 absolute TER scores, despite of the weak HMM-based word alignment model (the dotted lines with symbols, "HMMAlign"). It means that the anchor-based word alignment model successfully improves the performance by segmenting sentences and achieves better translation results. **(B)** If we focus on the anchor-based word alignment, we can find that it is more suitable for ORF-s based translation model, namely reducing 0.49 absolute TER scores compared to GIZA++. If we were only looking at the TER scores, the improvement is less pronounced. It should be noted that GIZA++ is a combination of various of alignment models (including the HMM word alignment model) and optimization techniques, while the anchor-based alignment model only use the HMM word alignment model. In this perspective, the improvement of the anchor-based word alignment model is remarkable.

(2) Translation Model: In Fig. 4, the TER scores of "RFs" and "ORFs" are significantly better than that of other approaches (about 1.0 absolute TER scores). If we fix the word alignment method, the overall performance of the RFs-based translation model is superior to the traditional off-line translation model labeled with "Baseline". The results lay a good foundation for further development of online learning methods. As a result, if we focus on the blue (■) and red (▲) lines, we can find that the performance of the ORFs-based model are comparable with the RFs-based off-line learning model as the number of feedback parallel sentences increasing, and better than that of the traditional translation model (more than 0.9 absolute TER scores). The gap between RFs- and ORFs-based translation model is very small (less than 0.2 TER scores) and can be ignored in practical applications. This means that we have achieved our goals of online learning from user feedback in real-time.

In summary, we can draw the conclusion that the proposed online framework significantly improves the performance of MT outputs by learning from user feedback as the number of training sentences increasing in the post-editing scenario.

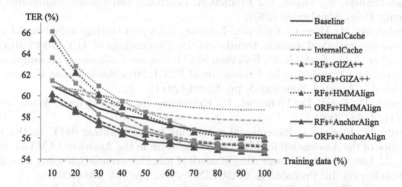

Fig. 4. TER scores with respect to the ratio of training data.

5 Conclusion

In this paper, we have presented an efficient framework for updating machine translation by learning from user feedback in real-time. This framework includes an online translation model based on the random forests, and an anchor-based word alignment model which combines phrase segmentation and HMM-based word alignment. It avoids repeating the same MT errors and significantly improves the translation quality as the number of feedback sentences increasing. The experimental results are promising.

Acknowledgements. The research work has been funded by the Natural Science Foundation of China under Grant No. 61303181.

References

1. Bertoldi, N., Simianer, P., Cettolo, M., Wäschle, K., Federico, M., Riezler, S.: Online adaptation to post-edits for phrase-based statistical machine translation. Mach. Transl. **28**(3–4), 309–339 (2014)
2. Blain, F., Schwenk, H., Senellart, J.: Incremental adaptation using translation information and post-editing analysis. In: International Workshop on Spoken Language Translation, pp. 234–241 (2012)
3. Bosch, A., Zisserman, A., Munoz, X.: Representing shape with a spatial pyramid kernel. In: Proceedings of the 6th ACM International Conference on Image and Video Retrieval, pp. 401–408 (2007)
4. Breiman, L.: Random forests. Mach. Learn. **45**(1), 5–32 (2001)
5. Brown, P.F., Pietra, V.J.D., Pietra, S.A.D., Mercer, R.L.: The mathematics of statistical machine translation: parameter estimation. Comput. Linguist. **19**(2), 263–311 (1993)
6. Carl, M., Dragsted, B., Elming, J., Hardt, D., Jakobsen, A.L.: The process of post-editing: a pilot study. In: Proceedings of the 8th International NLPSC Workshop. Special Theme: Human-Machine Interaction in Translation, vol. 41, pp. 131–142 (2011)
7. Cesa-Bianchi, N., Lugosi, G.: Prediction, Learning, and Games. Cambridge University Press, Cambridge (2006)
8. Denkowski, M., Dyer, C., Lavie, A.: Learning from post-editing: online model adaptation for statistical machine translation. In: Proceedings of ACL 2014 (2014)
9. Farajian, A.M., Bertoldi, N., Federico, M.: Online word alignment for online adaptive machine translation. In: Proceeding of EACL 2014 Workshop on Humans and Computer-Assisted Translation, pp. 84–92 (2014)
10. Geurts, P., Ernst, D., Wehenkel, L.: Extremely randomized trees. Mach. Learn. **63**(1), 3–42 (2006)
11. Hardt, D., Elming, J.: Incremental re-training for post-editing SMT. In: 9th Conference of the Association for Machine Translation in the Americas (AMTA) (2002)
12. He, Z., Liu, Q., Lin, S.: Improving statistical machine translation using lexicalized rule selection. In: Proceddings of COLING 2008, pp. 321–328 (2008)
13. Huang, G., Zhang, J., Zhou, Y., Zong, C.: A new input method for human translators: integrating machine translation effectively and imperceptibly. In: Proceedings of the IJCAI 2015 (2015)
14. Koehn, P.: Statistical significance tests for machine translation evaluation. In: Proceedings of EMNLP 2004 (2004)
15. Koehn, P.: Computer-added trasnlation. Machine Translation Marathon (2012)
16. Koehn, P., Och, F.J., Marcu, D.: Statistical phrase-based translation. In: Proceedings of HLT-NAACL 2003, pp. 48–54 (2003)
17. Li, L.J., Fei-Fei, L.: Optimol: automatic online picture collection via incremental model learning. Int. J. Comput. Vis. **88**(2), 147–168 (2010)
18. Liu, Q., He, Z., Liu, Y., Lin, S.: Maximum entropy based rule selection model for syntax-based statistical machine translation. In: Proceedings of EMNLP 2008, pp. 89–97 (2008)
19. Mccarley, J.S., Ittycheriah, A., Roukos, S., Xiang, B., Xu, J.M.: A correction model for word alignments. In: Proceedings of EMNLP 2011, pp. 889–898 (2011)

20. Nepveu, L., Lapalme, G., Langlais, P., Foster, G.F.: Adaptive language and translation models for interactive machine translation. In: Proceedings of EMNLP 2004, pp. 190–197 (2004)
21. Och, F.J., Ney, H.: Improved statistical alignment models. In: Proceedings of ACL 2000, pp. 440–447 (2000)
22. Och, F.J., Ney, H.: A systematic comparison of various statistical alignment models. Comput. Linguist. 29(1), 19–51 (2003)
23. Ortiz-Martínez, D., García-Varea, I., Casacuberta, F.: Online learning for interactive statistical machine translation. In: Proceedings of NAACL 2010, pp. 546–554 (2010)
24. Oza, N.C.: Online bagging and boosting. In: IEEE International Conference on Systems, Man and Cybernetics, vol. 3, pp. 2340–2345 (2005)
25. Saffari, A., Leistner, C., Santner, J., Godec, M., Bischof, H.: On-line random forests. In: IEEE International Conference on Computer Vision Workshops (2009)
26. Simard, M., Foster, G.: PEPr: post-edit propagation using phrase-based statistical machine translation. In: Proceedings of the XIV Machine Translation Summit 2013, pp. 191–198 (2013)
27. Snover, M., JDorr, B., Schwartz, R., Micciulla, L., Makhoul, J.: A study of translation edit rate with targeted human annotation. In: Conference of the Association for Machine Translation in the Americas (2006)
28. Stolcke, A., et al.: SRILM - an extensible language modeling toolkit. In: Proceedings of the International Conference on Spoken Language Processing, vol. 2, pp. 901–904 (2002)
29. Utgoff, P.E., Berkman, N.C., Clouse, J.A.: Decision tree induction based on efficient tree restructuring. Mach. Learn. 29(1), 5–44 (1997)
30. Vogel, S., Ney, H., Tillmann, C.: HMM-based word alignment in statistical translation. In: Proceedings of the 16th Conference on Computational Linguistics, vol. 2, pp. 836–841 (1996)
31. Xiong, D., Liu, Q., Lin, S.: Maximum entropy based phrase reordering model for statistical machine translation. In: Proceedings of COLING-ACL 2006 (2006)
32. Xu, P., Jelinek, F.: Random forests in language modeling. In: Proceedings of EMNLP 2004, vol. 4, pp. 325–332 (2004)
33. Zaidan, O.F.: Z-MERT: a fully configurable open source tool for minimum error rate training of machine translation systems. Prague Bull. Math. Linguist. 91, 79–88 (2009)
34. Zhang, Y., Vogel, S., Waibel, A.: Integrated phrase segmentation and alignment model for statistical machine translation. In: Proceedings of NLP-KE 2003 (2003)
35. Zhao, B., Vogel, S.: Adaptive parallel sentences mining from web bilingual news collection. In: Proceedings of IEEE International Conference on Data Mining 2002, pp. 745 (2002)
36. Zhechev, V.: Machine translation infrastructure and post-editing performance at autodesk. In: AMTA 2012 Workshop on Post-Editing Technology and Practice (WPTP 2012), pp. 87–96 (2012)

GuideRank: A Guided Ranking Graph Model for Multilingual Multi-document Summarization

Haoran Li[1,2], Jiajun Zhang[1,2], Yu Zhou[1,2], and Chengqing Zong[1,2(✉)]

[1] National Laboratory of Pattern Recognition,
Institute of Automation, Chinese Academy of Sciences, Beijing, China
{haoran.li,jjzhang,yzhou,cqzong}@nlpr.ia.ac.cn
[2] University of Chinese Academy of Sciences, Beijing, China

Abstract. Multilingual multi-document summarization is a task to generate the summary in target language from a collection of documents in multiple source languages. A straightforward approach to this task is automatically translating the non-target language documents into target language and then applying monolingual summarization methods, but the summaries generated by this method is often poorly readable due to the low quality of machine translation. To solve this problem, we propose a novel graph model based on guided edge weighting method in which both informativeness and readability of summaries are taken into consideration fully. In methodology, our model attempts to choose from the target language documents the sentences which contain important shared information across languages, and also retains the salient sentences which cannot be covered by documents in other language. The experimental results on our manually labeled dataset (It will be released to the public.) show that our method significantly outperforms other baseline methods.

1 Introduction

The explosion of multilingual news in the Internet provides users with the opportunity to capture richer information about a specific topic but also increases the difficulty to focus on the important information. Multilingual multi-document summarization aims to provide users with the summary in their own language from multilingual documents of the same topic, which will help users to obtain clear and brief information in a short time.

In this work, English and Chinese documents are considered as the input, and we perform extractive summarization experiments on two tasks: one is generating English summaries and the other is generating Chinese summaries. As the models for these two tasks are the same, we just introduce the model producing English summaries from English and Chinese documents.

A simple approach to this task is first translating the Chinese documents into English by machine translation (MT) and then regarding it as a general monolingual multi-document summarization task. However, as MT is still far from being perfect, translation errors are propagated to the summarization task and

C.-Y. Lin et al. (Eds.): NLPCC-ICCPOL 2016, LNAI 10102, pp. 608–620, 2016.
DOI: 10.1007/978-3-319-50496-4_54

can lead to less readable summaries. While in fact, the information of translated documents is also necessary.

This paper proposes a guided edge weighting graph model for multilingual multi-document summarization (GuideRank). An important component of our method is edge weights which can be learned. Through controlling the weights flow, we can guide the system to choose from target language documents more sentences which contain important shared information of documents in both languages, without ignoring the translated sentences which cannot be covered by target language documents. Our model is mostly inspired by CoRank model [16] which was proposed for cross-lingual summarization and the edges in CoRank model are equal in both the directions. Different from CoRank model, in our model, the cross-lingual edges connecting the related sentences in different languages are unidirection which invalidate the direction from original English sentences to translated sentences. In this way, the translated English sentences will contribute the weights to their related original English sentences but the opposite is not the case. This transformation brings two advantages: one is that the sentences in original English documents which contain the shared information expressed in both languages will tend to be chosen as the summary, the other is that the important translated sentences which cannot be covered by the original English documents also have the opportunity to appear in the summary. Note that the original English sentences sharing little information with Chinese sentences are not affected in our model. We also employ different measures to re-weight these cross-lingual edges in different languages.

We use Fig. 1 to illuminate our GuideRank model furtherly. Sentence S_1 is extracted from English documents and the sentence T_1 from Chinese documents. S_1 and T_1 express the information about the plane crash site, but the quality of T_1_mt, the machine translation version of T_1, is far from satisfactory. We tend to extract original English sentence S_1 rather than translated sentence T_1_mt considering the readability of the summary. Our GuideRank model attempts to

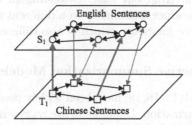

S_1: The plane crashed on to the Syria side of the Turkish-Syrian border.

T_1: 俄罗斯一架苏-24战机24日在土耳其和叙利亚边境叙利亚一侧坠毁。

T_1_mt: A Russian Su-24 fighter crashed 24 side of the Syrian border in Turkey and Syria.

Fig. 1. The simplified illustration of our GuideRank model. The vertices denote sentences and the edges reflect the relationships between sentences. The thickness of the edges connecting two parts indicates the strength of the relationships in which the strong connections are converted to unidirection.

achieve this goal through modifying the direction of the weight propagation in the process of random walk of graph model.

We make the following contributions:

- We propose GuideRank model which can generate the target language summaries with more target language sentences which contain shared information across language to enhance the readability.
- We employ several approaches to measure relevance between sentences across language and to re-weight the edges connecting cross-lingual sentences.
- The experiments show that we can outperform baselines on our dataset.

2   Related Work

2.1   Multilingual Multi-document Summarization

The Multilingual Summarization Evaluation (MSE) 2005 and 2006 aimed to create a 100-word English summary on documents consisting of English and Arabic news. Many researchers [1,3,13,20,22] participated the evaluation and they regarded the task as a general summarization from original English documents along with English documents translated from Arabic. Daumé III and Marcu [3] achieved the first place in MSE 2005 and they got the better performance when never extracting sentences from the Arabic MT documents. Although MT sentences are often largely incomprehensible, they failed to access effective means to take advantage of the Arabic documents which can provide useful information beyond English documents. Our GuideRank model can make full use of the information in both language documents.

The Text Analysis Conference (TAC) 2011 MultiLing [6] posed a multilingual summarization task which aimed to generate a summary from a set of documents in seven languages. The MultiLing task required language-independent summarization methods that the language of output summary is the same as input documents, which is different from our task. Cross-lingual document summarization [16,17,21] aims to produce a summary in a different target language for a set of documents in a source language, which is also different from our task.

2.2   Graph-Based Extractive Summarization Models

Graph-based methods [2,4,11,12,16,18] have been widely used to rank sentences for general document summarization. Documents are represented as a graph and sentences are represented as nodes. The edges reflect relations between nodes. The importance of the sentences are decided through random walk. Graph-based methods have the advantage in that they do not require training data and can be easily adapted to any languages, which is suitable for our task.

CoRank [16] is a graph model which is proposed to address cross-language summarization, in which the different language sentences are ranked simultaneously using a unified graph-based algorithm.

3   Methods

3.1   CoRank Model

The CoRank algorithm first needs to calculate three similarity matrices: M^{en} which denotes affinity matrix between the original English sentences, M^{c2e} which denotes affinity matrix between the translated English sentences from Chinese and $M^{en\text{-}c2e}$ which denotes affinity matrix between the original and the translated English sentences. The similarity matrices are computed as follows:

$$M_{ij}^{en} = \begin{cases} sim(s_i^{en}, s_j^{en}), & \text{if } i \neq j \\ 0 & \text{otherwise} \end{cases}$$

where s_i^{en} denotes English sentence which can be represented by TF-IDF vectors or averaging the embeddings of words (except stop-words) contained in the sentence. $sim(\cdot)$ denotes the similarity between two sentences, which is calculated with cosine measure. M^{c2e} and $M^{en\text{-}c2e}$ are computed in the same way. Note that these matrices are normalized to make the sum of each row equal to 1.

Next, the salience scores for the original and the translated English sentences, which are denoted by $u(s_i^{en})$ and $v(s_j^{c2e})$, are calculated iteratively until convergence using the following equations:

$$u(s_j^{en}) = \alpha \sum_i M_{ij}^{en} u(s_i^{en}) + (1 - \alpha) \sum_i M_{ij}^{en\text{-}c2e} v(s_i^{c2e})$$
$$v(s_i^{c2e}) = \alpha \sum_j M_{ji}^{c2e} v(s_j^{c2e}) + (1 - \alpha) \sum_j M_{ji}^{en\text{-}c2e} u(s_j^{en})$$

Finally, re-ranking is employed to remove the redundant information in the summary as Wan et al. [19] did and summary is generated by the sentences with highest scores.

3.2   GuideRank Model

The affinity matrices in CoRank model are symmetric, while for the task of multilingual document summarization, in consideration of the unsatisfactory quality of the translated English sentences, the symmetric affinity matrices is inappropriate. Specifically, for a translated English sentence, if there are some original English sentences which are related to it, we would prefer to choosing these original English sentences instead of the translated English sentence. In other words, the summarization system should be guided to control the direction of sentence salience score updating: when an original sentence is related to a translated sentence, the symmetric weighted edge between them should be transformed into unidirection in which we invalidate the direction from original sentences to translated sentences.

We use $M_{ij}^{en\text{-}c2e}$ to represent the weight pointing from the original English sentences to the translated English sentences, and use $M_{ij}^{c2e\text{-}en}$ to represent the weight pointing from the translated English sentences to the original English sentences. The similarity matrices representing relations between sentences across languages are changed in our GuideRank model as follows:

$$M_{ij}^{en\text{-}c2e} = \begin{cases} 0, & \text{if } s_i^{en} \text{ is related to } s_j^{c2e} \\ sim(s_i^{en}, s_j^{c2e}), & \text{otherwise} \end{cases}$$

$$M_{ij}^{c2e\text{-}en} = \begin{cases} relevance(s_i^{c2e}, s_j^{en}), & \text{if } s_i^{c2e} \text{ is related to } s_j^{en} \\ sim(s_i^{c2e}, s_j^{en}), & \text{otherwise} \end{cases}$$

where $relevance(\cdot)$ denotes the semantic relevance between two sentences from different languages. The motivation of our GuideRank model is that if there are some English sentences which are related to a Chinese sentence, we should guide the weight of this Chinese sentence to be transformed to its corresponding English sentences. Towards this objective, a requirement is to identify whether s_i^{en} is related to s_j^{c2e} and how to measure the semantic relevance between sentences across the languages. We propose the following three methods to achieve this goal.

Similarity (Sim) Evaluation. This method is a simple decision mechanism where cosine similarity of two sentence is leveraged. We propose three heuristic approaches to search for the related s_i^{en} for s_j^{c2e} using similarity evaluation.

The Maximum Similarity (SimMax).

$$s_i^{en} = \underset{s_i^{en^*}}{\operatorname{argmax}} \, sim(s_i^{en^*}, s_j^{c2e})$$

The Top-Five Similarity (SimTop5).

$$s_i^{en} \in \left\{ s_i^{en^*} \mid \underset{s_i^{en^*}}{\operatorname{arg\,top5}} \, sim(s_i^{en^*}, s_j^{c2e}) \right\}$$

where top5 denotes five highest values.

Higher than the Average Similarity (SimAve).

$$s_i^{en} \in \left\{ s_i^{en^*} \mid sim(s_i^{en^*}, s_j^{c2e}) > \frac{\sum_k sim(s_k^{en}, s_i^{c2e})}{N} \right\}$$

where s_k^{en} denotes the original English sentences and N is the total number of them.

$relevance(\cdot)$ in this method is equal to $sim(\cdot)$ which is introduced in Sect. 3.1.

Textual Entailment (TE) Evaluation. This method regards identification of semantic relevance as recognizing textual entailment (RTE) task where entailment and non-entailment relations are seen as judgments about semantic relevance.

RTE is a task to recognize, given two text fragments, whether one can be inferred by the other. For the following text-hypothesis pair:

Text: ... Obasanjo invited him to step down as president ... and accept political asylum in Nigeria.

Hypothesis: Charles G. Taylor was offered asylum in Nigeria.

After reading **T** we can infer that **H** is true, which means **T** entails **H**.

We use BIUTEE [14], a transformation-based TE system using various types of knowledge resources, to determine textual entailment. We train BIUTEE with 800 entailment or non-entailment text-hypothesis pairs of the RTE-3 [5] dataset for our task, and the possible inputs to BIUTEE are pairs of sentences consisting of any two sentences in which one is extracted from original English documents and the other from translated English documents. Since the size of the inputs is very large, in order to keep the whole summarization system efficient, we eliminate the sentence pairs which have no token (except stop-words) overlap. For the remaining pairs, the longer sentence is regarded as **T** and the other as **H**.

relevance(·) in this method is represented by textual entailment score, obtained by BIUTEE, between pairs of sentences determined as TE relation.

Translation (Trans) Evaluation. This method regards identification of semantic relevance as a translation evaluation where the probability of fully or partially translating a sentence into the other is seen as judgments about semantic relevance.

The translation probability is obtained based on the word alignment model. We use TsinghuaAligner[1] to perform word alignment. First, we train word alignment model on a large English-Chinese parallel corpus A which consists of two million sentence pairs. Then, another corpus B consisting of fully or partially translation English-Chinese pair run the word alignment model. Next, several features based on the word alignment are extracted for sentence pairs in B. Taking the features as input, an SVM classifier for determining translation relations is trained to fit the data B. The last step is to use the classifier to predict the translation probability for the candidate sentence pairs in summarization dataset in which the English sentence is from original English documents and the Chinese sentence is from original Chinese documents. The candidate sentence pairs are also obtained by the approach introduce in TE evaluation.

A preprocessing step to this method is to build the dataset to train the model detecting fully or partially translation English-Chinese pair. We construct the dataset in a straightforward way as follows:

We use an English-Chinese parallel corpus in FBIS corpus, which contains around 236 thousand English and Chinese sentence pairs as primary data. They come from the domain of news which is same as our summarization task. Then, we parse all the English and Chinese sentences using Stanford parser [7,9], and last, we randomly remove one of the verb phrases in the sentences except the following conditions:

(1) There will be no verb phrases in the sentence after removing the selected verb phrase;

---

[1] http://nlp.csai.tsinghua.edu.cn/~ly/systems/TsinghuaAligner/TsinghuaAligner.html.

(2) The length of the verb phrase is 1;
(3) The length of the verb phrase is longer than the half of sentence.

The constraints described above are expected to guarantee the removing operations effective and keep the generated sub-sentences meaningful. Note that both of the sentences in a English-Chinese parallel sentence pair have the chances to randomly remove a verb phrase or keep unchanged. We generate corrupted sentence pairs by random sampling.

To train the model for detecting fully or partially translation relation between the sentence pair (S_i, S_j), we extract 6 features based on proportions of aligned unigram and bigram as follows:

$$maxang = \max\left\{\frac{ang(S_i)}{L(S_i)}, \frac{ang(S_j)}{L(S_j)}\right\}$$

$$minang = \min\left\{\frac{ang(S_i)}{L(S_i)}, \frac{ang(S_j)}{L(S_j)}\right\}$$

$$aveang = \frac{ang(S_i) + ang(S_j)}{L(S_i) + L(S_j)}$$

where $ang(S_i)$ and $L(S_i)$ denotes the number of the aligned n-gram ($n = 1, 2$) and the number of the words (except stop-words) in the sentence S_i, respectively.

We evaluate the effectiveness of these features on our fully or partially translation English-Chinese pair dataset through the 10-fold cross-validation, and find that the F-scores using unigram and bigram features are 69% and 78%, respectively. When we combine unigram and bigram features, the F-score reaches up to 96%, which proves the robustness of these simple features to detect whether one text segment can be fully or partially translated by the other.

$relevance(\cdot)$ in this method is represented by the estimated probability of mutual translation, obtained by the SVM classifier, between pair of sentences determined as translation relation. Note that the $relevance$ scores are normalized to make the sum for each sentence equal to 1.

4   Experiment

4.1   Dataset

There is no benchmark dataset for multilingual multi-document summarization (the datasets in MSE 2005 and 2006 were not released by the organizers), and we construct a dataset as follows.

We first select 15 news topics in 2015, and collect 20 articles in Chinese and 20 in English about each topic within the same period using Google News[2]. The statistics of the corpus is shown in Table 1.

We employ 9 graduate students to write the English and Chinese reference summaries for the 15 topics after reading both English and Chinese documents

---

[2] http://news.google.com/.

Table 1. Corpus statistics.

	Topic number	Article number	Average sentence number per topic	Average word number per article
English	15	300	513.3	590.5
Chinese	15	300	447.7	556.6

for each topic. There are 3 reference summaries for each topic. For English reference summaries, we set the length limit to 250 words, and for Chinese the limit to 400 characters. The different length limits are set for considering the ratio of the lengths of translation English and Chinese text. We perform sentences and words tokenization and all the Chinese sentences are segmented by Stanford Chinese Word Segmenter [15].

4.2 Baseline Models

We compare our GuideRank model with the following baseline CoRank models without guidance.

Baseline-EN. This model generates summaries only using the original English documents.

Baseline-CN. This model generates summaries only using the translated English documents.

Baseline-ENCN. This models generate summaries using all the multilingual documents.

Replacement Models. Replacement strategy is adopted in the process of re-ranking. If a translated English sentence is chosen as summary, we will replace it with original English sentence with highest *relevance* score which is determined by Sim, TE and Trans evaluations introduced in Sect. 3.2.

4.3 Experimental Results

We use the ROUGE-1.5.5 [10] toolkit to evaluate the output summaries. Tables 2 and 3 show the averaged ROUGE-2 and ROUGE-SU4 scores regarding to the three reference summaries for each topic. The value of α is set to 0.5.

To evaluate the effectiveness of proposed GuideRank model, we conduct experiments using different sentence representations, i.e., TF-IDF vectors and averaging word embeddings.

The Results for English Summaries. For the first three lines in Table 2, *Baseline-EN* outperforms *Baseline-CN* and even *Baseline-ENCN*, which may due to the translation errors. This phenomenon has been also verified by Daumé III and Marcu [3].

Table 2. Experimental results (F-score) for English summaries. * denotes statistically significant better than the baselines, p <0.01, t-test.

		TF-IDF		Embeddings	
		ROUGE-2	ROUGE-SU4	ROUGE-2	ROUGE-SU4
Baselines	EN	0.13477	0.18904	0.13326	0.18071
	CN	0.10272	0.15812	0.09067	0.14504
	ENCN	0.11325	0.16671	0.10709	0.16156
Replacement models	Sim	0.12780	0.17977	0.14052*	0.18963*
	TE	0.13883	0.18832	0.14457*	0.19411*
	Trans	0.16471*	0.20798*	0.16805*	0.20813*
GuideRank models	SimMax	0.11279	0.16688	0.10749	0.16105
	SimTop5	0.11315	0.16699	0.11035	0.16304
	SimAve	0.12757	0.18104	0.13814	0.18384
	TE	0.13261	0.18357	0.14447	0.19477
	Trans	0.16863*	0.21122*	**0.18360***	**0.22215***

For *Replacement* models, when we replace the translated English sentences in summaries with original sentences using *Sim* evaluation, the system does not achieve the desirable results. The reason is that this simple strategy cannot accurately capture the sentences which are semantically related to the translated sentences. The performances of the *Replacement TE* and *Trans* models are much better which means better related English sentences to Chinese sentences are obtained.

GuideRank Trans model achieves the highest ROUGE score, and then GuideRank TE model. *GuideRank SimMax* and *GuideRank SimTop5* model do not perform well. The reason is that the strengths of the guidance for these two models are weak: for a certain topic document set which contains thousands of sentences, only changing one or five edges for every translated sentence seems to be negligible. By contrast, *GuideRank SimAve* model performs much better than other *GuideRank Sim* models. We also conduct experiments regarding different proportion of sentences with highest similarity score as related, and we get the similar results when the proportion ranging from 10–50%.

The advantage of *GuideRank* models over *Replacement* models is that the algorithms optimize the problem globally, which take the interactions between sentences across languages into account during the process of calculating the sentence weights. While *Replacement* models are post-processing methods which will prevent some important translated sentences which cannot be covered by English sentences.

The Results for Chinese Summaries. We evaluate the Chinese summaries on word and character level, and the results are similar to English summaries that *GuideRank Trans* model achieves the best performance. The performance using averaging word embeddings as sentence representation is worse than TF-IDF

Table 3. Experimental results (F-score) for Chinese summaries.

Models		Word level evaluation				Character level evaluation			
		TF-IDF		Embeddings		TF-IDF		Embeddings	
		Rouge-2	Rouge-SU4	Rouge-2	Rouge-SU4	Rouge-2	Rouge-SU4	Rouge-2	Rouge-SU4
Baselines	CN	0.12045	0.17581	0.11802	0.16145	0.23513	0.23314	0.22054	0.21797
	EN	0.07542	0.13666	0.05800	0.11497	0.17205	0.17946	0.14885	0.15827
	ENCN	0.09256	0.15273	0.08041	0.13528	0.19856	0.20189	0.18258	0.18388
Replacement models	Sim	0.12015	0.17094	0.10453	0.15212	0.22473	0.22312	0.20700	0.20792
	TE	0.11653	0.16634	0.09129	0.14234	0.22423	0.22369	0.19329	0.19694
	Trans	0.11253	0.16435	0.10186	0.15023	0.21950	0.21906	0.20402	0.20596
GuideRank models	SimMax	0.09386	0.15427	0.08094	0.13592	0.20110	0.20451	0.18256	0.18839
	SimTop5	0.09665	0.15698	0.08229	0.13640	0.20491	0.20816	0.18356	0.18883
	SimAve	0.12238	0.17680	0.10812	0.15664	0.22886	0.23175	0.21984	0.20182
	TE	0.11180	0.15908	0.11778	0.16365	0.22542	0.22250	0.23189	0.22666
	Trans	**0.13958***	**0.18999***	0.12323*	0.17349*	**0.25332***	**0.25148***	0.23507*	0.23343*

partially because we train the Chinese word embeddings with a relative small size corpus compared to English. When we use TE evaluation as the sentence relevance detection approach, the Rouge scores are lower than *GuideRank SimAve* model for the reason that the input to BiuTee toolkit must be two English sentences (Chinese sentences are translated into English), which will influence the TE recognition for Chinese sentences.

The Influence of the Parameter α. We evaluate the influence of the parameter α for *GuideRank Trans* model. The results are shown in Fig. 2. Note that larger α means the model relies more on the information of the same side of language. We can conclude that our model benefits from both sides of language and relies more on cross-language information from the observation that Rouge scores first increase with α, and after reach the peak value Rouge scores where α is 0.4, decrease with α. This conclusion accords with the motivation of our GuideRank model that we take advantage of the interaction between different languages to guide the system to generate better summaries.

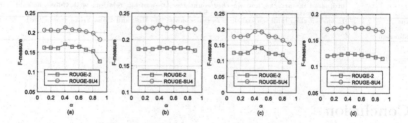

Fig. 2. Experimental results of *GuideRank Trans* models with different values of α. (a) English summaries taking TF-IDF as sentence feature. (b) English summaries taking embedding as sentence feature. (c) Word level evaluation for Chinese summaries taking TF-IDF as sentence feature. (d) Word level evaluation for Chinese summaries taking embedding as sentence feature.

5   Analysis

To explore the differences of the three methods in evaluating the relevance between sentences across languages, we show two examples about the three methods to search for the most related sentence in English documents for a given Chinese sentence in Table 4. We can come into the following conclusions:

The results for similarity evaluation are the sentences with some words overlap with the translated English sentences, which suggests similarity is not sufficient enough for evaluating the semantic relevance no matter what kind of sentence representations.

TE evaluation obtains real related sentence, but the rigidity of TE may restrain the further improvement upon the Sim evaluation. The partial TE [8] may remedy this problem.

Translation evaluation performs much better than other methods. To some degree, for Sim and TE evaluation, we need to translate the Chinese sentences into English, which will influence the downstream relevance detection. While there is no influence on this aspect for Translation evaluation.

For Trans, TE and SimAve evaluation, the proportion of target language sentences in the summaries is around 68%, 73% and 91%, which suggests that the more original target language sentences doesn't stand for higher performance. The best performance of Guide Trans model illuminates its ability to balance the informativeness and readability of summaries.

Table 4. Examples for searching for the most related English sentence to the Chinese sentences.

	Example 1	Example 2
Original	目前尚不清楚到周六早上是否⊠有其他⊠⊠者逃逃法外。	1961年1月5日，美国宣布与古巴断⊠外交⊠系。
Translation	It is unclear whether there are other Saturday morning to the attackers go unpunished.	January 5, 1961, the United States announced the severance of diplomatic relations with Cuba.
Sim Evaluation (embeddings)	It was unclear whether that term meant the terrorists were dead .	July 20 is the date when the United States and Cuba officially restore diplomatic ties
Sim Evaluation (tf-idf)	Paris terror attack: Everything we know on Saturday afternoon.	Obama announces re-establishment of U.S. Cuba diplomatic ties.
TE Evaluation	Many questions remain unanswered, including whether any accomplices are at large, who co-ordinated the attacks, and whether counterterrorism efforts could have foiled the plot.	In January of 1961 , the year I was born , when President Eisenhower announced the termination of our relations with Cuba , he said.
Trans Evaluation	It was not clear if all the attackers were accounted for.	The U.S. and Cuba broke ties in 1961.

6   Conclusion

In this paper, we constructed a multilingual summarization dataset and propose GuideRank model by considering the interaction between sentences in different languages. Our model is designed to generate the target language summaries by selecting sentences from the target language documents which contain shared information across languages, and also remaining the salient translated sentences beyond the content of target language documents. The experimental results show the effectiveness of our method.

Acknowledgments. The research work has been funded by the Natural Science Foundation of China under Grant No. 61333018 and supported by the Open Project Program of the State Key Laboratory of Mathematical Engineering and Advanced Computing.

References

1. Dalli, A., Catizone, R., Wilks, Y.: Clustering-based language independent multiple-document summarizer at MSE 2006. In: Proceedings of MSE (2006)
2. Daraksha Parveen, H.M.R., Strube, M.: Topical coherence for graph-based extractive summarization. In: EMNLP 2015 (2015)
3. Daumé III., H., Marcu, D.: Bayesian multidocument summarization at MSE. In: Proceedings of MSE (2005)
4. Erkan, G., Radev, D.R.: LexRank: graph-based lexical centrality as salience in text summarization. J. Qiqihar Jr. Teach. Coll. **22**, 2004 (2011)
5. Giampiccolo, D., Magnini, B., Dagan, I., Dolan, B.: The third pascal recognizing textual entailment challenge. In: ACL-PASCAL Workshop on Textual Entailment and Paraphrasing, pp. 1–9 (2007)
6. Giannakopoulos, G., El-Haj, M., Favre, B., Litvak, M., Steinberger, J., Varma, V.: TAC 2011 multiling pilot overview. Contribution in Book/report/proceedings (2011)
7. Klein, D., Manning, C.D.: Accurate unlexicalized parsing. In: Meeting on Association for Computational Linguistics, pp. 423–430 (2003)
8. Levy, O., Zesch, T., Dagan, I., Gurevych, I.: Recognizing partial textual entailment. In: Meeting of the Association for Computational Linguistics, pp. 451–455 (2013)
9. Levy, R., Manning, C.: Is it harder to parse Chinese, or the Chinese treebank? In: Proceedings of the 41st Annual Meeting of the Association for Computational Linguistics, pp. 439–446 (2003)
10. Lin, C.Y., Hovy, E.: Automatic evaluation of summaries using n-gram co-occurrence statistics. In: Conference of the North American Chapter of the Association for Computational Linguistics on Human Language Technology (2003)
11. Mihalcea, R.: Graph-based ranking algorithms for sentence extraction, applied to text summarization. In: Proceedings of the ACL 2004 on Interactive Poster and Demonstration Sessions, ACLdemo 2004 (2004)
12. Mihalcea, R., Tarau, P.: TextRank: bringing order into texts. UNT Scholarly Works, pp. 404–411 (2004)
13. Siddharthan, A., Evans, D.: Columbia University at MSE 2005 (2005)
14. Stern, A., Dagan, I.: BIUTEE: a modular open-source system for recognizing textual entailment. In: ACL 2012 System Demonstrations, pp. 73–78 (2012)
15. Tseng, H., Chang, P., Andrew, G., Jurafsky, D., Manning, C.: A conditional random field word segmenter (2005)
16. Wan, X.: Using bilingual information for cross-language document summarization. In: ACL 2011, pp. 1546–1555 (2011a)
17. Wan, X., Li, H., Xiao, J.: Cross-language document summarization based on machine translation quality prediction. In: Proceedings of the Meeting of the Association for Computational Linguistics, ACL 2010, Uppsala, Sweden, 11–16 July 2010, pp. 917–926 (2010)
18. Wan, X., Yang, J.: Improved affinity graph based multi-document summarization. In: Proceedings of the Human Language Technology Conference of the North American Chapter of the Association of Computational Linguistics, New York, USA, 4–9 June 2006, pp. 181–184 (2006a)

19. Wan, X., Yang, J., Xiao, J.: Using cross-document random walks for topic-focused multi-document. In: 2006 IEEE/WIC/ACM International Conference on Web Intelligence (WI 2006), Hong Kong, China, 18–22 December 2006, pp. 1012–1018 (2006b)
20. Wei, X., C.Y.: The THU/PolyU system at MSE 2006: an event-relevance based approach. In: Proceedings of MSE 2006 (2006)
21. Yao, J.G., Wan, X., Xiao, J.: Phrase-based compressive cross-language summarization. In: Conference on Empirical Methods in Natural Language Processing, pp. 1546–1555 (2015)
22. Zajic, D., Dorr, B., Lin, J., Schwartz, R., Zajic, D., Dorr, B., Lin, J.: UMD/BBN at MSE 2005. In: Proceedings of MSE (2005)

Fast-Syntax-Matching-Based Japanese-Chinese Limited Machine Translation

Wuying Liu and Lin Wang[✉]

Laboratory of Language Engineering and Computing,
Guangdong University of Foreign Studies, Guangzhou 510420,
Guangdong, China
wyliu@gdufs.edu.cn, wanglin@nudt.edu.cn

Abstract. Limited machine translation (LMT) is an unliterate automatic translation based on bilingual dictionary and sentence bank. This paper addresses the Japanese-Chinese LMT problem, proposes two syntactic hypotheses about Japanese texts, and designs a fast-syntax-matching-based Japanese-Chinese (FSMJC) LMT algorithm. In which, the fast syntax matching function, a modified version of Levenshtein function, can predict an approximate similarity of syntactic patterns between two Japanese sentences by a straightforward calculating of their formal occurrences. The experimental results show that the FSMJC LMT algorithm can obtain desirable effects with greatly reduced time costs, and prove that our two syntactic hypotheses are effective on Japanese texts.

Keywords: Limited machine translation · Fast syntax matching · Hiratoken · Syntactic pattern · Formal occurrence

1 Introduction

Limited machine translation (LMT) is a hybrid machine translation (MT) technique, which combines the techniques of example-based MT [1], information retrieval (IR), fast syntax matching (FSM), and supports the applications of skimming reading, translingual IR or filtering, computer-aided translation based on translation memory [2], statistical MT [3]. The effectiveness of the LMT technique is dependent on the efficient FSM function and big data resources of bilingual dictionary and sentence bank.

According to the syntactic pattern [4], the FSM, an efficient approximate string matching [5], aims to seek the most similar sentence from a big set of sentences for a given one. The traditional Levenshtein algorithm calculates an edit distance of two strings to estimate their formal similarity. Unfortunately, the calculating cost of the Levenshtein algorithm is too high, which defeats it in FSM. Subsequently, some index-based matching methods [6] can achieve the optimal result in approximate string matching.

© Springer International Publishing AG 2016
C.-Y. Lin et al. (Eds.): NLPCC-ICCPOL 2016, LNAI 10102, pp. 621–630, 2016.
DOI: 10.1007/978-3-319-50496-4_55

The MT problem between Japanese and Chinese [7] has been widely investigated since the early days of MT, and many effective algorithms have been proposed [8]. The total number of hiragana characters is 75 only, but their function is special and powerful. The hiragana characters are mainly used as accessory word, auxiliary verb, okurigana, or transliteration of Chinese characters. Just because the functional symbols are mainly made up of hiragana characters, the occurrence of sequential hiragana characters implicates the syntactic pattern of a Japanese sentence. The important feature allows readers to quickly understand Japanese texts by vision, and also allows a computer to simplify the Japanese information processing.

In this paper, we investigate the LMT problem from Japanese to Chinese. Based on statistical analysis from large-scale corpus, we propose two syntactic hypotheses to support the efficient FSM function. The first is that the formal occurrence implicates the similarity of syntactic pattern. The second is that the hiratoken, consisting of any sequential hiragana characters separated by katakana characters, Chinese characters, letters, Arabic numerals or punctuations, holds a post of syntactic identifier on Japanese texts. According to above hypotheses, we present an architecture for Japanese-Chinese LMT.

2 Architecture

Figure 1 shows our Japanese-Chinese LMT architecture, which mainly includes two parts: data preprocessing and limited translating. In the data preprocessing part, the **SenIndexer** receives Japanese-Chinese sentence pairs from *JCSenBank*, and indexes each pair of key-value <*JSen, CSens*> into a hash table *JCSenIndex*; the **HiraIndexer** receives the same sentence pairs, extracts hiratokens from each Japanese sentence, and

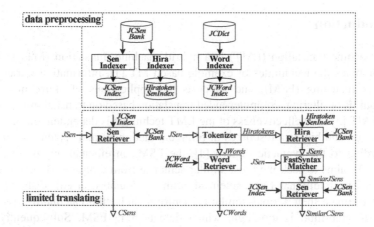

Fig. 1. Japanese-Chinese LMT architecture.

indexes each pair of key-value <*Hiratoken, JSens*> into a hash table *Hirato-kenSenIndex*; the **WordIndexer** receives Japanese-Chinese word pairs from *JCDict*, and indexes each pair of key-value <*JWord, CWords*> into a hash table *JCWordIndex*.

In the limited translating part, the **SenRetriever** receives an input Japanese sentence (*JSen*), and retrieves it in the *JCSenIndex*. If the *JCSenIndex* contains the key of *JSen*, the **SenRetriever**, supported by the *JCSenBank*, will output the value of *CSens* corresponding to the *JSen*. If the *JCSenIndex* does not contain the *JSen*, a similar Japanese sentence in the syntactic pattern and word-word translations as much as possible will be very helpful. At this time, the **Tokenizer** is triggered, which receives the input *JSen*, and extracts its Japanese words (*JWords*) and hiratokens (*Hiratokens*). The **WordRetriever** retrieves the *JWords* in the *JCWordIndex*, and outputs the corresponding Chinese words (*CWords*). The **HiraRetriever** retrieves the *Hiratokens* in the *HiratokenSenIndex*, and outputs Japanese sentences (*JSens*) supported by the *JCSenBank*. For the input *JSen*, the **FastSyntaxMatcher** calculates one Levenshtein distance to each sentence in the *JSens*, and outputs the most similar Japanese sentences (*SimilarJSens*). The *SimilarJSens* is a set of sentences, because multiple sentences may have the same shortest Levenshtein distance to the given *JSen*. The same **SenRetriever** will output the Chinese sentences (*SimilarCSens*) related to the *SimilarJSens*.

The **FastSyntaxMatcher** is only a loop version of the traditional Levenshtein function, which depends on the **HiraRetriever** to fast seek sentences with a similar syntactic pattern. In the **HiraRetriever**, there is a preset Top-n value to truncate the number of output Japanese sentences, which have a similar syntactic pattern for containing the same syntactic identifiers.

3 Algorithm

Figure 2 gives the pseudo-code for our fast-syntax-matching-based Japanese-Chinese (FSMJC) LMT algorithm consisting of two main functions: *translate* and *preprocess*. And the *translate* function calls a key *fastsyntaxmatch* function. The FSMJC LMT algorithm takes the translating as an index retrieving process and takes the preprocessing as an indexing process.

If we use N and n to denote the number of sentences in the *JCSenBank* and the preset Top-n value, respectively, the maximal complexity of the FSMJC LMT algorithm will be $O(n)$ and be independent of the N value. Usually, the n is a small integer and is far smaller than the N value. Thus, the FSMJC LMT algorithm is acceptable in practical applications.

```
1.      // FSMJC LMT Algorithm
2.      JCSenBank jcsb;
3.      JCDict jcd;
4.      JCSenIndex jcsi;
5.      HiratokenSenIndex hsi;
6.      JCWordIndex jcwi;
7.
8.      Function Result: translate(JSen js, Integer n)
9.      Result r;
10.     If (jcsi.contain(js))
11.     Then  r.add((CSen[]) jcsi.get(js, jcsb));
12.     Else   Hiratoken[] hs ← Tokenizer.htokenize(js);
13.            JWord[] jws ← Tokenizer.wtokenize(js);
14.            r.add((CWord[]) jcwi.get(jws));
15.            JSen[] jss ← hsi.get(hs, jcsb, n);
16.            JSen[] sjss ← fastsyntaxmatch(js, jss);
17.            r.add((CSen[]) jcsi.get(sjss, jcsb));
18.     End If
19.     Return r.
20.
21.     Function JSen[]: fastsyntaxmatch(JSen js, JSen[] jss)
22.     JSen[] sjss;
23.     Float min ← Float.max;
24.     For Integer i ← 1 To jss.size Do
25.         Float f ← levenshteindis(js, jss[i]);
26.         If (f < min)
27.         Then sjss.clear;
28.              sjss.add(jss[i]);
29.              min ← f;
30.         Else If (f = min)
31.         Then sjss.add(jss[i]);
32.         End If
33.     End For
34.     Return sjss.
35.
36.     Function void: preprocess()
37.     jcsi ← senindex(jcsb);
38.     hsi ← hiraindex(jcsb);
39.     jcwi ← wordindex(jcd).
```

Fig. 2. FSMJC LMT algorithm.

4   Experiment

In order to validate the effectiveness of our LMT technique, we do the following experiment. Firstly, we test the *preprocess* function to explain that the data structure of our indexes is space-time-efficient. Secondly, we implement a baseline syntax matcher based on the traditional Levenshtein algorithm. Finally, we compare our LMT result with the manual golden standard to discuss the performance of the FSMJC LMT algorithm.

4.1   Dataset

In the experiment, we use a public dataset of the Japanese-Chinese Sentence Bank (JCSB)[1] and our Japanese-Chinese dictionary. The JCSB dataset contains 371,712 pairs of Japanese-Chinese sentences. The Japanese-Chinese dictionary contains 436,199 pairs

---

[1] http://cbd.nichesite.org/CBD2014D002.htm.

of Japanese-Chinese words, which can be used as the *JCDict* in Fig. 1. We run the experiment on a computer with 4.00 GB RAM and Intel Core i5-2520 M CPU.

In order to construct the scientific test set (*TSet*) and the *JCSenBank* mentioned in Sect. 2, we use a simple random sampling method to extract 1,000 pairs of sentences from the JCSB dataset as a *TSet*, and the remaining 370,712 pairs as a *JCSenBank*. We run the simple random sampling 10 times, and get 10 pairs of <*JCSenBank, TSet*>. We do the experiment in each pair of <*JCSenBank, TSet*>, and will get 10 groups of experimental results. In the following discussions, we will report the mean value of performance among the 10 groups.

4.2 Preprocess Result and Discussion

We run the *preprocess* function to make three indexes. Table 1 shows the mean run-time and file space. Averagely, the raw plain text file of the *JCSenBank* occupies 33 MB space, and it will cost 6 s to make the *JCSenBank* into a *HiratokenSenIndex*, which will occupy 29 MB space.

Table 1. Time and space.

	Raw space (MB)	Indexing time (sec)	Index space (MB)	
JCSenBank	33	1	35	*JCSenIndex*
JCSenBank	33	6	29	*HiratokenSenIndex*
JCDict	17	2	21	*JCWordIndex*

Because there is not a repetitive item both in the *JCSenBank* and the *JCDict*, the size of raw file is close to that of corresponding index. It is equivalent to converting the file storage format, so the index structure is space-efficient. And each retrieving in an index has a constant time complexity according to a string hash function, so the index structure is also time-efficient.

4.3 FSM Result and Discussion

We focus more on the FSM issue, and ignore the exact-hit-based translation memory. There is just not an intersection between the *JCSenBank* and the *TSet*, so the *JCSenIndex* will not be hit during the experiment.

Supported by the above indexes, we run our *translate* function and output the similar Japanese sentences (*SimilarJSens*) for each sentence in the *TSet*. We also implement a baseline syntax matcher with no need for indexes. If the number of Japanese sentences is m in the *JCSenBank*, the baseline will calculate m Levenshtein distances and output the most similar Japanese sentences (*MSimilarJSens*) for a given sentence. Using the same *TSet*, we run the baseline and regard its result as the pseudo golden standard.

We report the runtime and the classical Precision, Recall, F1 measure to evaluate the experimental result. The value of Precision, Recall, F1 belongs to [0, 1], where 1 is optimal.

As expected, the runtime of the baseline in the *TSet* is the horrible 3,088 s. It will cost 3 s that the traditional Levenshtein function compares 370,712 times for a given Japanese sentence. Figure 3 shows the experimental result of our *translate* function under different Top-n value from 10 to 200. We find that the *translate* function can get the 37% precision at the time cost of 40 s, and it can reduce the time cost from 3,088 s to 40 s. On the situation of Top-n = 200, averagely each sentence costs 40/1,000 = 0.04 s. That is to say, in one second, the *translate* function can complete 25 FSM operations in a big set of 370,712 sentences.

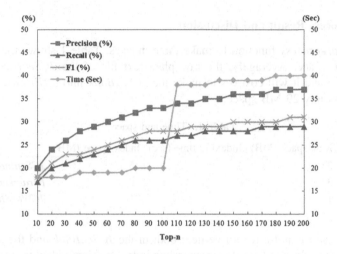

Fig. 3. Precision, recall, F1 and time.

Moreover, the 37% precision is dependent of the pseudo golden standard from full formal occurrence. The actual precision of our FSM is higher than 37%, because the full formal occurrence is stricter than the syntactic pattern. The result proves that Japanese texts have explicit syntactic identifiers, and this feature helps the FSM method to calculate part formal occurrence efficiently, which is the substantial clause of its success.

4.4 LMT Result and Discussion

Among MT evaluation measures, the BLEU4 is an effective one [9], which is based on the smoothed modified k-gram precision for multiple reference texts, and is computed as Eq. (1). Where the c denotes the length of candidate text, the r denotes the length of effective reference text, and the p_k denotes the smoothed modified k-gram precision.

$$BLEU4 = exp(min(0, 1 - \frac{r}{c}) + \frac{1}{4}\sum_{k=1}^{4} ln(p_k)) \tag{1}$$

Comparing with the golden standard, we calculate the BLEU4 value to evaluate our LMT result. The values of **BLEU4**.*JSens* are calculated from our candidate source *SimilarJSens* and the pseudo reference source *MSimilarJSens*. The values of **BLEU4**. *CSens* are calculated from our candidate translation *SimilarCSens* and the manual reference translation.

Table 2 shows the detailed experimental result. With the Top-n value from 10 to 200, the time cost only increases a little, while that of the baseline is 3,088 s. On the situation of Top-n = 200, the FSMJC LMT algorithm can achieve the performance (**BLEU4**.*JSens* = 0.4792, **BLEU4**.*CSens* = 0.1797).

Table 2. Time and BLEU4.

Top-n	Time (sec)	BLEU4. JSens	BLEU4. CSens	Top-n	Time (sec)	BLEU4. JSens	BLEU4. CSens
10	18	0.3248	0.1688	110	38	0.4455	0.1794
20	18	0.3627	0.1724	120	38	0.4492	0.1795
30	18	0.3835	0.1746	130	38	0.4549	0.1793
40	19	0.3956	0.1746	140	39	0.4562	0.1791
50	19	0.4075	0.1756	150	39	0.4619	0.1790
60	19	0.4198	0.1772	160	39	0.4652	0.1791
70	19	0.4278	0.1775	170	39	0.4704	0.1794
80	20	0.4348	0.1776	180	40	0.4713	0.1794
90	20	0.4408	0.1784	190	40	0.4756	0.1797
100	20	0.4422	0.1786	200	40	0.4792	0.1797

We select two example sentences randomly in the experiment to further expatiate the advantage of our algorithm. Table 3 shows the two Japanese sentences ([*JSen*]) and the corresponding Chinese translation sentences ([*CSen*]) in the JCSB, the sentence [*MSimilarJSens*] of pseudo golden standard, and the sentence recommended by our FSMJC LMT algorithm.

Table 3. Two example sentences.

	Example Sentence 1	Example Sentence 2
JCSB	[*JSen*]2003 年の環境汚染処理投資額は国内総生産の 1.39%を占めた。[*CSen*]2003 年环境污染治理投资占国内生产总值的 1.39%。	[*JSen*]彼は歌がへたなので人を静めることができず、聴衆はみな帰ってしまった。[*CSen*]他唱得不好，压不住人，听众都走了。
Pseudo Golden Standard	[*MSimilarJSens*]2006 年、環境汚染処理への投資は GDP の 1.15%を占めた。[*MSimilarCSens*]2006 年，环境污染治理投资占国内生产总值的 1.15%。	[*MSimilarJSens*]彼はみんなの意見に逆らうことができず、やむなく承知した。[*MSimilarCSens*]他拗不过大家的意见，只得依从。
FSMJC LMT Algorithm	[*SimilarJSens*]2006 年、環境汚染処理への投資は GDP の 1.15%を占めた。[*SimilarCSens*]2006 年，环境污染治理投资占国内生产总值的 1.15%。	[*SimilarJSens.0*]彼は様子がおかしいので、とんぼ返りに帰ってしまった。[*SimilarCSens.0*]他看情形不对，转身就走了。[*SimilarJSens.1*]彼は寝返りを一つうったが、また眠ってしまった。[*SimilarCSens.1*]他翻了一个身，又睡着了。[*SimilarJSens.2*]彼は不当な取り扱いを受けたと思い、ふてくされて帰ってしまった。[*SimilarCSens.2*]他觉得受了委屈，一赌气就走了。

For the example sentence 1, we find that the baseline Levenshtein algorithm and our algorithm can get the same result ([*MSimilarJSens*] and [*SimilarJSens*]), and there is only a few difference between sentences ([*JSen*] and [*SimilarJSens*]). If a Chinese person sends a Japanese sentence ([*JSen*]) of the example sentence 1 to a computer-aided translation system, and can get a pair of Japanese-Chinese sentences ([*SimilarJSens*] and [*SimilarCSens*]). We believe that the person will guess well.

For the example sentence 2, the baseline Levenshtein algorithm recommends a similar sentence ([*MSimilarJSens*]), while the FSMJC LMT algorithm recommends three similar ones ([*SimilarJSens*.0], [*SimilarJSens*.1], and [*SimilarJSens*.2]). Judging by the linguists, the three similar sentences have the most similar syntactic pattern to the given Japanese sentence [*JSen*]. Though the FSMJC LMT algorithm does not hit the pseudo golden standard for the sentence [*JSen*], the linguists believe that the sentence [*SimilarJSens*.0] is a fine recommendation especially.

We will further explain the belief of linguists by calculating a hit rate manually. Table 4 shows the token bitmap of the example sentence 2. There are three lines for each sentence: the first line is the symbol bitmap, the second line is the hiratoken bitmap, and the third line is the word bitmap segmented by linguists.

Table 4. Token bitmap of example sentence 2.

[JSen]

- Symbol: 彼(1) は(2) 歌(3) が(4) へ(5) た(6) な(7) の(8) で(9) 人(10) を(11) 静(12) め(13) る(14) こ(15) と(16) が(17) で(18) き(19) ず(20) 、(21) 聴(22) 衆(23) は(24) み(25) な(26) 帰(27) っ(28) て(29) し(30) ま(31) っ(32) た(33) 。(34)
- Hiratoken: は(1) がへたなので(2) を(3) めることができず(4) はみな(5) ってしまった(6)
- Word: 彼(1) は(2) 歌(3) が(4) へたな(5) ので(6) 人(7) を(8) 静める(9) こと(10) が(11) でき(12) ず(13) 、(14) 聴衆(15) は(16) みな(17) 帰(18) っ(19) てしま(20) った(21) 。(22)

[MSimilarJSens]

- Symbol: 彼(1) は(2) み(3) ん(4) な(5) の(6) 意(7) 見(8) に(9) 逆(10) ら(11) う(12) こ(13) と(14) が(15) で(16) き(17) ず(18) 、(19) や(20) む(21) な(22) く(23) 承(24) 知(25) し(26) た(27) 。(28)
- Hiratoken: は みんなの(1) に(2) らうことができず(3) やむなく(4) した(5)
- Word: 彼(1) は(2) みんな(3) の(4) 意見(5) に(6) 逆らう(7) こと(8) が(9) でき(10) ず(11) 、(12) やむなく(13) 承知(14) し(15) た。(16)

[SimilarJSens.0]

- Symbol: 彼(1) は(2) 様(3) 子(4) が(5) お(6) か(7) し(8) い(9) の(10) で(11) 、(12) と(13) ん(14) ぼ(15) 返(16) り(17) に(18) 帰(19) っ(20) て(21) し(22) ま(23) っ(24) た(25) 。(26)
- Hiratoken: は(1) がおかしいので(2) とんぼ(3) りに(4) ってしまった(5)
- Word: 彼(1) は(2) 様子(3) が(4) おかしい(5) ので(6) 、(7) とんぼ(8) 返り(9) に(10) 帰(11) っ(12) てしま(13) った。(14)

[SimilarJSens.1]

- Symbol: 彼(1) は(2) 寝(3) 返(4) り(5) を(6) 一(7) つ(8) う(9) っ(10) た(11) が(12) 、(13) ま(14) た(15) 眠(16) っ(17) て(18) し(19) ま(20) っ(21) た(22) 。(23)
- Hiratoken: は(1) りを(2) つうったが(3) また(4) ってしまった(5)
- Word: 彼(1) は(2) 寝返り(3) を(4) 一(5) つ(6) う(7) っ(8) た(9) が(10) 、(11) また(12) 眠(13) って(14) しまった。(15)

[SimilarJSens.2]

- Symbol: 彼(1) は(2) 不(3) 当(4) な(5) 取(6) り(7) 扱(8) い(9) を(10) 受(11) け(12) た(13) と(14) 思(15) い(16) 、(17) ふ(18) て(19) く(20) さ(21) れ(22) て(23) 帰(24) っ(25) て(26) し(27) ま(28) っ(29) た(30) 。(31)
- Hiratoken: は(1) な(2) り(3) いを(4) けたと(5) い(6) ふてくされて(7) ってしまった(8)
- Word: 彼(1) は(2) 不当(3) な(4) 取り(5) 扱い(6) を(7) 受け(8) た(9) と(10) 思い(11) ふてくされて(12) 帰(13) っ(14) てしま(15) った(16) 。(17)

According to the above token bitmap, we can easily calculate the hit rate for each sentence. Table 5 shows the detailed hit rate of various tokens. We can find that the sentence [*MSimilarJSens*] of pseudo golden standard has lower hit rates in three tokens and the top hit rate belongs to the sentence [*SimilarJSens*.0]. Especially the word hit rate of the sentence [*SimilarJSens*.0] is the top 0.714 among those of the four sentences, which proves that the sentence recommended by our algorithm has a more similar syntactic pattern to the given sentence [*JSen*].

Table 5. Hit rate of various tokens.

Token	Sentence	Hit number	Total number	Hit rate
Symbol	[*MSimilarJSens*]	15	28	15/28 = 0.536
	[*SimilarJSens*.0]	14	26	14/26 = **0.538**
	[*SimilarJSens*.1]	12	23	12/23 = 0.522
	[*SimilarJSens*.2]	14	31	14/31 = 0.452
Hiratoken	[*MSimilarJSens*]	0	5	0/5 = 0.000
	[*SimilarJSens*.0]	2	5	2/5 = **0.400**
	[*SimilarJSens*.1]	2	5	2/5 = **0.400**
	[*SimilarJSens*.2]	2	8	2/8 = 0.250
Word	[*MSimilarJSens*]	9	16	9/16 = 0.563
	[*SimilarJSens*.0]	10	14	10/14 = **0.714**
	[*SimilarJSens*.1]	9	15	9/15 = 0.600
	[*SimilarJSens*.2]	9	17	9/17 = 0.529

The above experiment validates the effectiveness of our LMT technique: (I) the data structure is space-time-efficient; (II) the two hypotheses are effective in the Japanese FSM method; and (III) the FSMJC LMT algorithm can obtain desirable effects with greatly reduced time costs.

5 Conclusion

This paper presents a novel bilingual LMT architecture, and validates that the two syntactic hypotheses are effective on Japanese texts. Currently, more finding similar sentence with manual translation and useful dictionary hints, than providing an imperfect translation will help us to make a tripping translation.

Further research will add some rules of probabilistic syntax frame to assemble our outputs of *CWords* and *SimilarCSens* into a fluent Chinese sentence. We also expect to discover explicit formal syntactic identifiers for other languages, and to transfer above research productions to the languages.

Acknowledgements. The research is supported by the Key Project of State Language Commission of China (Resource Construction and Application of Low-Resource Languages for the 21st Century Maritime Silk Road) and the Featured Innovation Project of Guangdong Province (No. 2015KTSCX035).

References

1. Brown, R.D.: The CMU-EBMT machine translation system. Mach. Transl. **25**(2), 179–195 (2011)
2. Biçici, E., Dymetman, M.: Dynamic translation memory: using statistical machine translation to improve translation memory fuzzy matches. In: Gelbukh, A. (ed.) CICLing 2008. LNCS, vol. 4919, pp. 454–465. Springer, Heidelberg (2008). doi:10.1007/978-3-540-78135-6_39
3. Callison-Burch, C., Talbot, D., Osborne, M.: Statistical machine translation with word- and sentence-aligned parallel corpora. In: Proceedings of ACL 2004, the 42nd Meeting of the Association for Computational Linguistics, Barcelona, Spain, Main Volume, pp. 175–182 (2004)
4. Vanallemeersch, T., Vandeghinste V.: Improving fuzzy matching through syntactic knowledge. In: Proceedings of the 36th Translating and the Computer Conference, Westminster, London, UK (2014)
5. Koehn, P., Senellart, J.: Fast approximate string matching with suffix arrays and A* parsing. In: Proceedings of AMTA 2010, the 9th Biennial Conference of the Association for Machine Translation in the Americas, Denver, Colorado, USA (2010)
6. Navarro, G., Baeza-Yates, R., Sutinen, E., Tarhio, J.: Indexing methods for approximate string matching. IEEE Data Eng. Bull. **24**(4), 19–27 (2001)
7. Dan, H., Sudoh, K., Wu, X., Duh, K., Tsukada, H., Nagata, M.: Head finalization reordering for Chinese-to-Japanese machine translation. In: Proceedings of the Sixth Workshop on Syntax, Semantics and Structure in Statistical Translation, Stroudsburg, PA, USA, pp. 57–66 (2012)
8. Chu, C., Nakazawa, T., Kawahara, D., Kurohashi, S.: Chinese-Japanese machine translation exploiting Chinese characters. ACM Trans. Asian Lang. Inf. Process. **12**(4), Article 16 (2013)
9. Lin, C.-Y., Och, F.J.: ORANGE: a method for evaluating automatic evaluation metrics for machine translation. In: Proceedings of the 20th International Conference on Computational Linguistics, Geneva, Switzerland (2004)

Value at Risk for Risk Evaluation in Information Retrieval

Meijia Wang[1], Peng Zhang[1(✉)], Dawei Song[1,2], and Jun Wang[3]

[1] Tianjin Key Laboratory of Congitive Computing and Application,
School of Computer Science and Technology, Tianjin University,
Tianjin, People's Republic of China
meigawang@163.com, {pzhang,dwsong}@tju.edu.cn
[2] Department of Computing and Communications,
The Open University, Bailrigg, UK
[3] Department of Computer Science, University College London, London, UK
jun_wang@acm.org

Abstract. In Information Retrieval (IR), evaluation metrics continuously play an important role. Recently, some risk measures have been proposed to evaluate the downside performance or the performance variance of an assumingly advanced IR method in comparison with a baseline method. In this paper, we propose a novel risk metric, by applying the Value at Risk theory (VaR, which has been widely used in financial investment) to IR risk evaluation. The proposed metric (VaR_IR) is implemented in the light of typical IR effectiveness metrics (e.g. AP) and used to evaluate the participating systems submitted to Session Tracks and compared with other risk metrics. The empirical evaluation has shown that VaR_IR is complementary to and can be integrated with the effectiveness metrics to provide a more comprehensive evaluation method.

Keywords: Risk · Evaluation · Value at Risk

1 Introduction

Risk is an important factor of uncertainties in both model design and system evaluation in Information Retrieval (IR). The uncertainties in IR include the uncertainty on document relevance, uncertainty on document ranking, and uncertainty on system stability, etc. From the model design perspective, given certain assumptions or loss functions, the probabilistic ranking principle (PRP) [6,7] and a risk minimization framework [8] estimate the document relevance precisely and obtain an optimal document ranking with minimal risks. From the system evaluation point of view, the concept of risk is different. It refers to the stability of the retrieval performance. In this paper, we focus on the evaluation perspective of risks and aim to develop a new risk evaluation metric.

In the literature, a number of risk measures have been proposed to evaluate the downside performance or the performance variance of an assumingly

© Springer International Publishing AG 2016
C.-Y. Lin et al. (Eds.): NLPCC-ICCPOL 2016, LNAI 10102, pp. 631–638, 2016.
DOI: 10.1007/978-3-319-50496-4_56

advanced IR method compared with a baseline method. The downside performance can be evaluated by the $R - Loss$ [2]), or the $<Init$ (the percentage of queries for which the retrieval performance is worse than that of a baseline method [1]). The robustness index (RI) [2] (reflecting the performance variance) calculates the difference between the number of queries that has achieved an improved performance and the number of queries whose performance gets hurt. In addition, the variance of retrieval performance (e.g., Variance of Average Precision, VAP) can be used as a risk metric to reflect the system stability [9]. More recently, U_{risk} was proposed by creating a win-loss distribution across all queries [3].

These existing risk metrics measure various stability aspects of a retrieval method. The design of these metrics, however, are mostly not based on a solid mathematical foundation. In addition, the aforementioned risk measures have some specific limitations. For instance, as shown in Table 1, the risk values are reported for the systems A and B against the baseline. Although the AP value of system A is equal to that of system B for each query, the document lists retrieved by the two systems are very different. Thus, we still want to analyze which system has the lower risk. However, based on the traditional risk metrics, the risk value for system A is the same as the risk value for system B, which means that the traditional risk metrics fail to test which system has a lower risk. In addition, even one can change the AP value of system B from 0.4 to 0.5, still, some existing risk metrics can not distinguish two systems, since they only take into account the number of improved queries and/or hurt queries and these numbers remains unchanged, thus they can't distinguish the risk between systems when systems have the same AP value. We will show in the experiments that the example in Table 1 is a common problem in Session search task.

In this paper, we propose a novel risk metric, by applying the Value at Risk (VaR, which has been widely used in financial investment) to IR risk evaluation. The proposed risk metric, namely VaR_IR, is different from the existing risk in the following aspects. First, VaR_IR is a formal quantitative analysis approach for risk estimation building upon a solid statistical basis, compared to existing risk metrics. VaR_IR can summarize potential risks at a given confidence level, which guarantees the reliability. Second, VaR_IR takes into account the variance of ranking, where the covariance matrix among returned document plays an important role (see Sect. 3.1). Third, VaR_IR is an integrated approach which naturally incorporates the effectiveness metrics and effectiveness improvements in its formulation (see Sect. 3.2). It can give a specific value of risk for each query (rather than across queries as in existing risk metrics) and mean of risk values over all queries can be used to evaluate the risk of a retrieval system.

We carry out experiments to evaluate the risks of different query reformulation methods in Session Track. We report the results for different query reformulation features, and the relationship between the effectiveness improvements. The formulation of VaR_IR and the experiments in Session track demonstrate the advantages of VaR_IR for the risk evaluation in a more comprehensive way.

Table 1. An example for different risk values

Model	Baseline		A		B	
Query	q1	q2	q1	q2	q1	q2
AP	0.3	0.2	0.2	0.4	0.2	0.4
$<Init$	0		0.5		0.5	
RI	0		0		0	
U_{risk}	0		0.2		0.2	
VAP	0.005		0.02		0.02	
VaR_IR	0.87		0.68		0.39	

2 Value at Risk in Finance

2.1 Concept of Value at Risk

In Finance, Value at Risk (VaR) is a method to formulate the magnitude of likely loss in a portfolio and measure the worst expected loss under normal market conditions over a specific time interval at a given confidence level [4].

2.2 General Formula of Value at Risk

To compute VaR of a portfolio, according to [5], we have:

$$VaR = E(W) - W^* \tag{1}$$

where $E(W)$ is expected value of portfolio, W is the portfolio value at the end, and W^* is the lowest portfolio value at a given confidence level.

Let W_0 denotes the initial investment and R denotes the rate of return. W can be defined as follows:

$$W = W_0 * (1 + R) \tag{2}$$

Likewise, let R^* denotes the lowest rate of return at given confidence level. We have

$$W^* = W_0 * (1 + R^*) \tag{3}$$

Based on the above equations, VaR can be calculated by:

$$
\begin{aligned}
VaR &= E(W) - W^* \\
&= E(W_0 * (1 + R)) - W_0 * (1 + R^*) \\
&= W_0(E(R) - R^*)
\end{aligned} \tag{4}
$$

It implies that VaR can be computed by the identification of the lowest rate of return at a given confidence level.

2.3   Variance-Covariance Method

In Finance, VaR can be calculated by four methods which are modified from general method, among which Variance-Covariance method is a widely used one and can be naturally applied in the IR task. Variance-Covariance method can be summarized into two steps: First, it calculates the variance, standard deviation, and covariance, respectively, in order to get the matrix of variance-covariance by historical data. Second, it computes the value of VaR at a fixed parameter of confidence interval. Following these steps, we have:

$$VaR = -S(\hat{\mu} + \phi^{-1}(\alpha)\hat{\sigma}) \tag{5}$$

where S depicts an investment which is corresponding to W_0 in Eq. 4, $\hat{\mu}$ is the estimator of the expected value of portfolio which is corresponding to $E(R)$ in Eq. 4, $\phi^{-1}(\alpha)$ is the quantile set by banks themselves, and $\phi^{-1}(\alpha)\hat{\sigma}$ is used to calculate the return R^* in Eq. 4. In Eq. 5, the negative sign reflects that you get the loss at the end.

3   Value at Risk in IR (VaR_IR)

In this section, we apply VaR to IR and propose a new evaluation method called VaR_IR. VaR_IR is used to measure the magnitude of risk in a IR system. A specific value of VaR_IR will be calculated for the document ranking list of a given query, and the mean of VaR_IR can be used to evaluate the overall risk of a system.

3.1   Estimation of Variance of Ranking

In Finance, one can calculate the variance term $\hat{\sigma}$ in Eq. 5, using variance-covariance matrix. We calculate VaR_IR based on the document ranking for each query. The equation is given as:

$$Var(a_n) = \sum_{i=1}^{n} w_i^2 c_{i,i} + \sum_{i=1}^{n} \sum_{j=i+1}^{n} w_i w_j c_{i,j} \tag{6}$$

where w_i denotes the weight of the position i in the document ranking, $c_{i,i}$ is the variance of the individual document, $c_{i,j}$ means the covariance of the documents at the position i and the document at the position j, and a_n means ranking of top n documents.

3.2   Incorporation of Effectiveness Metric and Effectiveness Improvement

In Finance, μ is the expected value of the portfolio in Eq. 5. We calculate μ on the basis of ranking positions. Four steps to compute μ are summarized as follows: First, the calculation of the expected value μ begins by identifying whether a document at each position in the rank list is relevant to the given query. Second, we compute the weight of position in a given rank list. Note that different effectiveness metrics result in different weight values as shown in the Table 2. Third, we calculate the effectiveness score of documents ranking by using aforementioned weights and relevance. Finally, we calculate the expected value by exploiting this score. We give the general formula for such an effectiveness score:

$$S_{a_n} = \begin{bmatrix} w_1 & w_2 & w_3 & ... & w_i & ... & w_n \end{bmatrix} \begin{bmatrix} r_1 \\ r_2 \\ ... \\ r_i \\ ... \\ r_n \end{bmatrix} \tag{7}$$

where w_i is the weight of the position i in the document ranking, r_i denotes the state of relevance of the corresponding document at the position i, n is the number of documents returned, and S_{a_n} denotes the result of matrix multiplication which refers to the effectiveness score of top n documents in the ranking list. Then, we calculate μ as:

$$\mu = (S_{a_{n'}} - S_{a_n})/S_{a_n} \tag{8}$$

where S_{a_n} is the effectiveness score of baseline, and $S_{a_{n'}}$ is the score of an assumingly advanced method to test. The value of μ in Eq. 8 computes the improvements of the retrieval effectiveness.

3.3 The Formula of VaR_IR

According to Eq. 5 and the above descriptions, the formula of VaR_IR is:

$$VaR\_IR = -S((S_{a_{n'}} - S_{a_n})/S_{a_n} + \phi^{-1}(\alpha)\sqrt{Var(a_n)}) \tag{9}$$

This is the final equation we proposed to calculate the risk in the information retrieval. In the above equation, S denotes the initial performance (i.e., the effectiveness score of the baseline), and $\phi^{-1}(\alpha)$ is the quantile which is decided by the confidence interval which can be set by the user according to their risk preference. $(S_{a_{n'}} - S_{a_n})/S_{a_n}$ is the improved effectiveness, and $Var(a_n)$ is the variance of document ranking list in Eq. 6.

Table 2. Effectiveness metrics and their weights

Metric	AP	P@M	DCG	RR
Weight	$\frac{1}{i}$	1	$\frac{1}{\log(1+i)}$	$\frac{1}{i}$

4   Empirical Evaluation

4.1   Evaluation Setup

Using VaR_IR we have proposed, we carry out an empirical evaluation on Session Track 2011, 2012. The goal of our experiments is to see the risk evaluation compared with different risk metrics and the relationship between VaR_IR and μ. Table 3 shows that different query reformulations contain different information, where RL1 is the baseline. We calculate VaR_IR of RL2, RL3 for participating systems based on effectiveness metric AP due to page limited.

Table 3. Different query formulation features

Types	Reformulation
RL1	Current query
RL2	Current query, previous queries
RL3	Current query, previous queries, URL
RL4	Current query, previous queries, URL, dwell time

4.2   Risk Evaluation Results in Session Track

Analysing Different Risk Measures. Recall that our goal is to compare the risk of different query reformulation features, by observing the risk values of different risk metrics. In this set of experiments, we actually tested ten systems participated in the Session Track 2011 and 2012, but only report the result of PITTSHQMsdm in Session Track 2012. The test queries are Q1-Q50, and the risk values of two query reformulation features (namely RL2 and RL3) are reported, with various risk metrics, in Table 4.

As shown in Table 4, for the three existing risk metrics, the risk values of RL2 are usually equal to the risk values of RL3. It shows the same problem as we observe from Table 1. To have a more systematic observation, we randomly choose a number of queries. This sampling process will repeat 30 times and the mean risk values are reported. Table 4 shows that the three existing risk metrics can not distinguish the risks between RL2 and RL3.

In order to explain this phenomenon in detail, we report the effectiveness scores (i.e., AP values) for RL2 and RL3 over five individual queries Q1–Q5 on the PITTSHQMsdm system. Table 5 shows that, for three out of five queries, the AP values are the same between RL2 and RL3. However, we find that the returned documents are different between RL2 and RL3. We also observe that 45 queries in 50 queries have the same cases, which lead to the fact that the risk values of RL2 are equal to those of RL3 for RI, $<Init$ and U_{risk}, like Table 4 shows.

Table 4. The value of different risk metrics

Query number	10		20		30		40		50	
Query type	RL2	RL3	RL2	RL3	RL2	RL3	RL2	RL3	RL2	RL3
$<Init$	0.2	0.2	0.1	0.1	0.07	0.07	0.05	0.05	0.04	0.04
RI	0	0	0	0	0	0	0	0	0	0
U_{risk}	0.03	0.04	0.02	0.02	0.01	0.01	0.01	0.01	0.01	0.01
VaR_IR	**1.13**	**1.58**	**1.32**	**1.51**	**1.31**	**1.58**	**1.25**	**1.57**	**1.48**	**1.64**

Table 5. AP of different query reformulations

Query	Q1	Q2	Q3	Q4	Q5
RL1	0.28	0.16	0.29	0.29	0.22
RL2	**0.27**	0.18	0.26	**0.29**	**0.28**
RL3	**0.27**	0.22	0.27	**0.29**	**0.28**

Table 6. The significance test for different risk metrics

Risk metric	$<Init$	RI	U_{risk}	VaR_IR
P value	1	1	0.92	0.01

We now observe the risk values evaluated by the proposed risk metric VaR_IR. Table 4 shows that using VaR_IR, we can distinguish RL2 and RL3, and observe that RL2 has the lower risk. VaR_IR shows significantly different risk values for RL2 and RL3 (see the significance test in Table 6). The reason is that VaR_IR does not only depend on the effectiveness score, but also takes into account the covariance matrix among returned documents. In other words, although two query formulation features (RL2 and RL3) have the same or close effectiveness scores, the different document lists lead to the different covariance matrices and hence the different risk values. Based on the above comparisons and discussions, VaR_IR can evaluate the risk more comprehensively, in the sense that VaR_IR can take into account the initial effectiveness, the effectiveness improvements and the variance of the retrieved documents, in a single metric.

Relationship Between μ and VaR_IR. We now analyze the correlation between μ which is the improved effectiveness scores (see Eq. 8) and the risk value of VaR_IR (see Eq. 9). In Fig. 1, we choose five systems which performs well in the Session Track 2012. From the Fig. 1, it shows that when the μ increases, the VaR_IR tends to decrease accordingly.

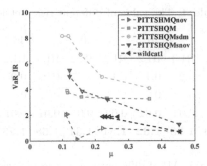

Fig. 1. VaR_IR and μ in Session Track 2012

5   Conclusions

In this paper, we propose a novel risk evaluation metric called VaR_IR on the basis of widely used Value at Risk theory in Finance. VaR_IR is not only a formal quantitative risk method but also integrates effectiveness metrics.

Acknowledgements. The work presented in this paper is sponsored in part by the Chinese National Program on Key Basic Research Project (973 Program, grant No. 2013CB329304, 2014CB744604), the Chinese 863 Program (grant No. 2015AA015403), the Natural Science Foundation of China (grant No. 61402324, 61272265), and the Research Fund for the Doctoral Program of Higher Education of China (grant No. 20130032120044).

References

1. Amati, G., Carpineto, C., Romano, G.: Query difficulty, robustness, and selective application of query expansion. In: McDonald, S., Tait, J. (eds.) ECIR 2004. LNCS, vol. 2997, pp. 127–137. Springer, Heidelberg (2004). doi:10.1007/978-3-540-24752-4_10
2. Collins-Thompson, K.: Reducing the risk of query expansion via robust constrained optimization. In: Proceedings of CIKM 2009, pp. 837–846. ACM (2009)
3. Collins-Thompson, K., Macdonald, C., Bennett, P., Diaz, F., Voorhees, E.M.: Trec 2014 web track overview. Technical report, DTIC Document (2015)
4. Linsmeier, T.J., Pearson, N.D.: Value at risk. Financ. Anal. J. **56**(2), 47–67 (2000)
5. Morgan, J.: Riskmetrics: Technical Document. Morgan Guaranty Trust Company of New York, New York (1996)
6. Robertson, S.E.: The probability ranking principle in IR. J. Documentation **33**, 294–304 (1977)
7. van Rijsbergen, C.J.: Information Retrieval. Butterworths, Oxford (1979)
8. Zhai, C., Lafferty, J.D.: A risk minimization framework for information retrieval. Inf. Process. Manag. **42**(1), 31–55 (2006)
9. Zhang, P., Song, D., Wang, J., Hou, Y.: Bias-variance decomposition of IR evaluation. In: Proceedings of SIGIR, vol. 2013, pp. 1021–1024 (2013)

Chinese Paraphrases Acquisition Based on Random Walk N Step

Jun Ma, Yujie Zhang[✉], Jinan Xu, and Yufeng Chen

School of Computer and Information Technology,
Beijing Jiaotong University, Beijing, China
{15125191,yjzhang}@bjtu.edu.cn

Abstract. Conventional "pivot-based" approach of acquiring paraphrasing from bilingual corpus has limitations, where only paraphrases within two steps were considered. We propose a graph based model of acquiring paraphrases from phrases translation table. This paper describes the way of constructing graph model from phrases translation table, a random walk algorithm based on N number of steps and a confidence metric for ranking the obtained results. Furthermore, we augment the model to be able to integrate more language pairs, for instance, exploiting English-Japanese phrases translation table for finding more potential Chinese paraphrases. We performed experiments on NTCIR Chinese-English and English-Japanese bilingual corpora and compared with the conventional method. The experimental results showed that the proposed model acquired more paraphrases, and performed more well after English-Japanese phrases translation was added into the graph model.

Keywords: Paraphrases acquisition · Random walk · Graph model

1 Introduction

Paraphrases are the different expressions of the same meaning [1]. Paraphrasing phenomena are common in natural language, which reflect the diversity and complexity of language. Paraphrasing is getting more attention in natural language processing and is used in many applications, including machine translation [2], automatic summarization [3, 4], information retrieve [5], natural language generation [6], question answering [7]. The key issues of paraphrasing are paraphrase recognition and paraphrase generation, which are all based on paraphrase knowledge. However, there are not enough resources for paraphrasing, compared to other language resources constructed for parsing and machine translation, such as lexical dictionary, Treebank and parallel corpora. Particularly, few paraphrase resources in Chinese have been constructed. The research on Chinese paraphrases resources construction, therefore, is of significance.

Conventional "pivot-based" approach considered two phrases to be paraphrases when the two phrases have the identical translation phrase [8]. For example, Chinese phrases "自行车" and "单车" are paraphrases each other because each of them has English phrase "bicycle" as translation. However, the conventional "pivot-based" approach has limitation in discovering more paraphrases. This paper proposes a new method to acquire more Chinese paraphrase phrases. The contributions of the work are as follows.

© Springer International Publishing AG 2016
C.-Y. Lin et al. (Eds.): NLPCC-ICCPOL 2016, LNAI 10102, pp. 639–647, 2016.
DOI: 10.1007/978-3-319-50496-4_57

(1) We design a graph based model for phrase translation table aiming at acquiring potential paraphrase phrases over two steps.
(2) We implement a random walk algorithm by which a random walking, started from a given node, is completed within the maximum step predefined.
(3) We propose a method of calculating confidence of the obtained paraphrases phrases based on expected number steps, which is used as a metric of similarity in meaning between the starting node and some node in the graph.

2 Background

Bannard and Callison Burch proposed the method based on large-scale bilingual corpora for acquiring paraphrases phrases [9]. The basic idea is that two phrases are paraphrases each other if they have the identical translation. The idea is demonstrated in Fig. 1. E1 and E2 present English phrases "motorway" and "highway", respectively, and F1 presents the French translation "autoroute" of both E1 and E2. We can acquire paraphrase phrases "motorway" and "highway" through their common French translation "autoroute", which is called "pivot". The "pivot-based" approach focuses on acquiring English paraphrases by regarding other foreign languages as "pivot". However, the approach only consider English phrase pairs connected by one identical French phrase, i.e. from E1 to F1 and then from F1 to E2, called as two steps in this paper. The approach therefore has limitation on acquiring more paraphrase.

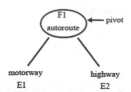

Fig. 1. "Pivot-based" approach f paraphrase phrase acquisition

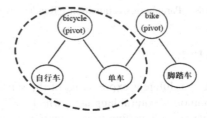

Fig. 2. Paraphrase phrases acquisition based on random walk with maximum number of steps

When we represent translation relations of all phrases using a graph, we can discover more potential paraphrase phrases. For instance, in Chinese-English translation relations, Chinese phrases "自行车", "单车", and "脚踏车" are connected with each other by English phrases "bicycle" and "bike", illustrated in Fig. 2. Conventional "pivot-based" approach considered the phrase "单车" as paraphrases for the phrase "自行车", but missed the phrase "脚踏车" that is far away from it over two steps. In this paper, we propose a graph model based method of acquiring paraphrases in which paraphrases are searched through random walk of N steps (N ≥ 2).

3 Paraphrases Acquisition Based on Graph Model

In this section, we introduce paraphrases acquisition method based on graph model and describe implementation using Chinese-English parallel corpora as an example, aiming at acquiring Chinese paraphrases. The proposed method can also be used for paraphrases acquisition of other language.

Phrases translation table is a product of statistical machine translation and can be extracted from bilingual parallel corpora using word alignment technology. Phrases translation table consists of phrase pairs and corresponding translation probability, hereafter referred as phrase table.

3.1 Graph Model Constructed for Phrase Table

Table 1 is an example of Chinese-English phrase table. As we can see, one Chinese phrase, for example "用作 阳极", may has more than one English translations. Also, one English phrase, for example "acts as an anode", may has more than one Chinese translations. There are more than one translations both for each Chinese phrase and for each English phrases, which enables random walk in a graph based model. We acquire potential paraphrases by discovering the Chinese-English translation relationship connected in the graph (Table 2).

Table 1. Samples of a Chinese-English phrase table

Chinese	English	P(C-> E)	P(E-> C)
充当 阳极	Acts as an anode	0.333333	0.25
用作 阳极	Acts as an anode	0.333333	1
用作 阳极	Serving as an anode	0.5	0.0416667
作为 阳极	Serving as an anode	1	0.03125

Table 2. Experiment evaluation result

Number of random walk N	Average number of candidate paraphrase	Average correct number of paraphrase	Average accuracy
N = 2	3.79	2.88	75.99 %
N = 12	11.56	7.18	62.11 %
N = 12 (Augmented method)	15.32	9.04	59.01 %

Figure 3 is an example of a graph constructed for a Chinese-English phrase table. In Fig. 3, there are three directed edges pointed out from C1, i.e. C1-> E1, C1-> E2, C1-> E3. Also, there are directed edges pointed from C2 and C3, respectively. We can see that C1 and C2 share the identical English translations E1, E2 and E3, and that C2

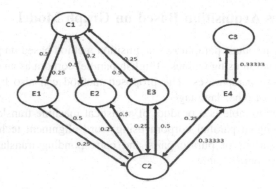

Fig. 3. A graph-based model constructed for a Chinese-English phrase table

and C3 also share the identical English translations E4. In addition to C2, C3 can also be considered as the potential paraphrases for C1. The method can also be used for acquiring English paraphrases by using Chinese phrase as pivot.

3.2   Paraphrases Acquisition Based on Random Walk

Next, we present paraphrases acquisition method based on graph model. In Fig. 3, we start from C1 and walk forward to arrive at E1. We call the walking C1-> E1 as one-step-walk. Then we continue to walk from E1 to C2, E1-> C2. So, we call the walking C1-> E1-> C2 as two-step-walk. C1 and C2 are considered as possible paraphrases because they share the identical translation E1. Because the conventional "pivot-based" method only considered phrases within this two-step-walk, only C2 was obtained as paraphrase for C1.

Actually, C3 may be a potential paraphrase for C1, which is connected to C1 through four-step-walk, i.e. C1-> E1-> C2-> E4-> C3. If we continue to walk from C2 and then arrive at C3, we may acquire C3 as the paraphrase for C1. Through this observation, we think that more potential paraphrases may be acquired if we walk more than two steps. Because searching all possible walking over two steps is not practical, we propose a paraphrase acquisition method based on random walk with N number of steps to solve this problem.

We assume that an ant walks in a graph, starting from a given node, randomly selects an adjacent node and then arrives at the node. Next, the ant takes the newly arrived node as the starting node and repeats the above process. The ant stops walking when some conditions are satisfied.

Figure 4 illustrates the process. We assume that there are M ants starting from the same node and then each ant walks independently in the graph. After walking in several steps, the node at which more ants arrive is considered to be related more closely to the starting node [10].

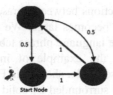
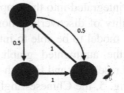

(a) Set off from start node   (b) Select next node arriving at second node

Fig. 4. The random walk process

3.3   Paraphrase Credibility Based on Expected Number Steps

After random walking N steps of M ants, the nodes at which the ants arrived are considered as candidate paraphrases. Considering the hitting confidence of the candidate paraphrases can be measured by the correlation between the nodes and the starting node, we propose a confidence metric based on expected number steps for ranking the obtained candidate paraphrases.

The expected number steps, denoted as $\hat{h}_{ij}^{N}$, which is defined as the average walking steps that M ants first arrived the node j starting from the node i after random walk N steps. Formula (1) shows how to calculate the expected number steps. After random walk N steps, if m ants arrived at node j, we record the number of steps by which m ants first arrived at the node j. For the (M-m) ants that do not arrive at the node j, we consider the walking steps taken as N.

$$\hat{h}_{ij}^{N} = \frac{\sum_{k=1}^{m} t_{j}^{k} + (M - m)N}{M} \tag{1}$$

$\hat{h}_{ij}^{N}$: the expected number steps between node i and j

M: the total number of ants

N: the maximum number of step

m: the number of ants that arrived at the node j

t_{j}^{k}: the number of step by which ant k arrive at the node j for the first time

It is required that $M \geq \frac{1}{2c^2}\log(\frac{2n}{\delta})$ and n is the number of nodes in the graph, δ and ε is the parameter for adjusting ants number, $0 \leq \delta, \varepsilon \leq 1$.

If more ants arrive at the node j with smaller steps, i.e. the value of t_{j}^{k} being smaller, the $\hat{h}_{ij}^{N}$ will be smaller, indicating the two nodes in graph are related more closely. In the case of our task, the smaller $\hat{h}_{ij}^{N}$ means that the two phrases are more closely in semantics and they are more likely to be paraphrases of each other.

3.4   Augmented Graph Based Model for Multiple Language Pairs

In the above described graph based model, phrases are connected by translation relations and paraphrases can be searched through random walk. We further consider that if more language pairs are integrated into the graph, more connections between phrases are set up and the possibility of discovering more paraphrases becomes large. We therefore augment the graph model to be able to integrate multiple language phrase table.

We illustrate the augmented graph model using the example of integrating Chinese-English phrase table and English-Japanese phrases table, showed in Fig. 5. As we can see from Fig. 5, the Chinese-English sub-graphs surrounded by solid lines are separated with each other. After integrating the English-Japanese phrase table, the English-Japanese sub-graphs are formed, showed by dotted lines. As a result, the separated Chinese-English sub-graphs are connected. Finally, the Chinese phrases C1, C3 and C4 are connected and the potential paraphrases between them may be possible to be discovered.

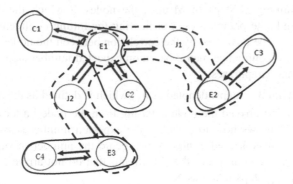

Fig. 5. Augmented graph model for Chinese-English-Japanese

4 Experiment

We present paraphrases acquisition method based on graph model and the confidence metric for ranking result candidate paraphrases. We augment the graph model for more language pairs. To compare with the conventional method and verify effectiveness of the method described above, we conducted three experiment by modifying maximum random walk step N and integrating English-Japanese phrase table into graph model.

(1) In experiment 1, we set maximum random walk steps as $N = 2$ (that is "pivot-based" method);
(2) In experiment 2, we modify the maximum random walk steps $N = 12$;
(3) In experiment 3, we add English-Japanese phrase table into the graph model and the maximum random walk steps $N = 12$ (same with experiment 2);

4.1 Experiment Data and Parameters

We conducted alignment using GIZA++ tool on NTCIR corpus, consisting of 1million Chinese-English sentence pairs and 3 million English-Japanese sentence pairs, and then extracted Chinese-English phrase table and English-Japanese phrase table by using grow-diag-final heuristic. Then, we filtered out noise data, such as special characters and stop words. We only used the phrases pairs whose translation probabilities are within the top 15. The final phrase tables consist of 21610194 pairs for Chinese-English and 34465517 pairs for English-Japanese.

Considering the restriction of the formula (1) and the computing feasibility, the parameter used for experiment are as follows.

(1) The graph is built by extending connection step by step from the given Chinese phrase by using the indexes. We allow the extension within 8 times, implying the distance between the farthest node and the given Chinese phrase node d = 8;
(2) Maximum number of nodes in graph n = 50000;
(3) Number of ants M = 1000000;
(4) Maximum steps of random walk N = 12 (N $\geq$ d);
(5) δ = 0.05, $\varepsilon \leq$ 0.03 (for formula (1))

4.2 Experiment Result

We randomly select 100 Chinese phrases regarded as test set from Chinese English phrase table. Then, we acquire the candidate paraphrases phrases for each Chinese phrase in test set, judge manually the correctness of the candidate paraphrases, and calculate the accuracy of the paraphrases phrases. The result is shown in Table 3.

Table 3. Example of paraphrase phrase and expected number of steps

No	Query phrases	Paraphrase expected number of steps
1	传送 给 远程 (send to the remote)	发送 给 远端 9.44202
		发送 到 远端 10.1433
		传送 到 远処 10.6529
		传输 到 远端 10.8738
		传送 到 远端 11.3424
		传输 给 远端 11.452
		朝向 该 远程 11.8415
		传输 到 远程 11.8629
		传递 到 远端 11.9333
		传递 给 远程 11.9999
2	微不足道 (not worth mentioning)	运输 至 遥远 11.9999
		无足轻重 11.9998
		无关紧要 11.9998
		忽略不计 11.9999
3	发送 图像 (send images)	传输 图像 11.3969
		图像 传输 11.9899
		传送 图像 11.9999
		医疗 材料 11.5707

From Table 3, we concluded that the paraphrases acquisition method based on random walk N step acquired more paraphrase phrases compared to the convolutional "pivot-based" method. Furthermore, the augmented graph model performed more well after English-Japanese phrases translation was added into the graph model. Although some noise caused lower accuracy, we think that it is more meaningful to discover greater number of paraphrases phrases in the paraphrase acquisition task.

Table 3 shows some examples of the Chinese paraphrases phrases and its expected number of steps acquired using the method presented in this paper. The smaller expected number of steps means the obtained phrases have higher probability to be the paraphrase for the given Chinese phrases.

Figure 6 is an instance of augmented graph model by adding English-Japanese phrase table. The sub-graph of Chinese-English phrases are surrounded by solid lines. The sub-graph of English-Japanese phrase are surrounded by dotted lines. The two sub-graphs in solid line are connected with each other by the help of the sub-graph dotted line. If we construct graph model only based on Chinese-English phrase table, we could not acquire the potential paraphrases phrases "对准" and "校正" for Chinese phrase "匹配". By adding more language pairs, i.e. English-Japanese phrase table, the Japanese phrase "整合" have translation relation with three English phrases "the matching", "matching" and "alignment" in Chinese-English sub-graph, which connects the two separated sub-graph. As a result, for the Chinese phrase "匹配", we acquired the potential paraphrase phrases "对准" and "校正".

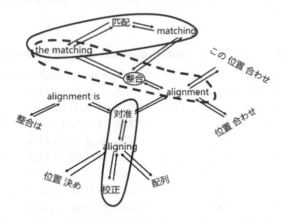

Fig. 6. Acquiring paraphrases instances by adding English phrase table

5   Conclusion

This paper proposed a paraphrases acquisition method based on graph model for resolving the problems of limitations in conventional "pivot-based" approach. We designed a random walk algorithm for searching candidate paraphrases and a confidence metric for ranking the obtained results. Furthermore, we augmented the graph model for integrating more language pairs. We performed experiments on NTCIR

Chinese-English and English-Japanese corpora and compared with the conventional method. The experimental results showed that the proposed model acquired more paraphrases, and achieved a more productive performance in discovering paraphrases after the English-Japanese phrases table was added into the graph model.

Acknowledgments. The research work has been partially funded by the International Science and Technology Cooperation Program of China under grant No. 2014DFA11350, National Nature Science Foundation of China (Contract 61370130 and 61473294), and the Fundamental Research Funds for the Central Universities (2015JBM033).

References

1. Barzilay, R., McKeown, K.R.: Extracting paraphrases from a parallel corpus. In: Proceedings of ACL/EACL, pp. 50–57 (2001)
2. Callison-Burch, C., Koehn, P'., Osborne, M.: Improved statistical machine translation using paraphrases. In: Proceedings of the HLT-NAACL, vol. 1, pp. 7–24. Association for Computational Linguistics, Morristown (2006)
3. Barzilay, R.: Information fusion for multi-document summarization: paraphrasing and generation. Ph.D. thesis, Columbia University (2003)
4. Zhou, L., Lin, C.Y., Munteanu, D.S., Hovy, E.: ParaEval: using paraphrases to evaluate summaries automatically. In: Proceedings of the HLT-NAACL, pp. 447–454. Association for Computational Linguistics, Morristown (2006)
5. Zukerman, I., Raskutti, B.: Lexical query paraphrasing for document retrieval. In: Proceedings of COLING, pp. 1–7. Association for Computational Linguistics, Morristown (2002)
6. Iordanskaja, L., Kittredge, R., Polguere, A.: Lexical selection and paraphrase in a meaning—text generation model. In: Paris, C.L., Swartout, W.R., Mann, W.C. (eds.) Natural Language Generation in Artificial Intelligence and Computational Linguistics, pp. 293–312. Springer, Heidelberg (1991)
7. McKeown, K.R.: Paraphrasing using given and new information in a question-answer system. In: Proceedings of the ACL, pp. 67–72. Association for Computational Linguistics, Morristown (1979)
8. 赵世奇.基于统计的复述获取与生成技术研究[学位论文].哈尔滨.哈尔滨工业大学, pp. 1–9 (2009)
9. Kok, S., Brockett, C.: Hitting the Right Paraphrases in Good Time, pp. 45–153. ACM (2010)
10. 徐晓华.图上的随机游走学习[学位论文].南京.南京航空航天大学 (2008)

A Micro-topic Model for Coreference Resolution Based on Theme-Rheme Structure

Xue-feng Xi[1,2] and Guodong Zhou[1(✉)]

[1] School of Computer Science and Technology, Soochow University, Suzhou, China
20114027008@suda.edu.cn, gdzhou@suda.edu.cn
[2] School of Electronic and Information Engineering,
Suzhou University of Science and Technology, Suzhou, China

Abstract. Coreference resolution is a major task of natural language processing. Although the mention-pair model is one of the most influential learning-based coreference models, it is hard to make any further improvements of the performance because of its inherent defects. From the perspective of discourse analysis, a micro-topic model based on the theme-rheme structure is proposed for coreference resolution in this paper. Compared with the traditional mention object recognition in text space, this model reduces problem space and complexity. The effectiveness of this model was evaluated by preliminary experimental in CoNLL-2012 shared task datasets and discourse topic corpus (DTC) tagged by us.

Keywords: Coreference resolution · Discourse topic · Theme-rheme theory

1 Introduction

The mention-pair model is a classifier that determines whether two NPs are coreferent. It was first proposed by [1,2], and is one of the most influential learning-based coreference models. Despite its popularity, this binary classification approach to coreference has two commonly cited defects to hinder the performance of these systems.

On the one hand, each anaphor must be combined with all candidate antecedents and constitute mention-pair instance, which leads to excessive mention-pair instance space. We name it FRS (Fully Referented Mention-pair Space), as shown in Fig. 1. Although there are various mentions [3–5] trying to reduce the number of mention-pair instance, these methods do not solve the problem in essence.

On the other hand, a skewed class distribution problem that surrounds the acquisition of the mention-pair is created. Specifically, a natural way to assemble a training set is to create one instance from each pair of NPs appearing in a training document. However, this instance creation method is rarely employed: as most NP pairs in a text are not coreferent, this method yields a training

© Springer International Publishing AG 2016
C.-Y. Lin et al. (Eds.): NLPCC-ICCPOL 2016, LNAI 10102, pp. 648–656, 2016.
DOI: 10.1007/978-3-319-50496-4_58

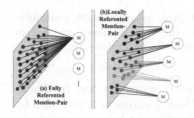
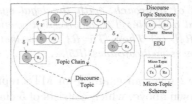

Fig. 1. Space(a) VS. Space(b).   **Fig. 2.** MTS representation of Example (1).

set with a skewed class distribution, where the negative instances significantly outnumber the positives.

To address these problems, we propose a new model to coreference resolution according to the Micro-Topic Scheme defined by us (see Sect. 2). According to some theories, coreference is a kind of discourse cohesion [6]. Firstly, the discourse can be split into Elementary Discourse Units (EDUs) via Rhetorical Structure Theory (RST) [7]. Secondly, each EDU can be represented as the theme and rheme structure based on theme-rheme theory [8]. Moreover, the theory of thematic progression [9] is proposed that there may be some kind of semantic association between the themes/rhemes in the upper and lower EDU, which can be represented by thematic progression. Furthermore, we find that semantic association is equivalent to discourse cohesion in a certain concept. In this case, discourse cohesions can be represented as these patterns of thematic progression. As mentioned before, coreference relationship is a kind of discourse cohesion, obviously, coreference are implied in these patterns. Therefore, it is easy to consider that mention-pair is likely to be included in the two theme-rheme object space, which is associated with one thematic progression pattern. In other words, we have found the reduced space (b). We named it Local Referented Mention-Pair Space (LRS).

Below we would discuss how to build this reduced space by our model. Section 2 presents the micro-topic scheme according to the theme-rheme theory. Section 3 describes this proposed model. Section 4 provides the preliminary experiment description and evaluate our model. Finally, Sect. 5 concludes our paper.

2   Micro-topic Scheme

In order to explore the discourse relationship, we propose a micro-topic scheme (MTS) to represent the discourse cohesion structure according to the theme-rheme theory [8].

Example 1. *(a) In spite of the fact that of the regulatory documents that the Pudong new region[T1] has formulated[R1], (b) some[T2=T1] are relatively "crude"[R2], and (c) some[T3=T2] are still only provisional regulations awaiting step - by - step completion as they are put into practice[R3], (d) nevertheless,* *this kind of approach, with the legal system tightly coupled with economic and social activities [T4], has received positive comments from domestic and foreign investors[R4]. (e) They [T5=R4] believe that in coming to the Pudong new region to invest there is methodicalness[R5]....*

Figure 2 gives an example of MTS representation, corresponding to Example (1) shown above, which consists of 5 clauses. Here, a clause is constituted by a theme and a rheme (see Subsect. 2.2), denoted by Tx and Rx, respectively.

According to the theme-rheme theory (see Subsect. 2.2), there is a reference relationship between the theme or rheme of current EDU and previous EDU. As shown in Fig. 2, an arrow is employed to indicate this reference by pointing to the theme or rheme in the EDU, such as T2 = T1, T3 = T2 and T5 = R4.

2.1   Elementary Discourse Units

As the basic unit of discourse analysis, EDUs are limited to clauses based on Rhetorical Structure Theory. In order to meet the requirements of our proposed model, we give the definition of EDU from three perspectives explicitly. Firstly, from the syntactic structure perspective, an EDU should contain at least one predicate and express at least one proposition. Secondly, from the functional perspective, an EDU should be related to other EDUs with some propositional function. Thirdly, from the morphological perspective, an EDU should be punctuated. Normally, it is easy to handle complex sentences and special sentence patterns (e.g. serial predicate sentences). For Example (2), (a) is a single sentence with serial predicate; (b) is a complex sentence with two EDUs (clauses).

Example 2. *(a) She started the car. (single sentence, serial predicate, one EDU) (b) She started the car, and drove off. (complex sentence, two EDUs).*

2.2   Theme-Rheme Structure

Derived mainly from the systemic-functional grammar [8], theme and rheme are two terms representing the way in which information is distributed in a clause. While theme indicates the given information serving as the departure point of a message, which has already been mentioned somewhere in text or shared as mutual knowledge from the immediate context, rheme is the remainder of the message in a clause in which theme is developed. That is to say, rheme typically contains unfamiliar or new information.

In order to improve the computational performance, we define that Theme Structure is the left part of the predicate in the EDU, and the remainder is Rheme Structure.

From the view point of discourse analysis, we are more interested in the developing sequences of thematic and rhematic choices creating certain kinds of thematic patterns instead of the actual individual choices of themes or rhemes. Subsect. 2.3 describes this development process.

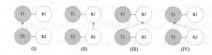

Fig. 3. Four major patterns of thematic progression.

Table 1. Inter-annotator consistency

Items	Agreement%	Kappa
EDU identification	96.0	0.91
TRS identification	92.0	0.83
MTL identification	90.5	0.88

2.3 Patterns of Thematic Progression

Previous studies [9,10] have claimed that the way in which lexical strings and reference chains interact with theme/rheme is not random; rather the patterns of interaction realize what they refer to as a texts thematic progression. Figure 3 shows four major patterns of thematic progression proposed in the literature:

(I) Constant Progression, where the theme of the subsequent clause is semantically equivalent to the theme of the first clause.

(II) Centralized Progression, where the rheme of the subsequent clause is semantically equivalent to the rheme of the first clause.

(III) Simple Linear Progression, where the theme of the subsequent clause is semantically equivalent to the rheme of the first clause.

(IV)Crossed Progression, where the rheme of the subsequent clause is semantically equivalent to the theme of the first clause.

As shown in Example (1), **pattern(I)** is suitable for the referent relationships among clauses 1–3, and **pattern(III)** is suitable for the referent relationship between clause 4 and clause 5.

2.4 Model Representation

Motivated by the theme-rheme theory, we propose MTS to represent our model's basic unit for coreference resolution, which can be formalized as a triple as below:

$$MTS = (S_n, S_{n+1}, \delta_n)$$

Where $S_n \in T \cup R$, $S_{n+1} \in T \cup R$, T represent the set of themes and R is the set of rhemes in the whole discourse. $\delta_n \in L$, L is a set of cohesion relationships between EDUs.

Based on this MTS model, we annotated a Discourse Topic Corpus (DTC) with 300 discourses from OntoNotes corpus English datasets (chtb_0001-chtb_0300). Table 1 illustrates a high consistency of inter-annotator specifically, which justifies the appropriateness of our tag items and their validation. The DTC corpus is also used for the experiment of Sect. 4.

3 Proposed Model

Our model framework is summarized in Fig. 4. This system takes an input discourse and output the confidence score of the mention-pair. It primarily consists of the following four components: Identifying the EDUs, Identifying the Theme-Rheme Structures (TRS), Recognizing the cohesion and Identifying mentions. Take Example (1) as an example, we will describe each components in our model as below.

3.1 Identifying the EDUs

According to the definition of Subsect. 2.1, the Example (1) has 5 EDUs, which include Clause(a),(b),(c),(d) and (e).

For the automatic identification of EDU, inspired by Li [11], we consider this as a binary classification for EDU's boundary and use some machine learning methods to solve this problem. We used various features adopted in [11,12]. Table 2 shows the performance of EDU identification on the DTC with 10-fold cross validation.

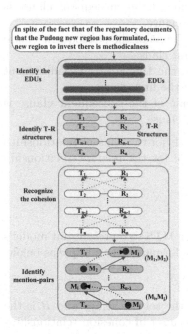

Fig. 4. Micro-topic model framework for coreference resolution.

Table 2. Performance of EDUs identification on the DTC

Classifier	Gold			Automatic		
	Pre.	Re.	F.	Pre.	Re.	F.
C45	90.6	**90.9**	90.5	89.3	90.3	88.6
NaiveBayes	90.3	89.6	89.4	88.5	89.2	87.8
MaxEnt.	**91.2**	90.3	**91.9**	90.2	**90.7**	**89.9**

Table 3. Performance of TRS identification on the DTC

Classifier	Gold			Automatic		
	Pre.	Re.	F.	Pre.	Re.	F.
C45	76.5	77.4	76.95	68.3	66.5	67.39
NaiveBayes	76.1	76.9	68.8	67.9	78.2	68.35
MaxEnt.	**79.8**	**80.3**	**80.05**	**72.5**	**71.8**	**72.15**

3.2 Identifying the TRS

According to the definition of Subsect. 2.2, the Example (1) has 5 themes and 5 rhemes, which are represented by T1-T5 and R1-R5, respectively.

For the automatic identification of TRS, according to our definition, predicate is used as a division sign, so the identification of TRS is equivalent to the predicate identification problem in a way. Besides those classical predicate features in previous studies [13–15], more features are derived from nominal and verbal

Table 4. Features of T-R structure identification

Name	Description
Predicate	A content word (lemma) of the predicate of each clause
Predicate class	The verb class that the predicate belongs to
Head word	String representation of head word of one clause
POS of Head word	Part of Speech of head word
Phrase type	Syntactic category of the constituent
Path of span	The path from the span to the nominal predicate
Position	The positional relationship of the span with the predicate, "left" or "right"
Focus word	First word and last word of the focus span
Focus span space	Is the focus span adjacent to the predicate? Yes or No
IsBrothers	Has the predicate brothers? Yes or No
IsRightBrother	Has the predicate right brother? Yes or No
Head word of right brother	The headword of the predicate's nearest right brother
POS of right brother	The POS of the predicate's nearest right brother
IVerb	Intervening verb itself
IVerb class	The verb class that contains IVerb
Path of IVerb	The path from the IVerb to the focus constituent
IsFocusSpArg	Is the focus span an argument for IVerb? Yes or No
Sematic Role of focus	The sematic role of the focus span for IVerb
IsHNPArg	Is HNP (Hightest NP headed by the nominal predicate) an argument for IVerb? Yes or No
Sematic Role of HNP	The semantic role of HNP for IVerb

SRL, such as the location to NP, the path features, intervening verb and the arguments. Using the Mallet toolkit [16] with features listed in Table 4. Table 3 shows the performance of TRS identification on the DTC corpus with 10-fold cross validation.

3.3 Recognizing Thematic Progression Patterns

According to the definition of Subsect. 2.3, the Example (1) has 3 cohesion relationships, which belong to two types of thematic progression pattern, Pattern (I) and Pattern (III), respectively. For the automatic recognition of thematic progression pattern between the upper and lower adjacent EDUs, according to our definition, this task can be considered as a sequence labeling problem. Therefore, we try to use the Markov Model to solve it.

In Markov Model tagging, we look at the sequence of thematic progression patterns in a text as a Markov chain. That is to say, we assume that a tag of thematic progression pattern only depends on the previous tag (limited horizon) and this dependency does not change over time (time invariance). Inspired by Charniak [17], we use the notation in Table 5. How to train a Markov Model tagger for recognition is not the focus of this paper, so we will discuss in detail

Table 5. Notational conventions for tagging

Notation	Thematic progression pattern
T	(I) Constant Progression
R	(II) Centralized Progression
L	(III) Simple Linear Progression
X	(IV) Crossed Progression
O	No relationship

Table 6. Performance of thematic progression pattern recognition

HMM (Benchmark)	Gold Precision	Recall	F-measure
Notation T	79.35	90.12	84.39
Notation R	66.68	80.16	72.80
Notation L	78.55	86.32	82.25
Notation X	76.68	90.37	82.96
Notation O	63.89	80.42	71.21

in another article. Table 6 shows the our benchmark systems performance of preliminary experimentation for recognition of thematic progression pattern on the DTC with 10-fold cross validation.

3.4 Identifying Mention-Pairs

As shown in the Example (1), when it reaches this step, we have been able to find space narrowed (b). Therefore, by using the traditional mention recognition method and classifier, we can get a good performance. Take the pronoun *"They"* in clause (e) of Example (1) as an example.

Obviously, the pronoun *"They"* is contained Theme Structre T5. According to Fig. 2, we can find that T5 is referented to R4 via thematic progression pattern. Here, R4 is *"has received positive comments from domestic and foreign investors"*. In other words, the pronoun *"They"* is very likely to be in the R4 module to look for the possible candidate antecedent. This greatly reduces the difficulty of the problem, which make it easy for us to find that *"domestic and foreign investors"* is the best candidate for the pronoun *"They"*.

4   Experiments and Results

We evaluated the system on the English part of the corpus provided in the CoNLL-2012 Shared Task and the DTC corpus tagged by ourselves (Subsect. 2.4). The corpus of CoNLL-2012 Shared Task contains 7 categories of documents (over 2 K documents, 1.3 M words). However, we just use an intersection of the official train/dev/test data sets and our DTC corpus data sets. In our experiments, the gold mentions are only considered by us. This is a rather idealized setting but our focus is on comparing various pairwise models rather than on building a full coreference resolution system.

To obtain the our model performance, we implemented three classic mention-pair models as competitors to be compared with our method in Table 7. These models are Soons Closest-First algorithm [3], Ngcardies Best-First algorithm [4] and Lassalle-Deniss Closest-First algorithm [5].

Table 7. Comparison baseline system on gold datasets

Models	Datasets (Gold)		
	Precision	Recall	F-measure
Soon	82.28	75.74	78.87
Ngcardie	76.55	89.12	82.36
LassalleDenis	80.02	**90.52**	84.95
Our model	**89.33**	90.36	**89.84**

Table 7 illustrates the macro-averaged F1 measure results for these competing methods along with the resources, features and classifier used by each method. Based on these results, we make the following observations:

(1) Our model achieves the highest score on the Precision's score and have a little difference from Recall's score, which showed that our model has a more balanced performance. The reason may be that our model reduces the problem space, which is a method to overcome the defects of traditional model in essence.

(2) Our model has achieved the highest score of F-measure, which was 4 points higher than the second model. This shows that our model has a prominent advantage.

(3) On the one hand, whichever NP extraction method is employed, it is clear that the use of gold NPs can considerably simplify the coreference task. This is also the reason why our experiments using gold datasets. On the other hand, although we only carry out the experiment on the basis of gold data and have no further confirmed on the whole automatic platform, the good results (see Sect. 3) from the independent experiments of each sub module also show the potential advantages of the development of the integrated system.

5 Conclusion and Further Work

The main contribution of this paper is to propose a new micro-topic model for coreference resolution based on Theme-rheme theory, which is to reduce the computational space to improve the performance of system. Different from the traditional coreference resolution model based on the level of words with the bottom-up approach, this system based on the discourse relationship have expanded the coreference resolution process through the top-down approach. In spite of building a model framework, we have just carried out a preliminary experiment. In the future we will further integrate the various modules, to carry out the optimization of the overall system for coreference resolution.

Acknowledgments. This work was supported by the National Natural Science Foundation of China (61673290).

References

1. Aone, C., Bennett, S.W.: Evaluating automated and manual acquisition of anophora resolution strategies. In: Proceedings of Annual Meeting Boston Association for Computational Linguistics, pp. 122–129 (1995)
2. Mccarthy, J.F., Lehnert, W.G.: Using decision trees for coreference resolution. In: Proceedings of the Fourteenth International Joint Conference on Artificial Intelligence, pp. 1050–1055 (1995)
3. Soon, W.M., Ng, H.T., Lim, D.C.Y.: A machine learning approach to coreference resolution of noun phrases. Comput. Linguis. **27**(4), 521–544 (2001)
4. Ng, V., Cardie, C.: Improving machine learning approaches to coreference resolution. In: Proceedings of the 40th Annual Meeting on Association for Computational Linguistics (2002)
5. Lassalle, E., Denis, P.: Improving pairwise coreference models through feature space hierarchy learning, pp. 497–506 (2013)
6. Halliday, M.A.K., Hasan, R.: Cohesion in English. Longman, London (1976)
7. Mann, W.C., Thompson, S.A.: Rhetorical structure theory: a theory of text organization. In: Polanyi C. (ed.) Discourse Structure (1987)
8. Halliday, M.A.K., Matthiessen, C.M.I.M.: An Introduction to Functional Grammar. Hodder Education, Arnold (2004)
9. Dañes, E.: Functienal sentenceperspective and te erganization of the texí. In: Papers on Functional Sentence Perspective, The Hague, Mouton (1974)
10. Zhu, Y.: Patterns of thematic progression and text analysis. Foreign Lang. Teach. Res. **3**, 6–12 (1995)
11. Li, Y., Feng, W., Sun, J., Kong, F., Zhou, G.: Building Chinese discourse corpus with connective-driven dependency tree structure. In: EMNLP, pp. 2105–2114 (2014)
12. Xue, N., Yang, Y.: Chinese sentence segmentation as comma classification. In: Meeting of the Association for Computational Linguistics: Human Language Technologies: Short Papers-Volume, pp. 631–635 (2011)
13. Jiang, Ng: Semantic role labeling of nombank: a maximum entropy approach. In: Proceedings of EMNLP, pp. 138–145 (2006)
14. Li, J., Zhou, G., Zhao, H., Zhu, Q., Qian, P.: Improving nominal SRL in chinese language with verbal SRL information, automatic predicate recognition. In: Proceedings of the 2009 Conference on Empirical Methods in Natural Language Processing, vol. 3, pp. 1280–1288 (2009)
15. Yang, H., Zong, C.: Multi-predicate semantic role labeling. In: Proceedings of 2014 Conference on Empirical Methods in Natural Language Processing, pp. 363–373 (2014)
16. McCallum, A.K.: Mallet: a machine learning for language toolkit (2002)
17. Charniak, E.: Statistical language learning. Language **27**(1), 146–148 (1993)

Learning from LDA Using Deep Neural Networks

Dongxu Zhang[1,3], Tianyi Luo[1], and Dong Wang[1,2(✉)]

[1] CSLT, RIIT, Tsinghua University, Beijing, China
wangdong99@mails.tsinghua.edu.cn
[2] Tsinghua National Lab for Information Science and Technology, Beijing, China
[3] PRIS, Beijing University of Posts and Telecommunications, Beijing, China

Abstract. Bayesian models and neural models have demonstrated their respective advantage in topic modeling. Motivated by the dark knowledge transfer approach proposed by [3], we present a novel method that combines the advantages of the two model families. Particularly, we present a transfer learning method that uses LDA to supervise the training of a deep neural network (DNN), so that the DNN can approximate the LDA inference with less computation. Our experimental results show that by transfer learning, a simple DNN can approximate the topic distribution produced by LDA pretty well, and deliver competitive performance as LDA on document classification, with much faster computation.

1 Introduction

Probabilistic topic models, for instance Latent Dirichlet Allocation (LDA) [2], have been extensively studied and widely used in applications such as topic discovery, document classification and information retrieval. Most of the successful probabilistic topic models are based on Bayesian networks [7,12], where the random variables and the dependence among them are carefully designed by people and so hold clear meanings in physics and/or statistics.

A particular problem of Bayesian topic models, however, is that when the model structure is complex, the inference for the latent topic distribution (topic mixture weights) is often untractable. Various approximation methods have been proposed, such as the variational approach and the sampling method, though the inference is still slow.

Recently, [3] proposed a transfer learning approach. In this approach, a complex model is used as a teacher model to supervise the training of a simpler model. The original proposal used a complex deep neural network (DNN) to train a simple shallow neural network and obtained performance very close to the complex DNN. This motivated our current research that attempts to use a Bayesian model to supervise the training of a neural model. By this approach, we hope to transfer the knowledge learned by the Bayesian model to the neural model, and combine the respective advantages of the two model families.

In this preliminary study, we use an LDA as the teacher model to guide the training of a DNN, so that the DNN can approximate the behavior and

© Springer International Publishing AG 2016
C.-Y. Lin et al. (Eds.): NLPCC-ICCPOL 2016, LNAI 10102, pp. 657–664, 2016.
DOI: 10.1007/978-3-319-50496-4_59

performance of LDA. The dropout technique [6] is utilized on the input layer, which endows the learned DNN with better generalizability. A big advantage of this transfer learning from LDA to DNN is that inference with DNN is much faster than with LDA. This solves a major difficulty of LDA on large-scale online tasks, meanwhile retaining the advantage of LDA in topic learning.

We tested the proposed method on document classification. The results show that a simple DNN model with dropout technique can approximate LDA pretty well and the inference speeds up tens or hundreds of times. Interestingly, a preliminary analysis shows that by the transfer learning, the DNN model seems can discover topics similar to those learned by LDA, although this information is not explicitly presented in the learning process.

2   Related Work

This work develops a neural model to approximate the function of LDA [2], with a direct goal of a fast inference. LDA is a generative probabilistic model and belongs to a large family of Bayesian topic models. LDA assumes that a document involves a mixture of latent topics, and each topic is characterized by a distribution over words. Compared with the early probabilistic models such as pLSI [7], LDA is a full generative model that can deal with new documents, but the inference is rather slow. The DNN-based LDA approximation presented in this paper attempts to solve this problem.

Our work is also closely related to the deep learning research which was largely initiated by [4]. DNN is a popular deep learning model and is capable of learning complex functions and inferring layer-wise patterns. This work leverages these advantages and uses DNNs to approximate LDA by learning its mapping function from the primary input (i.e., term frequency) to the high-level output (i.e., topic mixture). Interestingly, we find that topics can be discovered by DNN automatically with this transfer learning, which in turn demonstrates the power of DNN models. Note that deep learning has been employed in topic modeling, e.g., the approach based on deep Boltzmann machines (DBM) [5,10]. The difference of our work is that we focus on approximating a well-trained Bayesian model with a deep neural model, instead of learning the deep model from scratch.

Finally, this research is directly motivated by the dark knowledge distiller model [3] that employs the knowledge learned by a complex DNN to guide the training of a simpler DNN, or vice versa [13]. In this work, we extend this method to learn a neural model with the supervision of a Bayesian model, which is more ambitious and challenging.

3   Methods

For a particular document d, LDA takes the term frequency (TF) as the input, denoted by $v(d)$. The inference task is then to derive the topic mixture $\theta(d)$, which is actually the posterior probability distribution that the document belongs to the topics. In tasks such as document clustering or classification, $\theta(d)$

is a good representation for document d, with a low dimensionality and a clear semantic interpretation.

Exact inference with LDA is untractable and so various approximation methods are usually used. This work chooses the variational inference method proposed by [2], which involves iterative update of the document and word topic mixtures and hence time-consuming. The basic idea of the LDA to DNN knowledge transfer learning is to train a DNN model which can simulate the behavior of LDA inference, but with much less computation. More precisely, the DNN model learns a mapping function $f(v(d); w)$ such that $f(v(d); w)$ approaches to $\theta(d)$, where w denotes the parameters of the DNN. Note that $\theta(d)$ is a probability distribution. To approximate such normalized variables, a softmax function is applied to the DNN output and the cross entropy is used as the training criterion, given by:

$$\mathcal{L}(w) = -\sum_d \sum_{i=1}^{K} \theta(d)_i \log f(v(d); w)_i \tag{1}$$

where K denotes the number of topics and the subscript i indexes the dimension. Once the DNN is trained, the mapping function $f(v(d); w)$ learns the behavior of the LDA model and can be used to predict $\theta(d)$ for new documents. Compared to the LDA inference, $f(v(d); w)$ can be computed very fast and hence amiable to large-scale online tasks.

Here in the training process, we employ dropout technique [6] on the input $v(d)$ by randomly set each dimension of $v(d)$ to zero with 0.5 probability. After that, we re-normalize the input by dividing $v(d)$ with $\sum_i v(d)_i$.

We experimented with two DNN structures: a 2-layer DNN (DNN-2L) that involves one hidden layer, and a 3-layer DNN (DNN-3L) that involves two hidden layers. In DNN-2L, the number of hidden units is twice of the output units; in DNN-3L, the number of hidden units are three and two times of the output units for the first and second hidden layer, respectively. The hyperbolic function is used as the activation function. The training employs the stochastic gradient descent (SGD) method, and is implemented based on Theano [1][1].

4   Experiments

4.1   Database and Experimental Setup

The proposed methods are tested on the document classification task with two datasets. The first dataset is Reuters-21578 and we follow the 'LEWISSPLIT' configure to define the training and test data. The documents are labelled in 55 classes.[2]

---

[1] http://deeplearning.net/software/theano/.
[2] https://kdd.ics.uci.edu/databases/reuters21578/reuters21578.html.

The second dataset is 20 Newsgroups collected by Ken Lang, which contains about 20,000 articles evenly distributed over 20 UseNet discussion groups. These groups correspond to the classes in document classification.[3]

It has been known that LDA performs better with long documents [11]. To establish a strong LDA baseline, only long documents are selected for training and test in this study. Considering that 20 Newsgroups is much larger than Reuters-21578, different selection criteria are used to choose documents for the two datasets, as shown in Table 1. The table also shows the lexicon size in the LDA and DNN modeling, which corresponds to the dimensionality of the TF feature. Note that this seemingly tricky data selection is just for building a strong LDA model for the DNN to learn, rather than intensively selecting a working scenario for the proposed method. In fact, the DNN learning works well with any LDA teacher model, and the performance of the resultant DNN largely depends on the quality of the teacher LDA.

Table 1. Data profile of the experimental datasets.

	Reuters	20 News
Document length threshold	100	300
Training documents	3622	6312
Test documents	1705	1542
Word frequency threshold	30	200
Lexicon size (words)	2388	1910

4.2 Results

To evaluate the proposed transfer learning, we compare the classification performance with the document vectors inferred from the LDA-supervised DNN and the original LDA. The support vector machine (SVM) with a linear kernel is used as the classifier. Since LDA is the teacher model, its performance can be regarded as a upper bound of the DNN learning. Additionally, we choose the popular principle component analysis (PCA) [8] as another baseline and regard it as a low bound of the learning. All these three methods generate low-dimensional document vectors and are comparable in the sense of dimension reduction. Note that in many cases LDA does not outperform PCA, though it is not the focus of our study. What we are concerned with is that in the case where LDA is superior to PCA, the learned DNN can keep this superiority, but with much less computation cost.

Document Classification. The results in terms of classification accuracy on the two datastes are reported in Fig. 1, where the number of topics varies from

---

[3] http://www.cs.cmu.edu/afs/cs.cmu.edu/project/theo-20/www/data/news20.html.

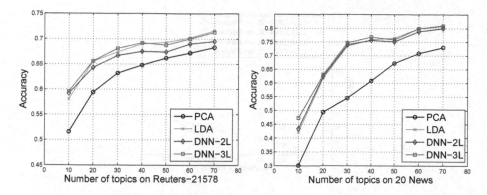

Fig. 1. The classification accuracy of PCA, LDA, 2-layer DNN (DNN-2L) and 3-layer DNN (DNN-3L).

10 to 70. We first observe that LDA obtains better performance than PCA on both the two datasets. Again, this is partly attributed to the long documents used in the study. The two DNN models obtain similar performance as LDA and outperform PCA, particularly with a small number of topics. This indicates that the DNNs indeed learned the behavior of LDA. If the number of topics is large, the DNN models work not as well, particularly on the Reuters task. This is probably because the limited amount of training data (just several thousands of training samples) can not afford learning complex models.

Note that the 3-layer DNN outperforms the 2-layer DNN. This indicates that deeper models can learn the LDA behavior more precisely. This is not surprising and has been widely demonstrated by the recent success of deep learning. This can be evaluated more directly in terms of KL divergence between the LDA output $\theta(d)$ and the DNN prediction $f(v(d); w)$, as shown in Fig. 2.

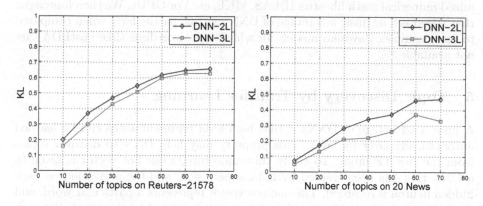

Fig. 2. The averaged KL divergency between the DNN and LDA output calculated on the test data of Reuters-21578 and 20 Newsgroups.

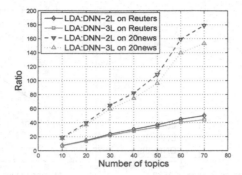

Fig. 3. The ratio of inference time of LDA to DNN.

Inference Speed. The comparative results on inference time are shown in Fig. 3. The experiments were conducted on a desktop with 43.4 GHz cores, and to alleviate randomness the experiments were conducted 10 times and the averaged numbers are reported. It can be seen that the DNN model is much faster (10 to 200 times) than the original LDA, and the superiority is more clear with a large number of topics. Comparing the results on the two datasets, we observe that DNN exhibits more advantages on 20 Newsgroups, because the long documents of this dataset are more difficult to infer with LDA. Additionally, the 3-layer DNN is not much slower than the 2-layer DNN, which means that using deeper models does not cause much additional computation.

We emphasize that the results here should not be over-interpreted. What we compared here is just the basic LDA implementation from [2]. There are quite some faster implementations that we did not compare with, e.g., FastLDA [9]. We expect that the margin between DNN and FastLDA is not as significant as reported here. Nevertheless, DNN inference involves only simple matrix manipulations and so are naturally amiable to large-scale computation, e.g., by optimized numerical math libraries (BLAS, MKL, etc.) or GPUs. We therefore argue that speed is a intrinsic advantage of DNN models, particularly when compared to more complex Bayesian models for which fast algorithms (like FastLDA) are not available.

5   Topic Discovery by Transfer Learning

A known advantage of DNNs is that high-level representations can be learned automatically layer by layer. This property may help DNN to discover topics from the raw TF input. To verify this conjecture, a one-hot vector is given to a DNN that has been trained by LDA supervision, and the activation on each hidden neuron is recorded. The one-hot vector represents a particular word, and the activation reflects how a particular neuron is related to this word. For each neuron, we record the activations of all the words and select the top-10 words that give the most significant activations, which forms the set of representative words for the neuron.

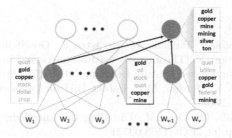

Fig. 4. Discovery for the topic 'mining' with DNN. The words in dark are topic related words.

Interestingly, we find that for each neuron, the representative words are generally correlated, forming a local topic. Figure 4 shows an example, where the topic 'mining' at the second hidden layer is formed by aggregating the related topics at the first hidden layer. This example shows clearly how words are clustered layer by layer to form semantic meaningful topics. Interestingly, we find that the topics derived from DNN and LDA are quite similar. As an example, the top-10 words for the topic 'mining' derived from LDA are **{gold, said, mine, copper, ounces, mining, tons, ton, silver, reuter}**, while the DNN-derived top-10 words are **{gold, copper, mine, mining, silver, zinc, minerals, metal, mines, ton}**.

This can be explained by the fact that the mixture weights generated by LDA and used as the DNN supervision are based on the same latent topics. We emphasize that the topic information is not transferred to DNN in the model training; it is the learning power of DNN that discovers the topics by itself.

6   Conclusion and Future Work

We proposed a knowledge transfer learning method that uses deep neural networks to approximate LDA. Results on document classification tasks show that a simple DNN can approximate LDA quite well, while the inference is significantly speeded up. This preliminary research indicates that transferring knowledge from Bayesian models to neural models is possible. The future work involves studying knowledge transfer between more complex probabilistic models and other neural models. Particularly, we are interested in how to use the knowledge of probabilistic models to regularize neural models so that the neurons are more interpretable.

Acknowledgments. The authors give great thanks to Dr. Shujie Liu (MSRA) for fruitful discussions. This research was supported by the National Science Foundation of China (NSFC) under the project No. 61371136, and the MESTDC PhD Foundation Project No. 20130002 120011. It was also supported by Huilan Ltd.

References

1. Bastien, F., Lamblin, P., Pascanu, R., Bergstra, J., Goodfellow, I.J., Bergeron, A., Bouchard, N., Bengio, Y.: Theano: new features and speed improvements. In: Deep Learning and Unsupervised Feature Learning NIPS 2012 Workshop (2012)
2. Blei, D.M., Ng, A.Y., Jordan, M.I.: Latent Dirichlet allocation. J. Mach. Learn. Res. **3**, 993–1022 (2003)
3. Hinton, G., Vinyals, O., Dean, J.: Distilling the knowledge in a neural network (2015). arXiv preprint arXiv:1503.02531
4. Hinton, G.E., Osindero, S., Teh, Y.W.: A fast learning algorithm for deep belief nets. Neural Comput. **18**(7), 1527–1554 (2006)
5. Hinton, G.E., Salakhutdinov, R.R.: Replicated softmax: an undirected topic model. In: Advances in Neural Information Processing Systems, pp. 1607–1614 (2009)
6. Hinton, G.E., Srivastava, N., Krizhevsky, A., Sutskever, I., Salakhutdinov, R.: Improving neural networks by preventing co-adaptation of feature detectors (2012). CoRR http://arxiv.org/abs/1207.0580
7. Hofmann, T.: Probabilistic latent semantic analysis. In: Proceedings of 15th Conference on Uncertainty in Artificial Intelligence, pp. 289–296. Morgan Kaufmann Publishers Inc. (1999)
8. Jolliffe, I.: Principal Component Analysis. Wiley Online Library, Hoboken (2002)
9. Porteous, I., Newman, D., Ihler, A., Asuncion, A., Smyth, P., Welling, M.: Fast collapsed Gibbs sampling for latent Dirichlet allocation. In: Knowledge Discovery and Data Mining (2008)
10. Srivastava, N., Salakhutdinov, R.R., Hinton, G.E.: Modeling documents with deep Boltzmann machines (2013). arXiv preprint arXiv:1309.6865
11. Tang, J., Meng, Z., Nguyen, X., Mei, Q., Zhang, M.: Understanding the limiting factors of topic modeling via posterior contraction analysis. In: Proceedings of 31st International Conference on Machine Learning, pp. 190–198 (2014)
12. Teh, Y.W., Jordan, M.I., Beal, M.J., Blei, D.M.: Hierarchical Dirichlet processes. J. Am. Stat. Assoc. **101**(476), 1566–1581 (2006)
13. Wang, D., Liu, C., Tang, Z., Zhang, Z., Zhao, M.: Recurrent neural network training with dark knowledge transfer (2015). arXiv preprint arXiv:1505.04630

Relation Classification: CNN or RNN?

Dongxu Zhang[1,3] and Dong Wang[1,2(✉)]

[1] CSLT, RIIT, Tsinghua University, Beijing, China
wangdong99@mails.tsinghua.edu.cn
[2] Tsinghua National Lab for Information Science and Technology, Beijing, China
[3] PRIS, Beijing University of Posts and Telecommunications, Beijing, China

Abstract. Convolutional neural networks (CNN) have delivered competitive performance on relation classification, without tedious feature engineering. A particular shortcoming of CNN, however, is that it is less powerful in modeling long-span relations. This paper presents a model based on recurrent neural networks (RNN) and compares the capabilities of CNN and RNN on the relation classification task. We conducted a thorough comparative study on two databases: one is the popular SemEval-2010 Task 8 dataset, and the other is the KBP37 dataset we designed based on MIML-RE [1], with the goal of learning and testing complex relations. The experimental results strongly indicate that even with a simple RNN structure, the model can deliver much better performance than CNN, particularly for long-span relations.

1 Introduction

This paper focuses on the task of sentence-level relation classification. Given a sentence X which contains a pair of nominals $\langle x, y \rangle$, the goal of the task is to predict relation $r \in R$ between the two nominals x and y, where R is a set of pre-defined relations [4]. Relation classification is a fundamental task in natural language processing (NLP) and plays an important role in information extraction and knowledge graph construction [9,11].

A multitude of studies have been conducted on deep neural models in relation classification. Most representative progress was made by Zeng et al. [15], who was motivated by the work of Collobert et al. [3] directly and used a CNN model to extract local semantic patterns and applied them to classify relations. The authors reported quite competitive results without utilizing any extra knowledge resource and NLP modules. Following this success, several CNN-based variants have been recently proposed, including multi-window CNN [5], CR-CNN [7] and NS-depLCNN [13].

The success of CNN models in relation classification can be largely attributed to its capability of learning local semantic patterns, thanks to the flexible convolutional structure of CNNs in multi-dimensional feature extraction. However, CNN possesses a clear shortage in modeling distant dependencies among words, due to the limited size of the convolution window. For the task of relation classification, the semantic meaning of a relation is often embedded in a long sequence

C.-Y. Lin et al. (Eds.): NLPCC-ICCPOL 2016, LNAI 10102, pp. 665–675, 2016.
DOI: 10.1007/978-3-319-50496-4_60

of contextual words. With CNN models, the long-span relation has to be split into local word fragments (the length equal to the size of the convolution window), and then the entire semantic is learned by merging the patterns learned from these fragments, where the simple max or mean pooling are often used as the merging algorithm. This splitting-and-pooling approach is certainly not ideal: the learning is separated in two stages and the behavior of the learned CNN is largely impacted by the size of the convolution window, i.e., whether the convolution size matches the length of the local patterns. Additionally, the max or mean pooling does not consider the order of the local patterns learned by the convolution layer.

A number of approaches have been proposed to improve CNN models in learning long-span relations. For example, Zeng et al. [15] proposed to use a position feature that specifies the position of each contextual word relative to the two target nominals. This position feature could provide order information of the contextual words, and was reported to offer significant performance improvement. Nguyen and Grishman [5] proposed a CNN structure with multiple convolution windows, which allows learning patterns of multiple levels of granularity. This approach, however, involves much more computation, and selecting the sizes of the convolution windows is not trivial. Another approach is to find the key path of the input sequence so that long-span relations can be learned on just a few key words on the key path. For example, the shortest dependency path approach presented in [9,13]. A shortcoming of this approach is that it depends on a parser that requires much computation and is error-prone. Moreover, if the dependency path is long, the problem associated with CNNs still exists.

In contrast to CNN-based methods, there are also a few work [11,14] using RNNs with long-short term memory (LSTM) units. Verga et al. [11] show that LSTMs outperforms CNNs in the knowledge base inferring task. But in the task of sentence-level relation classification, CNN-based models and basic RNN-based models have not been compared thoroughly with equal conditions.

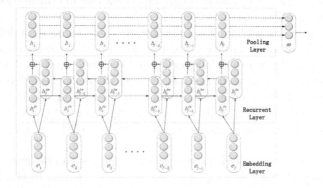

Fig. 1. The structure of the proposed RNN-based model.

In this paper, we analyse the capability of RNN on the relation classification task. Compared with CNN, RNN can memorize a long history and so is good at modeling sequential data [2]. To employ RNN in relation learning, a few modifications are proposed in our study, including a bi-directional architecture and a position indicator feature. The structure of the RNN-based model is shown in Fig. 1 and some details will be described in Sect. 2. The main contributions of this paper are as follows:

- Designed a new dataset based on the MIML-RE's annotated data [1] that involves more complex relations, and verified the advantage of RNN on the new dataset.
- Empirically analyzed the advantage of the RNN-based approach in learning long-span relations.
- Demonstrated that the position indicator feature proposed in this work is more effective than the position feature proposed by Zeng et al. [15].

2   Model

As has been shown in Fig. 1, the RNN-based model used in this paper contains three components: (1) a word embedding layer that maps each word in a sentence into a low dimension word vector; (2) a bidirectional recurrent layer that models the word sequence and produces word-level features (representations); (3) a max pooling layer that merges the word-level features of all the time steps into a sentence-level vector, by selecting the maximum value among all the word-level features for each dimension. The sentence-level vector is finally used for relation classification.

2.1   Model Training

The training objective is to let the produced sentence vectors maximize performance on the task of relation classification. To keep consistency between our model and CNN model proposed by Zeng et al. [15], here we use a simple softmax regression as the classifier and objective function is the cross entropy between the predictions and the labels. And we follow the training method proposed by Collobert et al. [3], and utilizes the stochastic gradient descent (SGD) algorithm. Specifically, the back propagation through time (BPTT) [12] is employed to compute the gradients layer by layer, and the fan-in technique proposed by Plaut and Hinton [6] is used to initialize the parameters.

2.2   Position Indicators

In relation learning, it is essential to let the algorithm know the target nominals. In the CNN-based approach, Zeng et al. [15] augment each word vector a position feature vector, i.e., the feature that indicates the distance from each word to the two nominals. This technique has been found highly important to gain high classification accuracy and was followed by a number of studies [5,7]. For RNN, since the model learns the entire word sequence, the *relative* position information for each word can be obtained automatically in the forward or backward recursive propagation. It is therefore sufficient to annotate the target nominals in the word sequence, without necessity to change the feature vector.

We choose a simple method that uses four position indicators (PI) to specify the starting and ending of the nominals. The following is an example: "<e1> **people** </e1> have been moving back into <e2> **downtown** </e2>". Note that **people** and **downtown** are the two nominals with the relation 'Entity-Destination (e1,e2)', and <e1>, </e1>, <e2>, </e2> are the four position indicators which are regarded as single words in model training and test. The position-augmented sentences are then used to train the RNN model as usual. Compared with the position feature approach, the position indictor approach is more straightforward. In Sect. 3.3, we will show that in most circumstances, the position indictor approach leads to better performance.

3   Experiments

3.1   Database

We use two datasets to evaluate the proposed RNN model. The first one is the dataset provided by SemEval-2010 Task 8. In this dataset, there are regular 9 relation types and an additional 'other' relation. Taking the direction into account (the order of the two nominals in the relation), this dataset involves 19 relation classes in total. The dataset is publicly available[1].

The second dataset is constructed by the authors based on the MIML-RE annotation dataset provided by Angeli et al. [1]. The original MIML-RE dataset involves the 2010 and 2013 KBP official document collections, plus a July 2013 dump of Wikipedia. There original data collection consists of 33811 annotated sentences. To make the dataset more suitable for relation classification tasks, we made several refinements:

1. First, we add two directions to each relation type, except the type 'no_relation'. For example, 'per:employee_of' is split into two relations 'per:employee_of(e1,e2)' and 'per:employee_of(e2,e1). To avoid incorrect accounting of errors associated with the directional relations[2], we replace 'org:parents(e1,e2)' with 'org:subsidiaries(e2,e1)' and replace 'org:member_of(e1,e2)' with 'org:member(e2,e1)'. After this arrangement, there are 76 relations in total.
2. Second, we compute the frequency of each relation type. Only the relation types with a frequency higher than 100 in both directions are retained. This

---

[1] http://docs.google.com/View?docid=dfvxd49s_36c28v9pmw.

[2] This is mainly caused by some relations that have been directional already in KBP. See the KBP manual at http://surdeanu.info/kbp2013/TAC_2013_KBP_Slot_Descriptions_1.0.pdf.

Table 1. Statistics of KBP37.

Number of training data	15917
Number of development data	1724
Number of test data	3405
Number of relation types	37
per:alternate_names	org:alternate_names
per:origin	org:subsidiaries
per:spouse	org:top_members/employees
per:title	org:founded
per:employee_of	org:founded_by
per:countries_of_residence	org:country_of_headquarters
per:stateorprovinces_of_residence	org:stateorprovince_of_headquarters
per:cities_of_residence	org:city_of_headquarters
per:country_of_birth	org:members
no_relation	

results in 19 relation types, including the 'no_relation' type. Each relation type (except 'no_relation') corresponds to two relation classes, by considering the relation direction. This leads to 37 relation classes in total. To gain better data balance, 80% of the sentences in the 'no_relation' type are randomly discarded.

3. Finally, the entire dataset is randomly split into three subsets: 70% for training, 10% for development, and 20% for testing. For a more strict test, sentences in the development and test set are removed if the nominal pairs *and* their relation have been both found in one training sentence.

In the rest of the paper, we will call the second dataset KBP37. Some statistics of this dataset and all the relation types are shown in Table 1. Notice that KBP37 is different from SemEval-2010 Task 8 in several aspects: First, there are more relation types in KBP37, and the relations are more 'specific' compared with those in SemEval-2010 task 8. For example, 'Member Collection' in SemEval-2010 task 8 can represent any 'member of' relation, while 'org:member' in KBP specifically refers to the relation between mother and child companies. Second, the nominal pairs in KBP37 are all entity names and so are more sparse than SemEval-2010 task 8 in both the domain-independent and task-specific corpus. Third, there are much more multi-word nominals in KBP37. Finally, the average length of the sentences in KBP37 is much longer than Semeval-2010 task 8, which will be discussed in details in Sect. 4.2.

It can be seen that the relation classification task on KBP37 is more difficult but also more realistic. We argue that SemEval-2010 Task 8 has been studied for a long time and the performance has been over-tuned. Therefore to evaluate a new algorithm, it would be more informative to test it on a new and more complex dataset. We design KBP37 to meet this request, particularly for learning and test on long-span relations. This dataset can be downloaded publicly[3].

3.2 Experimental Setup

In order to compare with the work by Socher et al. [8] and Zeng et al. [15], we use the same 50-dimensional word vectors proposed by Turian et al. [10] to initialize the embedding layer in the experiments.

Because there is no official development dataset in Semeval-2010 Task 8 dataset, we tune the hyper-parameters by 8-fold cross validation. Once the hyper-parameters are optimized, all the 8000 training data are used to train the model with the best configuration. With Turian's 50-dimensional word vectors, the best dimension of the sentence vector is 800. The number of iterations is set to 20. For fast convergence, we set the learning rate to 0.1 in the first five iterations, and then diminish it to 0.01.

For KBP37, the hyper-parameters are tuned based on the development set. The development data is also used to choose the best model among different iterations. With Turian's 50-dimensional word vectors, the best dimension of the sentence vector is 700. The training process is the same as the one used on the Semeval-2010 Task 8 dataset.

3.3 Results

The performance is evaluated in terms of F1 score defined by SemEval-2010 Task 8 [4]. Note that given a sentence and two target nominals, a prediction is counted as correct only when both the relation type and its direction are correct.

Table 2. F1 results with the proposed RNN model on SemEval-2010 Task 8 dataset, '+' means adding a new modification.

Model	RNN	+ max-pooling	+ position indicators	+ bidirection
F1	31.9	67.5	76.9	79.6

Table 2 presents the F1 results of the proposed RNN model on the SemEval-2010 Task 8 dataset, with the contribution offered by each modification. It can be seen that the basic RNN, which is single directional and with the output of the last step as the sentence vector, performs poorly. This can be attributed to the lack of the position information of target nominals and the difficulty in RNN training. The max-pooling offers the most significant performance improvement, indicating that local patterns learned from neighbouring words are highly important for relation classification. The position indicators also produce highly

---

[3] https://github.com/zhangdongxu/kbp37.

Table 3. Comparison of F1 scores with different neural models on different datasets. The 50-dimensional word vectors provided by Turian et al. [10] are used for pre-training. 'PF' stands for position features and 'PI' stands for position indicators. The numbers in the parentheses show the best dimensions of the hidden layer. Since Zeng et al. [15] did not release the source code, we reproduced their method, denoted by 'Our rep.'.

Model	MV-RNN (Socher, 2012)	CNN+PF (Zeng, 2014)	CNN+PF (Our rep.)	CNN+PI (Our rep.)	RNN+PF	RNN+PI
Semeval-2010 task8	79.1	78.9	78.3 (300 → 300)	77.4 (400 → 400)	78.8 (400)	**79.6** (800)
KBP37	-	-	51.3 (500 → 500)	55.1 (500 → 500)	54.3 (400)	**58.8** (700)

significant improvement, which is not surprising as without the position information, the model would be puzzled by which pattern to learn. The contribution of positional information has been demonstrated by Zeng et al. [15], where the positional features lead to nearly 10 percentiles of F1 improvement, which is similar as the gain obtained in our study.

The second experiment compares three representative neural models, especially CNN and RNN. The results are presented in Table 3, where the 50-dimensional word vectors are employed in the experiments. Since Zeng et al. [15] did not release the source code, we tried to reproduce their result and got a very close number although not identical (78.3 vs. 78.9), as shown in the third row of Table 3.

Comparing the results with different models and methods, it can be seen that the RNN model outperforms both the MV-RNN model proposed by Socher et al. [8] and the CNN model proposed by Zeng et al. [15]. This demonstrates that an RNN model is more appropriate for the relation classification task. An interesting observation is that the RNN model performs better than the MV-RNN model which uses syntactic parsing as extra resources. This indicates that relation patterns can be effectively learned by RNNs from raw text, without any explicit linguistic modules and knowledge.

Comparing the results on the two datasets, it can be observed that the F1 scores are much lower on KBP37 than on Semeval-2010 Task 8. This indicates that KBP37 is a more difficult dataset. Moreover, the RNN model beats the CNN by a larger margin on KBP37. This indicates that RNN possesses more advantage in learning more complex relations. More discussion will be given in Sect. 4.2.

From Table 3, we also find that with RNN, position indicators (PI) is more effective than position features (PF), and this is more evident on the KBP37 task. A possible reason is that the recurrent process can remember the PI vectors but may corrupt the PF information associated with each word. More discussion will be presented in Sect. 4.1.

4   Discussion

4.1   Impact of Long Context

We have argued that a particular advantage of the RNN model compared with the CNN model is that it can learn long-distance patterns more effectively, and so can better deal with long-span relations. To verify this argument, we split each test dataset (Semeval-2010 Task8 and KBP37) into 5 subsets according to the context length of the relations, i.e., the number of words between the two nominals, plus 2 words prior to the first nominal and 2 words after the second nominal, if they exist. The position indicators are not counted.

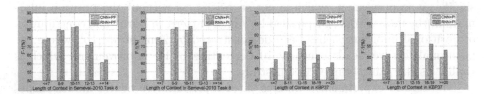

Fig. 2. F1 scores with different lengths of contexts on Semeval-2010 Task 8 and KBP37.

The F1 results on the 5 subsets are reported in Fig. 2. It can be seen that on both test datasets, if the context length is small, the CNN and RNN models perform similar with PI, whereas if the context length is large, the RNN model is clearly superior. This confirms that RNN is more suitable to learn long-distance patterns. If PF is used, this trend is not such clear. This seems to indicate that PF is more suitable for CNN and PI is more suitable for RNN. Nevertheless, PI performs much better than PF in KBP37 even with CNN (51.3 vs. 55.1 from Table 3), which suggests that PI tends to be more robust.

Note that with both the two models, the best F1 results are obtained with a moderate context length, no matter how the position information is used. This is understandable, as too small contexts involve limited semantic information, while too large contexts lead to difficulties in pattern learning.

4.2   Proportion of Long Context

Fig. 2 shows that the RNN model significantly outperforms the CNN model on almost all the configurations. This is a little different from the results presented in Table 3, where the discrepancy between the two models in SemEval-2010 dataset is not so remarkable (78.8 vs. 78.3 with PF and 77.4 vs. 79.6 with PI). This can be attributed to the small proportion of long contexts in test data of SemEval-2010 dataset.

To make it clear, the distribution of the context length is calculated on the two datasets. The statistics are shown in Table 4. It can be observed that long contexts exist in both datasets, but the proportion of long contexts in the

Table 4. The distribution of context lengths with two datasets.

Dataset	Context length			Proportion of long context (≥11)
	≤10	11–15	≥16	
SemEval-2010 task-8	6658	3725	334	0.379
KBP37	4719	7512	8815	0.776

SemEval-2010 task 8 dataset is much smaller than those in the KBP dataset. This suggests that the strength of a method can not be fully demonstrated on the SemEval-2010 task 8 dataset. This is the reason we release KBP37 and argue that it is a major contribution of this paper.

4.3 Semantic Accumulation

Another interesting analysis is to show how the 'semantic meaning' of a sentence is formed. First notice that with both the CNN and the RNN models, the sentence-level vectors are produced from local features (word-level for CNN and segment-level for RNN) by dimension-wise max-pooling.

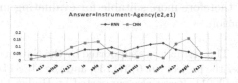

Fig. 3. Semantic distribution on words in the sentence "A <e1> witch </e1> is able to change events by using <e2> magic </e2>."

To measure the contribution of a particular word or segment to the sentence-level semantic meaning, for each sentence, we count the number of dimensions that the local feature at each word step contributes to the output of the max-pooling. This number is divided by the number of total dimensions of the feature vector, resulting in a 'semantic distribution' over the word sequence. Figure 3 shows an example of the semantic distribution with results from both the CNN and RNN models.

From Fig. 3, the correct relation is 'Instrument-Agency', but CNN gives wrong answer 'Other'. It can be seen that CNN matches two patterns 'is able to' and 'magic', while the RNN matches the entire sequence between the two nominals **witch** and **magic**, with the peak at 'by using'. Clearly, the pattern that the RNN model matches is more reasonable than that matched by the CNN model. We highlight that RNN is a temporal model which accumulates the semantic meaning word by word, so the peak at 'by using' is actually the contribution of all the words after 'witch'. In contrast, CNN model learns only local patterns, therefore it splits the semantic meaning into two separate word segments.

An interesting observation is that the RNN-based semantic distribution tends to be smoother than the one produced by the CNN model. In fact, we calculate the average variance on the semantic contribution of neighbouring words with all the sentences in the SemEval-2010 task 8 dataset, and find out that the variance with the RNN model is 0.0017, while this number is 0.0025 with the CNN model. The smoother semantic distribution is certainly due to the temporal nature of the RNN model.

5 Conclusion

In this paper, we compare CNN-based and RNN-based approaches for relation classification. Since the RNN model can deal with long-distance patterns, it is particular suitable for learning long-span relations. Several important modifications were proposed to improve the basic RNN model, including a max-pooling feature aggregation, a position indicator approach to specify target nominals, and a bi-directional architecture to learn both forward and backward contexts. Experimental results on two datasets demonstrated that the RNN-based approach can achieve better results than CNN-based approach, and for sentences with long-span relations, the RNN model exhibits clear advantage. Last but not least, we released a new dataset KBP37 that contains more complex patterns and long-span relations, therefore more suitable for evaluating models and methods for relation classification.

Acknowledgments. This research was supported by the National Science Foundation of China (NSFC) under the project No. 61371136, and the MESTDC Ph.D. Foundation Project No. 20130002 120011. It was also supported by Huilan Ltd.

References

1. Angeli, G., Tibshirani, J., Wu, J.Y., Manning, C.D.: Combining distant and partial supervision for relation extraction. In: Proceedings of the 2014 Conference on Empirical Methods in Natural Language Processing, October 2014
2. Boden, M.: A guide to recurrent neural networks and backpropagation. In: The Dallas project, SICS Technical report T2002:03 (2002)
3. Collobert, R., Weston, J., Bottou, L., Karlen, M., Kavukcuoglu, K., Kuksa, P.: Natural language processing (almost) from scratch. J. Mach. Learn. Res. **12**, 2493–2537 (2011)
4. Hendrickx, I., Kim, S.N., Kozareva, Z., Nakov, P., Ó Séaghdha, D., Padó, S., Pennacchiotti, M., Romano, L., Szpakowicz, S.: Semeval-2010 task 8: multi-way classification of semantic relations between pairs of nominals. In: Proceedings of the Workshop on Semantic Evaluations: Recent Achievements and Future Directions, pp. 94–99 (2009)
5. Nguyen, T.H., Grishman, R.: Relation extraction: perspective from convolutional neural networks. In: Proceedings of the 2013 Conference of NAACL Workshop on Vector Space Modeling for NLP (2015)
6. Plaut, D.C., Hinton, G.E.: Learning sets of filters using back-propagation. Comput. Speech Lang. **2**(1), 35–61 (1987)

7. dos Santos, C.N., Xiang, B., Zhou, B.: Classifying relations by ranking with convolutional neural networks. In: Proceedings of the 53rd Annual Meeting of the Association for Computational Linguistics, pp. 626–634 (2015)
8. Socher, R., Huval, B., Manning, C.D., Ng, A.Y.: Semantic compositionality through recursive matrix-vector spaces. In: Proceedings of the 2012 Conference on Empirical Methods in Natural Language Processing (2012)
9. Toutanova, K., Chen, D., Pantel, P., Poon, H., Choudhury, P., Gamon, M.: Representing text for joint embedding of text and knowledge bases. In: Proceedings of the 2015 Conference on Empirical Methods in Natural Language Processing (2015)
10. Turian, J., Ratinov, L., Bengio, Y.: Word representations: a simple and general method for semi-supervised learning. In: Proceedings of the 48th Annual Meeting of the Association for Computational Linguistics, pp. 384–394 (2010)
11. Verga, P., Belanger, D., Strubell, E., Roth, B., McCallum, A.: Multilingual relation extraction using compositional universal schema. In: Proceedings of the 2016 Conference of the North American Chapter of the Association for Computational Linguistics (2016)
12. Werbos, P.J.: Backpropagation through time: what it does and how to do it. Proc. IEEE **78**(10), 1550–1560 (1990)
13. Xu, K., Feng, Y., Huang, S., Zhao, D.: Semantic relation classification via convolutional neural networks with simple negative sampling. In: Proceedings of the 2015 Conference on Empirical Methods in Natural Language Processing (2015)
14. Yan, X., Mou, L., Li, G., Chen, Y., Peng, H., Jin, Z.: Classifying relations via long short term memory networks along shortest dependency path. In: Proceedings of the 2015 Conference on Empirical Methods in Natural Language Processing (2015)
15. Zeng, D., Liu, K., Lai, S., Zhou, G., Zhao, J.: Relation classification via convolutional deep neural network. In: Proceedings of COLING, pp. 2335–2344 (2014)

Shared Tasks

Ensemble of Feature Sets and Classification Methods for Stance Detection

Jiaming Xu[1(✉)], Suncong Zheng[1], Jing Shi[1], Yiqun Yao[1], and Bo Xu[1,2]

[1] Institute of Automation, Chinese Academy of Sciences (CAS), Beijing, China
{jiaming.xu,suncong.zheng,shijing2014,yaoyiqun2014,xubo}@ia.ac.cn
[2] Center for Excellence in Brain Science and Intelligence Technology,
CAS, Shanghai, China

Abstract. Stance detection is the task of automatically determining the author's favorability towards a given target. However, the target may not be explicitly mentioned in the text and even someone may refer some positive opinions to against the target, which make the task more difficult. In this paper, we describe an ensemble framework which integrates various feature sets and classification methods, and does not consist any handcrafted templates or rules to help stance detection. We submit our solution to NLPCC 2016 shared task: Detecting Stance in Chinese Weibo (Task A), which is a supervised task towards five targets. The official results show that our solution of the team "CBrain" achieves one 1st place and one 2nd place on these targets, and the overall ranking is 4th out of 16 teams. Our code is available at https://github.com/jacoxu/2016NLPCC_Stance_Detection.

Keywords: Stance detection · Ensemble framework · Text classification · Chinese Weibo

1 Introduction

Stance detection is the task of automatically determining from text whether the author of the text is in favor of, against, or neutral towards a given target [18], which has widespread applications in information retrieval, text summarization [9], and textual entailment [14]. This task can be viewed as a subtask of opinion mining and it stands next to the sentiment analysis [12].

Conventional techniques in stance detection generally follow topical text classification methods [11], where a text is regarded as a bag of words (BOW), and then classified by machine learning techniques. However, the given target, for stance detection, may not be explicitly presented in the text and even someone may refer other people's positive opinions to against the target, which has significant difference from the topical text classification task. From another perspective to detect stance, Hasan and Ng [19] employed additional linguistic features to train a stance classifier, and Xia and Zong [22] learned patterns of opinion expression in the texts. However, social media data are often event-driven temporal

© Springer International Publishing AG 2016
C.-Y. Lin et al. (Eds.): NLPCC-ICCPOL 2016, LNAI 10102, pp. 679–688, 2016.
DOI: 10.1007/978-3-319-50496-4_61

information. Extracting the accurate linguistic features and learning practicable patterns form these social media are also challenge tasks which may introduce additional noises to the current task.

Considering that integrating different types of features and classifications may overcome their individual drawbacks and benefit from each other's merits [22], we propose an ensemble framework to solve stance detection task. In particular, we first generated various types of semantic features to describe the stance representations, such as Paragraph Vector (Para2vec) [13], Latent Dirichlet Allocation (LDA) [2], Latent Semantic Analysis (LSA) [5], Laplacian Eigenmaps (LE) [1] and Locality Preserving Indexing (LPI) [8]. Then, these features are ranked and selected to train various classification methods, including Random Forest (RF) [3], Linear Support Vector Machines (SVM-Linear) [10], SVM with RBF Kernel (SVM-RBF) [21] and AdaBoot [7]. Finally, we use ensemble techniques to integrate multiple classification methods to further improve the performance.

Our contributions are three-fold: (1) We explore an ensemble framework by integrating various feature sets and classification methods to solve stance detection task. (2) Our framework can be successfully conducted without designing any handcrafted templates or rules to detect the author's stance. (3) Two feature selection strategies are exploited to help choose the best feature groups, and we further investigate the influence of these features.

2 Problem Description

The Detecting Stance in Chinese Weibo (Task A) at NLPCC 2016 is a supervised task to test stance towards five targets: #Firecracker ("春节放鞭炮"), #Iphone ("IphoneSE"), #Terrorism ("俄罗斯在叙利亚的反恐行动"), #Child ("开放二胎") and #Motorcycle ("深圳禁摩限电"). Participants were provided 600 labeled training Weibo texts as well as some unlabeled Weibo texts and 3,000 test Weibo texts for each target. The statistics of these datasets are summarized in Table 1, where the training Weibo texts are labeled with three stances: FAVOR, AGAINST and NONE. It can be seen that the distribution is not uniform and there is always a preference towards a certain stance. For example, 51.2% of Weibo texts about #Motorcycle are labeled as AGAINST.

We further report the vocabulary size of the original datasets in Table 2. It can be seen that the labeled data of each target dataset has a large vocabulary but still has a huge gap to cover the vocabulary of the test data. For example, for #Firecracker, the vocabulary sizes of labeled data and +Unlabeled are 5,543 and 8,220 respectively while the vocabulary size is rapidly extended to 19,268 by adding test data. In order to control the computational complexity and filter some nonsense words, it is necessary to limit the vocabulary to contain a smaller size of most meaningful words by using word selection methods, such as Mutual Information (MI), Information Gain (IG) and Chi-square test (CHI) [23].

Table 1. Statistics of the five target datasets. Note that we drop out 14 bad labeled samples (lack of texts or labels) in *#Motorcycle* and 1 bad unlabeled sample (lack of texts) in *#Child* from the raw datasets.

Dataset	#Firecracker	#Iphone	#Terrorism	#Child	#Motorcycle
FAVOR	250 (41.7%)	245 (40.8%)	250 (41.7%)	260 (43.3%)	160 (27.3%)
AGAINST	250 (41.7%)	209 (34.8%)	250 (41.7%)	200 (33.3%)	300 (51.2%)
NONE	100 (16.7%)	146 (24.3%)	100 (16.7%)	140 (23.3%)	126 (21.5%)
Labeled	600	600	600	600	586
Unlabeled	600	600	600	599	600
Test	3,000	3,000	3,000	3,000	3,000

Table 2. Original vocabulary size of the five target datasets after preprocessing. +Test means the vocabulary size of labeled data, unlabeled data and test data together.

Dataset	#Firecracker	#Iphone	#Terrorism	#Child	#Motorcycle
Labeled	5,543	3,409	4,076	5,334	4,475
+Unlabeled	8,220	5,461	5,992	7,882	6,632
+Test	19,268	13,302	10,318	15,969	8,787

3 Feature Engineering

The BOW model for text representation is simple and quite efficient in classification task. However, the texts in social media is very short and have a large vocabulary size which make the BOW based text representation, as a high dimensionality of feature space, is very sparse. In order to compress the native feature space, we use Chi-square test (CHI) to automatically remove the non-informative words and form a refined feature space. Nonetheless, BOW based representation has a semantic gap problem which fails to construct the latent semantic relevance, thus we also use some latent semantic techniques, such as Para2vec, LDA, LSA, LE and LPI, to capture the semantic representations of texts based on the native feature space and the refined feature space respectively. Furthermore, we extract some stance-lexicon features from two public subjectivity lexicons. More details are described in the following sections.

3.1 Text Preprocessing

For the Chinese Weibo texts, we process the raw texts via the following steps: (1) Removing all the hashtag #target by considering that the content in hashtag mostly just highlight the target and rarely contains the author's stance; (2) Removing all URLs and @tags, such as "http://t.cn/RqGPSED" and "@ChinaDaliy"; (3) Transferring the full-width characters into half-width characters and converting letters into lower case; (4) Removing all the special symbols; (5) Segmenting Chinese words using Ansj[1].

---

[1] https://github.com/NLPchina/ansj_seg.

3.2 Word Selection

As the comparative study of feature selection methods in [23], the results show that MI had relatively poor performance due to its bias towards favoring rare terms while IG and CHI showed most effective in aggressive term removal without losing categorization accuracy. In this paper, we choose CHI as the feature selection to reduce the vocabulary size. CHI test measures the lack of independence between the i-th word w_i and the j-th class C_j [6].

After obtaining the CHI statistic values of the words toward to the stances, the top 500 words in each stance of each target dataset are selected by ranking their Chi-square values to form the refined vocabulary as shown in Table 3. In our experiments, we use the refined vocabulary to construct BOW representations of the Weibo texts which are respectively weighted with term frequency (TF) and term frequency-inverse document frequency (TFIDF).

Table 3. Refined vocabulary size of the five target datasets, where the top 500 in each stance is selected by CHI. Null/Test means that the number of Weibo texts with empty content after word selection.

Dataset	#Firecracker	#Iphone	#Terrorism	#Child	#Motorcycle
Vocab size	1,227	1,234	1,216	1,218	1,219
Null/Labeled	1/600	1/600	6/600	0/600	2/586
Null/Unlabeled	1/600	1/600	49/600	2/599	0/600
Null/Test	2/3,000	19/3,000	243/3,000	1/3,000	43/3,000

3.3 Latent Semantic Features

Para2vec features. Paragraph Vector (Para2vec) is an unsupervised method to learn distributed representations of word and paragraphs [13]. The key idea is to learn a compact vector by predicting nearby words in a fixed context window. In our experiments, we use the open-source software released by Mesnil et al. [17]. The dimension of the embedding is set to 50, and the model is trained on the original datasets of each target, including labeled, unlabeled and test datasets.

LDA features. Latent Dirichlet Allocation (LDA), first introduced by Blei et al. [2], is a probabilistic generative model that can be used to estimate the multinomial observations by unsupervised learning [20]. The number of topic is set to 50 and the model is estimated on the original datasets of each target.

LSA features. Latent Semantic Analysis (LSA) [5] is the most popular global matrix factorization method, which applies a dimension reducing linear projection, Singular Value Decomposition (SVD), of the corresponding BOW matrix. For our task, we apply LSA on two matrices, one is constructed based on the original vocabulary and another is constructed based on the refined vocabulary, to map the BOW representations into two 50-dimensional subspaces, denoted as LSA features and LSA (CHI) features respectively in this paper.

LE and **LPI** features. Laplacian Eigenmaps (LE) [1] discover the manifold structure of the BOW features by extracting the top eigenvectors of graph Laplacian, that is the similarity matrix of texts. Locality Preserving Indexing (LPI) [8] can be seen as an extended version of LE to deal with the unseen texts by approximating a linear function. Here, we construct two local similarity matrices, using heat kernel measure, based on the original text representation and the refined text representation, which are all weighting with TFIDF. Finally, we get four 50-dimensional feature spaces, denoted as LE features, LE (CHI) features, LPI features and LPI (CHI) features respectively.

3.4   Lexical Features

The lexical features are extracted from two public subjectivity lexicons, one is an evaluation word set generated from HowNet and the other one is an emotion word set released by Li and Sun [15]. Both of these lexicons organize the subjective words into two groups: positive and negative. Take one Weibo text as an example, let P_{ev} be the number of the positive evaluation words in the text, N_{ev} be the number of the negative evaluation words, P_{em} be the number of the positive emotion words, and N_{em} be the number of the negative emotion words. The following four features are then generated:

(1) Positive evaluation feature: $(P_{ev} + 1)/(P_{ev} + N_{ev}{}^{\lambda} + 2)$;
(2) Negative evaluation feature: $(N_{ev}{}^{\lambda} + 1)/(P_{ev} + N_{ev}{}^{\lambda} + 2)$;
(3) Positive emotion feature: $(P_{em} + 1)/(P_{em} + N_{em}{}^{\lambda} + 2)$;
(4) Negative emotion feature: $(N_{em}{}^{\lambda} + 1)/(P_{em} + N_{em}{}^{\lambda} + 2)$.

In these features, the exponent λ is used to control the effect of the negative words, and λ is set to 1.3 in our experiments.

4   Model Training

Here, we first rank and select the above features to train various classification methods, including Random Forest (RF) [3], Linear Support Vector Machines (SVM-Linear) [10], SVM with RBF Kernel (SVM-RBF) [21] and AdaBoot [7]. Then, an ensemble framework is applied to further improve the performance.

4.1   Feature Ranking and Selection

In Sect. 3, we get 11 feature vectors in total. It is crucial to identify important features and remove the redundant features to reduce the train cost and noises [4, 23]. Inspired by [16], we exploit two feature selection strategies, one is top k based selection and the other one is leave-out k based selection. Before conducting the two selection methods, all features are ranked based on the results of each

classification method on each target dataset. As an example, Table 4 shows the
ACC (Accuracy) scores of RF method on five target training datasets via cross
validation. It can be seen that the features based on the refined vocabulary
space, such as TF, TFIDF, LSA (CHI), LE (CHI) and LPI (CHI), can achieve a
better performance, and lexical feature perform a worst results on the five target
datasets. We also observe the similar results of the other classification methods.
But due to the limit of space, they are not presented in this paper.

For top k based selection, we simply select the k best features, based on the
feature ranking results, as the best feature groups. For example, we apply top
3 selection for RF method on #Terrorism, the best feature group is generated
as {TF, TFIDF, LSA (CHI)}. For leave-out k based selection, we iteratively
evaluate the importance of each feature by leaving it out from all the current
feature group and remove the most insignificant feature, until k features are
removed. The optimal selection strategy and parameter k are tuned by using
each classification on each target training dataset via cross validation.

Table 4. ACC results obtained via 4-fold cross validation by using RF method on five
target training datasets. The three highest scores on each target are shown in bold.

Feature	#Firecracker	#Iphone	#Terrorism	#Child	#Motorcycle
Para2vec	66.83	48.50	47.33	60.83	61.26
LDA	63.83	42.00	47.83	49.67	57.85
LSA	68.67	51.83	49.33	61.33	66.21
LE	64.83	48.00	50.17	61.00	64.99
LPI	63.83	48.17	51.27	61.17	65.02
TF	71.00	52.50	**57.17**	61.83	64.69
TFIDF	71.50	53.16	**57.33**	61.33	64.34
LSA (CHI)	**72.33**	**58.83**	**61.00**	**68.33**	**74.06**
LE (CHI)	**73.17**	**61.67**	45.33	**68.33**	**68.95**
LPI (CHI)	**73.17**	**61.33**	54.50	**67.33**	**68.94**
Lex. Fea.	38.83	41.33	40.50	42.50	43.34

4.2 Model Ensemble

To further improve the performance, ensemble technique is utilized to integrate
the outputs of the various classification methods as $p(C|x) = \sum_{i=1}^{m} w_i \cdot p_i(C|x)$,
where $p(C|x)$ is the final probability that the author of a Weibo text x toward
to the stance C, $p_i(C|x)$ is the probability predicted by the i-th classification
method, m is the number of classification methods, and w is the weight parameter learned by a linear model.

5   A Performance Study

5.1   Importance of the Features

In this section, we evaluate the importance of all the features on each target training dataset via cross validation. Two feature selection strategies are conducted based on the ranked results of the features by using the classification methods. Figure 1 shows the ACC results obtained via 4-fold cross validation by using the classification method on five target training datasets. It can be seen that RF and SVM-Linear show the best performances and SVM-RBF not well deal with integrated features. The optimal feature selection strategies and the best feature groups for each classification are selected and reported in Table 5. Two feature selection strategies perform their respective advantages on different

Table 5. ACC results obtained via 4-fold cross validation on five target datasets.

Dataset	Method	Selection	Features	ACC
#Firecracker	RF	Top 3	LE (CHI), LPI (CHI), LSA (CHI)	74.17
	SVM-Linear	Top 2	LPI (CHI), LSA (CHI)	**76.50**
	SVM-RBF	Top 1	LPI (CHI)	76.00
	AdaBoost	Leave-out 3	TFIDF, LE (CHI), LSA	73.17
	Ensemble	–	–	73.83
#Iphone	RF	Leave-out 4	LPI, LSA, Para2vec, TF	63.33
	SVM-Linear	Leave-out 3	TFIDF, Para2vec, LE	61.83
	SVM-RBF	Top 1	LE (CHI)	59.83
	AdaBoost	Leave-out 1	TFIDF	61.67
	Ensemble	–	–	**63.67**
#Terrorism	RF	Top 4	LSA (CHI), TFIDF, TF, LPI (CHI)	62.00
	SVM-Linear	Leave-out 3	TFIDF, LPI (CHI), LE	61.50
	SVM-RBF	Top 1	LSA (CHI)	63.50
	AdaBoost	Leave-out 4	TFIDF, LPI (CHI), LSA, Para2vec	52.67
	Ensemble	–	–	**65.00**
#Child	RF	Top 3	LE (CHI), LSA (CHI), LPI (CHI)	70.17
	SVM-Linear	Top 1	LPI (CHI)	70.67
	SVM-RBF	Top 1	LSA (CHI)	69.50
	AdaBoost	Leave-out 4	TFIDF, Para2vec, LSA, LPI (CHI)	66.33
	Ensemble	–	–	**71.33**
#Motorcycle	RF	Top 1	LSA (CHI)	74.06
	SVM-Linear	Top 1	LSA (CHI)	72.87
	SVM-RBF	Top 1	LSA (CHI)	**74.92**
	AdaBoost	Top 2	LSA (CHI), LPI (CHI)	71.00
	Ensemble	–	–	74.24

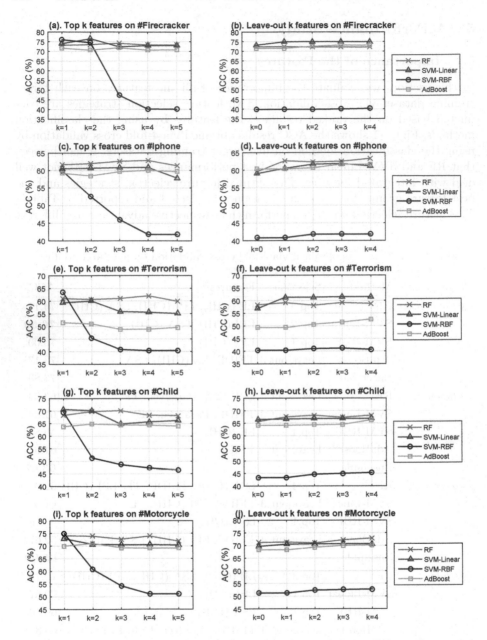

Fig. 1. ACC curves on five target training datasets via 4-fold cross validation by varying the parameter k of the two feature selection methods (top k selection and leave-out k selection). Note that leave-out 0 means that all features are reserved.

target datasets and different classification methods, and our ensemble framework improves upon the single models on 3 out of 5 target datasets. One interesting result as shown in Table 5 is that the lexical features, showing the worst performances, are not dropped by the leave-out k selection on all target datasets. An explanation maybe that leave-out k selection prefers to drop the redundant features from all feature groups, such as LE (CHI) and LPI (CHI).

5.2 Performance on Test Data

Part of the official ranking results on test datasets are summarized in Table 6. We can see that our solution of the team "CBrain" achieves one 1st place on #Child and one 2nd place on #Motorcycle, and the overall ranking is 4 out of all 16 teams, where the official metric of our solution is very close to the above two teams within 0.4%. Note that the official result of our solution on #Terrorism is lower than the top team about 10%. The reason to explain this problem maybe that, we empirically select top 500 words in each stance of each target dataset via CHI to form the refined vocabulary which leads to lots of null samples, as shown in Table 3, and lots of null samples may hurt the prediction of our system.

Table 6. Part of the official results (Official metric: (F_FAVOR + F_AGAINST)/2).

TeamID	#Firecracker	#Iphone	#Terrorism	#Child	#Motorcycle	Overall
RUC_MMC	77.30	57.80	**58.14**	80.36	76.52	71.06
TopTeam	74.49	57.64	52.32	76.61	**79.49**	68.94
SDS	**77.84**	**58.52**	53.32	79.48	68.83	68.61
CBrain	76.04	55.28	47.87	**81.35**	78.55	68.56
...	...	...	...	...	...	...
SCHOOL	34.22	42.22	39.03	46.13	36.76	39.95

6 Conclusion

This paper presents an ensemble framework for stance detection in Chinese Weibo hosted at NLPCC 2016 conference. In the framework, a lots of semantic features are captured from Weibo text and two feature selection strategies are exploited to generate the optimal feature groups. Moreover, we train various classification methods based on the optimal feature groups and integrate the results of these methods to further improve the performance. Our solution can be successfully conducted without designing any handcrafted templates or rules to detect the author's stance which has good scalability for other related tasks.

Acknowledgments. We thank the anonymous reviewers for their insightful comments, and this work was supported by the Strategic Priority Research Program of the Chinese Academy of Sciences (Grant No. XDB02070005), the National High Technology Research and Development Program of China (863 Program) (Grant No. 2015AA015402) and the National Natural Science Foundation (Grant No. 61602479 and 61403385).

References

1. Belkin, M., Niyogi, P.: Laplacian eigenmaps for dimensionality reduction and data representation. Neural Comput. **15**(6), 1373–1396 (2003)
2. Blei, D.M., Ng, A.Y., Jordan, M.I.: Latent Dirichlet allocation. J. Mach. Learn. Res. **3**, 993–1022 (2003)
3. Breiman, L.: Random forests. Mach. Learn. **45**(1), 5–32 (2001)
4. Chen, M., Jin, X., Shen, D.: Short text classification improved by learning multi-granularity topics. In: IJCAI, pp. 1776–1781. Citeseer (2011)
5. Deerwester, S., Dumais, S.T., Furnas, G.W., Landauer, T.K., Harshman, R.: Indexing by latent semantic analysis. JASIS **41**(6), 391 (1990)
6. Dunning, T.: Accurate methods for the statistics of surprise and coincidence. Comput. Linguist. **19**(1), 61–74 (1993)
7. Freund, Y., Schapire, R.E., et al.: Experiments with a new boosting algorithm. In: ICML, vol. 96, pp. 148–156 (1996)
8. He, X., Cai, D., Liu, H., Ma, W.Y.: Locality preserving indexing for document representation. In: SIGIR, pp. 96–103. ACM (2004)
9. Hu, M., Liu, B.: Mining and summarizing customer reviews. In: KDD, pp. 168–177. ACM (2004)
10. Joachims, T.: Learning to Classify Text Using Support Vector Machines: Methods, Theory and Algorithms. Kluwer Academic Publishers, Dordrecht (2002)
11. Kim, S.M., Hovy, E.H.: Crystal: analyzing predictive opinions on the web. In: EMNLP-CoNLL, pp. 1056–1064 (2007)
12. Krejzl, P., Steinberger, J.: UWB at SemEval-2016 task 6: stance detection. In: Proceedings of SemEval, pp. 408–412 (2016)
13. Le, Q.V., Mikolov, T.: Distributed representations of sentences and documents. In: ICML, vol. 14, pp. 1188–1196 (2014)
14. Lendvai, P., Augenstein, I., Bontcheva, K., Declerck, T.: Monolingual social media datasets for detecting contradiction and entailment. In: LREC (2016)
15. Li, J., Sun, M.: Experimental study on sentiment classification of Chinese review using machine learning techniques. In: NLPKE, pp. 393–400. IEEE (2007)
16. Liu, G., Nguyen, T.T., Zhao, G., Zha, W., Yang, J., Cao, J., Wu, M., Zhao, P., Chen, W.: Repeat buyer prediction for e-commerce. In: KDD. ACM (2016)
17. Mesnil, G., Mikolov, T., Ranzato, M., Bengio, Y.: Ensemble of generative and discriminative techniques for sentiment analysis of movie reviews (2014). arXiv preprint arXiv:1412.5335
18. Mohammad, S.M., Kiritchenko, S., Sobhani, P., Zhu, X., Cherry, C.: SemEval-2016 task 6: detecting stance in tweets. In: SemEval, vol. 16 (2016)
19. Ng, V., Hasan, K.S.: Predicting stance in ideological debate with rich linguistic knowledge. In: COLING, p. 451 (2012)
20. Phan, X.H., Nguyen, L.M., Horiguchi, S.: Learning to classify short and sparse text & web with hidden topics from large-scale data collections. In: WWW (2008)
21. Schölkopf, B., Smola, A.J.: Learning with Kernels: Support Vector Machines, Regularization, Optimization, and Beyond. MIT Press, Cambridge (2002)
22. Xia, R., Zong, C., Li, S.: Ensemble of feature sets and classification algorithms for sentiment classification. Inf. Sci. **181**(6), 1138–1152 (2011)
23. Yang, Y., Pedersen, J.O.: A comparative study on feature selection in text categorization. In: ICML, vol. 97, pp. 412–420 (1997)

Exploiting External Knowledge and Entity Relationship for Entity Search

Le Li[1,2]($\boxtimes$), Junyi Xu[1], Weidong Xiao[1], Shengze Hu[1], and Haiming Tong[2]

[1] College of Information System and Management,
National University of Defense Technology, Changsha, China
lile10@126.com

[2] China Satellite Maritime Tracking and Control Department, Jiangyin, China

Abstract. Entity search has received abroad attentions and researches that aim to retrieve entities matching the query. Conventional methods focus on entity search task on local dataset, e.g. INEX Wikipedia test collection, where the descriptions of entities are given and relationships between entities are also known. In this paper, we propose an entity search method to handle real-world queries, which need to crawl related descriptions of entities and construct relations between entities manually. By mining historical query records and offline data, our method builds an entity relationship network to model the similarity of entities, and converts the entity search problem to within-network classification problem, which can introduce many novel solutions. Then we use the entity relationship based approach as an offline solution and external knowledge based approach as an online solution to build an ensemble classifier for handling entity search problem. Comprehensive experiments on real-world dataset demonstrate that our method can deal with entity search task effectively and obtain satisfactory performance.

Keywords: Entity search · External knowledge · Entity relationship

1 Introduction

With the rapid development of mobile and web applications, personalized recommendation has received much attention. An intelligent recommendation system should contain many components, and one of the core components is entity search [1–3]. Entity search refers to: given a search query q and a set of candidate entities E, the participating system should automatically retrieve entities that match the query q from E. For instance, people may search for "restaurants with good environment suitable for kids' birthday parties". In order to meet the user's intent, the recommendation system needs to understand every restaurant, check which of them can be tagged as "good environment" and "suitable for kids' birthday parties" and index the restaurants with these tags for recommendation.

Conventional methods focus on entity search task on local dataset, e.g. INEX Wikipedia test collection [3,4], where the descriptions of entities are given and

C.-Y. Lin et al. (Eds.): NLPCC-ICCPOL 2016, LNAI 10102, pp. 689–700, 2016.
DOI: 10.1007/978-3-319-50496-4_62

well structured. The relationships between entities are also known as the pages are interconnected. However, in order to handle real-world queries, it needs to search related information of entities. Accurate descriptions of entities mainly exist in external knowledge bases (e.g. search engines, Wikipedia, reviews on shopping websites and so on), making these online-search methods rely heavily on the quality of external knowledge and development of semantic query. Moreover, different knowledge sources are suitable for queries of different domains. For example, searching movies on professional knowledge bases (Douban and IMDB) will obtain more accurate information than common knowledge bases (Wikipedia and Google). Therefore, these methods often require searching multiple knowledge sources to obtain better results. Furthermore, when network condition is poor or we need to make rapid prediction, these online-search methods will become ineffective. It will be useful to store the information of related entities in internal knowledge base. However, due to capacity constraints, we can only store a small part of entities' information. Furthermore, due to the high cost of online search, it is not possible to update these contents frequently, making such strategy only have limited effectiveness.

In addition, given an entity search query, the system tends to chooses m candidate entities randomly from the internal entity library, which are submitted to recommendation algorithm to calculate the similarities with query. Hence, some practical tasks, such as how to find m candidates with higher similarity from the entity library or how to make a fast and rough ranking of the m entities based on available information, have become more important in the personalized recommender system of big data era.

In this paper, we aim to handle above problems by proposing a method that utilizes historical query records and offline data effectively. The accurate descriptions of entities often exist in external knowledge bases, which cannot be read in real time. While, with the recommendation system widely used, it will accumulate large amounts of historical records that can also provide valuable information. In historical records, if two entities often occur in the same query results, it means that these entities have many of the same tags. Then we can assume that these entities have higher similarity, and we can use the characteristics of one entity to describe the other one. Based on this, we propose an entity search method by exploiting external knowledge and entity relationship. Inspired by the dependency of nodes in complex network, we use network to model the similarity of entities. First, we use the historical records to build an entity relationship network, in which the entities are represented as nodes, the queries are represented as labels of nodes, and the nodes with same labels are connected. Then given a specific query, the problem is converted to find nodes with specific labels, which is a typical problem of within-network classification. We use the entity relationship based approach as an offline solution and external knowledge based approach as an online solution to build an ensemble classifier for handling the entity search problem.

In summary, we make the following contributions:

1. We propose an entity search method that makes use of historical records and external knowledge effectively. Our method reduces the dependence on external knowledge, so it is able to handle the entity search problem when network condition is poor.
2. We convert the entity search problem to within-network classification problem, making many within-network classification algorithm can be applied for entity search.
3. We conduct comprehensive experiments to verify the effectiveness of our method on real-world entity search queries.

2   Related Works

Entity Search (also known as Entity Ranking) has received great concern in recent years [2,3,5]. In order to evaluate the ranking algorithm performance, INitiative for Evaluation of XML retrieval (INEX) setup an Entity Ranking track with the goal of creating a test collection for entity ranking. Based on this benchmark collection, many approaches have been proposed for handle the problem [4,6]. Researchers also have paid attention on the impact of different topics on the entity ranking performance [7,8], which distinguish easy and difficult queries. For example, Pehcevski et al. [2] used a combination of Wikipedia categories knowledge, link structure and topic difficulty prediction to improve the effectiveness of entity ranking.

However, above methods focus on different problem settings from ours. In their solutions, the query is constraint in the local dataset (e.g. Wikipedia), so the descriptions of entities are given and self-contained. The relationships between entities are also known as the pages are interconnected. While our method aim to handle the real-world queries. The related descriptions of entities are stored in external knowledge bases, and searching will consume much time; there are no obvious relations between entities, so we need to construct the network manually. Therefore, the conventional methods are not suitable for handling our problem.

We convert the entity search problem to within-network classification [9,10] problem in offline situation. Given a partially labeled network, in which the labels of some nodes are known, within-network classification aims to predict the labels of the rest nodes. wvRN [9,11] predicts the label of unknown nodes via a weighted average of the estimated class membership of the node's neighbors. Gallagher et al. [12] design an even-step random walk with restart (Even-step RWR) algorithm, which can mitigate the impact of network heterogeneity effectively. Heterogeneous networks often consist of various relations. Most existing approaches, however, treat these relations as the same type. In order to handle network heterogeneity, Tang and Liu [13] propose a novel classification framework, SocioDim, to learn a classifier which is based on social dimensions extracted from network structure.

Macskassy and Provost [9] provided an excellent review of within-network classification, which divides the classifier into three parts: local classifier, relational classifier and collective inference classifier. Our method is similar to this framework, in which solutions based on entity relationship can be treated as relational classifier and solutions based on external knowledge can be treated as local classifier. In conventional framework, local classifier is used as preprocess step and relational classifier makes the final prediction, while our method is different from this point of view. In entity search task, offline search operations are mostly rely on the internal knowledge base, which can produce preliminary prediction results quickly. However external knowledge bases store the latest entity information, so online search operations are often more accurate. Therefore, our method rely more on the online search component to make final prediction, and the offline search component is used with lower weight in the ensemble classifier, or as main classifier when network condition is poor.

3 Method

Internet data grow with remarkable speed while people focus on different points, so the description of an entity must be incomplete. For example, given a restaurant, we can know its current characteristics from following comments: "the salad is very good here", "that waitress was so friendly", "good environment". However, as the restaurant just opened a couple weeks ago, the comments are much fewer. Other characteristics, such as "a place best for lover" and "relaxed music", have not been reflected. Similar situations also appear in the movie recommendation, for instance, a "comedy" starred by "Jackie Chan" is certainly "suitable for the whole family to watch together", while the last tag may be missing due to fewer comments. We give the formal description of above phenomenon here, given the known description of entity $E1$ as $D'(E1) = \{d_1, ..., d_m\}$, and the true description of $E1$ as $D(E1) = \{d_1, ..., d_n\}$, then $D'(E1) \subset D(E1)$.

Recommendation of item with fewer comments is a typical "cold start" phenomenon [14]. When performing offline entity search, it is unable to get plenty of information and the description of the entity will be almost zero in some cases, making the offline search also encounter a cold start phenomenon. Our method tries to handle this problem. In historical records, if two movies are often described by same tags, or often appear in the same query results, then we believe that the two movies are of high similarity. Thus, when querying information of a movie with fewer tags, we can use the information of similar movie to enrich it. An Intuition is that for the entity with few descriptions, we can use the information of similar entities to make supplementary description.

We give the formal description here. Given descriptions of entity $E1$ and $E2$ are $D'(E1) = \{d_1, ..., d_{m1}\}$ and $D'(E2) = \{d_1, ..., d_{m2}\}$, if $\frac{|D'(E1) \cap D'(E2)|}{|D'(E1) \cup D'(E2)|}$ is large, then we assume that using supplementary description will make the result is close to reality, i.e. $D'(E1) \cup D'(E2) \to D(E1)$ and $D'(E1) \cup D'(E2) \to D(E2)$. Therefore, if $D'(E1)$ is not enough to describe E1, using $D'(E2)$ will be an effective mean to make supplementary description of $E1$. For example, if two hot pot restaurants $E1$ and $E2$ often co-occur in "hot pot", "delicious soup", "many spices", "spicy" and other queries, then the additional description of $E1$ "suitable for sichuan people" can also be applied to describe $E2$.

Network is suitable for describing the relationship of nodes, e.g., if two nodes are similar, we can use an edge to connect them. Inspired by this idea, we can build an entity relationship network based on historical data, in which the nodes are entities, the labels are queries and the nodes with same labels are interconnected. Given a query and candidate entities, we can infer possible labels of each entity based on the entity relationship network at first. And then, according to the similarity between query and labels, we can predict the rank of each candidate. This strategy is the offline prediction component of our method. When the network condition is poor, this strategy can still be able to yield ranking results quickly.

We propose an entity search method based on external knowledge and entity relationship, which consist of two core components:

1. **Online Prediction Component**. We search and crawl related information of entities from the external knowledge base, and make prediction based on text similarity.
2. **Offline Prediction Component**. We use historical query records and internal knowledge base to model similarity of entities, and making prediction based on entity relationship network.

The framework is shown in Fig. 1.

As shown in Fig. 1, given a query q and candidate entities $E = \{e_1, ...e_n\}$, our method will calculate the similarity of each entity with q, and output a ranked list of entities E that match q. In offline prediction component, we build an entity relationship network through historical records. And for each entity e, we use labels of similar nodes to describe e, and obtain offline descriptions; in online

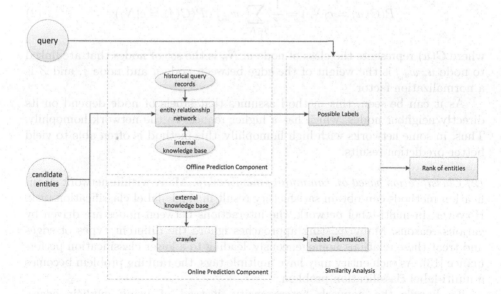

Fig. 1. Framework of our entity search method

prediction component, we search, crawl and extract related information of e. Both offline prediction component and online prediction component will predict the probability of e that match q: $P_{offline}$ and P_{online} respectively. Then the final result is calculated by using different weight to the above result, which is as shown in Eq. (1).

$$P_{(e,q)} = \alpha \times P_{offline} + (1 - \alpha) \times P_{online} \tag{1}$$

Since the offline prediction component does not rely on external knowledge, so it can either be used with online prediction component together to make final prediction, or it can also be used as a pre-sorting approach for extracting candidates from all entities library.

4   Implementation

4.1   Offline Prediction Component

According to the entity relationship network, we assume that nodes' labels rely on the similar nodes. The similarity can be measured from close range, e.g., the direct neighbors; or from a far range, e.g. the community membership. In this paper, we choose the two following methods to measure the similarity of nodes.

(1) Classification based on direct neighbors. Weighted-vote Relational Neighbor (wvRN) [9,11] is a recommended baseline method for comparison as it has shown surprisingly well performance in many real world dataset. Given an unknown node u, wvRN calculates the probability of each class c for node u as:

$$P(C(u) = c|N_u) = \frac{1}{Z} \sum_{j \in N_u} w_{u,j} \cdot P(C(j) = c|N_j) \tag{2}$$

where $C(u)$ represents the class of node u, N_u is the set of nodes that are linked to node u, $w_{u,j}$ is the weight of the edge between node u and node j, and Z is a normalization factor.

As it can be seen, this method assumes that labels of node depend on its directly neighbor nodes, which has a higher request to the network homophily. Thus, in some networks with high homophily, this method is often able to yield better prediction results.

(2) Classification based on community membership. Many within-network classification methods can obtain satisfactory result in single-label classification task. However, in multi-label network, the interactions between nodes are driven by various reasons. Many existing approaches ignore the different types of edges and treat these relations homogeneously, leading to a lower classification performance [13]. As each entity may have multiple tags, the ranking problem becomes a multi-label classification problem.

To handle the network heterogeneity, instead of using explicit edges, researchers try to mine the implicit relationships between nodes in various ways.

SocioDim [13,15,16] is one of the representative classification frameworks. Given a network in which some nodes to be labeled, SocioDim performs community discovery algorithm on the network first, and uses vector-format representation of nodes' involvement in different communities as the latent social dimensions, and then applies discriminative classifier to predict the unknown nodes. Spectral clustering [13] is a representative method to handle network heterogeneity. In SocioDim framework, spectral clustering is used to extract the latent social dimensions based on the network structure. Then by using the social dimensions as new features, it applies the SVM to classify the unknown nodes.

4.2   Online Prediction Component

Due to the rapid development of the Internet, accurate descriptions of entities are mostly stored in external knowledge bases. For instance, Wikipedia and Baidu Baike have contained large scale of entities with detailed descriptions. In addition, some professional descriptions often stored in multiple knowledge bases, e.g. comments about movie mainly exist in Douban and IMDB, and descriptions of restaurant can be found in Dianping. Different knowledge bases have different value for entity search problem, so we need to retrieve specific knowledge base according to the type of entity. The specific knowledge bases for searching Chinese entity in our system are listed in Table 1.

Table 1. Specific knowledge base for searching Chinese entity

Entity type	External knowledge base
Restaurants	Dianping (http://www.dianping.com/)
Movies	Douban (https://www.douban.com/)
TV shows	Douban (https://www.douban.com/)
Celebrities	Baidu Baike (http://baike.baidu.com/)

After extracting related descriptions from external knowledge base, we can perform text similarity analysis to measure whether the entity match the query. Commonly used approach for text similarity analysis are TFIDF, LSI, PLSA and LDA. As the query is generally a short text, we don't choose the latter methods, and use TFIDF for similarity analysis. Several preprocessing steps are applied for the related contents, such as making words segmentation, filtering noisy data and removing lower frequency words etc. And then, TFIDF technique is used to measure the importance of words and make prediction by cosine similarity.

In addition, in order to obtain more accurate result, we also extend the query by synonyms and try to handle the semantic query to some extent.

5   Experiment

During the 2015 Baidu World Summit, Baidu has unveiled the new virtual assistant "Duer" which is integrated into its latest mobile search app. Baidu Cup

2016 CCF nlp challenge (http://nlpcc.baidu.com/) asks participants to tackle the problem of entity search in the scenario of Duer. Here we use the dataset of this challenge to show the performance of our method.

5.1 Case Study

Here we will show the performance of our method when user conducts a specific query. For instance, people may search for: "movie about vampires" in Chinese, system provides 97 candidate entities for ranking. The top 20 ranking entities predicted by our method are shown in Table 2.

Table 2. Top 20 ranking entities predicted by our method

Ranking	Prediction result
1	吸血鬼2000(2000)
2	吸血鬼助理(2009)
3	吸血鬼之吻(1989)
4	吸血鬼助手(2009)
5	吸血鬼女王(2002)
6	最后一个吸血鬼(2001)
7	黑夜传说前传：狼族再起(2009)
8	吸血莱恩(2005)
9	吸血鬼猎人D(2001)
10	黑夜传说(2003)
11	暮光之城(2009)
12	刀锋战士(1998)
13	德古拉2000(2000)
14	驱魔者(2011)
15	血之猎手(2007)
16	黑暗阴影(2012)
17	新天师斗僵尸(2011)
18	唯爱永生(2013)
19	守夜人(2004)
20	三十极夜(2007)

As can be seen, our method makes very accurate prediction, and the top 20 movies are of high correlation with the query, indicating our method can effectively deal with entity search task. In addition, given ground truth dataset, the precision-recall curve is plotted in Fig. 2.

As can be seen from Fig. 2, with the improvement of recall, precision has been maintained at 1. This trend has been maintained for a long time and begins to decline until retrieving about 70% target entities. In addition to better result of top 20 recommendations, this curve indicates that our method can also make very satisfactory ranking performance for all the 97 candidate entities.

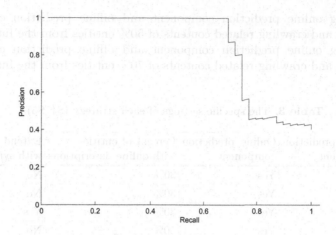

Fig. 2. Precision-recall curve of the ranking performance

5.2 Performance on Large-Scale Dataset

We evaluate the performance of our method by using the dataset of Baidu Cup 2016 challenges. The dataset contains four specified types of entities including restaurants, movies, TV shows and celebrities. For every type there are 1,000 entity queries along with 50–100 candidate entities for each query. All retrieved candidate entities will be collected and manually annotated to construct the gold-standard entity sets for each query. Right after the competition begins, 40% of data will be released as the development set for all participants. The rest 60% of data will be released two days before the submission deadline. All participants should finish processing the full dataset (including the development set) and submit their final results to the evaluation platform.

The challenge also released a manually annotated data for training model. For every type in the training set, there are 100 entity queries along with 50–100 candidate entities for each query.

We report the performance on development set by using different strategies, and also show the final result on the full dataset. Here we first introduce four strategies (S1–S4) used on the development set, and the strategy (S5) used on the full dataset when submitting final result. The specific settings of each strategy can be found in Table 3.

- S1. Using online prediction component and offline prediction component together, and crawling related contents of 30% entities from the Internet.
- S2. Using online prediction component only, and crawling related contents of 30% entities from the Internet.
- S3. Using online prediction component and offline prediction component together, and crawling related contents of 30% entities from the Internet. We also tried to use synonyms to extend the query when performing similarity analysis.

– S4. Using online prediction component and offline prediction component together, and crawling related contents of 50% entities from the Internet.
– S5. Using online prediction component and offline prediction component together, and crawling related contents of 70% entities from the Internet.

Table 3. The specific settings of each strategy (S1–S5).

	Offline prediction component	Online prediction component	Percent of entities with online descriptions	Extend the query with synonym
S1	Yes	Yes	30%	No
S2	No	Yes	30%	No
S3	Yes	Yes	30%	Yes
S4	Yes	Yes	50%	No
S5	Yes	Yes	70%	No

MAP (Mean Average Precision) based on the gold-standard entity set is used to measure the performance of different strategies, which are reported in Fig. 3.

From above results, we can see the impact of different strategies clearly.

As shown in Fig. 3(a), when we discard offline prediction component, the result decreases obviously (S2 yields lower performance than S1), indicating that the offline prediction component has important role for prediction when

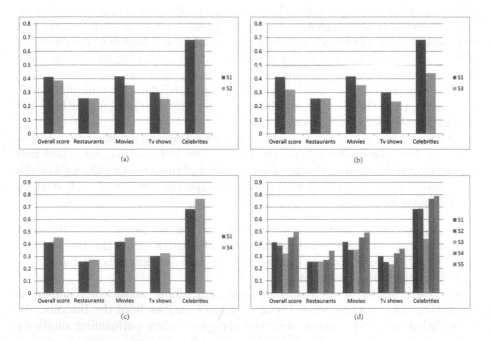

Fig. 3. Performance on real-world dataset

there are fewer descriptions about entities (only crawling related information of 30% entities). Therefore, we should use offline and online prediction component together to deal with the entity search task.

Then we want to verify whether semantic query can improve the results. We use synonyms to extend the query, and apply the extended query to calculate similarity with entity related descriptions. We find that in Fig. 3(b), contrary to our expectation, the experiment result decreases (the performance of S3 is lower than S1). After analyzing the error cases carefully, we find the reasons. The dictionary we used recognizes all the location information as synonyms. For some queries, such as "born in Hunan, Changsha", it will expand the query as "born, Hunan, Hubei, Guangdong, Shanxi, ...". This extended query will make the wrong prediction definitely. Such error cases occur in celebrities dataset frequently, resulting in significantly lower performance. Therefore, simply extending the query with synonyms won't improve the entity search quality. When performing semantic extension, it is necessary to use ontology or other semantic technology to improve the performance.

Next, we try to expand the scope of online search. The proportion of the entities crawled will be up to 50%. As shown in Fig. 3(c), descriptions on external knowledge base have a very significant role for entity search problem (S4 outperformed S1). Getting more online information can obtain more accurate prediction result.

It should be noted that, S5 is the strategy we adopted in the final submission. Compared to S1–S4, the performance of S5 is evaluated on the full dataset (1,000 entity queries for each type). As shown in Fig. 3(d), S5 yields best performance, and the result indicates that our method avoids over-fitting problem and gets very stable performance. By exploiting external knowledge and entity relationship together, our method obtains satisfactory performance in the final result. We win the third prize of the challenge due to the excellent performance.

6   Conclusion

We propose an entity search method based on external knowledge and entity relationship, which mainly consists of two components, online prediction component and offline prediction component. The accurate descriptions of entities are mainly stored on external knowledge bases, so in online prediction component, we crawl related information from multiple external knowledge bases and make prediction by text similarity analysis. Meanwhile, large amounts of historical records are utilized to build an entity relationship network, in which we can make offline prediction by performing multi-label classification. Experiments on real-world data set demonstrate that our method can handle the entity search task effectively and obtain satisfactory performance.

When there is a large amount of historical data, prediction based on entity relationship can obtain better results. In future studies, we also concern about how to improve the within-network classifier performance with less historical data. Moreover, due to the time limit of the competition, we have not crawled all entities' related information in the final submission, and there are various optimization strategies have not been applied either, which requires continued attention in future studies.

References

1. Cheng, T., Yan, X., Chang, K.C.C.: EntityRank: searching entities directly and holistically. In: Proceedings of the 33rd International Conference on Very Large Data Bases, pp. 387–398. VLDB Endowment (2007)
2. Pehcevski, J., Thom, J.A., Vercoustre, A.M., Naumovski, V.: Entity ranking in Wikipedia: utilising categories, links and topic difficulty prediction. Inf. Retr. **13**(5), 568–600 (2010)
3. Kaptein, R., Kamps, J.: Exploiting the category structure of Wikipedia for entity ranking. Artif. Intell. **194**, 111–129 (2013)
4. Demartini, G., Iofciu, T., Vries, A.P.: Overview of the INEX 2009 entity ranking track. In: Geva, S., Kamps, J., Trotman, A. (eds.) INEX 2009. LNCS, vol. 6203, pp. 254–264. Springer, Heidelberg (2010). doi:10.1007/978-3-642-14556-8_26
5. Kang, C., Yin, D., Zhang, R., Torzec, N., He, J., Chang, Y.: Learning to rank related entities in web search. Neurocomputing **166**(C), 309–318 (2015)
6. Wu, Y., Kashioka, H.: NiCT at TREC 2009: employing three models for entity ranking track. In: Eighteenth Text Retrieval Conference, TREC 2009, Gaithersburg, Maryland, USA, November 2009
7. He, B., Ounis, I.: Query performance prediction. Inf. Syst. **31**(7), 585–594 (2006)
8. Zhou, Y., Croft, W.B.: Query performance prediction in web search environments. In: SIGIR 2007: Proceedings of the International ACM SIGIR Conference on Research and Development in Information Retrieval, Amsterdam, The Netherlands, pp. 543–550, July 2007
9. Macskassy, S.A., Provost, F.: Classification in networked data: a toolkit and a univariate case study. J. Mach. Learn. Res. **8**, 935–983 (2007)
10. Sen, P., Namata, G., Bilgic, M., Getoor, L., Gallagher, B., Eliassi-Rad, T.: Collective classification in network data articles. AI Mag. **29**(3), 93–106 (2008)
11. Macskassy, S.A., Provost, F.: A simple relational classifier. In: The Workshop on Multi-relational Data Mining at KDD, pp. 64–76 (2003)
12. Gallagher, B., Tong, H., Eliassi-Rad, T., Faloutsos, C.: Using ghost edges for classification in sparsely labeled networks. In: ACM SIGKDD International Conference on Knowledge Discovery and Data Mining, pp. 256–264 (2008)
13. Tang, L., Liu, H.: Leveraging social media networks for classification. Data Min. Knowl. Discov. **23**(3), 447–478 (2011)
14. Lam, X.N., Vu, T., Le, T.D., Duong, A.D.: Addressing cold-start problem in recommendation systems. In: International Conference on Ubiquitous Information Management and Communication, ICUIMC 2008, Suwon, Korea, 31 January–01 February, pp. 208–211 (2008)
15. Tang, L., Liu, H.: Relational learning via latent social dimensions. In: ACM SIGKDD International Conference on Knowledge Discovery and Data Mining, Paris, France, 28 June–01 July, pp. 817–826 (2009)
16. Tang, L., Liu, H.: Scalable learning of collective behavior based on sparse social dimensions. In: CIKM 2009 Proceeding of ACM Conference on Information and Knowledge Management, pp. 1107–1116 (2009)

A Flexible and Sentiment-Aware Framework for Entity Search

Kerui Min[✉], Chenghao Dong, Shiyuan Cai, and Jianhao Chen

BosonData, Inc., Shanghai, China
{kerui.min,pierce.dong,carol.cai,jianhao.chen}@bosondata.com.cn

Abstract. As a sub-field of information retrieval, entity search which answers users' queries by entities, is very useful across various vertical domains. In this paper we propose a flexible and sentiment-aware framework for entity search. Our approach achieved the average MAP score of 0.7044 in the competition of NLPCC Baidu Challenge 2016, obtained the 3rd place among 174 teams.

1 Introduction

Search engine is arguably the most important and successful application in natural language processing. It has been studied and developed in academia and industry for a long time, *e.g.*, the famous SIGIR conference is nearly 40-year-old. Although the general search technology is still an interesting topic of research, nowadays, the holy grail is more than pure search, but to *answer* users' queries directly. Results should be semantically relevant to the queries instead of simply keyword-based match.

It can be seen that in certain vertical domains, the answer to a given query is a set of entities. Formally, this problem can be described as: given a pre-defined entity set $\mathcal{E}$ where each entity $e \in \mathcal{E}$ is associated with certain related meta data $m \in \mathcal{M}$. Then, given a query $q \in \mathcal{Q}$, we would like to compute a ranking function: $f : (q, e, m) \mapsto \mathbb{R}$, where $(q, e, m) \in \mathcal{Q} \times \mathcal{E} \times \mathcal{M}$, so that a loss function defined over $f(q, S)$ is minimized, where $S \subset \mathcal{E} \times \mathcal{M}$.

As a way towards semantically answers users' entity-related queries, NLPCC 2016 Baidu Challenge address this problem over four vertical fields–restaurants, movies, TV shows and celebrities, which requires ranking the entities of given queries.

This task is challenging since:

- There are only 100 training queries provided for each domain by the competition. Therefore, data-hungry machine learning algorithms are unlikely to be used in this scenario.
- In order to rank the given entities, we should not only know the entity names but also other important meta data $\mathcal{M}$, *e.g.*, we could not determine whether a restaurant is quiet or not from its name. Unfortunately, the competition doesn't provide the necessary meta data.

© Springer International Publishing AG 2016
C.-Y. Lin et al. (Eds.): NLPCC-ICCPOL 2016, LNAI 10102, pp. 701–710, 2016.
DOI: 10.1007/978-3-319-50496-4_63

– Certain queries are inherently ambiguous to answer. Again taking the "quiet restaurant" as an example, if five people said a restaurant is noisy and two people consider it very quiet, in whom should we trust?

In the following of this paper, we will decompose the problem into two stages: in the offline stage, we enrich meta data of entities by web-crawlers, and map the entities crawled from web to the entities provided by the competition; in the online stage, we rewrite given queries (including removing unnecessary words, query expansion, etc.) so that we can compute a similarity score between an entity and a query more accurately in semantic space. The similarity score will be used to rank the entities to produce the final result.

2   Related Work

Information Retrieval (IR) has been long studied and people have come up with many different models along these years. After the age of manual indexing, the first and simplest model used in search engine was Boolean Model (BM), which is still used in library search systems. Based on boolean logic and set operations, this model find documents satisfying boolean expressions. The terms and boolean logical rules, though not very friendly, can be entered directly by users.

Another basic and widely used model is Vector Space Model (VSM) [1]. In this model, words and documents are represented as vectors (e.g. tf-idf). Similarity between a query and a document could be measured by cosine similarity of two vectors. Compared with BM, it provides with more flexible partial matching. VSM is easy to implement and performs well, however, one should notice that it implicitly assumes the independence among terms, which is not the case apparently.

Later, Latent Semantic Indexing (LSI) [2] is incorporated into ranking process, which uses Singular Value Decomposition (SVD) to transform the vector space to generating latent semantic space and then defines relevance between queries and documents in that new space. Supervised Semantic Indexing (SSI) [3] pushes the direction further.

LSI tries to provide a solution to the fundamental problems in IR, namely, synonymy and polysemy. Query Expansion (QE) is another way to deal with those two fundamental problems, especially to the case of less-well-developed queries [4]. Hand-collected resource could be used, like WordNet or knowledge-base in general. Otegi et al. [5,6] modified specific words in queries as well as documents (in which case it becomes document expansion), to bring in more semantic richness, improved IR system's recall and robustness.

Effect of Word Sense Disambiguation (WSD) is discussed in [7]. They draw attention to reduce the negative impact of erroneous disambiguation. Pseudo Relevance Feedback (PRF) [8] is much like a local way to do QE, compared to the global aspect of previous methods.

As continuous space word embeddings such as word2vec or GloVe have shown to grasp term relatedness well, recent work [9,10] has claimed superiority of similarity based on global word embeddings to classic PRF techniques. Motivated by that, Diaz et al. [11] showed local-trained word embeddings would outperform the global one.

Learning to rank [12] is popular used in document retrieval, collaborative filtering and other tasks, which use a score or a scalar as a ranking problem. It is widely employed in commercial web search engines to significantly improve their search quality. Since more indices are considered as the indication of similarity, the weight of each index could be learned by optimizing a loss function, with which to minimize errors in ranking (e.g., measured by MAP or NDCG). The specific learning algorithms could be categorized into three approaches: the pointwise, pairwise and listwise approaches, based on their difference on training data formats and evaluation methods. This learning machine's feature vectors include documents' static features which are independent of queries, queries' features independent of documents and dynamic features which depend on both the documents and the queries.

Based on clickthrough data and deep learning methods, Huang et al. [13] proposed Deep Structured Semantic Models (DSSM) which significantly outperforms other latent semantic models.

3   System Design

The overall system consists of four components: data collection, data alignment, query rewriting and entity ranking.

As illustrated in Fig. 1, the offline system finds related meta information of entities related to this competition, including restaurants, movies, TV shows and celebrities. When a query is given, the online system tries to rewrite the given query, and ranks entities based on the rewritten query to produce the final ranking list. We will introduce each component in more details in the next few sections.

3.1   Data Collection and Data Alignment

As we mentioned before, the training data provided by the competition doesn't contain necessary meta information $\mathcal{M}$. Therefore, it is crucial that we can gather those information from online resources. We identified the following important sources for meta information:

- Restaurants: Dianping (http://www.dianping.com)
- Movies: Douban Movie (http://movie.douban.com)
- TV shows: Douban TV (http://movie.douban.com/tv)
- Celebrities: Baidu Baike (http://baike.baidu.com)

We use a Distributed Master-Slave Crawler Framework to collect data. The framework mainly consists of a distributed job queue, a distributed lock mechanism, a dedupe caching system, a backend storage system and around 100 crawler nodes.

Each slave crawler does the following repeatedly, as shown in Fig. 2:

704 K. Min et al.

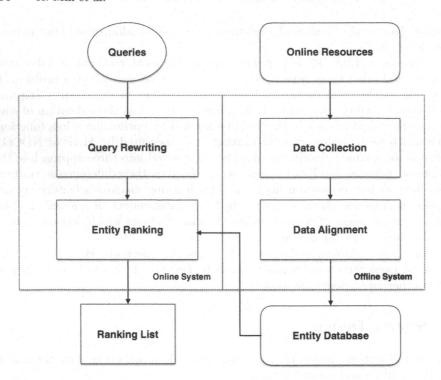

Fig. 1. User interaction flow diagram, the Entity Database contains meta information that can be used by Entity Ranking module to produce final ranking list.

1. Acquire the distributed job lock with a reasonable timeout, hence we don't need to release it after the job is done;
2. Pull a job from the queue if lock acquired;
3. Analyze job meta and get the function to execute;
4. Download resources (mainly HTML) from the Internet;
5. Extract documents and links to follow;
6. Store documents to database;
7. Dedupe the jobs to follow by the caching system;
8. Enqueue additional jobs if any.

With the help of the distributed framework, we collected around 60 millions information in 3 weeks, *i.e.* we collected all the relevant comments and reviews from Dianping and Douban, as well given celebrity pages from Baidu Baike.

Since our data are collected externally, we should notice that it corresponds to another entity set $\mathcal{E}'$. We need to find an alignment function $g : \mathcal{E}' \mapsto \mathcal{E} \cup \{\bot\}$ to either map $e' \in \mathcal{E}'$ to our target entity set, or indicate that it doesn't exist, *i.e.* $g(e') = \bot$. Preliminary experiment showed that a simple Levenshtein distance function performed reasonably well. Therefore, we choose it for entity data alignment for all of the four domains.

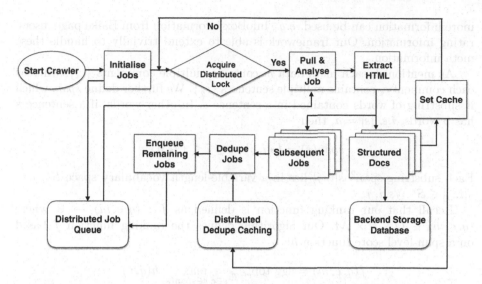

Fig. 2. The flowchart of the Distributed Master-Slave Crawler Framework

3.2 Query Rewriting

By observing the given training/development data, it is not difficult to find that certain words in queries are highly redundant. For example, in query "适合安静吃饭的地方", the suffix "的地方" can be removed since this vertical domain is all about finding restaurants. Similarly, degree adverbs can be removed without changing the semantics, but improve the recall of the system significantly. These rules can be designed once we pre-processed a query by obtaining its word segmentation, part-of-speech tagging and named entity recognition result using BosonNLP engine[1]. Finally, to further improve the recall, we expand the resultant query with a synonyms dictionary.

To summarize, the following three steps are involved:

- word segmentation, POS tagging and named entity recognition
- remove query words
- query expansion using a synonyms dictionary.

3.3 Entity Ranking

Entity ranking is arguably the most important component in the system, since it directly affects the ranking result.

Before getting into details, let us be more concrete about the meta data m associated with each entity e. We find that users' comments and reviews are the most useful information for restaurants, movies and TV shows domains, as for celebrities, we simply treat each Baike page as a single review. Admittedly,

---

[1] www.bosonnlp.com.

more information can be used, *e.g.*, InfoBox information from Baike page, users' rating information. Our framework is able to extend trivially to handle these meta information.

As mentioned, each meta data m contains multiple comments $\{c_i\}$, whereas each comment c_i contains multiple sentences $\{s_j\}$. We further define *span*, which is substring of words contained in a sentence s. In other words, if a sentence s has n words, *i.e.* $|s| = n$, then

$$\text{span}(s) = \{s[i..j] : 1 \leq i \leq j \leq n\}.$$

Each substring span[2] $s[i..j]$ lies in a variable-length vocabulary space $\mathcal{S}^*$, *i.e.*, $s[i..j] \in \mathcal{S}^* \ \forall s, i, j$.

Recall that our ranking function is defined as $f : (q, e, m) \mapsto \mathbb{R}$ where $(q, e, m) \in \mathcal{Q} \times \mathcal{E} \times \mathcal{M}$. Our algorithm defines the ranking function f based on a span-level score function h:

$$f(q, e, m) = \text{agg top}_{c \in m} \max_{s \in c, r \in \text{span}(s)} h(q, r)$$

It is a composition of four functions, which we explain as follows.

Operator	Description	Domain, range
agg	Aggregation function, either *sum* or *average*	$\mathbb{R}^k \rightarrow \mathbb{R}$
top	Get the top k values from a list	$\mathbb{R}^l \rightarrow \mathbb{R}^k$
max	Conventional max operator	$\mathbb{R}^d \rightarrow \mathbb{R}$
h	Span-level score function	$\mathcal{Q} \times \mathcal{S}^* \rightarrow \mathbb{R}$
f	Entity-level score function	$\mathcal{Q} \times \mathcal{E} \times \mathcal{M} \rightarrow \mathbb{R}$

With the above transformation, we reduce the problem to find an effective span-level score function h. Specifically, we can define various features between a span and a query to measure the score or similarity between them. We define it as a linear model:

$$h(q, r) = \mathbf{w} \cdot \mathbf{fea}(q, r),$$

where $\mathbf{fea}(q, r)$ is the feature vector defined on (q, r) and $\mathbf{w}$ is the corresponding weight vector.

In this competition, we defined the following features

- the length of the given span r;
- punctuation score in span r, defined as $1/(1 + \#\text{num of punctuation})$;
- the word order in span r, measured by the number of pair of words in reverse order between q and r;
- sentiment compatibility between q and r;

---

[2] We slightly abuse the notation span to represent the set of all substring of s as well a single substring, which should be clear from the context.

– can *must contain* words be found in r;
– cosine similarity between q and r (with *idf* word weighting).

Intuitively, the first two rules are designed to choose shorter and simpler spans, as the meaning is more clearly defined. Taking the query "安静，吃饭" as an example, a long span "安静的洒下来，照在小路上，我们来的这家餐馆非常热闹，菜不错，我们中午在这里吃饭" is found in our database. The score of h will be small, since it is a long span with many punctuation. In this case, the *cosine similarity* will be very small as well.

The sentiment compatibility is useful in cases where r and q convey opposite meaning, *e.g.* the span could be "不能安静吃饭". Assume a sentiment classifier return 1 for non-negative text and −1 for negative text, the compatibility can be defined as Sentiment(r) · Sentiment(s). In our actual implementation, however, we include two words before and after r as the contextual information together to determine the sentiment of the span with higher accuracy.

In terms of those words who have dominated *idf* value in a given query, it is reasonable that they should be always included in a target span r. For example, if the query is "有小提琴", "小提琴" (or it's synonyms) must be included in a matched span r. We say a word is a *must contain* word in q if the *idf* is at least 0.6.

4 Experiments

We validate the effectiveness of our framework by evaluating it on four vertical fields, as stated before, restaurants, movies, TV shows and celebrities. The dataset is provided by the competition. For each field, there are 1,100 (100 for training, 400 for development, and the remaining 600 for testing) queries along with 50–100 short-listed candidate entities for each query. The training data also contain ground-truth labels for each short-listed entity.

The competition consists of two stages. In the first stage, training data and development data were released. Each team is not able to get the ground-truth labels for development data directly, but can submit calculated result to an online evaluation system to get the evaluation score. In the second stage, test data was released but we can no longer calculate the evaluation score until the end of the competition.

Mean Average Precision (MAP) is used as the official evaluation metric. The final score is decided by the average MAP score of each query for all four domains on both development and testing data.

We fix the top operator to return the top 3 values during the experiment. Notice that the dimension of the weight **w** of the span-level score function h defined in the previous section is only 5, which is not prone to over-fitting. Therefore, instead of optimizing **w** using conventional convex optimization algorithms, we simply apply a grid search over the training data to obtain the set of weights in Fig. 3. It should be noted that the weight for *must contain* is infinity, as we enforce it as a hard constraint. In terms of the aggregation, we found

Feature	Length of Span	No. of Punctuation in Span	Words Order	IDF-based Cosine Similarity	Must Contain	Sentiment
Weight	0.07	0.1	0.4	0.4	$+\infty$	0.2

Fig. 3. Weights for each feature in the score function.

Field	Restaurants	Movies	TV shows	Celebrities	Total
MAP	0.6148	0.7977	0.5396	0.8653	0.7044

Fig. 4. The final score on each field, official release.

that the *average* operator worked better for restaurants and celebrities domains, while the *sum* operator worked better for movies and TV shows domains.

By inspecting the feature weights in Fig. 3, the *words order* and *cosine similarity* are the most important features, whereas the *span length* penalty only mildly influence the final score. We conjecture that this is because the feature is highly correlated with the *cosine similarity*.

We obtained the 3rd place among 174 teams in terms of the final average MAP score, 0.8% below the best team. The performance on each domain is given in Fig. 4.

There are several ideas which we believe could further improve the performance of the framework, but did not finish it during the competition. The most important one is probably the missing of meta data. Despite the effort we spent on crawling online resources, we still find that some entities don't contain any meta data at all, see Fig. 5 for details. It can be improved by crawling more resources, and using better data alignment algorithms.

We believe more meta data can improve the results significantly, especially in *Restaurants* domain. We conducted a simple test on training data. By reducing the missing data from 50% to 16%, the MAP of the system improved around 50%, from 0.392 to 0.593, demonstrating the importance of this issue.

Another general issue over all domains is caused by the lack of syntactical information in the current feature functions. Two typical examples are given in

Field	Restaurants	Movies	TV shows	Celebrities
Missing Data(%)	14.5%	1%	5%	0.2%

Fig. 5. Percentage of missing (meta) data of each domain.

Example 1:
Query：脑科专家
Entity：丽莎·库卓
Sentence：丽莎出生在一个富裕的家庭，父亲是脑科专家和内科医生

Example 2:
Query：县卫生局局长
Entity：高勇(吉林省扶余县政府副县长)
Sentence：给予县卫生局局长李纯辉撤销党内职务、行政撤职处分

Fig. 6. Errors that caused by the lack of syntactical information in the current feature functions.

Fig. 6. In the first example, it can be found that "脑科专家" does not refers to "丽莎·库卓" but her father, although the span "脑科专家" is a perfect match to the query. Similarly, in the second example, "县卫生局局长" is not "高勇" in the sentence. It can be improved by cooperating syntactical information, *e.g.*, extracting SVO information using a *dependency parser*.

5   Conclusion

We have developed a general and flexible framework for entity search, including data collection, data alignment, query rewriting and entity ranking. In particular, the entity ranking include a linear model which could incorporate various feature functions.

The framework successfully demonstrated its effectiveness in the competition. Nevertheless, there is large room for improvement, *e.g.* using syntactical information, which we believe is important if serving as a base for intelligent question-answer system.

References

1. Salton, G., Wong, A., Yang, C.-S.: A vector space model for automatic indexing. Commun. ACM **18**(11), 613–620 (1975)
2. Dumais, S.T., Furnas, G.W., Landauer, T.K., Deerwester, S., Harshman, R.: Using latent semantic analysis to improve access to textual information. In: Proceedings of the SIGCHI Conference on Human Factors in Computing Systems, pp. 281–285. ACM (1988)
3. Bai, B., Weston, J., Grangier, D., Collobert, R., Sadamasa, K., Qi, Y., Chapelle, O., Weinberger, K.: Supervised semantic indexing. In: Proceedings of the 18th ACM Conference on Information and Knowledge Management, pp. 187–196. ACM (2009)
4. Voorhees, E.M.: Query expansion using lexical-semantic relations. In: Croft, B.W., et al. (eds.) SIGIR '94, pp. 61–69. Springer, London (1994)

5. Agirre, E., Arregi, X., Otegi, A.: Document expansion based on WordNet for robust IR. In: Proceedings of the 23rd International Conference on Computational Linguistics: Posters, pp. 9–17. Association for Computational Linguistics (2010)
6. Otegi, A., Arregi, X., Agirre, E.: Query expansion for IR using knowledge-based relatedness. In: IJCNLP, pp. 1467–1471 (2011)
7. Zhong, Z., Ng, H.T.: Word sense disambiguation improves information retrieval. In: Proceedings of the 50th Annual Meeting of the Association for Computational Linguistics: Long Papers, vol. 1, pp. 273–282. Association for Computational Linguistics (2012)
8. Xu, J., Croft, W.B.: Query expansion using local and global document analysis. In: Proceedings of the 19th Annual International ACM SIGIR Conference on Research and Development in Information Retrieval, pp. 4–11. ACM (1996)
9. Sordoni, A., Bengio, Y., Nie, J.-Y.: Learning concept embeddings for query expansion by quantum entropy minimization. In: AAAI, pp. 1586–1592 (2014)
10. ALMasri, M., Berrut, C., Chevallet, J.-P.: A comparison of deep learning based query expansion with pseudo-relevance feedback and mutual information. In: Ferro, N., Crestani, F., Moens, M.-F., Mothe, J., Silvestri, F., Nunzio, G.M., Hauff, C., Silvello, G. (eds.) ECIR 2016. LNCS, vol. 9626, pp. 709–715. Springer, Heidelberg (2016). doi:10.1007/978-3-319-30671-1_57
11. Diaz, F., Mitra, B., Craswell, N.: Query expansion with locally-trained word embeddings (2016). arXiv preprint: arXiv:1605.07891
12. Liu, T.-Y.: Learning to rank for information retrieval. Found. Trends Inf. Retr. 3(3), 225–331 (2009)
13. Huang, P.-S., He, X., Gao, J., Deng, L., Acero, A., Heck, L.: Learning deep structured semantic models for web search using clickthrough data. In: Proceedings of the 22nd ACM International Conference on Information & Knowledge Management, pp. 2333–2338. ACM (2013)

Word Segmentation on Micro-Blog Texts with External Lexicon and Heterogeneous Data

Qingrong Xia, Zhenghua Li[(✉)], Jiayuan Chao, and Min Zhang

Soochow University, Suzhou, China
kirosummer.nlp@gmail.com, {zhli13,minzhang}@suda.edu.cn,
chaojiayuan.china@gmail.com

Abstract. This paper describes our system designed for the NLPCC 2016 shared task on word segmentation on micro-blog texts (i.e., Weibo). We treat word segmentation as a character-wise sequence labeling problem, and explore two directions to enhance our CRF-based baseline. First, we employ a large-scale external lexicon for constructing extra lexicon features in the model, which is proven to be extremely useful. Second, we exploit two heterogeneous datasets, i.e., Penn Chinese Treebank 7 (*CTB7*) and People Daily (*PD*) to help word segmentation on Weibo. We adopt two mainstream approaches, i.e., the guide-feature based approach and the recently proposed coupled sequence labeling approach. We combine the above techniques in different ways and obtain four well-performing models. Finally, we merge the outputs of the four models and obtain the final results via Viterbi-based re-decoding. On the test data of Weibo, our proposed approach outperforms the baseline by $95.63 - 94.24 = 1.39\%$ in terms of F1 score. Our final system rank the first place among five participants in the open track in terms of F1 score, and is also the best among all 28 submissions. All codes, experiment configurations, and the external lexicon are released at http://hlt.suda.edu.cn/~zhli.

1 Introduction

Chinese word segmentation (WS) is the most fundamental task in Chinese language processing. In the past decade, supervised approaches have gained extensive progress on canonical texts, especially on texts from domains or genres similar to existing manually labeled data[1]. However, the upsurge of web data imposes great challenges on existing techniques. The performance of the state-of-the-art systems degrades dramatically on informal web texts, such as micro-blogs, product comments, and so on. Driven by this challenge, NLPCC 2016 organizes a shared task with an aim of promoting WS on Weibo (*WB*, Chinese pinyin of micro-blogs) text [8].

This paper describes our system designed for the shared task in detail. We treat WS as a character-wise sequence labeling problem, and build our model

---

[1] Please refer to http://zhangkaixu.github.io/bibpage/cws.html for a long list of related papers.

© Springer International Publishing AG 2016
C.-Y. Lin et al. (Eds.): NLPCC-ICCPOL 2016, LNAI 10102, pp. 711–721, 2016.
DOI: 10.1007/978-3-319-50496-4_64

based on the standard conditional random field (CRF) [4] with bigram features. Our major contributions are three-fold. First, we employ a large-scale external lexicon for constructing extra lexicon features in the model, which is proven to be extremely useful.

Second, we exploit two mainstream approaches to exploit heterogeneous data, i.e.,the guide-feature based approach and the recently proposed coupled sequence labeling approach. The third-party heterogeneous resources used in the work are Penn Chinese Treebank 7.0 (*CTB7*, *50K*) and People's Daily (*PD*, *100K*). Since *CTB7* and *PD* have different annotation standards in word segmentation and part-of-speech (POS) tagging, *PD* has been automatically converted into the style of *CTB7*.

Third, we propose a merge-then-re-decode ensemble approach to combine the outputs of different base models.

On the test data of Weibo, our proposed approach outperforms the baseline by $95.63 - 94.24 = 1.39\%$ in terms of F1 score. Our final system rank the first place among five participants in the open track in terms of F1 score, and is also the best among all 28 submissions.

This paper is organized as follows. Section 2 introduces the baseline CRF-based word segmentation model. Section 3 describes how to employ external lexicon features into baseline CRF model. Section 4 briefly illustrates the guide-feature based approach while Sect. 5 briefly presents the coupled sequence labeling approach. Section 6 introduces the merge-then-re-decode ensemble approach. Section 7 presents the experimental results. We discuss closely related works in Sect. 8 and conclude this paper in Sect. 9.

2   The Baseline CRF-Based WSTagger

We treat WS as a sequence labeling problem and employ the standard CRF with bigram features. We adopt the $\{B, I, E, S\}$ tag set, indicating the beginning of a word, the inside of a word, the end of a word and a single-character word [13].

Figure 1 shows the graphical structure of the CRF model. Given an input sentence, which is a sequence of n characters, denoted by $\mathbf{x} = c_1...c_n$, WS aims to determine the best tag sequence $\mathbf{y} = y_1...y_n$, where $y_i \in \{B, I, E, S\}$. As a log-linear model, CRF defines the probability of a tag sequence as:

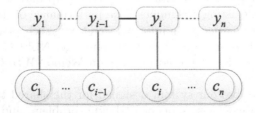

Fig. 1. Graphical structure of the baseline CRF model.

$$P(\mathbf{y}|\mathbf{x}; \theta) = \frac{e^{Score(\mathbf{x},\mathbf{y};\theta)}}{\sum_{\mathbf{y}'} e^{Score(\mathbf{x},\mathbf{y}';\theta)}}$$

$$Score(\mathbf{x}, \mathbf{y}; \theta) = \sum_{1 \leq i \leq n+1} \theta \cdot \mathbf{f}_{bs}(\mathbf{x}, i, y_{i-1}, y_i) \tag{1}$$

where $Score(\mathbf{x}, \mathbf{y}; \theta)$ is a scoring function; $\mathbf{f}_{bs}(\mathbf{x}, i, y_{i-1}, y_i)$ is the feature vector at the ith character and θ is the feature weight vector. Please note that c_0 and c_{n+1} are two pseudo characters marking the beginning and end of the sentence. We use the features described in Zhang et al. [16], as shown in Table 1.

Table 1. Feature templates for $\mathbf{f}_{bs}(\mathbf{x}, i, y_{i-1}, y_i)$ used in the baseline CRF model. $T(c_i)$ returns the type of the character c_i (time, number, punctuation, special symbols, else). $I(c_i, c_j)$ judges whether the two characters c_i and c_j are the same.

Unigram: $\mathbf{f}_{bs\_uni}(\mathbf{x}, i, y_i)$		Bigram: $\mathbf{f}_{bs\_bi}(\mathbf{x}, i, y_{i-1}, y_i)$
01: $y_i \circ c_k$	$i-2 \leq k \leq i+2$	09: $y_{i-1} \circ y_i$
02: $y_i \circ c_{k-1} \circ c_k$	$i-1 \leq k \leq i+2$	10: $y_{i-1} \circ y_i \circ c_i$
03: $y_i \circ c_{k-1} \circ c_k \circ c_{k+1}$	$i-1 \leq k \leq i+1$	11: $y_{i-1} \circ y_i \circ c_{i-1} \circ c_i$
04: $y_i \circ T(c_k)$	$i-1 \leq k \leq i+1$	
05: $y_i \circ T(c_{k-1}) \circ T(c_k)$	$i \leq k \leq i+1$	
06: $y_i \circ T(c_{i-1}) \circ T(c_i) \circ T(c_{i+1})$		
07: $y_i \circ I(c_i, c_k)$	$i-2 \leq k \leq i+2, k \neq i$	
08: $y_i \circ I(c_{i-1}, c_{i+1})$		

3   Exploring External Lexicon Features

Inspired by the work of Yu et al. [14] who have participated last year's shared task, we try to enhance the baseline CRF by using a large-scale word dictionary [15]. The dictionary we use is composed of two parts. The first part contains about $210K$ words, and is directly borrowed from Yu et al. [14].[2] The second part contains $217K$ words, and is collected by ourselves from the lexicon sharing website of Sogou (http://pinyin.sogou.com/dict/). In total, the external lexicon consists of $428,101$ words, and is denoted as $\mathcal{D}$ in this work.

Apart from the features used in Table 1, denoted as $\mathbf{f}_{bs}(\mathbf{x}, i, y_{i-1}, y_i)$, the enhanced model adds extra lexicon features to the feature vector, denoted as $\mathbf{f}_{lex}(\mathbf{x}, i, y_i, \mathcal{D})$. Thus, the scoring function becomes:

---

[2] We are very grateful for their kind sharing. Their dictionary is composed of several word lists, the SogouW word dictionary (http://www.sogou.com/labs/resource/w.php), and a few lists on different domains (finance, sports, and entertainment) from the lexicon sharing website of Sogou (http://pinyin.sogou.com/dict/).

$$Score(\mathbf{x}, \mathbf{y}; \theta) = \sum_{1 \le i \le n+1} \theta \cdot \begin{bmatrix} \mathbf{f}_{bs}(\mathbf{x}, i, y_{i-1}, y_i) \\ \mathbf{f}_{lex}(\mathbf{x}, i, y_i, \mathcal{D}) \end{bmatrix} \tag{2}$$

where the first term of the extended feature vector is the same as the baseline feature vector and the second term is the lexicon feature vector.

Table 2 lists the lexicon feature templates, which are mostly borrowed from Zhang et al. [15]. $F_B(\mathbf{x}, i, y_i, \mathcal{D})$ considers words beginning with c_i, and returns the maximum length m, so that the span $c_i c_{i+1}...c_{i+m-1}$ in $\mathbf{x}$ is a word in $\mathcal{D}$. "Maximum" means that there is no $r > m$ so that $c_i c_{i+1}...c_{i+r-1}$ in $\mathbf{x}$ is a word in $\mathcal{D}$. In contrast, $F_E(\mathbf{x}, i, y_i, \mathcal{D})$ considers words ending with c_i, and returns the maximum length m, so that the span $c_{i-m+1}...c_{i-1}c_i$ in $\mathbf{x}$ is a word in $\mathcal{D}$. Analogously, $F_I(\mathbf{x}, i, y_i, \mathcal{D})$ considers words containing c_i (absolutely inside), and returns the maximum length m, so that the span $c_{i-(m-j-1)}...c_i...c_{i+j}$ (where $m > 2$ and $0 < j < m - 1$) in $\mathbf{x}$ is a word in $\mathcal{D}$.

Table 2. Lexicon feature templates $\mathbf{f}_{lex}(\mathbf{x}, i, y_i, \mathbf{D})$.

01: $F_B(\mathbf{x}, i-1, y_i, \mathcal{D})$	04: $F_B(\mathbf{x}, i, y_i, \mathcal{D})$	07: $F_B(\mathbf{x}, i+1, y_i, \mathcal{D})$
02: $F_I(\mathbf{x}, i-1, y_i, \mathcal{D})$	05: $F_I(\mathbf{x}, i, y_i, \mathcal{D})$	08: $F_I(\mathbf{x}, i+1, y_i, \mathcal{D})$
03: $F_E(\mathbf{x}, i-1, y_i, \mathcal{D})$	06: $F_E(\mathbf{x}, i, y_i, \mathcal{D})$	09: $F_E(\mathbf{x}, i+1, y_i, \mathcal{D})$

4   The Guide-Feature Based Approach for Exploiting *CTB7* and *PD*

To use the heterogeneous data, we re-implement the guide feature baseline method [3]. The basic idea is to use one resource to generate extra guide features on another resource, as illustrated in Fig. 2. *PD* is converted into the style of *CTB*, as discussed in Sect. 7.1. First, we use *CTB7* and *PD* as the source data to train a source model $Tagger_{CTB7+PD}$. Then, $Tagger_{CTB7+PD}$ generates automatic tags on the target data *WB*, called *source annotations*. Finally, a target model $Tagger_{WB\leftarrow(CTB7+PD)}$ is trained on *WB*, using source annotations as extra guide features.

Table 3 lists the guide feature templates used in this work. Adding the guide features into the model feature vector, the scoring function becomes:

$$Score(\mathbf{x}, \mathbf{y}; \theta) = \sum_{1 \le i \le n+1} \theta \cdot \begin{bmatrix} \mathbf{f}_{bs}(\mathbf{x}, i, y_{i-1}, y_i) \\ \mathbf{f}_{guide}(\mathbf{x}, \mathbf{y}^S, i, y_i) \end{bmatrix} \tag{3}$$

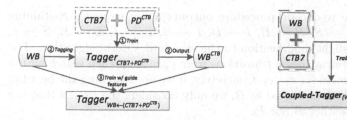

Fig. 2. Our model using guide feature   **Fig. 3.** Graphical structure of the coupled CRF

Table 3. Guide feature templates for $\mathbf{f}_{guide}(\mathbf{x}, \mathbf{y}^S, i, y_i)$. Where $\mathbf{f}_{bs\_uni}(\mathbf{x}, i, y_i) \circ y_i^S$ means that each feature template in $\mathbf{f}_{bs\_uni}(\mathbf{x}, i, y_i)$ is concatenated with y_i^S to produce a new feature template.

Guide features: $\mathbf{f}_{guide}(\mathbf{x}, \mathbf{y}^S, i, y_i)$	
01: $\mathbf{f}_{bs\_uni}(\mathbf{x}, i, y_i) \circ y_i^S$	05: $y_i \circ y_{i-1}^S \circ y_i^S$
02: $y_i \circ y_i^S$	06: $y_i \circ y_i^S \circ y_{i+1}^S$
03: $y_i \circ y_{i+1}^S$	07: $y_i \circ y_{i-1}^S \circ y_{i+1}^S$
04: $y_i \circ y_{i-1}^S$	08: $y_i \circ y_{i-1}^S \circ y_i^S \circ y_{i+1}^S$

5   The Coupled Approach for Exploring *CTB7* and *PD*

The coupled sequence labeling approach is proposed in our earlier work Li et al. [6], and aims to learn and predict two heterogeneous annotations simultaneously. The key idea is to bundle two sets of tags together, and build a conditional random field (CRF) based tagging model in the enlarged space of bundled tags with the help of *ambiguous labeling*. To train our model on two non-overlapping datasets that each has only one-side tags, we transform a one-side tag into a set of bundled tags by concatenating the tag with every possible tag at the missing side according to a predefined context-free tag-to-tag mapping function, thus producing ambiguous labeling as weak supervision. The bundled tag space contains $4 \times 4 = 16$ tags in our task of WS. Please refer to Chao et al. [2] for the detailed description of the coupled WS tagging model (Fig. 3).

6   The Merge-then-re-decode Ensemble Approach

In this section, we propose a merge-then-re-decode ensemble approach to combine the outputs of different base models, which is inspired by the work of Sagae and Lavie [10]. First, given a sentence $\mathbf{x} = c_1...c_n$, the outputs of several base models are treated as votes of character-wise tags with equal weights. For example, if three models assign B to the character c_i, and only one model assigns S to it, then the scores of tagging c_i as $\{B, I, E, S\}$ are $\{3, 0, 0, 1\}$ respectively. In such way, we can get all scores for all characters in $\mathbf{x}$. Then, we find the highest-scoring tag sequence using the Viterbi algorithm.

To avoid that the re-decode procedure outputs a tag sequence containing illegal transitions ($B \rightarrow S$, $B \rightarrow B$, $I \rightarrow B$, $I \rightarrow S$, $E \rightarrow I$, $E \rightarrow E$, $S \rightarrow I$, $S \rightarrow E$), we make a slight modification to the standard Viterbi algorithm. The basic idea is to throw away illegal transitions from c_{i-1} to c_i when searching the best partial tag sequences for $c_1...c_i$. Concretely, if we are searching the best tag sequences for $c_1...c_i$ with c_i tagged as B, we only considers the results that tag c_{i-1} as E or S (but neither B nor I).

7 Experiments

7.1 Datasets

Table 4 shows the datasets used in this work. "WB", short for Weibo, refers to the labeled data provided by the NLPCC 2016 shared task organizer. Actually, the organizer also provides a large set of unlabeled *WB* text, which is not considered in this work.

We adopt *CTB7* as a third-party resource and follow the suggestion in the data description guideline for data split.

We also use *PD* as another labeled resource. Since *PD* and *CTB7* have different word segmentation and POS tagging standards, we used a converted version of *PD* following the style of *CTB* for the sake of simplicity in this work.

Annotation Conversion: PD^{CTB}. We directly use the coupled WS&POS tagging model trained on *CTB5* and *PD* in Li et al. [5] for data conversion. As pointed in Li et al. [6], the coupled model can be naturally used for annotation conversion via constrained decoding with the *PD*-side tags being fixed. After conversion, if a sentence in *PD* contains a character with a very low marginal probability (<0.8), we throw away the sentence to guarantee the data quality. Finally, we get the $100K$ *PD* dataset in the same style of *CTB7*, denoted as PD^{CTB}.

For **evaluation metrics**, we adopt character-level accuracy, and the standard Precision (P), Recall (R), and F1 score.

Table 4. Data statistics

Dataset	Partition	Sentences	Words	Characters
WB	Train	20,135	421,166	688,734
	Dev	2,052	43,697	73,244
	Test	8,592	—	315,857
CTB7	Train	46,572	1,039,774	1,682,485
	Dev	2,079	59,955	100,316
	Test	2,796	81,578	134,149
PD	Train	106,157	1,752,502	2,911,489

Training with Multiple Training Datasets: For some models (such as $WSTagger_{CTB7+PD}$ and $CoupledWSTagger_{WB\&CTB7+PD}$), we use two or three training datasets simultaneously. To balance the contribution of different datasets, we adopt the simple corpus-weighting strategy proposed in Li et al. [6]. Before each iteration, we randomly select 5000 sentences from each training datasets. Then, we merge and shuffle the selected sentences, and use them for one-iteration training.

7.2 Heterogeneity of WB and CTB7

To investigate the heterogeneity of WB and CTB7, we use the baseline model trained on WB-train, denoted as $WSTagger_{WB}$, to process CTB7-dev/test, and also use the baseline model trained on CTB7-train, denoted as $WSTagger_{CTB7}$, to process WB-dev. Table 5 shows the results. It is obvious that CTB7 and WB differs a lot in the definition of word boundaries. In contrast, in the shared task of NLPCC 2015, we find that CTB7 and the provided WB are very similar in the word boundary standard [2].

Based on this observation, we employ the guide-feature based approach and the coupled approach to exploit CTB7, instead of directly adding CTB7 as extra training data.

Table 5. WS accuracy: an investigation of the heterogeneity of WB and CTB7.

	on CTB7		on WB
	Dev	Test	Dev
$WSTagger_{CTB7}$	**96.37**	**95.81**	91.77
$WSTagger_{WB}$	90.86	90.82	**94.66**

7.3 Results on CTB7-dev/test

To investigate the performance on canonical texts of the models trained on CTB7 (and PD), we evaluate the models on CTB7-dev/test. Table 6 shows the results on the task of WS. We can get several reasonable yet interesting findings. First, comparing the results in all four major rows, we can see that using PD as extra labeled data consistently improves the F1 score by about 0.5%. Second, comparing the results in the first two major rows, it is clear that jointly modeling WS&POS outperforms the pure WS tagging model by about 0.3–0.5%. Third, comparing the results in the bottom two major rows, we can see that lexicon features are useful and improves F1 score by about 0.5%. Fourth, comparing the results in the first and third major rows, we can see that using WB as extra labeled data leads with the coupled approach to slight improvement in F1 score (0.03–0.24%).

Table 6. Results on $CTB7$-dev/test.

	on Dev				on Test			
	Acc	P	R	F	Acc	P	R	F
$WSTagger_{CTB7}$	96.37	95.84	95.37	95.60	95.81	95.40	94.58	94.98
$WSTagger_{CTB7+PD}$	96.82	96.29	96.14	96.21	96.37	95.94	95.44	95.69
$WS\&POSTagger_{CTB7}$	96.70	96.21	95.78	96.00	96.25	95.92	95.13	95.52
$WS\&POSTagger_{CTB7+PD}$	**97.04**	**96.62**	**96.34**	**96.48**	**96.61**	**96.30**	**95.66**	**95.98**
$CoupledWSTagger_{WB\&CTB7}$	96.54	96.03	95.55	95.79	96.02	95.59	94.86	95.22
$CoupledWSTagger_{WB\&CTB7+PD}$	96.96	96.43	96.21	96.32	96.45	95.96	95.48	95.72
$CoupledWSTagger_{WB\&CTB7}$ w/ lexicon	96.82	96.29	95.96	96.12	96.42	95.95	95.39	95.67
$CoupledWSTagger_{WB\&CTB7+PD}$ w/ lexicon	**97.25**	**96.79**	**96.51**	**96.65**	**96.83**	**96.45**	**95.88**	**96.16**

Table 7. Performance of joint WS&POS tagging on $CTB7$-dev/test.

	on Dev			on Test		
	P	R	F	P	R	F
$WS\&POSTagger_{CTB7}$	91.28	90.86	91.04	90.91	90.16	90.54
$WS\&POSTagger_{CTB7+PD}$	**92.19**	**91.92**	**92.06**	**91.80**	**91.19**	**91.49**

Table 7 shows the results on the joint task of WS&POS. We can see that using PD as extra labeled data dramatically improves the word-wise F1 score by about 1%.

7.4   Results on WB-dev

In this part, we conduct extensive experiments to investigate the effectiveness of different methods for WS on WB-dev. Table 8 shows the results. From the results, we can obtain the following findings.

First, lexicon features are very useful. Comparing the first two major rows, we can see that using lexicon features leads to a large improvement of $94.88 - 93.65 = 1.23\%$ on F1 score over the baseline model. Comparing the third and fourth major rows, lexicon features boost F1 score by $95.15 - 94.16 = 0.99\%$ over the models with guide features. Comparing the fifth and sixth major rows, lexicon features boost F1 score by $95.30 - 94.64 = 0.66\%$ over the coupled models.

Second, the coupled approach is much more effective than the guide-feature based approach in exploiting multiple heterogeneous data. Comparing the third and fifth major rows, the coupled approach outperforms the guide-feature based approach by $94.64 - 94.16 = 0.48\%$ on F1 score. Comparing the fourth and sixth major rows, with the lexicon features, the coupled approach achieves higher F1 score by $95.30 - 95.15 = 0.15\%$ over its counterpart.

Third, looking into the third major row, we also get a few interesting findings: (1) using a joint WS&POS tagger to produce guide tags is better than using a WS tagger, indicating that jointly modeling WS&POS leads to better guide information, which is consistent with the results in Table 6; (2) PD is helpful by producing better guide tags, leading to higher F1 score on WB-dev by

Table 8. Results on *WB*-dev

	Approaches	Acc	P	R	F
Baseline	1. $WSTagger_{WB}$	94.66	93.30	93.99	93.65
w/ lexicon features	2. $WSTagger_{WB}$	95.74	94.45	95.31	94.88
w/ guide features	3. WS-tag from $WSTagger_{CTB7}$	94.52	93.21	93.93	93.58
	4. WS-tag from $WSTagger_{CTB7+PD}$	94.80	93.41	94.40	93.90
	5. WS-tag from $WS\&POSTagger_{CTB7}$	94.86	93.64	94.27	93.95
	6. WS-tag from $WS\&POSTagger_{CTB7+PD}$	**95.05**	93.76	**94.57**	**94.16**
	7. WS&POS-tag from $WS\&POSTagger_{CTB7}$	94.88	**94.33**	93.64	93.98
	8. WS&POS-tag from $WS\&POSTagger_{CTB7+PD}$	95.03	93.83	94.50	**94.16**
w/ lexicon &guide	9. WS&POS-tag from $WS\&POSTagger_{CTB7+PD}$	95.97	94.77	95.53	95.15
Coupled	10. $CoupledWSTagger_{WB\&CTB7}$	95.38	94.12	94.91	94.51
	11. $CoupledWSTagger_{WB\&CTB7+PD}$	**95.50**	**94.25**	**95.03**	**94.64**
Coupled w/ lexicon	12. $CoupledWSTagger_{WB\&CTB7}$	96.01	94.74	95.61	95.17
	13. $CoupledWSTagger_{WB\&CTB7+PD}$ (submitted)	95.98	94.78	95.56	95.17
	14. $CoupledWSTagger_{WB\&CTB7+PD}$	**96.11**	**94.80**	**95.82**	**95.30**
Merge-then-re-decode	On four models (2,9,12,13) (submitted)	96.14	95.03	95.72	95.37
	On four models (2,9,12,14)	**96.22**	**95.10**	**95.84**	**95.47**
	On all models (w/o 13)	95.88	94.76	95.48	95.12

about 0.2%; (3) using both WS&POS tags for guide achieves nearly the same performance as using only WS tags.

Finally, the proposed merge-then-re-decode ensemble approach improves F1 score by $95.47 - 95.30 = 0.17\%$ over the best single model. However, we find that the performance drops when we use all model during ensemble, which may be caused by the very bad performance of some models.

7.5   Reported Results on WB-test

Since we do not have the gold-standard labels for the test data, Table 9 shows the results provided by the shared task organizers. Our effort leads to an improvement on WS F1 score by $95.37 - 93.83 = 1.54\%$. And our results on test data rank the first place among five participants, and is also the best among all 28 submissions.

Table 9. Results on *WB*-test

	P	R	F
Baseline	93.53	94.14	93.83
Merge-then-re-decode (2,9.12,13)	95.05 (**+1.52**)	95.70 (**+1.56**)	95.37 (**+1.54**)

8   Related Work

Using external lexicon is first described in Pi-Chuan Chang et al. [1]. Zhang et al. [15] find the lexicon features are also very helpful for domain adaptation of WS models.

Jiang et al. [3] first propose the simple yet effective guild-feature based method, which is further extended in [7,11,12].

Qiu et al. [9] propose a model that performs heterogeneous Chinese word segmentation and POS tagging and produces two sets of results following *CTB* and *PD* styles respectively. Their model is based on linear perceptron, and uses approximate inference.

Li et al. [6] first propose the coupled sequence labeling approach. Chao et al. [2] make extensive use of the coupled approach in participating the NLPCC 2015 shared task of WS&POS for Webo texts. Li et al. [5] further improves the coupled approach in terms of efficiency via context-aware pruning, and first apply the coupled approach to the joint WS&POS task. In this work, we directly use the coupled model built in Li et al. for converting the WS&POS annotations in *PD* into the style of *CTB*.

9   Conclusion

We have participated in the NLPCC 2016 shared task on Chinese WS for Weibo Text. Our main focus is to make full use of an external lexicon and two heterogeneous labeled data (i.e., *CTB7* and *PD*). Moreover, we apply an merge-then-re-decode ensemble approach to combine the outputs of different base models. Extensive experiments are conducted in this work to fully investigate the effectiveness of methods in study. Particularly, this work leads to several interesting findings. First, lexicon features are very useful in improving performance on both canonical texts and WB texts. Second, the coupled approach is consistently more effective than the guide-feature based approach in exploiting multiple heterogeneous data. Third, using the same training data, a joint WS&POS model produces better WS results than a pure WS model, indicating that the POS tags are helpful for determining word boundaries. Our submitted results rank the first place among five participants in the open track in terms of F1 score, and is also the best among all 28 submissions.

For future work, we plan to work on word segmentation with different granularity levels. During this work, we carefully compared the outputs of different base models, and found that in many error cases, the results of the statistical models are actually correct from the human point view. Many results are considered as wrong answers simply because they are of different word granularity from the gold-standard references. Therefore, we are very interested in build statistical models that can output WS results with different granularities. And perhaps, we have to first construct some WS data with multiple-granularity annotations.

Acknowledgments. The authors would like to thank the anonymous reviewers for the helpful comments. This work was supported by National Natural Science Foundation of China (Grant No. 61502325, 61432013) and the Natural Science Foundation of the Jiangsu Higher Education Institutions of China (No. 15KJB520031).

References

1. Chang, P.C., Galley, M., Manning., C.D.: Optimizing Chinese word segmentation for machine translation performance. In: ACL 2008 Third Workshop on Statistical Machine Translation (2008)
2. Chao, J., Li, Z., Chen, W., Zhang, M.: Exploiting heterogeneous annotations for weibo word segmentation and POS tagging. In: Li, J., Ji, H., Zhao, D., Feng, Y. (eds.) NLPCC 2015. LNCS (LNAI), vol. 9362, pp. 495–506. Springer, Heidelberg (2015). doi:10.1007/978-3-319-25207-0_46
3. Jiang, W., Huang, L., Liu, Q.: Automatic adaptation of annotation standards: Chinese word segmentation and POS tagging - a case study. In: Proceedings of ACL, pp. 522–530 (2009)
4. Lafferty, J., McCallum, A., Pereira, F.C.: Conditional random fields: probabilistic models for segmenting and labeling sequence data (2001)
5. Li, Z., Chao, J., Zhang, M.: Fast coupled sequence labeling on heterogeneous annotations via context-aware pruning. In: Proceedings of EMNLP (2016)
6. Li, Z., Chao, J., Zhang, M., Chen, W.: Coupled sequence labeling on heterogeneous annotations: POS tagging as a case study. In: Proceedings of ACL (2015)
7. Li, Z., Che, W., Liu, T.: Exploiting multiple treebanks for parsing with quasisynchronous grammar. In: ACL, pp. 675–684 (2012)
8. Qiu, X., Qian, P., Shi, Z.: Overview of the NLPCC-ICCPOL 2016 shared task: Chinese word segmentation for micro-blog texts. In: Proceedings of the Fifth Conference on Natural Language Processing and Chinese Computing & the Twenty Fourth International Conference on Computer Processing of Oriental Languages (2016)
9. Qiu, X., Zhao, J., Huang, X.: Joint Chinese word segmentation and POS tagging on heterogeneous annotated corpora with multiple task learning. In: Proceedings of EMNLP, pp. 658–668 (2013)
10. Sagae, K., Lavie, A.: Parser combination by reparsing. In: Proceedings of NAACL, pp. 129–132 (2006)
11. Sun, W.: A stacked sub-word model for joint Chinese word segmentation and part-of-speech tagging. In: Proceedings of ACL, pp. 1385–1394 (2011)
12. Sun, W., Wan, X.: Reducing approximation and estimation errors for Chinese lexical processing with heterogeneous annotations. In: Proceedings of ACL, pp. 232–241 (2012)
13. Xue, N., et al.: Chinese word segmentation as character tagging. Comput. Linguist. Chin. Lang. Process. 8(1), 29–48 (2003)
14. Yu, Z., Dai, X.-Y., Shen, S., Huang, S., Chen, J.: Word segmentation of micro blogs with bagging. In: Li, J., Ji, H., Zhao, D., Feng, Y. (eds.) NLPCC 2015. LNCS (LNAI), vol. 9362, pp. 573–580. Springer, Heidelberg (2015). doi:10.1007/978-3-319-25207-0_54
15. Zhang, M., Deng, Z., Che, W., Liu, T.: Combining statistical model and dictionary for domain adaption of Chinese word segmentation. J. Chin. Inf. Process. 26, 8–12 (2012)
16. Zhang, M., Zhang, Y., Che, W., Liu, T.: Character-level Chinese dependency parsing. In: Proceedings of ACL, pp. 1326–1336 (2014)

Open Domain Question Answering System Based on Knowledge Base

Yuxuan Lai[1], Yang Lin[1], Jiahao Chen[3], Yansong Feng[2(✉)], and Dongyan Zhao[2]

[1] School of Electronics Engineering and Computer Science,
Peking University, Beijing, China
{erutan,linyang_}@pku.edu.cn
[2] Institute of Computer Science and Technology, Peking University, Beijing, China
{fengyansong,zhaody}@pku.edu.cn
[3] School of Mathematical Sciences, Peking University, Beijing, China
kaelchan@pku.edu.cn

Abstract. Aiming at the task of open domain question answering based on knowledge base in NLP&CC 2016, we propose a SPE (subject predicate extraction) algorithm which can automatically extract a subject-predicate pair from a simple question and translate it to a KB query. A novel method based on word vector similarity and predicate attention is used to score the candidate predicate after a simple topic entity linking method. Our approach achieved the F1-score of 82.47% on test data which obtained the first place in the contest of NLP&CC 2016 Shared Task 2 (KBQA sub-task). Furthermore, there are also a series of experiments and comprehensive error analysis which can show the properties and defects of the new data set.

Keywords: Chinese · Natural language question answering · Knowledge base · Information extraction

1 Introduction

Open-domain question answering (QA) is an important and yet challenging problem that remains largely unsolved. In recent years, a lot of works on QA in English have been published. But, to the best of our knowledge, the KBQA (question answering based on knowledge base) data set in NLP&CC 2016 evaluation task is the first large scale Chinese KBQA data set. In this paper we focus on answering single-relation factoid questions in Chinese, which is the main component of this data set. A SPE algorithm is proposed to translate a Chinese question to a KB querie. Logically, this algorithm can solve multiple-relation questions which can be expressed as a topic entity with a chain of predicates going from it. But limited by the data set, we did not carry out experiment about that.

Candidate predicate evaluation is the most important part of this algorithm, and a novel method based on word vector similarity and predicate attention

© Springer International Publishing AG 2016
C.-Y. Lin et al. (Eds.): NLPCC-ICCPOL 2016, LNAI 10102, pp. 722–733, 2016.
DOI: 10.1007/978-3-319-50496-4_65

is applied. To a certain extent, this method looks like a neural network with attention mechanisms but it is so shallow that no parameters need to be trained except word vectors. As a result, it is more concise, efficient, interpretable and can be combined with prior knowledge more flexibly but lost some advantages of deep neural networks like the strong representational ability. There are also attempts to deal with knowledge base error caused by spider, question classification and training data to improve performance. Our approach achieved the F1-score of 82.47% on test data which obtained the first place in the evaluation task.

In the rest of the paper, we first review related work in Sect. 2, and in Sect. 3, we introduce the architecture of our method in detail. Experimental setup, results and implementation tricks are discussed in Sect. 4. We conclude the whole paper and look forward to the future research in Sect. 5.

2   Related Work

Open domain question answering is a perennial problem in the field of natural language processing, which is known as an AI-complete problem. Traditional method to solve this problem is basically based on information retrieval, such as the Mulder system [1] and the AskMSR system [2,3]. Meeting with the requirement of answering questions more directly and accurately, some knowledge bases were built to structure facts. Large-scale knowledge bases (KB) like DBPedia [4] and Freebase [5] have become important resources for supporting open-domain question answering. Most approaches to KBQA map a question to its semantic representation (e.g. first-order logical form) based on some kinds of parsing method such as: Semantic Parsing [6], dependency parsing [7], and CCG (Combinatory Categorial Gramma) [8]. But these works hardly use KBs to help with parsing and they are bounded by the accuracy of the parsing method which is particularly severe while dealing with Chinese. To avoid these disadvantages, some approaches extract KB queries from questions with the help of knowledge bases like the recent works on WebQuestions [9–11]. The Ye's system [12], which achieved the best performance in NLP&CC 2015 Chinese QA task, also had a SPE algorithm, but it was only used as a supplement to their web knowledge extraction algorithm.

3   Architecture

The architecture of our system is shown in Fig. 1. Several hand-written patterns are used to find out the core of each question (See Appendix A). The interrogative structures such as "我想知道 ‖ I want to know that" and "吗 ‖ (modal particle)" are abandoned. There are some rules to reduce errors which are obviously caused by spider such as unexpected special symbols and heritage of html tags in knowledge base (See Appendix B). For each question, we use a simple topic entity linking method to extract possible KB entities. All the predicates after these entities are evaluated based on word vector similarity and predicate

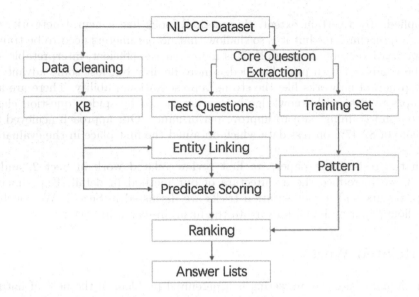

Fig. 1. Architecture of our KBQA system

attention. A linear combination of entity length and predicate score is used to rank the subject-predicate pairs as well as the answer patterns extracted from question-answer pairs in training set and a prior rule to deal with alternative questions.

3.1 Topic Entity Linking

Topic entities of questions are the core entities of the corresponding KB queries. In our system, all entities in KB which is a substring of a question and not overlapped by others are considered as potential topic entities. There is also a stop word list that consists of high frequency entities to reduce the noise entities (such as "是 ‖ is", "什么 ‖ what" and some auxiliary word) and improve efficiency. The length of entity is considered as a feature to use in the ranking stage.

For example, the potential topic entities of the question "做铁板鱼要用到哪些调料? ‖ What sauce will be used when you make iron fish (Chinese cuisine)?" are "铁板鱼 ‖ iron fish", "到 ‖ to" and "调料 ‖ sauce". "做 ‖ make", "要 ‖ will", "用 ‖ use", 哪 and "些" ("哪些" means "what") are ignored for they are high frequency entities.

3.2 Predicate Scoring

After topic entity linking, there are some potential entities and every entity has a few predicates in KB. From our perspective, a good predicate can handle the semantic of the rest of the question perfectly. Then the score of a candidate predicate is:

$$S_p = \frac{\sum_i (lp_i * \max_j Sim(wp_i, wq_j))}{\sum_i lp_i} \tag{1}$$

Where wp_i is the i_{th} word in predicate, wq_j is the j_{th} word in the question. lp_i is the length of wp_i. Sim is the semantic similarity of the two words, here the cosine similarity of word vectors is adopted. This score will be used in ranking stage.

The semantic similarity is considered to represent how much the words in predicate care about words in question. If the similarity between p_i and q_{j1} is higher than that between p_i and q_{j2}, then q_{j1} involves more semantic of p_i. Since only one question word is considered in evaluation for each predicate word, the attention is similar to a weighted alignment procedure. The most concerned question words constitute the attention of the whole predicate. The weighted average of word similarities using the length of predicate words as the weight measures whether the predicate is suitable to this question.

To get words from predicates and questions, we build a Chinese word segmenter which print all possible words based on a large word list. For example, the sequence "使用人数 ‖ number of users" is separated to "使 ‖ make", "使用 ‖ use", "用 ‖ use", "用人 ‖ choose a person for a job", "人 ‖ person", "人数 ‖ number of person" and "数 ‖ number". Several segmentation tools such as hanLP and NLPIR are attempted but the statements are so casual that these tools bring more errors than benefits. The performance of omni-segmentation mode is better than normal mode but still worse than our segmenter obviously. Furthermore, auxiliary words and punctuation are ignored here since they are meaningless.

There are two reasons why this segmenter performs better. Firstly, in Chinese, if one word covers another word, they usually have similar semantic, especially in oral language. For example, "这个东西怎么使 ‖ How to use it", "这个东西怎么用 ‖ How to use it", and "这个东西怎么使用 ‖ How to use it". Secondly, there often exists a relation like "kind of" between covering words, e.g. "人数 ‖ number of person" and "数 ‖ number", which is much useful when sentence structure are changed. As a result, this segmenter can deal with high flexible lexical in oral language. There are also a few word ambiguities such as "用人 ‖ choose a person for a job" caused by this segmenter, some of them can be solved in the predicate attention part for the greatly difference on semantic. Anyway, some errors still remain but it is not so significant as the benefit.

Using word vector to calculate semantic similarity has trouble in dealing with interrogative words. The cosine similarity between "什么时候 ‖ when" and "日期 ‖ date", "在哪儿 ‖ where" and "地点 ‖ place" are much lower than expected. So some hand-written pattern are used to finger out question types and some symbol words are added to the segmenter result directly. Since the statements are very flexible, only 3 types of questions are processed (Table 1), which cover about 10% among all questions. It is just a small attempt to combine the predicate scoring with some prior rules, which has much room for improvement.

Table 1. Question type rules

Question Type	Question Symbol	Added Words
when	什么时候, 何时	时间, 日期
where	在哪	地点, 位置
how much money	多少钱	价格

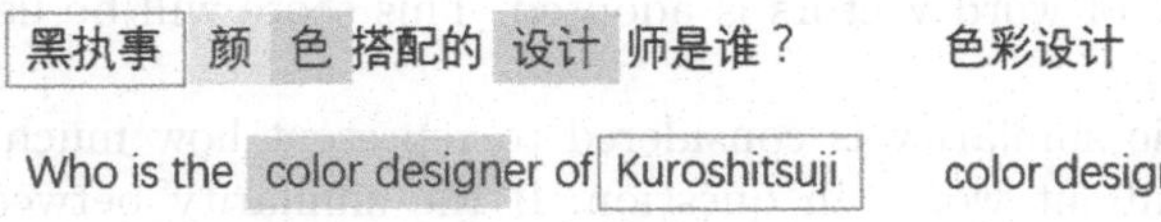

黑执事 颜 色 搭配的 设计 师是谁？   色彩设计

Who is the color designer of Kuroshitsuji   color design

Fig. 2. Predicate attention example

An example of the predicate attention is shown in Fig. 2, and the cosine similarity and mapping relations are shown in Table 2.

Table 2. Cosine similarity and mapping relations in Fig. 1

Words in Predicate	Words in Question	Cosine Similarity
色	色	1.0
色彩	颜色	0.60
彩	色	0.42
设	设	1.0
设计	设计	1.0
计	计	1.0

3.3 Answer Pattern

Answer patterns are rules extracted from labeled question-answer pairs which can reveal the connection between problem statements and the KB structures corresponding to true answers. For each question-answer pair, candidate triples are SPO (subject-predicate-object) triples in KB whose subject is a substring of the question and object is the same as the answer. Several simple rules are used to filter high confidence triples (mainly based on the length of match). There are also a few cases that no candidate triple left and these question-answer pairs are ignored in order to ensure the high precision of best triples.

Generalizing the subject, answer patterns are extracted from question-answer pairs and best triples. How many times a answer pattern generated from a test question and a candidate subject-predicate pair occurs in training answer patterns is used as a feature in ranking stage. An example of answer pattern extraction is shown in Table 3.

Table 3. Answer pattern example

Question	做铁板鱼要用到哪些调料?
	What sauce will be used when you make iron fish(Chinese cuisine)?
Answer	粗盐味精鸡精
	coarse salt, Monosodium glutamate, chicken bouillon
Best Triple	铁板鱼,调味品,粗盐味精鸡精
	iron fish, condiment, coarse salt Monosodium glutamate chicken bouillon
Answer Pattern	做(SUB)要用到哪些调料? -(SUB),调味品,(ANS)
	What sauce will be used when you make (SUB) - (SUB),condiment,(ANS)

3.4 Ranking

In ranking stage, a linear combination of features including entity length, predicate score and answer pattern occurrence is used to choose golden answers.

Some rules can be added here to deal with questions which are not suitable for this architecture. For example, alternative questions hardly involve the meaning of predicates and only have limited objects to choose. So rules make sure that the answers of these questions must occur between "是...还是... ‖ either ... or ...". But the statements of questions are so flexible that the improvement is limited.

4   Experiment

4.1   Dataset

The dataset is published by NLP&CC2016 evaluation task including a knowledge base and question-answer pairs for training and testing. There are about 43M SPO pairs in the knowledge, where about 6 M subjects, 0.6 M predicates and 16 M objects are mentioned. The training set contains 14,609 question-answer pairs and testing contains 9,870 question-answer pairs. The answers are labeled by human and most of them are objects in the KB (the rest are caused by human mistake or other unexpected reasons).

4.2   Experiment Settings

The entities which have occurred in both training and testing questions more than 150 times are considered as stop words during topic entity linking. There are 52,916 distinctive entities in 24,479 questions and only 496 high frequency entities, which is less than 1% of all.

We use word2vec software of Tomas Mikolov and his colleagues[1] to generate word vectors. The CBOW model [13–15] are used. The window size is 5, the desired vector dimensionality is 300 and threshold for downsampling the frequent words is 20. Sentences in Baidu baike are used as training data and 155,837 word vectors are generated, which is also the word list used in the segmenter.

---

[1] https://code.google.com/archive/p/word2vec.

The weights of the linear combination in ranking stage are assigned as follow: weight of entity length (an integer) is 1 (record as w_{el}), weight of predicate score (a float between 0 to 1) is 10 (record as w_{ps}), weight of answer pattern occurrence (an integer) is 100 (record as w_{po}). The confidence of answer patterns is naturally high to make sure the patterns will be followed as long as they matches. The combination is mainly a balance between the other two features. Let r be the rate of weights between predicate score and entity length. We tested the influence of r (fixing $w_{el} = 1$ and $w_{po} = 100$) alidation on training set. The results are shown in Fig. 3. The performance was robust when r is from 10 to 16, so we set $r = 10$, which means $w_{ps} = 10$.

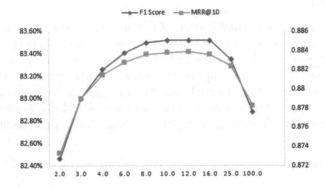

Fig. 3. Influence of tuning weight rate

4.3   Benchmark Systems

There are three benchmark systems. The first of them is provided by Duan Nan, which is basically based on the idea of two previous works [11,16] and is the official benchmark system of this KBQA task. So we just call it "NLPCC". The second one is called "PatternMatch", which only uses answer patterns extracted from training data to answer questions. Core question extraction is retained to improve hit rate. The precision of this benchmark system can be considered as the performance of the labeled answers in training data, which is also a sort of upper bound of this data set. The Third system is a naive SPE algorithm which just finds the longest subject-predicate pair in questions and the corresponding object is regarded as answers, the accuracy of which is the lower bound of all SPE algorithm. We call it "NaiveSearch".

4.4   Results

We compare our system with some benchmark systems, which is shown in Table 4. "Answered" means the rate of questions that the system can answer.

Table 4. Results compared with benchmarks

System	F1 Score	Pre@1	Pre@2	Pre@3	Pre@5	Pre@inf	Answered
NLPCC	52.48%	52.48%	60.46%	64.15%	67.33%	—	100%
PatternMatch	18.41%	88.59%	—	—	90.93%	90.93%	20.78%
NaiveSearch	47.39%	84.41%	—	—	88.19%	—	56.13%
PatternMatch+ NaiveSearch	52.99%	85.18%	—	—	—	—	62.21%
Ours	**82.47%**	82.47%	88.82%	91.17%	92.71%	95.08%	100%

So accuracy@N is equal to precision@N multiplied by the answered rate. "PatternMatch+NaiveSearch" is the combination of those two systems by adding the scores of candidate answers directly.

The F1 score of our system is much better than all baselines, which proves the effect of our approach. The accuracy@1 of our system is close to the precision@1 of PatternMatch and NaiveSearch system which are systems based on strong rules with high precision and poor recall, which means that our system is close to the theoretically best system on this data set.

We also test the performance of the core of our system and the influence of rule parts, which is shown in Table 5. Since all systems print ordered answers instead of parallel answers, the best strategy is to select the first answer, thus average F1 score is equal to accuracy@1. And because all of the "Answered" rates of these tests are 100%, we use accuracy@N to replace precision@N here.

Table 5. Contributions of each part

System	ACC@1	ACC@2	ACC@3	ACC@5	ACC@inf	MRR
Core	81.64%	88.37%	90.75%	92.33%	95.06%	0.8616
Core+Tr	81.77%	88.46%	90.82%	92.41%	95.06%	0.8627
Core+QCore	81.83%	88.47%	90.89%	92.46%	95.06%	0.8631
Core+Tr+QCore	82.16%	88.64%	91.07%	92.66%	95.08%	0.8657
Full-QClassify	82.18%	88.67%	91.09%	92.68%	95.08%	0.8660
Full-AQ	82.45%	88.79%	91.14%	92.68%	95.08%	0.8676
Full-Tr	82.33%	88.67%	90.99%	92.55%	95.06%	0.8663
Full	**82.47%**	88.82%	91.17%	92.71%	95.08%	0.8678

In Table 5, "Tr" means using answer patterns extracted from training data. "QCore" means using the core of questions instead of full questions. "QClassify" means adding question classification method to predicate scoring. "AQ" means posttreatment rules for alternative questions. "Full" equals to "Core + Tr + QCore + QClassify + AQ". The "Core" system is a unsupervised system using the basic SPE algorithm.

According to Table 5, the added methods improve the performance of the core system a little. There are two reasons why the influence is not significant. Firstly, all the added methods except "QCore" involve only few questions, and "QCore" is just a data cleaning method. Secondly, these rules improve some weakness which was found when making cross-validation in training data, but the distribution of questions in testing data is a little different, which makes the effect weaker. Details are shown in Table 6.

Table 6. Influence of each method

Method	Train-Influence		Test-Influence	
	Sphere	Improvement	Sphere	Improvement
AQ	0.21%	46.7%–63.3%	0.11%	72.7%–90.9%
Tr	22.35%	82.5%–84.4%	20.78%	88.4%–89.0%
QClassify	10.51%	71.0%–77.5%	8.74%	77.5%–80.9%

The results of NLP&CC2016 evaluation task are shown in Table 7 (the top 5 results of 21 submissions in total). Our system achieve the best performance in all teams. Compared with Table 5, even the core system is better than the second team in this evaluation task.

Table 7. Evaluation results in this evaluation task

Team	F1 score
Ours	**82.47%**
NUDT	81.59%
CCNU	79.57%
HIT-SCIR	79.14%
NEU (NLP Lab)	72.72%

4.5 Error Analysis

We randomly sampled 100 questions that our system did not generate the correct answer in order to analyze the room for improvement. Near half of errors are in fact due to label problems or question design which are not real mistakes. This includes unclarified entity in question (31%, e.g. "兴隆镇的邮编是多少‖ what is the postcode number of Xinglong Town", there are a lot of Xinglong Towns in China), contradictory in KB (5%) and questions whose intent are unable to understand (2%) or with wrong labeled answer (5%). 30% of the errors are because of the unsuccessful entity linking or predicate scoring, which is the foremost part of the room for improvement. There are 27% of the errors are caused by questions whose answer is not an object of a subject in question, which can not be handled by our architecture. This will be discussed later in Sect. 4.6.

4.6 Dataset Analysis

Since this data set is the first large scale Chinese KBQA data set, we performed a series of experiments to show properties and defects, which can be useful to those who want to use this data set or to build another one.

This data set is a "simple-question" data set where every question can be answered by only one SPO pair in KB. For most questions, there is a SPO pair that the subject is a substring of the question and the object is equal to the answer. But there are 788 exceptions (3.22%), 343 in training set (2.35%) and 445 in testing set (4.51%). We randomly sampled 100 of them and find that the reasons why their answers can not be represented as objects of their subjects. Reasons include format problems (26%, e.g. "胡椒基氯的分子量是什么 ‖ What is the molecular weight of piperonyl chloride", the labeled answer is "170.6", while the answer in KB is "170.60"), wrong answers (11%, e.g. ""钡d-3-三氟乙酰基樟脑酸的分子量是多少 ‖ what is the molecular weight of Barium D-3-trifluoroacetylcamphorate", the labeled answer is "9月22日 ‖ Sep 22nd"), typos in entities (29%), aliases of entities (14%), incomprehensible questions (2%). There are still 18% of them we cannot classify. The aliases of entities and some of the typos in entities can be solved in future works.

Some ambiguities are caused by entities with the same name and no clue in questions can help to distinguish them. There are 4773 such questions (19.50%), 3189 in training set (21.83%) and 1584 in testing set (16.05%). The original accuracy of our system on these questions is only 62.43%, 62.40% in training set and 62.50% in testing set. If the accuracy of these is judged by finding correct subject-predicate pair, the accuracy of our system on these questions in testing set is 82.07%. So with this change, our system performance will be up to 85.61%.

5 Conclusion

In this paper, we present a KBQA system which can answer simple-relation Chinese questions base on a SPE algorithm. We use this system to participate in the contest of NLP&CC 2016 Shared Task 2 (KBQA sub-task) and obtained the first place. Since this data set is the first large scale Chinese KBQA data set, we perform a series of experiments and comprehensive error analysis which can be useful to those who want to use this data set or to build another Chinese KBQA data set. In the future, we would like to extend our system to answer multi-relation questions and try some deeper models to improve the performance.

Acknowledgement. We would like to thank members in our NLP group and the anonymous reviewers for their helpful feedback. This work was supported by National High Technology R&D Program of China (Grant No. 2015AA015403, 2014AA015102), Natural Science Foundation of China (Grant No. 61202233, 61272344, 61370055) and the joint project with IBM Research. Any correspondence please refer to Yansong Feng.

732   Y. Lai et al.

Appendix A

The 8 regular expressions shown in Table 8 are used to capture the non-core parts. They are executed in order.

Table 8. Regular expressions for core question extraction

(啊|呀|(你知道)?吗|呢)?(? |\?)*$
来着$
^呃(……)?
^请问(一下|你知道)?
^(那么|什么是|我想知道|我很好奇|有谁了解|问一下|请问你知道|谁能告诉我一下)
^((谁|(请|麻烦)?你|请|)?(能|可以)?告诉我)
^((我想(问|请教)一下)，?)
^((有人|谁|你|你们|有谁|大家)(记得|知道))

Appendix B

The rules to clean KB are shown in Table 9.

Table 9. KB cleaning rules

Type	Times	e.g.	Disposal
Appendix labels in predicate	9110	性质[1]	Correct
Predicate prefix "-"	77332	- 社区数	Correct
Predicate prefix "•"	85953	• 密度	Correct
Space in predicate between Chinese characters	367218	国 籍	Correct
Predicate is the same as object	193716	陈祝龄旧居||| 天津市文物保护单位	Delete

References

1. Kwok, C.C.T., Etzioni, O., Weld, D.S.: Scaling question answering to the Web. In: Proceedings of the 10th International Conference on World Wide Web (2001)
2. Brill, E., Lin, J., Banko, M., Dumais, S., Ng, A.: Data-intensive question answering. In: Proceedings of TREC (2001)
3. Tsai, C.-T., Yih, W.-T., Burges, C.J.C.: Web-based question answering: revisiting AskMSR. Technical report MSR-TR-2015-20, Microsoft Research (2015)
4. Auer, S., Bizer, C., Kobilarov, G., Lehmann, J., Cyganiak, R., Ives, Z.: DBpedia: a nucleus for a web of open data. In: Aberer, K., Choi, K.-S., Noy, N., Allemang, D., Lee, K.-I., Nixon, L., Golbeck, J., Mika, P., Maynard, D., Mizoguchi, R., Schreiber, G., Cudré-Mauroux, P. (eds.) ASWC/ISWC -2007. LNCS, vol. 4825, pp. 722–735. Springer, Heidelberg (2007). doi:10.1007/978-3-540-76298-0_52

5. Bollacker, K., Evans, C., Paritosh, P., Sturge, T., Taylor, J.: Freebase: a collaboratively created graph database for structuring human knowledge. In: Proceedings of the 2008 ACM SIGMOD International Conference on Management of Data, SIGMOD 2008, pp. 1247–1250 (2008)
6. Berant, J., Chou, A., Frostig, R., Liang, P.: Semantic parsing on freebase from question-answer pairs. In: Proceedings of EMNLP (2013)
7. Liang, P., Jordan, M., Klein, D.: Learning dependency-based compositional semantics. In: Proceedings of ACL (2011)
8. Kwiatkowski, T., Zettlemoyer, L., Goldwater, S., Steedman, M.: Lexical generalization in CCG grammar induction for semantic parsing. In: Proceedings of the Conference on Empirical Methods in Natural Language Processing (2011)
9. Yao, X., Van Durme, B.: Information extraction over structured data: question answering with freebase. In: Proceedings of ACL (2014)
10. Yao, X., Berant, J., Van Durme, B.: Freebase QA: information extraction or semantic parsing? In: Proceedings of ACL (2014)
11. Yih, W.-T., Chang, M.-W., He, X., Gao, J.: Semantic parsing via staged query graph generation: question answering with knowledge base. In: Proceedings of ACL Association for Computational Linguistics (2015)
12. Ye, Z., Jia, Z., Yang, Y., Huang, J., Yin, H.: Research on open domain question answering system. In: Li, J., Ji, H., Zhao, D., Feng, Y. (eds.) NLPCC 2015. LNCS (LNAI), vol. 9362, pp. 527–540. Springer, Heidelberg (2015). doi:10.1007/978-3-319-25207-0_49
13. Mikolov, T., Chen, K., Corrado, G., Dean, J.: Efficient estimation of word representations in vector space. In: Proceedings of Workshop at ICLR (2013)
14. Mikolov, T., Sutskever, I., Chen, K., Corrado, G., Dean, J.: Distributed representations of words and phrases and their compositionality. In: Proceedings of NIPS (2013)
15. Mikolov, T., Yih, W.-T., Zweig, G.: Linguistic regularities in continuous space word representations. In: Proceedings of NAACL HLT (2013)
16. Junwei, B., Nan, D., Ming, Z., Tiejun, Z.: Knowledge-based question answering as machine translation. In: Proceedings of ACL (2014)

Recurrent Neural Word Segmentation
with Tag Inference

Qianrong Zhou[✉], Long Ma, Zhenyu Zheng, Yue Wang, and Xiaojie Wang

School of Computer, Beijing University of Posts and Telecommunications,
Beijing, China
{zhouqr,miss_longma,zzybuptzzy,wangyuesophie,xjwang}@bupt.edu.cn

Abstract. In this paper, we present a Long Short-Term Memory
(LSTM) based model for the task of Chinese Weibo word segmentation.
The model adopts a LSTM layer to capture long-range dependencies in
sentence and learn the underlying patterns. In order to infer the optimal
tag path, we introduce a transition score matrix for jumping between
tags of successive characters. Integrated with some unsupervised features, the performance of the model is further improved. Finally, our
model achieves a weighted F1-score of 0.8044 on close track, 0.8298 on
the semi-open track.

Keywords: Chinese Word Segmentation · LSTM · Weibo

1 Introduction

Word segmentation is a preliminary yet non-trivial procedure for Chinese natural language processing. Many tasks such as POS-tagging, syntax paring and
sentiment analysis could be expected to benefit by correctly treating a piece of
character sequence together as one Chinese word. Lots of researches have been
done to address this problem. The state-of-the-art segmentation systems can
perform well on formal text. However, the ability of those systems is restricted
by lots of finely engineered features and they perform poorly on informal text
such as micro-blog and forums. The problem of informal text segmentation has
gained more and more interests recently.

The NLPCC 2016 word segmentation shared task[1] [1] focuses on Chinese
word segmentation in informal text domain. The task is difficult due to the high
rate of Out-Of-Vocabulary (OOV) and conversational nature of the text. Most
previous systems address this problem by employing Conditional Random Fields
(CRFs) [2,3]. Usually, bootstrap aggregating is also used to further improve the
system performance.

Recently, neural network models have been investigated for Chinese word
segmentation. Pei et al. [4] presented a Max-Margin Tensor Neural Network

---

[1] Conference on Natural Language Processing and Chinese Computing. http://tcci.
ccf.org.cn/conference/2016.

© Springer International Publishing AG 2016
C.-Y. Lin et al. (Eds.): NLPCC-ICCPOL 2016, LNAI 10102, pp. 734–743, 2016.
DOI: 10.1007/978-3-319-50496-4_66

(MMTNN) that has the ability to model complicated interactions between tags and context characters. Chen et al. [5] proposed a Gated Recursive Neural Network (GRNN) to explicitly model the combinations of the characters. Chen et al. [6] firstly introduced the Long Short-Term Memory (LSTM) model for Chinese word segmentation. All these neural models are used to derive feature representations from input sentences, which then are fed to a CRF inference layer to decode the optimal tag sequences. However, most of them are not investigated or evaluated on informal datasets.

In this paper, we introduce a LSTM based model for Chinese Weibo word segmentation in the NLPCC 2016 shared task. The model consists of two main components: (1) a LSTM layer which captures long distance dependencies in the sentence, and (2) a tag inference layer stacked on LSTM which explicitly models interactions between tags. We also adopt unsupervised global features to further improve performance. For both close and semi-open tracks, our system won the first position with weighted F1-score[2] of 0.8044 on the close track, 0.8298 on the semi-open track respectively. Moreover, experimental results show that our model achieves better results than strong baselines and are well suitable for Weibo word segmentation.

The paper is structured as follows: Sect. 2 describes in detail the LSTM based model for word segmentation. Section 3 presents experimental results. Finally, Sect. 4 draws conclusions.

2   The Network Architecture

The overall architecture of our system is summarized in Fig. 1. The first layer accepts features in a window as inputs. The input features are projected to vectors respectively by lookup table operation in the second layer. Feature vectors in the window are then concatenated to one embedded feature. At each time, LSTM receives the embedded feature and output the probabilities of all possible tags for current character. Finally, a tag inference layer decodes an optimal tag sequence for this sentence. We introduce them in following subsections one-by-one.

2.1   Character Feature Vectors

Characters and their corresponding discrete features, including Character Type, Accessor Variety and Conditional Entropy (see Sect. 3.1 for details), are fed to the first layer of our model as indices. These indices are then mapped into vectors, by lookup table operations.

Formally, for each character c_t, its feature vector d_t is given by Eq. (1) and implemented by the lookup table layer.

$$d_t = LT_{M^0}(c_t) \oplus LT_{M^1}(f_t^1) \oplus \ldots \oplus LT_{M^K}(f_t^K), \tag{1}$$

---

[2] A weighted evaluation metric provided by organizers that gives more reasonable and distinguishable scores and correlates well with human judgment. More details in Qian et al. [8].

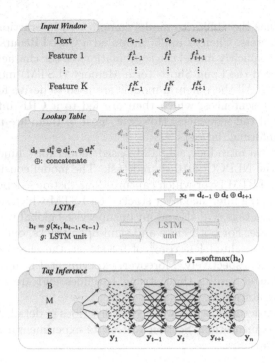

Fig. 1. The network architecture of our model.

where M^0 is character lookup table, f_t^k ($1 \leq k \leq K$) is k-th discrete feature of c_t and M^k is the corresponding feature lookup table. $LT(\cdot)$ denotes lookup table operation, $\oplus$ denotes the concatenation of two vectors. We use a classical window approach (window size s is set to 3) to get vector representation x_t of character c_t by concatenating the contextual lookup table outputs as in Eq. (2):

$$x_t = d_{t-1} \oplus d_t \oplus d_{t+1}. \tag{2}$$

2.2 LSTM

The Long Short-Term Memory (LSTM) model [7] has been widely used since it can capture temporal dependencies. It alleviates the problem of gradients exploding or vanishing in Recurrent Neural Network (RNN) by introducing a memory cell, which is composed of three gates to control how information is stored, forgotten and exploited inside the network.

At every time step t, LSTM unit takes above concatenated feature embedding x_t as input. It calculates the hidden state vector h_t as follows:

$$i_t = \sigma(W^i x_t + U^i h_{t-1} + V^i c_{t-1} + b^i), \tag{3}$$

$$f_t = \sigma(W^f x_t + U^f h_{t-1} + V^f c_{t-1} + b^f), \tag{4}$$

$$o_t = \sigma(W^o x_t + U^o h_{t-1} + V^o c_{t-1} + b^o), \tag{5}$$

$$c_t = f_t \odot c_{t-1} + i_t \odot tanh(W^u x_t + U^u h_{t-1} + b^u), \tag{6}$$

$$h_t = o_t \odot tanh(c_t), \tag{7}$$

where i_t, f_t, o_t are the gating vectors representing the input gate, the forget gate and the output gate respectively. σ denotes the sigmoid function and $\odot$ denotes elementwise multiplication. W^i, U^i, V^i, W^f, U^f, V^f, W^o, U^o, V^o, W^u, U^u are weight matrices associated with different gates. b^i, b^f, b^o, b^u are the bias items. The probability distribution over possible output tags is estimated as follows:

$$y_t = softmax(W h_t + b), \tag{8}$$

where W is a weight matrix for softmax classifier, b is a bias term.

2.3 Tag Inference

To model the tag dependency among the output tags, we follow Chen et al. [6] by introducing a tag transition matrix A. Let $c_{(1:n)} = (c_1, c_2, \ldots, c_n)$ be an input sentence. Every output tag sequence $y_{(1:n)} = (y_1, y_2, \ldots, y_n)$ is given a score by summing tag transition score and tagging score:

$$s(c_{(1:n)}, y_{(1:n)}) = \sum_{t=1}^{n} (A_{y_{t-1} y_t} + (y_t)_{y_t}). \tag{9}$$

Suppose the correct tag sequence of $c^{(i)}$ is $\hat{y}^{(i)}$. Let $Y(c^{(i)})$ be the set of all possible tag sequences. Then the predicted tag sequence $\bar{y}^{(i)}$ can be computed as:

$$\bar{y}^{(i)} = \arg \max_{y \in Y(c^{(i)})} (s(c^{(i)}, y) + \Delta(\hat{y}^{(i)}, y)), \tag{10}$$

where $\Delta(\hat{y}^{(i)}, y)) = \sum_{t=1}^{n} \gamma \mathbf{1}\{\hat{y}_t^{(i)} \neq y_t\}$ is a structured margin loss. γ is a discount parameter, the loss is proportional to the number of incorrect tags. However, it cannot be used to predict the most possible tag sequence during testing since the correct tag sequence is unknown, Eq. (10) is replaced by Eq. (11) then.

$$\bar{y}^{(i)} = \arg \max_{y \in Y(c^{(i)})} s(c^{(i)}, y). \tag{11}$$

The parameter set of our network is $\theta = \{W^i, U^i, V^i, W^f, U^f, V^f, W^o, U^o, V^o, W^u, U^u, A\}$ (bias items are omitted).

2.4 Model Training

Given a training set $\mathcal{D}$, the regularized objective function is the loss function $J(\theta)$ including a l_2-norm term:

$$J(\theta) = \frac{1}{|\mathcal{D}|} \sum_{i}^{|\mathcal{D}|} \frac{1}{n} l^{(i)} + \frac{\lambda}{2} ||\theta||_2^2, \tag{12}$$

738   Q. Zhou et al.

$$l^{(i)} = \max(0, s(c^{(i)}, \bar{y}^{(i)}) + \Delta(\hat{y}^{(i)}, \bar{y}^{(i)}) - s(c^{(i)}, \hat{y}^{(i)})). \quad (13)$$

We use AdaGrad [9] with mini-batches to minimize the objective function. Derivatives are calculated from standard back-propagation [10]. It is worth mentioning that inspired by the state transition matrix in Hidden Markov Model (HMM) [11], we enforce two constraints on A every time the parameters are updated:

$$A_{i,j} \geq 0, \quad (14a)$$
$$\sum_j A_{i,j} = 1, \quad (14b)$$

where i and j denote two successive tags.

We also apply dropout [12] to input layer and LSTM hidden layer to reduce overfitting. Feature embeddings are all randomly initialized, and fine-tuned during training. Hyper-parameters are listed in Table 1.

Table 1. Hyper-parameter settings in our model.

Type	Hyper-parameter
Network	$s = 3$
	$d(c) = 100$
	$d(f^k) = 30$
	$d(h) = 100$
Training	$p = 0.2, \alpha = 0.2$
	$\gamma = 0.2, \lambda = 10^{-4}$

3 Experiments

The data provided for the shared task is collected from Weibo[3]. It consists of micro-blogs from various topics, such as finance, sports, entertainment. The basic information of dataset is shown in Table 2. Participant systems are evaluated in three different categories depending on whether they make use of external sources of information. A weighted F1 measure method [8] is used for evaluation. Weighted-F1 measure is a new psychometric-inspired evaluation metric which takes difficulties of segmentation in test into considerations.

We participate in two tracks: close track and semi-open track. In both two tracks, we employ the same model but with different unsupervised features. The corpus is converted to 4-tag (B, M, E and S) labeling format. The model achieving best performance on the development set is used as the final model to be evaluated. Theano [13,14] is used.

Before we present results on two tracks, we give a brief description of features used in our system.

---

[3] http://weibo.com.

Table 2. Statistical information of dataset.

Dataset	Sents	Words	Chars	Word types	Char types	OOV rate
Training	20,135	421,166	729,013	43,634	4,504	-
Dev.	2,052	42,697	77,350	11,244	2,881	6.82%
Test	8,592	187,877	333,049	28,043	3,913	6.97%

3.1 Features

We refer to the following features as basic features. Same basic features are used in both two tracks.

Character feature: The characters in sentence. Inspired by Pei et al. [4], bigram of character is used as features as well.

Character Type (CT) feature: Each character is assigned one of 5 types by its Unicode code point. They are Chinese character, English character, number, punctuation and others respectively.

We also use the following unsupervised global features.

Accessor Variety (AV) feature: Accessor variety proposed by Feng et al. [15], which could be used to measure the possibility of whether two substrings join into one Chinese word. The way we derive AV feature from unlabeled corpus follows Wu et al. [16]. They introduced an improvement in AV feature, and achieved better results.

Conditional Entropy (CE) feature: Gao and Vogel [17] introduced conditional entropy feature to improve performance of segmentation. Continuous values of conditional entropy are mapped into discrete numeric values, following Gao et al.

For the close track, training data (ignoring labels) is used to obtain above two unsupervised features, while for semi-open track, the background data officially provided is used. All these features are represented by integer indices, which is the input to lookup table layer.

3.2 Feature Evaluation

Our first experiment is to evaluate the effectiveness of different features described in Sect. 3.1. The baseline model only uses character feature (i.e., only raw characters). Then other features are added one-by-one. The results are shown in Table 3.

As shown in Table 3, unsupervised features bring performance boosts in both two tracks. It is similar with the conclusions in Sun and Xu [18] and Wu et al. [16]. Reminded that the only difference between two tracks is that unsupervised features are derived from provided background data in the semi-open track, but from unlabeled training data in the close track instead. The features extracted from larger scale contribute much significantly to Weibo word segmentation. It is a helpful hint on how to achieve higher performance on this task.

Table 3. Performances on test data with different feature sets.

Track	Model	F1	Weighted-F1
Close	Base	0.9440	0.7951
	+ CT	0.9451	0.7957
	+ CT + AV	0.9446	0.7975
	+ CT + AV + EN	0.9441	0.8044
Semi-open	Base	0.9448	0.7971
	+ CT	0.9448	0.7953
	+ CT + AV	0.9483	0.8194
	+ CT + AV + EN	0.9517	0.8298

3.3 Model Evaluation

Results of our model and other top competitors in the shared task are shown in Table 4. Our model wins first place on both tracks by weighted-F1 measure, and has comparable performance by traditional F1 measure. According to weighted-F1 [8], it means our model correctly segments more hard words and wrongly segments fewer easy words. As we can see, the advantage of our model is extended from close track to semi-open track. Our model only outperforms second by 0.6% in close track, it is 1.2% in semi-open track.

Table 4. Close and semi-open track results in NLPCC 2016 shared task.

Track	Model	F1	Weighted-F1
Close	Our	0.9441	**0.8044**
	BJTU	**0.9476**	0.7996
	BUPT-1	0.9476	0.7981
Semi-open	Our	0.9517	**0.8298**
	BUPT-1	**0.9519**	0.8197
	DLUT-2	0.9505	0.8089

Most state-of-the-art systems apply CRF model to word segmentation. We provide a comparison with CRF model adopting same features in the close track. A CRF model[4] in Wu et al. [16] is used. The results are shown in Table 5. As can be seen from Table 5, with same features, our model is comparable to CRF model on F1 measure, and outperforms CRF model significantly on weighted-F1.

According to officially released weights, Chinese idioms are much more difficult to be segmented than other types of words[5]. We found our model performs

---

[4] https://github.com/wugh/CistSegment.
[5] https://github.com/FudanNLP/NLPCC-WordSeg-Weibo.

Table 5. Comparing with CRF model.

	F1	Weighted-F1
Wu et al. [16]	**0.9445**	0.7804
Our	0.9441	**0.8044**

better on idioms. In the test data, there exists 429 Chinese idioms[6]. Our model correctly finds 316 idioms, while only 256 idioms are found by CRF model. Some examples found by our model are listed in Fig. 2.

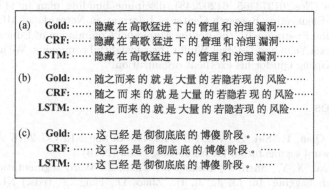

Fig. 2. Segmented sentences which have Chinese idioms.

To compare with other existing neural word segmentation systems, we evaluate the model proposed by Chen et al. [5], which is, to the best of our knowledge, the only published result specially for Chinese Weibo segmentation. They propose a GRNN for word segmentation, and evaluate it on NLPCC 2015 Weibo dataset[7] [19]. 10% of the training set is split into a development set. For a fair comparison, character type feature and unsupervised global features are not used in our model. Table 6 shows the comparison of our model with GRNN. As we can see from Table 6, our model gets better results compared with GRNN which achieves state-of-the-art performances on three popular datasets.

Table 6. Comparing with other neural model.

	F1
Chen et al. [5]	0.948[a]
Our	**0.949**

[a]They also use pre-trained character embeddings.

---

[6] Chinese idiom dictionary is used. https://github.com/sunflowerlyb/idiom.
[7] http://nlp.fudan.edu.cn/nlpcc2015/.

4 Conclusion

We have described a LSTM-based system for Chinese Weibo word segmentation. Our approach takes advantage of LSTM to keep long-range dependency information and preserves label transition information. We also combine unsupervised global features together to further improve performance on micro-blog text. Experimental results show the effectiveness of our model. We believe the proposed approach provides potential solutions for Weibo word segmentation and other sequence labeling tasks.

Acknowledgments. This work was partially supported by Natural Science Foundation of China (Nos. 61273365, 61202248), discipline building plan in 111 base (No. B08004) and Engineering Research Center of Information Networks of MOE, and the Co-construction Program with the Beijing Municipal Commission of Education. Many thanks to Caixia Yuan and Guohua Wu for their insightful comments. We are also very thankful to Xipeng Qiu for his excellent organization.

References

1. Qiu, X., Qian, P., Shi, Z., Wu, S.: Overview of the NLPCC 2016 shared task: Chinese word segmentation for micro-blog texts (2016)
2. Yu, Z., Dai, X.-Y., Shen, S., Huang, S., Chen, J.: Word segmentation of micro blogs with bagging. In: Li, J., Ji, H., Zhao, D., Feng, Y. (eds.) NLPCC 2015. LNCS (LNAI), vol. 9362, pp. 573–580. Springer, Heidelberg (2015). doi:10.1007/978-3-319-25207-0_54
3. Min, K., Ma, C., Zhao, T., Li, H.: BosonNLP: an ensemble approach for word segmentation and POS tagging. In: Li, J., Ji, H., Zhao, D., Feng, Y. (eds.) NLPCC 2015. LNCS (LNAI), vol. 9362, pp. 520–526. Springer, Heidelberg (2015). doi:10.1007/978-3-319-25207-0_48
4. Pei, W., Ge, T., Chang, B.: Max-margin tensor neural network for Chinese word segmentation. In: ACL, vol. 1, pp. 293–303 (2014)
5. Chen, X., Qiu, X., Zhu, C., Huang, X.: Gated recursive neural network for Chinese word segmentation. In: Proceedings of Annual Meeting of the Association for Computational Linguistics (2015a)
6. Chen, X., Qiu, X., Zhu, C., Liu, P., Huang, X.: Long short-term memory neural networks for Chinese word segmentation (2015b)
7. Hochreiter, S., Schmidhuber, J.: Long short-term memory. Neural Comput. **9**(8), 1735–1780 (1997)
8. Qian, P., Qiu, X., Huang, X.: A new psychometric-inspired evaluation metric for Chinese word segmentation. In: Proceedings of Annual Meeting of the Association for Computational Linguistics (ACL) (2016)
9. Duchi, J., Hazan, E., Singer, Y.: Adaptive subgradient methods for online learning and stochastic optimization. J. Mach. Learn. Res. **12**, 2121–2159 (2011)
10. Goller, C., Kuchler, A.: Learning task-dependent distributed representations by back propagation through structure. In: IEEE International Conference on Neural Networks, vol. 1, pp. 347–352. IEEE, June 1996
11. Ghahramani, Z.: An introduction to hidden Markov models and Bayesian networks. Int. J. Pattern Recogn. Artif. Intell. **15**(01), 9–42 (2001)

12. Srivastava, N., Hinton, G.E., Krizhevsky, A., Sutskever, I., Salakhutdinov, R.: Dropout: a simple way to prevent neural networks from overfitting. J. Mach. Learn. Res. **15**(1), 1929–1958 (2014)
13. Bastien, F., Lamblin, P., Pascanu, R., Bergstra, J., Goodfellow, I., Bergeron, A., Bengio, Y.: Theano: new features and speed improvements (2012). arXiv preprint arXiv:1211.5590
14. Bergstra, J., Breuleux, O., Bastien, F., Lamblin, P., Pascanu, R., Desjardins, G., Bengio, Y.: Theano: a CPU and GPU math expression compiler. In: Proceedings of Python for Scientific Computing Conference (SciPy), vol. 4, p. 3, June 2010
15. Feng, H., Chen, K., Deng, X., Zheng, W.: Accessor variety criteria for Chinese word extraction. Comput. Linguist. **30**(1), 75–93 (2004)
16. Wu, G., He, D., Zhong, K., Zhou, X., Yuan, C.: Leveraging rich linguistic features for cross-domain Chinese segmentation. In: CLP 2014, p. 101 (2014)
17. Gao, Q., Vogel, S.: A multi-layer Chinese word segmentation system optimized for out-of-domain tasks. In: Proceedings of CIPS-SIGHAN Joint Conference on Chinese Language Processing (CLP 2010), pp. 210–215 (2010)
18. Sun, W., Xu, J.: Enhancing Chinese word segmentation using unlabeled data. In: Proceedings of Conference on Empirical Methods in Natural Language Processing, pp. 970–979. Association for Computational Linguistics, July 2011
19. Qiu, X., Qian, P., Yin, L., Wu, S., Huang, X.: Overview of the NLPCC 2015 shared task: Chinese word segmentation and POS tagging for micro-blog texts. In: Li, J., Ji, H., Zhao, D., Feng, Y. (eds.) NLPCC 2015. LNCS (LNAI), vol. 9362, pp. 541–549. Springer, Heidelberg (2015). doi:10.1007/978-3-319-25207-0_50

Chinese Word Similarity Computing Based on Combination Strategy

Shaoru Guo[1], Yong Guan[1], Ru Li[1,2(✉)], and Qi Zhang[3]

[1] School of Computer and Information Technology,
Shanxi University, Taiyuan, China
guoshaoru0928@163.com, guanyong0130@163.com,
liru@sxu.edu.cn
[2] Key Laboratory of Ministry of Education for Computation Intelligence and
Chinese Information Processing, Shanxi University, Taiyuan, China
[3] College of Mathematics and Computer Science,
Fuzhou University, Fujian, China
zxq502528023@126.com

Abstract. Chinese word similarity computing is a fundamental task for natural language processing. This paper presents a method to calculate the similarity between Chinese words based on combination strategy. We apply Baidubaike to train Word2Vector model, and then integrate different methods, semantic Dictionary-based method, Word2Vector-based method and Chinese FrameNet (CFN)-based method, to calculate the semantic similarity between Chinese words. The semantic Dictionary-based method includes dictionaries such as HowNet, DaCilin, Tongyici Cilin (Extended) and Antonym. The experiments are performed on 500 pairs of words and the Spearman correlation coefficient of test data is 0.524, which shows that the proposed method is feasible and effective.

Keywords: Chinese word similarity computing · Combination strategy · Semantic dictionary · Word2Vector · Chinese FrameNet

1 Introduction

Chinese word similarity computing is one of the key technologies in Chinese information processing. Chinese word similarity computing provides a generic evaluation framework and is useful across applications like information retrieval, machine translation, semantic disambiguation, question answering etc.

Traditional methods that are normally used for computing words similarity can be divided into two categories: one is to calculate semantic similarity based on semantic dictionary; the other one is to calculate semantic similarity based on corpus. There is also recently developed word embedding (Mikolov et al. 2013) method, which apply large-scale corpus to train term vector, and then do the similarity calculation.

We participated in "Chinese Word Similarity Measurement" of the Fifth Conference on Natural Language Processing and Chinese Computing and The Twenty Fourth International Conference on Computer Processing of Oriental Languages

© Springer International Publishing AG 2016
C.-Y. Lin et al. (Eds.): NLPCC-ICCPOL 2016, LNAI 10102, pp. 744–752, 2016.
DOI: 10.1007/978-3-319-50496-4_67

(NLPCC-ICCPOL 2016) evaluation. For this task, we apply Baidubaike to train Word2Vector model, and then integrate different methods to calculate the similarity of Chinese word, Dictionary-based method, Word2Vector-based method and Chinese FrameNet (Liu 2011)-based method. The Dictionary-based method includes HowNet (Dong 2000), DaCilin, Tongyici Cilin (Extended) and Antonym dictionary. This paper presents a method to calculate the similarity between Chinese words based on combination strategy.

The rest of this paper is organized as follows: in Sect. 2, we describe the task of Chinese word similarity computing with combination strategy. Section 3 describes the method we used in the combination strategy. We present the results and observations in Sect. 4, followed by the conclusion in Sect. 5.

2 Combination Strategy

The semantic dictionary-based method to calculate the similarity of words depends on dictionaries. The method is efficient and accurate, but it is unable to calculate the unknown words. And the Word2Vector-based method is widely coverage, but it depends on the train corpus.

In our work, we attempt to address these concerns. Our approach uses a combination of semantic dictionary-based method and Word2Vector-based method to calculate the similarity between Chinese words. What's more, we also use semantic resource, Chinese FrameNet (CFN), to calculate similarity of two words. The method is illustrated in Fig. 1. If HowNet contains the two words, firstly we need to calculate the similarity with the method based on HowNet. Then, if Word2Vector contains the two words, we calculate the cosine similarity with the method based on Word2Vector. The Chinese FrameNet is used to calculate the semantic relation between two words. Besides, for the method base on semantic dictionary, we use DaCilin, Tongyici Cilin

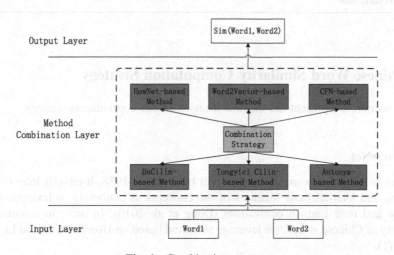

Fig. 1. Combination strategy

(Extended) and Antonym dictionary. The detailed steps are reported in Algorithm 1. This method both consider the words resemblance and the words relevance.

Algorithm1: Combination Strategy

Input: Word pair (Word1,Word2)
Output: Sim(Word1,Word2)
$Sim1$ = SimH(Word1,Word2)
$Sim2$ = SimW(Word1,Word2)
If $Sim1$ == 1.0
  $Sim = Sim2$
else if $Sim2$ == 1.0
    $Sim = Sim1$
  else
    $Sim = (Sim1 + Sim2) / 2.0$
  end if
end if
if Word1 AND Word2 evoke the same frame
  $Sim = (Sim + 10.0) / 2.0$
end if
if Word1 AND Word2 in DaCilin or Tongyici Cilin (Extended)
  $Sim = (Sim+10.0) / 2.0$
else if Word1 AND Word2 in Antonym dictionary
  $Sim = Sim / 2.0$
  else
    $Sim = Sim$
  end if
end if
return Sim

---

3   Chinese Word Similarity Computation Strategy

In this section, we present the method we used in our combination strategy.

3.1   HowNet

HowNet is a Chinese word dictionary built by Dong in 1988. It unveils inter-concept relations and inter-attribute relations of the concepts as connoting in lexicons of the Chinese and their English equivalents (Dong et al. 2010). In order to calculate the similarity of Chinese words, we leverage a method based on HowNet (Liu and Li 2002) in Eq. (1).

$$SimH(W_1, W_2) = \max_{i=1...n, j=1...m} SimH(S_{1i}, S_{2j}) \qquad (1)$$

Where $SimH(W_1, W_2)$ is the similarity of Word1 (W_1) and Word2 (W_2) base on HowNet; $S_{11}, S_{12}, ..., S_{1n}$ represent the sememe (concept) of Word1; $S_{21}, S_{22}, ..., S_{2m}$ represent the sememe (concept) of Word2.

For example, the similarity of "平凡" and "平庸" base on HowNet can be represented as

$$SimH(平凡，平庸) = 6.4 .$$

3.2 Word2Vector

Word2Vector is a Deep Learning toolkit which developed by Mikolov et al. (2013). Word2Vector takes a text corpus as input and produces the word vectors as output. It first constructs a vocabulary from the training text data and then learns vector representation of words (Xue et al. 2014). The resulting word vector file can be used as features in many natural language processing and machine learning applications. For our method, we apply the corpus of 12.6G Baidubaike to train Word2Vector model. The model has a window size of 5 and the dimension we adopted is 100. The resulting data set contains about 220 million words. With Word2Vector tool-set, we can define the cosine distance between two vectors in Eq. (2).

$$SimW(W_1, W_2) = \cos \theta = \frac{\overline{W_1} \bullet \overline{W_2}}{||\overline{W_1}|| \bullet ||\overline{W_2}||} \qquad (2)$$

Where $SimW(W_1, W_2)$ is the similarity of Word1 (W_1) and Word2 (W_2) base on Word2Vector; $\overline{W_1}$ represents the vector of Word1; $\overline{W_2}$ represent the vector of Word2.

For example, the similarity of "老气" and "土气" base on Word2Vector can be represented as

$$SimW(老气，土气) = 5.1 .$$

3.3 Chinese FrameNet (CFN)

Chinese FrameNet (CFN), which is a word semantic knowledge based on the frame semantics of Fillmore (Fillmore 1976, 1982; Fillmore et al. 2001) and takes Berkeley's FrameNet Project (Baker et al. 1998) as the reference. In Chinese FrameNet, the predicates, called word units (LU) (Hao et al. 2007), evoke frames which roughly correspond to different events or scenarios. Each frame defines a set of arguments called Frame Elements (FE). For example, the "锻炼" frame describes a common situation in which an agent actively maintains or improves their level of physical fitness. And is evoked by words such as "锻炼", "健身", "健", "运动", etc. We call these frame-evoking words are LUs in the "锻炼" frame.

Frame Semantics (Petruck 1996) is a research program in empirical semantics which emphasizes the continuities between language and experience, and provides a framework for presenting the results of that research. A FRAME is any system of concepts related in such a way that to understand any one concept it is necessary to understand the entire system; introducing any one concept results in all of them becoming available. Our approach for computing the similarity between two words base on CFN is described as follows. If two words evoke the same frame, we think they are related, and Table 1 illustrates this case. As the word units "锻炼" and "健身" evoke the "锻炼" frame, we can assume that two words are semantic equivalent.

Table 1. Example of frame and word units

Frame	Word units (LUs)
锻炼	锻炼 健身 健 运动
预订	预订 预约 预购 订 订购 定购 订阅
种植	种植 种 栽 栽种 栽植 栽培 植树 植 植苗 植根 根植 播种 移植 培植 插秧 插播

3.4 Other

In this paper we use the dictionary of Tongyici Cilin (Extended) and DaCilin, both of which are come from Research Center for Social Computing and Information Retrieval of Harbin Institute of Technology, to calculate the similarity between two words.

The methods mentioned above are all to pay attention to the similarity of two words. Besides, we also use Antonym dictionary to detect the antonym of the words. The Antonym dictionary come from Semantic Computing and Chinese FrameNet Research Center of Shanxi University. The Antonym dictionary contains about 17,000 pairs of words.

4   Experiments

We present our experimental results in this section by first introducing the data and evaluation metrics, followed by the results of our system.

4.1   Data and Evaluation Metrics

The Chinese word similarity computation test dataset we used was offered by NLPCC-ICCPOL: 2016 Shared Task (Wu and Li 2016). In order to capture word usages both in formal written documents and causal short texts, words mainly from news articles and Weibo text. There are together 10,000 pairs of words in the file, in which only 500 pairs will be selected as the final test data. In this paper, we do experiments on the final test data.

In order to keep consistent with NLPCC-ICCPOL: 2016 Shared Task Guideline, this paper uses Spearman's rank correlation coefficient to evaluate the statistical dependence between automatic computing results and the golden human labeled data, we denote the method in Eq. (3):

$$r_R = 1 - \frac{6 \sum_{i=1}^{n} (R_{Xi} - R_{Yi})^2}{n(n^2 - 1)} \tag{3}$$

Where n is the number of observations, R_{Xi} and R_{Yi} are the standard deviations of the rank variables.

4.2   Experiments Results

Based on the experimental methods described in the previous section, we have systematically evaluated our approach on the 500 pairs of words. We denote the HowNet-based method by H, the Word2Vector-based method by W, and the Chinese FrameNet (CFN)-based method by C. We denote the DaCilin-based method, Tongyici Cilin (Extended)-based method and Antonym dictionary-based method by D. We use superscripts d, t, and s to indicate the use of DaCilin, Tongyici Cilin (Extended) and Antonym dictionary for a particular method set.

The performance of different methods set on the 500 pairs of words is given in Table 2. The method of W + H + D + C achieves a Spearman score 0.524. We observer, from Table 2, that the result of H + W is better than H and W separate test results. This is because the HowNet-based method (H) depends on dictionary to calculate the similarity, so it is unable to calculate the unknown words. And the Word2Vector-based method (W) depends on the train corpus, NLPCC-ICCPOL selects words mainly from news articles and Weibo text, but this paper only applies Baidubaike to train Word2Vector models. As shown in Table 3, the similarity of "没辙" and "没戏" is 1.0 using the method of H. Meanwhile some pairs of words are not same totally, but the similarity is 10.0 using the method H as the description of the two words are same. For example, the Chinese word "踟蹰不前" is described as: "hesitate|犹豫, content = SelfMove|自移", and the Chinese word "犹豫" is described as: "hesitate|犹豫", so the similarity of this pair of words is 10.0, but the two words are not same.

Table 2. Performance of different method set

Methods	Spearman correlation
H	0.266
W	0.378
W + C	0.380
W + D	0.475
W + H	0.468
W + H+C	0.471
W + H+D	0.518
W + H+D + C	0.524

Table 3. Word similarity based on H and W

Word1	Word2	Similarity			
		Criterion	H	W	H + W + D + C
没戏	没辙	4.9	1.0	3.8	3.8
犹豫	踟蹰不前	8	10	1.0	6.0
GDP	生产力	6.5	1.0	1.0	1.0

Among the 500 pairs of words, there are 156 pairs of words appear in DaCilin, Tongyici Cilin (Extended) and Antonym dictionary, while only 16 pairs of words using the CFN-based method. So as shown in the Table 2, the results of W + H + D is better than W + H + C.

As evident from Table 4, higher accuracy is achieved with W + H + D. For example, the similarity of "高兴" and "兴奋" is 5.5 using the method of HowNet-based method (H) and Word2Vector-based method (W). While integrating CFN-based method (C), similarity of "高兴" and "兴奋" is 7.7, which is consistent with the criterion. This is because "高兴" and "兴奋" evoke the same semantic frame "情感反应". The definition of the frame is "The adjectives and nouns in this frame describe an Experiencer who is feeling or experiencing a particular emotional response to a Stimulus or about a Topic. There can also be a Circumstances under which the response occurs or a Reason that the Stimulus evokes the particular response in the Experiencer". Meanwhile, as shown in Table 5, higher accuracy is achieved with W + H + D than W + H. For example, the similarity of "振兴" and "建设" is 3.8 using the method of H + W. While integrating D, the similarity increase to 6.9.

Table 4. Performance of CFN-based method (C) on test data

Word1	Word2	Similarity		
		Criterion	W + H	W + H + C
种	栽	8.4	4.1	7.1
高兴	兴奋	7.7	5.5	7.7

Table 5. Performance of D on test data

Word1	Word2	Similarity		
		Criterion	W + H	W + H + D
振兴	建设	5.2	3.8	6.9
计算机	电脑	9.9	8.5	9.3

We also measure the contribution of each method by deleting it from the full method set. These ablation results are shown in Table 6. If we delete W, then correlation coefficient drops significantly. We find that using H contributes slightly more than D. When deleting the Antonym dictionary, the results almost has no change, because only 4 pairs of words appear in the Antonym dictionary. We observe, from Table 7, the Antonym dictionary has significant contributes to the Antonym words. For

Table 6. Ablation study of method type on test set

Method	Spearman correlation
W + H + D + C	0.524
−W (H + D + C)	0.385
−H (W + D + C)	0.465
−C (W + H + D)	0.519
−D (W + H + C)	0.471
−D − C (W + H)	0.468
−W − C (H + D)	0.381
−W − D (H + C)	0.282
−D^a(W + H + D^{t+d} + C)	0.523

Table 7. Deleting the antonym dictionary

Word1	Word2	Similarity		
		Criterion	W + H + D^{t+d} + C	W + H + D + C
缓慢	飞快	4.3	7.6	3.8
认真	马虎	4.1	7.7	3.9
君子	小人	4.1	6.9	3.5
积极	消极	4.1	8.7	4.4

example, the similarity of "积极" and "消极" is 8.7 without the antonym dictionary-based method. While with the full method set (W + H + C + D), similarity of the words is 4.1, which is consistent with the criterion.

5 Conclusion and Future Work

Apparently, Chinese word similarity computing is a fundamental task for Chinese information processing. We have present a study for computing similarity of Chinese words.

The paper proposed a method to calculate the similarity between Chinese words based on combination strategy. We integrate different ways of Chinese word calculating methods, Dictionary-based method, Word2Vector-based method and CFN-based method to calculate the similarity. The Dictionary-based method includes HowNet, DaCilin, Tongyici Cilin (Extended) and Antonym dictionary. The Spearman score of test data is 0.524.

The future work will be carried out in the following aspects. First, we would like to work on Frame-to-Frame relations, which could potentially further improve the performance of our proposed method. As the relations of Frame-to-Frame in FrameNet, serves as important information sources, to be calculating the similarity of words. Second, we are going to apply this method to question answering system.

Acknowledgements. This work is supported by the National 863 Project of China (2015AA015407), National Natural Science Foundation of China (61373082, 61673248, 61502287), Shanxi Platform Project (2014091004-0103), Scholarship Council (2013-015), Open Project Foundation of Information Security Evaluation Center of Civil Aviation, Civil Aviation University of China (CAAC-ISECCA-201402) and Shanxi Higher School Science and Technology Innovation Project (2015104, 201505).

References

Mikolov, T., Sutskever, I., Chen, K., Corrado, G.S., Dean, J.: Distributed representations of words and phrases and their compositionality. In: Advances in Neural Information Processing Systems, pp. 3111–3119 (2013)

Liu, K.: Research on Chinese FrameNet construction and application technologies. J. Chin. Inf. Process. **6**(006), 47 (2011)

Dong, Z., Dong, Q.: Introduction to hownet. HowNet (2000). http://www.keenage.com

Dong, Z., Dong, Q., Hao, C.: Hownet and its computation of meaning. In: Proceedings of 23rd International Conference on Computational Linguistics: Demonstrations, pp. 53–56. Association for Computational Linguistics, August 2010

Liu, Q., Li, S.: Word similarity computing based on How-net. Comput. Linguist. Chin. Lang. Process. **7**(2), 59–76 (2002)

Xue, B., Fu, C., Shaobin, Z.: A study on sentiment computing and classification of Sina Weibo with Word2vec. In: 2014 IEEE International Congress on Big Data, pp. 358–363. IEEE, June 2014

Fillmore, C.J.: Frame semantics and the nature of language. Ann. N.Y. Acad. Sci. **280**(1), 20–32 (1976)

Fillmore, C.: Frame semantics. In: Linguistics in the Morning Calm, pp. 111–137 (1982)

Fillmore, C.J., Wooters, C., Baker, C.F.: Building a large lexical databank which provides deep semantics. publisher not identified (2001)

Hao, X., Wei, L., Ru, L., Kaiying, L.: Description systems of the Chinese FrameNet database and software tools. J. Chin. Inf. Process. **21**(5), 96–100 (2007)

Baker, C.F., Fillmore, C.J., Lowe, J.B.: The Berkeley FrameNet project. In: Proceedings of 36th Annual Meeting of the Association for Computational Linguistics and 17th International Conference on Computational Linguistics, vol. 1, pp. 86–90. Association for Computational Linguistics, August 1998

Wu, Y., Li, W.: NLPCC-ICCPOL 2016 Shared Task 3: Chinese word similarity measurement. In: Proceedings of NLPCC 2016 (2016)

Petruck, M.R.L.: Frame semantics. Handbook of Pragmatics, pp. 1–13 (1996)

An Empirical Study on Chinese Microblog Stance Detection Using Supervised and Semi-supervised Machine Learning Methods

Liran Liu[1], Shi Feng[1,2(✉)], Daling Wang[1,2], and Yifei Zhang[1,2]

[1] School of Computer Science and Engineering,
Northeastern University, Shenyang, China
lyran_summer@sina.com, {fengshi,wangdaling,
zhangyifei}@cse.neu.edu.cn
[2] Key Laboratory of Medical Image Computing (Northeastern University),
Ministry of Education, Shenyang 110819, China

Abstract. Nowadays, more and more people are willing to express their opinions and attitudes in the microblog platform. Stance detection refers to the task that judging whether the author of the text is in favor of or against the given target. Most of the existing literature are for the debates or online conversations, which have adequate context for inferring the authors' stances. However, for detecting the stance in microblogs, we have to figure out the stance of the author only based on the unique and separate microblog, which sets new obstacles for this task. In this paper, we conduct a comprehensive empirical study on microblog stance detection using supervised and semi-supervised machine learning methods. Different unbalanced data processing strategies and classifiers, such as Linear SVM, Naive Bayes and Random Forest, are compared using NLPCC 2016 Stance Detection Evaluation Task dataset. Experiment results show that the method based on ensemble learning and SMOTE2 unbalanced processing with sentiment word features outperforms the best submission result in NLPCC 2016 Evaluation Task.

Keywords: Stance detection · Chinese microblog · Sentiment analysis · Supervised learning · Semi-supervised learning · Unbalanced classification

1 Introduction

With the rapid development of mobile Internet, the social media has played an increasingly important role in human's life. More and more people are willing to express their personal views towards the hot trends and events on Weibo, Twitter, and other platforms, where have aggregated huge amounts of people's various opinions on hot topics. Therefore, how to extract and analyze people's opinions on certain topic have become the major concern for both research and commercial communities. Stance detection is an emerging research task judging whether a person is in favor of, against, or neutral to the specific target or the degree he or she is in favor of the specific target

© Springer International Publishing AG 2016
C.-Y. Lin et al. (Eds.): NLPCC-ICCPOL 2016, LNAI 10102, pp. 753–765, 2016.
DOI: 10.1007/978-3-319-50496-4_68

Table 1. The examples of stance detection task for microblogs (translated from Chinese)

Microblogs	Stance
The two-child policy is an absolutely right decision. It can optimize the demographic structure, and increase the labor supply.	*Favor*
Are all of us easily arranged machines?!!	*Against*
I don't know whether it is right time to let every couple in China has two children. Time will prove all.	*None*
I think the Family Planning Policy is better. There are so many people in China!	*Against*

according to his or her microblogs. The target may be a celebrity, a government organization, a controversial policy, a political movement, or a commercial product. Several examples of stance detection for the target "the universal two-child policy" are shown in the Table 1 below.

We can see in Table 1 that the first two people are in favor of and against the target "the universal two-child policy" respectively. The third people's stance toward the target is *None*. Note that the given target may not be present in the Weibo text. For example, in the second microblog, the author did not explicitly use the topic words for the target "two-child policy". However, we can infer that the author's stance is against the given target.

As an emerging research direction, stance detection is different from the traditional sentiment analysis or opinion mining. The stance detection stresses the importance of the target topic when analyzing the text. However, the sentiment orientation analysis methods usually adopt a target-independent strategy, which may assign irrelevant sentiment orientations to the specific target. In Table 1 for the orientation analysis task, the fourth microblog is positive. Nevertheless, the author is implicitly against the "two-child policy". Therefore, the stance of this microblog is *Against*.

There are several critical new challenges for detecting the stance in microblogs. Firstly, the microblog usually has a length limitation of 140 characters, which leads to extremely sparse vectors for the learning based algorithms. On the other hand, people are used to employing a simple sentence, or even a few words to express their attitude towards a target. The free and informal writing styles of users also set obstacles for the stance detection in microblogs. Secondly, the target topic may not be explicitly included in the microblogs, such as the second microblog in Table 1. It is a tricky situation when analyzing the relationship between the target and microblogs. Thirdly, people may utilize negative orientation sentences to express *Favor* attitude towards the target or positive orientation sentences to express *Against* attitude towards the target, such as the fourth microblog in Table 1. At last, how to make full use of characteristics of Chinese microblog to get the author's stance towards that target is a brand new challenge in this field.

To tackle these challenges, in this paper, we regard the stance detection in Chinese microblogs as a classification problem. We utilize TFIDF and sentiment dictionary to represent the microblogs as the sparse vectors and leverage SVM, Naive Bayes, Random Forest and the ensemble classifier to detect stance in a supervised and a semi-supervised way. The comprehensive empirical studies were conducted on NLPCC 2016 microblog stance detection benchmark dataset task A. The experiment results show that TFIDF and the voting based classifier is a more stable combination in stance detection without unbalanced processing in most case. However, the method based on ensemble learning and SMOTE2 unbalanced processing with sentiment word features could achieve the best result in our experiments which slightly outperforms the best submission result in NLPCC 2016 Evaluation Task.

The remainder of this paper is organized as follows. Section 2 is related work. Section 3 describes our data preprocessing methods. Sections 4 and 5 introduce the supervised way and the semi-supervised way for stance detection separately. Section 6 reports the experimental dataset and the results. Finally, Sect. 7 draws the conclusion and outlines the future work.

2 Related Work

As an emerging research problem and a subfield of text mining, the stance detection stresses the importance on the given target, which differs from sentiment analysis.

Thomas et al. proposed a new framework for stance detection of Congress debates utilizing constraints based on speaker identity and on direct textual references between statements [1]. Walker et al. first applied Max-Cut in stance classification, which showed large performance improvements from modeling dialogic relations [2]. Recasens et al. studied the bias in Wikipedia which had implications for linguistic theory and computational linguistics by classifying bias in reference works into two classes, i.e. framing and epistemological [3]. Somasundaran et al. presented an unsupervised approach using ICA to accomplish stance classification [4]. Murakami et al. introduced a method for identifying the general positions of users in online debates by using a rule-based classifier to classify the replies and using these classifiers' results to determine the weights of the corresponding links in the link structure of the reply network [5]. Millen et al. pointed out the importance of supporting the participants in discussions and demonstrated the effectiveness of their methods in one of these jams [6]. Abbott et al. examined agreement and disagreement in quote/response pairs in ideological and nonideological online forum discussions, and showed that it was possible to distinguish the agreement relation with 68% accuracy [7]. Wang et al. showed that they could use a variant of LSA to identify a parent post, given a response post with approximately 70% accuracy [8]. Faulkner et al. investigated the problem of detecting document-level stance in student essays by making use of two sets of features that were supposed to represent stance-taking language [9]. Sobhani et al. extracted arguments used in online news comments to detect stance [10]. Rajadesingan et al. determined the stance at user-level based on the assumption that if several users retweeted one pair of tweets about a controversial topic, it was likely that they supported the same side of a debate [11].

Most of the existing literature on stance detection are for the debates or online conversations. It means that there are adequate context for inferring the stances of the authors. However, for microblog stance detection task, we have to figure out the stance of the author based only on the unique and separate microblog, which set new obstacles for this task. In this paper, we conduct a comprehensive empirical study on microblog stance detection using supervised and semi-supervised learning methods.

3   Data Preprocessing

Data preprocessing for microblogs plays an important role in stance detection, which can directly influence the quality of the detection results. In this paper, we adopt a few microblog preprocessing methods that can pave the way for the subsequent steps of the stance detection task. The method we adopt includes the following steps:

Handle Targets: Use regular expression matching to extract targets from microblogs. We think that the target can be treated as disturbing factors that can adversely affect the generation of the document matrix.

Remove Numbers: The numbers are usually without any stance information but appear frequently. Thus, numbers are removed in order to refine the microblog content.

Remove URLs: The URLs can lead us to new webpages, but they do not carry much information about the stance. Therefore, we remove them away to reduce the influence to none.

Remove '@' Mentions: The action to point out a specified bodies or organization in a microblog often start with '@', and what follows it is usually the name of people or organizations. This information is always unhelpful for the stance detection of the microblog. Hence, they are removed.

Remove Stop Words: Stop words are extremely common words but do not carry any stance related information. Thus, they are of no use. To solve this, we manually create a stop words list with which we decide whether to remove a word from the text.

After preprocessing of the dataset, we will use Bag of Words model and TFIDF to convert text data into vectors. Then a good classifier can be trained to predict test data. We will describe the algorithms that are used to predict the stance of Chinese microblog in different perspectives of supervision in Sect. 4 and semi-supervision in Sect. 5 respectively in this paper.

4   Stance Detection Based on Supervised Learning

In this section, we will describe in detail how to detect the stance of each microblog against specified target in a supervised way. After the preprocessing steps as described in Sect. 3, we segment the sentences with an open source tool Jieba[1]. Afterwards we take several actions to predict the stance using steps described below:

Utilizing BOW and Sentiment Dictionary Together to Generate Document-Word Matrix: We adopt unigram, bigram and trigram as features and TFIDF as weighting scheming based on Bag of Words model, and then normalize the weights with L2. With help of sentiment dictionary, we also consider the polarity of the word, the ratio of sentiment words, the punctuations and other features to form the vector space.

---

[1] https://pypi.python.org/pypi/jieba/.

Unbalanced Dataset Handle: We observe that the microblogs that are in favor of and against a given target are usually unbalanced. In this paper, we adopt different over-sample methods such as OverSampling, SMOTE [12], SMOTE1 [13], SMOTE2 [13], and SMOTE + Tomeklinks [14] to balance the training dataset. Different parameters are chosen for different targets. Moreover, we employ One-Vs-Rest (OVR) skills in this multiple-class unbalanced training process until the number of data with different labels is the same as each other, namely *FAVOR:NONE:AGAINST* = 1:1:1. This will be a help in the following stance detection.

χ^2 **Feature Selection:** For each feature and class, there is also a score to measure if the feature and the class are independent to each other. We use χ^2 to test it, which is a statistic method to check if two events are independent. The larger the score is, the higher dependency they have. At last, 32% is the most appropriate ratio we choose through which we achieve the best macro-F values in the cross validation experiments in supervised machine learning method.

Classification Algorithms: An appropriate classifier is extremely useful to obtain a good stance detection result. We empirically evaluate the performance of the classifiers such as linear SVM, Random Forest, and Naive Bayes in this task, and we also ensemble them together through voting strategy. In fact, we have also tried KNN and SVM with Gaussian kernel, but the results are unpromising. Figure 1 shows the final framework of our experiment.

Using the framework in Fig. 1, we conduct extensive experiments with different features, unbalanced data handle strategies and classifiers, and the results are shown in the experiment section.

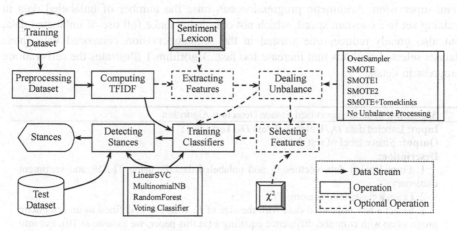

Fig. 1. The details of our supervised learning framework for stance detection

5 Stance Detection Based on Semi-supervised Learning

Semi-supervised learning has an advantage over supervised learning since it can make full use of all the data whether they are labeled or not. When taking difficulty of data annotation into account, we adopt the semi-supervised learning framework to update a semi-supervised classifier to complete stance detection.

758   L. Liu et al.

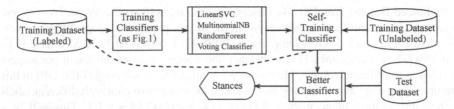

Fig. 2. The details of our proposed framework in a semi-supervised way

After preprocessing steps in Sect. 3, the microblog texts are represented as vectors. First, we create a classifier with labeled data. Then, we update the classifier trained from the first step through self-training. Finally, we predict the stance for test data. The detail of this scheme is shown in Fig. 2.

In self-training step, firstly we select a number of unlabeled data and put them into classifier to get predicted results. Secondly, we select half number of predicted results with higher probability, and combine them with the original labeled data as the new training dataset. Thirdly, we leverage the combined dataset to train a new classifier. Finally, we update the classifier using this self-training method again and again until there exists no unlabeled data.

During self-training, we use arithmetic progression as the method to select the number of unlabeled data for training this semi-supervised classifier. Moreover, in the paper the common difference of the arithmetic progression is set to be 10. It should be emphasized that the way of using arithmetic progression as the strategy to select unlabeled dataset in self-training can have a good effect on a large number of dataset in semi-supervision. Arithmetic progression can raise the number of unlabeled data in training set in a constant speed, which not only helps make full use of unlabeled data, but also greatly reduce time wasted in the semi-supervision compared with those dataset selected methods that increase too fast. Algorithm 1 illustrates the self-training progress in detail.

Algorithm 1. Semi-supervised Stance Detection Algorithm

Input: Labeled data D_1, Unlabeled data D_2, Test file T;
Output: Stance label of test data S;
Description:
  1. Form labeled data vectors V_1 and unlabeled data V_2 using TFIDF and sentiment dictionary.
  2. Learn a classifier clf_0 using V_1.
  3. Select a few unlabeled data with the size of K, where K is defined as an arithmetic progression with common difference equaling k (in this paper, we assume k=10). Put into clf_0 to get stance label S_K={$s_1, s_2, ..., s_K$}(s_i is the label of ith unlabeled data)
  4. Select top m stance labels with larger probabilistic and its corresponding vectors in V_2 (in this paper, m is equal to half of K), combine V_1 and top m selected data, and then remove that top m data which are added to V_1 away from V_2.
  5. Loop (2)(3)(4) for N times until there exists less unlabeled data than K. Then predict labels of those data, and add all of them to labeled data. Train classifier clf using V_1.
  6. Input test dataset to classifier clf and get S of these data. Output S.

Note that in the final unlabeled data selection, it is very likely that the remaining size of unlabeled data is not as big as the one we expected. Thus, we give up the above strategy and select all the unlabeled data to update the classifier.

As normal, we consider the different unbalanced data processing methods, feature selection and classifiers the same as what we do in supervised learning. We also consider the sentiment dictionary to improve the performance. Note that different classifier could not give a uniform label probability. Therefore, to ensemble several classifier, during the unlabeled data selection process, we randomly select higher probabilistic results instead of comparing the output of different classifiers.

6 Experiments and Results

6.1 Experiment Dataset

We conduct our experiments with the dataset of NLPCC 2016 Evaluation Task 4A - Stance Detection in Chinese Microblogs[2]. In this task, the training dataset contains 3,000 microblog sentences, and the testing dataset contains 1,000 microblog sentences. In the training set, each microblog contains three basic stance labels, i.e. *Against, None* and *Favor*. In training set, some microblogs are labeled *Unknown*. Moreover, both the training set as well as the test set contains five targets, and the number of microblogs towards each targets are equal to each other. Table 2 shows the statistics information of the datasets.

Table 2. The statics of microblogs in the datasets

Dataset	Usage	Learning method	Target	Size	Label	Size/target
Task A	Training set	Supervised semi-supervised	T1-T5	3000	Labeled	600
Task R	Training set	Semi-supervised	T1-T5	3000	Unlabeled	600
Test	Test set	Supervised semi-supervised	T1-T5	1000	Labeled	200

As described, we take the labeled dataset Task A as training set both in supervised learning and in semi-supervised learning. It is unusual that there are 14 microblogs in Task A with no labels. We pick up these 14 microblogs and add them into Task R for the self-training process.

The metric for evaluating the classifiers is shown below.

$$F_{avg} = \frac{F_{favor} + F_{against}}{2} \tag{1}$$

---

[2] http://tcci.ccf.org.cn/conference/2016/pages/page05_evadata.html.

where F_{favor} and $F_{against}$ are calculated as:

$$F_{favor} = \frac{2P_{favor}R_{favor}}{P_{favor} + R_{favor}} \tag{2}$$

$$F_{favor} = \frac{2P_{against}R_{against}}{P_{against} + R_{against}} \tag{3}$$

6.2 Experiment Results Based on Supervised Learning

After extensive empirical study, we get the experiment results as shown in Table 3. We compare different classifier using F_{avg} that is the macro-average of F-score (*Favor*) and F-score (*Against*) which are used as the standard evaluation metric for NLPCC 2016 Evaluation Task.

Note that we do not disregard the "*None*" class. Because falsely labeled "*None*" class as "*Favor*" or "*Against*" may affect the value of precision and recall which may affect F_{avg}. Table 3 shows the details of our experiment results.

In Table 3, **T-FS-LC** means that we utilize TFIDF to calculate the word weights in the vectors, the feature selection based on χ^2 is conducted, and the Linear SVM

Table 3. Microblog stance classification results on the dataset. -T is TFIDF. -SD refers to sentiment dictionary. -FS represents Feature Selection. -LC means Linear SVM classifier. -**NBC** is Naive Bayes classifier. -**RFC** is Random Forest classifier. -**VoC** is Voting Classifier. -**SMOTE + TLinks** represents SMOTE + Tomeklinks.

Experiment settings	Over-sampling	SMOTE	SMOTE1	SMOTE2	SMOTE+TLinks	No unbalanced processing
T-LC	0.6693	0.6676	0.6713	0.6712	0.6694	0.6705
T-NBC	0.6715	0.6707	0.6793	0.6842	0.6748	0.7001
T-RFC	0.6624	0.6653	0.6679	0.6703	0.6628	0.6689
T-VoC	0.6802	0.6813	0.6855	0.6924	0.7012	0.7003
T-FS-LC	0.6791	0.6756	0.6728	0.6796	0.6737	0.6637
T-FS-NBC	0.6694	0.6589	0.6718	0.6849	0.6599	0.6886
T-FS-RFC	0.6578	0.6622	0.6646	0.6674	0.6636	0.6673
T-FS-VoC	0.6837	0.6726	0.6802	0.6811	0.6752	0.6972
T-SD-LC	0.6782	0.6463	0.6694	0.6633	0.6582	0.6653
T-SD-NBC	0.5946	0.5598	0.5711	0.5987	0.5853	0.5273
T-SD-RFC	0.6784	0.6751	0.6824	0.6816	0.6777	0.6707
T-SD-VoC	0.6877	0.6599	0.6936	**0.7123**	0.6980	0.6940
T-SD-FS-LC	0.6548	0.6663	0.6659	0.6493	0.6527	0.6653
T-SD-FS-NBC	0.6358	0.6166	0.6208	0.6313	0.6259	0.5992
T-SD-FS-RFC	0.6737	0.6609	0.6794	0.6843	0.6782	0.6812
T-SD-FS-VoC	0.6857	0.6826	0.6792	0.6893	0.6808	0.6855

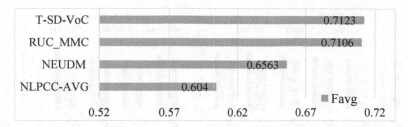

Fig. 3. The comparison of the results with F_{avg}. **T-SD-VoC** is the combination through which we get the best F_{avg} in this paper. **RUC_MMC** is the F_{avg} of the first place team in NLPCC 2016 evaluation task. **NEUDM** is our team score in NLPCC2016 evaluation task. **NLPCC-AVG** is the F_{avg} average of all teams participated in NLPCC 2016 evaluation task.

classifier is used. Similarly, **T-SD-FS-VoC** means that the sentiment dictionary is leveraged to enrich feature set, the TFIDF and feature selection methods are used, and the ensemble method based on voting strategy are chosen for the classifier. We also compare the best performance achieved in this paper with the 1st place team and our result in the NLPCC competition, as shown in Fig. 3.

First, let us analyze the role of sentiment dictionary in the experiments. From Fig. 3 and Table 3, we observe that the best performance **T-SD-VoC** is achieved when using

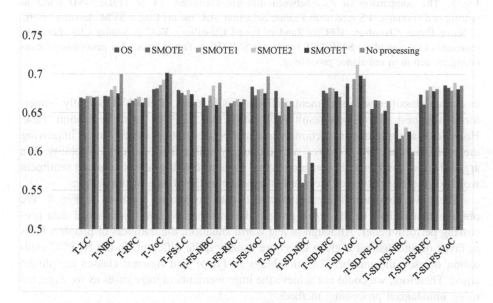

Fig. 4. The comparison of F_{avg} between several unbalanced processing. **-T** is TFIDF. **-SD** refers to sentiment dictionary. **-FS** represents Feature Selection. **-LC** means Linear SVM classifier. **-NBC** is Naive Bayes Classifier. **-RFC** is Random Forest Classifier. **-VoC** is Voting Classifier. **-OS** represents OverSampler. **-SMOTET** represents SMOTE + Tomeklinks. **-No processing** means taking no action in unbalance processing.

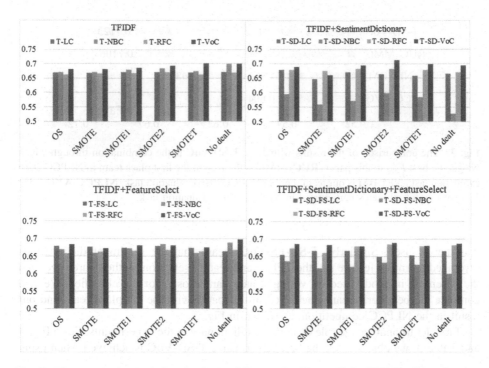

Fig. 5. The comparison of F_{avg} between different classifiers. **-T** is TFIDF. **-SD** refers to sentiment dictionary. **-FS** represents Feature Selection. **-LC** means Linear SVM classifier. **-NBC** is Naive Bayes Classifier. **-RFC** is Random Forest Classifier. **-VoC** is Voting Classifier. **-OS** represents OverSampler. **-SMOTET** represents SMOTE + Tomeklinks. **-No processing** means taking no action in unbalance processing.

ensemble classifier with sentiment dictionary as features. **T-SD-VoC** slightly outperforms the best submission result RUB_MMC in NLPCC 2016 Evaluation Task. However, adding sentiment dictionary as features does not necessarily mean improving the performances. The F-scores with dictionary suffer from extreme instability. We argue the reason of this phenomenon is that some microblogs do not contain sentiment words or the orientation of the word is opposite to the stance of the author.

Then, we compare different unbalanced data processing methods in Fig. 4. We observe that in half of the result groups, the methods without unbalanced data processing perform better. Although in real world situation, the numbers of people who is in favor of and against a given target are usually quite different. In the NLPCC evaluation dataset, the numbers of microblogs in *Favor* and *Against* classes are almost equal. Therefore, we could not achieve the improvements in most cases as we expected using unbalanced processing methods.

Based on Table 3, we also conclude that feature selection method could help us to get better F-scores when using words in dictionary as additional features. Thus, we argue that sentiment dictionary brings us lots of useless features for stance detection task and feature selection can alleviate this embarrassing situation.

Finally, we compare different classifiers for stance detection as shown in Fig. 5. It is clear that the ensemble method based on voting strategy could achieve the best performance in all the result groups.

6.3 Experiment Results Based on Semi-supervised Learning

Furthermore, we conduct extensive the experiment based on semi-supervised machine learning methods as described in Sect. 5. The results are shown in Table 4.

Compared with Table 3, we can easily get that the F-scores in Table 4 are generally smaller. We think this is because the multiple iteration of the self-training process which depends heavily on the inaccurate results predicted by the classifiers. What makes things worse is the instability of the classifiers, which works badly in the supervised learning. This also explains why the ensemble classifier performs so badly in the semi-supervised learning.

Moreover, from Table 4 we can conclude that Naïve Bayes and the ensemble classifier suffer more from the inaccurate results and the instability of the classifiers. Although the ensemble classifier is affected by Naïve Bayes, which is an instability classifier, the performance shouldn't be so bad. We think it is because we randomly selected unlabeled dataset to combine with labeled data to update semi-classifier in self-training step instead of through comparing. This inversely proves it is a good idea that selecting a number of results with higher probability to update classifier in semi-supervised learning.

Table 4. Microblog stance classification results on the dataset. -T is TFIDF. **-SD** refers to sentiment dictionary. **-FS** represents Feature Selection. **-LC** means Linear SVM classifier. **-NBC** is Naive Bayes classifier. **-RFC** is Random Forest classifier. **-VoC** is Voting Classifier.-**SMOTE + Tlinks** represents SMOTE + Tomeklinks.

Experiment settings	Over-sampling	SMOTE	SMOTE1	SMOTE2	SMOTE+TLinks	No unbalanced processing
T-LC	0.6525	0.6509	0.6501	0.6534	0.6536	**0.6627**
T-NBC	0.4921	0.4899	0.4282	0.4966	0.5028	0.4194
T-RFC	0.6232	0.5927	0.6591	0.6017	0.6212	0.6096
T-VoC	0.3815	0.3824	0.3869	0.3947	0.3778	0.3614
T-FS-LC	0.6457	0.6514	0.6521	0.6510	0.6547	0.6524
T-FS-NBC	0.5015	0.516	0.4910	0.4603	0.4566	0.4147
T-FS-RFC	0.6360	0.6117	0.5987	0.6231	0.6333	0.6096
T-FS-VoC	0.3768	0.3596	0.3681	0.3648	0.3622	0.3655
T-SD-LC	0.5752	0.631	0.6502	0.6606	0.644	0.6341
T-SD-NBC	0.3284	0.3363	0.3284	0.3284	0	0.3284
T-SD-RFC	0.6274	0.6196	0.6044	0.6062	0.6028	0.6121
T-SD-VoC	0.3284	0.3284	0.3284	0.3284	0.3284	0.3284
T-SD-FS-LC	0.6447	0.4988	0.4931	0.6489	0.6205	0.6231
T-SD-FS-NBC	0.334	0.334	0.3366	0.337	0.3368	0.334
T-SD-FS-RFC	0.6133	0.6356	0.6169	0.6065	0.5839	0.6346
T-SD-FS-VoC	0.337	0.3342	0.331	0.3314	0.3314	0.3314

7 Conclusions and Future Work

In this paper, we detect the stances in microblogs based on supervised and semi-supervised learning methods respectively. The comprehensive empirical experiments are conducted on NLPCC 2016 Stance Detection Evaluation Task dataset. In this paper, we regard the stance detection in Chinese microblogs as a classification problem. We utilize TFIDF and sentiment dictionary to represent the microblogs as the sparse vectors and leverage SVM, Naive Bayes, Random Forest and the ensemble classifier to detect the stance in a supervised and a semi-supervised way. In semi-supervised learning, we introduce self-training where we take arithmetic progression as the method to select the number of unlabeled data to update this semi-supervised classifier.

Based on the experiment results, we observe that TFIDF and ensemble classifier are good combination for stance detection task. Taking arithmetic progression as a strategy for selecting unlabeled data in self-learning will make worse results due to multiple iteration in unstable and inaccurate predicted results, though this strategy could work in a time saving way.

For the future work, we are interested in using word2vec and other deep learning algorithms to further improve the performance of stance detection in Chinese microblog.

Acknowledgements. The work is supported by National Natural Science Foundation of China (61370074, 61402091), the Fundamental Research Funds for the Central Universities of China under Grant N140404012.

References

1. Thomas, M., Pang, B., Lee, L.: Get out the vote: determining support or opposition from congressional floor-debate transcripts. In: EMNLP, pp. 327–335 (2006)
2. Walker, M.A., Anand, P., Abbott, R., Grant, R.: Stance classification using dialogic properties of persuasion. In: HLT-NAACL, pp. 592–596 (2012)
3. Recasens, M., Danescu-Niculescu-Mizil, C., Jurafsky, D.: Linguistic models for analyzing and detecting biased language. In: ACL (1), pp. 1650–1659 (2013)
4. Somasundaran, S., Wiebe, J.: Recognizing stances in online debates. In: ACL-IJCNLP, pp. 226–234 (2009)
5. Murakami, A., Raymond, R.: Support or oppose? Classifying positions in online debates from reply activities and opinion expressions. In: COLING (Posters), pp. 869–875 (2010)
6. Millen, D.R., Fontaine, M.A.: Multi-team facilitation of very large-scale distributed meetings. In: ECSCW, pp. 259–275 (2003)
7. Abbott, R., Walker, M., Anand, P., Tree, J.E.F., Bowmani, R., King, J.: How can you say such things?!?: recognizing disagreement in informal political argument. In: The Workshop on Languages in Social Media, 8 (2011)
8. Wang, Y., Rosé, C.P.: Making conversational structure explicit: identification of initiation-response pairs within online discussions. In: HLT-NAACL, pp. 673–676 (2010)
9. Faulkner, A.: Automated classification of stance in student essays: an approach using stance target information and the wikipedia link-based measure. In: FLAIRS (2014)

10. Sobhani, P., Inkpen, D., Matwin, S.: From argumentation mining to stance classification. In: The Workshop on Argumentation Mining (2015)
11. Rajadesingan, A., Liu, H.: Identifying users with opposing opinions in Twitter debates. In: Kennedy, W.G., Agarwal, N., Yang, S.J. (eds.) SBP 2014. LNCS, vol. 8393, pp. 153–160. Springer, Heidelberg (2014). doi:10.1007/978-3-319-05579-4_19
12. Chawla, N.V., Bowyer, K.W., Hall, L.O., Kegelmeyer, W.P.: SMOTE: synthetic minority over-sampling technique. J. Artif. Intell. Res. **16**(1), 321–357 (2002)
13. Han, H., Wang, W.-Y., Mao, B.-H.: Borderline-SMOTE: a new over-sampling method in imbalanced data sets learning. In: Huang, D.-S., Zhang, X.-P., Huang, G.-B. (eds.) ICIC 2005. LNCS, vol. 3644, pp. 878–887. Springer, Heidelberg (2005). doi:10.1007/11538059_91
14. Batista, G.E.A.P.A., Bazzan, A.L.C., Monard, M.C.: Balancing training data for automated annotation of keywords: a case study. In: WOB, pp. 10–18 (2003)

Combining Word Embedding and Semantic Lexicon for Chinese Word Similarity Computation

Jiahuan Pei[1], Cong Zhang[1], Degen Huang[1(✉)], and Jianjun Ma[2]

[1] School of Computer Science and Technology, Dalian University of Technology,
Dalian 116024, Liaoning, China
{p_sunrise,cccaaag}@mail.dlut.edu.cn, huangdg@dlut.edu.cn
[2] School of Foreign Languages, Dalian University of Technology, Dalian 116024,
Liaoning, China
majian@dlut.edu.cn

Abstract. Large corpus-based embedding methods have received increasing attention for their flexibility and effectiveness in many NLP tasks including Word Similarity (WS). However, these approaches rely on high-quality corpora and neglect the human's intelligence contained in semantic resources such as Tongyici Cilin and Hownet. This paper proposes a novel framework for measuring the Chinese word similarity by combining word embedding and Tongyici Cilin. We also utilize retrieval techniques to extend the contexts of word pairs and calculate the similarity scores to weakly supervise the selection of a better result. In the Chinese Lexical Similarity Computation (CLSC) shared task, we rank No. 2 with the result of 0.457/0.455 of Spearman/Pearson rank correlation coefficient. After the submission, we boost the embedding model by merging an English model into the Chinese one and learning the co-occurrence sequence via LSTM networks. Our final results are 0.541/0.514, which outperform the state-of-the-art performance to the best of our knowledge.

Keywords: Chinese word similarity · Word embedding · Semantic lexicon · LSTM networks

1 Introduction

Word similarity is a task of measuring the lexical similarity degree between word pairs, which has attracted much attention as a fundamental research in many NLP tasks. To date, numerous approaches have been proposed for computing lexical similarity, which can be briefly categorized into thesaurus-based methods [1], traditional corpus-based methods [2] and corpus-based embedding methods [3–6].

Typically, thesaurus-based strategies mainly rely on manual semantic resources and define the degree of similarities based on the distance between

© Springer International Publishing AG 2016
C.-Y. Lin et al. (Eds.): NLPCC-ICCPOL 2016, LNAI 10102, pp. 766–777, 2016.
DOI: 10.1007/978-3-319-50496-4_69

the two items in the structural semantic thesaurus, including Tongyici Cilin [1,7], Hownet [8,9] and Wordnet [10,11]. These semantic measures, while interpretable and effective, have the disadvantage that the computation only affects the pairs when both members are presented in the lexicons. Therefore, corpus-based methods tend to be more attractive to predict unknown words, especially the hot embedding approaches, such as skip-gram model [3–5] and GloVe model [6], which use the degree of replaceability between words to measure the similarity and prevent the learning process from *Data Sparsity* problem in the traditional corpus-based means.

However, limited to the *distributional hypothesis*, which assumes that similar words occur in similar context [12], basic embedding methods generally have three drawbacks in nature. Firstly, they can hardly distinguish *semantic similarity* from *conceptual association* [13]. For instance, the words in the pair (残疾/disability, 死亡/death, score = 2.8) may be regarded as similar by mistake because they can both occur in the X position of contexts like "An illness resulted in his X". Second, solely embedding technique cannot capture the differences between synonyms and antonyms [22]. For example, the words in (积极/positive, 消极/negative, score = 4.1) have a cosine similarity of approximately 0.76 in the *pre-train word2vec model* released by Mikolov et al. [3]. At last, context-dependent embedding methods are unable to differentiate distinct senses of a word [14]. One example of polysemy phenomenon is the pair (包袱/baggage; jokes in the crosstalk, 段子/joke, score = 2.6). To be specific, if the word "包袱" is assigned as the most direct meaning of "baggage", the two words are most probably unsimilar, but the other meaning "jokes in the crosstalk" draws the distance closer. In addition, for Chinese language, the challenge is also due to the lack of contexts for the single-character word in such pair as (面/face; noddles, 首/head, score = 4.7), because it is a rare utterance in general texts. Therefore, the drawbacks arouse people's recent interest in integrating lexicons into word embeddings to capture multiple semantics [15–19,23].

In this paper, we present a framework that combines word embedding and semantic lexicon for Chinese word similarity computation by simple but meaningful linear combination, which initially comes from the basic question that how does a person evaluate the similarity between a pair of words: He may search words in his knowledge base and compute a similarity score based on the distance between the two lexical items. Simultaneously, he will retrieve the words in search engines to find out the sentences containing these words and then estimate the score via the similarity of the contexts. At last, he may give the final result after balancing the previous two results. To demonstrate the performance, we participated in the Chinese Lexical Similarity Computation (CLSC) shared task [20], which provides a benchmark dataset to evaluate and compare different lexical similarity methods.

2 Methodology

Figure 1 briefly illustrates the general architecture of our Chinese word similarity computation system.

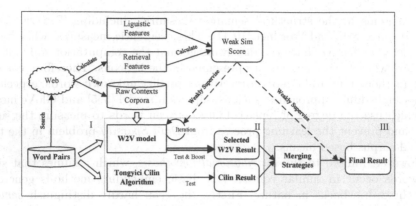

Fig. 1. The general architecture of Chinese word similarity computation

2.1 Similarity Computation Based on Tongyici Cilin

The *Cilin* model utilized in this paper is developed from the algorithm proposed in reference [1], which fully exploits the coding and structure information to estimate both similarity and relevance between the words.

The cilin dictionary is organized by a 5-layer hierarchical structure. Correspondingly, it supplies 5-layer patterns to generate coding for a group of words, which are joined by relationships like "synonym" or "relevance". For instance, the words in the pair (紫禁城/the Forbidden City, 故宫/the Imperial Palace, score = 10) are coded in the items "Bn23A03# 正殿...金銮殿 紫禁城" and "Bn23A02# 行宫 东宫...爱丽舍宫 故宫" respectively. Figure 2 shows the two example words represented in cilin's hierarchical structure.

Given two words w_a and w_b, let set $C_a = \{c_a^1, c_a^2, \ldots, c_a^A\}$ and $C_b = \{c_b^1, c_b^2, \ldots, c_b^B\}$ be concepts of w_a and w_b respectively. Set $\Lambda = \{\lambda_1, \lambda_2 \ldots, \lambda_6\} = \{0.65, 0.8, 0.9, 0.96, 0.5, 0.1\}$ denotes the parameters in the computation. The similarity between w_a and w_b can be computed as maximum value of every "sense" in set C_a and C_b respectively, which is denoted as:

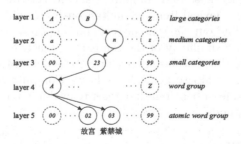

Fig. 2. The words "紫禁城" and "故宫" in the 5-layer hierarchical structure

$$SIM_{cilin}(w_a, w_b) = \max_{1 \leqslant i \leqslant A; 1 \leqslant j \leqslant B} \{sim(c_a^i, c_b^j)\} \tag{1}$$

where function $sim(c_a^i, c_b^j)$ defines the concept similarity between sense c_a^i and c_b^j as:

$$sim(c_a^i, c_b^j) = \begin{cases} 1.0, \ if \ code(c_a^i) = code(c_b^j) \ \& \ end \ with \ "=" \\ \lambda_5, \ elif \ code(c_a^i) = code(c_b^j) \ \& \ end \ with \ "\#" \\ \lambda_6, \ elif \ c_a^i, c_b^j \ not \ in \ the \ same \ tree \\ \lambda_{l-1} \times cos(n_{l-1} \times \frac{\pi}{180}) \times (\frac{n_{l-1}-k+1}{n_{l-1}}), \ else \end{cases} \tag{2}$$

where $l = 2, 3, 4, 5$ and it represents the number of layer in a hierarchical tree, n_{l-1} denotes the number of nodes in the branch layer l, k is the distance between two branches.

SIM_{cilin} is represented as a real number in domain [0,1]. Therefore, we transform original domain [0,1] into [1,10] via a simple linear function $f(x) = 9x + 1$.

2.2 Similarity Computation Based on Embedding Vectors

We introduce a general approach for improving word embeddings by weakly supervising the learning process with the *weak similarity score* (WSS), which is generated from some similarity-related retrieval statistics and linguistic features. We begin with reviewing the basic skip-gram model and then present our boosting method.

The Skip-Gram Model. The skip-gram model is a learning framework to learn continuous word vectors from text corpora [3,4]. It maps each word in the vocabulary into a continuous vector space by the method of looking up the embedding matrix $W^{(1)}$. $W^{(1)}$ is learned through maximizing the prediction probability of its neighbouring words within a context window, and the prediction probability is calculated using another embedding matrix $W^{(2)}$. For a sequence of training data: $w_1, w_2, \ldots, w_N$, this model aims at maximizing the following objective function:

$$Q = \frac{1}{N} \sum_{n=1}^{N} \sum_{-c \leq j \leq c, j \neq 0} \log p(w_{n+j}|w_n) \tag{3}$$

where N represents the number of words, c is the size of context windows, w_n denotes the input central word and w_{n+j} stands for its neighbouring word and the conditional probability $p(w_{n+j}|w_n)$ is defined as:

$$p(w_{n+j}|w_n) = \frac{\exp(\mathbf{w}_{n+j}^{(2)} \cdot \mathbf{w}_t^{(1)})}{\sum_{k=1}^{V} \exp(\mathbf{w}_k^{(2)} \cdot \mathbf{w}_t^{(1)})} \tag{4}$$

where $\mathbf{w}_n^{(1)}$ and $\mathbf{w}_k^{(2)}$ denote row vectors in matrices $W^{(1)}$ and $W^{(2)}$, corresponding to word w_n and w_k respectively.

Our Improved Model. The basic unsupervised skip-gram model can produce impressive results depending on the large contexts corpora. However, unsupervised learning may not be suitable for the task of interest as Yu and Dredze [21] stated. Therefore, they incorporate prior knowledge by supervised learning. But supervised learning highly relies on tagged resources. To avoid this limitation, we use weak supervising method in this paper, by which the automatically computed WSS can reflect the similarity between the word pair to some degree with the hypothesis – Not only the contexts of the words, but also similarity-related retrieval statistics and linguistic features can reflect the degree of the word similarity. So far, our objective function can be denoted as:

$$J = \max_{1 \leqslant iter \leqslant I} \{\Phi_{iter}(\overrightarrow{S_{pred}}, \overrightarrow{S_{wss}})\} \tag{5}$$

where $\overrightarrow{S_{pred}}$ is the sequence of prediction similarity scores of the word pairs, $\overrightarrow{S_{wss}}$ is the sequence of WSS scores, Φ is a task specific function like Spearman or Pearson index detailed in Sect. 4.1, and I is the maximum number of iterations. In each iteration, a new W2V model is trained and evaluated by the function J. And the model with highest performance is selected to be used in the merging stage.

As cosine similarity, which is used to measure the similarity degree in W2V, between vectors ranges from -1 to 1, we transform original domain $[0, 1]$ into $[1, 10]$ via a simple function $g(x)$ as:

$$g(x) = \begin{cases} 1, & x \leqslant 0 \\ 9x + 1, & x > 0 \end{cases} \tag{6}$$

Computation of WSS. We use 4 kinds of web features [24], including web-jaccard, web-overlap, web-dice, web-pmi and 3 kinds of linguistic features, pinyin-similarity, sequence-similarity and pattern-similarity to compute the value of WSS.

We use the notation P and Q to denote the 2 words in a word pair, $H(P)$ to denote the result counts for the query P in a search engine, $P \cap Q$ to denote the conjunction query P and Q. The retrieval statistics web-jaccard, web-overlap, web-dice and web-pmi can be defined as Eqs. 7–10:

$$web - jaccard(P \cap Q) = \begin{cases} 0, & H(P \cap Q) < c \\ \frac{H(P \cap Q)}{H(P)+H(Q)-H(P \cap Q)}, & H(P \cap Q) \geq c \end{cases} \tag{7}$$

$$web - overlap(P \cap Q) = \begin{cases} 0, & H(P \cap Q) < c \\ \frac{H(P \cap Q)}{min(H(P),H(Q))}, & H(P \cap Q) \geq c \end{cases} \tag{8}$$

$$web - dice(P \cap Q) = \begin{cases} 0, & 2H(P \cap Q) < c \\ \frac{H(P \cap Q)}{H(P)+H(Q)}, & H(P \cap Q) \geq c \end{cases} \tag{9}$$

$$web - pmi(P \cap Q) = \begin{cases} 0, & H(P \cap Q) < c \\ \log(\frac{\frac{H(P \cap Q)}{N}}{\frac{H(P)}{N}\frac{H(Q)}{N}}), & H(P \cap Q) \geq c \end{cases} \qquad (10)$$

where N stands for the number of documents indexed by the search engine. In the present work, we set $N = 10^{16}$.

Pinyin similarity is a feature which measures the similarity between Pinyin representations of 2 words, and it is defined as:

$$S_{py} = \frac{2n_{ps}}{L_{pp} + L_{pq}} \qquad (11)$$

where n_{ps} stands for the count of same character combinations in the representations of P and Q in Pinyin. L_{pp} and L_{pq} denote the length of the 2 Pinyin sequence. For example, the Pinyin representations of Chinese words (必须, 必需, score = 7.3) are (bi xu, bi xu), so the pinyin similarity between them is $(2 * 2)/(2 + 2) = 1.0$, which infers a high similarity in terms of pronunciation.

Sequence-similarity is a feature which measures the similarity between 2 Chinese words in the inspect of Chinese character sequences, and it is defined as:

$$S_s = \frac{2n_{sa}}{L_p + L_q} \qquad (12)$$

where n_{sa} stands for the count of same Chinese character at the same relative position in P and Q. L_p and L_q denote the length of the 2 words. For instance, the sequence similarity between "阿拉伯" and "阿拉伯人" is $(2 * 3)/(3 + 4) = 0.857$.

Pattern-similarity is a feature which measures the similarity between 2 Chinese words in the aspect of similar Chinese characters, and it is defined as:

$$S_{pa} = \frac{2n_{si}}{L_p + L_q} \qquad (13)$$

where n_{si} stands for the count of similar Chinese character in P and Q. Similar characters are judged by a similar-characters-dictionary. L_p and L_q denote the length of the 2 words. Taking the words "生命" and "性命" as an example, the Chinese character "生" and "性" are similar to each other, so the pattern similarity is $(2 * 2)/(2 + 2) = 1.0$, which indicates a high similarity from the perspective of word types.

As all the 7 features range in domain $[0, 1]$, we map each of them into $[1, 10]$ and compute their weighted average as the weak similarity score.

2.3 Combination Strategies

We utilize 6 strategies to merge the best results of Cilin and W2V model for the submission to CLSC task. For each similarity score in the two results, we calculate a merged score according to the merging strategy. We use the notation S_c and S_v to denote the scores in the two results respectively, and S_m to denote the merged score. The 6 merging strategies are defined as:

– Max:
$$S_m = max\{S_c, S_v\} \tag{14}$$

– Min:
$$S_m = min\{S_c, S_v\} \tag{15}$$

– Replace 1:
$$S_m = \begin{cases} S_c, & S_c \neq 1 \\ S_v, & S_c = 1 \end{cases} \tag{16}$$

– Replace 1 and 10:
$$S_m = \begin{cases} S_c, & S_c \neq 1, S_c \neq 10 \\ S_v, & S_c = 1 \; or \; S_c = 10 \end{cases} \tag{17}$$

– Arithmetic Mean:
$$S_m = \frac{S_c + S_v}{2} \tag{18}$$

– Geometric Mean:
$$S_m = \sqrt{S_c * S_v} \tag{19}$$

2.4   A-Posteriori Improvements

Boosting Embedding Model by Machine Translation. The *pre-train word2vec model*, which is trained on part of Google News dataset with 300-dimensional vectors for 3 million words and phrases, is adopted to improve our W2V model. Firstly, the Chinese words are translated into English words or phrases via Google Translation. Then, spelling checking and length filtering are utilized to guarantee the correctness of the translated texts. Finally, the embedding vectors of the remaining translated words, which are searched in the English model, are adopted to replace the corresponding vectors in the Chinese model.

Refitting by Sequence Learning via LSTM Networks. In the previous work, we train the W2V model with the paragraphs where the words occur. However, the contexts where the pair of words co-occur may reflect their relationship as well. For instance, the pair of words (孤单, 寂寞, score = 8.1) occur in the coordinate structure of texts like "寂寞和孤单的区别是什么" are more likely to be comparable. To refit W2V model based on this association, Long Short Term Memory (LSTM) networks are employed to perform similarity analysis for sentences that target words co-occurrence. For each sample sequence, the vector of each word is jointed by a 300-dimension word vector and a 300-dimension distance vector, which represents the distance between the current word and the 2 target words, the input tag is the round number of the word-pair's similarity and the final similarity score is the *mathematical expectation* of all probable prediction scores by the LSTM model.

3 Experiment Settings

3.1 Data Set

The proposed approach is evaluated on the dataset released by NLPCC-ICCPOL 2016 CLSC shared task [20]. The dataset contains 40 sample data and 500 test word pairs with their similarity scores, which are properly balanced in terms of the different factors including *Domain, Frequency, POS Tags, Word length* and *Senses*. The similarity score between the two words ranges from 1 to 10, and the higher the score is, the more similar the 2 words are.

3.2 Evaluation

The performance in our experiments is evaluated by the Spearman (ρ) and Pearson (r) rank correlation coefficient, which are widely used to test the consistency between automatic predicting results and the golden human labelled data. The Spearman correlation coefficient (ρ) is defined as:

$$\rho = 1 - \frac{6 \sum_{i=1}^{n} (R_{Xi} - R_{Yi})^2}{n(n^2 - 1)} \tag{20}$$

where R_{X_i} and R_{Y_i} are the standard deviations of the rank variables, which are converted from the raw scores X_i and Y_i, and n is the size of observations.

The Pearson correlation coefficient (r) is shown as:

$$r = \frac{\sum_{i=1}^{n} (X_i - \bar{X})(Y_i - \bar{Y})}{\sqrt{\sum_{i=1}^{n} (X_i - \bar{X})^2} \sqrt{\sum_{i=1}^{n} (Y_i - \bar{Y})^2}} \tag{21}$$

where X_i and Y_i are the raw score, $\bar{X}$ and $\bar{Y}$ are the mean value respectively, and n is the number of sample data.

In our experiment, we regard the Spearman ρ as the main index and the Pearson r as the second important index for evaluation. Limitation of space, all the resource utilized in this paper are listed at https://github.com/JiahuanPei/NLPCC-2016-CLSC.

4 Results and Analysis

4.1 Results of Submission

Table 1 shows the results of W2V models trained with 8 groups of different corpora, where ρ represents the Spearman ρ between the result and the golden score, and ρ' denotes that between the result and WSS, which is the main index used for weak supervision; r is the Pearson r between the result and the golden score, and r' stands for that between the result and WSS. For each W2V result, we train the W2V model under the weak supervision of WSS and choose the best one within 50 iterations.

Table 1. Results of W2V models based on different corpora

No.	Corpora	ρ	r	ρ'	r'
1	Xieso (62M)	0.205	0.203	0.249	0.230
2	Datatang (199M)	0.267	0.272	0.337	0.343
3	News (381M)	0.311	0.305	0.317	0.277
4	News + Xieso	**0.311**	**0.311**	**0.359**	**0.310**
5	Wiki (1.1G)	0.211	0.213	0.324	0.343
6	News + Xieso + Wiki	0.178	0.197	0.221	0.220
7	News + Xieso + Datatang	0.174	0.190	0.211	0.207
8	News + Xieso + DataTang + Wiki	0.214	0.239	0.314	0.308

As is shown in Table 1, both quantity and quality of corpora have a significant effect on performance of W2V model. Comparing the results No. 1–4 of corpora with different scale, we can see that larger quantity of corpora may enrich more contexts to improve the performance. To be specific, No. 4 achieves a ρ value of 0.311 and r value of 0.311, which performs 0.106 and 0.108 higher than No. 1. However, the larger scale does not absolutely mean the higher performance (See No. 5–8), we infer that the quality of the corpora leads to these phenomena. Specifically, there are some paragraphs offending against the rules of grammar in the Datatang and Wiki corpus. Finally, the approach No. 4 is selected as the best W2V model in this step.

Table 2 shows the comparison between the original and weakly supervised W2V models. The original model could be any W2V model which is generated randomly at one iteration. The weakly supervised model is the best one in all 50 iterations, which also illustrated in Table 1.

Table 2. Comparison between the original and weakly supervised W2V models

No.	Strategy	ρ	r	ρ'	r'
1	Original W2V	0.296	0.241	0.330	0.262
2	Weakly supervised W2V	**0.311**	**0.311**	**0.359**	**0.310**

Table 3 shows the results of 6 merging strategies, where the symbols ρ, ρ', r, r' share the same meanings with those of Table 1. According to Table 3, different merging strategies can greatly affect the final result. Given No. 5 achieves the best ρ' value of 0.335 and r' value of 0.306, which outperforms other results by weak supervision, No. 5 is selected with the 0.457/0.455 value of ρ and r. Although the results No. 4 and No. 6 perform better than No. 5 in terms of ρ and r, the results No. 1–3 can be remarkably differentiated from the results No. 4–6, which indicates that the weak supervision method can distinguish the good results from the bad ones.

Table 3. Merging results based on 6 strategies

No.	Strategy	ρ	r	ρ'	r'
1	Replace 1 and 10	0.104	0.090	0.096	0.074
2	Replace 1	0.457	0.446	0.258	0.223
3	Min	0.301	0.314	0.288	0.296
4	Max	0.469	0.464	0.290	0.254
5	Arithmetic mean	<u>0.457</u>	<u>0.455</u>	**0.335**	**0.306**
6	Geometric mean	**0.478**	**0.468**	0.326	0.285

Table 4 shows the comparison between the 2 single models and the best merging model. The result No. 3 achieves the 0.457/0.455 value of ρ/r, which performs 0.146 (47%) and 0.144 (46%) higher than No. 2. It illustrates the effectiveness of the merging approaches and is submitted as our final result to CLSC task.

Table 4. Comparison between single and merging models

No.	Strategy	ρ	r
1	Cilin	0.405	0.393
2	W2V	0.311	0.311
3	Cilin + W2V	**0.457**	**0.455**

4.2 Result of Improvement

Table 5 indicates the effectiveness of machine translation and sequence learning via LSTMs network, where the result of the best merging model is regarded as the baseline. Specifically, the result No. 3 achieves the 0.541/0.514 value of ρ/r, which performs 0.146 (47%) and 0.144 (46%) higher than baseline.

Table 5. Result of improvement by translation and LSTM networks

No.	Strategy	ρ	r
1	Baseline	0.457	0.455
2	Baseline + Translation	0.531	0.476
3	Baseline + Translation + LSTM	**0.541**	**0.514**

5 Conclusion

This paper proposes a novel framework for the CLSC task. In the final framework, our boosting tricks are as follows: (1) Utilizing Tongyici Cilin to compute the dictionary-based similarity scores and extend the corpora for corpus-based word embedding. (2) Using semantic similarity scores generated from retrieval statics and manual features to weakly supervise the model selection process. (3) Leveraging translation technique to improve the Chinese embedding model with an English model, which also reduce the effect of contexts shortage for Chinese single-character word. (4) Adopting similarity calculated by retrieval information to weakly supervise the skip-gram model. (5) Applying LSTM networks to build language model for the words co-occurrence sentences and return the embedding vectors in this process. The experiments on the CLSC shared task have demonstrated the effectiveness of our approach: we rank No. 2 with the result of 0.457/0.455 of Spearman ρ/Pearson r by merging the result of Cilin model and W2V model, where the W2V model is weakly supervised using scores generated from retrieval information and manual features. In our posteriori improvements after the submission, we strengthen the W2V model by merging an English model and refitting the word vectors through LSTM networks. Finally, we get a final result of 0.541/0.514 of Spearman ρ/Pearson r, which outperforms the state-of-the-art performance to the best of our knowledge.

Acknowledgements. This research is supported by National Natural Science Foundation of China (Nos. 61672127, 61173100) and National Social Science Foundation of China (No. 15BYY175). We also wish to thank NVIDIA Corporation for their donation of Tesla K40c GPU device.

References

1. Tian, J.L., Zhao, W.: Words similarity algorithm based on Tongyici Cilin in semantic web adaptive learning system. J. Jilin Univ. (Inf. Sci. Edn.) **28**(6), 602–608 (2010)
2. Zhao, J., Hu, S.Z., Fan, X.H.: Word similarity computation based on word link distribution. J. Chongqing Univ. Posts Telecommun. (Nat. Sci. Edn.) **4**, 021 (2009)
3. Mikolov, T., Chen, K., Corrado, G., Dean, J.: Efficient estimation of word representations in vector space. In: Proceedings of Workshop at ICLR (2013a)
4. Mikolov, T., Sutskever, I., et al.: Distributed representations of words and phrases and their compositionality. In: Proceedings of NIPS, pp. 3111–3119 (2013b)
5. Levy, O., Goldberg, Y.: Neural word embedding as implicit matrix factorization. In: Advances in Neural Information Processing Systems, pp. 2177–2185 (2014)
6. Pennington, J., Socher, R., Manning, C.D.: Glove: global vectors for word representation. In: Proceedings of EMNLP 2014, pp. 1532–1543 (2014)
7. Mei, J.J., Zhu, Y.M., et al.: Tongyici Cilin. Shanghai Lexicon Publishing Company, Shanghai (1983)
8. Dong, Z., Dong, Q.: HowNet and the Computation of Meaning, pp. 85–95. World Scientific, Singapore (2006)
9. Liu, Q., Li, S.: Word similarity computing based on How-Net. Comput. Linguist. Chin. Lang. Process. **7**(2), 59–76 (2002)

10. Wu, S.Y., Wu, Y.Y.: Chinese and English word similarity measure based on Chinese WordNet. J. Zhengzhou Univ. (Nat. Sci. Edn.) **42**(2), 66–69 (2010)
11. Ahsaee, M.G., Naghibzadeh, M., Naeini, S.E.Y.: Semantic similarity assessment of words using weighted WordNet. Int. J. Mach. Learn. Cybernet. **5**(3), 479–490 (2014)
12. Turney, P.D., Pantel, P.: From frequency to meaning: vector space models of semantics. J. Artif. Intell. Res. **37**(1), 141–188 (2010)
13. Hill, F., Reichart, R., Korhonen, A.: Simlex-999: evaluating semantic models with (genuine) similarity estimation. Comput. Linguist. **41**(4), 665–695 (2015)
14. Iacobacci, I., Pilehvar, M.T., Navigli, R.: SensEmbed: learning sense embeddings for word and relational similarity. In: Proceedings of ACL, pp. 95–105 (2015)
15. Mrkšić, N., Séaghdha, D.Ó, et al.: Counter-fitting word vectors to linguistic constraints (2016). arXiv preprint arXiv:1603.00892
16. Nguyen, K.A., Walde, S.S.I., Vu, N.T.: Integrating distributional lexical contrast into word embeddings for antonym-synonym distinction (2016). arXiv preprint arXiv:1605.07766
17. Chen, Z., Lin, W., et al.: Revisiting word embedding for contrasting meaning. In: Proceedings of ACL, pp. 106–115 (2015)
18. Rothe, S., Schütze, H.: AutoExtend: extending word embeddings to embeddings for synsets and lexemes. In: Proceedings of ACL-IJNLP, pp. 1793–1803 (2015)
19. Faruqui, M., Dodge, J., et al.: Retrofitting word vectors to semantic lexicons. In: Proceedings of NAACL (2015)
20. Wu, Y.F., Li, W.: NLPCC-ICCPOL 2016 shared task 3: Chinese word similarity measurement. In: Proceddings of NLPCC 2016 (2016)
21. Yu, M., Dredze, M.: Improving lexical embeddings with semantic knowledge. In: Proceedings of ACL, pp. 545–550 (2014)
22. Ono, M., Miwa, M., Sasaki, Y.: Word embedding-based antonym detection using thesauri and distributional information. In: Proceedings of NAACL (2015)
23. Liu, Q., Jiang, H., et al.: Learning semantic word embeddings based on ordinal knowledge constraints. In: Proceedings of ACL-IJCNLP, pp. 1501–1511 (2015)
24. Bollegala, D., Matsuo, Y., Ishizuka, M.: Measuring semantic similarity between words using web search engines. In: WWW, vol. 7, pp. 757–766 (2007)

Football News Generation from Chinese Live Webcast Script

Tang Renjun[1,2], Zhang Ke[1,2], Na Shenruoyang[1],
Yang Minghao[1,3(✉)], Zhou Hui[1,2], Zhu Qingjie[1,2], Zhan Yongsong[2],
and Tao Jianhua[1,3,4]

[1] National Laboratory of Pattern Recognition, Institute of Automation,
Chinese Academy of Sciences, Beijing, China
531415551@qq.com
[2] Guangxi Key Laboratory of Trusted Software, Guilin University of Electronic
Technology, Guilin, China
[3] CAS Center for Excellence in Brain Science and Intelligence Technology,
Institute of Automation, Chinese Academy of Sciences, Beijing, China
[4] School of Computer and Control Engineering, University of Chinese Academy
of Sciences, Beijing, China

Abstract. Challenges exist in the field of sports news generation automatically
from webcast that (1) finding hot events and sentences accurately; (2) organizing
the selected sentences with highly readability. This paper proposes a framework
to generate sports news automatically. First, to obtain accurate hot events and
sentences, we design a neural network to predict the probabilities that each
statement in live webcast script appears in the writing news, where the inputs of
the neural network are weighed word vectors obtained from football keywords
dictionary, and the outputs the similarity of statements in training live webcast
script and sentences in training news. In this way, the "good" sentences selected
from webcast contribute to the semi-finished sport news. To make the generated
news to be possibly similar to human writing, we adopt idioms often appeared in
football game to describe or summarize the games' development or turns
between the selected sentences, and come into being the final sport news. The
proposed framework are validated on the training and test data set proved by
"Sports News Generation from Live Webcast scripts" task of NLPCC 2016, the
experiments show that the proposed method present good performance.

Keywords: Football news generation · Neural network · Live webcast script

1 Introduction

Football news always are written by football news journalist after the game. So it is
necessary for a journalist to record the key events happened in the match. However, it
is inefficient to spend time on writing the report after the game. How to write and
publish football news immediately became a challenge for journalist and media website. Fortunately, many Chinese media provides football game live webcast script on
the websites. It is possible to generate a football news by using the live webcast script
and automatic summary technique.

© Springer International Publishing AG 2016
C.-Y. Lin et al. (Eds.): NLPCC-ICCPOL 2016, LNAI 10102, pp. 778–789, 2016.
DOI: 10.1007/978-3-319-50496-4_70

To generate a Chinese football news automatically, two problems should be solved: (1) extract appropriate information from the live webcast script and (2) improve the readability of the generated news. To solve the first problem, we applied keyword weight to evaluate the important of the sentences in the script, because a particular football game can be described through some important sentences. Furthermore, a football related keywords dictionary and a neural network are established to improve the performance of the information extraction. As for the second problem, we introduced a correlation sentence detection method to improve the description of the football news. Besides that, several event recognition methods and preinstall templates are designed to enhance the readability of the whole football news.

According to the experiment part and conclusion part in this paper, our system obtains quite well results in ROUGE evaluation and artificial scoring. Our system can be applied to generate Chinese football news from live webcast scripts. Due to the improvement we made, the generated news is able to descript the football game correctly and vividly. With the help of our system, journalists will be liberated from the repeated and heavy works.

2 Related Work

Recently years, news generation and automatic writing have made good progress in fields such as economy, finance, opening speech and so on [1, 2]. For example, Dixon implemented a financial news generation system which generates financial news automatically. Automated Insights, an American company, writes prose narrative of 150–300 words automatically according to the data of Zacks Investment Research [3]. A group from Capital Normal University implemented automatic writing of opening speech by their Chinese intelligent authoring system. The mentioned systems reflected the latest research progress of news generation and automatic writing. However, sports news generation is still a challenge for researchers in the field of Natural Language Processing.

Heretofore, automatic summarization technology has been developed for a long time, and is widely applied in generating news [4]. Two main methods are employed in this area, which are extraction method and generation method.

Generation method is mainly based on natural language understanding. It focuses on analyzing the grammar and meaning of the text. It uses the information fusion method to generate the summary. Comparing to generation method, extraction method is much simpler and easier for practical application. Extraction method tries to divide the original text into small units, and each unit is given a weight. Extraction method follows some rules to select the most important units and assemble them into summarization text. There are some famous automatic summarization systems in the world, such as *NeATS* [5, 6], *NewsBlaster* [7] and *NewsInEssence* [8]. In China, Tencent has developed an automatic summarization system called dreamwriter, which published financial news in September 2015.[1] As for the field of sports, an automated storytelling system called

---

[1] http://js.qq.com/a/20150911/016002.htm.

Heliograf is used by Washington Post for reporting the 2016 Rio Olympics. So far, it can only generated several short sentences about the key information.[2]

Our task for generating sports news report is similar to single document summary. Our method combines the advantages of these two methods, and we also make improvements on them. We adopt the concepts of extraction method to build the main structure of the news, which is easy to be realized. Furthermore, the generation method is applied to improving the readability of the news.

3   Sports News Generation

The proposed method consists of four steps: keyword processing, sentence selection, paragraphs writing and report refinement. On the first two steps, we focus on extracting information from webcast script accurately. As for the other two steps, our target is to improve the readability of the generated news (Fig. 1).

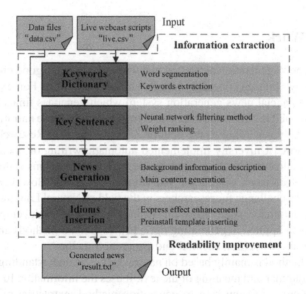

Fig. 1. Framework of the proposed method

3.1   Keywords Dictionary

This part mainly introduces the solutions for establishing keywords dictionary. In order to obtain the keywords, the words must be segmented in Chinese sentences first [9]. To ensure the football player names and team names are segmented correctly. We collect

---

[2] https://www.washingtonpost.com/pr/wp/2016/08/05/the-washington-post-experiments-with-automated-storytelling-to-help-power-2016-rio-olympics-coverage/.

plenty of data of proper names and the corresponding part-of-speech (POS) tags to enrich the word segmentation dictionary.

To evaluate the importance of keywords, Term Frequence-Inverse Document Frequency (TF-IDF) method was used to calculate words weight. TF-IDF is a statistical method which tends to filter common words and reserve important keywords. The weights are obtained from the following formula:

$$W_{i,j} = TF_{i,j} \times IDF_i = \frac{n_i}{\sum_k n_{k,j}} \times \log \frac{|d|}{|1 + \sum\{j|T_i \in D_j\}|}$$

In this formula, $W_{i,j}$ is the weight value of word T_i in document D_j. n_i is the sum of T_i, $\sum_k n_{k,j}$ is the total number of words in D_j. d means the total number of documents in corpus, $\sum\{j|T_i \in D_j\}$ means the sum of the document which contain T_i.

We extract the top 30 keywords from each reference news, then reserve verbs and football-specific words, which remove unrelated word and meaningless single-character word.

$$L = \{word_i|pos_i \in \{verb, noun\}\}$$

L is the extracted keywords dictionary. In this dictionary, the POS tag of word is verb or noun. However, the words such as red card, injury and own goal appear in low frequency. But these words are also important for football news. Therefore, these words are added to the keywords dictionary particularly. The weights of these words are set at the maximum value. Part of keywords dictionary is shown in the table below.

Table 1. Part of keywords dictionary

Word	Part of speech	Frequency	Weighting
起脚	v	18	0.5
绝杀	v	12	1.0
门框	n	43	0.5

3.2 Key Sentences

On sentence level, our work concentrates on calculating the importance of live webcast sentence. Two methods are employed to extract key sentences. One is basing on keyword weights, the other is neural network filtering method.

Sentence Weight Calculation

The importance of sentence depends on how many keywords it contains. Basically, sentence weight is the algebra sum of the weights of each word. The weight of the sentence is calculated as following:

$$W_{sentence} = \sum_k w_k, w_k \in sentence$$

w_k stands for the weight of k th word in sentence. Finally, key sentences are selected by weight ranking. Sentences of high weight usually descript an important event in football news.

Good Sentences Selected by Neural Network

However, it is unreliable to extract sentences or information only by weight ranking method. Therefore we try to train a neural network model to decide whether the sentence is the description of events which often appear in football news. Each sentence is a sequence of words, and the word embedding method is applied to represent the words in vector. The vectors of words are used to represent the sentence vector.

$$V_{sentence} = (V_{W_1}, V_{W_2}, \ldots, V_{W_n}), W_k \in sentence, k \leq 20$$

W_k is the k th keyword of sentence. V_{W_k} is the vector of W_k. $V_{sentence}$ is the vector representation of the sentence. The length of the vector of each word is 50. The vector of sentence is consisted of 20 vectors of the keyword. Stop words such as player names and team names are abandoned.

The neural network model is designed as Restricted Boltzmann Machines [10]. The input of network is the vector of sentence, the output of network is an estimated similarity which indicates the correlation degree between input sentence and reference news [11]. The structure of network is shown below (Fig. 2):

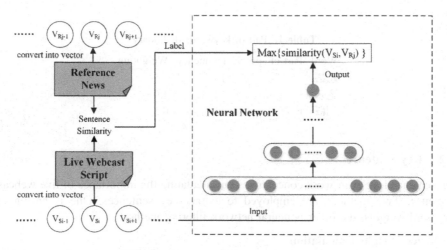

Fig. 2. Structure of the neural network

The network is trained by sentence in live webcast script and its corresponding similarity estimation. The similarity is evaluated by the cosine similarity between the sentence in the script and the sentence from reference news. In order to obtain enough reference sentences of football news, we collected 600 additional football news that contain nearly 24000 sentences. A threshold is set to extract important sentences. Some rules are built to improve the result of the network extraction. For example, if the sentence contains keywords of shooting or foul, then the weight of the sentence is increased. As a result, weights of all sentences have been adjusted and sentences could be ranked by weights to extract the most important one.

3.3   News Generation

Reference football news has a uniform format. The first part is the description of basic background information such as game time, place and teams. The second part is the description of the process of the game, and the third part is the starting line-up and player list.

In the first paragraph, sentence weights are ranked to extract the top sentences. In the main paragraph, the events may not be described completely only with the key sentences. Thus, a correlation sentence detection method is proposed to choose the correlating sentences of the key sentences [12, 13]. The correlating sentences are added as the supplement of the event. For example, a key sentence may possess very high weighting value, but it is an incomplete description of event. It is possible to calculate the correlation by using sentence vector. Sentence correlation can be represented by the following:

$$R_{n,k} = (1 - \log_d(|k - n| + 1))$$

In the formula, $R_{n,k}$ is the correlation value between sentence n and k. $|k - n|$ means the distant between sentence k and n. The correlation of two neighboring sentences depends on the distant between them. The $R_{n,k}$ above the certain threshold would be chose as the correlating sentences. Finally, the selected sentences are sorted by time to formulate a whole paragraph. What's more, the time information is added before each event to enrich the event completeness. In the final paragraph, the starting line-up and player list can be generated by extracting information from data file of the participating teams.

3.4   Readability Improvement

After the football news is generated, several phrases have to be inserted to improve the readability of news. According to the different type of events in the game, several kinds of templates are designed to generate colloquial phrases. The phrases are made up of preinstall text template whose subject is vacant. Those templates are classified as two different types, one type is motion action which contains shooting, foul, cutting and so on, the other type is score rewriting such as first goal, final-hitting, overtaking, draw, etc.

The motion action event is recognized by detect the motion keywords in the sentences. Thereby, the behavior body of the motion is extracted and added to the suitable templates. Score rewriting event is recognized by analyzing the data statistics file and score recording history. The templates are chose to describe the score events according to the different score changing conditions.

4 Experiments

This part, we will demonstrate some experiment results from three aspects.

4.1 Keywords Collection

As the number of the football news is increasing, the extracted number of keywords would converge to a certain value. In our experiment, the number of keywords would achieve 230 or so, when we extract more than 120 football news. All these keywords is stored in keywords dictionary. The relation between the scale of the keywords dictionary and the scale of the sports news is shown below. According to the result of Fig. 3, the number of keywords stored in our keywords dictionary is enough for information extraction.

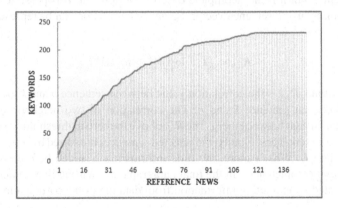

Fig. 3. The number of keyword changes with the total number of the reference news.

4.2 Weights Alignment Between Hot Events and Key Sentences

To test the accuracy of our method, we introduce time-weight graph to directly show the comparison between event and sentence's weight.

Figure 4(a) shows the relation between scoring event and weights of the sentences which are not adjusted by neural network and rules. The scoring event usually appears on the peak of the weight or near it. If sentence extraction is only based on weight, some important events will be missed. Figure 5(a) demonstrates the adjusted result by neural network and rules.

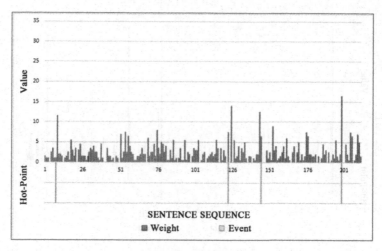

Fig. 4 (a)

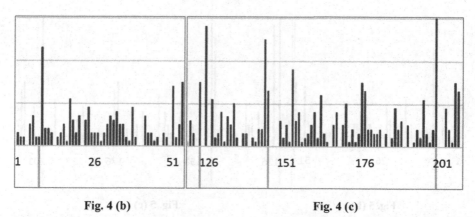

Fig. 4 (b)   Fig. 4 (c)

Fig. 4. (a) Sentences weight calculated by keyword weight summation and scoring event. (b) and (c) are the enlarge view of (a).

According to Figs. 4(a) and 5(a), our method is reliable for extracting important information. The other peaks of weight columns represent for special event such as foul, passing and attack.

We tested on 110 live webcast scripts, as a result, our method successfully extracts the hot point in the football game from live webcast scripts. The extracted high value sentences usually describe shooting, stealing, saving and so on, which are similar to normal news.

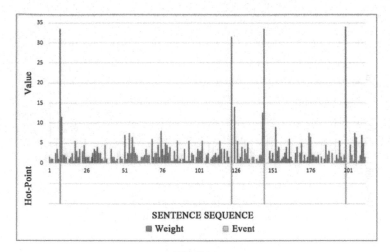

Fig. 5 (a)

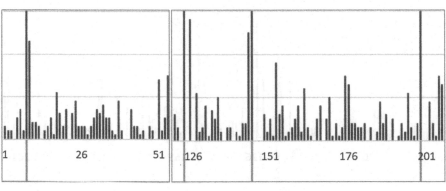

Fig. 5 (b)   Fig. 5 (c)

Fig. 5. (a) is the amendment of Fig. 4(a), (b) and (c) are the enlarge view of (a).

4.3 Scores of Automatic Evaluation

ROUGE toolkit is widely used for automatic evaluation of summaries. In this paper, ROUGE2.0 is chosen to evaluate our generated news [14, 15]. 30 football news are set as reference document and all these news are provided by NLPCC 2016 shared task. Therefore, this news is professional and typical. We use ROUGE toolkit to test the performance of initial generated news, final generated news and a manually writing version. Initial version is the result without any weight adjustment and readability improvement, Final version is the result for weight adjustment and readability improvement, manual version is one of the reference documents which are also provided by NLPCC 2016 shared task. In the properties file of the ROUGE toolkit, we set configuration parameter *ngram* as *1* and *2*, *pos_tagger_name* as *chinese-nodistsim.tagger*. Other configuration parameters are set as default. The performance is shown in the following tables:

According to Tables 2 and 3, our final version of generated news has a better performance than initial version. The improvement of final version is obviously. In the Table 1, the score of the generated news of our final version is close to the manual version. In the Table 2, our final version of generated news acquires a higher score than manual version.

Table 2. Average scores of the ROUGE-1

ROUGE-Type	System name	Avg recall	Avg precision	Avg F-score
ROUGE-1	*Initial version*	0.135278	0.531720	0.214376
ROUGE-1	*Final version*	0.494006	0.506041	0.496974
ROUGE-1	*Manual version*	0.501425	0.501036	0.497021

Table 3. Average scores of the ROUGE-2

ROUGE-Type	System name	Avg recall	Avg precision	Avg F-score
ROUGE-2	*Initial version*	0.069832	0.300113	0.112575
ROUGE-2	*Final version*	0.247545	0.385886	0.296926
ROUGE-2	*Manual version*	0.217605	0.211780	0.212743

Besides, Table 4 is automatic and manual evaluation results provided by organizers. Table 4 list the automatic evaluation results of 7 teams who participated in the share task5 of NLPCC2016 and Table 5 is the manual evaluation results of top 3 teams. IACAS_Human_HCI is our team.

Each team is permitted to submit two version, our results win three best one in Automatic evaluation results. In manual evaluation, results are evaluated by

Table 4. Automatic evaluation results

Team	Run	ROUGE-1		ROUGE-2		ROUGE-SU4	
		Recall	F-measure	Recall	F-measure	Recall	F-measure
IACAS_Human_HCI	1	**0.57782**	0.59846	0.24998	0.26293	**0.25464**	0.26652
	2	0.55643	**0.60331**	0.24448	0.26092	0.24777	0.26581
ICDD_SportsNews	1	0.56515	0.59261	0.25235	0.26444	0.25404	0.26613
	2	0.56768	0.59179	0.25059	0.26119	0.25438	0.26497
RDNH	1	0.55235	0.5865	**0.25527**	**0.27081**	0.25333	**0.26863**
BIT_Coder	1	0.49728	0.55851	0.22524	0.25333	0.22484	0.25263
CQUT_AC996	2	0.5222	0.55728	0.22182	0.23688	0.22689	0.2422
CCNU2016NLP	1	0.46105	0.52478	0.19486	0.22128	0.19322	0.21947
	2	0.4948	0.52425	0.20894	0.22123	0.21102	0.22325
BIT_Hunter	2	0.36532	0.47758	0.16072	0.2106	0.16504	0.21589

788   T. Renjun et al.

Table 5. Manual evaluation results

Team	Run	Aspect	Average
IACAS_Human_HCI	1	Read.	3.84444
		Cont.	3.54444
		Overall	3.63333
	2	Read.	**3.88889**
		Cont.	**3.64444**
		Overall	**3.73333**
ICDD_SportsNews	1	Read.	3.34444
		Cont.	3.32222
		Overall	3.24444
	2	Read.	3.46667
		Cont.	3.32222
		Overall	3.28889
BIT_Coder	1	Read.	2.55556
		Cont.	2.74444
		Overall	2.45556

three factors: readability (Read.), content coverage (Cont.) and overall score. Because of our efforts in the readability improvement, our results win the highest and the second-highest average scores in manual evaluation. In summary, our method has a good performance both in automatic evaluation and manual evaluation.

5 Conclusion

In this paper, a method of neural network and key weighting is proposed for football news generation. It utilizes live webcast scripts to generate a sport news automatically, all the data related to the game are available on the Internet. The football news is generated by the method in this paper has obtained a good evaluation in the competition of NLPCC2016 task5—Sports News Generation from Live Webcast Scripts, which is held by Technical Committee of Chinese Information, China Computer Federation. We obtained good performance both in automatic evaluation and manual evaluation.

Acknowledge. This work is supported by the National Key Research & Development Plan of China (No. 2016YFB1001404), the Strategic Priority Research Program of the CAS (Grant XDB02080006), the National High-Tech Research and Development Program of China(863 Program) (No. 2015AA016305), the National Natural Science Foundation of China (NSFC) (No. 61425017, No. 61332017, No. 61375027, No. 61203258, No. 61273288), the Strategic Priority Research Program of the CAS (Grant XDB02080006), and the Guangxi Science and Technology Development Project (No: 1598018-6), the Guangxi Key Laboratory of Trusted Software of Guilin University of Electronic Technology (KX201514).

References

1. Schiller, V.H.: System, report, and method for generating natural language news-based stories: US, US8494944 (2013)
2. Dixon, T.: Financial News Generation System: WO/2012/119247 (2012)
3. Tornoe, R.: Learn to Stop Worrying and Love Robot Journalists. Editor & Publisher (2014)
4. Wan, X., Yang, J., Xiao, J.: Manifold-ranking based topic-focused multi-document summarization. In: IJCAI, vol. 7, pp. 2903–2908 (2007)
5. Hovy, E., Lin, C.Y.: Automated text summarization and the SUMMARIST system. In: Proceedings of a Workshop on Held at Baltimore, Maryland, 13–15 October 1998, pp. 197–214. Association for Computational Linguistics (1998)
6. Lin, C.Y., Hovy, E.: From single to multi-document summarization: a prototype system and its evaluation. In: Proceedings of the 40th Annual Meeting on Association for Computational Linguistics, pp. 457–464. Association for Computational Linguistics (2002)
7. Evans, D.K., Klavans, J.L., McKeown, K.R.: Columbia newsblaster: multilingual news summarization on the web. In: Demonstration Papers at HLT-NAACL 2004, pp. 1–4. Association for Computational Linguistics (2004)
8. Radev, D., Otterbacher, J., Winkel, A., et al.: NewsInEssence: summarizing online news topics. Commun. ACM **48**(10), 95–98 (2005)
9. Min, K., Ma, C., Zhao, T., Li, H.: BosonNLP: an ensemble approach for word segmentation and POS tagging. In: Li, J., Ji, H., Zhao, D., Feng, Y. (eds.) NLPCC 2015. LNCS (LNAI), vol. 9362, pp. 520–526. Springer, Heidelberg (2015). doi:10.1007/978-3-319-25207-0_48
10. Chuang, W.T., Yang, J.: Extracting sentence segments for text summarization: a machine learning approach. In: Proceedings of the 23rd Annual International ACM SIGIR Conference on Research and Development in Information Retrieval, pp. 152–159. ACM (2000)
11. Zhang, Q., Huang, X., Wu, L.: A new method for calculating similarity between sentences and application on automatic text summarization. In: Proceedings of the First National Conference on Information Retrieval and Content Security (2004)
12. Conroy, J.M., O'leary, D.P.: Text summarization via hidden markov models. In: Proceedings of the 24th Annual International ACM SIGIR Conference on Research and Development in Information Retrieval, pp. 406–407. ACM (2001)
13. Zhang, P., Li, C.: Automatic text summarization based on sentences clustering and extraction. In: 2nd IEEE International Conference on Computer Science and Information Technology, ICCSIT 2009, pp. 167–170. IEEE (2009)
14. Lin, C.-Y.: ROUGE: a package for automatic evaluation of summaries. In: Proceedings of the Workshop on Text Summarization Branches Out (WAS 2004), Barcelona, Spain, 25–26 July 2004 (2004a)
15. Lin, C.Y., Hovy, E.: Automatic evaluation of summaries using n-gram co-occurrence statis-tics. In: Proceedings of the 2003 Conference of the North American Chapter of the Association for Computational Linguistics on Human Language Technology, vol. 1, pp. 71–78. Association for Computational Linguistics (2003)

Convolutional Deep Neural Networks
for Document-Based Question Answering

Jian Fu, Xipeng Qiu$^{(\boxtimes)}$, and Xuanjing Huang

School of Computer Science, Fudan University,
825 Zhangheng Road, Shanghai, China
{12307130136,xpqiu,xjhuang}@fudan.edu.cn

Abstract. Document-based Question Answering aims to compute the similarity or relevance between two texts: question and answer. It is a typical and core task and considered as a touchstone of natural language understanding. In this article, we present a convolutional neural network based architecture to learn feature representations of each question-answer pair and compute its match score. By taking the interaction and attention between question and answer into consideration, as well as word overlap indices, the empirical study on Chinese Open-Domain Question Answering (DBQA) Task (document-based) demonstrates the efficacy of the proposed model, which achieves the best result on NLPCC-ICCPOL 2016 Shared Task on DBQA.

1 Introduction

In this paper, we regard document-based question answering as a problem of semantic matching between two pieces of texts. Semantic matching is a critical task for many applications in NLP. It aims to model sentences and then compute the similarity or relevance. And it's central to many tasks such as question answering [8,15], answer sentence selection [19], textual entailment [12,13], and so on.

Recently, deep learning approaches have achieved a lot of success in many research due to its ability to automatically learn optimal feature representations for a given task, including modeling sentence pairs. Among neural network models, long short-term memory neural network (LSTM) [7] and convolutional neural network (CNN) [11] are two popular models to model sentences and sentence pairs. In this paper, we use CNN to model sentence, since CNN is good at extracting robust and abstract features and its capable of feature selection [10].

A successful sentence-matching algorithm need to not only primely model the internal structures of natural language sentences but also the interaction between them. The match score is supposed to be more accurate if the rich patterns in each pair of sentences can be well exploited. A proposed way to reach this target is to align the two sentences word by word just like ARC-II [8] or do similarity matching [17] to compute a similarity matrix. Apart from the alignment and similarity match, attention mechanism, a powerful mechanism in Neural Machine Translation [1], can also be applied for modelling sentence pair

© Springer International Publishing AG 2016
C.-Y. Lin et al. (Eds.): NLPCC-ICCPOL 2016, LNAI 10102, pp. 790–797, 2016.
DOI: 10.1007/978-3-319-50496-4_71

by taking into account the interdependence between the two sentences [16]. By the way, attention mechanism and similarity match can be put into the top or bottom or both top and bottom layer of the neural network [18]. Also, semantic matching with attention has variations like [6].

Besides these, additional features which not require external knowledge sources make contributions to the performance of neural network (see experiment results), such as word overlap indices [19] and IDF-weighted word overlap indices.

The contribution of this work lies in three folds:

1. We propose a CNN-based Semantic Match Architecture, which can not only model internal structure of sentence separately through layer-by-layer convolution and pooling, but also capture the rich matching patterns between query and document.
2. We perform empirical study on NLPCC-ICCPOL 2016 Shared Task on DBQA and put additional word overlap features, which can improve the performance without pre-processing or external resources into the neural network.
3. We apply attention mechanism to neural network and do evaluation by visualizing the attention matrices.

2   Convolutional Sentence Model

The convolutional sentence model of our ConvNet is shown on Fig. 1. It is inspired by many convolutional models [9], but the goal of our distributional model is to learn good intermediate feature representations for each pair of query and document, which are then used for semantic match. As illustrated, it takes input as the words embeddings in the sentence alignment sequentially, and then distill the meaning of each sentence through several layers (or just a single layer) of convolution and max-pooling, reaching a fixed length vectorial representation which is their final intermediate feature representations. To be mentioned, there could be many filters and its number is a hyperparameter to be tuned.

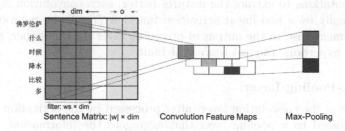

Fig. 1. The overall architecture of the convolution sentence model for mapping input sentences to intermediate feature representations.

In general, our sentence model consists of a single convolution layer which followed by non-linearity layer and max-pooling layer. There are 4 layers in detail as below and we now describe each in turn.

2.1 Embedding Layer

The input of the network is a sequence of words: $[w_1, ..., w_l]$, and each word is derived from a vocabulary $\mathbf{V}$. Words are represented by distributional vectors $\mathbf{w} \in R^d$ which are drawn from a word embedding matrice $\mathbf{W} \in R^{|V| \times d}$, a pre-trained word2vec [14] embedding.

Besides word2vec embedding, word overlap features is also added to the dimension of each word of a sentence which indicates essential matching information in Flatten layer and future match score computing (see Model Architecture in Fig. 1). For each question and answer, we get sentence matrix $S \in R^{L \times (d+1)}$.

2.2 Convolution Layer

The aim of convolution layer is to extract features or patterns. Given the sequence $q^{emb} = r^{w_1}, ..., r^{w_l}$, let us define the matrix $Z_q = [z_1, ..., z_l]$ as a matrice where each column contains a vector $\mathbf{z_i} \in R^{dw_s}$ which is the concatenation of a sequence of w_s word embeddings. The output of the convolution with c filters over the question q is computed as follows:

$$Q = WZ_q + b \tag{1}$$

where each row m in $Q \in R^{l \times c}$ contains features extracted in a context window around the m_{th} word of q. The matraces W and the vector b are parameters which to be learned. The number of convolution filters c, and the length or size of the word-level context window w_s are hyper-parameters that need be chosen manually by the user.

We then compute A in a similar manner (the neural network parameters can be the same or not).

2.3 Non-linearity Layer

To make the network enable to learn non-linear decision boundaries which make the representations to extract the features better, each convolution layer is followed typically by a non-linear activation function $f()$. To be mentioned, it is applied element-wise to the output of preceding layer. In this paper, activation function is hyperbolic tangent $tanh$ by default.

2.4 Max-Pooling Layer

The output of the convolution layer (after processed by the activation function) are then passed to a pooling layer that aggregate the information, and also, reduce the representation. Max pooling and average pooling, are commonly used to extract robust features from convolution. In this paper, we use max pooling, which selects the max of each filter, to extract patterns for future semantic matching.

3   Convolutional Matching Model

The sentence-pair matching model of our model is presented in Fig. 2. Our ConvNets-Based sentence models (described above), learn to map the input sentence pairs to vectors, which can proceed to be computed their similarity. It mostly take the conventional approach: firstly, it finds the representation matrice of each sentence, then deal with the representations for the two sentences with a multi-layer perceptron (MLP) [2], the Siamese architecture introduced in [3, 10].

However, different from previous work, we can compute more interaction between two sentences such as query-document similarity score or attentive pooling (see later).

In the following, we described how to computer similarity score by using the intermediate feature representations and some other remaining layers.

3.1   Interact Layer

Given the representations of our convNets after processing queries and documents, the resulting vector representations x_q and x_d, can be used to compute a similarity score between query-document pairs. Following the approach of [4], the similarity unit is defined as follows:

$$sim\_score(x_q, x_d) = x_q M x_d{}^T, \tag{2}$$

where $M \in R^{d \times d}$ is a similarity matrix and is optimized during the training.

3.2   Multi-layer Perceptron

Multi-layer perceptron (MLP) is composed of a hidden layer and a logistic regression (softmax layer). Hidden layer computes the following transformation:

$$f(w_h x + b), \tag{3}$$

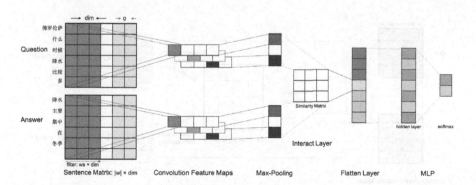

Fig. 2. Illustration of our whole convolutional deep neural network for semantice match.

where w_h is the weight vector of the hidden layer and f is the non-linearity activation function. After then, we apply a logistic regression to the vector, the softmax function computes the probability distribution over the labels:

$$p(y = j|x) = \frac{e^{y_j}}{\Sigma e^{y_k}}, \tag{4}$$

3.3 Training

The model is trained to minimise the cross-entropy cost function:

$$L(y, o) = -\frac{1}{N} \Sigma_{n \in N} y_n \log o_n \tag{5}$$

4 Attentive Pooling

Attentive pooling [5,16,18] is an approach which enables the pooling layer to be sensitive to the current input pair, in a way that the information from question q can directly influence the representation of the answer a r_a, and vice versa. It's an attention mechanism for model training to discriminate sentence pairs that can model sentence pairs into a common representation space where they can be computed and compared in a more plausible way.

In Fig. 3, we illustrate the application of attentive pooling over the output of the convolution layer to construct the representations r_q and r_a. After we compute the representation matrices $Q \in R^{c \times L_q}$ and $A \in R^{c \times L_a}$ by convolution (weights shared), we compute the attention matrix $G \in R^{L_q \times L_a}$ as follows:

$$G = tanh(QUA^T) \tag{6}$$

where $U \in R^{c \times c}$ is a matrix of parameters which to be learned by the NN. After the convolution is used to compute the representations of Q and A, the matrix G contains the scores of an alignment between the w_s-size context windows of q and a after convolution.

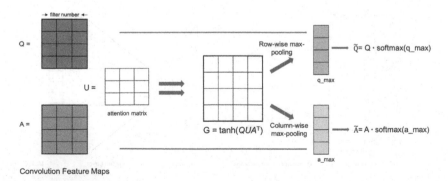

Fig. 3. Attentive pooling architecture which applys attention mechanism right after convolution layer.

Next, we apply row-wise and column-wise max-pooling over G to generate the vectors $g^q \in R^{L_q}$ and $g^a \in R^{L_a}$, respectively. And we apply the softmax function to the vectors g^q and g^a to create attention vectors σ_q and σ_a.

Finally, the representations of r^q and r^a are computed as dot product between the attention vectors σ_q and σ_a and the output of the convolution over q and a, respectively:

$$r^q = Q\sigma_q \tag{7}$$

$$r^a = A\sigma_a \tag{8}$$

5   Experiments

5.1   Dataset

We conduct experiments on Chinese Open-Domain Question Answering Task (document-based). The dataset is shown in Table 1. The QA-pairs of dbqa-train and dbqa-test is 181882 and 122531. After segmentation, the length of most question sentences is less than 20 and the one of most answer sentences is less than 40.

Table 1. Dataset of NLPCC DBQA Task, 2016

Dataset	QA-pairs
DBQA-train	181882
DBQA-test	122531

5.2   Evaluation Metrics

DBQA Task is formalized as a ranking problem. Therefore, we use Mean Reciprocal Rank (MRR) as evaluation metrics, but accuracy in validation.

5.3   Embedding

We use word2vec to train word embeddings on corpus Chinese Wikipedia (zhwiki), which contain more than 230 thousand Chinese articles. The pre-trained word embedding is much of importance to this task.

5.4   Results and Discussion

Our experiments results are illustrated as Table 2. The table shows the performance of the baseline (CNN), and the improvement of interact layer and additional features. The interaction and word overlap indices play important roles in the performance. And additionally, attentive pooling (with word overlap features) gives a comparable performance. Related research showed that adding attention mechanism before or after convolution layer may have better performance for longer sentences. We didn't tune the hyperparameters very much on both neural networks and we'll do more research on it.

Table 2. Experimental results on the NLPCC-DBQA Task

Model	MAP	MRR
CNN_base	36.41	36.42
+interact	59.14	59.21
+interact&overlap	85.86	85.92
AttentivePooling	84.90	84.96

5.5   Attentive Pooling Visualization

The Fig. 4 depict an attention heat map of a sample of QA-pair which is correctly answered by the NN. The darker of the color of a word in the question (answer), the larger the attention score in $\sigma_q(\sigma_a)$ of the trigram centred at that word. As shown in the pictures, the attentive pooling mechanism indeed puts more focus on the segments of the answer which have some relation or interaction with the question, and vice-verse.

Fig. 4. Attention heat map of a sample of QA-pair that correctly answered by the neural network

6   Conclusion

In this paper, we proposed a deep convolutional architecture for sentence semantic matching, which can nicely combine the hierarchical modelling of individual sentences and the patterns of their matching. Empirical study on DBQA Task shows that our model can perform well with word overlap features. Additionally, we apply attention mechanism to it and do evaluation by visualizing the attention matrices.

Acknowledgement. This work was partially funded by National Natural Science Foundation of China (Nos. 61532011 and 61672162), the National High Technology Research and Development Program of China (No. 2015AA015408).

References

1. Bahdanau, D., Cho, K., Bengio, Y.: Neural machine translation by jointly learning to align and translate. arXiv preprint arXiv:1409.0473 (2014)

2. Bengio, Y.: Learning deep architectures for AI. Found. Trends Mach. Learn. **2**(1), 1–127 (2009)
3. Bordes, A., Glorot, X., Weston, J., Bengio, Y.: A semantic matching energy function for learning with multi-relational data. Mach. Learn. **94**(2), 233–259 (2014)
4. Bordes, A., Weston, J., Usunier, N.: Open question answering with weakly supervised embedding models. In: Calders, T., Esposito, F., Hüllermeier, E., Meo, R. (eds.) ECML PKDD 2014. LNCS (LNAI), vol. 8724, pp. 165–180. Springer, Heidelberg (2014). doi:10.1007/978-3-662-44848-9_11
5. Chen, K., Wang, J., Chen, L.C., Gao, H., Xu, W., Nevatia, R.: ABC-CNN: an attention based convolutional neural network for visual question answering. arXiv preprint arXiv:1511.05960 (2015)
6. Cui, Y., Chen, Z., Wei, S., Wang, S., Liu, T., Hu, G.: Attention-over-attention neural networks for reading comprehension. arXiv preprint arXiv:1607.04423 (2016)
7. Hochreiter, S., Schmidhuber, J.: Long short-term memory. Neural Comput. **9**(8), 1735–1780 (1997)
8. Hu, B., Lu, Z., Li, H., Chen, Q.: Convolutional neural network architectures for matching natural language sentences. In: Advances in Neural Information Processing Systems, pp. 2042–2050 (2014)
9. Kalchbrenner, N., Grefenstette, E., Blunsom, P.: A convolutional neural network for modelling sentences. arXiv preprint arXiv:1404.2188 (2014)
10. LeCun, Y., Bengio, Y.: Convolutional networks for images, speech, and time series. Handb. Brain Theor. Neural Netw. **3361**(10), 1995 (1995)
11. LeCun, Y., Bottou, L., Bengio, Y., Haffner, P.: Gradient-based learning applied to document recognition. Proc. IEEE **86**(11), 2278–2324 (1998)
12. Liu, P., Qiu, X., Chen, J., Huang, X.: Deep fusion LSTMs for text semantic matching. In: Proceedings of Annual Meeting of the Association for Computational Linguistics (2016). http://aclweb.org/anthology/P/P16/P16-1098.pdf
13. Liu, P., Qiu, X., Huang, X.: Modelling interaction of sentence pair with coupled-LSTMs. arXiv preprint arXiv:1605.05573 (2016)
14. Mikolov, T., Sutskever, I., Chen, K., Corrado, G.S., Dean, J.: Distributed representations of words and phrases and their compositionality. In: Advances in Neural Information Processing Systems, pp. 3111–3119 (2013)
15. Qiu, X., Huang, X.: Convolutional neural tensor network architecture for community-based question answering. In: Proceedings of International Joint Conference on Artificial Intelligence (2015). http://ijcai.org/papers15/Papers/IJCAI15-188.pdf
16. Santos, C.D., Tan, M., Xiang, B., Zhou, B.: Attentive pooling networks. arXiv preprint arXiv:1602.03609 (2016)
17. Severyn, A., Moschitti, A.: Learning to rank short text pairs with convolutional deep neural networks. In: Proceedings of the 38th International ACM SIGIR Conference on Research and Development in Information Retrieval, pp. 373–382. ACM (2015)
18. Yin, W., Schütze, H., Xiang, B., Zhou, B.: ABCNN: attention-based convolutional neural network for modeling sentence pairs. arXiv preprint arXiv:1512.05193 (2015)
19. Yu, L., Hermann, K.M., Blunsom, P., Pulman, S.: Deep learning for answer sentence selection. arXiv preprint arXiv:1412.1632 (2014)

Research on Summary Sentences Extraction Oriented to Live Sports Text

Liya Zhu[1], Wenchao Wang[1], Yujing Chen[1], Xueqiang Lv[1(✉)],
and Jianshe Zhou[2]

[1] Beijing Key Laboratory of Internet Culture
and Digital Dissemination Research, Beijing Information Science
and Technology University, Beijing, China
lxq@bistu.edu.cn
[2] Beijing Advanced Innovation Center for Imaging Technology, Beijing, China
zhoujianshe@cnu.edu.cn

Abstract. In order to enable automatic generation of sports news, in this paper, we propose an extraction method to extract summary sentences from live sports text. After analyzing the characteristics of live sports text, we regard extraction of summary sentence as the sequence tagging problem, and decide to use Conditional Random Fields (CRFs) as the extraction model. Firstly, we expend the correlated words of keywords using word2vec. Then, we select positive correlated words, negative correlated words, time and the window of score changes as features to train the model and extract summary sentences. This method get good results on the evaluation indicators of ROUGE-1, GOUGE-2 and ROUGE-SU4. And it shows that this method has a meaningful influence on automatic summarization and automatic generation of sports news.

Keywords: Sports news · Live sports text · Conditional Random Fields · Word2vec

1 Introduction

With the rapid development of information technology, the internet information, as a brand new information communication platform, is now spreading its influence on every aspect of daily life. Under this circumstance, the information acquisition is becoming more and more convenient. Through the network media, sports news has become one of the main ways to know the sports games. However, compared with the live broadcasts of sports events, the sport news reports have a drawback of hysteresis. So how to improve the efficiency of the news writing, and handle the processing of information collection, news writing and news arrangement in a unified frame work, so to realize the two-step automatic news from "data extraction" to "document generation" will become a popular research direction in the future. At present, the "data extraction" of sports events includes game entity extraction, data mining and the events of dynamic information extraction. Among them, the events of dynamic information extraction is one of the hotspots in the current research, through the extraction of dynamic information, we can easily get the important events, such as the wonderful ball-passing, the goal-scoring, the interception and the foul goals in a football game. Text Summarization achieves the extraction of information through the text mining, and it is an important means of information filtering and effective way to solve the information overload in the field of Natural Language Processing.

Automatic Summarization was proposed by Luhn [1] in 1985, he put forward an automatic summarization method based on keyword frequency statistics. He weighted each keyword by the word frequency, graded and ranked for the sentences according to the word weights, and extracted the sentence as the summary sentence if it reach the threshold. Prasad Pingali and Varma [2] proposed a feature that separated from the query and another feature that depends on the query, and rated each of the two characteristics, then calculated the score of each sentence by the linear combination of the two characteristics and extracted the sentence as the summary sentence if its score reach the threshold. Lin et al. [3] proposed a method which combine a graph model with time-stamped and the MMR technique to extract the summary sentences. He et al. [4] proposed a strategy of summary sentence selection based on the multi-feature fusion, and they finally realized the extraction through the fusion of two features, the first feature is the correlation characteristics of sentences and query, the second is the correlation characteristics of global sentences. And their method achieved good results. Liu et al. [5] proposed a method based on the HMM model, in his method, the assumption of theme independent in LDA model has been eliminated, and a multi-feature fusion has been used to improve the quality of summary. Cheng et al. [6] built a weight function on multi-features, used a mathematical regression model to train the corpus, then removed the redundant sentences and realized the summaries generation.

In this paper a new method on the dynamic information extraction from the live sport text is been presented, it transforms the dynamic information extraction into summary sentences extraction. First, build a positive keywords set and a negative keywords set by hand, and extend this keywords in semantic level to get more related words. Then the positive correlated words, the negative correlated words, the time and the window of score changes are treated as features in the Conditional Random Fields model for model training. Finally use the model to extract the summary sentences from the live sport text.

2 Expanding Correlated Words Method Based on Word2vec

In this thesis, an efficient method of expanding the correlated words based on word2vec is presented. This method uses a vector model trained by word2vec to represent the words in corpus, and transforms the problem of text-processing into the vector operations in space vector. It computes the text similarity by using vector space model and the cosine distance to realize the expansion of related words, and to strengthen the indication role of keywords in the extraction of summary sentences.

2.1 Model Training on Word2vec

Word2vec is an open source released by Google in 2013, it can translate the words into vectors by using a deep learning algorithm. There are two kinds of training models in

Wrod2vec, the Continuous Bag-Of-Words Model (CBOW) [7] and Skip-gram model [8]. Both of them use a shallow neural networks training algorithm. The basic principle of CBOW is to predict the probability of the word according to the context, however the Skip-gram is to forecast the probability of context according to the word. This paper establishes a prediction model based on Skip-gram, and the model is optimized by the Hierarchical Softmax method. Assume that the training data is $w_1, w_2, w_3 \ldots w_t$, the objective function of Skip-gram is as follows:

$$J(\theta) = \frac{1}{T} \sum\nolimits_{t=1}^{T} \sum\nolimits_{-c \leq k \leq c} log\, p(w_{t+k}|w_t) \tag{1}$$

In the formula (1), $J(\theta)$ represents the objective function, T is the total number of data, c is an important parameter which determines the neighborhood size, and the bigger the value of c is, the longer it takes for data training, therefore the more accurate the results will be.

In respect of optimization, the paper adopts the Hierarchical Softmax algorithm which realizes the representation of characteristic words using the Huffman Binary Tree. It treats the words in output layer as leaf nodes, then weights the words according to the frequency and codes them. In the Huffman binary tree, high frequency words are assigned the shorter paths, low frequency words are assigned the longer paths, and each word has a unique path that can be accessed. So the function of $p(u|w)$ is defined as the formula (2):

$$p(u|w) = \prod\nolimits_{j=2}^{L(u)} p(d_j^u|v(w), \theta_{j-1}^u) \tag{2}$$

In the function, $L(u)$ is the path length of root node to u node, θ_j^u is the vector of the *jth* non-leaf node in the path of root node to u node, d_j^u is the code of jth node in the path of root node to u node, $v(w)$ is the vector of w. Finally, we use the algorithm of gradient descent to solve the objective function, and the word vector is generated.

2.2   Correlated Words Extension

Generally speaking, in the field of live sports text, the keywords can express the action theme of the sentence. For example, we can speculate a series of events through the words of "传中", "攻门", "出底线" in the sentence of "桑切斯右路的传中, 吉鲁俯身头球攻门打在冯特身上出底线". It can be seen that some keywords are decisive roles in judging whether a sentence is important or not. On the other hand, if some words co-occurrence frequently in the sentence, there must exist some relevance between them. Therefore, we propose to build a positive keywords set and a negative keywords set manually, and extend these keywords set according to the semantic relevance, finally use the keywords and the extended words to improve the extraction effect of summary sentences.

In the big data environment, the distance between two points in the vector space is exactly the correlation of these two words. So when the vector model training on word2vec is completed, we use cosine distance to measure the relevant weight of keywords in relation to other words, and the greater the cosine distance is, the more relevant the words are, so we can select Top N the most relevant words to realize words extension. In addition, the calculation formula of cosine function is shown as formula (3), and $distance(w_1, w_2)$ is the cosine distance between the word w_1 and word w_2, the v_{w_1}, v_{w_2} is the vector of w_1 and w_2 respectively.

$$distance(w_1, w_2) = v_{w_1} \cdot v_{w_2} \tag{3}$$

The Tables 1 and 2 shows the related words of "进球" and "拦截" respectively, which obtained by means of the method in this paper.

Table 1. The related words of "进球"

Related words	Cosine distance
射门	0.6894
直射	0.6828
攻门	0.6623
追回	0.6498
领先	0.6408
打门	0.6396
打破	0.6294
僵局	0.6251

Table 2. The related words of "拦截"

Related words	Cosine distance
截断	0.6529
断球	0.6397
挡出	0.6363
扑住	0.6256
扑出	0.6208
解围	0.6107
没收	0.6084
破坏	0.6053

3 Summary Sentence Extraction Based on CRFs

In this paper a new method of summary sentences extraction on live sport text is been presented, it transforms the summary sentences extraction into an equivalent sequence tagging problem, and builds up an automatic extraction model through the Conditional Random Fields. The output of automatic extraction model is a sequence of "1" and "0", if a sentence is judged as the summary sentence, its label is "1", otherwise "0". While it is affected by multiple factors to determine whether a sentence is a summary sentence or not, according to the characteristics of the live texts for football matches, we select four kinds of features for model training: the positive correlated words, the negative correlated words, the time and the window of score changes.

3.1 Conditional Random Fields

The Conditional Random Fields (CRFs) is a probability statistic model, which was first proposed by Lafferty [9] in 2001. It combines the advantages of the Maximum Entropy Model (MEM) and the Hidden Markov Model (HMM), which overcomes the limitation for the strong independence assumption in HMM, it has a strong ability of feature fusion and can accommodate rich contextual information. On the other hand, the CRFs adopts the global normalization method, and overcomes the making bias problem in MEM. CRFs is one of the best machine learning models which can effectively solve the problem of serialized data partitioning and data annotation, and has been widely applied in the field of Natural Language Processing, such as the task of Named Entity Recognition (NER), Chunk Parsing and Part-of-Speech Tagging, etc.

3.2 Extraction Model

In our method, we transform the problem into an equivalent sequence tagging problem, and build up the automatic extraction model through the Conditional Random Fields. The input of the model is a set of documents that composed of sentences, the output is a sequence of "0" and "1", the tag is "1" if the sentence can be summary sentence, otherwise "0". Assume that the input is $X = \{x_1, x_2, x_3, \ldots, x_n\}$, the output sequence is $Y = \{y_1, y_2, \ldots, y_n\}$, value of y_i is 1 or 0. From the basic principle of random field theory, the probability of y under the given conditions of x is shown as formula (4).

$$P(y|x; w) = \frac{1}{Z(x|w)} \exp(\sum_j w_j F_j(x, y)) \tag{4}$$

$Z(x|w)$ is the normalized constant to ensure the sum of probabilities is 1, the calculation formula is shown as formula(5). $F_j(x, y)$ is the jth feature of X, and its

$$Z(x|w) = \sum_y \exp \sum_j w_j F_j(x, y) \tag{5}$$

$$F_j(x, y) = \sum_i f_j(y_{i-1}, y_i, x, i) \tag{6}$$

Our goal is to find the weight vector w and make the formula (7) be workable. Finally, we use the gradient ascent method to estimate the CRF parameters and get the weight vector w.

$$y^* = \mathrm{argmax}\, P(y|x, w) \tag{7}$$

3.3 Feature Selection

- The positive correlated words
  The ultimate goal is to extract the sentences that reflect the key events in the live text of football match. Through the observation of the live text, we found that the words such as "进球", "犯规" can be used to identify the key actions, these words bring important guiding role for the extraction of summary sentences, we call them the positive correlated words. In our method, we collect the positive keywords from live text, then use the method of word2vec mentioned above to extend the keywords, thus to get the positive correlated words. Finally we statistics on the number of positive correlated words in every sentence, and treat the number as a training feature, join it into the training model.

- The negative correlated words
  Contrary to the positive correlated words, there also exist some words such as "收看", "嘉士伯" in the live text, these words will lead to the information redundancy, and reduce the accuracy of extraction, we call these words the negative correlated words. We get the negative correlated words through the same method as the positive correlated words, then statistics on the number of negative correlated words in every sentence, and treat the number as a training feature, join it into the training model.

- The time
  Through the comprehensive statistical analysis of the scoring time in soccer competition and live texts, we found that there exist important information and important comments in some periods of time, these periods are the minutes after game starting, the midfield time and a few minutes before match ending. So we select the time as a feature for the model training, and the functions of characteristic time are defined as follows (8).

$$F(s) = \alpha f_1(s) + \beta f_2(s) + \gamma f_3(s) \qquad (8)$$

$$f_1(s) = \begin{cases} 1, & 0 < x \leq T \\ 0, & else \end{cases} \qquad (9)$$

$$f_2(s) = \begin{cases} 1, & s\ in\ the\ break\ time \\ 0, & else \end{cases} \qquad (10)$$

$$f_3(s) = \begin{cases} 1, & endTime - T_3 \leq x \leq endTime \\ 0, & else \end{cases} \qquad (11)$$

In the above formulas, s is a sentence, $F(s)$ refers to the characteristic time of s, which consists of $f_1(s)$, $f_2(s)$, $f_3(s)$. $f_1(s)$ is the function to judge whether s is in the period of T_1 minutes after game starting, $f_2(s)$ is the function to judge whether s is in the midfield time, and $f_3(s)$ is the function to judge whether s is in the period of T_3 minutes before the match ending. endTime is the time of match ending in live text, and the weight of three periods is α, β, γ respectively. In our experiment, we set $\alpha = 0.18$, $\beta = 0.32$, $\gamma = 0.5$.

- The window of score changes

  The information is especially important before and after the goal, and the goal-scoring means the score changes between the two teams. So we propose to set context window according to the score changes in the live text, and judge whether the sentence is contained in a context window, if in, mark the sentence "1", otherwise mark "0". Finally, we treat the marks as a training feature and join it into the training model.

4 Experiment and Results

4.1 Data Set

The training data this experiment used are 900 live texts that crawled from web, the test data are the 30 sample files provided by NLPCC-ICCPOL 2016. Accordingly, we select key sentences from the standard news in the 30 sample files, and take them as the reference summary.

4.2 Evaluating Indicator

We use the ROUGE-1.5.5 toolkit [10] for evaluation, the toolkit uses multiple evaluation indexes to evaluate the results. It measures summary quality by counting overlapping units such as the n-gram, word sequences and word pairs between the summary results and the reference summary. Here we use the ROUGE metrics–Recall and F-scores in ROUGE-1、ROUGE-2 and ROUGE-SU4 to evaluate the result of this experiment comprehensively.

4.3 Result and Analysis

In the experiment, we manually constructed a positive keywords set and a negative keywords set, used the word2vec to build a word vector on training corpus, and used vector result and cosine distance to achieve the lexical semantic computation, we will select the top 8 words that ranking by the cosine value from big to small for each keyword, so we can get the related words set. Finally, we filtered both two related words set by removing the words that the semantic error are obvious, then got 179 positive correlated words and 43 negative correlated words. Some positive and negative correlated words are shown in Table 3. The next step, we put the positive correlated words, the negative correlated words, the time and the window of score changes as features in CRFs model for training, the trained model is used to the extraction of summary sentence on the test data set.

To verify the effect of related words extension at different number on experimental result, we conducted some comparative experiments while other experimental parameters being unchanged. In the comparative experiments 0, 5 and 15 correlated words are extended, the Baseline is the number of 8 that we extended, the comparison results are shown in Table 4:

Table 3. Positive and negative correlated words set

Word set classes	The words
Positive correlated words set	进球 球门 扑出 旋向 角球 边线 射门 没收 犯规 踢倒 解围 拦截 断球 推射 直射 打门 底线 攻门 挡出 绊倒 打飞 换人 换下 受伤 倒地 流血 包扎 冲撞 黄牌 警告 拉倒
Negative correlated words set	网友 进场 更正 回复 镜头 如何 办法 休息 直播 大家 感谢 收看 结束 再见 图文 关注

Table 4. Results in different number of extensions

Number of extensions	ROUGE-1		ROUGE-2		ROUGE-SU4	
	Recall	F-value	Recall	F-value	Recall	F-value
Baseline	0.587	0.674	0.252	0.269	0.248	0.275
0	0.328	0.362	0.117	0.163	0.212	0.197
5	0.504	0.513	0.146	0.175	0.233	0.247
15	0.556	0.603	0.245	0.254	0.263	0.243

The figures in Table 4 indicate that compared to Baseline, the extracting effect is poor when the keywords are not extended or the number of extensions is small, the reason is that many important words in sentences have not been found, so the accuracy and Recall rate are low. On the other hand, when extending too much of the correlated words, there will be a lot redundant information being extracted, therefore the Recall rate and F-value is low.

To verify the effect of CRF machine learning method on summary sentences extraction from the live sports text, we conducted some comparative experiments while other experimental parameters being unchanged. In the comparative experiments, the Hidden Markov Model (HMM) and the Maximum Entropy Model (MEM) are used to train the model on corpus, the extraction results are shown in Table 5:

Table 5. Results on different models

Method	ROUGE-1		ROUGE-2		ROUGE-SU4	
	Recall	F-value	Recall	F-value	Recall	F-value
CRFs	0.556	0.603	0.245	0.261	0.248	0.266
HMM	0.392	0.477	0.184	0.231	0.197	0.206
MEM	0.385	0.361	0.191	0.226	0.188	0.223

As seen in Table 5, the effect of HMM is not so good, that is because, in the HMM model, each sentence in the corpus is considered as an independent individual, it can not effectively use the complex features, however, there is a certain correlation between sentences in the corpus. And the effect of MEM is not so obvious also, although it can solve the complex problems which combine multi-characteristics well, but it can only use the feature of binarization which only records characteristics appear or not, there is no way to record the strength of the characteristics, so there exists biases in the annotation results.

Through the above comparing experiments, it can be concluded that the proposed method, which based on the correlated words extension and the CRFs machine learning method achieved a good result on the summary sentences extraction in the field of live sport text.

5 Conclusion

From the perspectives of the semantics, the vector representation of words and correlated words extension based on word2vec can effectively solve the synonym and correlated words problem. So the experimental result has a good performance by applying the word2vec to extend the keywords in the live sports text. On the other hand, the CRFs can transform the extraction problem into an equivalent sequence tagging and binary classification problem. In our method, we select positive correlated words, negative correlated words, time and the window of score changes as features to train a CRFs model, and use the model to extract the summary sentences. Experiment shows that it not only improves training efficiency, but also has high precision. And the proposed method has a meaningful influence on automatic summarization and automatic generation of sports news.

Acknowledgements. This work is supported by the National Natural Science Foundation of China under Grants Nos. 61271304, 61671070, Beijing Advanced Innovation Center for Imaging Technology BAICIT-2016003, National Social Science Foundation of China under Grants Nos. 14@ZH036, 15ZDB017, National Language Committee of China under Grants No. ZDA125-26.

References

1. Luhn, H.P.: The automatic creation of literature abstracts. IBM J. Res. Dev. **2**(2), 159–165 (1958)
2. Prasad Pingali, R.K., Varma, V.: IIIT Hyderabad at DUC 2007. In: Proceedings of DUC 2007 (2007)
3. Lin, Z., Chua, T.S., Kan, M.Y., et al.: NUS at DUC 2007: using evolutionary models of text. In: Proceedings of Document Understanding Conference (DUC) (2007)
4. He, T., Shao, W., Xiao, H.S., et al.: The implementation of a query-directed multi-document summarization system. In: 6th International Conference on Advanced Language Processing and Web Information Technology, ALPIT 2007, pp. 105–110. IEEE (2007)
5. Liu, J., Xu, J., Zhang, Y.: Summarization based on hidden topic Markov model with multi-features. Acta Scientiarum Naturalium Universitatis Pekinensis **1**, 027 (2014)
6. Cheng, Y., Silamu, W., Hasimua, M.: Automatic text summarization based on comprehensive characteristics of sentence. Comput. Sci. **42**(4), 226–229 (2015)
7. Mikolov, T., Chen, K., Corrado, G., et al.: Efficient estimation of word representations in vector space (2013). arXiv preprint arXiv:1301.3781
8. Mikolov, T., Dean, J.: Distributed representations of words and phrases and their compositionality. In: Advances in Neural Information Processing Systems (2013)

9. Lafferty, J., McCallum, A., Pereira, F.: Conditional random fields: probabilistic models for segmenting and labeling sequence data. In: Proceedings of 18th International Conference on Machine Learning, ICML, vol. 1, pp. 282–289 (2001)
10. Lin, C.Y.: Rouge: a package for automatic evaluation of summaries. In: Workshop Text Summarization Branches Out: Proceedings of ACL-2004, vol. 8 (2004)

Short Papers

Statistical Entity Ranking with Domain Knowledge

Xiao-Bo Jin[1], Guang-Gang Geng[2]([✉]), Kaizhu Huang[3], and Zhi-Wei Yan[4]

[1] Henan University of Technology, Zhengzhou, China
xbjin9801@gmail.com
[2] China Internet Network Information Center, Beijing, China
gengguanggang@cnnic.cn
[3] Xi'an Jiaotong-Liverpool University, Suzhou, China
kaizhu.huang@xjtlu.edu.cn
[4] National Engineering Laboratory for Naming and Addressing Technologies,
Beijing, China
yanzhiwei@cnnic.cn

Abstract. Entity search is a new application meeting either precise or vague requirements from the search engines users. Baidu Cup 2016 Challenge just provided such a chance to tackle the problem of the entity search. We achieved the first place with the average MAP scores on 4 tasks including movie, tvShow, celebrity and restaurant. In this paper, we propose a series of similarity features based on both of the word frequency features and the word semantic features and describe our ranking architecture and experiment details.

Keywords: Entity search · Similarity features · Statistical features · Domain knowledge

1 Introduction

The extraction of the feature vectors from the query-document is a critical step in learning to ranking. The main effort lies in mapping the query-document pair into a joint feature space which can precisely establish their relevance.

The common method is to extract the features for each of the input text pair and then rank them on the various similarity measures based on the lexical and semantic analysis. But the similarity defined in a different measure will lead to the different rank sequences. Surdeanu et al. [8] explore a wide range of classes of the features such as coarse word sense disambiguation, name-entity identification, syntactic parsing, and sematic role labeling. Although there is a large mount of text resource in the Web, but the labeled semantic resource for the supervised learning such as Penn Treebank is rare especially for the minority language, e.g. Chinese or Korean.

Deep learning especially the Convolutional Neural Networks (CNN) has been recently shown that it can efficiently learn to embed the sentences into a low

© Springer International Publishing AG 2016
C.-Y. Lin et al. (Eds.): NLPCC-ICCPOL 2016, LNAI 10102, pp. 811–818, 2016.
DOI: 10.1007/978-3-319-50496-4_73

dimensional vector space but preserve their syntactic and semantic relations in many NLP tasks [2,10]. Severyn and Moschitti [7] build the CNN on the sentences pair in an end-to-end manner, where their model on the TREC question answering task outperforms the state-of-art systems without the manual feature engineering and the additional syntactic parsers.

In Baidu Cup 2016 Challenge, the competition invites the participants to tackle the problem of the Chinese entity search on four tasks including restaurants, movies, TV shows and celebrities. Given a query on the entity and a set of candidate entities, the ranking system should rank the entities with their relevance to the query. It is similar to the question answering, but with one characteristic: the answering only contains the entity name, which is too short to express its hiding meanings. For example, when querying "President of U.S.A.", can we predict the relevance of the celebrity 'Isaac Newton' to the question without domain knowledge? It is impossible to achieve a good performance without the domain knowledge if we only focus on the lexical, the statistical, and the semantical feature information of the answer.

In this paper, we describe a novel ranking learning architecture for the ranking of the entity object to help us to achieve the champion of Baidu Cup 2016 challenges. The distinctive properties of our architecture are: (1) we crawl the domain knowledge automatically to extend the answers according to the different tasks; (2) the statistical relevance features are extracted to build ranking models, but we only use the simple frequency features since the syntax or the semantical resource on Chinese text is difficult to obtain; (3) we also define the new semantic relevance features by means of word2vec to handle the large scale of corpus, in contrast to the CNN [7] which is restricted to the short texts or sentences; (4) we adopt the simple point-wise method to take the relevance features as the input instead of directly computing their similarity.

We validate our architectures on the four tasks and analyze the effects of the components on the ranking performance, e.g. MAP or MRR. In the following, we describe the components of the ranking learning system and report our state-of-art experimental results. Finally, we conclude the paper and the outline the future work.

2   Framework of Learning to Rank Entity

The section briefly describes entity search problem, then discusses learning to rank, which will train a rank model to predict the order of the candidate answer.

2.1   Problem Formulation

The query is a set of keywords or key-phrases used by the users to express their desire. An entity is a thing with distinct and independent existence such as celebrity, restaurant, movie and tvShow in our tasks. The goal is to query the description targeting the entities, e.g. the review on some movie, the feeling in the restaurant environment.

Given an entity search query $q_i \in Q$ and a set of the candidate entities $E_i = (d_1, r_1), (d_2, r_2), \cdots, (d_{i_k}, r_{i_k}), (d_{i_n}, r_{i_n})$, where d_{i_k} is the entity object and r_{i_k} is the relevant label equal to 1 if relevant to the query and 0 otherwise. The objective is to retrieve entities that is relevant to the query q_i from E_i under the ranking function is:

$$h(\boldsymbol{w}, \phi(q, D)) \rightarrow R, \tag{1}$$

where $\phi(q, D)$ is a query-dependent features depending both on the entity and the query and $\boldsymbol{w}$ is the parameter of the ranking function.

2.2   Extending Entity Extension by External Resources

We have recently seen a rapid and successful growth of Baidu Baike[1], which is a largest open Chinese encyclopedia on the Web. It has now more than 13,000,000 word-items edited by approximate 6,000,000 free volunteers or professional personnel. The Baike aims to be a Chinese encyclopedia and the articles on the Baike is refer to all aspects of the Chinese culture. We extract the knowledge for each entity object from celebrity, movie and tvShow. Baike will be much easier than from raw texts or from usual Web texts because of its structure. The objectiveness of the Baike also help us to rank the entity according to the query precisely. In fact, many natural language processing studies try to exploit Wikipedia as a knowledge source [1,9] for the English language.

The restaurant tasks is an exception since there is no needs for each restaurant for the Baike which aims to provide the authoritative resources or knowledge. So we crawled the review pages from Dazhong review[2], which is the largest city life website guiding the mass consumption in China.

Finally, we also collected the information and the user reviews for the movie and the tvShow tasks from Douban website[3], which provides the information and reviews on the books, the movies (including tvShow) and the music generated by over 2 billions Chinese users.

2.3   Feature for Learning

In this section, we introduce the features extracted in our experiments which can be directly used by the learning algorithm. Each row of the matrix corresponding to the feature file represents a query-entity pair. The other files for each query-entity pair separately records the query id, the entity id, the answer id in the query and the label shows the entity is relevant to the query or not.

Word Features. In the following, We give some details of these features, the fore part of which is referenced to the dataset LETOR 3.0 [6].

---

[1] http://baike.baidu.com/.
[2] https://www.dianping.com.
[3] https://www.douban.com/.

Table 1. Statistical features on corpuses: the words streams come from the title, the body and the title + the body and it can be segmented phrase or 2-ngram words

No	Description
1	Sum of TF of the query in the stream
2	Sum of IDF of the query in the stream
3	Sum of TFIDF of the query in the stream
4	Sum of BM25 of the query in the stream
5	Sum of LMIR.JM of the query in the stream
6	Sum of LMIR.DIR of the query in the stream
7	Sum of LMIR.ABS of the query in the stream
8	Max of all SS distance in the stream
9	Max of all SWS distance in the stream
10	Max of all MS distance in the stream
11	Max of all MWS distance in the stream
12	Average of all SS distance in the stream
13	Average of all SWS distance in the stream
14	Average of all MS distance in the stream
15	Average of all MWS distance in the stream

In the corpus, we considered three types of streams: title, body and title + body. For the entity body, we cut the whole part into the sentences by the end mark of the Chinese language and the English language for convenience. We also removed all Chinese and English punctuation character (Table 1).

Word2vec [3] is a series of models used to produce the word embeddings, where the models are a two-layer neural networks that take as the input a large corpus of text and produce a corresponding vector for each unique word in the high-dimensional space. Although word2vec plays a part just for computing the similarity between the words, we have no knowledge about the computation of the sentence similarity. In the following, we first give some heuristic approaches to compute the similarity between any sentence based on the public available word2vec[4].

The similarity between the query word q_i and the sentence s is defined as the max value among the similarity between q_i and the word s_i in the sentence s

$$sim(q_i, s) = \max_{s_j \in s} q_i^T s_j, \tag{2}$$

where q_i and s_i is a normalized vector with the unit length and both of them are extracted on the trained model from all types of entity corpus by word2vec. We arrange all $q_i \in q(i = 1, 2, \cdots, m)$ into the matrix $Q = [q_1, q_2, \cdots, q_m]^T$ and $s_j \in s(j = 1, 2, \cdots, n)$ into the matrix $S = [s_1, s_2, \cdots, s_n]^T$, then

$$R = QS^T \tag{3}$$

---

[4] https://code.google.com/archive/p/word2vec/.

where $R = [r_1, r_2, \cdots, r_m]^T$ and $r_i = q_i^T s$. It is clear that

$$sim(q_i, s) = \|r_i\|_\infty \qquad (4)$$

The similarity computation of the query q and the sentence s is related to $sim(q_i, s)$ for all $q_i \in q$. With the sum and max operation, we can define the following four features including Sum of Similarity (SS), Sum of Weighted Similarity (SWS), Max of Similarity (MS) and Max of Weighted Similarity (MWS)

$$SS(q, s) = \sum_{q_i \in q} sim(q_i, s) \qquad (5)$$

$$SWS(q, s) = \sum_{q_i \in q} sim(q_i, s) * idf(q_i) \qquad (6)$$

$$MS(q, s) = \max_{q_i \in q} sim(q_i, s) \qquad (7)$$

$$MWS(q, s) = \max_{q_i \in q} sim(q_i, s) * idf(q_i) \qquad (8)$$

2.4 Word Segmentation and 2-Gram Words

Chinese Word segmentation is the problem of dividing a string into its component words. It is a critical step for Chinese language processing. But the performance of the algorithm depends the domain specific dict and the used corpus. The most word segmentation algorithm does not handle the ambiguous words and unregistered ones. In our work, we adopt the simple 2-gram representation to complement the deficiencies of the word segmentation considering most of Chinese phrases consist of two words.

2.5 Ranking Model Design

In our work, we chose the ensemble approaches to predict the similarity probability for each query-entity pair. Our experiment took three candidates including AdaBoost, Random Forest and ExtraTree Classifier [5]. Further, we also tried to fuse the posterior probabilities and the rankings from multiple classifiers although the improvement is subtle on the celebrity and the restaurant datasets.

3 Experiments

3.1 DataSet Description

Baidu Challenge 2016 includes four datasets including movies, tvShows, restaurants and celebrities. For each type, there are 100 entity queries for the training and 1,000 ones for the testing. Before the competition ends, 40% of the test queries were used as the development set for all participants. In our experiments, we do not consider the results on the development set. We extracted the feature vectors from all query-entity pairs, where Table 2 gives the detailed information.

Table 2. DataSet Information

Name	#Training queries	#Training examples	#Test queries	#Test examples
Movie	100	9,596	1,000	98,309
TvShow	100	10,264	1,000	103,409
Celebrity	100	9,939	1,000	99,785
Restaurant	100	9,983	1,000	99,796

3.2   Experiments Design and Results

Data Retrieval. We crawled Baike, Douban, Dazhong web sites by the Baidu crawler and Yahoo crawler. It is important to validate the correctness of the crawled pages. We saved the meta information in the front of the texts to check whether it is consistent with the corresponding entity or not.

Preprocessing. We preprocessed the Chinese texts by removing all Chinese punctuations after splitting the total texts into the sentences with the Chinese punctuations as the end mark. Further, the sentences were split into the single Chinese words by the Jieba open source[5] and by sliding on the text with the two-width window (2-gram), separately.

Word Embeddings. We initialized the word embeddings by running word2vec tool [4] on the Chinese corpus. The tvshow and movie tasks used the corpus contain roughly 2 million vocabularies, 1 million ones for the celebrity tasks and 0.8 million ones. To train the embeddings we used the continuous of bag words model with the window size 5 to generate a 50-dimensional vectors for each word. The embeddings vector not present in the word2vec model were randomly initialized with the equal length vector with each component taken from the uniform distribution $U[-0.25, 0.25]$. On both of word segmentation form and 2-ngram form, we extracted 33 features from each corpus and merged them into 66-dimensional features.

Experiment Setup. We evaluated the performance on the training dataset by 10-fold cross validation (cv-10). In particular, the query-entity pair from the same query would be put into the same fold for keeping the completeness of each query. The cross folds were kept invariant for all parameters settings.

In implementing the extra tree classifier, the parameter $n\_estimator$ were randomly drawn from the integer range $[100, 500]$ and another parameter max_depth was randomly from the enumeration range $\{4, 6, 8, 10, 12\}$. The models parameters were optimized in the space of the grid with the parameter $n\_estimator$ and max_depth by the cross-validation on the training data.

---

[5] https://github.com/fxsjy/jieba.

Evaluation Measures. The competition uses the Mean Average Precision (MAP) to evaluate the quality of the submission file, which is common in the information retrieval. MAP examines the ranks of all the related entities and computes the mean over the average precision scores for each query

$$MAP(q) = \frac{1}{|q|} \sum_{q_i \in q} avgprec(q_i). \tag{9}$$

Meanwhile, we computes $avgprec(q_i)$ as follows

$$avgprec(q_i) = \sum_{e \in q_i} \frac{rel(e, q_i)}{pos(e)} \tag{10}$$

where $rel(e, q_i)$ (1 or 0) shows whether the entity e is correlated with the query q and $pos(e)$ is the position of the entity e in the ranking sequence of the query q.

Finally, we achieve the first place of the Baidu Challenge 2016 competition as shown in the Table 3. Limited to the short readiness time, more experiments and analysis are ongoing in order to keep the integrity of the entire paper. In the further work, we will promptly give more detailed comparisons and comprehensive experimental analysis.

Table 3. Competition results on four tasks

Tasks	Celebrity	Movie	Restaurant	TvShow	Total
Results	0.8818	0.7759	0.5939	0.5978	0.7124

4   Conclusion

In this paper, we explore the merging of the simple word frequency features and the word2vcc-based sematic features to solve the entity search problem. The effectiveness of the features is shown on the Baidu Challenge 2016 competitions datasets. We explain the entire processing of the experiments. We achieved the best performance with the merging of the features and the extra tree ranker (point-wise ranker). In future work, we will improve and finish the experiment comparisons, furthermore, we will take these features as the preprocessing step of the deep learning and apply the CNN to learn the relation between the query and the entity.

Acknowledgment. This work was partially supported by the Fundamental Research Funds for the Henan Provincial Colleges and Universities in Henan University of Technology, the National Basic Research Program of China (2012CB316301), the National Natural Science Foundation of China (61103138, 61005029, 61375039 and 61473236).

References

1. Kazama, J., Torisawa, K.: Exploiting Wikipedia as external knowledge for named entity recognition. In: Proceedings of the Joint Conference on Empirical Methods in Natural Language Processing and Computational Natural Language Learning, pp. 698–707 (2007)
2. Yoon, K.: Convolutional neural networks for sentence classification. In: EMNLP 2014, August 2014. arXiv:1408.5882
3. Mikolov, T., Chen, K., Corrado, G., Dean, J.: Efficient estimation of word representations in vector space. arXiv:1301.3781, January 2013
4. Mikolov, T., Sutskever, I., Chen, K., Corrado, G., Dean, J.: Distributed representations of words and phrases and their compositionality. In: NIPS 2013. arXiv:1310.4546, October 2013
5. Pedregosa, F., Varoquaux, G., Gramfort, A., Michel, V., Thirion, B., Grisel, O., Blondel, M., Prettenhofer, P., Weiss, R., Dubourg, V., Vanderplas, J., Passos, A., Cournapeau, D., Brucher, M., Perrot, M., Duchesnay, E.: Scikit-learn: machine learning in python. J. Mach. Learn. Res. **12**, 2825–2830 (2011)
6. Qin, T., Liu, T.-Y., Jun, X., Li, H.: LETOR: a benchmark collection for research on learning to rank for information retrieval. Inf. Retrieval J. **13**(4), 346–374 (2010)
7. Severyn, A., Moschitti, A.: Learning to rank short text pairs with convolutional deep neural networks. In: Proceedings of the 38th International ACM SIGIR Conference on Research and Development in Information Retrieval, SIGIR 2015, pp. 373–382 (2015)
8. Surdeanu, M., Ciaramita, M., Zaragoza, H.: Learning to rank answers to non-factoid questions from web collections. Comput. Linguist. **37**(2), 351–383 (2011)
9. Torsten Z., Iryna G., Max M.: Analyzing and accessing wikipedia as a lexical semantic resource. In: Biannual Conference of the Society for Computational Linguistics and Language Technology (2007)
10. Zhang, X., Zhao, J., LeCun, Y.: Character-level convolutional networks for text classification. arXiv:1509.01626 [cs], September 2015

Study on the Method of Precise Entity Search Based on Baidu's Query

Teng Wang[1(✉)], Xueqiang Lv[1], Xun Ma[1], Pengyan Sun[1],
Zhian Dong[1], and Jianshe Zhou[2]

[1] Beijing Key Laboratory of Internet Culture and Digital Dissemination
Research, Beijing Information Science and Technology University,
Beijing, China
419684410@qq.com

[2] Beijing Advanced Innovation Center for Imaging Technology,
Capital Normal University, Beijing, China

Abstract. For a given query, searching for entities that conform to the description facts in the given set, in view of this goal, this paper proposes a matching method based on classification and semantic extension. The algorithm firstly to classify the query string into three categories, and extract the key word of different categories of query word. Then the keyword is extended to get the matching word set based on the word2vec word vector model. At last we calculate the score of every entity by the weighted matching method and get results according to the score ranking. After the experiment, the method get the correct rate of 63.2%, which has good applicability, and to a certain extent, it reduces the retrieval failure rate due to the query of the spoken language and diversification.

Keywords: Entity search · Word2vec · Precise matching · Similarity

1 Introduction

Developing more intelligent search engines [1] is a long-term common goal for both academia and industry. An intelligent search engine should meet either precise or vague requirements from users. Results that are semantically relevant [2] to the queries should be returned, other than those literally matching results. For instance, people may search for "restaurants with good environment suitable for kids' birthday parties". In order to meet the user's intent, the search engine needs to understand every restaurant, check which of them can be tagged as "with good environment" and "suitable for kids' birthday parties" and index the restaurants with these tags for retrieval.

This work is supported by the National Natural Science Foundation of China under Grants No. 61271304, 61671070, Beijing Advanced Innovation Center for Imaging Technology BAICIT-2016003, National Social Science Foundation of China under Grants No. 14@ZH036, 15ZDB017, National Language Committee of China under Grants No. ZDA125-26.

© Springer International Publishing AG 2016
C.-Y. Lin et al. (Eds.): NLPCC-ICCPOL 2016, LNAI 10102, pp. 819–827, 2016.
DOI: 10.1007/978-3-319-50496-4_74

The traditional method of researching is matching the query with all index pages, without analysis of the user's search intention. In a real environment the method is limited by the complex semantic representation or spoken query [3], and the entity search [4–8] results are often unsatisfactory. In order to realize the accurate matching [9] based on semantic analysis, a series of analysis of the query string is needed. Literature [5] proposes a general probabilistic framework for entity search to evaluate and provide insights in the many ways of using these types of input for query modeling. Literature [8] employs a probabilistic retrieval model for entity search in which term-based and category-based representations of queries and entities are effectively integrated. The word2vec was used in Literature [10] to map all the words into a more abstract word vector space, and then calculates the similarity between words based on the word vector, and finally obtains the article keyword by word clustering. But it all did not carry out a deeper classification of semantics and consider the context.

The analytical method of semantics are not the same in different application scenarios, so this paper take four basic scenarios of movies, TV shows, restaurants, names as the research object which is all based on Baidu's evaluation corpus. With analyzing of Content information of every entity and query, this paper put forward an accurate searching method based on extended query string which consists of three parts: query string parser, entity information collector and rule matching, and provides an important theoretical basis for research of entity search.

2 Query String Parsing

2.1 Movies, TV Shows Query String Classification

After analyzing the query string, while taking into account the complexity on the semantics of the query, this article will take the film query string into three categories: Basic information adaptive type (info), adapting the content type (content), complex and difficult to determine type (complex), details as follows:

- Info: this type represents user intents to search for the video basic attributes, including names, director, genre, running time, etc. This type of query string is represented as "Starring Xun Zhou", Directed by "Feng Xiao gang", etc.
- Content: this type represents the user intends to search for the information about the video content which can get information from reviews of movies, like "about the revenge", "on the witch", "people and animals", "the theme of war", etc.
- Complex: This type is difficult to judge the results obtained by analyzing basic information and plot summary with subjective factors, such as "80's like to watch", "Slow pace", "an unexpected ending", "very alternative", etc.

First (Info) Extraction. Take 1000 query string for analysis, statistics prefix and suffix word first class, get first class "attribute vocabulary". When the query of the first type is matched by the table, return to <type, matching word>. For example, if the query is about director, the extraction of Prefix and suffix in Chinese is like "主演、所演、出演、演、参演…", and return <info, the name of the director>.

Second (Content) and Third (Complex) Extraction. This experiment adopts the ways with machine expansion like the first extraction and manual annotation. With the increase of data, it can form a rich "complex query corpus", the manual annotation of the subsequent query string can be completely replaced by the machine.

2.2   The Extraction of the Matched Words in Restaurants' Query

Through the analysis of a large number of query strings, it is found that the query string can be represented by three nouns, verbs or adjectives. Dependency syntax can express the relationship of the internal structure of a sentence, and the dependency parsing of LTP is used in this paper. The query string is converted into the three tuple SAO structure.

2.3   The Extraction of the Matched Words in Name's Query

The name query string's content is the description of the term information, so without classification, directly extract nouns as the matching word set.

3   Semantic Extension and Matching Rules

3.1   Word2vec Word Vector Model and Semantic Extension

The word2vec [10] model is used to compute the similar words of query's basic matching words to extend that sense group sets of words. The vector space which is the output of the word2vec can be used to represent text semantic similarity. In this paper, word2vec was used to train the word vector model in field of film and television, and by cosine similarity to compute the similarity of the two words. For example, "Holmes" calculation of the high similarity of the word "Watson" "reasoning" "detective" "murder" "case" and so on, and the extended words can accurately represent the user's query intention.

3.2   Matching Rule

String Matching Rules for Movies and TV Series. Set the score of category X for query string Q as Score (X), then the calculation method for each category of query is as follows:

The first category is info, the extraction of key words can be directly matched. Set the number of hits as N, the weight as I, then

$$\text{Score}(X) = I * n, X = \text{Info} \tag{1}$$

For the Second category content and third category complex. Set content matching word vector as $\text{vec}(b_1, b_2, \ldots b_i, P_1, P_2, \ldots P_j)$, where the first i of the basic extraction of the query for the b_i, the weight is B, set the complex class matching word vector as vec $(m_1, m_2, \ldots m_i, Q_1, Q_2, \ldots Q_j)$, the first i manual annotation words for the m_i, the weight is M. The first j expansion word is x_j, corresponding to the weight of S_j (similarity), matching the number of hits is n_i, such as $n_i * b_i$ means the times of b_i hits, then

$$\text{Score}(X) = \begin{cases} B * \sum_{i=1}^{i} n(b_i) + \sum_{i=1}^{i} S_i * n(P_i), X = \text{content} \\ M * \sum_{j=1}^{j} n(m_j) + \sum_{j=1}^{j} S_j * n(Q_j), X = \text{complex} \end{cases} \tag{2}$$

Among them, for the content, b_i is the based matching keyword extracted from the query string, which is regarded as the accurate matching for target, given a higher weight; for the category of complex, m_i for manual annotation, is regarded as a non-deterministic matching, giving a smaller weight. All extended by word similarity descending take the first N, according to the similarity of each expansion word and the basic word to calculate the similarity S_j, which is calculated by word2vec. To sum up, entity E in the query string Q scores of:

$$\text{ScoreE} = \text{Score(info)} + \text{Score(content)} + \text{Score(complex)} \tag{3}$$

The optimum value of the parameter I, B, M is obtained by the experiment. Under normal circumstances the query string is only one of the three categories, the complex situation will be the intersection.

The Matched Rules for the Restaurants' Query String. With the analysis of the dependency syntax, the query string is converted into the three tuple SAO structure. Then by analyzing the relationship of the three tuple, the member is set different weights. Non three tuple structure is set as the default weight 1. Finally, the set $B\{c_1 : w_1; c_2 : w_2; c_3 : w_3\}$ that contains the basic word and the corresponding weight is gotten.

The weight formula is as follows:

$$w_{E1} = \begin{cases} 2, & (E1, REL) \text{ is } SBV(subjectverb) \\ 1, & others \end{cases} \tag{4}$$

$$w_{E2} = \begin{cases} 2, & (E2, REL) \text{ is } VOB(verbobject), POB \text{ or } ATT \\ 1, & others \end{cases} \tag{5}$$

The weight of the entity E1 is w_{E1}. The weight of the entity E2 is w_{E2}.

By extending the basic word with word2vec, getting the original word similarity from word2vec, computing the weight of word finally get the matched set.

$C\{c_1 : w_1; c_2 : w_2; \ldots \ldots; c_n : w_n\}$. The weight of extended words formula is as follows:

$$w_j = c_i * s_{ij} \tag{6}$$

c_i is the weight of original word. s_{ij} is the similarity between the extended word and the original word, which is obtained from word2vec. w_j is the weight of the extended word.

When calculating the correlation degree, this paper divides it into three parts, which are the basic information correlation, the label correlation, the comment correlation.

The comments correlation calculation formula is as follows:

$$Score = w_B * \left(\sum_i S_i + num(B) \right) + w_L * num(L) + n(Query) * 5000 +$$
$$min(n(C)) * 1000 + \sum_i (n(c_i) * w_i * w_R) \tag{7}$$

w_B is the predefined weight of the basic information. S_i is the corresponding score of a query string that the basic information contains. $num(B)$ is the number of matched words that name contains. w_L is a predefined label correlation weights. $num(L)$ is the number of matched words contained in restaurant reviews. $min(n(C))$ represents the number of all labels in the comments. w_i is the weight of the matched word c_i that is gotten from the similarity of word2vec and dependency syntax. w_R is the predefined weight of comments.

The Matched Rules for the Name's Query String.

(1) Whether the query segment for proper nouns, if yes, then match the proper person set. If not, all field match with the query segment. If all match, give a weight of α.
(2) Use the query segment label set match the entity data set. If all label set match, weight increased by β, plus the the number of occurrences of the label set, minus the total number of full match appears. If it not all label set match, weight increased by the number of each label occurrence number.
(3) Use the query segment label set match the person set. If all label set match, weight increased by γ, plus the the number of occurrences of the label set, minus the total number of full match appears. If it not all label set match, weight increased by the number of each label occurrence number.

At last, sort the data of name weight, obtain the result. Formula is as follows:

$$Weight_j = \alpha + \beta * min(n_1, \ldots, n_N) + \sum_i^N [n_i - min(n_1, \ldots, n_N)] +$$
$$\gamma * min(m_1, \ldots, m_N) + \sum_i^N [m_i - min(m_1, \ldots, m_N)] \tag{8}$$

Among them, n_i represent the numbers of the i'th label in the query segment label set matching to the physical properties of names; $min(n_1, \ldots, n_N)$ is the minimum of the times that all of these label matches the query segment label set; m_i means represent the numbers of the label i in the query segment label set matching to the Entity data set of names; $min(m_1, \ldots, m_N)$ means the minimum of these numbers. In this paper, in order to be able to ensure the right value of the parameter weights in α, β, λ, make the value divide into three groups, K1 {1000,10,10}, K2 {100,100,10}, K3 {100,10,10}, and test these method with data set.

4 Evaluation Method and Experimental Result Analysis

4.1 Evaluation Standard

This experiment uses the Mean Average Precision (MAP) as the evaluation standard, and more specific content about MAP can refer to Wikipedia.

4.2 Experimental Results and Analysis

Film, TV and Restaurant. In the film and television section, each query entity corpus (long reviews, commentaries and content outline for each 200) after data processing are about the size of 1 M. Adjust the weight parameter I, B, S based on the actual number of matches and three classification features. Divide the weight into absolute weight and general weight. The absolute weight indicates a hundred percent hit, applying to basic information class matches; the general weight is according to the actual situation and occurrence frequency to determine. The experimental results of observation obtained, the maximum number of hits of a query string expanded matching word set is about 130 times, with a matching weight of 10, the maximum score of the matching entity is 1300 points. So for the absolute weight, the result of the calculation is much higher than that of the score. I is the weight of info, just from the basic information matching to belongs to the absolute hit, so make I absolute weight values I = 3000; B is the weight of basic matching word of second type, which matching one time means a larger rate of a hit, make weight B = 100; S is the weight of extended term, is calculated by the cosine similarity of the extended term and basic term according to result of the word2vec training. Basis weight is in front of the establishment of the reference standard S = 10, such as expansion word J and basic word similarity for S_j, the corresponding weight $S_j = 10 * s_j$.

In the restaurant section, we conduct an experiment which add the dependency syntax and use word2vec to expand the number of synonyms. In the end, we adjust the number of the expansion words to make a better result, and use the traditional method which does not consider the relationship between the weight of the noun phrase and the adjective as a contrast experiment.

The result of different N values of the MAP on Film and TV and the result of traditional method and improved method on Restaurant is shown in Fig. 1.

In Film and TV section, the result shows that the MAP is the highest when the number of extended words is extended to 30. When the extension number is low, the matching set to query for the meaning expression is not complete, when the extension number is large, increasing the ratio of impurity word, dilute the ratio of real similar words, two cases the correct rate was decreased.

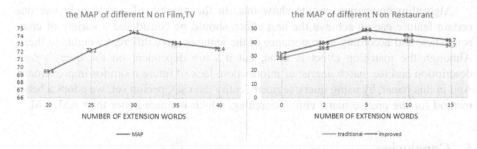

Fig. 1. The MAP of the different N

At the same time, the contrast test, using the traditional query string word segmentation - Extraction Keyword - direct full text matching method, get the MAP value is only about 0.45, it is proved that the physical search method in this paper has a good improvement.

In the restaurant section, the result by traditional method is much poor than improved method joining dependency syntax. The main reason is that the dependency syntax considers the weight of entity relationship, and reduces the non-key entities score, it enhances the accuracy of the correlation.

Celebrity

Traditional method

1. All Match: Based on the analysis of characteristics of query segment. In this paper, use it as a reference method AM.
2. Entity Match: This method uses the entity data set match with the query segment label set. This paper will use it as a reference method EM.

The result is shown in Table 1.

Table 1. Different methods and parameters' MAP

Method	MAP/%
AM	79.3
EM	71.2
K1	80.2
K2	82.9
K3	**83.2**

Experimental results showed that in this data set, the AM method is a little higher than EM method, but these two methods can't compare with this paper's methods. In this paper, K3 of α, β, γ is better than other method.

From the experiments above, we can see in the search experiments, after using the query, and name entity, this paper propose word weight to make the result's accuracy higher.

Algorithm comparing results show that, in the process of query, only use one certain feature cannot achieve the best effect, should be considered a variety of characteristics, and according to importance of the features, give different weights to them. Although the matching effect is good, but it's too dependent on the query's own description and the match degree of information, lack of future room for improvement. And in this paper, by using query segment, entity data set, person set, we adopt a better method for the precise name entity searching, which is much better than AM, EM.

5 Conclusion

This paper proposes a precise entity matching method by calculating the content correlation. According to the data analysis, different classification methods are used in different entities. In the field of film and television, use three levels of classification of the query string, consists of basic query, deterministic query and uncertainty query; In the field of restaurant, query string dependency parsing is the main method; In the celebrity search field, establish special name library for disambiguation. These methods can be obtained for a more accurate understanding of the semantics of the query. Word2vec based on the full text of the calculation of key words, to expand the basic matching words extracted from the query statement to reduce the language and diversification of the matching failure. Compared with the traditional search method, the method based on semantic understanding and retrieval results has higher accuracy. The next step is to build a more complete query string when you have more data, entirely by machines instead of manual annotation, to further improve the usability and search results.

References

1. Ping, J., Zhiming, C.: Intelligent search engine user interest model analysis and research. Microelectron. Comput. **11**, 24–26 (2004)
2. Xiuli, H., Qiaoming, Z., Li, P.F.: The combination of semantic analysis and word frequency statistics of Chinese text similarity measurement method. Appl. Res. Comput. **03**, 833–836 (2012)
3. Wolf, L., et al.: Joint word2vec networks for bilingual semantic representations. Int. J. Comput. Linguist. Appl. **5**(1), 27–44 (2014)
4. Cheng, T., Chang, K.C.C.: Entity search engine: towards agile best-effort information integration over the web. In: CIDR, vol. 2007 (2007)
5. Balog, K., Bron, M., De Rijke, M.: Query modeling for entity search based on terms, categories, and examples. ACM Trans. Inf. Syst. (TOIS) **29**(4), 22 (2011)
6. Neumayer, R., Balog, K., Nørvåg, K.: On the modeling of entities for ad-hoc entity search in the web of data. In: Baeza-Yates, R., Vries, A.P., Zaragoza, H., Cambazoglu, B.B., Murdock, V., Lempel, R., Silvestri, F. (eds.) ECIR 2012. LNCS, vol. 7224, pp. 133–145. Springer, Heidelberg (2012). doi:10.1007/978-3-642-28997-2_12

7. Bron, M., Balog, K., Rijke, M.: Example based entity search in the web of data. In: Serdyukov, P., Braslavski, P., Kuznetsov, S.O., Kamps, J., Rüger, S., Agichtein, E., Segalovich, I., Yilmaz, E. (eds.) ECIR 2013. LNCS, vol. 7814, pp. 392–403. Springer, Heidelberg (2013). doi:10.1007/978-3-642-36973-5_33

8. Balog, K., Bron, M., Rijke, M., Weerkamp, W.: Combining term-based and category-based representations for entity search. In: Geva, S., Kamps, J., Trotman, A. (eds.) INEX 2009. LNCS, vol. 6203, pp. 265–272. Springer, Heidelberg (2010). doi:10.1007/978-3-642-14556-8_27

9. Freitas, A., et al.: Treo: combining entity-search, spreading activation and semantic relatedness for querying linked data. In: Proceedings of 1st Workshop on Question Answering over Linked Data (QALD-1) at the 8th Extended Semantic Web Conference (ESWC 2011) (2011)

10. Rong, X.: word2vec parameter learning explained. arXiv preprint arXiv (2014)

Overview of the NLPCC-ICCPOL 2016 Shared Task: Chinese Word Similarity Measurement

Yunfang Wu[(⊠)] and Wei Li

Key Laboratory of Computational Linguistics,
Peking University, Beijing 100871, China
{wuyf,liweitj47}@pku.edu.cn

Abstract. Word similarity computation is a fundamental task for natural language processing. We organize a semantic campaign of Chinese word similarity measurement at NLPCC-ICCPOL 2016. This task provides a benchmark dataset of Chinese word similarity (PKU-500 dataset), including 500 word pairs with their similarity scores. There are 21 teams submitting 24 systems in this campaign. In this paper, we describe clearly the data preparation and word similarity annotation, make an in-depth analysis on the evaluation results and give a brief introduction to participating systems.

Keywords: Word similarity · Similarity computation · Semantic campaign

1 Introduction

Word similarity computation is to automatically predict the similarity degree of word pairs, which is a fundamental task for many natural language processing (NLP) systems, such as question answering, information retrieval, paraphrase detection and textual entailment. There are two kinds of ways to evaluate word similarities: (i) intrinsic evaluation: compute the correlation coefficient between the automatic predicted results with the human labelled similarity scores; (ii) extrinsic evaluation: apply the word similarities to a specific downstream task, like name entity recognition or relation extraction. The extrinsic evaluation is a valid method, but it does not allow us to understand the properties of lexical similarities without further analysis. Therefore, this paper focuses on the first method of intrinsic evaluation. There needs a benchmark dataset to evaluate and compare different systems on computing lexical similarity, and thus to encourage more researches on this problem.

In English, there are quite a few open datasets that are commonly used as benchmark for evaluating word similarity. The first data RG is from Rubenstein and Goodenough [1]. The data contains 65 pairs of nouns, and the human subjects were asked to order the pairs according to the amount of "similarity meaning" and give a similarity value from 0.0–4.0. Miller and Charles [2] selected 30 of those pairs (MC data), and studied semantic similarity as a function of contexts in which words are used. The most widely used dataset is WordSim-353 [3]. It selected out 353 pairs of nouns and asked 16 human annotators to assign a numerical similarity score between 0 and 10. In the recent time, Huang et al. [4] created a new dataset, where the word pairs were presented in sentential context rather than in isolation.

© Springer International Publishing AG 2016
C.-Y. Lin et al. (Eds.): NLPCC-ICCPOL 2016, LNAI 10102, pp. 828–839, 2016.
DOI: 10.1007/978-3-319-50496-4_75

However, such an open benchmark has been absent in Chinese for a long time, which becomes a bottleneck for Chinese word similarity computation. In the early and notable work of Liu and Li [5], only 39 word pairs were selected for evaluating. Jin and Wu [6] organized a campaign of evaluating Chinese word similarity at Semeval-2012. They translated the word pairs of WordSim-353 data to Chinese, and asked twenty human annotators to give a similarity score between 0 and 5. But only two teams submitted four systems in this campaign. Guo et al. [7] constructed a Chinese Poly-semous Word Similarity Dataset, which contains 401 word pairs selected from Hownet, but this data focuses on polysemous words and so the data diversity is limited.

We organize a campaign of Chinese word similarity measurement at NLPCC-ICCPOL 2016, and construct a benchmark dataset (namely PKU-500). The dataset contains 500 Chinese word pairs, which are assigned similarity scores by twenty subjects. Researchers have shown great interest in this problem and totally 49 teams registered in this task. Finally 21 teams participated in our campaign and submitted 24 systems.

In this paper, we make an overview of this task. In Sect. 2, we introduce the dataset construction, including the diverse criteria for data collection and the annotation scheme of similarity scores. Section 3 describes the task setup and the evaluation metrics. In Sect. 4, we report the evaluation results of 24 systems and make a detailed analysis on the experimental results. We analyze the following factors that may affect Chinese word similarity computation: (i) the inter-annotator agreement in assigning similarity scores, (ii) part of speech, (iii) word length and (iv) polysemous words. In Sect. 5, we make a brief introduction to the participating systems. Section 6 gives the conclusion.

2 Dataset Construction

2.1 Word Selection

The commonly-used WordSim-353 dataset [3] only contains nouns and tries to have word pairs with a diverse set of similarity scores. But in recent years, researchers pay more attention to the semantic representations of some special words, like rare words and polysemous words. Accordingly, more important and diverse criteria should be considered in constructing the dataset.

- **Domain.** Covering both the traditional formal language and the recent web language.
- **Frequency.** The high-frequency words, middle-frequency words and low-frequency words should all be included.
- **Part of Speech.** Not only nouns but also verbs and adjectives should be included. Not only the content words (noun, verb and adjective) but also the functional words (e.g., adverb, conjunction) should be considered.
- **Word Length.** A Chinese word may be composed of one character, two characters, three characters or four characters. All these different types of words should be considered.

- **Word Sense.** Ambiguous words with multiple meanings are the most difficult part for lexical semantic researches, so some polysemous words should be included.
- **Polarity.** Words with different semantic orientations (positive vs. negative) should be included.

According to the above criteria, we selected words in the following procedure.

1. The data comes from two domains: three month *People's Daily News* and a large collection of WeiBo data.
2. All the data was word segmented and POS tagged using the open software ANSJ.
3. We extracted words separately from the two domains according to their frequency, part of speech and word length.
4. The automatically extracted words were further picked out manually by the first author of the paper, according to the word senses and semantic polarities. Finally, we got 514 words and 202 words from *People's Daily News* and WeiBo data, respectively.

2.2 Word Pair Generation

In total we selected 716 single words from the corpus in the previous phrase. Now, we will generate word pairs for evaluating word similarity.

1. For each target word, we automatically extracted three candidate words from HIT-CIR Tongyici Cilin (Extended): the first word lies in the same synset; the second is one of the words belonging to the parent node; the third one is randomly selected from other words.
2. For each target word, the candidate words were further picked out manually by the first author of the paper. We removed some candidate words and add some new words by linguistic insight, according to the criteria described in Sect. 2.1. Finally, we got 470 word pairs.
3. We selected other 30 word pairs that were translated from the WordSim-353 data.
4. Finally, we got 500 word pairs for Chinese word similarity measurement.

2.3 Similarity Score Annotation

We asked twenty graduate students to annotate similarity scores of word pairs. All the students are Chinese native speakers and major in Chinese linguistics. The similarity score is set to [1, 10], where 1 means two words are totally different and 10 means two words carry the same meaning. We calculated the average value of twenty humans as the final similarity score of each pair.

We didn't give any annotation guidelines to the human annotators, so the annotators were encouraged to judge just by their intuition of language. We didn't make a clear distinction between semantic relatedness and semantic similarity, because it is a notorious problem in lexical semantics and it depends on the application task you will do.

Tables 1 and 2 give some examples of word pairs with their similarity scores. Table 1 lists the top 10 similar words and Table 2 lists the top 10 dissimilar words.

Table 1. The top 10 similar word pairs

Word 1	Word 2	Score
WTO	世界贸易组织	10
紫禁城	故宫	10
计算机	电脑	9.9
赢	胜	9.8
维他命	维生素	9.5
化肥	化学肥料	9.5
课程表	课表	9.5
互联网	因特网	9.5
假货	赝品	9.5

Table 2. The top 10 dissimilar word pairs

Word 1	Word 2	Score
讲价	打架	1
教授	黄瓜	1
控制	恐高	1
阻力	天花板	1
结盟	无理取闹	1.1
调查	努力	1.1
玻璃	魔术师	1.1
干扰	上网	1.1
课堂	美食	1.1

Table 3. The top 10 word pairs with low standard deviation

Word 1	Word 2	Score	Stad.
教授	黄瓜	1	0.00
控制	恐高	1	0.00
阻力	天花板	1	0.00
WTO	世界贸易组织	10	0.00
紫禁城	故宫	10	0.00
讲价	打架	1	0.22
玻璃	魔术师	1.1	0.30
干扰	上网	1.1	0.30
课堂	美食	1.1	0.30

Table 4. The top 10 word pairs with high standard deviation

Word 1	Word 2	Score	Stad.
没戏	没辙	4.9	3.03
只管	尽管	4	2.94
GDP	生产力	6.5	2.80
包袱	段子	2.6	2.71
日期	时间	6	2.67
由此	通过	3.4	2.66
爱面子	好高骛远	4	2.56
一方面	一边	5.4	2.54
托福	GRE	8	2.54

In assigning similarity scores, some word pairs have quite high inter-annotator agreement while some other word pairs have very low inter-annotator agreement. Tables 3 and 4 list the top 10 word pairs with low standard deviation and high standard deviation, respectively.

It can be seen that two types of word pairs are likely to have high inter-annotator agreement. (1) Word pairs that refer to the same entity. For example, the word pair "紫禁城" vs. "故宫" gets a standard deviation 0.0 that means all twenty annotators give it the same score 10. (2) Word pairs that are totally different. For example, all twenty annotators give the pair "教授" vs. "黄瓜" the same score 1. However, for the following word pairs, different annotators tend to give different similarity scores. (1) Two words are functional words (e.g., "只管" vs. "尽管", "由此" vs. "通过", "一方面" vs. "一边"). (2) Two words are sematic related (e.g., "GDP" vs. "生产力", "日期" vs. "时间", "托福" vs. "GRE"). Annotators handle semantic related words differently: some annotators assign them a high similarity score, while other annotators assign them a low score. It is an interesting topic to investigate why annotators give different similarity scores to a pair of word, so for further research Appendix A lists the 91 word pairs with standard deviation greater than 2.0.

3 Task Setup

All 500 word pairs serve as the test data, and no training data is provided. We first released 40 word pairs as the trial data before the evaluation phrase. All kinds of strategies are welcome, including the traditional corpus-based distributional similarity, dictionary-based similarity computation, as well as the recently developed word embedding methods and deep learning models. Also, the participating systems are encouraged to use external resources.

In order to avoid over-fitting on this small test dataset, we released a large collection of 10,000 word pairs in the testing phrase. Our 500 word pairs were mixed in the large data, and the other word pairs were randomly generated from a large dictionary.

We use Spearman's rank correlation coefficient to evaluate the statistical dependence between the automatic computing results and the golden human labelled scores:

$$\rho = 1 - \frac{6 \sum_{i=1}^{n} (R_{Xi} - R_{Yi})^2}{n(n^2 - 1)} \tag{1}$$

where n is the number of word pairs being evaluated, R_{Xi} and R_{Yi} are the standard deviations of the rank of automatic computing results and human labelled scores, respectively.

4 Evaluation Results and Analysis

4.1 Overall Results

Together 21 teams participated in our task and submitted 24 systems. Table 5 reports the evaluation results, listing the team ID, organizations and Spearman scores.

The best result of the wining team is 0.518, which is significantly better than the second best system by 6.1%. The last system gets a score 0.000, because it destroys the format of the testing data. Only the wining first system gets a Spearman score greater than 0.50; 16 systems are in 0.30–0.50; 7 systems are below 0.30. In the recent work of Schnabel et al. [8], they report a score of 0.640 on WordSim-353 data by using CBOW word embeddings. It demonstrates that there is still a large gap between Chinese and English word similarity computation.

4.2 Inter-annotator Agreement and Evaluation Results

We think those word pairs with low inter-annotator agreement in assigning similarity scores will have negative effects on evaluation results. To address the inconsistency of annotators, we remove those word pairs with a standard deviation greater than 2.0, and we get 401 word pairs with low standard deviation. Figure 1 reports the evaluation results of the top three systems on 401 word pairs.

Table 5. The overall evaluation results

Team ID	Organization	Spear.
SXUCFN-QA	Shanxi University	0.518
DLUT_NLPer	Dalian University of Technology	0.457
CQUT_AC996	Chongqing University of Technology	0.436
nlp_polyu	The Hong Kong Polytechnic University	0.421
BLCU_CNLR	Beijing Language and Culture University	0.414
Cbrain	Institute of Automation, Chinese Academy of Sciences	0.412
CIST	Beijing University of Posts and Telecommunications	0.405
wanghao.ftd	Shanghai Jiao Tong University	0.405
DUTNLP	Dalian University of Technology	0.372
BIT_CWSM	Beijing Institute of Technology	0.371
NJUST-CWS	Nanjing University of Science and Technology	0.365
TJIIP	Tongji University	0.357
SWJTU_CCIT	Southwest Jiaotong University	0.349
QLUNLP_1	Qilu University of Technology	0.327
QLUNLP_2		0.328
QLUNLP_3		0.314
QLUNLP_4		0.234
CCNU BeliefTeam	Central China Normal University	0.316
DM&S Lab	Beijing University of Technology	0.286
Zsw	University of South China	0.272
AngryXYZ	University of Beijing Science and Technology	0.268
Zutcsnlp2016	Zhongyuan University of Technology	0.206
whut_nlp	Wuhan University	0.014
USC	University of South China	0.000

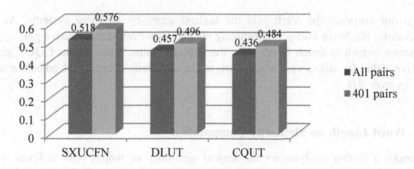

Fig. 1. The performances of top three systems on word pairs with low standard deviation

As our expectation, the performances of the top three systems are consistently improved on 401 word pairs, and the Spearman scores $\rho * 100$ are improved by 5.8, 3.9 and 4.8 for SXUCFN, DLUT and CQUT, respectively. For further research, Appendix A lists the 91 word pairs with high standard deviation.

4.3 Part of Speech on Similarity Computation

Both the RG and WordSim-353 dataset only contain nouns. We want to know whether different parts of speech will affect the automatic computation of word similarity, so we make a comparison on different parts of speech by the top three systems, as shown in Fig. 2. Those word pairs where both words are nouns constitute a set of Noun, and we compare the automatic scores of word pairs within this set with the golden human labelled score. In the same way, we compute the Spearman scores of Verb and Adjective. The Noun set includes 247 word pairs, and the Verb set includes 104 word pairs and Adjective set 52 word pairs. The other word pairs are: (i) two words have different parts of speech; (ii) both words are functional words. These three sets of word pairs will be released separately in the website of NLPCC-ICCPOL 2016 for further researches.

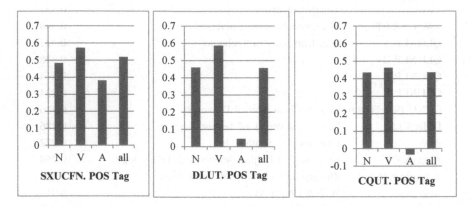

Fig. 2. The performances of top three systems on different parts of speech

To our surprise, the Verb gets the highest score by all three systems. As our expectation, the Noun also gets promising results. However, the Adjective gets a quite low score, which is much lower than the average value. The system CQUT gets a negative value for adjectives, which assigns the similarity score of 24 adjective word pairs as over 9.0.

4.4 Word Length on Similarity Computation

We make a further analysis on the lexical similarity of words with different word length. We regard a word pair as One Character if it contains a single-character word; we regard a word pair as Three Characters if it contains a three-character word. In the same way, we extract the word pairs of Two Characters and Four Characters. Please note that these different sets may have overlap. In our testing data, the One Character set includes 25 word pairs, and the Three Characters set includes 90 word pairs and the Four Characters set 43 word pairs. The majority part is the set of Two Characters, which includes 450 word pairs. These different sets of word pairs will be released in the

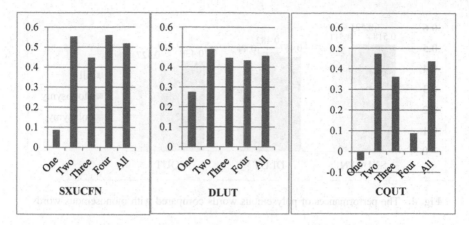

Fig. 3. The performances of word pairs with different word length

website of NLPCC-ICCPOL 2016 for more researches. The following Fig. 3 reports the evaluation results of the top three systems on different word length.

It can be seen that all three systems get very high scores for word pairs where one of the words is composed of two characters; however, they get quite low scores for word pairs that contain a single-character word. This is because (i) the character information is important to predict the meaning of a Chinese compound word while we can't make use of this knowledge for a single-character word; (ii) most of single-character words are ambiguous and have multiple senses.

4.5 Polysemous Words on Similarity Computation

The semantic representations of polysemous words have been a challenging task in natural language processing, and word sense disambiguation is a traditional hot topic in the research community. In recent years, there has been an increasing interest in learning sense embeddings from large corpus [4, 7, 9].

In our task, we want to investigate whether polysemous words pose more difficulties in word similarity computation. We divide our dataset into two subsets: both words are monosemous; one of the words is polysemous. Following the work of Guo et al. [7], we first extracted polysemous words based on HowNet (version 2000), but it ended up 415 word pairs, because most words in our data were assigned multiple senses by HowNet. Therefore, we resort to "Xiandai Hanyu Cidian (version 5)" to find polysemous words, and get 268 word pairs that contain at least one polysemous word in each word pair. To encourage more researches in this problem, these two subsets will be released in the website. Figure 4 reports the evaluation results of the top three systems on polysemous words compared with monosemous words.

It can be seen that all the three systems get a worse performance on polysemouswords than monosemous words, but only by a small margin. It drops 1%, 3.8%, and 1.2% for the wining system, the second system and the third system, respectively. It demonstrates that the effect of polysemous words on lexical similarity computation isn't as large as people thought.

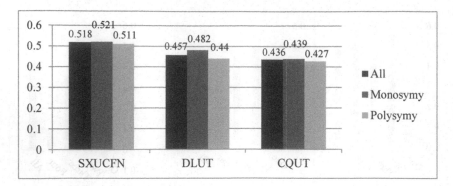

Fig. 4. The performances of polysemous words compared with monosemous words

5 Participating Systems

Our task has attracted much concern in the research community, and 21 teams participated in our task and submitted their results. Another one team submitted results after the deadline. In this section, we will make a brief introduction to the top three systems. We will introduce the methods and resources they used, and discuss the results they achieved.

Extensive researches have been conducted on lexical similarity computation. Theses work can be briefly clustered into three groups. (i) Thesaurus-based method. The similarity degree of a word pair is predicted based on the manually constructed dictionary, like WordNet [10, 11], HowNet [5] and Tongyici Cilin [12]. These methods rely heavily on the hierarchical structure of the dictionary, and can't deal with those out of vocabulary (OOV) words. (ii) Corpus-based method [13–15]. These methods are based on the distributional hypothesis which assumes that similar words occur in similar context. They represent the contextual features as vectors from a large corpus and then compute the similarity score between vectors. (iii) Corpus-based embedding method. These methods exploit neural networks to extract distributed representations of words based on a large corpus, and then compute the similarity of word embeddings, such as the work of Mikolov et al. [16] and Guo et al. [7]. Due to the limitations of single methods, most systems in our task exploit the combining strategy.

The wining first system comes from Shanxi University [17], which achieves a Spearman score 0.524. They propose a combining strategy that exploits different similarity computing methods based on a variety of semantic resources. Their work can be divided into three steps. (1) Compute the similarity score based on Hownet (*sim1*), and compute the cosine distance between two vectors that are pre-trained using the Word2Vector tool (*sim2*). Then the similarity score is set to be the average value $sim = (sim1 + sim2)/2$. (2) If both words of a pair evoke the same frame according to the Chinese FrameNet [18], the score should be $sim = (sim + 10.0)/2$. (3) If both words are in DaiCilin, Synonym dictionary (Tongyiic Cilin) and Antonym dictionary, the score is further updated according to heuristic rules. The experimental results show that (i) Combing the HowNet-based method and corpus-based embedding method gets a significant improvement over the individual methods; (ii) Adding the semantic resources of DaiCilin, Synonym dictionary and Antonym dictionary further improves the performance.

The second best system comes from Dalian University of Technology [19], which achieves a Spearman score 0.457. They propose a framework by combining word embeddings and Tongyiic Cilin. The similarity computation method based on Tongyici Clilin is developed from the algorithm of Tian and Zhao [12], which fully exploits the coding and hierarchical structure information to predict the similarity degree between two words. They employ the skip-gram model to learn the continuous word vectors from text corpora and then do similarity computation on embedding vectors. The interesting part is that they use the weak similarity score (WSS) to weakly supervise the learning process of word embedding, which is automatically computed based on some retrieval statistics and linguistic features. The combination strategy exploits different ensemble learning methods, including Max, Min, Replace, Arithmetic Mean and Geometric Mean. The Cilin method gets a Spearman value 0.405, the W2V method gets 0.311, and the combing method with Arithmetic Mean gets 0.457, which ranks the second in all participating systems. After the submission, they make further studies: (1) enhance the embedding model by merging equivalent English word embeddings; (2) learn the co-occurrence sequence via LSTM networks. They finally get a Spearman value 0.541, which is the best result on PKU-500 data to date.

The third best system is from Chongqing University of Technology. They adopt the lexicon-based method by using Tongyici Cilin, and their method is derived from the algorithm of Tian and Zhao [12], which takes advantage of the structure information and coding rules to estimate the similarity of a word pair. They propose two improvements. (1) For polysemous words, they take the average value of similarity scores across all senses rather than the biggest similarity score. (2) For OOV words that are not recorded in Tongyici Cilin, they split the words into characters and extract those words that contain the character. They then calculate the similarities of those words and take the average value. Their work gets a Spearman score 0.436. However, as shown in Figs. 1 and 2, their method is not robust and behaves badly for adjectives and single-character words.

6 Conclusion

This paper gives an overview of the NLPCC-ICCPOL 2016 shared task 3 "Chinese word similarity measurement". We describe clearly the diverse criteria in selecting words, the data preparation and similarity score annotation by twenty graduate students. In total 24 systems participated in our task. We make a detailed analysis in the evaluation results, considering the inter-annotator agreement, part of speech, word length and polysemous words.

The wining first system gets a Spearman score 0.518, which is much lower than the Spearman score 0.640 on WordSim-353 data reported in the work of Schnabel et al. [8], suggesting that there is much room to improve for Chinese word similarity computation. Most works employ the traditional methods (thesaurus-based method) and the simple corpus-based embedding method, therefore more advanced model and novel ways are encouraged to use. Besides the intrinsic evaluation based on our PKU-500 dataset, extrinsic evaluation is also welcome by applying it to real-world applications, such as question answering and machine translation.

Acknowledgement. This work is supported by National High Technology Research and Development Program of China (2015AA015403), National Natural Science Foundation of China (61371129, 61572245), Key Program of Social Science foundation of China (12&ZD227).

Appendix A: 91 Word Pairs with Standard Deviation Greater Than 2

[没戏 没辙] [只管 尽管] [**GDP** 生产力] [包袱 段子] [日期 时间] [由此 通过]
[爱面子 好高骛远] [一方面 一边] [托福 **GRE**] [严厉 严谨] [抄袭 克隆]
[悲喜 大悲大喜] [亏 幸亏] [老气 土气] [蹩脚 差强人意] [容易 顺利]
[狭隘 狭窄] [害臊 腼腆] [理解 理会] [的哥 司机] [娇艳 幽美] [幻境 红楼梦]
[自然 环境] [权限 权利] [几乎 差点儿] [酣睡 打鼾] [振兴 建设] [节日 假日]
[依稀 清晰] [伟大 壮烈] [典型 代表] [出神 发楞] [冷僻 晦涩] [面 首]
[发票 账单] [物品 物质] [回收站 垃圾篓] [必须 必需] [路子 后门]
[牛脾气 我行我素] [免费 便宜] [江湖 红尘] [塞车 拥挤] [要面子 虚荣心]
[琢磨 镂刻] [大小 多少] [候选人 备胎] [旅客 驴友] [多角度 多元化]
[信物 物件] [豆蔻年华 黄金时代] [血液 红细胞] [酷 爽] [质量 重量]
[牺牲 粉身碎骨] [隆重 重要] [天赋 技能] [身姿 身手] [事变 后院起火]
[鸣谢 酬答] [硅谷 中关村] [平凡 平庸] [了不得 好] [许可证 执照]
[线路 行程] [与 以及] [和谐 平安] [怯懦 胆小鬼] [是非 方圆] [大 高]
[手续 过程] [高峰 山巅] [崛起 凸起] [辛勤 夜以继日] [环境 生态]
[渣 废品] [杂事 闲事] [商标 符号] [右翼 左派] [实践 进行] [借口 理由]
[收费 缴纳] [享受 大快朵颐] [吸引力 地磁力] [工作日 开放日]
[合理 合理性] [违纪 贪污] [言语 语言] [买卖 营销] [光盘 硬盘]

References

1. Rubenstein, H., Goodenough, J.B.: Contextual correlates of synonymy. Commun. ACM **8** (10), 627–633 (1965)
2. Miller, G.A., Charles, W.G.: Contextual correlates of semantic similarity. Lang. Cogn. Neurosci. **6**(1), 1–28 (1991)
3. Finkelstein, L., Gabrilovich, E., Matias, Y., Rivlin, E., Solan, Z., Wolfman, G., et al.: Placing search in context: the concept revisited. TOIS **20**, 116–131 (2002)
4. Huang, E.H., Socher, R., Manning, C.D., Ng, A.Y.: Improving word representations via global context and multiple word prototypes. In: Proceedings of the Association for Computational Linguistics (2012)
5. Liu, Q., Li, S.: Word similarity computing based on HowNet. Int. J. Comput. Linguist. Chin. Lang. Process. **7**, 59–76 (2002)

6. Jin, P., Wu, Y.: SemEval-2012 task 4: evaluating Chinese word similarity. In: First Joint Conference on Lexical and Computational Semantics (2012)
7. Guo, J., Che, W., Wang, H., Liu, T.: Learning sense-specific word embeddings by exploiting bilingual resources. In: Proceedings of COLING 2014 (2014)
8. Schnabel, T., Labutov, I., Mimno, D., Joachims, T.: Evaluation methods for unsupervised word embeddings. In: Proceedings of Empirical Methods in Natural Language Processing (2015)
9. Trask, A., Michalak, P., Liu, J.: Sense2vec - a fast and accurate method for word sense disambiguation in neural word embeddings (2015). arXiv preprint: arXiv:1511.06388
10. Resnik, P.: Using information content to evaluate semantic similarity in a taxonomy. In: International Joint Conference on Artificial Intelligence (1995)
11. Meng, L., Huang, R., Gu, J.: A review of semantic similarity measures in WordNet. Int. J. Hybrid Inf. Technol. **6**, 1–12 (2013)
12. Tian, J.L., Zhao, W.: Words similarity algorithm based on Tongyici Cilin in semantic web adaptive learning system. J. Jilin Univ. **28**(06), 602–608 (2010)
13. Lin, D.: Automatic retrieval and clustering of similar words. In: Proceedings of Coling-ACL 2002 (2002)
14. Agirre, E., Alfonseca, E., Hall, K., Kravalova, J., Paşca, M., Soroa, A.: A study on similarity and relatedness using distributional and WordNet-based approaches. In: Proceedings of Human Language Technology (2009)
15. Shi, J., Wu, Y., Qiu, L., Lv, X.: Chinese lexical semantic similarity computing based on large-scale corpus. J. Chin. Inf. Process. **27**(1), 1–6 (2013)
16. Mikolov, T., Chen, K., Corrado, G., Dean, J.: Distributed representations of words and phrases and their compositionality. In: Advances in Neural Information Processing Systems (2013)
17. Guo, S., Guan, Y., Li, R., Zhang, Q.: Chinese word similarity computing based on combination strategy. In: Proceedings of NLPCC 2016 (2016)
18. Liu, K.: Research on Chinese FrameNet construction and application technologies. J. Chin. Inf. Process. **6**, 47 (2011)
19. Pei, J., Zhang C., Huang, D., Ma, J.: Combining word embedding and semantic lexicon for Chinese word similarity computation. In: Proceedings of NLPCC 2016 (2016)

Exploring Various Linguistic Features
for Stance Detection

Qingying Sun[1,2], Zhongqing Wang[3], Qiaoming Zhu[1(✉)],
and Guodong Zhou[1]

[1] Soochow University, Suzhou, Jiangsu, China
sunqingying.sun@gmail.com, {qmzhu,gdzhou}@suda.edu.cn
[2] Huaiyin Normal University, Huaian, Jiangsu, China
[3] Singapore University of Technology and Design, Singapore, Singapore
wangzq.antony@gmail.com

Abstract. In this paper, we describe our participation in the fourth shared task (NLPCC-ICCPOL 2016 Shared Task 4) on the stance detection in Chinese Micro-blogs (subtask A). Different from ordinary features, we explore four linguistic features including lexical features, morphology features, semantic features and syntax features in Chinese micro-blogs in stance classifier, and get a good performance, which ranks the third place among sixteen systems.

1 Introduction

Stance detection aims to automatically determine from text whether the author of the text is in favor of, against, or neutral towards a given target.[1] People explicitly or implicitly express their stance towards various targets through posts on social media, such as Weibo and Twitter. The target can be a person, an organization, an event, a movement, or a policy. The given target can be mentioned explicitly or implicitly. For example, consider the following <target, post> pair:

E1:   Target: 深圳禁摩限电 (*The ban on motorcycles in Shenzhen*)
Post: 从长远看，深圳禁摩限电也许没有错。但短时间内一棍子打死，未免太绝情了! (*In the long run, it is not wrong to say no to motorcycles and electric bicycles. However, it is unhuman to finish them in such a short time.*)

The poster is against the target on E1, since he expresses the negative opinion toward the target. However, the stance toward the target and the opinion of the post may be opposite in some posts. For example on E2, the poster is in favor of the given target although the post expresses the negative opinion. The targets on E1 and E2 are mentioned explicitly. In contrast, some targets may be mentioned implicitly. In E3, the entity mentioned on the post is 'iPhone4', while the given target is 'iPhone SE'. It also would involve the opposite between the opinion and stance. It is more difficult to automatically detect the stance for the implicit target.

---

[1] http://tcci.ccf.org.cn/conference/2016/pages/page05_CFPTasks.html.

© Springer International Publishing AG 2016
C.-Y. Lin et al. (Eds.): NLPCC-ICCPOL 2016, LNAI 10102, pp. 840–847, 2016.
DOI: 10.1007/978-3-319-50496-4_76

E2:   Target: 春节放鞭炮 *(set off firecrackers during Spring Festival)*
Post: 呼吁春节不放鞭炮的环保局都是奇葩。该管的不管， 不该管的偏要
管。 *(It is surprising that Environmental Protection Agency appealed to the public not to set off firecrackers during Spring Festival. They did not do well at their own duty work, but are concerned about the irrelevant things)*

E3:   Target: iPhone SE
Post: 还是喜欢苹果4的备忘录，会显示时间的长短。 *(I prefer iPhone 4's memo, which can display the length of time.)*

From the above discussion, we can find that there are two challenges in stance classification: (1) the stance may be opposite to the opinion, and (2) the target may be implicit. Thus, it is difficult to predict the stance using traditional classification model which only consider surface features such as bag-of-words. In this study, we explore various linguistic features to find deep and implicit information to solve this problem. In particular, four types of features which include Lexical, Morphology, Semantics, and Syntax are used to detect stance of the posts. The experimental results show that our method can effectively detect stance, and our system ranks 3rd on subtask A (among 16 teams).

This paper describes our participating system for the stance detection in Chinese micro-blogs shared task on NLPCC-ICCPOL 2016 in details.

2   Related Works

Early work on stance detection mainly focused on congressional debates [1]. In their work, the author used a simple method to identify cross-speaker references indicating agreement. Later, more work on detecting stance of debates in online forums emerge. One method is to mine the web to learn associations that are indicative of opinion stances in debates [2]. Subsequently, Murakami and Raymond [3] propose a method exploiting local information in user's remarks within the debate. [4] develop a novel collective classification approach to stance classification, which makes use of both structural and linguistic features, and capture the underlying relationships between posts and users.

Different from the previous research, we do not have any relation between the posts and the posters. And thus, to address this challenge, we focus on the use of the information contained in the post itself and design four types of features including Lexical, Morphology, Semantics, and Syntax to detect stance.

3   Approach

By considering the implicit and explicit target in stance classification, we use both surface and deep features to solve the problem. Lexical features such as n-gram and theme words are employed as surface features, and deep features include morphology, semantics, and syntax features. Table 1 illustrates an overview of the features which are used in this study. In the following of this section, we will discuss these features one by one.

Table 1. Feature sets, description, and examples

Features		Description/examples
Lexical features	Unigrams (UW)	Each word in the post
	Word with target (UWT)	Target with each word in the post
	Bigrams (BW)	Target_word1_word2
	Trigrams (TW)	Target_word1_word2_word3
	Theme word with target (TWT)	Use TF-IDF value to rank the words in each post, and select top-n words as the theme words
	Word position (PNW)	Use the previous or next word of current word
	Length of post (LOP)	The length of each post
Morphology	POS (POW)	Connect each word with its part of speech
Semantics	Polarity with target (TPOL)	Target_ the polarity of each post
	Polarity with bigram word and POS (BIPOL)	Combination polarity, bigram words and POS
	Polarity with trigram word and POS (TRPOL)	Combination polarity, trigram words and POS
	Number of sentiment/stance words (POLN)	Sentiment/stance_number
Syntax	Dependency tree (DPGD)	Connect two words in dependency relation
	Syntax tree (STPH)	Use the path of phrase labels from root to each leaf

3.1 Lexical Features

Lexical features can capture the surface representation of each document, it has been proved that lexical features are always useful for many NLP applications, such as sentiment classification, and emotion detection [5, 6].

N-gram. Since previous work shows that the stance classifier trained on n-gram is a relatively strong baseline [7–10]. We use the unigrams, bigrams, and trigrams features.

Theme Word. For extracting the theme words, we compute the TF-IDF value for each word in the post and use the value to rank the words, selecting top-5 words as the theme words.

Context Word. Besides we consider the previous or next word of the current word as the features.

Length of Post. We also use the length of each post as features to connect similar length posts.

Specially, by considering the target information, we connect the n-gram words and theme words with target word to build the <target, word> pair.

3.2 Morphology

Part-of-Speech. This feature concerns about the word's part-of-speech, and we select the noun, verb, adjective, adverb, name, location, interrogative pronoun, exclamation mark, and question mark to generate features. We connect selected word with its part of speech.

3.3 Semantics

Semantics information, such as sentimental information can influence the stance of document with the corresponding target. For example, a document with positive opinion may have the favor stance toward the target. We thus use various kinds of sentimental information to help stance classification.

Polarity of Target. This feature concerns about the sentiment polarity of the post. The sentiment towards different ideological topics normally influences the ideological stance of a person. Accordingly, we compute the sentiment polarity according the number of sentiment or stance words in a post (if positive words number is the biggest one, the sentiment polarity is positive, and so on.) and use this sentiment as a possible indicator of a post's stance. Besides, we combine the bigram/trigram words, part of speech and the polarity to generate features.

Sentimental Word. The sentimental words are extracted from the document using a sentimental lexicon. The lexicon is extended from the DUT Affective lexicon Ontology [11] by adding 435 stance words manually. Table 2 shows some examples of extended stance words in the lexicon.

Table 2. Example of stance related words about iPhone SE

Stance	Stance related words
FAVOR	首选, 风向标, 平民化, 白菜, 好看, 赞, 亲民, 易用性, 便宜, 新亮点, 福利, 坐等, 深得我心 *(top choice, vane, civilians, cabbage, good-looking, great, friendly, easy to use, cheap, highlights, welfare, wait for, deep in my heart)*
AGAINST	黄屏, 折腾, 嫌弃, 松动, 摆设, 装逼, 坑爹, 坑, 卡顿, 受不了, 入坑, 逼死, 下滑, 差评, 差, 傻 *(yellow screen, toss, abandon, loose, furnishings, loading force, cheating, pits, not smooth, can not stand, into the pit, fatal, decline, bad review, poor, stupid)*
NONE	小屏, 新机, 淘汰, 尝试 *(small screen, new machine, elimination, try)*

Degree of Sentiment/Stance. We count the number of sentimental and stance words in a document to measure the degree of sentiment and stance of each document.

3.4 Syntax

We generate the syntax feature from dependency and parse tree. The dependency and syntax parse tree are generated by Stanford Parser tool.

Dependency Features. Each post is represented as several triples (i.e., relation (government, dependent)) and all dependency pairs <government, dependent> are used as features.

Syntax Features. We use the path of phrase labels from root to each leaf to construct the syntax features.

4 Experiments

4.1 Datasets

We participate in NLPCC-ICCPOL 2016 Share Task 4 subtask A, and the task aims to detect the stance of each post into three categories: FAVOR, AGAINST, NONE. There are five targets in this task including IPhone SE (Target-1), setting off firework during Spring Festival (Target-2), Russia's anti-terrorist action in Syria (Target-3), two children policy (Target-4), and ban on motorcycles in Shenzhen (Target-5).

There are 3000 posts in the training dataset, 1000 posts in the testing dataset, and 15000 posts in submission dataset for measuring the performance of our system.

4.2 Experimental Setting

LIBSVM[2] with default parameters is used to build our classifier. We employ 'Jieba' Chinese text segmentation tool[3] to implement Chinese word segmentation, POS tagging and top TF-IDF word extraction. We also remove some special symbols such as: "@", "#". We obtain the syntax and dependency trees of the post text by using the Stanford parser[4].

We split the data into five subsets according to the five targets and train a separate classifier for each of these targets.

4.3 Experimental Results

We adopt the macro-average F score to evaluate the performance. For stance classification of Favor and Against categories, the macro-average F score is computed as the NLPCC-ICCPOL 2016 Shared Task 4 Guidelines[5] described.

Table 3 presents the performance of our system compared with the top-ranked, average-ranked and median-ranked system on the submission data set.

Our system ranks 3rd Rank in the share task, which is just 2.45% lower than the top one, and much higher than the averaged-ranked and median-ranked scores. It indicates that incorporating both surface and deep features are effective for stance classification.

---

[2] https://www.csie.ntu.edu.tw/~cjlin/libsvm/.

[3] https://github.com/fxsjy/jieba/.

[4] http://nlp.stanford.edu/software/lex-parser.shtml.

[5] http://tcci.ccf.org.cn/conference/2016/dldoc/evagline4.pdf.

However, more deep information, such as word embedding can be used to enhance our model, we will incorporate these information to our future work.

We then show the influence of different factors on Table 4. Note that, different from Table 3, we use the testing data set instead of submission data set, since we do not know the label of submission data set. From the table, we can obtain the following findings.

- Comparing UW with UW&TWT results, we can see that using theme word features (TWT) can outperform the basic n-gram features significantly in all targets. It indicates that people would focus on some key phrases when they judge a target.
- However, not all lexical features are effective. For example, comparing with UW results, the improvement by adding bigram (UW&BW), trigram (UW&TW), length (UW&LOP), and position (UW&PNW) features respectively is low. It may due to that most information has been learned in unigram language model. Moreover, there is looser relationship between the stance and the length, position of a post.
- Comparing UW with UW&UWT results, we can see that using extra target (UWT) information leads to worse performance. This indicates that given target information is not effective for this task. This may be due to that the target itself involves little information about stance.
- The part-of-speech features (POW) are also not very effective for this task. It may be because that we can get limited information about stance only from the part of speech.
- In the semantics type features, comparing with UW results, the improvement by adding the polarity feature (UW&TPOL) is high. This shows that the sentiment information is helpful to the detection of the stance. The performance by adding other three types of features (UW&BIPOL, UW&TRPOL, and UW&POLN) is low. The reason may be that there is too much overlap between these features and n-gram features.
- The dependency features (DPGD) are effective in some targets. Target-2 and Target-4 can improve 5%. It shows that the structural dependency features can get deeper information than the word sequence.
- Adding Syntax features (UW&STPH) improves the performance in most targets. Especially, Target-1 obtained the best F_{avg} value.

Table 3. Performance of our system and the top-ranked, average-ranked, and median-ranked system for subtask A offered by the organizer

Team ID	Overall			Target-1	Target-2	Target-3	Target-4	Target-5
	$F_{against}$	F_{favor}	F_{avg}	F_{avg}	F_{avg}	F_{avg}	F_{avg}	F_{avg}
RUC_MMC(top)	0.7243	0.6969	0.7106	0.7730	0.5780	0.5814	0.8036	0.7652
SDS(ours)	0.6965	0.6758	0.6861	0.7784	0.5852	0.5332	0.7948	0.6883
printf(median)	0.6702	0.6183	0.6443	0.7048	0.5769	0.5547	0.7150	0.6417
March*(average)	0.6244	0.5858	0.6051	0.6950	0.5466	0.4906	0.6442	0.6169

We then compare the effectiveness of different set of features on Table 5. It shows that: The lexical features are effective in Target-1 and Target-3, the syntax feature leads to best performance in Target-4 and Target-5, however the Target-2 obtains the best result by using all features.

Table 4. Contribution of different features over 5 targets on the test data

Features	Overall			Target-1	Target-2	Target-3	Target-4	Target-5
	$F_{against}$	F_{favor}	F_{avg}	F_{avg}	F_{avg}	F_{avg}	F_{avg}	F_{avg}
UW	0.6810	0.6273	0.6542	0.7848	0.4829	0.5429	0.7229	0.6725
UW&UWT	0.6760	0.6284	0.6522	0.7894	0.4829	0.5248	0.7229	0.6725
UW&BW	0.6875	0.6461	0.6668	0.7721	0.5158	**0.5564**	0.7546	0.6728
UW&TW	0.6878	0.6588	0.6733	0.7989	0.507	0.5271	0.7685	**0.7042**
UW&TWT	0.6931	**0.6699**	**0.6815**	0.8043	0.5318	0.5485	0.7675	0.6975
UW&PNW	0.6958	0.6307	0.6633	0.7922	0.4775	0.5385	0.7591	0.6781
UW&LOP	0.6803	0.6273	0.6538	0.7916	0.4826	0.5185	0.7371	0.6724
UW&POW	0.6831	0.6321	0.6576	0.7933	0.4829	0.5392	0.7336	0.6696
UW&TPOL	0.6947	0.6594	0.6771	0.8000	0.5165	0.5513	0.7744	0.6865
UW&BIPOL	0.6838	0.6307	0.6572	0.7322	0.5103	0.5213	0.7869	0.6730
UW&TRPOL	0.6871	0.6425	0.6648	0.7671	0.5207	0.5250	**0.7973**	0.6322
UW&POLN	0.6883	0.6496	0.6689	0.7738	0.5303	0.5421	0.7569	0.6886
UW&DPGD	**0.6967**	0.6564	0.6765	0.7860	0.5365	0.5504	0.7795	0.6679
UW&STPH	0.6948	0.6409	0.6678	**0.8121**	0.4873	0.5183	0.7667	0.7008
ALL	0.6884	0.6659	0.6772	0.7615	**0.5852**	0.5274	0.7785	0.6764

Table 5. performance of the unigram baseline combine each type of features respectively

Features	Overall			Target-1	Target-2	Target-3	Target-4	Target-5
	$F_{against}$	F_{favor}	F_{avg}	F_{avg}	F_{avg}	F_{avg}	F_{avg}	F_{avg}
UW	0.6810	0.6273	0.6542	0.7848	0.4829	0.5429	0.7229	0.6725
UW&Lexical	**0.6967**	0.6466	0.6717	**0.7933**	0.5070	**0.5523**	0.7652	0.6840
UW&Morphology	0.6831	0.6321	0.6576	**0.7933**	0.4829	0.5392	0.7336	0.6696
UW&Semantics	0.6791	0.6452	0.6621	0.7177	0.5736	0.5343	0.78	0.6576
UW&Syntax	**0.6967**	0.6538	0.6753	0.775	0.5461	0.4956	**0.7996**	**0.7057**
ALL	0.6884	**0.6659**	**0.6772**	0.7615	**0.5852**	0.5274	0.7785	0.6764

5   Conclusion

We explore and analyze the effectiveness of different features for stance detection. We find that base lexical feature is useful for all the targets and the effectiveness of other types of features are different in different targets. Our submission system gets a good performance and ranks the third place on the NLPCC-ICCPOL shared task 4. We will do more work to improve the system performance, such as using word embedding, and deep neural networks.

Acknowledgments. In building our system, we are grateful to all the people who have helped us. Sheng Li has helped us to parse the syntax tree; Jingjing Wang, Lu Zhang, Jinghang Gu, and Qing rong Xia have provided help in programing; Shoushan Li, Zhenghua Li, and Ziwei Fan have given us insight comments etc. We also would like to thank the organizer of this shared task for hard work, especially in data annotation and preparation.

This work is supported by the National Natural Science Foundation of China (61272260), Ministry of Education China Mobile Research Foundation (MCM20150602), Jiangsu Provincial Science and Technology Plan (SBK2015022101), Huaian Applied Research and Scientific Technology Project (HAG2014025), and Huaiyin Normal University Youth Talent Support Program (13HSQNZ07).

References

1. Thomas, M., Pang, B., Lee, L.: Get out the vote: determining support or opposition from congressional floor-debate transcripts. In: Proceedings of Conference on Empirical Methods in Natural Language Processing, pp. 327–335. EMNLP, Sydney (2006)
2. Somasundaran, S., Wiebe, J.: Recognizing stances in online debates. In: Proceedings of 47th Annual Meeting of the ACL and the 4th IJCNLP of the AFNLP, pp. 226–234. AFNLP, Suntec, Singapore (2009)
3. Murakami, A., Raymond, R.: Support or oppose? Classifying positions in online debates from reply activities and opinion expressions. In: Proceedings of International Conference on Computational Linguistics, pp. 869–875. COLING, Beijing (2010)
4. Sridhar, D., Getoor, L., Walker, M.: Collective stance classification of posts in online debate forums. In: Proceedings of Joint Workshop on Social Dynamics and Personal Attributes in Social Media, pp. 109–117. ACL, Baltimore (2014)
5. Jiang, L., Yu, M., Zhou, M., Liu X.H., Zhao, T.J.: Target-dependent Twitter sentiment classification. In: Proceedings of 49th Annual Meeting of the Association for Computational Linguistics, pp. 151–160. ACL, Portland (2011)
6. Kiritchenko, S., Zhu, X., Mohammad, S.: Sentiment analysis of short informal texts. J. Artif. Intell. Res. **50**, 723–762 (2014)
7. Anand, P., Walker, M., Abbott, R., Tree, J.E.F., Bowmani, R., Minor, M.: Cats Rule and Dogs Drool!: classifying stance in online debate. In: Proceedings of 2nd Workshop on Computational Approaches to Subjectivity and Sentiment Analysis, pp. 1–9. ACL, Portland (2011)
8. Somasundaran, S., Wiebe, J.: Recognizing stance in ideological on-line debates. In: Proceedings of NAACL HLT Workshop on Computational Approaches to Analysis and Generation of Emotion in Text, pp. 116–124. NAACL, Los Angeles (2010)
9. Hasan, K.S., Ng, V.: Stance classification of ideological debates: data, models, features, and constraints. In: Proceedings of 6th International Joint Conference on Natural Language Processing, pp. 1348–1356. IJCNLP, Nagoya (2013)
10. Mohammad, S.M., Kiritchenko, S., Sobhani, P., Zhu, X.D., Cherry, C.: SemEval-2016 Task 6: detecting stance in tweets. In: Proceedings of International Workshop on Semantic Evaluation, SemEval-2016, San Diego, pp. 31–41 (2016)
11. 徐琳宏, 林鸿飞, 潘宇.: 情感词汇本体的构造. 情报学报. **27**(2), 180–185 (2008). (Xu, H. L., Lin, H.F., Pan, Y.: The construction of affective lexicon ontology. J. China Soc. Sci. Tech. Inf. **27**(2), 180–185 (2008))

Overview of Baidu Cup 2016: Challenge on Entity Search

Ke Sun[1(⊠)], Tingting Li[1], Shiqi Zhao[1], Yajuan Lv[1], Yansong Feng[2],
Xiaojun Wan[2], and Dongyan Zhao[2]

[1] BAIDU Campus, NO. 10, Shangdi 10th Street, Haidian District,
Beijing 100085, People's Republic of China
{sunke,litingting03,zhaoshiqi,lvyajuan}@baidu.com
[2] Peking University, No. 5, Yiheyuan Road, Haidian District, Beijing 10087,
People's Republic of China
{fengyansong,wanxiaojun,zhaody}@pku.edu.cn

Abstract. Baidu Cup 2016 challenges participants to tackle the problem of entity search in the scenario of Duer. In this paper, we present the overview of this challenge, including the overview of participants, the definition of the task, how we prepare the challenge data and the final challenge result.

Keywords: Entity search · Baidu cup · Virtual assistant

1 Introduction

Developing more intelligent search engines is a long-term goal for both academia and industry. An intelligent search engine should meet either precise or vague requirements from users. Results that are semantically relevant to the queries should be returned, other than those literally matching results.

In particular, the technologies behind modern personal digital assistants and robots should accurately interpret requirements and intents from users, and retrieve answers automatically from the Web. During the 2015 Baidu World Summit, Baidu unveiled the new virtual assistant 'Duer' (度秘) which is now integrated into its latest mobile search app. The company's CEO Robin Li pointed out that there would be three core components involved in Duer: integration, indexing and delivery. Here indexing means the indexing of all integrated information and services to provide more intelligent services to users. In other words, we need better ways to model all these information and services. For instance, people may search for "restaurants with good environment suitable for kids' birthday parties". In order to meet the user's intent, the search engine needs to precisely understand every restaurant, to check which of them can be tagged as "with good environment" and "suitable for kids' birthday parties", and to index the restaurants with satisfied tags for retrieval.

This year, Baidu Cup 2016 challenges participants to tackle the problem of entity search in the scenario of Duer. Table 1 lists the 54 groups that participate (and at least submitted once) in BAIDU CUP 2016. The participating groups come from 27 organizations and include academic, commercial, and government institutions.

C.-Y. Lin et al. (Eds.): NLPCC-ICCPOL 2016, LNAI 10102, pp. 848–853, 2016.
DOI: 10.1007/978-3-319-50496-4_77

Organization list		
Harbin institute of technology (10 groups)	Tongji university (6 groups)	National university of defense technology (5 groups)
East China normal university (3 groups)	Chinese academy of sciences (2 groups)	Beijing information science and technology university (2 groups)
Meituan web (2 groups)	Baidu Inc.	BosonData Inc.
China internet network information center	Chitu Inc.	Fudan university
Henan university	The international centre for diffraction data	Institute of computing technology, Chinese academy of sciences
Institute of software, Chinese academy of sciences	Nanjing left-brain corporation	Nanjing university
Soochow university	South China university of technology	University of Chinese academy of sciences
Northeastern university	Cat eye	Inner mongolia university
Shandong university of finance and economics	Information and safety engineering school of zhongnan university of economics and law	Personal: INFO MISS (6 groups)

This paper serves as an introduction to the challenge. The next section provides a summary of the entity search task and the detail of how we collect the ground truth of the dataset. Section 3 presents the results of top10 teams, and the final section looks into future.

2 Entity Search Task

2.1 Task Definition

"Entity search" means the search behaviors targeting for entities, such as restaurants with elegant environment, movies recommended for lovers, yellow-flowered trees, etc. Where "entity" means something that exists in itself, including normal entities such as animals, plants and foods; named entities such as names of people, organization, movies, songs, etc. In this challenge, we define the "entity search task" as follows:

Given an entity search query q and a set of candidate entities E, retrieve entities that match the query q from E.

Where "entity search query *q*" means keywords or key-phrases used by users to express their intent, like "适合带孩子看的电影" (movies suitable for children), "日式装修的餐厅" (restaurants with Japanese style decoration) etc.

2.2   Dataset

In order to encourage participants to develop a generalizable and adaptive strategy, we prepared four specified types of entities in the task, including restaurants, movies, TV shows and celebrities. Participants need to complete *all* 4 types of entity search tasks to complete the challenge.

2.2.1   Query Preparation

For each entity type *t*, we prepare 1,100 queries, forming the query set **Q**.

For restaurants, movies, and TV shows, to ensure the entity search queries close to user's real demands, we extract queries from Baidu's search log during the second half of 2015. A pattern-based method is used to extract entity search queries, following are pattern examples for each type.

> *restaurant* :附近的 <*q*>的餐厅, 哪些餐厅 <*q*>, <*q*>主题的酒吧,适合 <*q*>的饭店.
> *movie*:推荐几部 <*q*>的电影, 最近有什么 <*q*>的电影, 有没有 <*q*>的影片.
> *tv_show*:有哪些 <*q*>的电视剧, 有 <*q*>的连续剧, 什么电视剧 <*q*>.

For each of the three types, we randomly select 2,000 queries from the high frequency portion of the extraction result.

For celebrities, we extract celebrity description phrases as queries from Wikipedia and Baidu Baike based on the parsing result of the celebrities' entries. Analogously, 2,000 high frequency descriptions, i.e. queries, are randomly selected.

The selected queries are finally refined by human annotation, forming the query set **Q**. Annotators are responsible for:

(a) Filtering invalid queries that are not really searching for entities;
(b) Keeping only one query among those semantically similar queries as far as possible.
(c) Keeping 1,100 queries for each type.

2.2.2   Association Entities Preparation

For each query *q* in the query set **Q**, we associate 100 candidate entities to it through the following steps:

First, we extract entities from Baidu Baike and vertical Web sites such as Douban.com, Mtime.com, and Dianping.com. Extracted entities with the same names need disambiguation. For movies and TV shows, we use their "release year" tags to distinguish them. For restaurants, we disambiguate them by their addresses. For celebrities, we distinguish them using the descriptions in their corresponding Baidu Baike entries, e.g., "李娜-中国女子网球名将 (LI Na–Chinese tennis star)".

Second, we find appropriate candidate entities for each *q*∈**Q**. With descriptions from Baidu Baike and comments from the vertical Web sites crawled beforehand, we regard an entity as a "relevant candidate" of q, if its descriptions or comments meet at least one of the following conditions:

(a) Contains all words or their synonyms of q in the same order

(b) Except stop words and common verbs, contains all other words or their synonyms of q with the same order.

For each q, $N(10–40)$ entities from q's relevant candidate set and **100-N** entities from the entire entity set are randomly selected as its final candidate set.

2.2.3 Annotation

The relevance between query q and its candidate entity e is judged manually based on annotators' knowledge and searching result of the query: $<q\ e>$ in Baidu. The annotation is binary, i.e., the entity e is either relevant or irrelevant to the query q. The 440,000 query-entity pairs are uploaded to BAIDU's crowd-sourcing platform, and about 500 annotators are invited to perform the annotation. The annotation interface is illustrated in Fig. 1.

Fig. 1. Annotation page for judging query-entity relevance

2.2.4 Dataset Arrangement

After human annotation, we can get the ground truth of the dataset for the challenge. We manually separate the dataset into **TRAINSET** (100 queries, each type), **DEVSET** (400 queries, each type) and **TESTSET** (600 queries, each type), as show in Table 2 shows.

Table 2. Dataset overview

Types	Trainset		Deveset		Testset	
	File name	# Queries	File name	# Queries	File name	# Queries
Restaurants	restaurant. TRAIN.TXT	100	restaurant. DEV.TXT	400	restaurant. TEST.TXT	600
Movies	movie.TRAIN. TXT	100	movie.DEV. TXT	400	movie.TEST. TXT	600
TV shows	tvShwo. TRAIN.TXT	100	tvShwo. DEV.TXT	400	tvShwo. TEST.TXT	600
Celebrities	celebrity. TRAIN.TXT	100	celebrity. DEV.TXT	400	celebrity. TEST.TXT	600

In the beginning of the challenge, the DEVSET and the entire TRAINSET were released for participants to tune their models. The participants could upload their ranking result upon our challenge website once a day to verify their model's performance by comparing with the ground truth of the DEVSET. Two days before the challenge ends, the TESTSET is released for participants to produce their final result.

The final results (including both DEVSET and TESTSET) of each team are pooled together. For each query, 5 extra entities (most co-retrieved by participants) are re-checked by our crowd-sourcing users and the relevance of the entities are merged into the ground truth.

Finally, the performance of each team was evaluated on the ground truth using the **MAP** [1] metric, and the final ranking score of each team is the average **MAP** scores over four types.

3   Challenge Results

Table 3 shows detailed final score of top 10 teams. The "Overall Score" column is the averaged **MAP** over the four types, and the "Average Score" row is the average **MAP** score of each column.

As Table 3 shows, most of the teams achieve a high score on celebrity type (Avg. MAP is 0.731), and a relatively low score on restaurant and TV show types (Avg. MAPs are 0.445 and 0.424 accordingly). We speculate that this is closely related to the dataset. We build celebrity's entity set mainly based on Baidu Baike, which is easier obtain. Moreover, the tags of celebrity are usually more objective, making the relationship between tags and entities clearer. By contrast, restaurant and TV show entities are more difficult to allocate from the Web, and the tags of entities are more subjective than that of celebrities, making them hard to handle.

Table 3. Final results (Top 10)

Team Alias	Overall score	Score on each type			
		Restaurant	Movie	tv_show	Celebrity
xbjin	0.712	0.594	0.776	0.598	0.882
fdusma	0.705	0.588	0.778	0.573	0.881
BosonNLP	0.704	0.615	0.798	0.540	0.865
flamingowt	0.633	0.490	0.732	0.476	0.833
I'm2009	0.550	0.444	0.495	0.398	0.862
NUDT5Y301	0.549	0.442	0.492	0.396	0.861
BetaGo	0.497	0.346	0.492	0.361	0.789
Tongji_DL	0.441	0.346	0.542	0.362	0.514
dx436	0.340	0.293	0.377	0.266	0.423
SteinsGate	0.334	0.293	0.377	0.266	0.402
Average score	–	0.445	0.586	0.424	0.731

4 Future Work

This year, we focus on the semantic relevance between tags and entities. However, in the real product of entity search, we should also consider some additional elements like, (1) user's personalization, and (2) the priori information of the given entity. (1) **User's personalization**, like user's current location, is an important feature for measuring the matching degree. For example, we should not recommend a restaurant in Paris for today's dinner to a user who lives in Beijing. (2) **The priori information of the given entity**, like the information on whether or not the restaurant is open, is also important for satisfying the users. For example, we should recommend a restaurant, which is at least open for business now. Therefore, in the future, we may consider involving more these elements into the challenge task. Also, as we found out, the ability to collect data (especially the entity-data) may largely affect participant's performance in the challenge, which may somehow limit the effort they put in the ranking algorithm. In the future, we will try to provide more data for the participants to lighten the burden of the data collection.

Acknowledgement. Thanks LI-Tingting's work on preparing the task dataset, developing the measurefunction and conclusion the final results. Thanks ZHANG Qian's organization work. Thanks CAO Zhuoran's work on developing the challenge website. Thanks the hard work of each member of organization committee. Thanks SUN Shuqi for the valuable advice given to this paper.

Reference

1. Voorhees, E.M.: Overview of TREC 2007. In: TREC (2007)

A Feature-Rich CRF Segmenter for Chinese Micro-Blog

Yabin Leng$^{(\boxtimes)}$, Weiwei Liu, Sheng Wang, and Xiaojie Wang

School of Computer Science, Beijing University of Posts and Telecommunications,
Beijing 100876, China
{lengyabin,liuww_victor,bupt10211677,xjwang}@bupt.edu.cn

Abstract. This paper describes our system for Chinese word segmentation of micro-blog text, one of the NLPCC-ICCPOL 2016 Shared Tasks [1]. The CRF (Conditional Random Field) model is employed to model word segmentation as a sequence labeling problem, 7 sets of features are selected to train the CRF model. The system achieves f_b 0.798144 on closed track, 0.81968 on semi-open track, and 0.82217 on open track with weighted measures [2].

Keywords: Chinese word segmentation on micro-blog · Sequence labeling · CRF

1 Introduction

Chinese word segmentation is the fundamental task of Chinese natural language processing [3]. Lots of models have been proposed for the task, such as ME (Maximum Entropy) [4], CRF (Conditional Random Field) [5] to deep learning such as LSTM (Long Short-Term Memory) [6]. The performance of traditional texts segmentation has been improved significantly. However, the results of previous methods on micro-blog is not as good as those in traditional texts. One of the main reasons is that micro-blog shows a very different wording style with traditional texts such as newspapers and radio reports. Sentences in micro-blog contain many new words, for instance, "木有", "棒棒哒". Not only the number of new words increases rapidly, but also they are constructed in very different way from those new words in traditional texts. It brings a big challenge for Chinese word segmentation.

In this paper, we take full advantages of both unsupervised features and supervised features to discover new words from unlabeled dataset. We explore some features especially for micro-blog, such as reduplication feature. The new words recognition is significantly improved with those features.

The remainders of this paper are organized as follows. In Sect. 2, we introduce the model and features. In Sect. 3, we show our experimental results and analysis on the evaluation data. Finally, we conclude the paper and discuss future work in Sect. 4.

© Springer International Publishing AG 2016
C.-Y. Lin et al. (Eds.): NLPCC-ICCPOL 2016, LNAI 10102, pp. 854–861, 2016.
DOI: 10.1007/978-3-319-50496-4_78

2   Our Method

We introduce the method in this section. There are mainly two parts including
the model and the features.

2.1   Model

Chinese word segmentations is often modeled as sequence labeling on Chinese
characters. Considering the great success that CRF has achieved in sequence
labeling and its capability of making use of different features, we use CRF as
basic model in our method.

A linear-chain CRF with parameters $\Lambda = \{\lambda_1, \ldots\}$ defines a conditional
probability for a label sequence $y = y_1 \ldots y_n$ given an input sequence $x = x_1 \ldots x_n$
to be

$$p_\Lambda(y|x) = \frac{exp(\sum_{i=1}^{n} \sum_k \lambda_k f_k(y_{i-1}, y_i, x, i))}{Z(x)} \tag{1}$$

where Z(x) is the normalization factor, $f_k(y_{i-1}, y_i, x, i)$ is a feature function
which is often binary-valued, but can be real-valued, λ_k is a learned weight
associated with feature f_k.

A 6-tag set including B, B_2, B_3, M, E and S is used in this paper to label
the position of characters in words. 6-tag set has been shown better performance
than other tag sets in Zhao et al. [7], Table 1 shows how to label the characters
in words with different lengths.

Table 1. Tagging for a word

Length of word	Tags for a word
1	S
2	BE
3	BB_2E
4	BB_2B_3E
5	BB_2B_3ME
>5	$BB_2B_3M\ldots E$

2.2   Features

Feature selection has a great influence on the performance of CRF model. Follows
are some features used in our CRF model. Feature templates we designed for all
features below (except AV) are shown in Table 2.

Basic Features. There are three types of basic features, including Character
Feature, Character Type Feature, and Reduplication Feature.

Table 2. The templates of CF

Feature	Instruction
C_{-1}	The previous character
C_0	The current character
C_1	The next character
$C_{-1}C_0$	The previous character and the current character
C_0C_1	The current character and the next character
$C_{-1}C_1$	The previous character and the next character

Character Feature (CF): 6 n-gram character feature are used, the templates are listed in Table 2.

Character Type Feature (CTF): The characters are divided into 7 categories, including numbers (0–9), unit of measurement, punctuations, English characters (a-zA-Z), Chinese numbers (零(zeor) – 十(ten)), Chinese characters and other characters.

Reduplication Feature (RF): Reduplication feature is special for micro-blog. There are many words with reduplication forms like "AAB", "ABAB", "AABB" or "AAA" in micro-blog. For example, "棒棒哒", "就是就是，"开开心心". There are also some long words consisting of punctuation marks or Chinese modal particle such as "哈" and "嘻". In order to better deal with these kinds of words, we propose reduplication feature shown in Table 3.

Conditional Entropy Feature (CEF). Conditional entropy feature is a kind of unsupervised feature. Gao and Vogel's [9] experiments proved that conditional entropy feature improves the performance of word segmentation model. Given a character C, the forward and backward conditional entropies are calculated by formulas (2) and (3) respectively. And continuous conditional entropies are then mapped into discrete labels as shown in Table 4.

$$H_f(C) := -\sum_{c_{ik}=C} \frac{n_k}{Z_f} log \frac{n_k}{Z_f} \qquad (2)$$

$$H_b(C) := -\sum_{c_{jk}=C} \frac{n_k}{Z_b} log \frac{n_k}{Z_b} \qquad (3)$$

Table 3. The description of RF

Type	Instruction
3	Shape like "AAA"
2	Shape like "ABA"
1	Shape like "ABB"
0	Others

Table 4. Mapping from conditional entropies to discrete labels

Conditional entropies	Labels
[0, 1.0)	0
[1.0, 2.0)	1
[2.0, 3.5)	2
[3.5, 5.0)	4
[5.0, 7.0)	5
[7.0, +∞)	6

where $Z_f = \sum_{c_{ik}=C} n_k$, $Z_b = \sum_{c_{jk}=C} n_k$ are the normalization factor, n_k denotes how many times the two consecutive characters c_{ik} and c_{jk} appear in corpus.

Location Feature (LF). Location feature indicates position information of characters in words. Some characters are often used alone, and others may often be used as prefixes or suffixes of words. Yan [8] proved that the position feature has a positive effect on the improvement of the performance on word segmentation models. The way we introduce location feature is same as Yan [8].

Accessor Variety Feature (AV). AV is used to measure the independence of a string by checking the variety of its left and right neighbors. How we use AV is similar to Wu [10], In their model, only the first character in words is used. It does not make good use of the boundary information at the end of a substring. Hence, we designed a new set of templates as shown in Table 5. For character C, we use both the AV value of the substring ending with C and the AV value of the substring starting with C in templates. Considering the length of the substring is

Table 5. The templates of AV

Length	Templates
1 char	$CAV1_{-1}$,$CAV1_0$,$CAV1_1$,$CAV1_{-1}CAV1_0$,$CAV1_0CAV1_1$,$CAV1_{-1}CAV1_1$
2 char	$CAV2_{-2}$,$CAV2_{-1}$,$CAV2_0$,$CAV2_1$,$CAV2_2$,$CAV2_{-2}CAV2_{-1}$, $CAV2_{-1}CAV2_0$,$CAV2_0CAV2_1$,$CAV2_{-1}CAV2_1$,$CAV2_1CAV2_2$
3 char	$CAV3_{-3}$,$CAV3_{-2}$,$CAV3_{-1}$,$CAV3_0$,$CAV3_1$,$CAV3_2$, $CAV3_{-3}CAV3_{-2}$, $CAV3_{-2}CAV3_{-1}$,$CAV3_{-1}CAV3_0$, $CAV3_0CAV3_1$,$CAV3_{-1}CAV3_1$,$CAV3_1CAV3_2$
4 char	$CAV4_{-4}$,$CAV4_{-3}$,$CAV4_{-2}$,$CAV4_{-1}$,$CAV4_0$,$CAV4_1$,$CAV4_2$, $CAV4_{-4}CAV4_{-3}$,$CAV4_{-3}CAV4_{-2}$,$CAV4_{-2}CAV4_{-1}$,$CAV4_{-1}CAV4_0$, $CAV4_0CAV4_1$,$CAV4_{-1}CAV4_1$,$CAV4_1CAV4_2$
5 char	$CAV5_{-5}$,$CAV5_{-4}$,$CAV5_{-3}$,$CAV5_{-2}$,$CAV5_{-1}$,$CAV5_0$,$CAV5_1$,$CAV5_2$, $CAV5_{-5}CAV5_{-4}$,$CAV5_{-4}CAV5_{-3}$,$CAV5_{-2}CAV5_{-1}$, $CAV5_{-1}CAV5_0$, $CAV5_0CAV5_1$,$CAV5_{-1}CAV5_1$,$CAV5_1CAV5_2$

less than 6, we use the marker CAV1 represents AV of a substring whose length equals to 1, and so on.

Character Vector Feature (CVF). Distributed representation of words (characters) in vector space has been shown to be able to capture semantic information which is also important for word segmentation. Two steps are taken for obtaining character vector feature. Firstly, each character is represented as a dense vector and trained by word2vec. Then we use K-means clustering to obtain its category information. Training for distributed representation usually needs a large-scale unsupervised data, so we only use the feature in the open track.

3 Experiment

There are three different tracks in this Shared Task. In closed and semi-open track, we only use the training data provided by organizer. MSRA and PKU data on Bakeoff-2005 [11] are joined in open track beside the data provided by organizer. Extra 1G Sina Weibo data is also used in open track, We combine those data with the training data to compute CEFs and AVs. CRF++[1] is used to implement our models.

3.1 Experimental Results

In this section, the official results of our models in different tracks are listed firstly. The models are evaluated by both standard measures [12] and weighted measures [2]. Since we have no official data of segmentation difficulty d_i for each word at that time, only standard measures (P, R, F1) are used to evaluate the efficiency of different features in our models latterly. Finally, we also present the results with weighted measures (p_b, r_b, f_b) when they were released by organizer.

The official results in different tracks are shown in Tables 6 and 7, and byu-1 is our model.

For the closed track, We obtained 3nd place by two measures, with weighted measures, there is only 0.006 difference with the best result. On the semi-open track our model achieves the best F1 (0.951935), and 2th place in f_b. Furthermore the f_b increased by 0.02 compared to the result on closed track. For the open track, our model achieves 4th place by standard measures but the best with weighted measures.

We also show a series of experimental results on semi-open track with different features in Table 8. It could be seen that the performance is greatly improved after adding AV on the baseline with basic features. We tried two different set of templates for AV. One is from Wu [10], another is ours. It could be also seen that our templates for AV are more effective than that in Wu [10].

---

[1] http://crfpp.googlecode.com/svn/trunk/doc/index.html.

Table 6. The official results with standard measures of our model on different tracks

Track	NickName (rank)	Standard measures		
		P	R	F1
Closed	panda-1 (1st)	0.939386	0.948021	0.947764
	bju (2st)	0.942164	0.953131	0.947616
	byu-1 (3st)	**0.943619**	**0.951535**	**0.94756**
Semi-open	**byu-1 (1st)**	**0.947689**	**0.956219**	**0.951935**
	byu-2 (2st)	0.948134	0.955356	0.951732
	dlu-2 (3st)	0.946183	0.954941	0.950542
Open	scu (1st)	0.950465	0.957007	0.953725
	bju (2st)	0.945906	0.955367	0.950613
	jj (3st)	0.935963	0.94659	0.941246
	byu-1 (4st)	**0.919183**	**0.914173**	**0.916671**

Table 7. The official results with weighted measures of our model on different tracks

Track	NickName (rank)	weighted measures		
		p_b	r_b	f_b
Closed	byu-2 (1st)	0.792917	0.816246	0.804412
	bju (2st)	0.781889	0.818178	0.799622
	byu-1 (3st)	**0.7834**	**0.813453**	**0.798144**
Semi-open	byu-2 (1st)	0.816755	0.843353	0.829841
	byu-1 (2st)	**0.804658**	**0.835274**	**0.81968**
	dlu-2 (3st)	0.793714	0.824671	0.808897
Open	**byu-1 (1st)**	**0.812359**	**0.832221**	**0.82217**
	scu (2st)	0.803946	0.830007	0.816769
	bju (3st)	0.788601	0.821837	0.804876

Table 8. Effect of features with standard measures of our model on semi-open tracks

Model	P	R	F1	P_{OOV}
Basic features (Baseline)	0.936	0.943	0.939	0.705
Basic features + AV (Wu [10])	0.943	0.953	0.948	0.702
Basic features + AV (Our) + LF, CEF	0.945	0.954	0.949	0.708
	0.946	0.955	0.950	0.711

Finally, with all of the features, the model gets an F1 of 0.95. We can also see that the precision of OOV recognition is also improved from 0.705 to 0.711 along with different features added at the same time.

For the open track, due to the CVF has the same effect on expressing character type compared to CTF, we do some comparative experiments on the open track shown in Table 9, and from the results we can see CVF is better than CTF.

The result also shows that the model with post processing gets F1 of 0.917 and gains improvement of 0.018. The post processing (PP) includes two aspects. One is non-Chinese character errors in micro-blog, like URL, E-mail address, decimals, percentages. Some regular expressions are designed for dealing with them. The other is the Segmentation errors of Chinese character, an idiom dictionary[2] including about 23000 idioms is used in the open track, and atomic words (words without segmentation ambiguity) generated from training dataset are also used in our task.

There are many spaces remained to be improved in our system. After the weighted measures were released by organizer, we do some experiments on semi-open track with weighted measures and the results are listed on Table 10, from the table we can see that the performance declined after LF and CEF are added, which is a little different with Table 8. And the result is also better than the result we submitted comparing the last two lines, the reason for this phenomenon is that maybe there have the difference between the two evaluation measures. In this task, we select features based on the standard measures instead of weighted measures, so there may exist a better combination of features.

Table 9. Effect of features with standard measures of our model on open tracks

Model	P	R	F1
Baseline[a]	0.891	0.897	0.894
Baseline + CTF	0.894	0.899	0.896
Baseline + CVF	0.896	0.901	0.899
Baseline + CVF + PP	0.919	0.914	0.917

[a]Features including: CF, RF, AV, LF, CEF

Table 10. The results with weighted measures of our model on semi-open tracks

Model	p_b	r_b	f_b
Basic features (Baseline)	0.726	0.753	0.739
Basic features + AV (Wu [10])	0.791	0.827	0.809
Basic features + AV (Our) + LF, CEF + PP (We submit)	0.799	0.833	0.815
	0.795	0.830	0.812
	0.805	0.835	0.820
Basic features + AV (Our) + PP	0.807	0.838	0.822

---

[2] https://github.com/sunflowerlyb/idiom.

4   Conslusion

This paper describes our system for Chinese micro-blog segmentation. We mainly explore some features to improve the performance of the model. There are still many spaces remained to be improved in our system. In future, we can improve our methods from several aspects including exploring new features and new models special for micro-blog.

Acknowledgments. This work was partially supported by Natural Science Foundation of China (No. 61273365), discipline building plan in 111 base (No. B08004) and Engineering Research Center of Information Networks of MOE, and the Co-construction Program with the Beijing Municipal Commission of Education.

References

1. Qiu, X., Qian, P., Shi, Z., Wu, S.: Overview of the NLPCC 2016 Shared Task: Chinese Word Segmentation for Micro-Blog Texts
2. Qian, P., Qiu, X., Huang, X.: A new psychometric-inspired evaluation metric for chinese word segmentation In: Meeting of the Association for Computational Linguistics (2016)
3. Sebastiani, F.: Machine learning in automated text categorization. ACM Comput. Surv. **34**(1), 1–47 (2002)
4. Jin, K.L., Ng, H.T., Guo, W.: A maximum entropy approach to Chinese word segmentation. In: Proceedings of 4th SIGHAN Workshop on Chinese Language Processing (2005)
5. Peng, F., Feng, F., Mccallum, A.: Chinese segmentation, new word detection using conditional random fields. In: Proceedings of COLING, pp. 562–568 (2004)
6. Chen, X., Qiu, X., Zhu, C., et al.: Long short-term memory neural networks for Chinese word segmentation. In: Conference on Empirical Methods in Natural Language Processing (2015)
7. Zhao, H., Li, M., Lu, B.L., et al.: Effective tag set selection in Chinese word segmentation via conditional random field modeling. In: 20th Pacific Asia Conference on Language, Information, Computation, pp. 87–94 (2006)
8. Yan, J.: Research and application of Chinese word segmentation based on conditional random fields (2009). (in Chinese)
9. Gao, Q., Vogel, S.: A multi-layer chinese word segmentation system optimized for out-of-domain tasks (2010)
10. Wu, G., et al.: Leveraging rich linguistic features for cross-domain Chinese segmentation. In: CIPS-SIGHAN Joint Conference on Chinese Language Processing (2014)
11. Emerson, T.: The second international Chinese word segmentation bakeoff. In: Proceedings of 4th SIGHAN Workshop on Chinese Language Processing, p. 133 (2005)
12. Goutte, C., Gaussier, E.: A probabilistic interpretation of precision, recall and F-score, with implication for evaluation. In: Losada, D.E., Fernández-Luna, J.M. (eds.) ECIR 2005. LNCS, vol. 3408, pp. 345–359. Springer, Heidelberg (2005). doi:10.1007/978-3-540-31865-1_25

NLPCC 2016 Shared Task Chinese Words Similarity Measure via Ensemble Learning Based on Multiple Resources

Shutian Ma[1], Xiaoyong Zhang[1], and Chengzhi Zhang[1,2(✉)]

[1] Department of Information Management, Nanjing University of Science
and Technology, Nanjing 210094, China
mashutian0608@hotmail.com, riyao95@qq.com
[2] Jiangsu Key Laboratory of Data Engineering and Knowledge Service
(Nanjing University), Nanjing 210093, China
zhangcz@njust.edu.cn

Abstract. Many Chinese words similarity measure algorithms have been introduced since it's a fundamental issue in various tasks of natural language processing. Previous work focused mainly on using existing semantic knowledge bases or large-scale corpora. However, knowledge base and corpus have limitations for broad coverage and data update. Thus, ensemble learning is then used to improve performance by combing similarities. This paper describes a Chinese word similarity measure using ensemble learning of knowledge and corpus-based algorithms. To be specific, knowledge-based methods are based on TYCCL and Hownet. Two corpus-based methods compute similarities via retrieving on web search engines and deep learning on large-scale corpora (news and microblog). All similarities are combined through support vector regression to get final similarity. Evaluation suggests that TYCCL-based method behaves best according to testing dataset. However, if tuning parameters appropriately, ensemble learning could outperform all the other algorithms. Besides, deep learning on news corpora is better than other corpus-based methods.

Keywords: Chinese word similarity · TYCCL · Hownet · Deep learning · Support vector regression

1 Introduction

Many tasks [1–3] in natural language processing reply on semantic similarity between words. Currently, there are two main ways to measure words similarity, e.g. knowledge-based and corpus-based methods [4]. Knowledge-based word similarity [5] is computed by identifying the degree of similarity between words using information derived from knowledge base or Ontology, such as semantic content or relative position within hierarchies. Since these artificial knowledge is not often updated, this method is unable to deal with unknown words, polysemy or some other issues. Without taking words' context into considerations, it will lead to semantic information loss as well. Apart from the choice of appropriate and large corpora, corpus-based method will take advantages over knowledge-based method which states that words occurring in the

© Springer International Publishing AG 2016
C.-Y. Lin et al. (Eds.): NLPCC-ICCPOL 2016, LNAI 10102, pp. 862–869, 2016.
DOI: 10.1007/978-3-319-50496-4_79

same contexts tend to have similar meanings [6]. However, when facing large-scale corpus, it often leads to curse of dimensionality. Machine learning methods are then proposed to solve this problem. Currently, high-quality word vectors can be obtained via deep learning which has been observed large improvements of accuracy in word similarity task [7]. Additionally, metrics are constructed by making use of page-counts retrieved from web search engines [8] for measuring word association [9].

More or less, all these methods have their own limitations. More and more researchers used ensemble learning to improve performance [10, 11]. This paper presents an algorithm using ensemble learning to combine similarities based on several resources. Although it performed moderately in NLPCC 2016 Task. Further experiments showed that it could get the best performance through parameters tuning. Moreover, it's optimized for general use and has great room to improve.

2   Related Work

There are many simple methods for word similarity computation, such as methods based on string sequences or character composition. It computes similarity by measuring distance between word strings, such as, longest common substring algorithm [12], Damerau-Levenshtein [13] and so on. However, these methods don't practically investigate semantic relationships between words and aren't suitable for Chinese words similarity measure. Currently, prevailing approaches have been divided into two parts, one is based on knowledge base or Ontology, and another is using large-scale corpora.

With the development of lexical knowledge base and Ontology, knowledge-based methods are proposed to measure similarity between words. As the fundamental resources, many Ontology or lexical knowledge bases, like WordNet [14], Eurowordnet [15], TongYiCi CiLin (TYCCL) [16], HowNet [17], etc. are all utilized to measure semantic distance between words. Information about depth of nodes, density in hierarchy structure, relation of links, weights of links, notion of information content are often applied to calculate words similarity [18, 19]. Obviously, knowledge-based method is a labor-intensive task that lacks context information and requires maintenance when new words and new word senses are coming out. Due to these limitations, corpus-based method is then proposed to take context around words into consideration. The meaning of words is modeled by using its distribution over contexts and the semantic similarity between two words is to compare these distributions [20]. There are many statistical models of distributional semantics but they can't avoid curse of dimensionality when facing large datasets. Therefore, machine learning is applied for distributed representation of words with low cost and similarity can be measured with cosine value [21]. Distributed representation is firstly proposed by Hinton in 1986 [22]. Then different architectures of neural network language model are represented to learn word vectors [23]. One well-known open tool, Word2Vec is developed by Mikolov et al. [7] which trains distributed representation in a skip-gram likelihood as the input for prediction of words from their neighbor words [24]. Apart from knowledge-based and corpus-based methods, popular co-occurrence measures such as, Jaccard [8], Pointwise mutual information [25] or Dice have also been adapted to compute semantic similarity. These coefficients use page counts when searching words on the search engines[26] which is more like to be word relevance.

Recently, hybrid strategies are raised to overcome limitations of different methods [10], similarities are combined via statistic or machine learning methods [11, 27]. Generally, combined multiple similarities are all based on single resource and word distributed representation methods haven't been employed too much in the integration of different strategies. In this paper, we use ensemble learning for Chinese words similarity measure. Several algorithms are integrated. Knowledge-based similarities are calculated based on two Chinese semantic knowledge bases. In corpus-based methods, deep learning is trained on news and microblog corpora, and web search engines are applied for retrieving words. All the similarities are combined for ensemble learning.

3   Methodology

3.1   Frameworks of Word Similarity Measure

In this paper, we calculate word similarities based on multiple resources and integrate them by machine learning method. As Fig. 1 shown, ensemble learning is constructed based on three different similarities. Semantic similarity is using knowledge-based algorithms based on TYCCL and Hownet. Corpus-based similarities contain distributed similarity and word relevance. News and microblog corpora are trained via deep learning to get cosine value between words distributed representations. Two web search engines, Baidu and Bing are chosen to retrieve words and calculate word relevance based on returned page counts. All these similarities are combined by an ensemble learning method to get final words similarity.

3.2   Word Similarity Computation via Different Algorithms

Semantic Similarity Computation. TYCCL organized words according to the structure of tree. Each word in this knowledge hierarchy can be assigned a hierarchical

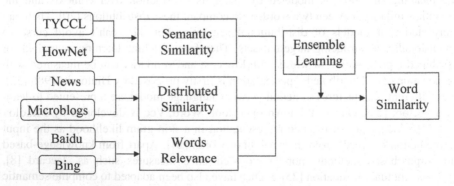

Fig. 1. Framework of word similarity measurement

ID. If two words have the same ID, then they are synonyms. This paper employs the algorithm which makes full use of the ID information [28]. Given two words with their ID information, judgment starts from the first level, if the encoding is the same, then multiply 1, different coefficients are multiplied according to the ID level where words have different encodings. Regulation parameter and controls parameter also need to multiply.

Different from TYCCL which build concept in a tree structure, HowNet uses different sememes to describe concepts. Similarity between words based on HowNet can be seen as the similarity between sememes describing the corresponding words. Algorithms applied in this paper come from previous work [29, 30]. Liu and Li [29] use set and structural characteristics to rewrite the semantic definition in HowNet, and proposed similarity measures based on sememes, set and structural characteristics. Xia [30] combined the depth of sememes, overlap degree to define the measure of similarity between sememes. He also solved problems about similarity of OOV words by segmenting words into two or more parts which exist in the HowNet.

Distributed Similarity Computation. There are many deep learning algorithms to learn distributed representation of words. However, most of the algorithms have large calculation cost. In order to minimize computational complexity, Mikolov et al. which constructed CBOW and skip-gram to learn concepts and semantic-syntactic relationships between words [31]. We applied this algorithm to learn distributed representation of words. The CBOW architecture predicts the current word based on the context, and the Skip-gram predicts surrounding words given the current word [7]. Open tool Word2Vec[1] is used which are developed by them. After training of word vectors, cosine value is calculated as the similarity between words and it ranges $[-1, 1]$.

Word Relevance Computation. Web search engines can provide large amount of available documents. Moreover, many commerce search engines offer shortcuts for users such as frequency counts, co-occurrence counts and context of retrieved results. To decrease computation complexity, page counts can be used to measure word relevance via four co-occurrence coefficients [26], such as Jaccard, Overlap, Dice and PMI. In this paper, we compute these four coefficients according to retrieval results from two web search engines. The final similarity based on Web search engines is calculated through ensemble learning on four coefficients of each engines respectively.

Ensemble Learning of Similarities. To integrate multiple similarities, we use support vector regression model (SVR). It has a very good performance in nonlinear regression and better implement of the structural risk minimization theory [32]. As Fig. 1 shown, ensemble learning is constructed based on different similarity methods mentioned above. Similarities under six methods are seen as eigenvalues and the given similarities labeled by human beings are corresponding regression values [33]. We use four kernel functions in the further experiments: linear, RBF, polynomial and sigmoid.

---

[1] Available at: https://code.google.com/p/word2vec/.

4 Experiments and Results Analysis

4.1 Task Dataset and Evaluation Method

This task provides a dataset of 500 Chinese words pairs and their golden human labeled similarities [34]. Sample data of 40 word pairs with similarities were firstly given. Test data of 10, 000 word pairs without similarities were given lately and 500 pairs are the one to evaluate. Spearman's rank correlation coefficient [35] is used to evaluate the statistical dependence between our automatic computing results and the golden human labeled data, formulation is shown below:

$$r_R = 1 - \frac{6 \sum_{i=1}^{n} (R_{Xi} - R_{Yi})^2}{n(n^2 - 1)} \tag{1}$$

Where, n is the number of observations, R_{Xi} and R_{Yi} are the standard deviations of rank variables. The bigger r_R is, computing results and labeled data are more related which means the results are better.

4.2 Multiple Resources

We utilized different resources for each kind of algorithm: Hownet and TYCCL, news and microblog corpora, Baidu and Bing. Referring to the corpora processing, word segmentation of Chinese sentence is done via ICTCLAS[2] and the stop words are then removed. We applied Word2vec model in Gensim[3] for word embedding. Open tool developed by Chang and Lin[4] is used to do ensemble learning. Detailed information of resources are given below.

HowNet[5] is a bilingual general knowledge base describing relations between concepts and relations between attributes of concepts. TYCCL was built by Mr. Mei [16] in 1983, which includes both synonym and similar words. Microblog corpora are from Sina Weibo, 1, 471, 919, 361 pieces of microblogs written from 2009 to 2014. News come from following resources: news.ifeng.com, www.chinanews.com, www. bwchinese.com, and other open news corpora[6]. Additionally, based on the website[7] which automatically crawls news URL, we download URL information from 2014.6.23 to 2016.4.24 and crawling the content of 18 websites[8]. Two search engines are Baidu and Bing. Baidu (https://www.baidu.com/) is a Chinese search engine for websites, audio files and images. Bing (http://cn.bing.com/) is a web search engine owned and operated by Microsoft.

---

[2] Available at: http://ictclas.nlpir.org/.
[3] Available at: http://radimrehurek.com/gensim/index.html.
[4] Available at: https://www.csie.ntu.edu.tw/~cjlin/libsvm/.
[5] Available at: http://www.keenage.com/.
[6] Available at: http://pennyliang.com/.
[7] Available at: http://lafnews.com/corpus/.
[8] 20 websites are selected based on the URL amount except two video websites.

4.3   Experimental Results and Analysis

During this task, 40 word pairs are training dataset while 500 pairs are test dataset. Spearman's rank correlation coefficients of different algorithms are shown in Tables 1 and 2. Besides, 40*p* and 500*p* represents training dataset of 40 word pairs and test dataset of 500 pairs. Deep learning trained corpora of Weibo, news, Weibo and news. Results of ensemble learning on four kernel functions are displayed in Table 2.

Table 1. Spearman's rank correlation coefficients of knowledge and corpus-based similarities

Method	Semantic similarity			Distributed similarity			Word relevance	
	TYCCL	Xia	Liu	Weibo	News	Weibo & news	Baidu	Bing
40p	0.2151	0.5296	0.4369	0.4985	**0.7514**	0.7210	0.5655	0.4503
500p	**0.3952**	0.3413	0.0298	−0.2413	0.3272	0.3136	0.1283	0.2205

Table 2. Spearman's rank correlation coefficients of ensemble learning-based similarities

Train-test	Kernel			
	Linear	RBF	Polynomial	Sigmoid
40p-40p	0.7864	**0.9366**	0.9172	−0.8942
40p-500p	0.3648	**0.3796**	0.2547	−0.9596
500p-500p	0.4735	**0.6931**	0.6613	−0.9596

Firstly, comparing highest spearman's rank correlation coefficients (bold) in Tables 1 and 2, we find that ensemble learning achieves the best performance if we can appropriately tune parameters. However, when we use 40 word pairs to predict 500 word pairs, spearman's rank correlation coefficient is lower than TYCCL-based method. Under fitting and poor parameter settings might lead to this. For knowledge-based algorithms, similarity based on TYCCL has the worst performance in training data which is totally opposite on test dataset. For corpus-based algorithms, similarity based on deep learning of news corpora performs best among all. News corpora is more suitable than microblogs to use in this task. Besides, referring to Hownet-based similarities, Xia's algorithm is better than Liu's for it solves OOV problem. Numbers of OOV in TYCCL, Xia's algorithm, Liu's algorithm, Weibo and News are 49, 84, 165, 249 and 49 respectively. It showed that the bigger number of OOV words is, Spearman's rank correlation is lower. Low coverage of lexical resources and wrong segmentations of corpora resources can be the reasons. Evaluation of web search engines differs on training and test data. When searching more words, Baidu behaved worse than Bing, different web page ranking algorithms might lead to this.

5 Conclusion and Future Works

In this paper, a similarity measure algorithm using ensemble learning on multiple resources is proposed. Although this algorithm behaves moderately in NLPCC 2016 task but evaluation of further experiments shows that ensemble learning could get best performance via parameters tuning. In the future, optimal strategy for ensemble learning should be investigated deeply, such as parameter setting, weak model filtering, adding other features. Besides, if we solve OOV problems by improving segmentation quality or user dictionary, great progress will make. Larger scale of corpora can also be used in corpus-based method. More room is there for improvement.

Acknowledgments. This work is supported by Major Projects of National Social Science Fund (13&ZD174), National Social Science Fund Project (No. 14BTQ033) and the Graduate Students Education Innovation Project of Jiangsu Province (No. KYLX16_0407).

References

1. Varelas, G., Voutsakis, E., Raftopoulou, P., Petrakis, E.G., Milios, E.E.: Semantic similarity methods in wordNet and their application to information retrieval on the web. In: Proceedings of the 7th Annual ACM International Workshop on Web Information and Data Management, pp. 10–16. ACM (2005)
2. Mikolov, T., Le, Q.V., Sutskever, I.: Exploiting similarities among languages for machine translation. arXiv preprint arXiv:1309.4168 (2013)
3. Karov, Y., Edelman, S.: Similarity-based word sense disambiguation. Comput. Linguist. **24**, 41–59 (1998)
4. Mihalcea, R., Corley, C., Strapparava, C.: Corpus-based and knowledge-based measures of text semantic similarity. In: AAAI, pp. 775–780 (2006)
5. Gan, M., Dou, X., Jiang, R.: From ontology to semantic similarity: calculation of ontology-based semantic similarity. Sci. World J. **2013**, 1–11 (2013)
6. Shi, J., Yunfang, W.U., Qiu, L., Xueqiang, L.V.: Chinese lexical semantic similarity computing based on large-scale corpus. J. Chin. Inf. Process. **27**, 1–461 (2013)
7. Mikolov, T., Chen, K., Corrado, G., Dean, J.: Efficient estimation of word representations in vector space. arXiv preprint arXiv:1301.3781, pp. 1–12 (2013)
8. Niwattanakul, S., Singthongchai, J., Naenudorn, E., Wanapu, S.: Using of Jaccard coefficient for keywords similarity. In: Proceedings of the International MultiConference of Engineers and Computer Scientists, pp. 13–15 (2013)
9. Manning, C.D., Schütze, H.: Foundations of Statistical Natural Language Processing. MIT Press, Cambridge (1999)
10. Li, Y., Bandar, Z.A., McLean, D.: An approach for measuring semantic similarity between words using multiple information sources. IEEE Trans. Knowl. Data Eng. **15**, 871–882 (2003)
11. Ittoo, A., Maruster, L.: Ensemble similarity measures for clustering terms. In: 2009 WRI World Congress on Computer Science and Information Engineering, pp. 315–319. IEEE (2009)

12. Bergroth, L., Hakonen, H., Raita, T.: A survey of longest common subsequence algorithms. In: Proceedings of the Seventh International Symposium on String Processing and Information Retrieval, SPIRE 2000, pp. 39–48. IEEE (2000)
13. Hall, P.A., Dowling, G.R.: Approximate string matching. ACM Comput. Surv. (CSUR) **12**, 381–402 (1980)
14. Fellbaum, C.: WordNet. Wiley Online Library (1998)
15. Vossen, P.: A Multilingual Database with Lexical Semantic Networks. Springer, Dordrecht (1998)
16. Mei, J.: Tongyici Cilin. Shanghai Cishu Publishing House, Shanghai (1984)
17. Dong, Z., Dong, Q.: HowNet and the Computation of Meaning. World Scientific, Singapore (2006)
18. Resnik, P.: Using information content to evaluate semantic similarity in a taxonomy. arXiv preprint arXiv:cmp-lg/9511007, pp. 1–6 (1995)
19. Jiang, J.J., Conrath, D.W.: Semantic similarity based on corpus statistics and lexical taxonomy. arXiv preprint arXiv:cmp-lg/9709008, pp. 1–15 (1997)
20. Miller, G.A., Charles, W.G.: Contextual correlates of semantic similarity. Lang. Cogn. Process. **6**, 1–28 (1991)
21. Bengio, Y., Courville, A., Vincent, P.: Representation learning: a review and new perspectives. IEEE Trans. Pattern Anal. Mach. Intell. **35**, 1798–1828 (2013)
22. Hinton, G.E.: Learning distributed representations of concepts. In: Proceedings of the Eighth Annual Conference of the Cognitive Science Society, Amherst, MA, pp. 1–12 (1986)
23. Bengio, Y., Ducharme, R., Vincent, P., Jauvin, C.: A neural probabilistic language model. J. Mach. Learn. Res. **3**, 1137–1155 (2003)
24. Taddy, M.: Document classification by inversion of distributed language representations. arXiv preprint arXiv:1504.07295, pp. 1–6 (2015)
25. Han, L., Finin, T., McNamee, P., Joshi, A., Yesha, Y.: Improving word similarity by augmenting PMI with estimates of word polysemy. IEEE Trans. Knowl. Data Eng. **25**, 1307–1322 (2013)
26. Bollegala, D., Matsuo, Y., Ishizuka, M.: Measuring semantic similarity between words using web search engines. WWW **7**, 757–766 (2007)
27. Neshati, M., Hassanabadi, L.S.: Taxonomy construction using compound similarity measure. In: Meersman, R., Tari, Z. (eds.) OTM 2007. LNCS, vol. 4803, pp. 915–932. Springer, Heidelberg (2007). doi:10.1007/978-3-540-76848-7_61
28. Jiu Le, T., Wei, Z.: Words similarity algorithm based on Tongyici Cilin in semantic web adaptive learning system. J. Jilin Univ. **28**, 602–608 (2010)
29. Liu, Q., Li, S.: Word simialrity computing based on How-net. Int. J. Comput. Linguist. Chin. Lang. Process. **7**, 59–76 (2002)
30. Xia, T.: Study on Chinese words semantic similarity computation. Comput. Eng. **33**, 191–194 (2007)
31. Mikolov, T., Sutskever, I., Chen, K., Corrado, G.S., Dean, J.: Distributed representations of words and phrases and their compositionality. In: Advances in Neural Information Processing Systems, pp. 1–9 (2013)
32. Smola, A.J., Schölkopf, B.: A tutorial on support vector regression. Stat. Comput. **14**, 199–222 (2004)
33. Cortes, C., Vapnik, V.: Support-vector networks. Mach. Learn. **20**, 273–297 (1995)
34. Wu, Y., Li, W.: NLPCC-ICCPOL 2016 shared task 3: Chinese word similarity measurement. In: Proceedings of NLPCC 2016 (2016)
35. Iman, R.L., Conover, W.-J.: A distribution-free approach to inducing rank correlation among input variables. Commun. Stat.-Simul. Comput. **11**, 311–334 (1982)

Overview of the NLPCC-ICCPOL 2016 Shared Task: Sports News Generation from Live Webcast Scripts

Xiaojun Wan[✉], Jianmin Zhang, Jin-ge Yao, and Tianming Wang

Institute of Computer Science and Technology,
The MOE Key Laboratory of Computational Linguistics,
Peking University, Beijing 100871, China
{wanxiaojun,zhangjianmin2015,yaojinge,
wangtm}@pku.edu.cn

Abstract. Live webcast scripts are valuable resources for describing the process of sports games. This shared task aims to automatically generate sports news articles from live webcast scripts. The task can be considered a special case of single document summarization. In this overview paper, we will introduce the task, the evaluation dataset, the participating teams and the evaluation results. The dataset has been released publicly.

Keywords: Sports news generation · Document summarization · Shared task · NLPCC-ICCPOL 2016

1 Task

It is an urgent demand to write and publish a sports news article immediately after a sports game ends. Till now, sports news articles are usually written by human experts or journalists. How to automatically generate sports news has always been a very challenging problem.

Many Chinese sports-related web sites (e.g. Sina Sports[1], NetEase Sports[2]) provide live webcast services to users for watching sports games. One popular service is based on live text webcast, and a webcast host frequently writes one or several short sentences (i.e. scripts) to describe the latest progress of a game in real-time. Users will know what happened in the game immediately after reading the latest scripts. The live webcast scripts are valuable resources for sports news generation, which are, however, neglected in the area of sports news generation and summarization. Note that we can also obtain live text scripts from live TV or video by using ASR technologies.

In this shared task, we aim to explore the possibility of generating Chinese sports news from live webcast scripts. The task can be treated as a special document summarization or text-to-text generation task. A very recent work has conducted a pilot study on this task [1]. In this year's task, we focus on football games. We encourage participants to consider the characteristics of live webcast scripts and develop more competitive sports news generation systems.

---

[1] http://sports.sina.com.cn.
[2] http://sports.163.com/.

© Springer International Publishing AG 2016
C.-Y. Lin et al. (Eds.): NLPCC-ICCPOL 2016, LNAI 10102, pp. 870–875, 2016.
DOI: 10.1007/978-3-319-50496-4_80

2   Data

We provided sample (training) data and test data for this shared task. For sample data, we provided a set of live webcast scripts and the corresponding human-written news stories for 30 football games. The live web cast scripts and the news stories were crawled from Sina Sports and NetEase Sports. For each sports game, we provided at least two news stories as the reference news. For test data, we provided a set of live webcast scripts for 30 other football games.

Part of the live webcast scripts for a football game (Chelsea vs Sunderland on 2015-12-19) is shown in Table 1. In each row in the table, the text scripts are provided along with the match time and match score.

Table 1. Part of live webcast scripts for the game of Chelsea vs Sunderland on 2015-12-19

伊万右路45度斜传球到禁区，科茨解围球直接停给了佩德罗，佩德罗将球一拨，左脚抽射，打进！！！	上半场 14'	2-0
威廉前场右路拿球，强突后分边给上来的伊万	上半场 14'	2-0
伊万没机会，回传给到小法	上半场 15'	2-0
小法拿球内切，斜塞禁区找插入的威廉	上半场 15'	2-0
球被回防的范安霍尔特抢先出脚碰出底线，角球	上半场 15'	2-0

In addition to the live webcast scripts, we also provided match statistics and players statistics of the game, as illustrated in Tables 2 and 3. The participants can optionally make use of the match statistics in developing their sports news generation systems.

Table 2. Match statistics for the game of Chelsea vs Sunderland on 2015-12-19

切尔西	项目	桑德兰
17	总射门	11
7	射正球门	3
10	射门偏出	8
0	击中门框	0
3	直塞球	1
0	越位	3
17	抢断	27
12	任意球	12
12	犯规	12
2	角球	2
26	界外球	22
69	超过25码长传	54
84.80%	传球成功率	69.60%
41.20%	传中成功率	33.30%
70.60%	抢断成功率	66.70%
40%	头球成功率	60%
67.50%	控球率	32.50%

Table 3. Players statistics for the game of Chelsea vs Sunderland on 2015-12-19

号码	位置	球员名	出场	时间	进球	助攻	威胁球	射门	射正	射正率	犯规	被犯	扑救
13	门将	库尔图瓦	首发	90'	0	0	0	0	0	0	0	0	2
28	后卫	阿斯皮利奎塔	首发	90'	0	0	0	0	0	0	3	0	0
2	后卫	伊万诺维奇	首发	90'	1	0	0	2	1	50%	2	0	0
26	后卫	特里	首发	90'	0	0	0	0	0	0	0	1	0
5	后卫	祖马	首发	90'	0	0	0	0	0	0	1	1	0
22	中场	威廉	首发	90'	0	1	4	3	2	66.70%	0	2	0
8	中场	奥斯卡	首发	82'	1	0	2	5	2	40%	1	1	0
21	中场	马蒂奇	首发	90'	0	0	2	0	0	0	2	1	0
4	中场	法布雷加斯	首发	71'	0	0	1	0	0	0	2	1	0
17	中场	佩德罗	首发	90'	1	0	3	3	1	33.30%	0	4	0
19	前锋	迭戈-科斯塔	首发	76'	0	0	0	2	0	0%	1	0	0
1	替补	贝戈维奇	替补	0'	0	0	0	0	0	0	0	0	0
24	替补	加里-卡希尔	替补	0'	0	0	0	0	0	0	0	0	0
12	替补	米克尔	替补	19'	0	0	0	0	0	0	0	1	0
18	替补	雷米	替补	14'	0	0	0	2	1	50%	0	0	0
7	替补	拉米雷斯	替补	8'	0	0	0	0	0	0	0	1	0
14	替补	特劳雷	替补	0'	0	0	0	0	0	0	0	0	0
6	替补	拉赫曼-巴巴	替补	0'	0	0	0	0	0	0	0	0	0

3 Participants

Each team is allowed to submit at most two runs of results. The length of each sports news is limited to 1000 Chinese characters and longer news articles will be truncated. The participants are allowed to use any NLP resources or toolkits, but it is NOT allowed to crawl and use any news articles related to the given games on the Web.

There are 7 teams participating in this shared task and they submitted a total of 10 valid runs of results. The participating teams are shown in Table 4. Various techniques have been used by the participating teams and several teams have crawled additional live scripts and sports news articles for other sports games to enhance the training data. For example, IACAS_Human_HCI mainly relies on key sentence extraction by considering various factors, including keywords, time, and so on. The team also designs

Table 4. Participating teams.

Team ID	Organization name
IACAS_Human_HCI	Chinese Academy of Sciences; Guilin University of Electronic Technology; Hebei University of Technology
ICDD_SportsNews	Beijing Information Science and Technology University
RDNH	Chongqing University of Technology
BIT Coder	Beijing Institute of Technology
CQUT_AC996	Chongqing University of Technology
CCNU2016NLP	Central China Normal University
BIT Hunter	Beijing Institute of Technology

and uses a few patterns to improve the readability of generated sports news. ICDD_-SportsNews uses different strategies for generating different parts of a sports news. The team generates the first paragraph of a sports news with patterns to briefly overview the sports game, and then applies supervised learning methods to extract key sentences to describe the process of the game, and finally provides statistics of players in the last paragraph. BIT Coder generates sports news with slot filling techniques.

4 Results

The generated sports news articles were evaluated both automatically and manually.

4.1 Automatic Evaluation

We used the ROUGE-1.5.5 toolkit [2] for automatic evaluation[3]. In order to make the ROUGE toolkit work well for evaluating Chinese news, the code related to text encoding in ROUGE-1.5.5.pl should be modified. The recommended options for the toolkit were -c 95 -2 4 -U -r 1000 -n 4 -w 1.2 –a –l 1000. Note that the length of each sports news was limited to 1000 Chinese characters, so we used –l 1000 for truncating longer news articles.

The recommended ROUGE metrics are Recall and F-measure scores of Character-based ROUGE-1, ROUGE-2 and ROUGE-SU4. Character-based evaluation means that we do not need to perform Chinese word segmentation when running the ROUGE toolkit. Instead, we only need to separate each Chinese character by using a blank space.

Table 5 gives the automatic evaluation results. We can see that the three teams of IACAS_Human_HCI, ICDD_SportsNews and RDNH perform better than the other four teams.

4.2 Manual Evaluation

We further performed manual evaluation, which is more reliable than the automatic evaluation for this special task. Three graduate students who are fluent in Chinese were asked to perform manual ratings for each news article with respect to three factors: readability (Read.), content coverage (Cont.) and overall score. The ratings were in the range of 1–5, with higher scores denoting better quality. Finally the scores were averaged across the 30 news articles, and then averaged across the three judges.

The results are shown in Table 6. We can see that the team of IACAS_Human_HCI performs the best over all the three factors, and the ICDD_SportsNews team also performs very well over the three factors. The two teams considered various factors for key sentence extraction, and they used both machine learning and pattern-based techniques for sports news generation.

---

[3] The ROUGE toolkit can be downloaded from http://www.berouge.com.

Table 5. Automatic evaluation results

Team	Run	ROUGE-1		ROUGE-2		ROUGE-SU4	
		Recall	F-measure	Recall	F-measure	Recall	F-measure
IACAS_Human_HCI	run1	0.57782	0.59846	0.24998	0.26293	0.25464	0.26652
	run2	0.55643	0.60331	0.24448	0.26092	0.24777	0.26581
ICDD_SportsNews	run1	0.56515	0.59261	0.25235	0.26444	0.25404	0.26613
	run2	0.56768	0.59179	0.25059	0.26119	0.25438	0.26497
RDNH	run1	0.55235	0.5865	0.25527	0.27081	0.25333	0.26863
BIT_Coder	run1	0.49728	0.55851	0.22524	0.25333	0.22484	0.25263
CQUT_AC996	run2	0.5222	0.55728	0.22182	0.23688	0.22689	0.2422
CCNU2016NLP	run1	0.46105	0.52478	0.19486	0.22128	0.19322	0.21947
	run2	0.4948	0.52425	0.20894	0.22123	0.21102	0.22325
BIT_Hunter	run2	0.36532	0.47758	0.16072	0.2106	0.16504	0.21589

Table 6. Manual evaluation results

Team	Run	Factor	Average score
IACAS_Human_HCI	run1	Read.	3.84444
		Cont.	3.54444
		Overall	3.63333
	run2	Read.	3.88889
		Cont.	3.64444
		Overall	3.73333
ICDD_SportsNews	run1	Read.	3.34444
		Cont.	3.32222
		Overall	3.24444
	run2	Read.	3.46667
		Cont.	3.32222
		Overall	3.28889
RDNH	run1	Read.	2.92222
		Cont.	1.85556
		Overall	2.17778
BIT Coder	run1	Read.	2.55556
		Cont.	2.74444
		Overall	2.45556
CQUT_AC996	run2	Read.	2.61111
		Cont.	2.21111
		Overall	2.30000
CCNU2016NLP	run1	Read.	2.06667
		Cont.	2.02222
		Overall	1.93333
	run2	Read.	2.24444
		Cont.	2.67778
		Overall	2.21111
BIT Hunter	run2	Read.	1.68889
		Cont.	1.94444
		Overall	1.60000

5 Conclusions

We proposed a new shared task of sports news generation from live webcast scripts for NLPCC-ICCPOL 2016, and 7 teams participated in this shared task. The evaluation dataset has been released publicly[4]. We expect more advanced text summarization and generation methods will be proposed for this special Chinese sports news generation task.

Acknowledgments. This work was supported by National Hi-Tech Research and Development Program (863 Program) of China (2015AA015403) and National Natural Science Foundation of China (61331011).

References

1. Zhang, J., Yao, J., Wan, X.: Toward constructing sports news from live text commentary. In: Proceedings of ACL (2016)
2. Lin, C.-Y.: Rouge: a package for automatic evaluation of summaries. In: Text Summarization Branches Out: Proceedings of the ACL-2004 Workshop, vol. 8 (2004)

---

4 http://www.icst.pku.edu.cn/lcwm/wanxj/files/NLPCC2016Eval-Task5-AllData.rar.

Sports News Generation from Live Webcast Scripts Based on Rules and Templates

Maofu Liu[1,2], Qiaosong Qi[1,2], Huijun Hu[1,2], and Han Ren[3(✉)]

[1] College of Computer Science and Technology, Wuhan University of Science
and Technology, Wuhan 430065, China
[2] Hubei Province Key Laboratory of Intelligent Information Processing
and Real-Time Industrial System, Wuhan University of Science
and Technology, Wuhan 430065, China
[3] Laboratory of Language Engineering and Computing,
Guangdong University of Foreign Studies, Guangzhou 510006, China
hanren@whu.edu.cn

Abstract. With the dramatic increase of the live webcast scripts about sports, it
is an urgent demand to write and publish a sports news article immediately after
a sports game. However, so far, the sports news articles are usually written by
human experts or journalists, and the manual writing of sports news is
time-consuming and inefficient. This paper describes our system on the sports
news generation from live webcast scripts task. On one hand, our system
extracts the important events occurring in the time period from the live webcast
scripts according to the rules, and on the other hand, our system generates a brief
summary from the live webcast scripts about the football matches. According to
the characteristic of live webcast scripts, we adopt an approach to sentence
extraction and template generation from live webcast scripts. The evaluation
results show that our system is feasible in sports news generation from live
webcast scripts.

Keywords: Sports news generation · Rules · Sentence extraction · Sentence
ranking

1 Introduction

With the increasing emphasis on sports events and the development of sports theme
websites, the automatic generation of sports news has become particularly important.
The sports fans do not have enough time to read all the live or replay due to the fast
pace of life, and thus they turn to read a short sports news. However, till now, sports
news articles are usually written by human experts or journalists. This paper attempts to
develop a competitive sports news generation system to replace the way of writing
news.

Different from the traditional single-document summarization, the sports news
article is produced from live webcast scripts in this paper. In single-document summarization, the important words or sentences will appear more frequently, and however, the exciting moments are often very rare and not replicable in a score game live

C.-Y. Lin et al. (Eds.): NLPCC-ICCPOL 2016, LNAI 10102, pp. 876–884, 2016.
DOI: 10.1007/978-3-319-50496-4_81

webcast. When the football fans read a sports news, some key messages might make a deep impression on them, such as the score, the intense rivalry in the penalty area, the overviews of the two teams. This requires that the system should be able to find the key information from the given live webcast scripts and generate one shorter sport news article. The length of the sports news is limited to 1000 Chinese characters in our system.

In this paper, we propose a hybrid approach based on the rules to extracting and generating sentences from the data set. Firstly, the system get data from the tec.csv file and summarize the performance of a team. Then, all the performance and visibility of the players are extracted from the home.csv and away.csv files. Finally, the important sentences will be located in live web script according to the rules and templates.

The remainder of this paper is organized as follows. Section 2 reviews related work. Section 3 introduces the proposed approach to generating the sport news. Section 4 presents the results of the evaluation and discussions. Finally, we conclude the paper and suggest the future work in the fifth section.

2 Related Work

The method of automatic generation based on extraction has been used for a long time. Ji et al. [1] proposed multiple approaches to information extraction based summarization. Wang and Tang [2] put forward a special Chinese automatic summarization method based on concept-obtained and hybrid parallel genetic algorithm. Kumar et al. [3] proposed a knowledge induced graph-theoretical model for extract and abstract single document summarization. Zhu et al. [4] presented a tag-oriented summarization method. Hirao et al. [5] gave a single-document summarization method based on the trimming of a discourse tree.

The single-document summarization has been turned to professional fields. Liu et al. [6] established a model based on feature combination to automatically generate summary for the given news article. Tran et al. [7] proposed a method to summarize a movie based on character network analysis. Sadiq et al. [8] gave system works by assigning scores to sentences in the document to be summarized. Li et al. [9] put forward a new keyword extraction method based on tf-idf for Chinese news documents.

In this paper, we make use of tec.csv to generate the evaluation of the whole game, and then summarize player performance and the team lineup from the away.csv and home.csv. The position, players, actions and other factors have been selected to determine the importance of live.csv in a series of sentences. Then, the extracted sentences are connected together in a format to form the final sports news article.

3 System Description

3.1 System Architecture

Our system consists of three main modules, i.e. data preprocessing, sentence extraction and generation, and sentence selection. We illustrate our system architecture in detail in Fig. 1.

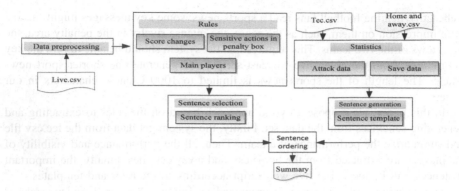

Fig. 1. System architecture

In data preprocessing, the main work is to segment the Chinese words and remove the stop words. We choose NLPIR Chinese words segmentation tools[1] and select Chinese stop word list from CCF (China Computer Federation) website[2].

In the Rules box of Fig. 1, the score changes mean that the third column of live.csv has changed in a row, and sensitive actions denote the foul, goal and other mentioned important activities. The players are ranked based on the statistics in the home.csv and away.csv, and the ranking determines the likelihood that a player will appear in the summary.

This system will use the number of shots and ball control rate to measure one team's offensive and ball possession, and generate a short game evaluation with templates for this team.

We use this rank list to score a sentence with the sum of all the players' scores in it.

3.2 Rules Based on Common Sense

Because of the particularity of the field in a football game, we introduce the common sense to this system, shown as follows.

(1) The score of the match is the most important.
(2) Appearance of yellow or red card is the key information.
(3) The readers will be concerned about the players who perform well.
(4) The offense, defense and foul in the penalty area constitute the main body of the article.

In order to enhance the readability and coherence of the generated sport news article, we divide the news article to be generated by the system into three parts, which are given in the following subsections.

---

[1] http://ictclas.nlpir.org/.

[2] http://www.ccf.org.cn/sites/ccf/ccfdata.jsp.

(1) **Time, match and teams**

In the first part, the news article tells the time of this competition, number of the match and history of confrontations. The following Example 1 illustrates this part.

Example 1: 北京时间2月3日凌晨3:45,英超第24轮一场焦点战,阿森纳主场出战南普顿。

The time and the match name can be found in the live scripts and the teams can be found in the tec.csv file. After obtaining these messages, this part can be generated.

(2) **The evaluation of players and the whole match**

In the second part, the article shows the general situation of the game and the players who perform well. The following Example 2 illustrates the form of this part.

Example 2: 本场比赛中,双方均有多次破门的机会。切尔西队门将库尔图瓦表现神勇,全场没收了4次射门。联赛首回合的交锋,切尔西也在客场0:1不敌对手。

The basis for the evaluation of the competition comes from the tec.csv, and the situation of the player can be summarized from the home.csv and away.csv. The following Tables 1 and 2 illustrate the format of the files.

Table 1. Part of tec.csv

切尔西	项目	桑德兰
17	总射门	11
7	射正球门	3
0	击中门框	0
67.50%	控球率	32.50%

Table 2. Part of away.csv

号码	位置	球员名	出场	进球	助攻	威胁球	犯规	扑救
13	门将	库尔图瓦	首发	0	0	0	0	2
28	后卫	阿斯皮利奎塔	首发	0	0	0	3	0
2	后卫	伊万诺维奇	首发	1	0	0	2	0
21	中场	佩德罗	首发	1	0	3	0	0
19	前锋	迭戈-科斯塔	首发	0	0	0	1	0

(3) **Exciting moments in the live**

The third part of the news article is the body of the match and this part will record the important moments in the live. The following Example 3 illustrates this part.

Example 3: 第53分钟,加布里埃尔横传被抢断,马内突破后射门被切赫得到。

In the live scripts, the system regards the sentences recorded in two minutes as a unit. According to the common sense mentioned above, we extract the units which record the goals, the fouls, the substitutions and the offenses or defenses in the penalty area. The following Table 3 presents the format of the live.csv.

Table 3. Part of live webcast scripts

威廉前场右路拿球,强突后分边上给上来的伊万	上半场14'	2-0
伊万没机会,回传给小法	上半场15'	2-0
小法拿球内切,斜塞禁区找插入的威廉	上半场15'	2-0
球被回防的范安霍尔特抢先出脚碰出底线,角球	上半场15'	2-0

In this part, we rank the player according to formula (1).

$$Rank_i = score_i + 0.5 \times assist_i + 0.1 \times threatball_i + 0.1 \times save_i \qquad (1)$$

Where the $score_i$, $assist_i$, $threatball_i$ and the $save_i$ denote the parameters of the scores, assists, threatening shots and saves in the football match. When the length of the article beyond the limit, the unit with lower total ranked players will be deleted.

3.3 Sentence Extraction and Generation

In order to enhance the readability of the sentence, the system has set up a variety of sentence templates. The following form describes a small sample of the template matching strategy in our system in detail.

The ctrlH and ctrlA in Table 4 represent the ball control time of the home team and the away team respectively.

Table 4. A sample of template matching strategy

ctrH/ctrA	Corresponding template
[1.5, +∞)	主队展现出惊人/压倒性的控球能力。
[1.3, 1.5)	本场比赛中,主队的控球能力略胜一筹。
$[\frac{1}{1.5}, \frac{1}{1.3})$	本场比赛中,客队的控球能力略胜一筹。
$(0, \frac{1}{1.5}]$	客队展示出了惊人/压倒性的控球能力。

By several sets of templates, the system will generate the first and second parts of the sport news article.

The third part of the news uses strategies for sentence extraction. The following Algorithm 1 describes the sentence extraction strategy in our system in detail.

Algorithm 1. Sentences extraction
Input: Sentence array *SenSet, rule1, rule2, professional noun*
Output: Key sentence extraction *result*
1: begin
2: foreach *Sen* in *SenSet*
3:    adddic.add(*professional noun*) // Add user dictionary
4:    nlpir(*sOutcell, Sen*) // Word segmentation
5:    if(*sOutcell* match *rule1*)
6:       connect(*connect, sOutcell*) //   Connect the sentences within 2 mins
7:       if(*sOutcell* match *rule2*)
8:        extract (*res, connect*) // Results are extracted in variable res.
9:       end if
10: end if
11:end for
12:Ranking (*ranklist, res*) // List of ranked sentences.
13:while(*res*.length>1000)
14:   delete *ranklist[ranklist.size()]* // Delete the lowest rank sentence
15:end while
16:Output key sentence extraction *result*
17:end

The matching rules means the system will detect the words which can express the rules in a sentence, such as "禁区", "手球", and "越位". The connecting means the sentences one minute before and after the words will be connected. The words can be represented by a tree diagram shown below (Fig. 2).

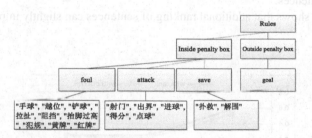

Fig. 2. Tree diagram of words

4   Evaluation Results and Discussions

In this paper, we use an approach based on the combination of extraction and generation to generating Chinese sports news from live webcast script. The length of the sports news is limited to 1000 Chinese characters. For automatic evaluation, we adopt the ROUGE toolkit and ROUGE-N F-measure is used as evaluation metric. The following Table 5 is the official evaluation results of our formal run.

Table 5. The official evaluation results of our formal runs

	ROUGE-1	ROUGE-2	ROUGE-3	ROUGE-4	ROUGE-SU4
NLP@WUST	0.57447	0.24894	0.11288	0.05540	0.24952

We compare our results to ones of the other seven groups who participated in Chinese sports news from live webcast script task and only select the best ROUGE evaluation result for each group shown in Fig. 3, and we can find that our system is at an intermediate level.

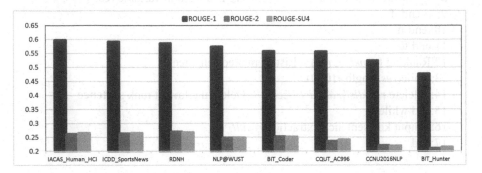

Fig. 3. ROUGE evaluation results for the formal runs of all task groups

In experiments, we also change some of the conditions and compare the different results. The following Fig. 4 can show the increase in the results after the additional ranking of sentences.

The Fig. 4 shows that additional ranking of sentences can slightly improve the final results.

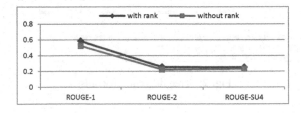

Fig. 4. The effect of sentences ranking on the results of the training set

As mentioned above, the system regards the sentences recorded in two minutes as a unit. The following Fig. 5 can illustrate the effect of the time span on the results.

From Fig. 5, we can find that the evaluation results will get a better F-measure when looking on the sentences recorded in two minutes as a unit.

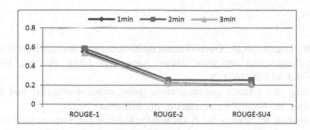

Fig. 5. The effect of time span on the results of the training set

But, the results of the system sometimes are not ideal for some of the training data. In the match of Dinamo versus Manchester on Feb. 25, 2015, our system only extracts four sentences to describe the offense and defense in the penalty area and this is obviously out of common sense. The possible causes of this issue are listed as follows.

(1) The two teams have done less offensive and defensive in this match.
    Sometimes, there are some unusual tactics in the game, and thus, the system needs to make adjustments to a variety of game lineup.
(2) Many synonyms of the words in the rules are adopted by the author of this live webcast script in this example.

In this paper, we refer to a number of football professional terms on the network[3]. In the 11.live.csv of the sample data, the author use "将球摁在身下" to express the save activity of the goalkeeper.

5   Conclusions and Future Work

In this paper, we present an approach to summarizing football sport news through rules and templates. We extract and generate the sentences in the final results by rules. The evaluation results show that our system ranks at an intermediate level in generating the sport news article from live webcast script.

Our system still has room to improve. In the future, we will introduce more rules and templates into the system with the guidance of professionals in the field of football in order to adjust various match situations. With the development of live webcast script standardization, some tags will be added to the script, and thus, the system can distinguish the type of each event with the tags. With a comprehensive thesaurus, the quality of summary will rise as expected as well.

Acknowledgments. The work presented in this paper is partially supported by the Major Projects of National Social Science Foundation of China under Grant No. 11&ZD189, Natural Science Foundation of China under No. 61402341, Natural Science Foundation of Education Department of Hubei Province under No. B2016010, and Open Foundation of Hubei Province Key Laboratory under No. 2016znss05A.

---

[3] http://edu.sina.com.cn/en/2007-11-26/135640034.shtml.

References

1. Ji, H., Favre, B., Lin, W., et al.: Open-domain multi-document summarization via information extraction: challenges and prospects. Theor. Appl. Nat. Lang. Process. 177–201 (2013). doi:10.1007/978-3-642-28569-1_9
2. Wang, M., Tang, X.: Extract summarization using concept-obtained and hybrid parallel genetic algorithm. In: Natural Computation, pp. 662–664 (2012)
3. Kumar, N., Srinathan, K., Varma, V.: A knowledge induced graph-theoretical model for extract and abstract single document summarization. In: Gelbukh, A. (ed.) CICLing 2013. LNCS, vol. 7817, pp. 408–423. Springer, Heidelberg (2013). doi:10.1007/978-3-642-37256-8_34
4. Zhu, J., Wang, C., He, X., et al.: Tag-oriented document summarization. In: Proceedings of the 18th ACM International Conference on World Wide Web, pp. 1195–1196 (2009). doi:10.1145/1526709.1526925
5. Hirao, T., Yoshida, Y., Nishino, M., et al.: Single-document summarization as a tree knapsack problem. In: Proceedings of the Conference on Empirical Methods in Natural Language Processing, pp. 1515–1520 (2013)
6. Liu, M., Wang, L., Nie, L.: Weibo-oriented chinese news summarization via multi-feature combination. In: Li, J., Ji, H., Zhao, D., Feng, Y. (eds.) NLPCC 2015. LNCS (LNAI), vol. 9362, pp. 581–589. Springer, Heidelberg (2015). doi:10.1007/978-3-319-25207-0_55
7. Tran, Q., Hwang, D., Lee, O., et al.: Exploiting character networks for movie summarization. Multimedia Tools Appl. 1–13 (2016). doi:10.1007/s11042-016-3633-6
8. Sadiq, A.T., Ali, Y.H., Fadhil, M.S.M.N.: Text summarization for social network conversation. In: International Conference on Advanced Computer Science Applications and Technologies, pp. 3–18 (2013)
9. Li, J., Zhang, K.: Keyword extraction based on tf-idf for Chinese news document. Wuhan Univ. J. Nat. Sci. 12(5), 917–921 (2007)

A Deep Learning Approach for Question Answering Over Knowledge Base

Linjie Wang[(⊠)], Yu Zhang[(⊠)], and Ting Liu[(⊠)]

Harbin Institute of Technology, Harbin, China
{linjiewang, zhangyu, tliu}@ir.hit.edu.cn

Abstract. With the increase of the scale of the knowledge base, it's important to answer question over knowledge base. In this paper, we will introduce a method to extract answers from Chinese knowledge base for Chinese questions. Our method uses a classifier to judge whether the relation in the triple is what the question asked, question-relation pairs are used to train the classifier. It's difficult to identify the right relation, so we find out the focus of the question and leverage the resource of lexical paraphrase in the preprocessing of the question. And the use of lexical paraphrase also can alleviate the out of vocabulary (OOV) problem. In order to let the right answer at the top of candidate answers, we present a ranking method to rank these candidate answers. The result of the final evaluation shows that our method achieves a good result.

1 Introduction

Answering question over a knowledge base is to extract the answers from knowledge base directly. In order to do this task, we have two methods to use. One is semantic parsing, and the other is information extraction based.

Semantic parsing methods try to convert question into a certain intermediate semantic representation and then convert the intermediate representation to a logic query. The results of semantic parsing based methods depend on the accuracy of the semantic parser. If the result of the semantic parser is wrong, we couldn't get the correct answer. Information extraction based methods take the question as a query to retrieve the candidate answers from the knowledge base and then try to find out which answer is the correct answer for the question.

Yao et al. [1] do the analysis of the two QA methods, semantic parsing and information extraction have shown no significant difference between them over Freebase. But in view of the fact that the knowledge triples in Chinese knowledge base used in our experiments crawled from the web. Same relation to two objects could be described in a different way. So we choose to use information extraction based method to answer the question over the Chinese knowledge base. The final result of the evaluation shows that our method can answer the most of the question correctly, and most of the right answers are in the first place. The F1 score of the evaluation is 0.7914.

In this paper, we will go through how to answer question over knowledge in the open domain. The steps to get answers include recognizing the entities mention in

© Springer International Publishing AG 2016
C.-Y. Lin et al. (Eds.): NLPCC-ICCPOL 2016, LNAI 10102, pp. 885–892, 2016.
DOI: 10.1007/978-3-319-50496-4_82

question, entities mention filters, retrieve the candidate triples from the knowledge base, judge which relation is what the question asks, and rank the candidate answers.

2 Background

The scale and quality of the knowledge base has an important influence on question answering. Some researchers use DBPedia [2], Freebase [3] and Yago2 [4] as the knowledge base in open domain question answering.

Answering question over knowledge base is an important task. The semantic parsing researchers try to do this task by using semantic parser parse these question. These works include combinatory categorial grammar [5–10], dependency trees [11–13] and string kernels [14, 15]. Most of these methods need use manually rules to train the semantic parser.

The information extraction researchers use the question as the query, and retrieve candidate triples from knowledge base, and the last step is to extract answers from candidate triples. Yao et al. [16] take the task of answering question over knowledge base as a binary classification problem. They use the dependency tree of the question as the representation of the question, and extract different features from question and the topic graph. These features will be fed into the logistic regression model. Some other methods use the summation the question word vectors as the representation of the question [17, 18], these works ignore the word order in question, so they will lose some information. Li et al. [19] propose a multi-column model to rank the candidate answers. They use a convolutional neural network to learn the representation of the question. Yih et al. [20] use convolutional neural network to answer the single relation question.

There are some other works on this task, for example, some researchers use manual templates to extract answers from knowledge triples [21].

We use the knowledge base released by the NLPCC 2016 open domain Chinese Question Answering task. In consideration of the quality of the knowledge base, we use the information extraction based method to do this task.

3 Approach

When our system receives one natural language question q, firstly, we will try to find out all entities mention in question, and take them as the candidate entities mention. It's obvious that there is lots of noise in the candidate entities mention, so we need to filter out these noises. In order to find out which entity mention is noise and which one is the topic of the question, we use a syntactic parser to parse the question and find out the name entities of the question. After filtering out the noise of candidate entities mention, we use these rest to retrieve relative triples in Chinese knowledge base. Once we get the candidate triples, the question and the relation of triples will be fed into the classifier. The classifier gives a score to each question-relation pair, if the score is less than θ, then this triple will be dropped. We will also compute the word overlap between the question and triple, and then combine the word overlap and the score given by the classifier to rank these candidate triples. Our system architecture is shown in Fig. 1.

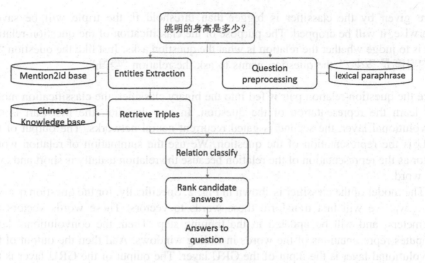

Fig. 1. System architecture

3.1 Entity Mention

The first step of the system is to find out the all entities mention of the question, and figure out which one is the topic of the question. We use the trie tree to help us find out the entities mention in question. But we don't know which entity mention is the topic of the question, if these all entities mention are used to retrieve the triples in Chinese knowledge base, we will get too much candidate triples, and too much noise will also affect our final result.

So we use a syntactic parser to parse the question and filter these candidate entities mention by the result given by parser. For instance, in a dependency tree, any word whose father node is the question word, we will drop it. In addition, we also think the focus of the question is not the topic of the question, so the focus in question will be dropped. Focus words are identified by the approach proposed by Zhang [22]. The name entity in question is very important, and we use LTP [23] to recognize the name entity in question, we will only save the name entity, and the other will be dropped.

3.2 Relation Classification

Retrieve Knowledge Triples. We use these entities mention of the question to retrieve all relative knowledge triples from the knowledge base. When we retrieve triples from the knowledge base, we only judge whether the subject of the triple is equal to the id of entity mention, if yes then we save it, if not then we drop it. For instance, for the question "姚明的身高是多少?", we use "姚明" to retrieve the candidate triples, finally, only the subject of triples is "姚明" will be saved.

Classification Model. In order to extract the correct answers from these candidate triples, we will put the question and the relation of the triple to a binary classifier, if the score given by the classifier is bigger than threshold θ, the triple will be saved, otherwise, it will be dropped. The purpose of the classification of the question-relation pair is to judge whether the relation is what the question asks. Just like the question "姚明的身高是多少?", the question wants to ask the relation "身高".

Once the question-relation pair is fed into the binary classifier, the classification model will learn the representation of the question. In our classifier, the first part is one convolutional layer, the second is gated recurrent neural networks. The output of the GRU is the representation of the question. We use the summation of relation words vector as the representation of the relation because the relation usually is short and even one word.

The model of the classifier is shown in Fig. 2. Specifically, for the question $q = w_1$, w_2, ...w_n, we will first transform these words to vectors. These words vectors are parameters, and will be updated in the training step. Then, the convolutional layer computes representations of the words in sliding windows. And then the output of the convolutional layer is the input of the GRU layer. The output of the GRU layer is the representation of the question. We use the summation of relation words vector as the representation of relation. The vector representation of question and the relation will be concatenated, and the concatenated result is the input to the fully connected layer. The fully connected layer can learn the relation between different dimensions of a vector. The last layer of the classifier is a logistic regression layer. An adaptive sigmoid function is used in this layer. The output of sigmoid is a value between 0 and 1, this value is used to represent the correlation degree between the question and relation.

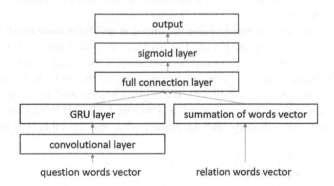

Fig. 2. The model of the binary classifier.

3.3   Ranking

After filtering the candidate triples by the binary classifier, in the rest of the candidate triples, some triples are more suitable as the answers than other triples. We need rank these candidate triples, and let the correct answer at the top of candidate answers. So it's important to rank these candidate answers. Actually, some researchers treat the answering question over knowledge base task as a ranking task [19].

Each question-triple pair will be given a score, the higher this score, the more likely the answer is the correct answer. We use Eq. (1) to compute the score.

$$\text{score}(q, \text{triple}) = \alpha * W_{score} + (1 - \alpha) * C_{score} \qquad (1)$$

W_{score} is the score given by word overlap between question and (subject, relation) of the triple. We need to let the word overlap score normalization, so for every question, the word overlap number of every candidate triple will divide the biggest word overlap of these candidate triples. Lastly, W_{score} is between 0 and 1. The reason we take W_{score} as a score is that we think the more word overlap number and the more likely the answer is the correct answer. C_{score} is the score given by the classifier. α indicates the proportion of the two score. We can modify the value of α to find a better value that let the final result is better. Table 1 shows that the step of ranking plays an important role in our method.

Table 1. Experimental results

Baseline	F1-score
Embedding similarity	0.3841
Our method	
CGRU	0.6964
CGRU + paraphrase	0.7185
CGRU + paraphrase + ranking	**0.7914**

4 Experiments

4.1 Datasets

We use NLPCC 2016 shared task open domain knowledge-based QA data. It contains 14609 question-answer pairs and 9870 questions that need to be answered. We then use entities of the question and the answer to extract the relation in the correct triple as positive sample, and also extract one relation in the wrong triple as the negative sample, and use question-relation pairs as the training set to train our model. We further randomly choose 11609 question-relation pairs for training and the 3000 question-relation pairs remained as a development set DEV. The organizers of shared tasked in NLPCC 2016 also offer a file that maps the entities mention in question to entities name in the knowledge base, and we use it in our experiments to transform entities mention to subject in the knowledge base.

4.2 Settings

The dimension of word vectors is set to 100, and they are initialized by the pre-trained word vectors provided by the tool word2vec [24]. The initial learning rate used in AdaGrad is set to 0.001. A mini-batch consists of 2000 question-relation pairs.

4.3 Search

We build a trie tree to store the total entities mention, and each node is one single word in Chinese. We use the trie tree to get all entities mention in question. These entities mention in question will be used to extract the triples in the knowledge base. Once we get the triples from the knowledge base, the properties in triples and question will be passed to the QA engine for classification and rank.

4.4 Model Tuning

We treat kbqa as a multi-task. Firstly, we need judge whether a relation is a right relation to the question and then we will rank the candidates. So we need to tune the parameters of the classifier and the ranking part.

The back-propagation algorithm is used to train the model. It back propagates errors from top to the bottom layer. Derivatives are calculated and gathered to update parameters. The AdaGrad algorithm is then employed to solve this non-convex optimization problem. Moreover, we use dropout in training.

We tune the threshold θ, the higher of θ, the lower the recall rate. In order to ensure high recall rate, we set threshold θ to 0.5. We also try to use the average of relation words vector as the representation of relation, but the final result shows that it's not as good as the summation of relation words. We found that different α in Eq. (1) gave a very different result over DEV set in the experiment. We took 0.1 as the step size to change the parameter α when the parameter α is 0.4, we got the best result in DEV set.

Also, in the preprocessing step of the question, we recognize the focus of the question, and then add the lexical paraphrase of the focus word to the question. After adding the lexical paraphrase of focus, we train the classifier again, and the result shows that we get a better result. In the final system, we got a good result in DEV set.

4.5 Results

The experimental results are given in Table 1. We use embedding similarity as our baseline, this method computes the cosine similarity of the question embedding and relation embedding and ranks these candidate answers by the similarity according to the similarity. CGRU is the method that only uses the classifier. CGRU + paraphrase uses the lexical paraphrase of the focus of the question. We then add the step of rank to our method, and our F1 score is 0.7914 in the final evaluation.

Model Analysis. The baseline uses the similarity between question and triple, and we only use the summation of the question words embedding as the representation of the question, and the summation of the triple words embedding as the representation of the triple. It can't learn the meaning of the question well. So the F1 score is only 0.3841.

CGRU employs a convolutional layer and GRU to learn the vector representation of the question. The F1 score is 0.6964. From the result, we can observe that CGRU can learn the question well, and the classifier gives a higher score to the right answer.

CGRU + paraphrase uses the lexical paraphrase extracted from monolingual corpus. We add the lexical paraphrase of focus word in question to the end of question sentence. The F1 score is 0.7185. The lexical paraphrase could alleviate the OOV problem. The focus of the question contains the main motivation of the question, the lexical paraphrase of focus could strengthen the information of the motivation.

CGRU + paraphrase + ranking will rank these candidate answers according to the score given by the Eq. (1). The F1 score is 0.7914, and the ranking step improves the F1 score by 10.1% compared with CGRU + paraphrase. This result indicates that the ranking step is necessary to this task, and word overlap between question and (subject, relation) of the triple can explain to some extent that the higher this score, the more likely the answer is right.

5   Conclusion

We proposed a method for answering question over Chinese knowledge base. Our method uses a Convolutional and GRU neural networks to learn the representation of the question, the summation of the relation words vectors is the representation of the relation accordingly, and then the classifier judge whether the relation is what the question wants to ask. We then rank these candidate answers. We recognize the focus of the question and add the lexical paraphrase of focus word to the question. These lexical paraphrase of focus can improve the accuracy of the results extracted from knowledge base, and give a higher score to the correct answers.

Acknowledgments. This work was supported by the National High Technology Development 863 Program of China (No. 2015AA015407), National Natural Science Foundation of China (No. 61472105 and No. 61472107).

References

1. Yao, X., Berant, J., Van Durme, B.: Freebase QA: information extraction or semantic parsing? In: ACL 2014, p. 82 (2014)
2. Auer, S., Bizer, C., Kobilarov, G., Lehmann, J., Cyganiak, R., Ives, Z.: DBpedia: a nucleus for a web of open data. In: Aberer, K., et al. (eds.) ASWC/ISWC -2007. LNCS, vol. 4825, pp. 722–735. Springer, Heidelberg (2007). doi:10.1007/978-3-540-76298-0_52
3. Bollacker, K., Evans, C., Paritosh, P., Sturge, T., Taylor, J.: Freebase: a collaboratively created graph database for structuring human knowledge. In: Proceedings of the 2008 ACM SIGMOD International Conference on Management of Data, pp. 1247–1250. ACM (2008)
4. Hoffart, J., Suchanek, F.M., Berberich, K., Lewis-Kelham, E., De Melo, G., Weikum, G.: YAGO2: exploring and querying world knowledge in time, space, context, and many languages. In: Proceedings of the 20th International Conference Companion on World Wide Web, pp. 229–232. ACM (2011)
5. Zettlemoyer, L.S., Collins, M.: Learning to map sentences to logical form: structured classification with probabilistic categorial grammars. Uncertainty in Artificial Intelligence (UAI) (2005)

6. Zettlemoyer, L.S., Collins, M.: Online learning of relaxed CCG grammars for parsing to logical form. In: Proceedings of EMNLP-CoNLL (2007)
7. Zettlemoyer, L.S., Collins, M.: Learning context-dependent mappings from sentences to logical form. In: Proceedings of ACLCoNLL (2009)
8. Kwiatkowski, T., Zettlemoyer, L., Goldwater, S., Steedman, M.: Inducing probabilistic CCG grammars from logical form with higher order unification. In: Proceedings of EMNLP, pp. 1223–1233 (2010)
9. Kwiatkowski, T., Zettlemoyer, L., Goldwater, S., Steedman, M.: Lexical generalization in CCG grammar induction for semantic parsing. In: Proceedings of EMNLP (2011)
10. Kwiatkowski, T., Choi, E., Artzi, Y., Zettlemoyer, L.: Scaling semantic parsers with on-the-fly ontology matching. In: Proceedings of EMNLP (2013)
11. Liang, P., Jordan, M.I., Klein, D.: Learning dependency-based compositional semantics. In: Proceedings of ACL (2011)
12. Berant, J., Chou, A., Frostig, R., Liang, P.: Semantic parsing on freebase from question-answer pairs. In: Proceedings of EMNLP (2013)
13. Berant, J., Liang, P.: Semantic parsing via paraphrasing. In: Proceedings of ACL (2014)
14. Kate, R.J., Mooney, R.J.: Using string-kernels for learning semantic parsers. In: Proceedings of ACL (2006)
15. Chen, D.L., Mooney, R.J.: Learning to interpret natural language navigation instructions from observations. AAAI 2, 1–2 (2011)
16. Yao, X., Van Durme, B.: Information extraction over structured data: question answering with freebase. In: Proceedings of ACL (2014)
17. Bordes, A., Chopra, S., Weston, J.: Question answering with subgraph embeddings. In: Proceedings of the 2014 Conference on Empirical Methods in Natural Language Processing (EMNLP), pp. 615–620. Association for Computational Linguistics (2014a)
18. Bordes, A., Weston, J., Usunier, N.: Open question answering with weakly supervised embedding models. In: Calders, T., Esposito, F., Hüllermeier, E., Meo, R. (eds.) ECML PKDD 2014. LNCS (LNAI), vol. 8724, pp. 165–180. Springer, Heidelberg (2014). doi:10.1007/978-3-662-44848-9_11
19. Dong, L., Wei, F., Zhou, M., Xu, K.: Question answering over freebase with multi-colum convolutional neural networks. In: Proceedings of ACL (2015)
20. Yih, W.-T., He, X., Meek, C.: Semantic parsing for single-relation question answering. In: Proceedings of the 52nd Annual Meeting of the Association for Computational Linguistics, vol. 2 (Short Papers), pp. 643–648. Association for Computational Linguistics (2014)
21. Chu-Carroll, J., Fan, J., Boguraev, B.K., Carmel, D., Sheinwald, D., Welty, C.: Finding needles in the haystack: search and candidate generation. IBM J. Res. Dev. 56, 6:1–6:12 (2012)
22. 张志昌, 张宇, 刘挺, 李生. 基于线索词识别和训练集扩展的中文问题分类. 高技术通讯, 19(2), 111–118 (2009)
23. Che, W., Li, Z., Liu, T.: LTP: a Chinese language technology platform. In: Proceedings of the COLING 2010: Demonstrations, Beijing, China, pp. 13–16, August 2010
24. Mikolov, T., Sutskever, I., Chen, K., Corrado, G., Dean, J.: Distributed representations of words and phrases and their compositionality. In: NIPS, pp. 3111–3119 (2013b)

Stance Detection in Chinese MicroBlogs with Neural Networks

Nan Yu, Da Pan, Meishan Zhang[(✉)], and Guohong Fu

School of Computer Science and Technology, Heilongjiang University,
Harbin 150080, China
yunan_v@outlook.com, pandacs@live.cn, mason.zms@gmail.com, ghfu@hotmail.com

Abstract. In this paper, we presents a stance detection system for NLPCC-ICCPOL 2016 share task 4. Our Stance Detection System can determinate whether the author of Weibo text is in favor of the given target, against the given target, or neither. We exploit LSTMs model and the average F score of our system is 56.56%. In contrast to the traditional target/aspect sentiment, the given target may not be preserved in Weibo text. We model the task as a classification problem, exploiting LSTMs as the basic part of classifier.

1 Introduction

Stance detection aims to extract the stances of user-generated texts towards a certain target. The target can be a product, a person, an event and etc. Table 1 shows several examples in Chinese, which is the main goal of this paper, while most of past work focuses on the English language.

The task can be useful in a number of practical applications. It can facilitate the public sentiment monitoring, social management, business decisions and etc., upon on the collecting stance detection results for specific target.

Typically, stance detection can be formulated as a classification problems. Given a piece of user text and a target expression, we determine the user's distance by three categories favor, against or none, where favor denotes the author supports the author supports the target, against denotes the author express a negative attitude towards the target and none denotes the author does not express any sentiment towards the target.

There are two main stream methods to achieve the above classification problem. One method exploits the traditional discrete models, which uses manually-crafted one-hot features, and this method has been studied for stance detection already. While the other method exploits the recently wide-concerned neural models, which uses low-dimensional dense features. This method does not require manually-designed features, and it uses deep neural layers to extract features automatically.

Our model follows the line of work of neural models. We exploit bare word embedding to represent sentential words, and first use convolution neural layers to extract local n-gram features, and then use bi-directional long-short-term-memory (LSTM) neural networks to extract latent global syntactic features.

© Springer International Publishing AG 2016
C.-Y. Lin et al. (Eds.): NLPCC-ICCPOL 2016, LNAI 10102, pp. 893–900, 2016.
DOI: 10.1007/978-3-319-50496-4_83

Table 1. The examples of stance

Target	Text	Stance
iPhone SE (iPhone SE)	很想尝试下iPhonese...... (I do want to try iPhoneSE)	FAVOR
iPhone SE (iPhone SE)	买了se感觉得买个平板 (After buying iphone SE, it's necessary to buy a tablet)	AGAINST
iPhone SE (iPhone SE)	iPhoneSE的上市，新款也应运而生 (iPhone SE listing, the other new phone also has emerged)	NONE

Base on these features, we represent the author texts an the given by fixed-dimensional feature vectors respectively. Finally, we combine the two vectors, and feed them into a classification layer to get the output labels.

Our paper is organized as follow. First, we briefly introduce the related work. Second we describe our neural stance detection model in detail. Third, we introduce the experiments. And finally we make conclusions and future work.

2   Related Work

Stance detection has been studied by several work. Most of these work focus on the English language [1–4]. In particular, thanks to the dataset of [5] the task is greatly promoted. The task is generally treated as a text classification problem, using different based on supervised learning and also semi-supervised methods such as distance supervision.

Discrete and neural models both have achieved successes for stance detection. Typical discrete models exploit manually-designed features and then employ classifiers for example SVM to perform the task. Typical features includes word ngrams, word embedding, word associations, hash tags and etc. [6] applies both character-level and word-level convolution neural networks to stance detection

Our work is closely related to the neural network models for stance detection. And we use those neural network models to extract context syntax features automatically [7] exploits a similar network structure based on LSTM. Our work differs with their work in neural network building and several detailed pro-processes.

3   Model Based Neural Network Overview

As shown in Fig. 1, our neural network contains several layers, and each layer can extract the special features. Features are important for classification task,

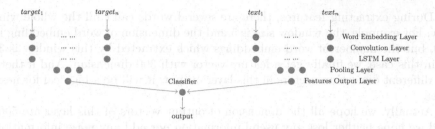

Fig. 1. Overview of neural network for stance detection

and they can influent the accuracy of classifier. But it's impossible to extract all effective features of the entity which need to be classified. In this task, we think the ngram features and latent global syntax features are essential, so we choose the convolution layer to extract the ngram features and LSTM layer for extracting global syntax features. Other layers have their own functions. Pooling layer can extracted the sentence features, and the tanh layer as the features output layer can combine those features.

3.1 Word Embedding Layer

The first layer of our neural network is word embedding layer. This layer maps Chinese words into k-dimensional space, and we can get a set of vectors which contain context information. In this layer, the word embeddings are learned by the word2vec. We sample tweets from Weibo platform and segment them. Then we use this unlabeled Weibo text as training corpus to generate word embeddings. But it is impossible that the training corpus cover all words, so we may be can't query the word embeddings of words which don't present in training corpus. About those words, we just use the symbol "-unk-" to represent them.

Word embeddings will be loaded in the lookup table when our system launch as initial input. But the lookup table is not static, it will be later tuned by back propagation during training of neural network.

3.2 Convolution Neural Layer

Second layer is convolution layer, and this layer can extract ngram features. The ngram features mean the features are collected by successive words information. We need to decide the how many successive words extracted features at a time. So we assign a window to extract local ngram word features successively by sliding over the entire word embeddings of text or target of Weibo. Here, the window size decides the number of words extracted features at a time. Then, we feed the word embedding of each of the words resulting in a set of vectors as this layer input.

During extracting features, there are several words can't fill the whole window. For example, the window size is 5 and the dimension of word embedding is 100, but the number of word embeddings which extracted by this window is 3. So in this case, we finally get a feature vector with 300 dimension. And if there are different dimension vectors in this layer output, it will be a big deal for next layer.

Actually, we hope all the dimension of output vectors of this layer are 500. And we hope neither loss any useful information nor add any noise information into those feature vectors. We use zero vector to fill the those low dimension vectors and transfer them into 500 dimensional vectors. After extracting features, the number of input vectors is same as output vectors, and such convolution method called isometric convolution.

3.3   Bi-Directional LSTM

The next layer of our network is composed of Bi-directional LSTM. And this layer can extract the global syntax information automatically. Actually, most of the sentences of Chinese Weibo are short, so we can see the same stance of sentences have similar syntactic structure. And this is why we chose the Bi-directional LSTM to extract features. Such neural model have been proved the validity of solving the stance detection task [7]. What's more, this layer is a special RNN model, but it require less fine-tuning of the weight to collect contextual information.

$$I_i = \sigma(W_{xi} \cdot X_i + W_{hi} \cdot H_{i-1} + W_{ci} \cdot C_{i-1} + b_i)$$

$$F_i = \sigma(W_{xf} \cdot X_i + W_{hf} \cdot H_{i-1} + W_{cf} \cdot C_{i-1} + b_f)$$

$$C_i = \sigma(W_{xc} \cdot X_i + W_{hc} \cdot H_{i-1} + b_c) \cdot I_i + C_{i-1} \odot F_i$$

$$O_i = \sigma(W_{xo} \cdot X_i + W_{ho} \cdot H_{i-1} + W_{co} \cdot C_i + b_o)$$

$$H_i = \tanh(C_i) \odot O_i$$

Here, X_i is an input vector at time step i, and H_i is an output vector. $\odot$ denotes element wise multiplication. I_i, F_i, C_i and O_i represent the input gate, forget gate, cell and output gate respectively.

Those blocks have their own functions. Cell is LSTM memory, which used to store the long short time information. Those gates provide some operation for cell to deal with the information which through it. More precisely, the information input to the cell is processed by input gate, and the output information is processed by output gate. Forget gate deal with the previous information in cell.

Bi-directional LSTM will output two set of vectors, and we concatenate them as following, so in this layer just output one vector sequence finally.

$$H = \tanh(W \cdot (concat(H_{left}, H_{right})) + b)$$

3.4   Pooling Layer

After convolution layer and Bi-directional LSTM layer, the features will be stored into a set of vectors, and we can't just use those vectors to predict the stance of Weibo. So we need to reduce the number of features. Using those a set of vector to generate one vector to represent the feature is our goal. Pooling layer extracted features by grouping together the feature vectors. And this is why we chose pooling layer. In this layer, we choose three type pooling functions. They are max pooling, min pooling and min pooling respectively. And every function will output one vector at a time, so we need to concatenate those three vectors into one vector and through a tanh layer to compose the final feature vector.

$$V = tanh(W \cdot (MaxPooling(H) \odot MinPooling(H) \odot AvgPooling(H)) + b)$$

3.5   Training

In this paper, we choose cross-entropy loss as objective function. The expression presents as following and minimizing the it is our goal.

$$H(\xi) = -\sum \log(P_{yi})$$

Here the P_{yi} denotes the probability of the Weibo is number i stance. Those P_{yi} computed by our above neural model. The probabilities can't give certain answers, so the output of our neural model always contain error. And we use those error to update the parameters of our model to minimize the objective function. And this method called error-driven.

About updating parameter, we choose AdaGrad [8] as the update method. The following expression shows the process of AdaGrad in our system. Here, W means the parameters of models, and the $\nabla Q(W)$ denote the gradient of W. And α and reg are constants.

$$g = \nabla Q(W) + W \cdot reg$$

$$G_{j,j} = \sum g_j^2$$

$$W_j = W_j - g_j \cdot \alpha / \sqrt{G_{j,j}}$$

4   Experiment

The NLPCC2016 Task 4 corpus is offered by sponsor. About pre-process, we use the stanford-segmenter-3.6.0 to segment the text of corpus. Table 2 shows the instances number and words number of corpus.

The following sections, we will present the details of experiment, including parameter settings, evaluation metrics and results analysis.

Table 2. The number of corpus instance

Corpus	Training	Development	Test
Sents	2980	20	15000
Words	142708	4493	673054

4.1 Parameter Settings

The unlabeled training corpus fed into the word2vec are collected in Chinese WeiBo platform. We normalized the special symbols in Weibo such as URLs, emojis. Then we use stanford-segmenter-3.6.0 to segment them. Finally we feed this training corpus to word2vec to train skip-gram 50 dimension word embeddings.

There are several parameters in our model, including the parameters of the those layers and the parameters of AdaGrad. The Table 3 shows parameter information. The $W_{WindowSize}$ decides convolution layer extract how many word embedding at one time. We will drop out some word embeddings, and p_{drop} is the probability of dropping out. $h_{HiddenSize}$ is the hidden layer output size.

Table 3. Parameter Settings

Type	Parameters
Hyper parameter	$W_{WindowSize} = 5$, $h_{HiddenSize} = 50$, $e_{word} = 50$, $p_{drop} = 0.5$
AdaGrad parameter	$reg = 10^{-8}$, $\alpha = 0.01$

4.2 Result Analysis

The results of system are evaluated by F-scores. The F-Score of the stance "Against" and "Favor" are 0.6729, 0.4584 respectively, and the average F score is 0.5656.

And Table 4 presents the given target F scores. The most high F-Score of given target is "开放二胎(separate two children)".

The system predicts error stances because of several reasons. If some pieces of Weibo are hard to classify by manual classification, they're also difficult for our system to classify. And it is make sense that our system output incorrect results for those hard classification Weibo.

In Table 5, we can see some pieces of Weibo are hard to classify even by manual classification.

In Table 4, we can see the average F1 score of some specific target is below 0.5. Such consequence was caused by many reasons, and we think word embedding layer is most important factor. Some words are emerge frequently in corpus but we can't find the word embedding of them, just like "iPhone" and "SE". This is one important reason why the average F1 score on "iPhoneSE" is too low. And other reason is the segmentation of targets and tweets. The segmentation result

Table 4. Given target F-Score

Target	F AVG Score
春节放鞭炮 (Set off firecrackers in the Spring Festival)	0.5281
iPhone SE (iPhone SE)	0.4494
俄罗斯在叙利亚的反恐行动 (Russia's anti terrorist operations in Syria)	0.5126
开放二胎 (separate two children)	0.7553
深圳禁摩限电 (Banning the motorcycle and electro-mobile in Shenzhen)	0.4355

Table 5. Hard to classify

Target	Text	Gold Answer
俄罗斯在叙利亚的反恐行动 (Russia's anti terrorist operations in Syria)	无耻国家，没有之一。 (Most shameless country.)	FAVOR
俄罗斯在叙利亚的反恐行动 (Russia's anti terrorist operations in Syria)	我当然相信。世界不就是它搅乱的吗！ (I do believe, it messes the world up！)	AGAINST
开放二胎 (separate two children)	如果有二胎，就给我生个哥哥吧——BY SN (If separate two children, please give me a old brother— BY SN)	FAVOR
开放二胎 (separate two children)	呵呵呵 ((Hehehe)	AGAINST

of the target "深圳禁摩限电" is "深圳 禁 摩 限 电", it will change the meaning of target. The word embedding layer may output unsuitable word embeddings because of this case, and finally caused low average F1 score.

Another reason is about corpus. The number of instances in training corpus is less than test corpus, so the model parameters may over fit in training corpus easily.

5   Conclusion and Future Work

We build a stance detection system with neural network which can extract the features of Weibo automatically and determine the stance of them.

The results of experiment demonstrated that the features extracted by convolution layer and LSTM neural network are useful for the stance detection. Our future work can be improved by many ways. First one is improving the structure of our neural network. Our system just extracted two kinds of features, and maybe extracting other discrete features can up our system accuracy. And second one is about the input method. Another input method is input characters, then system transfers those characters into character embeddings. Third one is collecting more training corpus. As we can see the instances number of our training corpus is less than test corpus. And a extended training corpus can avoid the over fitting.

Acknowledgements. This study was supported by National Natural Science Foundation of China under Grants Nos. 61672211 and 61602160, the Natural Science Foundation of Heilongjiang Province under Grant No. F2016036, and the Returned Scholar Foundation of Heilongjiang Province, respectively.

References

1. Hasan, K.S., Ng, V.: Stance classification of ideological debates: data, models, features, and constraints. In: IJCNLP, pp. 1348–1356 (2013)
2. Walker, M.A., Anand, P., Abbott, R., Grant, R.: Stance classification using dialogic properties of persuasion. In: Proceedings of 2012 Conference of the North American Chapter of the Association for Computational Linguistics: Human Language Technologies, pp. 592–596. Association for Computational Linguistics (2012)
3. Rajadesingan, A., Liu, H.: Identifying users with opposing opinions in Twitter debates. In: Kennedy, W.G., Agarwal, N., Yang, S.J. (eds.) SBP 2014. LNCS, vol. 8393, pp. 153–160. Springer, Heidelberg (2014). doi:10.1007/978-3-319-05579-4_19
4. Mohammad, S.M., Kiritchenko, S., Sobhani, P., Zhu, X., Cherry, C.: A dataset for detecting stance in tweets. In: Proceedings of 10th edition of the the Language Resources and Evaluation Conference (LREC), Portoroz, Slovenia (2016)
5. Zhu, X., Kiritchenko, S., Mohammad, S.M.: NRC-Canada-2014: recent improvements in the sentiment analysis of tweets. In: Proceedings of 8th International Workshop on Semantic Evaluation (SemEval), pp. 443–447. Citeseer (2014)
6. Vijayaraghavan, P., Sysoev, I., Vosoughi, S., Roy, D.: Deepstance at SemEval-task 6: detecting stance in tweets using character and word-level CNNS (2016). arXiv preprint arXiv:1606.05694
7. Augenstein, I., Rocktäschel, T., Vlachos, A., Bontcheva, K.: Stance detection with bidirectional conditional encoding (2016). arXiv preprint arXiv:1606.05464
8. Duchi, J., Hazan, E., Singer, Y.: Adaptive subgradient methods for online learning, stochastic optimization. J. Mach. Learn. Res. **12**(7), 2121–2159 (2011)

Overview of the NLPCC-ICCPOL 2016 Shared Task: Chinese Word Segmentation for Micro-Blog Texts

Xipeng Qiu[✉], Peng Qian, and Zhan Shi

School of Computer Science, Fudan University,
825 Zhangheng Road, Shanghai, China
{xpqiu,pqian11,zshi16}@fudan.edu.cn

Abstract. In this paper, we give an overview for the shared task at the 5th CCF Conference on Natural Language Processing & Chinese Computing (NLPCC 2016): Chinese word segmentation for micro-blog texts. Different with the popular used newswire datasets, the dataset of this shared task consists of the relatively informal micro-texts. Besides, we also use a new psychometric-inspired evaluation metric for Chinese word segmentation, which addresses to balance the very skewed word distribution at different levels of difficulty. The data and evaluation codes can be downloaded from https://github.com/FudanNLP/NLPCC-WordSeg-Weibo.

1 Introduction

Word segmentation is a fundamental task for Chinese language processing. Benefiting from the developments of the machine learning techniques and the large scale shared corpora, Chinese word segmentation has achieved a great progress. The state-of-the-art method is to regard this task as sequence labeling problem. However, their performances are still not satisfying for the practical demands to analyze Chinese texts, especially for informal texts. The key reason is that most of annotated corpora are drawn from news texts. Therefore, the system trained on these corpora cannot work well with the informal or specific-domain texts. To address this, we introduce a new large corpus and a new evaluation metric [3]. We hope that our corpus and metric can provide a valuable testbed for Chinese word segmentation on informal texts.

In this shared task, we wish to investigate the performances of Chinese word segmentation for the micro-blog texts. Different with the former task in NLPCC 2015 [4], we just focus on word segmentation and introduce a new evaluation metric [3] this year.

2 Data

Different with the popular used newswire dataset, we use relatively informal texts from Sina Weibo[1]. The training and test data consist of micro-blogs from various

---

[1] http://weibo.com/.

Table 1. Statistical information of dataset.

DataSet	Sents	Words	Chars	Word types	Char types	OOV rate
Train	20135	421166	688743	43331	4502	-
Develop	2052	43697	73246	11187	2879	6.82%
Test	8592	187877	315865	27804	3911	6.98%
Total	30779	652740	1077854	56155	4838	-

topics, such as finance, sports, entertainment, and so on. Both the training and test files are UTF-8 encoded. To reduce the cost of data annotation, we use FudanNLP[2] [5] to obtain the initial segmentations. Then two annotators modify the errors in the initial segmentation. When two annotators disagree, a third annotator gives a final decision.

The information of dataset is shown in Table 1. The out-of-vocabulary (OOV) rate is slight higher than the other benchmark datasets.

2.1 Background Data

Besides the training data, we also provide the background data, from which the training and test data are drawn. The purpose of providing the background data is to find the more sophisticated features by the unsupervised way.

3 Description of the Task

Word is the fundamental unit in natural language understanding. However, Chinese sentences consists of the continuous Chinese characters without natural delimiters. Therefore, Chinese word segmentation has become the first mission of Chinese natural language processing, which identifies the sequence of words in a sentence and marks the boundaries between words.

3.1 Tracks

Each participant will be allowed to submit the three runs for each subtask: **closed track** run, **semi-open track** run and **open track** run.

1. In the **closed** track, participants could only use information found in the provided training data. Information such as externally obtained word counts, part of speech information, or name lists was excluded.
2. In the **semi-open** track, participants could use the information extracted from the provided background data in addition to the provided training data. Information such as externally obtained word counts, part of speech information, or name lists was excluded.
3. In the **open** track, participants could use the information which should be public and be easily obtained. But it is not allowed to obtain the result by the manual labeling or crowdsourcing way.

---
[2] https://github.com/FudanNLP/fnlp.

4   Evaluations

4.1   Evaluation Metric

After the successive improvements, the standard metric is becoming hard to distinguish state-of-the-art word segmentation systems. In this shared task, we use a new psychometric-inspired evaluation metric for Chinese word segmentation, which addresses to balance the very skewed word distribution at different levels of difficulty. The performance on a real evaluation shows that the proposed metric gives more reasonable and distinguishable scores and correlates well with human judgement. The detailed information can be found in [3].

To show the difference between the standard and new evaluation measures, we report both metrics for each system.

4.2   Results

There are 19 submitted systems. The results on three tracks are shown in Tables 2, 3 and 4 respectively.

Table 2. Performances on closed track.

Systems	Standard scores			Weighted scores		
	p	r	f_1	p_b	r_b	f_b
S1	94.13	94.69	94.41	**79.29**	81.62	**80.44**
S2	94.21	**95.31**	**94.76**	78.18	**81.81**	79.96
S3	**94.36**	95.15	94.75	78.34	81.34	79.81
S4	93.98	94.78	94.38	78.43	81.2	79.79
S5	93.93	94.8	94.37	76.24	79.32	77.75
S6	93.9	94.42	94.16	75.95	78.2	77.06
S7	93.82	94.6	94.21	75.08	77.91	76.47
S8	93.74	94.31	94.03	74.9	77.14	76
S9	92.89	93.65	93.27	71.25	73.92	72.56
S10	93.31	93.83	93.57	71.22	73.32	72.25
S11	93.52	94.14	93.83	70.12	72.55	71.31
S12	90.78	91.88	91.33	68.29	71.93	70.06
S13	87.93	89.82	88.86	61.05	66.06	63.46
S14	85.08	87.18	86.12	55.04	59.77	57.31
S15	66.39	73.6	69.81	50	63.84	56.08
S16	80.53	80.53	80.53	41.3	43.61	42.42
Average	90.16	91.42	90.8	69.04	72.72	70.8

904   X. Qiu et al.

Table 3. Performances on semi-open track.

Systems	Standard scores			Weighted scores		
	p	r	f_1	p_b	r_b	f_b
S1	**94.81**	95.53	95.17	**81.67**	**84.33**	**82.98**
S3	94.76	**95.62**	**95.19**	80.46	83.52	81.96
S8	94.61	95.49	95.05	79.37	82.46	80.88
S7	94.56	95.35	94.95	78.98	81.8	80.36
S2	94.23	95.32	94.77	78.2	81.87	79.99
S9	90.49	91.76	91.12	68.3	72.24	70.21
S16	80.32	79.91	80.12	41.64	43.55	42.57
AVG	91.97	92.71	92.34	72.66	75.68	74.14

Table 4. Performances on open track.

Systems	Standard scores			Weighted scores		
	p	r	f_1	p_b	r_b	f_b
S3	91.91	91.41	91.66	**81.23**	**83.22**	**82.21**
S11	**95.04**	**95.7**	**95.37**	80.39	83	81.67
S2	94.59	95.53	95.06	78.86	82.18	80.48
S6	93.59	94.65	94.12	75.86	79.42	77.6
S9	90.78	91.88	91.33	68.29	71.93	70.06
AVG	93.18	93.83	93.51	76.93	79.95	78.41

4.3   Some Representative Systems

In this section, we give brief introductions to some representative system.

– The **S1** system [7] uses Long Short-Term Memory (LSTM) for Chinese Weibo word segmentation. In order to infer the optimal tag path, a transition score matrix is used for jumping between tags in successive characters. By integrating unsupervised features, the performance is further improved.
– The **S3** system [2] uses sequence labeling for CWS with CRF model. It takes full advantages of both unsupervised features and supervised features to discover new words from unlabeled dataset. The new words recognition is significantly improved with those features. Accessor variety (AV) [1] features are used to measure the possibility of whether a substring is a Chinese word. They report that the ability of OOV detection can be improved by integrating unsupervised global features extracted from the provided background data.
– The **S11** system [6] also treats word segmentation as a character-wise sequence labeling problem, and explores two directions to enhance the CRF-based baseline. First, a large-scale external lexicon is employed for constructing extra lexicon features in the model, which is proven to be extremely useful. Second,

two heterogeneous datasets, i.e., Penn Chinese Treebank 7 (CTB7) and People Daily (PD) are used to help word segmentation on Weibo.

5   Analysis

The analyses of the participant systems are as follows.

1. The best system on semi-open track is better than that on closed track, which shows the large scale unlabeled data from the same domain are useful for Chinese word segmentation.
2. The neural network based model shows a distinct advantage. The **S1** system adopts LSTM to model the sequence and achieves the best results on both closed and semi-open tracks.
3. The new evaluation metric gives more distinguishable score than the standard metric.

6   Conclusion

After years of intensive researches, Chinese word segmentation has achieved a quite high precision. However, the performances of state-of-the-art systems are still relatively low for the informal texts, such as micro-blogs, forums. The NLPCC 2016 Shared Task on Chinese Word Segmentation for Micro-blog Texts focuses on the fundamental research in Chinese language processing. It is the first time to use the micro-texts to evaluate the performance of the state-of-the-art methods. Besides, we also wish to extend the scale of corpus and add more informal texts.

Acknowledgement. We are very grateful to the students from our lab for their efforts to annotate and check the data. We would also like to thank the participants for their valuable feedbacks and comments. This work was partially funded by National Natural Science Foundation of China (No. 61532011 and 61672162), the National High Technology Research and Development Program of China (No. 2015AA015408).

References

1. Feng, H., Chen, K., Deng, X., Zheng, W.: Accessor variety criteria for Chinese word extraction. Comput. Linguist. **30**(1), 75–93 (2004)
2. Leng, Y., Liu, W., Wang, S., Wang, X.: A feature-rich CRF segmenter for chinese micro-blog. In: Proceedings of the Fifth Conference on Natural Language Processing and Chinese Computing and the Twenty Fourth International Conference on Computer Processing of Oriental Languages (2016)
3. Qian, P., Qiu, X., Huang, X.: A new psychometric-inspired evaluation metric for Chinese word segmentation. In: Proceedings of Annual Meeting of the Association for Computational Linguistics (2016). http://aclweb.org/anthology/P/P16/P16-1206.pdf

4. Qiu, X., Qian, P., Yin, L., Wu, S., Huang, X.: Overview of the NLPCC 2015 shared task: Chinese word segmentation and POS tagging for micro-blog texts. In: Li, J., Ji, H., Zhao, D., Feng, Y. (eds.) NLPCC 2015. LNCS (LNAI), vol. 9362, pp. 541–549. Springer, Heidelberg (2015). doi:10.1007/978-3-319-25207-0_50
5. Qiu, X., Zhang, Q., Huang, X.: FudanNLP: a toolkit for Chinese natural language processing. In: Proceedings of Annual Meeting of the Association for Computational Linguistics (2013)
6. Xia, Q., Li, Z., Chao, J., Zhang, M.: Word segmentation on micro-blog texts with external lexicon and heterogeneous data. In: Proceedings of the Fifth Conference on Natural Language Processing and Chinese Computing & the Twenty Fourth International Conference on Computer Processing of Oriental Languages (2016)
7. Zhou, Q., Ma, L., Zheng, Z., Wang, Y., Wang, X.: Recurrent neural word segmentation with tag inference. In: Proceedings of the Fifth Conference on Natural Language Processing and Chinese Computing & the Twenty Fourth International Conference on Computer Processing of Oriental Languages (2016)

Overview of NLPCC Shared Task 4: Stance Detection in Chinese Microblogs

Ruifeng Xu[1,2(✉)], Yu Zhou[1], Dongyin Wu[1], Lin Gui[1], Jiachen Du[1],
and Yun Xue[2]

[1] School of Computer Science and Technology, Harbin Institute of Technology,
Shenzhen Graduate School, Shenzhen, China
xuruifeng@hitsz.edu.cn, zhouyu.nlp@gmail.com,
wudongyin@foxmail.com, guilin.nlp@gmail.com,
dujiachen@stmail.hitsz.edu.cn
[2] Guangdong Provincial Engineering Technology Research Center
for Data Science, Guangzhou, China
happyhuashida@sina.com.cn

Abstract. This paper presents the overview of the shared task, stance detection in Chinese microblogs, in NLPCC-ICCPOL 2016. The submitted systems are expected to automatically determine whether the author of a Chinese microblog is in favor of the given target, against the given target, or whether neither inference is likely. Different from regular evaluation tasks on sentiment analysis, the microblog text may or may not contain the target of interest, and the opinion expressed may or may not be towards to the target of interest. We designed two tasks. Task A is a mandatory supervised task which detects stance towards five targets of interest with given labeled data. Task B is an optional unsupervised task which gives only unlabeled data. Our shared task has had sixteen team participants for Task A and five results of Task B. The highest F-score obtained was 0.7106 for Task A and 0.4687 for Task B, respectively.

1 Introduction

With the rapidly growth of subjective text on the internet, sentiment analysis (Gui et al. 2016; Tang et al. 2014) or opinion mining (He et al. 2012; Gui et al. 2014) became a hot topic problem in nature language processing. The proposed techniques aim to detect the sentiment or opinion from the text. However, in many cases, we care more about the attitude of the author to a specific topic (Anand et al. 2011; Boltužić et al. 2014). For example, in the topic of American election, we may care about if the author of a text support Trump or not. We call this attitude as stance in a topic.

For more details, stance detection aims to determine the author's stance towards a certain target from given text. The target here may be an issue, a government policy, a social phenomenon, and a product. The target may or may not be mentioned explicitly in the text. Meanwhile, the stance could be in favor of, against, or neutral towards the target of interest (Mohammad and Kiritchenko 2016). For instance, it is reasonable for people to predicate that a woman is in favor of "Two-child policy" if she always wants the second kid. Nowadays people express their attitude towards almost everything through online websites or mobile Apps. Detecting the stance of the authors towards certain target should be helpful to many applications.

© Springer International Publishing AG 2016
C.-Y. Lin et al. (Eds.): NLPCC-ICCPOL 2016, LNAI 10102, pp. 907–916, 2016.
DOI: 10.1007/978-3-319-50496-4_85

We formulate the task data as below:

<ID><Tab><Target><Tab><Text><Tab><Stance>

The IDs are unique for each microblog, and the Targets are specified. The Text contains everything that author has posted in the microblog, including pure text, emotion faces, address information, the original source, etc.

For example:

<ID> 1884
<Target>开放二胎 *Two child policy*
<Text>二胎了，小伙伴们替我想个名字 *My second child is coming. Please think of name for me, my friends.*
<Stance>FAVOR

The automatic stance detecting system is required determine whether the author is in favor of or against the given target, or neither of those. To support the evaluation for stance detection, we manually labeled 4000 microblogs of targets of "iPhone SE", "春节放鞭炮 *Set off firecrackers in the Spring Festival*", "俄罗斯在叙利亚的反恐行动 *Russia's anti terrorist operations in Syria*", "开放二胎政策 *Two child policy*", and "深圳禁摩限电 *Prohibition of motorcycles and restrictions on electric vehicles in Shenzhen*" for Task A. For each target, we use 75% as training data and 25% as testing data, respectively. For Task B, we provide 2000 unlabeled microblogs for "转基因食品 *Genetically modified food*" and "朝鲜核试验 *The Nuclear Test in DPRK*" as training data. The participants may use unlabeled data from other sources in Task B. For both Task A and Task B, we provide 300 sample data for each target as trial data.

Sixteen team participants submitted their result of Task A and the highest F-score achieved was 0.7106. The best classification system actually used five separate classifiers for each target. That should be a very important factor that improves the performance. Meanwhile, most teams bi-gram, TF-IDF, word vector and sentiment lexicons features. Some teams used ensemble learning frameworks while other teams used relatively simple classifiers due to the amount of dataset. Although this task is to determine stance towards certain target, only about half of the participants have considered the specific target related features.

Five teams submitted their results experiment result of Task B. The highest achieved F-score was 0.4687. Generally speaking, the achieved performances of Task B are lower than the performances of Task A. Furthermore, it seems that these five teams did not use extra data to train their models for Task B.

Stance detection is a new challenge task. In this evaluation, the participated system achieved acceptable performance. The dataset for NLPCC Stance Detection are published online now. More effective features and learning methods are expected to handle this problem in the future.

The rest of this paper is organized as follows. Section 2 describes the definition of stance in this evaluation. Section 3 presents the dataset preparation. Section 4 presents the evaluation setting and evaluation metrics. Section 5 provides the evaluation results and discussions. Finally, Sect. 6 concludes this paper.

2   Stance Detection

In this section we present the definition of stance detection in this evaluation and the relationship between stance detection and sentiment analysis.

2.1   Stance Detection

Stance detection can be formulated in different ways. In the context of this task, stance detection is defined as automatically determining whether the author is in favor of the given target, against the given target, or whether neither inference is likely from the text. Consider the following target-microblog pair:

> Target: 俄罗斯在叙利亚的反恐行动 *Russia's anti terrorist operations in Syria*
> Microblog: 9月30日开始至今，俄空爆叙利亚，共死亡1331人，其中403人是一般的民
> 众……其中的三分之一是无辜平民陪葬。 *Since September 30th, a total of 1331 persons
> dead in the Russian air strikes in Syria, of which 403 people are the general public…… 1/3 of
> them are innocent civilians.*

Humans can deduce from the microblog that the speaker is likely against the target, namely *Russia's anti terrorist operations in Syria*. The corresponding stance label is AGAINST.

The aim of this task is to evaluate the performance on the systems which deduces the stance of the microblog. To successfully detect stance, the automatic systems normally have to identify relevant bits of information that may not be present in the focus text. In the above example microblog, if one emphasizes the death of innocent civilians, and then he or she is likely against the air strikes by Russia. Thus, we provide microblogs corresponding to each of the targets, from which systems can gather information to help the detection of stance.

Automatically detecting stance has widespread applications in information retrieval, text summarization, and textual entailment. In fact, one can argue that stance detection can often bring complementary information to sentiment analysis, because we often care about the author's evaluative outlook towards specific targets and propositions rather than simply about whether the speaker was angry or happy.

2.2   Stance Detection and Sentiment Analysis

Stance detection has some shared points with sentiment analysis. Actually they are distinct from each other. Sentiment analysis always aims to either classify a piece of text into a label of "Positive", "Negative", or "Neutral". In stance detection tasks, a target of interest is given to a collection of related microblogs. Based on this target, the system detects the stance/favorability of the author stance towards this target. The stance could be "FAVOR", "AGAINST", or "NONE". Notice that the target may be mentioned in the microblogs and it also may not be mentioned. Furthermore, there could be another target (or entity) mentioned in microblogs. For example, consider the following target-microblog pairs:

E.g. 1   Target 春节放鞭炮 *Set off firecrackers in the Spring Festival*

Microblog: 今天是大年初一，传统意义上的春节，放鞭炮接财神吃饺子一样不能少。 *Today is the first day of lunar New Year. Setting off firecrackers, welcoming the god of wealth, eating dumplings, a traditional Chinese Spring Festival will not go without one of these.*

E.g. 2   Target: 深圳禁摩限电 *Prohibition of motorcycles and restrictions on electric vehicles in Shenzhen*

Microblog: 主题执法日迟迟不来，笋岗片区多了好几部崭新的三轮。 *Law enforcement day has been slow to come. A few new tricycle appeared in Sungang.*

E.g. 3   Target: 转基因食品 *Genetically modified food*

Microblog: 崔永元那帮人一点科学证据也不拿，问问美国民众就算证明了？ *Cui Yongyuan guys do not provide a little bit of scientific evidence. Ask the American people to prove it?*

E.g. 4   Target: 深圳禁摩限电 (*Prohibition of motorcycles and restrictions on electric vehicles in Shenzhen*)

Microblog: 规范电瓶车的违章行驶是最合理的好事，要不出事儿太大了，人命关天。 *Correcting the illegal driving of electric vehicles is the most reasonable thing. Otherwise, traffic accident brings big trouble. People's life is serious.*

In E.g. 1, the target is explicit, and people can easily deduce that the author support the act of setting off fireworks in Spring Festival. In E.g. 2, the target is not mentioned, but people can deduce that the author is talking about the target because it contains a place name in Shenzhen and the transportation related to the target. In E.g. 3, the direct opinion target is "Cui Yongyuan", and apparently the author is satirizing Cui, while we know that Cui is famous for his against genetically modified food (GM food). Thus, the author tends to be support GM food.

Now consider E.g. 4, it has the same target of interest as E.g. 2. In sentiment analysis task, E.g. 2 will be classified into Negative while E.g. 4 into Positive. The sentiment polarities in those two examples are different. However, in stance detection, they will both be classified into FAVOR for the given target "深圳禁摩限电 *Prohibition of motorcycles and restrictions on electric vehicles in Shenzhen*". These examples show the difference between sentiment analysis and stance detection.

3   Dataset for Stance Detection in Chinese Microblogs

Sina Weibo is a popular microblogs platform in China where people express stance implicitly or explicitly. Thus, the dataset for stance detection is constructed based on microblogs from Sina Weibo. The target-microblog pairs are firstly identified. In the second step, the stance of the microblog author to the target is annotated.

3.1　Dataset Construction and Annotation

The target-microblog pairs selection followed the guideline as given below:

1. The discussions and opinions on the target are hot, that is to say there are enough amounts of stances of FAVOR, AGAINST, and NONE.
2. The microblogs consists of complete sentences.
3. The dataset must contains sufficient microblogs covering different kinds of target mention situations, namely target are explicitly mentioned in microblogs/target are not explicitly mentioned or referred to/and others.

Totally, six targets are selected. The corresponding raw microblogs are retrieved from Sina Weibo. These microblogs are manually selected to cover different kinds of target mention situations.

The annotation of this dataset is manually conducted by a group of research students. The major instructions in stance labeling including:

1. Possible stance labels are FAVOR, AGAINST, NONE.
2. If the target of interest is explicitly expressed in the microblog, then directly give stance towards the target of the author.
3. If the target of interest is not explicitly expressed or inferred to in microblog while this microblog indeed is talking about the target, then give stance towards the target of the author based on the combination of comprehension of the microblog and understanding of the issue related to this target.
4. If another target is mentioned in microblog, carefully consider what the opinion is and what the opinion towards to in the microblog, with sound reasoning we can give proper stance towards the target of interest of the author.

The stance of each target-microblog pair is duplicated annotated by two students individually. If these two students provide the same annotation, the stance of this microblog-target pair is then labeled. If the different annotation is detected, the third student will be assigned to annotate this pair. Their annotation results will be voted to obtain the final label.

Table 1. Statistics of NLPCC stance detection dataset

Target	Instances in training dataset				Instances in testing dataset			
	Total	FAVOR	AGAINST	NONE	Total	FAVOR	AGAINST	NONE
Data for Task A								
iPhone SE	600	245	209	146	200	75	104	21
春节放鞭炮	600	250	250	100	200	88	94	18
俄罗斯在叙利亚的反恐行动	600	250	250	100	200	94	86	20
开放二胎政策	600	260	200	140	200	99	95	6
深圳禁摩限电	600	160	300	140	200	63	110	27
Data for Task B								
转基因食品	1000	-	-	-	200	55	97	48
朝鲜核试验	1000	-	-	-	200	39	98	63

912 R. Xu et al.

3.2 Statistics of the Dataset

Table 1 lists the statistics of instances in the training and the testing datasets for Task A and Task B, respectively.

The stance distribution of instances is roughly the same as in real situations. Since we empirically selected the hot targets, the discussions from different points of views which lead to different stances, are collected and annotated. Meanwhile, there are many discussions with neutral stance or even lack of concern.

4 Evaluation Settings

The stance detection evaluation consists of two sub-tasks: Task A (supervised framework) and Task B (unsupervised framework). Task A is a mandatory task. Each participant is required submit the results for this task. Task B is an optional task. Each participant is allowed to submit only one running result for each task. In the running result, each microblog should be classified into three classes:

FAVOR: The author is in favor of the target (e.g., directly or indirectly by supporting someone/something, by opposing or criticizing someone/something opposed to the target, or by echoing the stance of somebody else).
AGAINST: The author is against the target (e.g., directly or indirectly by opposing or criticizing someone/something, by supporting someone/something opposed to the target, or by echoing the stance of somebody else).
NONE: None of the above.

Notice that NONE could be either the cases that the author has a neutral stance towards the target or the cases that there is no clue about what stance the author holds.

4.1 Sub-tasks

The microblogs corresponding to five targets are selected in Task A, including "iPhone SE", "春节放鞭炮 Set off firecrackers in the Spring Festival", "俄罗斯在叙利亚的反恐行动 Russia's anti terrorist operations in Syria", "开放二胎政策 Two child policy", and "深圳禁摩限电 Prohibition of motorcycles and restrictions on electric vehicles in Shenzhen". For each target, there are 600 labeled training data instances and 3000 testing data instances.

The two targets, "转基因食品 Genetically Modified Foods" and "朝鲜核试验 The Nuclear Test of DPRK" are selected for Task B. Participants were provided 6000 related instances without any label.

4.2 Evaluation Metrics

Macro-average of F-score (FAVOR) and F-score (AGAINST) is employed as the bottom-line evaluation metric for both Task A and Task B, as shown below:

$$F_{AVG} = \frac{F_{FAVOR} + F_{AGAINST}}{2} \tag{1}$$

where F_{FAVOR} and $F_{AGAINST}$ are calculated as follows, respectively:

$$F_{FAVOR} = \frac{2 * P_{FAVOR} * R_{FAVOR}}{P_{FAVOR} + R_{FAVOR}} \tag{2}$$

$$F_{AGAINST} = \frac{2 * P_{AGAINST} * R_{AGAINST}}{P_{AGAINST} + R_{AGAINST}} \tag{3}$$

where, P and R are the for precision and recall, respectively. Note that only 'FAVOR' class and 'AGAINST' class are considered in evaluation metrics, because we take 'NONE' class as the negative class in this information retrieval case. Although 'NONE' class was not shown in evaluation metric, it was not disregarded since it affects the scores of recalls in the evaluation metric if falsely labeled. The macro F-scores of F_{FAVOR} and $F_{AGAINST}$ is equivalent to the micro F-scores over all the targets. Alternatively, macro F-scores could be determined by the mean of the F_{AVG} scores for each target. To reveal the performance in the whole dataset, the former was chosen as the official evaluation metric.

5 Submission Results and Discussions

There are two tasks in evaluation. 16 participants submitted valid results for Task A. Among them, 5 participants submitted valid results for Task B.

5.1 Submission Result for Task A

As mentioned before, Task A is a supervised task which aims to detect stance towards five targets. Here, Target-1 to Target are in turn corresponding to "iPhone SE", "春节放鞭炮 Set off firecrackers in the Spring Festival", "俄罗斯在叙利亚的反恐行动 Russia's anti terrorist operations in Syria", "开放二胎政策 Two child policy", and "深圳禁摩限电 Prohibition of motorcycles and restrictions on electric vehicles in Shenzhen", respectively. The achieved performances on the overall and each target are listed in Table 2, respectively.

It is shown that the highest performance achieved in Task A is submitted by RUC_MMC. The achieved F_{FAVOR}, $F_{AGAINST}$, F_{AVG} are 0.6969, 0.7243, 0.7106, respectively. This system trained five separate models corresponding to five targets. In their model, five types of features including unigram, TFIDF, synonym, word vector and character vectors are employed. These features are adopted in the classifier based on Support Vector Machine (SVMs) and Random Forest with grid search of parameters.

Furthermore, it is shown that, generally speaking, the achieved F-value performance on Target-2 (iPhone SE) and Target-3 (俄罗斯在叙利亚的反恐行动 Russia's anti terrorist operations in Syria) are much lower than other targets. This may partially due to the fact that target-2 and target-3 have little related Hashtags in the corpus.

Table 2. Evaluation results for Task A

Team ID	OVERALL			Target-1	Target-2	Target-3	Target-4	Target-5
	F_{FAVOR}	$F_{AGAINST}$	F_{AVG}	F_{AVG}	F_{AVG}	F_{AVG}	F_{AVG}	F_{AVG}
RUC_MMC	0.6969	0.7243	0.7106	0.7730	0.5780	0.5814	0.8036	0.7652
TopTeam	0.6601	0.7186	0.6894	0.7449	0.5764	0.5232	0.7661	0.7949
SDS	0.6758	0.6965	0.6861	0.7784	0.5852	0.5332	0.7948	0.6883
CBrain	0.6618	0.7094	0.6856	0.7604	0.5528	0.4787	0.8135	0.7855
nlp_polyu	0.6476	0.6870	0.6673	0.7354	0.5312	0.5584	0.7708	0.7090
Scau_SDCM*	0.6304	0.7027	0.6666	0.7033	0.5493	0.5780	0.7639	0.7138
NEUDM	0.6268	0.6858	0.6563	0.7173	0.5485	0.5240	0.7497	0.7052
Printf	0.6183	0.6702	0.6443	0.7048	0.5769	0.5547	0.7150	0.6417
CQUT_AC996	0.5897	0.6557	0.6227	0.7015	0.4646	0.5280	0.7661	0.5879
March*	0.5858	0.6244	0.6051	0.6950	0.5466	0.4906	0.6442	0.6169
BIT_NLP_FC*	0.5573	0.5833	0.5703	0.7444	0.3460	0.3769	0.5888	0.4195
HLJUNLP	0.4584	0.6729	0.5656	0.5281	0.4494	0.5126	0.7553	0.4355
CIST-BUPT	0.4660	0.6136	0.5398	0.4754	0.4579	0.5003	0.6867	0.5048
Lib1010	0.4636	0.4944	0.4790	0.4551	0.4420	0.4934	0.4946	0.5045
USCGreenTree*	0.3609	0.5904	0.4756	0.4799	0.4052	0.4586	0.5288	0.3871
SCHOOL	0.3329	0.4662	0.3995	0.3422	0.4222	0.3903	0.4613	0.3676

The team ID with * means late submission.

Meanwhile, more named entities in the microblogs of these two targets affected the stance detection.

Most participators used textual features such as TF-IDF, word Uni-grams, word Bigrams, word embedding vectors, and sentiment lexicons like Boson lexicon, HowNet sentiment lexicon, etc. We noticed that two participators constructed target related lexicons for stance detection. TopTeam constructed an Internet-Sentiment dictionary and a Domain-Sentiment dictionary. BIT_NLP_FC employed a domain-dictionary and sentiment patterns. It seems that domain related sentiment lexicon brings few improvement contributions.

Many participators employed multiple classifiers in this evaluation. RUC_MMC employed multiple target-dependent classifiers to handle target-dependent stance problem. CBrain and nlp_polyu adopted ensemble learning framework which incorporates multiple base classifiers for stance detection.

5.2   Submission Result for Task B

Task B is an unsupervised task which aims to detect stance towards two targets without manually labeled data. Target-6 and Target-7 are corresponding to "转基因食品 *Genetically modified food*" and "朝鲜核试验 *The Nuclear Test in DPRK*", respectively. The achieved performances on the overall and each target are listed in Table 3, respectively.

It is observed that the achieved performances in Task B are evidently lower than performances achieved in Task A. Even though the lower performance is foreseeable

Table 3. Evaluation results for Task B

Team ID	OVERALL			Target-6	Target-7
	F_{FAVOR}	$F_{AGAINST}$	F_{AVG}	F_{AVG}	F_{AVG}
March*	0.3707	0.5667	0.4687	0.5173	0.4165
BIT_NLP_FC*	0.2706	0.6137	0.4421	0.4485	0.4289
CQUT_AC996	0.2985	0.5455	0.4220	0.4562	0.3815
TopTeam	0.0000	0.6555	0.3277	0.3266	0.3289
NEUDM	0.2478	0.3987	0.3232	0.1730	0.3628

The team ID with * means late submission.

for no training data, the achieved performance is still lower than expectation. The system with highest performance is submitted by March. The achieved F_{FAVOR}, $F_{AGAINST}$, F_{AVG} are 0.3707, 0.5667 and 0.4687, respectively. Such F-value is even lower than the second lowest performance in Task A.

Another phenomenon is that the achieved $F_{AGAINST}$ performances are much higher than F_{FAVOR} performances for most participant systems. This partially attributes to the fact that the stance of favor is much less than that of against in the microblogs in Task B. March has gained the highest F_{FAVOR} of 0.3707.

5.3 Discussions

Generally speaking, it is observed that the performances for both Task A and Task B have a lot of room for improvement, especially for Task B. The analysis on the evaluation results show that a good sentiment analysis system cannot ensure a high performance in stance detection task. It means that determining the stance side of mentioned named entity is important to stance detection. For example, for Target 3 (俄罗斯在叙利亚的反恐行动 *Russia's anti terrorist operations in Syria*), the named entities like 俄罗斯 *Russia*, 俄国 *Russia*, 老毛子 *Russian*, 普京 *Putin*, 战斗民族 *Fighting nation*, 医生 *Doctor* (*referred to President of Syria*) and 政府军 *Government troops* are in the side of Russia while the named entities like 美国 *U.S.A*, 米国 *U.S.A*, 反政府军 *Rebel forces* and ISIS are on the opposite side. Thus, the sentiment polarity of the sentence "反政府军真汉子 *The rebel forces are true men*" is positive but the stance of this microblog is AGAINST because it opposite the Russia's anti terrorist operations. How to obtain such knowledge is a big challenge.

Furthermore, in many cases, the microblogs do not mention the target of the interest explicitly at all. For an example sentence, "七十二个处女也不管用 *Seventy-two virgin are not helpful*", its stance determination is hard. If we know the saying that a dead Islam martyr will get seventy-two virgins as wives, we will know that this sentence opposite the Islam fighters. It means that the stance for Russia's anti terrorist operations described in this sentence is FAVOR. This example shows that the collection, understanding and utilization of background knowledge are important to stance detection. Meanwhile, the reasoning based on natural language understanding is helpful.

We hope the works in the future bring inspirations and show more possibilities in stance detection.

6 Conclusions

In this paper, we present the overview of the NLPCC shared task on stance detection in Chinese microblogs. The microblogs related to seven pre-defined targets were collected from Sina Weibo. The stance corresponding to the targets are then annotated to construct a corpus for stance detection task, namely whether the author is in favor of the given target, against the given target, or whether neither inference is likely. This corpus is divided to training dataset and testing dataset for the NLPCC stance detection evaluation. In this evaluation, we designed two tasks. Task A is a mandatory supervised task and Task B is an optional unsupervised task. Sixteen team participants and five team participants submitted their results for Task A and Task B, respectively. The highest F-score achieved was 0.7106 for Task A and 0.4687 for Task B, respectively. This shared task is the first attempt on stance detection in Chinese microblogs. It is expected to promote the research on stance detection.

Acknowledgment. We thank the hard work of Feng Shi, Qikang Wei, Jiannan Hu, Yao Yan, and Zhishan Zhao for preparing the dataset. This work was supported by the National Natural Science Foundation of China 61370165, 61632011, National 863 Program of China 2015AA015405, Shenzhen Peacock Plan Research Grant KQCX20140521144507925 and Shenzhen Foundational Research Funding JCYJ20150625142543470, Guangdong Provincial Engineering Technology Research Center for Data Science 2016KF09.

References

Gui, L., Xu, R., He, Y., Lu, Q., Wei, Z.: Intersubjectivity and sentiment: from language to knowledge. In: Proceedings of International Joint Conference on Artificial Intelligence, pp. 2789–2795 (2016)

Tang, D., Wei, F., Yang, N., et al.: Learning sentiment-specific word embedding for Twitter sentiment classification. In: Proceedings Annual Meeting of the Association for Computational Linguistics, pp. 1555–1565, 23–25 June 2014

He, Y., Saif, H., Wei, Z., Wong, K.-F.: Quantising opinion for political tweets analysis. In: LREC 2012, Eighth International Conference on Language Resources and Evaluation, Istanbul, Turkey, pp. 3901–3906 (2012)

Gui, L., Xu, R., Lu, Q., Xu, J., et al.: Cross-lingual opinion analysis via negative transfer detection. In: Proceedings Annual Meeting of the Association for Computational Linguistics, pp. 860–865, 23–25 June 2014

Anand, P., Walker, M., Abbott, R., Tree, J.E.F., Bowmani, R., Minor, M.: Cats rule and dogs drool!: classifying stance in online debate. In: Proceedings of the 2nd Workshop on Computational Approaches to Subjectivity and Sentiment Analysis, pp. 1–9, June 2011

Boltužić, F., Šnajder, J.: Back up your stance: recognizing arguments in online discussions. In: Proceedings of the First Workshop on Argumentation Mining, pp. 49–58, 26 June 2014

Mohammad, S.M., Kiritchenko, S.: SemEval-2016 task 6: detecting stance in tweets. In: International Workshop on Semantic Evaluation (2016)

Combining Deep Learning with Information Retrieval for Question Answering

Fengyu Yang[✉], Liang Gan, Aiping Li, Dongchuan Huang,
Xiaohui Chou, and Hongmei Liu

Department of Computer, National University of Defense Technology,
Changsha, China
yangfengyu_nudt@126.com, huangdongchuan@yahoo.com

Abstract. This paper presents a system which learns to answer single-relation questions on a broad range of topics from a knowledge base using a three-layered learning system. Our system first learning a Topic Phrase Detecting model based on a phrase-entities dictionary to detect which phrase is the topic phrase of the question. The second layer of the system learning several answer ranking models. The last layer re-ranking the scores from the output of the second layer and return the highest scored answer. Both convolutional neural networks (CNN) and information retrieval (IR) models are included in this models. Training our system using pairs of questions and structured representations of their answers, yields competitive results on the NLPCC 2016 KBQA share task.

Keywords: Question answering · Deep learning · Information retrieval · Knowledge base

1 Introduction

Aiming at open domain question answering system evaluation task in the NLPCC-ICCPOL 2016 Knowledge-based QA task, called KBQA task, this paper presents a solution of single-relation question answering. The system contains three layers learning models. The first layer which we called Topic Phrase Detecting model learning a topic detect model to detect which phrase is the topic phrase for a giving question. After detecting the topic phrase, we could get one or several topic entities from the phrase-entities dictionary and extract all triples which the subjects are topic entities from knowledge base. Each triple is regarded as a candidate answer. The key of get the correct answer is to ranking all candidate answers. The second layer which we called Base Ranking models learning several base ranking model. Inspired by Wang and Manning [1], we propose a NBSVM-based answer ranking model, and like what [2] do, convolutional neural networks (CNN) also used in this work. However, most traditional approaches ignore the words POS-tagging feature. In this step, we both use word sequences, and POS-tagging sequences to train different models. The last layer is an ensemble layer which used to re-rank the output of different ranking models from the second layer. In our experience, re-ranking layer obtained a great improvement in performance.

C.-Y. Lin et al. (Eds.): NLPCC-ICCPOL 2016, LNAI 10102, pp. 917–925, 2016.
DOI: 10.1007/978-3-319-50496-4_86

2 Related Work

Most previous knowledge-based QA system use WebQuestion [3] as they evaluation benchmark and using Freebase as they KB. The WebQuestion dataset is built using Freebase as the KB and contains 5,810 question-answer pairs. The existing knowledge-based QA technologies can be divided into three approaches: (1) Information Retrieval Approach [4, 5, 8, 9]; (2) Semantic Parsing Approach [3, 10–13]; (3) Deep Learning Approach [6, 7]. Bast et al. [5] use three pre-defined templates to generate answer candidates, more rich linguistics features like number of overlapping words, derived words, word vector embedding cosine similarities were used for training a question-relation alignment model. Berant et al. [3] was the semantic parsing system that first introduced the WebQuestions dataset and remains a popular baseline. It builds a lexicon mapping from phrases to predicates by aligning Freebase to Clue-Web and producing co-occurrence based features. Dong et al. [7] use multi-column convolutional neural networks (MCCNNs) to understand questions from three different aspects (namely, answer path, answer context, and answer type) and learn their distributed representations.

3 Framework

In this paper, we focus on using knowledge base to answer single-relation questions. A single-relation question is defined as a question composed of an entity mention and a binary relation description. Figure 1 illustrates the intuition of our method by an example: "我想知道小行星605是什么时候发现的?".

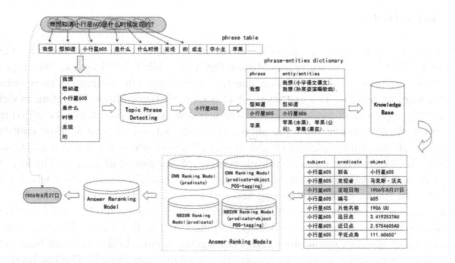

Fig. 1. System overview

3.1   Topic Phrase Detecting

Giving a single-relation question, we first use the phrase-entities dictionary to detect all phrases which appear in the question. In our example, "我想", "想知道", "小行星 605", "是什么时候", "发现", "的" can be first detected. We use the question-answer pairs to make a training set. The training set is in the format of <question, phrase, label>. We generate rich linguistics features from the training set, and training a GBDT (Gradient Boost Decision Tree) model. The GBDT's output is a probability value between 0-1, we choose the highest ranked phrase as the topic phrase of each question.

We generate rich features from each candidate (question-phrase pair). Consider there are n question-phrase-label samples: $< question_i, phrase_{i,j}, label_k >$, $phrase_{i,j}$ means the j-th phrase of $question_i$, $label_k$ is 0 or 1, $question_i$ is a sequence of words.

Pre-word Feature. We use the all of training samples to make a Pre-word Probability Dictionary. A pre-word is a word that precedes the head word in a phrase. If the phrase is the head of question, just use a special string like "HEAD" as the phrase's pre-word. We extract pre-words from all phrases. These pre-words compose all keys of Pre-word Probability Dictionary. Let $<k_i, v_i>$ be the i-th element of Pre-word Probability Dictionary, k_i be the i-th pre-words, pos_i be the number of positive samples which the pre-word is k_i for each sample, neg_i be the number of negative samples which the pre-word is k_i for each sample. We define v_i as follow:

$$v_i = ln\left(\frac{\frac{pos_i+1}{pos_i+neg_i+1}}{\frac{neg_i+1}{pos_i+neg_i+1}}\right) = ln\left(\frac{pos_i+1}{neg_i+1}\right)$$

Post-word Feature. Do the same things as we generate pre-word feature except that pre-words replaced with post-words. A post-word is a word that follows the last word in a phrase. If the phrase is at the end of question, just use a special string like "END" as the phrase's post-word.

Pre-word POS-Tagging Feature. Do the same things as we generate pre-word feature except that pre-words replaced with pre-word POS-Tagging. Pre-word POS-Tagging is the POS-Tagging of a word that precedes the head word in a phrase.

Post-word POS-Tagging Feature. Do the same things as we generate pre-word feature except that pre-words replaced with post-word POS-Tagging. Post-word POS-Tagging is the POS-Tagging of a word that follows the last word in a phrase.

Average Inverse Document Frequency (Average IDF) in Questions Corpus. The question corpus is made by <question_1, question_2, ..., question_i> from all training question. We compute the average word's IDF score of $phrase_{i,j}$ in questions corpus.

Average Inverse Document Frequency (Average IDF) in Relations Corpus. The relations corpus is made by <predicate_1, predicate_2, predicate_i...> from all triples. We compute the average word's IDF score of $phrase_{i,j}$ in relations Corpus.

Other Features. We also consider phrase length, phrase position as important features when detecting topic phrases.

3.2   NBSVM-Based Ranking

After detecting the topic phrase, we get one or several entities from the phrase-entities dictionary and extract all triples which the subjects are these entities from knowledge base. In our example, there is only one entity "小行星605" for the phrase "小行星605". All relevant triples, like <小行星605, 别名, 小行星605>, <小行星605, 发现者, 马克斯·沃夫>, <小行星605, 发现日期, 1906年8月27日>, are extracted from knowledge base. Each triple is regarded as a candidate answer. In this subsection we describe four answer ranking models in detail.

NBSVM. NBSVM is a simple but novel SVM variant proposed by Wang and Manning [1] which using Naïve Bayes(NB) log-count ratios as feature values. It outperforms most published results on sentiment analysis datasets.

N-gram Co-occurrence Feature Between Question and Predicate (N-gram Q-P Feature). To use NBSVM model for our answer ranking task, we consider correspondences between words(uni-grams) or phrases (bi-grams or tri-grams) in the question and the predicate in the candidate triple. For example, the question "…什么时候…" almost always asks for the "…时间". For each question with corresponding predicate in training samples, we generate all unigrams, bigrams and trigrams of the words of question. The topic phrase is replaced with a special string "ENTITY". For each question n-gram and predicate n-gram, we then create an indicator feature by appending the question n-gram to the predicate n-gram. In our example, one of the features would be "什么\时候 + 发现\日期" for the question bi-gram "什么\时候" and predicate bi-gram "发现\日期".

N-gram Co-occurrence Feature Between Question and Predicate + Object POS-Tagging (N-gram Q-P-OPOS Feature). We also consider correspondences between words(uni-grams) or phrases (bi-grams or tri-grams) in the question and POS-Tagging sequence of object. For example, for the question "…什么时候…", its answer almost always is a time phrase, and its POS-Tagging always like "…/t/t…". We add this POS-Tagging sequence to generate N-gram co-occurrence feature. In our example, there are two features "什么/时候 + 发现/日期", "什么/时候 +/t/t" for the question bi-gram "什么/时候" and predicate bi-gram "发现/日期" and its corresponding object POS-Tagging bi-gram "/t/t".

We use the N-gram Q-P-POS feature to make the log-count ratio and train a NBSVM ranking model (predicate), and use the N-gram Q-P-OPOS feature to make another log-count ratio and train another NBSVM ranking model (predicate + object POS-Tagging).

3.3   CNN-Based Ranking

Besides the NBSVM-based Answer Ranking, we also consider convolutional neural networks for answer ranking.

Yih et al. [2] propose using a convolutional neural network (CNN) framework to handle the huge variety of the semantically equivalent ways of stating the same

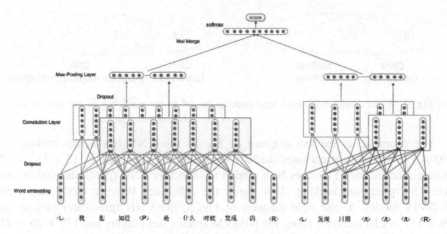

Fig. 2. The architecture of the convolutional neural networks (CNN) used in this work.

question as well as the mismatch of the natural language utterances and predicates in the knowledge base. In our work, we use a convolutional neural network framework to handle the mismatch of the natural language utterances and predicates. Figure 2 illustrates our convolutional neural network framework.

The first layer is the word embedding layer, we use all questions from the training set to pre-train word2vec model and use the pre-trained word2vec embedding to initializing word vectors of questions. We also use all predicates from the training set to pre-train another word2vec model and use the pre-trained word2vec embedding to initializing word vectors of predicates. Then, a 1-D convolution layer with multiple filter widths and feature maps used to extract some semantic feature. A max-pooling layer apply a max-pooling operation over the feature map. We use "mul" [14] model to merge the two output vectors and then use a softmax [15] for the network output.

We use binary cross-entropy as the loss function and use Adam optimizer to train the convolutional neural networks. We also use dropout for over-fitting. The question sequence length is set to 20 and predicate sequence length is set to 10, if the number of words is smaller than the sequence length, just use a special string like "\t" to fill to the full. The embedding dim is set to 64. There are two type filters with width 3 and 5 used for capture different n-gram features. Each type has 200 filters. So, both the question CNN and predicate CNN has 400-dim vector after max-pooling.

Like what we do at Subsect. 3.2, we also consider "predicate + object POS-Tagging" for ranking.

3.4   Re-ranking

We consider re-ranking in this step because each base ranking model use different structures and features, this may cause some differences between base ranking models. We training these base models using the same training set and test these well trained models in the same testing set. Figure 3 shows the error numbers for each base ranking model while predicting at the testing set.

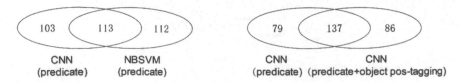

Fig. 3. Error numbers for each base ranking model while predicting at the testing set.

For example, at the left diagram of Fig. 3, the CNN (predicate) ranking has 103 + 113 = 216 incorrect cases, the NBSVM (predicate) ranking has 113 + 112 = 225 incorrect cases, only 113 cases both predict incorrect by CNN (predicate) ranking and NBSVM (predicate) ranking. This shows the difference between CNN model and NBSVM model. At the right diagram of Fig. 3, the CNN (predicate) ranking has 79 + 137 = 216 incorrect cases, the NBSVM (predicate) ranking has 137 + 86 = 223 incorrect cases, only 137 cases both predict incorrect by CNN (predicate) ranking and NBSVM (predicate) ranking. This shows the difference between CNN (predicate) model and CNN (predicate + object pos-tagging) model.

We use stacking method to ensemble base models and train a GBDT model for re-ranking.

4   Experiment

4.1   Train

The NLPCC-ICCPOL 2016 Knowledge-based QA task provide every participant a Chinese knowledge base, a training set and a phrase-entities dictionary for entity linking. The training set contains 14609 question-answer pairs. After we remove some noise data. There are left 14033 question-answer pairs. We first learn a Topic Phrase Detecting model (see Sect. 3.1 for in detail).

At the ranking steps. We use 11370 question-answer pairs for training and 2663 question-answer pairs for testing. To avoid over-fitting, we use 5-fold stacking to training 4 base ranking models. The output of each base ranking model in validation data with some ranking features, string similarity feature are used to train the re-ranking models (GBDT).

4.2   Experimental Results

Topic Phrase Detecting. We use 10-fold cross-validation to test our Topic Phrase Detecting model. Table 1 shows the mean accuracy, recall, F1 score of 10 folds.

Ranking and Re-ranking. We use the 2663 question-answer pairs to test all of our ranking model (base ranking model and re-ranking model). Table 2 shows the ACC@1, ACC@2, MRR score of each ranking models.

Table 1. 10-fold cross-validation of Topic Phrase Detecting model

accuracy	recall	F1 score
0. 9910	0. 9899	0. 9904

Table 2. ACC@1, ACC@2, MRR score of each ranking models.

Models	ACC@1	ACC@2	MRR
Levenshtein Distance	0. 705	0. 851	0. 809
NBSVM(predicate)	0. 842	0. 938	0. 909
NBSVM(predicate+object pos-tagging)	0. 850	0. 923	0. 905
CNN(predicate)	0. 849	0. 942	0. 912
CNN(predicate+object pos-tagging)	0. 847	0. 939	0. 908
Re-ranking	0. 899	0. 970	0. 941

Levenshtein Distance is an algorithm that calculate string edit distance of two different string. We use this to calculate the similarity of question and predicate. We consider this is a baseline for our ranking system. We can see from Table 2 that the four base ranking models have very little performance difference. But when ensemble these four ranking model with string similarity score feature, we get ACC@1 0.899, ACC@2 0.970, MRR 0.941.

Table 3. Evaluation result in NLPCC 2016 KBQA

KBQA Submissions	F1 Score	Rank(by F1 Score)
Team-1	0. 8247	1
Team-2	0. 8159	2
Team-4	0. 7957	3
Team-5	0. 7914	4
Team-6	0. 7272	5
Team-7	0. 7251	6
...	...	...

The results of our methods proposed in the evaluation task in NLPCC 2016 KBQA task are shown in Table 3:

Our system gets competitive performance that F1 score is 0.8159 while the best F1 score in all participants is 0.8247.

5   Conclusion

This paper describes a new end-to-end system that combining deep learning with information retrieval method for question answering which obtained high performance. The system gets competitive performance on the NLPCC 2016 KBQA share task. However, the system handles only for singe relation question answering. But the framework described in the paper can also be adapted to multi-relation question answering like what [5] do. Our system use a Topic Phrase Detecting model to detect the topic phrase from a giving question. But we do nothing for entity disambiguation. However, there are remains some works to do.

Acknowledgment.   The work is supported by National Basic Research and Development Program (Nos. 2013CB329601, 2013CB329604) and National Natural Science Foundation of China (No. 61502517, No. 61472433, No. 61372191, No. 61572492).

References

1. Wang, S., Manning, C.D.: Baselines and bigrams: simple, good sentiment and topic classification. In: Meeting of the Association for Computational Linguistics (2012)
2. Yih, W., Chang, M., He, X., et al.: Semantic parsing via staged query graph generation: question answering with knowledge base. In: Meeting of the Association for Computational Linguistics (2015)
3. Berant, J., Chou, A., Frostig, R., et al.: Semantic parsing on freebase from question-answer Pairs. In: Empirical Methods in Natural Language Processing (2013)
4. Yao, X., Van Durme, B.: Information extraction over structured data: question answering with freebase. In: Meeting of the Association for Computational Linguistics (2014)
5. Bast, H., Haussmann, E.: More accurate question answering on freebase. In: Conference on Information and Knowledge Management (2015)
6. Bordes, A., Chopra, S., Weston, J., et al.: Question answering with subgraph embeddings. In: Empirical Methods in Natural Language Processing (2014)
7. Dong, L., Wei, F., Zhou, M., et al.: Question answering over freebase with multi-column convolutional neural networks. In: Meeting of the Association for Computational Linguistics (2015)
8. Fader, A., Zettlemoyer, L., Etzioni, O., et al.: Open question answering over curated and extracted knowledge bases. In: Knowledge Discovery and Data Mining (2014)
9. Yao, X.: Lean question answering over freebase from scratch. In: North American Chapter of the Association for Computational Linguistics (2015)
10. Berant, J., Liang, P.: Semantic parsing via paraphrasing. In: Meeting of the Association for Computational Linguistics (2014)

11. Reddy, S., Lapata, M., Steedman, M., et al.: Large-scale semantic parsing without question-answer pairs (2014)
12. Pasupat, P., Liang, P.: Compositional semantic parsing on semi-structured tables. In: Meeting of the Association for Computational Linguistics (2015)
13. Wang, Y., Berant, J., Liang, P., et al.: Building a semantic parser overnight. In: Meeting of the Association for Computational Linguistics (2015)
14. https://keras.io/layers/core/#merge
15. http://ufldl.stanford.edu/wiki/index.php/Softmax_Regression

A Hybrid Approach to DBQA

Fangying Wu, Muyun Yang$^{(\boxtimes)}$, Tiejun Zhao, Zhongyuan Han,
Dequan Zheng, and Shanshan Zhao

Harbin Institute of Technology, Harbin, China
yangmuyun@hit.edu.cn

Abstract. Document-based question answering (DBQA) is a sub-task of open-domain question answering, targeted at selecting the answer sentence(s) from the given documents for a question. In this paper, we propose a hybrid approach to select answer sentences, combining existing models via the rank SVM model. Specifically, we capture the inter-relationship between the question and answer sentences from three aspects: surface string similarity, deep semantic similarity and relevance based on information retrieval models. Our experiments show that an improved retrieval model out-performs other methods, including the deep learning models. And, applying a rank SVM model to combine all these features, we achieve 0.8120 in mean reciprocal rank (MRR) and 0.8111 in mean average precision (MAP) in the opening test.

Keywords: QA · String similarity · Information retrieval · Deep learning · Rank SVM · Hybrid approach

1 Introduction

Document-based question answering (DBQA) is a sub-task of the open-domain question answering. For each question, the target is to select sentences as answers from given relevant document(s). Classic open-domain QA system usually involved three parts: (i) question analysis; (ii) relevant document retrieval; (iii) answer sentence extraction. DBQA is different from open-domain QA in that it just focuses on selecting answer sentences from candidate answer sentences in provided documents.

Previous works on answer selection of QA are dependent on linguist analysis tools and various external resources (Ravichandran 2002). Analyzing sentence structure by such techniques as name entity taggers and shallow parser (Srihari and Li 2000). External knowledge covers semantic resources such as WordNet, QA typology (Hovy et al. 2001), and Wiki pages. A clear limitation of them is that the results are substantially affected by the quality of external resources and parse tools.

Recently, different architectures of deep learning (DL) models are emerging as a new solution to QA task. DL models are either claimed to extract semantic information from texts, or directly adopted to rank candidates by training the distributed representation of question and candidates to find their semantic relevance (Wang and Nyberg 2015; Yin et al. 2015; Severyn and Moschitti 2015).

In another aspect, QA can be naturally regarded as the relevance estimation between question and candidates. For relevance measure, information retrieval circle provides abundant successful solutions. Although IR models have already been

© Springer International Publishing AG 2016
C.-Y. Lin et al. (Eds.): NLPCC-ICCPOL 2016, LNAI 10102, pp. 926–933, 2016.
DOI: 10.1007/978-3-319-50496-4_87

adopted to retrieve relevant documents in QA, they are not well examined for sentence level answer identification yet. Simply treating question as query, candidates as collection, various IR models could be directly applied for DBQA.

Therefore, as an effort in the DBQA evaluation campaign organized by NLP&CC 2016, we focus on examining existing approaches for their efficiency, and then try to combine them for an optimized result. To get a quick and robust method for DBQA, we capture the inter relationship between question and answer sentences from three aspects: surface string similarity, semantic relevance based on DL models and relevance based on IR models. Our experiment results show that features based on IR models perform better than DL models. By applying a rank SVM model to combine all these features, the test results in opening test data set are 0.8120 in mean reciprocal rank (MRR) and 0.8111 in mean average precision (MAP).

The remainder of this paper is organized as follows: Sect. 2 describes the related work. Section 3 describes the detail of different features in our model. In Sect. 4, we present our experiment results, and finally, we draw a conclusion in Sect. 5.

2 Related Work

Many methods have been applied to find the relationship between sentence pairs. Ranking candidate sentences according to bag-of-word matching have been regarded as baseline in many works (Tan et al. 2015; Wang and Nyberg, 2015). But they have a relatively low performance on answer selection. Tran et al. (2015) combine multiple features to rank answers and get the best result in SemEval-2015 Task 3, in which word match is still indispensable. These works show that surface word matching features are necessary for answers selection.

As for the recent efforts to apply DL methods on QA task, the straight-forward idea is to learn the distributed representation of question and answer sentences, then calculate the (cosine) similarity between two sentence vectors (Ming Tan et al. 2015). The more ambitious effort is to train a specialized DL model for similarity estimation. But the best results have been, so far, reported as combination with other features like keywords matches by a machine learning method (Wang and Nyberg 2015; Yin et al. 2015; Severyn and Moschitti 2015).

As for the IR circle, language model is the state-of-the-art model. Compared with learning to rank, the best performed machine learning techniques in web search experiments, language model are still deemed enough to prove a new feature or new strategy designed for the retrieval process. Therefore, in this paper, we do not exhaust variants of learning to rank methods in search, but simply choose two classic forms of language model, the query likelihood model and the KL divergence model.

3 Hybrid Approach via Rank SVM

In this paper, our work focuses on mining the inter relationship between question and candidate answer sentences from three perspectives: surface string similarity, sentence relevance based on retrieval model and relations based on DL text distribution representation. In order to find a quick and robust answer selection model which doesn't depend on extra resources to train, we use linear rank SVM model to combine all features of the three types for ranking candidate answer sentences.

3.1 Measures for Surface String Similarity

Various methods have been used to compare the matching between two sentences (Turney 2006). Especially, the recent success of automatic machine translation evaluation circle also provides another group of string similarity metrics based on n-gram matching (Kondrak 2005), e.g, BLEU, ROUGE and NIST (Papineni et al. 2002; Lin et al. 2004). In our work, we collect the following measures to capture surface string matching between question and the answer sentences:

- Recall and precision of n-gram: Recall and precision of n-gram matches for question and candidate answer sentences.
- MT evaluation metrics: BLEU-1, BLEU-2, BLEU-3, BLEU-4 and NIST5.
- Longest Common Sub-sequence(LCS): The sum of all the same sub-sequence length between question and candidate sentences.
- Edit distance: Defined as the least steps to transform the question sentence to candidate sentence using insertion, deletion and substitution.
- Tf-isf sum: For each matched n-gram, we multiply its frequency by its "reverse sentence frequency" to get a new weight. Then add all the value for each n-gram.
- Words match: The number of same words in question and candidate sentences.
- Nouns match: The number of same nouns in question and candidate sentences.
- Verbs match: The number of same verbs in question and candidate sentences.
- Cosine similarity: Question and candidate sentences are assumed to be two vectors in a $|V|$-dimensional vector space. $|V|$ is the number of unique terms in the corpus. Calculate the cosine of the angle between two vectors.

In addition, the organizer of the evaluation provided another kind of metric: the translation probability of each candidate sentence given the question. We add it to our system to measure the similarity of question and answer sentences.

3.2 Features Based on Retrieval Models

Here we apply IR-based techniques (Lavrenko et al. 2001; Manning et al. 2008; Huerta 2010) to estimate the relevance between two sentences.

Query Likelihood Model. Given a query sentence Q, we rank the candidate answer sentences according to probability $P(C_i|Q)$. According to Bayes' Rule, we can calculate this by:

$$P(C_i|Q) = \frac{P(C_i)P(Q|\theta_{C_i})}{P(Q)} \qquad (1)$$

where θ_{C_i} is the distribution of candidate sentence C_i. We set the prior probability of each candidate sentence C_i equally, so $P(C_i|Q) \propto P(Q|\theta_{C_i})$. $P(Q|\theta_{C_i})$ is the probability that the query text could be generated by the candidate sentence language model and calculated by:

$$P(Q|\theta_{C_i}) = \prod_{j=1}^{n} P(q_j|\theta_{C_i}) \tag{2}$$

where q_j is a query word and question sentence Q contains n query words. We need estimate the language model for each candidate sentence.

According to the maximum likelihood estimator, we estimate the sentence language model $P(w|\theta_{C_i})$ by $\frac{f_{w,C_i}}{|C_i|}$. f_{w,C_i} is the number of times word w occurs in candidate sentence C_i. $|C_i|$ is the total number of words in C_i.

For a word w who doesn't occur in candidate C_i, we apply Dirichlet smoothing method to mitigate the zero-probability problem:

$$P(w|\theta_{C_i}) = (1 - \lambda)\frac{f_{w,C_i} + \mu P_{ml}(w|C)}{|C_i| + \mu} + \lambda P_{ml}(w|C) \tag{3}$$

By analyzing all the queries, question words like what and who occur frequently and they put forward questions. Other words in a question sentence are called query words. The query words nearer to a question word are more important. So we re-estimate the sentence language model by:

$$P'(q_j|\theta_{C_i}) = \frac{1}{Z} * \lambda * e^{-\lambda|pos(q_j)-pos(q_c)|} \tag{4}$$

where $pos(q_j) - pos(q_c)$ is the distance between word q_j and word q_c. Z is the regularization term which is the sum of $\lambda * e^{-\lambda|pos(q_j)-pos(q_c)|}$ for all q_j.

3.3 Features Based on Deep Learning

Word Embedding. One of the baseline systems provided by the task trains a word embedding model (Mikolov et al. 2013). It represents a sentence as vector by computing the average of word vectors that occur in this sentence. The cosine of candidate and query sentence vectors is regarded as the probability that the candidate would be an answer.

BLSTM Model. In this paper, we use BLSTM architecture for answer selection (Wang and Nyberg 2015) because it can learn from context information. Figure 1, without attention module within the dashed box, shows the main structure of this model.

Putting embeddings transformed from words into the LSTM sequentially, then we get a matrix that represents semantic of the question or answer sentence. After max-pooling, a vector are generated, which represents the semantic of a sentence. finally, we put the two sentence vectors into a softmax layer to compute the relation of the two sentences. Output of the architecture is a probability that presents the possible of candidate sentence being an answer. We train our model to maximize the probability of answer sentence.

Attention based BLSTM Model Attention model is always used to make the predicate representation matched with predicate-focused sentence representation more effectively (Yin et al. 2015; Zhou et al. 2016; Severyn 2015). Answer sentences use specific words to answer specific question such as name of people to who, words that represent time to when. To better utilize the relationship among words in question and answer sentence, we multiply hidden units by an alignment matrix to generate attention and add it to input question's BLSTM units. Figure 1 as a whole shows the structure of this model.

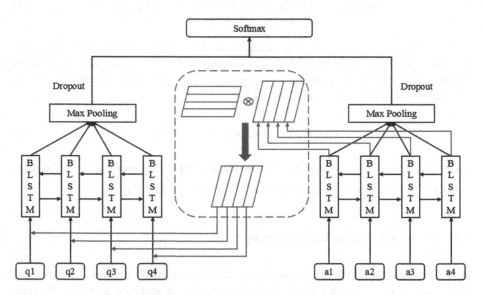

Fig. 1. BLSTM model (with attention)

4 Experiments

4.1 Evaluation Metrics

The evaluation metrics of DBQA system are mean reciprocal rank (MRR) and mean average precision (MAP). MRR and MAP are defined as formulas (5) and (6):

$$MRR = \frac{1}{|Q|} \sum_{i=1}^{|Q|} \frac{1}{rank_i} \qquad (5)$$

$$MAP = \frac{1}{|Q|} \sum_{i=1}^{|Q|} AveP(C_i, A_i) \qquad (6)$$

where $|Q|$ is the total number of questions in evaluation set and $rank_i$ is the position of the first answer sentence in your sorted candidate answer sentences set, and $AveP(C_i, A_i) = \frac{\sum_{k=1}^{n} (P(k) \cdot rel(k))}{\min(m,n)}$ denotes the average precision.

4.2 Experiments Results and Analysis

The provided training data set contains 8772 questions and a document for each question. We perform 4-fold cross validation to examine the hybrid approach. And we also set 4 different conditions with different feature combination:

- Group 1: features based on surface word matching.
- Group 2: features in group 1 plus features based on query likelihood models.
- Group 3: features in group 1 plus features based on deep learning models.
- Group 4: all features we proposed.

Evaluation results of four group features are showed in Table 1. And contribution of each typical single feature for three aspects is in Table 2. It reveals that the most effective features are that based on query likelihood models and BLSTM model. MRR of these features reach up to 0.65 while others are almost not larger than 0.5.

Table 1. Evaluation of different feature sets

Feature set	MRR	MAP
Group 1	0.6151	0.6126
Group 2	0.7320	0.7292
Group 3	0.6870	0.6848
Group 4	0.7854	0.7822

Features based on string similarity don't make a considerable effect individually. Putting them together, we have gained 0.1 improvement for both MRR and MAP evaluate metrics. It generates a remarkable result after adding features based on query likelihood models to group 2. The value of MRR is 0.7320 and of MAP is 0.7292.

Features based on DL models are somewhat inferior to the IR model. And for DL models, BLSTM model with attention has lower evaluation results compared with that without attention. This situation is strange as related work having showed an opposite result. We think this may arise from the very limited training data provided for the deep training, which usually depends on a very large corpus.

Table 2. Typical single feature of three aspects

Feature	MRR	MAP	Feature	MRR	MAP
2-gram match recall	0.5259	0.5239	Bleu-2	0.4974	0.4961
2-gram match precision	0.4763	0.4755	Bleu-4	0.4221	0.4208
TFISF sum for 2 g	0.4531	0.4517	NIST5	0.4995	0.4981
Word match recall	0.5193	0.5173	LCS	0.5079	0.5058
Cosine similarity	0.4502	0.4493	Edit distance	0.2098	0.2097
Nouns match	0.4929	0.4905	Verbs match	0.4317	0.4293
Translation probability	0.2617	0.2615	Word embedding	0.4769	0.4754
Query likelihood model	0.6536	0.6514	BLSTM	0.6634	0.6615
Re-estimate query likelihood model	0.6936	0.6907	BLSTM with attention	0.5743	0.5720

For candidate answer sentences among which models of feature group four and five give a highest score to the real answer, we analyze their corresponding questions. Query likelihood models perform differently from BLSTM models. Generally speaking, language model performs better than DL models in training data set. But when question sentences contain specific question words like how many, DL models perform better than language model.

Finally, we combine all these features of three types. The results of four-fold cross validation are 0.7854 and 0.7822 for MRR and MAP, respectively. That is, all the features are utilized and training over the whole provided data to be tested by the final open text, achieving a result of 0.8120 in MRR and 0.8111 in MAP.

5   Conclusion

In this paper, we examine the existing question-answer sentence methods from three perspectives, and propose a hybrid solution by ranking SVM. We reveal that the surface word similarity doesn't work well in selecting answer sentences. In contrast, an improved IR model performs best in this task, better than the state-of-the-art deep learning techniques. Combing all these model results under the rank SVM framework, we achieve in the open test with 0.8120 in MRR and 0.8111 in MAP.

Acknowledgments. This paper is supported by the project of Natural Science Foundation of China (Grant Nos. 61272384, 61402134, and 61370170).

References

Srihari, R.K., Li, W.: A question answering system supported by information extraction. In: Proceedings of the 1st Meeting of the North American Chapter of the Association for Computational Linguistics (ANLP-NAACL-2000), Seattle, WA, pp. 166–172 (2000)

Hovy, E., Hermjakob, U., Lin, C., et al.: The use of external knowledge of factoid QA. In: TREC, vol. 2001, pp. 644–652 (2001)

Ravichandran, D., Hovy, E.: Learning surface text patterns for a question answering system. In: Meeting of the Association for Computational Linguistics (2002)

Severyn, A., Moschitti, A.: Learning to rank short text pairs with convolutional deep neural networks. In: International ACM SIGIR Conference on Research and Development in Information Retrieval (2015)

Tran, Q.H., Tran, V., Vu, T., et al.: JAIST: combining multiple features for answer selection in community question answering. In: Proceedings of the 9th International Workshop on Semantic Evaluation, SemEval, vol. 15, pp. 215–219 (2015)

Tan, M., Santos, C.N., Zhou, B., et al.: LSTM-based deep learning models for non-factoid answer selection. arXiv preprint arXiv:1511.04108 (2015)

Wang, D.W., Nyberg, E.: A long short-term memory model for answer sentence selection in question answering. In: Meeting of the Association for Computational Linguistics (2015)

Yin, W., Yu, M., Zhou, B., et al.: Simple question answering by attentive convolutional neural network. arXiv preprint arXiv:1606.03391 (2016)

Papineni, K., Roukos, S., Ward, T., et al.: BLEU: a method for automatic evaluation of machine translation. In: Meeting of the Association for Computational Linguistics (2002)

Kondrak, G.: N-gram similarity and distance. In: Consens, Mariano, Navarro, Gonzalo (eds.) SPIRE 2005. LNCS, vol. 3772, pp. 115–126. Springer, Heidelberg (2005). doi:10.1007/11575832_13

Lin, C., Och, F.J.: Automatic evaluation of machine translation quality using longest common subsequence and skip-bigram statistics. In: Meeting of the Association for Computational Linguistics (2004)

Huerta, J.M.: An information-retrieval approach to language modeling: applications to social data. In: North American Chapter of the Association for Computational Linguistics (2010)

Manning, C.D., Raghavan, P., Schutze, H., et al.: Introduction to information retrieval. In: Proceedings of the International Communication of Association for Computing Machinery Conference (2008)

Lavrenko, V., Croft, W.B.: Relevance based language models. In: International ACM SIGIR Conference on Research and Development in Information Retrieval (2001)

Turney, P.D.: Similarity of semantic relations. J. Comput. Linguist. 32(3), 379–416 (2006)

Mikolov, T., Sutskever, I., Chen, K., et al.: Distributed representations of words and phrases and their compositionality. In: Neural Information Processing Systems (2013)

Yin, W., Schütze, H., Xiang, B., et al.: ABCNN: attention-based convolutional neural network for modeling sentence pairs. arXiv preprint arXiv:1512.05193 (2015)

A Chinese Question Answering Approach Integrating Count-Based and Embedding-Based Features

Benyou Wang[1], Jiabin Niu[1], Liqun Ma[1], Yuhua Zhang[1], Lipeng Zhang[1], Jingfei Li[1], Peng Zhang[1(✉)], and Dawei Song[1,2]

[1] Tianjin Key Laboratory of Cognitive Computing and Application, School of Computer Science and Technology, Tianjin University, Tianjin, People's Republic of China
{waby,niujiabin,liqun,yuhuazhang,jingfeili,pzhang}@tju.edu.cn, zh583007354@qq.com
[2] Department of Computing and Communications, The Open University, Milton Keynes, UK
dawei.song2010@gmail.com

Abstract. Document-based Question Answering system, which needs to match semantically the short text pairs, has gradually become an important topic in the fields of natural language processing and information retrieval. Question Answering system based on English corpus has developed rapidly with the utilization of the deep learning technology, whereas an effective Chinese-customized system needs to be paid more attention. Thus, we explore a Question Answering system which is characterized in Chinese for the QA task of NLPCC. In our approach, the ordered sequential information of text and deep matching of semantics of Chinese textual pairs have been captured by our count-based traditional methods and embedding-based neural network. The ensemble strategy has achieved a good performance which is much stronger than the provided baselines.

Keywords: Question Answer · DBQA · Semantic matching · Chinese text

1   Introduction

Question Answering (QA) has attracted great attention with the development of Natural Language Processing (NLP) and Information Retrieval (IR) techniques. One of the typical tasks named document-based question answering (DBQA) focuses on finding answers from the question's given document candidates. Compared with the traditional document retrieval task, DBQA system usually usWes fluent natural language to express the query intent and desires an accurate result which has discarded most unmatching candidates.

Due to the short length of the text in DBQA task, data sparsity have become more serious problems than those of the traditional retrieval task. The relevance-based IR methods like TFIDF or BM-25 cannot solve these semantic matching

© Springer International Publishing AG 2016
C.-Y. Lin et al. (Eds.): NLPCC-ICCPOL 2016, LNAI 10102, pp. 934–941, 2016.
DOI: 10.1007/978-3-319-50496-4_88

problems effectively. Thus, word embedding technology [1] has been applied in some English QA system as well as the Chinese QA system. Moreover, the question text is natural language with complete syntax structures instead of some keywords in document-retrieve task. A sentence should be considered as a sequence or a tree instead of an unordered word bag, and each components has different semantic contributions to the whole sentence. In summary, an effective QA system should consider the following problems simultaneously.

(1) Matching the semantics-similar texts which is synonymous paraphrased.
(2) Taking the sequential information of the question text into consideration, instead of an unordered set of words.

For the first problem, enumerating all the paraphrase rules of text seems to be impossible. We usually adopt the embedding-based method in which two words have a closed embedding representations when they usually appear in the similar context. These representation can capture the semantic link between independent terms to some extent in a distributed way. For the second problem, people are more likely to firstly elaborate the premise and then ask the related issues under such premise according to the Chinese expression habit. In the bag-of-words model, an unordered set of words in questions will lose the information to distinguish the premise and issues. We utilize the position-aware information in our count-based model and keep the order of the word or character sequence in the neural network during the row-pooling and col-pooling operations.

This paper elaborates an approach for the Open Domain Question Answering shared sub-task of Document-based QA task in NLPCC-ICCPOL 2016. We combine the count-based and embedding-based method with an ensemble strategy. In order to adapt to the Chinese expression habit, we integrate the features of Chinese into both the count-based method and embedding-based method, which achieves significant improvement upon baselines in the final evaluation.

2   Related Work

QA task focuses on automatically understanding natural language questions and selecting or generating one or more answers which can match semantically the question. Due to the shorter text than the traditional task of document retrieval, structured syntactic information and the lexical gap are two key points for QA system. For the first point, tree [2] and sequential [3] structure have been proposed to utilize the syntactic information instead of an unordered bag-of-word model. Some efforts like lexical semantics [4], probabilistic paraphrase or translation [5] have been made to alleviate the problem of lexical gap. Moreover, feature-based ensemble method [6] tries to combine both the semantic and syntactic information to rank the answers by the data-driven learning mechanism.

Recently, the end-to-end strategy motivates researchers to build a deep symantic matching model which can also model the sequential text. With the development of the embedding-based neural network, deep learning has achieved a good performance in the QA task [7]. Severyn et al. propose a shallow convolutional neural network (CNN) which combines the ordered overlapped information into the hidden layer [8]. Recurrent neural network (RNN) and the following long short-term memory neural network (LSTM) [9,10] which can model the sequential text are also applicable for the textual representation and matching of question and answers. Santos et al. propose an attentive pooling networks with two-way attention mechanism for modelling the interactions between two sequential text, which can easily integrating a CNN or RNN network [11].

3   Methods

3.1   Data Exploration

The provided dataset of the DBQA task contains a training dataset and a testing dataset. There are 181882 question-answer pairs with 8772 questions in the training set, and 122532 pairs with 5997 questions in the testing set.

Word-Level and Character-Level Overlap. Intuitively, The question-answer pair with more overlapped words seems to be more topic-relevant, which means a higher matching probability. In the whole training test, we get the trend as showed in the Fig. 1. It is easily found in the range from 0 to 13 of the x-axis that the more overlapped words between the question-answer pairs, the more likely the QA pairs match. Data are dispersed in the range between 15 and 28 because the samples are not enough. Moreover, the information of character-level overlap showed in Fig. 2 will cover many paraphrased patterns of Chinese.

Sequential Structure Information. Traditional IR model like TF-IDF or BM25 model treats a query or a document as a bag of words, in which the

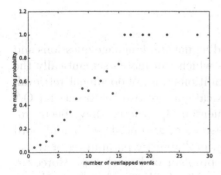
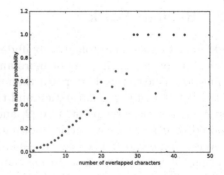

Fig. 1. The x-axis means the number of overlapped words in both question and answer sentences. y-axis refers to the probabilities of becoming the target answers.

Fig. 2. The x-axis means the number of overlapped characters in both question and answer sentences. While y-axis refers to the probability of becoming the target answer.

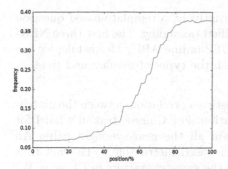 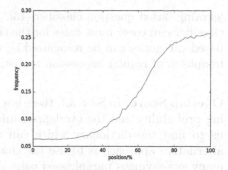

Fig. 3. The x-axis refers to the relative position of the overlapped word in the question sentence. the y-axis means the question-answer matching probability

Fig. 4. Similar to Fig. 3, it shows the relationship between the relative position of the overlapped characters in question sentences and the matching probabilities.

sequential information of structure is ignored. In the scenario of QA system with a shorter length of questions and answers, sequential information may help a lot for the matching of the question-answer pairs and a more elaborate model which takes the sequential information into consideration is needed. Roughly speaking, the words in different positions of a sentence may reflect different syntactic and semantic structures. For the example of the question "中央大学的首任校长是谁?", the word "中央大学" in the forward position is the limited premise of the issues of the latter words "首任" and "校长" while the rearward word may be more relevant to the issues. In the training and testing set, we easily find the positive statistical correlation between the overlapped position and its corresponding probability of question-answer matching in Fig. 3 for word-level overlap and Fig. 4 for character-level overlap.

3.2 Data Preprocessing

Due to the lack of the obvious boundaries of Chinese, we use the pynlpir[1] [12] to segment the Chinese text. Stopwords are removed for dropping the useless high-frequency words which are not discriminative and have little semantic meaning. The 300-dimention word embedding is provided by the NLPCC competition. Moreover, we have trained an embedding model of some crawled pages from the site of Baidu Baike (http://baike.baidu.com/).

3.3 Feature Extraction

Questions' Categories and Answers' Classification. The questions is divided into 5 categories in our paper. 3 of them are concerned with name entity, which are *person*, *place* and *organization*. The remaining two are *time* and *number*. Due to the lack of large-scale labeled data, we can not adopt a

---

[1] https://github.com/tsroten/pynlpir.

learning-based question classifier [13]. Alternatively, a template-based question classifier can cover most cases for the simplified taxonomy. The first three NER-based categories can be recognized by the LTP online API[2]. Meanwhile, we use templetes of regular expression to distinguish the types of *number* and *time*.

Overlap Score. In Sect. 3.1, there is a statistical correlation between the matching probability and the overlapped information. For Chinese text, it's hard for us to find the dictionary which can contain all the near-synonym pairs. An alternative approach is to use the character-based metric due to the fact that many synonymous paraphrased pairs share the same characters in Chinese. We calculate both the word-level and character-level scores of overlap as follows:

$$Score_{overlap}(Q, A) = \sum_{q_i \in Q}^{n} freq_A(q_i) \cdot weight(q_i) \tag{1}$$

where a question Q has n words (characters) and the answer A has m words (characters). The weighted model is based on the position of q_i in the sentence. $freq_A(q_i)$ is denoted as the smoothed frequency of the q_i in the answer A.

BM25 Score. The BM25 model is implemented as Eq. 2.

$$Score_{bm25}(Q, A) = \sum_{q_i \in Q}^{n} IDF(q_i) \cdot \frac{freq_A(q_i) \cdot (k+1)}{freq_A(q_i) + k \cdot (1 - b + b \cdot \frac{Length_A}{Lenght_{avg}})} \tag{2}$$

where $freq_A(q_i)$ is the frequency of the q_i in the answer A. k and b are adjustable parameters for the specific task. $Length_A$ and $Lenght_{avg}$ are the length of the answers A and the average length of the whole answers, respectively.

Weighted Embedding. Embedding technology embeds words into a uniform semantic space, which makes it possible to find the relationship between words. Sentence is simply considered to have been lapped by words linearly. Different words can contribute different weights for the whole meaning of a sentence, which depends on their position, semantic structure and IDF. We get the representation of a word or a Chinese character as Eq. 3

$$Representation(S) = \frac{\sum_{i=0}^{n} weight(s_i) \cdot \overrightarrow{embedding(s_i)}}{\sum_{i=0}^{n} weight(s_i)} \tag{3}$$

s_i is the character or word in a sentence (question or answer), and $embedding(s_i)$ is the corresponding embedding vector. Then we calculate the inner product between the representation of questions and answers as the final score.

---

[2] http://www.ltp-cloud.com/.

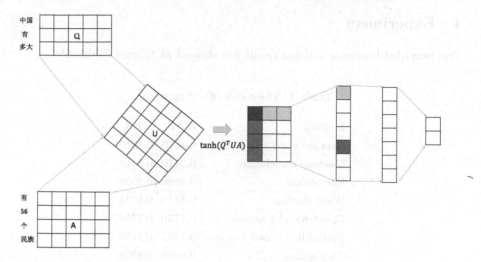

Fig. 5. The structure of our neural network

Neural Network. Besides the weighted combination of the inside word embedding, we have built a neural network which is showed as Fig. 5. In our approach, both word-level embedding and character-level embedding have been adopted to form the sentence matrices of question and answers. A trainable matrix U is used for bridging the question embedding matrix and the answer embedding matrix. The following *tanh* function can avoid the explosion of the previous activated value. The information of the ordered position can still be remained in the full-connection layer by the operation of row-pooling and col-pooling instead of max-pooling [11]. After the softmax layer, the last output layer contains two floating numbers which represent the probabilities of question-answer matching and unmatching respectively. Cross-entropy loss function is used for the optimization process.

Other Features. Edit distance is usually used to measure the similarity of textual strings. While Jaccard index gives the similarity of morphemic sets between the textual pairs. The length of answer is often considered as a significant feature.

3.4   Model Ensemble

We have presented various fundamental features in last chapter, which will directly affect the degree of how question and answer matches. We adopt a linear regression model, learn-to-rank model[3] and tree-based boost model to integrate those features after the normalization of Z-score.

---

[3] https://sourceforge.net/p/lemur/wiki/RankLib/.

4   Experiment

The provided baselines and our result are showed as follows (Table 1):

Table 1. The result of our approach.

Method	MAP	MRR
Average word embedding	0.4610	0.4610
Machine translation	0.2410	0.2412
Paraphrase	0.4886	0.4906
Word overlap	0.5114	0.5134
Count-based features	0.7750	0.7756
Embedding-based features	0.7467	0.7470
All features	0.8005	0.8008

Due to the fact that the above baselines are based on the bag-of-word model and do not have a learn-based mechanism, the performance is rather poor. In the final evaluations, our approach gets the MRR of 0.8008 and ranks 5th among the 18 submissions (4th among the 15 teams).

In our approach, the final scores of some models are treated as features of the ensemble method. As mentioned in the Sect. 3.1, features which can effectively model both syntax and semantic information may be more likely to be correlated to matching labels. In the syntax of Chinese expression, for example, the key words which are related to the issues of question usually appear in the latter positions of the question sentence, while the words in the front positions are more related to the indiscriminative premise which are satisfied by most candidate answers. Moreover, an effective semantic match strategy is also needed. We adopt both the character-level and word-level models in our approach, and a deep neural network may help a lot while our network is a little shallow and compact.

In our experiment, the traditional models like BM25 do not have the potential to do the semantic matching, while the character-based model outperforms the word-character in Chinese. A position-aware deep neural network with the end-to-end strategy may be the trend for the QA tasks. Due to the low-dimension features space, the linear regression has achieved a pretty good performance comparing to the learn-to-rank method or the tree-based boosting methods.

5   Conclusion and Future Work

In this paper, we report technique details of our approach for the sub-task of NLPCC 2016 shared task Open Domain Question answering. Some traditional methods and neural-network based methods have been proposed. In our approach, we combine the characteristics of Chinese text with our models and achieve a good performance by an ensemble learning strategy. Our final performance is not so great due to the shallow structure of the neural network. In our opinions, an effective representation which contains the sequential (or tree-based) information of short text and the corresponding effective semantic matching are the two key factors of the QA system. Both a RNN network which can directly models sequential texts and a CNN network which is more flexible have the potential to get better performances after some adaptions in the textual data. Moreover, although there are many shared characteristics between English and Chinese text, an end-to-end system which is specifically applicable for Chinese can also be the trend for Chinese Question-Answering system.

Acknowledgements. The work presented in this paper is sponsored in part by the Chinese National Program on Key Basic Research Project (973 Program, grant Nos. 2013CB329304, 2014CB744604), the Chinese 863 Program (grant No. 2015AA015403), the Natural Science Foundation of China (grant Nos. 61402324, 61272265), and the Research Fund for the Doctoral Program of Higher Education of China (grant No. 20130032120044).

References

1. Mikolov, T., Chen, K., Corrado, G., Dean, J.: Efficient estimation of word representations in vector space. arXiv preprint arXiv:1301.3781 (2013)
2. Yao, X., Durme, B.V., Callison-Burch, C., Clark, P.: Answer extraction as sequence tagging with tree edit distance. In: Conference of the North American Chapter of the Association for Computational Linguistics (2013)
3. Wang, Z., Ittycheriah, A.: FAQ-based question answering via word alignment (2015)
4. Yih, W.T., Chang, M.W., Meek, C., Pastusiak, A.: Question answering using enhanced lexical semantic models, In: Meeting of the Association for Computational Linguistics, pp. 1744–1753 (2013)
5. Zhou, G., Cai, L., Zhao, J., Liu, K.: Phrase-based translation model for question retrieval in community question answer archives. In: The Meeting of the Association for Computational Linguistics, pp. 653–662 (2011)
6. Severyn, A.: Automatic feature engineering for answer selection and extraction. In: EMNLP (2013)
7. Yu, L., Hermann, K.M., Blunsom, P., Pulman, S.: Deep learning for answer sentence selection. arXiv preprint arXiv:1412.1632 (2014)
8. Severyn, A., Moschitti, A.: Learning to rank short text pairs with convolutional deep neural networks. In: SIGIR, pp. 373–382. ACM (2015)
9. Wang, D., Nyberg, E.: A long short-term memory model for answer sentence selection in question answering. In: Meeting of the Association for Computational Linguistics and the International Joint Conference on Natural Language Processing (2015)
10. Tan, M., Xiang, B., Zhou, B.: LSTM-based deep learning models for non-factoid answer selection. arXiv preprint arXiv:1511.04108 (2015)
11. Santos, C.D., Tan, M., Xiang, B., Zhou, B.: Attentive pooling networks (2016)
12. Liu, T., Che, W., Zhenghua, L.I.: Language technology platform. In: COLING 2010, pp. 13–16 (2010)
13. Li, X., Roth, D.: Learning question classifiers. In: COLING, vol. 12, no. 24, pp. 556–562 (2003)

Overview of the NLPCC-ICCPOL 2016 Shared Task: Open Domain Chinese Question Answering

Nan Duan[(✉)]

Microsoft Research Asia, Beijing, China
nanduan@microsoft.com

Abstract. In this paper, we give the overview of the open domain Question Answering (or open domain QA) shared task in the NLPCC-ICCPOL 2016. We first review the background of QA, and then describe two open domain Chinese QA tasks in this year's NLPCC-ICCPOL, including the construction of the benchmark datasets and the evaluation metrics. The evaluation results of submissions from participating teams are presented in the experimental part.

Keywords: Question Answering · Knowledge-based QA · Document-based QA

1 Background

Question Answering (or QA) is a fundamental task in Artificial Intelligence, whose goal is to build a system that can automatically answer natural language questions. In the last decade, the development of QA techniques has been greatly promoted by both academic field and industry field.

In the academic field, with the rise of large scale curated knowledge bases, like Yago, Satori, Freebase, etc., more and more researchers pay their attentions to the knowledge-based QA (or KBQA) task, such as semantic parsing-based approaches [1–7] and information retrieval-based approaches [8–16]. Besides KBQA, researchers are interested in document-based QA (or DBQA) as well, whose goal is to select answers from a set of given documents and use them as responses to natural language questions. Usually, information retrieval-based approaches [18–22] are used for the DBQA task.

In the industry field, many influential QA-related products have been built, such as IBM Watson, Apple Siri, Google Now, Facebook Graph Search, Microsoft Cortana and XiaoIce etc. These kinds of systems are immerging into every user's life who is using mobile devices.

Under such circumstance, in this year's NLPCC-ICCPOL shared task, we call the open domain QA task that cover both KBQA and DBQA tasks. Our motivations are two-folds:

1. We expect this activity can enhance the progress of QA research, esp. for Chinese;
2. We encourage more QA researchers to share their experiences, techniques, and progress.

© Springer International Publishing AG 2016
C.-Y. Lin et al. (Eds.): NLPCC-ICCPOL 2016, LNAI 10102, pp. 942–948, 2016.
DOI: 10.1007/978-3-319-50496-4_89

The remainder of this paper is organized as follows. Section 1 describes two open domain Chinese QA tasks. In Sect. 2, we describe the benchmark datasets constructed. Section 3 describes evaluation metrics, and Sect. 4 presents the evaluation results of different submissions. We conclude the paper in Sect. 5, and point out our plan on future QA evaluation activities.

2 Task Description

The NLPCC-ICCPOL 2016 open domain QA shared task includes two QA tasks for Chinese language: knowledge-based QA (KBQA) task and document-based QA (DBQA) task.

2.1 KBQA Task

Given a question, a KBQA system built by each participating team should select one or more entities as answers from a given knowledge base (KB). The datasets for this task include:

- **A Chinese KB**. It includes knowledge triples crawled from the web. Each knowledge triple has the form: <Subject, Predicate, Object>, where 'Subject' denotes a subject entity, 'Predicate' denotes a relation, and 'Object' denotes an object entity. A sample of knowledge triples is given in Fig. 1, and the statistics of the Chinese KB is given in Table 1.

```
新还珠格格 ||| entity.primaryName ||| 新还珠格格
新还珠格格 ||| 中文名 ||| 新还珠格格
新还珠格格 ||| 外文名 ||| New my fair Princess
新还珠格格 ||| 出品时间 ||| 2011年和2014年
新还珠格格 ||| 出品公司 ||| 上海创翊文化传播有限公司
新还珠格格 ||| 制片地区 ||| 中国大陆，中国台湾
新还珠格格 ||| 拍摄地点 ||| 横店影视城
新还珠格格 ||| 发行公司 ||| 上海创翊文化传播有限公司
新还珠格格 ||| 首播时间 ||| 2011年7月16日
新还珠格格 ||| 导演 ||| 李平，丁仰国
新还珠格格 ||| 编剧 ||| 琼瑶，黄奕媛
新还珠格格 ||| 主演 ||| 李晟，海陆，张睿，李佳航，潘杰明，赵丽颖，邱心志，邓萃雯，刘雷华
新还珠格格 ||| 集数 ||| 总共98集→第一部1至37集→第二部37至74集→第三部74至98集
新还珠格格 ||| 每集长度 ||| 前三部：45分钟 第四部：48分钟
新还珠格格 ||| 类型 ||| 古装，爱情，励志，喜剧
新还珠格格 ||| 上映时间 ||| 前三部：2011年07月16日至2011年9月8日第四部：2016年暑期档
新还珠格格 ||| 在线播放平台 ||| 芒果TV,PPTV,暴风影音，优酷，搜狐。
新还珠格格 ||| 总策划 ||| 杨文红，苏晓
新还珠格格 ||| 出品人 ||| 欧阳常林
新还珠格格 ||| 总监制 ||| 魏文彬
新还珠格格 ||| entity.description ||| 《新还珠格格》翻拍自琼瑶经典之作《还珠格格》，由李晟、海
```

Fig. 1. An example of the Chinese KB.

Table 1. Statistics of the Chinese KB.

# of subject entities	8,721,640
# of triples	47,943,429
# of averaged triples per subject entity	5.5

- **A training set and a testing set**. We assign a set of knowledge triples sampled from the Chinese KB to human annotators. For each knowledge triple, a human annotator will write down a natural language question, whose answer should be the object entity of the current knowledge triple. The statistic of labeled QA pairs and an annotation example are given in Table 2:

Table 2. Statistics of the KBQA datasets.

# of labeled Q-A pairs (training set)	14,609	
# of labeled Q-A pairs (testing set)	9,870	
An example	Triple	<微软, 创始人, 比尔盖茨>
	Labeled question	微软公司的创始人是谁?
	Golden answer	比尔盖茨

In KBQA task, any data resource can be used to train necessary models, such as entity linking, semantic parsing, etc., but answer entities should come from the provided KB only.

2.2 DBQA Task

Given a question and its corresponding document, a DBQA system built by each participating team should select one or more sentences as answers from the document. The datasets for this task include:

- **A training set and a testing set**. We assign a set of documents to human annotators. For each document, a human annotator will (1) first, select a sentence from the document, and (2) then, write down a natural language question, whose answer should be the selected sentence. The statistic of labeled QA pairs and an annotation example are given in Table 3:

Table 3. Statistics of the DBQA datasets.

# of Labeled Q-A Pairs (training set)	14,609
# of Labeled Q-A Pairs (testing set)	9,870
An Example	俄罗斯贝加尔湖的面积有多大? \t 贝加尔湖, 中国古代称为北海, 位于俄罗斯西伯利亚的南部。 \t 0
	俄罗斯贝加尔湖的面积有多大? \t 贝加尔湖是世界上最深, 容量最大的淡水湖。 \t 0
	俄罗斯贝加尔湖的面积有多大? \t 贝加尔湖贝加尔湖是世界上最深蓄水量最大的淡水湖。 \t 0
	俄罗斯贝加尔湖的面积有多大? \t 它位于布里亚特共和国(Buryatiya)和伊尔库茨克州(Irkutsk)境内。 \t 0
	俄罗斯贝加尔湖的面积有多大? \t 湖型狭长弯曲, 宛如一弯新月, 所以又有"月亮湖"之称。 \t 0
	俄罗斯贝加尔湖的面积有多大? \t 湖长636公里, 平均宽48公里, 最宽79.4公里, 面积3.15万平方公里。 \t 1
	俄罗斯贝加尔湖的面积有多大? \t 贝加尔湖湖水澄澈清冽, 且稳定透明 (透明度达40.8米), 为世界第二。 \t 0

As shown in the example in Table 3, a question (the 1st column), question's corresponding document sentences (the 2nd column), and their answer annotations (the 3rd column) are provided. If a document sentence is the correct answer of the question, its annotation will be 1, otherwise its annotation will be 0. The three columns will be separated by the symbol '\t'.

In DBQA task, any data resource can be used to train necessary models, such as paraphrasing model, sentence matching model, etc., but answer sentences should come from the provided documents only.

3 Evaluation Metrics

The quality of a KBQA system is evaluated by **Averaged F1**, and the quality of a DBQA system is evaluated by **MRR**, **MAP**, and **ACC@1**.

- **Averaged F1**

$$Averaged\ F1 = \frac{1}{|Q|} \sum_{i=1}^{|Q|} F_i$$

F_i denotes the F1 score for question Q_i computed based on C_i and A_i. F_i is set to 0 if C_i is empty or doesn't overlap with A_i. Otherwise, F_i is computed as follows:

$$F_i = \frac{2 \cdot \frac{\#(C_i, A_i)}{|C_i|} \cdot \frac{\#(C_i, A_i)}{|A_i|}}{\frac{\#(C_i, A_i)}{|C_i|} + \frac{\#(C_i, A_i)}{|A_i|}}$$

where $\#(C_i, A_i)$ denotes the number of answers occur in both C_i and A_i. $|C_i|$ and $|A_i|$ denote the number of answers in C_i and A_i respectively.

- **MRR**

$$MRR = \frac{1}{|Q|} \sum_{i=1}^{|Q|} \frac{1}{rank_i}$$

$|Q|$ denotes the total number of questions in the evaluation set, $rank_i$ denotes the position of the first correct answer in the generated answer set C_i for the ith question Q_i. If C_i doesn't overlap with the golden answers A_i for Q_i, $\frac{1}{rank_i}$ is set to 0.

- **MAP**

$$MAP = \frac{1}{|Q|} \sum_{i=1}^{|Q|} AveP(C_i, A_i)$$

$AveP(C, A) = \frac{\sum_{k=1}^{n} (P(k) \cdot rel(k))}{min(m,n)}$ denotes the average precision. k is the rank in the sequence of retrieved answer sentences. m is the number of correct answer sentences.

n is the number of retrieved answer sentences. If $min(m, n)$ is 0, $AveP(C, A)$ is set to 0. $P(k)$ is the precision at cut-off k in the list. $rel(k)$ is an indicator function equaling 1 if the item at rank k is an answer sentence, and 0 otherwise.

- **ACC@N**

$$Accuracy@N = \frac{1}{|Q|} \sum_{i=1}^{|Q|} \delta(C_i, A_i)$$

$\delta(C_i, A_i)$ equals to 1 when there is at least one answer contained by C_i occurs in A_i, and 0 otherwise.

4 Evaluation Results

There are totally 99 teams registered for the above two Chinese QA task, and 39 teams submitted their results. Tables 4 and 5 lists the evaluation results of KBQA and DBQA tasks respectively.

Table 4. Evaluation results of the KBQA task.

	Averaged F1	Rank (by averaged F1)
Team 1	0.8247	1
Team 2	0.8159	2
Team 3	0.7957	3
Team 4	0.7914	4
Team 5	0.7272	5
Team 6	0.7251	6
Team 7	0.7022	7
Team 8	0.6956	8
Team 9	0.6809	9
Team 10	0.5537	10
Team 11	0.5237	11
Team 12	0.5119	12
Team 13	0.4923	13
Team 14	0.3808	14
Team 15	0.3584	15
Team 16	0.0015	16
Team 17	0.0005	17
Below are results of LATE submissions		
Team 18	0.6234	–
Team 19	0.5930	–
Team 20	0.3172	–
Team 21	0.0044	–

Table 5. Evaluation results of the DBQA task.

	MRR	MAP	ACC@1	Rank (by MRR)
Team 1	0.8592	0.8586	0.7906	1
Team 2	0.8269	0.8263	0.7385	2
Team 3	0.8120	0.8111	0.7144	3
Team 4	0.8114	0.8105	0.7135	4
Team 5	0.8005	0.8008	0.7139	5
Team 6	0.7811	0.7804	0.6659	6
Team 7	0.7612	0.7607	0.6640	7
Team 8	0.7593	0.7588	0.6373	8
Team 9	0.7526	0.7519	0.6390	9
Team 10	0.7428	0.7422	0.6287	10
Team 11	0.7051	0.7047	0.5907	11
Team 12	0.6932	0.6925	0.5731	12
Team 13	0.6605	0.6576	0.5912	13
Team 14	0.6412	0.6409	0.5145	14
Team 15	0.6392	0.6386	0.5045	15
Team 16	0.6123	0.6120	0.4628	16
Team 17	0.5873	0.5864	0.4430	17
Team 18	0.5840	0.5834	0.4042	18

5 Conclusion

This paper briefly introduces the overview of this year's two open domain Chinese QA shared tasks. Comparing to last year's results (19 teams registered and only 3 teams submitted final submissions), in this year, we have 99 teams registered and 39 teams submitted final submissions, which has been a great progress for the Chinese QA community. In the future, we plan to provide more QA datasets and call for new QA tasks for Chinese. Besides, we plan to extend the QA tasks from Chinese to English as well.

References

1. Wang, Y., Berant, J., Liang, P.: Building a semantic parser overnight. In: ACL (2015)
2. Pasupat, P., Liang, P.: Compositional semantic parsing on semi-structured tables. In: ACL (2015)
3. Pasupat, P., Liang, P.: Zero-shot entity extraction from web pages. In: ACL (2014)
4. Bao, J., Duan, N., Zhou, M., Zhao, T.: Knowledge-based question answering as machine translation. In: ACL (2014)
5. Yang, M.-C., Duan, N., Zhou, M., Rim, H.-C.: Joint relational embeddings for knowledge-based question answering. In: EMNLP (2014)
6. Berant, J., Chou, A., Frostig, R., Liang, P.: Semantic parsing on freebase from question-answer pairs. In: EMNLP (2013)

7. Kwiatkowski, T., Choi, E., Artzi, Y., Zettlemoyer, L.: Scaling semantic parsers with on-the-fly ontology matching. In: EMNLP (2013)
8. Bordes, A., Usunier, N., Chopra, S., Weston, J.: Large-scale simple question answering with memory network. In: ICLR (2015)
9. Weston, J., Bordes, A., Chopra, S., Mikolov, T.: Towards AI-complete question answering: a set of prerequisite toy tasks, arXiv (2015)
10. Dong, L., Wei, F., Zhou, M., Xu, K.: Question answering over freebase with multi-column convolutional neural networks. In: ACL (2015)
11. Yih, W.-T., Chang, M.-W., He, X., Gao, J.: Semantic parsing via staged query graph generation: question answering with knowledge base. In: ACL (2015)
12. Yao, X.: Lean question answering over freebase from scratch. In: NAACL (2015)
13. Berant, J., Liang, P.: Semantic parsing via paraphrasing. In: ACL (2014)
14. Yao, X., Van Durme, B.: Information extraction over structured data: question answering with freebase. In: ACL (2014)
15. Bordes, A., Weston, J., Chopra, S.: Question answering with subgraph embeddings. In: EMNLP (2014)
16. Bordes, A., Weston, J., Usunier, N.: Open question answering with weakly supervised embedding models. In: ECML-PKDD (2014)
17. Yang, Y., Yih, W.-T., Meek, C.: WIKIQA: a challenge dataset for open-domain question answering. In: EMNLP (2015)
18. Miao, Y., Yu, L., Blunsom, P.: Neural variational inference for text processing, arXiv (2015)
19. Wang, D., Nyberg, E.: A long short term memory model for answer sentence selection in question answering. In: ACL (2015)
20. Yin, W., Schütze, H., Xiang, B., Zhou, B.: ABCNN: attention-based convolutional neural network for modeling sentence pairs. In: ACL (2016)
21. Yu, L., Hermann, K.M., Blunsom, P., Pullman, S.: Deep learning for answer sentence selection. In: NIPS Workshop (2014)
22. Yan, Z., Duan, N., Bao, J., Chen, P., Zhou, M., Li, Z., Zhou, J.: DocChat: an information retrieval approach for chatbot engines using unstructured documents. In: ACL (2016)

Author Index

Printed in the United States
By Bookmasters